Lecture Notes in Computer Science 3280

Commenced Publication in 1973
Founding and Former Series Editors:
Gerhard Goos, Juris Hartmanis, and Jan van Leeuwen

Editorial Board

David Hutchison
 Lancaster University, UK
Takeo Kanade
 Carnegie Mellon University, Pittsburgh, PA, USA
Josef Kittler
 University of Surrey, Guildford, UK
Jon M. Kleinberg
 Cornell University, Ithaca, NY, USA
Friedemann Mattern
 ETH Zurich, Switzerland
John C. Mitchell
 Stanford University, CA, USA
Moni Naor
 Weizmann Institute of Science, Rehovot, Israel
Oscar Nierstrasz
 University of Bern, Switzerland
C. Pandu Rangan
 Indian Institute of Technology, Madras, India
Bernhard Steffen
 University of Dortmund, Germany
Madhu Sudan
 Massachusetts Institute of Technology, MA, USA
Demetri Terzopoulos
 New York University, NY, USA
Doug Tygar
 University of California, Berkeley, CA, USA
Moshe Y. Vardi
 Rice University, Houston, TX, USA
Gerhard Weikum
 Max-Planck Institute of Computer Science, Saarbruecken, Germany

Cevdet Aykanat   Tuğrul Dayar
İbrahim Körpeoğlu (Eds.)

Computer and Information Sciences – ISCIS 2004

19th International Symposium
Kemer-Antalya, Turkey, October 27-29, 2004
Proceedings

 Springer

Volume Editors

Cevdet Aykanat
Tuğrul Dayar
İbrahim Körpeoğlu
Bilkent University
Department of Computer Engineering
06800 Bilkent, Ankara, Turkey
E-mail: {aykanat, tugrul, korpe}@cs.bilkent.edu.tr

Library of Congress Control Number: 2004113696

CR Subject Classification (1998): H, C, B, D, F, I

ISSN 0302-9743
ISBN 3-540-23526-4 Springer Berlin Heidelberg New York

This work is subject to copyright. All rights are reserved, whether the whole or part of the material is
concerned, specifically the rights of translation, reprinting, re-use of illustrations, recitation, broadcasting,
reproduction on microfilms or in any other way, and storage in data banks. Duplication of this publication
or parts thereof is permitted only under the provisions of the German Copyright Law of September 9, 1965,
in its current version, and permission for use must always be obtained from Springer. Violations are liable
to prosecution under the German Copyright Law.

Springer is a part of Springer Science+Business Media

springeronline.com

© Springer-Verlag Berlin Heidelberg 2004
Printed in Germany

Typesetting: Camera-ready by author, data conversion by Christian Grosche, Hamburg
Printed on acid-free paper   SPIN: 11335832   06/3142   5 4 3 2 1 0

Preface

The series of ISCIS (International Symposium on Computer and Information Sciences) symposia have been held each year since 1986, mostly in Turkey and occasionally abroad. It is the main computer science and engineering meeting organized by Turkish academics and was founded by Erol Gelenbe. Each year ISCIS attracts a significant number of international participants from all over the world. The 19th ISCIS was organized by Bilkent University, Department of Computer Engineering, and was held in Kemer-Antalya, Turkey during 27–29 October 2004.

For ISCIS 2004, a total of 335 papers went through the review process and a large number of high-quality papers competed for acceptance. This volume of the Springer Lecture Notes in Computer Science (LNCS) series contains 100 of those papers that broadly fall into the following areas of interest: artificial intelligence and machine learning, computer graphics and user interfaces, computer networks and security, computer vision and image processing, database systems, modeling and performance evaluation, natural language processing, parallel and distributed computing, real-time control applications, software engineering and programming systems, and theory of computing.

The symposium contained three invited talks. The first talk titled "An Approach to Quality of Service" was given by Erol Gelenbe of Imperial College London. The second talk titled "Modeling Assumptions in Mobile Networks" was given by Satish Tripathi of State University of New York at Buffalo. The third talk titled "Combinatorial Scientific Computing: The Role of Computer Science Algorithms in Scientific Simulation" was given by Bruce Hendrickson of Sandia National Laboratories. The symposium also contained the following special sessions: Advanced Real-Time Applications, All Optical Networks, Component-Based Distributed Simulation, Mobile Agents: Mechanisms and Modeling, and Performance Evaluation of Complex Systems.

ISCIS 2004 would not have taken place without the contributions of many people. We first thank the 60 program committee (PC) members who did an excellent job in publicizing the symposium and in helping to attract a large number of high-quality submissions. We thank all the authors who contributed papers. We especially acknowledge the time and efforts of Maria Carla Calzarossa, Ivo De Lotto, Jean-Michel Fourneau, Jane Hillston, Giuseppe Iazeolla, and Salvatore Tucci that went into organizing special sessions. We are also very much grateful to the PC members and the external referees who provided thorough reviews in a short time frame.

Among the people who contributed locally, we thank Selim Çıracı for setting up the Web server used in the submission process, and Barla Cambazoglu and Bora Uçar for, among other things, their meticulous work in the proof reading process.

We greatly appreciate the financial support from the Scientific and Technical Research Council of Turkey (TÜBİTAK) and the Turkey Section of the Institute of Electrical and Electronics Engineers (IEEE) that was used towards the costs of printing, inviting speakers, and registering local IEEE members.

Finally, we thank all who contributed to the planning and realization of the symposium.

October 2004

Cevdet Aykanat
Tuğrul Dayar
İbrahim Körpeoğlu

Organization

Chairs

Honorary Chair: Erol Gelenbe (Imperial College London, UK)
Conference and PC Chairs: Cevdet Aykanat (Bilkent University, Turkey)
Tuğrul Dayar (Bilkent University, Turkey)
İbrahim Körpeoğlu (Bilkent University, Turkey)

Program Committee

Bülent Abalı (USA)
Sibel Adalı (USA)
Varol Akman (Turkey)
Reda Alhajj (Canada)
Ethem Alpaydın (Turkey)
Volkan Atalay (USA)
Fevzi Belli (Germany)
Semih Bilgen (Turkey)
Arndt Bode (Germany)
Peter Buchholz (Germany)
Maria Carla Calzarossa (Italy)
K. Selçuk Candan (USA)
Gabriel Ciobanu (Romania)
Ümit Çatalyürek (USA)
Erdal Çayırcı (Turkey)
Uğur Çetintemel (USA)
İlyas Çiçekli (Turkey)
Andrea D'Ambrogio (Italy)
David Davenport (Turkey)
Ivo De Lotto (Italy)
Asuman Doğaç (Turkey)
Uğur Doğrusöz (Turkey)
Susanna Donatelli (Italy)
Jack Dongarra (USA)
Iain S. Duff (UK, France)
Cem Ersoy (Turkey)
Pierre Flener (Sweden)
Jean-Michel Fourneau (France)
Uğur Güdükbay (Turkey)
Attila Gürsoy (Turkey)

Jane Hillston (UK)
Giuseppe Iazeolla (Italy)
Carlos Juiz (Spain)
Eser Kandoğan (USA)
Ezhan Karasan (Turkey)
Çetin Kaya Koç (USA)
Albert Levi (Turkey)
Kemal Oflazer (Turkey)
Yavuz Oruç (USA)
Füsun Özgüner (USA)
Gültekin Özsoyoğlu (USA)
M. Tamer Özsu (Canada)
Ali Pınar (USA)
Ramon Puigjaner (Spain)
Guy Pujolle (France)
A. Aydın Selçuk (Turkey)
Koshrow Sohraby (USA)
Abdullah Uz Tansel (USA)
Bedir Tekinerdoğan (The Netherlands)
Miklos Telek (Hungary)
Miroslav Tuma (Czech Republic)
Daniel Thalmann (Switzerland)
Salvatore Tucci (Italy)
Gökhan Tür (USA)
Özgür Ulusoy (Turkey)
Mustafa Uysal (USA)
Alper Üngör (USA)
Chris Walshaw (UK)
Adnan Yazici (Turkey)
Uri Yechiali (Israel)

Local Organizing Committee

B. Barla Cambazoglu
Selim Çıracı
Bora Uçar

Referees

B. Abalı
H. Acan
N. Adabala
S. Adalı
Y. Ahmad
N. Akar
L. Akarun
E. Akçalı
S.F. Akgül
D. Aksoy
S. Aksoy
A. Akyamaç
R. Alhajj
D.N. Alparslan
E. Alpaydın
İ.S. Altıngövde
E. Arsal
V. Atalay
A. Ayaz
Ö. Aydemir
T. Aydın
M. Aydos
C. Aykanat
Ö. Babür
E. Bahçeci
F. Balazs
A. Bargteil
A. Barili
D. Barth
T. Batu
F. Bause
B. Bayoğlu
A.G. Bayrak
F. Belli
S. Bernardi
A. Bertolino
M. Besta

A. Biancardi
V. Biçer
S. Bilgen
H. Bingöl
S.İ. Birbil
A. Bode
D. Bozağaç
D. Bozdağ
P. Buchholz
G. Buttazzo
K. Bür
M.C. Calzarossa
B.B. Cambazoglu
F. Can
K.S. Candan
A. Cervin
A.E. Cetin
D.-P. Chi
N. Chiba
S. Chung
J. Ciger
G. Ciobanu
V. Ciubotariu
R. Civanlar
T. Czachorski
A. Çakmak
Ü. Çatalyürek
H. Çelikkanat
U. Çetintemel
S. Çıracı
İ. Çiçekli
A. D'Ambrogio
D. Davenport
T. Dayar
Z. Dayar
P. de Heras
E. de Sevin

I. De Lotto
V. De Nitto Personé
M. De Pierro
Y. Dedeoğlu
Emek Demir
Engin Demir
İ. Demirkol
M. Dimitrijevic
A. Doğaç
E. Doğan
U. Doğrusöz
S. Donatelli
M.Y. Donmez
I.S. Duff
D. DuVarney
P. Duygulu-Şahin
M. Eltayeb
A. Erçil
E. Erdem
U. Ermiş
E.Z. Erson
C. Ersoy
L. Ertaul
P. Flener
J.-M. Fourneau
G. Franceschinis
S. Fukuda
R. Gaeta
S. Galmes
D. Gianni
K. Gilly
S. Gilmore
E. Giral
P. Glardon
B. Gökberk
M. Gribaudo
G. Guidi

O. Gusak
M. Gutierrez
U. Güdükbay
T.D. Güney
A. Gürsoy
H.A. Güvenir
R. Hamzaoui
İ. Haritaoğlu
V. Hayward
B. Herbelin
J. Hillston
G. Horvath
G. Iazeolla
S. Isik
S.P. Iyer
G. Jeney
C. Juiz
K. Kahraman
E. Kandoğan
A. Kara
H. Karaata
M. Karahan
E. Karasan
S. Katzenbeisser
K. Kaya
M. Keckeisen
M. Kıraç
A. Koca
Ç.K. Koç
V. Koltun
C. Komar
R. Koşar
T. Küçükyılmaz
F. Kuru
M.A. Kutay
İ. Körpeoğlu
A. Lerner
A. Levi
D. Lucanu
A. Maciel
M. Marinoni
K. Mitchell
S. Narayanan
Z. Nemeth
J. Nichols

S. North
M. Novotni
R. Nuray
O. Oanea
K. Oflazer
C. Okutan
M. Olduz
E. Onur
Y. Oruç
S.G. Öğüdücü
T. Önel
F. Özgüner
E. Özkural
S. Özler
G. Özsoyoğlu
M.T. Özsu
C. Özturan
T. Pan
A. Panchenko
M.R. Pariente
L. Patrick
F. Pekergin
A. Pınar
J. Pilet
D. Pisinger
R. Puigjaner
G. Pujolle
F. Quessette
A. Rasin
F. Rodriguez-Henriquez
G. Ruffo
S. Saginbekov
E. Sağbaş
G. Saldamlı
S. Sarni
E. Savaş
B. Say
E. Şahin
E. Şaykol
S. Schertenleib
A.A. Selçuk
M. Sereno
T. Sevilmiş
M. Sharghi
J. Smith

K. Sohraby
H. Sözer
O. Soysal
R. Sugar
B. Sunar
A.U. Tansel
M. Taşan
B. Tekinerdoğan
M. Tekkalmaz
M. Telek
C. Tepper
D. Tessera
D. Thalmann
A. Thummler
M. Tuma
A. Turk
G. Tür
B. Uçar
E. Uğur
B. Ulicny
Ö. Ulusoy
M. Uysal
E. Uzun
A. Üngör
K. Varga
A. Velingkar
F. Vexo
C. Walshaw
R. Wildes
W. Xu
F. Yarman-Vural
G. Yavaş
A. Yazici
T. Yılmaz
Y. Yılmaz
P. Yolum
M. Yüksel
D. Yüret
M. Zachariasen
M. Zeren
E. Zhang
N. Zhang
Xi Zhang
Xinwen Zhang
T. Zimmerman

Sponsoring Institutions

Bilkent University, Department of Computer Engineering
Institute of Electrical and Electronics Engineers (IEEE), Turkey Section
International Federation for Information Processing (IFIP), Working Group 10.3
Scientific and Technical Research Council of Turkey (TÜBİTAK)

Table of Contents

Invited Talk

An Approach to Quality of Service 1
Erol Gelenbe

Artificial Intelligence and Machine Learning

A New Classifier Based on Attribute Weighted Artificial Immune
System (AWAIS)... 11
Seral Şahan, Halife Kodaz, Salih Güneş, Kemal Polat

Investigating the Effects of Recency and Size of Training Text on
Author Recognition Problem 21
Ebru Celikel, Mehmet Emin Dalkılıç

Model Based Intelligent Control of a 3-Joint Robotic Manipulator:
A Simulation Study Using Artificial Neural Networks 31
Rasit Koker, Abdullah Ferikoglu

Knowledge Incorporation into ACO-Based Autonomous Mobile Robot
Navigation 41
Mehtap Kose, Adnan Acan

The Effects of Data Properties on Local, Piecewise, Global, Mixture of
Experts, and Boundary-Optimized Classifiers for Medical Decision Making   51
Nilgün Güler, Fikret S. Gürgen

Learning Interestingness of Streaming Classification Rules 62
Tolga Aydın, Halil Altay Güvenir

Using Fuzzy Petri Nets for Static Analysis of Rule-Bases 72
Burcin Bostan-Korpeoglu, Adnan Yazici

Protein Structural Class Determination Using Support Vector Machines . 82
Zerrin Isik, Berrin Yanikoglu, Ugur Sezerman

Computer Graphics and User Interfaces

Flexible and Interactive Crack-Like Patterns Presentation on 3D Objects   90
Hsien-Hsi Hsieh, Wen-Kai Tai, Cheng-Chin Chiang, Mau-Tsuen Yang

An Occlusion Culling Approach Based on Exploiting Multiple
Hardware-Accelerated Occlusion Queries for Dynamical Scenes 100
Wen-Kai Tai, Chih-Kang Hsu, Hsien-Hsi Hsieh

Acceleration of Perspective Volume Rendering Using Depth-Subsampling   110
Byeong-Seok Shin, Yu Sik Chae

An Efficient Camera Path Computation Using Image-Space Information in Virtual Endoscopy 118
Koo-Joo Kwon, Byeong-Seok Shin

Hair Motion Simulation 126
Yusuf Sahillioğlu, Bülent Özgüç

Interactive Mouse Systems Providing Haptic Feedback During the Exploration in Virtual Environment 136
Ki-Uk Kyung, Heejin Choi, Dong-Soo Kwon, Seung-Woo Son

Developing Finite State NLP Systems with a Graphical Environment 147
Kemal Oflazer, Yasin Yılmaz

Computer Networks and Security

Bandwidth-Aware Scaling for Internet Video Streaming 157
Turhan Tunalı, Nükhet Özbek, Koray Anar, Aylin Kantarcı

The Abnormal Traffic Control Framework Based on QoS Mechanisms ... 167
Kwangsun Ko, Eun-kyung Cho, Taekeun Lee, Yong-hyeog Kang, Young Ik Eom

Proximity-Based Overlay Routing for Service Discovery in Mobile Ad Hoc Networks 176
Hyeon-Ju Yoon, Eun-Ju Lee, Hyunku Jeong, Jin-Soo Kim

Multicast Routing for Ad Hoc Networks with a Multiclass Scheme for Quality of Service 187
Kaan Bür, Cem Ersoy

HVIA-GE: A Hardware Implementation of Virtual Interface Architecture Based on Gigabit Ethernet 198
Sejin Park, Sang-Hwa Chung, In-Su Yoon, In-Hyung Jung, So Myeong Lee, Ben Lee

Modeling TCP Loss Recovery Latency with the Number of Retransmissions   207
Beomjoon Kim, Jaesung Park, Yong-Hoon Choi

A Two-Step EM Algorithm for MAP Fitting 217
Peter Buchholz, Andriy Panchenko

Performance Evaluation of the 802.16 Medium Access Control Layer 228
Oleg Gusak, Neal Oliver, Khosrow Sohraby

Fixed Size and Variable Size Packet Models in an Optical Ring
Network: Complexity and Simulations 238
*Dominique Barth, Johanne Cohen, Lynda Gastal, Thierry Mautor,
Stéphane Rousseau*

A Tabu Search Algorithm for Sparse Placement of Wavelength
Converters in Optical Networks 247
Namik Sengezer, Ezhan Karasan

Mixed Routing for ROMEO Optical Burst 257
Jean-Michel Fourneau, David Nott

A Fast Hardware-Oriented Algorithm for Cellular Mobiles Positioning ... 267
Muhammed Salamah, Evgueni Doukhnitch, Deniz Devrim

Relay Attacks on Bluetooth Authentication and Solutions 278
*Albert Levi, Erhan Çetintaş, Murat Aydos, Çetin Kaya Koç,
M. Ufuk Çağlayan*

Reliable Delivery of Popular Data Services in WIDE 289
Sinan Isik, Mehmet Yunus Donmez, Cem Ersoy

Wireless Interworking Independent CAN Segments 299
Cuneyt Bayilmis, Ismail Erturk, Celal Ceken

Real-Time Admission Control Supporting Prioritized Soft Handoff
Calls in Cellular DS-CDMA Systems 311
Kuo-Chung Chu, Frank Yeong-Sung Lin

Voice Traffic Integration in Wireless Data Networks with Channel State
Information 321
Jin-Ghoo Choi, Saewoong Bahk

Blind Collision Resolution Using Retransmission Diversity under
Quasi-static Fading Channels 331
Barış Özgül, Hakan Deliç

CRAM: An Energy Efficient Routing Algorithm for Wireless Sensor
Networks 341
Zeng-wei Zheng, Zhao-hui Wu, Huai-zhong Lin, Kou-gen Zheng

An Approach for Spam E-mail Detection with Support Vector Machine
and n-Gram Indexing 351
Jongsub Moon, Taeshik Shon, Jungtaek Seo, Jongho Kim, Jungwoo Seo

Finding Breach Paths Using the Watershed Segmentation Algorithm in
Surveillance Wireless Sensor Networks 363
Ertan Onur, Cem Ersoy, Hakan Deliç, Lale Akarun

Biometric Authentication Using Online Signatures 373
Alisher Kholmatov, Berrin Yanikoglu

Computer Vision and Image Processing

Moving Region Detection in Compressed Video 381
B. Uğur Töreyin, A. Enis Cetin, Anil Aksay, M. Bilgay Akhan

Shape Recognition with Generalized Beam Angle Statistics 391
Ömer Önder Tola, Nafiz Arıca, Fatoş Yarman-Vural

3D Cognitive Map Construction by Active Stereo Vision in a Virtual
World 400
Ilkay Ulusoy, Ugur Halici, Kemal Leblebicioglu

3D Real Object Recognition on the Basis of Moment Invariants and
Neural Networks 410
Muharrem Mercimek, Kayhan Gulez

A Novel Watermarking for Image Security 420
Jun Zhang, Feng Xiong

Boosting Face Recognition Speed with a Novel Divide-and-Conquer
Approach 430
Önsen Toygar, Adnan Acan

A New Document Watermarking Algorithm Based on Hybrid
Multi-scale Ant Colony System 440
Shiyan Hu

An Image Retrieval System Based on Region Classification 449
Özge Can Özcanlı, Fatoş Yarman-Vural

Database Systems

Temporal Data Modeling and Integrity Constraints in Relational
Databases... 459
Abdullah Uz Tansel

Query Builder: A Natural Language Interface for Structured Databases .. 470
Jim Little, Michael de Ga, Tansel Özyer, Reda Alhajj

Situation-Aware Coordination in Multi-agent Filtering Framework 480
Sahin Albayrak, Dragan Milosevic

A Study on Answering a Data Mining Query Using a Materialized View . 493
Maciej Zakrzewicz, Mikolaj Morzy, Marek Wojciechowski

Efficient Methods for Database Storage and Retrieval Using
Space-Filling Curves.. 503
Srinivas Aluru, Fatih Erdogan Sevilgen

Modeling and Performance Evaluation

Modelling Mobility with PEPA Nets................................ 513
Jane Hillston, Marina Ribaudo

Modelling Role-Playing Games Using PEPA Nets 523
Stephen Gilmore, Leila Kloul, Davide Piazza

Fault-Tolerant and Scalable Communication Mechanism for Mobile Agents 533
JinHo Ahn

CSL Model Checking for the GreatSPN Tool 543
Davide D'Aprile, Susanna Donatelli, Jeremy Sproston

Performance and Dependability Analysis of Fault-Tolerant Memory
Mechanisms Using Stochastic Well-Formed Nets 553
Paolo Ballarini, Lorenzo Capra, Guiliana Franceschinis

UML Design and Software Performance Modeling 564
Salvatore Distefano, Daniele Paci, Antonio Puliafito, Marco Scarpa

Stubborn Sets for Priority Nets 574
Kimmo Varpaaniemi

Model-Driven Maintenance of QoS Characteristics in Heterogeneous
Networks 584
Andrea D'Ambrogio, Vittoria de Nitto Personé, Giuseppe Iazeolla

A Performance Study of Context Transfer Protocol for QoS Support..... 594
*Novella Bartolini, Paolo Campegiani, Emiliano Casalicchio,
Salvatore Tucci*

A Methodology for Deriving Per-Flow End-to-End Delay Bounds in
Sink-Tree DiffServ Domains with FIFO Multiplexing 604
Luciano Lenzini, Linda Martorini, Enzo Mingozzi, Giovanni Stea

Performance Analysis of a Predictive and Adaptive Algorithm in
Cluster-Based Network Servers with Resource Allocation.............. 615
Katja Gilly, Carlos Juiz, Ramon Puigjaner, Salvador Alcaraz

ARTÌS: A Parallel and Distributed Simulation Middleware for
Performance Evaluation 627
*Luciano Bononi, Michele Bracuto, Gabriele D'Angelo,
Lorenzo Donatiello*

Comparison of Web Server Architectures: A Measurement Study 638
Davide Pagnin, Marina Buzzi, Marco Conti, Enrico Gregori

Modelling Dynamic Web Content 648
Antonio Barili, Maria Carla Calzarossa, Daniele Tessera

Behavioral Intrusion Detection 657
Stefano Zanero

Biological Metaphors for Agent Behavior 667
Erol Gelenbe, Varol Kaptan, Yu Wang

The Effects of Web Logs and the Semantic Web on Autonomous Web
Agents 676
*Michael P. Evans, Richard Newman, Timothy A. Millea,
Timothy Putnam, Andrew Walker*

Social Network of Co-occurrence in News Articles 688
Arzucan Özgür, Haluk Bingol

Using CORBA to Enhance HLA Interoperability in Distributed and
Web-Based Simulation 696
Andrea D'Ambrogio, Daniele Gianni

Designing and Enacting Simulations Using Distributed Components 706
Alberto Coen-Porisini, Ignazio Gallo, Antonella Zanzi

Semi-formal and Formal Models Applied to Flexible Manufacturing
Systems 718
Andrea Matta, Carlo A. Furia, Matteo Rossi

New Computer Model of a Dipolar System with Hexagonal Geometry
in Presence of an External Electric Field 729
*Rafaella Turri, M. Buscaglia, Giovanni Danese, Ivo De Lotto,
Francesco Leporati*

Natural Language Processing

A Linguistically Motivated Information Retrieval System for Turkish 741
F. Canan Pembe, Ahmet Celal Cem Say

SmartReader: An NLP-Based Interactive Reading Application for
Language Learning 751
Kemal Oflazer, Meryem Pınar Dönmez

A Preprocessor for Turkish Text Analysis 761
Kemal Oflazer, Özlem Çetinoğlu, Orhan Bilgin, Bilge Say

The Effect of Part-of-Speech Tagging on IR Performance for Turkish 771
B. Taner Dinçer, Bahar Karaoğlan

Parallel and Distributed Computing

A New Pareto-Based Algorithm for Multi-objective Graph Partitioning .. 779
Raul Baños, Concolación Gil, M.G. Montoya, Julio Ortega

Parkway 2.0: A Parallel Multilevel Hypergraph Partitioning Tool........ 789
Aleksander Trifunovic, William J. Knottenbelt

Data-Parallel Web Crawling Models 801
Berkanat Barla Cambazoglu, Ata Turk, Cevdet Aykanat

Parallel Implementation of the Wave-Equation Finite-Difference
Time-Domain Method Using the Message Passing Interface............. 810
Omar Ramadan, Oyku Akaydin, Muhammed Salamah, Abdullah Y. Oztoprak

A Parallel Genetic Algorithm/Heuristic Based Hybrid Technique for
Routing and Wavelength Assignment in WDM Networks 819
A. Cagatay Talay

Static Mapping Heuristics for Tasks with Hard Deadlines in Real-Time
Heterogeneous Systems 827
Kavitha S. Golconda, Atakan Doğan, Füsun Özgüner

An Advanced Server Ranking Algorithm for Distributed Retrieval
Systems on the Internet... 837
Byurhan Hyusein, Joe Carthy

Real-Time Control Applications

Energy-Aware Strategies in Real-Time Systems for Autonomous Robots . 845
Giorgio Buttazzo, Mauro Marinoni, Giacomo Guidi

Multirate Feedback Control Using the TINYREALTIME Kernel.......... 855
Dan Henriksson, Anton Cervin

An Educational Open Source Real-Time Kernel for Small Embedded
Control Systems 866
Michele Cirinei, Antonio Mancina, Davide Cantini, Paolo Gai, Luigi Palopoli

Coordinating Distributed Autonomous Agents with a Real-Time
Database: The CAMBADA Project 876
Luis Almeida, Frederico Santos, Tullio Facchinetti, Paulo Pedreiras, Valter Silva, L. Seabra Lopes

Software Engineering and Programming Systems

A Static Approach to Automated Test Data Generation in the Presence of Pointers 887
Insang Chung

A Use-Case Based Component Identification Approach for Migrating Legacy Code into Distributed Environment 897
Hyeon Soo Kim, Heung Seok Chae, Chul Hong Kim

Software Testing via Model Checking 907
Fevzi Belli, Barış Güldalı

Mutation-Like Oriented Diversity for Dependability Improvement: A Distributed System Case Study 917
Daniel O. Bortolas, Avelino F. Zorzo, Eduardo A. Bezerra, Flavio M. de Oliveira

JAWIRO: Enhancing Java with Roles 927
Yunus Emre Selçuk, Nadia Erdoğan

A Survey of Public-Key Cryptography on J2ME-Enabled Mobile Devices 935
Stefan Tillich, Johann Großschädl

Thread-Sensitive Points-to Analysis for Multithreaded Java Programs ... 945
Byeong-Mo Chang, Jong-Deok Choi

Theory of Computing

Correctness Requirements for Multiagent Commitment Protocols 955
Pınar Yolum

Generating Equiprobable Superpositions of Arbitrary Sets for a New Generalization of the Deutsch-Jozsa Algorithm 966
Elton Ballhysa, Ahmet Celal Cem Say

Proof of the Basic Theorem on Concept Lattices in Isabelle/HOL 976
Barış Sertkaya, Halit Oğuztüzün

System BV without the Equalities for Unit 986
Ozan Kahramanoğulları

Comparison of Different Variable and Value Order Strategies for the Optimum Solution of a Single Machine Scheduling Problem with Sequence-Dependent Setups 996
Seyda Topaloglu, Irem Ozkarahan

Author Index 1007

An Approach to Quality of Service

Erol Gelenbe

Dennis Gabor Chair, Intelligent Systems and Networks
Department of Electrical and Electronic Engineering
Imperial College, London, SW7 2BT, UK
e.gelenbe@imperial.ac.uk

Abstract. Network Quality of Service (QoS) criteria of interest include conventional metrics such as throughput, delay, loss, and jitter, as well as new QoS criteria based on power utilization, reliability and security. In this paper we suggest a theoretical framework for the characterization and comparison of adaptive routing algorithms which use QoS as the criterion to select between different paths that connections may take from sources to destinations. Our objective is not to analyze QoS, but rather to provide routing rules which can improve QoS. We define a QoS metric as a non-negative random variable associated with network paths which satisfies a sub-additivity condition along each path. Rather than a quantity to be minimised (such as packet loss or delay), our QoS metrics are quantities that should be maximised (such as the inverse of packet loss or delay), similar in spirit to utility functions. We define the QoS of a path, under some routing policy, as the expected value of a non-decreasing measurable function of the QoS metric. We discuss *sensitive* and *insensitive* QoS metrics, the latter being dependent on the routing policy which is used. We describe routing policies simply as probabilistic choices among all possible paths from some source to some given destination. *Sensible* routing policies are then introduced: they take decisions based simply on the QoS of each available path. We prove that the routing probability of a sensible policy can always be uniquely obtained. A hierarchy of m–sensible probabilistic routing policies is then introduced and we provide conditions under which an $(m+1)$–sensible policy provides better QoS on the average than an m–sensible policy.

1 Introduction

Quality of Service (QoS) has now become a central issue in network design, and there is a vast and significant literature on the problem of *estimating certain specific quality of service parameters* (e.g., loss or delay) for *given traffic characteristics* and a given network topology [2,13]. Typically such work has considered single buffer models (finite or infinite), or models of cascaded nodes with or without interfering traffic. There has also been much work on schemes for obtaining better QoS through routing [11,12], on scheduling techniques in routers to achieve desired QoS objectives [9], as well as on the analysis of QoS resulting from the detailed behavior of protocols such as TCP/IP.

The mixed wired and wireless network topologies that are becoming common, including fixed and ad-hoc connections, create the need to rationally exploit dynamically variable routing as a function of network conditions, since the applications that use such networks have QoS requirements such as delay, loss or jitter, as well as reliability and low power utilization.

Motivated by our prior work on adaptive network routing algorithms [3]–[7], in this paper we investigate some basic mathematical problems concerning QoS driven routing. The aim of this work is not to analyze QoS, but rather to show that certain randomized routine policies can improve QoS.

We define QoS metrics as non-negative random variables associated with network paths which satisfy a sub-additivity condition along each path. We then describe routing policies simply as probabilistic choices among all possible paths from some source to some destination. Incremental routing policies are defined as those which can be derived from independent decisions along each sub-path. We define the QoS of a path, under some routing policy, as the expected value of a measurable function of the QoS metric. We discuss *sensitive* and *insensitive* QoS metrics, the latter being dependent on the routing policy which is used. *Sensible* routing policies are then introduced; these policies take decisions based simply on the QoS of each allowable path. Finally, a hierarchy of m–sensible probabilistic routing algorithms is introduced. The 0–sensible ruting policy is simply a random choice of routes with equal probability, while the 1–sensible policy uses the relative QoS for each alternate route to make select a path. An m–sensible policy uses the mt power of the QoS for each alternate path, rather than just the 1st power. Thus it simply uses the same information in a different manner. It is particularly interesting that we can prove that an $(m+1)$–sensible policy provides better resulting average QoS than an m–sensible policy, provided that the QoS metric is insensitive. We also prove that under certain sufficient conditions, the same result holds for sensitive QoS metrics.

1.1 Quality of Service (QoS) Metrics

A QoS metric relates to some specific *data unit*, the most obvious example being a *packet*. However more broadly, a data unit may be a significant sequence of packets which belong to the same connection. A QoS metric q can be illustrated by the following examples:

- q_D may be the inverse of the delay D experienced by a packet as it traverses some path in the network, or
- it may be the inverse of the binary variable $q_r = 1[\text{the-path-is-connected}]$, or
- $q_{LR} = (n/L)$ may be the number of packets sent n divided by the number of packets lost L for a sequence of packets, or
- q may be the inverse of the average jitter experienced by n successive packets:

$$q_J = \left[\frac{1}{n-1} \sum_{l=2}^{n} |(R_l - R_{l-1}) - (S_l - S_{l-1})| \right]^{-1},$$

where S_l is the date at which packet l was sent from the source, and R_l is the time at which packet l arrives to its destination, etc., or
- q may be one over the number of hops a packet has to traverse, or
- q may be one over the power expended by the network nodes to service and forward a packet as it travels through a path in the network, or
- q may be the inverse of the "effective delay" obtained by composing some of these values, such as

$$q = [(1 - q_{LR})q_D + q_{LR}(T_o + q_D)]^{-1} = [q_D + q_{LR}T_o]^{-1},$$

where T_o is the (large) timeout delay that triggers a packet's retransmission.

1.2 Routing Policies

Let the nodes in a network be denoted by a fine set of natural numbers $\{0, 1, 2, \ldots, N\}$.

Definition 1. *A path in the network starting at node i and ending at node v_d is denoted by $V_i = (i, \ldots, v_d)$. It is a sequence of nodes such that the first node is i, the last node is v_d, and no node in the sequence V_i appears more than once.*

We associate QoS metrics with paths in the network.

Let $FV_i(v_d) = \{V_i^1, V_i^2, \ldots, V_i^m\}$ be the set of all distinct, but not necessarily disjoint, paths from node i to node v_d in the network.

Definition 2. *A routing policy for source-destination pair (i, v_d) is a probability distribution $\pi^{FV_i(v_d)}$ on the set $FV_i(v_d)$, that selects path $V_i^j \in FV_i(v_d)$ with probability $\pi^{FV_i(v_d)}(V_i^j)$ for each individual data unit which is sent from node i to node v_d.*

For any $V_i^j \in FV_i(v_d)$, we may write $V_i^j = (i, \ldots, l, n, \ldots, v_d)$ as a concatenation of a prefix path and a suffix path: $V_i^j = P_i^p.S_n^s$ where $P_i^p = (i, \ldots, l)$, $S_n^s = (n, \ldots, v_d)$. Consider now the sets of paths from i to l, $FV_i(l)$ and from n to v_d, $FV_n(v_d)$. Whenever needed, Π will denote the routing policy for the network as a whole, i.e., the set of rules that assign unique paths for each data unit moving from any source node to any destination in the network. FV will denote the set of all paths from all possible source to destination nodes in the network.

2 QoS Metrics

Definition 3. *A QoS metric for path V is a random variable $q^{\Pi}(V)$ which takes values in $\{0, +\infty\}$, such that for $V = V_1.V_2$ (i.e., V is composed of path V_1 followed by path V_2)*

$$q^{\Pi}(V) \leq q^{\Pi}(V_1) + q^{\Pi}(V_2) \quad a.s.$$

Note that the requirement that the QoS metric be *sub-additive* covers many strictly additive metrics of interest such as packet or cell loss rates, delay, path length (number of hops), and power dissipation. Other metrics such as path reliability and available bandwidth are sub-additive, and are also covered by our definition. For a path V composed of two successive sub-paths $V = V_1.V_2$, the following are obviously sub-additive:

$$q_{available-BW}(V) = inf(q_{available-BW}(V_1), q_{available-BW}(V_2)) \text{ a.s.,}$$
$$\leq q_{available-BW}(V_1) + q_{available-BW}(V_2) \text{ a.s.,}$$
$$q_r(V) = [q_r(V_1) \text{ and } q_r(V_2)] \text{ a.s.,}$$
$$\leq q_r(V_1) + q_r(V_2) \text{ a.s.,}$$

where $q_r(.)$ is treated as a logical binary random value in the third equation, and as a numerical (binary) random value in the last equation.

2.1 QoS Metrics and QoS

In the sequel $q^{\pi^{FV_i(v_d)}}(V_i^j)$ will denote the *QoS metric q measured on path V_i^j*, when the policy $\pi^{FV_i(v_d)}$ is applied to data units travelling from node i to v_d using the set of paths $FV_i(v_d)$, $V_i^j \in FV_i(v_d)$.

We sometimes write q with a subscript, e.g., $q_D^{\pi^{FV_i(v_d)}}(V_i^j)$ or $q_{LR}^{\pi^{FV_i(v_d)}}(V_i^j)$ to indicate that it designates some specific metric such as packet delay or packet loss rate.

Definition 4. *Let u be a non-decreasing measurable function and q be a QoS metric. The QoS for data units sent on the path V_i^j using policy $\pi^{FV_i(v_d)}$, from source i to destination v_d along the set of paths $FV_i(v_d)$ is simply the expected value $E[u(q^{\pi^{FV_i(v_d)}}(V_i^j))]$, i.e., the expected value of a measurable function of a QoS metric.*

The reason for assuming that u is an increasing function (i.e., non-decreasing) is that we want to the QoS to reflect the trend of the QoS metric. If the QoS metric has a larger value reflecting improvement in the path, we want the QoS also to reflect this improvement, or at least not to reflect a degradation.

2.2 Sensitive QoS Metrics

The value for some path of a *routing sensitive*, or simply *sensitive* QoS metric q increases when the probability of directing traffic into that path increases; examples include path delay and path loss ratio. An example of an *insensitive* QoS metric is the number of hops along a path; the power dissipated per data unit on a path may also be insensitive. Even when the probability of sending traffic down a given path is zero, we may assume that the path can be infrequently tested to obtain the value of the QoS metric of that path, or the path QoS may be known via prior information (e.g., available bandwidth, number of hops, or the path's power dissipation).

Definition 5. *We will say that the QoS metric q is sensitive on the set $FV_i(v_d)$, if for any two routing policies $\pi^{FV_i(v_d)}$ and $\pi'^{FV_i(v_d)}$ and any path $V_i^j \in FV_i(v_d)$, for all $x > 0$:*

$$\{\pi^{FV_i(v_d)}(V_i^j) < \pi'^{FV_i(v_d)}(V_i^j)\} \Rightarrow$$
$$P[q^{\pi^{FV_i(v_d)}}(V_i^j) > x] > P[q^{\pi'^{FV_i(v_d)}}(V_i^j) > x].$$

Thus a QoS metric is sensitive if, when the load is increased on the path then the resulting QoS gets worse (is smaller). We say that q is *insensitive on the set* $FV_i(v_d)$ if for any path V_i^j and any two routing policies such that $\pi^{FV_i(v_d)}(V_i^j) \neq \pi'^{FV_i(v_d)}(V_i^j)$:

$$P[q^{\pi^{FV_i(v_d)}}(V_i^j) > x] = P[q^{\pi'^{FV_i(v_d)}}(V_i^j)], \text{ for all } x > 0.$$

3 Sensible Routing Policies

A *sensible routing policy* is one which:

- selects paths only using the *expected value of the QoS*, i.e., the expected value of a function u of the QoS metric q for each path, as the criterion for selecting the *probability* that a path is chosen;
- selects the path for a new data unit independently of the decision taken for the previous data unit.

The practical motivation for considering sensible routing policies is that (1) averages of QoS metrics, or of functions of QoS metrics, are typically easy to estimate, and (2) decisions which are successively independent for successive data units are easier to implement.

Definition 6. *Let u be a non-decreasing measurable function. A sensible routing policy (SRP) from node i to destination v_d based on the QoS metric q is a probability distribution $\pi^{FV_i(v_d)}$ on the set $FV_i(v_d)$ such that:*

$$\pi^{FV_i(v_d)}(V_i^j) =$$
$$f_i^j(E[u(q^{\pi^{FV_i(v_d)}}(V_i^1), u(q^{\pi^{FV_i(v_d)}}(V_i^2), \ldots, u(q^{\pi^{FV_i(v_d)}}(V^{|FV_i(v_d)|}))]), \quad (1)$$

for a function $f_i^j : R^m \to [0,1]$, for each $V_i^j \in FV_i(v_d)$, such that

–

$$\sum_{V_i^j \in FV_i(v_d)} \pi^{FV_i(v_d)}(V_i^j) = 1, \quad (2)$$

- *and for each path V_i^j, the function $f_i^j(y_1, \ldots, y_j, \ldots, y_{|FV_i(v_d)|})$ defined in (1) is strictly decreasing in its argument y_j, with*

$$\lim_{y_j \to +\infty} f_i^j(y_1, \ldots, y_{|FV_i(v_d)|}) = 0.$$

Remark 1. Thus a SRP is a routing policy which decides on routing based only on the QoS of each path, such that whenever the value of the QoS for any path increases then the probability of selecting that path decreases.

Example 1. A simple example of a SRP is the following:

$$\pi^{FV_i(v_d)}(V_i^j) = \frac{\frac{1}{E[q_D^{\pi^{FV_i(v_d)}}(V_i^j)]}}{\sum_{all\ s} \frac{1}{E[q_D^{\pi^{FV_i(v_d)}}(V_i^s)]}}, \qquad (3)$$

which says that packets are directed to the paths with a probability which is inversely proportional to the average delay.

In a sensible routing policy, the probability that a specific path is selected will depend on the QoS of that path, which in general depends on the policy itself, i.e., on the probability that the path is selected, unless the policy is insensitive. Thus there is the question of whether we are able to compute the routing probabilities. The following theorem provides sufficient conditions for being able to do this.

Theorem 1. *If $\pi^{FV_i(v_d)}$ is a sensible routing policy on $FV_i(v_d)$, then the solution to (1) exists and is unique for each path V_i^j.*

Proof. For any path V_i^j, consider the function $f_i^j(y_1,\ldots,y_j,\ldots,y_{|FV_i(v_d)|})$ of equation (1), which (strictly) decreases when y_j increases, and the path QoS $y_j(\pi^{FV_i(v_d)}) = E[u(q^{\pi^{FV_i(v_d)}}(V_i^j)]$. Since

$$\{\pi^{FV_i(v_d)}(V_i^j) > \pi'^{FV_i(v_d)}(V_i^j)\} \Rightarrow P[q^{\pi^{FV_i(v_d)}}(V_i^j) > x] \geq P[q^{\pi'^{FV_i(v_d)}}(V_i^j) > x]$$

for all $x > 0$, the path QoS is an increasing function (not strictly) $y_j(\pi)$ of its argument, the probability π, because of (1), and because u is an increasing function. Thus the solution of equation (1) for any V_i^j is obtained at the intersection of a non-negative, strictly decreasing function f_i^j of y_j which tends to zero, and an increasing non-negative function y_j of f_i^j. □

4 m–Sensible Routing Policies (m–SRP)

In this section we extend the concept of a sensible policy to more sophisticated usage of QoS to make routing decisions. We construct a hierarchy of m-sensible policies, where the 1–sensible policy is just the sensitive policy defined earlier, and the 0–sensible policy is a random uninformed choice between paths with equal probability. What is particularly interesting is that, just by increasing the value of m we are guaranteed to achieve better overall QoS, when the QoS metric is insensitive. The same result can be obtained in the sensitive case as well under certain sufficient conditions.

Definition 7. *For a natural number m, an m–sensible routing policy (m–SRP) from node i to destination v_d based on the QoS metric q is a probability distribution $\pi^{FV_i(v_d)}$ on the set $FV_i(v_d)$ such that*

$$\pi^{FV_i(v_d)}(V_i^j) = \frac{\frac{1}{E[(u(q^{\pi^{FV_i(v_d)}}(V_i^j))^m]}}{\sum_{all\ s} \frac{1}{E[u(q^{\pi^{FV_i(v_d)}}(V_i^s))^m]}}. \quad (4)$$

We will use the notation $\pi^{m-SRP[FV_i(v_d)]}$ to denote the fact that the policy π on the set of paths $FV_i(v_d)$ is m–sensible, and the corresponding QoS value will be denoted by $q^{\pi^{m-SRP[FV_i(v_d)]}}(V_i^s)$ for path V_i^j. Note that a 0–SRP is just a random choice among paths, with equal probability.

4.1 The m–Sensible Routing Theorem when the QoS Metric Is Insensitive

In this section we assume that q is insensitive on the set $FV_i(v_d)$, and consider m-SRP routing policies as defined in (4).

To simplify the notation, let us associate the index j with the path V_i^j and write

$$W_j(m) = E[u(q^{\pi^{m-SRP[FV_i(v_d)]}}(V_i^j))]. \quad (5)$$

When q is insensitive, we will simply write W_j. Using (4) and (5) we have

$$Q^{\pi^{m-SRP[VF_i]}} = \frac{\sum_{j=1}^n \frac{W_j}{W_j^m}}{\sum_{j=1}^n \frac{1}{W_j^m}}. \quad (6)$$

We first prove the following simple result.

Lemma 1. *For any $W_j \geq 0$, $W_k \geq 0$,*

$$\tfrac{1}{2}(W_j + W_k) \geq \frac{2}{\frac{1}{W_j} + \frac{1}{W_k}}$$

or

$$\frac{W_j}{W_k} + \frac{W_k}{W_j} \geq 2.$$

Proof. Since $(W_j - W_k)^2 \geq 0$, we have $(W_j^2 + W_k^2) \geq 2W_j W_k$, and therefore $(W_j + W_k)^2 \geq 4 W_j W_k$, or

$$\tfrac{1}{2}(W_j + W_k) \geq \frac{2}{\frac{1}{W_j} + \frac{1}{W_k}},$$

and therefore

$$(W_j + W_k)(\tfrac{1}{W_j} + \tfrac{1}{W_k}) \geq 4,$$

which can be written as

$$2 + (\tfrac{W_k}{W_j} + \tfrac{W_j}{W_k}) \geq 4,$$

thus completing the proof. □

We will call the following result the *m–SRP theorem* (*m*-sensible routing theorem) for insensitive metrics.

Theorem 2. *If q is insensitive on the set $FV_i(v_d)$, the policy $(m+1)$–SRP is better than m–SRP for $m \geq 1$, i.e.,*

$$Q^{\pi^{m-SRP[VF_i]}} \geq Q^{\pi^{(m+1)-SRP[VF_i]}}.$$

Proof. From Lemma 1, we have that for any $W_j \geq 0, W_k \geq 0$,

$$\frac{W_j}{W_k} + \frac{W_k}{W_j} \geq 2,$$

and multiplying both sides by $1/(W_j^m W_k^m)$ we obtain

$$\frac{1}{W_j^{m-1} W_k^{m+1}} + \frac{1}{W_j^{m+1} W_k^{m-1}} \geq \frac{2}{W_i^m W_j^m}.$$

Summing for $j, k = 1, \ldots, n$ and adding identical terms on both sides, we have

$$\sum_{j=1}^{n} \frac{1}{(W_j^m)^2} + \sum_{j,k=1; j \neq k}^{n} \{\frac{1}{W_j^{m-1} W_k^{m+1}} + \frac{1}{W_j^{m+1} W_k^{m-1}}\} \geq$$
$$\sum_{j=1}^{n} \frac{1}{(W_j^m)^2} + \sum_{j,k=1; j \neq k}^{n} \frac{2}{W_j^m W_k^m},$$

or

$$(\sum_{j=1}^{n} \frac{1}{W_j^{m-1}})(\sum_{j=1}^{n} \frac{1}{W_j^{m+1}}) \geq (\sum_{j=1}^{n} \frac{1}{W_j^m})^2.$$

This can be written as

$$\frac{\sum_{j=1}^{n} \frac{1}{W_j^{m-1}}}{\sum_{j=1}^{n} \frac{1}{W_j^m}} \geq \frac{\sum_{j=1}^{n} \frac{1}{W_j^m}}{\sum_{j=1}^{n} \frac{1}{W_j^{m+1}}},$$

or in the final form

$$\frac{\sum_{j=1}^{n} \frac{W_j}{W_j^m}}{\sum_{j=1}^{n} \frac{1}{W_j^m}} \geq \frac{\sum_{j=1}^{n} \frac{W_j}{W_j^{m+1}}}{\sum_{j=1}^{n} \frac{1}{W_j^{m+1}}},$$

which completes the proof. □

It is obvious that for an *insensitive* QoS metric, selecting m to be very large is good, since this will lead to choosing the path with the best QoS if such a path exists. We summarize this point in the following remark. However, if the QoS metric is *sensitive* then the matter is quite different, as will be discussed in the next section.

Remark 2. Suppose that q is *insensitive* on the set $FV_i(v_d)$, and that path V_i^1 is best in the following sense:

$$W_1 < W_2, \ldots, W_n.$$

Then $\lim_{m \to \infty} Q^{\pi^{m-SRP[VF_i]}} = W_1$.

Proof. Using

$$Q^{\pi^{m-SRP[VF_i]}} = \frac{\sum_{j=1}^{n} \frac{W_j}{W_j^m}}{\sum_{j=1}^{n} \frac{1}{W_j^m}} \qquad (7)$$

$$= \frac{W_1 + \sum_{j\neq 1}^{n} W_j (\frac{W_1}{W_j})^m}{1 + \sum_{j\neq 1} (\frac{W_1}{W_j})^m} \qquad (8)$$

yields the result when we take $m \to \infty$. □

4.2 The Sensible Routing Theorem for Sensitive QoS Metrics

When the QoS metric is sensitive, the QoS varies with the load on the paths. This is of course the most common situation in practice, e.g., for QoS metrics such as delay, packet or cell loss, etc. Thus we cannot generalize Theorem 2 to the case where the QoS metric is sensitive. However we can provide necessary and sufficient conditions which will yield a similar result.

Theorem 3. *If q is sensitive on the set $FV_i(v_d)$, the policy $(m+1)$–SRP is better than m–SRP for $m \geq 0$:*

$$Q^{\pi^{m-SRP[VF_i]}} \geq Q^{\pi^{(m+1)-SRP[VF_i]}},$$

provided that the following condition holds:

$$[\sum_{j=1}^{n} \frac{1}{(W_j(m+1))^{m-1}} - \sum_{j=1}^{n} \frac{1}{(W_j(m))^{m-1}}] \sum_{j=1}^{n} \frac{1}{(W_j(m+1))^{m+1}}$$
$$\leq [\sum_{j=1}^{n} \frac{1}{(W_j(m+1))^{m}} - \sum_{j=1}^{n} \frac{1}{(W_j(m))^{m}}] \sum_{j=1}^{n} \frac{1}{(W_j(m+1))^{m}}.$$

5 Conclusions

In this paper we suggest a theory of routing based on QoS. We have distinguished between QoS metrics, and QoS. Variable and adaptive routing have again become of interest in networking because of the increasing importance of mobile ad-hoc networks. In this paper we have developed a framework for the study of adaptive routing algorithms which use the expected QoS to select paths to their destination. Our objective is not to analyze QoS, but rather to design randomized routing policies which can improve QoS. We define QoS metrics as non-negative random variables associated with network paths that satisfy a sub-additivity condition along each path. We define the QoS of a path as the expected value of a non-decreasing measurable function of the QoS metric. We discuss *sensitive* and *insensitive* QoS metrics, the latter being dependent on the routing policy which is used. An example of an insensitive QoS metric is the number of hops on a path, since it will not change with the fact that this particular path is selected by the route selection. We describe routing policies as probabilistic choices among all possible paths from some source to some given destination. *Sensible* routing policies are then introduced: they take decisions based simply on the QoS of each possible path. Sensible policies, which make decisions based on the QoS of the paths, are introduced. We prove that the routing probability of a sensible policy can always be uniquely determined. A hierarchy of m-sensible probabilistic routing policies is then introduced. A 0-sensible policy is simply a random choice of routes with equal probability, while a 1-sensible policy selects a path with a probability which is inversely proportional to the (expected) QoS of the path. We prove that an $(m+1)$-sensible policy provides better QoS on the average than an m-sensible policy, if the QoS metric is insensitive. We also show that under certain conditions, the same result also holds for sensitive QoS metrics.

References

1. Chaintreau, A., Baccelli, F., Diot, C.: Impact of TCP-Like Congestion Control on the Throughput of Multicast Groups. IEEE/ACM Transactions on Networking **10** (2002) 500–512
2. Gelenbe, E., Mang, X., Feng, Y.: Diffusion Cell Loss Estimates for ATM with Multiclass Bursty Traffic. Computer Systems–Science and Engineering: Special Issue on ATM Networks **11** (1996) 325–334
3. Gelenbe, E., Xu, Z., Seref, E.: Cognitive Packet Networks. In: Proceedings of the 11th IEEE International Conference on Tools for Artificial Intelligence (ICTAI'99), Chicago, Illinois. IEEE Computer (1999) 47-54
4. Gelenbe, E., Lent, R., Xu, Z.: Towards Networks with Cognitive Packets. In: Proceedings of the 8th International Symposium on Modeling, Analysis, and Simulation of Computer and Telecommunication Systems (MASCOTS 2000), Keynote Paper, San Francisco, California. IEEE Computer (2000) 3–12
5. Gelenbe, E., Lent, R., Xu, Z.: Measurement and Performance of Cognitive Packet Networks. Journal of Computer Networks **37** (2001) 691–701
6. Gelenbe, E., Lent, R.: Mobile Ad-Hoc Cognitive Packet Networks. In: Proceedings of the 2nd IEEE Workshop on Applications and Services in Wireless Networks (ASWN 2002), Paris, France. (2002)
7. Gelenbe, E., Lent, R., Montuori, A., Xu, Z.: Cognitive Packet Networks: QoS and Performance. In: Proceedings of the 10th International Symposium on Modeling, Analysis, and Simulation of Computer and Telecommunication Systems (MASCOTS 2002), Keynote Paper, Forth Worth, Texas. IEEE Computer (2002) 3–12
8. Guérin, R., Ahmadi, H., Nagshineh, M.: Equivalent Capacity and Its Application to Bandwidth Allocation in High Speed Networks. IEEE Journal on Selected Areas in Communications **9** (1991) 968–981
9. Hao, F., Zegura, E.W., Ammar, M.H.: QoS Routing for Anycast Communications: Motivation and an Architecture for Diffserv Networks. IEEE Communications Magazine **40** (2002) 48–56
10. Kodialam, M., Lakshman, T.V.: Restorable Quality of Service Routing. IEEE Communications Magazine **40** (2002) 72–81
11. Lin, Y.-D., Hsu, N.-B., Hwang, R.-H.: QoS Routing Granularity in MPLS Networks. IEEE Communications Magazine **40** (2002) 58–65
12. Nelakuditi, S., Zhang, Z.-L.: A Localized Adaptive Proportioning Approach to QoS Routing Granularity. IEEE Communications Magazine **40** (2002) 66–71
13. Srinivasan, V., Ghanwani, A., Gelenbe, E.: Block Cell Loss Reduction in ATM Systems. Computer Communications **19** (1996) 1077-1091

A New Classifier Based on Attribute Weighted Artificial Immune System (AWAIS)

Seral Şahan[1], Halife Kodaz[2], Salih Güneş[1], and Kemal Polat[1]

[1] Selcuk University, Eng.-Arch. Fac. Electrical & Electronics Eng.
42031, Konya, Turkey
{seral,sgunes,kpolat}@selcuk.edu.tr

[2] Selcuk University, Eng.-Arch. Fac. Computer Eng.
42031, Konya, Turkey
hkodaz@selcuk.edu.trs

Abstract. 'Curse of Dimensionality' problem in shape-space representation which is used in many network-based Artificial Immune Systems (AISs) affects classification performance at a high degree. In this paper, to increase classification accuracy, it is aimed to minimize the effect of this problem by developing an Attribute Weighted Artificial Immune System (AWAIS). To evaluate the performance of proposed system, aiNet, an algorithm that have a considerably important place among network-based AIS algorithms, was used for comparison with our developed algorithm. Two artificial data sets used in aiNet, Two-spirals data set and Chainlink data set were applied in the performance analyses, which led the results of classification performance by means of represented network units to be higher than aiNet. Furthermore, to evaluate performance of the algorithm in a real world application, wine data set that taken from UCI Machine Learning Repository is used. For the artificial data sets, proposed system reached 100% classification accuracy with only a few numbers of network units and for the real world data set, wine data set, the algorithm obtained 98.23% classification accuracy which is very satisfying result if it is considered that the maximum classification accuracy obtained with other systems is 98.9%.

1 Introduction

A new artificial intelligence area named as Artificial Immune Systems (AISs) is going forward gradually. There are many AIS algorithms in which recognition and learning mechanisms of immune system were modeled. As a representation method of immune system cells, shape-space approach is used in many of the AIS classification algorithms. Shape-space model, which was proposed by Perelson and Oster in 1979 [1], is used as a representation mechanism modeling the interactions between two cells in the immune system.

'Curse of Dimensionality' is among the main problems of classification systems in which distance criterion is used as a metric [2,3]. One attribute value in shape space can cause two data in the same class to be distant from each other and therefore to be recognized and classified by different system units. In this paper, it was aimed to reach higher classification accuracy by assigning weights to important attributes in classification. This was done with some modifications to affinity measures of AISs and then a new system named AWAIS (Attribute Weighted Artificial Immune System) has come into existence.

AiNet, one of the algorithms in which shape-space representation is used, is both a network-based and population-based AIS algorithm to be used in data mining and classification applications [4]. For effects of novelties obtained by AWAIS on classification performance to be analyzed, the artificial data sets used by aiNet were applied to AWAIS and resulted system performance was evaluated comparatively with aiNet. According to the results of performance analyses, it was observed that AWAIS showed a higher performance with respect to the minimum number of system units at which classification can be done at a high accuracy and less processing time of the algorithm. Besides of these comparison data sets, a real world application of the algorithm is performed with wine data set which consists of the data taken from the results of a chemical analysis of wines grown in the same region in Italy but derived from three different cultivars [5]. Performance results for this application showed considerably satisfying classification accuracy, 98.23%, with respect to the other classifiers.

This paper is organized as follows. In Section 2, natural and artificial immune systems are introduced and shape-space representation is explained. Section 3 is allocated for the comparison algorithm, aiNet, and its deficiencies. The AWAIS algorithm is proposed in Section 4. Section 5 contains the experimental results and analyses. In Section 6, experimental results are discussed and future works are emphasized.

2 Natural and Artificial Immune System

The natural immune system is a distributed novel-pattern detection system with several functional components positioned in strategic locations throughout the body [6]. Immune system regulates defense mechanism of the body by means of innate and adaptive immune responses. Between these, adaptive immune response is much more important for us because it contains metaphors like recognition, memory acquisition, diversity, and self-regulation. The main architects of adaptive immune response are Lymphocytes, which divide into two classes as T and B Lymphocytes (cells), each having its own function. Especially B cells have a great importance because of their secreted antibodies (Abs) that takes very critical roles in adaptive immune response. For detailed information about immune system refer to [7].

Artificial Immune Systems emerged in the 1990s as a new computational research area. Artificial Immune Systems link several emerging computational fields inspired by biological behavior such as Artificial Neural Networks and Artificial Life [8].

In the studies conducted in the field of AIS, B cell modeling is the most encountered representation type. Different representation methods have been proposed in that modeling. Among these, shape-space representation is the most commonly used one [1].

The shape-space model (S) aims at quantitatively describing the interactions among antigens (Ags), the foreign elements that enter the body like microbe, etc., and antibodies (***Ag-Ab***). The set of features that characterize a molecule is called its *generalized shape*. The ***Ag-Ab*** representation (binary or real-valued) determines a distance measure to be used to calculate the degree of interaction between these molecules. Mathematically, the generalized shape of a molecule (*m*), either an antibody or an antigen, can be represented by a set of coordinates $m = <m_1, m_2,...m_L>$, which can be regarded as a point in an *L*-dimensional real-valued shape-space ($m \in S^L$). In this work, we used real strings to represent the molecules. Antigens and antibodies were considered of same length *L*. The length and cell representation depends upon the problem [6].

3 AiNet and Its Deficiencies

In the aiNet algorithm proposed by De Castro and Von Zuben [4,9], antibodies represent the internal image of the input space. Antibodies, the system units, are named as *'nodes'* which have connections with some other nodes. In connected node pairs called *'edges'*, connection weights define the strength of the interaction between the nodes in that edge.

aiNet was developed as a data mining approach and the responsibility of the algorithm was to represent input data with less memory units carrying the same class distribution with original data before the classification. So, for the algorithm to be used as a classification system alone, some class-analysis methods must be used after training to determine the system units of each class. In the test phase, the class of memory unit with smallest distance to presented data is given as the class of this data. So, determination of system units is sensitive to 'curse of dimensionality' problem due to the distance criteria.

The main evident deficiencies of aiNet as emphasized by the authors in [4] are the high number of parameters determined by the user and the processing overhead of each iteration. Besides, shape-space representation makes some class-analysis methods like *MST, Dendogram* necessary if the algorithm is to be used for classification.

4 AWAIS (Attribute Weighted Artificial Immune System)

As mentioned before, most of network-based AIS algorithms use shape-space representation and 'curse of dimensionality' problem inevitably appeared in turn affects the system performance [4,10,11]. The AWAIS algorithm proposed for minimizing the effect of this problem is a supervised Artificial Immune System based on attribute weighted distance criteria. The supervision in the algorithm shows itself while determining the weights of attributes and during the process of developing memory cells in the training by taking the class of the input data into account. AWAIS is a two-level classification system in which attribute weights of each class are formed in one level and a training procedure with these weights takes place at the other.

4.1 Attribute Weighting

In most real valued shape-space representations, the distance between two points is calculated by the Euclidean distance criteria (Eq. (1)):

$$D = \sqrt{\sum_{i=1}^{L} (ab_i - ag_i)^2}. \qquad (1)$$

Where **ab** and **ag** are the two points in the shape-space represented by a vector respectively and L is the length of these vectors. According to this formula, all of the attributes have same effect in determining distance. However, there are such data sets that some attributes of them have no effect on the class of data while some other attributes are more important in determining class. So, if it is assigned higher weights to the attributes that are more important in determining one class and if these weights are used in calculation of distance, it can be prevented to make a misclassification of the two distant data according to the Euclidean norm in the same class. Starting from this point, the proposed attribute weighting depends on the following base: if one attribute doesn't changing very much among the data of one class, this attribute is one of the characteristic attributes of related class and it must have a higher weight than others.

The applied attribute weighting procedure in the AWAIS is as follows:
(1) Normalization of each attribute in data set between 0-1.
(2) Determine the antigens of each class→ Ag_class_j ($j:1,....n$, $n:$ number of class)
(3) For each class do:
   For $Ag\_class_{(LxNc)}$ to be a matrix that involves the antigens of that class;
   (L: attribute num., Nc: ag num. of that class);
   (3.1) For i^{th} attribute do:($i:1,...,L$)
      Evaluate standard deviation of ith attribute with Eq. (2):

$$std\_dev_i = \sqrt{\frac{1}{Nc}\sum_{k=1}^{Nc}(Ag_{k,i} - mean(Ag_i))^2}. \qquad (2)$$

Here $Ag_{k,i}$ is the ith attribute of kth Ag in j^{th} class; $mean(Ag_i)$ is the mean of ith attribute of all Ags in j^{th} class.
Calculate the weights as follows:

$$w_{j,i} = 1/std\_dev_i, (i=1,...L; j=1,...n) \qquad (3)$$

(3.2) normalize the weights of jth class.

The calculated w_{nxL} matrix is a normalized weight matrix involving the weights of each attribute for each class and this matrix is used in distance calculations of the training algorithm of AWAIS.

Here, in the attribute weighting procedure, a means of normalization of attributes for each class by standard deviation is performed. By doing so, each class has its own set of attribute weights.

4.2 AWAIS Training Algorithm

The originality of AWAIS lies in formation of memory Antibodies through using the attribute weights and in knowing the classes of formed memory Antibodies.
The training procedure of the algorithm conducts the following steps:
(1) For each Ag_i do :($i: 1,...N$)
   (1.1) Determine the class of Ag_i. Call memory Abs of that class and calculate the distance between Ag_i and these memory Abs with Eq. (4):

$$D = \sqrt{\sum_{k=1}^{L} w_{j,k} \left(Ab_{j,k} - Ag_{i,k} \right)^2}. \qquad (4)$$

Here $Ab_{i,k}$ and $Ag_{i,k}$ are the kth attribute of Ab_j and Ag_i respectively; $w_{j,k}$ is the weight of kth attribute that belongs to the class of Ab_j.
   (1.2) If the minimum distance among the calculated distances above is less than a threshold value named as suppression value ($supp$) then return to step 1.
   (1.3) Form a memory Ab for Ag_i:
      At each iteration do:
      (1.3.1) Make a random Ab population with $Ab=[Ab\_mem ; Ab\_rand]$ and calculate the distances of these Abs to Ag_i.
      (1.3.2) Select m nearest Abs to Ag_i; clon and mutate these Abs (Ab_mutate).
      (1.3.3) Keep the m nearest Abs in the Ab_mutate population to Ag_i as Ab_mem temporary memory population.
      (1.3.4) Define the nearest Ab to Ag_i as Ab_cand, candidate memory Ab for Ag_i and stop iterative process if the distance of Ab_cand to Ag_i is less that a threshold value named as stopping criterion (sc).
      (1.3.5) Concatenate Ab_cand as a new memory Ab to memory matrix of the class of Ag_i.
   (1.4) Stop training.

The mutation mechanism in the algorithm which is used in many AIS algorithms and named as *hypermutation* is performed proportional to distance between two cells (Eq. (5)):

$$Ab_{j,k}' = Ab_{j,k} \pm D_{j,i} * (Ab_{j,k}) \qquad (5)$$

Here $Ab_{j,k}'$ is the new value and $Ab_{j,k}$ is the old value of kth attribute of jth Ab. $D_{j,i}$ stands for the distance between Ag_i and Ab_j.

The used affinity measure is no more a pure Euclidean Distance and the attribute weights are used in distance criteria. As another important point, the classes of memory Abs in the AWAIS after training are known with the aid of a labeling vector that contains the information about which memory Abs belong to which class. This makes us to get rid of the problem of using extra class-analysis methods after training unlike aiNet.

5 AWAIS Performance Analysis

The classification performance of AWAIS was analyzed in three data sets. Among these, two data sets were selected to compare the proposed algorithm with an other AIS, aiNet, that is in the same category with AWAIS. These selected artificial data sets are Two-spirals and Chainlink data sets which were used in the performance analysis of aiNet [4]. In the analyses, classification accuracy and memory cell number are given with respect to the suppression parameter (*supp* or *s*) in tabulated and graphical forms. Also, compression rates are determined according to the memory cell number (*m*) that represents the input data set and compared with the compression rates reached by the aiNet algorithm for same data sets. Other than these data sets, one more application with wine data set was performed to see the real world performance of the algorithm.

5.1 Two-Spirals Data Set

This data set consists of 190 data [12]. 130 of these were used for training and the remaining 60 were used as test set. The data in the set contains two classes. The classification performance of AWAIS for this set is given in Table 1. The classification accuracy and memory cell number with respect to the *supp* parameter in test set is given in Fig. 1(a) and Fig. 1(b) respectively.

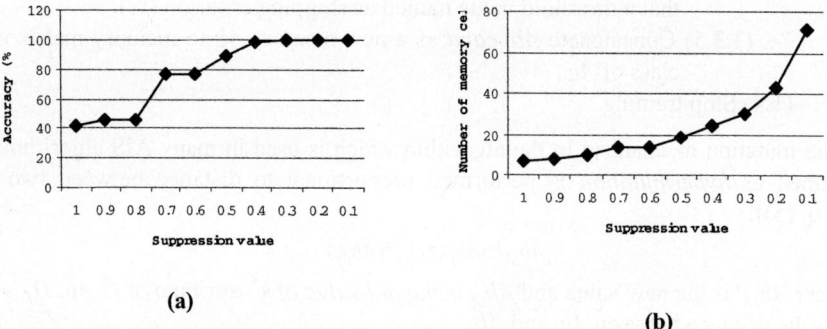

(a)

(b)

Fig. 1. Performance analysis of AWAIS for test data set of Two-spirals data set: (a) Classification accuracy versus suppression value, (b) Number of memory cell versus suppression value

In the Fig. 3(a), Two-spirals data set and memory cells that give the best classification performance are presented.

Table 1. Performance analysis of AWAIS for Two-Spirals data set

Suppression Value(s)	Number of Memory Cell(m)	Compression Rate(%)	Accuracy (%)
1	7	96.31	42
0.8	10	94.73	45
0.6	14	92.63	77
0.4	24	87.36	98
0.36	27	85.78	100
0.2	43	77.36	100

5.2 Chainlink Data Set

1000 data are used in this data set [12]. 500 of these data were allocated for training with using other 500 data for testing. Again, two classes exist in the set. The performance results of AWAIS for Chainlink data set are given in Table 2. The Chainlink data set and memory cells giving the best classification accuracy are shown in Fig. 2. The classification accuracy and memory cell number versus suppression value are given in graphical form in Fig. 3(b) for the test set.

Table 2. Performance of AWAIS analysis for Chainlink data set

Suppression Value (s)	Number of Memory Cell (m)	Compression Rate (%)	Accuracy (%)
1	2	99.8	86.2
0.8	4	99.6	100
0.6	6	99.4	100
0.4	9	99.1	100
0.2	30	97.0	100

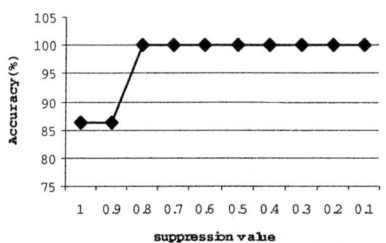
(a)

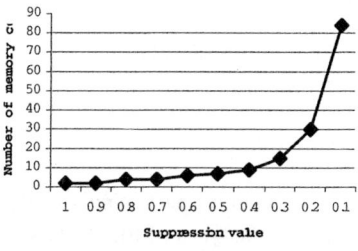
(b)

Fig. 2. Performance analysis of AWAIS for test data set of Chainlink data set: (a) Classification accuracy versus suppression value, (b) Number of memory cell versus suppression value

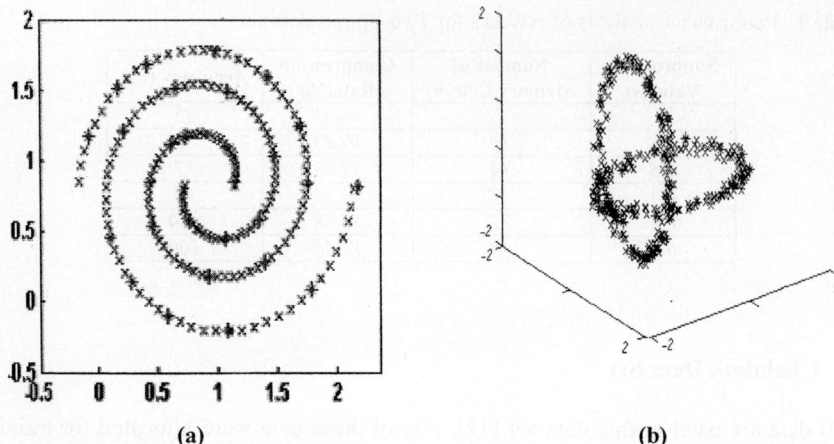

Fig. 3. (a)Two-spirals data set and memory cells (b) Chainlink data set and memory cells

According to the experimental results, it is hopeful for us to see the system reached 100% classification accuracy with remarkable small number of network units. When it comes to the processing time of the system, it was able to form memory units in 4 *sec* for Two-spirals and 11 *sec* for Chainlink data set in Matlab 6.5 programming language conducted on Intel Pentium II processor computer. This is also an advantage of the system with regard to the aiNet's processing time 14 *sec* and 23 *sec* respectively for the same problems conducted on the same computer.

It is seen in Table 3 that the compression rates of aiNet and AWAIS for Two-spirals and Chainlink data set. As can be seen from the Table, AWAIS can classify the data sets in the same accuracy with aiNet by less system units.

Table 3. The Comparison for compression rates of aiNet and AWAIS algorithms for Chainlink and Two-spirals data sets

Data Set	aiNet (%)	AWAIS(%)
Chainlink	94.5 *((1000-55)/1000)*	**99.6** *((1000-4)/1000)*
Two-spirals	74.21 *((190-49)/190)*	**85.78** *((190-27)/190)*

5.3 Wine Data Set

In the experimental part of this study, the artificial data sets above were used for the performance analyses of the proposed algorithm as well as for comparison with aiNet. To analyze the behavior of AWAIS in a real world problem, wine data set was also used in the experiments. This data set consists of the results of a chemical analysis of wines grown in the same region in Italy but derived from three different cultivars [5]. The analysis determined the quantities of 13 constituents found in each of the three types of wines. This data set was applied to AWAIS with 10-fold cross validation (10 CV) method and the classification accuracies of the algorithm were analyzed for different values of supp parameter. The maximum classification accuracy reached by AWAIS was 98.23% for 0.1 value of supp parameter.

Various methods were also used for this classification problem and they obtained the following classification accuracies shown in Table 4 with the result that reached by AWAIS [13]. All of these methods used 10 CV scheme as AWAIS. As can be seen from the table, the classification accuracy of AWAIS is comparable with other classification methods for this problem and this result may be improved by some modifications on the algorithm resulting in a higher accuracy than all of the methods.

Table 4. Classification accuracies obtained by different methods for wine data set with AWAIS performance result

Method:	Classification Accuracy (%):
kNN, Manhattan, auto k=1-10	98.9±2.3
10 CV SSV, opt prune	98.3±2.7
AWAIS	**98.2±3.0**
kNN, Euclidean, k=1	97.8±2.8
IncNet, 10CV, def, bicentral	97.2±2.9
FSM a=.99, def	96.1±3.7
kNN, Euclidean, k=1	95.5±4.4
10 CV SSV, opt node, BFS	92.8±3.7
10 CV SSV, opt node, BS	91.6±6.5
10 CV SSV, opt prune, BFS	90.4±6.1

6 Conclusions

Shape-space representation, especially used in many network-based AIS algorithms is a means of representing immune system units as system units and this representation scheme also defines the interactions of the system units with the environment by means of distance criteria. The 'curse of dimensionality' problem appeared in the distance-based classification systems affects the classification performance in negative manner especially for nonlinear data sets. In this paper, by proposing an Attribute Weighted Artificial Immune System (AWAIS), this problem of shape-space representation was tried to be minimized. The key concepts and mechanisms in the AWAIS are; assigning weights to attributes proportional to their importance in determining classes, usage of these weights in calculations of distance measures between the system units and input data, clonal selection and hypermutation mechanism similar to those that were used in other AIS algorithms. Two artificial data sets, Chainlink and Two-spiral data sets and one real world data set, wine data set were used in the performance analyses of AWAIS. The obtained results for artificial data sets were compared with other important AIS, aiNet. With regard to the performance results both in terms of classification accuracy and the number of resulted system units, the proposed system performs classification at 100% accuracy with less system units than aiNet. To analyze AWAIS classification accuracy for a real world problem, another data set, wine data set was used for   classification and 98.23% classification accuracy was reached for optimum parameter values. With regard to the classification systems used for the same data, this result is very satisfactory for now because it gives us a support that we are on correct way to develop supervised artificial immune networks based on shape-space representation with high accuracies.

Due to the fact that the study aims at elimination of problems caused by shape-space representation, the training procedure have similarities with aiNet in respect to the main metaphors of the immune system inspired from. One of the future works related to this system is improving the attribute weighting procedure such that the algorithm performs very well in a great variety of data sets. Besides, the attribute weighting scheme can be applied other AIS algorithms that use shape-space representation and performance of these algorithms can be improved by this way. For one more thing, attribute weighting itself can be done by AISs, too, by adding some adaptation. Nevertheless, a new branch of classification field is improving day by day toward high performance classification systems with Artificial Immune Systems.

References

1. Perelson, A.S., Oster, G.F.: Theoretical Studies of Clonal Selection: Minimal Antibody Repertoire Size and Reliabilty of Self-Nonself Discrimination. Journal of Theoretical Biology **81** (1979) 645–670
2. Mitchell, T.M.: Machine Learning. The McGraw-Hill Companies Press (1997) 234–236
3. Hart, E.: Immunology as a Metaphor for Computational Information Processing: Fact or Fiction? PhD. Thesis, Artificial Intelligence Applications Institute, Division of Informatics, University of Edinburgh (2002) 28–34
4. De Castro, L.N., Von Zuben, F.J.: AiNet: An Artificial Immune Network for Data Analysis. In: Abbas H.A., Sarker R.A., Newton C.S. (eds.): Data Mining: A Heuristic Approach. Idea Group Publishing, USA (2001)
5. Blake, C.L., Merz, C.J.: UJI Repository of Machine Learning Databases. http://www.ics.uci.edu./~mlearn/MLRepository.html (1996)
6. De Castro, L.N., Von Zuben, F.J.: Artificial Immune Systems: Part I-Basic Theory and Applications. Technical Report, TR-DCA 01/99 (1999) 3–14
7. Abbas, A.K., Lichtman, A.H., Pober, J.S.: Cellular and Molecular Immunology. Fourth edition. W.B. Saunders Company (2000)
8. De Castro, L.N., Timmis, J.: Artificial Immune Systems: A New Computational Intelligence Approach. Springer-Verlag (2002)
9. De Castro, L.N., Von Zuben, F.J: Immune and Neural Network Models: Theoretical and Empirical Comparisons. International Journal of Computational Intelligence and Applications **1**(3) (2001) 239–257
10. Knight, T., Timmis, J.: Assessing The Performance of The Resource Limited Artificial Immune System AINE. Technical Report, Computing Laboratory, University of Kent at Canterbury (2001)
11. De Castro, L.N., Von Zuben, F.J., De Deus Jr,, G.A.: The Construction of of a Boolean Competitive Neural Network Using Ideas from Immunology. Neurocomputing **50** (2003) 51–85
12. http://www.dca.fee.unicamp.br/~lnunes
13. http://www.phys.uni.torun.pl/kmk/projects/datasets.html

Investigating the Effects of Recency and Size of Training Text on Author Recognition Problem

Ebru Celikel and Mehmet Emin Dalkılıç

Ege University, International Computer Institute, 35100 Bornova, Izmir, Turkey
{celikel,dalkilic}@ube.ege.edu.tr

Abstract. Prediction by partial match (PPM) is an effective tool to address the author recognition problem. In this study, we have successfully applied the trained PPM technique for author recognition on Turkish texts. Furthermore, we have investigated the effects of recency, as well as size of the *training text* on the performance of the PPM approach. Results show that, more recent and larger *training texts* help decrease the compression rate, which, in turn, leads to increased success in author recognition. Comparing the effects of the recency and the size of the training text, we see that the size factor plays a more dominant role on the performance.

1 Introduction

Today, with widespread availability of documents on the Internet, author recognition attains higher importance. Author recognition is the process of determining the author of unknown or disputed texts. It not only dissolves the ambiguity to reveal the truth, but also resolves the authorship attribution and plagiarism claims [1].

Discriminating among authors can be accomplished through various techniques. Most of the author recognition methods are lexically based in that, they exploit information about variety of words, consistency among sentences, use of punctuations, spelling errors, frequency and average of words, usage of filler words within the text, etc. These techniques extract the stylometry (wordprints) of disputed texts [2]. One of the fundamental notions in stylometry is the measurement of what is termed the richness or diversity of an author's vocabulary. Mathematical models exist for the frequency distributions of the number of vocabulary items as well as once-occurring words (*hapax legomena*) and twice occurring-words (*hapax dislegomena*) as stylometric tools [3]. Another lexically based technique proposed by Burrows is to use a set of common *function* (context-free) *word* frequencies in the disputed text [4]. This method requires the selection of the most appropriate set of words that best distinguish a given set of words.

All the lexically based style markers are so highly author and language dependent that, they frustrate the result of such measures to be applied to other authors and languages. As a result, syntax-based approach, which exploits the frequencies of the rewrite rules as they appear in a syntactically annotated corpus, has been proposed. Whether used with high-frequent or low-frequent rewrite rules, the syntax based approach yields accuracy results that are comparable to lexically based methods. Yet, the syntactic annotation required to prepare the text for this method itself is highly complicated, which makes it less common [5].

Another approach used by Khmelev considers a sequence of letters of a text as a Markov chain and calculates the matrices of transition frequencies of letter pairs to get the transition probabilities from one letter to the other for each disputed author [6]. Exploiting the principle of maximal likelihood, the correct author is determined to be the one with the maximal corresponding probability (or the minimal *relative entropy* which is inversely proportional to the probability) [7]. This technique has been successfully applied on determining the authorship for disputed Russian texts [8].

A slightly different approach in the area is entropy based: It uses compression tools for author recognition. Teahan lead some compression based experiments on text categorization, which is the basis for authorship attribution [9]. Although until that time it was believed that compression based techniques yield inferior results compared to the traditional machine learning approaches, Teahan and Harper obtained competitive results with compression models on text categorization [10].

With some compression algorithms using another text (called the *training text*) to extract symbol frequencies before compression, it is possible to determine the author of disputed texts. The idea is that, when the *training text* belongs to the same author as that of the disputed text, the symbol statistics gathered by the model on the *training text* will highly resemble that of the disputed text, which in turn will help the disputed text to be compressed better. No other text that was written by some other writer is expected to compress the disputed text better. Prediction by partial match (PPM)[11] is such an algorithm. In PPM, first a statistical model is constructed from the symbol counts in the *training text* and then the target text is compressed using these statistics.

There exists some authorship detection studies carried on Turkish texts: One is that of Tur's study, which uses word-based, stem-based and noun-based language models for determining the correct author [12]. Among the three methods, word-based model yields the best performance.

In the following section, we introduce our approach that we used for author recognition problem. In Section 3, we present the results of our implementations and in the last section, conclusion together with suggestions for future work are given.

2 Our Approach

In this study, we used a compression based approach employing PPMD+, a derivative of the PPM algorithm which uses *training text* to compress files, for author recognition on sample Turkish texts. The idea is that determining the correct author of the text T, is just a matter of calculating θ(T) in Eq. 1, where H(T|S) is some approximation to the relative entropy of text T with respect to text S [13]:

$$\theta(T) = \min_i H(T|S_i) \tag{1}$$

In our implementation, T is the disputed text whose author is to be determined and S_i is the *training text* belonging to the ith candidate author. From theory, we know that compression rate is a measure of entropy, i.e. the higher the entropy of a source text, the harder it is to compress it. Hence, we can use compression rate (measured in *bits per character – bpc*) and entropy interchangeably to evaluate our experiment results. If there are *m training texts* as S_1, S_2, ..., S_m, using each S as the *training text*, we compress the disputed text T with PPMD+ and then rank the resulting *bpc* values. At the end of *m* runs we conclude that the disputed text T belongs to the author whose *training text* (say S_i) yields the lowest *bpc* rate, i.e. highest compression.

Besides author recognition attempts, we further investigated the effect of two factors, namely recency and size of the *training text* to the recognition performance. Intuitively, more recent, as well as larger *training text* should be more successful in determining the right author. To test the correctness of this argument and to determine to which extend each factor, i.e. recency and size, affects the rate of success of the author recognition attempts, we applied several tests.

2.1 Prediction by Partial Match (PPM) Algorithm

A statistics based compression algorithm needs a model to determine how to represent the input stream. It then uses this model to encode the input sequence. PPM is such a modeling technique, which provides symbol statistics to the encoder [5]. It blends together several fixed-order context models to predict the next symbol in the input sequence. These distributions are effectively combined into a single one, and Arithmetic Coding [14] is used to encode the unit that actually occurs, relative to that distribution. The length of the context determines the order of the PPM model. In case the current order cannot determine the probability for the upcoming symbol, a special sequence called the *escape sequence* is issued and the control is transferred to a lower order model.

PPM model takes different names according to the probabilities assigned to escape events. What we used for our author recognition studies is PPMD+, i.e. PPM model with method D. In this algorithm, *escape* (*e*) and symbol probabilities ($p(\phi)$) are calculated as below (Eq. 2), where $c(\phi)$ is the number of times the context was followed by the symbol ϕ, *n* is the number of tokens that have followed, i.e. the sum of the counts for all symbols, $\sum_\phi c(\phi)$; and *t* is the number of types.

$$e = \frac{t}{2n} \quad \text{and} \quad p(\phi) = \frac{2c(\phi) - 1}{2n} \quad (2)$$

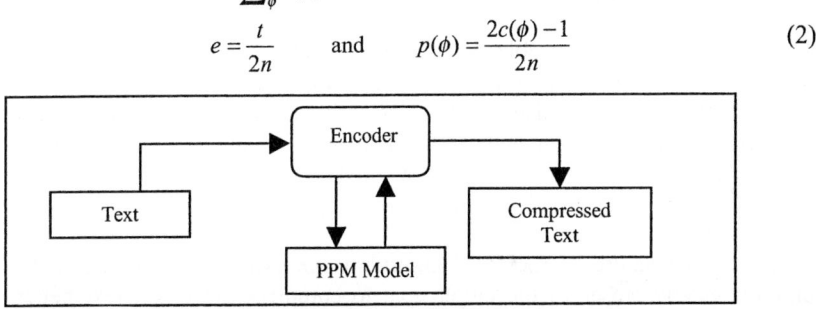

Fig. 1. Compression via PPM model

The PPM model is depicted in Figure 1 above. As seen from Figure 1, the input text is fed into the encoder which interacts with the adaptive PPM model. The model estimates a probability distribution for the upcoming symbol based on the symbols previously seen in the text. The symbol is then encoded using this probability distribution and the model is revised for better estimating the upcoming symbols.

PPM is flexible enough to let those symbols to be either characters, or words or parts of speech (PoS) tags. In our implementation, we choose symbols to be characters. This makes the PPM model independent of the source language.

2.2 Corpus

As for the corpus, we compiled daily articles of four journalists (namely Mehmet Ali Birand, Cetin Altan, Emin Colasan and Melih Asik) on Turkish newspapers (Hurriyet, Milliyet and Sabah) via Internet. For each author, we created six files: One file consisting of the author's articles before 2000, and five more belonging to years between 2000 and 2004, inclusively. For 2004, we only have the authors' articles written during the first four months of the year.

The authors we selected are among the daily columnists, each of whom has his own writing style. As a side note, Melih Asik frequently allows his column to be partially shared by other authors or even readers. Very frequently, he quotes reader letters which may expectedly lead to a much less stable writing style.

3 Results

In order to determine the correct author of disputed texts, we employed PPMD+ on our Turkish corpus. Besides, we investigated the effect of two factors to the recognition performance: One being the chronological distance, i.e. recency of the *training text* to the disputed text and the other being the size of the *training text*. In the following subsections, these experiments are explained and their results are given.

3.1 Author Recognition

The author recognition problem may arise in two different flavors. We either know the authors of older texts and using these texts, we are required to determine the correct author of a newer disputed text. The other case is that, we already have current texts belonging to known authors at hand, and we are required to determine the correct author of an older disputed text. These cases are reflected to our implementation as disputed text being the compressed text and known text being the *training text*.

Due to the nature of the PPM algorithm, we expect the *training text*, which is chronologically closer to the target text, to compress the target text better. To see whether this is the case in actual implementation or not, we run PPMD+ algorithm on yearly organized Turkish newspaper articles of the four different columnists. To calculate the classification accuracy for author recognition tests we use Eq. 3:

$$\text{accuracy} = \frac{\text{\# of correctly identified texts}}{\text{\# of total texts}} \quad (3)$$

Assume that we have older texts belonging to years before 2000 of the four journalists (Birand, Altan, Colasan and Asik) and we are required to determine correct author of these journalists' newer (belonging to years between 2001 and 2004) articles. This is an instantiation of the first case for author recognition problem, as mentioned above, where we use the older texts of each author as the *training text* to compress these authors' newer texts with PPMD+. For that, we use the full size of each article.

Table 1. Author recognition on sample Turkish texts with PPMD+ using full file sizes

Compressed text (approx. size)	Training text size (bytes)	Birand_19XX_2000 (1.7MB) Compression rate (bpc)	Altan_19XX_2000 (3.3MB) Compression rate (bpc)	Colasan_19XX_2000 (2.3MB) Compression rate (bpc)	Asik_19XX_2000 (1.5MB) Compression rate (bpc)	Identification margin (bpc)
Birand	2001 (0.3MB)	**1.98**	2.27	2.22	2.20	0.22
	2002 (1.2MB)	**1.87**	1.99	1.94	1.91	0.04
	2003 (1.1MB)	**1.86**	1.98	1.93	1.90	0.04
	2004 (0.4MB)	**1.91**	2.07	2.01	1.98	0.07
Altan	2001 (0.3MB)	2.27	**1.96**	2.25	2.17	0.21
	2002 (1.1MB)	2.11	**1.96**	2.10	2.03	0.07
	2003 (1.3MB)	2.09	**1.95**	2.08	2.01	0.06
	2004 (0.4MB)	2.24	**2.03**	2.22	2.13	0.10
Colasan	2001 (0.4MB)	2.15	2.17	**1.94**	2.03	0.09
	2002 (1.2MB)	2.04	2.08	**1.92**	1.97	0.05
	2003 (1.1MB)	2.06	2.10	**1.94**	1.99	0.05
	2004 (0.5MB)	2.17	2.21	**2.01**	2.07	0.06
Asik	2001 (0.3MB)	2.44	2.41	2.35	**2.20**	0.15
	2002 (1.1MB)	2.20	2.21	2.16	**2.05**	0.11
	2003 (1.3MB)	2.13	2.15	2.10	**2.00**	0.10
	2004 (0.5MB)	2.24	2.25	2.18	**2.05**	0.13

According to Table 1, correct author of each article is successfully determined (depicted as bold *bpc* values at each row) yielding an accuracy rate of 16/16=100%.

To observe the recency effect, we used the identification margin measure (last column in Table 1), which we define as the absolute difference between the correct author's *bpc* value and the value nearest to it at each row. In Table 1, as the size of the compressed (disputed) text becomes larger (years 2002 and 2003), the identification margin gets narrower. This means that the compression performance is highly affected by the size factor. In order to remove this size effect, we equalized the file sizes to the lowest file size in the test set: ~0.25MB for the disputed texts and ~1.5MB for the *training texts* and repeated the above experiment, with results given in Table 2.

Table 2. Author recognition on sample Turkish texts with PPMD+ using equal file sizes

Compressed text (approx. size)	Training text size (bytes)	Birand_19XX_2000 (1.5MB) Compression rate (bpc)	Altan_19XX_2000 (1.5MB) Compression rate (bpc)	Colasan_19XX_2000 (1.5MB) Compression rate (bpc)	Asik_19XX_2000 (1.5MB) Compression rate (bpc)	Identification margin (bpc)
Birand	2001 (0.25MB)	**1.98**	2.42	2.26	2.20	0.22
	2002 (0.25MB)	**1.92**	2.29	2.10	2.02	0.10
	2003 (0.25MB)	**1.96**	2.31	2.12	2.04	0.08
	2004 (0.25MB)	**1.93**	2.28	2.09	2.01	0.08
Altan	2001 (0.25MB)	2.27	**2.32**	2.29	2.17	0.03
	2002 (0.25MB)	2.33	**2.39**	2.35	2.20	0.04
	2003 (0.25MB)	2.25	**2.31**	2.27	2.11	0.04
	2004 (0.25MB)	2.28	**2.34**	2.29	2.15	0.05
Colasan	2001 (0.25MB)	2.18	2.40	**2.04**	2.06	0.02
	2002 (0.25MB)	2.19	2.40	**2.07**	2.08	0.01
	2003 (0.25MB)	2.19	2.40	**2.08**	2.09	0.01
	2004 (0.25MB)	2.22	2.43	**2.10**	2.10*	0.00
Asik	2001 (0.25MB)	2.44	2.63	2.42	**2.20**	0.22
	2002 (0.25MB)	2.43	2.59	2.43	**2.22**	0.21
	2003 (0.25MB)	2.25	2.44	2.25	**2.05**	0.20
	2004 (0.25MB)	2.29	2.49	2.27	**2.07**	0.20

*: Slightly less than 2.10 bpc.

We calculate the accuracy rate for Table 2 as 11/16=68.75%. The difference in the accuracy rates in Table 1 and Table 2 (as 100% and 68.75%, respectively) reveals the size effect: In case we have limited *training text* and/or disputed text sizes, the performance of the author recognition attempts decrease considerably.

Results in Table 2, where the size factor is neutralized, show that (except for Altan's case where recognition fails) as the text in question becomes less recent to the *training text*, the identification margin gets narrower. This feature, which is valid for all of the four authors, can be attributed to the recency effect.

3.2 Recency Effect

Table 3. The effect of recency of the *training text* on Birand's articles – full sizes

Filename	Size (KB)	Training text					
		Birand_19XX bpc	Birand_2000 bpc	Birand_2001 bpc	Birand_2002 bpc	Birand_2003 bpc	Birand_2004 bpc
Birand_19XX	1,036		← 1.44	1.43	1.45	1.46	1.44
Birand_2000	646	2.17 →		← 2.01	1.95	1.97	2.02
Birand_2001	267	2.34	1.96 →		← 2.01	2.03	2.10
Birand_2002	1,120	1.99	1.85	1.89 →		← 1.79	1.85
Birand_2003	1,125	1.98	1.84	1.88	1.77 →		← 1.82
Birand_2004	444	2.10	1.88	1.94	1.78	1.76 →	

Table 3 shows the effect of recency of the *training text*. While compressing each year's articles with PPMD+, the articles except for that year's articles are used as the *training text*. It makes no sense to compress a particular year's article by using this text itself as the *training text*. This is why the compressed article at each row is denoted by a shaded cell in the table. The arrows in the table indicate the nearest neighbors (upper and lower) of the compressed text on each row. What we expect out of this experiment is that, each year's article is best compressed with *training text* being the nearest neighbor. In four out of six cases, our expectation is met. Whereas in two cases, it is not. This anomaly may be due to the different size of texts available for each year. To see if this was the reason, we normalized the text sizes for each year and repeated the measurements. For that, we chopped each year's text size to year 2004's size for that particular author. We also excluded the years having texts less than year 2004's size. The reduction has been done beginning from the end of each year's texts, because newer texts are nearer to year 2004's articles and hence would compress better. The results are presented between Tables 4 through 7:

Table 4. The effect of recency of the *training text* on Birand's articles – equal sizes

Filename	Size (KB)	Training text				
		Birand_19XX bpc	Birand_2000 bpc	Birand_2002 bpc	Birand_2003 bpc	Birand_2004 bpc
Birand_19XX	444		← 1.49	1.51	1.51	1.51
Birand_2000	444	2.20 →		← 2.01	2.02	2.02
Birand_2002	444	2.13	1.92 →		← 1.89	1.90
Birand_2003	444	2.13	1.93	1.89 →		← 1.87
Birand_2004	444	2.09	1.90	1.86	1.84 →	

As seen on Table 4, removing the size effect, we can better realize that recency plays a significant role in the performance of the PPMD+ algorithm. For each year's article of Birand, with *training text* being the nearest neighbors, the best performances are obtained. Tables 5 through 7 show similar results for the authors, as well.

Table 5. The effect of recency of the *training text* on Altan's articles – equal sizes

Filename	Size (KB)	Training text				
		Altan_19XX bpc	Altan_2000 bpc	Altan_2002 bpc	Altan_2003 bpc	Altan_2004 bpc
Altan_19XX	436		← 1.58	1.60	1.61	1.61
Altan_2000	436	2.31 →		← 2.08	2.12	2.12
Altan_2002	436	2.31	2.08 →		← 2.08	2.09
Altan_2003	436	2.26	2.06	2.02 →		← 2.05
Altan_2004	436	2.29	2.09	2.07	2.07 →	

For Altan's articles, whenever the nearest neighbor is the *training text*, the best compression performance is obtained (Table 5). In three out of the five cases, previous articles and two out of five cases the following year's articles as *training texts* give the best compression. In all cases, the best results are obtained via the most recent *training texts*. Table 6 shows that a similar tendency exists for Colasan's articles.

Table 6. The effect of recency of the *training text* on Colasan's articles – equal sizes

Filename	Size (KB)	Training text				
		Colasan_19XX bpc	Colasan_2000 bpc	Colasan_2002 bpc	Colasan_2003 bpc	Colasan_2004 bpc
Colasan_19XX	398		← 1.85	1.86	1.86	1.86
Colasan_2000	398	2.24 →		← 2.03	2.04	2.05
Colasan_2002	398	2.25	2.04 →		← 2.01	2.02
Colasan_2003	398	2.26	2.05	2.01 →		← 2.00
Colasan_2004	398	2.26	2.05	2.02	2.01 →	

According to Table 7, in three out of four cases, the most recent texts as *training text* provide the best compression. In one case only (the last row of Table 7), a non-most recent text yields slightly better compression. This can be due to the idiosyncrasy of this specific author as was explained in section 2.2.

Considering the whole recency experiments, the most recent *training text* compresses consistently better, but only with a small margin.

Table 7. The effect of recency of the *training text* on Asik's articles – equal sizes

Filename	Size (KB)	Training text			
		Asik_2000 bpc	Asik_2002 bpc	Asik_2003 bpc	Asik_2004 bpc
Asik_2000	456		← 2.16	2.17	2.16
Asik_2002	456	2.19 →		← 2.17	2.20
Asik_2003	456	2.11	2.07 →		← 2.10
Asik_2004	456	2.13	2.14	2.14 →	

The recency effect is not only a matter of same topics being discussed in the articles, which are close in time, but also the variation in the author's writing style. For the former factor, since the articles under consideration are the texts from daily newspapers, it is quite expected that they are highly effected by the current politic, economic and social climate. For the latter factor, the authors do develop their writing style with time: There are some "hot" words, sayings changing with time and authors get effected by those trends while writing. This effect has already been investigated on the writings of two famous Turkish writers: Cetin Altan and Yasar Kemal by Can and Patton [15]. Results of this study support with statistical evidence that the change of writing style for these authors change with time.

3.3 Size Effect

We have investigated the effect of *training text* size on the performance of the compression with PPMD+. For that, we have used the articles of each author written before year 2004 as the *training text* to compress his articles written in 2004. In order to observe the effect of gradually changing the *training text* size, we measured the compression performance of the PPMD+ algorithm under ten different *training text* sizes. By employing *training texts* of size 1K, 5K, 10K, 50K, 100K, 250K, 500K, 1000K, 2000K and 4000K, we compressed each author's year 2004 articles. With results of each run are given in the charts below:

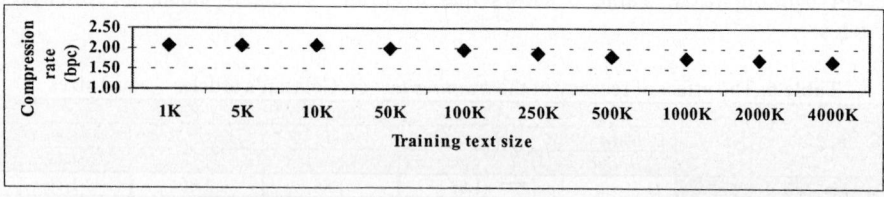

Fig. 2. Effect of training text size on Birand's articles

As seen from Figure 2, increasing the *training size* gradually improves the compression performance of Birand's articles, as expected. The rate of improvement, calculated as the difference percentage between the largest (2.08 bpc with 1K *training text*) and the smallest (1.70 bpc with 4000K *training text*) *bpc* values, is 18.25% for Birand's case. This represents a considerable performance improvement.

We also plotted the compression performance variation with changing *training text* size for Altan's articles. This plot is shown in Figure 3. According to Figure 3, *bpc* rates for Altan's articles improves with increasing *training text* size as was the case with Birand's articles. The rate of improvement with Altan's articles is 19.30%.

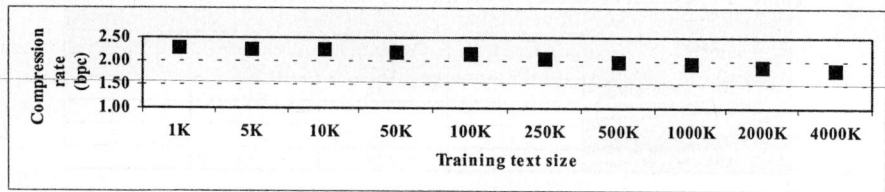

Fig. 3. Effect of training text size on Altan's articles

The compression rate vs. *training text* size charts for Colasan and Asik (Figure 4 and Figure 5) have the same trend as that of the other journalists, i.e. using larger *training text* helps improve the compression rate. The improvement rates are 19.60% and 18.40% for Colasan and Asik, respectively.

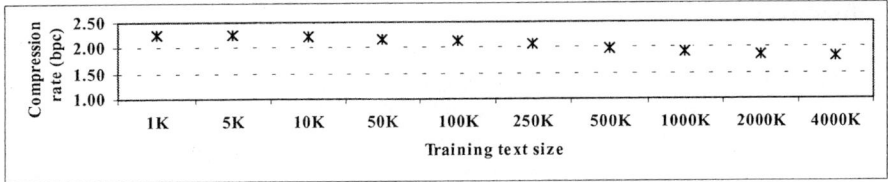

Fig. 4. Effect of training text size on Colasan's articles

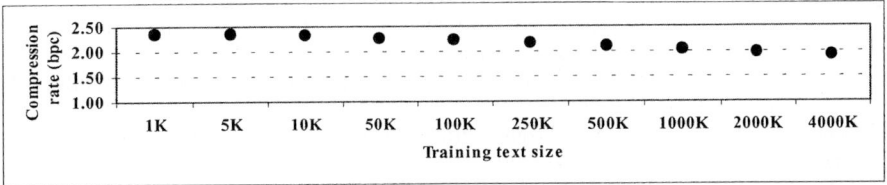

Fig. 5. Effect of training text size on Asik's articles

Above experiments clearly indicate that employing larger *training text* yields better compression. Evaluating the *training text* size experiments for all four authors, we note that the performance gain from the smallest size to the largest size is very consistent at around 19%. Addressing the author recognition problem, this property can be used to improve the performance of the recognition studies implemented with compression tools: Selecting larger *training texts* increase the success of determining the right author.

4 Conclusion

Using the trained PPM algorithm for author recognition was introduced in [11] for English texts. In this work, we have applied this approach on Turkish texts. With larger texts the approach resulted in 100% accuracy. On the other hand, when the *training text* and/or disputed text sizes are limited, classification accuracy drops significantly to 68.75%.

We have also investigated the effect of recency and size of *training text* on the success of the author recognition. What we obtained is that, the more recent and the larger the *training text* is, the better gets the compression rate. This, presumably leads to higher possibility of correctly recognizing the right author.

Comparing the effects of recency and size of the *training text*, we see that as compared to recency, size plays a more dominant role on the performance of author recognition.

Further tests with more distant writings, together with larger *training text* sizes will be possible as more and more texts are available online. Experiments on the data set used in this study can further be carried on with Support Vector Machine (SVM) classifier to compare the performances of the two. PPM has already reached and even outperformed the SVM performance on English texts [10]. The same experiments can be carried out on our Turkish data set.

References

1. Clough, P.: Plagiarism in Natural and Programming Languages: An Overview of Current Tools&Techs. Dept. of Comp. Sc., Univ. of Sheffield, UK (2000)
2. Stylometry Authorship Analysis: http://www.lightplanet.com/response/style.htm
3. Rudman, J., Holmes D.I., Tweedie F.J., Baayen R.H.: The State of Authorship Studies: (1) The History and the Scope; (2) The Problems – Towards Credibility and Validity. In: Joint Int'l Conf. of the Assoc. for Comp. & the Humanities and the Assoc. for Literary & Linguistic Computing, Queen's Univ., Canada. (1997)
4. Burrows, J.F.: Word-Patterns and Story-Shapes: The Statistical Analysis of Narrative Style. Literary & Linguistic Computing **2**(2) (1987) 61–70
5. Stamatatos, E., Fakotakis, N., Kokkinakis, G.: Automatic Authorship Attribution. In: Proceedings of EACL. (1999)
6. Khmelev, D.V., Tweedie, F.J.: Using Markov Chains for Identification of Writers. Literary and Linguistic Computing **16**(4) (2001) 299–307
7. Khmelev, D.V.: Disputed Authorship Resolution through Using Relative Empirical Entropy for Markov Chains of Letters in Human Language Texts. Journal of Quantitative Linguistics **7**(3) (2000) 201–207
8. Kukushkina, O., Polikarpov, A., Khmelev, D.V.: Using Letters and Grammatical Statistics for Authorship Attribution. Problems of Information Transmission **37**(2) (2001) 172–184
9. Teahan, W.J.: Modeling English Text. PhD. Thesis, Univ. of Waikato, NZ (1998)
10. Teahan, W.J., Harper, D.J.: Using Compression-Based Language Models for Text Categorization. In: Workshop on Language Modeling and Information Retrieval, Carnegie Mellon University. (2001) 83–88
11. Teahan, W. J.: Text Classification and Segmentation Using Minimum Cross-Entropy. In: Proceedings of RIAO'2000, Paris, France. (2000) 943–961
12. Tur, G: Automatic Authorship Detection. (unpublished) (2000)
13. Khmelev, D.V., Teahan, W.J.: A Repetition Based Measure for Verification of Text Collections and for Text Categorization. In: SIGIR 2003, Toronto, Canada. (2003)
14. Witten, I., Moffat, A., Bell, T.C.: Managing Gigabytes. San Fransisco (1999)
15. Can, F., Patton, J. M.: Change of Writing Style with Time. Computers and the Humanities **38**(1) (2004) 61–82

Model Based Intelligent Control of a 3-Joint Robotic Manipulator: A Simulation Study Using Artificial Neural Networks

Rasit Koker[1] and Abdullah Ferikoglu[2]

[1] Computer Engineering Department, Sakarya University, Sakarya, Turkey
rkoker@sakarya.edu.tr
[2] Electronics and Computer Education Department, Sakarya University, Sakarya, Turkey
af@sakarya.edu.tr

Abstract. Recently, there has been a great deal of interest in intelligent control of robotic manipulators. Artificial neural network (ANN) is a widely used intelligent technique on this way. Using ANN, these controllers learn about the systems to be online controlled by them. In this paper, a neural network controller was designed using traditional generalized predictive control algorithm (GPC). The GPC algorithm, which belongs to a class of digital control methods and known as Model Based Predictive Control, require long computational time and can result in a poor control performance in robot control. Therefore, to reduce the process time, in other words, to avoid from the highly mathematical computational structure of GPC, a neural network was designed for a 3-Joint robot. The performance of the designed control system was shown to be successful using the simulation software, which includes the dynamics and kinematics of the robot model.

1 Introduction

Robotic manipulators have become increasingly important in the field of flexible automation. To get an autonomous robot controller to be useful, it must operate in real time, pick up novel payloads, and be expandable to accommodate many joints. One of the indispensable capabilities for versatile applications of the mechanical robotic manipulators is high speed and high precision trajectory [1,2]. Recently, artificial neural networks have been successfully used to model linear and nonlinear systems. In process control applications the controller makes explicit use of the neural network based process model to determine the k-step ahead prediction of the process outputs [3]. There has also been much interest in learning the form of simple models of networks of neurons. The overall complexity of robot control problems, and ideal of a truly general robotic system, have led to much discussion on the use of artificial neural networks to learn the characteristics of the robot system, rather than having to specify explicit robot system models.

Artificial neural networks-based predictive control has been studied in several papers [1,4-6]. Arahal et al. [6] have presented a study on neural identification applied to predictive control of a solar plant. In their paper, an application of general identification methodology to obtain neural network predictors for use in a nonlinear predictive control scheme is derived from the generalized predictive controller structure. Gupta and Sinha [1] have designed an intelligent control system using PD controller and artificial neural network. They have found the algorithm successful. On the other hand, they mentioned, as "the learning system used does not suffer from the restriction of repetitive task since the training information is in the form of the system transfer characteristics at individual points in the state space, and is not explicitly associated with the trained trajectories. Obviously, it would be difficult to train a system to generate correct control outputs for every possible control objective." Similarly, the same event as stated above is observed in this study.

In this paper, a three-joint robotic manipulator was controlled to prepare data by using Generalized Predictive Control algorithm [7–9]. A simulation software, which includes all the dynamics and kinematics equations of the defined robot model, was used. The simulation software was previously developed in a study involving the attitude of robot depending on the different vision-based trajectories [10]. Robotic manipulator was controlled for different trajectories with GPC, and during these simulations a training set was prepared for neural network. The aim of this paper is to reduce the process time due to the on-line working feature of neural networks instead of highly mathematical structure of GPC algorithm.

2 The Dynamic and Kinematics Model of the Robot

A three-joint robot model shown in Figure 1 was used in the simulation. The simulation software includes dynamics and kinematics equations for the given robot model. As it is well known, the dynamics of a robot arm [11] can be expressed by the following general set of equations given in Eq. (1):

$$\sum_{j} d_{kj}(q)\ddot{q}_j + \sum_{i,j} c_{ijk}(q)\dot{q}_i\dot{q}_j + f_k(q) = \tau_k \qquad (1)$$

k = 1, ... n, i = 1, ..., n, j = 1, ..., n and where;

q_j	jth generalized coordinate
q	generalized coordinate vector
τ_k	kth generalized force
n	number of joints
d_{kj}	inertial coefficients
c_{ijk}	centrifugal and Coriolis coefficients
f_k	loading item due to gravity

The parameters of the robotic manipulator [12] used in the simulations were given in Table 1. The simulation software was developed in order to observe the movements of robot model visually using Open GL program, and a view of the robot model was given in Fig. 1. So, the simulation software gives the result of speed and position at the end of control process to take information about the obtained control system accuracy. The robot control and neural networks software was coded using Delphi Programming Language.

In this study, the robotic manipulator was modeled using its dynamic equations. However, the disturbances, which exist in a real robot implementation, were also expressed in the dynamic model equations with a coefficient. The aim of this is to see the affects of some disturbances in real life such as rusting, friction and other effects.

Table 1. The parameters of the used robotic manipulator

I	Joint-1	Joint-2	Joint-3	Units
m_i	13.1339	10.3320	6.4443	kg.
a_i	0.1588	0.445	0.10	m.
α_i	$\pi/2$	0.0	$\pi/2$	Radian
X_i^*	-0.0493	-0.1618	0.0	m.
Z_i^*	0.0	0.0	0.2718	m.
k_{i11}	5.6064	3.929	82.0644	$m^2 x10^{-3}$
k_{i22}	8.9196	47.8064	81.9353	$m^2 x10^{-3}$
k_{i33}	13.2387	45.4838	1.400	$m^2 x10^{-3}$

In Table 1;
- m_i The weight of arm 'i'
- a_i Shift distance of the ith coordinate system along the rotating axis of X_{i-1}
- α_i The orientation of z_i axis according to Z_{i-1} axis
- X_i^*, Z_i^* The coordinates of gravity center of arm 'i' according to ith coordinate frame
- k_{ijj} Jiration radius ($I_{ij} = m_i k_{ijj}^2$)

In Figure 1 the kinematics structure of the robotic manipulator was given. This figure gives us information about the cartesian position of end effector according to joint angles. This figure is also named as direct kinematics solution. On the other hand, it is necessary to compute the joint angles according to a given cartesian coordinates especially for a vision based applications [13]. This solution is known as inverse kinematics solution. The aim of this paper is to obtain a neural network control based on training with obtained data from GPC algorithm. Therefore, inverse kinematics problem is not detailed here.

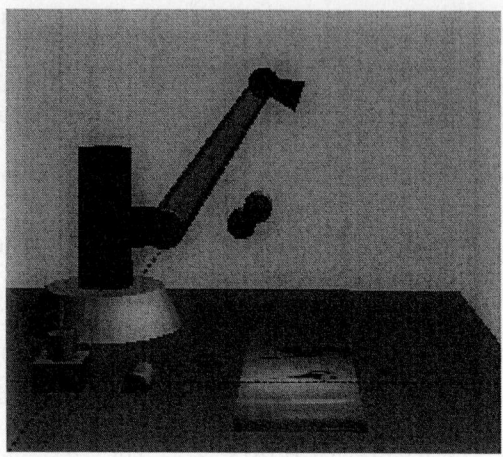

Fig. 1. A view from the 3-D simulated robotic manipulator

3 Design of the Neural Network Controller

Artificial Neural Network (ANN) is a parallel-distributed information processing system. The main idea of the ANN approach resembles the human brain functioning [14]. It has a quicker response and higher performance than a sequential digital computer. The learning feature of the neural network is used in this study.

In this section, it is firstly aimed to present the design of the neural network, which is working online to produce applied torque values for each joint in the system. A Back-Propagation neural network that uses gradient descent error learning algorithm with sigmoid activation function was used to model GPC algorithm. The data prepared during the implementation of traditional GPC algorithm was used to train neural networks. The training process has been implemented just for some areas in the work volume of robot. To design a controller generalized for whole area of work volume of robot is a very time consuming study due to the training difficulty.

3.1 Data Preparation

To train the neural network, a training set has been prepared by using the results of implementation of GPC. The manipulator has been controlled for different trajectories to generate the data for the training set. The designed neural network has 12 inputs and 3 outputs. To obtain the torque value at time "t" as an output, the torque values at time (t-1), (t-2), and y and y-references at time (t-1) are used in input stage as 12 elements. These data has been generated using GPC controller for different trajectories. These trajectories have been selected uniformly to model the GPC algorithm. In the preparation of training set, care has also been taken of payload variations. Payload variations are taken between 0 gram and 10000 gram. Due to the characteristic feature of sigmoid activation function used in the training of backpropagation neural network model, all data in training set has been normalized between "0" and "1".

3.2 Training of the Neural Network

In the off-line training of the backpropagation neural network, 13000 input and output vector sets are generated using simulation software. 12000 of these are used as learning set, and others are used in test. Learning rate and the momentum rate are experimentally chosen as 0.3 and 0.85, respectively. Error at the end of the learning is 0.007895. The error is computed based on mean square error (MSE) [15].

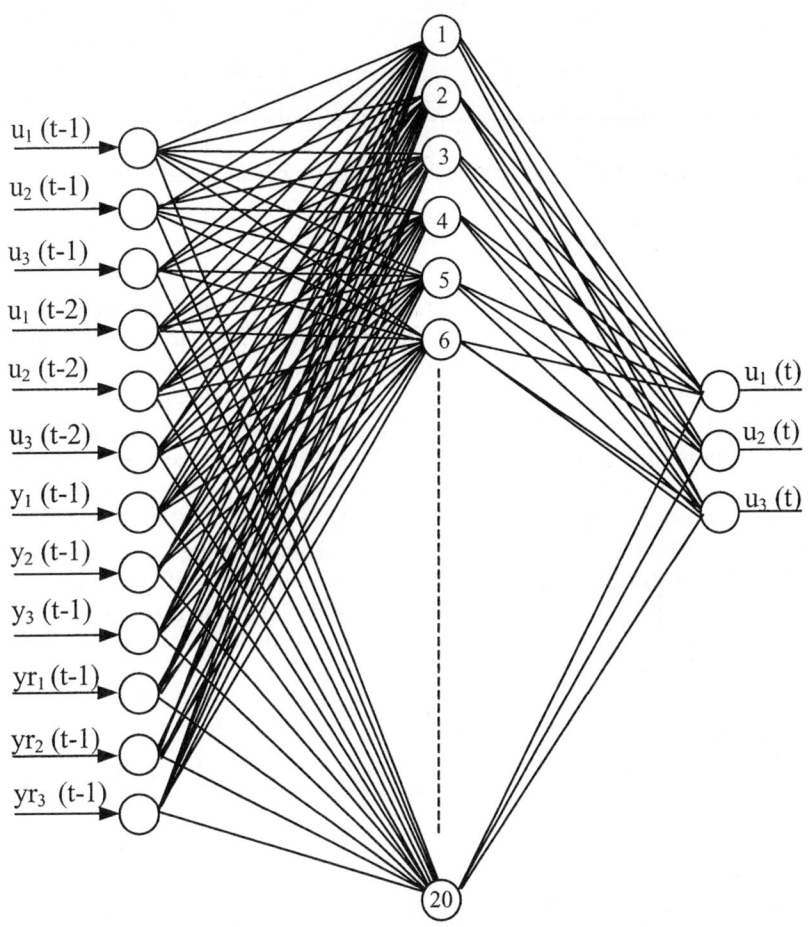

Fig. 2. The topology of the designed neural network

The training process has been completed approximately in 7.500.000 iterations. After the off-line neural network training is finished, the neural network, which works online, is coded with obtained synaptic weights as seen in Figure 2. The neural network includes 20 neurons in the hidden layer, and it has been tried to obtain the neural network controller with the least number of perceptron in the hidden layer. An example of the obtained torque curve has been given in Figure 3.

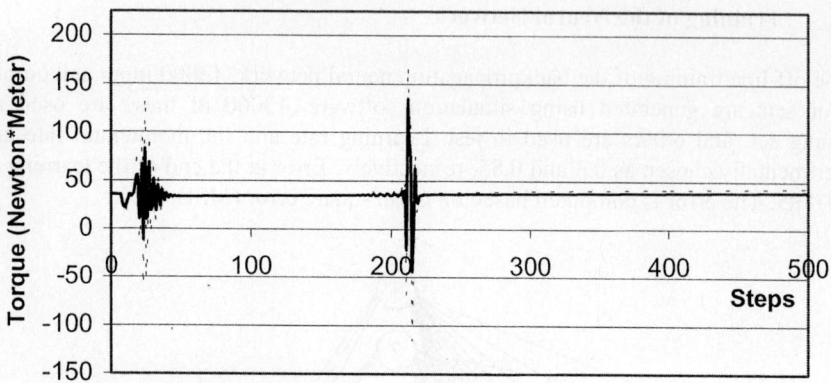

Fig. 3. Obtained torque curve from the neural network with actual torque curve

4 Simulation Results

The designed neural network controller, which is the obtained by modeling GPC controller, is implemented by using simulation software for a trajectory. The block diagram of the neural network control implementation has been shown in Fig. 4. The results have been compared with the results obtained from GPC to have information about the success of the neural network controller. The simulation results have been given for both traditional GPC controller and the designed neural network controller in Fig.5 and Fig. 6 respectively. The same trajectory has been used for both controllers to observe the accuracy of the ANN controller compared to GPC controller. In these simulations, cubic trajectory planning is used as a path-planning algorithm. Its equation, which has been used in the computation of reference position and speed values, is given in eq. (2) below. The speed equation can be obtained from this equation by a derivation process. A second derivation process will give acceleration equation.

$$\theta_i(t) = \theta_{i0} + \frac{3}{t_f^2}(\theta_{if} - \theta_{i0})t^2 - \frac{2}{t_f^3}(\theta_{if} - \theta_{i0})t^3 \quad (i=1, 2, 3) \quad (2)$$

where

t_f : Total simulation time,

θ_{if} : The final angular position for ith joint,

θ_{i0} = The starting position of ith joint,

t = Time,

n = The number of joints.

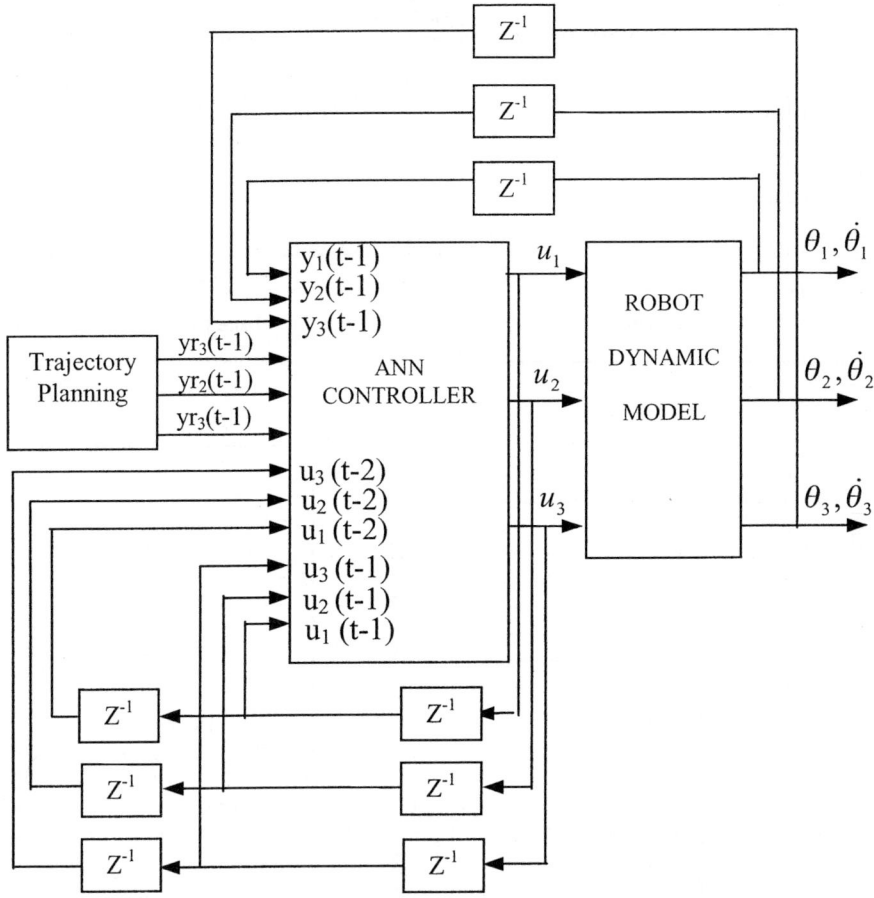

Fig. 4. The block diagram of the trajectory control implemented by using the designed ANN controller

The result of GPC controller is found successful. On the other hand, the error is too much at the starting points in speed curves. But, the GPC algorithm has taken the system under control a few iterations later. The same error has been also observed in ANN controller results in the same way.

The strongest way of GPC is the acceptances on the future control trajectories. However, it has a complex computational structure and needs too much computation time. On the other hand, a neural network can give results rather quickly.

In the simulation studies, it is observed that the training process is too much important for the accuracy of the obtained ANN control system. Generalization is also made through the reproduction of a situation that was absent from the training sct. On the other hand, the system is more successful for the trajectory, which is in training set than one, which is not in training set. In Fig. 6, the result is taken from the trajectory that is not in training set, to demonstrate the generalization of the designed ANN controller.

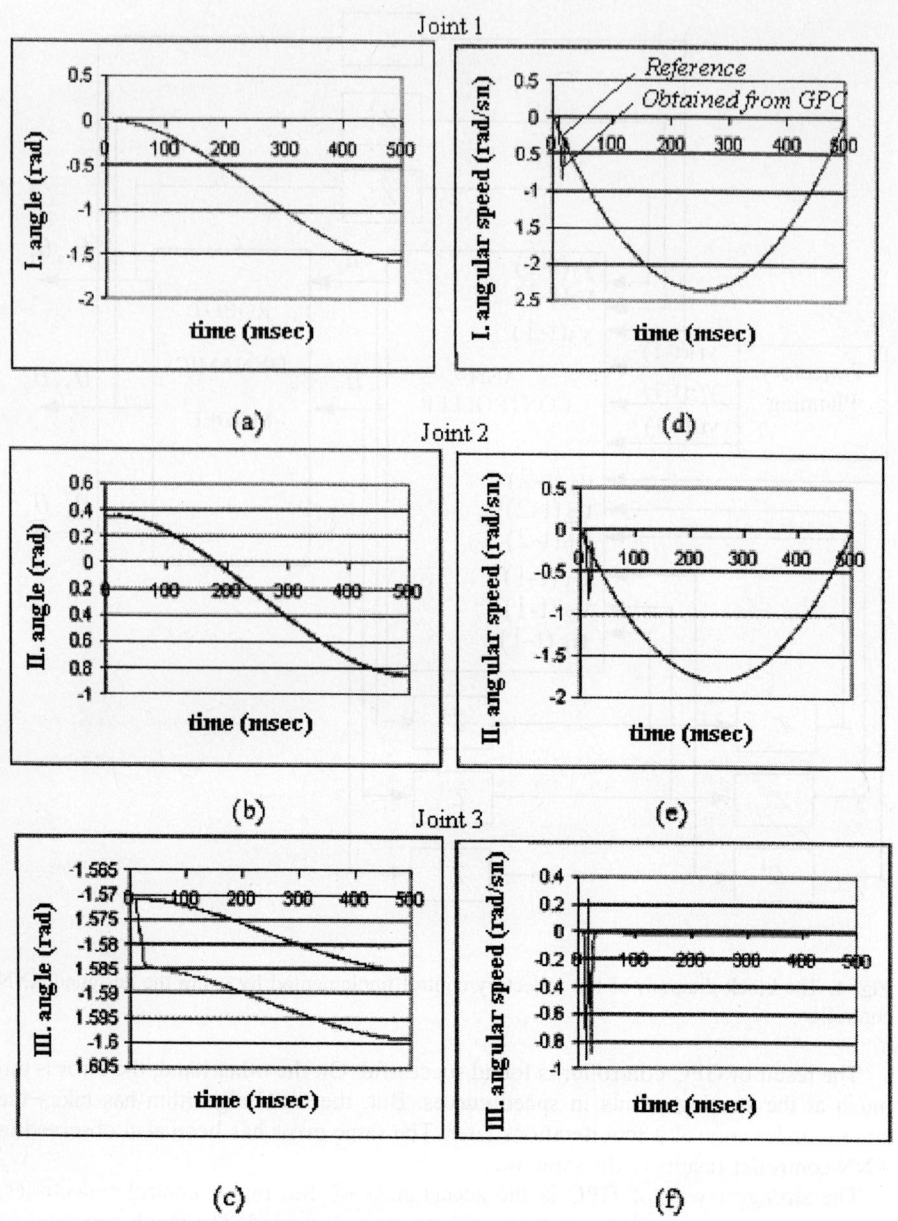

Fig. 5. The results of the GPC controller. Joint position and references are shown in (a), (b), and (c); Joint speed and references are shown in (d), (e), and (f)

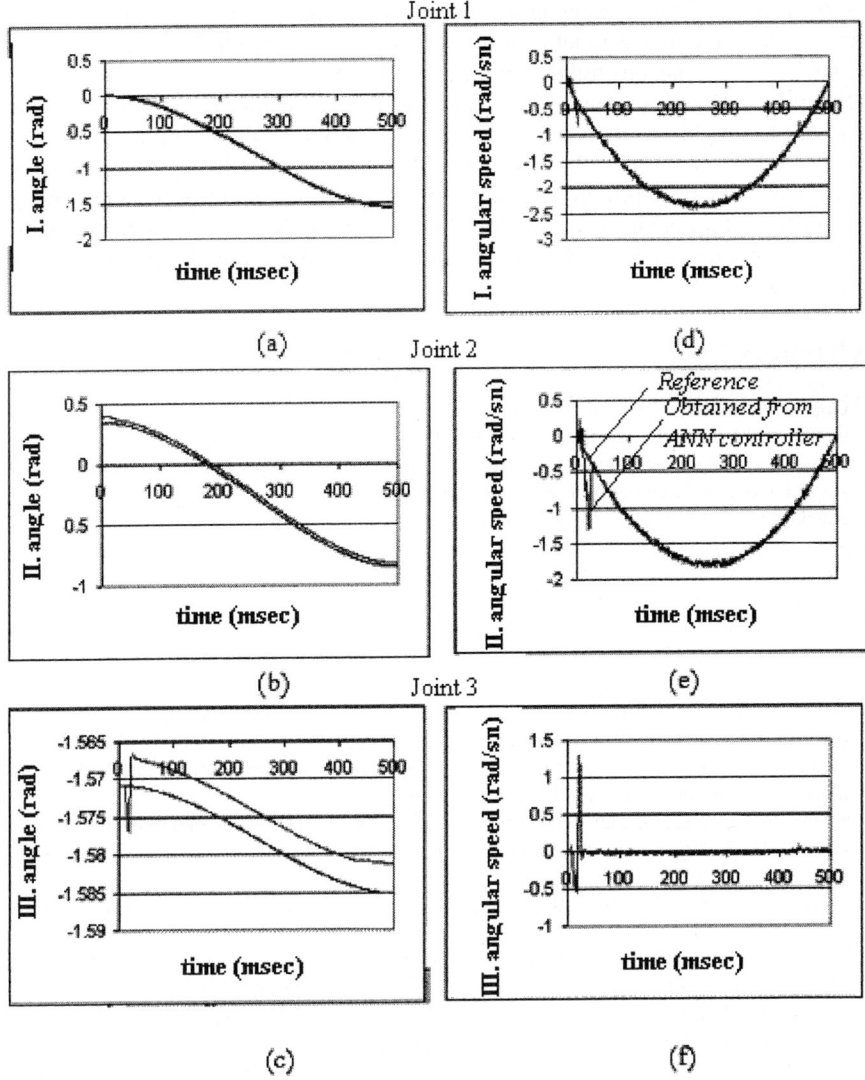

Fig. 6. The results of the neural network controller. Joint position and references are shown in (a), (b), and (c). Joint speed and references are shown in (d), (e), and (f)

5 Conclusions

Through the simulation studies, it was found that robotic manipulators can be controlled by learning. In this study, GPC algorithm was modeled by using artificial neural networks. The performance of the neural network controller, used instead of GPC, was found successful. It was observed that, the prepared training set and the training sensitivity of the neural network much affects the system performance. However, it is also difficult to imagine a useful non-repetitive task that truly involves making random motions spanning the entire control space of the mechanical system. This results an intelligent robot concept as being one is trained for a certain class of operations, rather than one trained for virtually all-possible applications.

The most important idea of this study is that Generalized Predictive Control algorithm has highly mathematical computations; where as the neural networks have the capability of fast and on-line working feature. Modeling GPC by neural networks can have an important role in real time systems in the viewpoint of reducing process time. In the future studies, the developed control algorithm can be examined with a real robot to observe its real time accuracy, and to compare the results those of simulations.

References

1. Gupta, P., Sinha, N.K.: Intelligent control of robotic manipulators: Experimental study using neural networks. Mechatronics **10** (2000) 289–305
2. Jang, J.O.: Implementation of indirect neuro-control for a nonlinear two robot MIMO system. Control Engineering Practice **9** (2001) 89–95
3. Kasparian, V., Batur, C.: Model reference based neural network adaptive controller. ISA Transactions **37** (1998) 21–39
4. Willis, M., Montague, G., Massimo, C., Tham, M., Morris A.: Artificial neural networks in process estimation and control. Automatica **28**(6) (1992) 1181–1187
5. Soloway, D., Haley, P.: Neural/generalized predictive control, a Newton-Raphson implementation. In: Proceeding of The Eleventh IEEE International Symposium on Intelligent Control. (1996) 277–282
6. Arahal, M.R., Berenguel, M., Camacho, E..F.: Neural identification applied to predictive control of a solar plant. Control Engineering Practice **6** (1998) 333–344
7. Clarke, D.W., Mohtadi, C., Tuffs, P.S.: Generalized predictive control, part-1: The basic algorithm. Automatica **23** (2) (1987) 137–148
8. Koker, R., Oz, C., Kazan, R.: Vision based robot control using generalized predictive control. In: Intern. Conf. on Electrics and Electronics Engineering, Bursa, Turkey. (2001) 236–240
9. Omatu, S., Khalid M., Yusof, R.: Neuro-control and its applications. 2nd edition. Springer-Verlag (1996)
10. Koker, R.: Model Based intelligent control of 3-joint robotic manipulator with machine vision system. PhD. Thesis, Sakarya University, Science Institute (2002)
11. Acosta, L., Marichal, G.N., Moreno, L., Rodrigo, J.J., Hamilton, A., Mendez, J.A.: A robotic system based on neural network controllers. Artificial Intelligence in Engineering **13** (1999) 393–398
12. Kao, C.K., Sinha, A., Mahalanabis, A.K.: A digital algorithm for near-minimum-time control of robotic manipulators. Journal of Dynamic Sys., Measurement and Control **109** (1987) 320–327
13. Koker, R. Ekiz, H., Boz, A.F.: Design and implementation of a vision based control system towards moving object capture for a 3-joint robot. In: 11th Mediterranean Conf. on Control and Automation, Rhodes, Greece. (2003)
14. Köker, R., Oz, C., Ferikoglu, A.: Development of a vision based object classification system for a robotic manipulator. In: 8th IEEE International Conference on Electronics, Circuits and Systems, Malta. (2001) 1281–1284
15. Haykin, S.: Neural networks. Macmillan College Publishing Company (1994)

Knowledge Incorporation into ACO-Based Autonomous Mobile Robot Navigation

Mehtap Kose and Adnan Acan

Eastern Mediterranean University, Computer Engineering Department
Gazimagusa, TRNC, Via Mersin 10, Turkey
{mehtap.kose,adnan.acan}@emu.edu.tr

Abstract. A novel Ant Colony Optimization (ACO) strategy with an external memory containing horizontal and vertical trunks from previously promising paths is introduced for the solution of wall-following robot problem. Ants construct their navigations by retrieving linear path segments, called trunks, from the external memory. Selection of trunks from lists of available candidates is made using a Greedy Randomized Adaptive Search Procedure (GRASP) instead of pure Greedy heuristic as used in traditional ACO algorithms. The proposed algorithm is tested for several arbitrary rectilinearly shaped room environments with random initial direction and position settings. It is experimentally shown that this novel approach leads to good navigations within reasonable computation times.

1 Introduction

Wall-following autonomous robot (WFAR) navigation is a well-known problem in the field of machine learning and different metaheuristics are used for its solution. The goal of a wall-following robot is to navigate along the walls of an environment at some fairly constant distance. The advantage of the wall-following domain is that it provides a simple test case to tell whether an autonomous robot is actually succeeding the given task or not. Genetic Programming (GP), Genetic Algorithms (GAs), Fuzzy Logic, and Neural Networks are commonly used methods to obtain wall-following behavior for an autonomous mobile robot. Mataric [1] has implemented a subsumption architecture in which one complex behavior is decomposed into many simple layers of increasingly more abstract behaviors such that a lover layer can overrule the decision of its overlaying layer. Mataric used the subsumption architecture for autonomous mobile robot control for the achievement of four different tasks: strolling, collision avoidance, tracing convex boundaries, and tracing general boundary of a room. The main difficulty of subsumption architecture in writing a composition of task achieving behaviors that are able to solve a particular problem is the requirement of considerable programming skills and ingenuity. Koza [2] used Genetic Programming (GP) for the evolution of wall-following behavior. Tree-structured computer programs consisting of robot instructions and environmental parameters are evolved to achieve the wall-following behavior. Ross et al. [3] improve the work of Koza by adding automatically defined functions (ADF's) in their GP implementation. ADF's allow the representation of more complicated robot behavior and flexibility in program development since problem-adapted instructions are developed by evolution. Braunstingl et al. [4] used Fuzzy Logic Controllers and GA's for the navigation of an autonomous mobile robot. The perceptual information of the sensors are passed to the fuzzy system without modeling the walls or obstacles of an environment. The rule base of the fuzzy system is designed by manually and then a GA is used to find the optimum membership functions.

Ant Colony Optimization (ACO) algorithm is one of the most popular metaheuristic approaches for the solution of complex optimization problems [5–7]. Ant algorithms have been inspired by the behavior of real ants. In particular, Argentine ants are capable of selecting the shortest path, among a set of alternative paths, from their nest to food sources [8]. Ants deposit a chemical trail (or pheromone trail) on the path that they follow, and this trail attracts other ants to take the path that has the highest pheromone concentration. Pheromone concentration on a path plays a key role in the communication medium between real ants. Since the first ants coming back to the nest are those that took the shortest path twice, more pheromone concentration is presented on the shortest path. Over a finite period of time, this reinforcement process results in the selection of the shortest pathway [9].

In this paper, an external memory supported ACO approach is presented for WFAR navigation problem. When classical ACO algorithm is applied to WFAR problem, two important observations that form the main inspiration behind the proposed approach are made: Firstly, a particular point inside the room may be simultaneously on low- and high-quality paths. Hence, pheromone deposition on single nodes over 2D plane may be misleading, because pheromone updates due to low-quality paths will hide the visibility due to a smaller number of high-quality navigations. Secondly, one should incorporate knowledge from previous iterations to exploit accumulated experience-based knowledge for the generation of correct decisions for future moves. The proposed approach overcomes these two difficulties by using a trunk-based path construction methodology, rather than the node-based approach, and using an external-memory of trunks, extracted from high-quality path of previous iterations, for knowledge accumulation. The details of implementation and algorithmic description of the proposed approach are given in Section 3.

This paper is organized as follows. A brief description of traditional ACO algorithms is given in Section 2. In Section 3, implementation details of the proposed external memory-based ACO strategy are discussed. Experimental results are reported in Section 4. Section 5 concludes the paper.

2 Traditional ACO Algorithms

ACO metaheuristic can be applied to any discrete optimization problem where some solution construction mechanisms can be described [5]. The ants in ACO implement a greedy construction heuristic based on pheromone trails on the search space. The main task of each artificial ant in the simple ant colony optimization algorithm is simply to find a shortest path between a pair of nodes on a graph on which the problem representation is suitably mapped. Each ant applies a step-by-step constructive decision policy to construct problem's solutions.

At each node of the graph, where the search space of the problem is mapped, local information maintained on the node itself and/or outgoing arcs is used in a stochastic way to decide the next node to move. The decision rule of an ant k located in node i uses the pheromone trails τ_{ij} to compute the probability of choosing node $j \in N_i$ as the next node to move to, where N_i is the set of one-step neighbors of node i. The probability of P_{ij}^k is calculated as follows [6]:

$$P_{ij}^k = \begin{cases} \tau_{ij}, & \text{if } j \in N_i \\ 0, & \text{otherwise} \end{cases} \tag{1}$$

At the beginning of the search process, a small amount of pheromone τ_0 is assigned to all the arcs on the graph. When all ants built their solutions, they deposit a constant amount $\Delta\tau_{ij}$ of pheromone information on the arcs they used. Consider an ant that at time t moves from node i to node j, it will change the pheromone values τ_{ij} as follows [6]:

$$\tau_{ij}(t+1) \leftarrow \tau_{ij}(t) + \Delta\tau_{ij}, \quad \text{where} \quad \Delta\tau_{ij} \leftarrow \sum_{k=1}^{all\_ants} \Delta\tau_{ij}^k \tag{2}$$

$$\Delta\tau_{ij}^k = \begin{cases} Q, & \text{if the ant used this line} \\ 0, & \text{otherwise} \end{cases} \tag{3}$$

The constant Q is computed according to the quality of the ant's solution. In this way, an ant using the arc connecting node i to node j increases the probability that ants will use the same arc in the future. Initially given pheromone trail τ_0 avoids a quick convergence of all the ants towards a sub-optimal path. An exploration mechanism called pheromone evaporation process is added by decreasing pheromone concentrations in an exponential way, as given in Equation 4, at each iteration of the algorithm [6, 9].

$$\tau \leftarrow (1-\rho)\tau, \rho \in (0,1] \tag{4}$$

3 Use of Trunk-Based External Memory in ACO

The room environment is represented as a two dimensional NxM grid, where N is the number of rows and M is the number of columns. Single integer codes are used to identify walls, restricted minimum safe distance cells, obstacles, and free cells.

The ideas forming the basis of the proposed approach are developed based on the results of two-phase studies. In the first phase, a simple ACO algorithm is applied for the solution of WFAR problem without any external memory. In its practical implementation, ants construct their navigations by moving cell-to-cell based on the pheromone concentrations within each cell and ants are also allowed to deposit pheromone inside cells that are visited during their navigations. The quality of the obtained solution was not sufficiently high due to two reasons: first, pheromone concentrations within individual cells are not informative enough because a particular cell may be simultaneously on both a high-quality and a low-quality path. Secondly, node visibility causes confusion in the calculation of node selection probabilities. As a result of these two observations that are supported by several experimental evaluations [10], two important conclusions are generated. First, an ant's decision on the selection of the next node to move must be effected from its previous selections, and secondly, if the moves to be taken can be made along linear trunks, interpretation of pheromone concentration will be much more meaningful because it will remove the first confusion mentioned above. These two conclusions form the main inspirations behind the proposed approach and the details of which described below.

The algorithm is started with an initialization process. Initial positions of ants are randomly set and a library of variable size linear path segments, called trunks, is generated. These trunks are used in the path construction phase of artificial ants. Trunks in the external memory are stored in a linked list structure. Each trunk in the trunk memory has a trunk *id*, its associated *start* and *end* coordinates, a *direction*, a *trunk fitness*, a *path fitness*, a flag for *best ant's use*, and *in use* information. In order to avoid the selection of the same path segments, ants are not allowed to use Greedy heuristics in their construction phase as used in traditional ACO algorithms. Fitness value of a trunk is calculated and recorded after its creation, which shows the quality of the trunk in its environment. The trunk *id* is used to follow the trunks that are used by each ant. At the end of each iteration, the fitness values of the constructed paths are calculated and a path's fitness value is also recorded with all the related trunks on this path. If more than one ant uses same trunk, then the highest one' path fitness is kept with this trunk. If the path fitness of a trunk is less than the average path fitness of the current iteration, then it is replaced by another randomly generated trunk.

At the beginning of the algorithm, initial random positions are assigned to each ant. Each ant uses its initially assigned position throughout all iterations. The proposed ACO algorithm is iterated until the *max-iteration* has been reached. At the beginning of all iterations, the list of used trunks for each ant is initialized in order to provide diversification in the construction of new paths in the coming iterations.

In order to construct a path, an ant first finds the set of memory elements having a start position attribute equal to the ant's initial position. Path construction consists of two repeatedly iterated tasks until it is terminated. Firstly, based on the latest end point coordinates on which the robot resides, the memory is searched for trunks having appropriate starting point coordinates. If there are such trunks available, then one of them is selected using the Greedy Randomized Adaptive Search Procedure (GRASP) method. If no such trunks are available, then γ new ones are generated such that their starting position coincides with the robot's latest coordinates. Consequently, one element of the newly created list of trunks is selected and it is added to the path under construction. The robot's position is updated after each trunk addition. Secondly, the memory is updated by replacing all unused trunks so far by with a best subset of the newly created ones. In case that there are no unused trunks, the subset of newly created elite trunks are inserted at the end of the trunk library. The structure of the trunk memory and the ant's path construction phase is illustrated in Figure 1.

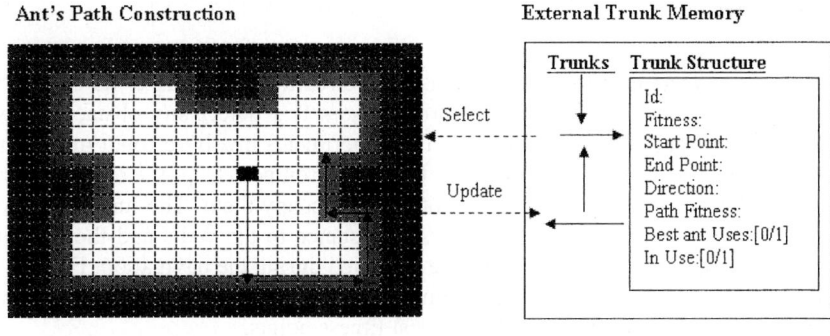

Fig. 1. Ant's path construction phase and structure of the trunk memory

Ants continue to construct new paths until no improvement is achieved in their navigations. This criterion is applied by using Euclidean distance measurement: path construction process is stopped when the length of the average Euclidean distance of the last three trunks is less than a threshold β; this means that the ant is stuck at around a localized region, hence its path construction is terminated. General description of the proposed ACO algorithm is given below:

Step 1. Initialization
    1.1 Initialize the trunk library with a number of randomly generated variable-size trunks
    1.2 Set initial random position of each ant
Step 2. Loop until *max-iteration* has been reached
Step 3. ACO Algorithm
    3.1 Initialize the used trunk list of each ant
    3.2 Loop for each ant in the population
        3.2.1 Search the memory for trunks having an appropriate start position
        3.2.2 If selected number of trunks < threshold γ then
            - Generate γ new random trunks with appropriate starting positions and directions
            - Select one trunk from this list by using GRASP algorithm
        Else
            - Select one trunk from the memory by using GRASP algorithm
        3.2.3 If termination criteria met for the current ant, then go to step 3.2
        Else go to step 3.2.1
    3.3 Evaluate Ants' fitness, and set path fitness' of each trunk
    3.4 Update best ant's navigation
    3.4 Update trunks that have less path fitness than the average path fitness
Step 4. Go to Step 2

4 Results

The robot is programmed to move only forward direction according to its current position. Therefore, it is enough to use three sensors that detect any obstacle or wall cells located in front, left, and right of it. The experiments involve a robot moving in a world that consists of a 16x16 cells map. In the environment map, the outer cells represent the walls of the room and the robot cannot occupy them. The inner cells adjacent to the walls represent the minimum safe distance to the walls and the fitness of the robot is penalized when these cells are occupied during the navigation. Finally, the inner cells that are adjacent to the minimum safe distance cells signify the desired cells where the robot is picking up the highest fitness points.

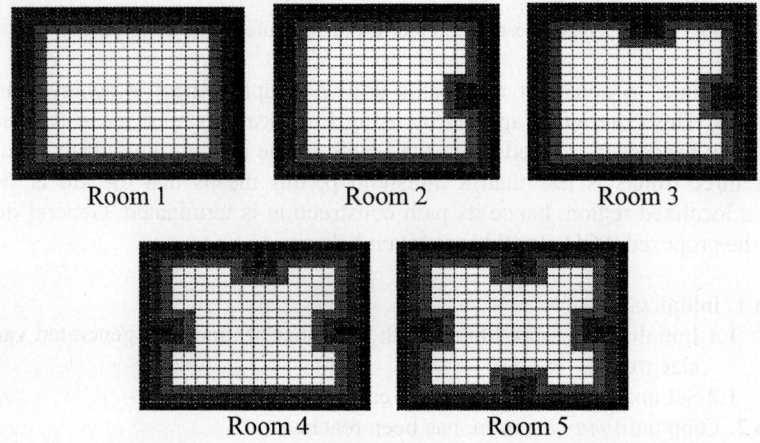

Fig. 2. Five different room types used in the experiments

For each run of the proposed ACO algorithm for wall-following behavior, ants are randomly placed within the allowable cells. The experiments were run independently from each other in five different rooms, with none to four protrusions from the walls. The shapes of the rooms are illustrated in Figure 2.

The maximum number of iterations for each ACO run is set to 300. The ants' population is kept as constant and the number of ants is selected as 100. The termination of an ant's navigation is controlled by checking the average of the Euclidean distance to the last three end positions. The minimum traveled distance required is taken as 3 on the average. Throughout the construction of ants' navigation, each ant selects its next position from the trunk memory by using a GRASP algorithm. The algorithm is stopped when 300 iterations have been passed. All these parameters are summarized in Table 1. The hit histograms that provide an overall picture of the number of hits to the desired cells through the best ant's navigation in each room are presented in Figure 3. These results are obtained from twelve consecutive runs of the algorithm.

Table 1. List of used parameters in ACO algorithm

Objective	To evolve a wall-following robot behavior for rooms having increasing complexity.
Fitness Cases	(500×number of traveled desired cells) - (10×number of crashes) - total number of visited cells Room 1: number of desired cells are 60 Room 2: number of desired cells are 64 Room 3: number of desired cells are 68 Room 4: number of desired cells are 72 Room 5: number of desired cells are 76
Selection	GRASP having candidate list length of γ at least
Hits	The number of times the robot occupies the desired cells. The robot is penalized if it occupies the cell already visited before, or minimum safe distance cell.
Parameters	Number of ants: 100, max-iteration: 300 Greedy α =0.5, γ=7, β = 3.
Success predicate	Room 1: 60 hits Room 4: 72 hits Room 2: 64 hits Room 5: 76 hits Room 3: 68 hits

The horizontal axis of each histogram refers to the number of hits in the corresponding room. The vertical axis is the frequency of runs for which the best ant's navigation achieved the specified number of hits during the execution. The details of the successful navigations in five different rooms are summarized in Table 2. Since the program parameters and the desired number of cells are given in Table 1; these informations are not included in Table 2.

Table 2. Characteristic of best runs in each room

Rooms	Iteration found	Visited desired cells	No of crashes	Visited cells
Room1	74	60	0	60
Room2	32	64	0	64
Room3	92	68	2	72
Room4	113	72	6	80
Room5	244	76	40	123

The required wall-following behavior in this study is organized as follows. The autonomous mobile robot is forced to visit all of the desired cells in the room environment without occupying minimum safe distance cells, wall cells, and previously already visited cells. The robot can only distinguish the desired cells by using sensor information. The robot navigation is penalized when it tries to occupy wall cells, or minimum safe distance cells, or already visited cells in its fitness assignment. The already visited nodes are distinguished from the list of used trunks of an ant.

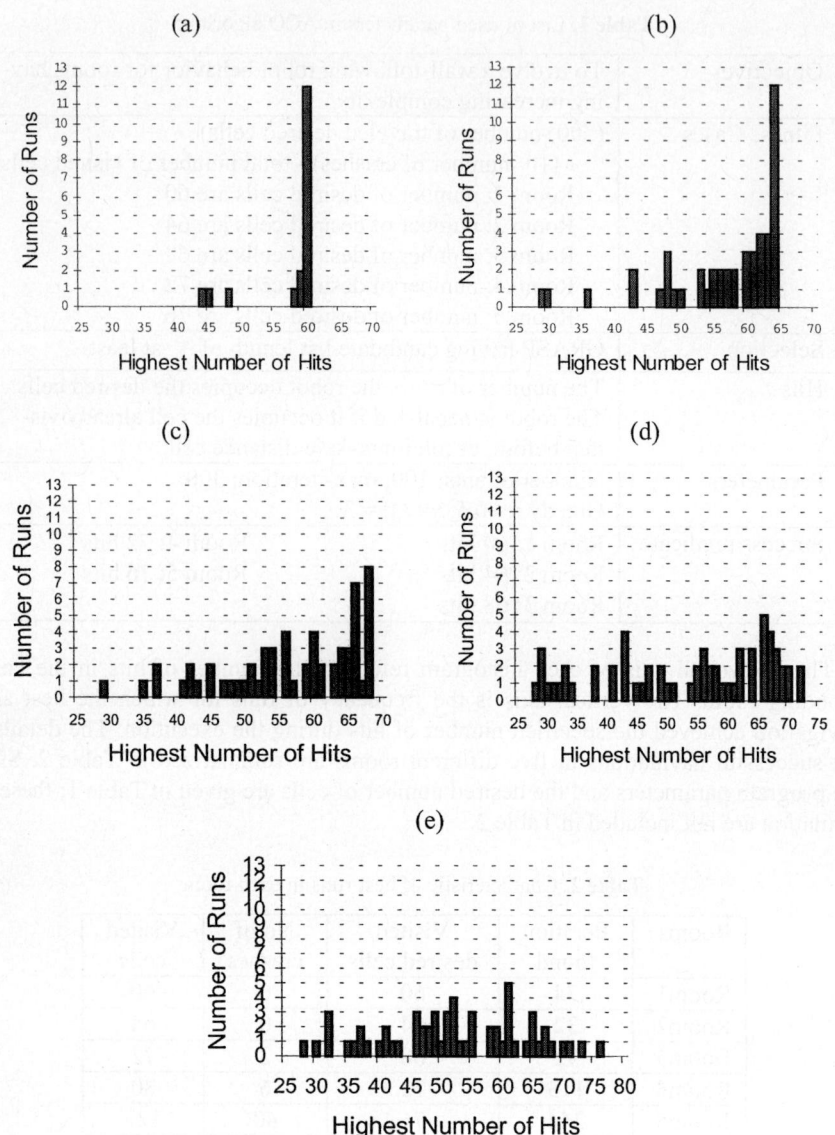

Fig. 3. Hits histogram. (a) Room 1, (b) Room 2, (c) Room 3, (d) Room 4, (e) Room 5

The hit histograms of the proposed algorithm demonstrate that the proposed ACO algorithm does not get stuck at locally optimal navigations in the wall-following domain and it visits all of the desired cells for all rooms. None of the previously performed studies are as good as our implementation. Nevertheless, the overall algorithm performances in room 3 are comparable with the results obtained by [3]. Our proposed algorithm found 8 successful solutions out of 12 trials where 6 successful solutions were reported out of 61 trails in [3]. Moreover, even we used similar type of environments in our simulations with the ones used in [11], the problem domain they studied is different. They aimed to evolve one GP program to be used in all rooms without considering the measures of already visited cells and smallest number of cell occupation.

5 Conclusions

A novel ACO strategy for the WFAR navigation problem is introduced. The proposed approach uses an external trunk library to allow ants to exploit their accumulated past experience and to remove the confusions caused by node-based pheromone deposition strategies.

The algorithm is tested on five different room environment where all of the desired cells are visited with smallest number of occupation on inner room redundant cells. As illustrated in Table 2, the number of crashes for the first two rooms is zero while only the desired cells are visited during the navigations. Considering rooms 3 and 4, all the desired cells are visited with very few number of crashes and quite small number of redundant cell occupations. Room 5 is the most complicated problem environment where there are four protrusions, still all the desired cells are visted, however, the number of crashes and the number of occupied redundant cells are comparably high. Higher number of crashes and redundant cell occupations for Room 5 can be caused by weakness of our stopping criteria. However, it can be noted that, the proposed approach did not get stuck at locally optimal solutions for any of the tested problem instances.

This approach needs futher investigation form the following points:
- Application in dynamic problem environments,
- Adaptive stopping criteria,
- Using separate trunk libraries on individual ants.

References

1. Mataric, M.: A Distributed Model for Mobile Robot Environment-Learning and Navigation. MIT Artificial Intelligence Laboratory technical report, AI-TR-1228 (1990)
2. Koza, J.R.: Genetic Programming: On the Programming of Computers by Means of Natural Selection. MIT Press, Cambridge, Massachusetts (1993)
3. Ross, S.J., Daida, J.M., Doan, C.M., Bersano-Begey, T.F., McClain, J.J.: Variations in Evolution of Subsumption Architectures Using Genetic Programming: The Wall Following Robot Revisited. In: Genetic Programming: Proceedings of the First Annual Conference, The MIT Press, Stanford University (1996) 28–31
4. Braunstingl, R., Mujika, J., Uribe, J.P.: A Wall Following Robot with a Fuzzy Logic Controller Optimized by a Genetic Algorithm. In: Fuzz-IEEE / IFES'95 Fuzzy Robot Competition, Yokohama. (1995) 77–82
5. Dorigo, M., Stützle, T.: The Ant Colony Optimization Metaheuristic: Algorithms, Applications, and Advances. In: Glover, F., Kochenberger, G. (eds.): Handbook of Metaheuristics (to appear)

6. Dorigo, M., Caro, G.D.: The Ant Colony Optimization Meta-Heuristic, New Ideas in Optimization. McGraw-Hill, London (1999)
7. Yan, Z., Yuan, C.W.: Ant Colony Optimization for Navigating Complex Labyrinths. Springer-Verlag, Berlin Heidelberg (2003) 445–448
8. Goss, S., Aron, S., Deneubourg, J.L., Pasteels, J.M.: Self-Organized ShortCuts in the Argentine Ant. Naturwissenschaften **76** (1989) 579–581
9. Botee, H.M., Bonabeau, E.: Evolving Ant Colony Optimization. Adv. Complex Systems (1998) 149–159
10. Kose, M., Acan, A.: Ant Colony Optimization for the Wall-Following Problem. IEEE Looking Forward Magazine (2003)
11. Lazarus, C., Hu, H.: Using Genetic Programming to Evolve Robot Behaviors. In: Third British Conference on Autonomous Mobile Robotics & Autonomous Systems, Manchester (2001)

The Effects of Data Properties on Local, Piecewise, Global, Mixture of Experts, and Boundary-Optimized Classifiers for Medical Decision Making

Nilgün Güler[1] and Fikret S. Gürgen[2]

[1] Yıldız Technical University, Math. Eng. Dept., Davutpasa, 34210 Esenler, Istanbul, Turkey
guler@yildiz.edu.tr
[2] Boğaziçi University, Comp. Eng. Dept., 34342 Bebek, Istanbul, Turkey
gurgen@boun.edu.tr

Abstract. This paper investigates the issues of data properties with various local, piecewise, global, mixture of experts (ME) and boundary-optimized classifiers in medical decision making cases. A local k-nearest neighbor (k-NN), piecewise decision tree C4.5 and CART algorithms, global multilayer perceptron (MLP), mixture of experts (ME) algorithm based on normalized radial basis function (RBF) net and boundary-optimized support vector machines (SVM) algorithm are applied to three cases with different data sizes: A stroke risk factors discrimination case with a small data size N, an antenatal hypoxia discrimination case with a medium data size N and an intranatal hypoxia monitoring case with a reasonably large data size individual classification cases. Normalized RBF, MLP classifiers give good results in the studied decision making cases. The parameter setting of SVM is adjustable to various receiver operating characteristics (ROC).

1 Introduction

In the past decade, there has been great activity in machine learning and intelligent techniques for the development of *models, applications etc.* These ideas have further led to reinterpretation of existing network structures; proposals of new net structures; and novel learning algorithms based on optimization techniques, principles, and criteria from these areas. In this field, there has also been a special interest in the development of classification, clustering, regression, prediction, etc. of medical data analysis problems. Remarkable efforts can be observed in the applications such as ECG, EEG, gynecology and obstetric, neurology, etc. with new ideas such as *neural and fuzzy combinations* [1], *mixture of experts, ensembles of neural networks, support vector machines (SVM), Bayesian nets,* and much more.

This study investigates the issues of purely local, piecewise and global, ME and boundary-optimized classification techniques in application to medical decision making cases with small, medium and large sample *(N)* sizes. By purely local models such as k-NN, the input space is hard partitioned into regions and decision outcome for each individual sample is obtained from this certain region. The piecewise classification function like in C4.5 and classification and regression tree (CART) consists of patchwork of local classifiers that collectively cover input space. In C4.5 classifier, individual features are considered for partition, but in CART, a combination of features decides the boundaries of class regions in the input space. By contrast, in global classification as in MLP, a single classification function that is generated by sigmoidal units of hidden layer must fit the data well everywhere with no explicit partitioning of input space or no subdivision of the parameter set. In the single perceptron case, the classification function becomes a single hyperplane that partitions input space into two regions. As a ME model, RBF net combines local experts' classification functions and makes a decision that is optimized in the minimum mean squared error sense (MMSE). RBF net also interprets the individual local classification functions of experts with a natural probabilistic association (conditional expectation) through output unit [2, 3]. Recently, boundary-optimized classification model, support vector machines (SVM) have been proposed and used in various applications [4]. The SVM maximizes the distance (margin) between the closest data points (support vectors) to the decision hyperplane and thus optimizes the decision rule for a better performance.

In our study on medical data analysis, we consider three cases: risk factors of stroke for a small population of size N, hypoxia decision for antenatal cases for a medium population of size N and intranatal decision making for normal and hypoxic conditions for a fairly large population of size N. In the stroke case, a total of N=44 diabetes mellitus (DM) patients are considered with 22 non-embolic stroke cases and 22 without stroke. In antenatal follow up, a total of N=210 patients are observed, there was 67 hypoxic cases and the rest (143) were normal cases. In intranatal monitoring, the total number of patients was 1537. Only 48 of them were observed to be hypoxic and the rest were normal delivery cases.

The rest of the paper is organized as follows: In the next section, a general classification model is described and examples of local, global and piecewise classifiers are reviewed. In the third section, we present the details of three medical cases that employ the decision-making procedure. The fourth section describes the performance and time complexity results of the classifiers and discusses issues of sample size N near the other effects. In the final section concluding remarks for the study are given.

2 Classification Models: k-NN, C4.5, CART, MLP, RBF, and SVM

In this work we discuss classifier choice with regards to the data sizes in medical decision making applications. Typically classifier design problem can be formulated as follows: Given a set of input-output pairs $T = \{(x_i, y_i)\}$, where $x_i \in R^n$, $y_i \in R^m$, we would like to design a mapping $f: R^n => R^m$ that minimizes the classification error, which, in the case of squared error, is given by $E[(y-f(x,w))^2]$. Note that the value of m changes according to the number of classes.

A purely local classifier such as k-NN employs local information by using the nearby samples of unknown sample, thus it may be considered for a small number of samples that describe the features of a region fairly good enough. Class belongingness decision is obtained from a local input space. In a k-NN with no weight case, the minimized mean squared-error cost can be defined as

$$E = \frac{1}{N}\sum_i \|y_i - x_i\|^2 \qquad (1)$$

where E shows the error of the optimization process according to given classes. A minimum total distance to a particular class defines the class identity of the unknown sample. Various windows may be used as the weight of the distance such as parzen window, etc. For medium and large size of data populations, local approaches can be considered as simple and effective classifiers and they produce the overall decision by the local decisions that use no specific rule. Local classifiers use no specific parametric model, they only depend on prescribed distances between regional samples.

Piecewise classifiers such as C4.5 and CART consider the partition of decision feature space by a patchwork of local decision functions. Overall decision collectively covers the total input space. In the C4.5 case, individual features draw class borders in a staircase shape. There is no effect of the rest of the features on the particular decision border drawn by a specific feature. In the CART case, a combination of the features is used to construct the class decision regions. In both cases, the overall class decision is obtained in a piecewise continuous manner; in fact local borders between classes represent sub-regional rules. There is no specific unknown sample (center) for the border description. In summary, piecewise models fit the data in local regions and patch the local parameters in a divide-and-conquer sense.

Global models like MLP employs a single classification function that must fit the data well everywhere with no explicit partitioning of the input space and no subdivision of the parameter set. It thus becomes more difficult to describe the role of individual parameters.

Popular MLP architecture with d inputs, h hidden units and one output is formulized as follows:

$$y(x) = f(\sum_{j=1}^{h} V_j * f(\sum_{i=1}^{d} w_{ji} * x_i + w_{j0}) + V_0) \qquad (2)$$

$f(.)$ is typically a smooth function such as the sigmoid function $\frac{1}{1+e^{-x}}$, w and V are the weights, parameters of the system. Back propagation (BP) algorithm and variations are used to train the structure (to optimize the weights of the system) [5, 6]. Sample population N must be large enough to train a MLP with a number of hidden units. A single global parametric model is described for the overall region.

The statistically based ME model can be described for the classification problems as follows: we first define *local expert's* classification function $f(x,w_j)$, where w_j is the set of model parameters for the local model j. The local experts may be constant, linear or nonlinear (polynomial of any degree) function of x. The overall classification function of the ME model is

$$f(x,w) = \sum_j P[j/x] f(x, w_j) \qquad (3)$$

where *P[j/x]* is a nonnegative weight of association between the input *x* and the expert (or local model) *j* and it determines the degree to which expert *j* contributes to the overall model output. These weights are often called *gating units* [2, 3] and are imposed $\Sigma_j P[j/x]=1$, which is parametric function determined by a parameter set w_{gating}. Statistical interpretation of the model is as follows: input-output pair *(x_i, y_i)* is randomly selected by an input density and by a local model according to probability mass function *{P[j/x]}*. For a selected local model *k*, the output is generated as a random variable whose *mean* is *f(x,w_k)*. With this viewpoint, *f(x,w)* represents the expected value of the output for a given input *x*. It is well known that the conditional expectation is the minimum mean-squared error (MMSE) classifier.

One main advantage of the ME model is creating a compromise among the purely local model such as that of k-NN, that is valid on a particular region of input space, the piecewise model such as that of a combination of rules for successive regions, and the global models such as that of MLP. The hard partition of regions of input space in "purely local" models is extended by piecewise functions of successive linear classifiers. In global models like MLP, a single classification function must classify the data everywhere with no explicit partitioning of the input space. Here, one can see the connection between ME models and the piecewise models: the piecewise models divide the data into local regions and conquer the local parameters in a divide-and-conquer sense. ME model also decomposes classification problem into the learning set of local (expert) models, but none of them claims exclusive ownership of the region unlike piecewise models. By using *P[j/x]* weights that is restricted to the values {0,1}, the parameters are added only the fit in the local region needs to be improved. Thus, the overall problem is simplified in terms of learning and modeling. Furthermore, unlike the piecewise modeling that generates discontinuous regions at boundaries, ME functions are smooth everywhere due to the averaging in equation (3).

In our study, we implemented normalized radial basis function (RBF) net as the ME structure. The normalized RBF uses a number of Gaussian functions to model the local regions and summarizes the overall region at the output nodes with a class decision. The normalized RBF net is an extension of the basic two-layer RBF net: in the hidden layer, we compute the hidden outputs by

$$P[k/x] = \frac{R_k(x)}{\sum_l R_l(x)} \qquad (4)$$

where $R_k(x) = \exp\left[-\|x - m_k\|^2 / 2\sigma^2\right]$ are the commonly used gaussian basis functions with m_k center (*prototype*) vectors and σ bandwidth. The *k* index is assigned to specify the hidden node and *l* ranges over all hidden node indices in the network. The second layer generates a linear combination

$$g(x) = \sum_{l=1}^{K} P[k/x] f(x, w_l) \qquad (5)$$

This architecture may be interpreted as a ME model where the weights $\{P[k/x]\}$ represent the probabilities of association with the corresponding local models $\{f(x,w_l)\}$.

Support vector machines (SVM) have been successfully employed for a number of real life problems [7]. They directly implement the principle of structural risk minimization [7] and work by mapping the training points into a high dimensional feature space where separating hyperplane (w, b) is found by maximizing the distance from the closest data points (boundary-optimization). Hyperplanes can be represented in feature space, which is a Hilbert space, by means of kernel functions such as Gaussian kernels $K(x',x) = \exp\left[-\|x - m_k\|^2 / 2\sigma^2\right]$. Kernel functions are dot products between mapped pairs of input points x_i, i=1,...,p. For input points x_i, mapping to targets y_i (i=1,...,p), the decision function is formulated in terms of these kernels $f(x) = sign\left(\sum_{i=1}^{p} \alpha_i y_i K(x,x_i) + b\right)$ where b is the bias and α_i are the coefficients that are maximized by the Lagrangian:

$$L = \sum_{i=1}^{p} \alpha_i - \frac{1}{2}\left(\sum_{i=1}^{p} \alpha_i \alpha_j y_i y_j K(x_i, x_j)\right) \qquad (6)$$

subject to the constraints: $\alpha > 0$ and $\left(\sum_{i=1}^{p} \alpha_i y_i = 0\right)$. Only those points that lie closest to the hyperplane have $\alpha_i > 0$ (support vectors). Linear (inner product) and gaussian kernel functions are selected in our experiments.

3 Medical Cases: Major Risk Factors of Stroke, Antenatal, and Intranatal Risk Assessment

Various sizes of medical databases are used in today's medical decision making applications [8, 9]. Each data set requires a proper choice of classifier due to the specific features such as size, application properties, etc. Using the classifiers that we discussed above, we present three medical cases with different features and with different sample sizes. A stroke risk factors discrimination case with small size N, an antenatal hypoxia discrimination case with medium size N and an intranatal hypoxia monitoring case with reasonably large size N are considered.

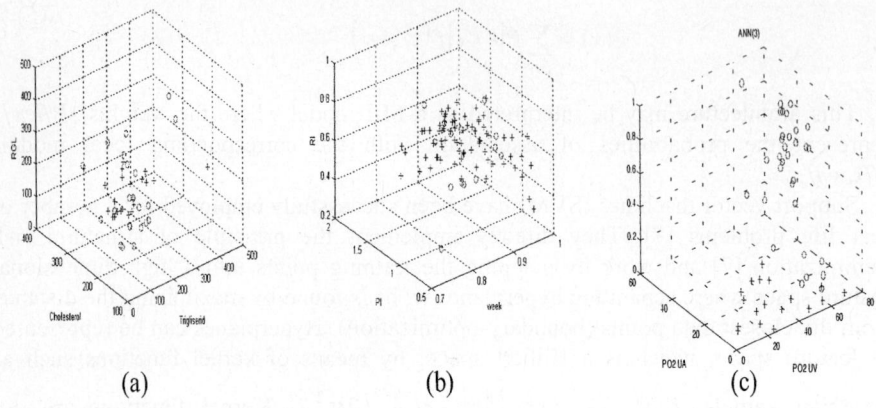

Fig. 1. 3-dimensional appearance of (a) stroke data, (b) antenatal data, (c) intranatal data.

3.1 A Small Population (N) Case: Diabetic Patients with and without Non-embolic Stroke

Using various diagnostic tests to search for evidence of disease is generally routine for monitoring patients with diabetes mellitus (DM) [10, 11] (Figure 1(a)). Measuring major risk factors of ischemic stroke in patients with DM can also provide reasons for the attending physician to initiate preventive measures adapted to particular case. Typical microvascular complications are neuropathy, nephropathy, retinopathy, macrovascular complications are coronary artery diseases (CAD) and peripheral vascular diseases (PVD). Abnormal test results of cholesterol, HDL, triglycerides levels, FGL and RGL and systolic and diastolic blood pressures are considered risk factors of nonembolic-ischemic stroke for DM patients.

The study population of 44 patients was chosen with these glucose levels. Diabetes mellitus (DM) is diagnosed by a fasting glucose level higher than 140 mg/dl and random glucose levels higher than 200 mg/dl in repeated measurements. The follow-up data of 22 diabetic patients with ischemic stroke (non-embolic) and 22 diabetic patients without stroke were collected over several years [11]. We use 7 metric components (cholestrol, HDL, triglyserides, FGL, RGL, systolic and diastolic pressures) in the experiments.

3.2 A Medium Size (N) Population Case: Antenatal Hypoxic Risk Assessment

In normal pregnancy, impedance to flow in the Umbilical Artery (UA) decreases with advancing gestation [12–14] (Figure 1(b)). Several studies have already demonstrated the possibilities and limits of using umbilical Doppler for the assesment of fetal growth. Some of these studies have used the systolic/diastolic (S/D) ratio, the resistance index RI=((S-D)/D). or pulsatility index PI=((S-D)/mean velocity), measurement on the UA Doppler velocity waveform. All of these UA resistance indices, when greater than the upper limit of normal range (>2 SD), are frequently associated with growth retarded pregnancy or intrauterine growth retardation (IUGR).

The 4 input values for classifiers are weekly ultrasound values that are PI, RI, S/D ratio from UA and WI. The WI is the normalized gestational age in terms of weeks between 0 to 40. In the antenatal hypoxia experiments, we employ a total of the 210 ultrasound measurements WI [14]. 67 of them are hypoxic and the other 143 are normal.

3.3 A Fairly Large (N) Population Case: Intranatal Acidosis Monitoring

Persistent fetal hypoxemia can lead to acidosis and neurologic injury and current methods to detect fetal compromise are indirect and nonspecific. Theoretically, direct continuous noninvasive measurement of fetal oxygenation is desirable to improve intrapartum fetal assesment and the specificity and detecting fetal compromise. The development of reflectance pulse oximetry has made it possible to measure fetal oxygen saturation during labor [15, 16].

The data of this study (Figure 1(c)) consist of umbilical cord blood samples of 1537 live-born singleton neonates (48 of them are hypoxic). 6 dimensions of input consists of two oxygen saturation values (measured by spectrophotometry), two pH values and two base excess values (from UA and UV) (measured by a pH and blood gas analyzer). Preductal oxygen saturation was calculated with an empirical equation [17]. Acidosis was defined as below the value of 7.09 for UA pH or −10.50 mmol/L for base excess.

4 Implementation Issues and Experimental Results

The study populations contain three medical cases: a stroke database with 44 diabetic patients, an antenatal hypoxia database with 210 cases and an intranatal database with 1537 cases. The performances are measured in terms of sensitivity and specificity. In this evaluation, test samples fall into one of 4 categories: *false positive (FP)* if the system decides as a positive while it is a negative, *false negative (FN)* if the system decides as a negative while it is a positive. Those decisions are false decisions and FP becomes vital error and is expected to be avoided. The others are *true positive (TP)* and *true negative (TN)* if the system decides correctly.

In the small population size stroke case with two classes, we observe a good success rate of piecewise C4.5 and global MLP and boundary-optimized SVM approaches over all input space. The specificity and sensitivity results of the other classifiers become inferior to C4.5, MLP and SVM. Multi-parameter classifiers were found to significantly improve upon the classification performance of single parameter designs. Instead of single parameter based conclusions, we employed the decision produced by major risk factors. The method gives the study stronger arguments on the distinctive factors. The small sample population size has an acknowledgable potential effect on the statistical power of the study, but we use classification techniques like C4.5 and MLP to help overcome this drawback. SVM's performance is not good in linear kernel case, it also can not find optimized values with gaussian kernels. Since CART considers a combination of individual features, it was not very successful for an input space with small size. Normalized RBF was also unsuccessful since it summarizes the local regions of input space at the output. In the case of C4.5, CART, MLP, normalized RBF, SVM, we implement a leave-n-out (n=4, 4 samples for testing of classifier trained with the rest of N=40 samples) method (jacknife, cross-validation) and repeat the experiments 4 times. The average performance is reported. The results are shown in Table 1.

It is an overall observation that the given stroke data which is used in our study is a difficult case of classification with a small sample size N and nonlinear separation function. This is also observed by the classifier performances.

Table 1. The test performance values and time complexities of the algorithms for diabetic patients with and without non-embolic stroke

	Sensitivity	Specificity	TP	TN	CPU-time (secs)
k-NN	%40	%40	%40	%40	0.05
C4.5	%63	%63	%63	%63	0.7
CART	%43	%45	%38	%50	0.78
MLP	%63	%63	%63	%63	0.65
Norm. RBF	-	-	-	-	-
SVM(linear)	%50	%50	%50	%50	0.057
SVM(Gaussian)	-	-	-	-	-

In the medium size (N) antenatal case with two classes (Table 2), MLP and RBF net yielded good results. k-NN has a close performance to MLP and normalized RBF net. The performance of CART is weak since it does not include the effect of combination of parameters. It is furthermore observed that the antenatal data is fairly easily classifiable and the performance results support this conclusion.

Table 2. The test performance values and time complexities of the algorithms for antenatal hypoxic risk assessment

	Sensitivity	Specificity	TP	TN	CPU-time (secs)
k-NN	%89	%98	%96	%95	0.05
C4.5	%87	%97	%92	%94	0.7
CART	%86	%90	%70	%95	0.98
MLP	%95	%98	%96	%98	0.65
Norm. RBF	%96	%98	%95	%98	0.70
SVM(linear)	%97	%61	%69	%95	0.065
SVM(Gaussian)	%90	%51	%60	%86	0.068

In the large size (N) intranatal data with two classes (Table 3), MLP and normalized RBF net perform well. CART has difficulty of learning the space because the number of hypoxic samples was not enough to train the CART structure. Finally k-NN and C4.5 perform weak compared to MLP and normalized RBF. The normalized RBF net describes input space better since it first makes a summary of local spaces at the first layer and then optimizes them at the output layer in the Bayesian sense. SVM with used parameter settings (56 support vectors for linear kernels and 93 support vectors for Gaussian kernels) gives inferior results. The intranatal data has fewer hypoxic samples: a total of 48 hypoxic cases exist among a total of 1537. This creates an unbalanced classification problem. The information on the borders of classes becomes valuable. The problem may be reduced to a different size classification case by clarifying the samples that have no information in the input space.

Finally, we compare the time complexities of the classifiers. The performances are given in 5th columns of Table 1, 2, 3. k-NN and SVM algorithms are observed to run fast compared to the other algorithms.

Table 3. The test performance values and time complexities of the algorithms for intranatal acidosis monitoring

	Sensitivity	Specificity	TP	TN	CPU-time (secs)
k-NN	%92	%94	%95	%90	0.10
C4.5	%92	%94	%95	%90	0.76
CART	-	-	-	-	-
MLP	%95	%100	%100	%97	0.65
Norm. RBF	%97	%93	%94	%96	0.75
SVM(linear)	%98	%83	%98	%82	0.07
SVM(Gaussian)	%95	%91	%99	%53	0.07

5 Discussion

We have studied three cases in medical decision making with the six classifiers with different properties: a k-NN that considers local feature vectors and defines a local decision hyperplane, an C4.5 that considers individual features for a piecewise hyperplane, a CART that considers the combination of the features for a linear hyperplane, a MLP that considers overall features and introduces a global, nonlinear decision surface, a normalized RBF that considers local, smoothed-piecewise models (ME) with Bayesian conditional probabilities for an overall decision and a SVM that considers support vectors of hyperplane for a Lagrangian optimization.

It is known that a MLP generates a nonlinear decision surface. In our study this is supported by our experiments. When sample size N is small, a training problem occurs. But this problem is also handled by strategies such as leave-n-out.

A normalized RBF net as a ME model offers new aspects over the classifiers such as k-NN, C4.5, CART and MLP, as it covers local feature space regions and patches these regions with Bayesian probabilities. For example, a set of parameters of MLP that defines the nonlinear decision surface can be divided into partial sets of parameters by a normalized RBF net. Each parameter set claims representation of a part of the decision surface. It can not be efficiently used for the stroke case since N is very small. For large N, it is still a problem to efficiently employ a normalized RBF net when class sizes are unequal and the size of one class is small. In intranatal hypoxia case, we face very small N values (48 for hypoxic cases) which is a typical situation since the most of the fetuses are healthy (1489 healthy cases). As a result, the ME model (norm. RBF) also becomes useful since it defines individual set of parameters for each subspace. Also, a specific ME structures [18] other than normalized RBF are useful for various applications.

The advantageous aspect of SVM is that it introduces boundary-optimization through a Lagrangian method using various kernel functions and thus, it produces good decision regions by optimizing data points that are closest to decision hyperplane. Various kernels such as linear, gaussian, polynomial, etc are available. In the application of three medical decision making cases, we observe the following: In the stroke case with small and medium N with equal size of samples in each class, the SVM works only for linear kernels with a poor performance. In the intranatal case with fairly large data size N and with also unequal number of data points in each class, it produces a good training performance, but the test performance was not very good when compared to a MLP or a normalized RBF.

As a result, nonlinear MLP, normalized RBF (ME structure) and boundary-optimized SVM are valuable in medical decision making applications when enough data is available. For small size N, the drawback of small N can be mitigated for a MLP by training strategies in our case. Statistically-based normalized RBF net needs more data.

One advantage of SVM structure is that we can control the sensitivity of the structure for individual classification performances. In many medical applications, medical specialists do not want to miss the false positive: FP (decision system labels it as positive while it is negative) cases. This makes SVM based system useful in many medical decision making applications.

Acknowledgements

This study is supported by Yildiz Technical University Research Fund 23-7-03-01 and Boğazici University Research Fund 03A103 project. We express our sincere thanks for their support.

References

1. Guler, N., Gurgen, F.S., Arikan, G.M.: The Accuracy and Reliability of Oxygen Saturation Prediction in Neurofuzzy Intranatal Risk Assessment Decision. In: Proceedings of ICANN/ICONIP. (2003)
2. Rao A.V., et al.: Mixture of Experts Regression Modeling by Deterministic Annealing. IEEE Trans. Signal Processing 45(11) (1997)
3. Jacobs, R.A., Jordan, M.I., Nowlan, S.J., Hinton, G.E.: Adaptive Mixture of Local Experts. Neural Computation 3 (1991) 79–87
4. Heckerman, D.: A Tutorial on Learning with Bayesian Networks. MIT Press Cambridge, MA, USA (1999)
5. Fukunaga, K.: Introduction to Statistical Pattern Recognition. Academic Press, Inc (1990)
6. Ripley, B.D.: Pattern Recognation and Neural Networks. Cambridge Press (1996)
7. Nuller, K.R., Smola, A.J., Ratsch, G., Scholkopf, B., Kohlmorgen, J., Vapnik, V.: Predicting Time Series with Support Vector Machine. In: Proceedings of ICANN'97. LNCS, Vol. 1327, Springer-Verlag (1997) 999–1004

8. Rudiger, B.: Medical Data Analysis. Springer-Verlag, Berlin Heidelberg New York (2000)
9. Hand D.J., Kok, J.N., Bertholt, M.R.: Advances in Intelligent Data Analysis. Springer-Verlag, Berlin Heidelberg New York (1999)
10. Aydın, N., Esgin, H., Yılmaz, A., Gözeten, F., Utku, U.: Diabetes Mellitus'lu Non-Embolik Stroklu Olgularda Retinopati ve Diğer Risk Faktörleri. In: Türk Beyin Damar Hastalıkları Derneği 3. Symposium (1999)
11. Gurgen, F.S., Gurgen, N.: Intelligent Data Analysis to Interpret Major Risk Factors for Diabetic Patients with and without Ischemic Stroke in a Small Population. Biomedical Engineering, http://www.biomedical-engineering-online.com/content/2/1/5 (2003)
12. Mari G., Copel J.A.: Doppler Ultrasound: Fetal Physiology and Clinical Application. In: Sonography in Obstetrics and Gynecology: Principal and Practice. London (1996)
13. Resnik C.J.A.: Doppler Ultrasound Assessment of Blood Flow. In: Maternal-Fetal Medicine. Philadelphia, W.B. Saunders (1999) 216–229
14. Gürgen, F., Güler, N., Varol, F.: Antenatal Fetal Risk Assessment by Blood-Flow Velocity Waveforms. IEEE Engineering in Medicine and Biology Magazine **19** (2000) 88–93
15. Arikan, G.M., Scholz, H.S., Haeusler, M.C.H., Giuliani, A., Haas, J., Weiss, P.A.M.: Low Fetal Oxygen Saturation at Birth and Acidosis. Obstetrics & Gynecology **95**(4) (2000) 565–571
16. Dildy, G.A., Clark, S.L., Loucks, A.: Intrapartum Fetal Pulse Oximetry: Past, Present, and Future. Am J Obstet Gynecol. **175** (1996) 1–9
17. Dildy, G.A., Thorp, J.A., Yeasti J.D., Clark, S.L.: The Relationship Between Oxygen Saturation and pH in Umbilical Blood: Implications for Intrapartum Fetal Oxygen Saturation Monitoring. Am J Obstet Gynecol. **175** (1996) 682–687
18. Shawe-Taylor, J., Cristianini, N.: Kernel Methods for Pattern Kernel Methods for Pattern Analysis. Cambridge University Press (2004)

Learning Interestingness of Streaming Classification Rules

Tolga Aydın and Halil Altay Güvenir

Department of Computer Engineering, Bilkent University
06800 Ankara, Turkey
{atolga,guvenir}@cs.bilkent.edu.tr

Abstract. Inducing classification rules on domains from which information is gathered at regular periods lead the number of such classification rules to be generally so huge that selection of interesting ones among all discovered rules becomes an important task. At each period, using the newly gathered information from the domain, the new classification rules are induced. Therefore, these rules stream through time and are so called streaming classification rules. In this paper, an interactive rule interestingness-learning algorithm (IRIL) is developed to automatically label the classification rules either as "interesting" or "uninteresting" with limited user interaction. In our study, VFP (Voting Feature Projections), a feature projection based incremental classification learning algorithm, is also developed in the framework of IRIL. The concept description learned by the VFP algorithm constitutes a novel approach for interestingness analysis of streaming classification rules.

1 Introduction

Data mining is the efficient discovery of patterns, as opposed to data itself, in large databases [1]. Patterns in the data can be represented in many different forms, including classification rules, association rules, clusters, sequential patterns, time series, contingency tables, and others [2]. However, for example, inducing classification rules on domains from which information is gathered at regular periods lead the number of such classification rules to be generally so huge that selection of interesting ones among all discovered rules becomes an important task. At each period, using the newly gathered information from the domain, the new classification rules are induced. Therefore, these rules stream through time and are so called streaming classification rules.

In this paper, an interactive rule interestingness-learning algorithm (IRIL) is developed to automatically label the classification rules either as "interesting" or "uninteresting" with limited user interaction. In our study, VFP (Voting Feature Projections), a feature projection based incremental classification learning algorithm, is also developed in the framework of IRIL. The concept description learned by the VFP algorithm constitutes a novel approach for interestingness analysis of streaming classification rules. Being specific to our concerns, VFP takes the rule interestingness factors as features and is used to learn the rule interestingness concept and to classify the newly learned classification rules.

Section 2 describes the interestingness issue of patterns. Section 3 is devoted to the knowledge representation used in this study. Sections 4 and 5 are related to the training and classifying phases of the VFP algorithm. IRIL is explained in the following section. Giving the experimental results in Section 7, we conclude.

2 Interestingness Issue of Patterns

The interestingness issue has been an important problem ever since the beginning of data mining research [3]. There are many factors contributing to the interestingness of a discovered pattern [3-5]. Some of them are coverage, confidence, completeness, action ability and unexpectedness. The first three factors are objective, action ability is subjective and unexpectedness is sometimes regarded as subjective [6-8] and sometimes as objective [9,10]. Objective interestingness factors can be measured independently of the user and domain knowledge. However, subjective interestingness factors are not user and domain knowledge independent. The measurement of a subjective interestingness factor may vary among users analyzing a particular domain, may vary among different domains that a particular user is analyzing and may vary even for the same user analyzing the same domain at different times.

An objective interestingness measure is constructed by combining a proper subset of the objective interestingness factors in a suitable way. For example, objective interestingness factor x can be multiplied by the square of another objective interestingness factor y to obtain an objective interestingness measure of the form xy^2. It is also possible to use an objective interestingness factor x alone as an objective interestingness measure (e.g. *Confidence*). Discovered patterns having *Confidence* ≥ *threshold* are regarded as "interesting". Although the user determines the threshold, this is regarded as small user intervention and the interestingness measure is still assumed to be an objective one.

The existing subjective interestingness measures in the literature are constructed upon unexpectedness and action ability factors. Assuming the discovered pattern to be a set of rules induced from a domain, the user gives her knowledge about the domain in terms of fuzzy rules [8], general impressions [7] or rule templates [6]. The induced rules are then compared with user's existing domain knowledge to determine subjectively unexpected and/or actionable rules.

Both types of interestingness measures have some drawbacks. A particular objective interestingness measure is not sufficient by itself [8]. They are generally used as a filtering mechanism before applying a subjective measure. On the other hand, subjective measures are sometimes used without prior usage of an objective one. In the case of subjective interestingness measures, user may not be well in expressing her domain knowledge at the beginning of the interestingness analysis. It'd be better to automatically learn this knowledge based on her classification of some presented rules as "interesting" or "uninteresting". Another drawback of a subjective measure is that the induced rules are compared with the domain knowledge that addresses the unexpectedness and/or action ability issues. Interestingness is assumed to depend on these two issues. That is, if a rule is found to be unexpected, it is automatically regarded as an interesting rule. However, it would be better if we learned a concept description that dealt with the interestingness issue directly and if we benefited from unexpectedness and action ability as two of the factors used to express the concept description. That is, interestingness of a pattern may depend on factors other than unexpectedness and action ability issues.

The idea of a concept description that is automatically determined and directly related with the interestingness issue motivated us to design IRIL algorithm. The concept description learned by the VFP algorithm, which was also developed in this framework, constitutes a novel approach for interestingness analysis of classification rules.

To ensure that the concept description is directly related to the rule interestingness issue, some existing and newly developed interestingness factors that have the capability to determine the interestingness of rules were used instead of the original attributes of the data set. Current implementation of IRIL does not incorporate unexpectedness and action ability factors, leading to no need for domain knowledge. Although the interestingness factors are all of type objective in the current version of IRIL, the thresholds of the objective factors are learned automatically rather than expressing them manually at the beginning. The values of these thresholds are based upon the user's classification results of some presented rules. So, although in the literature subjectivity is highly related to the domain knowledge, IRIL differs from them. IRIL's subjectivity is not related with the domain knowledge. IRIL makes use of objective factors (actually the current version makes use of only objective factors) but for each such a factor, it subjectively learns what ranges of factor values (what thresholds) lead to interesting or uninteresting rule classifications if only that factor is used for classification purposes. That is, IRIL presents a hybrid interestingness measure.

IRIL proceeds interactively. An input rule is labeled if the learned concept description can label the rule with high certainty. If the labeling or classification certainty factor is not of sufficient strength, user is asked to classify the rule manually. The user looks at the values of the interestingness factors and labels the rule accordingly. In IRIL, concept description is learned or updated incrementally by using the interestingness labels of the rules that are on demand given either as "interesting" or "uninteresting" by the user.

3 Knowledge Representation

We think of a domain from which information is gathered at regular periods. For each period p, classification rules are induced from the gathered information and these streaming rules' interestingness labeling seems to be an important problem. This labeling problem is modeled as a new classification problem and a *rule set* is produced for these rules. Each instance of the rule set is represented by a vector whose components are the interestingness factors having the potential to determine the interestingness of the corresponding rule and the interestingness label of the rule.

The classification rules used in this study are probabilistic and have the following general structure:

If $(A_1\ op\ value_1)$ AND $(A_2\ op\ value_2)$ AND ...AND $(A_n\ op\ value_n)$ THEN
$(Class_1: vote_1, Class_2: vote_2,...,Class_k: vote_k)$

A_i's are the features, $Class_i$'s are the classes and $op \in \{=, \neq, <, \leq, >, \geq\}$.

The instances of the rule set have either "interesting" or "uninteresting" as the interestingness label, and have the interestingness factors shown in Table 1. In this new classification problem, these factors are treated as determining features, and interestingness label is treated as the target feature (class) of the rule set.

Table 1. Features of the rule set

Feature	Short description and/or formula
Major Class	$Class_i$ that takes the highest vote
Major Class Frequency	Ratio of the instances having $Class_i$ as the class label in the data set
Rule Size	Number of conditions in the antecedent part of the rule
Confidence with respect to Major Class	$\|Antecedent\ \&\ Class_i\| / \|Antecedent\|$
Coverage	$\|Antecedent\| / \|N\|$
Completeness with respect to Major Class	$\|Antecedent\ \&\ Class_i\| / \|Class_i\|$
Zero Voted Class Count	Number of classes given zero vote
Standard Deviation of Class Votes	Standard deviation of the votes of the classes
Major Class Vote	Maximum vote value distributed
Minor Class Vote	Minimum vote value distributed
Decisive	True if Std.Dev.of Class.Votes > s_{min}

Each feature carries information of a specific property of the corresponding rule. For instance, letting $Class_i$ to take the highest vote makes it the *Major Class* of that classification rule. If we shorten the representation of any rule as "If *Antecedent* THEN $Class_i$" and assume the data set to consist of N instances, we can define *Confidence*, *Coverage* and *Completeness* as in Table 1. Furthermore, a rule is decisive if the standard deviation of the votes is greater than s_{min}, whose definition is given in the following equation:

$$s_{min} = \frac{1}{(Class\ Count - 1)\sqrt{Class\ Count}} \qquad (1)$$

If a rule distributes its vote, '1', evenly among all classes, then the standard deviation of the votes becomes zero and the rule becomes extremely indecisive. This is the worst vote distribution that can happen. The next worst vote distribution happens if exactly one class takes a zero vote, and the whole vote is distributed evenly among the remaining classes. The standard deviation of the votes that will occur in such a scenario is called s_{min}.

4   Training in the VFP Algorithm

VFP (Voting Feature Projections) is a feature projection based classification-learning algorithm developed in this study. It is used to learn the rule interestingness concept and to classify the unlabeled rules in the context of modeling rule interestingness problem as a new classification problem.

The training phase of VFP, given in Figure 3, is achieved incrementally. On a nominal feature, concept description is shown as the set of points along with the numbers of instances of each class falling into those points. On the other hand, on a numeric feature, concept description is shown as the gaussian probability density functions for each class. Training can better be explained by looking at the sample data set in Figure 1, and the associated learned concept description in Figure 2.

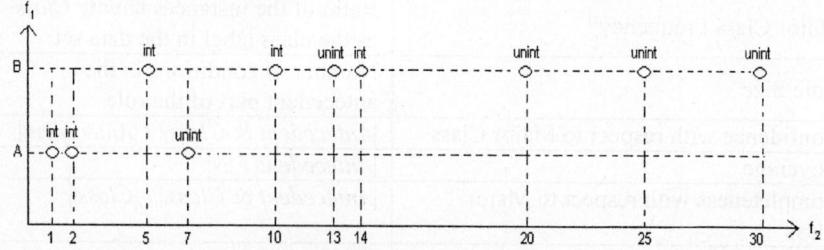

Fig. 1. Sample data set

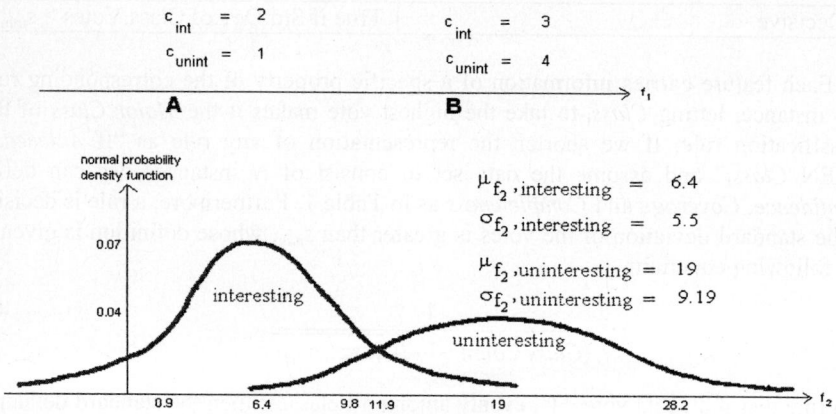

Fig. 2. Concept description learned for the sample data set

The example data set consists of 10 training instances, having nominal f_1 and numeric f_2 features. f_1 takes two values: 'A' and 'B', whereas f_2 takes some integer values. There are two possible classes: "interesting" and "uninteresting". f_2 is assumed to have gaussian probability density functions for both classes.

```
VFP_train (t)           /* t: newly added training instance */
begin
    let c be the class of t
    let others be the remaining classes
    if training set = {t}
        for each class s
            class_count[s] = 0
    class_count[c]++

    for each feature f

        if f is nominal
            p = find_point(f, t_f)
            if such a p exists
                point_class_count [f,p,c] ++
            else    /* add new point for f */
                add a new p' point
                point_class_count [f,p',c] = 1
                point_class_count [f,p',others] = 0

        else if f is numeric
            if training set = {t}
```
$\mu_{f,c} = t_f$, $\mu_{f,others} = 0$
$\mu^2_{f,c} = t_f^2$, $\mu^2_{f,others} = 0$
$\sigma_{f,c}$ = Undefined
norm_density_func.$_{f,c}$ = Undefined
```
            else
                n = class_count[c]
```
$\mu_{f,c} = (\mu_{f,c} * (n-1) + t_f) / n$ /*update*/
$\mu^2_{f,c} = (\mu^2_{f,c} * (n-1) + t_f^2) / n$ /*update*/
$\sigma_{f,c} = \sqrt{\frac{n}{n-1}(\mu^2_{f,c} - (\mu_{f,c})^2)}$

norm_density_func.$_{f,c}$ = $\frac{1}{\sigma_{f,c}\sqrt{2\pi}} e^{-\frac{(x-\mu_{f,c})^2}{2\sigma_{f,c}^2}}$

```
    return  { For numeric features:
              norm_density_func._f,c (∀f, c)
              For nominal features:
              point_class_count[f, p, c] (∀f, p, c)
end.
```

Fig. 3. Incremental train in VFP

In Figure 3 for a nominal feature f, *find_point* (f, t_f) searches t_f, the new training instance's value at feature f, in the f projection. If t_f is found at a point p, then *point_class_count* [f, p, c] is incremented, assuming that the training instance is of class c. If t_f is not found, then a new point p' is constructed and *point_class_count* [$f, p', class$] is initialized to 1 for *class* = c, and to 0 for *class* = *others*. In this study, features used in VFP are the interestingness factor values computed for the classification rules, and the classes are "interesting" and "uninteresting".

For a numeric feature f, if a new training instance t of class c is examined, the previous training instances of class c is let to construct a set P and $\mu_{f,c}$ and $\sigma_{f,c}$ are let to be the mean and the standard deviation of the f feature projection values of the instances in P, respectively. $\mu_{f,c}$ and $\sigma_{f,c}$ are updated incrementally. Updating $\sigma_{f,c}$ incrementally requires $\mu^2_{f,c}$ to be updated incrementally, as well.

5 Classification in the VFP Algorithm

Classification in VFP is shown in Figure 4. The query instance is projected on all features If a feature is not ready to querying, it gives zero, otherwise normalized votes. Normalization ensures each feature to have equal power in classifying the query instances. For a feature to be ready to querying, it requires to have at least two different values for each class.

The classification starts by giving zero votes to classes on each feature projection. For a nominal feature f, $find\_point$ (f, q_f) searchs whether q_f exists in the f projection. If q_f is found at a point p, feature f gives votes as given in equation 2, and then these votes are normalized to ensure equal voting power among features.

$$feature\_vote\ [f, c] = \frac{point\_class\_count\ [\ f, p, c\ ]}{class\_count\ [\ c\ ]} \qquad (2)$$

In equation 2, the number of class c instances on point p of feature projection f is divided by the total number of class c instances to find the class conditional probability of falling into the p point. For a linear feature f, each class gets the vote given in equation 3. Normal probability density function values are used as the vote values. These votes are also normalized.

$$feature\_vote\ [f, c] = \lim_{\Delta x \to 0} \int_{q_f}^{q_f + \Delta x} \frac{1}{\sigma_{f,c}\sqrt{2\pi}} e^{-\frac{(q_f - \mu_{f,c})^2}{2\sigma_{f,c}^2}} dx \qquad (3)$$

Final vote for any class c is the sum of all votes given by the features. If there exists a class c that uniquely gets the highest vote, then it is predicted to be the class of the query instance. The certainty factor of the classification is computed as follows:

$$C_f = \frac{final\ vote\ [c]}{\sum_{i=1}^{\#Classes} final\ vote\ [i]} \qquad (4)$$

```
VFP_query(q)                /* q: query instance*/
begin
   for each feature f and class c
      feature_vote[f,c] = 0
      if feature_ready_for_query_process(f)
         if f is nominal
            p = find_point(f,q_f)
            if such a p exists
               for each class c
```
$$feature\_vote\ [f,c]\ =\ \frac{point\_class\_count[f,p,c]}{class\_count[c]}$$
```
                  normalize_feature_votes (f)
         else if f is numeric
            for each class c
               feature_vote [f,c]=
```
$$lim_{\Delta x \to 0} \int_{q_f}^{q_f + \Delta x} \frac{1}{\sigma_{f,c}\sqrt{2\pi}} e^{-\frac{(q_f - \mu_{f,c})^2}{2\sigma_{f,c}^2}} dx$$
```
                  normalize_feature_votes (f)
   for each class c
```
$$final\_vote\ [c]\ =\ \sum_{f=1}^{\#Features} feature\_vote\ [\ f,c\ ]$$
```
   if  min_{i=1}^{#Classes} final_vote[i] < final_vote [k] = max_{i=1}^{#Classes} final_vote[i]
         classify q as "k" with a certainty factor C_f
         return C_f
      else return -1
end.
```

Fig. 4. Classification in VFP

6 IRIL Algorithm

IRIL algorithm, shown in Figure 5, needs two input parameters: R_p (The set of streaming classification rules of period p and $MinC_t$ (Minimum Certainty Threshold). It tries to classify the rules in R_p. If $C_f \geq MinC_t$ for a query rule r, this rule is inserted into the successfully classified rules set (R_s). Otherwise, two situations are possible: either the concept description is not able to classify r ($C_f = -1$), or the concept description's classification (prediction of r's interestingness label) is not of sufficient strength. If $C_f < MinC_t$, rule r is presented, along with its computed eleven interestingness factor values such as *Coverage*, *Rule Size*, *Decisive* etc., to the user for classification. This rule or actually the instance holding the interestingness factor values and the recently determined interestingness label of this rule is then inserted into the training rule set R_t and the concept description is reconstructed incrementally.

All the rules in R_p are labeled either automatically by the classification algorithm, or manually by the user. User participation leads rule interestingness learning process to be an interactive one. When the number of instances in the training rule set increases, the concept description learned tends to be more powerful and reliable.

IRIL executes on classification rules of all the periods and finally concludes by presenting the labeled rules in R_s.

```
IRIL (R_p, MinC_t)
  begin
        R_t ← ∅,    R_s ← ∅
        if p is the 1st period              //Warm-up Period
           for each rule r ∈ R_p
                   ask the user to classify r
                   set C_f of this classification to 1
                   insert r into R_t
                   VFP_train (r)
        else
           for each rule r ∈ R_p
                C_f ← VFP_query (r)
                   if C_f < MinC_t
                      ask the user to classify r
                      set C_f of this classification to 1
                      insert r into R_t
                      VFP_train (r)    //Update Concept Description
                   else
                      insert r into R_s
        return rules in R_s
  end.
```

Fig. 5. IRIL algorithm

7 Experimental Results

IRIL algorithm was tested to classify 1555 streaming classification rules induced from a financial distress domain between years 1989 and 1998. Each year has its own data and classification rules induced by using a benefit maximizing feature projection based rule learner proposed in [11]. The data set of the financial distress domain is a comprehensive set consisting of 25632 data instances and 164 determining features (159 numeric, 5 nominal). There are two classes: "DeclareProfit" and "DeclareLoss". The data set includes some financial information about 3000 companies collected during 10 years and the class feature states whether the company declared a profit or loss for the next three years. Domain expert previously labeled all the 1555 induced rules by an automated process to make accuracy measurement possible. Rules of the first year are selected as the warm-up rules to construct the initial concept description.

The results for $MinC_t$ = 51% show that 1344 rules are classified automatically with $C_f > MinC_t$. User participation is 13% in the classification process. In the classification process, it is always desired that rules are classified automatically, and user participation is low.

The accuracy values generally increase in proportion to the $MinC_t$. Because higher the $MinC_t$, higher the user participation is. And higher user participation leads to learn a more powerful and predictive concept description.

Table 2. Results for IRIL

	$MinC_t$ 51%	$MinC_t$ 53%	$MinC_t$ 55%	$MinC_t$ 57%
Number of rules	1555	1555	1555	1555
Number of rules classified automatically with high certainty	1344	1286	1196	1096
User participation	13%	17%	23%	29%
Overall Accuracy	80%	82%	86%	88%

8 Conclusion

IRIL feature projection based, interactive rule interestingness learning algorithm was developed and gave promising experimental results on streaming classification rules induced on a financial distress domain. The concept description learned by the VFP algorithm, also developed in the framework of IRIL, constitutes a novel approach for interestingness analysis of classification rules. The concept description differs among the users analyzing the same domain. That is, IRIL determines the important rule interestingness factors for a given domain subjectively.

References

1. Fayyad, U., Shapiro, G., Smyth, P.: From data mining to knowledge discovery in databases. AI Magazine **17**(3) (1996) 37–54
2. Hilderman, R.J., Hamilton, H.J.: Knowledge discovery and interestingness measures: a survey. Technical Report, Department of Computer Science, University of Regina (1999)
3. Frawely, W.J., Piatetsky-Shapiro, G., Matheus, C.J.: Knowledge discovery in databases: an overview. Knowledge Discovery in Databases. AAAI/MIT Press (1991) 1–27
4. Major, J.A., Mangano, J.J.: Selecting among rules induced from a hurricane database. In: Proceedings of AAAI Workshop on Knowledge Discovery in Databases. (1993) 30–31
5. Piatetsky-Shapiro, G., Matheus, C.J.: The interestingness of deviations. In: Proceedings of AAAI Workshop on Knowledge Discovery in Databases. (1994) 25–36
6. Klemettinen, M., Mannila, H., Ronkainen, P., Toivonen, H., Verkamo, A.I.: Finding interesting rules from large sets of discovered association rules. In: Proceedings of the 3rd Int. Conf. on Information and Knowledge Management. (1994) 401–407
7. Liu, B., Hsu, W., Chen, S.: Using general impressions to analyze discovered classification rules. In: Proceedings of the 3rd Int. Conf. on KDD (1997) 31–36
8. Liu, B., Hsu, W.: Post-analysis of learned rules. AAAI (1996) 828–834
9. Hussain, F., Liu, H., Suzuki, E., Lu, H.: Exception rule mining with a relative interestingness measure. In: Proc. Pacific-Asia Conf. on Knowledge Discovery and Data Mining. (2000) 86–97
10. Dong, G., Li, J.: Interestingness of discovered association rules in terms of neighborhood-based unexpectedness. In: Proceedings of the 2nd Pacific-Asia Conference on Knowledge Discovery and Data Mining. (1998) 72–86
11. Güvenir, H.A.: Benefit maximization in classification on feature projections. In: Proc. 3rd IASTED Int. Conf. on Artificial Intelligence and Applications (AIA 2003). (2003) 424–429

Using Fuzzy Petri Nets for Static Analysis of Rule-Bases

Burcin Bostan-Korpeoglu and Adnan Yazici

Department of Computer Engineering
Middle East Technical University, TR-06531, Ankara, Turkey
burcin.bostan@tcmb.gov.tr, yazici@ceng.metu.edu.tr

Abstract. We use a Fuzzy Petri Net (FPN) structure to represent knowledge and model the behavior in our intelligent object-oriented database environment, which integrates fuzzy, active and deductive rules with database objects. However, the behavior of a system can be unpredictable due to the rules triggering or untriggering each other (non-termination). Intermediate and final database states may also differ according to the order of rule executions (non-confluence). In order to foresee and solve problematic behavior patterns, we employ a static analysis on the FPN structure that provides easy checking of the termination property without requiring any extra construct. In addition, with our proposed fuzzy inference algorithm, we guarantee confluent rule executions. The techniques and solutions provided in this study can be utilized in various complex systems, such as weather forecasting applications and environmental information systems.

1 Introduction

Knowledge intensive applications require an intelligent environment with deduction capabilities. In such an application, there may be two reasons for deduction; One is user queries and the other is events occurring inside or outside the system. We introduce an intelligent object-oriented database environment in order to fulfill the requirements of knowledge-intensive applications. In that, we integrate fuzzy active and deductive rules with their inference mechanism in a fuzzy object-oriented database environment. After the incorporation of rules, our database system gains intelligent behavior. This allows objects to perceive dynamic occurrences or user queries after which they produce new knowledge or keep themselves in a consistent, stable and up-to-date state. We use Fuzzy Petri Nets (FPNs) to represent the knowledge and model the behavior of the system.

Petri nets are considered as a graphical and mathematical modeling tool. They are powerful in describing and studying information processing systems that are characterized as being concurrent, asynchronous, distributed, parallel and nondeterministic [8]. Several kinds of Petri nets have been investigated as tools for representing rules in knowledge based systems. The main advantage of using Petri nets in rule-based systems is that they provide a structured knowledge representation in which the relationships between the rules in the knowledge base are easily understood and they render a systemic inference capability [4]. Considering the uncertain and imprecise knowledge existing in various knowledge-intensive applications, the degree of truth of rules and facts represented in a knowledge base is expressed as a real number in interval [0,1]. Fuzzy Petri Nets (FPNs) are formed [4] to handle such fuzzy expressions.

There have been a couple of approaches on alternative formulations of FPNs to model the behavior of the system. However, due to the unstructured and unpredictable nature of rule processing, rules can be difficult to program and the behavior of the system can be complex and sometimes unpredictable. In an active database, rules may trigger and untrigger each other, and the intermediate and final states of the database can depend upon which rules are triggered and executed in which order. In order to determine these undesirable behavior patterns of the rule base, static rule analysis should be performed [1]. Such analysis involves identifying certain properties of the rule base at compile-time, which gives programmer an opportunity to modify the rule base.

Two important and desirable properties of active rule behavior are termination and confluence. These properties are defined for user-defined changes and database states in a given rule set.

– *Termination:* A rule set is guaranteed to terminate if, for any database state and initial modification, rule processing does not continue forever.
– *Confluence:* A rule set is confluent if, for any database state and initial modification, the final database state after rule processing is unique, i.e., it is independent of the order in which activated rules are executed.

Static analysis techniques only give sufficient conditions for guaranteeing the property searched for. For example, the identification of potential non-termination in a set of rules indicates the possibility of infinite loops at run time, while the identification of potential non-confluence indicates that a rule base may exhibit nondeterministic behavior.

In this paper, we check properties of our system using the FPN structure. Our FPN structure already contains the Triggering Graph information and supports the static analysis of the rule base. Therefore, there is no need to do extra work to construct Triggering Graph as required in other studies [1,5–7,9], which use different structures other than FPN for studying rule analysis. In addition, while performing termination analysis, we do also care about the event and condition compositions. We also guarantee confluent rule execution with the fuzzy inference algorithm that we introduce in this paper.

The organization of this paper is as follows. In Section 2, we briefly define our Fuzzy Petri Net model for fuzzy rules. In Section 3, after we give the assumptions and understandings in Termination Analysis, we explain the details of how we perform termination analysis on the FPN. These are followed by a summary of the earlier work on confluence analysis in Section 4. We also explain how we guarantee confluence in our model in this section. Finally, we make our conclusions and state future work in Section 5.

2 A Fuzzy Petri Net Model for Fuzzy Rules

We introduce the following Fuzzy Petri Net (FPN) structure to model the fuzzy rules: (P,P_s,P_e,T, A, TT, TTF, AEF,PR,PPM,TV) where

i. P is a finite set of *places*, in which
   - $P_s \subset$ P is a finite set of *input places* for primitive events or conditions.
   - $P_e \subset$ P is a finite set of *output places* for actions or conclusions.
ii. T is a finite set of *transitions*.
iii. A $\subset$ (PxT $\cup$ TxP) is a finite set of *arcs* for connections between places and transitions.
iv. TT is a finite set of *token(color) types*.
v. TTF:P $\rightarrow$ TT is *token type function*, mapping each place $\in$ P to a token type $\in$ TT.
vi. AEF: Arc $\rightarrow$ expression, is *arc expression function* mapping each arc to an expression.
vii. PR is a finite set of *propositions*, corresponding to either events or conditions or actions/conclusions.
viii. PPM: P $\rightarrow$ PR , is *place to proposition mapping*, where | PR |=| P |.
ix. TV: P$\rightarrow$ [0,1] is *truth values of propositions* assigned to places.

The FPN is represented as directed arcs with two types of nodes (places and transitions) connected by arrows that specify the direction of information flow. Places represent storage for input or output. Transitions represent activities (transformations). A token represents a fragment of information which has a type. Tokens are used to define the execution. An assignment of tokens to places is called marking. We model the dynamic behavior of fuzzy rule-based reasoning with evaluation of markings. Every time an input place of the FPN is marked, whether the corresponding transition(s) can fire has to be checked. A transition *t* can fire if and only if all its input places are marked. Since we provide parameter passing, token value of an output place is calculated from that of its input places using the transition function. The firing of a transition leads to removal of tokens from the input places and calculation and insertion of tokens into output places. Since we employ fuzziness, each token has a membership value to the place it is assigned. This is part of the token and gets calculated within the transition function. Figure 1 shows how we realize the steps of Fuzzy Inference using the FPN structure that we present above. During the FPN construction, first the rule definitions are obtained from the user. For each rule, a rule object is created, and event, condition, action parts of the rule is examined. While doing that, Fuzzy Petri Net places are created. Then, the fuzzy inference groups, which are the concurrent rule sets that gets triggered at the same time, are determined according to their event, condition and action parts. Finally, transitions are constructed over these FPN places. In order to determine which rule triggers another one (i.e. which action execution or condition evaluation generates new events), unification of condition and action calls with event specifications is performed. During the FPN construction, the attributes of the rule objects are updated to hold the related links on FPN. Also each FPN place has a *rule_set* attribute in order to hold the rule objects that uses the FPN place.

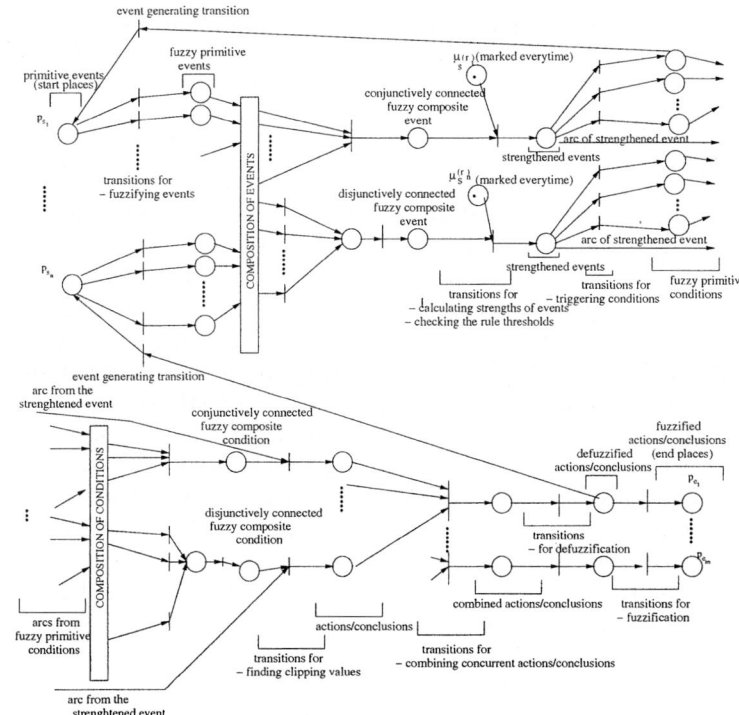

Fig. 1. Modeling fuzzy inference using fuzzy petri nets.

3 Termination Analysis

Termination for a rule set is guaranteed if rule processing always reaches a state in which no rule is triggered. Several methods have been proposed in the literature to perform termination analysis. One of them is building a triggering graph by considering the type of triggering events and events generated by the execution of the rule actions [1,5,7]. A Triggering Graph [1] is a directed graph $\{V, E\}$, where each node in V corresponds to a rule in the rule base and each edge $r_i \rightarrow r_j$ in E means that the action of the rule r_i generates events that trigger r_j. If there are no cycles in the triggering graph, then processing is guaranteed to terminate. The triggering graph, however, fails to take account the details of the interaction between the conditions and the actions of potentially non-terminating rules. That is, although triggering graph has a cycle, there may be the case that when a rule in the cycle gets triggered, the condition of that rule is not true. As a result, the rule is not executed and the cyclic chain is broken. Consider for example the following rule:

```
R1:
  ON update to attribute A of T
  IF new value A > 10
  THEN set A of T to 10
```

The triggering graph for the rule base involving R_1 contains a cycle, as the action of R_1 updates the attribute A of T, which in turn triggers R_1. However, non-termination does not result as the action of R_1 assigns A a value for which the condition of R_1 never becomes true. It is to overcome this limitation in triggering graphs that activation graphs have been introduced.

An Activation Graph [2] is built upon the semantic information contained in the rule conditions and actions. It is a directed graph $\{V,E\}$, where each node in V corresponds to a rule in the rule base, each edge $r_i \rightarrow r_j$ ($i \neq j$) in E means that the action of the rule r_i may change the truth value of the condition of r_j from false to true, and each edge $r_i \rightarrow r_i$ means that the condition of r_i may be true after the execution of its own action. If there are no cycles in the activation graph, then processing is guaranteed to terminate. Some studies [3] mostly rely on the Activation Graph while making termination analysis.

Other studies [2] try to detect the potential non-termination by using both triggering graph and activation graph together in which a rule set can only exhibit nonterminating behavior when there are cycles in both the triggering and the activation graphs that have at least one rule in common. Returning to the example given above, the activation graph for rule R_1 contains no cycle. Because its condition can not be true after the execution of its action. Thus, even though the triggering graph contains a cycle, execution of the rule terminates.

While triggering graph arcs are syntactically derivable, it is very difficult to precisely determine the arcs of an activation graph. In [2], it is assumed that conditions and actions are both represented by relational algebra expressions. Unfortunately, for the host languages that are not based on relational algebra or relational calculus, it is difficult to infer the truth value of a condition from the imperative code of a rule's action.

Most of the existing studies on rule analysis only deal with simple rule languages; i.e. languages that support only a limited set of constructs for specifying active behavior. If the rules become complex (like having composite events, supporting complex conditions/actions, etc.), their analysis also becomes complex. The reason is, there are more elements on which the triggering of a rule depends. For example, a rule defined on a complex event is triggered only when all component events occur. Therefore, compared to a simple rule language, it is more difficult to decide when rules may generate an infinite loop during execution. That is , in a system having only primitive events, an edge in the triggering graph indicates that one rule can generate an event that can in turn trigger another. However, where a rule r has a composite event, it may be that no other single rule in the rule base can trigger r, but that a subset of the rules together may be able to trigger r. Only a very few studies consider compositions while performing termination analysis [6, 9].

3.1 Termination Analysis on the FPN

Before we check termination property of the system, we construct the FPN. In that, during the transition construction, we obtain the triggering graph information from the *event generating transitions*. (An *event generating transition* is an indication of one rule triggering another.) During the termination analysis, once a cyclic path is detected, it may not be a true cycle due to one or more rules in the cycle having composite events. That is, not all composing events of a composite event may be triggered. We eliminate these type of false cycles in the termination analysis. The algorithm whose explanation and pseudecode given below finds the true cycles.

An Algorithm for Determining True Cycles. We hold an $m \times m$ matrix of rules, which is D. Each d_{ij} entry holds the connectivity information about the rules. d_{ij} entry is 1 if rule r_i triggers r_j, meaning there is an *event generating transition* from r_i to r_j. Otherwise, its value is 0. Let D_k be an $m \times m$ matrix holding the matrix composition result of k number of D matrices. It holds the connectivity information at k edges (or *event generating transitions*) distance. Assuming there is a cycle, if we have *number_of_rules* rules in the rule base, we can have at most *number_of_rules* distinct *event generating transitions* to go through in our FPN. This is due to the fact that, there may be at most *number_of_rules event generating transitions* that connect these rules. If the ith diagonal at D_k holds a value greater than 0, this means that there is a cycle in k steps (or k *event generating transitions* distance). Notice that all rules taking place in that cycle have values greater than 0 in their diagonal entry. Comparing with the previous matrices which indicates a cyclic path, if the same diagonal elements having values greater than 0 are obtained at some k steps, the matrix composition should be terminated. Or if 0 is obtained for all entries of a matrix, again the matrix composition should be terminated. This means that all edges have been consumed and there is no further edge to go through, which is an indication of no cyclic behavior.

By the time these D matrices have been calculated, a linked list of rules which have been gone through the path is held in the L matrix. This means that $l_k[i][j]$ holds a linked list of rules which is passed through the path from rules r_i to r_j. If the ith diagonal at D_k holds a value greater than 0, we can obtain the cyclic path elements at $l_k[i][i]$. Now it is easy to find true cycles by checking the $[i][i]$ entry of L_k. If all the rules in the path have only primitive events, this is certainly a true cycle. Otherwise (if any of them has a composite event) the rule set of the primitive events of the rules is examined. If they are all included in the cycle, again the cycle is a true cycle. Otherwise it is not a true cycle. If there is at least one true cycle, the user is informed about the situation together with the rules taking place inside the cycle. Then it is the user's choice to change the definitions of these rules. After that, the termination analysis is repeated.

```
DETERMINE_TRUE_CYCLES ALGORITHM
BEGIN
calculate L1
DO{
   FOR each place i
   { IF Dk(ii) is >= 1 where i is the index of the rule ri
        IF rules in the Lk(ii) is distinct
           IF none of the rules contains composite event
              RETURN cyclic rules (Lk(ii))
```

```
        ELSE
            IF all rule sets of the primitive events of the the rules
                (which have composite event) is included in the Lk(ii)
                RETURN cyclic rules (Lk(ii))
        ELSE
            RETURN no cycle}
    k=k+1
    calculate Dk
    calculate Lk }UNTIL (Dk = 0) OR (k > number_of_rules)
RETURN no cycle
END
```

Example 1. Suppose there are the following two rules:

R1:   R2:
ON (e11 and e21) threshold R1   ON e12 threshold R2
IF c1   IF c2
THEN a1   THEN a2

In these rules, a_1 unifies with crisp event e_1 (which has e_{11} and e_{12} as its fuzzy primitive events) and a_2 unifies with crisp event e_2 (which has e_{21} as its fuzzy primitive event). The dependencies and the triggering graph are shown in Figure 2. Dashed arcs show the partial triggering due to composite events and solid arcs show the total triggering. Figure 3 shows the FPN constructed according to this rule set. For this example, D_1 and L_1 are as follows:

$$D_1 = \begin{bmatrix} 1 & 1 \\ 1 & 0 \end{bmatrix} L_1 = \begin{bmatrix} 1,1 & 1,2 \\ 2,1 & 0 \end{bmatrix}$$

Since $D_1[1][1]$ entry has the value 1, this means that there is a cycle. The rules taking place in the cycle are found at $l[i][i]$ entry, which is $\{1,1\}$, meaning the rule r_1. The rules that pass through the primitive event places of the rules in the cycle (which can be found at $r_1.PN\_primitive\_event.rule\_set$), are the rules r_1 and r_2. Since the cyclic set $\{1,1\}$ does not contain r_2, this is not a true cycle. Therefore it is excluded. Then D_2 is calculated and at the same time L_2 is obtained:

$$D_2 = \begin{bmatrix} 2 & 1 \\ 1 & 1 \end{bmatrix} L_2 = \begin{bmatrix} 1,1,1;1,2,1 & 1,1,2 \\ 2,1,1 & 2,1,2 \end{bmatrix}$$

Since $D_2[1][1]$ entry has a value greater than 0, there is a possibility of a cycle. $r_1.PN\_primitive\_event.rule\_set$ is the rules r_1 and r_2. Since the cyclic set $\{1,2,1\}$ contains both r_1 and r_2, it is a true cycle. Termination analysis returns the rules r_1 and r_2, which take place inside the cycle. These rules should be changed in order to break the cycle.

4 Confluence Analysis

On each execution of the scheduling phase of rule processing, multiple rules may be triggered. A rule set is confluent if the final state of the database doesn't depend on which eligible rule has been chosen for execution.

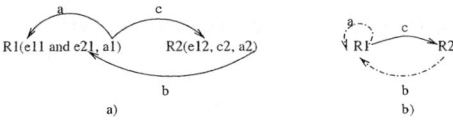

Fig. 2. Dependencies and the Triggering Graph for Example 1

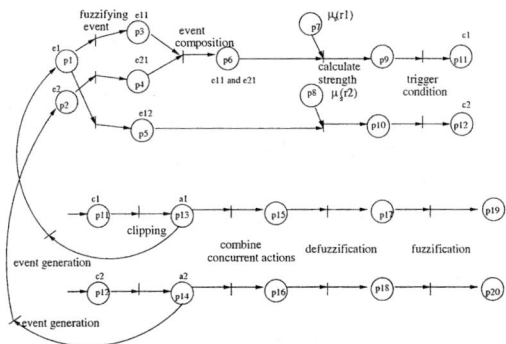

Fig. 3. Fuzzy petri net of Example 1

The rule execution process can be described by the notions of *rule execution state* and *rule execution sequence*. Consider a rule set R. A rule execution state S has two components: 1. a database state d, and 2. a set of triggered rules $R_T \subset R$. When R_T is empty, no rule is triggered and the rule execution state is quiescent. A rule execution sequence consists of a series of rule execution states linked by (executed) rules. A rule execution state is complete if its last state is quiescent. A rule set is confluent if, for every initial execution state S, every complete rule execution sequence beginning with S reaches the same quiescent state. Then confluence analysis requires the exhaustive verification of all possible execution sequences for all possible initial states. This technique is clearly unfeasible even for a small rule set.

A different approach to confluence analysis is based on the *commutativity* of rule pairs. Two rules r_i and r_j commute if, starting with any rule execution state S, executing r_i followed by r_j produces the same rule execution state as executing r_j followed by r_i. If all pairs of rules in a rule set R commute, any execution sequences with the same initial state and executed rules have the same final state. Then, it is possible to state a sufficient condition to guarantee confluence of a rule set: A rule set R is confluent if all pairs of rules in R commute [3].

Confluence may be guaranteed by imposing a total ordering on the active rule set [2]. If a total ordering is defined on the rules, when multiple rules are triggered only one rule at a time is eligible for evaluation. This provides a single rule execution sequence, which yields a unique final state, and confluence is guaranteed.

4.1 Guaranteeing Confluent Executions in Our FPN Model

Our fuzzy inference algorithm based on our FPN is given below. In that, if the rules triggered are in the same fuzzy inference group, their execution is carried at the same time and the total outcome is computed. On the other hand, if the rules triggered are not in the same fuzzy inference group, total ordering is achieved according to their $\mu_s(r)$ (similarity to the current scenario) values. Therefore, our inference algorithm based on FPN guarantees confluent rule execution. The algorithm uses the following data structures:

a. M is an m x 1 column vector of places p_i, where $i = 1, ..., m$. Each of its entries holds a data structure of two elements:
   - the 1st element holds the number of tokens, (*current_marking*),
   - the 2nd element holds a linked list of current_marking many token values, which works with FIFO queuing mechanism (*token_values*)
b. N is an n x 1 column vector of transitions t_j, where $j = 1, ..., n$. Each of its entries holds a transition function. Each transition function uses the head elements of the input places token_values and produces an output to be added to the tail of the output places token_values.
c. $C^+ = (c_{ij}^+)$ and $C^- = (c_{ij}^-)$ represent the output and input incidence matrices respectively, where c_{ij}^+ is 1 if there is an arc from the transition t_j to place p_i and c_{ij}^- is 1 if there is an arc from the place p_i to the transition t_j and their values are 0 if there is no connection.

```
INFERENCE ALGORITHM
INPUT: start place Psi
OUTPUT: a set of end places Pe as the result of the inference
BEGIN
find the index of the start place in M vector
increase the number of tokens in the start place
add a new token to the tail of the start place
IF the rules triggered are in the same fuzzy inference group THEN
    set the active rule to any one of the rules triggered.
ELSE
   order the triggered rules according to their scenario similarity
   set the linked list of active rules according this order
WHILE ordered rules (i.e. linked list of active rules)
                are not consumed yet
{ check the transitions in N where the current place
    is connected as an input in input incidence matrix cij-
  DO for each one of them
  { If the rules that uses the transition
        is a subset of the ordered rules' head
      Check the other input places of the transition in cij-
      If they also have tokens to use
        Fire the transition
        Mark the output places in M using cij+
        remove the tokens from the input places in M using cij-
}UNTIL an end place Pex is reached
```

```
        add the end place reached (Pex) to the set of outputs Pe
        update the ordered rules' head to the next }
RETURN(Pe)
END
```

5 Conclusion

FPNs analytic capability can help with checking the properties of a system, which provides deeper insights into that system. In this paper, having observed this ability of the FPNs, we study the static analysis of our rule base. When we construct our FPN, we inherently also contain the triggering graph information. When the assumptions and the theories regarding the termination analysis were put forward, event and condition compositions have been neglected. Recently, only a limited number of studies have considered compositions. However, in these studies, in order to perform termination analysis together with compositions, extra effort is involved in dealing with complex structures and algorithms. On the other hand, we can handle event and condition compositions easily by the structures provided by our FPN. As a result, our termination analysis algorithm is simple and easy to understand. In addition, our fuzzy inference algorithm working on our FPN assures confluent rule executions. This assurance comes from the fact that our inference algorithm provides a total order within the rules using the similarity of the rules to the current active scenario.

The techniques and solutions provided in this study can be utilized in various complex systems, such as weather forecasting applications and environmental information systems.

References

1. Aiken, A., Hellerstein, J., Widow, J.: Static analysis techniques for predicting the behavior of active database rules. ACM TODS **20**(1) (1995) 3–41
2. Baralis, E., Ceri, S., Paraboschi, S.: Improved rule analysis by means of triggering and activation graphs. In: Proc. of RIDS'95. LNCS, Vol. 985. Springer-Verlag (1995) 165–181
3. Baralis, E., Widow, J.: An algebraic approach to rule analysis in expert database systems. In: Proc. of VLDB'94. (1994) 475–486
4. Chun, M., Bien, Z.: Fuzzy petri net representation and reasoning methods for rule-based decision making systems. IECE Trans. Fundamentals **E76** (A/6) (1993)
5. Ceri, S., Widow, J.: Deriving production rules for constraint maintenance. In: Proc. of VLDB'90. (1990) 566–577
6. Dinn, A., Paton, N., Williams, H.: Active rule analysis in the rock and roll deductive object-oriented database. Information Systems **24**(4) (1999) 327–353
7. Karadimce, A., Urban, S.: Refined triggering graphs: A logic-based approach to termination analysis in an object-oriented database. In: ICDE. (1996) 384–391
8. Murata, T.: Petri nets: Properties, analysis and applications. In: Proc. IEEE **77**(4). (1989) 541–540
9. Vaduva, A., Gatziu, S., Dittrich, K.: Investigating termination in active database systems with expressive rule languages. Technical Report, Institut für Informatik (1997)

Protein Structural Class Determination Using Support Vector Machines

Zerrin Isik, Berrin Yanikoglu, and Ugur Sezerman

Sabanci University, 34956, Tuzla, Istanbul, Turkey
zisik@su.sabanciuniv.edu, {berrin,ugur}@sabanciuniv.edu

Abstract. Proteins can be classified into four structural classes (all-α, all-β, α/β, $\alpha+\beta$) according to their secondary structure composition. In this paper, we predict the structural class of a protein from its Amino Acid Composition (AAC) using Support Vector Machines (SVM). A protein can be represented by a 20 dimensional vector according to its AAC. In addition to the AAC, we have used another feature set, called the Trio Amino Acid Composition (Trio AAC) which takes into account the amino acid neighborhood information. We have tried both of these features, the AAC and the Trio AAC, in each case using a SVM as the classification tool, in predicting the structural class of a protein. According to the Jackknife test results, Trio AAC feature set shows better classification performance than the AAC feature.

1 Introduction

Protein folding is the problem of finding the 3D structure of a protein, also called its native state, from its amino acid sequence. There are 20 different types of amino acids (labeled with their initials as: A, C, G, ...) and one can think of a protein as a sequence of amino acids (e.g. AGGCT...). Hence the folding problem is finding how this amino acid chain (1D structure) folds into its native state (3D structure). Protein folding problem is a widely researched area since the 3D structure of a protein offers significant clues about the function of a protein which cannot be found via experimental methods quickly or easily.

In finding the 3D structure of a protein, a useful first step is finding the 2D structure, which is the local shape of its subsequences: a helix (called α-helix) or a strand (called β-strand). A protein is classified into one of four *structural classes*, a term introduced by Levitt and Chothia, according to its secondary structure components: all-α, all-β, α/β, $\alpha+\beta$, [1, 2]. An illustration of two of these (all-α, all-β) is given in Figure 1.

The structural class of a protein has been used in some secondary structure prediction algorithms [3–5]. Once, the structural class of a protein is known, it can be used to reduce the search space of the structure prediction problem: most of the structure alternatives will be eliminated and the structure prediction task will become easier and faster.

During the past ten years, much research has been done on the structural classification problem [6–18]. Chou [12] used the amino acid composition of a protein and Mahalanobis distance to assign a protein into one of the four structural

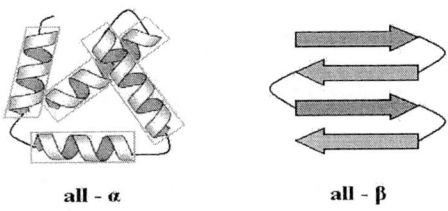

Fig. 1. The illustration of two structural classes. The one on the left is a protein composed of only α-helices whereas the one on the right is composed of what is called a β-sheet (formed by strands of amino acids).

classes. Due to the high reported performance, Wang et al. tried to duplicate Chou's work using the same data set, without success [19]. More recently, Ding and Dubchak compare the classification performance of ANNs and SVMs on classifying proteins into one of 27 fold classes, which are subclasses of the structural classes [17]. Tan and coworkers also work on the fold classification problem (for 27 fold classes), using a new ensemble learning method [18].

These approaches typically use the *Amino Acid Composition* (AAC) of the protein as the base for classification. The AAC is a 20 dimensional vector specifying the composition percentage for each of the 20 amino acids. Although the AAC largely determines structural class, its capacity is limited, since one looses information by representing a protein with only a 20 dimensional vector. We improved the classification capacity of the AAC by extending it to the *Trio AAC*. The Trio AAC records the occurrence frequency of all possible combinations of consecutive amino acid triplets in the protein. The frequency distribution of neighboring triplets is very sparse because of the high dimensionality of the Trio AAC input vector (20^3). Furthermore, one also should exploit the evolutionary information which shows that certain amino acids can be replaced by the others without disrupting the function of a protein. These replacements generally occur between amino acids which have similar physical and chemical properties [20]. In this work, we have used different clusterings of the amino acids to take into account these similarities and reduce the dimensionality, as explained in Section 2.

In the results section we compare the classification performance of two feature sets, the AAC and the Trio AAC. The classification performance of a Support Vector Machine with these feature sets is measured on a data set consisting of 117 training and 63 test proteins [12]. The comparison of two different feature sets have proved that the high classification capacity of SVMs and the new feature vector (Trio AAC) lead to much better classification results. Most work in this area is not directly comparable due to different data sets or different number of classes the proteins are classified into. We use the same data set used by Chou [12] and Wang et al. [19], in order to be able to compare our results to some extent.

2 Protein Structural Class Determination

We have tried two approaches to classify a protein into one of the four structural classes (all-α, all-β, α/β, $\alpha+\beta$). A Support Vector Machine is used with the feature sets of AAC and Trio AAC, which incorporates evolutionary and neighborhood information to the AAC.

We preferred to use a SVM as the classification tool because of its generalization power, as well as its high classification performance on the protein structural classification problem [21, 16, 17]. The SVM is a supervised machine learning technique which seeks an optimal discrimination of two classes, in high dimensional feature space. The superior generalization power, especially for high dimensional data, and fast convergence in training are the main advantages of SVMs. Generally, SVMs are designed for 2-class classification problems whereas our work requires the multi-class classification. Multi-class classification can be achieved using a one-against-one voting scheme, as we have done using the one-against-one voting scheme of the LIBSVM software [22]. In order to get good classification results, the parameters of SVM, especially the kernel type and the error-margin tradeoff (C), should be fixed. In our work, the Gaussian kernels are used since, they provided better separation compared to Polynomial and Sigmoid kernels for all experiments. The value of the parameter C was fixed during the training and later used during the testing. The best performance was obtained with C values ranging from 10 to 100 in various tasks.

We used two different feature sets, the AAC and the Trio AAC, as the input vectors of the SVM. The PDB files were used to form both the AAC and the Trio AAC vectors for the given proteins [23]. After collecting the PDB files of proteins, we extracted the amino acid sequence of each one. The amino acid sequences were then converted to the feature vectors as described in the following sections.

2.1 AAC

The AAC represents protein with a 20 dimensional vector corresponding to the composition (frequency of occurrence) of the 20 amino acids in the protein. Since the frequencies sum up to 1, resulting in only 19 independent dimensions, the AAC can be used as a 19 dimensional vector.

$$X = \begin{bmatrix} x_1 & x_2 & \ldots & x_{20} \end{bmatrix}, \tag{1}$$

where x_k is the occurrence frequency of the kth amino acid.

2.2 Trio AAC

The Trio AAC is the occurrence frequency of all possible consecutive triplets of amino acids in the protein. Whereas the AAC is a 20-dimensional vector, the Trio AAC vector, consisting of the neighborhood composition of triplets of amino acids, requires a 20x20x20 dimensional vector (e.g. AAA, AAC, ...).

We reduce the dimensionality of the Trio AAC input vector using various different clusterings of the amino acids, also taking into account the evolutionary information. The amino acid clusters are constructed according to hydrophobicity and charge information of amino acids given by Thomas and Dill [20]. We experimented with different number of clusters: 5, 9, or 14 clusters of the amino acids, giving Trio AAC vectors of 125 (5^3), 729 (9^3), and 2744 (14^3) dimensions, respectively.

3 Results

We have measured the performance of two algorithms: SVM with the AAC and SVM with the Trio AAC. We have also compared our test results to another structural classification work which also applied the AAC feature set on the same data set [19]. In all these tests, we have used a data set consisting of 117 training proteins (29-α, 30-β, 29-α/β, 29-$\alpha + \beta$) and 63 (8-α, 22-β, 9-α/β, 24-$\alpha + \beta$) test proteins [12].

A protein is said to belong to a structural class based on the percentage of its α-helix and β-sheet residues. In our data set, the data is labeled according to the following percentage thresholds:

- α class proteins include more than 40% α-helix and less than 5% β-sheet residues
- β class proteins include less than 5% α-helix and more than 40% β-sheet residues
- α/β class proteins include more than 15% α-helix, more than 15% β-sheet, and more than 60% parallel β-sheets
- $\alpha+\beta$ class proteins include more than 15% α-helix, more than 15% β-sheet, and more than 60% antiparallel β-sheets.

Note that the remaining, less-structured parts of a protein, such as loops, are not accounted in the above percentages.

3.1 Training Performance

The term *training performance* is used to denote the performance of the classifier on the training set. Specifically, the training performance is the percentage of the correctly classified training data, once the training completes, and is an indication of how well the training data is learned. Even though what is important is the generalization of a classifier, training performances are often reported for this problem, and we do the same for completeness.

The SVM achieved a near 99.1% training performance for for both sets of features (96.% for β, 100% for the rest). Not achieving a 100% separation on the training data is quite normal and just indicates that the data points may not be linearly separable in the feature space, due to the input space mapping done by the kernel function.

3.2 Test Performance

Table 1 summarizes the test performance of the classifier on the test set (63 proteins), after being trained on the training set (117 other proteins). The AAC and the Trio AAC are used as feature vectors for the SVM.

The average test performances of the SVM using the AAC and the Trio AAC are 71.4% and 66.6%, respectively. The performance of the SVM with Trio AAC feature was found to be lower compared to the AAC feature. This is likely to be due to the high dimensionality of the input data, compared to the size of the training set: if there are points in the test set which are not represented in the training set, they could be misclassified. In this and all the other tables, we report the performance of the Trio AAC using 9 clusters, as that gave the best results.

Class Name	SVM^{AAC}	$SVM^{TrioAAC}$
all-α	100%	100%
all-α	62.5%	62.5%
all-β	77.2%	77.2%
α/β	100%	77.7%
$\alpha+\beta$	58.3%	54.1%
$Average$	71.4%	66.6%

Table 1. Performance of the classifier on the test set. The AAC feature and the Trio AAC (9 clusters) are used for the SVM

3.3 Test Performance Using the Jackknife Method

The *Jackknife test*, also called the leave-one-out test, is a cross-validation technique which is used when there is a small data set. In the Jackknife test, training is done using all of the data (train + test) leaving one sample out each time; then the performance is tested using that one sample, on that round of train-test cycle. At the end, the test performance is calculated as the average of the test results obtained in all the cycles. This method uses all of the data for testing, but since the test data is not used for the corresponding training phase, the testing is unbiased.

Table 2 displays the results of a Jackknife experiment using both the train and test sets (117 + 63), in conjunction with the AAC and the Trio AAC. According to this Jackknife test results, the performance of the SVM is quite successful. The average classification rates are 85% and 92.7% for the AAC and the Trio AAC, respectively. We achieved the 92.7% classification rate using the Trio AAC which is constructed using 9 amino acid clusters.

Class Name	SVM^{AAC} %	#	$SVM^{TrioAAC}$ %	#
all-α	72.9	(27/37)	72.9	(27/37)
all-β	100	(52/52)	98	(51/52)
α/β	84.2	(32/38)	94.7	(36/38)
$\alpha+\beta$	79.2	(42/53)	100	(53/53)
Average	85.0	(153/180)	92.7	(167/180)

Table 2. Jackknife test performance on (117+63) proteins, using the SVM with the AAC and the Trio AAC (9 clusters) features

A second Jackknife test has been performed on only the 117 training proteins in order to compare our results to the previous work of Wang and Yuan [19], who also used the AAC feature as a base classifier. The results for both works are shown in Table 3. According to these results, the average classification performance of the SVM (using the AAC) is significantly better than the other work. The average classification rate of the Trio AAC (84.6%) is even better than that of the AAC (74.3%).

Class Name	Wang et.al.	SVM^{AAC}	$SVM^{TrioAAC}$
all-α	66.7%	75.8%	82.7%
all-β	56.7%	93.3%	93.3%
α/β	43.3%	71.4%	89.2%
$\alpha+\beta$	46.7%	55.1%	72.4%
Average	53.3%	74.3%	84.6%

Table 3. Jackknife test performance on 117 proteins (the training set only). This experiment was done to compare our results to a previous work of Wang and Yuan (given on the first column), who also used the AAC feature in the Jackknife test on the same proteins [19]. Our results, obtained by the SVM method using the AAC or the Trio AAC, are given on the second and third columns

4 Summary and Discussion

Despite years of research and the wide variety of approaches that have been utilized, the protein folding problem still remains an open problem. Today the problem is approached in many different directions and divided up into smaller tasks, such as secondary structure prediction, structural class assignment, contact map prediction etc.

In this study, we addressed the structural classification problem and compared the performance of Support Vector Machines using the AAC and the Trio AAC features. The comparison of two feature sets shows that the Trio AAC provides 8-10% improvement in classification accuracy (see Tables 2 and 3). We experimented with different number of clusters, 5, 9, and 14 clusters of the amino acids, giving Trio AAC vectors of increasing lengths. The experiment with 9 clusters of the amino acids has the highest classification performance. The better performance of the Trio AAC proves our assumption: the neighborhood and evolutionary information positively contributes on the classification accuracy. We have also obtained better classification rates using more training data, which is as expected. the second Jackknife test (Table 4), using both the AAC and the Trio AAC features.

In literature, there are two studies which use feature vectors similar to the Trio AAC on different domains; however they are on remote homology detection problem and amino acid neighboring effect [24, 25]. We recently became aware of two other studies: Markowetz et al. uses feature vectors similar to the Trio ACC, however the idea of using amino acid clusters (to reduce dimensionality) has not been applied [26]. In this work, 268 protein sequences are classified into a set of 42 structural classes with a 78% performance in cross-validation tests. Cai et al. uses a Support Vector Machine as the classification method and the amino acid composition as feature set and report an average classification performance of 93%, for a set of 204 proteins [16]. However these results are not directly comparable to ours due to the differences in the number of structural classes or in the data sets.

In summary, we devised a new and more complex feature set (Trio AAC) incorporating neighborhood information in addition to the commonly used amino acid composition information. The higher classification rates indicate that the combination of a powerful tool and this new feature set improves the accuracy of the structural class determination problem.

References

1. Levitt, M., Chothia, C.: Structural patterns in globular proteins. Nature **261** (1976) 552–558
2. Richardson, J.S., Richardson, D.C.: Principles and patterns of protein conformation. In: Fasman, G.D. (ed.): Prediction of protein structure and the principles of protein conformation. New York, Plenum Press (1989) 1–98
3. Deleage, G., Dixon, J.: Use of class prediction to improve protein secondary structure prediction. In: Fasman, G.D. (ed.): Prediction of protein structure and the principles of protein conformation. New York, Plenum Press (1989) 587–597

4. Kneller, D.G., Cohen, F.E., Langridge, R.: Improvements in protein secondary structure prediction by an enhanced neural network. J Mol Biol **214** (1990) 171–182
5. Eisenhaber, F., Persson, B., Argos, P.: Protein structure prediction: recognition of primary, secondary, and tertiary structural features from amino acid sequence. Crit Rev Biochem Mol Biol **30** (1995) 1–94
6. Nakashima, H., Nishikawa, K., Ooi, T.: The folding type of a protein is relevant to the amino acid composition. J Biochem (Tokyo) **99** (1986) 153–162
7. Klein, P., Delisi, C.: Prediction of protein structural class from the amino acid sequence. Biopolymers **25** (1986) 1659–1672
8. Chou, P.Y.: Prediction of protein structural classes from amino acid composition. In: Fasman, G.D. (ed.): Prediction of protein structure and the principles of protein conformation. New York, Plenum Press (1989) 549–586
9. Zhang, C.T., Chou, K.C.: An optimization approach to predicting protein structural class from amino acid composition. Protein Sci **1** (1992) 401–408
10. Metfessel, B.A., Saurugger, P.N., Connelly, D.P., Rich, S.S.: Cross-validation of protein structural class prediction using statistical clustering and neural networks. Protein Sci **2** (1993) 1171–1182
11. Chandonia, J.M., Karplus, M.: Neural networks for secondary structure and structural class predictions. Protein Sci **4** (1995) 275–285
12. Chou, K.C.: A novel approach to predicting protein structural classes in a (20-1)-d amino acid composition space. Proteins **21** (1995) 319–344
13. Bahar, I., Atilgan, A.R., Jernigan, R.L., Erman, B.: Understanding the recognition of protein structural classes by amino acid composition. Proteins **29** (1997) 172–185
14. Chou, K.C.: A key driving force in determination of protein structural classes. Biochem Biophys Res Commun **264** (1999) 216–224
15. Cai, Y., Zhou, G.: Prediction of protein structural classes by neural network. Biochimie **82** (2000) 783–787
16. Cai, Y.D., Liu, X.J., Xu, X., Chou, K.C.: Prediction of protein structural classes by support vector machines. Comput Chem **26** (2002) 293–296
17. Ding, C.H., Dubchak, I.: Multi-class protein fold recognition using support vector machines and neural networks. Bioinformatics **17** (2001) 349–358
18. Tan, A.C., Gilbert, D., Deville, Y.: Multi-class protein fold classification using a new ensemble machine learning approach. Genome Informatics **14** (2003) 206–217
19. Wang, Z.X., Yuan, Z.: How good is prediction of protein structural class by the component-coupled method. Proteins **38** (2000) 165–175
20. Thomas, P.D., Dill, K.A.: An iterative method for extracting energy-like quantities from protein structures. Proc Natl Acad Sci USA **93** (1996) 11628–11633
21. Vapnik, V.: Statistical learning theory. NY: Wiley, New York (1998)
22. Chang, C.C., Lin, C.J.: LIBSVM: A library for support vector machines. (2002)
23. Berman, H.M., Westbrook, J., Feng, Z., Gilliland, G., Bhat, T.N., Weissig, H., Shindyalov, I.N., Bourne, P.E.: The protein data bank. Nucleic Acids Res **28** (2000) 235–242
24. Leslie, C., Eskin, E., Noble, W.S.: The spectrum kernel: A string kernel for svm protein classification. In: Pacific Symposium on Biocomputing, Hawaii, USA. (2002)
25. Vishwanathan, S.V.N., Smola, A.J.: Fast kernels for string and tree matching. In: Neural Information Processing Systems: Natural and Synthetic, Vancouver, Canada. (2002)
26. Markowetz, F., Edler, L., Vingron, M.: Support vector machines for protein fold class prediction. Biometrical Journal **45** (2003) 377–389

Flexible and Interactive Crack-Like Patterns Presentation on 3D Objects

Hsien-Hsi Hsieh, Wen-Kai Tai, Cheng-Chin Chiang, and Mau-Tsuen Yang

Department of Computer Science and Information Engineering,
National Dong Hwa University, Taiwan, R.O.C.
hsi@game.csie.ndhu.edu.tw, {wktai,ccchang,mtyang}@mail.ndhu.edu.tw

Abstract. In this paper a novel approach is proposed to present crack-like patterns on the surface of 3D objects. Instead of simulating the physical processes or using texturing techniques, the vectorized crack-like pattern is used. Given a crack-like pattern, basic image processing operations are applied to extract the feature pattern, and the redundant vertices are removed in the simplification process. The pattern is transformed onto the surface of paraboloid bounding volume of the input 3D object and then projected to the object's surface according to a set of given projection reference points. Based on reference points generation mechanism, crack-like patterns can be effectively and flexibly presented on the 3D objects. By the proposed hardware accelerated mechanism using stencil buffer, the interactivity of pattern presentation can be achieved on the fly.

1 Introduction

Natural things are difficult to formulate. Crack pattern is also one of them. There are many methods focusing on generating crack patterns. Approximate simulation demonstrates good visual results but exhausts huge amount of computation time. Alternatively, texturing is used to map the crack pattern on a given 3D object. However, some inherent problems associated with texturing such as memory space requirement for texture libraries, orientation and scale consistency, the demands of seamless texturing, and animation of cracking propagation make this approach not a straight and easy solution. In order to quickly generate various cracks on 3D objects for non-scientific purposes such as games and art, an approach for interactive crack-like pattern presentation on 3D objects is proposed in this paper.

Our approach is a non-physical approach, which means it is not going to simulate the cracking propagation with physical models. A feature pattern is extracted from various crack-like patterns ranging from natural patterns, manual drawing patterns, procedural patterns, and so forth, by using basic image processing operations. By tracking the pixel connectivity in the pattern image, the input one could be vectorized and simplified as a planar graph, called feature pattern. To present the crack pattern on the object's surface, the planar graph is transformed onto the surface of paraboloid bounding volume of the target object first. Then the transformed graph is projected on the surface of the 3D object. Projection is to calculate the intersections between the 3D object and the quads, which are formed by edges of the transformed graph on the paraboloid bounding volume and corresponding projecting reference points. With the proposed hardware acceleration technique, feature patterns can be presented on the surface of the object without additional intersection calculations.

Briefly, we summarize the contributions of the proposed approach as follows.
-Crack Pattern: In our approach, input is simply a 2D image. The crack pattern can be any crack-like patterns, such as realistic crack patterns from natural patterns, various sets of crack-like patterns from man-made patterns, and procedural patterns. Also, we propose a simple mechanism to efficiently obtain the feature crack pattern automatically. However, crack textures used in the non-physical approach need more labor works to have ideal ones. For the physical approach, simulated crack patterns are probably realistic. But the physical model used for simulation is computation intensive.
-Reference Points Generation: Reference points are automatically generated according to the shape distribution of the target 3D object for approximating a suitable projection. With three user-controlled parameters, user can interactively specify the distribution of reference points to produce the desired 3D object's crack pattern presentation on the fly.
-Rendering: Interactive presentation and control of feature pattern on the surfaces of 3D objects are feasible by using hardware-accelerated mechanism. The feature pattern can be carved on the 3D object's surface to change the visual geometric appearance of object.

The rest of paper is organized as follows. Some related works are surveyed in Section 2. In Section 3, we present the framework and describe each stage in the framework specifically. The experimental results are illustrated in Section 4. Finally, we conclude the proposed approach and point out some future works.

2 Related Work

There are two classes of research on cracks. One is the physical approaches. These approaches propose realistic models but are largely restricted by huge computation time and often result in poor images. The proposed simulations focus on the models of energy, forces, and structure of fractures, such as [1, 2] using finite element method, [3] studying crack pattern of mud, [4] using spring network, and [5] animating fracture by physical modeling.

Another class is the semi-physical or non-physical approaches. They focus on the lower computational propagation of cracks or visual effects. Semi-physical approaches simplify the stress model of objects and use simple rules to simulate the propagation of cracks. For example, Gobron and Chiba [6] simulated the crack pattern based on a special structural organization and rules of propagation. Non-physical approaches analyze the crack patterns or sample a lot of images, and use some methods such as texture mapping techniques to render the crack patterns. Dana et al. [7] and Chiba et al. [8] could display crack patterns

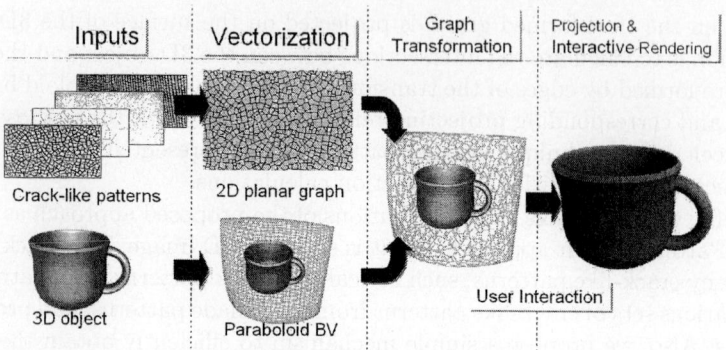

Fig. 1. Conceptualized framework

realistically using texture mapping. Neyret and Cani [9] produced predefined crack pattern on 3D object using texturing. This approach created almost seamless 3D crack pattern. Soler et al. [10] could synthesize textures on arbitrary surface from only one texture pattern such as crack pattern. Wyvill et al. [11] generated and rendered cracks in batik on clothes for art.

3 Pattern Extraction and Presentation

The framework of crack-like pattern presentation is conceptualized in Figure 1. It consists of the following stages:

- Vectorizing the input 2D crack-like pattern and generating the corresponding planar graph, called feature pattern,
- Transforming the planar graph onto the surface of paraboloid bounding volume of the target 3D object,
- Generating a set of references points according to the shape distribution of the target 3D object,
- Projecting feature pattern on the 3D object's surface to corresponding reference points,
- Interactively modifying projection parameters and rendering on the fly.

3.1 Vectorizing Crack-Like Pattern

Various crack-like patterns can be input images. For example, they can be natural patterns, such as tree branches, veins of leaves, fracture of rocks, dry mud, and china. They can be manual drawing patterns, such as artistic patterns and maps. Even procedural patterns, such as Voronoi diagrams, Koch curves and fractal patterns also can be inputs. Basic image processing operations [12], like bi-leveling, segmentation, and thinning mechanism [13], are applied to extract the raw feature pattern which consists of discrete pixels. Then a simple greedy

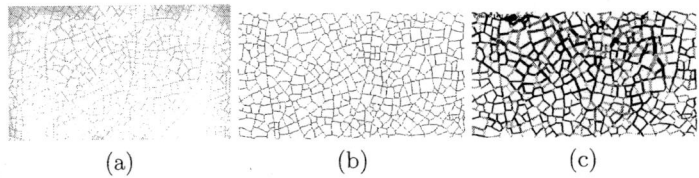

Fig. 2. Vectorizing crack-like pattern. (a) A sample input image. (b) The raw feature pattern (thinned image). (c) A vectorized planar graph shown by associating width with each edge. Note that each edge is randomly assigned with a color

algorithm is proposed to construct planar graph (feature pattern) from the raw feature pattern (thinned input pattern).

The feature extraction process consists of two stages. In the first stage, pixels in the raw feature pattern are grouped into short and straight line segments, called raw edges. This grouping process starts from seed pixels with degree ≥ 3, and then for seed pixels with degree 1 and 2. Pixels in a raw edge (line segment) are all adjacent and with degree 2 except two end pixels, and the number of pixels, i.e., the length of a raw edge, is bounded. These raw edges form the raw planar graph which is usually full of tiny edges and needs to be simplified.

In the stage 2, redundant edges are removed. Let V_q be a vertex with degree 2 and E_{pq} and E_{qr} be two edges connected to V_q, edges E_{pq} and E_{qr} can be substituted as edge E_{pr} if the bending angle between these two edges is less than a given threshold. All vertices in the raw graph are checked to see if the edge substitution mechanism is applicable.

After the vectorization, some attributes, like edge width, vertex degree, user-defined values, etc., can be associated with vertices and edges of the graph for facilitating the presentation of crack pattern even the animation of cracking propagation. An input crack-like pattern, a raw feature pattern, and the corresponding planar graph is shown in Figure 2. It shows that the crack-like pattern reconstructed from the vectorized graph is similar to original input image.

3.2 Graph Transformation

To wrap the 3D object in the planar graph, $G = (V, E)$, the planar graph needs to be transformed to a 3D object enclosing the target object. This idea is similar to the paraboloid mapping [14]. Prior to undergo the graph transformation, we set up a normalized coordinate system for all vertices in V so that the origin is at the center of the planar graph. Then all normalized vertices $v(s,t)$ in G, where $s, t \in [-1, 1]$, are transformed onto the surface of the paraboloid bounding volume of the target object with a rotation vector $U(u,v)$, where $u, v \in [-4, 4]$, as shown in Figure 3, by

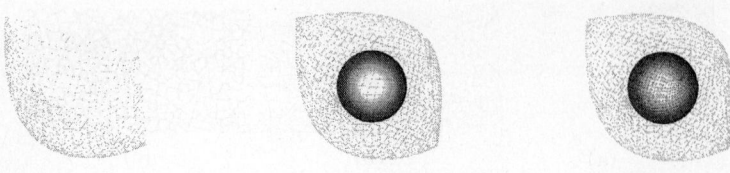

(a) Paraboloid   (b) Paraboloid bounding volume   (c) Edge projection

Fig. 3. Graph transformation and edge projection

$$\begin{bmatrix} x \\ y \\ z \\ 1 \end{bmatrix} = \begin{bmatrix} \cos(\frac{u\pi}{2}) & \sin(\frac{u\pi}{2})\sin(\frac{v\pi}{2}) & \sin(\frac{u\pi}{2})\cos(\frac{v\pi}{2}) & 0 \\ 0 & \cos(\frac{v\pi}{2}) & -\sin(\frac{v\pi}{2}) & 0 \\ -\sin(\frac{u\pi}{2}) & \cos(\frac{u\pi}{2})\sin(\frac{v\pi}{2}) & \cos(\frac{u\pi}{2})\cos(\frac{v\pi}{2}) & 0 \\ 0 & 0 & 0 & 1 \end{bmatrix} \begin{bmatrix} r\sin(\frac{s\pi}{2}) \\ -r\sin(\frac{t\pi}{2}) \\ r\cos(\frac{s\pi}{2})\cos(\frac{t\pi}{2}) \\ 1 \end{bmatrix},$$

where r is the radius of bounding sphere of the target object; u and v are rotation factor against axes Y and X respectively which indicates where the feature pattern should be projected. The paraboloid bounding volume is composed of two co-mirroring paraboloids. Figure 3 shows an example of paraboloid transformation.

Many mechanisms can be employed to perform this transformation. The proposed paraboloid transformation is simple but effective, and preserves angles for almost all edges, i.e., less distortion except a few edges near the corner regions. Note that there is no guarantee that the projected cracks-like pattern on a 3D object is the same as its input image. The degree of distortion depends on the projection and how the target object is fit to the paraboloid.

3.3 Generating Reference Points and Projecting Crack-Like Pattern

Now, all edges of the planar graph are transformed into the surface of paraboloid bounding volume. These edges are then mapped onto the target object by projecting them to the surface of the object. To conduct the projection, a set of reference points is used. For uniform distributed projection, reference points are generated according to the shape distribution of the target object: we use the vertex mean of the target object, $M(x_m, y_m, z_m)$, vertex variances in three main axes, $\{x_v, y_v, z_v\}$, and a user-controlled weight $W(w_x, w_y, w_z)$ to generate reference points for approximation of proper shape distribution. Each normalized vertex $v_i(s,t) \in V$ generates a reference point $p_i(x, y, z)$ with the same rotation vector U in the graph transformation by

$$\begin{bmatrix} x \\ y \\ z \\ 1 \end{bmatrix} = \begin{bmatrix} \cos(\frac{u\pi}{2}) & \sin(\frac{u\pi}{2})\sin(\frac{v\pi}{2}) & \sin(\frac{u\pi}{2})\cos(\frac{v\pi}{2}) & 0 \\ 0 & \cos(\frac{v\pi}{2}) & -\sin(\frac{v\pi}{2}) & 0 \\ -\sin(\frac{u\pi}{2}) & \cos(\frac{u\pi}{2})\sin(\frac{v\pi}{2}) & \cos(\frac{u\pi}{2})\cos(\frac{v\pi}{2}) & 0 \\ 0 & 0 & 0 & 1 \end{bmatrix} \begin{bmatrix} x_m + w_x \times x_v \sin(\frac{s\pi}{2}) \\ -y_m - w_y \times y_v \sin(\frac{t\pi}{2}) \\ z_m + w_z \times z_v \cos(\frac{s\pi}{2})\cos(\frac{t\pi}{2}) \\ 1 \end{bmatrix}.$$

Eventually, the projected edge is the intersection between the object's facets and the quad formed by two endpoints of the projecting edge and the corresponding reference points, as shown in Figure 4(a). The user-controlled weight W dominates the result of intersection: if W is $(0, 0, 0)$, then all edges in E are

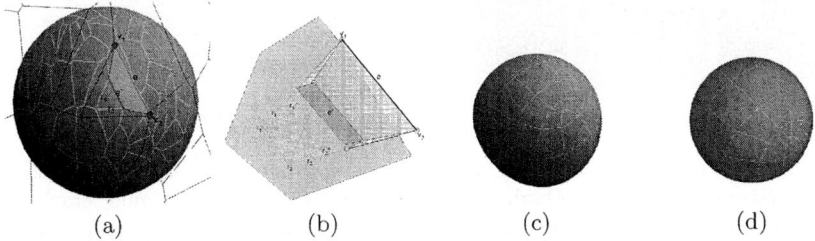

Fig. 4. Projection: (a) A quad is formed by an edge $e(v_1, v_2)$ and the corresponding reference points r_1 and r_2. Edge e' is the intersection between the object and the quad. (b) An octahedron is constructed by an edge $e(v_1, v_2)$ and four jittered vertices $\{r'_1, r''_1, r'_2, r''_2\}$ of the reference points r_1 and r_2. Edge e' is the area in green that will be rendered by graphics hardware. (c) Projecting a 6×6 regular grid on a ball to the center of object. (d) Projecting a 6×6 regular grid on a ball with $W=(2,0,0)$.

projected toward M, the center of target object, as shown in Figure 4(c); if W is anisotropic, it will lead different deformation of projected pattern, as shown in Figure 4(d). If all reference points are inside the target object, projected pattern will have the same topology as the feature pattern; otherwise, some edges or some portions of feature pattern will not appear on the surface of the target object. The projection is not distortionless, but the intuition between input 2D crack-like patterns and presented 3D cracks on objects is high for most objects, especially for convex-like objects.

3.4 Pattern Presentation

After constructing quads for all pairs of edges and reference points, the intersections between quads and the object need to be calculated for obtaining projected edges. However, computing the intersections is time consuming. Instead, a mechanism with hardware acceleration to quickly visualize the intersections and make the interactive control feasible is proposed. Once the view, feature pattern, target object, graph transformation or distribution of reference points is changed, the projected crack pattern will be re-rendered on the fly to get the correct visual result of intersections. We exploited the stencil buffer. The target 3D object is rendered into only z-buffer first, and then both Z-buffer and color buffer writing are temporally disabled. Then the stencil buffer is enabled, and initialized by

$$stencil(x) = \begin{cases} 2, \text{ if } x \in proj(obj) \\ 0, \text{ otherwise} \end{cases},$$

where $proj(obj)$ is the projected area of the target object. As Figure 4(b) shows, for each quad, an octahedron constructed by a projecting edge and four jittered points of the two reference points along the normal direction of the quad is rendered for updating the stencil buffer. For each pixel being rasterized, if its stencil value is greater than or equal to 2 and its z-value is smaller than the value in z-buffer, the LSB of its stencil value inverts. This can be implemented

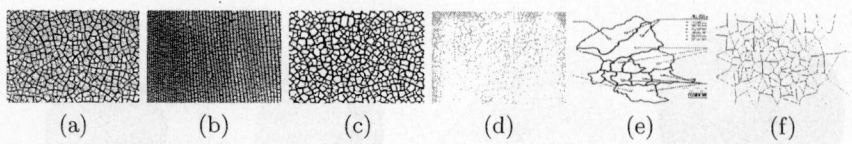

Fig. 5. Six crack-like patterns: (a) a natural Aluminum Oxide crack pattern, (b) another natural Aluminum Oxide crack pattern, (c) a natural mud crack pattern, (d) a crack-like pattern captured from a real cup, (e) a map pattern, (f) a Voronoi diagram pattern. Patterns (a) and (b) are obtained from website http://www.physics.utoronto.ca/nonlinear/gallery.html

by increasing stencil value with a writing mask that all bits are 0 except the LSB. After the above processing, cracks are rendered in the stencil buffer where the stencil values are 3. To show carving effect on the surface of the target object on the frame buffer, we just need a few simple steps. First, we clear the z-buffer and set the stencil function to test for equality to 2 and set the stencil operations to do nothing. Second, we draw the object again, so the object is rendered on frame buffer except pixels whose stencil values are 3. Then we set the stencil test again for equality to 3, and draw the object with a different material and a scaling value $s(s<1, s\approx 1)$. Then the smaller object will appear on where the cracks should be. We can not only control how the material of cracks is, but also change the geometric appearance of the target object. Because the constructed octahedron is closed, the projections of its front faces and back faces may completely overlay each other in stencil buffer. In our method, only the fragments that are visible and bounded by the tetrahedron will be marked as 3 in the stencil buffer. The entire process can be described as a function:

$$stencil(x) = \begin{cases} M_2(\sum_{t \in T} V(t,x)), & \text{if } x \in proj(obj) \\ 0, & \text{otherwise} \end{cases},$$

and

$$V(t,x) = \begin{cases} 1, & \text{if } x \in proj(obj) \text{ and } Z_t(x) < Z_{Buffer}(x) \\ 0, & \text{otherwise} \end{cases},$$

where x is a pixel in the stencil buffer, t is a triangle of octahedron T, $proj(obj)$ is a function projecting a 3D object obj onto the screen space, $M_2()$ is a function to module input by 2, $Z_t(x)$ is the z value for a rasterized triangle t at pixel x, and $Z_{Buffer}(x)$ is the z value at pixel x in z-buffer.

This idea is similar to a mechanism used in the shadow volume [15], but our technique requires only a 2-bit stencil buffer. The advantages of the proposed mechanism are (1) an efficient hardware acceleration method without z-fighting problem, (2) easy to dynamically change or reposition the crack pattern and adjust width of projected crack edges, and (3) independent of view, which means there is no need to determine the front or back face for each triangle, and triangles can be rendered in an arbitrary order. There is a drawback that some insignificant errors may occur between connections of crack edges caused by over flipping at overlapped areas.

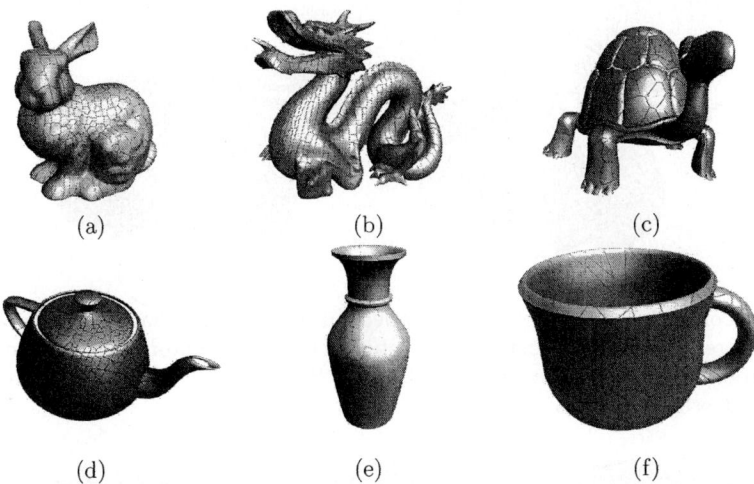

Fig. 6. Presenting crack-like patterns on 3D objects: (a) an Aluminum Oxide crack pattern presented on bunny, (b) another Aluminum Oxide crack pattern presented on dragon, (c) a mud crack pattern presented on turtle, (d) a captured crack-like pattern presented on teapot (e) a map pattern presented on vase, (f) a Voronoi diagram presented on teacup

4 Experimental Results

There are many crack-like patterns that can be used to present on 3D objects. As shown in Figures 5 and 6, two Aluminum Oxide crack patterns are presented on bunny and dragon, one crack pattern of dry mud is presented on turtle, one crack-like pattern captured from a real cup is presented on teapot, one map pattern is presented on Chinese utensil, and one Voronoi diagram pattern is presented on teacup. The fragments of surface where cracks are on are cut out so that the surface geometry is displaced to reveal carving effect, as shown in Figure 8(a). As experimental results show, a presented pattern will look like real if the crack-like pattern is from real natural one.

For convex-like object, one reference point is enough to get good result. However, for the model with irregular shape like a dragon, only one reference will result in a highly distorted crack pattern, as shown in Figure 7(a). To estimate how many reference points are needed and to where should they be projected is not easy, we propose the automatic reference points generation. Using the mechanism with some user interaction, we can get a visually good crack pattern on an arbitrary object, as shown in Figure 7(b).

Although we don't need to compute the 3D information of the projected feature pattern, we might have better visual effect by using the 3D information of the projected feature pattern for lighting the surface around the crack edges to produce more rich bumping or carving effects on 3D object, as shown in Figure 8(b) and 8(c). Besides, because the feature pattern consists of graph, it is

Fig. 7. Comparison of reference points selections for irregular shaped object: (a) Using only reference points at center of the object. (b) Using automatic reference points generation with a little user interaction, where $W = (1.5, 1.3, 0)$. Both of them use the crack pattern in Figure 5(a) as input

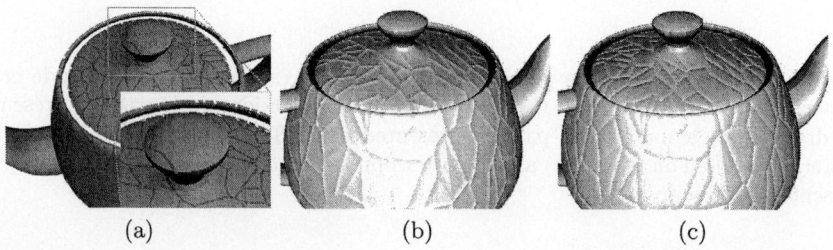

(a) (b) (c)

Fig. 8. Visual effects: (a) Geometric carving effect by using stencil technique. Right-bottom corner of the image enlarge the area in orange rectangle for showing carving effect. (b) Bumping and (c) carving visual effects in our previous work by changing luminance around the crack edges of 3D graph constructed from the 3D information of projected feature pattern [16]

feasible to demonstrate the animation of cracking propagation on the surface of 3D objects with proper traversal schemes. Figure 9 shows a cracking animation simulating a cracking propagation of drying mud due to high temperature based on edge priority based traversal scheme.

5 Conclusion

In this paper, we introduce an approach for interactive crack-like pattern presentation on the surface of 3D objects. The proposed approach is an automatic process from processing images of various crack-like patterns, constructing graph from feature crack patterns, for presenting the graph of feature crack patterns on the surface of 3D objects with a set of corresponding reference points. Due to hardware stencil buffer, a feature pattern can be rendered on the 3D object's surface without expensive intersection computation. Interactive rendering provides a quick snapshot of a set of specific reference points and the feature pattern setting.

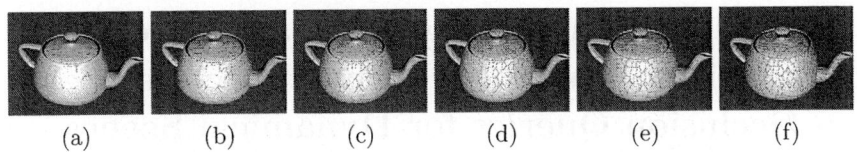

(a)　　　　(b)　　　　(c)　　　　(d)　　　　(e)　　　　(f)

Fig. 9. Six representative snapshots selected from an animation of priority based traversal scheme in our previous work [16]

In the near future, the presentation of crack pattern on a 3D object will be improved. The visual effect of cracks can be presented more realistically by exploring an illumination model of crack. Furthermore, we consider re-tessellating the object according to the crack pattern for demonstrating an animation of object breaking or peeling effect.

References

1. O'Brien, J.F., Hodgins, J.K.: Graphical modeling and animation of brittle fracture. In: Proc. of ACM SIGGRAPH'99. (1999) 137–146
2. O'Brien, J.F., Hodgins, J.K.: Graphical modeling and animation of ductile fracture. In: Proc. of ACM SIGGRAPH 2002. (2002) 291–294
3. Neff, M., Fiume, E.: A visual model for blast waves and fracture. In: Proc. of the Graphics Interface Conference. (1999) 193–202
4. Hirota, K., Tanoue, Y., Kaneko, T.: Simulation of three-dimensional cracks and animation. The Visual Computer **16** (2000) 371–378
5. Norton, A., Turk, G., Bacon, B., Gerth, J., Sweeney, P.: Animation of fracture by physical modeling. The Visual Computer **7** (1991) 210–219
6. Gobron, S., Chiba, N.: Crack pattern simulation based on 3D surface cellular automata. The Visual Computer **17** (2001) 287–309
7. Dana, K.J., van Ginneken, B., Nayar, S.K., Joenderink, J.J.: Reflectance and texture of real-world surface. ACM Transaction on Graphics **18** (1999) 1–34
8. Chiba, N., Wada, S., Kaino, K., Muraoka, K.: A behavioral model of cracks and its applications to CG. Systems and Computers in Japan **22** (1991) 82–91
9. Neyret, F., Cani, M.P.: Pattern-based texturing revisited. In: Proc. of ACM SIGGRAPH'99. (1999) 235–242
10. Soler, C., Cani, M.P., Angelidis, A.: Hierarchical pattern mapping. ACM Transaction on Graphics **21** (2002) 673–680
11. Wyvill, B., van Overveld, K., Carpendale, S.: Rendering cracks in batik. In: Proc. of NPAR 2004, ACM Press (2004) 61–149
12. Gonzalez, R.C., Woods, R.E.: Digital Image Processing. 2nd edition. Addison-Wesley (2002)
13. Cychosz, J.M.: Efficient binary image thinning using neighborhood maps. Graphics Gems IV (1994)
14. Heidrich, W., Seidel, H.P.: View-independent environment maps. In: Proc. of SIGGRAPH/Eurographics Workshop on Graphics Hardware. (1998) 39–45
15. Heidmann, T.: Real shadows real time. Iris Universe, Silicon Graphics Inc. **18** (1991) 28–31
16. Hsieh, H.H., Tai, W.K., Wang, H.W.: A novel approach for crack pattern synthesis and animation. In: IWAIT 2003. (2003)

An Occlusion Culling Approach Based on Exploiting Multiple Hardware-Accelerated Occlusion Queries for Dynamical Scenes

Wen-Kai Tai, Chih-Kang Hsu, and Hsien-Hsi Hsieh

Department of Computer Science and Information Engineering
National Dong Hwa University, Hualien, Taiwan, R.O.C.
wktai@mail.ndhu.edu.tw

Abstract. Occlusion culling has been studied extensively in computer graphics for years. In this paper, an occlusion culling approach based on exploiting multiple hardware-accelerated occlusion queries using the concept of eye-siding number for dynamic scene is proposed. Organizing the regular grid with overlapping voxels for the scene as an octree-like hierarchy, the actual position of dynamical objects can be updated efficiently. Based on the eye-siding number, the nodes occlusion front-to-back order enumeration can be done efficiently and the number of parallelizable occlusion queries for nodes in the hierarchy while traversing can be maximized efficiently and effectively. As experimental results shown, for all frames of the test walk-through in a dynamical environment, our approach does improve the overall performance.

1 Introduction

Occlusion culling (OC) has been studied extensively in computer graphics in recent years. In this paper, we propose an OC approach based on exploiting multiple hardware-accelerated occlusion queries (HaOQs) for the dynamical scene in a hierarchical representation. In our approach the space of the scene is divided into a regular grid with overlapping voxels and organized as an octree. In each frame, we efficiently update the positions of dynamic objects and build the object list for each voxel. Then, the hierarchy traversal proceeds in an occlusion front-to-back (ftb) order and hidden nodes are culled away according to the results of parallelized occlusion queries (OQs). Finally, objects contained in a visible voxel are rendered. The proposed approach exploits the eye-siding number of the nodes in the hierarchy so that we are capable of efficiently providing an occlusion ftb order while traversing and effectively maximizing the number of parallelizable OQs for nodes in the hierarchy.

Below we summarize contributions of our approach.
-Efficient Hierarchy Construction and Update: Hierarchical spatial data structures have been used for accelerating OQs. The cost of hierarchy construction and update for dynamical objects is high. In this paper, we use the regular grid with overlapping voxels to uniformly partition the scene. With the regular grid

the octree-like hierarchy is simple and rapid to construct, and with the overlapping voxels the hierarchy update for dynamical objects can be done efficiently.
-Fast Occlusion Front-To-Back Order Enumeration: While traversing the hierarchy for OC, an occlusion ftb traversal order improves the performance. We propose an efficient scheme to provide an occlusion ftb order using the eye-siding number of nodes in the hierarchy. The concept of the eye-siding number can be further explored to classify nodes into parallel units for multiple HaOQs.
-Maximizing the Utilization of HaOQs: The visibility culling will be tending to use the HaOQ. However, setting up and waiting for the OQ stalls the rendering pipeline. The more multiple queries sent for occlusion evaluation at a time, the better performance can be gained. Nodes with the same eye-siding number in an occlusion ftb order sequence can be grouped into a parallel unit and can be sent for occlusion evaluation at a time. Maximizing the number of parallelizable OQs for nodes in the hierarchy speeds up the performance.

There are three approaches similar to our method. Govindaraju et al. [8] switched roles of two GPUs for performing OC in parallel between successive frames. The parallelism of OQs is exploited by sending all possible OQs for the nodes at a given level in the hierarchy at a time. However, they are not guaranteed in an occlusion ftb order, and the occlusion representation from the previous frame may not be a good occlusion approximation for the current frame. Hillesland et al. [11] decomposed the static scene using uniform grid and nested grid and made use of HaOQ to evaluate the visibility in ftb order determined by a variant of the axis aligned slabs. To reduce the setup cost, the pipeline is kept busy by submitting n cells in a slab at a time, and recursively traverse the contained subgrids of a visible cell. This method is simple and fast. But, too many OQs are sent for visibility evaluation in the scene represented by the uniform grid. Also, it is less effective on reducing the pipeline stalls that multiple OQs are only selected from a single subgrid of a visible cell for the nested grid traversal. Staneker et al. [22] proposed the software-based Occupancy Map to significantly reduce the overhead of HaOQs and to arrange multiple OQs in a static scene browsing. The proposed method is useful for scenes with low occlusion. However, the screen space bounding rectangle is too conservative such that it tends to obtain low occlusion effectiveness, especially in a dense environment.

The rest of this paper is organized as the follows. In Section 2, a survey of OC is presented. The proposed methods are specified in Section 3. In Section 4 we show the experimental results. Finally, the conclusion and future works are given in Section 5.

2 Related Works

A recent survey of OC is given in [6]. OC algorithms, [4, 5, 7, 10, 13, 16, 19, 20, 24], are conservative. A few approaches [2, 14, 21] were proposed to approximate the rendering. The approximation technique sacrifices visibility conservativeness for the performance and simplicity of implementation. Region-based visibility techniques [7, 16, 17, 20, 24], compute the visibility and record visible objects in each region. In rendering, the view-cell where the viewpoint locates is found and its visible objects are rendered. Point-based visibility methods [1,4,5,14], relying on the identification of large occluders, compute the visibility on the fly. Region-based techniques work well for the scene with large convex objects as occluders and benefit viewpoint coherence. However, they take long preprocessing time, require large storage space, and result in low culling effectiveness. Point-based methods address moving objects but with less effective in occlusion fusion. Object-based approach [5] evaluates the occlusion by comparing the occlusion volumes formed with raw 3D objects. These approaches utilize spatial hierarchies, but they suffer from performing occlusion fusion for small occluders. Projection-based schemes [1,3,4,14,20] evaluate occlusion by testing the projected region of objects to the maintained occlusion information. Approaches of analytic visibility [10,13,16] exploit the geometry information of special domains to determine the visibility. Projection-based and analytic approaches can fuse the occlusion in their space of the overlap tests.

Sudarsky and Gotsman [23] update dynamic objects using temporal coherence only for potentially visible objects and expired TBV (Temporal Bounding Volume). The output-sensitivity is provided, but assumes that the motion of objects is predictable. Besides, the update of hierarchies may be still too expensive. Batagelo and Wu [3] adapted [20] to dynamic scenes using [23]. The scene is discretized into voxels which maintain volumetric characteristics: occluder, occlusion, identifiers and TBVs matrix. To reduce the spanning voxels computation, TBVs is used for hidden dynamic objects. Batagelo can take care of truly dynamic environments and output-sensitivity is provided. Although the voxel traversal approximates the ftb order, it cannot exploit the advantages of hierarchy schemes like methods given in [5,12,16,23]. In a densely occluded scene, this may result in more traversals. Algorithms proposed in [2,8,9,11,15,18,22] evaluate the occlusion by performing the HaOQs. These techniques do have faster performance if the bounding boxes contain a large number of objects, and the effectiveness of OQ depends on the underlying hardware and input models.

3 Proposed Approach

3.1 Scene Organization and Dynamic Object Update

A spatial data structure, regular grid, is used to organize the scene so that the construction simply computes the object list for each cell (axis-aligned voxel). The size of voxel is set as a multiple of the average size of objects' bounding boxes which are the majority in a scene so that the voxel can contain several objects. If most of objects are small but a few are large, we divide large objects into small ones to increase the probability of considering them as hidden.

So far, solutions for handling cross-node objects might not be feasible for dynamic objects, require large memory space when the cross-node object increases, or suffer from low OC effectiveness. To address cross-node objects, we conceptually extend every voxel up to a given constrained size in each axis's positive direction such that each object being located in a node can be fully contained in the extended voxel, called overlapping voxel. The constrained size is the maximum of the dimensions of bounding box of dynamic objects in majority. Of course, it is smaller than the size of voxel which is set to contain several objects.

To minimize the update time for dynamic objects, the scene is scaled such that each voxel is a unit cube so that the minimal vertex of the bounding box of an object can be used to represent its position. The object's owner voxel is simply determined using the integral parts of its position. Let the minimal vertex of the bounding box of an object be (1.23, 8.0, 7.96), then the owner voxel is indexed by (1, 8, 7), and the object is inserted into the object list of the voxel. With the overlapping voxel, every dynamic object can be exactly assigned to a voxel. Besides, scaling voxel to a unit cube speeds up the dynamic object update.

Organizing the space of a scene as a hierarchy makes traversal efficient. We build a hierarchy based on the voxels and render the scene while traversing. In the special case, the grid can be treated as an octree. In general cases, dimensions of the grid are arbitrary. We can treat a grid as an octree-like hierarchy. The root of the hierarchy holds the whole grid. The subdivision starts from the root, and proceeds to partition from the spatial median along each axis.

If there is only one voxel left in an axis, the partition stops in the axis. If there is no divisible axis, the division terminates and the node is a leaf.

3.2 Occlusion Front-to-Back Order

With ftb order, distant nodes tend to be hidden so the number of visited nodes can be reduced. Although Bernardini et al. [4] determines the ftb order by looking up a pre-constructed table based on the viewpoint, the look-up result might not be further used in maximizing the number of parallelizable OQs in our approach.

To efficiently enumerate an occlusion ftb order for the nodes, octants in a node are encoded using 3-bit codes. The bits represent the partition planes, orthogonal to x, y, and z axes, respectively. A bit is set if the octant is in the positive half-space of the corresponding partition plane. Figure 1(a) shows an example of the encoded octants. Then, we sort the octants into an occlusion ftb order, $O_0, O_1, ..., O_7$, by the eye-siding number. The eye-siding number indicates how many times the node lies at the same half-space of partition planes with the viewpoint. The 3-eye-siding octant, O_0, containing the viewpoint is the first node. The 0-eye-siding octant, O_7, which is not at the same half-space with the viewpoint for all partition planes, is the last node. Three 2-eye-siding octants, O_1, O_2, and O_3, which are at the same half-space with the viewpoint with respect to two partition planes out of three partition planes, are the second order, and the three 1-eye-siding octants, O_4, O_5, and O_6, which locate at the same half-space for one partition plane out of three partition planes, are the third order. The proposed algorithm for occlusion ftb order enumeration is described as follows:

```
DetermineFront2BackOrder(Node) // Node: an internal node of the octree
{ SetBit= 1;
    for i in {x, y, z} {
        if(Ei > Node.Centeri) {// E: eye position, Node.Center: center of the node
```

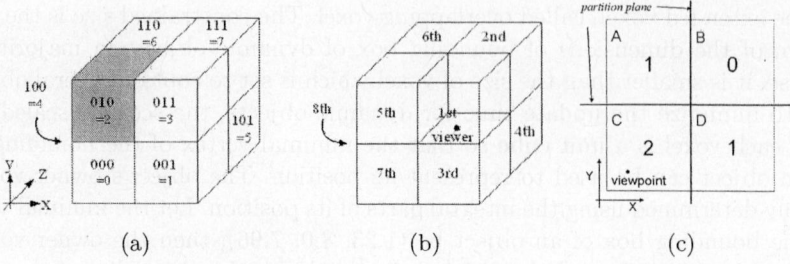

Fig. 1. (a) An encoded octants. The gray octant is in the positive half-space of y axis but in negative one of both x and z axes. (b) An occlusion ftb order for the viewpoint located in octant 011. (c) The eye-siding number for four children in a quad-tree node

```
    eyesidei = SetBit; // eyesidei: indicate the eye side for three axes
    oppsidei = 0;      // oppsidei: indicate the opposite side
  }
  else {
    eyesidei = 0;
    oppsidei = SetBit;
  }
  SetBit = SetBit << 1;          // <<: shift left bitwise operator
}// end of for i in {x, y, z}
O0 = eyesidex | eyesidey | eyesidez;  // |: bitwise OR operation
O1 = eyesidex | eyesidey | oppsidez;
O2 = eyesidex | oppsidey | eyesidez;
O3 = oppsidex | eyesidey | eyesidez;
O4 = eyesidex | oppsidey | oppsidez;
O5 = oppsidex | eyesidey | oppsidez;
O6 = oppsidex | oppsidey | eyesidez;
O7 = oppsidex | oppsidey | oppsidez;
return O;   // O: the front-to-back order array
}// end of DetermineFront2BackOrder(Node)
```

Figure 1(b) shows an occlusion ftb order for the viewpoint in octant 011. Let $Node.Center$ be $(0, 0, 0)$, the eyeside and oppside vectors are $(1, 2, 0)$ and $(0, 0, 4)$ respectively. Therefore, an occlusion ftb order, i.e., O_0, O_1, O_2, O_3, O_4, O_5, O_6, O_7, is $O_0 = 1|2|0 = 011 = 3$, $O_1 = 1|2|4 = 111 = 7$, $O_2 = 1|0|0 = 001 = 1$, $O_3 = 0|2|0 = 010 = 2$, $O_4 = 1|0|4 = 101 = 5$, $O_5 = 0|2|4 = 110 = 6$, $O_6 = 0|0|0 = 000 = 0$, and $O_7 = 0|0|4 = 100 = 4$. Notice that the order of selection of partition plane will influence the produced node sequence of ftb order, but the actual occlusion order is equivalent. It's easy to adapt this algorithm to the hierarchies of voxels with arbitrary dimensions, not just with power of 2.

While traversing the hierarchy in an occlusion ftb order, the visibility of each node is evaluated using the HaOQ for the bounding box of node which consists of its descendant overlapping voxels. If a node is invisible, its recursion stops. If a visible leaf node is found, its contents have to be rendered.

3.3 Maximizing Parallelizable Occlusion Queries

While using HaOQ, the parallelism must be exploited to reduce the stalling. To maximize the number of parallelizable OQs while traversing the hierarchy,

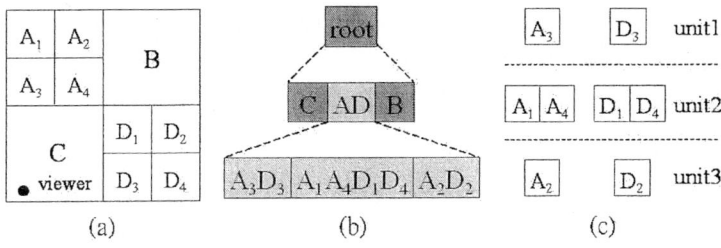

Fig. 2. A 2D example of the parallel unit hierarchy. (a) A node hierarchy where nodes A and D are partitioned into four subnodes respectively. (b) The children of the root node are grouped into three parallel units by the eye-siding number, C, A, D, and B. Similarly, the parallel unit A, D can be further divided into three parallel units: $\{A_3, D_3\}, \{A_1, A_4, D_1, D_4\}$, and $\{A_2, D_2\}$. (c) A *ftb* order of parallel unit $\{A, D\}$

the nodes are divided into parallel units. The eye-siding number encoded for octants of a node benefits the exploration of parallelizable nodes. The nodes with the same eye-siding number are parallelizable because the rendering order doesn't affect the occlusion result. Hence, the eight child octants of a node can be classified into parallel units by their eye-siding number. There are four parallel units for octants in a node. The 3-eye-siding unit includes only one octant in which the viewpoint lies. The 0-eye-siding unit includes only one octant that is at the opposite side of the 3-eye-siding octant. The 2-eye-siding unit has three octants which locate at the eye side of two partition planes out of three partition planes. The 1-eye-siding unit also has three octants which locate at the eye side of one partition plane out of three partition planes. Figure 1(c) shows a quad-tree case. Node C is 2-eye-siding because it contains the viewpoint. Both node A and D are 1-eye-siding since this two nodes are at the eye side of x and y partition planes respectively. Node B is not at the eye side for two partition planes, so it is 0-eye-siding. Hence, there are three parallel units; $\{C\}, \{A, D\}$, and $\{B\}$. For each parallel unit the eye-siding numbers of its descendent are determined by their corresponding partition planes respectively, and all children in a level can be classified into parallel units. For example, as shown in Figure 2, the children nodes of parallel unit $\{A, D\}$ are divided into $\{A_3, D_3\}, \{A_1, A_4, D_1, D_4\}$, and $\{A_2, D_2\}$ parallel units according to their eye-siding number.

During the hierarchy traversal, the parallel units are examined one-by-one recursively rather than visiting the nodes. The parallel unit on the top of the scene graph contains the root node only. For each visited unit, nodes in it is evaluated using parallel OQs, and the hidden ones are excluded in further processing. The children of the visible nodes are classified into four eye-siding sets, parallel units: P_i, $i = 3, 2, 1, 0$. These four units are recursively traversed in depth first order until the leaf node is reached. Eventually, the number of parallel queries is not unlimited due to the hardware implementation. If the number of the parallelizable OQs exceeds the bound, then the queries are divided into multiple passes. The algorithm of multi-pass parallel OQ is described as follows:

```
MultipassParallelOcclusionQuery(pNodes)// pNodes: the set of parallelizable nodes
{
  V= empty;
  While (pNodes is not empty) {
    Get nNodes={Node1, Node2,..., NodeN} out of pNodes //N:the max. no. of parallelizable OQs
    // switching hardware setting
    UpdateColorBuffer(DISABLE);
    UpdateDepthBuffer(DISABLE);
    // sent n(<= N) nodes for occlusion query at a time
    for i = 1 to Cardinality(nNodes){
      BeginOcclusionQuery(Qi); // Qi is the occlusion query identifier for Nodei
      Draw(nNodes.Nodei);
      EndOcclusionQuery(Qi);
    }
    UpdateColorBuffer(ENABLE);
    UpdateDepthBuffer(ENABLE);
    // get the pixel count of occlusion evaluation back
    for i = 1 to Cardinality(nNodes)
      V= V union (RequestPixelCount(Qi)> 0 ? Nodei : empty);
    pNodes= pNodes- nNodes;
  }// end of while (pNodes is not empty)
  return V; // V: the set of visible nodes
}// end of MultipassParallelOcclusionQuery(pNodes)
```

Furthermore, we must keep the ftb order while OQs are requested for parallel units. A ftb order for children of a node is determined using procedure *DetermineFront2BackOrder()*. The returned array O contains an occlusion ftb order of the children nodes, and elements in array O reveal the eye-siding order. Namely, the parallel unit traversal sequence, $P_3 = O_0, P_2 = O_1, O_2, O_3, P_1 = O_4, O_5, O_6, P_0 = O_7$, is in ftb order. Figure 2 shows an example of the hierarchy of parallel units and their occlusion ftb order. We summarize the traversal scheme with ftb order as follow:

```
ParallelUnitOcclusionQueryTraversal(P)   // P: the parallel unit
{
P3= P2= P1= P0= empty;  // Pi: i-eye-siding parallel unit
V = MultipassParallelOcclusionQuery(P.Nodes); // V: the set of visible nodes
while (Nodei in P.Nodes && Nodei in V && Nodei != LeafNode){
// determine the front-to-back order for children of Nodei
O= DetermineFront2BackOrder(Nodei); // O: the front-to-back order array
  // insert children of Nodei with eye-siding number i into parallel unit Pi
P3= P3 union {Nodei.Child00};
P2= P2 union {Nodei.Child01, Nodei.Child02, Nodei.Child03};
P1= P1 union {Nodei.Child04, Nodei.Child05, Nodei.Child06};
P0= P0 union {Nodei.Child07};
}
ParallelUnitOcclusionQuery(P3);
ParallelUnitOcclusionQuery(P2);
ParallelUnitOcclusionQuery(P1);
ParallelUnitOcclusionQuery(P0);
return;
}// end of ParallelUnitOcclusionQueryTraversal(P)
```

4 Experimental Results

We have implemented and tested our approach on a PC, running Windows XP, with one CPU, P4 2.4G, and 1GB main memory. The graphics card is based on the chipset of GeForce 4 Ti 4400. All the scenes are rendered by Gouraud shading with one directional light at screen resolution 1024x768 pixels.

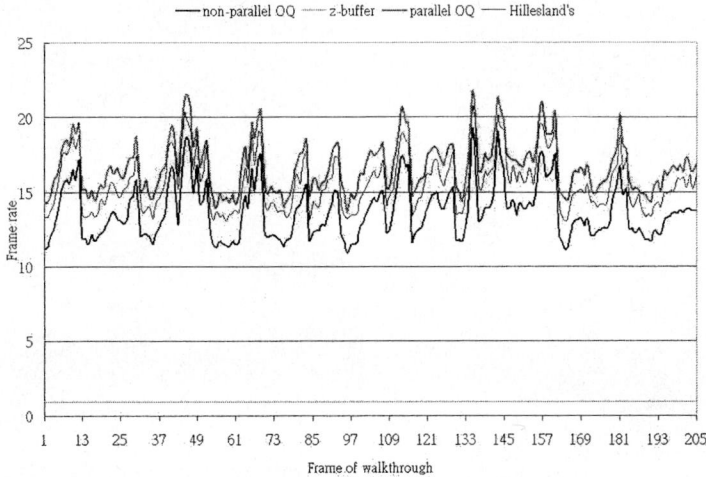

Fig. 3. The statistics of frame rates in an walk-through for the proposed approach using parallel and non-parallel OQs, Hillesland's, and Z-buffer

To show the overall performance of our approach for an interactive walk-through, we constructed a scene consisting of one million objects (778,497,348 polygons), of which one half is dynamic and other half is static. Objects consist of static type: torus knot (1920 polygons), hose (920 polygons), and hollow box (135 polygons) and dynamic type: teapot (1024 polygons), torus (576 polygons), star (96 polygons). The 16x16x16 voxels are used to represent the scene, and the grid is scaled such that all voxels in the grid are unit cubes for speeding up the position update for dynamic objects. A snapshot of the test walk-through environment is shown in Figure 4. The initial position and velocity of dynamic objects are generated randomly. While objects are in dynamics, the collision detection is only performed for objects against the scene boundary to prevent objects from moving away. If an object collides the boundary, a new velocity is assigned.

Figure 3 shows the frame rate statistics of proposed approach using parallel OQ, non-parallel OQ, Hillesland's method [11], and Z-buffer. We implemented the nested grid decomposition version of Hillesland's method to compare with our approach. For all frames of the walk-through, it shows that the performance of using parallel OQ is the best. On the average, we have 16.8434 fps for parallel OQ, 13.7902 fps for non-parallel OQ, 15.6917 fps for Hillesland's method, and 0.95 fps for z-buffer. Namely, we have 18.13% speed-ups of parallel OQ over the non-parallel OQ and 7.48% speed-ups of parallel OQ over Hillesland's method.

5 Conclusion

In this paper, we proposed an OC approach based on exploiting multiple parallelizable HaOQs. The regular grid with overlapping voxel is used to organize the

Fig. 4. The snapshot of the scene used for the overall performance test

spatial data for efficiently updating the actual position of objects in dynamics, and the grid is easy to be represented as an octree-like hierarchy for hierarchical traversal. By exploiting the eye-siding number of nodes in the hierarchy, we can easily traverse the nodes in an occlusion ftb order. Also, nodes with the same eye-siding number in a ftb order sequence can be grouped into a parallel unit and sent for OQs at a time. As experimental results show, maximizing the number of parallelizable OQs for nodes in the hierarchy makes the utilization of HaOQ even better, and it leads to a better overall performance.

Currently, objects in a visible voxel are all sent for rendering. Eventually, objects could be sorted into an approximate ftb order for occlusion evaluation in a node if the rendering time of objects is much higher than that of performing OQs. In the near future, a mechanism that can decide whether or not the OQ is worth applying for objects in a visible node is to be explored. The grid resolution is empirically selected, i.e., independent upon the number and size of objects in this research. In addition, with experiments we have made, the hierarchy traversal time, the time for performing node OQ, and the actual position update time for dynamic objects are relevant to the grid resolution. An automatic grid resolution determination scheme should be studied for improving or even optimizing the overall performance.

References

1. Bartz, D., Klosowski, J., Staneker, D.: K-dops as Tighter Bounding Volumes for Better Occlusion Performance. In: SIGGRAPH Visual Proceedings. (2001)
2. Bartz, D., Meibner, M., Huttner, T.: OpenGL Assisted Occlusion Culling for Large Polygonal Models. C&G. **23**(3) (1999) 667–679
3. Batagelo, H.C. Wu, S.T.: Dynamic Scene Occlusion Culling Using a Regular Grid. In: XV Brazilian Symp. on Comp. Graph. & Image Proc. (2002) 43–50
4. Bernardini, F., El-Sana, J., Klosowski, J.T.: IDirectional Discretized Occluders for Accelerated Occlusion Culling. In: EUROGRAPHICS. (2000)
5. Bittner, J., Havran, V., Slavk, P.: Hierarchical Visibility Culling with Occlusion Trees. In: Comp. Graph. Int.'98. (1998) 207–219
6. Cohen-Or, D., Chrysanthou, Y.L., Silva, C.T., et al.: Survey of Visibility for Walkthrough Applications. IEEE TVCG **9**(3) (2003)
7. Durand, F., Drettakis, G., Thollot, J., and Puech, C.: Conservative Visibility Preprocessing Using Extended Projections. In: SIGGRAPH. (2000)
8. Govindaraju, N.K., Sud, A., et al.: Interactive Visibility Culling for Complex Environments Using Occlusion-Switches. In: Symp. I3D. (2003)
9. Greene, N.: Occlusion Culling with Optimized Hierarchical Z-buffering. ACM SIGGRAPH Course Notes on Visibility **30** (2001)
10. Heo, J., Kim, J., Wohn, K.: Conservative Visibility Preprocessing for Walkthroughs of Complex Urban Scenes. In: ACM Symp. on VRST. (2000)
11. Hillesland, K., Salomon, B., Lastra, A., Manocha, D.: Fast and Simple Occlusion Culling Using Hardware-Based Depth Queries. Technical report TR02-039, Dep of Comp Sci, Univ of North Carolina (2002)
12. Ho, P.C., Wang, W.: Occlusion Culling Using Minimum Occluder Set and Opacity Map. In: Int. IEEE Conference on Information Visualisation (1999)
13. Kim, J., Wohn, K.: Conservative Visibility Preprocessing for Complex Virtual Environments. In: VSMM. (2001)
14. Klosowski, J.T., Silva, C.T.: The Prioritized-Layered Projection Algorithm for Visible Set Estimation. IEEE TVCG **6**(2) (2000)
15. Klosowski, J.T., Silva, C.T.: Efficient Conservative Visibility Culling Using the Prioritized-layered Projection Algorithm. IEEE TVCG **7**(4) (2001) 265–379
16. Koltun, V., Chrysanthou, Y., Cohen-Or, D.: Hardware-Accelerated From-Region Visibility Using a Dual Ray Space. In: Eurographics Workshop on Rendering. (2001) 205–216
17. Koltun, V., Chrysanthou, Y., Cohen-Or, D.: Virtual Occluders: An Efficient Intermediate PVS Representation. In: Eurographics Workshop on Rendering. (2000)
18. Meissner, M., Bartz, D., et al.: Generation of Subdivision Hierarchies for Efficient Occlusion Culling of Large Polygonal Models. Computer and Graphics (2002)
19. Pastor, O.E.M.: Visibility Preprocessing using Spherical Sampling of Polygonal Patches. In: Eurographics, Short/Poster Presentations. (2002)
20. Schaufler, G., Dorsey, J., Decoret, X., Sillion, F.X.: Conservative Volumetric Visibility with Occluder Fusion. In: SIGGRAPH. (2000)
21. Shou, L., Huang, Z., Tan, K.L.: Performance Guaranteed Rendering Using The HDoV Tree. In: GRAPHITE. (2003)
22. Staneker, D., Bartz, D., Meibner, M.: Improving Occlusion Query Efficiency with Occupancy Maps. In: Symp. on Parallel and Large-Data Vis. and Graph. (2003)
23. Sudarsky, O., Gotsman, C.: Dynamic Scene Occlusion Culling. IEEE TVCG **5**(1) (1999) 13–29
24. Wonka, P., Wimmer, M., Schmalstieg, D.: Visibility Preprocessing with Occluder Fusion for Urban Walkthroughs. In: Eurographics Workshop on Rendering. (2000) 71–82

Acceleration of Perspective Volume Rendering Using Depth-Subsampling

Byeong-Seok Shin and Yu Sik Chae

Inha University, Department of Computer Science and Engineering
253 Yonghyeon-Dong, Nam-Gu, Inchon, 402-751, Korea
bsshin@inha.ac.kr, g2011143@inhavision.inha.ac.kr

Abstract. In volume visualization, a high-speed perspective rendering algorithm that produces accurate images is essential. We propose an efficient rendering algorithm that provides high-quality images and reduces rendering time regardless of viewing condition by using depth-subsampling scheme. It partitions image plane into several uniform pixel blocks, then computes minimum depth for each pixel block. While conventional ray casting starts ray traversal from its corresponding pixel, rays in our method can jump as the amount of the minimum z-value calculated. It can also be applied to space-leaping method. Experimental results show that our method produces high-quality images as those of volume ray casting and takes less time for rendering.

1 Introduction

The most important issue in recent volume visualization is to produce high-quality perspective-projection images in real time. Real-time volume rendering is highly related to hardware-based approaches such as 3D texture mapping hardware [1,2], specialized volume rendering hardware [3,4]. Although they achieve 30 *fps* without preprocessing, it is too expensive to be used in common applications and difficult to manipulate large volume data due to limitation of dedicated memory size. In addition, some of the hardware cannot support perspective rendering.

Volume ray casting is the most famous software-based rendering algorithm [5]. Although it produces high-quality images, it takes long time due to randomness in memory reference pattern. In order to speed up, several optimized methods have been proposed [7-9]. They have mainly concentrated on efficiently skipping over transparent or homogeneous regions using coherent data structures such as octrees [10], *k*-d trees [11], and Run-Length Encoded (RLE) volume [6]. However these methods require long preprocessing time and extra storage to maintain the data structures. Template-based method improves rendering speed by using spatial coherence such that the sampling pattern on each ray is identical in parallel projection [12]. However, it is not suited to perspective projection.

In this paper, we propose an efficient method that produces high-quality images and reduces rendering time regardless of viewing condition by applying depth subsampling scheme to volume ray casting. Also it does not require preprocessing or additional data structures. It partitions image plane into several uniform pixel blocks, and determines the minimum depth for each pixel block. While the original method fires a ray from its corresponding pixel in view plane, our method moves forward the starting point of ray traversal as the amount of the minimum depth value calculated.

Our method can also be used for accelerating the space leaping. Space leaping is regarded as an efficient rendering method that skips over empty space using distance information [7,8]. Much work has been done to devise efficient space leaping. Sharghi and Ricketts proposed a method that exploits a pre-processed visibility determination technique and considers only a potentially visible set of boundary cells [13]. Vilanova *et al.* presented how to identify empty region of a tubular shaped organ as a series of cylindrical structures [14]. Although it is possible to accelerate volume rendering by skipping over those cylindrical regions, it requires some human intervention for cylindrical approximation. Wan *et al.* devised a method that exploits distance information stored in the potential field of the camera control model [15]. After that, Wan *et al.* presented a Z-buffer-assisted space-leaping method, which derives most of the pixel depth at the current frame by exploiting the temporal coherence during navigation with cell-based reprojection scheme [16].

However, the space leaping does not always provide speed-up as we expect. Its performance might be declined according to the viewing condition. Our method can solve the problem with depth-subsampling. It computes and stores z-depth only for some pixels (one per pixel block) rather than all pixels. It does not require complex cell reprojection to calculate the distance from the image plane to visible cells. Also it can rapidly produce images even when we cannot exploit temporal coherence.

In Section 2, we present our algorithm in detail. Extension to space leaping is mentioned in Section 3. Experimental results and remarks are shown in Section 4. Lastly, we summarize and conclude our work.

2 Efficient Volume Ray Casting Using Depth-Subsampling

The main drawback of volume ray casting is to take a long time for rendering due to randomness in memory reference pattern. We propose a method to reduce the rendering time by identifying empty space with depth-subsampling scheme and skipping over the empty region. Assume that a view plane P has a resolution of $N \times N$. During rendering we can compute z-value (depth value), d_{ij} for a pixel, p_{ij} without extra cost. The volume between image plane ($z = 0$) and object surfaces to be displayed ($z = d_{ij}$) is defined as *exactly empty space* (*EES*). We do not have to consider the value of voxels that lie on this volume. However, calculating z-value for all pixels does not contribute to reduce the rendering time for the current frame. Instead, it requires more storage to keep the z-value for all pixels.

Our method computes z-values for some pixels rather than all pixels, so we call it *depth subsampling*. In the first step, our method divides a view plane P into several uniform pixel blocks G_{uv} as depicted in Figure 1. Given the size of pixel block as $S \times S$, rays emanate from its four corner pixels. It performs full range ray traversal and shading to determine colors for those pixels. At the same time, it stores z-depth values into the depth buffer of which size is $(N / S)^2$. Since four adjacent pixel blocks share a corner pixel, we have to store only a single depth value for one pixel per pixel block. The minimum depth of G_{uv}, d_{uv}^{min} can be determined by comparing four depth values.

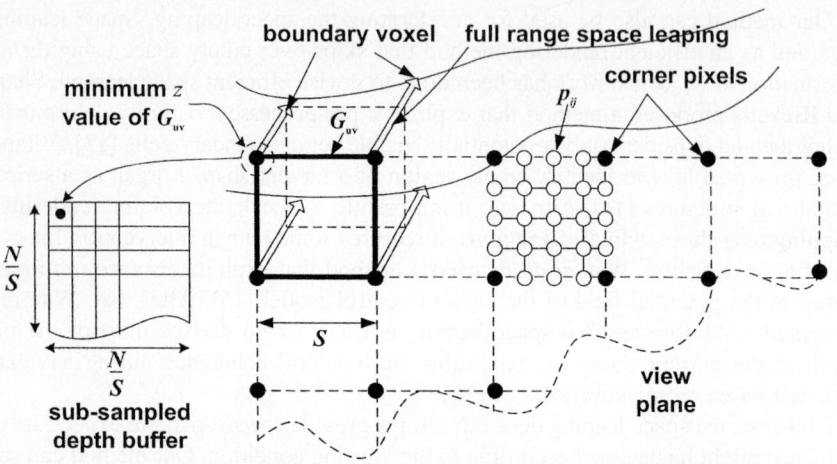

Fig. 1. Depth-subsampling procedure. Our method samples depths of corner pixels for each pixel block, determines the minimum depth, and saves them into a subsampled depth buffer

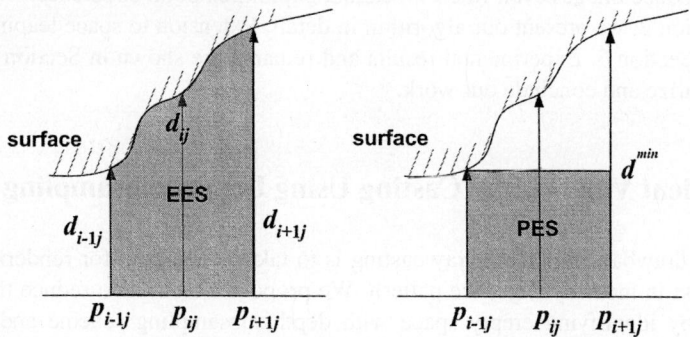

Fig. 2. A comparison of exactly empty space and potentially empty space for the same region

Using depth-subsampling, we can identify *potentially empty space* (PES). Figure 2 shows the difference of EES and PES for the same region.

The depth values calculated in the previous step can be used for accelerating rendering process. In conventional ray casting, a ray emanates from its corresponding pixel. On the other hand, in our method, all the rays that belong to a pixel block G_{uv} start to traverse at the point apart from their corresponding pixels as the value of d_{uv}^{min}.

Figure 3 shows how original ray casting and our method differ in rendering process. A black circle stands for a pixel whose color and z-value are already calculated in the depth-subsampling step (that is, a corner pixel). A white one means a non-corner pixel. A gray circle is a starting point of ray traversal. So we can reduce the rendering time as the amount of potentially empty space (hatched region).

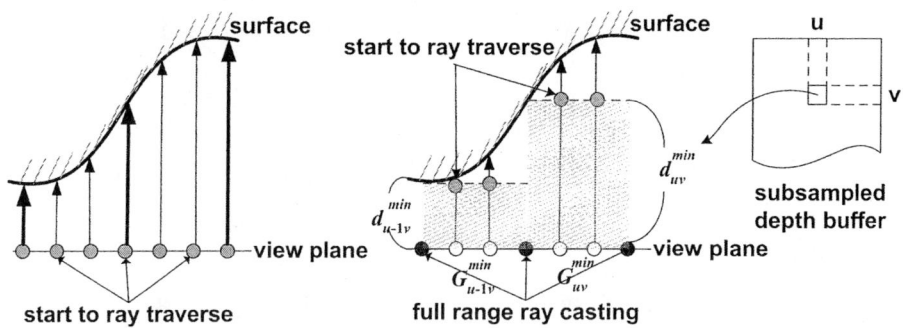

Fig. 3. A comparison of original ray casting (left) and our method (right) in ray advance

The most important factor in this method is the pixel block size, S. It directly affects rendering speed and image quality, so we have to choose optimal values for S to achieve maximum performance without deteriorating image quality. Let the average time to compute the color and z-value for each corner pixel be t_{minz}, the time for traversing a ray in the original method be t_{rt}, and that for our method be t_{minrt}, then rendering time of original ray casting t_{old} and our method t_{new} can be defined as follows:

$$t_{old} = t_{rt} N^2$$
$$t_{new} = t_{\min z}(\frac{N}{S})^2 + t_{\min rt}(N^2 - (\frac{N}{S})^2) \;. \tag{1}$$

Since the additional time to determine minimum depth value and store it into Z-buffer is negligible, t_{minz} is almost the same as t_{rt}. We can estimate the average time to reduce t_{save} as follows.

$$\begin{aligned} t_{save} &= t_{old} - t_{new} \\ &= t_{rt} N^2 - t_{\min z}(\frac{N}{S})^2 - t_{\min rt}(N^2 - (\frac{N}{S})^2), \\ &\cong (t_{rt} - t_{\min rt})(1 - \frac{1}{S^2})N^2 \end{aligned} \tag{2}$$

where $t_{rt} - t_{minrt}$ is regarded as the average gain for each ray using our method and it is denoted as t_{gain}. Assume that t_{gain} is a constant, t_{save} is proportional to the value of S. However, as the value of S gets larger, spatial coherence decreases and t_{gain} becomes smaller as shown in Figure 4. Since ray traversal is performed only in the gray region, we can reduce the time as the amount of hatched region (*PES'*). So, in this case, t_{gain} is inversely proportional to the value of S. Consequently, we have to choose the optimal value of S so as to minimize the rendering time.

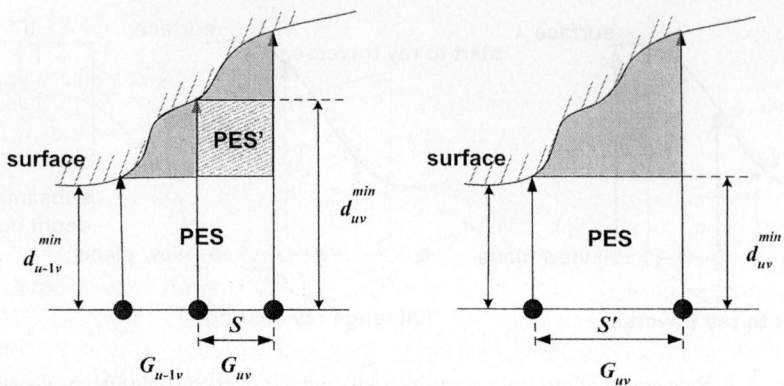

Fig. 4. Relationship between the pixel block size and the average time to be reduced

3 Efficient Space-Leaping Using Depth-Subsampling

Performance of space leaping might be degraded according to viewing specification. When the camera is close to object boundary, and the camera orientation is almost parallel to surface's tangent, rendering time gets longer since a ray cannot jump over empty space with single leaping. Instead, the ray has to jump several times to access the surface boundary as depicted in Figure 5. This is because original space leaping relies only on the distance between a voxel and its nearest boundary voxel. We can solve the problem of the performance degradation by taking into account image-space information (subsampled Z-buffer) as well as object-space information (distance map).

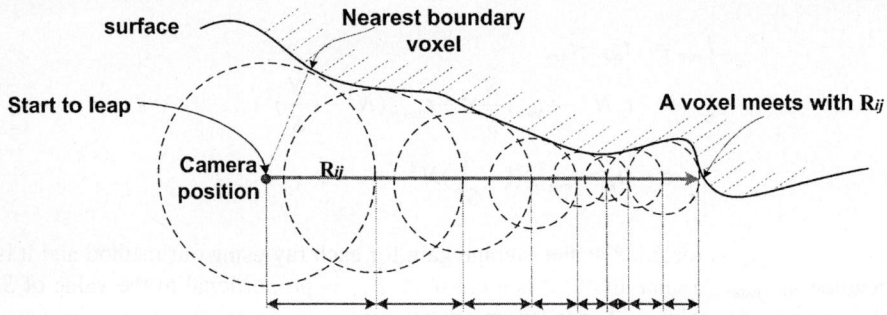

Fig. 5. An example of inefficient space-leaping. A ray has to jump several times to access the object in this viewing situation

It partitions image plane into several uniform pixel blocks, then determines minimum depth of four corner pixels for each pixel block just as the accelerated ray casting. While original method start to jump from its corresponding pixel in view plane, our method moves forward the starting point of leaping as the amount of the minimum depth value.

4 Experimental Results

Virtual endoscopy is a non-invasive diagnosis method based on computer processing of 3D image data sets such as CT scans in order to provide visualizations of inner structures of the human organ cavity [17-19]. It is a very good example to verify the performance enhancement of a perspective volume rendering method since it requires real-time generation of high-quality perspective images.

We compare the rendering time and image quality of original volume ray casting (*RC*), space leaping (*SL*) and our algorithm. All of these methods are implemented on a PC equipped with a Pentium IV 2.2GHz CPU, 1GB main memory, and NVIDIA GeForce4 graphics accelerator. The volume dataset is obtained by scanning a human abdomen with a multi-detector CT of which resolution is 512×512×541.

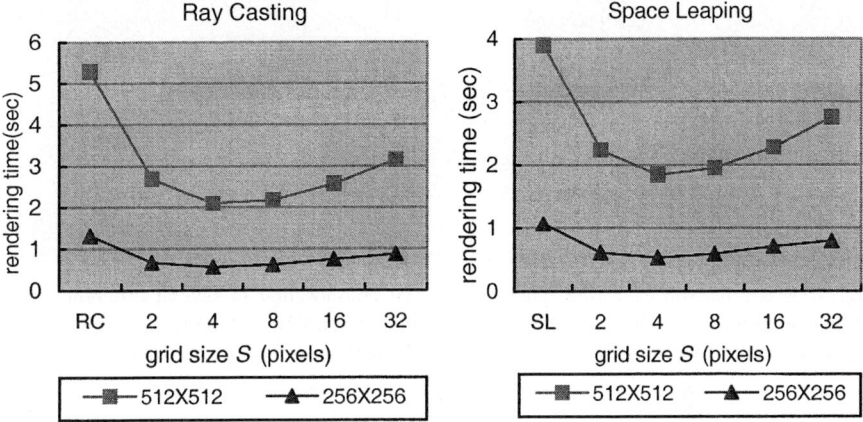

Fig. 6. Left graph shows rendering time of original ray casting (*RC*) and our method (*S*=2~32), and right graph shows that of space leaping (*SL*) and our enhanced method

We measure the rendering time on several different points in colon cavity under fixed viewing conditions. In order to estimate the influence of image resolution upon rendering speed and image quality, we render the dataset with resolutions of 256×256 and 512×512. Figure 6 (left) shows a comparison of average rendering time of original ray casting and our method. As the value of *S* increases, rendering time gets shorter since t_{save} is proportional to the pixel block size. However when the size of pixel block becomes larger than specific value (*S* = 4), the rendering time increases slightly due to the lack of spatial coherence as mentioned in Section 2. So we have to determine the optimal value of *S* according to volume data and final image size. For example, when we set the size of pixel block as 4 and image size as 512×512, rendering time of our method is only about 39% of that of original ray casting. Figure 6 (right) shows the comparison of average rendering time for conventional space leaping (*SL*) and our method. As the value of *S* increases, rendering speed increases until it reaches specific value. When we set the value of *S* as 4, rendering time of our method is about 47% of that of original space leaping. So we can conclude that our method can double up the rendering speed in comparison to conventional rendering methods.

Figure 7 shows the quality of images produced by original ray casting method and ours as the pixel block size increased from 4 to 16 under fixed viewing condition. It is very hard to recognize the difference between images from the two methods. Therefore we conclude that our method renders volumetric scene without loss of image quality.

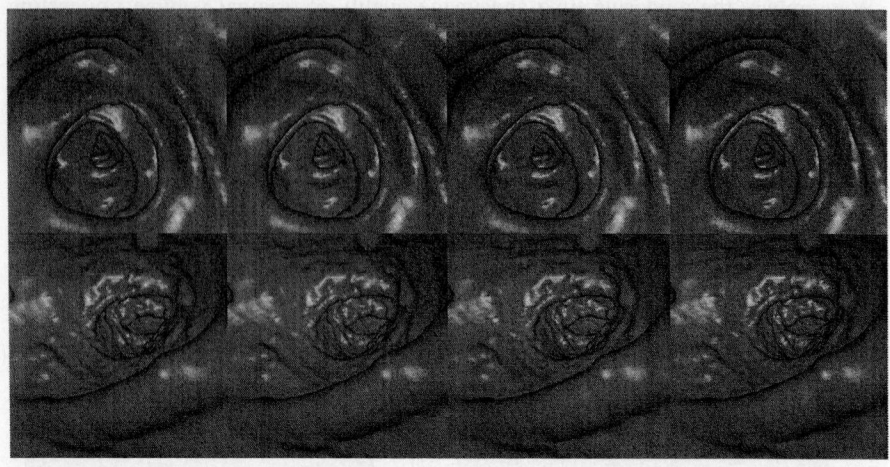

Fig. 7. A comparison of image quality of virtual colonoscopy in several different regions: leftmost column shows images produced by original ray casting and the remaining ones depict images produced by our method when $S = 4$, $S = 8$, and $S = 16$ from left to right

5 Conclusion

The most important issue in volume rendering for medical image viewing is to produce high quality images in real time. We propose an efficient ray casting and space-leaping method that reduces the rendering time in comparison to the conventional algorithms in any situation without loss of image quality. Using depth-subsampling scheme, our method moves forward the starting point of ray traversal as the amount of the minimum depth value calculated in subsampling step. This method reduces rendering time of space leaping even when a camera is close to object surface and its direction is most parallel to tangent vector of the surface. It can be applied to generate endoscopic images for any kind of tubular-shaped organs. Experimental results show that it normally produces high-quality images as in ray casting and takes less time for rendering.

Acknowledgement

This research was supported by University IT Research Center Project.

References

1. Van Gelder, A., Kim, K.: Direct volume rendering with shading via three-dimensional textures. In: Proc. of Volume Visualization Symposium, San Francisco, CA. (1996) 23–30
2. Meissner, M., Hoffmann, U., Strasser, W.: Enabling classification and shading for 3D texture mapping based volume rendering using OpenGL and extensions. In: Proc. of IEEE Visualization'99, San Francisco, CA. (1999) 207–214
3. Guenther, T., Poliwoda, C., Reinhard, C., Hesser, J., Maenner, R., Meinzer, H., Baur, H.: VIRIM: A massively parallel processor for real-time volume visualization in medicine. In: Proc. 9th Eurographics Workshop on Graphics Hardware, Oslo, Norway. (1994) 103–108
4. Pfister, H., Hardenbergh, J., Knittel, J., Lauer, H., Seiler, L.: The VolumePro real-time raycasting system. In: SIGGRAPH 99, Los Angeles, CA. (1999) 251–260
5. Levoy, M.: Display of surfaces from volume data. IEEE Computer Graphics and Applications **8**(3) (1988) 29–37
6. Lacroute, P., Levoy, M.: Fast volume rendering using a shear-warp factorization of the viewing transformation. In: SIGGRAPH 94, Orlando, Florida. (1994) 451–458
7. Yagel, R., Shi, Z.: Accelerating volume animation by space-leaping. In: Proc. of IEEE Visualization . (1993) 62–69
8. Zuiderveld, K.J., Koning, A.H.J., Viergever, M.A.: Acceleration of ray-casting using 3D distance transforms. In: Proc. Visualization in Biomedical Computing. (1992) 324-335
9. Udupa, J.K., Odhner, D.: Shell rendering. IEEE Computer Graphics and Applications **13**(6) (1993) 58–67
10. Levoy, M.: Efficient ray tracing of volume data. ACM Transactions on Graphics **9**(3) (1990) 245–261
11. Subramanian, K., Fussell, D.: Applying space subdivision techniques to volume rendering. In: IEEE Visualization'90, San Francisco, CA. (1990) 150–159
12. Yagel, R., Kaufman, A.: Template-based volume viewing. In: Eurographics'92, Cambridge, UK. (1992) 153–167
13. Sharghi, M., Ricketts, I.W.: Further acceleration of the visualization process used in virtual colonoscopy. In: Proc. 2nd IASTED International Conference on Visualization, Imaging and Image Processing, Malaga, Spain. (2002) 730–735
14. Vilanova, A., Groller, E., Konig, A.: Cylindrical approximation for tubular organ for virtual endoscopy. In: Proc. Computer Graphics and Imaging. (2000) 283–289
15. Wan, M., Tang, Q., Kaufman, A., Liang, Z., Wax, M.: Volume rendering based interactive navigation within the human colon. In: Proc. IEEE Visualization. (1999) 397–400
16. Wan, M., Sadiq, A., Kaufman, A.: Fast and reliable space leaping for interactive volume rendering. In: Proc. IEEE Visualization. (2002) 195–202
17. Hong, L., Kaufman, A., Wei, Y., Viswambharan, A., Wax, M., Liang, Z.: 3D virtual colonoscopy. In: IEEE Symposium on Biomedical Visualization. (1995) 26–32
18. Hong, L., Muraki, S., Kaufman, A., Bartz, D., He, T.: Virtual voyage: Interactive navigation in the human colon. In: ACM SIGGRAPH (1997) 27–34
19. Shin, B.S., Lim, S.H.: An efficient navigation method for virtual endoscopy using volume ray casting. LNCS, Vol. 2659. Springer-Verlag (2003) 60–69

An Efficient Camera Path Computation Using Image-Space Information in Virtual Endoscopy

Koo-Joo Kwon and Byeong-Seok Shin

Inha University, Department of Computer Science and Engineering
253 Yonghyeon-Dong, Nam-Gu, Inchon, 402-751, Korea
g2012154@inhavision.inha.ac.kr, bsshin@inha.ac.kr

Abstract. In virtual endoscopy, fast and accurate path generation and navigation is the most important feature. Previous methods made a center line of organ cavity by connecting consecutive points maximally distant from organ wall. However they have some problems to demand a lot of computation and extra storage for spatial data structures. We propose an efficient path computation algorithm. It determines camera direction for the next frame identifying a ray that has maximum depth in current frame. Camera position is determined by using the center of gravity of organ's cross-section. Entire camera path can be constructed by applying the operation in every frame. It doesn't require preprocessing and extra storage since it depends only on image-space information generated in rendering time.

1 Introduction

Optical endoscopy is a less-invasive diagnosis method. We can directly examine the pathologies of internal organs by putting endoscopy camera into human body. It offers higher quality images than any other medical imaging methods. However it has some disadvantages of causing patients discomfort, limited range of exploration and serious side effect such as perforation, infection and hemorrhage.

Virtual endoscopy provides visualizations of inner structure of the human organ, which has pipe-like shape such as colon, bronchus and blood vessel [1]. Since virtual endoscopy is non-invasive examination, there is no discomfort and side effects. In order to implement virtual endoscopy, we should devise a method that produces high quality perspective images within short time. However, it is more important to avoid collision between virtual camera and organ wall, and let the camera smoothly move through the human cavity. Therefore, fast and accurate path generation is essential for efficient diagnosis using virtual endoscopy. Previous methods mainly depend on object-space information such as distance map and potential field. Since entire volume data should to be considered to produce those spatial data structures, a lot of computation in preprocessing step and extra storages are required.

In this paper, we propose an efficient camera path generation and navigation algorithm that computes camera position and orientation for the next frame while rendering a scene in current frame. It determines camera orientation for the next frame using a ray that has maximum distance in current frame, and it calculates camera position in the next frame using center of gravity of organ region on cross-sectional image. Since this process can be done without extra cost during ray casting, it computes accurate camera path in real-time.

Related work is summarized in the next section. In Section 3, we present our method in detail. Experimental results and remarks are shown in Section 4. Lastly, we summarize and conclude our work.

2 Related Works

Volume ray casting is the most famous rendering method [2]. After firing a ray from each pixel on a view plane, it computes color and opacity on sample points along the ray and determines final color by blending those sample values. Although it takes a long time to make an image due to randomness in memory reference pattern, it can produce high-quality images in comparison to the other methods and provide perspective rendering for generating endoscopic scene.

In order to implement realistic virtual environment, several kinds of interactions between objects should be considered. Especially, collision avoidance and fly-through along center line are more important than any other components in virtual endoscopy. Some spatial data structures can be used for collision avoidance. Occupancy map has the same resolution as the volume dataset and each cell of the map stores identifiers for objects that occupy the cell [3]. As an object changes its position or size, the value of each cell should be updated. If a cell has two or more identifiers, it is regarded as collision of those objects. Since the method should update cell data whenever an object changes its position and size it is not adequate for real-time application. A distance map [4] is a 3D spatial data structure that has the same resolution of its volume data and each point of the map has the distance to the nearest boundary voxel. The smaller the distance values the larger the collision probability. However this method requires long preprocessing time for 3D distance transformation.

Navigation method for virtual endoscopy can be classified into three categories; manual navigation [5], planned navigation [6] and guided navigation [7,8]. In manual navigation, we can directly control the virtual camera to observe anywhere we want to examine. However the user might feel discomfort since camera movement is entirely dependent on user's control, and collision may occur if the user misleads the camera. Planned navigation calculates entire path in preprocessing time using several path generation algorithms, then moves the camera along the pre-calculated path. It can fly through the desired area without user intervention. It requires a lot of computation in preprocessing step and it doesn't allow users to control the camera intuitively. Guided navigation is a physically-based method, which makes a spatial data structure such as potential field in preprocessing step and determines camera orientation by considering attractive force that directs to target point, repulsive force from organ surface, and user's input. It guarantees that a camera arrives to target point and move the camera to anywhere the user want to place without collision against organ wall. However it is hard to implement and it demands a lot of cost to make and maintain the potential field.

3 Navigation Method Using Image-Space Information

Guided navigation methods mentioned in the previous section are regarded as *object-space* approach as it exploits overall information of entire volume dataset while building spatial data structures. Even though it guarantees to generate reliable navigation path, it takes a lot of preprocessing time. In virtual endoscopy, in general, information for a small part of entire volume is required since field of view is restricted in cavities of a volume dataset. Our method computes camera position and orientation considering only some voxels in view frustum, thus we call it *image-space* approach.

A navigation path can be defined as a pair of functions, $P = \{\delta(t), \varphi(t)\}$, where $\delta(t)$ returns camera direction at a specific frame t, and $\varphi(t)$ returns camera position. Our method determines camera orientation for the next frame t_{i+1} using depth information obtained in rendering step of current frame t_i and camera position for the next frame by using the center of gravity in cross-section of organ cavity. Figure 1 shows the procedure for determining entire navigation path of our method. Rendering pipeline is the same as in the conventional volume ray casting method. Our method has another pipeline to specify the center-line of organ cavity.

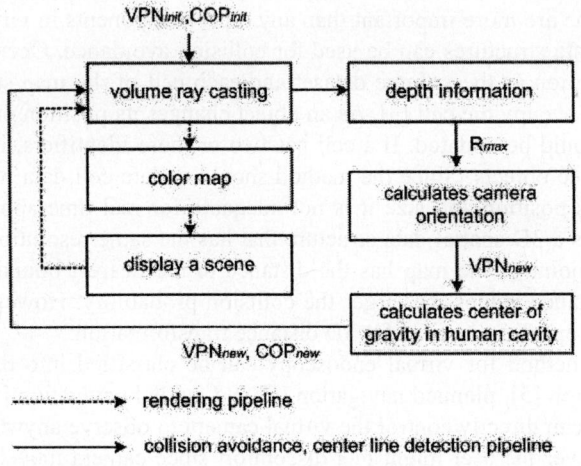

Fig. 1. A procedure for determining navigation path

Figure 2 shows a procedure to the determine camera position and orientation in the next frame in detail. Volume ray casting fires a ray from each pixel on the view plane, then it computes color and opacity on sample points along the ray and determines final color by blending them. During traversing a ray we can compute the distance to the nearest non-transparent voxel multiplying the number of samples by unit distance between two consecutive samples. The distance can be regarded as the depth value to organ wall. Let d_{ij} be the depth value of a pixel p_{ij}, we find the direction of a ray R_{max}, fired from a pixel that has the maximum depth value as follows :

$$R_{max} = f\left(\max_{i,j=0}^{M,N}(d_{ij})\right). \quad (1)$$

Where M and N are horizontal and vertical resolution of an image and f is a mapping function of a depth value for a pixel to its corresponding ray vector R_{ij}. We set the direction of a ray fired from a pixel that has the maximum depth value d_{max} as a form of unit vector, which is denoted as R_{max} (see Figure 2 (top)).

Depth values reflect the possibility of collision in organ cavity. Larger depth value means that obstacles are located far away from the current camera position. On the contrary, smaller the depth value, higher the collision possibility since the camera is close to the organ wall. VPN_i is a unit vector that represents a view plane normal for current frame t_i. We set the view plane normal for the next frame VPN_{i+1} as R_{max} to minimize the probability of collision. Then move the view plane as the amount of unit distance (Δ) toward the direction as depicted in Figure 2 (middle).

After determining viewing direction of the next frame, we have to calculate new camera position, COP_{i+1} as shown in Figure 2(bottom). That is the center of gravity on organ cavity, which is composed of connected pixels has minimum intensity in view plane. In the following equation $COG(x,y)$ calculates the center of gravity on the next frame.

$$COG\left(\frac{1}{N}\sum_{i=0}^{N-1}x_i, \frac{1}{N}\sum_{i=0}^{N-1}y_i\right). \qquad (2)$$

Where, N is a number of pixels corresponding organ cavity on projected area and x_i, y_i are coordinates for each pixel. We can calculate the center of gravity point on projection plane by averaging of all pixels on organ cavity area.

4 Experimental Results

In order to check whether our method generates a camera path along center line and provides reliable navigation through organ cavity, we compare navigation paths made by object-space method using 3D distance field and our image-space method. These methods are implemented on a PC equipped with Pentium IV 2.6GHz CPU, 1GB main memory, and ATi RADEON 8500 graphics accelerator. The volume data used for the experiment is a clinical volume obtained by scanning a human abdomen with a multi detector CT of which the resolution 512×512×541. Since human colon has complex pipe-like structure, virtual colonoscopy is a good example to apply our method.

Figure 3 shows how different the paths generated by object-space method using 3D distance transformation (denoted as DIST) [9] and our method (denoted as OURS). Since DIST is known as an accurate center-line computation method, difference between those paths can reflect the accuracy of our method.

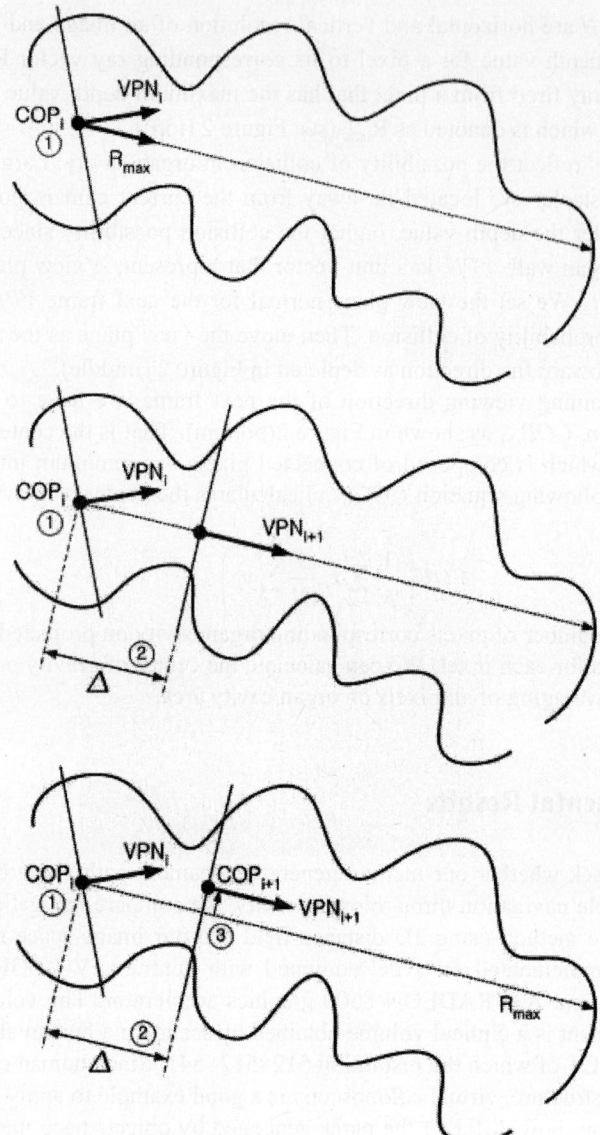

Fig. 2. A procedure to the determine camera position and orientation in the next frame. (top) calculates a maximum depth value and set R_{max} as the ray that has the maximum depth on current frame. (middle) moves the view plane foward as the amount of unit distance (Δ) along R_{max} and set VPN_{i+1} as R_{max}. (bottom) compute center of gravity and set it as COP_{i+1} for the next frame

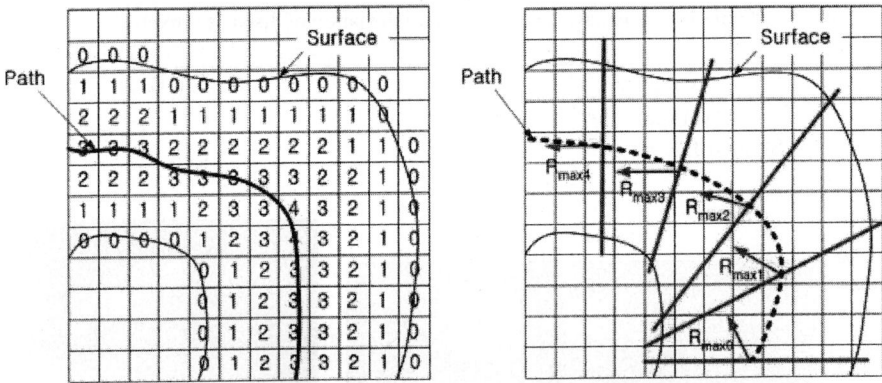

Fig. 3. A comparison of navigation paths produced by DIST (left) and OURS (right)

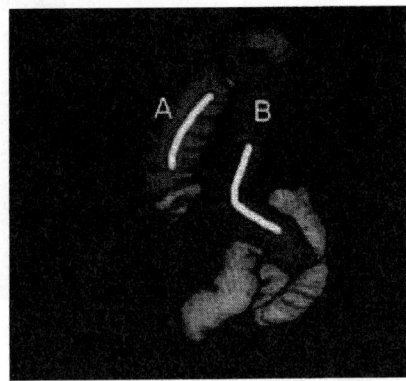

Fig. 4. Test region in colon. A straight region (A) and a curved region (B)

In case of DIST, distance based path generation method takes 260 sec in preprocessing step. Our image-space based method need no preprocessing.

Several regions are carefully selected for accuracy test. As shown in Figure 4, we made navigation paths on a straight region and a curved region using two methods. Our method is adequate to any pipe-like structure without branch.

Two graphs in Figure 5 show the difference between center of gravity (OURS) and maximum distance point (DIST) on region A and region B in the colon. Average radius of colon cavity in cross-sectional image is about 20 to 30 voxels. Experimental results show that center of gravity points are very close to the center-line of organ cavity generated by distance-based method. The average of distance between a center of gravity and colon center is 1.7 voxels in straight region and 1.9 voxels in curved region. This means that our method guarantees to generate a camera path on center-line of organ cavity.

Table 1. The average and the standard deviation of distance (voxels)

	Region A	Region B
Average	1.7	1.9
Standard deviation	0.8	1.5

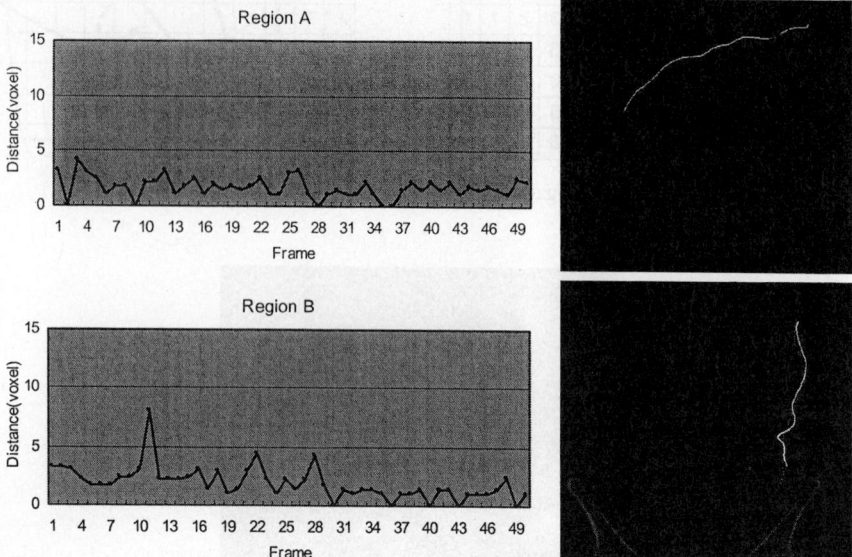

Fig. 5. A distance between center of gravity (in OURS) and a position maximally distant from organ wall (in DIST) is measured in consecutive frames on a straight region (top) and a curved region in colon (bottom). A path for DIST is represented as yellow line, and that for OURS is depicted as red line in cross-section images on right column

Figure 6 shows consecutive frames for region A while applying our navigation method. It can allow users to control the virtual camera conveniently and examine wider area in colon since the camera lies on center point of colon cavity.

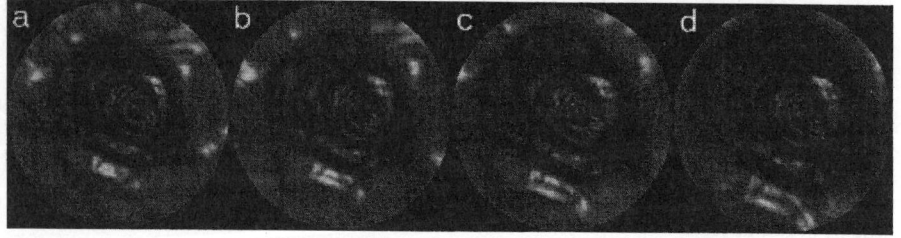

Fig. 6. Virtual navigation in human colon with our method

5 Conclusion

We proposed an efficient path generation method using depth values and the center of gravity in cross-section. We can get camera direction of the next frame using the ray that has maximum distance in current frame. And the camera position is calculated using the center of gravity in cross-section. Our method can generate a reliable camera path and it doesn't require preprocessing stage and extra storage for maintaining spatial data structures. Consequently it helps doctors to perform fast and accurate diagnosis.

Acknowledgement

This research was supported by University IT Research Center Project.

References

1. You, S., Hong, L., Wan, M., Junyaprasert, K., Kaufman, A., Muraki, S., Zhou, Y., Wax, M., Liang, Z.: Interactive volume rendering for virtual colonoscopy. In: IEEE Visualization Proceedings of the 8th conference on Visualization. (1997)
2. Levoy, M.: Display of surfaces from volume data. IEEE Computer Graphics and Applications 8(3) (1988) 29–37
3. Gibson, S.: Beyond volume rendering: visualization, haptic exploration, and physical modeling of voxel-based objects. In: 6th Eurographics Workshop on Visualization in Scientific Computing. (1995)
4. De Assis Zampirolli, F., De Alencar Lotufo, R.: Classification of the distance transformation algorithms under the mathematical morphology approach. In: Proceedings XIII Brazilian Symposium on Computer Graphics and Image Processing. (2000) 292–299
5. Gleicher, M., Witkin, A.: Through the lens camera control. In: ACM SIGGRAPH. (1992) 331–340
6. Hong, L., Kaufman, A., Wei, Y., Viswambharan, A., Wax, M., Liang, Z.: 3D virtual colonoscopy. In: IEEE Symposium on Biomedical Visualization. (1995) 26–32
7. Hong, L., Muraki, S., Kaufman, A., Bartz, D., He, T.: Virtual voyage: Interactive navigation in the human colon. In: ACM SIGGRAPH. (1997) 27–34
8. Wan, M., Tang, Q., Kaufman, A., Liang, Z., Wax, M.: Volume rendering based interactive navigation within the human colon. IEEE Visualization (1999)
9. Datta, A., Soundaralakshmi, S.: Fast parallel algorithm for distance transforms. In: The 15th International Symposium on Parallel and Distributed Processing. (2001) 1130–1134

Hair Motion Simulation

Yusuf Sahillioğlu and Bülent Özgüç

Bilkent University, Department of Computer Engineering
Bilkent, 06800 Ankara, Turkey
sahilli@ug.bilkent.edu.tr, ozguc@bilkent.edu.tr

Abstract. Hair motion simulation in computer graphics has been an attraction for many researchers. The application we have developed has been inspired by the related previous work as well as our own efforts in finding useful algorithms to handle this problem. The work we present uses a set of representations, including hair strands, clusters and strips, that are derived from the same underlying base skeleton, where this skeleton is animated by physical, i.e. spring, forces.

1 Introduction

One of the most exciting and challenging research areas in CG is the hair motion simulation. The challenge is due to the fact that a human head has up to 160,000 individual hair strands and simulating each of them in a straightforward manner is quite costly and tedious. Therefore, one should come up with efficient algorithms.

One idea is using level of detail (LOD) approach, a popular method in CG modeling. The hair can be represented as segments where each segment might be either a hair strand, a cluster or a strip. Depending on the distance between the viewer and animated head, the corresponding level switches will be performed.

In addition to the LOD usage, there is also another useful idea: The structure behind the modeling of these segments. All the segments are derived from the same base hair skeleton structure and the dynamics of this structure is based on the applied physical forces, such as spring, gravitation, friction, absorption and repulsion force.

This paper aims to present the work we have carried out to add these features to our hair motion simulation application. We should also produce a human head which is ready to host the hair. Thus, this problem can be described as the modeling, dynamics and rendering of human hair and head in real time.

2 Solution and Design Decisions

The solution to this problem consists of two parts, namely, modeling, rendering and animating human head, and modeling, rendering and animating human hair. While deciding on the design issues, a human head model for hair placement is prepared, making use of an auxiliary software package called 3DS Max [1]. Then, use of the physical laws and the base skeleton structure for hair is prepared. Finally, the hair part is implanted on the scalp of the head part.

2.1 Human Head

The procedure to obtain a human head requires modeling and rendering it. Making use of an existing head model in 3DS Max software environment, the head is loaded into the software and some transformations and a crucial operation, scalp mesh separation are added to it. Having seperated the scalp mesh and added some basic transformations, i.e. rotation and translation to the head, the hair can be implanted and moved.

Tasks of Scalp Mesh Triangles. Each scalp mesh triangle is associated with the following tasks:
1. Determining the implanting point of the hair segment (rooting)
2. Determining the density of hair (density)
3. Detecting collision between scalp and hair segment (collision)

Rooting: The root of each hair segment will be the center of gravity (COG) of the corresponding scalp mesh triangle [2]. Having obtained the scalp mesh triangles, new hair segments originating from the COG of these triangles are generated. Since each hair segment will be long enough, the segments originating from a higher triangle, will also cover regions of some lower triangles. As the number of segments increases, some of the lower level triangles will be automatically hidden by the long hairs originating from above. Hence, for the sake of performing less computation in real-time, the rooting of hair from lower triangles is sometimes omitted.

Density: If the number of hair segments is equal to the number of scalp mesh triangles, rooted hair might be sparce. In order to handle this problem, a given triangle is recursively subdivided and new hair segments are originated from the COG of the newly created ones [2], as demonstrated in Figure 1.

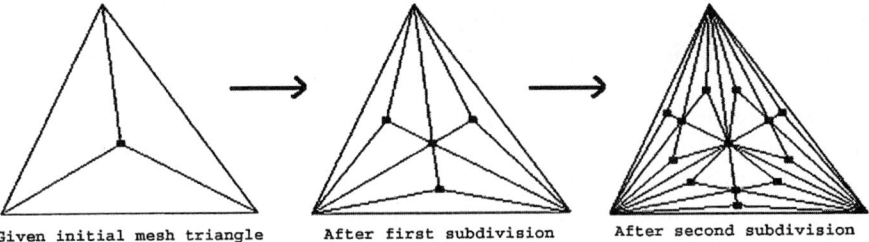

Fig. 1. Increasing number of roots via subdivision process

It should be noted that when the type of the triangle is close to an equal-sided triangle (well-proportioned), the rooting points are fairly and logically distributed over the shape. However, when the triangle sides are badly proportioned then the rooting points will stack on one region of the shape dominantly. The latter case is undesirable and therefore while generating the scalp mesh triangles, it should be tried to create as proportioned triangles as possible.

Collision: The last task of the scalp mesh triangles is the collision detection between themselves and the corresponding hair segment. To do this the normal –to decide collision- and some physical constants (i.e. absorption, friction, repulsion) -to decide the response forces in case of a collision- of each triangle are necessary. Since each hair segment is recognized by their masses[1], the location of all masses is compared with a single scalp triangle. In case of a collision between a given triangle and a hair segment mass point, the following collision response operations are performed:

1. Copy and omit the velocity component of the mass in each axis, set v_x v_y v_z to 0, in order to prevent it from going further towards to the inside of head.
2. Apply the friction force, using the physical friction constant of triangle material, to the mass. The force will be proportional to the magnitude of velocity (which is copied before setting initial velocity to 0) of the collided mass and be applied in the direction of the velocity vector of the mass to reduce repulsion effect.
3. Apply the absorption force, using the physical absorption constant of triangle material, to the mass. The force will be proportional to the magnitude of velocity of the collided mass and be applied in the direction of the velocity vector of the mass to reduce repulsion effect.
4. Apply the repulsion force, using the physical repulsion constant of triangle material, to the mass. The force will be proportional to the magnitude of velocity of the collided mass and be applied in the *opposite* direction of the velocity vector of the collided mass to make mass go away from triangle.

Considering that there are roughly 80 mass points for one hair segment and each of these points must be compared with candidate triangles for collision detection process, the cost of computation becomes expensive if the number of triangles in scalp increases. Therefore, some sparseness in the scalp is left and those sections are treated as rough bounding rectangles.

2.2 Human Hair

There are three main aspects in human hair simulation which are stated as hair shape modeling, hair dynamics (animation) and hair rendering in [3].

Hair modeling involves the exact or fake creation of individual hairs. Since there are approximately 160.000 individual hair strands on a given human scalp, the modeling should be performed in such a way that the resulting animation of the selected model will be efficient and fast.

Hair dynamics involves the animation of the hair. Several forces are applied to the particular parts of the hair in order to accomplish the animation.

Hair rendering is involved with the appearance of simulated hair from the viewer's point of view. Several rendering techniques are applied to the hair for realism.

Hair Modeling. There are three hair modeling schemes dominant in this research area: Strand Hair Model (SHM) introduced in [4, 5]; Multiresolution Hair Model (MHM) introduced in [6]; Modeling with Level-of-Detail Representations (LOD) introduced in [7–9].

Strand Hair Model (SHM): SHM is the simplest way to model the hair. Each individual hair strand is explicitly designed by this scheme [5]. The details can be seen in Figure 2.

---

[1] Masses are the nodes of the base skeleton structure.

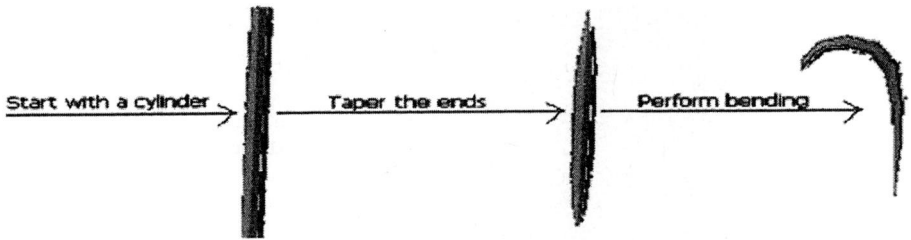

Fig. 2. The process of modeling an individual hair strand in SHM

After applying the related transformations, namely tapering and bending respectively to the initial cylinder object, an individual hair strand is obtained.

Multiresolution Hair Model (MHM): MHM is an admissible model to represent hair since it is based on the multiresolution concept whose major benefit is the user's freedom to choose the appropriate level of detail for a desired model manipulation. Multiresolution manipulations for hair modeling are achieved with a hierarchy of a set of generalized cylinders. Hair design is created with a small set of clusters, roughly 30 clusters per human head. Subdividing these clusters yields the submodel of MHM, which is Cluster Hair Model (CHM). Putting all together, MHM combines the benefits of CHM and SHM by allowing local control as well as global control. MHM is too complex to model since it allows for interactive hair modeling. Considering that our project does not deal with interactively creating complex hair models, we have concentrated on the following method instead of using the MHM.

Modeling with LOD Representations: Getting the basic idea from [7], we introduced some new algorithms. The preferred approach, LOD, uses three novel representations based on a base skeleton to create levels-of-detail (LODs) for hair. These are strips, clusters and individual strands:

Strips: Strip is the coarsest (lowest) LOD used for hair modeling. It is typically used to represent the inner most layers of hair and it is responsible for the global physical behavior and the volume of the hair during the simulation. The transition (switching) to this LOD representation is performed when the viewing distance to the human head is increased.

In order to model the strip, the base skeleton structure is used. Starting from the top skeleton node, it is proceeded towards to the bottom by putting 2 control points for each of the node point encountered. It is important to notice that, the 2 control points and the related node point are collinear. Obtaining the global surface by this way, we subdivide it to obtain a smooth representation. The subdivision surface that is obtained for one strip is shown in Figure 3.

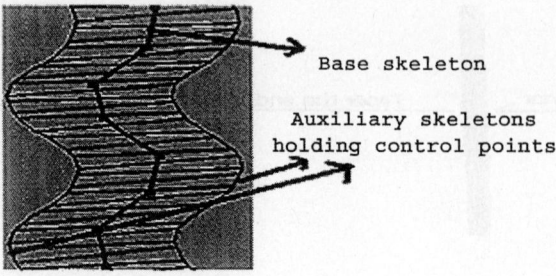

Fig. 3. Strip represented as a subdivision surface

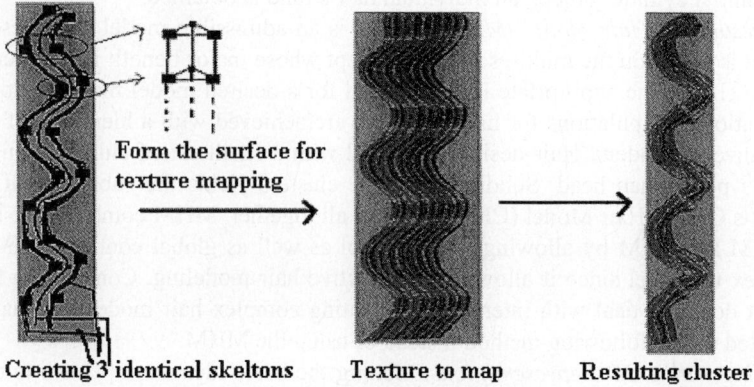

Fig. 4. Process of obtaining a cluster

Clusters: Cluster is used to represent a group of hair. This LOD improves performance since instead of animating lots of hair strands close to each other; we will animate just one object that represents the total behavior.

In addition to the use of base skeleton structure, the generalized cylinder concept arises in order to model a cluster. The generalized cylinder is obtained as follows: Initially three identical base skeletons are created; one on the left, one on the right and the other on the back (Figure 4). The corresponding nodes of each skeleton are joined, forming a surface to which our texture can be easily mapped. The texture gives the illusion of a group of strands, roughly 30 strands. Hence, by applying forces to just 3 skeletons, a group motion consisting of 30 strands is obtained. It will gain a volume to hair and reduce the sparseness with the cost of animating just three skeletons.

Individual Strands: An individual strand is used to model the hair strand and can be seen only when the viewer is very close to the head. Switching to this LOD will take place when distance between the viewer and the head is sufficiently decreased.

As in all other LODs, individual strands are based on the base skeleton. Actually, the base skeleton itself is directly the hair strand. By combining two consequent masses of the skeleton via a line segment, the hair strand is automatically obtained (Figure 5).

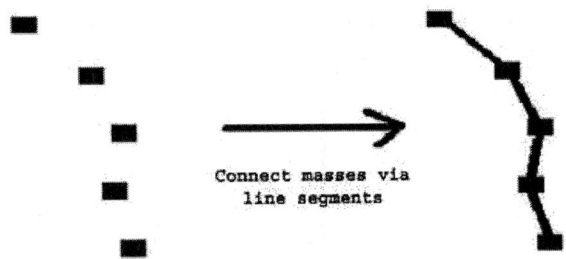

Fig. 5. Process of obtaining an individual strand

Hair Dynamics. Hair dynamics (animation) is closely related to the base skeleton structure. The base skeleton is defined as the structure consisting of point-like masses connected to each other via line segments (Figure 5). The hair dynamics is performed by applying forces to each mass of the base skeleton structure, where the term mass seems logical since the Newton forces ($F = ma$) is applied to those masses. The applied forces will change the position of each mass accordingly. Changing the positions of masses will change the position of the base skeleton and therefore the position of the active LOD representation derived from the moved base skeleton.

Moving Base Skeleton. Moving the base skeleton corresponds to moving the derived LOD representation as well. Thus, the understanding of the idea of moving this skeleton resolves the dynamics involved.

The source of a movement is the applied forces. The net force applied on a mass, F, changes its acceleration, by $F = ma$ where m is predefined. By new acceleration, the new velocity is obtained and by new velocity the displacement that should be added to the current position for that particular mass is obtained.

There are two types of forces (main forces) that are always applied regardless of the animation state. *Spring forces*: Two consequent masses introduce to each other spring forces. *Gravitation forces*: The traditional gravitational force is applied to each mass.

Besides, there are four more forces (extra forces) that are applied when necessary:
1. Air Friction: As long as a mass is moving (velocity is not 0), an air friction force is applied in the opposite direction of velocity vector and with the magnitude proportional to velocity of the mass.
2. Scalp Friction: As long as a mass is colliding to a triangle, or a bounding rectangle of scalp mesh, a friction force is applied in the direction of velocity vector and with the magnitude proportional to velocity of the mass.
3. Scalp Absorption: As long as a mass is colliding to a triangle, or a bounding rectangle of scalp mesh, an absorption force is applied in the direction of velocity vector and with the magnitude proportional to velocity of the mass.
4. Scalp Repulsion: As long as a mass is colliding to a triangle, or a bounding rectangle of scalp mesh, a repulsion force is applied in the *opposite* direction of velocity vector and with the magnitude proportional to velocity of the mass.

The visualization of the forces mentioned above is given in Figure 6.

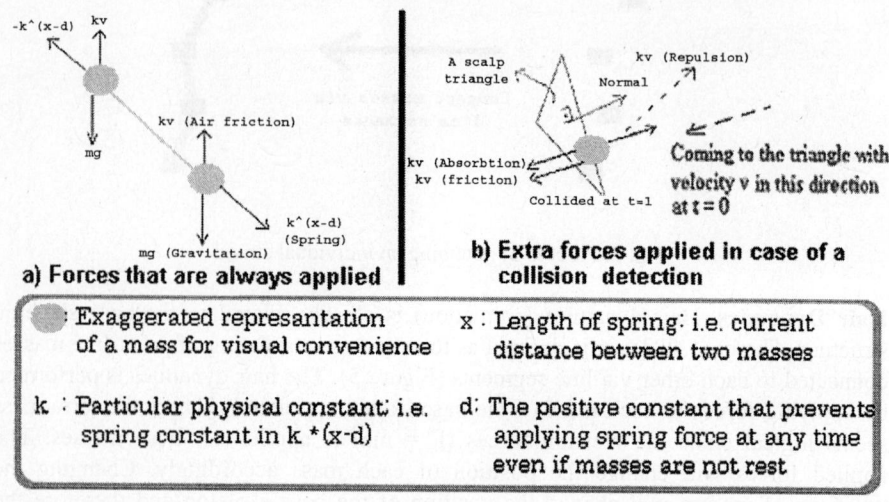

Fig. 6. Visualized representation of forces

In each frame of the animation, the current total force acting on corresponding mass is simulated by using the Newton law, $F = ma$. Since F is known, by the result of Figure 6, and m, the predefined constant is known, acceleration, a, is computed. Knowing the acceleration, the amount of change in velocity is computed by using $v = ad_t$, where a is the acceleration just found and d_t is the predefined change in time. Adding this new v, the velocity gained/lost, to current v, new velocity is obtained.

Knowing the new velocity, the amount of change in displacement is computed by using equation $x = vd_t$, where v is the velocity just found and d_t is the change in time. Adding this new x, the road taken, to current x, the desired new position is obtained.

The scalp friction-absorption-repulsion forces need to detect collision. Another collision detection is necessary between the hair segments themselves. All of these collisions will change the net force when they are detected and the changing net force will obviously change the dynamics (movement) of the hair.

Collision Detection. There are two types of collisions to be detected. When they are detected, the specified response forces of Figure 6 are applied to the collided mass.

In *scalp collision*, it is required to detect collision between a scalp mesh triangle and a mass of the hair segment. This is done in two steps. First, the mass must reside on the "infinite" plane of the candidate triangle. If not, then there is no need to apply the second step since the mass cannot hit the triangle. However, if the mass is on the plane then the second step takes place to decide whether the mass is inside the boundaries of the candidate triangle. To perform this inside-the-boundary test, we create three planes for each edge of the candidate triangle with their normals all pointing in. The mass is decided to hit the triangle if and only if it is inside all of the three planes. Applying these two steps to all of the mesh triangles reduces the real-time running performance significantly. Therefore, *binary search* approach is used to find the candidate triangle. This is done by a bounding box approach where the far left triangles are ignored if the mass is on the right side with respect to the center of gravity of current region of head and vice versa (Figure 7).

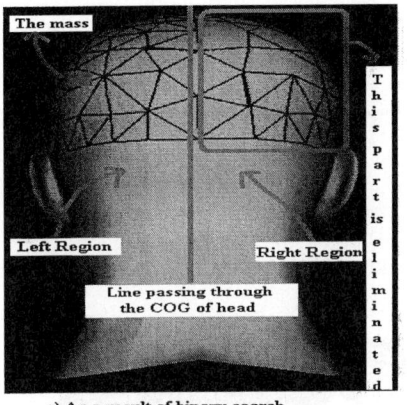
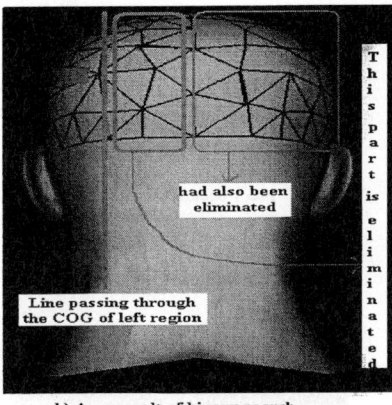

a) As a result of binary search iteration1, eliminate right region

b) As a result of binary search iteration2, eliminate specified region

Fig. 7. Eliminating irrelevant triangles before deciding the one being hit by the mass

In *hair collision*, the simplest algorithm is the detection of collision of every mass of each hair strand with all the masses of the remaining hair segments exhaustively. This is done by comparing the nearness of the two mass coordinates; i.e. by tolerating some amount of error. This tolerance is necessary since it is almost impossible to match two coordinates exactly when many forces are acting on each mass in each refresh cycle.

This approach is computationally expensive. For only one mass of N masses of the given segment, all N masses of the other hair strands are tested, leading to the cost of $O(N^2)$ for just one hair collision. If we assume that there are N such segments on the scalp, this cost increases to $O(N^3)$. In short, we will be forced to apply this $O(N^3)$ algorithm in each frame, which is done in periods of 0.33 seconds for 15 strands with 80 masses each. The bounding boxe idea can help. Instead of testing the given mass with all of the N masses of the candidate hair segment all the time, we put that candidate segment into a bounding box and make a test only once, just for the intersection between mass and box. Only if this initial test is passed, i.e. intersection is detected, then we try the test of one mass with all others. The boxing of a given hair segment will be done using the min/max of axis values as Figure 8 illustrates.

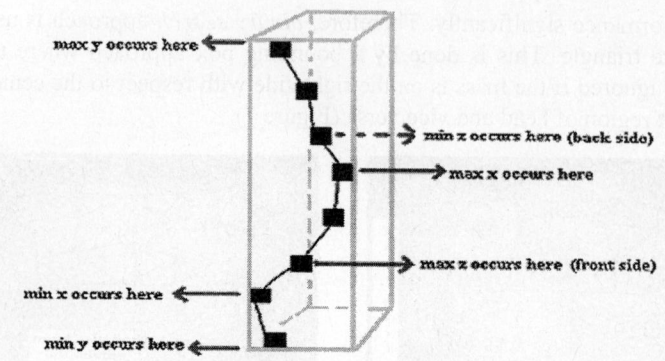

Fig. 8. Bounding box of a given hair segment

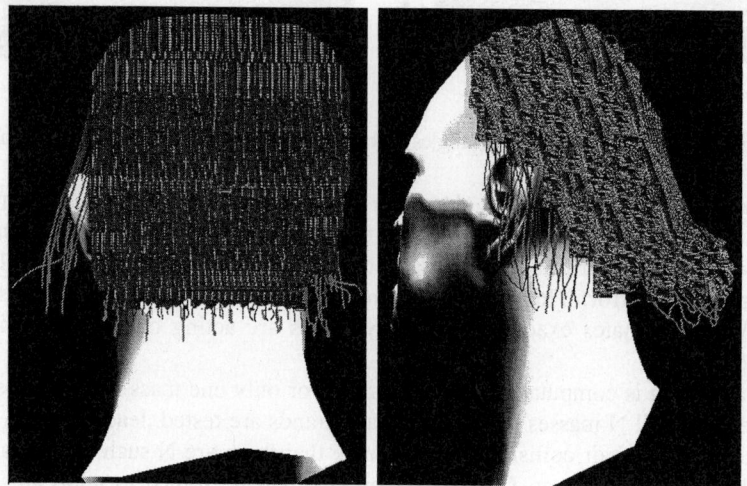

Fig. 9. Rendered versions of cluster representation

Hair Rendering. According to the active LOD, several techniques of rendering are applied. When the viewing distance is very large, we switch to strip representation. Since strip is a subdivision surface, it has well-defined surface normals. Hence, bump texture maps are easily applied. Clusters are also bump-mapped since they have similar properties (Figure 9). Strands are just lines, thus they are drawn with a single shaded color.

3 Results and Future Work

Hair motion simulator is tested on a PC having 512MB of RAM and 2.4GHz processor speed. In order to evaluate the program several tests, whose results are given in Table 1, have been applied. (SC: Scalp to hair collision; HC: hair to hair collision)

Table 1. Frame process time measured in seconds

	no collision	SC	HC	SC + HC
1 Hair Strand	0.04	0.04	n/a	0.04
100 Hair Strands	0.08	0.27	0.88	>2.0
1 Hair Cluster	0.05	0.05	n/a	0.05
100 Hair Clusters	0.09	0.44	0.94	>3.0

The model used for the table consists of 17064 vertices for the head mesh that make up 5688 head mesh triangles, 312 scalp mesh vertices for 104 scalp mesh triangles and 80 masses for each hair strand. Real time animation for a denser hair placement than what is given in Table 1 is not achieved yet and we are improving some of the techniques used so that a more realistic head (Figure 9) can be animated close to real time.

References

1. Ben, D.: Game programming with a personality. http://gametutorials.com
2. Usher, J.: Computer Science Honours Dissertation 499: Dynamic Hair Generation. Curtin University of Technology, http://www.vhml.org/theses/usher/
3. Thalmann, N., Hadap, S., Kalra, P.: State of the art in hair simulation. In: Int. Workshop on Human Modeling and Animation, Seoul, Korea. (2002) 3–9
4. Anjyo, K., Usami Y., Kurihara, T.: A simple method for extracting the natural beauty of hair. In: Proc. SIGGRAPH'92. (1992) 111–120
5. Tomwool, H.: Growing hair by tutor Tomwool. http://luna.spaceports.com/~inferno/tu_hair.htm
6. Kim, T., Neumann, U.: Interactive multiresolution hair modeling and editing. ACM Transactions on Graphics 21(3) (2002) 620–629
7. Ward, K., Lin, M., Lee, J., Fisher, S., Macri, D.: Modeling hair using level-of-detail representations. In: Proc. of Computer Animation and Social Agents, New Brunswick, New Jersey. (2003) 41–47
8. Ward, K., Lin, M.: Adaptive grouping and subdivision for simulating hair dynamics. In: Proc. of 11th Pacific Conference on Computer Graphics and Applications, Canmore, Canada. (2003) 234–243
9. Ward, K., Fisher, S., Lin, M.: Simplified representations for modeling hair. UNC Technical Report #TR02-020 (2002)

Interactive Mouse Systems Providing Haptic Feedback During the Exploration in Virtual Environment

Ki-Uk Kyung[1], Heejin Choi[2], Dong-Soo Kwon[1], and Seung-Woo Son[1]

[1] Telerobotics & Control Laboratory, Dept. of Mechanical Engineering, KAIST
Guseong-dong, Yuseong-gu, Daejeon, 305-701, Korea
{kyungku@robot,kwonds@,sons@robot}.kaist.ac.kr
[2] Mechatronics Research Laboratory, Dept. of Mechanical Engineering, MIT
77 Massachusetts Avenue, Cambridge MA 02139, USA
choihj@mit.edu

Abstract. This paper presents two kinds of novel haptic mouse systems as new human computer interfaces, which have a force and tactile feedback capability. The first one can reflect 1 dof grabbing force as well as 2 dof translation force. Five-bar mechanism has been adapted to realize the 2 dof translation force feedback, and double prismatic joint mechanism has been used to implement the grabbing force feedback. This system helps the user to feel grabbing force, contact force and weight while picking up and moving an object in virtual environment. The second system can simulate the surface roughness as well as contact force. This system consists of two parts: a 2 DOF force feedback device for kinesthetic display and a tactile feedback unit for displaying the normal stimulation to the skin and the skin stretch. The proposed systems are expected to be used as new human computer interfaces by presenting realistic haptic interaction in e-commerce or VR environment.

1 Introduction

Since the advent of the first modern computer "ENIAC" in 1946, many types of computer interface have been developed to facilitate the use of computer. Punch card and high-speed magnetic tape had been developed in an early stage of computer interface history. Mouse and touch screen were developed in 1963 and 1970 respectively. Most recently, touch pad was developed in 1988. However, the computer interfaces developed so far have been used unilaterally only as input devices to transfer information to computer, and could not play an interactive role. In addition as the demand for more realistic communication method with the computer is growing, haptics has emerged as the new element in the computer interfaces. As stated in an article of MIT's Technology Review, the haptic interface will become "an expected part of interfaces of all kinds of computing devices." Especially in the area of telepresence and virtual presence, the demand for communication with haptic information is ever growing and the forthcoming of haptic interface as the third interface is self-evident beyond the visual and audio interfaces [19].

So far, many types of haptic interfaces with the computer have been developed. PHANToM™ of SensAble Technologies [17], and CyberForce™ of Immersion Corporation [11] are typical examples of commercial haptic devices. However, these haptic devices are inadequate as a computer interfaces since it gives fatigue when people use them for a long time. Among the possible types of interfaces, mouse-type interfaces have received much attention. Since people have been used the mouse as a main computer interface for a long time, adding haptic functionality to the mouse will be the natural extension of an existing computer interface. A number of research works have proposed several mouse-type haptic interfaces with the computer. Since the operating system of a computer has changed to Windows-based environment, research on mouse-type haptic interface, here we define it as haptic mouse, have been focused on delivering interactions with the GUI to human in the form of haptic sense. Akamatsu developed multi-modal mouse that presents tactile sense via a small pin driven by solenoid on the index finger and the kinesthetic sense via an electromagnet on the bottom of the mouse [1,2]. Through the button clicking experiments with the help of haptic cue, he demonstrated the usefulness of haptic information in computer interfaces. Kelly and Salcudean developed MagicMouse system, which receives position input through the PSD sensor and feedback 2 dof forces through the electromagnetic voice coil actuator in the X Windows environment. With the MagicMouse they made a haptic modeling of elements such as button, menu bar, and icons in Windows and asserted that inclusion of force feedback increases the efficiency of work with the computer [12]. In addition to mentioned devices, many other types of interfaces to implement the grabbing force feedback exist [4,5].

The objective of this paper is to present two kinds of new haptic mouse systems which are able to convey the virtual environment to human more realistically with the grabbing force feedback and tactile feedback respectively. In Section 2, we explain a haptic mouse which provides 2dof translational forces and grabbing force feedback. Overall structure, design specification and evaluation of the system are described in this section. In Section 3, we suggest an integrated tactile display mouse that provides kinesthetic force, pressure distribution, vibration and skin stretch. It helps user to feel the shape of virtual object and the roughness of contact surface simultaneously. In Section 4, we will briefly mention the proposed haptic mouse's application to the e-commerce and 3d CAD (Computer Aided Design) system.

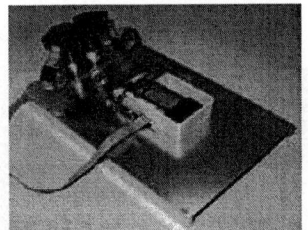

Fig. 1. A motor is embedded into mouse body which is laid on the holed plate. A special mechanism is controlled by other two motors and mouse body is connected to the mechanism under the plate

2 Grabbing Force Feedback Mouse System

A new haptic mouse system is designed by adding force feedback to the conventional mouse. Virtual environment, for example, icons and menu bar of the Windows system as well as graphically rendered object can be felt through the touch senses. Figure 1 shows the overall configuration of the haptic mouse system.

2.1 Overall Structure

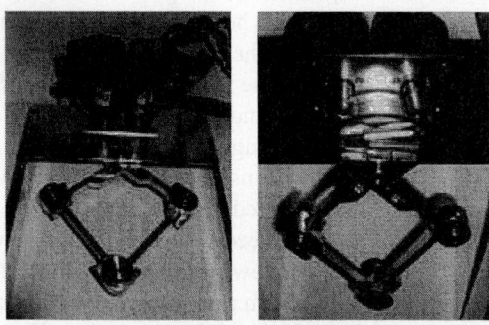

Fig. 2. Two motors and five bar mechanism provide 2 dof translational forces

Hardware of the proposed haptic mouse system can be divided into two parts. The first part is to provide 2 dof translation force feedback. Five bar mechanism is adapted for this purpose with the ground link length to be zero, as shown in Fig. 2. The workspace of the five bar linkage is mapped one-to-one to each pixel of the computer screen. Wire-driven mechanism is used to provide back-drivability as well as to eradicate problems aroused from backlash.

The second part is to provide grabbing force feedback, as shown in Fig. 3. Pulley is attached to the axis of the DC motor, which provides actuating force to the bar tangent on the pulley. Users feel the grabbing force by pressing the finger pad on each sides of the mouse. Wire-driven mechanism is also used and linear motion of the finger pads are guided by the ball bush bearings.

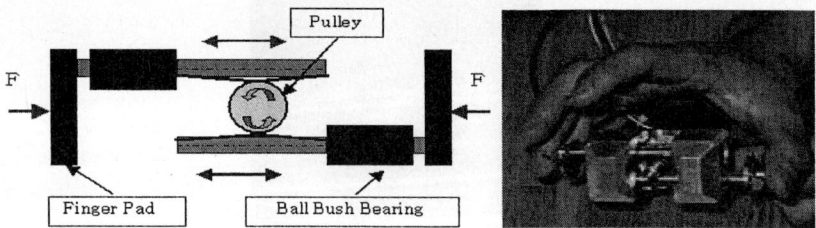

Fig. 3. This device adapts wire-driven mechanism for the actuation. Two prismatic joint are tangentially attached to the pulley with wire. Two prismatic joint moves inward and outward together, so that it transmits one dof grabbing force generated from the motor

2.2 Design Specifications

To find out the design specification for the new haptic mouse, we performed three experiments. In the first experiment, we measured the force and stiffness combination to give a hard wall feeling to the user's wrist that holds the haptic mouse with precision grasping. To provide a similar environment as the haptic mouse, mouse is attached to the stylus of PHANToM^{TM}. Precision grasping is assumed for mouse manipulation. 8 subjects participated in the experiments. Each subject felt the virtual wall with a mouse attached to PHANToM^{TM} by tapping the virtual wall. Virtual wall is modeled with spring where its stiffness varies from 1.0N/mm to 2.4N/mm at 0.2 N/mm intervals. Maximum force output of PHANToM^{TM} varies from 1N to 5N at 1N intervals. Each subject felt the 40 combinations of the virtual wall, and the subjects were required to answer whether they felt the hard wall or not. This test was repeated two times, and only subject's answers that showed consistency in both times were recorded. From this experiment, we concluded that five bar mechanism should be able to present at least 4N in all direction and the stiffness of a virtual wall should be at least 2.4N/mm to be perceived as a hard wall by the user's wrist.

In the second experiment, we measured the force and stiffness combination to give a hard object feeling to the thumb and ring finger that are used to grab the virtual object. Likewise, we concluded that grabbing force feedback mechanism should be able to present at least 3.5N at each finger and the stiffness of a virtual object should be a least 2.2N/mm to be perceived as a hard object by the fingers.

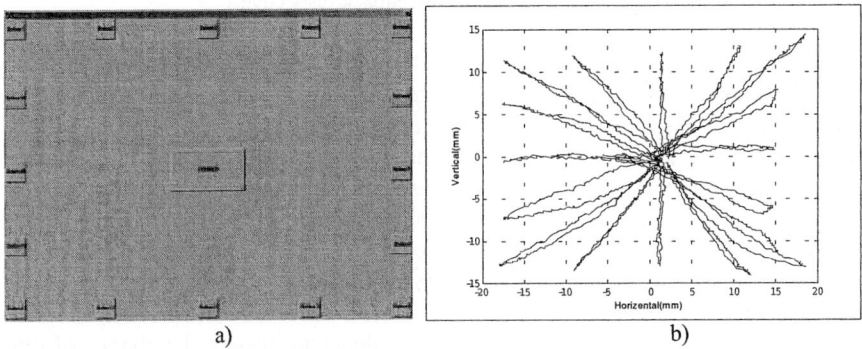

Fig. 4. a) Subjects are required to click buttons on the edge and button on the center by turns until they click all the buttons on the edge. b) The figure shows the measurement result of a subject

In the third experiment, we measured the average mouse workspace required to manipulate it under the condition that subject uses mouse the most comfortably. The workspace needed to complete a given task was measured with magnetic position tracker (Flock of Bird-FOB). The task to be completed is designed to measure the motion range of the point in the mouse, to which the end-effector of the five-bar will be attached. As shown in Fig. 4(a), buttons are placed along the edge of the monitor to obtain the maximum range of motion of the mouse manipulation. Subjects are required to click buttons on the edge and button on the center by turns until they click all the buttons on the edge. Before performing the task, subjects were allowed to adjust the resolution of the mouse until they feel the mouse is comfortable to use. 10 subjects are participated in the experiment and Fig. 4(b) shows the measurement result of a subject. Except the two extreme cases, the results of the 8 subjects are averaged. As a result, 32mm by 22mm rectangular area is obtained, which is used as the workspace of the mouse bounded by the hole of the plate under the mouse.

2.3 Comparison of Point Force with Grabbing Force

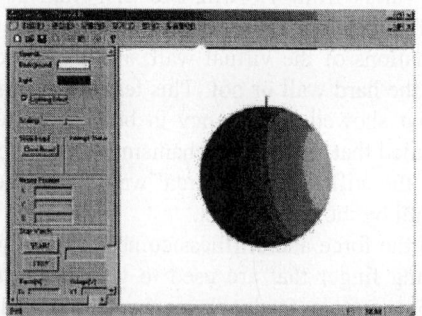 

Fig. 5. One of the five different shapes of objects which are triangle, square, diamond, circle and ellipse is randomly presented and the subjects are expected to tell the shape of an object by point force feedback and grabbing force added feedback respectively

We performed an experiment to evaluate the usefulness of the grabbing force feedback. As shown in Fig.5, a circular area indicated by an arrow is located in the computer screen. In this area, one of the five different shapes of objects which are triangle, square, diamond, circle and ellipse is randomly presented and the subjects are expected to tell the shape of an object. The visual information is shut off and only haptic information is provided. The subjects performed the experiment in two modes, one with point force interaction with only five bar force feedback mechanism to mouse body and the other with grabbing force interaction with both of grabbing force feedback mechanism and five bar mechanism. With the stated experimental condition above we measured the time taken for the subject to answer the shapes of objects correctly.

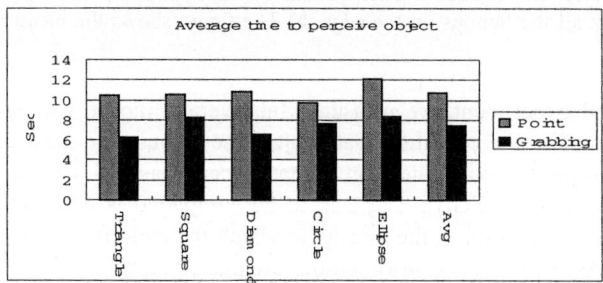

Fig. 6. Grabbing force feedback helps user to recognize the shape more intuitively

Figure 6 shows the experimental result of 8 subjects. As we have expected, answering correctly the shape of an object with grabbing force interaction takes less time than that with point force interaction. From this result, we can say that the concurrent feedback of grabbing force and translational force can produce more intuitive and effective haptic interaction than the ordinary point force feedback by only translational force.

3 Integrated Tactile Display Mouse System

Tactile sensation is essential for many manipulation and exploration tasks not only in a real environment but also in a virtual environment. While touching or feeling the surface of an object with their fingers, human can perceive complex shapes and textures through physical quantities such as pressure distribution, vibrations from slipping and stretching of the finger and temperature on the finger. Based on these tactile information, human can understand the features of an object and can precisely manipulate it

In this section, we introduce a mouse type tactile display that provides physical quantities related to tactile sense, for example contact force, small-scale shape, vibration, skin stretch. Contact force is related to the recognition of shape and stiffness of an object and small-scale shape on the surface is represented by distributed pressure. Vibration is related to surface roughness and skin stretch is caused by active touch (rubbing) [6,13,16]. Since tactile sensation is related to several kinds of sensing elements stated above, several preliminary studies on the tactile display have been conducted.

There have been many researches on the tactile display. Ikei et al. designed a vibrotactile device [8]. Hayward and Cruz-Hernandez focused on the tactile sensation of lateral skin stretch [7] and suggested a tactile display device for stimulating a small displacement of distributed lateral skin stretching up to several kilohertz. Asamura et al. studied a tactile display that stimulates the skin receptors selectively [3]. However previous tactile display devices sometimes involve user discomfort and are too big to be embedded into mouse system.

In this section, we propose a new type of tactile display and an integrated tactile display system that can simultaneously provide kinesthetic and tactile feedback. The tactile display unit that can display contact force, small-scale shape on the surface, normal vibration and lateral skin stretch is small enough to be embedded into the mouse.

3.1 Overall Structure and Design Specifications

Previous physiological and psychophysical studies on the human sense of touch show the change of sensitivity by frequency variation [11,12,17] and rubbing method [16]. We determined the principal requirements of a tactile display device for simulating a realistic sense of touch based on the literature survey. The requirements are as follows:

o Normal stimulus to skin in the frequency range of 0Hz to 500Hz
o 10 times displacement of threshold value of nerve system [13]
  - 60dB μm (about 1 mm) in low frequency band
  - At least 35dB μm (about 56.2 μm) in high frequency band
o Distributed pressure for displaying the static small-scale shape
o Sufficient ability to deform the skin's normal direction up to 1mm
o Small size to be embedded into PC mouse
o Mechanical structure to provide force and tactile feedback simultaneously
o Selectively providing an active touch mode and a passive touch mode

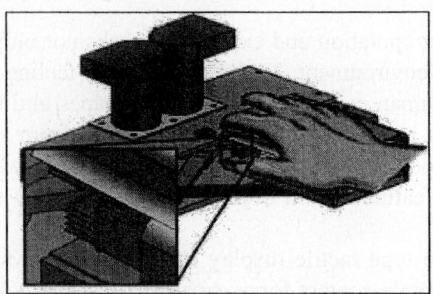

Fig. 7. We use the 2 DOF translation force feedback mechanism mentioned in section 2.1 for an integrated tactile display system. In addition, the tactile display unit substitutes for the grabbing force feedback part

Figure 7 shows the design drawing and an implemented assembly of an integrated tactile display mouse that simultaneously presents the shape and the texture. The proposed tactile display unit is attached to the joint of two link manipulators. The translational forces from the five-bar mechanism describe the shape and stiffness, and the tactile information from the tactile display unit describes the texture. The tactile display unit is designed to meet the requirement stated above. More details on design parameters are described in [14].

Tactile display unit is designed to simulate the small static shape by distributed pressure, vibration and lateral movement across the contact region. Although the finger pad on the tactile display surface is immobile, it can be passively moved across the contact area of the skin. As a result, the hardware of the tactile display unit consists of two parts: one for normal vibrotactile stimulation and the other for lateral movement of the display region that triggers the skin stretch. The size of mouse body is approximately 80x35x60 mm and that of the tactile display unit is 50x14x18 mm. While user is grabbing the mouse, 2dof translational force is transmitted to mouse body and tactile display unit stimulates the finger pad of thumb.

The tactile display unit is composed of two main parts. The first part is comprised of a pin array and eight piezoelectric bimorphs for normal vibrotactile stimulation (see Fig.8). Each piezoelectric bimorph has a displacement larger than 1 mm and a low operating input voltage (60V). In addition, its response time is on the order of millisecond and it can provide force up to 0.5N. Srinivasan has studied these skin mechanics and found the perceivable condition of stimulus [18]. The specifications of the tactile stimulator with piezoelectric bimorphs were verified to meet those requirements.

Hence, the tactile stimulator is adequate for normal vibrotaction satisfying required frequency range and stimulation intensity. We also confirmed that the actuator does not deflect by the normal rubbing on the surface to sense the texture.

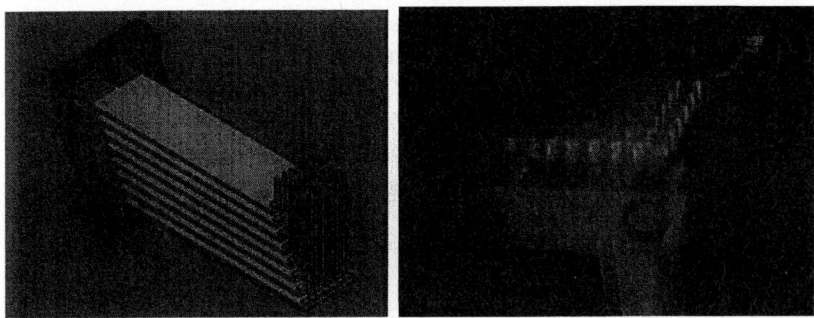

Fig. 8. Piezoelectric bimorphs are clamped with 1 mm spacing and the 6 x 1 pin array is attached to the tip of each bimorph. The pin spacing is 1 ~ 1.5 mm and the diameter of each pin is 0.5 or 0.7 mm enabling the display of a texture of 8 mm wide

The second part is a 1 DOF translation mechanism with a small rotary motor with a ball screw for the lateral movement of the tactile display unit, which triggers the lateral skin stretch. The tactile display unit is fixed on this mechanism for linear motion. The range of linear motion and maximum velocity is 50mm and 150mm/sec respectively.

3.2 Concurrent Stimulation of Kinesthetic Force Feedback and Tactile Feedback

In this section, the concurrent feedback of the kinesthetic force and the tactile display are investigated to verify the effectiveness of tactile feedback in transmitting the surface properties. For the objective and absolute comparison of touch feeling, we designed four specimen prototypes with different degrees of surface roughness. Figure 9 shows the design specification of the specimens used in the experiment.

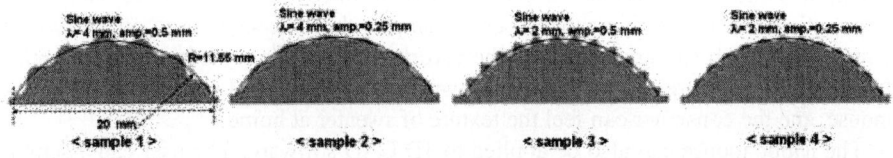

Fig. 9. The specimens have an identical rounded shape, however each one has different surface properties represented by changes in the height and the wavelength. The material used in each of the specimens was identical to the material used in the pins of each tactile display

Real specimen prototypes were given to participants and a simulated stimulus among them was presented through the integrated tactile display mouse. The stimulus was randomly presented twice and each participant was instructed to check the closest stimulus without any given chance of changing his or her answer. As shown in Fig. 10, the concurrent feedback of force and a tactile stimulus can more effectively simulate virtual objects than force feedback only. Although, participants matched the same surface texture relying solely on tactile feelings from the beginning, the ratio of correct answer is higher than 80 percent for sample 2 and 3. Kinesthetic feedback produced a high ratio of correct answer for sample 4; this result, however, could be unreliable because the participants were closer to the judgment that sample 4 was being suggested whenever they feel relatively smooth.

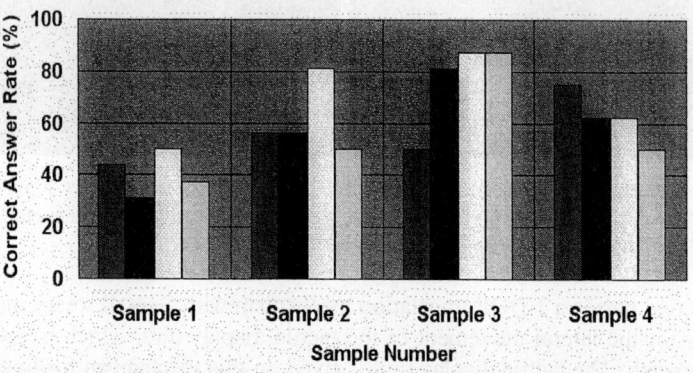

Fig. 10. ■ Force feedback only ■ Force feedback + static small-scale shape display ☐ Force feedback + static small-scale shape with rubbing ☐ Force feedback + normal vibration. Four kinds of stimulating methods are applied. Force feedback which is generated by 2dof link mechanism helps user to recognize the shape and the stiffness of virtual object and tactile feedback which stimulates the finger pad of thumb helps user feel the roughness on the surface by static small-scale shape, vibration and lateral movement

4 Application Areas

Major drawback of current Internet shopping mall is that we cannot actually touch goods. If haptic information such as surface texture and weight is additionally provided, the consumers can make a better judgment. In reality, e-commerce with haptic information can be partly realized. For example, the consumer logs on the virtual sweater shop web site and clicks on the favorite fabric. Then, the haptic information file containing textures of the fabric is downloaded on the local computer with haptic mouse, and the consumer can feel the texture of sweater at home.

The haptic mouse can also be applied to 3D CAD software. The user can assemble the parts while feeling the contact force. Haptic mouse helps the user to determine whether the parts can be assembled or not. In addition, the touch sense can contribute the user to determine suitable clearance of assembled parts.

5 Conclusion

In this paper, we introduced two kinds of haptic mouse systems. They are optimally designed based on the psychophysical and physiological studies. Grabbing force feedback mouse can provide grabbing force as well as translational force, which help users to feel the shape intuitively. The integrated tactile display system can simulate the shape and roughness simultaneously by several stimulating methods. We verified the effectiveness of the proposed systems compared to previous methods. Haptic mouse introduced in this paper potentially can overcome the limitations of the existing haptic interfaces by adding kinesthetic and tactile feedback to the mouse. As a future work, the combination of two kinds of mouse will be carried out.

Acknowledgements

This research has been supported by 'Smart Haptic Interface Project (2004-S-030, KMIC)' and 'Tangible Space Interface Project (NN44710, KIST)'.

References

1. Akamatsu, M.: Movement Characteristics Using a Mouse with Tactile and Force Feedback. International Journal of Human-Computer Studies **45** (1996) 483–493
2. Akamatsu, M., Sato, S.: A Multi-modal Mouse with Tactile and Force Feedback. International Journal of Human-Computer Studies **40** (1994) 443–453
3. Asamura, N., Yokomu, N., Shinoda, H.: Selectively Stimulating Skin Receptors for Tactile Display. IEEE Computer Graphics and Applications (1998) 32–37
4. Budea, G.C.: Force and Touch Feedback for Virtual Reality. John Wiley & Sons, New York (1996)
5. Burdea, G.C.: Haptic Issues in Virtual Environment. In: IEEE Proceeding of Computer Graphics International. (2000) 295–302
6. Essick, G.K.: Factors Affecting Direction Discrimination of Moving Tactile Stimuli. Morley, J.W. (ed.): Neural Aspect of Tactile Sensation. Elsevier Science, B.V. (1998) 1–54
7. Hayward, V., Cruz-Hernandez, M.: Tactile Display Device Using Distributed Lateral Skin Stretch. In: Proc. ASME, Vol.DSC-69-2. (2000) 1309–1314
8. Ikei, Y., Yamada, M., Fukuda, S.: A New Design of Haptic Texture Display-Texture Display-and Its Preliminary Evaluation. In: Proc. IEEE Virtual Reality Conf. (2001) 21–22
9. Immersion Corporation. http://www.immersion.com
10. Johansson, R.S., Vallbo, A.B.: Tactile Sensibility in the Human Hand: Relative and Absolute Densities of Four Types of Mechanoreceptive Units in Glabrous Skin. Journal of Physiology **286** (1979) 283–300
11. Johnson, K.O.: The Roles and Functions of Cutaneous Mechanoreceptors. Current Opinion in Neurobiology **11** (2001) 455–461
12. Kelley, A.J., Salcudean, S.: On the Development of a Force-feedback Mouse and its Integration into a Graphical User Interface. ASME Dynamic Systems and Control, Vol. 1, DSC-vol.55-1 (1994) 287–294

13. Kruger, L.: Pain and Touch. Academic Press, San Diego (1996)
14. Kyung, K.U., Son, S.W., Kwon, D.S., Kim, M.: Design of an Integrated Tactile Display System. In: IEEE International Conference on Robotics and Automation. (2004) 776–781
15. Lederman, S.J.: The Perception of Surface Roughness by Active and Passive Touch, Bulletin of the Psychonomic Society **18** (1981) 253–255
16. Morley, J.W.(ed.): Neural Aspects in Tactile Sensation. Elsevier Science B.V. (1998)
17. SensAble Technologies, Inc. http://www.sensable.com
18. Srinivasan, M.A.: Surface Deflection of Primate Fingertip under Line Load. Journal of Biomechanics **22**(4) (1989) 343–349
19. Technology Review. MIT's Magazine of Innovation. March (2002)

Developing Finite State NLP Systems with a Graphical Environment

Kemal Oflazer and Yasin Yılmaz

Faculty of Engineering and Natural Sciences
Sabancı University, Istanbul, 34956 Turkey
oflazer@sabanciuniv.edu, yyilmaz@su.sabanciuniv.edu

Abstract. Developing finite state natural language processing resources (such as morphological lexicons) and applications (such as light-parsers) is also a complex software engineering enterprise which can benefit from additional tools that enables to developers to manage the complexity of the development process. We describe visual interface and a development environment, for developing finite state language processing applications using the Xerox Finite State Tool, *xfst*, to address some of these engineering concerns. *Vi-xfst* lets a user construct complex regular expressions via a drag-and-drop visual interface, treating simpler regular expressions as "Lego Blocks." It also enables the visualization of the topology of the regular expression components at different levels of granularity, enabling a user to easily understand and track the structural and functional relationships among the components involved.

1 Introduction

Finite state machines are widely used in many natural language processing applications to implement components such as tokenizers, morphological analyzers/generators, shallow parsers, etc. Large scale finite state language processing systems built using tools such as the Xerox Finite State Tool [1–3], van Noord's Prolog-based tool [4] or the AT&T weighted finite state machine suite [5], involve tens or hundreds of regular expressions which are compiled into finite state transducers that are interpreted by the underlying run-time engines of the (respective) tools. Developing such large scale finite state systems are currently done without much of a support for the "software engineering" aspects. Regular expressions are constructed manually by the developer with a text-editor and then compiled, and the resulting transducers are tested. Any modifications have to be done afterwards on the same text file(s) and the whole project has to be recompiled many times in a development cycle. Visualization, an important aid in understanding and managing the complexity of any large scale system, is limited to displaying the finite state machine graph (e.g., Gansner and North [6]). However, such visualization (sort of akin to visualizing the machine code of a program written in a high-level language) is not very helpful, as developers rarely, and possibly never, think of such large systems in terms of states and transitions. The relationship between the regular expressions and the finite state machines they are compiled into are opaque except for the simplest of regular expressions. Further, the size of the resulting machines, in terms of states and transitions, is *very large*, usually in the thousands to hundreds of thousands states, if not more, making such visualization meaningless.

This paper describes the salient features and the use of a graphical environment for developing finite state natural language processing resources and applications. The paper is organized as follows: In the next section we provide an overview of the functionalities provided by the graphical environment *Vi-xfst* [7], demonstrating the functionality by running through a simple example. We then discuss selective compilation and finally end with some closing remarks.

2 Vi-xfst

Vi-xfst is developed as a visual front end to for the Xerox Finite State Tool, *xfst* [2], a sophisticated command-line-oriented interface developed by Xerox Research Centre Europe, for building large finite state transducers for language processing resources and applications. Users of *xfst* employ a high-level regular expression language which provides an extensive repertoire of high-level operators.[1] Such regular expressions are then compiled into finite state transducers and interpreted by a run time engine built into the tool. *xfst* also provides a further set of commands for combining, testing and inspecting the finite state transducers produced by the regular expression compiler.

To motivate the examples that will be coming later we provide here a very simple finite state description of a (synthetic) phonological phenomena that can be described by a sequence of two finite state transducers that implement the top-down contextual replace operations, which are then composed to give a single transducer.

In this example, an abstract lexical string *kaN* with an abstract (nasal) phoneme *N*, is concatenated to the suffix *pat*.[2] As it happens, when these morphemes are concatenated, phonemes at the morpheme boundaries undergo changes. The *N* changes to an *m* when it is followed by a *p* at a morpheme boundary. This is captured by a replace rule

```
define Rule1 [ N -> m || _ p ];
```

expressed in the *xfst* regular expression language. This rule describes finite state transducer which maps the symbol *N* in the upper string of the transducer to an *m* in the lower string, provided it is followed by a *p* in the upper string, that is *N* is obligatorily replaced by *m* when it appears in the context before *p*. Figure 1 shows the traditional representation of this transducer compiled from this rule.

For instance the lexical upper string *kaNpat* would be transformed into *kampat* as a lower string by this transducer.

---

[1] Details of the operators are available at http://www.xrce.xerox.com/competencies/content-analysis/fsCompiler/fssyntax.html and http://www.xrce.xerox.com/competencies/content-analysis/fsCompiler/fssyntax-explicit.html.
[2] This example is from Beesley and Karttunen [3].

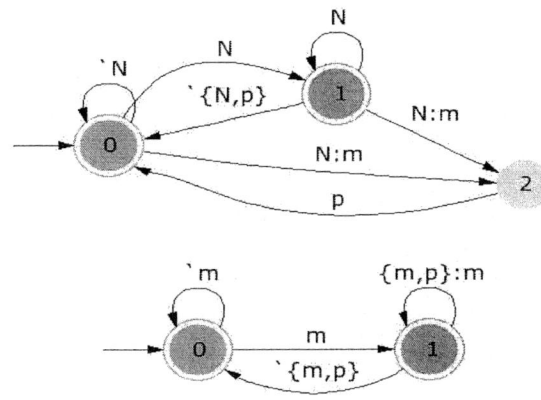

Fig. 1. The transducers for the replace rule Rule1 on the left and for the replace rule Rule2 on the right

A second rule in this language states that a *p* that occurs just after an *m* gets realized as *m*. This is formalized as a second replace rule

```
define Rule2 [ p -> m || m _ ];
```

Thus for example when the output string *kampat* is applied to this transducer as the upper string, it would produce *kammat*.

As usual with finite state transducers, the transducers for these rules can be composed at "compile" time to get a single transducer

```
define CombinedRules Rule1
                     .o.
                     Rule2;
```

We have intentionally written this combination so that Rule1 is the upper rule and Rule2 is the bottom rule and that the output of Rule1 feeds into Rule2. Thus when the string *kaNpat* is applied to the combined transducer, the output that is produced is *kammat*. Figure 2 shows the traditional representation of the composed transducer compiled from this combination of rules.

Obviously this is a very simple example transducer; real finite state systems usually get very complex with transducers combined in various ways to compile into a single very large transducer. For instance, a large scale finite state pronunciation lexicon developed for Turkish [8], uses about 700 regular expressions in addition to various lexicons, distributed to over 115 files. The resulting finite state transducer has over 6 million states and 9 million transitions.[3]

---

[3] A demo of this pronunciation lexicon is at http://www.hlst.sabanciuniv.edu.

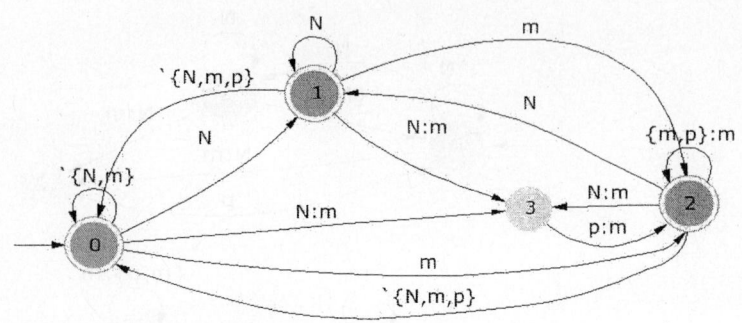

Fig. 2. The transducer for the composed sequence of rules

2.1 Using Vi-xfst

Vi-xfst enables incremental construction of complex regular expressions via a drag-and-drop interface, treating simpler regular expressions as "Lego Blocks". *Vi-xfst* also enables the visualization of the topology of the regular expression components, so that the developer can have a bird's eye view of the overall system, easily understanding and tracking the relationships among the components involved. Since the structure of a large regular expression (built in terms of other regular expressions) is now transparent, the developer can interact with regular expressions at any level of detail, easily navigating among them for testing and debugging.

When we start developing a new project with *xfst* the interface looks like as shown in Figure 3. The window on the left hand side displays the regular expressions already defined (none yet here since we have not defined any), the top right window is where a regular expression is visualized and the bottom right window is used for debugging and other operations.

To start, we select an operator template from the operator palette above (or from the *Insert* menu and extend it if necessary (with more operands, conditions, etc.) This brings up a visualization template to the screen. We then enter the operands by either selecting from the palette of already defined regular expressions on the left window or just directly enter a regular expression and save it by optionally giving it a name. For example, when `Rule1` above is entered, the top right window looks like as in Figure 4. The regular expression for `Rule2` can similarly be defined. Once these transducers are defined, we now bring in a template for the composition operator `.o.` where the layout for the operand transducers are positioned in vertical manner. We then select from the *Definitions* palette on the left, the two rules, and just drop them on their respective slots in the composition template. The result of this is depicted in Figure 5. At

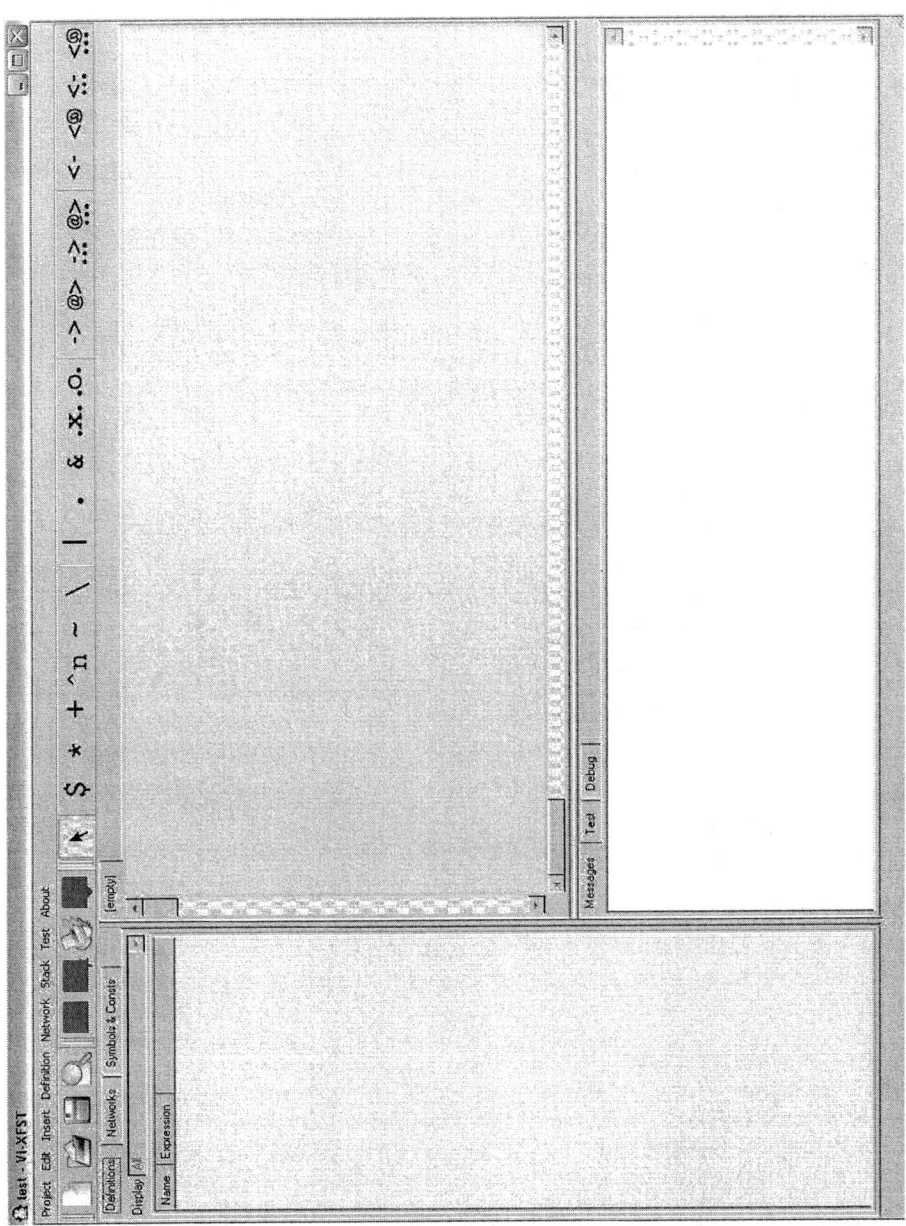

Fig. 3. The initial layout of the *Vi-xfst* screen

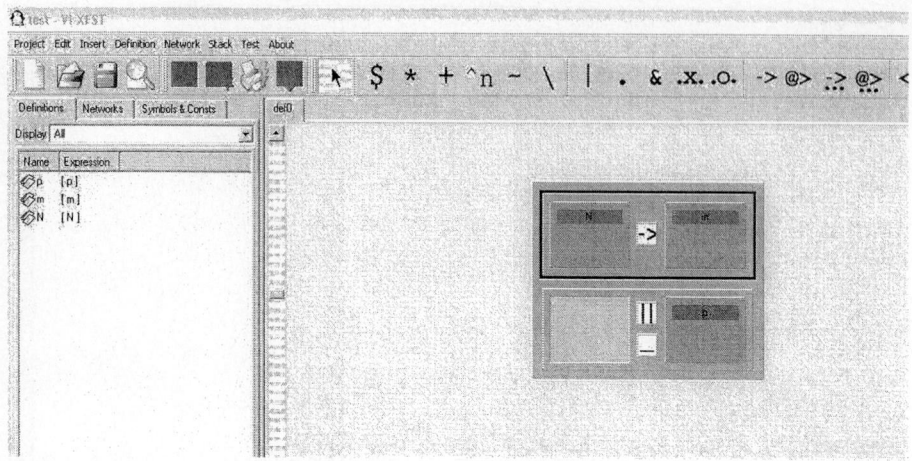

Fig. 4. Constructing the first rule

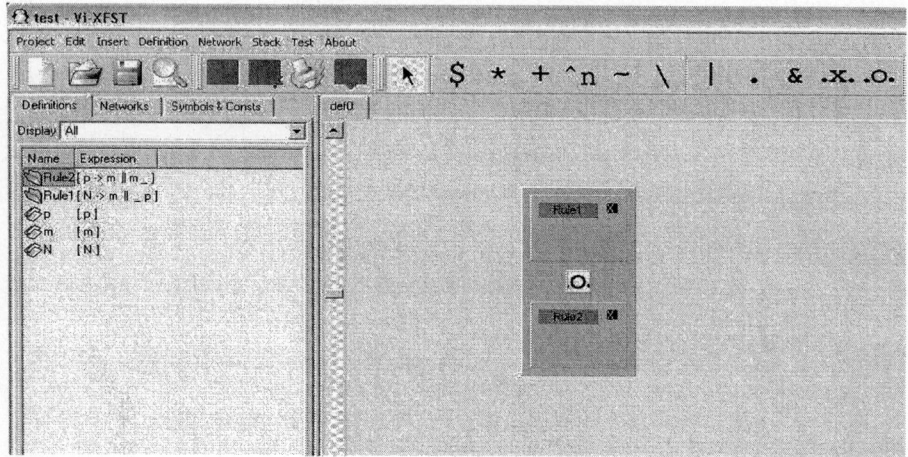

Fig. 5. Constructing the combined rule

this point one can visualize the combined rule also by fully expanding each of its components as shown in Figure 6.

Although this is a very simple example, we believe it shows important aspects of our functionality. A visualization of a complex network employing a different layout of the replace rules is shown in Figure 7. Here we see a portion of a Number-to-English mapping network[4] where different components are visualized at different structural resolutions.

---

[4] Due to Lauri Karttunen; see http://www.cis.upenn.edu/ cis639/assign/ assign8.html for the *xfst* script for this transducer. It maps numbers like 1234 into English strings like *One thousand two hundred and thirty four*.

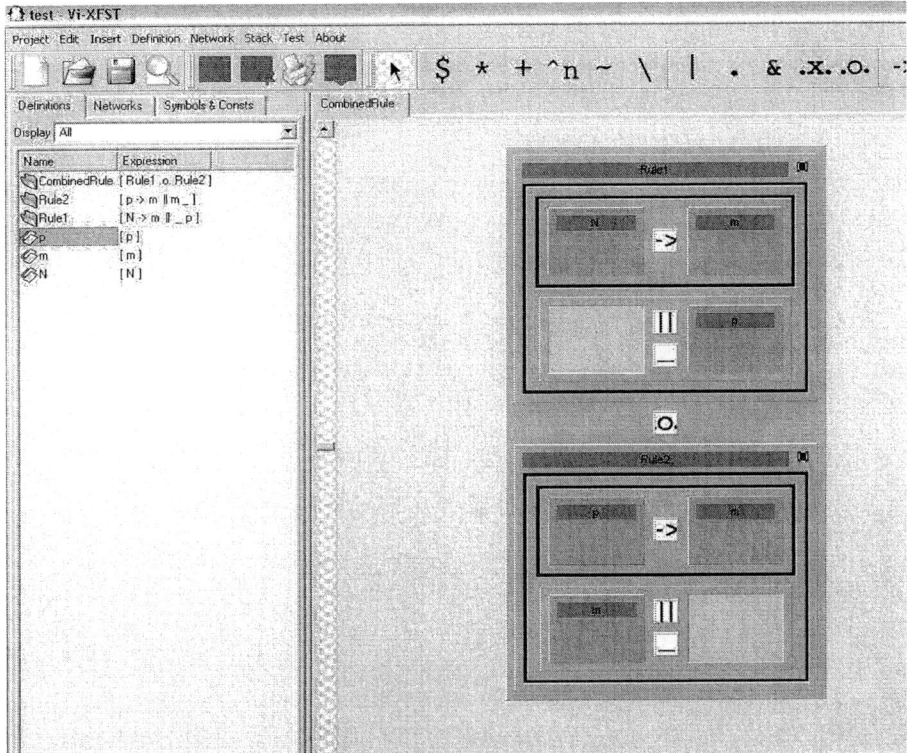

Fig. 6. Fully expanded visualization of the combined regular expression

3 Maintaining Regular Expression Dependency and Selective Compilation

Selective compilation is one of the simple facilities available in many software development environments. A software development project uses selective compilation to compile modules that have been modified and those that depend (transitively) in some way (via say header file inclusion) to the modified modules. This selective compilation scheme, typically known as the *make* operation, depends on a manually or automatically generated *makefile* capturing dependencies. It can save time during development as only the relevant files are recompiled after a set of modifications.

In the context of developing large scale finite state language processing application, we encounter the same issue. During testing, we recognize that a certain regular expression is buggy, fix it, and then have to recompile all others that use that regular expression as a component. *Vi-xfst* provides a selective compilation functionality to address this problem by automatically keeping track of the regular expression level dependencies as they are built via the drag-and-drop

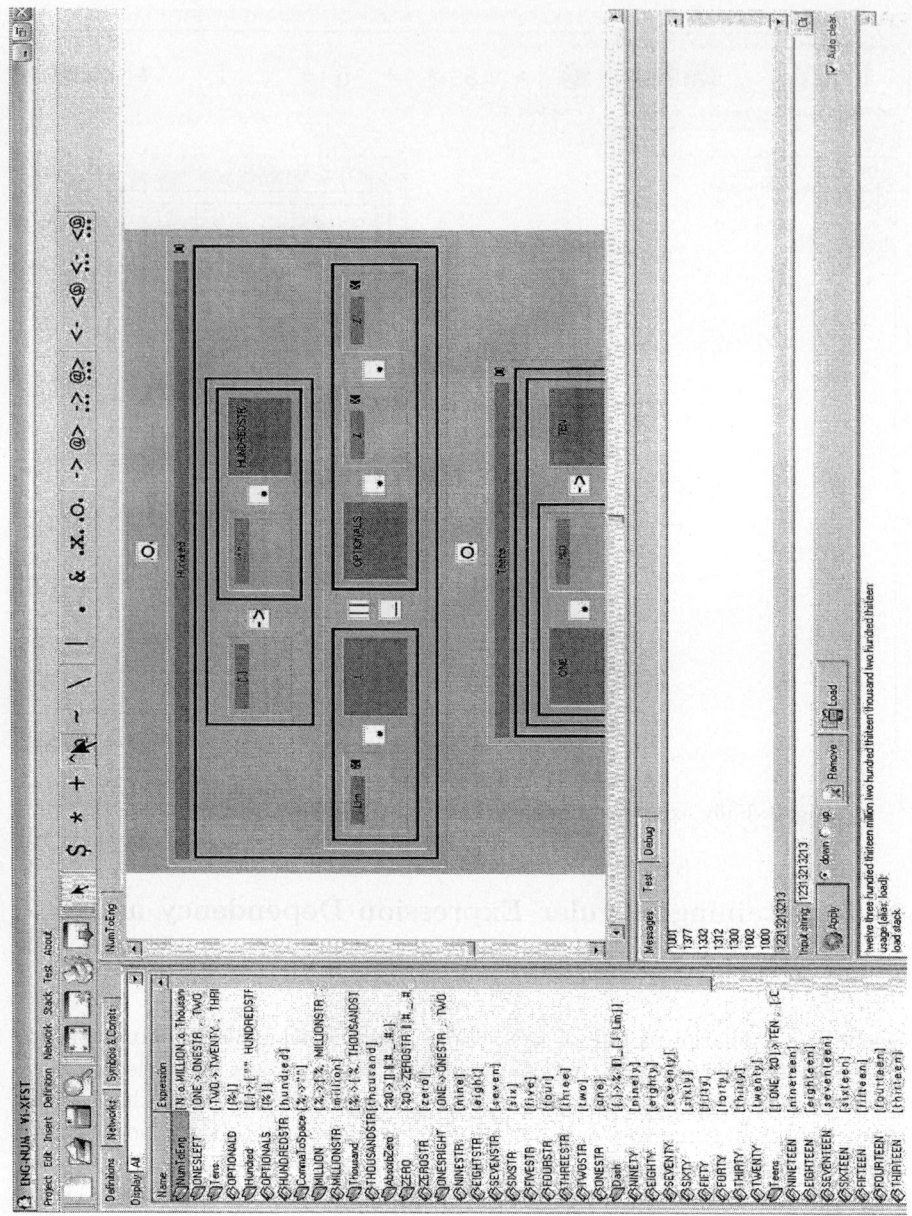

Fig. 7. Mixed visualization of a complex regular expression

interface. This dependency can then be exploited by *Vi-xfst* when a recompile needs to be done.

After one or more regular expressions are modified, we first recompile (by sending a *define* command to *xfst*) those regular expressions, and then recompile all regular expressions starting with immediate dependents and traversing systematically upwards to the regular expressions of all "top" nodes on which no other regular expressions depend, making sure:

- all regular expressions that a regular expression depends on and have to be recompiled, are recompiled before that regular expression is recompiled, *and*
- every regular expression that needs to be recompiled is recompiled only once.

To achieve these, we compute the subgraph of the dependency graph that has all the nodes corresponding to the modified regular expressions and any other regular expressions that transitively depends on these regular expressions. Then, a topological sort of the resulting subgraph gives a possible linear ordering of the regular expression compilations. For instance in the simple example, if we have to change the right context of `Rule1`, to say `p t`, then the transducer `Rule1` would have to be recompiled and then the `CombinedRule` need to be recompiled since it depends on `Rule1`.

4 Conclusions

We have described *Vi-xfst* a visual interface and a development environment for the development of finite state language processing resources and application components, using the Xerox Finite State Tool *xfst*. In addition to a drag-and-drop user interface for constructing regular expressions in a hierarchical manner, *Vi-xfst* can visualize the structure of a regular expression at different levels of detail. It also keeps track of how regular expressions depend on each other and uses this dependency information for selective compilation of regular expressions when one or more regular expressions are modified during development.

Acknowledgments

We thank XRCE for providing us with the *xfst* and other related programs in the finite state suite.

References

1. Karttunen, L., Chanod, J.P., Grefenstette, G., Schiller, A.: Regular expressions for language engineering. Natural Language Engineering **2** (1996) 305–328
2. Karttunen, L., Gaal, T., Kempe, A.: Xerox finite-state tool. Technical report, Xerox Research Centre Europe (1997)
3. Beesley, K.R., Karttunen, L.: Finite state morphology. CSLI Publications, Stanford University (2003)

4. van Noord, G.: FSA utilities: A toolbox to manipulate finite state automata. In: Raymond, D., Wood, D., Yu, S. (eds.): Automata Implementation. LNCS, Vol. 1260. Springer-Verlag (1997)
5. Mohri, M., Pereira, F., Riley, M.: A rational design for a weighted finite-state transducer library. LNCS, Vol. 1436. Springer-Verlag (1998)
6. Gansner, E.R., North, S.C.: An open graph visualization system and its applications to software engineering. Software–Practice and Experience (1999)
7. Yılmaz, Y.: Vi-XFST: A visual interface for Xerox finite state toolkit. M.Sc. Thesis, Sabancı University (2003)
8. Oflazer, K., Inkelas, S.: A finite state pronunciation lexicon for Turkish. In: Proceedings of the EACL Workshop on Finite State Methods in NLP. (2003)

Bandwidth-Aware Scaling for Internet Video Streaming

Turhan Tunalı[1], Nükhet Özbek[1], Koray Anar[1], and Aylin Kantarcı[2]

[1] International Computer Institute, Ege University
35100, Bornova, İzmir, Turkey
{tunali,ozbek,kanar}@ube.ege.edu.tr
[2] Department of Computer Engineering, Ege University
35100, Bornova, İzmir, Turkey
kantarci@bornova.ege.edu.tr

Abstract. In this study, we propose a bandwidth-aware scaling mechanism for rate adaptive video streaming. This mechanism involves estimation of the capacity of the network dynamically by measuring *bottleneck bandwidth* and *available bandwidth* values. By taking the available bandwidth as an upper limit, the sender adjusts its output rate accordingly. While increasing the quality of the video, using a bandwidth estimator instead of probing prevents the congestion generated by the streaming application itself. The results of the bandwidth-aware algorithm are compared with that of a similar algorithm with no bandwidth-aware scaling and the improvement is demonstrated with measurements taken over WAN.

1 Introduction

In Internet video streaming applications, compressed video streams need to be transmitted over networks that have varying bandwidth conditions. At any time, making best use of available network resources and guaranteeing maximum level of perceptual video quality from the end-user's perspective require utilization of rate control mechanisms in video streaming systems [1]. Over-rating the output of a video streamer can cause an undesirable traffic explosion and can lead to congestion in the network. On the other hand, uncontrolled reduction of the output bit rate of a video streamer leads to unnecessary quality degradation and inefficient use of available bandwidth resources. Therefore, to achieve the best trade-off between quality and congestion, adaptive strategies have to be developed [2, 3].

In many of the studies, rate adaptation algorithms are based on observed variables such as packet loss rate and delay. These variables provide some information about congestion in classical wired networks. However, particularly loss rate can not be a good indicator of congestion in wireless networks. On the other hand, to eliminate jitter, efficient receiver buffer management policies should be developed [4]. Another important parameter that can efficiently be used is available bandwidth. A good estimate of available bandwidth can provide preventive congestion control. However, integration of a bandwidth estimation algorithm into an adaptive video streamer is not an easy task. Firstly, bandwidth estimation requires sending extra burst packets that brings a considerable overhead into the system. Secondly, these burst packets have to be transmitted over the path of the streamer. Finally, to meet real-time limitations of the streaming system, as opposed to the proposed methods in the literature, the bandwidth estimator should be very fast.

In this paper, we propose a bandwidth-aware rate control algorithm which is modified from our previously developed adaptive rate control algorithm that did not contain any bandwidth estimator [5]. In [5], quality increases until loss occurs which means that congestion must have already started. Embedding a bandwidth estimator into our rate control algorithm avoids this congestion that is merely caused by our streamer. Another improvement is optimal selection of video quality during initial buffer filling period. This minimizes number of changes of video parameters which, in turn, improves perceived video quality.

The paper is organized as follows: In Section 2, a brief review of our adaptation algorithm is given. In Section 3, the bandwidth estimator module developed for our algorithm is introduced. In Section 4, our bandwidth-aware scaling algorithm and initial quality detection method are examined in detail. In Section 5, performance results on WAN environment are given. Finally, in Section 6, concluding remarks are made.

2 Rate Adaptive Streaming Algorithm

In this section, we briefly review our previously developed streaming algorithm [5]. Rate adaptation is achieved by video scaling in a seamless manner via frame dropping or switching to another encoding rate or changing the packet interval. The video is encoded in multiple encoding rates and stored in the database. A metadata file is prepared by packetization module for every encoding rate of the video. Packetization module determines the number of packets to be sent per video file for each encoding rate and frame discard level pair. The transmission interval between consecutive packets is calculated as video duration divided by the number of packets for each pair. Packet interval values are also stored in the metafile.

Frame dropping is performed in levels. Considering the dependency among frame types, the adaptation module drops first B frames then P frames if necessary from the current GOP pattern. Each encoding rate (ER) and frame discard level (FDL) pair corresponds to a different transmission rate in the network. Encoding rates have values as 1000, 500, 200, 100 kbps. Frame rates have values as 30, 20, 10, 5, 1 fps. A grid is formed by using ER and FDL combinations. On this grid, depending on the receiver buffer and the network congestion status, the appropriate ER-FDL pair is chosen for adaptation that follows an AIMD (Additive Increase Multiplicative Decrease) strategy to preserve TCP-friendliness.

Table 1. Observed and controlled variables of the algorithm

Observed variables	Source	Controlled variables	Source
Loss rate	RTCP RR feedback	Encoding rate (ER)	Sender
ttp	UDP receiver feedback	GOP pattern (FDL)	Sender
dttp	UDP receiver feedback	Packet interval (PI)	Sender

Table 1 shows the observed and controlled variables of the rate control algorithm. The receiver periodically sends loss rate, current stored video duration, denoted *ttp*, and rate of change of *ttp*, denoted dttp, to the sender. Examining these data and current values of the controlled variables ER, FDL and PI, the algorithm running at the sender decides on the trade off between the video quality and congestion. Further details can be found in [4, 5].

Our algorithm follows a conservative approach by allowing quality degradations after two adaptation requests and quality increases after 5 adaptation requests. We observed that a non-conservative approach that reacts to adaptation requests immediately resulted in frequent rate oscillations, displeasing the viewer. The conservative approach based on a hysteresis model preserved the prevailing quality until an indicator of persistent behaviour in congestion and buffer status is available, thereby eliminating the disturbance of the viewer.

Another property of our algorithm is that it has a content-aware media scaling system. When adaptation is required, quality scaling is used by switching to a version at a lower encoding rate during the transmission of the video segments which contain high motion whereas temporal scaling (i.e. frame dropping) takes precedence over quality scaling during the transmission of the video portions with low motion content.

Since there is no bandwidth estimator in [5], when all goes fine, i.e. the receiver buffer level is within the desired interval and there is no packet loss in the network, the algorithm probes for bandwidth by increasing video quality until it experiences packet loss. Then, it decreases quality but some packets have already been lost in the network. To prevent this negative effect of probing particularly at the initial buffer filling phase, a good estimation of the available bandwidth could be of great help. However, such an estimator may bring in considerable overhead to the streaming algorithm and it may degrade overall performance. In the next section, we will introduce a bandwidth estimator that is suitable for embedding into our algorithm.

3 Estimation of Available Bandwidth

In recent years, there has been significant progress in the area of bandwidth estimation. Several papers related to this area discuss capacity (i.e. bottleneck bandwidth) and available bandwidth estimation methodologies. Among them, Van Jacobson's Pathchar [6], determines per hop based capacity by using variable packet sizes. Another study by Lai and Baker's Nettimer [7], determines end-to-end path capacity via Packet Pairs. These two measure only bottleneck bandwidth. For our purposes, there is another measure called *available bandwidth* which provides better feedback for our streamer. Cprobe [8], Pathload [9], IGI [10] and Pathchirp [11] develop available bandwidth measurement methods.

Cprobe is the first tool to attempt to measure available bandwidth. However, it ignores the fact that bottleneck bandwidth is not same as the available bandwidth. It also requires some privileges on routers such as ICMP messaging. Cprobe is not useful especially nowadays because network administrators are very concerned about attacks based on ICMP messages. For wide area network measurement, it is useful to work with other packet types.

Pathload is based on Self Loading Periodic Streams (SLoPS) methodology. SLoPS consists of K packets of size L, sent to destination at constant rate R. If the stream rate R is higher than the available bandwidth, one way delay of successive packets at receiver shows an increasing trend. By trying different probing speeds, estimation for the available bandwidth can be found. Pathload implementation uses UDP packets that require no privileges on router. Main disadvantage is reported to be low estimation speed [10].

IGI and Patchirp are the new tools that use modified Train of Packet Pairs (TOPP) [11] and SLoPS. They use different packet pair streams and they can achieve similar accuracy in small measurement times [9]. Packet Pair Technique (PPT) is a common approach for bandwidth estimation [12]. Since the approach basically depends on observation of active probing packets' dispersion at receiver, it is also referred to as Packet Pair Dispersion. The active measurement probes are injected to the network by sender for the attention of receiver. By measuring the space changing between consecutive packets at destination, the network path properties can be estimated. The model used in PPT is given in Fig. 1 [13].

Our Packet Pair Model is similar to IGI/TOPP model except that we send single train of packet pairs in each experiment and use small constant initial gaps rather than increasing amount of initial gaps. This is due to the fact that determining a good value for the initial probing gap is much more difficult. It is possible to determine a better gap value by making several experiments in which a sequence of packet trains with increasing initial probing gaps is sent. However, these experiments take some time, and it may be possible to miss instant available bandwidth. Another important property in our algorithm is that it is 2-5 times faster than IGI method in estimating bandwidth.

In each experiment, the sender injects probe packets into network at regular intervals denoted by ΔTs_n and the destination receives them in intervals denoted by ΔTr_n. To get more accurate results, packet pair train is formed from fixed-size packets represented as P.

If there is no additional traffic on the path, bottleneck bandwidth is also called "path capacity" that is the maximum throughput that the path can provide. We denote it as B_BW. Bottleneck bandwidth should not be confused with the available bandwidth of a path. Available bandwidth is the redundant capacity that is not used by the existing traffic.

We assume that there is no cross traffic in the path and the complete path is formed of K links. We measure the smallest bottleneck bandwidth of the present links [12]:

$$B\_BW = \min_{i=0\ldots K-1} \{B\_BW_i\}. \tag{1}$$

Amount of competing traffic ratio represented by α is the ratio of increased gaps to received gaps. Motivated by [10], the competing traffic represented by C_BW is given as

$$C\_BW = B\_BW * \alpha. \tag{2}$$

Finally, we estimate the available bandwidth by subtracting competing traffic throughput from bottleneck bandwidth,

$$A\_BW = B\_BW - C\_BW. \tag{3}$$

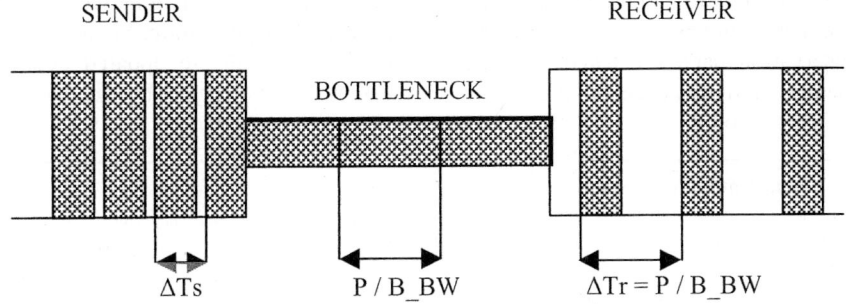

Fig. 1. Packet Pair Model without any competing traffic

4 A Bandwidth-Aware Streaming Algorithm

We developed and implemented a bandwidth-aware streaming algorithm that can efficiently operate on both local and wide area networks. This algorithm is integrated to our previously developed rate adaptive algorithm that utilizes the loss statistics and receiver buffer status.

First, the channel bandwidth estimator module is implemented stand-alone and its performance is optimized to meet our streaming environment requirements. Then the module is embedded into the rate adaptive streaming algorithm. Combining available bandwidth estimation with rate adaptation has two important advantages. First, available bandwidth is used to decide on the initial video quality to be sent during pre-buffering period. The estimated bandwidth value lets the algorithm choose the most appropriate encoding rate to start streaming. Hence, heavy load during initial buffer filling period is avoided. Second, when the quality is to be increased, available bandwidth is very useful to understand whether the current channel capacity meets the new bandwidth requirement. By this way, the unnecessary quality increases in the adaptation algorithm, which may cause packet loss and congestion, are avoided.

Depending on the observed measures of loss rate, ttp, dttp, video dynamics and current values of ER-FDL-PI, the algorithm determines new values for ER-FDL-PI. If conditions impose a decrease in quality, than no further step is taken and new values of ER-FDL-PI are applied to streaming. Since RTCP reports are at least as fast as our bandwidth estimator in informing the congestion to the sender, the estimated bandwidth value is not used when the quality is to be decreased. Hence, no advance information is available in this particular case.

If new adaptation is not in the direction of decreasing data rate, than new proposed data rate (*put_bw*) is compared with estimated available data rate. If *put_bw* is less than the available bandwidth, then the chosen ER-FDL-PI is applied to streaming. If *put_bw* is more than available bandwidth, the current ER-FDL-PI values remain the same. This last case occurs when the streaming application is already using up a hefty bandwidth and there is no more bandwidth available for quality increase. A sketch of the algorithm is given in Fig. 2 where the procedures *down_scale_video* and *up_scale_video* correspond to the original adaptation algorithm [5] with rate decrease and increase respectively.

It is important to note that the bandwidth estimator module is run at the receiver and it operates in full synchronization with other modules of the algorithm. In particular, the observation parameters and estimated available bandwidth are updated every five seconds and the decision process at the sender is not delayed by the bandwidth estimator module.

```
bandwidth_aware_scale( )
{
     observe loss_rate, ttp, dttp, video_dynamics, available_bw;
     if (congestion)
          down_scale_video(loss_rate, ttp, dttp, video_dynamics);
     else
          compute put_bw;
          if (put_bw < available_bw)
               up_scale_video(ttp, dttp, video_dynamics);
          else
               no_scale;
}
```

Fig. 2. Bandwidth-aware video scaling algorithm

5   Experimental Results

The bandwidth-aware scaling algorithm introduced in the previous section has been tested with the video streaming system that we have implemented. In the system, RTP has been used for data transfer and RTCP has been used to collect network statistics. Control messages are exchanged over UDP. Our streaming system has client-server architecture. The clients request video from the server. Server streams video to the client in a unicast manner. Both the server and client software are multithreaded. Pipelined architecture of the client software further increases the performance of the whole system. Detailed explanation of our testbed can be found in [4, 5].

Experiments have been performed in the actual Internet environment between two Sun Ultra 5 workstations. The workstation which acts as the streaming server is located in Koc University Campus in Istanbul. The client workstation is located in Ege University Campus. *Traceroute* command shows that the number of hops between the two workstations is 9.

We carried out two sets of experiments to observe the performance of our bandwidth-aware scaling algorithm. The first set of experiments was carried out late at night when the amount of traffic on the network was low, while the second set of experiments was conducted during busy working hours when the load was higher. In both sets of experiments, to be able to evaluate the benefits of our bandwidth-aware scaling algorithm, we collected performance results under two configurations. In the first configuration, bandwidth-aware scaling is turned off, while in the other, it is turned on.

Results presented in Fig. 3 and Fig. 4 which belong to an example in the first set of experiments. Figure 3 shows system variables when adaptation is performed without bandwidth considerations. As seen in Fig. 3.b, during pre-buffering period, transmitted video quality can reach its highest level in which the encoding rate is 1000 kbps (ER = 0) and the frame rate is 30 fps (FDL = 0). However, the estimated available bandwidth is around 550 kbps. Therefore, our system overloads the network, available bandwidth decreases sharply and congestion develops soon after streaming begins. Our adaptation module decreases video quality by following our content-aware scaling algorithm. As the video quality decreases, congestion alleviates and available bandwidth increases. As a consequence, the adaptation module increases video quality by adjusting the encoding rate and frame rate. At sample=35, encoding rate rises to 1000 kbps. This bit rate overloads the network and congestion develops again. In response, the adaptation module decreases video quality again. This cycle repeats itself throughout the transmission, generating a self-similar traffic in the network. Frequent quality switches have been observed as the streaming proceeds.

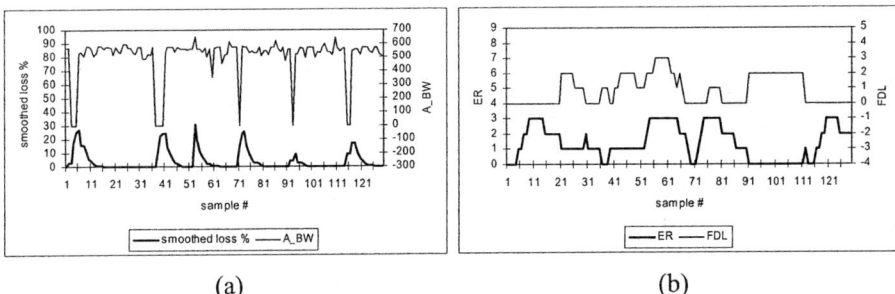

(a) (b)

Fig. 3. System variables in lightly loaded network without bandwidth aware scaling

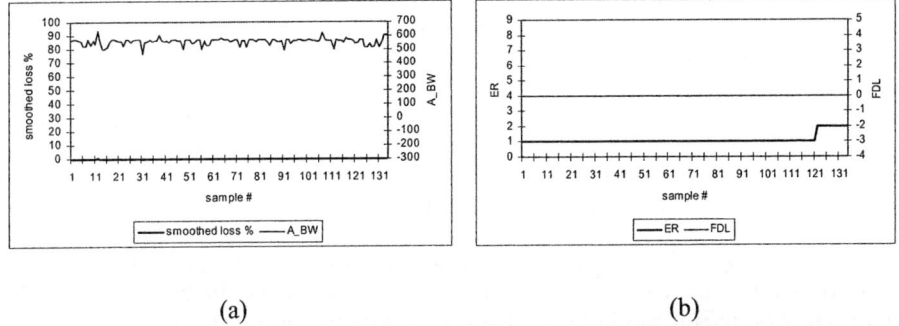

(a) (b)

Fig. 4. System variables in lightly loaded network with bandwidth aware scaling.

Fig. 4 shows system variables when our bandwidth-aware scaling algorithm is applied. Prior to streaming, initial network bandwidth is estimated and proper quality level is determined by comparing available bandwidth with encoding rates of pre-encoded streams. According to Fig. 4a, available bandwidth is between 500 and 600 kbps and the highest encoding rate that is closest to the available bandwidth is 500 kbps. Therefore, transmission starts with this encoding rate (500 kbps) with a frame rate of 30 fps (FDL = 0). Before switching to a higher quality video, our streaming system calculates the bit rate requirement and compares this value with the available bandwidth. Since the available bandwidth does not exceed 600 kbps, we observed that the adaptation module does not increase video quality. Since this experiment is conducted late at night when the Internet is lightly loaded and our system transmits video packets at a rate in compliance with the available bandwidth, no loss has been conveyed through RTCP reports and transmission proceeds at the initial video quality throughout the experiment, without invoking the adaptation module. At sample=120, buffer level has fallen below a predetermined threshold. The decrease in buffer level has been compensated by decreasing the video quality to 200 kbps. Low quality video results in less number of packets in the network leading to fewer packets with smaller end-to-end delays which increases input rate to the buffer, increasing the buffer occupancy in turn.

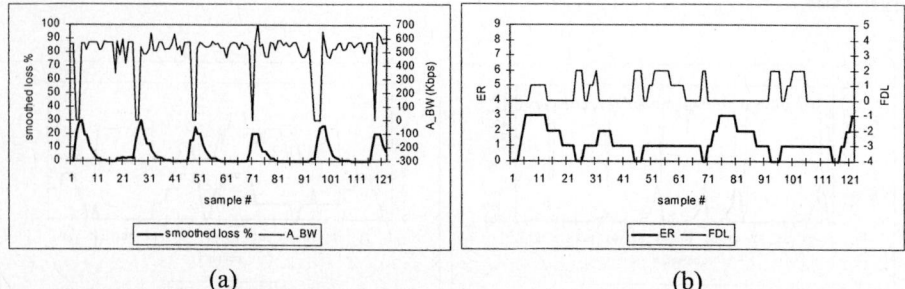

(a) (b)
Fig. 5. System variables in periodically loaded network without bandwidth aware scaling.

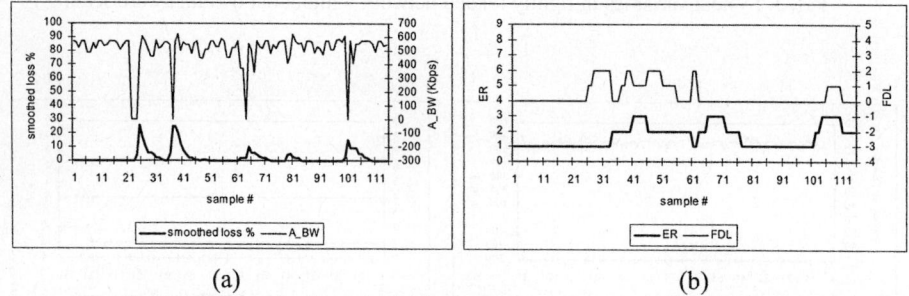

(a) (b)
Fig. 6. System variables in periodically loaded network with bandwidth aware scaling.

Figure 5 and Fig. 6 demonstrate the behavior of our system in a periodically loaded network. When these figures are examined, it is seen that the available bandwidth has more variation than it had in lightly loaded network scenarios. This is because of the fact that, compared to the lightly loaded case, the competing traffic on the Internet is varying considerably in this case. Figure 5 shows the status of system variables when the bandwidth-aware scaling algorithm is switched off. Behavior of the system is very similar to the case given in Fig. 3. Figure 6 presents the performance results when bandwidth-aware scaling is applied. We observed that the number of congested intervals is reduced when bandwidth is taken into account in rate control decisions. When quality changes given in Fig. 6.b are examined, it is seen that congestion is caused by the traffic generated by the other sources on the Internet rather than by our streaming software. This is best observed during the initial buffer filling periods.

Upon detecting the congestion, our adaptation module reacted properly by decreasing video quality. When Fig. 5.b and Fig. 6.b are compared, it is seen that inclusion of the bandwidth estimation module decreased the number of quality changes, resulting in more stable video quality settings. Additionally, overall quality was higher when bandwidth aware algorithm was applied. For example, the encoding rate was decreased to the worst level (ER = 100 kbps) at sample = 6 in Fig. 5.b. On the other hand, prevailing encoding rate was 500 kbps until sample = 33 in Fig. 6.b, thanks to the employment of initial bandwidth estimation procedure.

To summarize, experimental results justify our hypothesis that bandwidth awareness may prevent the occurrence of congestion due to probing and reduces the effects of congestion due to the traffic generated by the external sources. It also reduces the quality fluctuations by avoiding unnecessary invocations of the adaptation module. Similarly, initial bandwidth detection eliminated congestions at the start of the streaming process. Finally, overall perceptual quality was higher with bandwidth-awareness, resulting in a positive effect on the disturbance of the viewer.

6 Conclusions

In this study, we developed a bandwidth-aware streaming algorithm and reported performance results. A mechanism is proposed to measure available bandwidth in the network. By using Pair Packet Dispersion technique, the channel bandwidth is estimated. Our adaptive streaming system checks available bandwidth before performing any increase in quality and/or transmission rate. We have particularly observed that our algorithm is effective during initial buffer filling period. We compared test results of the algorithms with and without bandwidth estimator, which are both taken in WAN environment. It has been shown that the bandwidth-aware streaming algorithm does not allow packet loss and congestion due to the quality increase. However, it can robustly react to the congestion caused by other factors while maintaining acceptable and interrupt-free perceptual quality.

Acknowledgement

The authors are indebted to Koc University for allowing remote use of their workstations while onducting streaming experiments.

References

1. Wang, L.: Rate Control for MPEG Video Coding. Signal Processing: Image Communications **15** (2000) 493–511
2. Girod, B.: Scalable Video for Multimedia Systems. Computers & Graphics **17**(3) (1993) 269–276
3. Sadka, A.H.: Compressed Video Communications. John Wiley & Sons, Ltd. (2002)
4. Tunalı, T., Kantarcı, A., Özbek, N.: Robust Quality Adaptation for Internet Video Streaming. Accepted to be published in Journal of Multimedia Tools and Applications. Kluwer Academics.

5. Kantarcı, A., Özbek, N., Tunalı, T.: Rate Adaptive Video Streaming Under Lossy Network Conditions. Elsevier Science Image Communications 19(6) (2004) 479–497
6. Jacobson, V.: Pathchar-a Tool to Infer Characteristics of Internet Paths. Presented at the Mathematical Sciences Research Institute (MSR1). (1997)
7. Lai, K., Baker, M.: Nettimer: A Tool For Measuring Bottleneck Link Bandwidth. In: Proceedings of the USENIX Symposium on Internet Technologies and Systems. (2001)
8. Carter, R.L., Crovella, M.E.: Measuring Bottleneck Link Speed in Packet-Switched Networks. Performance Evaluation 27(28) (1996) 297-318
9. Jain, M., Dovrolis, C.: Pathload: A Measurement Tool for End-to-end Available Bandwidth. In: Proceedings of Passive and Active Measurements (PAM) Workshop. (2002)
10. Hu, N., Steenkiste, P.: Evaluation and Characterization of Available Bandwidth Probing Techniques. IEEE Journal on Selected Areas in Communications 21(6) (2003)
11. Ribeiro, V., Riedi, R., Baraniuk, R., Navratil, J., Cottrell, L.: PathChirp: Efficient Available Bandwidth Estimation for Network Paths. In: Proceedings of Passive and Active Measurements (PAM) Workshop. (2003)
12. Dovrolis, C., Ramanathan, P., Moore, D.: What Do Packet Dispersion Techniques Measure? In: Proceedings of IEEE INFOCOM. (2001)
13. Jacobson, V., Karels, M.J.: Congestion Avoidance and Control. In Proceedings of the ACM SIGCOMM Conference. (1988)

The Abnormal Traffic Control Framework Based on QoS Mechanisms*

Kwangsun Ko[1], Eun-kyung Cho[1], Taekeun Lee[1],
Yong-hyeog Kang[2], and Young Ik Eom[1]

[1] School of Information and Communication Eng., Sungkyunkwan University
300 Cheoncheon-dong, Jangan-gu, Suwon, Gyeonggi-do 440-746, Korea
{rilla91,iuno,tedlee,yieom}@ece.skku.ac.kr
[2] School of Business Administration, Far East University
5 San Wangjang, Gamgok, Eumseong, Chungbuk 369-851, Korea
yhkang@mail.kdu.ac.kr

Abstract. Recently various hacking tools that dig out the vulnerabilities of hosts on a network are easily accessible through the Internet, and large-scale network attacks have been increased during last decades. To detect these network attacks, a variety of schemes are developed by several companies and organizations. But, many previous schemes are known to have some weakness in protecting important hosts from network attacks because of their inherent unconditional filtering mechanisms. This means that they unconditionally filter out doubtful network traffic in spite of its being normal network traffic. Therefore, to filter out only abnormal network traffic, step-by-step filtering capabilities are required. In this paper, we propose a framework for controlling abnormal network traffic. This framework is implemented through the CBQ and iptables mechanisms in Linux kernel.

1 Introduction

Along with the widespread use of the Internet, abnormal network traffic that wastes useful network bandwidth has been increased considerably [10]. Many schemes for detecting network attacks have been developed, but they are known to have some weakness in protecting hosts from network attacks because they have undesirable features such as an unconditional filtering mechanism. This means that they unconditionally filter out doubtful network traffic in spite of its being normal network traffic. Therefore, to filter out only abnormal network traffic, more active responding capabilities are required.

In this paper, we propose a framework for controlling abnormal network traffic. This framework was implemented in the Linux-based routing system, and it partially limits the network bandwidth against the alerted network traffic by the CBQ mechanism and drops the attack traffic by the iptables mechanism [6, 3].

The rest of the paper is organized as follows. Section 2 outlines background information and mechanisms that are used by our framework. Section 3 describes

---

* This research was supported by University IT Research Center Project.

the overall architecture of our framework and the detailed algorithms of each component in the framework. Section 4 describes in detail how our framework works and discusses the performance comparison with other security systems. Section 5 concludes our proposed scheme and outlines future work.

2 Background

2.1 Netfilter

Netfilter can be regarded as a set of hooks inside the Linux kernel 2.4.x's network stack that allows kernel modules to register callback functions that should be called whenever a network packet traverses one of those hooks [4]. In our proposed framework, the specific functions that are required to disassemble and analyze packets are registered at the appropriate hooks. All network packets are analyzed with these functions before they can continue their traversals or can be dropped according to the results. The hooks of netfilter are illustrated in Figure 1.

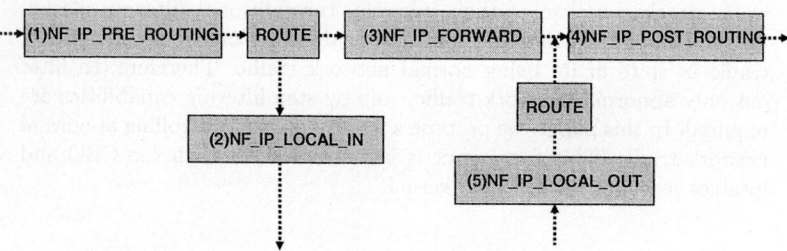

Fig. 1. The hooks of netfilter

2.2 Kernel Module and Kernel Thread

The kernel module programming is the technology that can be used to support various hardware devices in Linux systems [11]. According to the needs of device drivers or file systems, the corresponding module can dynamically be inserted or removed without the modification of the kernel and system shutdown.

The kernel thread concept can be implemented in the kernel module. When it is adopted in the kernel module programming, the kernel module can have many useful features that the application-level processes have [1, 2]. Accordingly, once a program is appropriately implemented as a kernel module with the kernel thread concept, it can improve the system performance, increase the execution speed, and simplify the programming process.

2.3 The Iptables and the CBQ Mechanisms

The iptables is a generic table structure for the definition of IP packet filtering rule sets. Each rule within an IP table consists of a number of classifiers (matches) and one connected action (target) [4]. Packets are filtered after they are compared with the rules in an IP table. The CBQ is one of the classful qdiscs(queueing disciplines) that are very useful when there are different kinds of traffic which should have different treatments [5]. With this mechanism, specific network traffic can be prevented from monopolizing the whole network bandwidth.

In this paper, when the abnormal network traffic is detected, the traffic can be placed on a special output queue that the network bandwidth of it is restricted by the CBQ mechanism or can be dropped by the iptables mechanism.

3 Implementation

We describe the system architecture of our framework and the detailed algorithms of the proposed anomaly traffic control system. The overall architecture of our framework and the description of each component are shown in Figure 2.

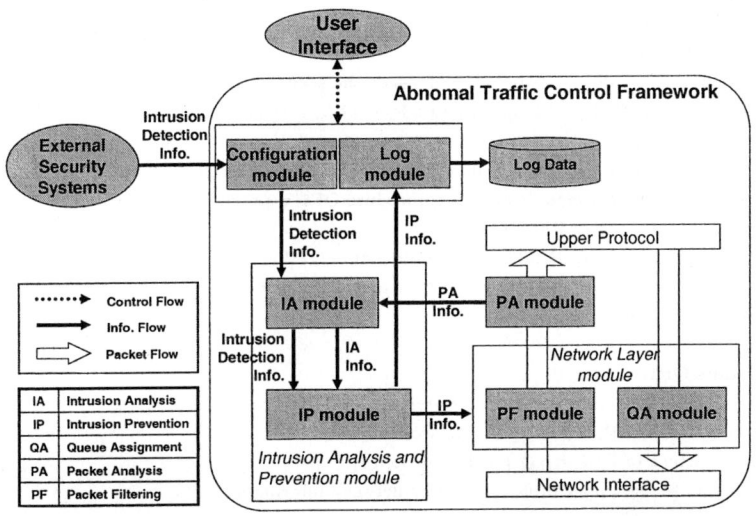

Fig. 2. The architecture of the framework

3.1 Network Layer Module

The network layer module consists of the PF (Packet Filtering) module and the QA(Queue Assignment) module. The PF module, with the iptables mechanism, drops the packets that are matched to the filtering rules. The QA module, with the CBQ mechanism, places network traffic to the output queues according to the queuing rules. When network traffic is alerted as an abnormal traffic by the IA (Intrusion Analysis) module, the QA module can restrict the output bandwidth of the traffic. Also, when network traffic is matched to filtering rules or when alerted network traffic is confirmed as attack traffic by the IA module, the PF module can drop it with filtering rules. The filtering and queuing rules consist of S (source address), D (destination address), P_s(the port of source address), and P_d(the port of destination address).

The filtering rules can be adopted at (1) NF_IP_PRE_ROUTING hook, and the queuing rules can be adopted at (4) NF_IP_POST_ROUTING hook as shown in Figure 1. These rules can be made automatically by the IP module or manually by the network security manager.

3.2 Packet Analysis Module

The PA (Packet Analysis) module disassembles the header of the network packets passing the PF module and queues them for IA module. The algorithm for the PF/PA module is illustrated in Figure 3.

```
/* R_ie: ingress/egress filtering rules */
/* R_ipt: filtering rules made by IP modules or the security manager */
/* M_tcp={F,S,D,P_s,P_d}, M_udp={S,D,P_s,P_d}, M_icmp={S,D,T,C} */

/* When a packet P arrives, it is hooked at the NF_IP_PRE_ROUTING position */
P is passed to the PF module and the procedure OP1 is processed;
if (P successfully passes PF module) {
    P is passed to the PA module and the procedure OP2 is processed;
    P is passed to the upper protocol layer or network interfaces;
} else {   P is dropped;   }

Procedure OP1:
/* P is checked whether its pattern matches to the filtering rules */
if ((the pattern of P) ∈ R_ie) {    P is dropped;    }
if ((the pattern of P) ∈ R_ipt) {    P is dropped;    }
P is passed to the upper protocol layer or network interfaces;

Procedure OP2:
/* When PA module receives network packet P that successfully passed the PF module */
switch(the protocol of P) {
    case TCP:      sends M_tcp to the Q_tcp in the IA module;    break;
    case UDP:      sends M_udp to the Q_udp in the IA module;    break;
    case ICMP:     sends M_icmp to the Q_icmp in sthe IA module;    break;
}
```

Fig. 3. The algorithm of the PF/PA module

When network packets that normally passed through the PF module arrive at the PA module, the headers of them are disassembled and queued for IA module. The message format of the disassembled packet headers are M_{tcp}, M_{udp}, and M_{icmp} for TCP, UDP, and ICMP, respectively. The meaning of each M's component is illustrated in Table 1.

Table 1. The meaning of each M's component

Component	Meaning
F	URG, PSH, SYN, FIN, ACK, RST
S (or D)	Source (Destination) IP address of the packet
P_s (or P_d)	Source (Destination) port number of the packet
T (or C)	ICMP message type (code) of the packet

The messages such as M_{tcp}, M_{udp}, and M_{icmp} and the disassembled packet headers are queued into the queues Q_{tcp}, Q_{udp}, and Q_{icmp} of the IA module, respectively. Afterwards, the information in each queue is used for intrusion analysis.

3.3 Intrusion Analysis and Prevention Module

The intrusion analysis and prevention module consists of the IA module and the IP (Intrusion Prevention) module. The IA module analyzes the disassembled packet headers in the queues, and alerts them as abnormal network traffic or detects attack traffic. Because the IA module is registered in the kernel timer, this module periodically reads the messages in the queues, analyzes them, and updates the state information of the network traffic. On the basis of the statistical method, the state information is used for judging abnormal or attack network traffic with the thresholds and variances that must be already defined in the configuration file. This module generally analyzes the messages at the predefined time T, and it also analyzes the state information at the time 4T, 16T, 64T, 128T, and 256T in order to detect the traffic that continuously tries to attack a host for a long time [7-9]. The analysis result of the IA module is passed to the IP module, the IP module sets up filtering or queuing rules according to the results, and those rules are applied to the QA module. Additionally, the IA module can accept the intrusion detection information from external security systems through the configuration module. This information is sent to the IP module and is used for filtering attack traffic.

Accordingly, when normal network traffic using the normal queue is alerted as abnormal traffic, the traffic is allocated to the alert queue by queuing rules. When alerted network traffic using the alert queue is detected as attack traffic or when normal traffic is matched to the filtering rules, the traffic is dropped by the filtering rules. Figure 4 shows the treatment of network traffic by the filtering and queuing rules.

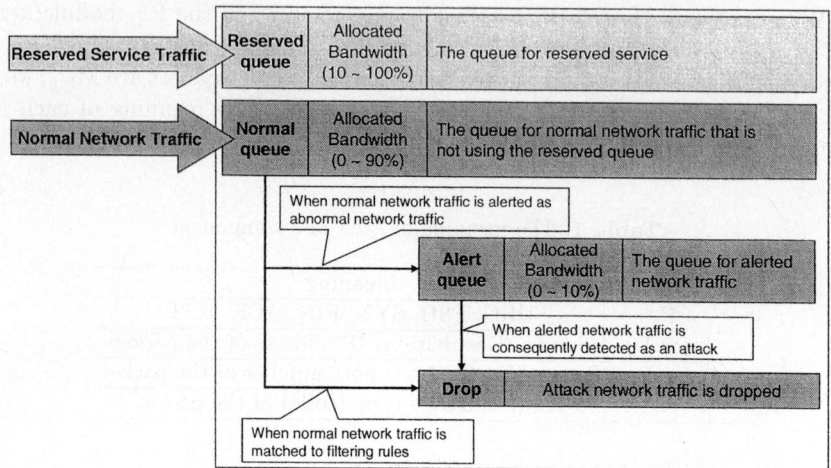

Fig. 4. The treatment of network traffic by filtering and queuing rules

3.4 Configuration and log Modules

The configuration module can accept the intrusion analysis information from the external security systems to detect a variety of new attacks, can check the sanity of the information, and can directly pass them to the IA module. The log module logs the information on the filtering and queuing rules made by IP module. A network security manager can monitor the system of our framework and configure the filtering rules with the web-based user interface.

4 Test and Performance Comparison

In order to test the functionality of our framework, we adopt the framework into the Linux-based routing system, mclab, and monitors the packets from attackers (192.168.x.2) to the target network (192.168.1.0). Our testbed is illustrated in Figure 5. As illustrated in Figure 6, the CBQ configuration adopted in the QA module is set up in mclab.

The output results generated at the mclab are looked into after artificial attack traffic is generated with some attacking tools (knocker, tfn2k). We used output messages recorded in '/var/log/messages' of the mclab. In Figure 5, when network traffic comes from attacker-1 to the target network, it passes through the normal queue of the mclab and can use the maximum 90% output bandwidth because the rest bandwidth (10%) is allocated for reserved network traffic. When abnormal network traffic comes from attacker-1 to the target network, the mclab analyzes the traffic and alerts the traffic as abnormal network traffic. This alerted network traffic is passed to the alert queue of the mclab. When alerted network traffic is alerted by the mclab again, it is dropped. When attack network traffic

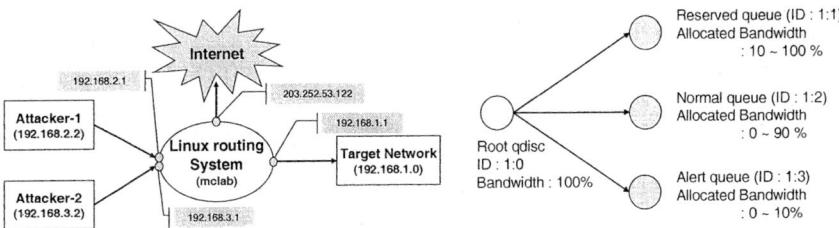

Fig. 5. Testbed   Fig. 6. The CBQ configuration

matched to the filtering rules in mclab comes from attacker-1, it can be directly dropped. This step-by-step response against abnormal network traffic with the CBQ and iptables mechanisms makes it possible to decrease false positive rate and to dynamically control the network traffic. Figure 7 shows the detection process of the DoS attack and we can see that the attack traffic is dropped. Figure 8 shows the state information of three queues that the output bandwidth of the system is divided into by the CBQ mechanism.

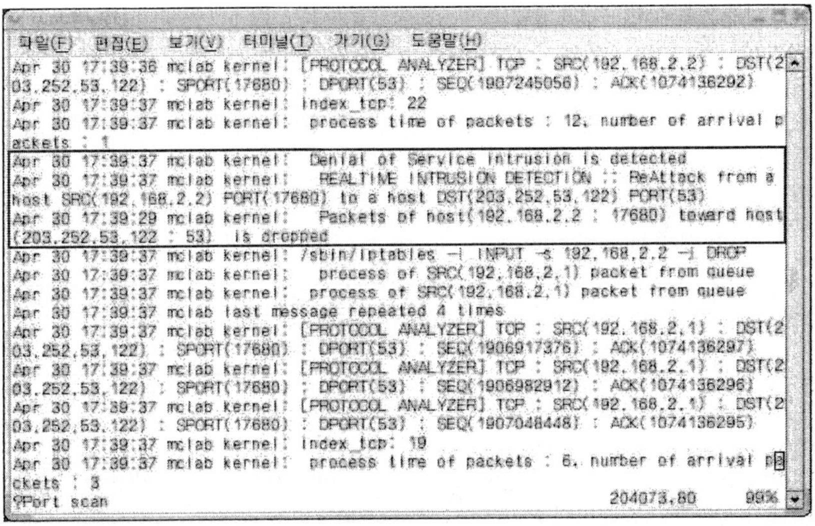

Fig. 7. The detection of the DoS attack

Table 2 shows the performance comparison with NIDS, NIPS (Network-based Intrusion Prevention System), and NTMS (Network Traffic Management System) from the viewpoint of some performance aspects such as intrusion detection capabilities, traffic control capabilities, false positive rates, and so on. NIDS offers the high detection rate of attack traffic because it is developed in order to detect a variety of attacks, but the system may be passive to intrusion because it

```
V root@mclab /
파일(F)  편집(E)  보기(V)  터미널(T)  가기(G)  도움말(H)
[root@mclab /]# tc -s class show dev eth3
class cbq 1: root rate 100Mbit (bounded,isolated) prio no-transmit
 Sent 72700882 bytes 56271 pkts (dropped 0, overlimits 0)
 borrowed 0 overactions 0 avgidle 0 undertime 0
class cbq 1:1 parent 1: rate 10Mbit (isolated) prio no-transmit
 Sent 0 bytes 0 pkts (dropped 0, overlimits 0)
 borrowed 0 overactions 0 avgidle 9 undertime 0
class cbq 1:2 parent 1: rate 80Mbit prio no-transmit
 Sent 28014436 bytes 21683 pkts (dropped 0, overlimits 0)
 borrowed 0 overactions 0 avgidle 0 undertime -1996
class cbq 1:3 parent 1: rate 10Mbit (bounded) prio no-transmit
 Sent 44686404 bytes 34587 pkts (dropped 0, overlimits 0)
 borrowed 0 overactions 0 avgidle 9 undertime 0
[root@mclab /]# []
```

Fig. 8. The state information of the three output queues

focuses only on intrusion detection. NIPS offers an active prevention mechanism, but it incurs high packet loss eventually increasing false positive rate. In general, NTMS offers a QoS mechanism to spread network traffic load. In the security area, NTMS can control network traffic that seems to be malicious by allocating limited bandwidth to the network traffic, but it has no intrusion detection capabilities. Our proposed framework adopts the strength of NTMS and overcomes the weakness of it by implementing the IA module. This framework can decrease the false positive rate and can control the network traffic dynamically.

Table 2. The performance comparison with NIDS, NIPS, and NTMS

Section	NIDS	NIPS	NTMS	Our framework
Intrusion detection	High	High	No	High
Attack traffic control	No	Medium	High	High
False positive rate	No	High	Medium	Medium
Strength	Detection of various attack traffic	Dynamic prevention of attack traffic	Various traffic control policies	Detection of various attack traffic and dynamic traffic control policies
Weakness	No network traffic control	Packet loss and high false positive rate	No intrusion detection	Portable only on the Linux-based routing system

5 Conclusion and Future Work

In this paper, we proposed an anomaly traffic control framework based on Linux netfilter and CBQ routing mechanisms. The concepts of kernel module and kernel thread are used for real-time detection of abnormal network traffic at the kernel level rather than at the application level, and the iptables and CBQ mechanisms are used for step-by-step filtering in order to decrease false positive rate. To detect a variety of new abnormal network traffic, the intrusion detection information from external security systems can be accepted through the configuration module. This information is sent to the IP module and is used for filtering attack traffic.

In the future, performance evaluation and analysis will be performed in order to prove that our framework has the capability of faster detection and more realtime response than other systems implemented on the application level, and that the mechanism of step-by-step filtering is very effective in controlling abnormal network traffic. The performance evaluation will be performed to compare the performance of the pre-existing security systems with our proposed framework.

References

1. Beck, M., et. al.: Linux Kernel Programming, 3rd edn. Addison Wesley, (2001)
2. Bovet, D.P., Cesati, M.: Understanding the Linux Kernel. O'Reilly, (2002)
3. Chang R.K.C.: Defending Against Flooding-Based, Distributed Denial-of-Service Attacks: A Tutorial. IEEE Communications Magazine **40**(10) (2002) 42–51
4. http://www.netfilter.org/documentation/index.html#whatis
5. http://www.lartc.org/lartc.pdf
6. Kargl, F., Maier, J., Weber, M.: Protecting Web Servers from Distributed Denial of Service Attacks. In: Proc. of the 10th International Conference on World Wide Web (WWW10). Hong Kong (2001) 514–524
7. Lee, W.: Applying Data Mining to Intrusion Detection: The Quest for Automation, Efficiency, and Credibility. ACM SIGKDD Explorations Newsletter **4**(2) (2002) 35–42
8. Lee, W., Stolfo, S.J., Chan, P.K., Eskin, E., Fan, W., Miller, M., Hershkop, S., Zhang J.: Real Time Data Mining-Based Intrusion Detection. In: Proc. of the DARPA Information Survivability Conference & Exposition II (DISCEX 2001). Vol.1 (2001) 89–100
9. Mutaf, P.: Defending Against Denial-of-service Attack on TCP. In: Web Proc. of the 2nd International Workshop on Recent Advances in Intrusion Detection (RAID '99). (1999)
10. Northcutt, S., Novak, J.: Network Intrusion an Analyst's Handbook, 2nd edn. New Riders, (2001)
11. Rubini, A., Corbet, J.: Linux Device Driver, 2nd edn. O'Reilly, (2002)

Proximity-Based Overlay Routing for Service Discovery in Mobile Ad Hoc Networks*

Hyeon-Ju Yoon[1], Eun-Ju Lee[2], Hyunku Jeong[1], and Jin-Soo Kim[1]

[1] Computer Science Division
Korea Advanced Institute of Science and Technology
373-1, Gusong-Dong, Yusong-Gu, Daejeon 305-701, S. Korea
{juyoon,hkjeong}@camars.kaist.ac.kr, jinsoo@cs.kaist.ac.kr
[2] R&D Lab., Mobile Communication Division
Samsung Electronics Co. Ltd.
Dongsuwon P.O. Box 105, Suwon-City, Gyeonggi-Do, 442-600, S. Korea
osis.lee@samsung.com

Abstract. We propose a proximity-based overlay routing algorithm for accelerating the service discovery using the distributed hash table (DHT)-based peer-to-peer (P2P) overlay in mobile ad hoc networks (MANET). DHT systems are useful for resource restrained MANET devices due to the relatively low communication overhead. However, the overlay routing for service discovery is very inefficient, since overlay structure is independent of physical network topology. Our proximity-based overlay routing utilizes the wireless characteristics of MANETs. The physically closer node to destination is preferred to the logical neighbors, using information collected by 1-hop broadcast between a node and its physical neighbors. More enhancement is achieved by the shortcut generated from the service description duplication. In a detailed ns-2 simulation study, we show that the proposed scheme achieves approximately shortest physical path without additional communication overhead, and also find that it works well in the mobile environment.

1 Introduction

Mobile ad hoc network (MANET) is a network of self-organized wireless mobile hosts, which is formed without help of the fixed infrastructure. Service discovery protocol (SDP) enables services (which may be network devices, applications or resources) to advertise themselves, and clients to issue queries and discover appropriate services needed to properly complete specified tasks. SDP is an important and challengeable component in the application layer for ad hoc communication and collaboration, because the MANET does not assume any centralized or publicly known fixed server, and the network topology incessantly varies during the lifetime. SDP for MANETs are usually based on the network-wide broadcasting and matching algorithms, and some improving mechanisms, such

---

* This research was supported by University IT Research Center Project and Brain Korea 21 Project, The school of information technology, KAIST in 2004.

as caching and grouping, have been developed because the broadcasting cost is very high when the size of network gets larger.

On the other hand, peer-to-peer (P2P) overlay networks, which have been proposed for the mutual information exchange among Internet users, are very similar to the MANET in the nature of self-organized and distributed networks. Early stage P2P protocols were based on the all-to-all broadcasting like SDPs in MANETs, but they suffered from the data redundancy, large amount of traffic, and so on. Now, the structured approach using distributed hash table (DHT) is gaining the popularity in the research community, and the P2P strategy has been being accepted as a novel technique for distributed resource management. We consider the structured P2P protocols as a good candidate for the SDP for MANETs to alleviate the redundancy and performance degradation.

On applying the DHT-based system to the MANETs, there are some difficulties caused by MANET's dynamic property, resource restraints, and wireless characteristics. Of those problems, we focus on the routing inefficiency of service query and retrieval process. The DHT overlay structure and its routing algorithm don't take the physical topology into account at all, so the shortest logical path may be a longest physical path. Some topology-aware DHT routing algorithms [1] have been proposed, but they are not applicable for MANETs because they usually exploit the fixed Internet topology information.

In this paper, we propose an overlay routing scheme on the DHT-based overlay in MANETs to reduce the length of physical routing path using the dynamic feature and wireless characteristics.

2 Related Work

Service discovery protocols for distributed environments have been mainly designed for the static networks including Internet, and they usually adopted the centralized directory-based approach as shown from SLP (Service Location Protocol), UDDI (Universal Description, Discovery & Integration), and Jini. In MANETs, every node including server nodes and directory nodes has possibility to change its location and the state, so the assumption for the designated centralized component is not appropriate or reasonable.

The simplest approach for the distributed service discovery is flooding-based algorithm, such as SSDP (Simple Service Discovery Protocol) of UPnP (Universal Plug and Play) and JXTA. Every node advertises its own services to all other nodes periodically (push model), or every query message floods into the network whenever a service is requested (pull model). The push model suffers from the requirement for large storage and outdated advertisements, and the pull model has to pay for the excessive communication overhead. These drawbacks are more problematic in MANETs because devices in MANETs usually have the limitations in the storage, computing and communication capability, and power capacity.

Some works have been proposed to reduce the storage or communication overhead by compromising the pull and push model. One approach is caching and the other is grouping. In caching approaches [2, 3], some intermediate nodes satisfying specific conditions store the service advertisements in their storage. The request message outside the range arrives at a cache node, the service description can be returned to the requester without reaching the service providers. Lanes [4] follows the grouping approach under the assumption of IPv6 addressing. A group of nodes forms a Lane, and the members of a lane share their service descriptions and have the same anycast address. Search message floods from a Lane to another Lane by anycasting. GSD [5] is another grouping method using ontology information of service description.

On the other hand, P2P networking mechanism, which has been developed for the mutual information exchange among Internet users, is emerging as a MANET SDP or resource sharing method because it is very similar to the MANET in the nature of self-organized, distributed, and ever-changing topology. Early stage P2P protocols based on the directory server approach (e.g. Napster) or all-to-all broadcasting (e.g. Gnutella) also have the resemblance and the same problems with the SDPs for MANET.

The DHT-based P2P system constructs an application level overlay network on top of the physical network. Each resource or service is associated with a key, and each DHT node is responsible for a certain range of keys (zone). The basic function of DHT is efficient key lookups, thus to route the query to the node that stores the corresponding resource of a key. This involves the construction and maintenance of topology among peers, routing in the overlay network. Several topologies such as ring (e.g. Chord), hypercube (e.g. CAN), and tree (e.g. Pastry, Tapestry) and the overlay routing algorithm based on each topology were proposed. Most of them maintain the information of $O(\log N)$ neighbors and logical route length of $O(\log N)$ hops for N participating peers. Participating nodes periodically exchange control messages with the neighbors and keep the overlay routing table up-to-date. When a node joins or departs the overlay network, some special process should be performed to maintain the structure in order to support full virtual key space. A query message travels the route established on the logical structure, though each overlay hop may consist of a number of hops in underlying IP network.

There have been some previous attempts to use DHT-based overlay for resource sharing in MANETs [4, 7–9], paying attention to the similarities of two networks - both are self-organizing and decentralized. [7] proposed an integrated architecture for P2P and mobile applications, and investigated the expected challenges. They pointed out the logical versus physical routing is a critical issue in the integration. In [4] and [8], the cost for maintaining the strict overlay structure is said as the biggest obstacle, because of highly dynamic feature and resource limited devices. [4] weakened the condition of overlay structure, and [8] proposed an on-demand structuring and routing. [9] proposed an IP layer routing protocol integrating a representative MANET routing algorithm DSR and an application layer P2P protocol, Pastry.

3 Proximity-Based Overlay Routing

Distributed service trading process in MANETs consists of service advertisement and discovery. Each node advertises its own services to be shared to the other nodes by sending messages with service descriptions, and the client nodes flow service request messages into the network. The nodes that own the matching service or store the advertised service descriptions reply with the requested service descriptions, so that the client node can access the server node.

In DHT-based P2P overlay networks, the basic functions are *join, leave, insert, update*, and *lookup* as described in Sec. 2. Our DHT-based service discovery follows the same process and rules as the given overlay structure except a few differences. Main resource to be shared is not service itself, but service description (SD). Each SD generates a key by hashing, and each node stores and maintains the (key, SD) pairs as well as the overlay routing table. *Service advertisement* is performed by the insertion of (key, SD) to the node that takes charge of a zone. Participating nodes exchange routing information periodically, and keep the routing table updated just as the way of overlay maintenance. When a service is requested, the overlay routing table is referred and the requesting message travels along the route constructed from the overlay routing table. *Service discovery* is performed by the lookup process on the overlay.

The logical overlay routing does not consider the physical topology at all, so unnecessarily longer paths often introduce the inefficiency and waste of limited resource of MANET devices. We propose a scheme to shorten the route utilizing the wireless characteristics of MANETs.

In the wired networks, only a part of nodes joins in the P2P overlay networks and the overlay construction and routing are performed among the participating peers only, while the underlying IP networking enables the real communication. However, every node which dwells in a MANET takes part in the overlay network, we assume, because each node in a MANET functions as a router as well as a working peer. Service description language and the hashing mechanism are not described because they are beyond the scope of this paper.

3.1 Consult Physical Neighbors

The first modification of overlay routing uses information from physical neighbors. The wireless devices in MANETs have limited radio range, so only the devices within the transmission range can hear the messages. Before forwarding a service discovery request message, a node sends a request for neighbor information to its own physical neighbors by 1-hop broadcast. The neighbors look up their routing table, compute the logical distance between the destination and each entry in the routing table, and reply with the information on the closest node and the distance. If one of the neighbors is responsible for the requested key, then it replies with its own address and the distance 0. The requester collects the replies for certain period, and selects the node that declares the shortest distance. That is, each node considers the physical neighbors' routing information prior to its own logical neighbors, so increases the possibility of choosing the physically shorter routes. We call this scheme as **CPN** (Consult Physical Neighbors).

Figure 1 shows a very simple example. The distance is computed based on the structure of key space, and a threshold is set to prevent too many replies in the case that the node density is high. In this example, the threshold value is 0.2. Though node B and E send the same response, E is chosen because the packet from E contains E as a source address. If the CPN is not used, the physical path length is 3 (A → B → A → E).

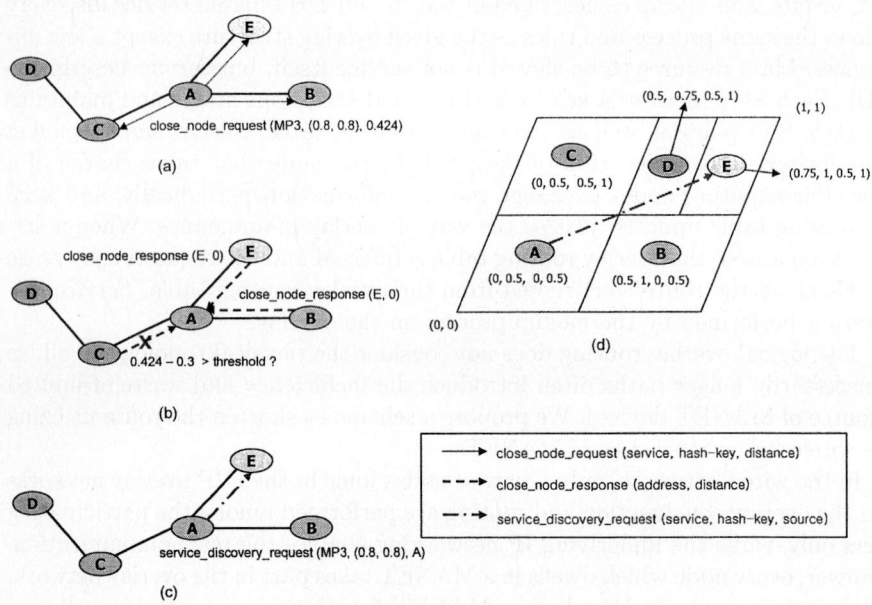

Fig. 1. Use of physical neighbors' routing information

3.2 Use Duplicated Description

The second modification utilizes the fact that the service descriptions are duplicated and stored in the node in charge of the key zone as well as the service provider. In addition to the advertised (key, SD) pairs (*Ad_SD_table*), each node maintains the (key, SD) directory of its own services (*My_SD_table*). When a SD request message arrives, the node looks up the *My_SD_table* first. So, the requester can be replied by the physically closer SD of the duplicated ones (see Fig. 2). We call this scheme as **UDD** (Use Duplicated Description). UDD can be used with the usual overlay routing, but more effective with CPN. In usual overlay structure of N nodes, the possibility to meet the service provider on the route to the designated key space is $1/N'$, where N' is $N-$(number of predecessors). In CPN routing, all physical neighbors are checked before forwarding so the possibility goes up to k/N'', where N'' is $N-$(total number of predecessors and their neighbors) and k is the number of current neighbors. The higher node density gives the higher possibility.

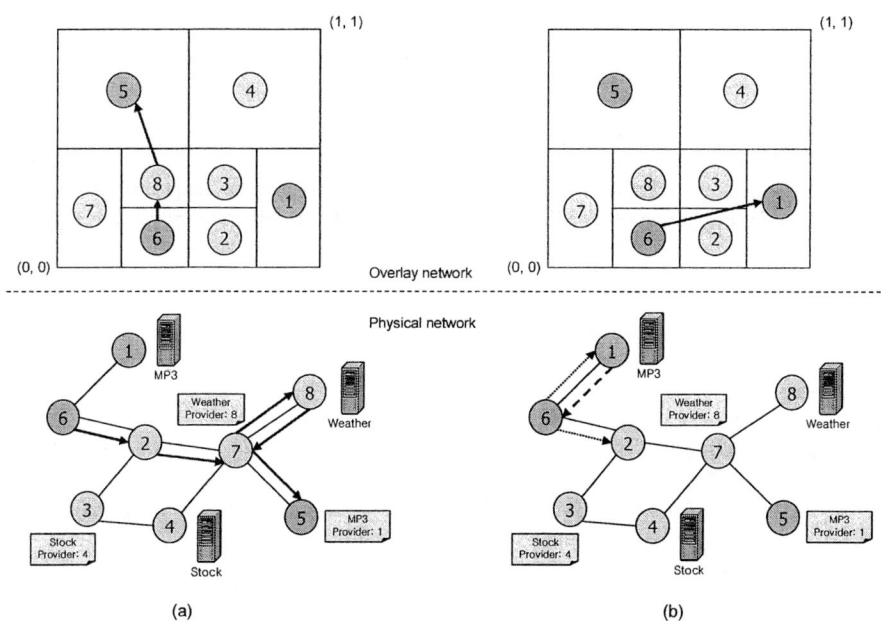

Fig. 2. Shortcut to physically close service descriptions

Integrating both acceleration methods, each node performs following algorithms as a sender or a receiver.

```
void retrieveService (char *serviceRequest) {
  ...
  key = makeKey(serviceRequest);
  if (zone.IsContain(key) || lookupMyService(serviceRequest)) {
     retrievalSuccess();
  } else if (neighbor = zone.isNeighborContain(key) >= 0) {
     forwardTo(neighbor, msg);
  } else {
     logicalDistance = zone.distance(key);
     sendCloseNodeRequest(serviceRequest, key, logicalDistance);
     setBroadcastTimer();
  }
  ...
}
```

```
void broadcastTimerExpire(Event *) {
  ...
  closest = selectCloseNode();
  forwardTo(closest, msg);
  ...
}

void recMsg(int size, char *msg) {
  ...
  switch(msgType) {
    case SERVICE_RETRIEVAL_REQUEST:
      if (zone.isContain(key) || lookupMyService(serviceRequest) {
        sendRetrievalResponse (serviceRequest, serviceDescription);
      } else if (neighbor = zone.isNeighborContain(key) >= 0) {
          forwardTo (neighbor, msg);
      } else {
          sendCloseNodeRequest (serviceRequest, key, logicalDistance);
      }
      break;
    case SERVICE_NODE_REQUEST:
      if (lookupMyService (serviceRequest)) {
        sendRetrievalResponse (serviceRequest, serviceDescription);
      } else if (neighbor = zone.isNeighborContain (key) >= 0) {
          sendCloseNodeReponse (serviceRequest, neighbor, 0);
      } else {
          myDistance = zone.distance (key);
          if (myDistance < msg->logicalDistance - threshold)
            sendCloseNodeResponse (serviceRequest, address, myDistance);
      }
      break;
    case CLOSE_NODE_RESPONSE:
      addReply (msg);
      break;
      ...
  }
}
```

4 Simulation Results and Discussion

We implemented the prototype of our scheme based on the IEEE 802.11 MAC and AODV [10] routing protocol in the ns-2 simulator with the CMU wireless extension. Two-dimensional CAN [6] was chosen as the basic construction algorithm for peer-to-peer structure. In DHT-based P2P overlay, periodical exchange of routing information is essential for the structure maintenance, but it is a large burden for limited communication capacity of MANET wireless channel. Whereas most of DHT structures maintain $O(\log n)$ neighbors, d-dimensional CAN requires only $2d$ neighbors. For implementation simplification and efficiency, we chose 2-dimensional CAN.

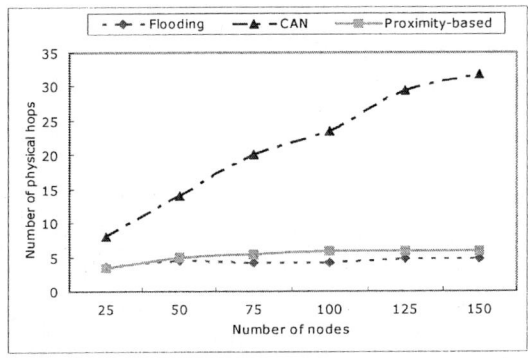

Fig. 3. Route length with respect to the number of nodes

For comparison, we also implemented the basic flooding approach and the original CAN algorithm which doesn't use proximity-based acceleration in the retrieval. The transmission range of each node is 250m, and the channel bit rate is 2 Mbps. The simulation area of 1500m x 1500m is used, and the number of nodes varies from 25 to 150 increased by 25, which are randomly placed in the area. In the initial stage, every node configures a MANET and an overlay, and 50% of nodes registers 3 services with 60 second interval. During the total simulation time of 20000 seconds, they periodically reregister their services and 30% of nodes discovers randomly selected 10 services in every 50 seconds.

Figure 3 shows the route length of service discovery. The more nodes join the network, the longer routes are needed in the original CAN algorithm, because the request message flows according to only the logical structure. In the case of flooding, a request message reaches all other nodes, so the shortest route was established between the requester and the service provider. Our algorithm achieves the similar route length with the flooding because the physically close node is chosen first and the logical structure is inspected next.

We estimated the communication overhead by counting the number of messages. Fig. 4(a) shows the number of received messages by all nodes, and (b) the number of sent messages from all nodes. As the number of nodes increases, the number of messages in the flooding scheme increases in geometrical order. Structured schemes show the superiority in reducing the number of messages. The interesting point is that the number of messages of our algorithm is not more than that of original CAN in spite of the 1-hop broadcast overhead. The reduced route length also reduces the total number of messages, so our algorithm can achieve the shorter routes without excessive communication overhead.

Figure 5 depicts the probability of meeting the service owner in the middle of routing. As we predicted, our UDD scheme raises the probability as the number of nodes increases.

The next result shows the effect on the route length in the mobile environment, for 100 nodes. Random waypoint mobility model is used with the maxi-

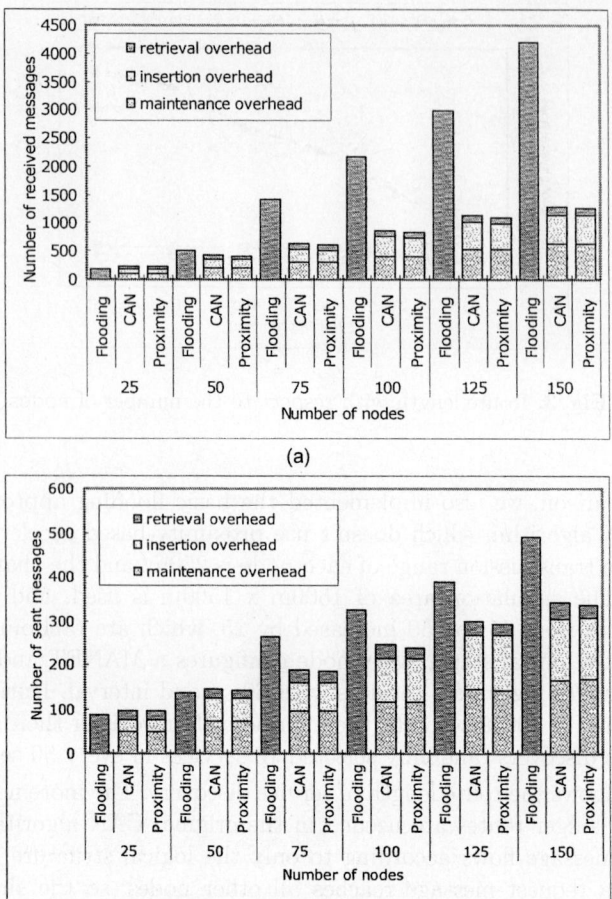

Fig. 4. Communication overhead

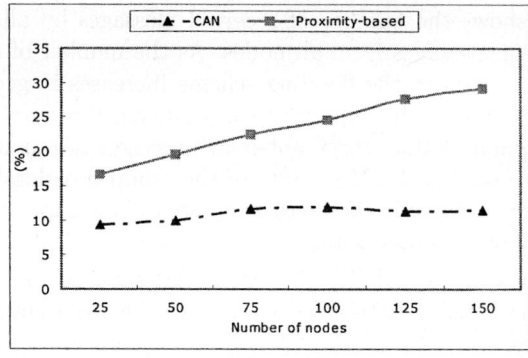

Fig. 5. Probability of meeting service provider in the mid of routing

mum speed of 40 m/s, and the maximum pause time varies from 0 to 40 seconds. Regardless of the degree of mobility, all 3 schemes show the similar result with that of the static network. The number of messages doesn't show any difference either because the messages for maintenance are counted for only logical structure, but the underlying IP routing messages increased due to the node mobility.

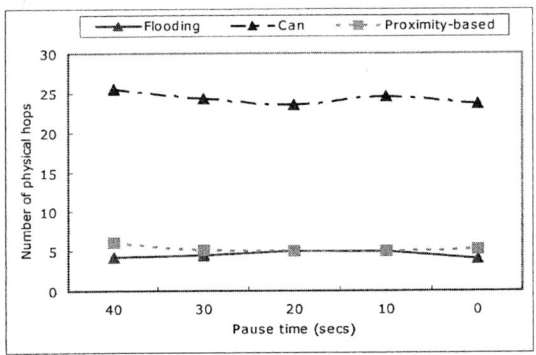

Fig. 6. Route length in the mobile environment

5 Conclusion

We proposed a scheme for accelerating the service discovery based on the DHT-based P2P overlay network in MANETs. Using the physical neighbor information which can be easily obtained in MANETs, the proposed algorithm could achieve the significant performance gain in terms of the routing distance. The overhead due to the 1-hop broadcast messages could be offset by the decreased number of hops. Our algorithm was implemented and evaluated with the CAN overlay network, and also applicable for other DHT-based P2P overlay structures.

References

1. Castro, M., Druschel, P., Hu, Y.C., Rowstron, A.: Topology-aware routing in structured peer-to-peer overlay networks. Tech. Rep., MSR-TR-2002-82, Microsoft Research (2002)
2. Motegi, S., Yoshihara, K., Horiuchi, H.: Service discovery for wireless ad hoc networks. In: Int. Symp. on Wireless Pers. Multimedia Comm. (2002)
3. Koubaa, H. Fleury, E.: Service location protocol overhead in the random graph model for ad hoc networks. In: 7th Int. Symp. on Comp. and Comm. (2002)
4. Klein, M. Konig-Ries, B. Obreiter, P.: Lanes - A lightweight overlay for service discovery in mobile ad hoc networks. In: 3rd Workshop on Applications and Services in Wireless Networks. (2003)

5. Chakraborty, D., Joshi, A., Yesha Y., Finin, T.: GSD: A novel group-based service discovery protocol for manet. In: IEEE Conf. on Mobile and Wireless Comm. and Net. (2002)
6. Ratnasamy, S., Francis, P., Handley, M., Karp, R., Shenker, S.: A scalable content-addressable network. In: ACM SIGCOMM'01. (2001)
7. Datta, A.: MobiGrid: P2P overlay and MANET rendezvous - A data management perspective. In: CAiSE 2003 Doc. Symp. (2003)
8. Klemm, A., Lindemann, C., Waldhorst, O. P.: A Special-purpose peer-to-peer file sharing system for mobile ad hoc networks. In: IEEE VTC2003-Fall. (2003)
9. Hu, Y. C., Das, S. M., Pucha, H.: Exploiting the synergy between peer-to-peer and mobile ad hoc networks. In: HotOS-IX: Ninth Workshop on Hot Topics in Op. Sys. (2003)
10. Perkins, C., Belding-Royer, E., Das, S.: Ad hoc on-demand distance vector (AODV) routing. IETF RFC 3561 (2002)

Multicast Routing for Ad Hoc Networks with a Multiclass Scheme for Quality of Service

Kaan Bür and Cem Ersoy

NETLAB, Department of Computer Engineering
Bogaziçi University, Bebek 34342, Istanbul, Turkey
{burk,ersoy}@boun.edu.tr

Abstract. As multimedia- and group-oriented computing becomes increasingly popular for the users of wireless mobile networks, the importance of features like quality of service (QoS) and multicasting support grows. Ad hoc networks can provide users with the mobility they demand, if efficient QoS multicasting strategies are developed. The ad hoc QoS multicasting (AQM) protocol achieves multicasting efficiency by tracking resource availability within a node's neighbourhood and announces it at session initiation. When nodes join a session of a certain QoS class, this information is updated and used to select the most appropriate routes. AQM is compared to a non-QoS scheme with emphasis on service satisfaction of members and sessions in an environment with multiple service classes. By applying QoS restrictions, AQM improves the multicasting efficiency for members and sessions. The results show that QoS is essential for and applicable to multicast routing in ad hoc networks.

1 Introduction

The increasing popularity of video, voice and data communications over the Internet and the rapid penetration of mobile telephony have changed the expectations of wireless users. Voice communication is accompanied by multimedia and the need for group-oriented services and applications is increasing. Therefore, it is essential that wireless and multimedia be brought together [1]. Ad hoc networks are communication groups formed by wireless mobile hosts without any infrastructure or centralised control, which can accompany these developments.

Quality of service (QoS) support for multimedia applications is closely related to resource allocation, the objective of which is to decide how to reserve resources such that QoS requirements of all the applications can be satisfied [2]. However, it is a significant technical challenge to provide reliable high-speed end-to-end communications in these networks, due to their dynamic topology, distributed management, and multihop connections [3]. In this regard, multicasting is a promising technique, the advantage of which is that packets are only multiplexed when it is necessary to reach two or more receivers on disjoint paths.

This work was supported in part by the State Planning Organisation, Turkey, under Grant No. DPT98K120890 and OPNET Technologies University Research Program.

It is not an easy task to incorporate QoS to ad hoc multicasting. Incremental changes on existing schemes cannot address the critical issues mentioned above efficiently. In this paper, the ad hoc QoS multicasting (AQM) protocol is presented to improve multicasting efficiency through QoS management. AQM tracks availability of QoS within a node's neighbourhood based on previous reservations in a network of multiple service classes, and announces it at session initiation. During the join process, this information is updated and used to select routes which can satisfy the QoS requirements of the session. Thus, AQM significantly improves the multicasting efficiency for members and sessions. The rest of this paper is organised as follows. Previous research related to ad hoc multicasting is summarised in Chapter 2. AQM is introduced in Chapter 3. The performance of the proposed system is evaluated in Chapter 4. Concluding remarks and future work are presented in Chapter 5.

2 An Overview to Ad Hoc Multicasting Protocols

Several protocols have been developed to perform ad hoc multicast routing. However, they do not address the QoS aspect of ad hoc communication, which is becoming increasingly important as the demand for mobile multimedia increases.

Associativity-based ad hoc multicast (ABAM) builds a source-based multicast tree [4]. Association stability, which results when the number of beacons received consecutively from a neighbour reaches a threshold, helps the source select routes which will probably last longer and need fewer reconfigurations. The tree formation is initiated by the source, whereby it identifies its receivers. To join a multicast tree, a node broadcasts a request, collects replies from group members, selects the best route with a selection algorithm, and sends a confirmation. To leave a tree, a notification is propagated upstream along the tree until a branching or receiving node is reached.

Neighbour-supporting multicast protocol (NSMP) utilises node locality to reduce route maintenance overhead [5]. A mesh is created by a new source, which broadcasts a flooding request. Intermediate nodes cache the upstream node information contained in the request, and forward the packet after updating this field. When the request arrives at receivers, they send replies to their upstream nodes. On the return path, intermediate nodes make an entry to their routing tables and forward the reply upstream towards the source. In order to maintain the connectivity of the mesh, the source employs local route discoveries by periodically sending local requests, which are only relayed to mesh nodes and their immediate neighbours to limit flooding while keeping the most useful nodes informed.

Differential destination multicast (DDM) lets source nodes manage group membership, and stores multicast forwarding state information encoded in headers of data packets to achieve stateless multicasting [6]. Join messages are unicast to the source, which tests admission requirements, adds the requester to its member list, and acknowledges it as a receiver. The source needs to refresh its member list in order to purge stale members. It sets a poll flag in data packets and forces its active receivers to resend join messages. Leave messages are also unicast to the source. Forwarding computation is based on destinations encoded in the headers, where each node checks the header for any DDM block or poll flag intended for it.

Multicast ad hoc on demand distance vector (MAODV) routing protocol is derived from AODV [7]. The multicast group leader maintains a group sequence number and broadcasts it periodically to keep fresh the routing information. A node wishing to join a multicast group generates a route request. Only the leader or members of the multicast group may respond to a join request by unicasting a route reply back to the requester, which selects the best from several replies in terms of highest sequence numbers and lowest hop count, and enables that route by unicasting a multicast activation message to its next hop. Intermediate nodes receiving the activation message unicast it upstream along the best route according to the replies they received previously. Nodes wishing to leave a group unicast a multicast activation message to their next hop with its prune flag set.

The on-demand multicast routing protocol (ODMRP) introduces the concept of a forwarding group [8]. Sources periodically broadcast join query messages to invite new members and refresh existing membership information. When a node receives a join query, it stores the upstream node address in its routing table. If the maximum hop count is not exceeded, it updates the join request using this table and rebroadcasts the packet. When a node decides to join a session, it broadcasts a join reply. When a node receives a join reply, it checks the table of next nodes to see if it is on the path to the source. If this is the case, it sets its forwarding group flag and broadcasts its own join reply after updating the table of next nodes. Periodic join requests initiated by the source must be answered by session members with join replies to remain in the group.

3 The Ad Hoc QoS Multicasting Protocol

As mobile multimedia applications and group communication become popular for wireless users, ad hoc networks have to support QoS for multicasting. A QoS strategy should handle the reservation of resources, the optimisation of loss and delay to acceptable levels, and the implementation of QoS classes efficiently. In the following sections, the structural components of AQM are defined, which address these issues. Design details include the usage of QoS classes and levels, session initiation and destruction, membership management, and neighbourhood maintenance.

In this work, four QoS classes are suggested to represent a sample set of applications to be supported by the ad hoc network. Defining QoS classes limits the amount of information to be transmitted. It is otherwise impossible to forward a best QoS combination without making some assumptions or losing some valuable data. It is preferable that nodes inform others on the availability of certain QoS conditions and send updates only when they change.

3.1 Session Initiation and Destruction

A session is defined by its identity number, application type, QoS class and, if predictable, duration and cost. A node starts a session by broadcasting a session initiation packet (SES_INIT). Thus, it becomes a session initiator (MCN_INIT). A table of active sessions (TBL_SESSION) is maintained at each node to keep the information on the session definitions. Figure 1 shows the phases of session initiation.

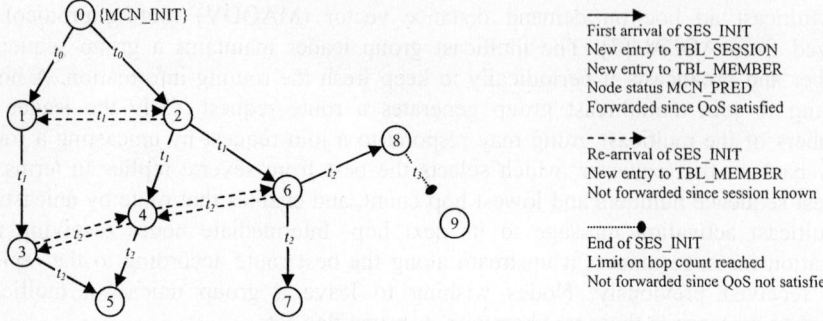

Fig. 1. The AQM session initiation process: SES_INIT is broadcast by MCN_INIT n_0 for a new session. It propagates through the network, informing all nodes from n_1 to n_8, which update their TBL_SESSION and TBL_MEMBER. n_9 is not informed since it is beyond the QoS limits in terms of hop count, which is used as a measure of end-to-end delay. $t_i < t_{i+1}$, $0 \leq i \leq 3$, represent the relative timing of the messages

Using their session tables, nodes forward initiation packets of new sessions. A membership table (TBL_MEMBER) is used to denote the status of the predecessors (MCN_PRED) which have informed the node about a particular multicast session, and the QoS status of the path from the session initiator up to that node via that predecessor. Session initiation packets are forwarded as long as QoS requirements are met. Before a packet is rebroadcast, each node updates its QoS information fields with the current QoS conditions. The packet is dropped if QoS requirements cannot be met any more, avoiding flooding the network unnecessarily. Hop count information in the packets is used to prevent loops. Successful propagation of session initiation data is an important factor for the efficiency of subsequent session joining processes.

The session is closed by its initiator with a session destruction (SES_DESTROY) message. Upon receiving it, all nodes clean their tables. Member nodes forwarding multicast data also free their resources allocated to that session. A node receiving a session destruction packet forwards it if it has also forwarded the corresponding initiation packet or is currently forwarding session data to at least one active session member. Thus, receivers of a closed session are forced to leave the session.

3.2 Membership Management

A node can directly join a session if it is already a forwarding node in that session. Otherwise, it broadcasts a join request packet (JOIN_REQ) containing the session information. The predecessors of the requester propagate it upstream as long as QoS is satisfied. Ad hoc networks are highly dynamic, and available resources may change considerably since the arrival of the QoS conditions with the session initiation packet. Therefore, QoS conditions are checked at each node to make sure that current available resources allow the acceptance of a new session. Intermediate nodes maintain a temporary request table (TBL_REQUEST) to keep track of the requests and replies they have forwarded and prevent false or duplicate packet processing.

The forwarded request reaches nodes which are already members of that session and can directly send a reply (JOIN_REP). Members of a session are the initiator, the forwarders, and the receivers. Downstream nodes, having initiated or forwarded join requests, thus waiting for replies, aggregate these and forward only the reply offering the best QoS conditions towards the requester. The originator of the join request selects the one with the best QoS conditions among possibly several replies it receives. It changes its status from predecessor to receiver (MCN_RCV) and sends a reserve message (JOIN_RES) to the selected node which has forwarded the reply.

Intermediate nodes check the reserve packet to see whether they are forwarders on the path from the selected replier to the requester. If this is the case, they change their status from predecessor to forwarder (MCN_FWD), reserve resources, and update their membership tables to keep a list of successors. They send the message upstream.

Eventually, the reserve message reaches the originator of the reply, which can be the session initiator with some or without any members, a forwarder, or a receiver. If the replier is the session initiator and this is its first member, it changes its status from initiator to server (MCN_SRV). If it is a receiver, it becomes a forwarder. In both cases, the replier records its successor in its member table and reserves resources to start sending multicast data. If the node is an active server or forwarder, it has already reserved resources. It only adds the new member to its member table and continues sending the regular multicast data. Figure 2 shows the phases of joining a session.

Each time a request-reply-reserve process succeeds, intermediate nodes have enough routing and membership data to take part in the packet forwarding task. When a node sends multicast packets, its neighbours already know if they are involved in the session by checking their tables, one with information on their own membership status, and another with a list of multicast sessions they are responsible of forwarding.

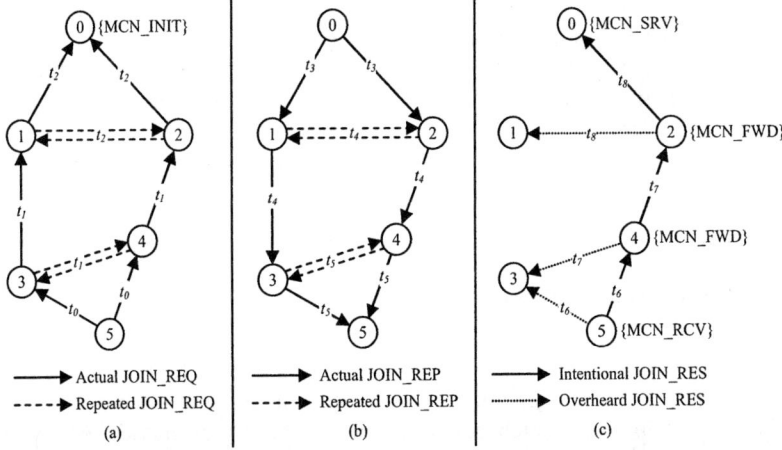

Fig. 2. The AQM session joining process: (a) JOIN_REQ is issued by n_5. It propagates through the network as long as QoS can be satisfied, until it reaches some members of the session. Nodes from n_1 to n_4 update their TBL_REQUEST as they forward the packet since they are not session members. (b) JOIN_REP is sent back from MCN_INIT n_0 to n_5. It is forwarded by n_1, n_2, n_3, n_4. (c) n_5 sends JOIN_RES along the selected QoS path via n_4, n_2, n_0, which reserve resources and update their status. Other nodes ignore the message. $t_i < t_{i+1}$, $0 \leq i \leq 8$, represent the relative timing of the messages

A node needs to inform its forwarder on the multicast graph upon leaving a session. After receiving a quit notification (SES_LEAVE), the forwarding node deletes the leaving member from its member table. If this has been its only successor in that session, the forwarding node checks its own status. If the forwarding node itself is not a receiver, it frees resources and notifies its forwarder of its own leave.

3.3 Neighbourhood Maintenance

The nodes in an ad hoc network have to maintain their connectivity information with as much accuracy as possible to support QoS. This includes the ability to keep track of available bandwidth within their transmission range, and provide their neighbours with valid routes when asked to take part in a request-reply-reserve process of a node wishing to join a multicast session.

Each node broadcasts periodic greeting messages (NBR_HELLO), informing its neighbours on its bandwidth usage determined by the QoS classes of the sessions being served or forwarded by that node. To reduce overhead, greeting messages can be piggybacked to control or data messages. Each node aggregates the information in these messages to its neighbourhood table (TBL_NEIGHBOUR). This table is used to calculate the total bandwidth currently allocated to multicast sessions in the neighbourhood, which is the sum of all used capacities of the neighbouring nodes for that time frame. Neighbourhood tables also help nodes with their decisions on packet forwarding. Session initiation packets are forwarded only if a node has neighbours other than its predecessors for that session. If a node does not receive any greeting messages from a neighbour for a while, it considers that neighbour lost and deletes it from neighbourhood, session and membership tables.

Due to the broadcasting nature of the wireless medium, free bandwidth is node-based, i.e. a node's available bandwidth is the residual capacity in its neighbourhood. A node can only use the remaining capacity not used by itself and its immediate neighbours. This approach provides a sufficient method to measure bandwidth availability within a neighbourhood.

4 Performance Evaluation

Simulations are repeated multiple times in a network with four service classes as defined in Table 1. Nodes generate their own sessions or join other nodes' sessions with certain probabilities, which belong to one of these four classes. All simulation parameters are given in Table 2. The simulations are conducted using OPNET Modeler 10.0 Educational Version and Wireless Module [9]. The usage scenarios consist of open-air occasions such as search and rescue efforts or visits to nature in an area with boundaries, where a wired network infrastructure is not available. A node can take part at only one application at a time as a server or receiver. However, it can participate in any number of sessions as a forwarder as long as QoS conditions allow.

AQM nodes are modelled in three layers with application, session, and network managers. The application manager is responsible for selecting the type of application to run, setting its QoS class, and making decisions on session initiation/destruction or join/leave. The session manager is responsible for declaring new sessions initiated by its application manager, sending requests for sessions it wishes to join, keeping lists of sessions, members and requests of other nodes, processing and forwarding their messages, and taking part in their join processes when necessary. The network manager is responsible for packet arrival and delivery, and for broadcasting periodic greeting messages to make the derivation of free bandwidth information possible.

Table 1. QoS classes and requirements

QoS Class	Bandwidth Requirement	Average Duration	Delay Tolerance	Application Type
0	128 Kbps	1,200 s	10 ms	High-quality voice
1	256 Kbps	2,400 s	100 ms	CD-quality streaming audio
2	3 Mbps	1,200 s	10 ms	TV-quality video conference
3	4 Mbps	4,800 s	90 ms	High-quality video

Table 2. Simulation parameters

Parameter Description	Value
Area size	400 m x 400 m
Greeting message interval	10 s
Maximum available bandwidth	10 Mbps
Node distribution (initial)	Uniform
Node idle times	Exponential (300 s; 600 s; 900 s; 1,200 s)
Service class distribution	0: 40%; 1: 20%; 2: 30%; 3: 10%
Session generation / joining ratio	1 / 9
Simulation duration	8 h
Wireless transmission range	200 m

Previous research efforts have mostly been evaluated through the use of important metrics which give a notion about the internal efficiency of a protocol. Two of these are data delivery ratio and control overhead [10]. However, the evaluation of QoS performance in ad hoc networks necessitates additional metrics. The main concern of this work is to evaluate the efficiency of AQM in providing multicast users with QoS and satisfying application requirements. Therefore, two new performance metrics, member- and session-level satisfaction grades, are introduced.

4.1 The Grade of Member Satisfaction

An important aspect of the QoS-related multicasting decisions made by AQM is the improvement in the ratio of overloaded member nodes, which has a direct impact on the satisfaction of session members regarding the multicasting service provided. On the other hand, the same decisions lead the network to reject more join requests than a non-QoS scheme. The member satisfaction grade S_{Member} is defined as the weighted sum of these two components to evaluate the member-level success ratio of AQM:

$$S_{Member} = \beta\left(1 - \frac{o}{s + \alpha f}\right) + (1-\beta)\frac{r}{q} . \tag{1}$$

In (1), o represents the number of overloaded nodes, which have decided to serve and forward more sessions than is possible without exceeding the maximum available bandwidth. s is the total number of session servers, and f is the total number of session forwarders. The streaming nature of multimedia applications and the broadcasting nature of the wireless medium necessitate that session servers and forwarders have different bandwidth requirements within their neighbourhood. A server only takes its successors into consideration whereas a forwarder deals with its predecessor as well as its successors in terms of overload. Thus, the impact of overloaded neighbours on these nodes is not the same. To reflect this difference, f is multiplied by a coefficient α, which is set to 1.5 in the simulations. The division $o/(s+\alpha f)$ gives the ratio of overloaded nodes to all serving and forwarding nodes. Thus, the first term of the summation, multiplied by a relative weight coefficient β, represents a member overload prevention rate. Continuing with the second term, r is the number of receivers, and q is the total number of join requests issued by all mobile nodes. Their ratio reflects the success of the scheme in satisfying a node's request to join a session. The purpose of β, which can be varied between 0 and 1, is to adjust the relative weight of one term over the other according to the preferences of the ad hoc network. To give equal weights to overload prevention and member acceptance, β is set to 0.5 in the simulations. Other values are possible to change the network preferences.

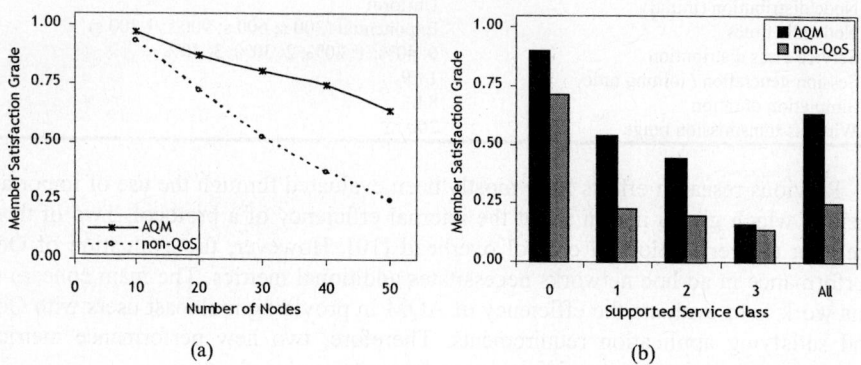

Fig. 3. Comparison of the member satisfaction grades of AQM and a non-QoS scheme: (a) Under support for multiple service classes. (b) Under support for single vs. multiple service classes with 50 nodes

Figure 3(a) compares the member satisfaction grades of AQM to a non-QoS scheme. In AQM, nodes do not accept more traffic than the bandwidth available in their neighbourhood. However, overloaded members still occur due to the hidden terminal problem. When QoS support is deactivated, nodes do not check their bandwidth limitations before replying to join requests. As a result of this, some of the serving or forwarding nodes become heavily overloaded, and their successors start suffering from collisions and packet losses. As the number of nodes grows, more requests are accepted per node without considering the available bandwidth, which causes a drastic decrease in member satisfaction grades. It can be concluded that the application of QoS restrictions significantly increases member satisfaction.

Figure 3(b) compares AQM to the non-QoS scheme with regard to the supported QoS class in a 50-node network. In each of the first four simulation pairs, all generated sessions belong to a single QoS class. AQM outperforms the non-QoS scheme in all of these classes. Moreover, AQM's overall performance increases as the network starts supporting multiple QoS classes. The reason for this improvement is that in AQM, sessions of lower classes can still be managed efficiently even if a join request for a higher-class has been rejected due to QoS restrictions. While the application of QoS causes more users to be rejected, the lack of these restrictions forces users to experience difficulties in getting any service as network population grows and bandwidth requirements increase.

4.2 The Grade of Session Satisfaction

Rejection of some join requests and excessive bandwidth occupation by single nodes in a session affects all its members. It is necessary to observe the implications of these events on sessions. The session satisfaction grade $S_{Session}$ is defined as the weighted sum of these two components to evaluate the session-level success ratio of AQM:

$$S_{Session} = \gamma\left(1 - \frac{l}{m}\right) + (1 - \gamma)\left(1 - \frac{j}{m}\right). \qquad (2)$$

In (2), l is the number of sessions with at least one overloaded member, j is the number of sessions with at least one rejected join request, and m is the total number of sessions. The first term is the ratio of sessions without any overloaded members, whereas the second term reflects the success of AQM with regard to sessions without any rejections. The purpose of γ, which can be varied between 0 and 1, is to adjust the relative weight of one term over the other according to the preferences of the ad hoc network. To explicitly stress the effect of overloaded sessions on AQM, γ is set to 0.8 in the simulations. Other values are possible to change the network preferences.

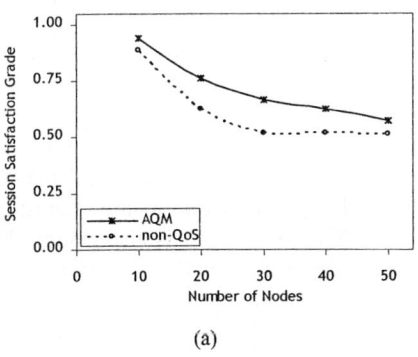
(a)

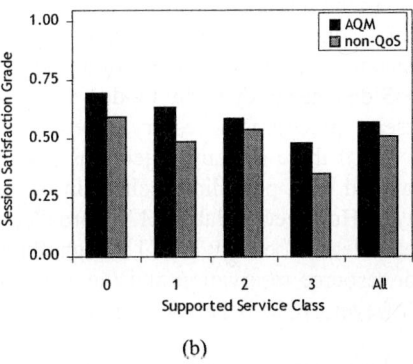
(b)

Fig. 4. Comparison of the session satisfaction grades of AQM and a non-QoS scheme: (a) Under support for multiple service classes. (b) Under support for single vs. multiple service classes with 50 nodes

Figure 4(a) compares the session satisfaction grades of AQM to the non-QoS scheme. Since AQM prevents single nodes from being overloaded more efficiently, it also achieves improvements in session satisfaction. However, unsatisfied sessions still occur. Some nodes become overloaded as a result of the allocations made by their neighbours that cannot be aware of each other's reservations due to the hidden terminal problem. When QoS support is deactivated, on the other hand, the lack of bandwidth restrictions causes more nodes to become overloaded, and as the network grows, more sessions are affected and session satisfaction decreases.

Figure 4(b) compares AQM to the non-QoS scheme with regard to the supported QoS class in a 50-node network. In each of the first four simulation pairs, all generated sessions belong to a single QoS class. AQM outperforms the non-QoS scheme in all of these classes. Thus, AQM achieves better performance by decreasing the number of overloaded members and sessions, at the cost of an acceptably increased number of rejected nodes.

5 Conclusion

AQM is designed to improve multicasting efficiency through the management of resources within each node's neighbourhood. It is compared to a non-QoS scheme in a realistic network scenario where multiple application service classes are supported. The primary evaluation criteria for AQM are service satisfaction grades defined both for members and sessions. Simulations show that, by applying QoS restrictions to the ad hoc network, AQM achieves significantly better results than a non-QoS scheme. Without QoS support, users experience difficulties in getting the service they demand as the network population grows and bandwidth requirements increase. AQM proves that QoS is essential for and applicable to ad hoc multimedia networks. It is not a realistic assumption that a mobile network can afford a pure on-demand scheme if it has to support QoS. AQM proposes a hybrid method in terms of multicasting with table-driven session management and on-demand verification of QoS information.

An important research direction is keeping the QoS data up-to-date, which is a major concern for a node in AQM, and involves the handling of lost neighbours, data exchange, and interpretation of a node's QoS status. A second issue closely related to QoS data accuracy is the hidden terminal problem. An extension to the request-reply-reserve process is necessary, whereby each replying node consults its neighbourhood to see if there are any objections. Neighbour awareness and discovery are typically handled by a periodic mechanism of beacons at the medium access control (MAC) layer. However, reliable MAC broadcast is a challenging task due to the request-to-send/clear-to-send (RTS/CTS) signalling problem. The MAC layer is also responsible for resource reservation and the acquisition of available link bandwidth information. However, AQM is independent of the design of lower layers.

References

1. Van Nee, R, Prasad, R.: OFDM for Wireless Multimedia Communications. Artech House Publishers, (2000)
2. Zhang, Q, Zhu, Wang, G.J., Zhang, Y.Q.: Resource Allocation with Adaptive QoS for Multimedia Transmission over W-CDMA Channels. In: Proceedings of IEEE WCNC, Chicago, USA. (2000)
3. Walrand, J., Varaiya, P.: High-Performance Communication Networks. 2nd edn. Morgan Kaufmann Publishers, (2000)
4. Toh, C.K.: Ad Hoc Mobile Wireless Networks. Prentice-Hall, (2002)
5. Lee, S., Kim, C.: A New Wireless Ad hoc Multicast Routing Protocol. Elsevier Science Computer Networks **38** (2002) 121-135
6. Ji, L., Corson, M.S.: Explicit Multicasting for Mobile Ad Hoc Networks. Mobile Networks and Applications (MONET) **8**(5) (2003) 535-549
7. Royer, E.M., Perkins, C.E.: Multicast Ad Hoc On-Demand Distance Vector (MAODV) Routing. IETF MANET WG Internet Draft, work in progress, (2000)
8. Lee, S.J, Su, W., Hsu, J., Gerla, M.: On-Demand Multicast Routing Protocol (ODMRP) for Ad Hoc Networks. IETF MANET WG Internet Draft, work in progress, (2000)
9. OPNET Technologies Inc, Bethesda, MD, USA. available at http://www.opnet.com.
10. Corson, S., Macker, J.: Mobile Ad Hoc Networking (MANET): Routing Protocol Performance Issues and Evaluation Considerations. RFC 2501, (1999)

HVIA-GE: A Hardware Implementation of Virtual Interface Architecture Based on Gigabit Ethernet

Sejin Park[1], Sang-Hwa Chung[1], In-Su Yoon[1], In-Hyung Jung[1], So Myeong Lee[1], and Ben Lee[2]

[1] Department of Computer Engineering
Pusan National University, Pusan, Korea
{sejnpark,shchung,isyoon,jung,smlee3}@pusan.ac.kr
[2] School of Electrical Engineering and Computer Science
Oregon State University, USA
benl@eecs.orst.edu

Abstract. This paper presents the implementation and performance of the HVIA-GE card, which is a hardware implementation of the Virtual Interface Architecture (VIA) based on Gigabit Ethernet. VIA is a user-level communication interface for high performance PC clustering. The HVIA-GE card is a 32-bit/33MHz PCI adapter containing an FPGA for the VIA Protocol Engine (VPE) and a Gigabit Ethernet chip set to construct a high performance physical network. HVIA-GE performs virtual-to-physical address translation, doorbell, and send/receive completion operations in hardware without kernel intervention. In particular, the Address Translation Table (ATT) is stored on the local memory of the HVIA-GE card, and the VPE efficiently controls the address translation process by directly accessing the ATT. As a result, the communication overhead during send/receive transactions is greatly reduced. Our experimental results show a minimum latency of 12.2 μs, and a maximum bandwidth of 96.3 MB/s. In terms of minimum latency, HVIA-GE performs 4.7 times and 9.7 times faster than M-VIA, a software implementation of VIA, and TCP/IP, respectively, over Gigabit Ethernet. In addition, the maximum bandwidth of HVIA-GE is 52% and 60% higher than M-VIA and TCP/IP, respectively.

1 Introduction

As cluster computing becomes more popular due to the increase in network speed and the enhanced performance of computing nodes, a significant effort has been made to reduce the communication overhead between cluster nodes to maximize the overall performance. In particular, there have been much research efforts in user-level communication to minimize the kernel intervention, such as context switching and data copy between protocol layers. Examples include Active Messages, Fast Messages, U-Net, and VIA [8]. Among them, Virtual Interface Architecture (VIA) was proposed to standardize different features of existing user-level protocols for System Area Network. VIA can be implemented in either software or hardware. The software implementations include M-VIA [3] and Berkeley VIA [4], and the hardware implementations include ServerNet II [6], and cLAN [5].

In this paper, Gigabit Ethernet is adopted as an underlying network to construct a VIA-based PC cluster. Since Gigabit Ethernet is a standard high-speed network for LAN and WAN, it has an advantage in terms of cost when compared with proprietary high performance networks, such as Myrinet and SCI. Moreover, when VIA is adopted as a user-level interface on Gigabit Ethernet based clusters, most of the low-level bandwidth can be redeemed at the application level by removing the time consuming TCP/IP protocol. Currently, there are a number of efforts to implement software versions of VIA based on Gigabit Ethernet using either M-VIA or Berkeley VIA [2],[1],[7],[9]. Meanwhile, Tandem/Compaq developed ServerNet II, a hardware version of VIA using Gigabit Ethernet as a physical network. ServerNet II uses its own switch, which supports wormhole routing with 512-byte packets, to connect cluster of nodes. ServerNet II shows a minimum latency of 12 μs for 8-byte data and a bandwidth of 92MB/s for 64 KB data using RDMA writes on a single Virtual Interface channel. Although, the specific details of the implementation were not reported, the address translation table was not implemented in hardware because there is no memory on the card. cLAN is also implemented as a hardware VIA, and shows a minimum latency of 7 μs and a maximum bandwidth of 110MB/s. Although cLAN shows better performance than ServerNet II, it is based on an expensive proprietary network, similar to Myrinet and SCI.

This paper presents the design and implementation of HVIA-GE, which is a *H*ardware implementation of *VIA* based on *G*igabit *E*thernet. HVIA-GE is a PCI plug-in card based on 33MHz/32-bit PCI bus. An FPGA was used to implement the VIA Protocol Engine (VPE) and a Gigabit Ethernet chip set was used to connect the VPE to Gigabit Ethernet. HVIA-GE performs virtual-to-physical address translations, send/receive operations including RDMA, and completion notifications fully in hardware without any intervention from the kernel. In particular, the Address Translation Table (ATT) is stored in the local memory of the HVIA-GE card, and the VPE efficiently performs the virtual-to-physical address translation. The PCI logic was directly implemented on the FPGA instead of using a commercial chip to minimize the latency of DMA initialization. The HVIA-GE cards can be connected to Gigabit Ethernet switches developed for LANs to form a cluster; therefore, a high performance but low cost cluster system can be easily constructed.

2 VIA Overview

VIA uses the Virtual Interfaces (VIs) to reduce the communication overhead. A VI for each node functions as a communication endpoint, and VIs generated between two nodes establish a virtual communication channel. Each VI contains a Work Queue (WQ), which consists of a Send Queue and a Receive Queue.

A send/receive transaction is initiated by posting a VI descriptor on the WQ, and the Network Interface Card (NIC) is notified of the send/receive transaction using a doorbell mechanism. Each VI descriptor contains all the information the NIC needs to process the corresponding request, including control information and pointers to data buffers. Then, the NIC performs the actual data transfer using DMA without any interference from the kernel. The send/receive transaction is completed when the VI descriptor's done bit is set and the Completion Queue (CQ) is updated by setting the corresponding VI descriptor handle.

3 Implementation of HVIA-GE

Our implementation of the major components of VIA is highlighted as follows. First, WQ is stored in the host memory but the VI descriptors that are currently being processed are copied and stored in the HVIA-GE card until the corresponding send/receive transactions are completed. Second, the send/receive completion notification mechanism is implemented only using the "done bit" in the status field of the VI descriptor. Third, the doorbell mechanism that notifies the start of a send/receive transaction is implemented using registers in the HVIA-GE card. Finally, since every send/receive operation requires a virtual-to-physical address translation, ATT is stored on the local memory implemented on the HVIA-GE card for efficient address translation. The VPE controls the address translation process directly based on the ATT.

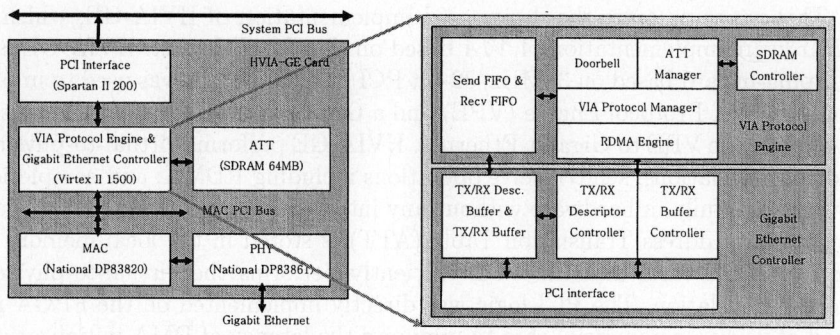

Fig. 1. HVIA-GE Card block diagram

Figure 1 shows the block diagram of the HVIA-GE card, which is a network adapter based on 33MHz/32-bit PCI bus. The PCI interface logic, VPE, the SDRAM controller, and the Gigabit Ethernet Controller (GEC) are all implemented using FPGA running at 33 MHz. The PCI interface logic is implemented directly on the FPGA, rather than using a commercial chip, such as PLX9054, to minimize the latency of the DMA initialization. National Semiconductor's MAC (DP83820) and PHY (DP83861) are used to connect the card to Gigabit Ethernet. On the software side, the Virtual Interface Provider Library (VIPL) and the device driver were developed based on Linux kernel 2.4. The following subsections provide the specifics of the HVIA-GE implementation.

3.1 VIA Protocol Engine and Gigabit Ethernet Controller

As shown in Fig. 1, VPE and GEC are the core modules of HVIA-GE. VPE consists of Send/Receive FIFOs, ATT Manager, Protocol Manager, RDMA Engine, Doorbells, and local memory controller. It processes VIPL functions delivered to HVIA-GE through the PCI bus. In the case of **VipRegisterMem**, which is the VIPL function used to register a user buffer, the user buffer's virtual address, physical address, and size are sent to HVIA-GE as function parameters. The ATT manager receives information regarding the user buffer (i.e., virtual and physical addresses) and stores them on ATT.

When a send/receive request is posted to a send/receive queue, HVIA-GE is notified through the doorbell mechanism, and obtains the corresponding VI descriptor via DMA. Then, the VIA Protocol Manager reads the physical address of the user data through the ATT Manager. If the current transaction is a send, it initiates a DMA read operation for the user data in the host memory and transfers the data to the Tx buffer in the GEC via the Send FIFO. A send/receive transaction can also be implemented using RDMA, which enables a local CPU to read/write directly from/to the memory in a remote node without intervention of the remote CPU. For example, a RDMA can be implemented as either RDMA read or RDMA write. If RDMA read is used, the local CPU must first send the request and then wait for the requested data to arrive from the remote node. Therefore, the RDMA Engine in HVIA-GE is based on RDMA write, which is more advantageous in terms of latency.

Since HVIA-GE directly drives the Medium Access Control (MAC), GEC basically functions as a device driver for the MAC. GEC processes the initialization, transmit/receive, MAC management routines, and interfaces with the MAC using PCI. The operations of GEC are as follows: When a send transaction is executed, Tx Descriptor Controller receives the size of the data to be transmitted and the address of the remote node from VPE, and produces a Tx descriptor. Meantime, Tx Buffer Controller adds the header information to the data received from the Send FIFO, stores the packet on the Tx Buffer, and informs the MAC of the start of a transmission. Then, the MAC reads the packet from the Tx Buffer and transfers it to the PHY.

3.2 Address Translation

During a VIA send operation, the user data is transmitted directly from the sender's user buffer to the receiver's user buffer without producing a copy in the kernel memory. To support this zero copy mechanism, the following features must be implemented. First, once a user buffer is allocated for a send/receive operation, the virtual and physical addresses of the user buffer must be obtained and sent to ATT on the HVIA-GE card using PIO. Second, a user buffer area must be pinned down when it is registered so that it is not swapped out during send/receive operations. In our implementation, one of the Linux kernel's features, `kiobuf`, is used to pin down the user buffer. The virtual address and the corresponding physical address of the user buffer obtained during the pin down process are saved on ATT.

ATT is divided into ATT Level 1 and ATT Level 2. Each 24-byte entry of ATT Level 1 corresponds to one of the allocated user buffers, which includes the number of the physical pages of the user buffer, the virtual address and the size of the first page, and ATT Level 2 pointer. ATT Level 2 stores the physical addresses (4-byte each) of all the allocated pages for the corresponding user buffer. Since ATT is implemented on the HVIA-GE card, it is important to acquire enough space for the table and provide an efficient access mechanism. In our implementation, a 64 MB SDRAM is used to store the ATT. If the ATT supports 1024 VIs and each VI uses one user buffer, then the SDRAM can support up to 60 MB of user buffer for each VI. If only one page (4 KB) is allocated for each user buffer, the SDRAM can support more than 3 million user buffers. Therefore, the capacity of the ATT should be sufficient to support most practical applications.

The access mechanism to ATT operates as follows. The kernel agent assigns a unique memory handle number to each user buffer in a linear fashion when it is allocated. An ATT Level 1 entry is also assigned in the same fashion by consulting the memory handle of the user buffer. Thus, the address of the entry can be calculated by multiplying the memory handle number by the entry size. The current ATT Level 2 pointer is calculated by adding the previous ATT Level 2 pointer to the number of the pages of the previous entry.

After a send/receive request is posted, HVIA-GE obtains the corresponding VI descriptor from WQ via DMA. The VI descriptor includes the corresponding memory handle and the virtual address of the user data. Then, the VPE reads the corresponding ATT Level 1 entry using the memory handle. This requires only one SDRAM access to read the entire entry, which is 24 bytes, in burst mode. The target address for the physical address at ATT Level 2 is determined by adding the ATT Level 2 pointer in the entry to the offset of the given virtual address. When a user buffer is allocated on the host memory, the start address of the user buffer can be at any place in the first page, which is indicated by the size of the first page in the entry. Thus, the size of the first page in the entry must be considered to properly determine the correct target address of ATT Level 2. Finally, the physical address of the user data is obtained by adding the physical address found at ATT Level 2 to the offset of the given virtual address. Therefore, the virtual-to-physical address translation can be processed using two SDRAM accesses.

Unlike the approach described here, it is also possible to implement ATT on the host memory. In this case, VPE has to access ATT via DMA reads. Although this method has an advantage in terms of the hardware cost, it takes about 3 times longer to access the ATT on the host memory than on SDRAM of the HVIA-GE card. Since ATT needs to be accessed for each send/receive operation, this overhead is significant, particularly when an application involves frequent communications between nodes in a cluster.

4 Experimental Results

The performance of the HVIA-GE card was evaluated using two 800 MHz Pentium III PCs with 32-bit/33MHz/PCI bus. The PCs were running RedHat 7.2 with Linux kernel 2.4. Also, for comparison purposes, the performances of TCP/IP and M-VIA were measured using AceNIC's Gigabit Ethernet card. The latency and bandwidth of HVIA-GE were measured by using a ping-pong program developed using VIPL. The performance of M-VIA was measured using the vnettest program included with the M-VIA distribution. The performance of TCP/IP was measured by modifying the vnettest program using the socket library.

4.1 Performance Comparison of HVIA-GE, M-VIA, and TCP/IP

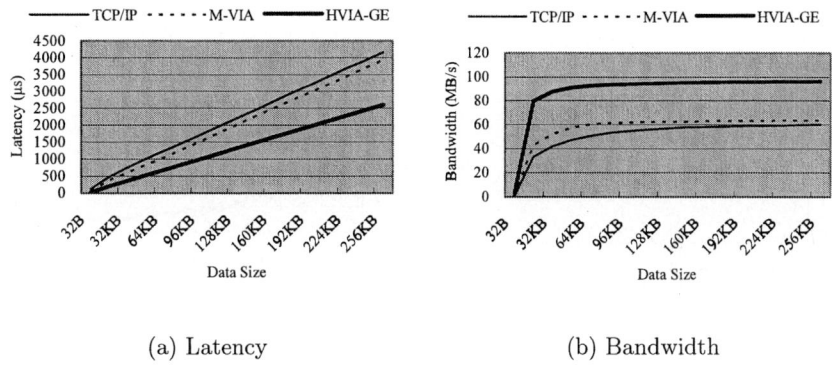

(a) Latency (b) Bandwidth

Fig. 2. Latency and Bandwidth Comparisons

Fig. 2 shows the latencies and the bandwidths results of HVIA-GE, M-VIA, and TCP/IP with the Ethernet MTU size of 1,514 bytes. The latency reported is one-half the round-trip time and the bandwidth is the total message size divided by the latency. The latency and bandwidth of HVIA-GE are measured using the RDMA write on a single VI channel. The minimum latency results of HVIA-GE, M-VIA, and TCP/IP for 4 bytes of user data are 12.2 μs, 57.6 μs, and 117.9 μs, respectively. Thus, the minimum latency of HVIA-GE is 4.7 and 9.7 times lower than M-VIA and TCP/IP, respectively. The maximum bandwidth results for 256 KB of user data are 96.3 MB/s, 63.5 MB/s, and 60 MB/s for HVIA-GE, M-VIA, and TCP/IP, respectively. Thus, HVIA-GE achieves 50% and 59% higher bandwidth than M-VIA and TCP/IP, respectively.

The minimum latency of H-VIA can be analyzed as follows. In the sender, the processing time required by the VPE and GEC is approximately 5.6 μs, and the data transmission time from Tx Buffer of the sender to Rx Buffer of the receiver is approximately 4.1 μs. In the receiver, the time required to transfer data from Rx Buffer via GEC and the VPE to the PCI bus is approximately 1.5 μs. Thus, in our implementation, the time spent in the host to call the send VIPL function, update WQ, and post the corresponding transaction is less than 1 μs.

4.2 Performance Comparison of Send/Receive and RDMA Write on HVIA-GE

Latency and Bandwidth. Fig. 3 shows the performance difference between RDMA write and send/receive. As shown in Fig. 3-a, the latency difference is on average 2.9 μs regardless of data size. Fig. 3-b represents the difference in bandwidth. These improvements are obtained because RDMA write does not require a VI descriptor to be created and posted to WQ at the target node. Thus, the completion mechanism that sets the done bit in the VI Descriptor's status field is also not necessary at the target node. Although the improvement is not significant for large data, it is meaningful to the applications that communicate using data size below 10 to 20 KB.

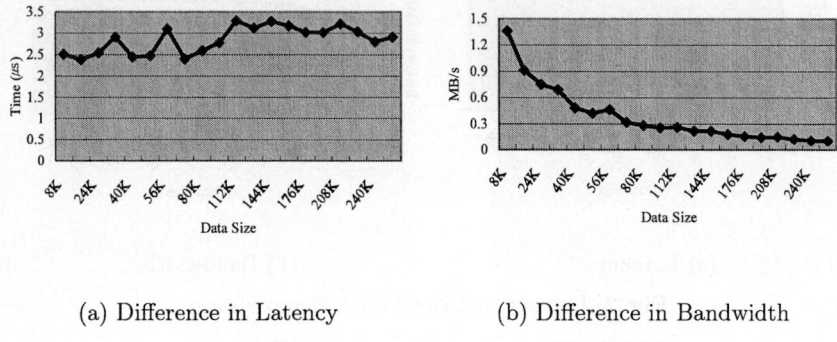

(a) Difference in Latency (b) Difference in Bandwidth

Fig. 3. Differences in Latency and Bandwidth

CPU Utilization. Unlike the RDMA write, a send/receive requires some VIPL functions such as VipPostRecv and VipRecvWait at the receiver. VipPostRecv generates a VI descriptor, posts it to WQ and waits for HVIA-GE to read it. VipRecvWait waits for the message to arrive and completes the transaction when the message is DMAed to the user buffer. Fig. 4 shows the CPU times spent for VipPostRecv and VipRecvWait. The CPU time spent for VipPostRecv is about 6.1 μs regardless of data size. However, the CPU time spent for VipRecvWait increases in proportion to the data size. Thus, this represents a significant portion of the latency for applications that communicate using large data. In the case of RDMA write, VipPostRecv and VipRecvWait are not necessary, thus the RDMA write is superior to the send/receive in terms of CPU utilization.

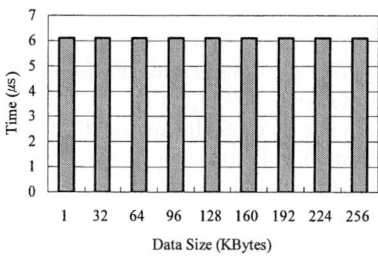 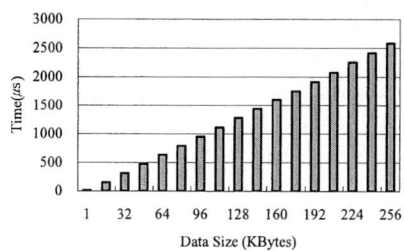

(a) CPU time for VipPostRecv   (b) CPU time for VipRecvWait

Fig. 4. CPU time in Receive Node.

5 Conclusions and Future Work

In this paper, we presented the design and performance of HVIA-GE that implements the VIA protocol in hardware. The HVIA-GE card contains VPE and GEC, and supports virtual-to-physical address translation, doorbell, RDMA write, and send/receive completion operations completely in hardware without intervention from the kernel. In particular, ATT is stored in the local memory on the HVIA-GE card and VPE directly and efficiently control the address translation process.

Our experiment with HVIA-GE shows a minimum latency of 12.2 μs, and a maximum bandwidth of 96.3 MB/s. These results indicate that the performance of HVIA-GE is much better than M-VIA and TCP/IP, and is comparable with that of ServerNet II. If applications with frequent send/receive transactions are executed, the performance of HVIA-GE will be better than that of ServerNet II because of the hardware implementation of ATT. In addition, it is easier to construct a low-cost, high performance cluster system compared to ServerNet II because HVIA-GE is connected to Gigabit Ethernet using the general Gigabit Ethernet switches developed for LAN. In our experiment with HVIA-GE, the RDMA write is better than the send/receive in terms of latency and bandwidth, particularly with data size below 10 to 20 KB. In addition, the RDMA write is superior to the send/receive in terms of CPU utilization for applications that communicate using large data.

As a future work, the HVIA-GE card will be further tested with real applications such as video streaming server. We also plan to make the HVIA-GE card support 64-bit data width. This means that the HVIA-GE card will support the 64-bit/66MHz PCI bus for the system and the MAC, and all the data paths of VPE and SDRAM will be 64 bits. The PCI interface of the HVIA-GE card can be further upgraded to support PCI-X and PCI Express. With these enhancements, the performance of the HVIA-GE card will be significantly improved.

References

1. Baker, M., Farrell, P.A., Ong H., Scott, S.L.: VIA Communication Performance on a Gigabit Ethernet Cluster. In: Proc. of the Euro-Par 2001. (2001)
2. Banikazemi, M., Liu, J., Kutlug, S., Ramakrishna, A., Sadayappan, P., Sah, H., Panda, D.K.: VIBe: A Micro-benchmark Suite for Evaluating Virtual Interface Architecture (VIA) Implementations. In: Int'l Parallel and Distributed Processing Symposium (IPDPS). (2001)
3. Bozeman, P., Saphir, B.: A Modular High Performance Implementation of the Virtual Interface Architecture. In: Proc. of the 2nd Extreme Linux Workshop. (1999)
4. Buonadonna, P., Geweke, A., Culler. D.E.: An Implementation and Analysis of the Virtual Interface Architecture. In: Proc. of the Supercomputing'98. (1998)
5. Emulex Corporation: Hardware-based (ASIC) implementation of the Virtual Interface (VI) standard. http://www.emulex.com/products/legacy/index.html
6. ftp://ftp.compaq.com/pub/supportinformation/papers/tc000602wp.pdf
7. Ong H., Farrell, P.A.: Performance Comparison of LAM/MPI, MPICH, and MVICH on a Linux Cluster connected by a Gigabit Ethernet Network. In: Proc. of 4th Annual Linux Showcase & Conference. (2000)
8. Virtual Interface Architecture Specification. http://www.viarch.org/
9. Yoon I.S., Chung, S.H., Lee, B., Kwon, H.C.: Implementation and Performance Evaluation of M-VIA on AceNIC Gigabit Ethernet Card. In: Proc. of the Euro-Par 2003. (2003)

Modeling TCP Loss Recovery Latency with the Number of Retransmissions

Beomjoon Kim, Jaesung Park, and Yong-Hoon Choi

LG Electronics Inc., LG R&D Complex, 533
Hogye-1dong, Dongan-gu, Anyang-shi, Kyongki-do, 431-749, Korea
{beom,4better,dearyonghoon}@lge.com

Abstract. So far, several analytic models have been proposed to predict the performance of transmission control protocol (TCP) such as steady-state throughput. However, for more detailed performance analysis of various TCP implementations, the fast recovery latency during which packet losses are retransmitted should be considered based on the relevant strategy. In this paper, we derive the loss recovery latency of three TCP implementations including TCP Reno, NewReno, and when selective acknowledgement (SACK) option is used. Specifically, the number of lost packets each TCP sender detects and retransmits during fast recovery is considered. Thereby, the proposed model can differentiate the loss recovery latency of TCP using SACK option from TCP NewReno. By numerical results verified by simulations, we evaluate that the proposed model can capture the precise latency of TCP loss recovery period.

1 Introduction

As a reliable transport layer protocol in the Internet [15], transmission control protocol (TCP) provides a function of congestion control to avoid the performance degradation, so-called 'congestion collapses' [6]. In TCP congestion control, a function for detecting and recovering a packet loss is implemented and called *loss recovery* in simple. The loss recovery mechanism works based on two basic algorithms of fast retransmit and fast recovery [1]. If loss recovery is successful, the sender need not wait for retransmission timeout (RTO). Generally, the frequency of RTO has an crucial effect on overall TCP performance and preventing unnecessary RTOs is also a very important issue [9, 10].

The original fast recovery algorithm implemented in TCP Reno [1] has a problem that RTO occurs frequently when multiple packets are lost in a window at the same time. To overcome this problem, the fast recovery algorithm has been modified in accordance with so-called *partial acknowledgement*, which is usually called as TCP NewReno [5]. Another alternative to this end is using selective acknowledgement (SACK) option [7, 2]. [1]

---

[1] In this paper, our scope is limited to TCP implementations and relevant mechanisms widely approved and released by Internet Engineering Task Force (IETF). For simplicity, we call TCP using SACK option as TCP SACK in the rest of this paper.

There have been a lot of works to analyze and predict TCP performance through modeling TCP window's evolution based on its cyclic characteristic [14, 3, 9, 10]. Two well-known papers [14, 3] derive the expected duration of loss recovery period to approximate TCP throughput. In the derivation of the loss recovery duration in [3], only successive RTOs are considered. In the extended model [3], it is assumed that fast recovery always continues for a single round-trip-time (RTT) regardless of the number of packet losses recovered by retransmissions. The assumption may be true because they consider only TCP Reno that can hardly recover more than two packet losses without RTO [9].

However, the fast recovery behaviors of TCP NewReno and SACK has a large difference from TCP Reno in that multiple packet losses in a window can be recovered without RTO if fast retransmit is successful [4]. The duration of fast recovery of TCP NewReno and SACK may last for several RTTs in accordance with the number of retransmissions, which means that the assumption of 'a single RTT fast recovery' does not fit these two TCPs. Especially, there is no difference between TCP NewReno and TCP SACK in the capability of handling multiple packet losses under the assumption of successful fast retransmit initiation. The only difference is that TCP SACK can recover *at least* a packet loss per RTT [2] while TCP NewReno can recover *at most* a single packet loss per RTT [5]. Consequently, under the assumption that fast recovery always continues for a single RTT, it is impossible to reflect the benefit coming from using SACK option. Therefore, we extend the previous works again, and propose a new model based on the model developed in [9, 10]. Based on the proposed model, we can derive the expected fast recovery latency of TCP Reno, NewReno, and SACK with the consideration of the number of retransmissions.

The remainder of this paper is organized as follows. Section 2 provides a brief presentation of TCP loss recovery behaviors and derive its loss recovery probability in terms of the number of retransmissions. In Section 3 we derive the loss recovery latency of TCP based on the loss recovery probability derived in Section 2. Section 4 contains the numerical results and their discussion. Finally, some conclusions are summarized in Section 5.

2 TCP Loss Recovery Model

2.1 Cyclic Behavior of TCP Congestion Window

During a TCP connection is maintained, the evolution of congestion window (*cwnd*) can be modeled as if it is comprised of successive cycles [14, 9, 10]. Each cycle ends with packet loss detection as shown in Fig. 1.

After a TCP connection is established, TCP sender starts to transmit packets in slow start phase. If there is no packet loss until *cwnd* reaches slow-start-threshold (*ssthresh*) [5], it continues to increase in congestion avoidance phase. As long as packet is not lost, *cwnd* keeps on increasing, which leads to an eventual packet loss(es), and the current cycle comes to an end. When a packet loss occurs, there are two different ways to recover it; one is by retransmission and the other

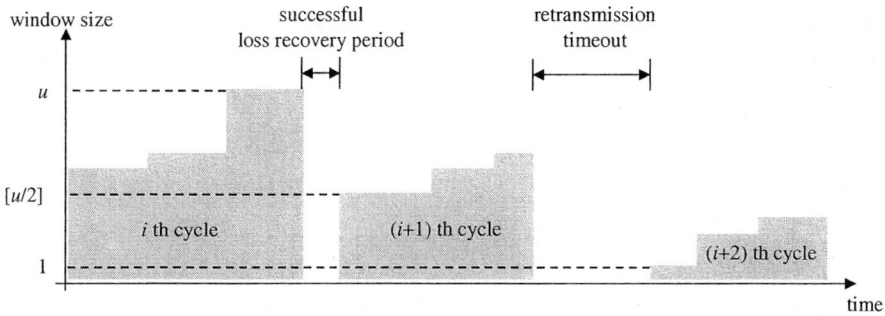

Fig. 1. Cyclic evolution of TCP congestion window

one is by RTO. If the sender can detect the packet loss and retransmit it, the next cycle starts in congestion avoidance with the halved *cwnd* as the $(i+1)$th cycle in Fig. 1. However, if the sender cannot recover the packet loss by retransmission, it should wait for RTO expiry and restart the next cycle in slow start again with the initial value of *cwnd*.

The total latency of a connection can be grouped into two types of period; one is a period of good packet transmission and the other one is a period of loss recovery. The term 'loss recovery period' in this paper means the time duration spent on recovering a lost packet; i.e., either fast recovery period or RTO period. The average throughput of the connection can be approximated by the ratio of the number of packets (or bytes) transmitted well to the total latency [14]. Since the fast recovery algorithm of each TCP adopts a different strategy, the frequency of RTO invocation is also different for the same rate of packet losses. In the rest of this paper, details of this feature are addressed.

2.2 Loss Recovery Probability

Before deriving the loss recovery latency, it is necessary to obtain each TCP's loss recovery probability in terms of the number of retransmissions. For modeling the evolution of congestion window and obtaining its stationary distribution, we mainly follow the procedures presented in [13] under the same assumptions such as fixed packet size, random packet losses with probability p, no ACK loss, and infinite packet transmission. We also follow some notations in [13] such as W_{max} for receiver's advertised window and K for *ssthresh*.

In modeling the loss recovery behaviors of each TCP, we adopt the concept of 'round' defined in [14] and 'loss window' in [9, 10, 13]. If we denote a loss window by Ω and the ith packet loss in Ω by l_i, the first packet that Ω includes is always l_1. Additionally, we define Φ_k as the number of packets that are transmitted newly in the kth round during loss recovery. For n packet losses in Ω that includes u packets, Φ_0 is always equal to $u - n$.

TCP Reno. For Ω whose size is equal to u packets and a single packet loss ($n = 1$), RTO does not occur if $\Phi_0 \geq K$ and the retransmission of l_1 is not lost. Therefore, for $u \geq K + 1$, its probability is given by

$$R_R^{(1)}(u) = (1-p)^{\Phi_0}(1-p) = (1-p)^u \tag{1}$$

where Φ_0 is equal to $u - 1$.

In the same way, l_2 can be recovered without RTO if $\Phi_1 \geq K$ and there is no packet loss during fast recovery. Since Φ_1 is equal to the number of new packets transmitted by the inflation of the *usable window* after the retransmission of l_1 [4], $\Phi_1 = \lfloor u/2 \rfloor + \Phi_0 - u = \lfloor u/2 \rfloor - 2$. When Ω is large enough to content $\lfloor u/2 \rfloor - 2 \geq K$, the recovery probability for $n = 2$ is given by

$$R_R^{(2)}(u) = \binom{u-1}{1} p(1-p)^{u-2}(1-p)^{\Phi_1}(1-p)^2. \tag{2}$$

For TCP Reno, over three packet losses are assumed to always invoke RTO.[2]

TCP NewReno. TCP NewReno can retransmit n packet losses if l_1 can be recovered by fast retransmit and there is no retransmission loss.[3] Therefore, for Ω whose size is equal to u packets, the recovery probability for n packet losses is given by

$$R_N^{(n)}(u) = \binom{u-1}{n-1} p^{n-1}(1-p)^{u-n}(1-p)^n \tag{3}$$

where $1 \leq n \leq u - K$.

TCP SACK. We consider 'Sack1' [4] [4] as a TCP implementation using SACK option. It uses a variable, `pipe`, during fast recovery to estimate the number of packets outstanding in the path.

For n packet losses out of u packets in Ω, the sender sets `pipe` to n ($=u-\Phi_0$) when all duplicate ACKs for l_1 are received. If n is greater than or equal to

---

[2] Three packet losses may be recovered without RTO under a strict condition that there are at least $u - \lfloor u/4 \rfloor + (K - 1)$ packets between l_1 and l_2 and Ω is large enough to content $\lfloor u/4 \rfloor - 3 \geq K$ [9, 10]. However, its probability is negligibly low so that we do not consider the situation (i.e., $R_R^{(3)}(u) = 0$).

[3] We have proposed an algorithm for lost retransmission detection for each TCP in [11, 12]. Also, note that the effect of retransmission losses is not considered in [13], which leads to overestimating the loss recovery probability of TCP NewReno as will be shown in Fig. 3.

[4] In [2], 'Sack1' is refined in terms of maintaining *additive-increase-multiplicative-decrease* (AIMD) principle of TCP congestion control specified in [1]. However, due to its complexity (e.g., the conditions to determine which packet is transmitted first), we consider only the part presented in [4]. As mentioned in [2], since the modified 'Sack1' is largely based on the previous version, we believe that it would not make large differences to the results.

halved cwnd ($=\lfloor u/2 \rfloor$), then $\Phi_1 = 0$. When the sender receives a partial ACK by retransmitted l_1, it decreases pipe by two [2] so that it is equal to $n-2$. If $n-2 \geq \lfloor u/2 \rfloor$, then $\Phi_2 = 0$ as well. In this case, the sender should wait RTO expiry. Considering it, the recovery probability of TCP SACK for n packet losses is given by

$$R_S^{(n)}(u) = \binom{u-1}{n-1} p^{n-1}(1-p)^{u-n}(1-p)^n \qquad (4)$$

where $1 \leq n \leq m(= min(u - K, \lfloor u/2 \rfloor + 1))$.

Normalized Loss Recovery Probability. We define the normalized loss recovery probability of each TCP as follows:

$$R_{tcp} = \sum_u \left(\sum_n R_{tcp}^{(n)}(u) \right) \pi_{tcp}(u) \qquad (5)$$

where $R_{tcp}^{(n)}(u)$ is the loss recovery probability of each TCP derived above and $\pi_{tcp}(u)$ is the stationary distribution of window obtained from the analysis using Markov Chain as in [13].

3 Loss Recovery Latency

If we denote the expected loss recovery duration of each TCP by $E[Z_{tcp}]$, it is given by combining a successful fast recovery period denoted by $E[Z_{tcp}^{fr}]$ and a RTO period denoted by $E[Z^{to}]$ as follows:

$$E[Z_{tcp}] = (1 - R_{tcp}) \cdot E[Z^{to}] + R_{tcp} \cdot E[Z_{tcp}^{fr}]. \qquad (6)$$

Each TCP has the same value of a RTO period as derived in [11] as follows:

$$E[Z^{to}] = \frac{f(p)T_0}{1-p} \qquad (7)$$

where T_0 is the average duration of the first RTO and $f(p) = 1+p+2p^2+4p^3+8p^4+16p^5+32p^6$.

On the other hand, the expected duration of successful fast recovery is different according to each TCP's fast recovery strategy and the number of retransmissions.

For TCP Reno, the expected duration of the fast recovery period is given by

$$E[Z_R^{fr}] = \sum_{u=1}^{W_{max}} \left(R_R^{(1)}(u) + 2 \cdot R_R^{(2)}(u) \right) \cdot \pi_R(u) \cdot T_1 \qquad (8)$$

where T_1 is the average value of RTT.

For TCP NewReno, it takes n RTTs for n retransmissions [5,4] so that its expected duration of the fast recovery period is given by

$$E[Z_N^{fr}] = \sum_{u=1}^{W_{max}} \sum_{n=1}^{u-K} n \cdot R_N^{(n)}(u) \cdot \pi_N(u) \cdot T_1. \qquad (9)$$

Since SACK option informs a sender about all of the packets that have arrived successfully [7], it needs to retransmit only the packets that have been lost. Therefore, the duration of fast recovery of TCP SACK may be different according to the position as well as the number of lost packets.

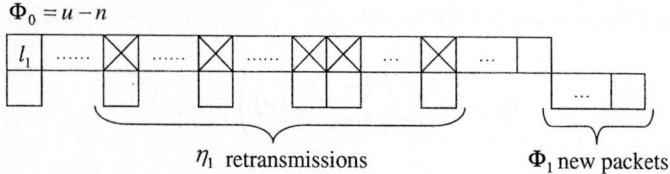

Fig. 2. Model of loss recovery behaviors of TCP SACK when the retransmission of n packet losses is completed within a round

In Fig. 2, we show the loss recovery behaviors of TCP SACK when all packet losses may be recovered by retransmission before a partial ACK arrives to acknowledge l_2. For n packet losses among u packets included in Ω, if we denote the number of retransmissions sent by the decrement of pipe in the kth round by η_k, then we have

$$n = \eta_1 + 1. \qquad (10)$$

When all duplicate ACKs are received for l_1, the values of cwnd and pipe are equal to $\lfloor u/2 \rfloor$ and n, respectively. Therefore, total number of packets that can be transmitted during the first round is given by

$$\eta_1 + \Phi_1 = \lfloor u/2 \rfloor - n. \qquad (11)$$

For simplicity, as long as pipe permits, a retransmission is assumed to be always transmitted first regardless of its position. Then, n retransmissions can be completed in a round if $\Phi_1 \geq 1$. From (10) and (11), the condition is given by

$$1 \leq n \leq \lfloor u/4 \rfloor.^5 \qquad (12)$$

Again, if we assume that the recovery period of TCP SACK is always finished within two rounds, [6] then the expected duration of fast recovery period of TCP

---

[5] If the last packet in Ω is lost, even if the condition of (12) is satisfied, the retransmission of n packet losses cannot be completed within a single round. However, its probability is negligibly low.

[6] The accurate condition for this assumption is $n \leq 0.75\lfloor u/2 \rfloor + 0.5$ [12]. The assumption can be justified by the fact that about 3/8 of packets in a window are rare to be lost at the same time unless packet loss rate is quite high.

SACK can be approximated by

$$E[Z_S^{fr}] = \sum_{u=1}^{W_{max}} \left(\sum_{j=1}^{\lfloor u/4 \rfloor} R_S^{(j)}(u) + \sum_{k=\lfloor u/4 \rfloor+1}^{m} 2 \cdot R_S^{(k)}(u) \right) \cdot \pi_S(u) \cdot T_1 \quad (13)$$

where $m = min(u - K, \lfloor u/2 \rfloor + 1))$.

4 Numerical Results and Discussion

In Fig. 3, we show the normalized loss recovery probability of each TCP derived in Section 2 compared to the simulation results.[7] We assume that K is always three as its typical value and W_{max} is set to 32.[8]

The loss recovery probability of all TCP starts to drop rapidly when p exceeds 10^{-2}. The higher recovery probability of TCP SACK reflects that it can recover multiple packet losses without RTO. As long as roughly half of the packets in Ω are not lost at the same time, which is a very uncommon event when packets are lost randomly, there is no difference in the conditions for successful loss recovery between TCP NewReno and SACK. Therefore, it can be seen that the loss recovery probabilities of the two overlap perfectly.

In Fig. 4, we compare the expected latency of the loss recovery period of each TCP derived in Section 3. It is observed that the loss recovery latency of all TCP starts to increase rapidly when p exceeds 10^{-2}, which corresponds to the result of the loss recovery probability shown in Fig. 2. When p is low, especially below 10^{-2}, most of fast recovery is for a single packet loss so that its period would likely be completed in a single RTT. Therefore, the loss recovery latency of all TCP has a similar value as $T_1 (= 100\ msec)$ until p reaches 10^{-2}.

In [14] and [3], the authors have made an assumption that packet losses in the same round are correlated so that packets transmitted after a lost packet may also be lost. The assumption underestimates the fast retransmit and fast recovery feature, which leads to lowering loss recovery probability and subsequent higher loss recovery latency than our prediction as shown in Fig. 4.

While simulations are running, the value of T_0 varies; as p increases, it also increases. It is because, for such a high p, there are few chances for T_0 to decrease due to frequent RTO expiry and its successiveness. Therefore, we averaged the first timeout during each simulation was running and reflected it as T_0 in the calculation of the timeout period of (7). It can be seen that the model agrees quite closely to the simulated results.

---

[7] In our simulations, a sender and receiver are connected with a long-fat link of 1 Mbps and 100 msec where packets are dropped in random. Using FTP, the sender transmits data consist of 10^5 packets whose size is 1 kbytes, and the loss recovery probability is defined as the ratio of the number of the packets recovered by retransmissions to the total number of packet losses.
[8] We have plotted the normalized loss recovery probability and latency for a smaller W_{max} of 8. However, for the same reason as addressed in [10], the variation of W_{max} makes no significant differences so that we do not include the figures for the case.

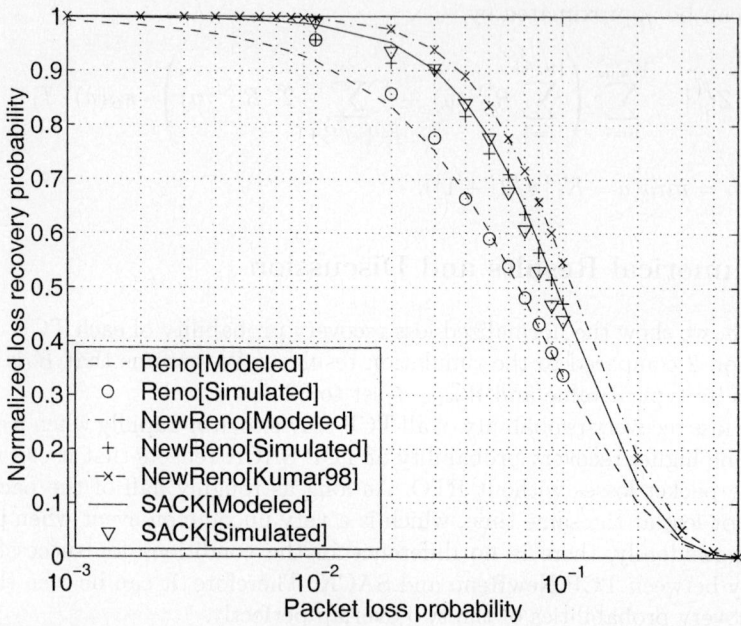

Fig. 3. Comparison of the normalized loss recovery probability predicted by the proposed model for each TCP ($W_{max} = 32$)

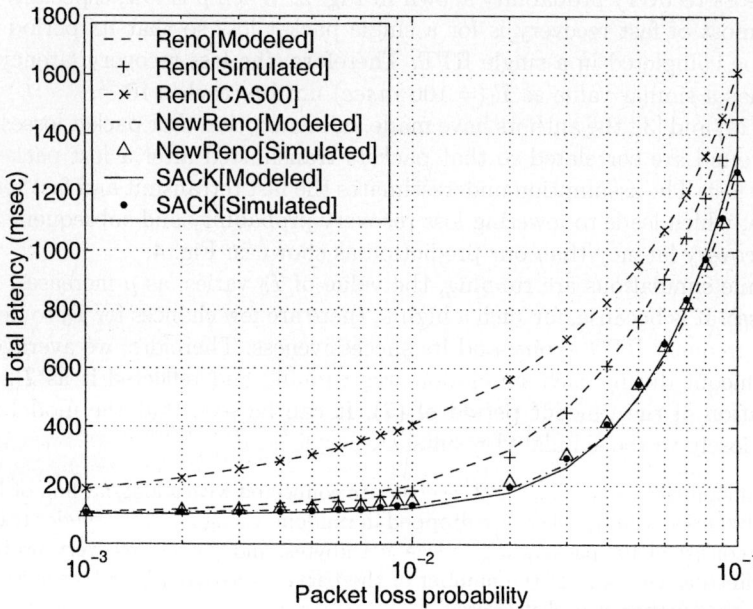

Fig. 4. Comparison of the expected loss recovery duration predicted in Section 3 ($W_{max} = 32$, initial $T_0 = 1,500$, and $T_1 = 100$ msec)

The loss recovery latency of TCP NewReno and SACK shown in Fig. 4 cannot be discriminated clearly but two lines almost overlap. As can be seen in Fig. 3, there is little difference in loss recovery capability between the two TCPs. It means that the difference appears only when fast recovery is successful for two or more number of packet losses. However, because T_1 has much smaller values compared to T_0, it makes no significant difference if they are averaged together. For the reason, we have isolated each TCP's fast recovery period when it is successful as shown in Fig. 5.

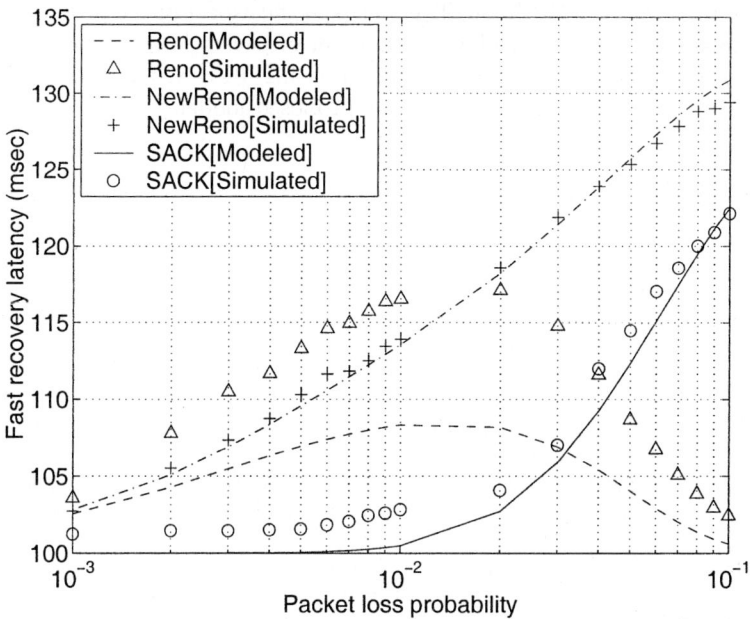

Fig. 5. Comparison of the expected fast recovery duration when it is successful ($W_{max} = 32$, initial $T_0 = 1,500$, and $T_1 = 100$msec)

The successful loss recovery latency shown in Fig. 5 reflects the difference between TCP NewReno and SACK clearly. Also, it reveals that TCP SACK always experiences lower latency than TCP NewReno throughout p. Unlike TCP NewReno and SACK, Reno's fast recovery latency rather decreases as p exceeds a certain value. It is because most of its successful fast recovery corresponds to retransmission of a single packet loss. On the other hand, it can be seen that the latency of TCP NewReno and TCP SACK continues to increase.

The practical latency for TCP Reno to recover two packet losses must be longer than $2 \cdot T_1$ because it should receive another three duplicate ACKs for the second lost packet. Because it is not considered in our model, the latency obtained from the simulations shows somewhat higher values. Also, the assumption that fast recovery continues at most two RTTs when SACK options is used makes a little lower predictions compared to the simulation results.

5 Conclusion

In this paper, we have proposed a model for analyzing the loss recovery performance and latency of various TCP implementations.

The proposed model is basically dependent upon the previous models. However, unlike the previous models that consider only TCP Reno, the proposed model provides a good prediction of the loss recovery latency of TCP NewReno and SACK as well as TCP Reno. The most specific aspect of the proposed model to be stressed is that it considers the number of packet losses recovered during fast recovery, which is essential for differentiating TCP SACK from NewReno. This point is also the contribution of the proposed model.

References

1. Allman, M., Paxson, V., Stevens, W.: TCP Congestion Control. RFC 2581, (1999)
2. Blanton, E., Allman, M., Fall, K., Wang, L.: A Conservative Selective Acknowledgement (SACK) -based Loss Recovery Algorithm for TCP. RFC 3517, (2003)
3. Cardwell, N., Savagem, S., Anderson, T.: Modeling TCP Latency. IEEE INFOCOM 2000. (2000) 1742–1751
4. Fall, K., Floyd, S.: Simulation-Based Comparisons of Tahoe, Reno, and SACK TCP. ACM Computer Communication Review **26**(3) (1996) 5–21
5. Hoe, J.C.: Improving Start-Up Behavior of a Congestion Control Scheme for TCP. ACM SIGCOMM'96. (1996)
6. Jacobson V.: Congestion Control and Avoidance. ACM SIGCOMM'88. (1988)
7. Mathis, M., Mahdavi, J., Floyd, S., Romanow, A.: TCP Selective Acknowledgement Options. RFC 2018, (1996)
8. Kim, B., et al.: Lost Retransmission Detection for TCP Part 2: TCP using SACK option. Lecture Notes in Computer Science, Vol. 3042. Springer-Verlag, Berlin Heidelberg New York (2004) 88–99
9. Kim, B., Lee J.: Analytic Models of Loss Recovery of TCP Reno with Packet Losses. Lecture Notes in Computer Science, Vol. 2662. Springer-Verlag, Berlin Heidelberg New York (2003) 938–947
10. Kim, B., Lee, J.: A Simple Model for TCP Loss Recovery Performance over Wireless Networks. Int'l Journal of Communications and Networks (JCN) published by Korean Institute of Communication and Science (KICS) **6**(3) (2004)
11. Kim B., Lee, J.: Retransmission Loss Recovery by Duplicate Acknowledgement Counting. IEEE Communications Letters **8**(1) (2004) 69–71
12. Kim, B., Kim, D., Lee, J.: Lost Retransmission Detection for TCP SACK. accepted for publication in IEEE Communications Letters (2004)
13. . Kumar, A.: Comparative Performance Analysis of Versions of TCP in a Local Network with a Lossy Link. IEEE/ACM Transactions on Networking **6**(4) (1998) 485–498
14. Padhye, J., Firoiu, V., Towsley, D.F., Kurose, J.F.: Modeling TCP Reno Performance: A Simple Model and Its Empirical Validation. IEEE/ACM Transactions on Networking **8**(2) 133–145
15. Postel J.: Transmission Control Protocol. RFC 793, (1981)

A Two-Step EM Algorithm for MAP Fitting

Peter Buchholz[1] and Andriy Panchenko[2]

[1] Informatik IV, Universität Dortmund
D-44221 Dortmund, Germany
peter.buchholz@cs.uni-dortmund.de
[2] Institute of Applied Computer Science, TU Dresden
D-01307 Dresden, Germany
ap28@mail.inf.tu-dresden.de

Abstract. In this paper we propose a two-step expectation-maximization (EM) algorithm to fit parameters of a Markovian arrival process (MAP) according to measured data traces. The first step of the EM algorithm performs fitting of the empirical distribution function to a phase type (PH) distribution, and the second step transforms the PH distribution into a MAP and modifies the MAP matrices to capture the autocovariance of the trace. In the first step of the algorithm a compact presentation of the distribution function is used and in the second step statistical properties of measured data traces are exploited to improve the efficiency of the algorithm. Numerical examples show that even compact MAP models yield relatively good approximations for the distribution function and the autocovariance.

1 Introduction

Modeling of network traffic processes and generation of adequate and compact workload descriptions is a challenging task since the workload model is one of the most important elements in performance models of computer networks. Modern network and multimedia applications generate complicated traffic processes which exhibit properties like heavy tailed distributions and self-similarity. An adequate traffic model has to capture both, the form of the distribution and the autocovariance function.

Processes like fractional Gaussian noise and fractional Brownian motion [11] have self-similarity properties by definition, but unfortunately such models are analytically almost intractable and their further application to performance analysis requires the development of new analysis methods. Existing techniques for performance analysis often use Markovian processes for the description of network processes since most analytical solution methods require such traffic models. Markovian arrival process (MAP), Batch MAP (BMAP) and Markov Modulated Poisson Process (MMPP) are different variants of Markov processes used as models for traffic processes. In this paper we consider the class of MAPs which includes the other types as special cases.

Fitting of the free parameters of a MAP to capture the behavior of a real trace is a complicated problem. Available fitting approaches may be classified into direct and iterative (numerical) methods.

In *direct* methods a system of equations is solved with expressions for the moments or the autocovariance at one side and with the statistical parameters obtained directly from the trace on the other side. Due to complex expressions for MAP properties, the solution of such systems is non-trivial. Available analytical solutions are restricted to MAPs with 2 or in some specific cases 3 states [8]. Several methods [2, 10, 14] perform separate fitting steps at different time scales and superpose afterwards the resulting MAPs.

Iterative methods are based on a maximum likelihood (ML) estimation and are implemented as expectation-maximization (EM) algorithms. The principle of EM algorithms is to maximize the likelihood of trace generation by changing the free parameters of the MAP. Starting with some MAP, in the first step of the EM algorithm a sufficient statistics is estimated that describes the properties of the trace and from the sufficient statistics new values of the free parameters of the MAP are computed. The existing fitting methods [3, 5, 7, 12, 13] applied to real data traces containing more than 10^4 elements often require fitting times in the order of days to complete the parameter estimation or yield a large state space as result of MAP superposition.

In this paper we present a new and more efficient fitting algorithm as an extension of the approach presented in [5]. The outline of the paper is as follows. In the next section we introduce some basic definitions and results. Afterwards our new fitting algorithm is presented and then the quality of the algorithm is experimentally shown by means of some examples.

2 Markovian Arrival Processes and PH Distributions

A trace t is a sequence of m values $t_1, \ldots, t_m$ which describe, for instance, inter-arrival times. We assume that the sequence is scaled such that its mean value equals $E[t] = 1$. For analytical performance analysis, traces are represented by Markovian Arrival Processes (MAPs) which have been introduced by Neuts [9]. A MAP can be described as a CTMC with finite state space $\mathcal{S} = \mathcal{S}_T \cup \mathcal{S}_A$, where $\mathcal{S}_T = \{1, 2, \ldots, n\}$ is a set of transient states and $\mathcal{S}_A = \{n+1, \ldots, 2n\}$ is a set of absorbing states. The absorption of the process can be interpreted as generation of an event (e.g., the arrival of a packet).

MAPs are formally represented by two square matrices $\mathbf{D_0}$ and $\mathbf{D_1}$ of order n, whose sum is an irreducible infinitesimal generator $\mathbf{Q} = \mathbf{D_0} + \mathbf{D_1}$. Matrix $\mathbf{D_0}$ describes transitions between transient states and all off-diagonal entries of $\mathbf{D_0}$ are non-negative and diagonal elements are chosen such that $\mathbf{Q}\mathbf{e}^T = \mathbf{0}$. Matrix $\mathbf{D_1}$ contains transition rates from $\mathcal{S}_T$ into $\mathcal{S}_A$ and describes implicitly how the transient states are immediately re-entered once an absorption occurs.

For a MAP $\langle \mathbf{D_0}, \mathbf{D_1} \rangle$ the stationary distribution $\boldsymbol{\pi}$ is obtained as solution of $\boldsymbol{\pi}\mathbf{Q} = \mathbf{0}$ and $\boldsymbol{\pi}\mathbf{e}^T = 1$. The distribution vector immediately after reentering the transient states is computed as $\boldsymbol{\tau} = \boldsymbol{\pi}\mathbf{D_1}/\boldsymbol{\pi}\mathbf{D_1}\mathbf{e}^T$.

The interarrival time distribution function of a MAP is given by $F(t) = 1 - \boldsymbol{\tau} \exp(\mathbf{D}_0 t)\mathbf{e}^T$ and the probability density function (pdf) is expressed as $f(t) = \boldsymbol{\tau} \exp(\mathbf{D}_0 t)\mathbf{D}_1 \mathbf{e}^T$. The column vectors of the l-th conditional moment $\boldsymbol{m}^{(l)}$ are given as the solution of the set of equations $\mathbf{D}_0 \boldsymbol{m}^{(l)} = -l\boldsymbol{m}^{(l-1)}$ with initial conditions $\boldsymbol{m}^{(0)} = \mathbf{e}^T$. The absolute l-th moment is defined by $\mathbb{E}[X^{(l)}] = \boldsymbol{\tau}\boldsymbol{m}^{(l)}$. The coefficient of autocorrelation of lag k ($k \geq 1$) for interarrival times equals

$$r(k) = \frac{Cov(X_i, X_{i+k})}{Var(X)} = \frac{\mathbb{E}\left[X^{(1)}\right] \boldsymbol{\pi} \left(\left(-\mathbf{D}_0^{-1}\mathbf{D}_1\right)^k \boldsymbol{m}^{(1)} - \mathbf{e}^T \mathbb{E}\left[X^{(1)}\right] \right)}{\mathbb{E}\left[X^{(2)}\right] - (\mathbb{E}\left[X^{(1)}\right])^2}. \quad (1)$$

PH distributions can be interpreted as specific cases of MAPs with $\mathbf{D}_1 = \boldsymbol{d}_1(\boldsymbol{\tau})^T$ and is completely defined if $\mathbf{D}_0$ and $\boldsymbol{\tau}$ are known since $\boldsymbol{d}_1 = -\mathbf{D}_0 \mathbf{e}^T$. In contrast to general MAPs, PH distributions describe uncorrelated events.

Analysis of MAPs requires the computation of the matrix exponential $\mathbf{D}_0[t] = \exp(\mathbf{D}_0 t)$ as basic step. Since this step is also used in our fitting procedure, we briefly present the randomization approach as a technique for this computation:

$$\exp(\mathbf{D}_0 t_i) = \sum_{k=0}^{\infty} \beta(k, \alpha t_i) \cdot (\mathbf{P}_0)^k \text{ with } \beta(k, \alpha t_i) = (-\alpha t_i)\frac{(\alpha t_i)^k}{k!}, \quad (2)$$

where α is the discretization rate such that $\alpha \geq \max_{1 \leq j \leq n} |\mathbf{D}_0[j,j]|$ and $\mathbf{P}_0 = \mathbf{I} + \mathbf{D}_0/\alpha$. In an implementation of Eq. (2), the infinite sum is bounded by left and right truncation points to provide calculation up to machine precision [6].

In a similar way, we define the matrix $\mathbf{P}_1 = \mathbf{D}_1/\alpha$, which contains probabilities of transitions into the set of absorbing states $\mathcal{S}_A$. Since $\mathbf{D}_0 + \mathbf{D}_1$ is an infinitesimal generator matrix, $\mathbf{P}_0 + \mathbf{P}_1$ is a stochastic matrix. For PH distributions we define the column vector $\boldsymbol{p}_1 = \boldsymbol{d}_1/\alpha$. Observe that $\mathbf{P}_0 \mathbf{e}^T + \boldsymbol{p}_1 = \mathbf{e}^T$.

3 Two-Step Algorithm

In contrast to the fitting algorithm proposed by Buchholz [5] where the distribution and autocovariance is considered in each step, the new algorithm performs fitting in two steps. The first step adjusts the parameters of a PH distribution to approximate the empirical distribution, and in the second step, the PH distribution is transformed into a MAP to reflect the autocovariance properties of the trace. Such an approach reduces the effort drastically. First, because of the reduced sample size which is necessary to perform pdf fitting and secondly due to repeated usage of transient probabilities matrices within the routine to capture the autocovariance. The fitting algorithm modifies the probability matrices of underlying DTMC $\mathbf{P}_0$ and $\mathbf{P}_1$. The iterative procedure stops if convergence is reached which means that matrices $\mathbf{P}_0$ and $\mathbf{P}_1$ differ elementwise by less than ε between two successive iterations.

3.1 Fitting of the PH Distribution with Fixed τ

The fitting problem of a PH distribution is the problem of adjusting the free parameters of the PH distribution such that the pdf of a PH distribution approximates the empirical pdf of the trace. The task can be restated as maximizing the density function $f(t)$ over all values t_i, $i = 1, \ldots, m$. To evaluate the quality of the approximation the likelihood function $L(\tau, \mathbf{D}_0; t) = \prod_{i=1}^{m} \tau \exp(\mathbf{D}_0 t_i) d_1$ is used. The goal of all fitting algorithms is the maximization of $L(\tau, \mathbf{D}_0; t)$.

Based on the general PH fitting problem using algorithms of the expectation-maximization type [4], the presented algorithm is a modified particular case of the procedure presented in [5]. The algorithm performs fitting for a fixed initial distribution τ by modifying the matrix $\mathbf{P}_0$ to achieve a good approximation of the empirical distribution.

Usually large traces t can be represented in a more compact form, which will be denoted as an aggregated representation. However, one has to take care to capture the relevant information of the whole trace in its aggregated representation. We represent an aggregated trace as a set of tuples $< \hat{t}_i, g(\hat{t}_i) >$, where $\hat{t}_i$ is the mean value of the interval $(\Delta_{i-1}, \Delta_i]$ and $g(\hat{t}_i)$ is the probability of finding a value from the interval $(\Delta_{i-1}, \Delta_i]$ in the trace.

The aggregated representation can be built in two different ways.

1. Divide the sample into r intervals of identical width and compute the average value and weight of each interval. Thus, interval $[\min(t), \max(t)]$ is divided into r subintervals $(\Delta_{i-1}, \Delta_i]$, $i = 1 \ldots r$ with $0 \leq \Delta_0 < \min(t)$, $\Delta_r = \max(t)$ and $\Delta_i = \Delta_{i-1} + (\max(t) - \min(t))/r$. Define r sets $\mathcal{T}_i$ (classes of elements) such that $t_j \in \mathcal{T}_i$ if $t_j \in (\Delta_{i-1}, \Delta_i]$. The average value of the elements in class i is defined as $\hat{t}_i = (1/|\mathcal{T}_i|) \sum_{j \in \mathcal{T}_i} t_j$, where $|\mathcal{T}_i|$ is the number of elements in the i-th class. For each element $\hat{t}_i$ define the corresponding weight $g(\hat{t}_i) = |\mathcal{T}_i|/m$ which equals the probability $P(t_j \in \mathcal{T}_i)$. The uniform division of the complete range may lead to rather bad approximations, if not enough intervals are defined or the distribution has a heavy tail such that the main part where most values are concentrated is captured by one or two subintervals.

2. Consequently, for heavy tailed distributions we consider l logarithmic scales and perform the approach of 1. within each scale. Define $L_{min} = \lfloor \log_{10}(\min(t)) \rfloor$ as a minimal log scale and $L_{max} = \lceil \log_{10}(\max(t)) \rceil$ as a maximal one. Then divide each interval $(10^l, 10^{l+1}]$ into r subintervals and define r classes of elements as stated above. Such a description captures the main part of the pdf as well as the tail of the distribution. Elements with $g(\hat{t}_i) = 0$ are ignored in subsequent computations. Denote as R the overall number of elements which are used for fitting. If all weights of the elements in the aggregated trace are nonzero, we have $R = r$ for the first method and $R = r(L_{max} - L_{min})$ for the second method.

EM algorithms estimate the value of the likelihood L in the expectation step and compute new values for the free parameters $\langle \tau^{(s+1)}, \mathbf{D}_0^{(s+1)} \rangle$ in the maximization step such that $L(\tau^{(s+1)}, \mathbf{D}_0^{(s+1)}; t) \geq L(\tau^{(s)}, \mathbf{D}_0^{(s)}; t)$.

If the initial probability distribution τ is fixed, then the likelihood function depends only on $\mathbf{D}_0$ and therefore the computation is reduced to the computation of $L(\mathbf{D}_0^{(s)}; t)$. The corresponding steps are realized in Algorithm 1.

Algorithm 1 Fitting of the PH distribution with fixed τ

Input: $<\hat{t}, g>$ Aggregated trace
τ Initial probability distribution
$\mathbf{P}_0$ Matrix of transition probabilities

Output: $\mathbf{P}_0$ Modified matrix of transition probabilities

$p_1 = \mathbf{e}^T - \mathbf{P}_0 \mathbf{e}^T$
REPEAT // perform fitting process

$\quad v^k = \tau(\mathbf{P}_0)^k;\ w^k = (\mathbf{P}_0)^k p_1$
$\quad$ FOR $i = 1 : R$

$$\mathbf{X}_0^{(i)}(x,y) = \sum_{k=l_i}^{r_i} \beta(k, \alpha \hat{t}_i) \cdot \sum_{l=0}^{k-1} v^l(x) \mathbf{P}_0(x,y) w^{k-l-1}(y)$$

$$x_1^{(i)}(x) = \sum_{k=l_i}^{r_i} \beta(k, \alpha \hat{t}_i) \cdot v^l(x) p_1(x)$$

$\quad$ END

$$\mathbf{Y}_0 = \sum_{i=1}^{R} g(\hat{t}_i) \cdot \mathbf{X}_0^{(i)};\ \mathbf{y}_1 = \sum_{i=1}^{R} g(\hat{t}_i) \cdot x_1^{(i)}$$

$\quad <\hat{\mathbf{Y}}_0, \hat{y}_1> $ = normalized$<\mathbf{Y}_0, \mathbf{y}_1>$
$\quad$ check convergence criteria $maxdiff(p_1, \hat{y}_1)$; $maxdiff(\mathbf{P}_0, \hat{\mathbf{Y}}_0)$
$\quad \mathbf{P}_0 = \hat{\mathbf{Y}}_0;\ p_1 = \hat{y}_1$
$\quad$ perform next iteration $iter = iter + 1$

UNTIL convergence

For the realization of the maximization step, we can exploit the randomization technique which is used for the calculation of $\exp(\mathbf{D}_0 t_i)$. The computation of the likelihood value for element t_i is split into two parts. Define forward likelihood vectors $v^k = \tau(\mathbf{P}_0)^k$, so that element $v^k(x)$ contains the likelihood of being in transient state x after starting with τ and going over k internal jumps among transient states. In a similar way, define a backward likelihood vector $w^k = (\mathbf{P}_0)^k p_1^T$ where the y-th element denotes the likelihood of ending in the absorbing state after k jumps starting in state y. If we consider the sequence of l transitions within $\mathcal{S}_T$ according to the transition probability matrix $\mathbf{P}_0$, then the expression $v^k(x) \cdot \mathbf{P}_0(x,y) \cdot w^{l-k-1}(y)$ denotes the likelihood of $l-1$ transitions in the set of transient states followed by a transition into the absorbing state.

Maximization is done with respect to the transition probabilities in one step, here $k+1$ (i.e., the values in $\mathbf{P}_0$ are chosen to maximize the resulting likelihood values). The elements computed during the maximization steps are multiplied with the probability to perform l jumps before absorption and are collected in the matrix $\mathbf{X}_0^{(i)}$ for element $\hat{t}_i$. As a result we obtain a sequence of $n \times n$ matrices $\mathbf{X}_0^{(i)}$, $i = 1, \ldots, R$. The matrix of integrated transition likelihoods $\mathbf{Y}_0$ is built as a sum of all $\mathbf{X}_0^{(i)}$ with the corresponding probabilities $g(\hat{t}_i)$; so element $\mathbf{Y}_0(x, y)$ contains a weighted sum of likelihoods.

Analogously, we define the column vector $x_1^{(i)}$, where the x-th element contains the likelihood of an event generation out of state x, after reaching state x with k internal jumps. The integrated likelihoods are accumulated in a column vector $y_1 = \sum_{i=1}^{R} g(\hat{t}_i) x_1^{(i)}$ according to their weights. Hence,

$$\mathbf{X}_0^{(i)}(x,y) = \sum_{k=l_i}^{r_i} \beta(k, \alpha \hat{t}_i) \cdot \sum_{l=0}^{k-1} v^l(x) \mathbf{P}_0(x,y) w^{k-l-1}(y), \tag{3}$$

$$x_1^{(i)}(x) = \sum_{k=l_i}^{r_i} \beta(k, \alpha \hat{t}_i) \cdot v^l(x) p_1(x). \tag{4}$$

The normalized matrix $\mathbf{Y}_0$ and vector y_1 define the transition and arrival probabilities in Eqs. (5) and (6) respectively, and can afterwards be used as $\mathbf{P}_0$ and p_1 in the subsequent iteration:

$$\hat{\mathbf{Y}}_0(x,y) = \frac{\mathbf{Y}_0(x,y)}{\mathbf{e}_x \mathbf{Y}_0 \mathbf{e}^T + y_1(x)}, \tag{5}$$

$$\hat{y}_1 = \mathbf{e}^T - \hat{\mathbf{Y}}_0 \mathbf{e}^T. \tag{6}$$

As local convergence criterion we use the maximum value of the absolute difference of all matrix elements $maxdiff(\mathbf{P}, \mathbf{Y}) = \max_{i,j} |\mathbf{P}(i,j) - \mathbf{Y}(i,j)|$, where $\mathbf{P}$ is the value of the matrix of the previous iteration and $\mathbf{Y}$ is the current matrix.

3.2 Approximation of the Autocovariance

The values in real traces are measured with some predefined precision which limits the number of different values in a trace. The analysis of pAug89 and LBL3 traces in [1] shows that they contain only 4% and 6% different elements. This observation can be exploited to reduce the computational effort of the fitting procedure.

In Algorithm 2, to capture the autocovariance we build an array u which includes the different elements from trace t, and define function $idx(t_i)$ which returns the index of t_i in an array of the different elements u (i.e., $u[idx(t_i)] = t_i$). Matrix $\mathbf{P}_0$ and consequently $\mathbf{D}_0$, which have been computed to match the pdf of the trace, remain unchanged such that matrices $\mathbf{T}_j = \mathbf{D}_0[u_j]$, $j = 1 \ldots |u|$ can be precalculated and stored to be used within the fitting iteration to calculate forward (see Eq. (7)) and backward likelihoods. In this way we can expect to save within one iteration cycle about 95% of the effort for computing $\mathbf{D}_0[t_i] = \mathbf{T}_{idx(t_i)}$.

For the representation of the autocovariance, only matrix $\mathbf{P}_1$ is modified. Again the quality of the resulting $\langle \mathbf{D}_0, \mathbf{D}_1 \rangle$ is measured in terms of the likelihood that the MAP generates trace t. For ease of notation we define a row vector of forward likelihood $a^{(i)}$, where element x of the normalized vector $a^{(i)}$ denotes the conditional probability of state x observing the sequence $t_1, \ldots, t_i$, $(i \leq m)$:

$$a^{(i)} = a^{(i-1)} \mathbf{D}_0[t_i] \mathbf{P}_1 \text{ with } a^{(0)} = \tau. \tag{7}$$

Algorithm 2 Capturing of the autocovariance

Input:	$t, u, idx()$ Trace sample, different elements, index function
	$\langle \mathbf{P}_0, \mathbf{P}_1 \rangle$ MAP probability matrices
Output:	$\mathbf{P}_1$ Modified matrix of transitions into absorbing states

calculate $\mathbf{T}_j = \mathbf{D}_0[u_j] \,\forall\, j = 1 : |u|$
REPEAT // capture autocovariance

    calculate $\boldsymbol{\pi}, \boldsymbol{\tau}$
    $a^{(0)} = \boldsymbol{\tau};\ b^{(M)} = \mathbf{e}^T$
    FOR $i = 1 : m\ \ a^{(i)} = a^{(i-1)} \mathbf{T}_{idx(t_j)} \mathbf{P}_1$ END // forward likelihoods
    FOR $i = m : 1\ \ b^{(i)} = \mathbf{T}_{idx(t_j)} \mathbf{P}_1 b^{(i+1)}$ END // backward likelihoods
    FOR $i = 1 : m$
        $v^{(i),k} = a^{(i)} (\mathbf{P}_0)^k$
        $\mathbf{X}_1^{(i)}(x,y) = \sum_{k=l_i}^{r_i} \beta(k, \alpha t_i) \cdot v^{(i),l}(x) \cdot \mathbf{P}_1(x,y) \cdot b^{(i+1)}(y)$
    END
    $\mathbf{Y}_1 = \sum_{i=1}^m \mathbf{X}^{(i)}$
    $\hat{\mathbf{Y}}_1 =$ normalize $\mathbf{P}_0 + \mathbf{Y}_1 = $ stochastic // do NOT modify $\mathbf{P}_0$
    check convergence criteria $maxdiff(\mathbf{P}_1, \hat{\mathbf{Y}}_1)$
    $\mathbf{P}_1 = \hat{\mathbf{Y}}_1$
    perform next iteration $iter = iter + 1$

UNTIL convergence // capture autocovariance

In a similar way, the column vector of backward likelihood $b^{(i)}$ is defined as $b^{(i)} = \mathbf{D}_0[t_i] \mathbf{P}_1 b^{(i+1)}$ with $b^{(m)} = \mathbf{e}^T$. Element $b^{(i)}(x)$ contains the likelihood of observing the sequence $t_i, \ldots, t_m$ before absorption after starting in state x. The complete likelihood of generating t from MAP $\langle \mathbf{D}_0, \mathbf{D}_1 \rangle$ is given by Eq. (8), and has to be maximized:

$$L(t, \langle \mathbf{D}_0, \mathbf{D}_1 \rangle) = \boldsymbol{\tau} \left(\prod_{i=1}^m \mathbf{D}_0[t_i] \mathbf{P}_1 \right) \mathbf{e}^T. \tag{8}$$

Analogously to pdf fitting, we define a row vector $v^{(i),k} = a^{(i)} (\mathbf{P}_0)^k$ and use this likelihood to define elementwise the likelihood matrix $\mathbf{X}_1^{(i)}$ for transitions with arrival (see Eq. (9)). Element $\mathbf{X}_1^{(i)}(x,y)$ contains the likelihood that sequence $t_1, \ldots, t_{i-1}$ was generated and after several internal transitions in the interval $[0, t_i)$ the CTMC generates an arrival event and changes the state from x to y. Matrices $\mathbf{X}_1^{(i)}$ are calculated for all trace elements t_i and the likelihood values of the complete trace are collected in the matrix $\mathbf{Y}_1 = \sum_{i=1}^n \mathbf{X}_1^{(i)}$, which is normalized in Eq. (10) such that $\mathbf{P}_0 + \hat{\mathbf{Y}}_1$ is a stochastic matrix. The normalized matrix $\hat{\mathbf{Y}}_1$ is used later as an estimate for the transition probability matrix $\mathbf{P}_1$:

$$\mathbf{X}_1^{(i)}(x,y) = \sum_{k=l_i}^{r_i} \beta(k, \alpha t_i) \cdot v^{(i),l}(x) \cdot \mathbf{P}_1(x,y) \cdot b^{(i+1)}(y), \tag{9}$$

$$\hat{\mathbf{Y}}_1(x,y) = \frac{\mathbf{Y}_1(x,y)}{\mathbf{e}_x (\mathbf{P}_0 + \mathbf{Y}_1) \mathbf{e}^T}. \tag{10}$$

Algorithm 3 Modified main fitting algorithm

Input: t Trace sample
$\quad\quad\quad\langle \mathbf{D}_0, \mathbf{D}_1 \rangle$ MAP (random initial values)
Output: $\langle \mathbf{D}_0, \mathbf{D}_1 \rangle$ Fitted MAP

Build aggregated trace $< \hat{t}, g(\hat{t}) >$
Build array u with different elements from t and define $idx(t_i)$, $\forall i = 1 \ldots m$
Encode MAP matrices $\mathbf{P}_0 = \mathbf{D}_0/\alpha + \mathbf{I}$, $\mathbf{P}_1 = \mathbf{D}_1/\alpha$
$\epsilon = 10^{-1}$
WHILE $(\epsilon > \varepsilon)$

$\quad$ REPEAT
$\quad\quad\quad \mathbf{P}_0^{(old)} = \mathbf{P}_0$, $\mathbf{P}_1^{(old)} = \mathbf{P}_1$
$\quad\quad\quad$ Calculate π, τ
$\quad\quad\quad$ Algorithm 1 ($\mathbf{P}_0, <\hat{t}, g(\hat{t})>, \alpha, \tau, \epsilon$);
$\quad\quad\quad$ Normalize $\mathbf{P}_0 + \mathbf{P}_1 = stochastic$
$\quad\quad\quad$ Algorithm 2 ($\langle \mathbf{P}_0, \mathbf{P}_1 \rangle, t, u, idx(), \alpha, \epsilon$);
$\quad\quad\quad$ Check convergence $maxdiff(\mathbf{P}_0^{(old)}, \mathbf{P}_0)$, $maxdiff(\mathbf{P}_1^{(old)}, \mathbf{P}_1)$
$\quad$ UNTIL convergence
$\quad \epsilon = \epsilon \cdot 10^{-1}$

END // while ϵ
Decode MAP matrices $\mathbf{D}_0 = \alpha(\mathbf{P}_0 - \mathbf{I})$, $\mathbf{D}_1 = \alpha \mathbf{P}_1$

3.3 Improvements

The two algorithms to fit the MAP according to the pdf and the autocovariance are used in simple form in Algorithm 3. Different modifications can be used to improve the efficiency of the algorithm. One possibility is to start with a larger value of ε in the first iteration and reduce it during the iterations.

Since an iteration of the algorithm to capture the autocovariance requires much more time than an iteration for pdf fitting, we try to reduce the number of autocovariance iterations to speed up convergence. To reduce the number of autocovariance steps, in each iteration the measure of relatively convergence speed $100 \cdot |diff1^{(old)} - diff1(\mathbf{P}_1, \hat{\mathbf{Y}}_1)|/diff1^{(old)}\%$ is calculated, and if this measure is less than 10%, the algorithm steps back to PH fitting.

A specific feature of the proposed algorithm is that matrix elements which are initially zero remain zero till the end of the fitting process. Based on this feature matrices with specific non-zero structures can be generated.

4 Experiments

In this section we empirically analyze the algorithm by fitting three different example traces. For the first trace a sample of 5000 elements is generated from a MAP which exhibit autocorrelation dependencies up to lag 50. As real traces we take sequences of interarrival times from pAug89 and LBL3 traces consisting of 10^6 and $2 \cdot 10^6$ elements respectively, and scale them to mean value 1.

4.1 Influence of Matrix Type

In this series of experiments we try different forms of MAP matrices to find a combination for D_0 and D_1 that captures the pdf and autocovariance with appropriate quality and keeps the effort of fitting low. For the experiments we denote dense matrices as Type 1, matrices with non-zeros in the main and first upper diagonal as Type 3, upper and lower triangular matrices as Type 4 and 5, respectively.

Fitting experiments are conducted with precision $\varepsilon = 10^{-3}$ and randomization rate $\alpha = 5$ for MAPs with 5 states. Values are considered in the interval $[10^{-2} : 10^2]$ with 5 values for each logarithmic scale.

To distinguish different matrix types, we use the notation Cx,Dy for the matrix types of $\langle D_0, D_1 \rangle$. For example C3,D1 means that D_0 is of Type 3 with non-zeros in the main and first upper diagonal and D_1 is a dense matrix. To avoid cluttering up the figures, we exclude the results for MAPs which failed to capture the autocovariance behavior.

Table 1. Likelihood values and fitting time (sec) for different matrix forms

C (D_0)	1	1	1	3	3	4	4	5	5
D (D_1)	1	4	5	1	5	1	5	1	4
corrmap L	-3.087e3	-3.163e3	-3.244e3	-2.951e3	-3.033e3	-2.977e3	-3.037e3	-2.977e3	-3.115e3
fit time	464	58	129	304	103	411	117	164	556
pAug89 L	-8.209e5	-8.31e5	-9.985e5	-8.277e5	-8.295e5	-8.264e5	-8.236e5	-8.559e5	-8.53e5
fit time	2080	2786	98.39	1629	847	704.5	940	4365	1222
lbl3 L	-1.661e6	-1.650e6	-1.654e6	-1.627e6	-1.638e6	-1.667e6	-1.634e6	-1.666e6	-1.675e6
fit time	5023	1512	3009	4889	4046	5366	4056	2672	2297

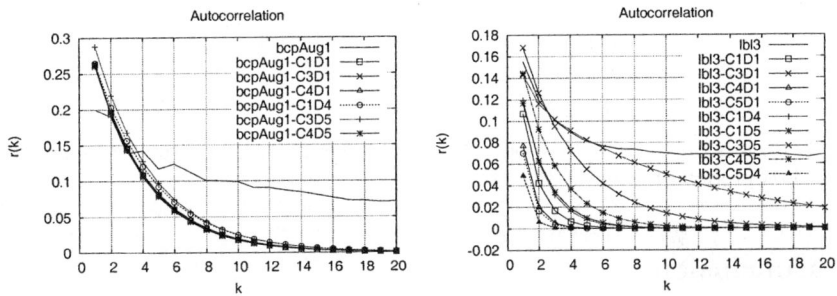

Fig. 1. Influence of the matrix form on autocovariance behavior

The likelihood values for each trace presented in Table 1 are all of the same order and larger values of the likelihoods correspond to better representations of the trace. The differences of fitting quality are also distinguishable in the autocovariance plots in Figure 1. For corrmap and LBL3 traces the distribution function has a simple decaying form which is approximated by a PH distribution adequately. For the pAug89 trace, the combination C1D4 provides a good approximation of the autocovariance, but the distribution approximation is not good. The likelihood value takes both into account, the autocovariance and the pdf fitting quality, and has a value less than for C3D1 or C1D1.

4.2 Queue Performance Analysis

The quality of the approximation is evaluated using performance results for a simple $\cdot/D/1/k$ queuing system. The model is analyzed with trace-driven simulation with NS-2. For the experiments we use the pAug89 trace and fit a MAP with $n = 10$ states and matrix combination C3,D1. From the resulting MAP, a trace is generated and used in the trace driven simulation.

Figure 2 shows results for the example model, namely the loss probability and the probability that the queue contains more than l customers. In all cases, the MAP-model slightly underestimates the real value up to $\rho = 1.0$. For larger utilization, the MAP model overestimates the real value. However, the difference is in most cases relatively small and might be explained by the fact that the MAP captures the autocovariance behavior relatively good up to lag 10, whereas the original trace still exhibits autocovariance dependencies for lag 100.

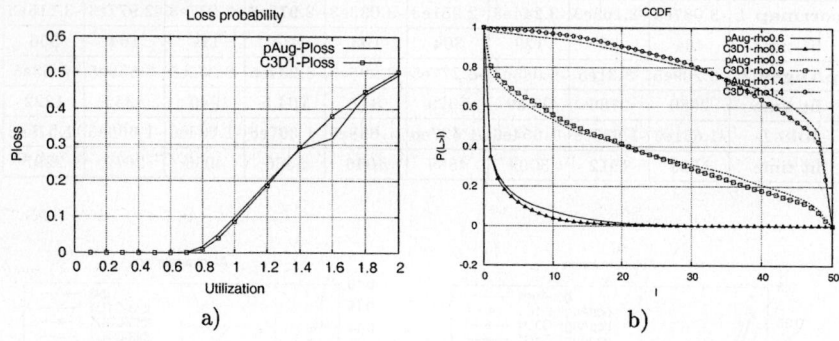

Fig. 2. Results for the queuing system with the original trace and the C3D1 model for a) the loss probability and b) P(L>l)

5 Conclusion

We propose a two step fitting algorithm for capturing the distribution and autocovariance of measured data traces. The algorithm is based on ML estimations and improves common EM algorithms used in the field of MAP fitting. The fitting procedure consists of separate steps for the fitting of the distribution and the autocovariance, and exploits several properties of real data traces. The resulting MAP shows relatively good approximations of the pdf as well as of the autocovariance up to lags of 10-20.

References

1. The internet traffic archive. http://ita.ee.lbl.gov/html/traces.html.
2. Allan Theodor Andersen. *Modelling of Packet Traffic With Matrix Analytic Methods*. PhD thesis, Technical University of Denmark, 1995.
3. Sofia Andersson. *Hidden Markov Models - traffic modeling and subspace methods*. PhD thesis, Lund University, Centre for Mathematical Sciences, 2002.
4. S. Asmussen, O. Nerman, and M. Olsson. Fitting phase type distributions via the EM algorithm. *Scandinavian Journal of Statistics*, 23:419–441, 1996.
5. Peter Buchholz. An EM-algorithm for MAP fitting from real traffic data. In P. Kemper and W. H. Sanders, editors, *Computer Performance Evaluation Modelling Techniques and Tools*, volume 2794 of *LNCS*, pages 218–236. Springer, 2003.
6. Bennett L. Fox and Peter W. Glynn. Computing Poisson probabilities. *Communications of the ACM*, 31(4):440–445, April 1988.
7. Alexander Klemm, Christoph Lindemann, and Marco Lohmann. Modeling IP Traffic Using the Batch Markovian Arrival Process (extended version),. *Perf. Eval.*, 54:149–173, 2003.
8. K. Mitchell and Appie van de Liefvoort. Approximation models of feed-forward G/G/1/N queueing networks with correlated arrivals. *Performance Evaluation*, 51(1), 2003.
9. Marcel F. Neuts. *Structured Stochastic Matrices of M/G/1 Type and Their Applications*. Marcel Dekker, Inc., 1989.
10. António Nogueira, Paulo Salvador, Rui Valadas, and António Pacheco. A hierarchical approach based on MMPP's for modelling self-similar traffic over multiple time scales. In *HET-NETs 2003 Technical Proceedings*, 2003.
11. Sidney Resnick. Modeling data networks. Tr-1345, School of Operations Research and Industrial Engineering, Cornell University, August 2002.
12. Alma Riska, Vesselin Diev, and Evgenia Smirni. An EM-based technique for approximating long-tailed data sets with ph distributions. *Performance Evaluation*, 55:147–164, 2004.
13. T. Ryden. An EM algorithm for estimation in Markov-modulated Poisson processes. *Computational Statistics and Data Analysis*, 21:431–447, 1996.
14. T. Yoshihara, S. Kasahara, and Y. Takahashi. Practical Time-scale Fitting of Self-similar Traffic with MMPP. *Telecommunication Systems*, 17:185–211, 2001.

Performance Evaluation of the 802.16 Medium Access Control Layer[*]

Oleg Gusak, Neal Oliver, and Khosrow Sohraby

School of Computing and Engineering, University of Missouri – Kansas City
5100 Rockhill Rd, Kansas City, MO 64110, USA
{gusako,sohrabyk}@umkc.edu
Intel Europe, 1515 Route 10 Parsippany, NJ 07054
Neal.Oliver@intel.com

Abstract. In this work we investigate performance of the medium access control layer of an 802.16 wireless network consisting of 100 subscriber stations (SSs) and a single base station (BS). Experimental results show that the average packet queuing delay was virtually the same for weighted round robin and weighted fair queuing scheduling algorithms. Another interesting finding is that adapting the uplink/downlink ratio plays a crucial role in performance as the network load increases and channel conditions change. On the other hand, experiments show that for a higher network load, segmentation of large packets is a necessity in order to achieve performance and QoS conformance. We also observed a smaller average queuing delay for smaller values of frame duration.

1 Introduction

The newly developed IEEE 802.16 standard for wireless broadband communications currently receives wide attention from the telecommunications industry as well as from researchers [1,3,5]. The high interest from the industry is mainly based on the ability of 802.16 networks to provide high speed telecommunication service to subscribers which is relatively inexpensive comparing to existing cable and satellite technologies. The interest for the researchers mainly lies in the flexibility of the standard which leaves implementation of performance sensitive parts of the network to the vendor.

In this work we investigate the performance of the Medium Access Control (MAC) layer of a relatively large 802.16 network. In particular, we consider various algorithms for packet scheduling and media access of subscriber stations (SSs) to the network.

In contrast to packet scheduling algorithms operating in a wired network, scheduling algorithms in 802.16 networks operate in a framing (i.e., discrete) environment. Moreover, conditions of the transmitting channel may change over time. Hence, an application of existing wired environment schedulers may not be that straightforward

---

[*] Copyright © 2004 Intel Corporation. All rights reserved.

and therefore requires a thorough performance analysis. The existing research in the wireless scheduling algorithms mainly concentrates on designing fair compensation algorithms for the case of changing channel conditions [1] or address QoS issues coupled with the resource allocation in the physical channel [3].

In this paper we resort to a simulation modeling which most of the time is the only option in performance analysis of complex telecommunication systems. Using the implemented simulation model, we investigate performance of scheduling algorithms which operates in the base station (BS) and subscriber stations (SSs) of the network. Based on preliminarily experiments with the basic configuration of the network, we propose an algorithm for adaptive frame partitioning for downlink and uplink channel and investigate its performance. Finally, we also study performance of the network as a function of the changing transmitting environment, maximum segment size, and the duration of the 802.16 frame.

In the next section, we briefly describe the 802.16 MAC layer and introduce our model. In section 3, we describe experiments we carried out with the model, give the algorithm for frame splitting and grant scheduling, and discuss results of experiments. In section 4, we summarize our findings.

2 802.16 MAC Layer Model

An 802.16 wireless network [2] consists of a BS and a number of SSs. Transmission occurs over a radio channel which is divided into intervals of uniform duration called frames. A number of alternate physical layer protocols are defined in the standard to encode data into frames; in this paper, we only consider systems using orthogonal frequency domain multiplexing (OFDM), in which the frame is divided into a time sequence of OFDM symbols, each of which in turn is composed of a collection of *modulation symbols* multiplexed in frequency, into which data are encoded.

The channel quality, as measured by the signal interference to noise ration (SINR), dynamically changes due to changing weather, obstacles between the BS and an SS, and other effects. In order to maintain the bit error rate below a given threshold, the transmitting node (either the BS or the SS) adjusts the modulation schema used to encode data into the frame. The standard defines a protocol by which the receiving node may request a change of modulation scheme, although a node may apply other proprietary rules to make further adjustments. The modulation schemes in use are encoded in a data structure called a *burst profile*, which is transmitted by the BS to all SSs and used to determine how to decode data from the frame.

The network may operate in time division duplex (TDD) mode, in which the frame is divided into a downlink and uplink subframe, or in frequency division duplex (FDD) mode, in which the separate downlink and uplink channels, each with their own frame structures, are used. In this paper, we consider the case of TDD mode. The channel carries multiple *service flows* of data between users on the BS and SSs, each with their own connection ID, quality of service (QoS) class, and other flow-specific parameters. In the downlink, the BS transmits packets to the SSs, which include both data from the service flows and control messages. It also transmits a *downlink map*, which describes to the SSs where their data is to be found in the downlink subframe, and which burst profile should be used to decode it, and an *uplink map*, which describes to the SSs the bandwidth and location in the uplink subframe that has been reserved for their uplink transmission in the frame. In the uplink, the SSs transmit packets to the BS in the regions of the uplink subframe described to them in the uplink map. The packets contain data from service flows and control messages, including additional bandwidth requests.

The BS scheduler is responsible for scheduling packet transmission in the downlink, and bandwidth grants for the uplink. It therefore must manage queues of service flow data from higher-level protocols and queues of bandwidth requests received from SSs; construct the uplink and downlink maps; and assemble the frame data structure which is subsequently encoded by the physical layer.

Research on physical channel modeling [7] has shown that the change of the SINR level over time can be described by a stochastic process which follows an exponential distribution. Each burst profile defined by the 802.16 standard corresponds to a range of SINR level. Therefore, the entire space of SINR values can be discretized with respect to the burst profiles. Now let each SINR range have an associated state called the channel state. Recall that the SINR changes according to an exponential distribution. Hence, the entire system which describes the state of the channel can be modeled as a discrete-time Markov chain (MC). In our model, we assume that the states of the MC are numbered starting from 0 and that the larger state index correspond to a poorer SINR range. We also assume that p_{ij}, the probability of transition from state i to j, is zero for all i and j such that $|i-j|>1$.

In the next section, we discuss the implementation of the 802.16 model and results of experiments with it. We also introduce an algorithm for adaptive partitioning of the frame between downlink and uplink.

3 Simulation Model and Experiments

The model of an 802.16 network we consider was implemented in OPNET Modeler and consists of 100 SSs and a single BS. Besides these elements there is a node which simulates behavior of the transmission channels each of which corresponds to a burst profile associated with a BS-SS link. Each station is capable of generating packets according to a user specified distribution. The behavior of each channel is controlled by a probability transition matrix P, which is also specified by the user. The BS and SSs are linked together by two broadcast buses (e.g., Ethernet bus) which correspond to downlink and uplink channels. Since we do not operate the channel in a contention mode (e.g., carrier detection multiple access mode), we set the propagation delay in the transmission channel to zero.

In the first set of experiments, we set the physical transmission rate of the downlink and uplink channels to 100 Mb/s, frame duration is set to 5 msec, out of which 4.8 msec are allocated for payload, and the load to the network is set to 80% of the network capacity. The load to the network is symmetric and consists of 100 flows originating in the BS and destined to SSs, one flow per SS, and 100 flows originating in SSs (a single flow per SS) and destined to the BS. In each experiment, the flows can be either data flows or voice flows. Data flows are modeled with exponential packet interarrival time. The distribution of the packet size is truncated Pareto with alpha parameter set to 81 (which is the smallest packet size in bytes), shape parameter set to 1.1 and the maximum packet size set to 1500 bytes. Voice flows are modeled with exponential packet interarrival time. The packet size is uniformly distributed in the range of integer numbers [31..50] (see [4,6] for the explanation of the chosen parameters). For this set of experiments we assume that the channel always stays in a single state (i.e., the physical transmission rate stays at 100 Mb/sec). We also assume that the frame is divided evenly among the downlink and the uplink channels and this division does not change during a simulation run.

In Table 1 we give results for the average queuing delay, which we define as the time elapsed from arrival of a packet until selection for transmission in the current frame. We assume that the packet processing time and hence the frame assembly takes zero time. Hence, all packets selected for transmission in a given frame have the same departure time. We give results for the average queuing delay for packets of the data and voice flows in the queues of the BS arbitrated by the weighted round robin (WRR) algorithm and the weighted fair queuing algorithm (WFQ) [8]. We also give results for the average queuing delay for the packets sent by SSs for the cases when the grant requests submitted by SSs to the BS are arbitrated by WRR or WFQ. Recall that WFQ uses the arrival time of the packet to compute the virtual finishing time [8]. The arrival time of the grant requests is the same since they arrive in the same uplink subframe. Hence, to make the scheduler fair with respect to the packets for which the grant request is issued, as the arrival time of the grant request we take the smallest packet arrival time among the packets in the corresponding SS.

Table 1. Queuing delay (msec) of WRR and WFQ schedulers for BS and a SS[1]

	BS		SS			
	Data	Voice	Data	Voice	Data (-5)	Voice (-5)
WRR	2.53	2.49	7.90	7.56	2.90	2.56
WFQ	2.51	2.49	7.84	7.56	2.84	2.56
Difference	0.63%	0%	0.76%	0%	2.07%	0%

The results show that there is no difference in the average queuing delay for the voice packets scheduled by WRR or WFQ, and that this difference is negligible for the data packets (compare WRR row with WFQ row for each column of the table). This is mainly caused by the discrete environment in which the schedulers operate. According to our assumption, all packets scheduled for transmission in the given

---

[1] 95% confidence intervals for all results on the average queuing delay reported in this paper do not exceed 1% of the measured value.

frame have the same departure time, which is the departure time of the frame. Hence, even though the packets may be selected by WFQ in a different order than in WRR, the set of packets selected for the given frame is more likely to be the same in both cases and hence the queuing delay of the packets is the same. This is more evident for the voice flows in which packet size variability is limited. The size of the data packets varies over a longer interval, and while we observe some difference in the average queuing delay for WRR and WFQ, the difference is insignificant.

Another observation is that the framing environment is the main contributor to the packet queuing delay. Thus, the average queuing delay of the packets processed by the BS is just slightly higher than the half of the frame duration (2.5 msec). On the other hand, the average queuing delay of the packets processed by the SSs has a constant component in it, the frame duration (5 msec), which is the shortest time needed for the grant request to arrive to the BS and for the BS to grant opportunity for the SS to transmit the packet. Hence, in the last two columns of Table 1, we have actually subtracted 5 msec from the measured average queuing delay for the packets processed in SSs; these values we refer to as the net average queuing delays. Note that the net average queuing delay in the SSs for WRR and data flows is 13% higher than in the BS and 11% higher in the SSs for WFQ than in BS; the difference for the voice flows for either algorithm is 3% (compare last two columns with the first two columns, respectively).

Having conducted these preliminary experiments, we turn our attention into how efficiently the frame space is used. On Figure 1, we plot the difference of the frame occupancy between the downlink subframe and the uplink subframe as a fraction of the subframe duration (i.e., 2.5 msec). In other words, let $D(t)$ and $U(t)$ be the time required to transmit the payload of the downlink and uplink subframe, respectively. Then the function we plot in Figure 1 is $\Delta(t) = (D(t)-U(t))/0.0025$.

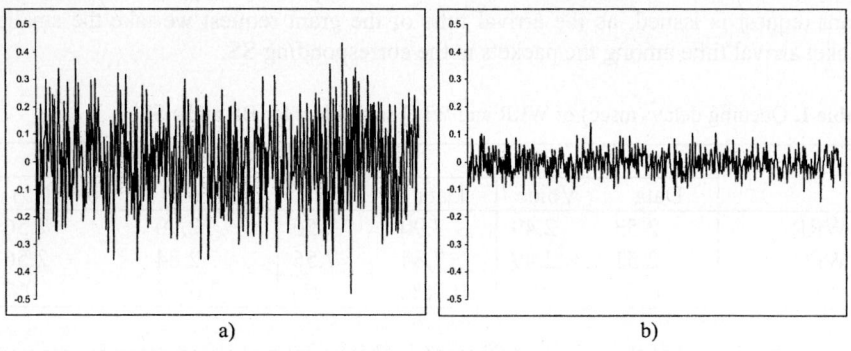

Fig. 1. $D(t)$ for data flows (a) and voice flows (b)

An inspection of Figure 1 shows that for data flows, a significant portion (up to 50 %) of either subframe may be unused while the other subframe can be fully occupied. This suggests using an algorithm which would allow a flexible split point which defines duration of the downlink and uplink subframes. In other words, based on the demand for packet transmission in the base station and the subscriber stations, the algorithm should suggest the duration for the downlink and uplink subframes. Note however, that we do not expect to obtain significant gains in the average queuing delay for voice flows since the unused space of the frame for this case rarely exceeds 10% (see Figure 1, (b)).

We propose the following algorithm which determines duration of the downlink and uplink subframes to be executed every time a new frame is formed at the BS. For this algorithm, we assume that the grant requests submitted by SS to the BS are of aggregate type and that the sum of the grant requests expressed in seconds, U_r, is available at the time a new frame is to be formed at the BS.

Algorithm for adaptive frame partitioning

Input:
- U_r – required duration of the uplink subframe
- F_d – frame duration
- w – average downlink data rate as a percentage of total downlink rate plus uplink data rate

Output:
- D, duration of the downlink subframe formed
- U_g, granted duration of the uplink subframe
  1. if $U_r > F_d \cdot w$, then $D_g = F_d \cdot w$, else $D_g = F_d - U_r$
  2. Form the downlink subframe with duration $D \leq D_g$.
  3. $U_g = F_d - D$

Note that according to this algorithm, the granted duration for the uplink subframe can be larger than the required duration of the uplink subframe. If this is the case, then the unused portion of the uplink subframe can be used for contention intervals specified in the 802.16 standard which can further improve utilization of the frame and reduce the average queuing delay in the queues of SSs. We leave implementation and investigation of this possibility for our future work.

Results with the implemented algorithm are given in Table 2 where we give the net average queuing delay for the data and voice packets scheduled in SSs. Note that due to symmetric load to the network, w of the algorithm is equal to 0.5.

Table 2. Average packet queuing delay for data flows scheduled in SSs

	Fixed Partitioning	Adaptive Partitioning	Difference
WRR	2.90	2.80	3.39%
WFQ	2.84	2.79	1.50%
Difference	2.07%	~0%	

As we predicted in the analysis of Figure 1, the data flow would benefit from the adaptive frame partitioning. The average queuing delay of the packets arbitrated by WRR is almost 3.4% less than in the case of fixed frame partitioning and is 1.5% less for WFQ. Note also that the difference in the average queuing delay between WRR and WFQ is diminished for the case of adaptive frame partitioning. This observation can be exploited if WFQ, which is a computationally intensive algorithm, cannot be run on SSs due to a limited processing power.

In the next set of experiments we consider the effect of changing channel conditions on the performance of the network. Each channel (out of 100) corresponds to a burst profile associated with a SS and is modeled by a 4 state Markov chain that is defined by a probability transition matrix P. We set the transmission rates corresponding to states 0,1,2,3 to 100 Mb/s, 80 Mb/s, 60 Mb/s, and 40 Mb/s, respectively. The transition probabilities of the matrix P are chosen such that the steady state vector π, $P \pi = \pi$, is π =(0.6332, 0.3166, 0.0452, 0.005). We leave all other parameters of the network the same as in the previous experiments and assume that the frame is evenly split between the downlink and uplink. Note that the average capacity of the network under changing channel conditions is about 92 Mb/s, i.e., smaller than in the previous experiments, where it is 100 Mb/s. Therefore, since we left the average arrival rate of the flows the same, the load to the network is higher in this set of experiment and is about 87% of the average network capacity.

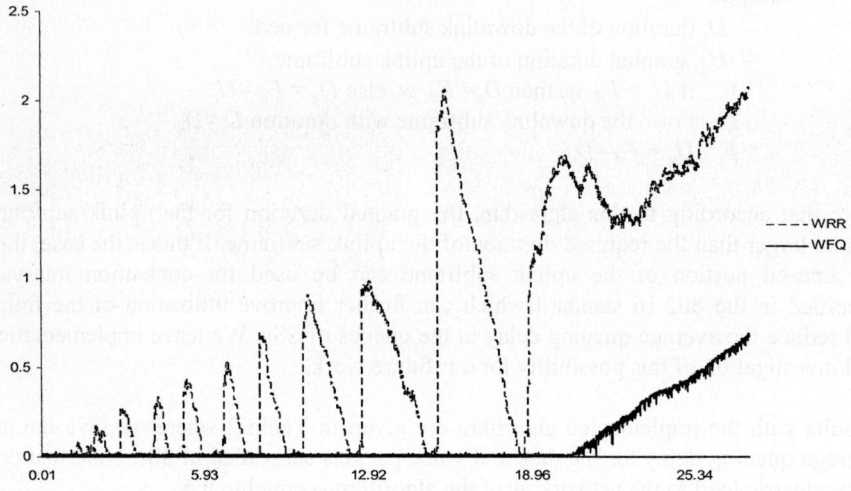

Fig. 2. Transient behavior of the packet queuing delay for WRR and WFQ in a SS

Our first observation is that, in experiments with the data flows the network was not stable in the uplink direction for either the WRR or the WFQ grant requests schedulers. After an initialization period, the SS queues were steadily building up. We demonstrate this observation on Figure 2 by plotting the queuing delay of packets scheduled in a subscriber station. We plot the queuing delay for the case when the grant requests are scheduled by WRR or WFQ.

First, we remark on an "ugly" oscillation behavior of the WRR which is caused by the round robin nature of the algorithm: when queues of the SSs are backlogged, it takes a noticeable amount of time for the scheduler to make a round and to start processing any given queue. During the duration of the round, queue size and hence queuing delay grows until the scheduler visits the queue again. Second, even though WFQ showed a better performance than WRR at the start of the simulation run, it also could not cope with the changing channel conditions.

On the other hand, we observed that in the experiments with the voice flows, in which the network load is the same, the network was stable in the downlink and uplink direction. Hence, we may guess that the problem with the data flows is the size of the data packets which can be as large as 1500 bytes. To support this idea, we plot in Figure 3 utilization of the uplink subframe over the simulation run.

The plot in the Figure 3 shows that at the time when the queues in the SSs start to build up, the uplink subframe utilization drops to about 77% on average, which is quite below the network load of 87%. Thus, even though the SSs are backlogged, the uplink subframe is 23% empty on average. This is caused by the large maximum packet size, and consequently the large maximum size of the grant requests. When the queues in SSs are backlogged, the SSs send grant requests of the maximum possible size. Hence, the unused portion of the frame can be as large as the time required to transmit a 1500 byte packet. The situation gets even worse due to the degrading quality of the channel, during which more time is needed to transmit the large packet.

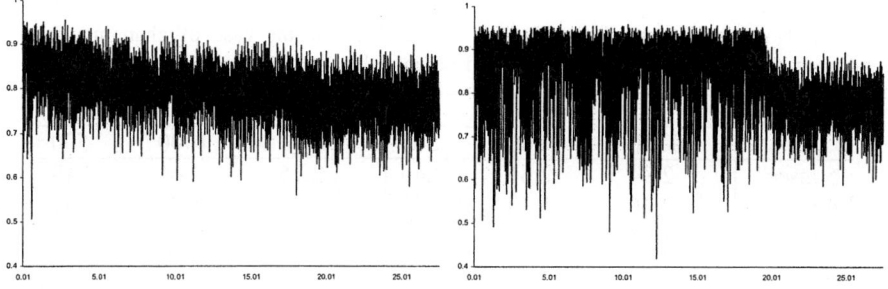

Fig. 3. Frame utilization over a simulation run for WRR and WFQ grant requests schedulers

Thus, a straightforward solution to the situation with the unstable uplink channel is a segmentation of the large data packets. Since this problem can also be addressed by applying the adaptive frame partitioning algorithm, the system operator has alternate solutions to this problem.

Table 3. Net average packet queuing delay for the case of changing channel conditions

	Fixed partitioning		Adaptive Partitioning		
	1000	500	1500	1000	500
WRR	2.83	2.51	2.94	2.66	2.49
WFQ	2.77	2.49	2.75	2.61	2.48

In Table 3, we give the net average packet queuing delay for the experiments with the changing channel conditions, adaptive frame partitioning, and data packet segmentation, with the largest segment size equal to 1000 and 500 bytes.

The results of Table 3 show that the net average queuing delay gets smaller with decreasing maximum segment size. On the other hand, a network which implements adaptive frame partitioning algorithm always provides smaller net average queuing delay than the network with the fixed frame partitioning for the same scheduling algorithm and the maximum segment size. Note also that the difference in the average queuing delay for the adaptive and the even partitioning becomes smaller as the maximum segment size decreases.

In the final set of experiment, we consider the influence of frame duration on the average packet queuing delay in the queues of the SSs. As we already noted, the average queuing delay of the packets sent by SSs has a constant term which is the duration of the frame. Hence, for smaller frame sizes, we would expect a smaller average queuing delay, which we verify in our experiments. However, not only is the average packet queuing delay smaller for smaller duration of the frame, but the net queuing delay is as well. This can be seen in Table 4, in which we give results for the net average queuing delay for various values of the frame duration and the maximum segment size for the adaptive frame partitioning and changing channel conditions.

Table 4. Net average queuing delay for data packets for the case of changing channel conditions, adaptive frame partitioning, and different values of the frame duration

	WRR			WFQ		
	1500	1000	500	1500	1000	500
5 msec	2.94	2.66	2.49	2.75	2.61	2.48
4 msec	2.46	1.92	1.82	2.26	1.89	1.81
3 msec	1.95	1.54	1.47	1.76	1.50	1.44

The results of Table 4 also show that the difference in the net average queuing delay between WRR and WFQ is larger for smaller values of frame duration. Thus, for 5 msec frames, the difference is 6% whereas for the 3 msec frame the difference is 10%. Finally we would like to note that the difference in the absolute average queuing delay for the "best case" (3 msec frames, 500 bytes maximum segment size, WFQ) and the "worst case" (5 msec frames, 1500 bytes maximum segment size, WRR) is 43%. Hence, a smaller frame size and the smaller maximum segment size can be suggested to decrease the average queuing delay in the queues of SSs. Obviously, the choice of the frame size duration and the maximum segment size are subjects to constraints of the processing power of the BS and the SSs.

4 Concluding Remarks

In this work we considered performance of the medium access control layer of an 802.16 wireless network consisting of 100 subscriber stations (SSs) and a single base station (BS). Our first finding is that due to the framing transmitting environment, the average packet queuing delay is virtually the same for weighted round robin and weighted fair queuing scheduling algorithms. Having analyzed utilization of the frame, we proposed an algorithm for adaptive partitioning of the 802.16 frame. We have shown that adapting the uplink/downlink ratio plays a crucial role in performance as the network load increases and channel conditions change. On the other hand, our experiments show that for a higher network load, segmentation of large packets is a necessity in order to achieve performance and QoS conformance. In addition to that, we observed a smaller average packet queuing delay for smaller values of frame duration.

References

1. Cao, Y., Li, V.O.K.: Scheduling Algorithms in Broadband Wireless Networks. Proceedings of the IEEE **89**(1) (2001) 76 – 87
2. Draft IEEE Standard for Local and Metropolitan Area Networks. Part 16: Air Interface for Fixed Broadband Wireless Access Systems, REVd/D3-2004
3. Ergen, M., Coleri, S., Varaiya, P.: QoS Aware Adaptive Resource Allocation Techniques for Fair Scheduling in OFDMA Based Broadband Wireless Access Systems. IEEE Transactions on Broadcasting **49**(4) (2003) 362–370
4. Gusak, O., Oliver, N., Sohraby, K.: Efficient Approximation of Multiplexed Voice Traffic, In: 15th IASTED International Conference on Modelling and Simulation (MS 2004), Marina del Rey. (2004) 475-479
5. Hawa, M., Petr, D. W.: Quality of Service Scheduling in Cable and Broadband Wireless Access Systems. In: Tenth International Workshop on Quality of Service (IWQoS 2002), Miami Beach. (2002)
6. IP transport in UTRAN Work Task. Technical Report 25.933 v1.0.0. Third Generation Partnerhip Project (3GPP) (2001)
7. Razavilar, J, Liu, K.J. Ray, Marcus, S. I.: Jointly Optimized Bit-Rate/Delay Control Policy for Wireless Packet Networks with Fading Channels. IEEE Transactions on Communications **50**(3) (2002) 484–494
8. Zhang, H.: Service Disciplines for Guaranteed Performance Service in Packet-Switching Networks. Proceedings of the IEEE **83**(10) (1995) 1374–1396

Fixed Size and Variable Size Packet Models in an Optical Ring Network: Complexity and Simulations

Dominique Barth[1], Johanne Cohen[2], Lynda Gastal[3], Thierry Mautor[1], and Stéphane Rousseau[1]

[1] PRiSM, UVSQ, 45 Av. des Etats-Unis, F-78035 Versailles, France
{Dominique.Barth,Thierry.Mautor,Stephane.Rousseau}@prism.uvsq.fr
[2] LORIA, Campus Scientifique BP2039, F-54506 Vandoeuvre les Nancy, France
Johanne.Cohen@loria.fr
[3] LRI, Bt 490 Université Paris Sud, 91405 Orsay Cedex, France
gastal@lri.fr

Abstract. In this paper, we compare the use of two packet models in slotted optical ring networks: a model where each packet has to be routed in consecutive slots, and a model where the slots that form a packet can be routed independently. We first focus on the algorithmic complexity of the related problems. Then, we give the results we obtain with an OMNET simulator in terms of packets' overdelay and jitter.

1 Introduction

All optical packet networks represent a challenging and attractive technology to provide a large bandwidth for future networks. Convergence between Internet and optical networks is also a major key point in the conception of the future telecommunication networks [7]. As mentioned by the ITU [5], the architectural choices for the interaction between IP and optical network layers, particularly the routing and signaling aspects are keys to the successful deployment of next generation networks (NGN). This is also a major topic of some working groups of the IETF [6]. This study concerns the DAVID project[4] we participate in. The DAVID optical network is a WAN interconnecting optical MANs, each one consisting of disjoint optical slotted rings [1]. Metropolitan optical rings have also been studied in the IST-1999-10402 European project METEOR. One of the question addressed in the DAVID project and in some other studies was the choice of the packet format and size transported by the slotted ring [2,10,9,8]. In this context, we compare here the communication efficiencies of a simple optical ring network under two packet models: a fixed size and a variable size packet models. A packet to be emitted by a node on the ring consists here of a sequence of slots. At each communication step, each node accesses the slot of the ring located on him. If the data contained by this slot is intended for him, the

---

[4] Data and Voice Integration over DWDM, European project of the 5th PCRD.

node reads it and removes the data from the slot (it becomes empty). If the slot is empty, the node can use it to send a new slot of a packet to be sent to a given destination. We consider two models to be compared here. In the *fixed size packet* model, all the slots composed of the same packet can be sent independently on the ring (i.e., each slot is considered as an independent packet of fixed size 1). In the *variable size packet* model, the sequence of slots corresponding to a packet have to be sent contiguously on the ring. The advantage of this second model is that there is a jitter equal to $sz(P) - 1$ and thus no need of memory in the destination node to reconstitute each packet. But, the sending protocol in each node needs to be much more complex.

The purpose of this study is to compare variable size packet and fixed size packet models from three points of view:

- Determining the complexity of obtaining an optimal scheduling in these two models;
- Evaluating performances of each model in terms of packet overdelay and jitter;
- Giving a distributed management algorithm for the variable size model.

Regarding the first two points, as we want the difficulty to be linked only to the models behaviors and not to the network control, we assume slotted rings with only one wavelength. We focus here on a network consisting of one only ring. We also give some results about two rings connected by a switch.

2 Models and Problems

Let us consider a ring network R connecting N nodes with only one slotted wavelength (with K slots on each link). Each node on this ring could have some packets to send to another nodes. Each such packet P is characterized by the origin node: $or(P)$, the destination node: $dest(P)$, the size in number of slots: $sz(P)$, the time at which it becomes available in $or(P)$: $dispo(P)$ and the distance (number of slots = number of steps) from $or(P)$ to $dest(P)$: $dist(P) = K * ((dest(P) - or(P)) \mod N)$. We also consider the time $First(P)$ (respectively, $Last(P)$) of packet P at which its first slot (respectively, last slot) is sent on the ring. Different measures can be defined and applied on each packet P. The delay, defined by $Delay(P) = (dist(P) + Last(P) - dispo(P))$, represents the time between the arrival of the packet on the origin node and the end of its transmission, i.e., the end of its reading on the destination node. The jitter, defined by $Jitter(P) = (Last(P) - First(P))$, represents the time between the beginning and the end of the emission of a packet. The overdelay, defined by $OvDel(P) = Last(P) - Dispo(P) - sz(P) + 1$, represents the difference between the delay of P and its minimal possible delay (equal to $dist(P) + sz(P) - 1$). This measure, inspired from some works on scheduling, is interesting to compare the delays of packets of different sizes.

The variable size packet (VSP) model has a jitter constraint: for each packet P, we want $Jitter(P) = sz(P) - 1$. This implies that all the slots of a packet have to be sent contiguously on the ring. Let us remark that, in this model, the overdelay of a packet P is equal to: $OvDel(P) = First(P) - Dispo(P)$. In the fixed size packet (FSP) model there is no such constraint and all the slots of a same packet can be sent independently of the others. Thus, the jitter is in this case an evaluation parameter of the behavior of the network.

As previously indicated, several objective functions can be considered for this problem ($Overdelay$, $Jitter$, $Cmax$). In this section, we have decided to focus on two of these objectives. The first criterion ($Cmax$) is the classical MS makespan criterion that consists of minimizing the number of steps needed to send all packets to their destination, and thus the time of reception of the last packet. The second criterion called MD $OvDel$ consists of minimizing the maximal overdelay of the packets. In order to formalize these two problems, we consider static instances: each node contains a finite and given set of packets. Moreover, we consider a centralized model where each node has a global vision of the network. In terms of complexity, we have thus to consider the following problems:

Problem 1. MS-VSP-Scheduling. Let there be a ring R, a set S of packets, an integer B. Does there exist a scheduling of S on R such that all the packets have reached their destinations after at most B steps, with the constraint $Jitter(P) = sz(P) - 1$ for each packet P?

Problem 2. MD-VSP-Scheduling. Let there be a ring R, a set S of packets, an integer B. Does there exist a scheduling of S on R such that the maximal OverDelay $OvDel(P)$ over all packets P is less than or equal to B, with the constraint $Jitter(P) = sz(P) - 1$ for each packet P?

Of course, we have the same problems for the FSP model called MS-FSP-Scheduling and MD-FSP-Scheduling (with the constraint on the jitter is removed).

2.1 Problem Complexity

Now, we focus on the complexity of MS-VSP-Scheduling problem.

Theorem 1. *The MS-VSP-Scheduling problem is NP-complete.*

Proof. It is easy to see that MS-VSP-Scheduling problem belongs to NP since a nondeterministic algorithm needs only to guess a scheduling S on R and check in polynomial time that the delay of all packets in S is less than or equal to B.

We reduce 3-PARTITION to MS-VSP-Scheduling problem. 3-PARTITION is defined as follows [3].

Problem 3. 3-PARTITION Problem. Let there be a finite set C of $3m$ elements $\{a_1, \ldots, a_{3m}\}$, a bound $\beta \in Z^+$ and a size $s(a) \in Z^+$ such that $\sum_{a \in C} s(a) = m\beta$. Can C be partitioned into m disjoint sets $C_1, C_2, \ldots, C_m$ such that, for $1 \leq i \leq m$, $\sum_{a \in C_i} s(a) = \beta$? Recall that 3-PARTITION is NP-complete in the strong sense. Let there be a finite set C of $3m$ elements, a bound $\beta \in Z^+$

and a size $s(a) \in Z^+$ such that $\sum_{a \in C} s(a) = m\beta$ be an arbitrary instance of 3-PARTITION denoted by I. We transform instance I into an instance I' of MS-VSP-Scheduling problem. Instance I' is composed of a ring R with 4 nodes numbered $1, 2, 3, 4$ with K slots on each link, where $K = m(\beta+1) - 1$. The set S of packets has $3m$ elements $p_1, \ldots, p_{3m}$ such that for $1 \leq i \leq 3m$, $sz(p_i) = s(a_i)$, $dispo(p_i) = 0$, $or(p_i) = 2$, $dest(p_i) = 3$. At time 0, ring R contains some packets that are already transmitted.

- The link connecting node 4 and node 1 contains K slots called $slot^{4 \to 1}(1), \ldots,$ $slot^{4 \to 1}(K)$ and there exists a packet z_0 of size 1 such that packet z_0 is contained by slot $slot^{4 \to 1}(K)$.
- The link connecting node 1 and node 2 such that it contains K slots called $slot^{1 \to 2}(1), \ldots, slot^{1 \to 2}(K)$ and there are m packets $z_1, \ldots, z_m$ of size 1 such that for $1 \leq i \leq m$, packet z_i is contained by slot $slot^{1 \to 2}(K - i \times (\beta + 1))$.

The construction of our instance of MS-VSP-Scheduling problem is completed by setting $K = m(\beta + 1) - 1$ and $B = m(\beta + 1) - 1$. It is easy to see how this construction can be accomplished in polynomial time. All that remains to be shown is that the desired partition exists if and only if there exists a scheduling having all the stated properties.

First, assume that there exists a partition $C' = \{C_1, C_2, \ldots, C_m\}$ such that for $1 \leq i \leq m$, $\sum_{a \in C_i} sz(a) = \beta$. Let i be an integer such that $1 \leq i \leq m$. We consider the partition C_i. Without losing generality, we set $C_i = \{a_{i^1}, \ldots, a_{i^t}\}$, where t depends on the C_i, we will construct a scheduling such that

for each $j \in [1, \ldots, t]$, $First(p_{ij}) = (\beta + 1) \times (i - 1) + \sum_{\alpha=1}^{j-1} sz(p_{i^\alpha})$.

Note that the overdelay of packet p_{ij} is $Last(p_{ij}) = First(p_{ij}) + sz(p_{ij})$. Since $Last(p_{ij}) < B$, we construct a scheduling having all the stated properties. Figure 3 is an example considering only nodes 1 and 2 and the link between them. In this example, $m = 3$, $\beta = 4$, $B = 14$.

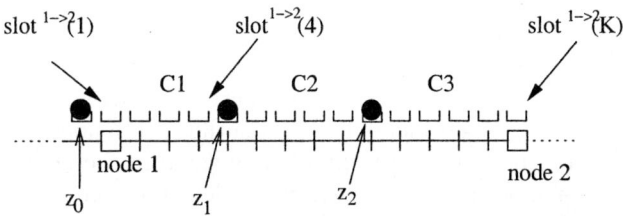

Fig. 1. Proof of transformation in Theorem 1 for $m = 3$ and $\beta = 4$

Conversely, assume that there exists a scheduling S on R such that the overdelay over all packets of S is less or equal to B. Now, we will construct a partition of m elements $C_1, C_2, \ldots, C_m$ such that for $1 \leq i \leq m$, $\sum_{a \in C_i} s(a) = \beta$. First, we focus on the property of such a scheduling. Each packet p_i, $1 \leq i \leq 3m$

satisfies the following property: $OvDel(p_i) \leq B$. It implies that all packets p_i, $1 \leq i \leq 3m$, are inserted before the slot containing packet z_0 arrives at node n_2.

Now, we construct set C_i, $1 \leq i \leq m$: a_j belongs to C_i if $(\beta+1) \times (i-1) < First(p_j) < i \times (\beta+1)$. First assume that $i > 2$. By construction, packets z_{i-1} and z_i arrive at time $(i-1) \times (\beta+1)$ and $i \times (\beta+1)$ respectively. Since, for all packets P have $sz(P) - 1$ as jitter, all slots containing a part of p_j should be contiguous: they must be between slots containing packets z_{i-1} and z_i. Thus, we get the following property $\sum_{j:a_j \in C_i} sz(p_j) \leq \beta$ and $\sum_{a_j \in C_i} s(a_j) \leq \beta$. We apply the same argument for the case where $i = 1$. So set $\{C_1, C_2, \ldots, C_m\}$ is partition of C such that for $1 \leq i \leq m$, $\sum_{a \in C_i} s(a) = \beta$.

So, we have shown that the desired partition exists if and only if there exists a scheduling having all the stated properties. This concludes the proof. □

3 One Ring Distributed Model

Let us consider the ring network presented in Section 2. In an off-line model, with a centralized management, finding a scheduling that minimizes either the delay or the jitter cannot be obtained in a polynomial time. From now on, we study a distributed management protocol in an on-line model. Quite obviously, in such a model, minimizing the criteria previously defined, cannot be obtained in polynomial time. Considering the two models (FSP and VSP) we present a management protocol in order to send packets contained in nodes to their destinations. But first, we present an access control strategy in each node to decide which packet can be sent and which one first.

In a distributed model, each node sees only the slot upon it at each step. If this slot indicates the number of slots in the free zone, the node knows if it can send a packet of a given size or not. Thus, the node knows the maximal packet length that can be put into this free zone. The access control protocol has to choose which packet or which subset of packets to put into it, if it is possible. When a slot contains data (or packets) it is considered as taken. In this case, when a node meets such a slot, it takes the packet if this packet is destined for it. The slot becomes free again and the node can use it. Thus, when a node is in front of a free zone, it tries to put one of its packets into it. However, this free zone could not be large enough to send any packet. In such a case, the node can reserve this zone in order to merge it with another contiguous one. Thanks to this reservation, the node is sure to find it free again in the next turn. For the other nodes, the slot seems to be taken but it does not contain any packet. In such a packet, the origin node is also the destination.

Because the constraint on the jitter does not occur in the FSP scheduling model, there is no need to have a free zone as large as a packet to send it. Indeed, a packet can be sent using severals disjoint free zones. Thus, in the distributed management protocol, a packet is put in the first possible free slot. However, in the VSP scheduling model, we assume that a node receiving a packet of S slots creates a free zone of S slots. Similarly, a node putting a packet of L slots into a free zone of $S > L$ slots creates after it a free zone of $S - L$ free slots. The consequence of such a basic distributed control is that the ring can become a cyclic sequence of free zone steps, each one being too short to be used by any node. Consequently, we have to enhance this distributed control in order to be able to merge consecutive free zones.

We now present our distributed management protocol in the VSP model.

3.1 Distributed Management Protocol in the VSP Model

In the VSP model, packets have to be sent so that the constraint on the jitter is respected. Before putting a packet, the node has to be sure to access a free zone large enough to put the packet in it. A free zone is made of a set of free slots. Each free slot of a free zone indicates the number of consecutive free slots left. Then when a node receives the first slot of a free zone, it is informed of the length of the free zone. However, as we said before, the ring can become a cyclic sequence of small free zones in which none of the packets can be put without being split.

First Part of the Distributed Management Protocol in the VSP Model.

1. When a node receives a taken slot:
   (a) If the packet inside the zone is destined for this node, then it takes it and considers the slot as free.
   (b) If the packet inside the zone is not destined for itself, then it does nothing.
2. When a node receives a reserved slot:
   (a) If the slot has been reserved by this node, then it makes it free again and considers this slot as such. It updates the length of the whole free zone, in the case where several reserved zones are adjacent.
   (b) If the packet has not been reserved by this node, then it considers this slot as not free.
3. When a node receives a free slot:
   (a) If the node has packets to send and the free zone indicated by the slot is large enough to put in one of its packets, then it sends a packet according to the $FIFO$ strategy. It updates the length of the free zone remaining.
   (b) If the node has packets to send but the free zone indicated by the slot is not large enough to put in one of its packets, then:
      i. If this free zone is just after with a free zone reserved by this node then it reserves it.
      ii. If the node has not reserved a free zone yet then it reserves this one.
      iii. In other cases, the node lets this free zone go as it is.
   (c) If the node does not have packets to send, then it lets the slot free.

When a node reserves a free zone, it is able to know the number of adjacent free zones and so the total length of the reserved zone. Then when this reserved zone reaches again the node, each slot has the same number of free slots as before.

One problem remains using this protocol. Some packets cannot be sent because they are too long. It is possible to have packets remaining in nodes and to be not able to send them to their destination. For example, consider a two node ring network with two free zones of length one. Assume that each node has to send one packet of length two. Then they have to reserve at least two contiguous slots and merge them in one free zone of length two. But they reserve one slot each other and this prevents them from reserving two contiguous slots. This is a deadlock problem.

Second Part of the Protocol. At each time slot, a single node has the highest priority. This priority allows it to reserve a zone that belongs to another node if and only if this zone follows a free zone. The priority changes periodically among nodes in order to ensure some fairness. In an off-line VSP distributed model, the distributed management protocol, using the priority, ensures each packet to reach its destination and, by using the priority, it ensures to merge at least two contiguous free zones in two turns, or at least three contiguous zones in $3 + [\#nodes - 1]/(\#nodes)$ turns. Proofs are available in [4].

3.2 Simulation Results

In this section, we present results from simulations. We have considered a ring of 10 nodes and 9 slots between each pair of nodes. Thus, the nodes can use 90 slots to send their packets. We focus on three kinds of traffic. The first one, called *traffic C*, is characterized by a long period of small packets and a short period of large packets. The second one, called *traffic G*, is characterized by a short period of small packets and a long period of large packets. The third one, called *traffic I*, is characterized by a short period of small packets and a short period of large packets.

Results Analysis. Even if many measures can be investigated with such a simulation model, we have focused on two parameters. The first one is the average overdelay of the packets in order to study the influence of the length of packets on the average overdelay. The second one is the average jitter. In Figure 2, we compare the average overdelay average in the FSP and the VSP models. We study the average jitter value according to traffic type.

As it can be seen in Figure 2, the overdelay is better in the FSP model than in the VSP model. Also, the FSP model accepts a larger data flow than the VSP model before the network is saturated. The network is saturated when the delay increases indefinitely. Then the average overdelay is not bounded. In the VSP model, when the data flow is over 0.13 amount of packets per time unit, the network is saturated, whereas in the FSP model the network can accept at least 0.2 amount of packets per time unit before being saturated. The amount of packets per time unit is the number of packet of size 1 generated by time unit. Referring to Figure 2, the average jitter increases as a function of the data traffic. In fact, as expected, the average jitter is better in traffic C where there are smaller packets and deteriorates as the number of large packets increases.

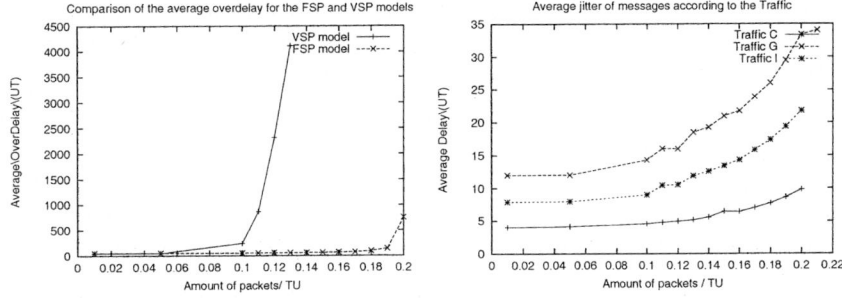

Fig. 2. Comparison of average overdelay in FSP and VSP models and average jitter under different types of traffic

4 Conclusions and Perspectives

We have shown that finding optimal packets scheduling is difficult in both FSP and VSP models. For this last one, in an online and distributed context, there is also the problem of merging consecutive free zones to avoid live-locks. The cost of a protocol realizing this concatenation can be evaluated in terms of resource use, and the one we give here ensures that at each step, about 80% of the slots are used to carry data, and this is not to the detriment of the overdelay of large packets.

References

1. Barth, D., Cohen, J., Fragopoulou, P., Hébuterne, G.: Wavelengths Assignment on a Ring All-Optical Metropolitan Area Network. In: Proceedings of the 3rd Workshop on Approximation and Randomization Algorithms in Communication Networks (ARACNE 2002), Rome Italy. (2002)
2. Bianco, A., Bonsignori, M., Leonardi, E., Neri, F.: Variable-Size Packets in Slotted WDM Ring Networks. Optical Network Design and Modelling (ONDM 2002), Torino, Italy. (2002)
3. Garey, M.R., Johnson, D.S.: Computers and Intractability: A Guide to the Theory of NP-Completeness. Series of Books in the Mathematical Sciences. W.H. Freeman and Company (1979)
4. Gastal, L., Mautor, T., Rousseau, S., Barth, D., Cohen, J.: Comparison of Fixed Size and Variable Size Packet Models in an Optical Ring Network. Technical report, PRiSM, UMR 8144, University Versailles-Saint Quentin, 45 avenue des Etats Unis, 78035 Versailles Cedex, France. (2004)
5. International Telecommunications Union. Convergence between Internet and Optical Networks. ITU News Magazine **2** (2002)
   http://www.itu.int/itunews/issue/2002/06/convergence.html
6. Jain, R., et al.: IP over Optical Networks: A Summary of Issues. IPO and MPLS Working Groups Internet Draft for IETF. (2001)
   http://www.cse.ohio-state.edu/~jain/ietf/ftp/draft-osu-ipo-mpls-issues-01.pdf

7. Rajagopalan, B., Pendarakis, D., Saha, D., Ramamoorthy, R.S., Bala, K.: IP over Optical Network: Architectural Aspects. IEEE Communications Magazine **38** (2000) 94–102
8. Yao, S., Yoo, S.J.B., Mukerjee, B.: A Comparison Study between Slotted and Unslotted All-Optical Packet-Switched Network with Priority-Based Routing. In: Proceedings of OFC 2001, Anaheim, California (2001)
9. Yu, X., Cheng, Y., Qiao, C.: A Study of Traffic Statistics of Assembled Burst Traffic in Optical Burst Switched Networks. In: Proceedings of the IEEE Optical Networking and Communications Conference (OPTICOMM), Boston, Massachusetts (2002) 149-159
10. Zapata, A., Düser, M., Spencer, J., de Miguel, I., Bayvel, P., Breuer, D., Hanik, N., Gladisch, A.: Investigation of Future Optical Metro Ring Networks Based on 100-Gigabit Ethernet (100GbME). ITG Fachbericht, Vol. 175. VDE, Berlin, Germany (2003) 89-98

A Tabu Search Algorithm for Sparse Placement of Wavelength Converters in Optical Networks*

Namik Sengezer and Ezhan Karasan

Electrical and Electronics Engineering Dept.
Bilkent University, 06800 Bilkent, Ankara, Turkey
{namik,ezhan}@ee.bilkent.edu.tr

Abstract. In this paper, we study the problem of placing limited number of wavelength converting nodes in a multi-fiber network with static traffic demands and propose a tabu search based heuristic algorithm. The objective of the algorithm is to achieve the performance of full wavelength conversion in terms of minimizing the total number of fibers used in the network by placing minimum number of wavelength converting nodes. We also present a greedy algorithm and compare its performance with the tabu search algorithm. Finally, we present numerical results that demonstrate the high correlation between placing a wavelength converting node and the amount of transit traffic passing through that node.

1 Introduction

All optical WDM networks, providing extremely large bandwidths, is one of the most promising solutions for the increasing need for high-speed data transport. In all optical networks, data is transmitted solely in the optical domain from source to destination without being converted into the electronic form [1]. This is achieved with the use of optical cross-connects (OXCs) which can optically switch the data from an incoming fiber to an outgoing fiber. There are two types of OXCs: wavelength-selective cross-connects (WSXCs) and wavelength-interchanging cross-connects (WIXCs). Any signal passing through a WSXC should occupy the same wavelength on the incoming and outgoing fibers. In WIXCs, the wavelength of the signal can be changed during switching [2].

Transmissions between nodes are done by establishing lightpaths that are direct optical connections between their source and destination nodes. In a wavelength selective network, which is comprised of WSXCs only, the same wavelength must be used on all the links along a lightpath. This is called the wavelength continuity constraint. This constraint can be removed by using WIXCs. The high cost of WIXCs leads to the idea of optical networks with sparse wavelength conversion where only a limited number of nodes in the network are equipped with WIXCs [3-9].

---

* This work was partially supported by the EU-FP6 IST-NoE e-Photon/ONe and by The Scientific and Technical Research Council of Turkey (TUBITAK) under projects EEEAG-101E048 and EEAG-199E005.

In sparse wavelength conversion, the main objective is to locate the limited number of WIXCs to achieve the optimum performance. It is shown that the problem of finding the locations of the minimum number of WIXCs so that no more wavelengths are needed than if there were WIXCs at all nodes is NP-complete [10].

The performance measures considered in the literature change with the type of traffic. In the dynamic traffic case, the overall blocking probability and in the static traffic case the number of WIXCs or the total cost of the network are generally used as performance measures. There are a number of studies in the literature focusing on each of these cases. In [3] and [4], the paths are divided into segments by WIXCs, and it is shown that the end-to-end blocking probability of a path is minimized when each segment has equal blocking probability. The optimal placement of WIXCs minimizing the overall network blocking probability for arbitrary network topologies is obtained by using an exhaustive search method employing auxiliary graphs in [5]. The relationship between the Routing and Wavelength Assignment (RWA) algorithms and the WIXC placement algorithm is investigated in [6], and two different WIXC placement heuristics minimizing the overall blocking probability are proposed. An optimization model for WIXC placement is presented in [7] based on the formulation of the end-to-end success probability between a pair of nodes as a function of WIXC locations. The issue of designing transparent optical networks minimizing the network cost while establishing all the lightpaths is studied in [8], and three heuristics are proposed for wavelength assignment and WIXC placement. A scalable solution technique for optimum placement of WIXCs is presented in [9]. The overall problem is modeled by a sequence of Integer Linear Programming (ILP) formulations with the objective of minimizing the number of WIXCs necessary to achieve the minimum fiber usage in the network.

In this paper, we assume static traffic demands in a multi-fiber network with fixed number of wavelengths on each fiber. The main objective is to place the minimum number of WIXCs necessary for achieving the minimum fiber usage which is obtained in a network having full wavelength conversion capability. We utilize an ILP based solution using path formulation for the routing problem and an iterative heuristic for the wavelength assignment. For the WIXC placement, we propose a tabu search based algorithm. This algorithm can find solutions in a reasonable amount of time and can be used in conjunction with different routing and wavelength assignment algorithms. We also implement a greedy search algorithm for WIXC placement and use its performance as a basis for comparison with the tabu search algorithm.

The remainder of the paper is organized as follows. In Section 2, the routing and wavelength assignment algorithms used in this study are presented. The greedy and tabu search algorithms proposed for the WIXC placement problem are introduced in Section 3. Section 4 presents some numerical results and the performance comparison of these algorithms. Finally, the conclusions are discussed in Section 5.

2 Routing and Wavelength Assignment

Although the routing and wavelength assignment problems can be solved jointly, the two subproblems are decoupled in this paper in order to reduce the computational complexity of the overall problem.

2.1 Routing Problem

The final objective in this work is to use the same number of fibers obtained with the full wavelength conversion while WIXCs are placed only at selected nodes. Concluding from this point of view, the routes to be used in conjunction with the sparse conversion network are obtained considering full wavelength conversion.

The network is represented by an undirected graph where the links and the connections are bidirectional. The set of k shortest paths between all node pairs is given by P. Let Z denote the set of all node pairs and L represent the set of links. For a node pair $z = (m, n) \in Z$, d_z denotes the number of lightpath requests between nodes m and n. The decision variable f_l denotes the number of fibers on link l and the routing variable X_{pz} represents the number of lightpaths for node pair z that are assigned to path p. The number of wavelengths on each fiber is denoted by W. The link-path incidence matrix is given by $J = [j_{lp}]$, where

$$j_{lp} = \begin{cases} 1 & \text{if link } l \text{ is on path } p, \\ 0 & \text{otherwise.} \end{cases}$$

The ILP formulation for the routing problem which minimizes the total number of fibers with full conversion is given by

$$\text{Minimize} \sum_{l \in L} f_l$$

Subject to

$$\sum_{p \in P} X_{pz} = d_z, \ \forall z \in Z, d_z \in D \quad \text{(demand constraints)}$$

$$\sum_{z \in Z} \sum_{p \in P} X_{pz} j_{lp} \leq W \times f_l, \ \forall l \in L \quad \text{(capacity constraints)}$$

$$f_l \in Z^+, \forall l \in L$$

$$X_{pz} \in Z^+, \forall z \in Z, \forall p \in P$$

The set of routing variables $\{X_{pz}\}$ in the optimum solution indicates paths used by the lightpaths.

2.2 Wavelength Assignment Problem

Next, we consider the wavelength assignment problem in optical networks with sparse wavelength conversion. For the wavelength assignment subproblem, an iterative heuristic algorithm based on the longest path first approach is used. For a given lightpath, each segment corresponds to the portion of the lightpath lying between two subsequent WIXCs along that lightpath. For the full wavelength conversion case in Section 2.1, segments correspond to individual links. All lightpaths obtained as the solution of the routing problem are divided into segments. These segments are sorted according to their lengths in a descending order. Starting from top of the list, the first available wavelength is assigned to each segment. When no available wavelength is found along a segment, that segment is placed at the top of the list, and all wavelength assignments are done from the beginning. This procedure is repeated for a maximum number of iterations, and when there is no available wavelength along a segment, the wavelength which is unavailable on the minimum number of links along that segment is determined, and the number of fibers on these links are incremented.

The pseudo-code for this algorithm is given below. The maximum number of times the list is reordered is represented by the variable *iteration_limit*.

```
1. set n=1,i=1
2. divide the lightpaths assigned to each node pair into segments
3. order the segments according to their lengths
4. while (i<number of segments)
     determine the first available wavelength for the segment in the
        i-th place in the list
     if (no available wavelength is found)
        if (n<iteration_limit)
           set n=n+1
           place this segment to the first place in the list
           undo all the wavelength assignments made so far
           set i=1
        else
           find the wavelength w which is unavailable on minimum number
              of links along the segment
           increase the number of fibers on the links for which
              wavelength w is not available along segment i
           set i=i+1
     else
        assign this wavelength on all links along the segment
        set i=i+1
5. stop
```

3 WIXC Placement

Our objective is to minimize the number of WIXCs in the network necessary to satisfy all the lightpath requests with the same total number of fibers as in the case of full wavelength conversion and to find the optimal locations for these WIXCs. To this end, we propose a tabu search algorithm and also implement a greedy search algorithm for comparison purposes that is used as the initial solution for the tabu search algorithm.

3.1 Greedy Search (GS) Algorithm

The target minimum number of fibers and the routes of the lightpaths are calculated beforehand using the ILP formulation described in Section 2 assuming full conversion. The flowchart of the GS algorithm is shown in Figure 1. The algorithm starts with no WIXCs. Each move in the algorithm consists of adding a WIXC to one of the nodes with no WIXCs. The node at which placing the WIXC reduces the total number of fibers most is determined. If there are multiple such nodes, the node to place next WIXC is chosen randomly among such nodes. When the target minimum number of fibers is reached, the algorithm stops. In order to determine the number of fibers on each link for each WIXC placement configuration, the wavelength assignment algorithm described in Section 2 is used. In our numerical studies, GS algorithm is executed a number of times in order to generate multiple solutions and the best solution is reported.

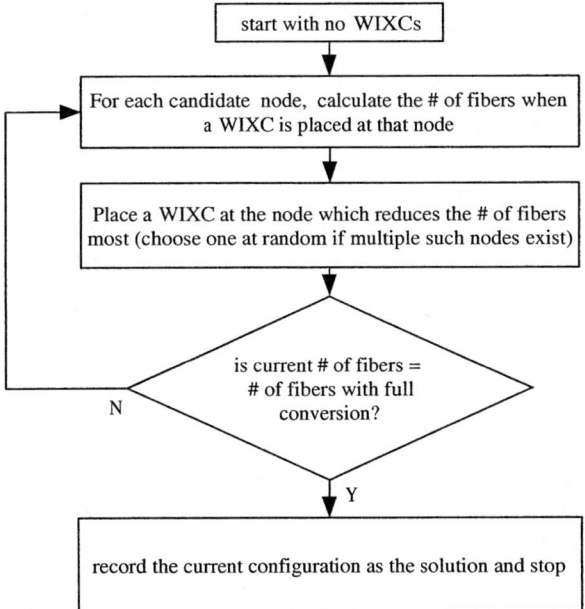

Fig. 1. Flowchart of the GS algorithm

3.2 Tabu Search (TS) Algorithm

Tabu search is an iterative improvement procedure which starts from an initial solution and gradually improves the objective function by a series of moves [12]. Its main difference from other iterative search techniques is that it allows non-improving moves to escape from local optima. Previously made moves are forbidden for a number of iterations by declaring these moves as tabu in order to avoid cycles.

The search space consists of all possible WIXC placements achieving the target number of fibers. The objective function is the number of nodes where a WIXC is placed. We consider three types of possible moves: addition of a WIXC to one of the nodes (add move), dropping one of the WIXCs (drop move) and adding a WIXC to a node while dropping another at the same time (exchange move).

The initial solution for the TS algorithm can be the full conversion case (since the minimum number of fibers is attainable by full conversion) or one of the solutions generated by the GS algorithm. The best solution generated by the GS algorithm is used as the initial solution for TS algorithm in this paper.

At each step, the list of all possible moves is calculated. If there exist possible drop moves, next move is chosen randomly among them. Otherwise, if possible, the next move is chosen among the exchange moves. If neither a drop nor an exchange move is possible, the next move is chosen among the possible add moves. Whenever a move is made, the move together with the existing configuration of WIXCs is added to the tabu list. The tenure of each entry in the tabu list is chosen randomly. The best solution, which is the configuration with the minimum number of WIXCs found so far, is stored. There are two stopping criteria for the algorithm: the conditions of no possible non-tabu moves and no improvement in the objective function for a number of iterations which is denoted by the parameter *no_imp_limit*.

With this state of the TS algorithm described so far, when a solution is found the algorithm has a tendency to return to that solution after a number of iterations since drop moves always have a higher priority than others. In order to overcome this problem and find other solutions that are not in the close neighborhood, a diversification step is introduced so that unvisited regions of the solution space are also visited. This diversification step is executed when no improvement in the objective function is achieved for a certain number of iterations denoted by the parameter *diverse_start*. In the diversification step, the drop and exchange moves are not considered for a number of iterations, represented by *diversification_limit*, leading to an escape from the local minima. The flowchart of the TS algorithm is given in Figure 2.

4 Numerical Results

The WIXC placement algorithms are tested using the 19-node European Optical Network (EON) [11]. The experiments are performed for different number of

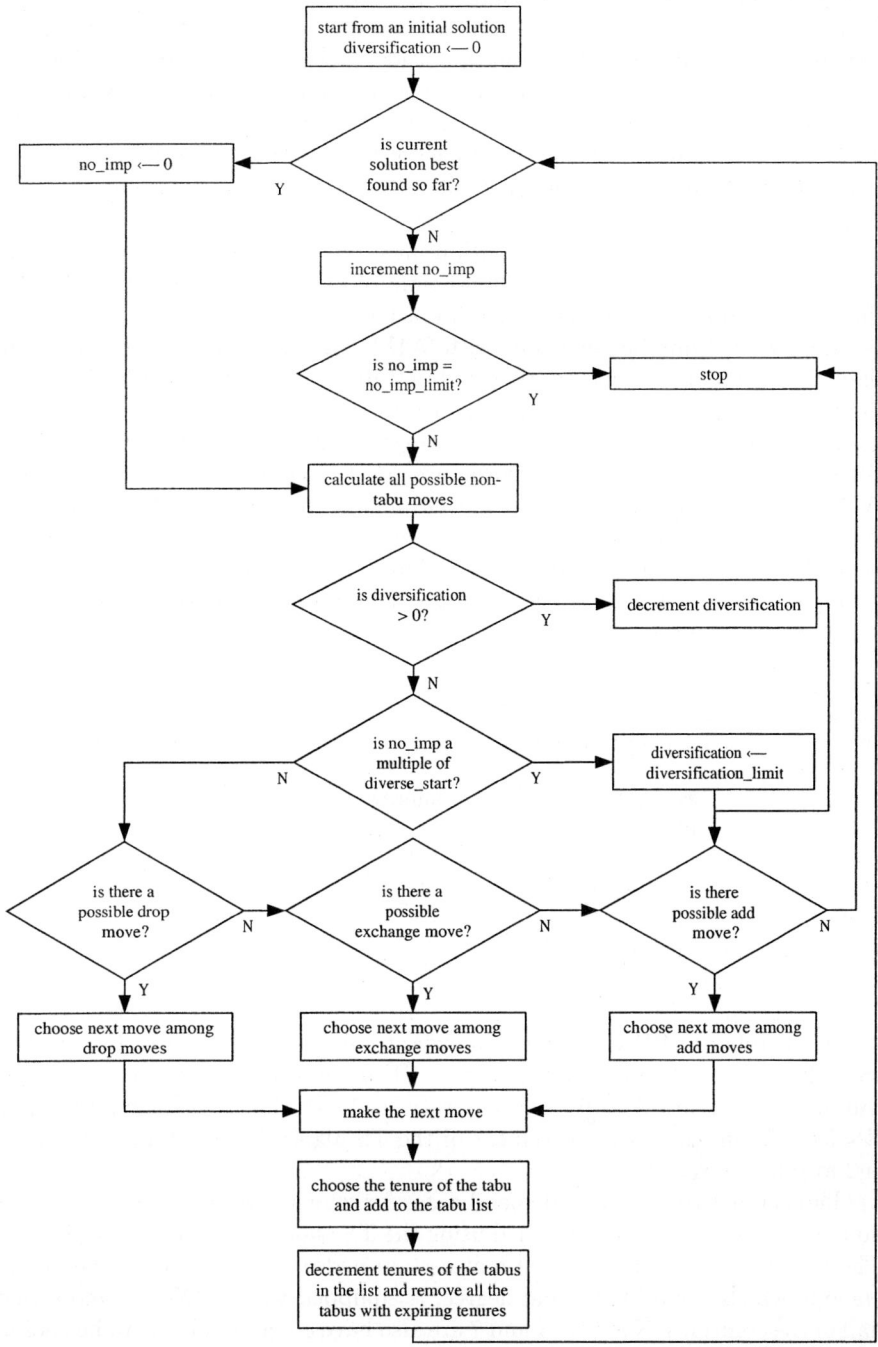

Fig. 2. Flowchart of the TS algorithm

wavelengths per fiber: $W=16$, 32 and 64. For each value of W, 50 different traffic demand matrices are generated, and the average values over these runs are reported. In the traffic model used in this study, lightpath demands exist between each pair of nodes. The number of demands between each node pair is randomly selected between [1-3], [2-6] and [4-12] for 16, 32 and 64 wavelengths, respectively. First, the GS algorithm is run a number of times in order to provide multiple solutions, then the TS algorithm is run starting from the best solution generated by the GS algorithm as initial the solution. The following values are used for the parameters in the TS algorithm: $no\_imp\_limit=100$, $diverse\_start=25$, $diversification\_limit=10$. The tenure time of each entry in tabu tabu list is chosen at random between 20 and 40 iterations.

The average number of nodes with WIXCs in the best solutions found by the GS and TS algorithms are reported in Table 1. The TS algorithm improves the best solution found by the GS algorithm in approximately 6% of the trials for 16 wavelengths, in 12% for 32 wavelengths and in 22% for 64 wavelengths. For small W, full conversion performance can be achieved with less number of WIXCs and it is more likely that the GS algorithm gives the same number of WIXCs as the TS algorithm. As W increases, it becomes more likely that the TS algorithm improves the results of the GS algorithm. In the cases for which the TS algorithm does not improve the initial solution found by the GS algorithm, it may generate alternative solutions.

Table 1. Average number of WIXCs obtained by the GS and TS algorithms, max. improvement of TS algorithm and percentage of the cases with no improvement

W	Average # of WIXCs		Max improvement in # of WIXCs	percentage of cases with no improvement
	GS	TS		
16	1.90	1.82	2	94
32	2.38	2.22	2	88
64	2.76	2.50	2	78

The number of WIXCs needed in order to obtain the same number of fibers with the full conversion case increases as W increases: about 9.6% of all nodes contain WIXCs for $W=16$, and this ratio is 11.7% for $W=32$ and 13.2% for $W=64$. The maximum improvement of the TS algorithm in number of WIXCs is 2 for all values of W.

The percentage of traffic demand cases for which a WIXC is placed at each node in the best solutions obtained using the TS algorithm is shown in Figure 3. The frequencies of placing WIXCs at certain nodes are higher than the others. Node 9, which has a high nodal degree, is equipped with WIXCs in more than half of the solutions. Nodes 1, 4 and 7 are also have a high tendency to be chosen. The total numbers of demands passing through each node are shown in Figure 4. We observe that there is a high correlation between the number of demands passing through a node and the probability that node is assigned a WIXC in the solution given by the TS algorithm. The five nodes that carry the largest number of lightpaths, namely nodes 1, 2, 4, 7 an 9, have the largest likelihood of placing a WIXC. Taking into account that the demands are uniformly distributed with equal parameters for all node pairs, the WIXC placement depends on the network topology and the routing algorithm used.

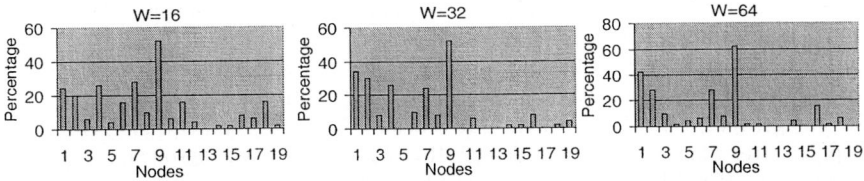

Fig. 3. The distribution of WIXCs at the nodes

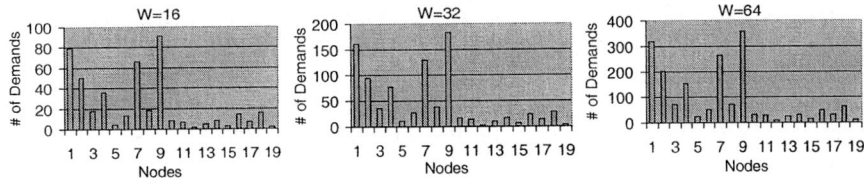

Fig. 4. The number of demands passing through the nodes

5 Conclusions

In this paper, a tabu search algorithm for placing limited number of WIXCs in a multi-fiber network under static traffic demands is presented. The objective of the algorithm is to achieve the performance of full wavelength conversion in terms of total number of fibers by placing minimum number of WIXCs. An iterative wavelength assignment algorithm is used in the tabu search algorithm giving satisfactory results in a reasonable amount of time.

The average percentage of nodes with WIXCs to all nodes in the best solution generated by the TS algorithm slightly increases with the number of wavelengths, but it is less than 14% on the average. We also observe that WIXCs are mostly concentrated at a small number of nodes and there is a significant correlation between the probability that a node is assigned a WIXC in the best solution and the number of demands passing through that node. The distribution of the WIXCs and the number of demands passing through the nodes can be used in order to form strategies that may improve the performance of the TS algorithm. One possibility is that certain nodes can be given a higher probability of WIXC assignment while making the movement decisions.

The TS algorithm can be studied further using different RWA algorithms. An important issue to be considered while choosing the wavelength assignment algorithm is the running time which is the determining factor for the overall run time since wavelength assignment is done for every WIXC placement configuration considered for each move of the TS algorithm.

References

1. Ramaswami, R., Sivarajan, K.N.: Optical Networks, A Practical Perspective. Morgan Kaufmann Publishers, San Francisco, CA (1998)
2. Karasan, E., Ayanoglu, E.: Performance of WDM Transport Networks. IEEE Journal on Selected Areas in Communications **16**(7) (1998) 1081–1096
3. Subramaniam, S., Azizoglu, M.: On Optimal Converter Placement in Wavelength-Routed Networks. IEEE/ACM Transactions on Networking **7**(5) (1999) 754–766
4. Li, L., Somani, A.K.: Efficient Algorithms for Wavelength Converter Placement. SPI/Kluwer Optical Networks Magazine **3**(2) (2002)
5. Thiagarajan, S., Somani, A.K.: An Efficient Algorithm for Optimal Wavelength Converter Placement on Wavelength-Routed Networks with Arbitrary Topologies. In: Proc. IEEE INFOCOM'99. (1999) 916–923
6. Chu X., Li, B., Chlamtac, I.: Wavelength Converter Placement Under Different RWA Algorithms in Wavelength-Routed All-Optical Networks. IEEE Transactions on Communications **51**(4) (2003) 607–617.
7. Gao, S., Jia, X., Huang, C., Du, D.: An Optimization for Placement of Wavelength Converters to Minimize Blocking Probability in WDM Networks. Journal of Lightwave Technology **21**(3) (2003)
8. Zymolka, A., Koster, A., Wessaly, R.: A Transparent Optical Network Design with Sparse Wavelength Conversion. In: Proc. ONDM 2003. (2003) 61–80
9. Karasan, E., Karasan, O.E., Erdogan, G.: Optimum Placement of Wavelength Interchanging Nodes in Optical Networks with Sparse Conversion. In: Proc. of the 9th European Conference on Networks and Optical Communications, Eindhoven, Netherlands. (2004) 525–532
10. Wilfong, G., Winkler, P.: Ring Routing and Wavelength Translation. In: Proc. of the 9th Annual ACM-SIAM Symposium on Discrete Algorithms. (1998) 333–341
11. Venugopal, K.R., Shivakumar, M., Kumar, P.S.: A Heuristic for Placement of Limited Range Wavelength Converters in All-optical Networks. Computer Networks **35**(2-3) (2001) 143–163
12. Glover, F. Laguna, M.: Tabu Search. Kluwer Academic Publishers, Boston, MA (1997)

Mixed Routing for ROMEO Optical Burst*

Jean-Michel Fourneau and David Nott

PRiSM, Université de Versailles Saint-Quentin
45 Av. des Etats Unis, 78000 Versailles, France
{Jean-Michel.Fourneau, David.Nott}@prism.uvsq.fr

Abstract. We show how a mixed routing strategy can be used for burst switching in all-optical networks. This new routing strategy combines deflection routing and convergence routing. Deflection routing is known to avoid deadlocks but livelocks may occur (packets move but never reach their destination) while convergence routing provides deterministic transport delays but has a very low network utilization. The convergence routing is based on a decomposition of the grid into two Eulerian directed cycles. The routing strategy permits the shortening of the ending guarantee; it is almost as efficient as deflection routing and it is consistent with the bursts we consider in the ROMEO project. We also compute the probability of failure insertion.

1 Introduction

Burst Switching in all-optical packets networks represents a challenging and attractive technology to provide a large bandwidth for future networks. But a lot of technical questions have to be solved first. With current optical technology, optical switches do not have large buffers or even have buffers at all. Delay loops are not designed to store a large number of packets. Because of this, routing algorithms are quite different of the algorithms designed for store and forward networks based on electronic buffering.

As part of the ROMEO project (a French research consortium of Alcatel and several research laboratories) we study an Electronic and Optic router which may become the last step before the spreading of All Optical technology. ROMEO follows the ROM project where the all optical technology has been extensively studied (for an overview of the results of the ROM project, see [5]). Pursuing their conclusions, we consider that the square *2D-mesh* $N \times N$ network is an sufficiently realistic topology for the *core network*. Of course, the access networks will certainly be more sparse. Here, we consider burst switching at the routing and access level for a system without intermediate storage. The routing strategy combines deflection routing [4,9] and convergence routing [1,2,6]. It is an improvement of the mixed routing strategy based on an Eulerian cycle which has been previously introduced in [3]. The improvements are twofold:

– the algorithm is now consistent with bursts as they have been defined in the ROMEO project,

---

* This work has been supported by the French RNRT project *ROMEO*.

– it uses a decomposition of the topology (a grid) into *two Eulerian cycles* to reduce the upper bound of the transport delay (i.e., the ending guarantee).

As we do not have buffer overflows, optical routing strategies do not suffer packet losses. However, these strategies keep the packets inside the network and reduce the bandwidth. The usable bandwidth (i.e., the goodput) of the network and the routing protocol is therefore a major measure of interest. The second performance measure of interest is related to the burst.

Optical Burst Switching (OBS) is known in the literature as one-way reservation paradigm where a control packet is sent first to reserve an appropriate amount of bandwidth and configure the switches along the path, followed by a data burst without waiting for an acknowledgment for the connection establishment [8, 10]. A burst is guaranteed to follow its path as long as the control packet successfully reserves the resources on the path and is entirely dropped if not. In order to avoid the optical-to-electrical-to-optical (OEO) bottleneck, OBS has been conceived to provide fast switching to the network by reducing the amount of work in the switches by eliminating the OEO conversion. However, OBS is valuable as long as the traffic of control packet is significantly inferior with the traffic of information packet and as long as the network load is light in order to keep a low burst losses ratio. For facing the OEO bottleneck, the ROMEO approach is to propose a fixed long duration packet which permits the electronic parts of the switches to have enough time to process the routing. Consequently, ROMEO packets are expected to be aggregations of smaller packets and to be the essential part of the ROMEO traffic. Thus, OBS networks are bursts dedicated networks while ROMEO is designed to support either bursts and single packets. In the ROMEO network, resources along the path are not reserved. So the access and routing algorithms must ensure that a burst will not be cut into two parts. At the time being, if such an event occurs, the burst would be considered as lost.

Here, we show how these mechanisms may cut bursts and we characterize the situation where this may happen. For instance, bursts routing with different algorithms may collide or the insertion of a burst at the interface of the optical part of the network may fail. We fix the first problem by a more complex specification of the routing algorithm and a partition of the spectral space. We also compute this failure probability and we show that under some simple assumptions about the load and the burst size, it can be kept as low as required by the QoS contract. The last performance measure we wish to obtain is the ending guarantee. It is an upper bound on the transport delay (i.e., the worst case). It does not take into account the waiting time before entering the optical part of the network. This guarantee implies that there is no livelock in the network. The decomposition of the 2D-mesh into two Eulerian cycles implies a significant reduction of the worst case (i.e., a much better guarantee). The rest of the paper is organized as follows. In Section 2, we introduce several routing strategies for optical networks. Then in section 3, we describe our new routing algorithm based on deflection and a two Eulerian cycles decomposition of the grid. We also show how it can manage bursts and we give the ending guarantee. Section 4 is devoted to the access of a burst to the network and probability of the insertion failure.

2 Routing Algorithm

Let us first recall the two basic strategies we want to mix: the deflection and the convergence algorithms. In shortest-path Deflection Routing, switches attempt to forward packets along a shortest path to their destination. Each link can send a finite number of packets per time-slot (the link capacity). The packets have a constant size and they are not queued. At each slot, incoming packets have to be sent to their next switch along the path. If the number of packets which require a link is larger than the link capacity, only some of them will receive the link they ask for and the other ones have to be misdirected or deflected. Some recirculation delay loops can be used to retain packets instead of sending them in a wrong direction. Using recirculation delay loops will be defined as an internal deflection while going in a wrong direction is an external deflection. Of course the real effect of the deflection on the path lengths depends on the topology. But clearly, deflected packets experience larger delays to reach their destination. Deflection routing has several advantageous properties: it avoids deadlocks and simulations show that the goodput is appreciable. However it has several drawbacks.

- Packets follow independent paths. Therefore the transport is not FIFO. Clearly, the algorithm must be adapted for ROMEO type of bursts.
- The number of deflections may be not negligible, especially if the traffic is unbalanced. The mean number of deflection is not that large but a significant number of packets are heavily deflected. We have observed several packets with more than 1000 deflections during a simulation of a 10×10 2D-mesh. These packets are a real problem for a network protocol because they are considered as lost due to large delays and they increase significantly the loss rates at heavy load with unbalanced traffic. The lack of ending guarantee is a real problem.

Convergence routing techniques permits the obtainment of a finite ending guarantee [7]. They are based on a global sense of direction that packets must follow. Such a property may be found using some decompositions of the network topology into directed cycles [11]. For instance in the Eulerian routing, the packets follow an Eulerian directed cycle [1, 2, 6]. Remember that an Eulerian cycle is a cycle which uses all the edges of the graph once only. Convergence routing techniques studied so far have several good properties but one major drawback:

- We can prove the ending guarantee.
- If we use a static decomposition (rather than a dynamic one like the Shortcut convergence routing) and a proper access algorithm, the FIFO property is ensured.

- By simulation, we have found goodput for various Eulerian directed cycles from 3 up to 6 packets per slot for a 10×10 2D-mesh [1]. For similar networks and traffic, deflection routing algorithms provide a goodput of more than 32 packets per slot [1]. This is due to the large average transport delay experienced with Eulerian routing.

Thus, in [3] we have designed and studied the performance of a new routing algorithm (the Mixed Routing) which combines the ending guarantee of the Eulerian routing with the goodput efficiency of deflection routing that we now improve to allow burst switching and better performances. The Mixed Routing strategy is based on a threshold S on the deflection number experienced by a packet. Each packet carries a deflection counter. When it is emitted, it uses deflection routing. After each deflection, the counter is increased. When the counter is larger than S, the packet switches to Eulerian routing mode and keeps this mode until its destination. As the packets in Eulerian mode are routed in a first phase, they have a higher priority to access the output links. And by definition, two Eulerian packets in a same node at a same step never ask for a same output link. Moreover any packet can be switched at any moment to the Eulerian routing mode without any additional delay. This is simply due to the fact that all the edges of the network belong by definition to the Eulerian circuit. Thus, a message is always on a portion of the Eulerian circuit, and uses the next edge in the Eulerian circuit. The ending guarantee of the Eulerian routing strategy ensures that the message will reach its destination, whatever the network load is. Unfortunately some of these properties will not be satisfied when we consider bursts instead of packets.

3 Improved Routing Algorithm

The packets and bursts may be routed using several modes: Deflection, Convergence or Mixed. All the packets in the same burst have the same routing mode (the information is carried by the header of the first packet of a burst). First, we show how two bursts may collide. It must be clear that all the packets within a burst must follow the same route. Thus, the routing decision computed for the head packet, must be used for the complete burst.

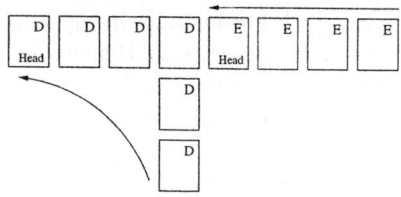

Fig. 1. Collision between a deflection burst and an Eulerian burst

Assume that a burst in deflection mode arrives in a node at time t (see Figure 1). The routing algorithm sends the head to the left. Now, at time $t + 3$, a new burst in Eulerian mode arrives in that node and requires also the same direction. Objects in Eulerian mode must have a higher priority to prove the ending guarantee. Thus, if we do not have enough wavelengths available, the deflection burst will be cut to let the Eulerian burst follow its path. Note that it is also true if we consider an Eulerian packet instead of an Eulerian burst. Clearly, it is not possible to have Eulerian bursts and Deflection bursts competing for the same wavelengths without burst collision. Therefore if we specify that the bursts cannot be divided during the transport, the deflection burst must be separated from the Eulerian packets or bursts. Thus we divide the spectral space into two sets: DF and ME and assign them to objects with different service requirements. The set DF is used by packets and bursts in Deflection mode while in set ME, packets use the Mixed routing and bursts follow the Convergence routing based on two Eulerian circuits that we will introduce in the following. Thus, we avoid any competition between bursts in Eulerian mode and burst in Deflection mode. Note that there is no collision between bursts in Eulerian mode.

For the set DF, the routing algorithm is based on the types of objects we have to route: a single packet, the head of the burst, the body of a burst. At each time slot, in each router, the routing algorithm performs the following steps in sequence :

1. First consider the packets which are in the body of a burst. Route them to follow exactly the head of the burst.
2. Consider the burst head. We give higher priority to bursts against packets in order to provide shorter delays to bursts.
3. Finally, route the packets in deflection mode.

It must be clear that once the burst has been inserted in the optical part of the net, collisions between bursts are impossible. However, during the insertion it is still possible that a burst entering the net will suffer from wavelength contention affecting one of its own packets.

In the ME set, bursts are emitted in Convergence mode while packets enter the network in Deflection mode (they use the Mixed Routing strategy). Packets and bursts in Convergence mode follow one of the two Eulerian circuits we will present in the following. Before the insertion (for burst) or the transition between deflection and convergence (for packets), we compute the free direction associated with the shortest Eulerian path to destination. The routing has three steps which must be performed in that order:

1. Route the bursts in Eulerian mode.
2. Route the packet in Eulerian mode
3. Route the packets in deflection mode.

The header of the message has to be increased in order to code the number of deflections a message can afford before using the Eulerian routing strategy. This modification of the header of a packet is compatible with optical technology, where all the headers are globally regenerated at each router (see [5] for technical details of optical technologies). In [3], we have proved the following theorem:

Theorem 1. *Let $G = (V, E)$ a graph and C an Eulerian circuit of G. Using the mixed routing strategy with threshold $S > 0$, any message reaches its destination in at most $D(G, S, C)$ steps, with: $D(G, S, C) = diam_G + 2S + stretchW_C - 3$., where $diam_G$ is the diameter (maximal distance) of G and $stretchW_C$ is the maximal distance along the Eulerian cycle C. When $S = 0$ (for Eulerian routing), we simply have $D(G, 0, C) = stretchW_C$.*

We can note immediately that once the network is known, we have two ways of shortening the ending guarantee: decrease the threshold S or decrease the value of $stretchW_C$ by a clever selection of the Eulerian circuit which covers the network. Now, remember that we consider a 2D-mesh as our network topology. The diameter of the $N \times N$ mesh is $2N - 2$. It has been proved in [2] that the stretch of an Eulerian circuit can be as bad as the number of the edges minus 3 (i.e., $m - 3$) and cannot be less than the number of edges of the corresponding graph divided by the minimum degree of the graph (more precisely, $\frac{m}{\delta} - 1$). Therefore, for a $N \times N$ 2D-mesh, the stretch lies between $2N(N - 1) - 1$ and $4N(N - 1) - 3$.

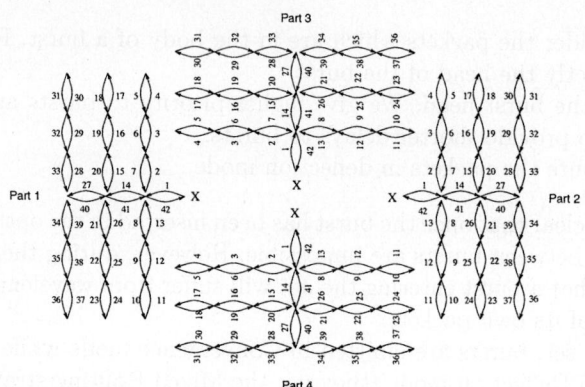

Fig. 2. The antenna Eulerian circuit

Unfortunately, most of the Eulerian cycles seem to have a large stretch. For instance, in Figure 2 we depict one of the cycles we have studied. This Eulerian tour starts from the central vertex X, then goes to part 1, part 2, part 3 and ends using part 4. In each part, the order of edges are shown on Figure 2. In [6], the $stretchW_C$ was shown to be $4N(N - 1) - 2N + 1$ for this particular circuit. Clearly it merely reaches the upper bound of the stretch.

We now propose another convergence technique. Instead of one Eulerian circuit, we cover the graph with two circuits. More precisely, we decompose the

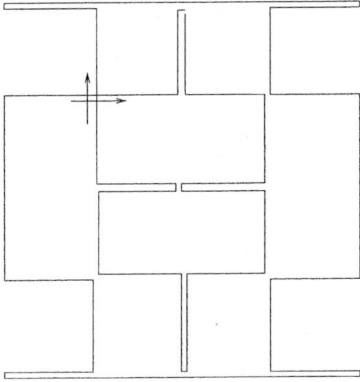

Fig. 3. The Chinese Eulerian circuit

mesh (V, E) into two graphs (V,E1) and (V,E2) such that $E1$ and $E2$ are a partition of the set of edges and both graphs $(V, E1)$ and $(V, E2)$ are Eulerian. In Figure 3, we present one of the two Eulerian circuits, the other one can be deduced by a rotation.

Note that the selection of the best free direction does not help to obtain a smaller upper bound for the transportation delay. In the worst cases, the only free direction is the worst one.

Theorem 2. *For the mesh, with the decomposition into 2 Eulerian cycles, the ending guarantee is:*

- *for the mixed routing with threshold S, $D(G, S, C) = 2S + 2N^2 - 5$.*
- *for the convergence routing, $D(G, S, C) = 2N(N - 1) - 3$.*

Thus the new routing algorithm provides a better bound for the ending guarantee. However, the only packets which take advantage of this new algorithm are the ones which suffers more than S deflections along their path. The number of these packets is small compared to those which reach their destination using the deflection mode only. Thus it does not affect significantly the mean thruput and their influence may be slightly observed on the tail of the transportation delay distribution. In order to make the new routing algorithm effect readable, we plot in Figure 4 the static distribution of the number of hops between all nodes and on all paths in a 7 × 7 grid of the antenna and the Chinese circuit. The transportation delay in Eulerian mode is divided by two for the worst case.

4 Probability of Collision During Admission

In this section, we first compute the insertion failure probability of a burst in deflection mode and then the insertion failure probability of a burst in Eulerian mode.

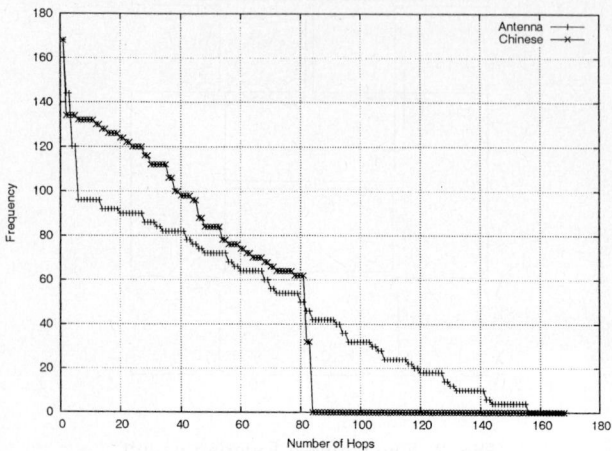

Fig. 4. Hops distribution

Consider a bufferless switch with D input and output ports, λ wavelengths per link. We assume independent arrivals at the input ports and uniform destination for each packet. Assume that packets from the network have a higher priority level than packets entering the network. In the case of contention between network packets and entering packets, the entering packets are rejected. In order to make routing decisions easier in each node on the path, we assume that burst packets are sent one by one in the network. When a burst enters the network, the entrance node has no future knowledge of incoming packets. So when the first packet from a burst enters the network, the packets following are not guaranteed to enter. Therefore, if the burst size is L, the probability of successful insertion is $p_L = p^{L-1}$, and p is the probability of successfully insertion of a packet in one particular direction (the one selected by the head packet). We need to compute the probability that at least one available wavelength in a link exists. Let ρ be the load on the output ports. Precisely, ρ is the load of incoming packets once the departure of arrived packets has taken place. Because of the independence assumption, the probability of packet arrival which is retained inside the net is ρ for every wavelength. Thus, the number of incoming packets on a link is given by a binomial distribution with parameters ρ and λ and the number of incoming packets from all links is given by a binomial distribution with parameters ρ and $D \times \lambda$:

$$\mathcal{P}(X = k) = \binom{D\lambda}{k} \rho^k (1-\rho)^{D\lambda - k}.$$

And the number of incoming packets with destination of a given output port a is, by conditioning on the number of incoming packets:

$$\mathcal{P}(X_a = k) = \sum_{i=k}^{D\lambda} \binom{D\lambda}{i} \rho^i (1-\rho)^{D\lambda-i} \binom{i}{k} \left(1 - \frac{1}{D}\right)^{i-k} \left(\frac{1}{D}\right)^k.$$

And after some algebraic manipulations,

$$\mathcal{P}(X_a = k) = \binom{D\lambda}{k} \left(\rho\left(\frac{1}{D}\right)\right)^k \left(1 - \rho\left(\frac{1}{D}\right)\right)^{D\lambda-k}.$$

The probability p to successfully insert a packet is

$$p = \mathcal{P}(X_a < \lambda) = \sum_{k=0}^{\lambda-1} \mathcal{P}(X_a = k) = \sum_{k=0}^{\lambda-1} \binom{D\lambda}{k} \left(\frac{\rho}{D}\right)^k \left(1 - \left(\frac{\rho}{D}\right)\right)^{D\lambda-k}.$$

Similarly, we compute the insertion failure probability of a burst in Eulerian mode. In Eulerian mode, the only packets which may ask a given output are the ones which come from the precedent input on the Eulerian circuit. Except the packets which may leave the network at this node, all the packets coming from this link ask the given output. Thus the successful insertion probability is

$$p_L = \left(1 - \rho^\lambda\right)^{L-1}.$$

Figures 5 and 6 show the probability of insertion failure for a node of degree 4 with 8 and 16 wavelengths per link. One may observe that Eulerian mode permits a lower burst loss probability at a given load or a higher network load at a given burst loss probability.

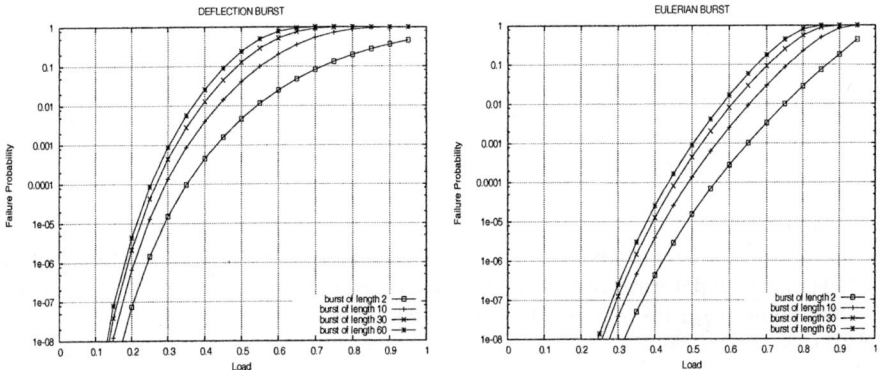

Fig. 5. Probability of insertion failure with 16 wavelengths

Thus, the failure probability can be decreased by reducing the burst length or the load using an access control based on a time-window estimate.

5 Conclusion

In this paper, we have shown how to modify the mixed routing strategy for burst switching all optical packet networks. We obtain an ending guarantee for some packets and bursts. The performance loss for packets is small: the goodput is only slightly reduced. For bursts, the price is higher but we can choose: using DF part of spectral space, we obtain high thruput but no guarantee while the Eulerian routing in set ME provides an ending guarantee but a low bandwidth.

References

1. Barth, D., Berthomé, P., Borrero, A., Fourneau, J.-M., Laforest, C., Quessette, F., Vial, S.: Performance Comparisons of Eulerian Routing and Deflection Routing in a 2D-Mesh All Optical Network. In: Proceedings of the 15th European Simulation Multiconference. (2001) 887–891
2. Barth, D., Berthomé, P., Cohen, J.: The Eulerian Stretch of a Digraph and the Ending Guarantee of a Convergence Routing. Technical Report A00-R-400, LORIA, BP 239, F54506 Vandoeuvre-ls-Nancy, France (2000)
3. Barth, D., Berthomé, P., Czachorski, T., Fourneau, J.-M., Laforest, C., Vial, S.: A Mixed Deflection and Eulerian Routing Algorithm: Design and Performance. In: EuroPar 2002. Lecture Notes in Computer Science, Vol. 2400 (2002) 767–774
4. Brassil, J.C., Cruz, R.L.: Bounds on Maximum Delay in Networks with Deflection Routing. IEEE Transactions on Parallel and Distributed Systems **6** (1995) 724–732
5. Gravey, P., Gosselin, S., Guillemot, C., Chiaroni, D., Le Sauze, N., Jourdan, A., Dotaro, E., Barth, D., Berthomé, P., Laforest, C., Vial, S., Atmaca, T., Hébuterne, G., El Biaze, H., Laalaoua, R., Gangloff, E., Kotuliak, I.: Multiservice Optical Network: Main Concepts and First Achievements of the ROM Program. Journal of Ligthwave Technology **19** (2001) 23–31
6. Laforest, C., Vial, S.: Short Cut Eulerian Routing of Datagrams in All Optical Point-to-Point Networks. In: Proceedings of the 16th International Parallel and Distributed Processing Symposium (IPDPS 2002), Fort Lauderdale, FL, USA. IEEE Computer Society (2002)
7. Ofek, Y., Yung, M.: Principles for High Speed Network Control: Loss-Less and Deadlock-Freeness, Self-routing and a Single Buffer per Link. In: ACM Symposium on Principles of Distributed Computing. (1990) 161–175
8. Qiao, C., Yoo, M.: Optical Burst Switching (OBS) - A New Paradigm for an Optical Internet. Journal of High Speed Networks **8** (1999) 69–84
9. Schuster, A.: Bounds and Analysis Techniques for Greedy Hot-Potato Routing. In: Berthomé, P., Ferrira, A. (eds.): Optical Interconnections and Parallel Processing: The Interface. Kluwer Academic Publishers (1997) 284–354
10. Xu, L., Perros, H.G., Rouskas, G.: Techniques for Optical Packet Switching and Optical Burst Switching. IEEE Communications Magazine **39** (2001) 136–142
11. Yener, B., Matsoukas, S., Ofek, Y.: Iterative Approach to Optimizing Convergence Routing Priorities. IEEE/ACM Transactions on Networking **5** (1997) 530–542

A Fast Hardware-Oriented Algorithm for Cellular Mobiles Positioning

Muhammed Salamah, Evgueni Doukhnitch, and Deniz Devrim

Computer Engineering Department
Eastern Mediterranean University, Gazimağusa, Cyprus
{muhammed.salamah,evgueni.douknitch,deniz.devrim}@emu.edu.tr

Abstract: Finding the location of a cellular mobile phone is one of the important features of the 3G wireless communication systems. Many valuable location based services can be enabled by this new feature. All location determination techniques which are based on cellular system signals and global positioning system (GPS) use standard trigonometric complex computation methods that are usually implemented in software. In this paper, we propose a new algorithm that uses only simple add and shift operations in the computation and therefore can be implemented in hardware. Our results show improvements of our algorithm in computation time, implementation simplicity and location accuracy over the traditional used method.

1 Introduction

The mobile cellular communication services industry is expected to continue growing rapidly in the next decade. One interesting aspect that exploits the possibilities of modern cellular communication technologies is to provide customers with location-based services [1,2]. These services include security, emergency rescue, resource tracking and management, tour guide, location sensitive billing, location-aided handover and others [2-5]. The US Federal Communications Commission (FCC) has made Emergency 911 (E911) a mandatory requirement for wireless communications services such as cellular phones and other personal communication services. The European Commission (EC) has a similar goal for their wireless emergency calls, E112. The common aim of these systems is to estimate the location of the mobile phone within an acceptable accuracy.

Generally, location determination schemes can be divided into two main classes, network-based and mobile-based schemes. In the network-based case, one or several base stations (BS) receive the mobile station (MS) signals and determine the location in a network server. These methods do not require any change to the existing handsets, but they have high network cost (because of high message exchange between the MS and BSs) and low accuracy [1,3]. In the mobile-based or handset-based case, the MS makes the necessary measurements using the received signals and determines the location itself. The MS reports its location to the service provider over the wireless network. Although these methods do not support legacy handsets, they have higher position accuracy. According to Phase II operation of E911, the accuracy requirements for network-based solutions are 100 m for 67% of calls and 300 m for 95% of calls; whereas for handset-based solutions, they are, 50 m for 67% of calls and 150 m for 95% of calls.

Many methods for locating MSs have been proposed and discussed in the literature [1,2,5-9]. These include cell identification [1,3,6], angle of arrival (AOA) [1,2,5,6,8,10], time of arrival (TOA) [1,2,6,8-11], time difference of arrival (TDOA) [1,2,5,6,8,10], assisted global positioning system (AGPS) [1,5,6,9], enhanced observed time difference (EOTD) [1,4,9], received signal strength (RSS) [6], and more [1,7,8]. All of these methods are mainly based on trigonometric computation. Comparisons and survey of these methods are given in [8] and [6].

TOA method is very popularly used. It determines the mobile phone position based on the intersection of the distance (or range) of three circles as seen in Figure1. Under ideal conditions the propagation time of the radio wave is directly proportional to its traversed distance. Hence, multiplying the speed of light to the time obtains the range from the MS to the communicating BS. The same principle is used by GPS, where the circle becomes the sphere in 3D space.

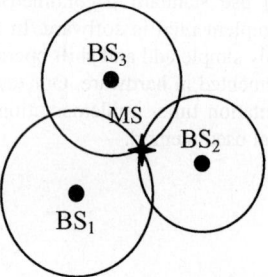

Fig. 1. Time of arrival (TOA) position determination method

As mentioned previously, mobile-based location schemes seem to be more attractive than the network-based schemes. However, since the MS has limited energy source, in the form of the battery pack, energy consumption should be minimized. An important factor in achieving this is to minimize and simplify the instructions that the MS has to execute in the location determination process. In fact the energy dissipation reduction is carried out at different levels of abstraction: from the algorithm level down to the implementation [12]. Motivated with this argument, we propose a new algorithm for location determination that we named as SDD algorithm. The major advantages of our SDD algorithm over the traditional one are its speed-up, low computation and communication overhead, and implementation simplicity. That is, since all operations in our SDD algorithm are simple add, subtract and shift operations, it can be implemented in hardware using a simple field programmable gate array (FPGA) chip. It should be noted that our algorithm is based on the assumption that we have a local coordinate system and location determination is done in 2D space.

The organization of this paper is as follows. In section 2, we give description of the traditional algorithm used for location determination. In section 3, we propose a new fast algorithm for determining the mobile location along with the detailed description. In section 4, the performance of the proposed algorithm is evaluated and compared with the traditional scheme. Conclusions are presented in section 5.

2 The Traditional Algorithm

Usually the traditional positioning algorithm uses three base stations to determine the mobile location. Assume that the coordinates of BS_1, BS_2 and BS_3 in Figure1 are (x_1,y_1), (x_2,y_2) and (x_3,y_3) respectively. Therefore according to the TOA or RSS by the MS from each of the three base stations the MS location is the intersection of the three circles centered at BS_1, BS_2 and BS_3 with radiuses d_1, d_2 and d_3 respectively. The traditional algorithm is illustrated in Figure 2 below.

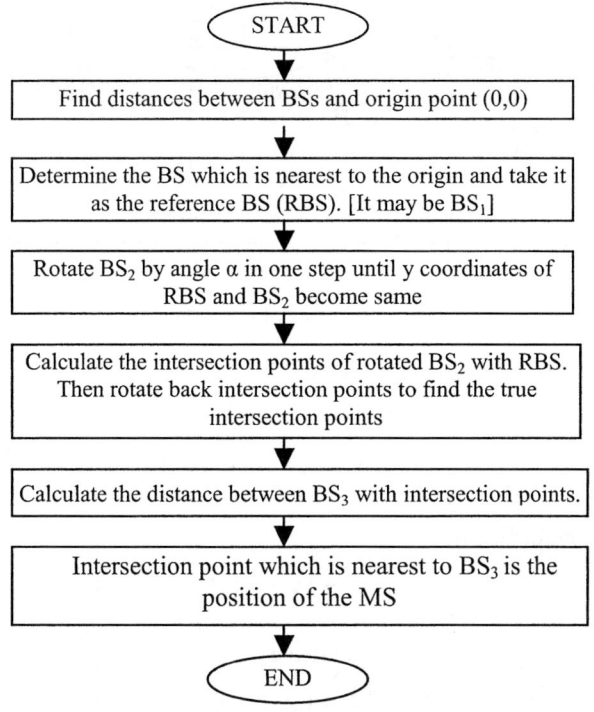

Fig. 2. The traditional algorithm

To illustrate the algorithm, Figure 3 shows a detailed drawing. Accordingly, BS_1 is the RBS, and we need to rotate BS_2 until its $y_2 = y_1$. The rotation angle (α) can be easily found to be

$$\alpha = \sin^{-1}\left(\frac{y_2 - y_1}{d}\right) \qquad (1)$$

Where the d is distance between RBS and BS_2. Hence, the new coordinates of BS_2 are:

$$x_2^1 = x_1 + d \quad \text{and} \quad y_2^1 = y_1 \qquad (2)$$

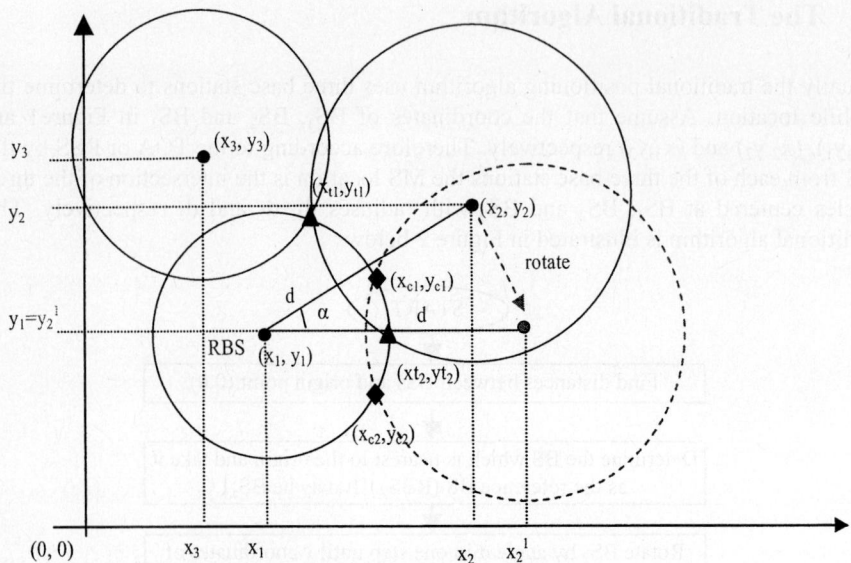

Fig. 3. Positions of Base Stations

Using the equation of a circle, the equation for RBS is:

$$(x-x_1)^2 + (y-y_1)^2 = d_1^2$$
$$(y-y_1)^2 = d_1^2 - (x-x_1)^2 \qquad (3)$$

and the equation for BS_2 is:

$$(x-x_2^1)^2 + (y-y_2^1)^2 = d_2^2. \qquad (4)$$

Since $y_1 = y_2^1$, equation (3) can be rewritten as:

$$(x-x_2^1)^2 + (y-y_1)^2 = d_2^2. \qquad (5)$$

Combining equations (5) and (3), we can find the x coordinate of the intersection points as:

$$x = \frac{d_2^2 - d_1^2 + x_1^2 - x_2^{1\,2}}{2(x_1 - x_2^1)}. \qquad (6)$$

Substituting (6) in (3), the y coordinates of the intersection points will be:

$$y = \pm \sqrt{d_1^2 - x_1^2 - x^2 + 2xx_1} + y_1. \qquad (7)$$

We need to rotate back these two intersection points (x_{c1}, y_{c1}) and (x_{c2}, y_{c2}) by α to get the true intersection points (x_{t1}, y_{t1}) and (x_{t2}, y_{t2}).

Since we have two intersection points, we need the third BS to find the unique position. We compare the distances of BS_3 with the intersection points and the nearest intersection point gives us the position of the mobile. The minimum distance d_{min} can be found as:

$$d_{min} = \min\left(\sqrt{(x_{t1} - x_3)^2 + (y_{t1} - y_3)^2}, \sqrt{(x_{t2} - x_3)^2 + (y_{t2} - y_3)^2} \right). \quad (8)$$

3 The SDD Algorithm

Our SDD algorithm is also based on TOA and it uses the same source of information as the traditional one. However, the way of finding the mobile location is performed in a completely different way as illustrated in the flowchart of Figure 5 below. The main idea is to take a fixed step rotation angle $\sigma = \arcsin 2^{-k}$, where k depends on the needed accuracy and do the rotation recursively step by step. To illustrate the algorithm, one should look back to Figure3 again. However, before rotating BS_2, the RBS coordinates (BS_1) should be transferred to the origin point (0,0) and the other BSs coordinates will be changed accordingly. The BS_2 will be rotated step by step (with step size σ) until its y coordinate becomes zero.

The rotation matrix M is as follows:

$$M = \begin{bmatrix} \cos\sigma & \sin\sigma \\ -\sin\sigma & \cos\sigma \end{bmatrix}. \quad (9)$$

We took the *sin* function as:

$$\sin\sigma = 2^{-k}, \quad (10)$$

and we approximate the *cos* function as follows[13]:

$$\cos\sigma = 1 - 2^{-(2k+1)} \quad (11)$$

Therefore, BS_2 coordinates are recursively rotated as follows:

$$x_{i+1} = x_i - x_i a + y_i b \quad (12)$$

$$y_{i+1} = y_i - y_i a - x_i b \quad (13)$$

Where, $a = 2^{-(2k+1)}$, and $b = 2^{-k}$.

So, it's clearly seen from the above equations we are not doing any trigonometric calculations. Instead, simple add, subtract and shift operations are used which are necessary requirement for hardware implementation.

Figure 5 shows the resultant configuration after rotating BS_2. The same figure illustrates the idea of positioning the MS. We rotate the vectors of BS_1 (d_1) and BS_2 (d_2), until their heads intersect each others. An equivalent rotation is illustrated in Figure 6. Initial positions of vectors heads are:

$x_1 = d_1$ and $y_1 = 0$ (14)

$x_1' = d_2$ and $y_1' = 0$ (15)

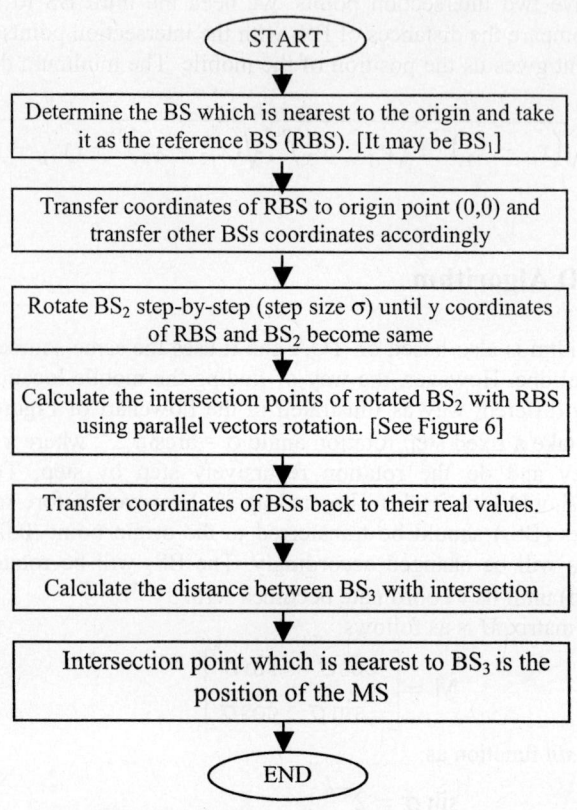

Fig. 4. The SDD algorithm

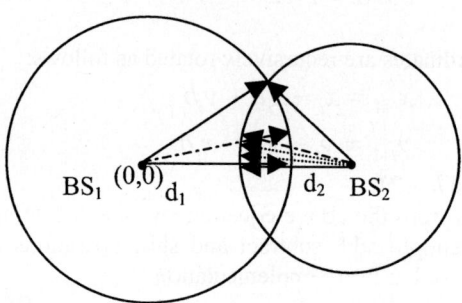

Fig. 5. Idea of Positioning

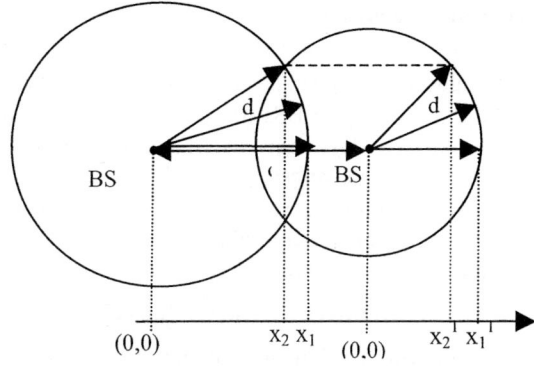

Fig. 6. Parallel rotations of vectors

Before starting vector rotations, we have to check which radius is larger. The smaller radius needs more rotations than the other one. If we assume that RBS (BS_1) has larger radius (i.e. $d_1 > d_2$), the conditions of rotation should be as follows;

```
While( xᵢ+xᵢ¹ > d)
        Rotate d₁
        While(yᵢ>yᵢ¹)
                Rotate d₂
        End while
End while
```

Rotation equations for d_1 are:

$$x_{i+1} = x_i - x_i a - y_i b \qquad (16)$$

$$y_{i+1} = y_i - y_i a + x_i b \ . \qquad (17)$$

And rotation equations for d_2 are:

$$x_{i+1}^{\ 1} = x_i^{\ 1} - x_i^{\ 1} a - y_i^{\ 1} b \qquad (18)$$

$$y_{i+1}^{\ 1} = y_i^{\ 1} - y_i^{\ 1} a + x_i^{\ 1} b \ . \qquad (19)$$

As shown in Figure 6, when x coordinates of vectors d_1 and d_2 heads are x_1 and x_1^1; we need to rotate because $x_1 + x_1^1 > d$. However, when x coordinates are x_2 and x_2^1, we don't need to rotate because $x_2 + x_2^1 = d$.

The first intersection point (x_{c1}, y_{c1}) can be found as a result of these rotations. Then, since we assumed that RBS is at the origin, the second intersection point is:

$$x_{c2} = x_{c1} \quad \text{and} \quad y_{c2} = -y_{c1} \ . \qquad (20)$$

The obtained intersection points are rotated ones. We have to rotate them back by a number of steps equals to the number of steps used in the rotation of BS_2. To obtain the real intersection points we should transfer BSs back to their original values.

Finally, we compare the distances of BS_3 with the intersection points and the nearest intersection point gives us the position of the mobile.

3.1 Convergence and Accuracy

Convergence of our algorithm is guaranteed because of the following two facts:
- Since the nearest three BSs are used for the MS positioning, the largest radius is always less than the distance between BSs. Therefore our algorithm always converges.
- In the parallel rotation of vectors we rotate the larger one first.

To estimate the accuracy of our algorithm and under the assumption that d_1 is the larger radius, we can obtain the accuracy as follows

$$\max|\Delta y_1| = \max|d_1|\sin\sigma \tag{21}$$

where Δy_1 is the increment of coordinate y in one step of rotation.
Using equation (10), we have

$$\max|\Delta y_1| = \max|d_1|2^{-k}. \tag{22}$$

In practice, a macro cell of a cellular system usually has a radius of 20km, and if the required accuracy is approximately 40m, we have

$$2^k = \frac{\max|d_1|}{\max|\Delta y_1|} = \frac{20\times 10^3}{40} = 500. \tag{23}$$

Therefore, $k = \log_2 500 \approx 9$.

4 Simulation Results and Analysis

We used Matlab 6.5 package in our analysis. We wrote programs for both traditional and our SDD algorithms. We run our programs to find the location of a mobile in the coverage area of the three BSs. The experiments were repeated for many arbitrary positions of the mobile. These arbitrary positions were taken using Matlab random number generator for each of the axes.

For the purpose of comparing our algorithm with the traditional one, we calculated the number of required operations to find the location of the mobile in each case. We used the Table 1 for the weights of the operations for 20 bits accuracy [14].

Table 1. Weights of the Operations

Operation	Add	Subtract	Shift	Multip.	Division	Square Root	Sin	Arcsin	Cos	Tan	Arctan
Weight	1	1	1	40	40	100	404	404	404	1448	1448

It is worth to mention that parallel vector rotations in our algorithm can be implemented in hardware in such a way that rotations are done simultaneously (SDD with parallel implementation: SDD-P).

Figure 7 shows the number of operations needed by each of the algorithms versus $\sin(\sigma)$ (which explicitly specifies the step rotation angle σ, and implicitly specifies the accuracy level). Note that $\sin(\sigma)$ is listed on the x axes in descending order to reflect an ascending order of the accuracy level.

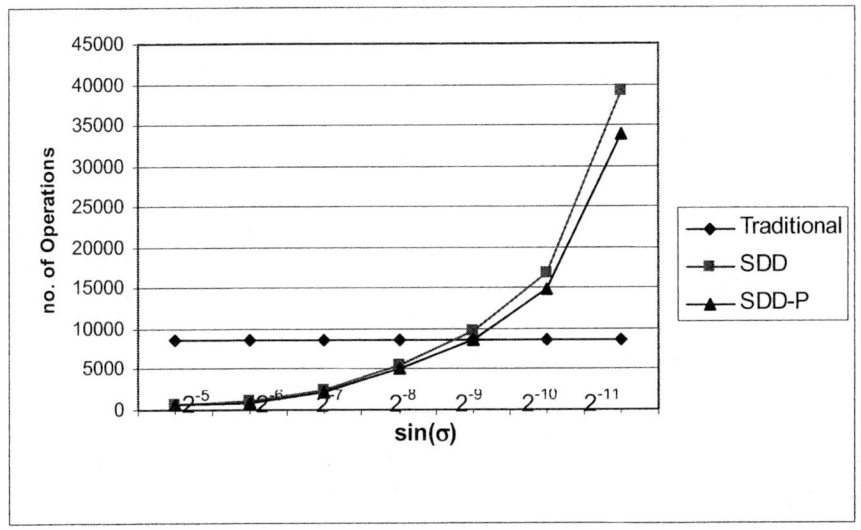

Fig. 7. Number of operations versus sin(σ) for the traditional and our algorithms

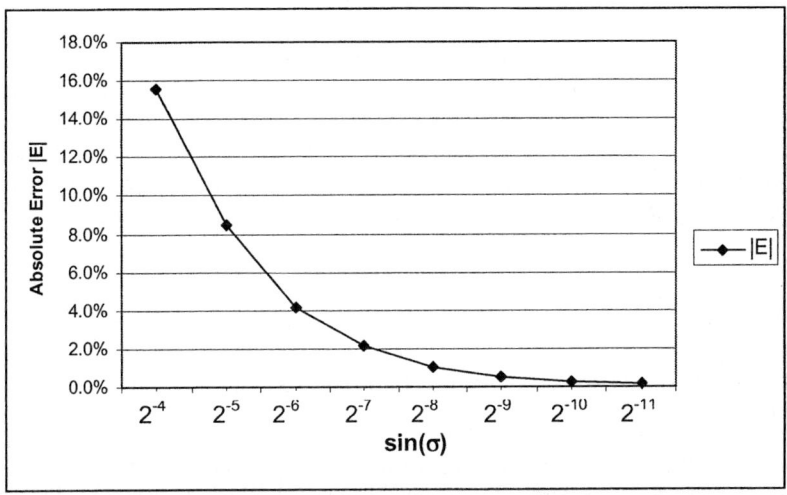

Fig. 8. Absolute rrror of mobile location versus sin(σ) for our algorithm

The traditional algorithm shows a constant performance, because rotation in traditional algorithm is done in one step, and therefore the number of operations is fixed and does not depend on the step rotation angle. For our algorithms the required number of operations increases as the step angle decreases (i.e. accuracy level increases). It is clear from the figure that for step rotation angle σ with sin(σ) greater than 2^{-9} our algorithm shows better performance than the traditional one for software and hardware implementations. For sin(σ) less than 2^{-9}, software implementation of traditional algorithm gives better performance however if the implementation is done in hardware (best approach) our algorithm will outperform the traditional one, because of its simple add and shift operations. Since the number of operations for SDD-P is reduced, this result in more superiority of our algorithm compared to the traditional one.

Figure 8 shows the absolute error in determining the mobile location against $\sin(\sigma)$. The absolute error decreases when the accuracy increases (step rotation angle decreases). For $\sin(\sigma)=2^{-9}$ a very good level of accuracy can be achieved. Referring to the accuracy calculations given in section 3.1 before, this corresponds to an accuracy of approximately 40m which is within the E-911 standards. Note that an accuracy of approximately 10m can be achieved for $\sin(\sigma)=2^{-11}$.

5 Conclusion

This paper presents a new hardware oriented algorithm (SDD) based on TOA measurements to determine the position of a mobile phone. Since all operations in our algorithm are simple add and shift operations, it can be implemented in hardware using a simple FPGA chip. Our results show that for an accuracy level of up to $\sin(\sigma)=2^{-9}$, our algorithm outperforms the traditional one in terms of both software and hardware implementations. It should be noted that such an accuracy level is sufficient to satisfy E-911 standards. For better accuracy levels, our algorithm maintains its superiority from the hardware implementation point of view.

Our proposed algorithm ignores the properties of the signal propagation environment which we plan to carry out in the future work. Currently, we are working on the use of this algorithm for mobile phone tracking. Another possible direction of study could be to modify this algorithm for finding the position of a mobile phone in 3-D space. Integrating our algorithm with the GPS system is noteworthy.

References

1. Laitinen. H., et al.: Cellular Location Technology. CELLO Project Technical Report, CELLO-WP2-VTT-D03-007-Int, (2001)
2. Roos, T., Myllymaki, P., Tirri, H.: A Statistical Modeling Approach to Location Estimation. IEEE Transactions on Mobile Computing **1**(1) (2002) 59–69
3. Chi, H., Jan, R.: Cell-Based Positioning Method for Wireless Networks, Parallel and Distributed Systems. In: Proc., Ninth Int. Conf. on 17-20. (2002) 375–380
4. Spirito, M.A.: On the Accuracy of Cellular Mobile Station Location Estimation. IEEE Transactions on Vehicular Technology **50**(3) (2001) 674–685
5. Koshima, H., Hoshen, J.: Personal Locator Services Emerge. IEEE Spectrum **37**(2) 41–48
6. Zhao, Y.: Standardization of Mobile Phone Positioning for 3G Systems. IEEE Communications Magazine **40**(4) (2002) 108–116
7. Weiss, A.J.: On the Accuracy of a Cellular Location System Based on RSS Measurements. IEEE Transactions on Vehicular Technology **52**(6) (2003) 1508–1518
8. Jami, I., Ali, M., Ormondroyd, R.F.: Comparison of Methods of Locating and Tracking Cellular Mobiles. Novel Methods of Location and Tracking of Cellular Mobiles and Their System Applications (Ref.No.1999/046). IEE Colloquium, London UK, 1/1-1/6.

9. Lopes, L, Villier, E., Ludden, B.: GSM Standards Activity on Location, Novel Methods of Location and Tracking of Cellular Mobiles and Their System Applications (Ref.NO.1999/046). IEE Colloquium on 05/17/1999, London UK, 7/1-7/6.
10. Messier, G.G., Nielsen, J.S.: An Analysis of TOA-Based Location for IS-95 Mobiles. Vehicular Technology Conference, Vol. 2. (1999) 1064–1071
11. Caffery, J.J.: A New Approach to the Geometry of TOA Location. Vehicular Technology Conference, Boston, MA USA, Vol.4. (2000) 1943-1949
12. Nannarelli, A., Lang, T.: Low-Power Divider, IEEE Transactions on Computers **48**(1) (1999) 2–14
13. Hekstra, G. J., Deprettere, F.A.: Fast Rotations: Low-cost Arithmetic Methods for Orthonormal Rotation. In: Proc. of the 13th Sym. on Computer Arithmetic. (1997) 116–126
14. Muller, J.-M.: Elementary Function Algorithms and Implementation. Birkhauser, (1997)

Relay Attacks on Bluetooth Authentication and Solutions

Albert Levi[1], Erhan Çetintaş[2], Murat Aydos[3],
Çetin Kaya Koç[4], and M. Ufuk Çağlayan[5]

[1] Sabanci University, Fac. of Eng. & Nat. Sci., Orhanli, Tuzla, TR-34956, Istanbul, Turkey
levi@sabanciuniv.edu
[2] TUBITAK – UEKAE, National Research Institute of Electronics and Cryptology
Gebze, TR-41470, Kocaeli, Turkey
cetintas@uekae.tubitak.gov.tr
[3] Pamukkale University, Dept. of Computer Engineering, Denizli, TR-20020, Turkey
maydos@pamukkale.edu.tr
[4] Oregon State Univ., School of Electr. Eng. & Comp. Sci., Corvallis, OR 97331 USA
koc@ece.orst.edu
[5] Boğaziçi University, Dept. of Computer Engineering, Istanbul, TR-34342, Turkey
caglayan@boun.edu.tr

Abstract. We describe relay attacks on Bluetooth authentication protocol. The aim of these attacks is impersonation. The attacker does not need to guess or obtain a common secret known to both victims in order to set up these attacks, merely to relay the information it receives from one victim to the other during the authentication protocol run. Bluetooth authentication protocol allows such a relay if the victims do not hear each other. Such a setting is highly probable. We analyze the attacks for several scenarios and propose practical solutions. Moreover, we simulate attacks to make sure about their feasibility. These simulations show that current Bluetooth specifications do not have defensive mechanisms for relay attacks. However, relay attacks create a significant partial delay during the connection that might be useful for detection.

1 Introduction and Background

Bluetooth [1] is a promising short-range radio link technology for wireless connectivity of portable electronic devices, such as mobile phones, laptop computers, palm computers and digital cameras. The Bluetooth system operates in the 2.4 GHz ISM (Industrial Scientific Medicine) band. In order to avoid interference with other piconets (piconet is Bluetooth's personal/local area network) and/or other devices using the ISM band, the master of a piconet synchronizes its slaves to hop among several RF channels in a pseudo-random sequence.

Bluetooth specification defines link level security mechanisms to provide confidentiality, integrity and authentication between Bluetooth devices. However, there are some vulnerabilities in the Bluetooth security as proposed in [2, 3, 4].

In this paper, we point to relay attacks on Bluetooth authentication protocol. In relay attacks, the attacker places itself in two distinct piconets and picks two victims, one in each piconet. The attacker impersonates those victims by forwarding authentication messages generated by one of them to another between the piconets. As opposed to the man-in-the-middle attacks described in [2], the attacker does not need to know any shared secret between the victims in order to set up our relay attacks. We simulate relay attacks to assess their feasibility. Moreover we use simulation to evaluate the delays caused by the attack and to see if these delays could be used as a detection mechanism. We propose two other low-cost solutions as well.

The rest of Section 1 gives an overview of Bluetooth key management and authentication scheme. Relay attacks are explained in Section 2. Mechanisms to detect relay attacks are proposed in Section 3. Simulation results are presented in Section 4. Conclusions and some discussions are in Section 5.

1.1 Key Management and Authentication in Bluetooth

There are several key types in Bluetooth, but the attacks described here depend on the initialization and combination keys. Initialization key (K_{init}) is calculated at both sides of communication using a pre-shared PIN, a random number and a Bluetooth Device Address (BD_ADDR). K_{init} is used to exchange the *Combination Key*, which is one of the members of the Bluetooth "Link Key" family. These keys are used for authentication. Both ends of communication, say A and B, contribute to the combination key (K_{AB}) in a secure way by encrypting some random numbers. Current link key or K_{init} is used as the key for this encryption. Link keys are stored in Bluetooth devices and they are reused whenever necessary.

Bluetooth uses a simple challenge-response authentication scheme. The verifier sends a 128-bit random number called AU_RAND to the claimant. Claimant calculates the authentication response called SRES, which is a cryptographic function of AU_RAND, its own BD_ADDR, and the current link key. Claimant sends SRES to the verifier. Meanwhile the verifier computes the same SRES and checks whether the computed one is equal to the received one. If so, that means the claimant is really who it claims to be.

2 Relay Attacks

In this section, we describe relay attacks proposed in the paper. In the relay attacks, adversary C talks to victim A posing as victim B, and to B posing as A. All authentication messages that C needs are generated by real A and B. C conveys these messages from A/B to B/A. We present two types of relay attacks: (i) two-sided, and (ii) one-sided. In a two-sided relay attack, both victims are impersonated. In a one-sided attack, only one victim is impersonated.

In [2], some man-in-the-middle and impersonation type of attacks are proposed where the attacker knows or can guess the PIN or existing link key between victims. Relay attacks are similar to man-in-the-middle attacks. There exists an adversary located between the sender and receiver, but the only activity of the adversary is to relay information that it receives from one to another without changing the content. Unlike the attacks in [2], the adversary does not need to know a shared secret.

2.1 Special Conditions of Bluetooth and Attack Settings

Relay attacks are possible if:
(i) actual communication between the real sender and receiver is disconnected and they cannot listen to each other anymore,
(ii) network infrastructure does not have a global infrastructure for routing and locating its users, and
(iii) adversary is capable enough to impersonate each of the victims to the other, even if the victims are located in distant locations.

As an example attack setting, suppose the victims A and B have communicated for some time and then terminated the communication. They may easily end up in different locations due to their mobile and ad-hoc behavior. In this example, we assume two users working in the sales department of a Bluetooth-enabled office. These two users exchange their data using a service configured in Bluetooth Security Mode 3 that requires only authentication. It is assumed that no encryption and application layer security are employed for this service. The users' laptops are normally part of a piconet within their department, but whenever one of them moved to conference room for a meeting, it becomes a part of the piconet in the conference room. Even if they might be close to each other, they cannot listen to each other since every piconet has a different frequency hopping order. Once the attacker impersonates the users, it can, for example, transfer fraudulent data or alter sales reports.

Although there are valuable efforts in the literature for forming and routing for Bluetooth Scatternets [7, 8, 9], the short-range characteristics of Bluetooth devices would not enable to have a Bluetooth-based global ad hoc network, thus satisfying the feasibility of the conditions (i) and (ii) above. One may argue that some application layer Bluetooth profiles, such as IP over Bluetooth, could provide global connectivity. However, such applications should be implemented over L2CAP (Logical Link Control and Adaptation Protocol) and consequently the LMP (Link manager Protocol) layers of Bluetooth at which relay attacks are implemented. Thus, such global connectivity does not help to avoid relay attacks since packets used in the relay attacks remain local and do not pass through the gateways.

In order to satisfy condition (iii), the adversary, C, should contain two different Bluetooth units, Ac and Bc (Ac and Bc denote A and B impersonated by C), with adjustable BD_ADDRs. Ac should be located close to B, and Bc close to A. The adversary C is also equipped with a special communication interface between Ac and Bc. This interface is not necessarily a Bluetooth interface; actually Bluetooth is not useful for communication between Ac and Bc if they are far apart. Some other wireless or wired methods can be used for communication between distant Ac and Bc. Moreover, C should know the pseudo-random frequency hopping order of real A and B in order to eavesdrop on their communication. Jakobsson and Wetzel proposed a method to determine this order in [2].

Each Bluetooth device is identified using an overt and fixed Bluetooth Device Address (BD_ADDR). It is embedded in the device and normally not changeable. However, a hostile manufacturer can build a Bluetooth device with an adjustable BD_ADDR. With the current trend of increased Bluetooth deployment in almost all type of mobile devices, attacks on Bluetooth may create a spying market and such manufacturers may come into sight.

2.2 Two-Sided Relay Attack

This attack is shown in Figure 1. Here, C must wait for a real request for connection from either A or B. Suppose real A wants to establish connection to B. The connection establishment process starts with the paging procedure. A first pages Bc thinking that it is real B. After the paging procedure, A sends *LMP_host_connection_req* command to Bc. Bc accepts the connection request by sending back *LMP_accepted*. Meanwhile, Ac pages B and initiates a connection establishment procedure posing as A.

The above connection establishment process is valid if victims A and B are distant. If they are close to each other, in order A to connect Bc instead of B, the attacker's Bc interface must respond to the paging request faster than B. The details of such a setting are described by Kügler [4]. In addition, Kügler [4] also discusses that the attacker's Ac interface must use a clock value different from the clock of A. Thus, both A and B use the same frequency hopping order with different offsets and do not hear each other.

The current link key between A and B may or may not be changed at each connection. The attacker does not need to know this key. Thus, changing the link key or using the current one do not cause any problem in attack setting. If the link is to be changed, then the next step is the exchange of combination key contributions (the random numbers which are encrypted by XORing with the current link key). A sends its encrypted random number, RAND_NR$_A$, to Bc in an *LMP_comb_key* command. C, using its Ac interface, relays this encrypted random number to real B as if it is sent by A. After receiving this number, B sends out its encrypted random number RAND_NR$_B$ to Ac, and C forwards it to real A while wearing its Bc hat. After these message rounds, both real A and real B compute the same combination key K$_{AB}$ and this key is assigned as new link key.

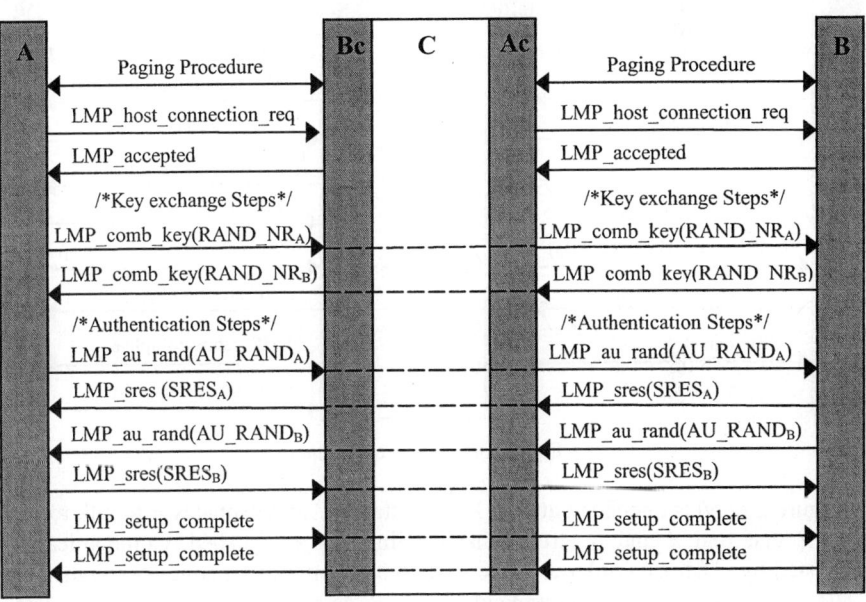

Fig. 1. Two-sided relay attack

The next steps are for authentication. A sends *LMP_au_rand* command to Bc (thinking that it is B) along with a 128 bit random number called AU_RAND_A. After sending AU_RAND_A, A expects the corresponding authentication response $SRES_A$. Bc cannot calculate $SRES_A$, since it does not know the current link key, but C (using its Ac interface) can forward AU_RAND_A to real B in another *LMP_au_rand* command as if A requests authentication of B. The response of real B to this command is an *LMP_sres* command that contains $SRES_A$. C forwards $SRES_A$ to A in another *LMP_sres* command as the authentication response of Bc. After that A thinks that B is authenticated, but the truth is that Bc is authenticated. Similar steps are taken in the case of mutual authentication where B requests authentication of Ac thinking that it is A. At the end, both A and B think that they authenticated each other, but the fact is that C impersonated both of them. C exploits both real A and B to generate authentication responses $SRES_B$ and $SRES_A$.

If there is no existing link key established beforehand or the link key is somehow unavailable (e.g. lost, compromised, expired, etc.), then A and B should initiate K_{init} generation before combination key generation steps. Two-sided attack works in such a setting too, because the attacker would only need to relay some messages as in combination key generation steps.

2.3 One-Sided Relay Attack

The adversary C can make use of this attack by initiating communication with one of the victims impersonating the other one. This attack is possible only when the victims can be convinced to use the existing link key.

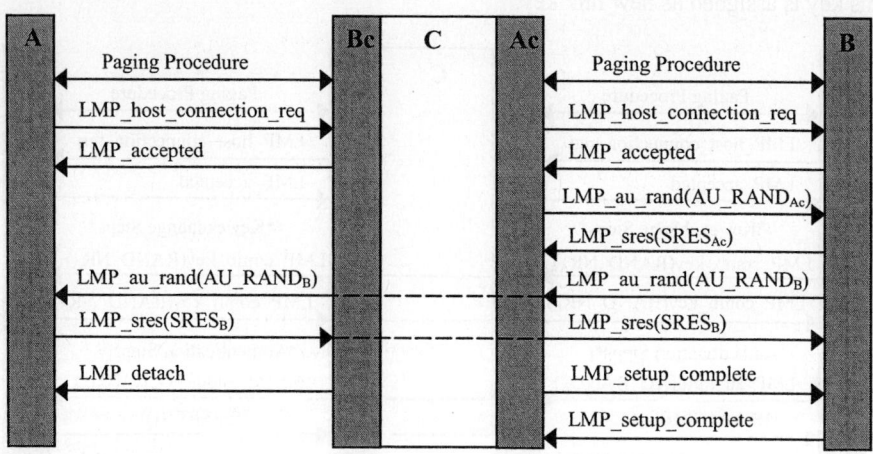

Fig. 2. One-sided relay attack

Figure 2 depicts one-sided attack. In this attack, C impersonates A to talk to B. We assume that real A and B already have a link key established. Communication is requested by C (Ac). In order to make new connection Ac first pages B and then sends *LMP_host_connection_req* command to B. B accepts the connection request by sending back *LMP_accepted*. At the same time Bc pages A and starts the connection establishment procedure with A. After the first step, Ac sends LMP_au_rand to B. In this command Ac includes a dummy random number AU_RAND_{Ac}. B wrongfully thinks that real A requests authentication and sends back the corresponding authentication response $SRES_{Ac}$. Ac has no way to check the correctness of $SRES_{Ac}$, so it implicitly assumes that real B is indeed genuine. Having sent $SRES_{Ac}$, B sends its authentication challenge AU_RAND_B to Ac. Ac should obtain $SRES_B$, which is the SRES corresponding to AU_RAND_B, so C sends out AU_RAND_B to real A using its Bc interface. Real A mistakenly thinks that B requests authentication, and calculates and sends $SRES_B$ to Bc. Then Ac forwards $SRES_B$ to real B. The connection setup is completed by mutually sending $LMP\_setup\_complete$. These steps authenticate Ac to B as if Ac were the real A. At the end Bc sends an LMP_detach command to end its communication with real A, since A is not needed anymore.

Although the above attack explanation is for distant victims, it also works for close ones by using different clock values as explained in Section 2.2 for two-sided attack.

3 Proposed Solutions

In this section, we propose three practical solutions to detect relay attacks.

3.1 Solution 1: For Victims in Close Piconets

One method for preventing the relay attacks is to include unforgeable piconet-specific information in SRES calculation. Such information could be hop sequence parameters, channel access code, which is added to each packet sent within the piconet, and the sync word, which is part of the channel access code. Unfortunately all of them are based on LAP (lower address part) of master's BD_ADDR and/or master's clock. Since the attacker is the master in one of the piconets, it can enforce those parameters that are learned from the other piconet where the attacker is a slave. The only exception is when these two piconets are close to each other. Channel access code, sync word, hop sequence and phase cannot be the same for those piconets due to interference problems. That means piconet specific information based relay attack control works for close piconets.

Implementation of this control is easy. It is sufficient to consider master's clock and LAP values in SRES calculation. To do so, the least significant 42 bits of the AU_RAND values could be XORed with the concatenation of clock and LAP values at each piconet for SRES calculation and verification. Real A and B use different clock and/or LAP values since the attacker cannot enforce the same values, because otherwise messages of two piconets mix up. The updated authentication mechanism is shown in Figure 3. The original Bluetooth authentication scheme does not have the XOR part, i.e. AU_RAND is directly fed into E1 boxes.

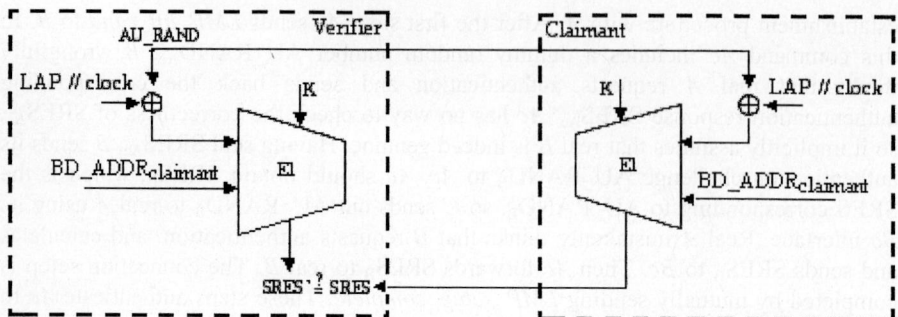

Fig. 3. Updated Bluetooth challenge-response authentication scheme that is sensitive to piconet (master) clock and LAP

3.2 Solution 2: For One-Sided Relay Attack

In the original Bluetooth scheme, mutual authentication is performed exclusively between master and slave. First, one is authenticated with AU_RAND (challenge) and SRES (response) exchange. Then the other is authenticated again using a challenge/response mechanism. We propose to change this authentication message exchanges in a nested form such that first both parties exchange their AU_RAND values and claimant does not send its SRES before getting the legitimate SRES from the verifier. This message exchange is shown in Figure 4.

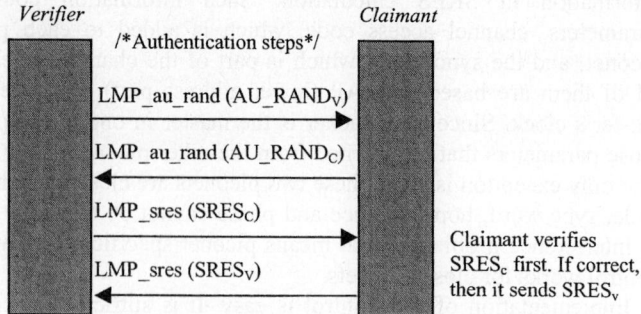

Fig. 4. Nested mutual authentication

In this method, which is effective against one-sided attack, the attacker cannot obtain SRES values from the victims, since both victims first wait for the SRES value from the other party (i.e. from the attacker). Since the attacker acts as a verifier in both piconets, its authentication challenge is responded with another authentication challenge from the genuine entities; SRES values are not sent and protocol eventually times out. Unfortunately, nested mutual authentication does not solve the problems associated with two-sided attacks. One of the victims is the verifier in that scenario, so the attacker can obtain the SRES from it.

3.3 Solution 3: Variance in Delays

This solution is based on consideration of variance in end-to-end delays between normal connection cases and attack cases, as will be discussed in Section 4.

4 Simulation Results

In order to analyze the effectiveness of the proposed relay attacks, we developed a simulator using C++ programming language that simulates baseband link connection and authentication procedures according to the baseband, security and LMP specifications.

First, we implemented the attack scenarios in our simulation environment and Link Manager transactions of the simulated Bluetooth devices are compared in normal connection and attack cases. During this analysis, we have realized that there is absolutely no difference in terms of transaction outputs between attacked victims and a non-attacked ones. Thus, we conclude that victim devices cannot be aware of the relay attacks by checking connection establishment transactions. These transaction outputs are not shown here because of space restrictions.

4.1 Timing Analysis

In our attack scenarios, one victim waits for receiving the authentication response SRES while the attacker is getting this SRES from the other victim. If this duration is too much, LMP response timeout may exceed. In addition, due to relay attacks the connection establishment process may take long time and one of the victims may be aware of the attack. Thus, in our experiments we measure the connection establishment time and the latency in receiving LMP_SRES. Here only the timings of successful transmissions are taken into account. In case of retransmissions, which are probable in Bluetooth, the baseband layer should inform link manager so that the corresponding timers are reset.

We first measured connection establishment times during normal connection cases and attack cases. Particular increase has been noticed in the connection time of an attacked victim as compared to non-attacked one. However, as discussed in [5], connection time can vary between devices which are produced by different manufacturers or whose clocks are not initially well synchronized. Thus we conclude that the increase was not big enough in order to conclude that connection time increase could be used as an attack detection mechanism.

In our experiments, we also considered how our relay attacks affect the duration between sending LMP_AU_RAND command and receiving LMP_SRES response in victim devices A and B. Figure 5 shows a histogram of the latency in receiving LMP_SRES in the normal connection establishment. A obtains the link key from *Host A* before receiving LMP_AU_RAND from B. However, B gets the link key after receiving LMP_AU_RAND from A. Therefore, A waits longer than B to receive LMP_SRES. The average waiting time is 10.378 ms for A and 2.008 ms for B.

Figure 6 and Figure 7 show the histograms of the waiting times for receiving LMP_SRES response in two-sided and one-sided relay attacks.

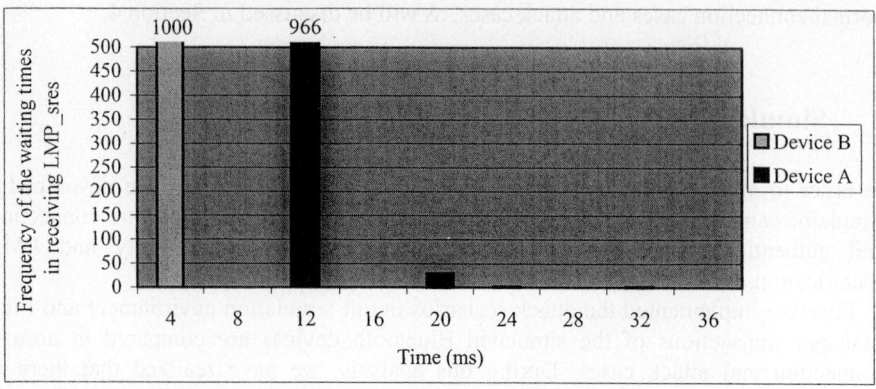

Fig. 5. Histogram for the waiting times for receiving LMP_sres in the normal connection

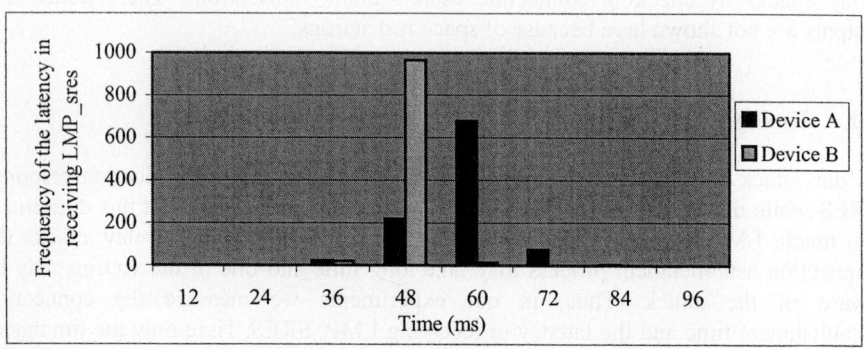

Fig. 6. Frequency of the latency in receiving LMP_sres in two-sided relay attack

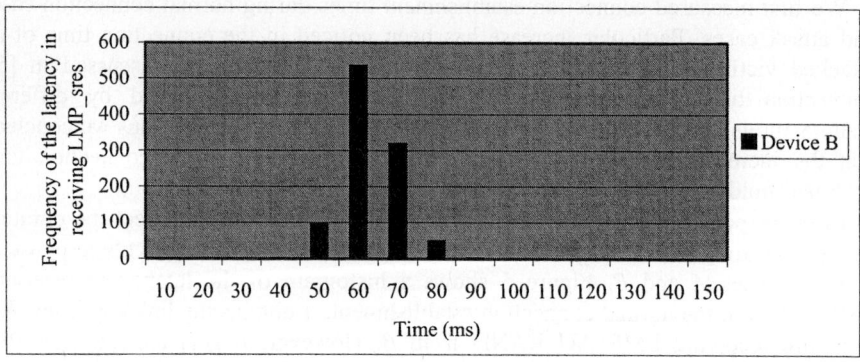

Fig. 7. Frequency of the latency in receiving LMP_sres in one-sided relay attacks

In two-sided relay attack, the average latency in receiving LMP_SRES for A and B is 50.978 and 39.625 ms respectively. As we see in Figure 7, most of the waiting times are between 50 ms and 80 ms (on average 62.578 ms) in one-sided relay attack. Thus we conclude that relay attacks increase the latency in receiving LMP_SRES response; two-sided relay attack increases this latency 5 times in A and 20 times in B. Similarly, the latency in one-sided relay attack is 30 times more than the latency in the normal connection. According to Bluetooth Link Manager Protocol specification, the time between receiving an LMP PDU and sending a valid response PDU must be less than the LMP response timeout, which is 30 seconds. Therefore, the LMP response timeout does not expire due to relay attacks. However, if enough intelligence is added to LMP protocol, the victims may detect the relay attacks by checking the considerable increase in latency of getting LMP_SRES response. For example, one device measures average delays in connection establishment processes and stores these values in its memory. During each connection, it estimates the current delay by considering a sequence of previous delays and then compares the estimated delay with new measured one. If there is a major difference, then the device may decide that there is an attack going on. One possible method for estimating the current delay would be simply to compute arithmetic average of stored delays. Since it is not necessary to store all past delays, this method is appropriate for devices with limited memory resources. Another method for the current delay estimation would be to compute exponential average delay by using the smoothing procedure as in the TCP protocol. With this method, we can give the most recent measurements a greater weight than the older ones. Dynamically estimating the current delay reduces the impact of transmission errors in decisions about the relay attacks.

5   Conclusion and Discussions

We present two important relay attacks on Bluetooth authentication method for impersonation purposes. The adversary need not obtain any secret (like PINs or current keys) of the victims. He/she simply relays some protocol messages from one victim to another without alteration.

Relay attacks are to make fail only Bluetooth authentication, not encryption. The attacker cannot continue its attack if the victims prefer to have encrypted communication. However, in Bluetooth specification [1], having no encryption is a valid option, and during negotiation the adversary can indeed convince the victims not to have encrypted communication. Bluetooth authentication is performed to authenticate entities, not messages, mostly for access control decisions. Traditionally access control does not require encrypted communications, once the access is granted. Thus, message encryption and entity authentication need not coexist all the time. As suggested in [6], it is conceivable that a device might want to perform only-authentication because it was not using encryption on the link, but it still wants to check if it is communicating with the correct device. The processing power limitations of a device might not let it use encryption that requires constant processing. However, authentication is once-per-session and can be tolerated even for restricted devices.

Relay attacks are based on a deception: both victims think they are in the same piconet. However, they are not. They are actually in different piconets. If the victims can include some information about their actual piconets in SRES, then relay attacks could be detected. As discussed in this paper, such piconet-specific information is unfortunately forgeable by the attacker, if the piconets are not close to each other. If they are close, then inclusion of LAP (lower address part) of the master BD_ADDR and master clock in SRES messages solves the problem. Such a solution is of limited use, but does not cause a remarkable load on the entities; the extra processing is just an XOR computation. Another limited use, but efficient precaution could be to exchange the challenge messages (AU_RAND) before sending out the responses (SRES). The claimant waits for the SRES for its challenge first. In this way, it does not give out the SRES to be relayed. This solution works only if the attacker is the verifier in both piconets. This situation corresponds to the one-sided attack described in this paper.

In the simulations of the attacks, we have realized that the victims cannot detect relay attacks if they strictly follow Bluetooth specifications. On the other hand, our analysis of the simulation results demonstrates that there is a perceptible variation in some end-to-end delays between the normal and the attacked connections. One device can estimate the current delay by observing the pattern of delay for recent connection establishments, and then compare the estimated delay with new measured one. A significant increase means that there may be an attack going on. Simple average or exponential average methods would be used for the current delay estimation. Such an intelligent adaptive mechanism can be incorporated in Bluetooth connection establishment procedure at LMP level to determine both types of relay attacks in a low-cost and effective way.

References

1. Bluetooth SIG. Specification of the Bluetooth System – Bluetooth Core Specification, Vol. 0-3, Version 1.2. http://www.bluetooth.org. (2003)
2. Jakobsson, M., Wetzel, S.: Security Weaknesses in Bluetooth. Lecture Notes in Computer Science, Vol. 2020. Springer-Verlag, (2001) 176–191
3. Vainio. J.T.: Bluetooth Security. http://www.niksula.cs.hut.fi/~jiitv/bluesec.html. (2000)
4. Kügler, D.: Man in the Middle Attacks on Bluetooth. Lecture Notes in Computer Science, Vol. 2742. Springer-Verlag, (2003) 149–161
5. Welsh, E., Murphy, P., Frantz, P.: Improving Connection Times for Bluetooth Devices in Mobile Environments. International Conference on Fundamentals of Electronics, Communications and Computer Sciences (ICFS). Tokyo, Japan (2002)
6. Bray, J., Sturman, C.F.: Bluetooth: Connect Without Cables. Prentice-Hall, (2000)
7. Bhagwat, P., Segall, A.: A Routing Vector Method (RVM) for Routing in Bluetooth Scatternets. In: IEEE International Workshop on Mobile Multimedia Communications (MoMuC'99). (1999)
8. Wang, Z., Thomas, R.J., Haas, Z.: Bluenet - A New Scatternet Formation Scheme. In: 35th Annual Hawaii International Conference on System Sciences. (2002)
9. Kapoor, R., Gerla, M.: A Zone Routing Protocol for Bluetooth scatternets. In: WCNC. (2003)

Reliable Delivery of Popular Data Services in WIDE*

Sinan Isik, Mehmet Yunus Donmez, and Cem Ersoy

NETLAB, Department of Computer Engineering, Bogazici University, Istanbul, Turkiye
{isiks,donmezme,ersoy}@boun.edu.tr

Abstract. Wireless Information Delivery Environment (WIDE) is a distributed data dissemination system, which uses IEEE 802.11b technology. WIDE aims to deliver popular information services to registered mobile clients in WLAN hot spots. Data delivery is based on broadcasting and multicasting. System specific reliability mechanisms are needed because of the unreliable medium and transport protocol. Reliability is assured with a combination of the Forward Error Correction (FEC), the data carousel and the ARQ techniques. This paper presents the proposed system architecture with the details of reliable data delivery mechanisms. Performance evaluation results of the proposed reliability mechanisms using the implemented prototype are also included in this paper.

1 Introduction

The dominant use of IEEE 802.11b WLANs is to provide Internet access for mobile users as distributed hot spots. However, WIDE (Wireless Information Delivery Environment) [1] is a system intended to offer data services other than Internet access to its users. WIDE aims to deliver popular information services, which appeals general interest such as entertainment, shopping and education in distributed hot spots. WIDE hot spots can be found in locations where there is the appropriate user density, but users have to walk through the service area in order to access the service, and then take their service away for later consumption. As users walk through the coverage area, the most recent version of the subscribed information services will be automatically downloaded to their mobile terminals without any user intervention.

Since the system offers popular data services, it should perform in an acceptable level in terms of reception time for individual clients when there are many users demanding the same service. Hence, the design is based on data multicasting to provide scalability and efficient use of the wireless channel. However, since TCP does not support multicasting, we used UDP with a specific reliability mechanism.

In this paper, we concentrate on the reliability mechanisms in WIDE system. ARQ techniques are generally used in unicast environments. Especially in a multicast environment, it might be highly inefficient because of uncorrelated losses at different groups of receivers. In these cases, Forward Error Correction (FEC) [2] techniques, possibly combined with ARQ may be useful [3]. Here the sender prevents losses by

---

* This work is partially supported by the State Planning Organization of Turkey under the grant number 98K120890, and by the Bogazici University Research Projects under the grant number 02A105D.

transmitting some amount of redundant information, which allows the reconstruction of missing data at the receiver without further interactions. FEC is also attractive for multicast since different loss patterns can be recovered from the same set of data.

The data carousel or the broadcast disk [4] is another approach to eliminate the need for retransmission and to allow receivers to access data asynchronously, ensuring full reliability. In this approach, the source repeatedly loops through transmission of all data packets. Receivers may join the stream at any time and listen until they receive all distinct packets comprising the transmission. Clearly, the reception overhead at a receiver, measured in terms of unnecessary receptions, can be extremely high using this approach. WIDE system employs a reliability mechanism, which is a mixture of the data carousel, the FEC and the ARQ techniques.

In Section 2, we give a brief overview of the WIDE system architecture and the data delivery mechanism. The details of the reliability mechanism are presented in Section 3. Section 4 presents the performance results evaluated on implemented WIDE prototype. Section 5 concludes the paper, suggesting some future works.

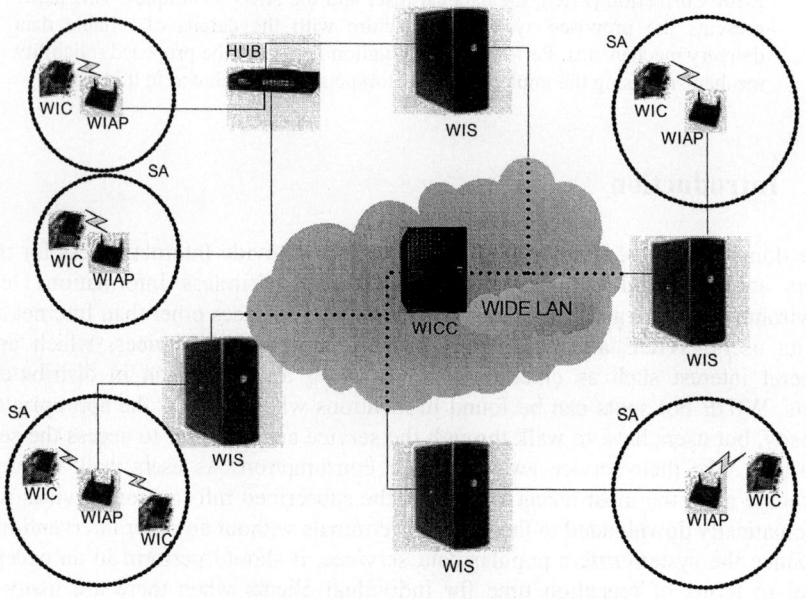

Fig. 1. Building blocks of WIDE

2 Wireless Information Delivery Environment

WIDE is a system, which is designed for delivering popular information services in moderate-sized environments. There are components having specific tasks in WIDE design, which form the WIDE network. The network is composed of both wired and wireless mediums. Two main system components, called WIDE cluster controller (WICC) and WIDE servers (WIS) are located in the wired part of the system and they communicate through WIDE LAN. WIDE servers are responsible for preparing and delivering information services to clients. WIDE cluster controller deals with the system administration. WIDE access points (WIAPs) are located at the end-points of the wired network to provide wireless connectivity of WIDE clients (WIC) to the servers. The geographical area covered by WIAPs that are connected to a server is called the service area (SA). The building blocks of the WIDE are shown in Figure 1.

Client-server communication in WIDE is divided into periodic time frames, which are also divided into sub frames. Each sub frame is a time period, which is dedicated to a certain communication task. This frame structure is formed to organize the message and data transfers, which decreases the number of collisions and provides efficient use of the channel. Periodic time frames are called Communication Cycles (CCs). Figure 2 illustrates the structure of the CC.

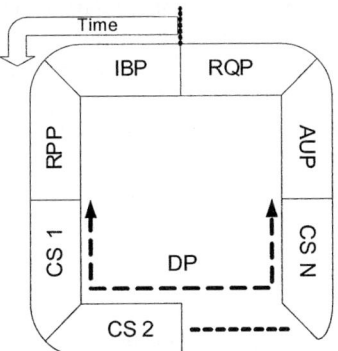

Fig. 2. Communication cycle

The sub frames, which are named as index broadcast period (IBP), reception preparation period (RPP), data period (DP), authentication period (AUP) and request period (RQP), sequentially follow each other in this order in a CC. DP is also divided into sub frames, called communication slots (CS).

A scheduler running in the server decides data to transmit during each CC and prepares the index. The scheduling of an information service in a server requires at least one client in the service area of that server who previously subscribed or has just subscribed to that service. If the client has just subscribed to that information service or a retransmission is requested for that service from the server due to incomplete reception, then that service is queued for delivery. In addition, if the client has made an authentication or polling request and if there is a version newer than the one recorded in the user profile of that client, then that service is queued for delivery. At the time of delivery, the service appears on the index.

When a client is within the service area of that server, it listens to the index sent on IBP to see which information services are offered by the server during that CC. This index message also informs the clients about the multicast group of transmission, the version and the size of the information service to be transmitted. Each multicast group is coupled with a CS in DP. The client examines the index and determines whether there are any available items of interest by looking up the user profile in the mobile terminal. If items of interest are available, the client joins to the announced multicast group and prepares the buffers for receiving an information service in the RPP.

Services are delivered to clients in the form of packets of fixed size. Data packets of each item announced for that CC are delivered in the corresponding CS. The client receives data packets of the interested service by listening to the multicast group.

3 Reliable Data Delivery in WIDE

Wireless data delivery systems require reliability mechanisms to ensure that all the intended recipients receive the service intact. The reliability mechanism in WIDE is designed to employ a mixed type of the carousel, FEC and the ARQ techniques. A pure carousel technique provides full reliability by delivering the data multiple times. However, this increases the number of unnecessary receptions caused by duplicate packets on the client side. Also, carousel mechanisms cause to increase the average reception time of an information service in unreliable mediums. Hence, the number of carousel cycles for each information service is kept limited. In addition, erasure code mechanisms [5] are employed to decrease the reception time.

The reliability mechanism in WIDE starts with the preparation of the requested information services for delivery. The preparation phase consists of three steps, namely packetization, encoding and security steps. In the packetization step, the service is sequentially buffered in memory in the form of equally sized blocks of data. The size of these blocks is a configuration parameter of the system. In our studies, we set the value of this parameter to 1400 bytes because the maximum throughput of UDP on wireless medium is achieved when the packet size is 1472 bytes including headers [6]. The number of data blocks, n, is determined by the size of the service.

In the encoding step, data packets are processed by the FEC module, which outputs $n+k$ packets. The k packets correspond to redundancy of the FEC applied in WIDE. The value of k is determined by the redundancy parameter of the system, which is set as a percentage of the number of whole packets. After the encoding process, a packet number is given to each packet. Security operations are performed on the encoded packets and the scheduler is informed that the service is ready for delivery (RFD).

The scheduler collects the RFD messages of each ready information service. These RFD messages are classified and queued according to some specific criteria to be able to inform Communication Cycle Manager whenever it is consulted. The current scheduler in WIDE operates in an FCFS manner.

In the data delivery step, another reliability mechanism of WIDE, namely data carousel, is employed. The data carousel is controlled by the CC Manager. At the beginning of each CC, the CC Manager consults the scheduler for any RFDs to be assigned to empty communication slots. Depending on the size of the assigned slot, the complete delivery of information services may take one or more CCs. The CC Manager keeps track of necessary data and makes necessary calculations for a complete delivery of an information service. Information services are delivered on the assigned CSs repeatedly, which is called a carousel cycle. The number of carousel cycles, nCAR, is a system parameter, and its default value is two. The details of the CC Manager will be given in Section 3.2.

A client can reconstruct an encoded information service by receiving of any n packets out of $n+k$ transmitted packets. When enough number of packets is received for the FEC decoding process, packets are decoded to form the actual data packets in sequential order. If the number of packets is not enough to reconstruct the actual data, the missing packets can be captured in the next cycle, if exists. If there are still missing packets, then an ARQ request is prepared by the client.

Since the packets to be requested may vary from client to client, the number of ARQ requests made for individual packets creates congestion on the server side. The ARQ mechanism in WIDE is used to make requests for the delivery of whole packets of an information service to decrease the risk of feedback implosion [7].

3.1 FEC Mechanism in WIDE

The FEC mechanism in WIDE uses the FEC schema proposed by Luigi Rizzo [8] based on the Galois Field Theory. It is noted that the algorithm most efficiently operates when the number of packets including the redundancy is smaller than 2^8, i.e. $n+k \leq 256$. There is another version of this FEC schema for higher number of packets, which is based on $GF(2^{16})$ instead of $GF(2^8)$. However, in the $GF(2^{16})$ polynomial space, the degrees of polynomials are at most 15. In this case, operation complexity is higher, since matrix sizes increase with the maximum polynomial degree, and operations mostly involve matrix multiplications and inversions. For the cases where the number of packets including redundancy is above 256, packets are divided into blocks of sizes smaller than 256.

FEC schema assumes a constant rate of redundancy packets per block. This rate is a percentage of the number of packets in each block. As this percentage increases to 100, the behavior of this schema converges to the data carousel. On the other hand, as this percentage decreases to zero, the schema will be less tolerant to errors. The aim of FEC schema in WIDE is to keep the number of blocks as small as possible. As the number of blocks increases, the size of the blocks decreases and the number of redundant packets per block decreases. As a result, this makes blocks less tolerant to packet losses. The number of blocks is minimized by either keeping the size of blocks except the last one as big as possible to leave some small portion of packets to the last block, or keeping the block sizes as equal as possible. In the former case, the loss tolerance of the bigger blocks is higher but the last block has a poor loss tolerance. In the latter case each block has almost equal tolerance. Therefore, the FEC schema in WIDE is designed to keep the block sizes as equal as possible. The number of packets to be encoded in each block is determined using the algorithm in Figure 3.

```
NumberOfBlocks = 1;
AvailableBlockSize = Floor(256*(1-Redundancy/100));
BlockSize = Ceil(TotalNumberOfPackets/NumberOfBlocks);
While BlockSize > AvailableBlockSize
        NumberOfBlocks = NumberOfBlocks + 1;
        BlockSize=Ceil(TotalNumberOfPackets/NumberOfBlocks);
```

Fig. 3. FEC block size algorithm

The information service packets are grouped into blocks of size determined by BlockSize in Figure 3. The result of application of FEC schema to each block is a new block of size `BlockSize*(1+ Redundancy/100)`. These blocks are sequentially buffered to form the encoded information service to be transmitted.

3.2 Communication Cycle Manager

The delivery of an information service may not be completed in one CC because of the limitations on the data period. These limitations are on the number of communication slots and total number of packets that can be delivered in a DP. The total number of packets is divided among the information services that are scheduled for delivery in that CC according to the partitioning algorithm. This algorithm decides the number of packets to be delivered for each information service considering the total remaining packets of it. In the first delivery, the number of remaining packets are nCAR * size in packets. If the number of packets scheduled to be transmitted for an information service is smaller than the total number of packets of it, the delivery of that service cannot be completed in that CC. The CC Manager keeps delivery status records necessary for the complete delivery of an information service. The manager controls the carousel cycles of each information service by making necessary calculations on the total number of remaining packets.

CC Manager communicates with the scheduler at the beginning of each CC and receives required number of RFDs to utilize the empty CSs whose data delivery have finished in a previous CC. Using these inputs, the manager forms a list of RFDs that represents the information services scheduled to be delivered in that CC. This list is processed by the partitioning algorithm, which outputs the numbers of packets to be sent corresponding to each RFD. Then the multiplexer assigns a distinct empty CS to each information service in the RFD list. Partitioning and multiplexing outputs, together with the RFD list are used to create the index message. After this point the manager executes the CC by delivering the appropriate packets informing clients about the start and end points of the periods.

Partitioning Algorithm. The aim of this algorithm is to determine the number of packets to be delivered in a CC for each information service, which is listed in RFD. There are two parameters used in this algorithm. These parameters are *nPACK* and *nCS*, which corresponds to the maximum total number of packets that can be delivered in a DP and the number of communication slots in a CC respectively. Partitioning algorithm works over sizes of sets. It gets the size of the whole set and outputs the sizes of the partition sets whose sum gives at most the size of the whole set. Figure 4 gives the partitioning algorithm used in WIDE.

Algorithm starts with summing up the number of remaining packets of each information service for delivery in the RFD list. If the sum is less than *nPACK*, then the result of the algorithm is an array containing the numbers of packets. Otherwise, it gets *nPACK* as the whole set size. If there are less than *nCS* information services, *nPACK* is divided into this many partitions. If there are more than *nCS* information services, only *nCS* many of them are delivered.

```
TotalPackets = 0;
For all RFD in RFD list
   TotalPackets = TotalPackets + RFD->NumberOfPackets;
If TotalPackets <= nPACK
   For all RFD in RFD list
      RFD->NumberOfScheduledPackets=RFD->NumberOfPackets;
Else
   Sort RFD list wrt NumberOfPackets;
   RFDCount = 0;
   For all RFD in RFD list
      SlotSize = Floor(nPACK/(RFDList length - RFDCount));
      If RFD->NumberOfPackets < SlotSize
            RFD->NumberOfScheduledPackets = RFD->NumberOfPackets;
      Else
            RFD->NumberOfScheduledPackets = SlotSize;
      nPACK = nPACK - RFD->NumberOfScheduledPackets;
      RFDCount = RFDCount + 1;
```

Fig. 4. Partitioning algorithm in CC Manager

4 Performance of Reliability Mechanisms on a WIDE Prototype

A "proof of concept" prototype of the proposed system is implemented and deployed as part of the Mobile Applications and Services Testbed (MAST) [9] of Bogazici University. The prototype provided a testbed for the evaluation of the performance of the proposed data delivery mechanisms and for further studies. Performance tests in this paper are not large-scale tests. We mainly concentrate on finding the effects of reliability mechanisms on the system performance. The behavior of the FEC schema is analyzed in terms of processing times measured for varying file sizes. In addition, the effect of the carousel and the FEC mechanisms on file reception is investigated in existence of background traffic.

For these analyses, the client is placed indoor, to five meters apart from the WAP, in the line of sight. The experiments were repeated 15 times and average values are reported. The client prototype is executed on a laptop computer with a Pentium III processor operating at 500 MHz and 192 MB RAM with Windows 2000 Professional Edition. The server and the controller applications are executed on the same desktop computer with a Pentium IV processor operating at 1800 Mhz and 1 GB RAM with Windows 2000 Advanced Server Edition operating system. The wireless connectivity between the server and the client is provided with a Cisco AiroNet 350 Series WAP connected to the server computer via an Ethernet adapter and a 3Com AirConnect WLAN PCMCIA card installed on the client.

4.1 Performance of FEC Schema

In this analysis, $nCAR$ parameter value was set to 1. The Server-WAP connection type was direct cable connection. No background traffic is employed on the adapter connecting the server to the WAP. Each information service is requested from the server in a way that only one file was delivered in a CC and the processing times of

FEC for these files are measured after every file reception. Figure 5.a presents the behavior of the FEC algorithm presented in Section 3.1.

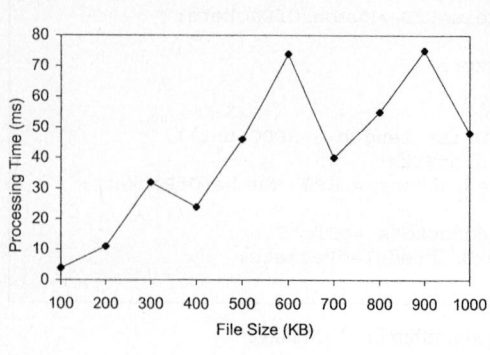

File Size	Packets	Block Size	Blocks
100	74	74	1
200	147	147	1
300	220	220	1
400	293	147	2
500	366	183	2
600	439	220	2
700	512	171	3
800	586	196	3
900	659	220	3
1000	732	183	4

(a) Performance of FEC for different file sizes

(b) FEC information

Fig. 5. FEC schema on client for different file sizes

Figure 5.b gives the information about the number and the size of FEC blocks for each file size used in the experiments. Table shows that the increase on the number of FEC blocks results with a decrease on the number of packets in each block, which is the behavior of the algorithm. Although the number of blocks increases, the decrease in the block size decreases the total processing time. The processing times for the files having the same FEC block size are observed to be nearly the same.

4.2 Effect of Background Traffic on Reliability

In this analysis, $nCAR$ parameter value was set to 1 to be able to detect the number of cycles elapsed for the completion of the reception. The Server-WAP connection was established via a 10 Mbps HUB. Background traffic is created by transferring data from another desktop computer connected to the HUB to a wireless capable laptop computer associated to the WAP.

Under this traffic condition, file reception statistics of subscribed information services are recorded with and without employing the FEC mechanism. Table 1 summarizes the statistics obtained in these experiments. The third, fourth and the fifth columns represent the number of trials in which the information services were received in one, two or three cycles respectively. The sixth column represents the average number of duplicate packets of the trials where reception of the information services was completed in more than one cycle. Similarly, the seventh column represents the average number of packet losses of the trials where reception of the information service was completed in more than one cycle. We can observe that the background traffic on the radio significantly affects the performance of information reception. The completion of reception may finish in more than one cycle, which increases the reception time. As the size of information service to be delivered increases, the average number of packet losses increases. The reason may be the congestion on the WAP caused by the traffic, which is created by both WIDE system communication and the background traffic.

Table 1. The statistics of information reception in case of background traffic on the radio

File Size (KB)	Packets	Without FEC			Duplicates	Loss	With FEC	
		One Cycle	Two Cycles	Three Cycles			Redundancy	Loss
100	74	11	4	0	42.75	3.5	0	2.22
200	147	5	10	0	104.7	6.1	0	7
300	220	6	9	0	139.44	7	0	6
400	293	2	13	0	196.31	10.77	12.07	4.53
500	366	0	15	0	291.73	11.27	14.33	7.6
600	439	1	14	0	341.43	20.07	15.93	11.4
700	512	2	12	1	337.08	19	28.07	9.53
800	586	0	14	1	527.53	21.07	31.67	9.2
900	659	0	10	5	667	33.13	39.73	6.07
1000	732	0	10	5	794.33	34.33	45.6	13.27

In the second part, the FEC mechanism is employed with 10% redundancy. We observed that all of the receptions completed in the cycle following the subscription. The eighth column in the table gives the average number of redundant packets received and discarded until the completion of reception. The last column gives the average number of packet losses. Employing FEC decreases the number of cycles for reception when there is background traffic on the radio. Consequently, the average reception time decreases and hence the performance of data reception increases.

It can be observed that without FEC mechanism, the increase in the average number of the packet losses results with an increase in the number of cycles for the reception. By comparing with and without FEC cases, we observe that the increase in the number of cycles also results with an increase in the number of packet losses which means that packet losses and number of retransmissions trigger each other in a cyclic way. This behavior repeats in the cases where the packet losses in a cycle coincide with the packets that could not be received in previous cycles. The high values of average loss in without FEC case are outcomes of this condition.

Another advantage of employing FEC can be observed by comparing the duplicates column with the redundancy column. We can state that employing FEC not only reduces the reception time, but also reduces the number of unnecessary receptions. We also compared the FEC case with FTP/TCP for different file sizes and observed that complete reception times in one cycle are similar to corresponding FTP results. We can state that the reception overhead of FEC does not add considerably more overhead than TCP. However FEC provides an effective usage of multicast mechanism.

5 Conclusion

The design of an information delivery system, namely WIDE, and the mechanisms required for reliable data dissemination are presented in this paper. Data delivery of WIDE is based on data multicasting to provide scalability and efficient use of the wireless channel. Since TCP does not support multicasting, UDP is used as the transport protocol in the system specific reliability mechanism. Proposed reliability mechanisms are tested on a prototype and some preliminary results achieved.

The test results show that although the pure carousel technique is known to provide full reliability, even a single packet loss dramatically increases the reception time together with the number of unnecessary receptions caused by duplicate packets. This proves that the carousel should be supported by another reliability mechanism. FEC mechanism in WIDE is shown to decrease the average reception time and number of unnecessary receptions by transmitting some amount of redundant information.

However, extensive tests have to be performed to decide on the optimal FEC schema in terms of power conservation of clients by considering the tradeoff between the processing time and the reception time of services. In addition, future tests should be realized with many users instead of single user to correctly measure the effectiveness of the proposed reliability mechanisms. Furthermore, different decision criteria [10] should be applied in the scheduling and the partitioning algorithms to observe their effects on overall system performance.

References

1. Donmez, M. Y., Isik, S., Ersoy, C.: WIDE: Wireless Information Delivery Environment in Distributed Hot Spots. Lecture Notes in Computer Science, Vol. 2928. (2004) 315–328
2. Luby, M., Vicisano, L.: Forward Error Correction (FEC) Building Block. IETF RFC 3452, (2002)
3. Rizzo L., Vicisano L.: RMDP: An FEC-based Reliable Multicast Protocol for Wireless Environments. Mobile Computing and Communications Review **2**(2) (1998) 1–10
4. Acharya, S.: Broadcast Disks: Dissemination-based Data Management for Asymmetric Communication Environments. Ph.D. Dissertation, Brown University, (1997)
5. Rizzo, L.: Effective Erasure Codes for Reliable Computer Communication Protocols. ACM Computer Communication Review **27**(2) (1997) 24–36
6. Vasan, A., Shankar, A.U.: An Empirical Characterization of Instantaneous Throughput in 802.11b WLANs. http://www.cs.umd.edu/~shankar/Papers/802-11b-profile-1.pdf, (2003)
7. Nonnenmacher J., Biersack E.W.: Optimal Multicast Feedback. In: Proceedings of IEEE INFOCOM, San Francisco, CA, USA, Vol. 3. (1998) 964–971
8. Rizzo, L.: FEC Code. http://info.iet.unipi.it/~luigi/vdm98/vdm980702.tgz. (1998)
9. Mobile Applications Testbed (MAST), NETLAB. Bogazici University. http://netlab.boun.edu.tr/mast.html.
10. Aksoy, D., Franklin, M.: RxW: A Scheduling Approach for Large-Scale On-Demand Data Broadcast. IEEE/ACM Transactions on Networking **7**(6) (1999) 846–860

Wireless Interworking Independent CAN Segments

Cuneyt Bayilmis, Ismail Erturk, and Celal Ceken

Kocaeli University, Technical Education Faculty
Electronics and Computer Education Department
41300 Kocaeli, Turkey
{bayilmis,erturk,cceken}@kou.edu.tr

Abstract. The CAN is used in many distributed real-time control applications in industrial environments where basically there are two main problems. These are namely the size of distributed area and the need for communication with other LANs and with independent CAN segments. A practical solution is to use interworking devices with wireless support to extend CAN segments, utilizing an IEEE 802.11b WLAN. Main objective of this research work is to design and implement such an interworking device called Wireless Interworking Unit enabling remote CAN2.0A nodes to communicate over IEEE 802.11b WLAN using encapsulation method. Computer modeling and simulation of the new approach are realized by using OPNET Modeler and analysis of the simulation results obtained are also presented.

1 Introduction

The Controller Area Network (CAN) is a serial communication bus with high performance, high speed, high reliability, and low cost for distributed real–time control applications in both the automotive and the industrial control. The CAN communication protocol is a contention–based serial communication. As an access method, it uses the CSMA/CR (Carrier Sense Multiple Access with Collision Resolution) with a bit–wise arbitration. Its common applications include intelligent motor control, robot control, intelligent sensors/counters, laboratory automation and mechanical tools [1].

Extensive use of several CAN networks (e.g., each dedicated to a portion of an industrial plant, connected by suitable devices) in automotive and other control applications in modern industrial plants results in also need for interworking between CAN networks as well as between CAN and other major public/private networks. Interworking Units (IUs) are high–performance devices that are used to interconnect similar or dissimilar LANs. While a pass–through forwarding process is sufficient for the interconnection of similar LANs, both a translation process and a forwarding process are required for the interconnection of dissimilar LANs [2]. It is used for extending CAN segments and for interworking between independent CAN segments.

In this research work a new Wireless Interworking Unit (WIU) is proposed to build interconnected independent CAN segments. As indicated in [3] the IEEE 802.11 standard possesses a centralized access mechanism capable of minimizing the time required to transfer the time–critical information exchanged between different interconnected FieldBus systems. This paper focuses on interworking independent CAN2.0A segments over an IEEE 802.11b WLAN.

The paper describes CAN and IEEE 802.11 briefly in Section 2. Section 3 introduces the proposed approach for interconnection of the CAN segments, using IEEE 802.11b WLAN over radio links. Section 4 presents simulation modeling of the proposed system. Finally simulation results of the proposed scheme are discussed in Section 5.

2 The CAN and the IEEE 802.11 WLAN

The Controller Area Network (CAN) employs a high performance and high reliable advanced serial communication protocol which efficiently supports distributed real-time control (in the field of automotive and industrial control) with a very high level of security. As CAN semiconductors produced by many different manufacturers are so inexpensive, their widespread use has found a way into such diverse areas as agricultural machinery, medical instrumentation, elevator controls, public transportation systems and industrial automation control components [4–9].

[4] and [5] supply a detailed overview of the CAN features that can be summarized as high speed serial interface, low cost physical medium, short data lengths, fast reaction times and high level of error detection and correction. The CAN uses the CSMA/CR (Carrier Sense Multiple Access with Collision Resolution) with a bit–wise arbitration. Therefore, the maximum data rate that can be achieved depends on the bus length. For example, the maximum data rates for 30 meter and 500 meter buses are 1 Mbit/s and 100 Kbit/s respectively. As CAN employs a priority based bus arbitration process, the node with the highest priority will continue to transmit without any interruption. Thus CAN has a very predictable behavior and in fact CAN networks can operate at near 100% bus bandwidth.

CAN messages include 0–8 bytes of variable data and 47 bits of protocol control information (i.e., the identifier, CRC data, acknowledgement and synchronization bits, Figure 1) [1], [4], [6–9]. Note that two versions of CAN exist, and they only differ in the size of the identifier (i.e., 11 and 29 bit identifiers with CAN 2.0A and with CAN 2.0B, respectively). The identifier field serves two purposes: assigning a priority for the transmission and allowing message filtering upon reception.

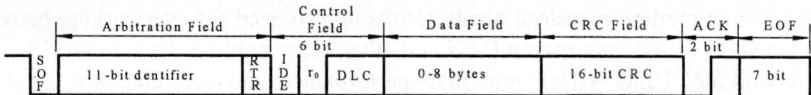

Fig. 1. CAN 2.0 A message format

IEEE 802.11 WLAN is a local area network implemented without wires. The main advantages of WLAN are the mobility and cost–saving installation. Any WLAN aims to offer all the features and benefits of traditional LAN technologies (e.g., Ethernet and Token Ring) but without the limitations of being tethered to a cable.

IEEE 802.11 supports two different topologies, namely independent Basic Service Set (BSS or ad-hoc network) and infrastructure BSS. The stations can communicate directly with each other in an independent BSS which is the simplest type of IEEE 802.11 LAN. In access point (AP) based networks (or infrastructure BSS) all mobile stations communicate through an AP that is connected to a wired network.

IEEE 802.11 employs Carrier Sense Multiple Access/Collision Avoidance (CSMA/CA) as the channel access method and operates in the 2.4 GHz unlicensed ISM (Industrial, Scientific and Medical) band. IEEE 802.11 WLAN standards are usually based on three physical layer (PHY) specifications: two for radio frequency (RF–Direct Sequence Spread Spectrum, DSSS and Frequency Hopping Spread Spectrum, FHSS) and one for infrared (IR). Each technique provides a different data transfer rate. Generally radio frequency technology is preferred in WLANs due to the limitations of the infrared medium. WLAN packet types vary according to the PHY employed [10–14]. The PHY layer is the interface between Medium Access Control (MAC) layer and wireless media. It consists of two sublayers, namely Physical Layer Convergence Procedure (PLCP) sublayer and Physical Medium Dependent (PMD) sublayer. The PLCP Protocol Data Unit (PPDU) is unique to the DSSS PHY layer. The PPDU frame consists of a PLCP preamble, PLCP header, and MAC Protocol Data Unit (MPDU) (Figure 2) [12].

IEEE 802.11 family consists of several substandards such as IEEE 802.11a operating in 5 GHz unlicensed U–NII (Unlicensed National Information Infrastructure) band with 54 Mbps data rate, and IEEE 802.11b operating in 2.4 GHz ISM band with 11 Mbps data rate and IEEE 802.11g (built on IEEE 802.11b) operating in 2.4 GHz ISM band with 54 Mbps data rate.

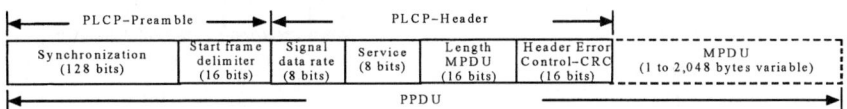

Fig. 2. IEEE 802.11b DSSS PLCP packet format

3 Designing and Modeling a CAN/IEEE 802.11 Wireless Interworking Unit for Independent CAN Segments

Interworking Units (IUs) are high–performance devices that are used to interconnect similar or dissimilar LANs. While a pass–through forwarding process is sufficient for the interconnection of similar LANs, both a translation process and a forwarding process are required for the interconnection of dissimilar LANs [2]. In this work, the proposed Wireless Interworking Unit (WIU) interconnects independent CAN2.0A networks communicating through IEEE 802.11b WLAN; therefore, both the translation and forwarding processes are required.

An important function of the WIU is that the Protocol Data Units (PDU) of the CAN2.0A messages are encapsulated within those of the IEEE 802.11b DSSS frames to be carried over wireless channels. Since a CAN 2.0A message is 108 bits, it can easily be fitted into one IEEE 802.11b frame MPDU (Figure 3). Thus, neither segmentation/reassembly of CAN messages nor data compression is necessary for carrying a CAN message in one IEEE 802.11 frame. At the destination WIU, preamble and header parts of the IEEE 802.11b frames are stripped off, and the CAN2.0A messages extracted from the IEEE 802.11b MPDUs can be processed.

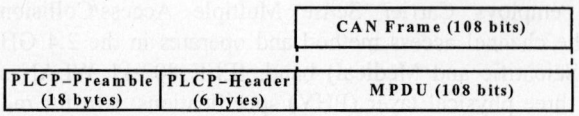

Fig. 3. Encapsulation of a CAN2.0A frame into an IEEE 802.11b DSSS frame

The proposed WIU has two ports which are capable of interconnecting independent CAN segments using an IEEE 802.11b WLAN. Its network model and layered system architecture are shown in Fig.4 and Fig.5, respectively.

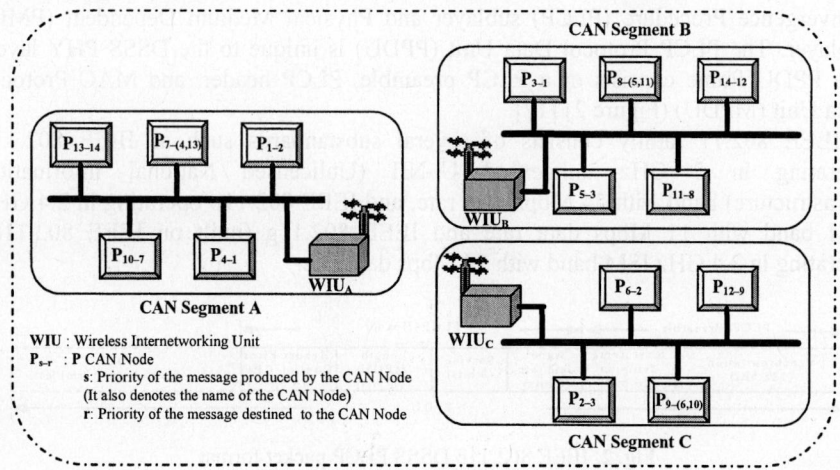

Fig. 4. The proposed network model

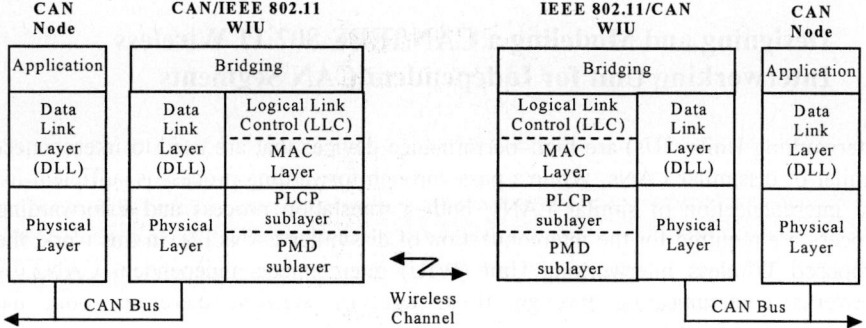

Fig. 5. Layered system architecture of WIU

The functional model of the WIU shown in Fig.6 contains following entities:
- The CAN Interface Entity (CIE) provides the means for communication with CAN bus and has a bus receiver and a bus transmitter.
- The WLAN Interface Entity (WIE) provides the necessary functions for communication over wireless medium and has a wireless receiver and a wireless transmitter.
- The CAN Bus Receiver is a buffer that stores CAN messages delivered from the CIE.
- The WLAN Receiver is a buffer that stores WLAN IEEE 802.11b frames delivered from the WIE.
- The Look-up Table (LT) is the most important part of a WIU. It is built up during a Learning Process (LP) in which every WIU finds out its own attached CAN nodes' local messages and remote messages destined from/to any other CAN segment. After that the messages with certain priorities are associated with the address of the relevant WIU connected to the destination CAN segment.
- The CAN Learning, Filtering, and Translating Entity (CLFTE) contains the CAN-LP. It also compares identifiers of the messages received from the CAN bus with the ones in the LT to realize whether the messages are local or remote. If the CAN message identifier has a match in the LT (i.e., it is destined to another CAN segment) then it is converted to WLAN frame format and sent to CAN Translating Buffer. Otherwise the CAN message is filtered as it is a local message.
- The WLAN Learning, Filtering and Translating Entity (WLFTE) contains the WLAN-LP. It is also used to realize if any WLAN frame received is destined to the WIU. If so, the CAN message is extracted from the WLAN frame delivered from the WIE, and it is sent to the WLAN Translating Buffer. Otherwise it is filtered as not destined to this WIU.
- FIFO2 and FIFO3 are the CAN Translating and the WLAN Translating buffers, respectively.

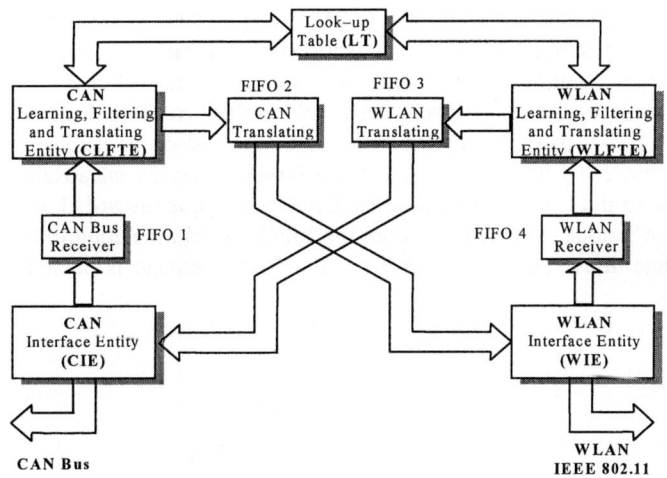

Fig. 6. Functional block diagram of a WIU

In the proposed WIU model, each port has a different protocol with a different frame and message format, and a different frame and message reception/transmission mechanism. Thus, the processes to be performed at each port of the WIU are different. The flowchart of CAN to WLAN data transfer process and flowchart of WLAN to CAN data transfer process of the proposed WIU are shown in Fig.7, in Fig.8, respectively.

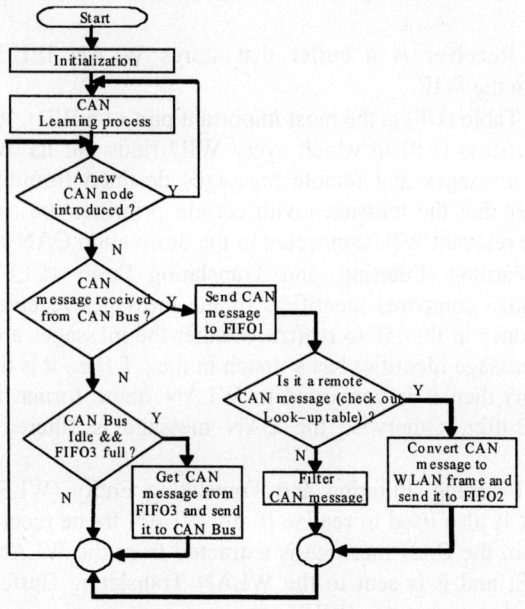

Fig. 7. Flowchart of the WIU–CAN to WLAN data transfer process

Learning processes are used to determine remote messages in every CAN segment and it works in conjunction with the LT. The LT is updated when either a new CAN node or WIU is introduced to the network as this is a very common case in an industrial process control environment.

All CAN messages received from the CAN bus through the CIE are checked for a match in the LT. If there is a match with this CAN message identifier then the CAN message is converted into the WLAN frame format using the encapsulation method, and it is sent to the FIFO2. Otherwise the CAN message is discarded as it is destined to a local CAN node. Meanwhile, when the FIFO3 is full, meaning that it contains a CAN message delivered from the WFTE, the CAN message is passed to the CAN bus (Fig.7).

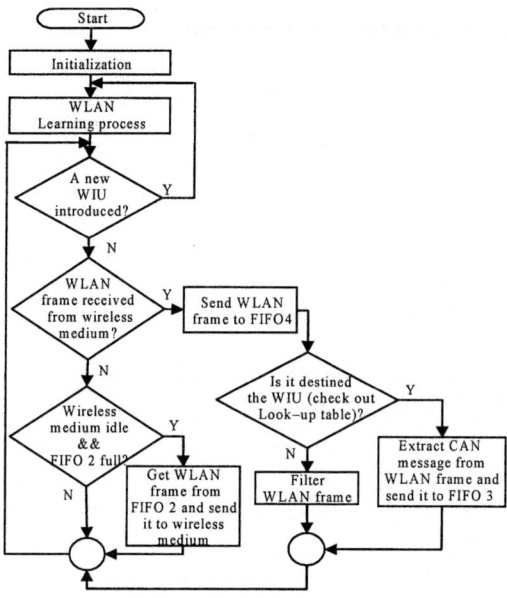

Fig. 8. Flowchart of the WIU–WLAN to CAN data transfer process

Processes in the WLAN part of the WIU (Fig.8) contain receiving and sending WLAN frames from/to the wireless medium. If there is an incoming WLAN frame then the CAN message is extracted from it. After that its identifier checked out in the LT and if there is a match the CAN message is sent to the FIFO3; otherwise, it is discarded. Meanwhile, when the FIFO2 is full, meaning that it contains a WLAN frame encapsulating a remote CAN message delivered from the CLFTE, and the wireless medium idle then the WLAN frame is sent to wireless medium as broadcast.

3.1 Learning Process

The main objective of the learning process is to create a look–up table (LT) that is used for filtering CAN messages and WLAN frames. It consists of a CAN-LP and a WLAN-LP. In the former, any CAN node informs its WIU about the remote and local CAN message identifiers to be received and sent when the initialization process takes place. After that all WIUs exchange their local LTs to build a global LT that is used to form a networking environment with fully connected independent CAN segments. On the other hand the latter is used to match any remote CAN message identifier with the relevant WIU. Both processes are repeated if a new CAN node or WIU is introduced to (or excluded from) the interworking system.

4 Simulation of the Proposed System

The node model of the proposed CAN2.0A/IEEE 802.11b WIU shown in Fig. 9 is realized using OPNET 10.5 Modeler Radio Module. The *CAN_proc* executes functions of the CAN Interface Entity (CIE), CAN Bus Receiver, and CAN Learning, Filtering and Translating Entity (CLFTE), which are shown in the functional block diagram (Fig.6). Similarly, the *WLAN_proc* executes functions of the WLAN Interface Entity (WIE), WLAN Receiver, and WLAN Learning, Filtering and Translating Entity (WLFTE). *CAN_buffer* and *WLAN_buffer* are used as CAN Translating buffer and WLAN Translating buffer, respectively.

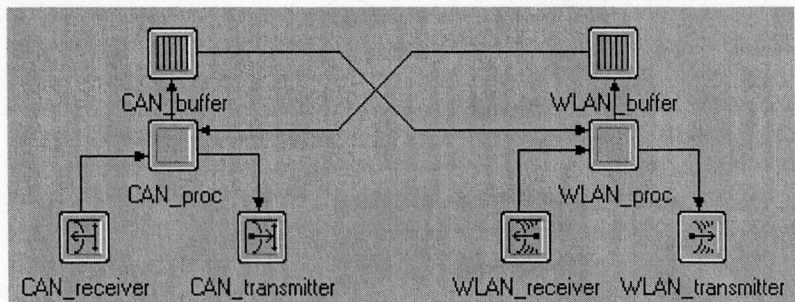

Fig. 9. Node model of the proposed WIU

The ranges of CAN implementations are so versatile that there is neither a general model for a CAN application nor even a benchmark [1]. Despite this drawback, a CAN network example can be used to illustrate the communication behavior and to discuss the system performance where the proposed WIU is employed.

The network model to be simulated (shown in Fig. 4) consists of three independent CAN segments. Every node introduces a single CAN message with a certain priority to the network. The CAN messages used in the simulation model are given in Table 1 for the CAN Segments A, B and C.

Performance evaluation of the simulation model is carried out depending upon such parameters as local/remote end to end message delay and processing times of a WIU. The performance of designed WIU is evaluated under diverse network load conditions formed varying the local/remote message ratios such as 70%/30% (respectively), 50%/50%, and 30%/70%. This ratio is same in all simulations for entire CAN segments. Message traffic with different load of the system is created by changing mean value of exponential distribution.

5 Simulation Results

The preliminary simulation results included are the end to end message delays (EEMDs) for the remote message of P_1 node, the EEMDs for the same message normalized with the EEMDs of its local message counterpart, and total processing time of the designed WIU. As three key factors affecting the system performance, it should be noted that depending on their message priorities (the lower the identifier number of a CAN message the higher its priority) CAN nodes have right for access to the CAN bus, that CAN2.0A bus data rate is 1 Mbps and that IEEE 802.11b WLAN data rate is 11 Mbps. Especially, the first one is reflected into the simulation results as erratic changes in the graphics.

Table 1. Local (L) and remote (R) messages of the CAN Segments

	SN	MT	DL	ML	DN L	DN R	WFA SS	WFA DS
Segment A	P_1	L/R	8	14	P_4	P_3	A	B
Segment A	P_4	L	6	14	P_7	–	–	–
Segment A	P_7	L	8	14	P_{10}	–	–	–
Segment A	P_{10}	R	7	14	–	P_9	A	C
Segment A	P_{13}	L	8	14	P_7	–	–	–
Segment B	P_3	L/R	8	14	P_5	P_2	B	C
Segment B	P_5	L	5	14	P_8	–	–	–
Segment B	P_8	L	8	14	P_{11}	–	–	–
Segment B	P_{11}	L	6	14	P_8	–	–	–
Segment B	P_{14}	L	8	14	–	P_{13}	B	A
Segment C	P_2	L/R	8	14	P_6	P_1	C	A
Segment C	P_6	L	7	14	P_9	–	–	–
Segment C	P_9	L	8	14	P_{12}	–	–	–
Segment C	P_{12}	R	8	14	–	P_{14}	C	B

SN: Source Node
MT: Message Type
  L: Local
  R: Remote
DL: Data Length (byte)
ML: Message Length (byte)
DN: Destination Node
WFA: WLAN Frame Address
  SS: Source Segment
  DS: Destination Segment

Fig. 10 illustrates the normalized mean EEMD results for the remote message of P_1 CAN node (with priority 1) destined to the CAN node P_3, where the mean EEMDs of its local message counterpart destined to P_4 is 1, as a function of varying network load for three different local/remote message ratios. Remote P_1 CAN messages experience 9.6 to 33.1 times higher mean EEMDs when the offered network loads are 100 message/second with 70/30% local/remote messages ratio and 400 message/second with 50/50% local/remote messages ratio, respectively. In the former, as local messages constitute most of the light network load, mean EEMDs for the remote messages are expectedly low regardless of the local/remote messages ratios. On the other hand, the latter represents the worst case scenario where half of the heavy network load is formed by the remote messages. This is not only due to the heavy network load or composition of the network load but also as a consequence of the random nature of the CSMA/CA access mechanism of the WIUs. The only explanation for the decreasing mean EEMDs when the network load is 400 message/second and above is also a direct result of the wireless medium access mechanism employed by all of the WIUs.

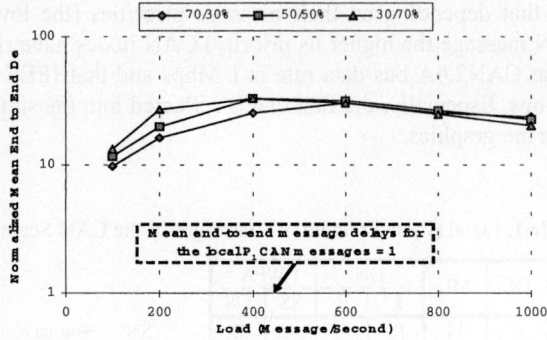

Fig. 10. Normalized mean end-to-end message delays for the remote P_1 CAN messages under varying network loads with different local/remote (L/R%) message ratios

Fig. 11 shows the mean EEMD results for the remote message of P_1 node, which is destined to the CAN node P_3 in the CAN Segment B, for three different local/remote message ratios. As it can be seen from the graphs, the mean EEMD result is the lowest (i.e., 100 ms) when the network load is 100 message/second with 70/30% local/remote ratio. On the other hand, the highest mean EEMD result is 217.5 ms for the network load 800 message/second. This is basically due to priority based nature of the CAN bus access mechanism and on top of that due to the random nature of the CSMA/CA access mechanism of the WIUs. This figure is normally expected to have been 1000 message/second where the mean EEMD obtained is 202 ms with 30/70% local/remote ratio. It can also be concluded that the more the ratio of the remote messages is the more the mean EEMDs.

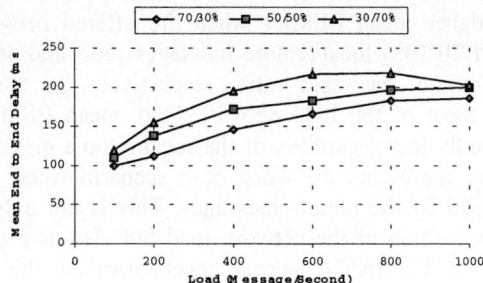

Fig. 11. Mean end-to-end message delays for the remote P_1 CAN messages under varying network loads with different local/remote (L/R%) message ratios

The rate at which CAN messages and IEEE 802.11b WLAN frames are processed and forwarded for transmission from one port to another in a WIU is called "the forwarding rate". The WIU forwarding rate and WIU process time are affected by high message traffic flowing in the WIU. Fig. 12 demonstrates the WIU total mean process time of the CAN to IEEE 802.11b WLAN transmission and IEEE 802.11b WLAN to CAN transmission as a function of varying network load with different local/remote message ratios. The WIU process time reaches a minimum value (98.6 ms) at 100 message/second with 70/30% local/remote message ratio and a maximum value (200 ms) at 600 message/second with the 30/70% local/remote message ratio. As a result of heavy network load and high remote message ratios, as much as twice processing time is required in the latter

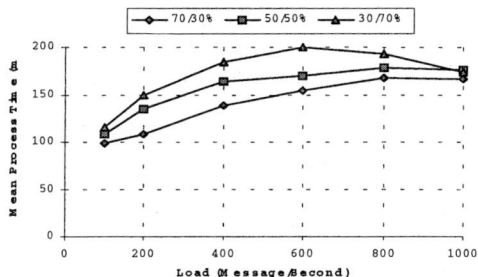

Fig. 12. The CAN/IEEE 802.11b WIU total mean process time under varying loads with different local/remote (L/R%) message ratios

6 Conclusion

An interworking unit must provide a selective frame retransmission function and interface operation allowing communication between similar and/or dissimilar systems. The aim of this work has been to design a WIU that provides a service to achieve the wireless interconnection of independent CAN2.0A segments over IEEE 802.11b WLAN. Considering their easy usage in many industrial areas, CAN nodes emerge inevitably to need this type of wireless interworking for greater flexibility for their applications to be controlled and/or programmed remotely.

The proposed WIU has fulfilled the design objectives and overcome the limitations mentioned in the previous sections. In summary, the functional model of the designed CAN/IEEE 802.11b WLAN WIU includes four phases of operation. First, it receives a CAN message or a WLAN frame from one of its ports, i.e. the CAN side or the IEEE 802.11b side, respectively. Second, it decides whether or not to forward the message/frame using its global LT built-up during a learning process. Third, the message/frame is reformatted into the required type that is then to be, lastly, transmitted to the other system.

The simulation results show that all parameters regarding the performance of the WIU are satisfactory in meeting the overall requirements considering the CAN message arrival time. The WIU provides the required services for interconnected independent CAN segments.

References

1. Erturk, I.,: Transporting CAN Messages over WATM. Lecture Notes in Artificial Intelligence, Vol. 2639. Springer-Verlag, Berlin Heidelberg New York (2003) 724–729
2. Ozcelik, I., Ekiz, H.: Design, Implementation and Performance Analysis of the PROFIBUS/ATM Local Bridge. Computer Standards & Interface (2004) 1–14
3. Cavalieri, S., Pano, D.: A Novel Solution to Interconnect FieldBus Systems Using IEEE Wireless LAN Technology. Computer Standards & Interfaces (1998) 9–23
4. Lawrenz, W.: CAN System Engineering: From Theory to Practical Applications. Springer-Verlag, New York (1997) 1–289
5. Farsi, M., Ratckiff, K., Babosa, M.: An Overview of Controller Area Network. Computing and Control Engineering Journal 10(3) (1999) 113–120
6. Pinho, L., M., Vasques, F.,: Reliable Real–Time Communication in CAN Networks. IEEE Transactions on Computers 52(12) (2003) 1594–1607
7. Navet, N.: Controller Area Network [Automotive Applications]. IEEE Potentials 17(4), (1998) 12–14
8. Ekiz, H., Kutlu, A., Powner, E., T.: Design and Implementation of a CAN/Ethernet Bridge. In: Proceedings of the ICC'96 3rd Int. CAN Conference, France. (1996) 1117–1126
9. Erturk, I.: Remote Access of CAN Nodes Used in a Traffic Control System to a Central Management Unit over Wireless ATM. In: IEEE 4th International Workshop on Mobile and Wireless Communications Networks, Stockholm, Sweden. (2002) 626–630
10. Aad, I., Castelluccia, C.: Priorities in WLANs. Computer Networks (2003) 505–526
11. Varshney, U.: The Status and Future 802.11 Based WLANs. IEEE Computer Communications (2003) 102–105
12. Part 11: Wireless LAN Medium Access Control (MAC) and Physical Layer (PHY) Specifications. IEEE Standards 802.11 (1999) 195–200
13. Lindgren, A., Almquist, A., Schelen, O.: QoS Schemes for IEEE 802.11 Wireless LANs-An Evaluation. Mobile Networks and Applications 8(3) (2003) 223–235
14. Eshghi, F., Elhakeem, A., K.: Performance Analysis of Ad Hoc Wireless LANs for Real–Time Traffic. IEEE Journal on Selected Areas in Communications 21 (2003) 204–215

Real-Time Admission Control Supporting Prioritized Soft Handoff Calls in Cellular DS-CDMA Systems

Kuo-Chung Chu[1,2] and Frank Yeong-Sung Lin[1]

[1] Department of Information Management, National Taiwan University
[2] Department of Information Management, Jin-Wen Institute of Technology
Taipei, Taiwan
d5725003@im.ntu.edu.tw

Abstract. This paper proposes a prioritized real-time admission control algorithm to support soft handoff calls with QoS assurance in both uplink and downlink signal to interference ratio (SIR) requirement. Admission control is formulated as a performance optimization model, in which the objective is to minimize handoff forced termination probability. The algorithm is based upon dynamic reserved channels (guard channels) scheme for prioritized calls, it adapts to changes in handoff traffics where associated parameters (guard channels, new and handoff call arrival rates) can be varied. To solving the optimization model, iteration-based Lagrangian relaxation approach is applied by allocating a time budget. We analyze the system performance, and computational experiments indicate that proposed dynamic guard channel approach outperforms other schemes.

1 Introduction

Demand for wireless communications and Internet applications is continuously growing. Due to the advantages in system capacity and soft handoff, direct sequence code division multiple access (DS-CDMA) provides a high-capacity mobile communications service. Capacity analysis by call admission control (CAC) has been conducted for the uplink connection, because the non-orthogonality leads to the limited capacity is in the uplink [1]. However, asymmetric Internet traffic has increased, and power allocation in a downlink is an important issue. Theoretically, capacity is unbalanced on the downlink and uplink [2]. Thus, both links analysis are required in admission control.

Soft handoff is another characteristic in DS-CDMA system. Admitting a call request with soft handoff consideration, mobile station (MS) maintains simultaneous connections with more than one base station (BS). The MS is allocated a downlink channel at each BS, and the information transmitted on each channel is the same. The MS performs diversity combining of the downlink paths, regardless of their origin. Rejection of a soft handoff request results in forced termination of an ongoing service. To reducing the blocking of handoff calls, several channel reservation researches have been conducted [3-5]. These researches focused on general cellular mobile networks but not CDMA system. For CDMA, the admission control problem has been proposed in literature [6-9], these articles are based on uplink analysis. Although [7,9] consider channel reservation for handoff calls, a fixed number of channel at each BS is reserved. Generally, these schemes give priority to handoff call over new call, so-called cutoff priority scheme (CPS), and do not adapt to changes in the handoff traffics. Unlike [7,9], Huang and Ho [5] proposed a dynamic guard channel approach which adapts the number of guard channels in each BS according to the estimate of the handoff calls arrival rate. In [5] non-CDMA admission control was considered.

In this paper, considering integrated voice/data traffics in CDMA system we propose a prioritized real-time admission control model for supporting soft handoff calls with QoS assurance in both uplink and downlink signal to interference ratio (SIR) requirement. For simplicity, we only focus on voice call requests to optimize the handoff call performance. To effectively manage system performance, a real-time admission control algorithm conducted by Lagrangian relaxation approach and subgradient-based method is proposed. The remainder of this paper is organized as follows. In Section 2, the background of DS-CDMA admission control is reviewed which consists of soft handoff, SIR models, as well as problem formulation. Solution approach is described in Section 3. Section 4 illustrates the computational experiments. Finally, Section 5 concludes this paper.

2 Prioritized Real-Time Admission Control

2.1 Soft Handoff

Considering the MS in soft-handoff zone, it applies maximum ratio combining (MRC) of contributions coming from the involved BSs, the addition of energy to interference (E_b/I_0) coming from involved BSs must be larger than the (E_b/I_0) target at the MS. A diversity gain has to be taken into account for those MSs in soft handoff zone. Two assumptions are possible to representing handoff gain. First one assumes the same transmission power from each involved BS, while the other considering those (E_b/I_0) contributions from involved BSs are the same [10–12]. For example, if MS t is in the handoff zone in which two BSs (BS 1 and 2) are involved, the first assumption denote P_{jt} the transmitted power from BS j to MS t in soft handoff situation, then $P_{1t} = P_{2t}$ is assigned by each BS. For second one, the total (E_b/I_0) calculated at MS t is expressed as $(E_b/I_0) = (E_b/I_0)_1 + (E_b/I_0)_2$ and $(E_b/I_0)_1 = (E_b/I_0)_2$ where $(E_b/I_0)_1$ and $(E_b/I_0)_2$ is contributed from BS 1 and 2, respectively. In this paper, both assumptions are applied. Denote Λ_t the soft handoff factor (SHOF), which is number of base stations involved in soft handoff process for mobile station t. With perfect power control, it is required that P_{jt} should be proportional to the interference. The transmitted power P_{jt} for MS t from BS j can be adjusted to have the same shape as the total interference. Then P_{jt} changes by power adjustment factor as interference changes with high P_{jt} for large interference.

2.2 SIR Model

In CDMA environment, since all users communicate at the same time and same frequency, each user's transmission power is regarded as a part of other users' interfer-

2.2 SIR Model

In CDMA environment, since all users communicate at the same time and same frequency, each user's transmission power is regarded as a part of other users' interference. CDMA is a kind of power-constrained or interference-limited system. With perfect power control and the interference-dominated system, we ignore background noise. The signal to interference ratio (SIR) to be considered is uplink (*UL*) and downlink (*DL*) interference, as shown in Fig. 1, which is coming from MS to BS and from BS to MS, respectively.

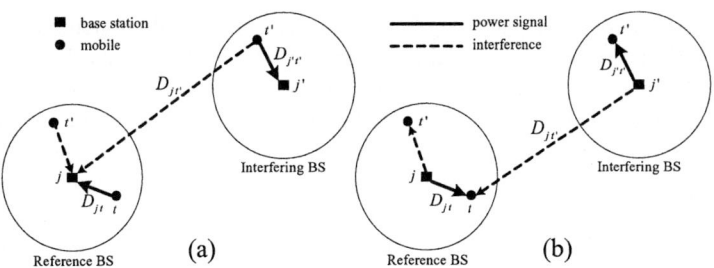

Fig. 1. The interference scenario: (a) uplink interference; (b) downlink interference

Let W^{UL} (W^{DL}) and d^{UL} (d^{DL}) be the system bandwidth and the traffic data rate for uplink (downlink), respectively. Given z_{jt}^N and z_{jt}^H ($z_{jt} = z_{jt}^N + z_{jt}^H$) is decision variable of new and handoff calls, respectively, which is 1 if mobile station t is admitted by base station j and 0 otherwise. We assume that the uplink power is perfectly controlled, it assures the received power at the BS j, $\forall j \in B$ where B is the BS set, is the same (constant value) for all MSs in the same traffic class-c. Denote $S_{c(t)}^{UL}$ the received uplink power signal at BS from MS t with traffic class $c(t)$, $\forall t \in T$ where T is the MS set. And denote D_{jt} the distance from MS t to BS j. The received SIR $SIR_{j,c(t)}^{UL}$ in uplink is given by (1), where θ^{UL} is the uplink orthogonality factor and $\alpha_{c(t)}^{UL}$ is uplink activity factor of traffic class-c(t), and attenuation factor $\tau = 4$. The uplink processing gain is given $G^{UL} = W^{UL}/d^{UL}$. The first and second term of denominator is intra-cell and inter-cell interference, respectively. A very large constant value V in numerator is to satisfying constraint requirement if MS t is rejected ($z_{jt}=0$).

$$SIR_{j,c(t)}^{UL} = \frac{W^{UL}}{d_{c(t)}^{UL}} \frac{S_{c(t)}^{UL} + (1-z_{jt})V}{(1-\theta^{UL})\left(\sum_{\substack{t' \in T \\ t' \neq t}} \alpha_{c(t')}^{UL} S_{c(t')}^{UL} z_{jt'}\right) + \left[\sum_{\substack{j' \in B \\ j' \neq j}} \sum_{\substack{t' \in T \\ t' \neq t}} \alpha_{c(t')}^{UL} S_{c(t')}^{UL} \left(\frac{D_{j't'}}{D_{jt'}}\right)^\tau\right] z_{j't'}} \quad (1)$$

In downlink case, notations used are similar to uplink model. Applying soft handoff factor (SHOF) $\Lambda_t = \sum_{j \in B} \delta_{jt}^H$ and downlink perfect power control is assumed, the received SIR $SIR_{j,c(t)}^{UL}$ in uplink is given by (2).

$$SIR_{j,c(t)}^{DL} = \frac{W^{DL}}{d_{c(t)}^{DL}} \frac{\Lambda_t S_{c(t)}^{DL} + (1-z_{jt})V}{(1-\theta^{DL})\sum_{\substack{t' \in T \\ t' \neq t}} \alpha_{c(t')}^{DL} S_{c(t')}^{DL} \left(\frac{D_{jt'}}{D_{jt}}\right)^\tau z_{jt'} + \sum_{\substack{j' \in B \\ j' \neq j}} \sum_{\substack{t' \in T \\ t' \neq t}} \alpha_{c(t')}^{DL} S_{c(t')}^{DL} \left(\frac{D_{j't'}}{D_{j't}}\right)^\tau z_{j't'}} \quad (2)$$

2.3 Traffic Model and Performance Measure

In this paper, we focus on voice traffic which consists of new and handoff call type. For each BS j, denote $\lambda_j = \lambda_j^N + \lambda_j^H$ total arrivals, where the arrivals of new and hand-off calls are Poisson distributed with rates λ_j^N and λ_j^H, respectively. The call holding time of both types is assumed to be exponentially distributed with mean μ. Location of MSs is generated in uniform distribution. Thus, the traffic intensity (in Erlangs) of new and handoff call is given $\varphi_j^N = \lambda_j^N \times \mu$ and $\varphi_j^H = \lambda_j^H \times \mu$, respectively. To investigating the effect of traffic intensity on performance analysis, denote ξ_j the ratio of φ_j^N to φ_j^H in BS j. Admission control is based on SIR measurement. Providing guaranteed QoS for ongoing calls is more important than admitting new call requests. Due to the soft handoff advantage in CDMA system, we would like to focus on minimization of handoff/ongoing call forced termination (blocking) probability subject to given new call blocking probability. For each admission control architecture in Fig. 2, admission control applying dynamic guard channel (DGC) approach is useful since it gives priority to handoff requests. The proposed approach dynamically reserves channels for prioritized handoff calls, it not only reserves different number of guard channels for each BS in terms of BS scenario (heterogeneous handoff arrival rate), but also provides runtime channel reservation. The reserved channels C_j^g ($=\lceil C_j \cdot f_j \rceil$, a ceiling function) among available channels C_j in BS j are referred to as the guard channels, where f_j is a reserved fraction of C_j and it is be determined. The remaining C_j^o ($=C_j - C_j^g$) channels, called the ordinary channels, are shared by both call types. When a new call attempt is generated in BS j, it is blocked if the number of free channels is less than or equal to C_j^g. Then the blocking probabilities of new and handoff calls in the BS j are given by $BN_j(g_j^N, g_j^H, C_j^o, C_j^g)$ and $BH_j(g_j^N, g_j^H, C_j^o, C_j^g)$ [3,4], respectively, where $\mu \sum_{t \in T} z_{jt}^N = g_j^N$ and $\mu \sum_{t \in T} z_{jt}^H = g_j^H$, and $g_j = g_j^N + g_j^H$.

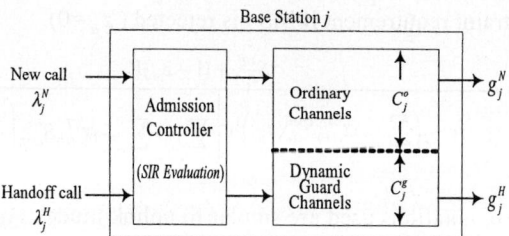

Fig. 2. Admission control architecture

2.4 Problem Formulation

In this section, we propose a prioritized real-time admission control algorithm to support soft handoff calls with QoS assurance in both uplink and downlink signal to interference ratio (SIR) requirement. The objective function (IP) is to minimize the weighted handoff call blocking probability, where the weighted probability is given by $w_j = g_j^H / \sum_{j \in B} g_j^H$.

Objective function:

$$Z_{IP} = \min \sum_{j \in B} w_j BH_j(g_j^N, g_j^H, C_j^o, C_j^g) \tag{IP}$$

s.t.

$$\left(\frac{E_b}{I_0}\right)_{c(t)}^{UL} \leq SIR_{j,c(t)}^{UL} \qquad \forall j \in B, t \in T \tag{3}$$

$$\left(\frac{E_b}{I_0}\right)_{c(t)}^{DL} \leq SIR_{j,c(t)}^{DL} \qquad \forall j \in B, t \in T \tag{4}$$

$$\mu \sum_{t \in T} z_{jt}^N = g_j^N \qquad \forall j \in B \tag{5}$$

$$\mu \sum_{t \in T} z_{jt}^H = g_j^H \qquad \forall j \in B \tag{6}$$

$$z_{jt}^N D_{jt} \leq \delta_{jt}^N R_j \qquad \forall j \in B, t \in T \tag{7}$$

$$z_{jt}^H D_{jt} \leq \delta_{jt}^H R_j \qquad \forall j \in B, t \in T \tag{8}$$

$$z_{jt}^N + z_{jt}^H \leq 1 \qquad \forall j \in B, t \in T \tag{9}$$

$$z_{jt}^N \leq (1 - \delta_{jt'}^H) + z_{jt'}^H \qquad \forall j \in B, t, t' \in T, t \neq t' \tag{10}$$

$$BN_j(g_j^N, g_j^H, C_j^o, C_j^g) \leq \beta_j \qquad \forall j \in B \tag{11}$$

$$\Omega_j \leq \frac{\sum_{t \in T} z_j^N}{\sum_{t \in T} \delta_j^N} \qquad \forall j \in B \tag{12}$$

$$\Phi_j \leq \frac{\sum_{t \in T} z_j^H}{\sum_{t \in T} \delta_j^H} \qquad \forall j \in B \tag{13}$$

$$C_j^o + C_j^g \leq C_j \qquad \forall j \in B \tag{14}$$

$$f_j \in F \qquad \forall j \in B \tag{15}$$

$$z_{jt}^N = 0 \text{ or } 1 \qquad \forall j \in B, t \in T \tag{16}$$

$$z_{jt}^H = 0 \text{ or } 1 \qquad \forall j \in B, t \in T \tag{17}$$

In CDMA system, each traffic demand is served with base station in the required QoS in both uplink and downlink connections. For uplink connection with perfect power control, the SIR value $SIR_{j,c(t)}^{UL}$ of each call class-c in its homing BS j must be greater than the pre-defined threshold $(E_b/I_0)_c^{UL}$, as shown in constraint (3). Again perfect power control is assumed in downlink, for each call request t in BS j QoS is required with threshold $(E_b/I_0)_{c(t)}^{DL}$ in (4). Constraint (5) and (6) check aggregate flow (in Erlangs) of new and handoff calls for BS j, which is based upon all granting mobile stations. Constraint (7) and (8) require that the MS would be in the coverage (power transmission radius R_j) area of a base station it is to be served by that base station. For each call request z_{jt} in BS j, in constraint (9), it must belong to only one of call types, either new (z_{jt}^N) or handoff call (z_{jt}^H). Constraint (10) guarantees the prioritized handoff calls. For each BS j, any new call z_{jt}^N can be granted only if all handoff calls $z_{jt'}^H$ are admitted if it initiates ($\delta_{jt}^H=1$ which is indicator function if MS t initiates a call request to BS j), or z_{jt}^N is admitted directly if there is no more handoff call initiates ($\delta_{jt}^H=0$). Constraint (11) requires that any base station can serve its slave MS under pre-defined new call blocking probability β_j. Constraint (12) and (13) require that the service rate for new and handoff calls is fulfilled in BS j. For channel reservation, total available channel is bounded by (14), and decision variable f_j is applied which belongs to the set F in (15). Constraint (16) and (17) are to enforce the integer property of the decision variables.

3 Solution Approach

3.1 Lagrangian Relaxation

The approach to solving problem (IP) is Lagrangian relaxation [13], which including the procedure that relax complicating constraints, multiple the relaxed constraints by corresponding Lagrangian multipliers, and add them to the primal objective function. Based on above procedure, the primal optimization problem (IP) can be transferred to Lagrangian relaxation problem (LR) where constraints (3)-(6), (10) are relaxed. LR can be further decomposed into two independent subproblems. All of them can be optimally solved by proposed algorithms. In summary, problem (IP) is transferred to be a dual problem (D) by multiplying the relaxed constraints with corresponding Lagrangian multipliers v_{jt}^1, v_{jt}^2, v_j^3, v_j^4, $v_{jtt'}^5$ and add them to the primal objective function. According to the weak Lagrangian duality theorem, for any v_{jt}^1, v_{jt}^2, v_j^3, v_j^4, $v_{jtt'}^5 \geq 0$, the objective value of $Z_D(v_{jt}^1, v_{jt}^2, v_j^3, v_j^4, v_{jtt'}^5)$ is a lower bound of Z_{IP}. Thus, the following dual problem (D) is constructed to calculate the tightest lower bound by adjusting multipliers.

$$Z_D = \max Z_D(v_{jt}^1, v_{jt}^2, v_j^3, v_j^4, v_{jtt'}^5) \qquad \text{(D)}$$

subject to: $v_{jt}^1, v_{jt}^2, v_j^3, v_j^4, v_{jtt'}^5 \geq 0$.

Then, subgradient method is applied to solving the dual problem. Let the vector S is a subgradient of $Z_D(v_{jt}^1, v_{jt}^2, v_j^3, v_j^4, v_{jtt'}^5)$ at $v_{jt}^1, v_{jt}^2, v_j^3, v_j^4, v_{jtt'}^5 \geq 0$. In iteration k of subgradient optimization procedure, the multiplier vector π is updated by $\pi^{k+1} = \pi^k + \zeta^k S^k$, the step size ζ^k is determined by $\varepsilon\left(Z_{IP}^* - Z_D(\pi^k)\right)/\|S^k\|^2$, where

Z_{IP}^* is an upper bound on the primal objective function value after iteration k, and ε is a constant where $0 \leq \varepsilon \leq 2$. Solutions calculated in dual problems need to be checked if solutions satisfy all constraints relaxed in (LR). A heuristic for getting primal feasible solutions is also developed [†].

3.2 Real-Time Admission Control Algorithm

Based upon Lagrangian relaxation approach, a predefined time budget η, 5 seconds is given to solving Lagrangian dual problem and getting primal feasible solutions iteratively. Number of call request admitted is depended on the time budget, as illustrated in Fig. 3. Assuming existing calls (in Erlangs) are still held after time Γ_n, at the same time call admission control starts when both calls arrived ($\lambda_j^N + \lambda_j^H$). After time budget η is used up, admission control is also well done, i.e. z_{jt}^N and z_{jt}^H are decided. On the other hand, initial value of Lagrangian multipliers and upper bound affects the solution quality on algorithm convergence. If we appropriately assign initial values, algorithm will be speeded up to converge in stead of more iterations are required. Fortunately, Lagrangian multipliers associated with users left can also be reused in next time interval. Besides, updating ε in the iteration process is carefully controlled by the error gap in previous iteration. The tighter gap is calculated, the smaller ε is assigned. For each real-time processing is on behalf of changing the number of both users arrived and users left in next time period. Overall procedure of real-time admission control is shown in Fig. 4.

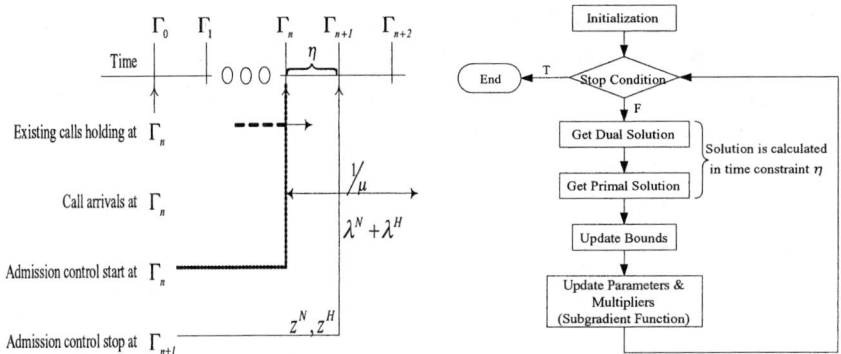

Fig. 3. The timing diagram of real-time admission control

Fig. 4. Procedure of Lagrangian relaxation based real-time admission control

---

[†] Associated algorithms to solving the subproblems and to getting primal feasible solutions are omitted due to the length limitation of the paper. A complete version of the paper is available upon request.

4 Experiment Analysis

For simplicity, we consider a cellular consisting of 9 BSs arranged as a two-dimensional array, and the voice call requests are analyzed. For statistic analysis, 500 time slots are experimented. After first 100 of them, the system is expected in the steady state. Final analysis report is based upon last 400 time slots. All experiments are coded in C. Given $\lambda_j = 12$ per η, the analysis is to examine the effect of traffic load ξ_j on handoff call blocking probability (Z_{IP}) with respect to several channel reservation schemes.

The system bandwidth allocated to both uplink (W^{UL}) and downlink (W^{DL}) is 6 MHZ, and the voice activity (α^{UL}, α^{DL}) and orthogonality (θ^{UL}, θ^{DL}) for both link is (0.3, 0.3) and (0.7, 1), respectively. It assumes ($S_{c(t)}^{UL}, S_{c(t)}^{DL}$) = (7dB, 10dB), available channel $C_j = 120$, as well as $R_j = 5$km. The required bit energy-to-noise density E_b/I_0 for both links is 5 dB. The bit rate of both links is 9.6KHZ. The requirements of service rate Φ_j and Ω_j are given 0.3. For comparison purpose, traditional complete sharing scheme (CSS) [9] and cutoff priority scheme (CPS) with fixed number of guard channels are implemented.

The effects of traffic load on handoff call blocking probability with $\beta_j = 0.01, 0.02$, and 0.03 are shown in Fig. 5, 6, and 7, respectively. They all illustrate that the number of reserved channel significantly affects the performance with respect to pre-defined threshold β_j. Theoretically, the more channels are reserved, the less blocking Z_{IP} is calculated. However, the minimization of Z_{IP} is constrained by β_j. As we can see, if we apply CPS with fixed number of reserved channels, the fraction (f_j) of reserved channel is up to 0.2, 0.3, and 0.4 in case of $\beta_j = 0.01, 0.02$, and 0.03, respectively. In summary, proposed dynamic guard channel (DGC) approach outperforms other schemes. For the analysis of performance improvement, under constraint of $\beta_j = 0.01$, DGC is compared to CSS and CPS with $f_j = 0.4$. Fig. 8 shows the reduction of blocking probability is up to 20% with CPS in $\xi_j = 1/3$, and up to 90% with CSS in the case of $\xi_j = 3/1$.

Applying Lagrangian relaxation and subgradient method to solve the problem (IP), the better primal feasible solution is an upper bound (UB) of the problem (IP) while Lagrangian dual problem solution guarantees the lower bound (LB). Iteratively, both solving Lagrangian dual problem and getting primal feasible solution, we get the LB and UB, respectively. The error gap is defined by (UB-LB)/LB*100%. Concerning about the solution quality of Lagrangian relaxation approach, we list the statistic of error gap in Table 1. All gaps are less than 10%. Actually, we also calculated the solution quality without applying multipliers technique as described in section 3.2, in most cases the gaps are larger than 80%. Experiments show that the proposed admission control scheme jointly considers real-time processing and dynamic channel reservation is valuable for further associated investigation.

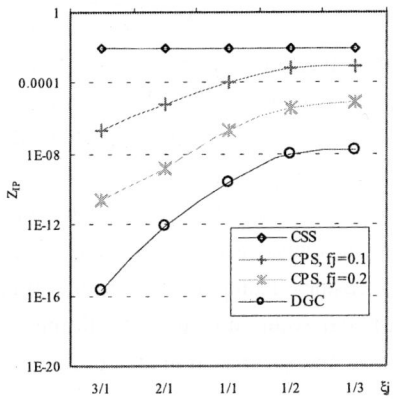

Fig. 5. Effect of traffic loads on handoff call blocking probability with $\beta_j=0.01$

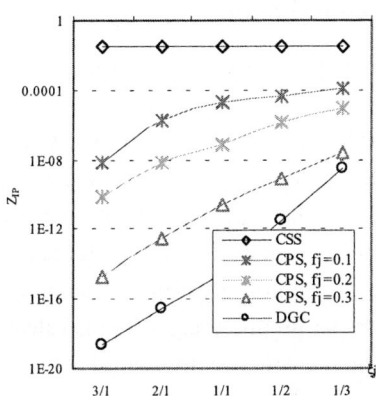

Fig. 6. Effect of traffic loads on handoff call blocking probability with $\beta_j=0.03$

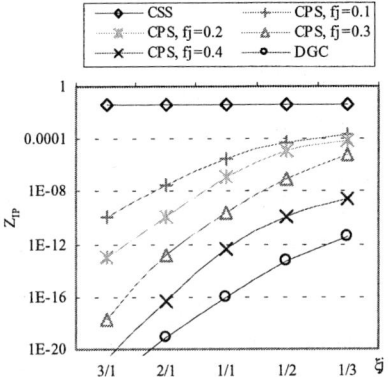

Fig. 7. Effect of traffic loads on handoff call blocking probability with $\beta_j=0.05$

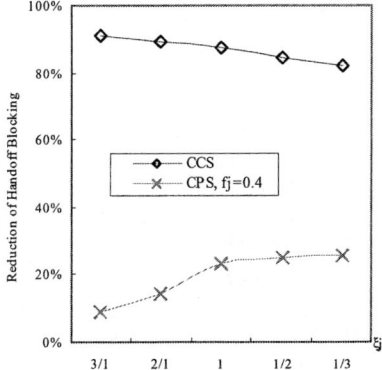

Fig. 8. Reduction of handoff blocking probability compared with two schemes in $\beta_j=0.01$

Table 1. Statistic of error gap with different traffic loads in $\beta_j=0.01$

Scheme	ξ_j				
	3/1	2/1	1/1	1/2	1/3
CSS	7.81%	8.50%	8.05%	7.70%	7.76%
CPS, $f_j=0.1$	8.73%	9.48%	7.78%	7.67%	9.12%
CPS, $f_j=0.2$	9.54%	9.97%	8.32%	9.27%	6.70%
CPS, $f_j=0.3$	8.59%	7.94%	7.98%	8.85%	7.05%
CPS, $f_j=0.4$	8.79%	9.47%	9.42%	6.99%	8.26%
DGC	8.82%	9.65%	8.19%	8.14%	8.86%

5 Conclusion

This paper proposes a prioritized real-time admission control model for DS-CDMA system. We jointly consider uplink/downlink, new/handoff calls. The algorithm is based upon dynamic reserved channels (guard channels) scheme for prioritized calls, it adapts to changes in handoff traffics where associated parameters (guard channels, new and handoff call arrival rates) can be varied. We express our achievements in terms of formulation and performance. Experiment analyzes the performance of admission control algorithm in terms of real-time manner. Computational results illustrate that proposed algorithm is calculated with better solution quality. To fitting real world scenario, jointly analysis of voice/data traffic and sectorization are considerable. They will be investigated in the future research.

References

1. Vitervi, A.M., Vitervi, A.J.: Erlang Capacity of a Power Controlled CDMA System. IEEE J. Select. Area Commun. **11**(6) (1993) 892–900
2. Jeon, W.S., Jeong, D.G.: Call Admission Control for Mobile Multimedia Communications with Traffic Asymmetry Between Uplink and Downlink. IEEE Trans. Veh. Technol. **59**(1) (2001) 59–66
3. Oh S.-H., Tcha D.-W.: Prioritized Channel Assignment in a Cellular Radio Network. IEEE Trans. Commun. **40** (1992) 1259–1269
4. Chang, K.-N., Kim, D.: Optimal Prioritized Channel Allocation in Cellular Mobile Systems. Computers & Operations Research **28** (2001) 345–356
5. Haung, Y.-R., Ho, J.-M.: Distributed Call Admission Control for a Heterogeneous PCS Network. IEEE Trans. Comput. **51**(12) (2002) 1400–1409
6. Soleimanipour, M., Zhung, W., Freeman, G.H.: Optimal Resource Management in Wireless Multimedia Wideband CDMA Systems. IEEE Trans. Mobile Computing **1**(2) (2002) 143–160
7. Chang, J.W., Chung J.H., Sung, D.K.: Admission Control Scheme for Soft Handoff in DS-CDMA Cellular Systems Supporting Voice and Stream-Type Data Services. IEEE Trans. Veh. Technol. **51**(6) (2002) 1445–1459
8. Singh, S., Krishnamurthy, V., Vincent P.H..: Integrated Voice/Data Call Admission Control for Wireless DS-CDMA Systems. IEEE Trans. Signal Processing **50**(6) (2002) 1483–1495
9. Liu Z., Zarki M. E.: SIR-Based Call Admission Control for DS-CDMA Cellular Systems. IEEE J. Select. Areas Commun. **12** (1994) 638–644
10. De Hoz A., Cordier C.: W-CDMA Downlink Performance Analysis. In: Proc. IEEE VTC. (1999) 968–972
11. Pistelli, W.-U., Verdone R.: Power Allocation Strategies for the Downlink in a W-CDMA System with Soft and Softer Handover: The Impact on Capacity. In: Proc. IEEE PIMRC. (2002) 5–10
12. Lee C.-C., Steele R.: Effect of Soft and Softer Handoffs on CDMA System Capacity, IEEE Trans. Veh. Technol. **47**(3) (1998) 830–841
13. Fisher M. L.: The Lagrangian Relaxation Method for Solving Integer Programming Problems. Management Science **27** (1981) 1–18

Voice Traffic Integration in Wireless Data Networks with Channel State Information*

Jin-Ghoo Choi and Saewoong Bahk

School of Electrical Engineering & Computer Science
Seoul National University, Seoul, Korea
{cjk,sbahk}@netlab.snu.ac.kr

Abstract. The knowledge for channel states can improve the performance of wireless access networks. The fast feedback of channel information was realized in the downlink of cdma2000 1xEV-DO system and it showed great enhancement in terms of total average throughput. Many schedulers have been proposed in this architecture, but they concentrate mainly on data users. The famous proportional fair (PF) scheduler, for instance, is not proper for voice services since it does not consider delay and packet drop constraints of sessions. In this paper, we accommodate voice traffic by the virtual frame structure and propose a simple admission control scheme. It accepts just the users who will be served with satisfaction, which prevents slots from being wasted by voice users with poor channels. Then, the voice service region is enlarged by two-level power control.

1 Introduction

In wireless environments, signals travel along multiple different paths and their interaction causes the multipath fading at the receiving point. As a result the channel gain fluctuates rapidly as time goes. Traditionally, unpredictable variation of channels is regarded as a major source of random error, so various techniques such as diversity and channel coding have been adopted to mitigate its adverse effect. While realtime traffic must be served within a bounded time, data applications can sustain some amount of packet delay. So, some recent researches proposed to exploit channel variation to increase average throughput in wireless data networks [3][9]. They utilized the fact that, when channel gains of users are statistically uncorrelated, some users are in good channel conditions while others suffer from deep fading. This effect is called the multi-user diversity.

In the cdma2000 1xEV-DO system, a base station (BS) broadcasts pilot symbols periodically and each mobile terminal (MT) measures the channel gain and feedbacks the information to it. Then, the central scheduler selects one user with the best channel condition and serves it [2]. By giving the priority to favorable users, system throughput grows significantly with the increase of users in number. Many opportunistic schedulers based on this architecture have been

---

* This work was supported by NRL Program of KISTEP, Korea.

proposed to balance the system throughput and user fairness [3][9]. However, they do not address how to accommodate realtime traffic such as Voice-over-IP (VoIP). We found some previous works discussing the delay issue in wireless networks. The Shortest Remaining Processing Time (SRPT) scheduling guarantees the shortest average delay but it might cause some jobs to starve [8]. [1] used the concept of stretch, a kind of normalized delay. In [7] the performance of SRPT is presented and a stretch-based algorithm is introduced for CDMA data networks. However, very limited works addressed the quality of service (QoS) issues in the cdma2000 1xEV-DO system. [5] proposed a scheduling scheme reducing the packet delay, but it does not guarantee the delay requirement and packet drop probability of realtime sessions.

In this paper, we support voice sessions by the virtual frame overlayed on the flat slot structure. We first enhance the PF scheduler to give higher priority to voice users, but it still experience frequent packet drops when the number of users is large. So we propose an admission control scheme which estimates the drop probability and does not accept voice users who cannot be served satisfactorily. Moreover, we adopt two-level power control scheme which differentiates the quality of slots by using different transmit power for each slot. We extend the voice service region by accommodating the voice users located around the cell boundary in high power slots

This paper is organized as follows. At first, we give a brief explanation on the considered system and PF scheduler. Then, the proposed scheme is described in section 3. In section 4, we introduce two-level power control as a means of extending service region for voice traffic, and the proposed scheme is modified for that environment. Section 5 presents the simulation results, followed by conclusions in Section 6.

2 Preliminary

2.1 System Model

We consider a wireless access network where a BS is located at the center and several MTs (or users) are within its coverage supporting a voice or data application. We concentrate on downlink for simplicity, but the proposed scheme can be applied for the uplink communication also. The considered downlink channel structure is similar to that of cdma2000 1xEV-DO systems. It is a single broadband channel shared by all users in a time division multiplexing manner. By exploiting the pilot signal from the BS, each mobile measures channel gain and the results are fed back to the BS. Based on this information the scheduler selects a user among the backlogged to be served in the following slot. The BS transmits a packet for the user with fixed power, which is equal for all users. The BS adapts the transmission rate according to channel gain and utilizes the wireless resource efficiently.

We use the frame structure to accommodate voice traffic. The frame is a group of consecutive time slots and its size, included slots in number, is determined considering the delay requirement of voice sessions. A voice codec generates a packet per frame so that it should be allocated a time slot every frame. Otherwise, the corresponding packet is dropped. The probability should be less than the desired value to satisfy the QoS requirement of voice users. The size of voice packets is fixed. So the scheduled voice user must have a feasible rate larger than a certain value to transmit the packet. Representing the maximum delay by D_v and the packet size by S_v, the frame size n_f is given by $\lceil D_v/t_{slot} \rceil$ and the minimum rate r_v is S_v/t_{slot}, where t_{slot} is the slot duration.

2.2 PF Scheduler

Various schedulers have been proposed on this architecture, but we concentrate on the PF scheduler since it is very simple to implement and achieves the well defined fairness criterion [6]. Its operation is as follows. In time slot n, every backlogged users are included in the candidate set $C[n]$. If the feasible rate of user k is $R_k[n]$ and its moving average is $T_k[n]$, then user $k^* = \arg\max_{k \in C[n]} R_k[n]/T_k[n]$ is served in the slot, and the average throughput of each user is updated by

$$T_k[n+1] = \begin{cases} (1 - \frac{1}{t_c})T_k[n] + \frac{1}{t_c}R_k[n], & k = k^* \\ (1 - \frac{1}{t_c})T_k[n], & k \neq k^* \end{cases} \quad (1)$$

where t_c is the time constant for the moving average. We omit the slot index n henceforth if it does not cause confusion.

The PF scheduler was mainly designed for best effort traffic. So we consider the slightly modified version in this paper. That is, a voice user does not become a candidate for scheduling if its feasible rate is less than r_v in the slot, and we use r_v in calculating the average rather than R_k.

3 Voice Traffic Integration

The PF scheduler allocates very similar portion of time slots to every user though it prefers users in good channel condition a little. Therefore, as the number of users grows, a voice user is hard to be assigned a slot every frame and its drop rate increases rapidly. As a partial solution, we first consider the priority PF (PPF) scheduler which gives a high priority to voice traffic.

3.1 PPF Scheduler

We define the voice candidate set C_v and data candidate set C_d. Every voice user is included in C_v at the beginning of a frame and excluded from it when assigned a slot. C_d consists of data users backlogged in the slot as in PF scheduler. First, a voice user $k_v^* = \arg\max_{k \in C_v} R_k/T_k$ is selected temporarily. If $R_{k_v^*} \geq r_v$, the user is served in the current slot. Otherwise, we consider another voice user with the next largest ratio for transmission. If no voice user is eligible, a data user $k_d^* = \arg\max_{k \in C_d} R_k/T_k$ is served then.

The PPF scheduler gives the absolute priority to voice users so that it serves them better than PF scheduler. However, they still suffer frequent packet drops when the number of voice users is large. Besides, the users with harsh channel conditions are assigned a slot sometimes, which degrades the data throughput without satisfying voice users.

3.2 Proposed Scheme

We cannot serve all the voice users with satisfaction when they are large in number and/or have poor channel conditions. So, we need an admission control to accommodate voice traffic, which will be performed considering the number of users and channel qualities.

Suppose that $i-1$ voice users are being served now. i-th voice user must pass the following admission test before being accepted into the system:

$$d_i = (1-g_i)^{\phi_i} \leq \tau_v, \qquad (2)$$

where d_i is the upper bound of drop probability of i-th voice, g_i is the good slot probability (GSP) of user i, ϕ_i is the number of remaining slots in a frame, and τ_v is the maximum endurable drop threshold. We say that a slot is *good* for a voice user when the channel gain is large enough so that it can receive a packet without corruption. ϕ_1 is initially set to the size of a frame since there is no voice user, and reduced by one when a user is accepted because it will be used by that user. That is, $\phi_{i+1} = \max\{0, \phi_i - 1\}$ if i-th user is admitted and, otherwise, ϕ_i does not change. A voice user is granted a priority number when accepted, which will be used by the scheduler in determining its service order. Since there are $i-1$ voice users already, the newcomer receives number i that indicates the lowest priority.

We give a second chance to a voice user who failed to pass the admission test. First, the priorities of existing users are rearranged, which may change the number of remaining slots for the current user. Then, the admission test is performed again for all voice users. The increasing order of GSP enables us to make room for the novice while serving the existing users since that ordering maximizes voice capacity in the following sense. We represent a voice user with k-th service priority in an arbitrary order o by V_k^o, and the increasing order of GSP is denoted by $o*$.

Property: If a sequence of N voice users $< V_1^o, V_2^o, ..., V_N^o >$ is accepted by the system, $< V_1^{o*}, V_2^{o*}, ..., V_N^{o*} >$ is permitted also.

Proof: Suppose that $g_i^o > g_j^o$ for a certain $i < j$, where the superscript represents the ordering. Then, we obtain another sequence $o+ = < V_1^o, ..., V_j^o, ..., V_i^o, ..., V_N^o >$ by changing them. Now, we show that $o+$ is accepted also.

For $1 \leq k < i$, $\phi_k^{o+} = \phi_k^o$ and $d_k^{o+} = (1-g_k^o)^{\phi_k^o} = d_k^o \leq \tau_v$. So, $\phi_i^{o+} = \phi_i^o$ and $d_i^{o+} = (1-g_j^o)^{\phi_i^o} < (1-g_j^o)^{\phi_j^o} = d_j^o \leq \tau_v$. For $i < k < j$, $\phi_k^{o+} = \phi_k^o$ and $d_k^{o+} = d_k^o \leq \tau_v$. So, $\phi_j^{o+} = \phi_j^o$ and $d_j^{o+} = (1-g_i^o)^{\phi_j^o} < (1-g_i^o)^{\phi_i^o} = d_i^o \leq \tau_v$. For $j < k \leq N$, $\phi_k^{o+} = \phi_k^o$ and $d_k^{o+} = d_k^o \leq \tau_v$.

$o*$ can be obtained from o by applying this operation finite times. This is clear from the well-known *insertion sort* or *bubble sort* algorithm, which completes the proof.

The scheduler plays a role of allocating time slots to accepted voice users and backlogged data users. Two candidate sets, C_v and C_d, are defined as PPF scheduler. All the accepted voice users are included in C_v at the beginning of a frame and C_d consists of data users backlogged in each slot. The scheduler temporarily selects the voice user who received the smallest priority number by the admission controller. If the feasible rate of the user is larger than r_v, it is served in the current slot and excluded from C_v. Otherwise, the next priority user will be considered for transmission. When there is no voice user eligible, the slot becomes available for data users. The PF or another scheduler designed for data traffic chooses a user to be served among the backlogged ones.

4 Extending Service Region

Users in the cell boundary have the poor channel condition owing to intercell interference as well as background noise. So, they are not liable to be accepted for voice service, which contracts the service region and causes frequent handoff drops. BS can utilize larger transmit power to break through the situation, but the benefit is limited since it increases the intercell interference also.

4.1 Two-Level Power Control

We differentiate the quality of slots by using different powers at each slot rather than the fixed power. Users experience a large signal-to-noise ratio (SNR) in slots using the high power (or *superior* slots) and, in other slots (or *inferior* slots), they suffer a small SNR. A BS sets its power to αP_t $(0 < \alpha \leq 1)$ in the first half of a frame and $(2-\alpha)P_t$ in the last half of it. So the average becomes P_t. The start time of a frame is staggered by half a frame between adjacent BSs. Then the first half of a frame becomes inferior slots and the last half superior ones. We can enlarge the service region when we serve the voice users close to BS in inferior slots and those far from BS in superior slots.

4.2 Modified Admission Control

We present another version of the proposed admission control, which was modified for systems utilizing two-level power control scheme. When a new voice user comes, the admission phase starts. We represent the GSP of user k in inferior slots by g_{ik}, and that in superior slots by g_{sk}. All the voice users including the newcomer are arranged in the increasing order of GSP, and their drop probabilities are calculated.

Let us denote the number of remaining inferior slots by ϕ_k and that of remaining superior slots by ψ_k for user k. Initially, they are set to the half size of a frame, $n_f/2$, respectively. Each voice user must pass the following admission test,

$$d_k = (1 - g_{ik})^{\phi_k}(1 - g_{sk})^{\psi_k} \leq \tau_v. \qquad (3)$$

The accepted user either can be served in the inferior slots or in the superior slots. The probability of being served in inferior slots is given as $a_k = 1 - (1 - g_{ik})^{\phi_k}$ and that in superior slots is $b_k = (1 - g_{ik})^{\psi_k}(1 - (1 - g_{sk})^{\psi_k})$. So, when user k is admitted, ϕ_{k+1} is set to $\max\{0, \phi_k - a_k(1 - d_k)^{-1}\}$ and $\psi_{k+1} = \max\{0, \psi_k - b_k(1 - d_k)^{-1}\}$. The new user is accepted into the system if every voice user passes the test.

5 Simulation Results

We model the cell as $L \times L$ square considering the metropolitan areas, and the cell layout consists of $5 \times 5 = 25$ cells or BSs. All simulation results were obtained in the center cell. Simulation parameters are as follows. The system bandwidth W is 1 (MHz), noise spectral density is -110 (dBm/Hz), the slot duration t_{slot} is 1.67 (msec), the frame size n_f is 30, and the cell size is 1000×1000 (m^2). The number of data users is 10 and their position is fixed at the distance of 300 (m) from BS. The number of voice users is 10 or 25 depending on the case. Every voice user is located at the same distance from BS, and the distance is varied from 50 to 600 (m). The packet drop probability should be less than 10.0 (%)

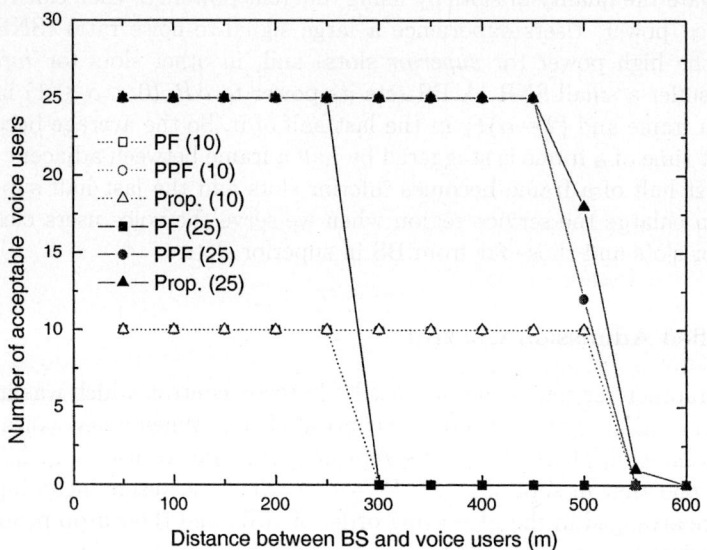

Fig. 1. Number of acceptable voice users

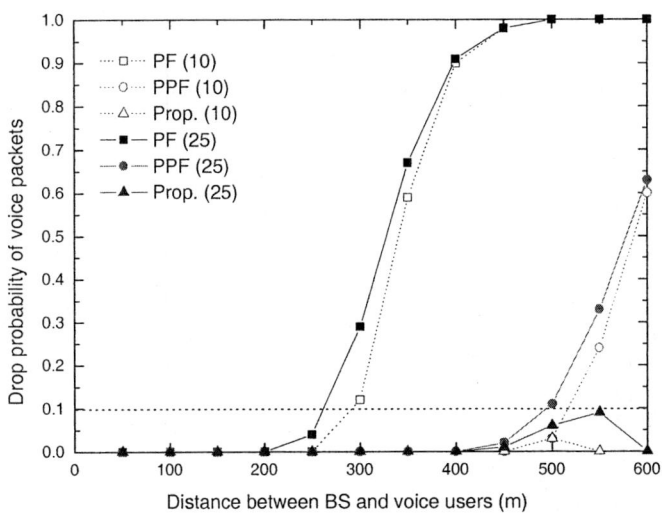

Fig. 2. Drop probability of voice packets

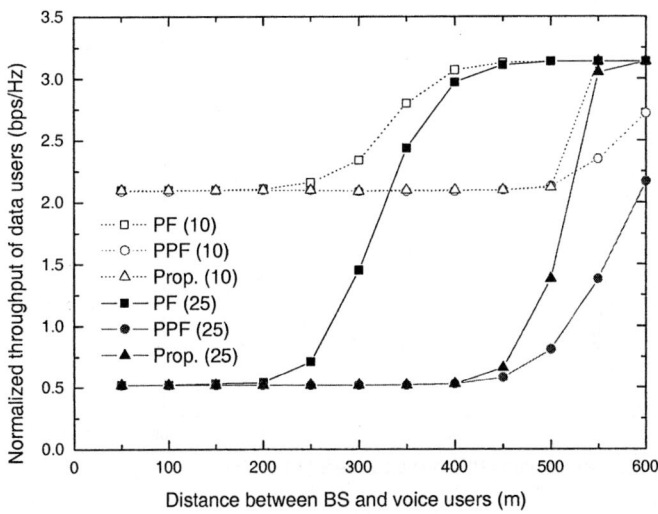

Fig. 3. Normalized throughput of data users

for voice users. The feasible rate R is related to SNR, Z, by $R = W \log_2(1 + \frac{Z}{K})$ where K is constant set to 8 (dB) [4].

Fig. 1 shows the acceptable number of voice users in PF, PPF, and the proposed scheme. We say that a voice user is acceptable when it experiences the drop rate less than 10.0 (%). The number of offered voice users is written

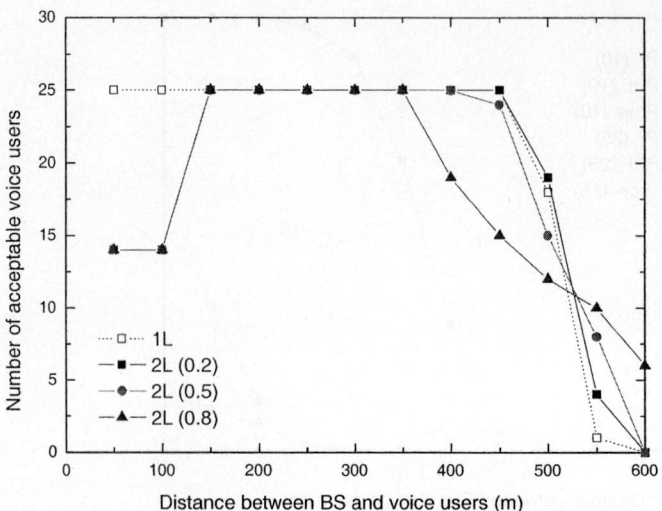

Fig. 4. Comparison of 1L and 2L systems: number of accepted voice users

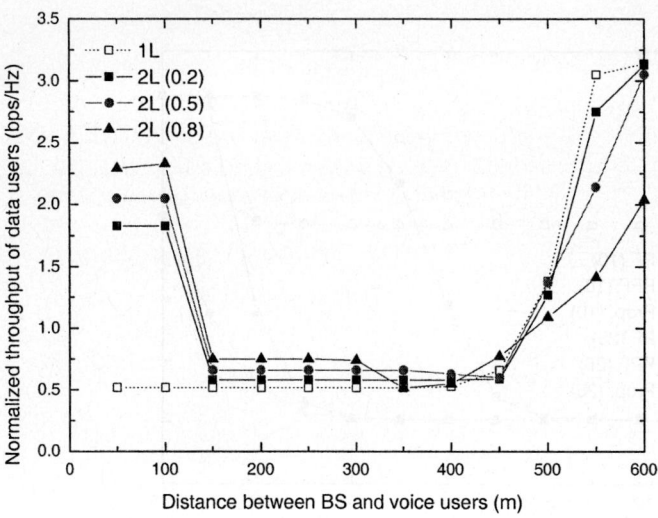

Fig. 5. Comparison of 1L and 2L systems: normalized throughput of data users

in the parenthesis. For PF scheduler, the number decreases to zero at 300 (m) while other two schemes serve some voice users even at 550 (m). Fig. 2 shows the drop probability of voice packets. We counted just the packet drops of accepted users for the proposed scheme. In PF and PPF scheduler, a voice user suffers from frequent packet drops as the distance increases because its channel becomes worse then. On the other hand, the proposed scheme abandons such a user and, if it were accepted, it always has the drop rate less than the required value. Fig. 3 presents the throughput of data users, which are normalized by the system bandwidth. The PF scheduler gives the best throughput at the cost of violating the QoS requirements of voice users. In general, the proposed scheme shows similar throughput to PPF scheduler, and it outperforms the latter when the distance of voice users is large. The PPF scheduler serves too many voice users and smaller time slots are assigned to data users compared with the proposed scheme.

Then, we compare the performance of the proposed scheme in one-level power control (1L) systems and two-level power control (2L) systems. Fig. 4 shows the number of accepted voice users. The used power adaptation factor α is written in the parenthesis, and the number of offered voice users is fixed to 25. The voice capacity decreases gradually in 2L systems and more users are accepted in the cell boundary. The cost is the capacity drop around the BS. Considering the entire cell, the center area is so small and the reduced capacity will be enough for the voice service. Fig. 5 presents the normalized data throughput. When the voice users are close to BS, 2L systems have the small voice capacity and the time slots are given to data users, which makes the data throughput increase. Similarly, the enhanced voice capacity at the cell edge leads to the throughput reduction.

6 Conclusion

In this paper, we investigated methods to support voice traffic in wireless data networks with channel state information. The proposed admission control scheme increases the number of voice users served with satisfaction while enhancing the average data throughput by eliminating wasted slots by voice users in poor channel condition. Sometimes voice users cannot be served in the cell edge owing to intercell interference and background noise. We applied two-level power control to enlarge the service region for voice traffic and modified the proposed scheme for that environment. The performance of proposed schemes was confirmed by computer simulations.

References

1. Bender, M., Chakraborti, S., Muthukreshman, S.: Flow and Stretch Metrics for Scheduling Continuous Job Streams. In: Proc. IX Ann. ACM SIAM Symp. Discrete Algorithms. (1998) 270–279
2. Bender, P., Black, P., Grob, M., Padovani, R., Sindhushyana, N., Viterbi, S.: CDMA/IIDR: A Bandwidth Efficient High Speed Wireless Data Service for Nomadic Users. IEEE Commun. Mag. **38**(7) (2000) 70–77
3. Borst, S., Whiting, P.: Dynamic Rate Control Algorithms for HDR Throughput Optimization. In: Proc. IEEE INFOCOM 2001. (2001) 976–985
4. Catreux, S., Driessen, P.F., Greenstein, L.J.: Data Throughputs using Multiple-input Multiple-output (MIMO) Techniques in a Noise-Limited Cellular Environment. IEEE Trans. Wireless Commun. **1**(2) (2002) 226–234

5. Choi, Y. Bahk, S.: Scheduling for VoIP Service in cdma2000 1xEV-DO. to appear in Proc. IEEE ICC 2004, Paris, France. (2004)
6. Jalali, A., Padovani, R., Pankaj, R.: Data Throughput of CDMA-HDR: A High Efficiency High Data Rate Personal Communication Wireless System. In: Proc. IEEE VTC 2000. (2000) 1854–1858
7. Joshi, N., Kadaba, S., Patel, S., Sundaram, G.: Downlink Scheduling in CDMA Data Packets. In: Proc. ACM MOBICOM 2000. (2000)
8. Karger, D., Stein, C., Wein, J.: Handbook of Algorithms and Theory of Computation. CRC Press, (1999)
9. Liu, X., Chong, E.K.P., Shroff, N.B.: Opportunistic Transmission Scheduling with Resource-Sharing Constraints in Wireless Networks. IEEE J. Select. Areas Commun. **19**(10) (2001) 2053–2064

Blind Collision Resolution Using Retransmission Diversity under Quasi-static Fading Channels*

Barış Özgül and Hakan Deliç

Signal and Image Processing Laboratory (BUSIM)
Department of Electrical and Electronics Engineering
Boğaziçi University, Bebek 34342 Istanbul, Turkey
{ozgulbar,delic}@boun.edu.tr

Abstract. Wireless multiple access protocols with retransmission diversity resolve packet collisions through source separation techniques. The number of retransmissions to achieve the necessary diversity level equals the collision multiplicity, whose proper detection is essential for good performance. The so-named network-assisted diversity multiple access (NDMA) resolves the collisions under quasi-static fading, but it is a non-blind approach. Moreover, the blind version of NDMA (B-NDMA) requires tight transmitter phase control and static channels. As another blind method, NDMA with independent component analysis (ICA-NDMA) performs under quasi-static channels, but its multiplicity detection technique suffers at low SNRs. In this paper, efficient collision resolution is achieved by employing a new multiplicity detection technique for ICA-NDMA, where both theoretical and experimental results are presented.

1 Introduction

Network-assisted diversity multiple access (NDMA) [10], blind version of NDMA (B-NDMA) [12], and NDMA with independent component analysis (ICA-NDMA) [8] are introduced to have high throughput and low delay performances in case of bursty data transmissions. The main contribution is to allow mobile users to transmit at any time slot without channel allocation, where the collided packets are not simply discarded, such as the case in slotted Aloha and many other random access algorithms. The diversity is achieved by retransmitting the collided packets for a certain number of channel slots. After the collision multiplicity is detected, the packets are separated using the appropriate signal processing tools. In the event of underestimation of the multiplicity, fewer packets are separated than the actual quantity, usually with bit errors, which causes a deterioration in the throughput performance. In case of overestimation, some channel slots are wasted by unnecessary retransmissions, and therefore the delay performance suffers. Bit errors are encountered, as well. Thus, the quality of the

---

* This work was supported by the Boğaziçi University Research Projects under grant no. 01A203.

collision multiplicity detection process has quite an impact on the performance of such protocols.

In quasi-static fading, the channel is constant during a whole data block, but changes independently block by block [6]. NDMA and ICA-NDMA achieves the diversity using the virtues of quasi-static frequency-flat fading, where a different channel coefficient is multiplied with the transmitted packet at each retransmission. The channel is assumed to be static in B-NDMA, and the diversity gain is achieved by changing the transmitter's phase properly during the retransmissions. Although NDMA resolves a K-packet collision in K transmissions, it is a non-blind method which requires user-specific orthogonal ID sequences in the packet headers [10]. As the population grows longer id sequences result in increased overhead, which has a negative impact on the bandwidth that carries the packet payload. Moreover, the system is sensitive to synchronization losses and multipath effects, due to the orthogonality assumption.

In B-NDMA and ICA-NDMA collided packets are retransmitted for a certain number of time-slots until the collision multiplicity is detected, and then the packets are separated, blindly. At each retransmission, the received packet at the base station (BS) is actually the summation of the additive noise and the linear combination of the collided packets. Therefore, for K collided packets with N symbols, the data observed at the BS after T transmissions ($T-1$ retransmissions) can be modeled as

$$\mathbf{Y}_{T\times N} = \mathbf{A}_{T\times K}\mathbf{S}_{K\times N} + \mathbf{V}_{T\times N}, \qquad (1)$$

where each row of the matrix $\mathbf{Y}_{T\times N}$ denotes the received data at the corresponding transmission, $\mathbf{A}_{T\times K}$ is the channel mixing matrix, $\mathbf{S}_{K\times N}$ is the packet data matrix with K collided packets in its rows, and the matrix $\mathbf{V}_{T\times N}$ stands for the additive white Gaussian noise. Both of B-NDMA and ICA-NDMA achieve the collision multiplicity detection using the eigenvalues of the covariance matrix of $\mathbf{Y}_{T\times N}$ in (1), which is

$$\mathbf{R}_T = \mathbf{Y}_{T\times N}(\mathbf{Y}_{T\times N})^H/N. \qquad (2)$$

After each transmission, size of the matrix $\mathbf{Y}_{T\times N}$ grows since a new row is appended, and a new covariance matrix is obtained. Retransmissions continue until the collision multiplicity is detected.

B-NDMA determines the multiplicity using the rank-test (RT) method, and resolves the packets by employing parallel factor analysis (PARAFAC) [12]. In case of a K-packet collision, the resolution is achieved in $K+1$ transmission slots, ideally. However, $\mathbf{A}_{T\times K}$ in (1) is guaranteed to be in Vandermonde structure by assuming tight control of the transmitter phase, and static channel fading throughout retransmissions. If these assumptions do not hold, RT method suffers from the underestimation/overestimation of the collision multiplicity, and PARAFAC cannot be applied for resolution. B-NDMA and ICA-NDMA results in similar throughput and delay performances, but ICA-NDMA can work under quasi-static channel conditions without any transmitter phase control, where the collision multiplicity is detected by using Akaike information criteria (AIC) in the expense of one additional retransmission slot, and the packets are resolved using independent component analysis (ICA). The noisy ICA algorithm given in [4] is used for collision resolution because of the additive Gaussian noise term in (1), and the application of the algorithm for ICA-NDMA is available in [8].

Detecting the number of mixed sources using information theoretic criteria, such as AIC and minimum description length (MDL), is a well investigated research area. In [11], the eigenvalue forms of AIC and MDL are derived to determine the model order of a mixture presented as (1), depending on the assumptions that the matrix $\mathbf{A}_{T \times K}$ is full-column rank $(T > K)$, sources in $\mathbf{S}_{K \times N}$ and additive noise terms in $\mathbf{V}_{T \times N}$ are zero-mean stationary complex Gaussian processes. Under these assumptions, MDL is shown to be asymptotically consistent, whereas AIC tends to overestimate the number of sources [11,13,7]. The performance is almost similar for BPSK, QPSK, and 16QAM sources [1]. In ICA-NDMA, it is assumed that AIC does not result in any detection, while the matrix $\mathbf{A}_{T \times K}$ is not full-column rank. However, this assumption does not hold and AIC results in false detections, especially in case of low SNR and high collision multiplicity [8]. Since it is more likely to overestimate, AIC results in fewer false detections with respect to MDL. Thus, AIC is preferred for ICA-NDMA.

In this paper, MDL is combined with the RT method [9] to replace the AIC-based collision detection [8] in ICA-NDMA, and it is shown to have much better performance than ICA-NDMA or ICA-NDMA with RT based collision detection, under quasi-static frequency flat fading. In Sect. 2, the signal model for the collision problem in (1) is given, and the multiplicity detection method is described in Sect. 3. Following the analytical procedure regarding the mean delay and throughput in Sect. 4, the simulation results are presented in Sect. 5. The conclusions can be found in Sect. 6.

2 Signal Model

The observed data matrix $\mathbf{Y}_{T \times N}$ in (1) contains the collided data packets after matched filtering and sampling at the bit rate, for all T transmissions. The content of $\mathbf{A}_{T \times K}$ is depicted as

$$\mathbf{A}_{T \times K} = \begin{bmatrix} a(1,1) & \cdots & a(1,K) \\ \vdots & \ddots & \vdots \\ a(T,1) & \cdots & a(T,K) \end{bmatrix}$$

and
$$a(t,k) = f(t,k)e^{j\varphi(t,k)}, \tag{3}$$

where $f(t,k)$ is the fading coefficient for the kth user, and $\varphi(t,k)$ is the phase difference between the kth transmitter and the receive antenna at the BS, during the tth transmission. All $\varphi(l,k)$ have a uniform distribution over $[-\pi,\pi)$, and they are independent and identically distributed (i.i.d.) across all packets and observations. The fading coefficient $f(t,k)$ is complex-valued and can be expressed by

$$f(t,k) = \alpha(t,k)e^{j\phi(t,k)}. \tag{4}$$

It is assumed that the amplitudes $\alpha(t,k)$ are Rayleigh-distributed with unit variance and i.i.d. across all users and observations. All $\phi(t,k)$ have uniform distribution over $[-\pi,\pi)$, and they are i.i.d. across all users and observations. The fading process is flat in frequency and constant during one transmission slot for each mobile. $\mathbf{V}_{T\times N}$ denote the noise matrix, whose elements are represented by $v(t,n)$, which is the complex white Gaussian noise term added to the nth symbol of the packet observed in the tth transmission. The Gaussian noise is i.i.d. across all observations with zero mean and variance of σ_v^2. The matrix $\mathbf{S}_{K\times N}$ contains the N-bit data packets transmitted by the K independent sources. Each packet is stationary with unit variance, and contains bits that are drawn from an equiprobable BPSK constellation. If the expression for $\mathbf{Y}_{T\times N}$ in (1) is put into (2),

$$\mathbf{R}_T = \mathbf{A}_{T\times K}(\mathbf{A}_{T\times K})^H + \sigma_v^2 \mathbf{I}_{T\times T}, \tag{5}$$

by assuming that the packets are mutually independent, and the noise process and the packets are uncorrelated.

3 MDL with RT Method for Collision Multiplicity Detection

The RT method is a blind multiplicity detection technique, which is used by B-NDMA in the presence of static channel conditions [12]. In this method, the eigenvalues of the covariance matrix $\mathbf{R}_T$ in (2) are estimated after every transmission and sorted in decreasing order as $\lambda_1 \geq \lambda_2 \geq \ldots \geq \lambda_t \geq \ldots \geq \lambda_T$. Then the eigenvalues are compared with a tolerance threshold τ, and if

$$\lambda_t < \tau, \qquad t = 1, \ldots, T,$$

the collision multiplicity is detected as $K = t - 1$. Otherwise, the packets are retransmitted, and the same procedure is applied. Thus, the multiplicity is determined in $K+1$ transmissions (which is also called as resolution epoch), ideally. It is not easy to select an appropriate threshold for the system, especially in quasi-static channels given in (3) when the additive noise is not perfectly white. In order to avoid the underestimations, τ can be chosen smaller, but this obviously results in more overestimations.

In [8], the AIC-based detector is employed to determine the collision multiplicity under quasi-static channel conditions, without any threshold selection. After every transmission, AIC is estimated by putting the eigenvalues $\lambda_1 \geq \lambda_2 \geq \ldots \geq \lambda_T$ of $\mathbf{R}_T$ in [7]

$$\mathrm{AIC}(t) = -2(T-t)N \ln \frac{G(\lambda_{t+1},\ldots,\lambda_T)}{A(\lambda_{t+1},\ldots,\lambda_T)} + 2t(2T-t) \tag{6}$$

where $t = 0,\ldots,T-1$, and A and G denote the arithmetic and the geometric means of their arguments, respectively. Then, the condition $\mathrm{AIC}(t) < \mathrm{AIC}(t+1)$ is checked for $t = 0,\ldots,T-2$, and if it is satisfied, the collision multiplicity is decided to be $K = t$. Otherwise, the collided packets are retransmitted and the above steps are repeated. Thus, epoch length is $K + 2$, ideally. However, AIC makes false detections when the number of observations are insufficient ($\mathbf{A}_{T \times K}$ in (1) is not full-column rank), especially at low SNRs when the collision multiplicity is high [8].

The proposed detector replaces the AIC-based detector in [8], by combining MDL with the RT method [9]. The eigenvalues of $\mathbf{R}_T$ are estimated after every transmission and sorted in decreasing order. The last two eigenvalues are decided to belong to noise, if

$$\lambda_{T-1} + \lambda_T < 2\tau.$$

If the above condition is satisfied, MDL is estimated by putting the eigenvalues $\lambda_1 \geq \lambda_2 \geq \ldots \geq \lambda_T$ of $\mathbf{R}_T$ in [7]

$$\text{MDL}(t) = -(T-t)N \ln \frac{G(\lambda_{t+1}, \ldots, \lambda_T)}{A(\lambda_{t+1}, \ldots, \lambda_T)} + 0.5t(2T-t)\ln N. \quad (7)$$

Then, the condition $\text{MDL}(t) < \text{MDL}(t+1)$ is checked for $t = 0, \ldots, T-2$, and if it is satisfied, the collision multiplicity is decided to be $K = t$. RT is only used to determine the sufficient number of observations for MDL, which is actually employed to detect the collision multiplicity. Thus, the new method suffers less from the overestimations with respect to the RT method. Moreover, underestimation rate also decreases since the sum of the last two eigenvalues are compared with the threshold instead of one eigenvalue, and MDL do not always result in multiplicity detection, although the RT may determine insufficient number of observations ($T < K + 2$). MDL is preferred for the proposed detector since it is asymptotically consistent, whereas AIC tends to overestimate the multiplicity.

4 Theoretical Analysis

Since the covariance matrix for the white noise is diagonal, the eigenvalues of $\mathbf{R}_T$ in (5) can be expressed as, $\lambda_i = \lambda_{c,i} + \sigma_v^2$, $i = 1, \ldots, T$, where $\lambda_{c,i}$ denotes the ith eigenvalue of

$$\mathbf{C} = \mathbf{A}_{T \times K}(\mathbf{A}_{T \times K})^H. \quad (8)$$

Therefore, to test whether $\lambda_{c,i} < (\tau - \sigma_v^2)$ is same as to check λ_i against the threshold value τ. Similarly, for the MDL with RT, the condition $\lambda_{c,T-1} + \lambda_{c,T} < (2\tau - 2\sigma_v^2)$ can be used to determine the sufficient number of observations. The entries of $\mathbf{A}_{T \times K}$ can be considered as complex Gaussian with unit variance, depending on the definition of the fading coefficients in (4). For such matrices, the joint eigenvalue distributions of $\mathbf{C}$ in (8) are derived both for $T \leq K$ (the Wishart distribution) in [3,5] and $T > K$ (the anti-Wishart distribution) in [5].

In [9], depending on the white noise assumption, underestimation probabilities for the RT method, and the insufficient observation probabilities for the MDL with RT are expressed analytically using Wishart distribution, and Wishart and anti-Wishart distributions, respectively. Ideally, the theoretical covariance matrix has equal eigenvalues of σ_v^2. However, for the time-average case, deviations are encountered for the eigenvalues with increasing noise variance [2]. Thus, in [9], higher experimental underestimation rates are observed for the RT method are with respect to the analytical underestimation probabilities, as the signal-to-noise ratio (SNR) decreases. Moreover, overestimation performance worsens with decreasing SNR, as well. Thus, it is hard to decide on an appropriate threshold for RT, especially at low SNRs. On the other hand, MDL with RT has superior underestimation and overestimation performances [9]. This is because the MDL does not always underestimate the collision multiplicity although the number of observations are insufficient, especially at high SNRs [9]. Moreover, it results in negligible overestimations irrespective of SNR if there are adequate number of symbols N in the packets [9,13].

If the matrix $\mathbf{A}_{T \times K}$ in (1) is full-column rank $(T > K)$, the overestimation and underestimation probabilities for MDL can be asymptotically expressed [13]. If we denote the estimated collision multiplicity as $\hat{K}$, the underestimation and overestimation take place, when $\hat{K} < K$ and $\hat{K} > K$, respectively. In [13] the underestimation and overestimation probabilities are approximated as $P(\hat{K} < K) \approx P(\hat{K} = K - 1)$, and $P(\hat{K} > K) \approx P(\hat{K} = K + 1)$. The underestimation probability is [13]

$$P(\hat{K} = K - 1) = \int_{-\infty}^{\gamma} \exp(-z^2/2) dz, \qquad (9)$$

where the integral upper limit is

$$\gamma = \{(\alpha(N)/\sqrt{N})(2T - 2K + 1) - F_K \sqrt{N}\} / \{a(1 + 1/(T - K))^{1/2}\} \qquad (10)$$

$$F_K = \ln\left\{(\sigma_v^2/\lambda_K)\left[\frac{\lambda_K/\sigma_v^2 - 1}{T - K + 1} + 1\right]^{T-K+1}\right\}, \qquad (11)$$

$$a = \{(T - K)(\lambda_K/\sigma_v^2 - 1)\} / \{\lambda_K/\sigma_v^2 + (T - K)\}. \qquad (12)$$

In (11), σ_v^2 denotes the variance of the noise process in (1), and λ_K is the Kth eigenvalue of $\mathbf{R}_T$ (2), in the decreasing order. The term $\alpha(N)$ in (10) is equal to $1/2 \ln N$ for MDL. For constant N, as $\lambda_K/\sigma_v^2 \to \infty$, $F_K \to \infty$ and $a \to (T - K)$, yielding $\gamma \to -\infty$. Hence, $P(\hat{K} = K - 1)$ goes to 0 or 1 as the ratio λ_K/σ_v^2 goes to infinity or zero, respectively [13]. Thus, the underestimation probabilities for MDL go to zero, as SNR goes to infinity. The overestimation probability is [13]

$$P(\hat{K} = K + 1) = 1 - \int_{-Y}^{Y} p(y) dy, \qquad (13)$$

$$Y = [2\alpha(N)(2T - 2K - 1)(T - K - 1) / (T - K)]^{1/2}, \qquad (14)$$

and $p(y)$ is the pdf for random variable y, which does not depend on λ_K or σ_v^2 [13]. Since $\alpha(N) = 1/2 \ln N$ for MDL, and as $N \to \infty$, $Y \to \infty$ resulting in $P(\hat{K} = K+1) \to 0$ [13]. Since $\alpha(N) = 1$ for AIC, it always tends to overestimate, as N increases.

In the following section, the analytical expressions are given for the delay and throughput performances of ICA-NDMA, when it uses MDL with RT.

4.1 Throughput and Delay Analyses

Let's assume that the total number of mobiles in the system is denoted by J, and each user stores the incoming packets in an infinite buffer, where the packets in the queue wait to be processed by the transmission channel. The number of packets arriving at each user's buffer is generated by a Poisson process which is independent for every user and has a per-user arrival rate of λ packets/slot. The traffic load of the system is λJ packets/slot.

Given a user k is either active or inactive, the corresponding probabilities for a K-packet collision can be expressed as

$$P_a(K) := P(K\text{-packet collision} \mid \text{user } k \text{ active})$$
$$= \binom{J-1}{K-1}(1-P_e)^{K-1}P_e^{J-K}, \quad K = 1, \ldots, J, \tag{15}$$
$$P_{ia}(K) := P(K\text{-packet collision} \mid \text{user } k \text{ inactive})$$
$$= \binom{J-1}{K}(1-P_e)^K P_e^{J-1-K}, \quad K = 0, \ldots, J-1, \tag{16}$$

respectively, where P_e is the probability that a user is not active at the beginning of the epoch. Ideally, the epoch length to detect a K-packet collision is $K+2$ for MDL with RT. However, in case of insufficient observations by the RT method, MDL may underestimate and result in smaller epoch lengths. Moreover, due to excessive number of observations by RT or overestimations by MDL, longer epoch lengths may be encountered, as well. In [9], it is both analytically and experimentally observed that the number of insufficient observations (or the insufficient epoch length) for a K-packet collision can be regarded as $K+1$. Similarly, the exceeded epoch length for a K-packet collision can be considered as $K+3$.

A user transmits in a relevant epoch (H_r) and is inactive in an irrelevant epoch (H_{ir}). The epoch length is a random variable which depends on the number of collided users at the beginning of that epoch. Using (15) and (16), and denoting the probability of encountering an insufficient epoch length and exceeded epoch length for a K-packet collision as $P_{ee}(K)$ and $P_{ie}(K)$, respectively, the probability mass function (pmf) for the relevant epoch is

$$P(H_r = h) = P_a(h-3)P_{ee}(h-3) + P_a(h-2)[1 - P_{ee}(h-2) - P_{ie}(h-2)]$$
$$+ P_a(h-1)P_{ie}(h-1), \quad h = 2, \ldots, J+3, \tag{17}$$

where $P_a(K) = 0$ for $K < 1$ and $K > J$. Similarly, the pmf for the irrelevant epoch is

$$P(H_{ir} = h) = P_{ia}(h-3)P_{ee}(h-3) + P_{ia}(h-2)[1 - P_{ee}(h-2) - P_{ie}(h-2)]$$
$$+ P_{ia}(h-1)P_{ie}(h-1), \quad h = 2, \ldots, J+3, \tag{18}$$

where $P_{ia}(K) = 0$ for $K < 0$ and $K > J-1$. The values for $P_{ie}(K)$ and $P_{ee}(K)$ are obtained by running simulations for each K and averaging the instantaneous values. During the simulations, (9) and (13) can be employed to get analytical results. Using the results in [12], P_e can be expressed as

$$P_e = \frac{1 - \lambda E[H_r]}{1 + \lambda E[H_{ir}] - \lambda E[H_r]}. \tag{19}$$

Then, P_e can be numerically computed using (19). Modelling each user's packet buffer as an M/G/1 queue with server vacation, and considering the relevant and irrelevant epochs as the service and vacation times, respectively, the mean delay D for a user's packet is expressed approximately as [10]

$$D = E[H_r] + \frac{\lambda E[H_r^2]}{2(1 - \lambda E[H_r])} + \frac{E[H_{ir}^2]}{2E[H_{ir}]}. \tag{20}$$

After finding P_e, D is plotted for different SNR scenarios in Fig. 1, using (20).

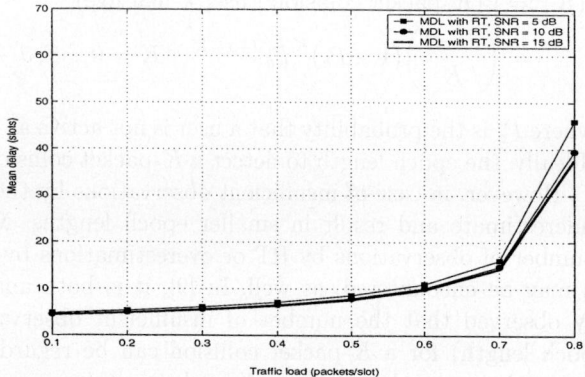

Fig. 1. Mean delay vs traffic load (λJ), $J = 10$

The maximum throughput can be regarded as the case where $P_{ee}(K)$ and $P_{ie}(K)$ are zero for all K and all the packets are resolved without bit errors at the end of the epoch. In such a case, it is found that $E[H_r] = (J-1)(1-P_e) + 3$ and $E[H_{ir}] = (J-1)(1-P_e) + 2$. If we put these in (19), and solve for P_e [8]

$$P_e = 1 - 2\lambda/(1 - \lambda J). \tag{21}$$

If P_e in (21) is zero, the maximum sustainable packet arrival rate per user is found as $\lambda_{\max} = 1/(J+2)$ packets/slot so that the maximum throughput is $J/(J+2)$. For $J = 10$, the maximum throughput is $0.8\overline{3}$. In Fig. 1, D is plotted up to 0.8 packets/slot traffic load not to exceed the maximum sustainable limit.

5 Simulations

During the simulations, the threshold value RT is set as $\sigma_v^2 + 0.005$, where it is two times this value for MDL with RT. Signal model in Sect. 2 is considered.

There are $J = 10$ users in the system and $N = 300$ bits in the packets. Each user's infinite buffer is independently fed by a Poisson process with a per-user arrival rate of λ packets/slot. The experimental results reflect the averages of three 100000-slot Monte-Carlo simulations. Throughput is estimated as the ratio of average number of packets resolved with no bit errors at the end of an epoch and the average epoch length. Average delay for a user packet includes the waiting time in the buffer and the transmission time in the channel. In Fig. 2a and Fig. 2b, the average delay and throughput performances of ICA-NDMA are observed, respectively, where the AIC-based detector is replaced with RT and the MDL with RT. Although ICA-NDMA with RT results in lower average delay (Fig. 2a), its throughput performance is worse, especially at 5 and 10 dBs. This is due to bit errors and packet losses since RT has higher underestimation rate with respect to MDL with RT, as SNR decreases [9]. RT has higher overestimation rate, and MDL with RT is more likely to exceed the ideal epoch length, at lower SNRs [9]. Thus, the average delay for ICA-NDMA using both detectors

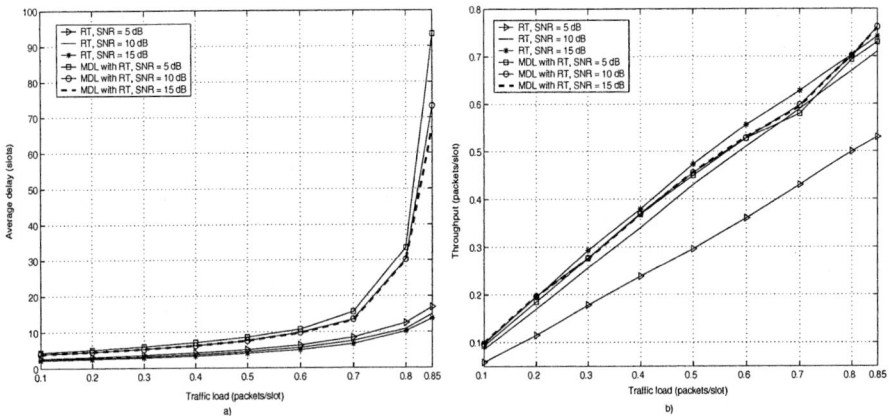

Fig. 2. a) Throughput vs traffic load (λJ), b) Average delay vs traffic load (λJ)

increases with decreasing SNR. Although the delay performance worsens after 0.8 packets/slot, ICA-NDMA using MDL with RT results in superior throughput performance, even at low SNR values, with respect to ICA-NDMA with RT, and ICA-NDMA in [8]. Its average delay performance in Fig. 2a is consistent with the mean delay results in Fig 1, as well.

6 Conclusion

In wireless multiple access protocols using retransmission diversity, correct detection of the collision multiplicity is essential to obtain high resolution performance. In this paper, a blind multiple access protocol which works efficiently under quasi-static channel conditions is introduced. AIC-based multiplicity detector of ICA-NDMA is replaced by a new method combining MDL with rank-test in [9]. The modified protocol has superior performance with respect to ICA-NDMA and ICA-NDMA with rank-test, as SNR decreases.

References

1. Fishler, E., Grossman, M., Messer, H.: Detection of Signals by Information Theoretic Criteria: General Asymptotic Performance Analysis. IEEE Transactions on Signal Processing **50** (2002) 1026–1036
2. Grouffaud, J., Larzabal, P., Clergeot, H.: Some Properties of Ordered Eigenvalues of a Wishart Matrix: Application in Detection Test and Model Order Selection. In: Proceedings of the IEEE International Conference on Acoustics, Speech, and Signal Processing, Vol. 5. Atlanta, USA (1996) 2463–2466
3. Haagerup, U., Thorbjornsen, S.: Random Matrices with Complex Gaussian Entries. Technical Report 4. Center for Mathematical Statistics, Aarhus University, Denmark (1998)
4. Hyvärinen, A.: Independent Component Analysis in the Presence of Gaussian Noise by Maximizing Joint Likelihood. Neurocomputing **22** (1998) 49–67
5. Janik, R.A., Nowak, M.A.: Wishart and Anti-Wishart Random Matrices. Journal of Physics A: Mathematical and General **36** (2003) 3629–3637
6. Li, Y., Georghiades, C.N., Huang, G.: Transmit Diversity Over Quasi-Static Fading Channels Using Multiple Antennas and Random Signal Mapping. IEEE Transactions on Communications **51** (2003) 1918–1926
7. Liavas, A.P., Regalia, P.A.: On the Behaviour of Information Theoretic Criteria for Model Order Selection. IEEE Transactions on Signal Processing **49** (2001) 1689–1695
8. Özgül, B., Deliç, H.: Blind Collision Resolution for Mobile Radio Networks in Fast-Fading Channels. Record of the IEEE International Conference on Communications. Anchorage, USA (2003) 1228–1332
9. Özgül, B., Deliç, H.: Blind Collision Multiplicity Detection for Wireless Access Using Retransmission Diversity. In: Proceedings of the 60th IEEE Semiannual Vehicular Technology Conference. Los Angeles, USA (2004)
10. Tsatsanis, M.K., Zhang, R., Banerjee, S.: Network-Assisted Diversity for Random Access Wireless Networks. IEEE Transactions on Signal Processing **48** (2000) 702–711
11. Wax M., Kailath, T.: Detection of Signals by Information Theoretic Criteria. IEEE Transactions on Acoustics, Speech, and Signal Processing **33** (1985) 387–392
12. Zhang, R., Sidiropoulos, N.D., Tsatsanis, M.K.: Collision Resolution in Packet Radio Networks Using Rotational Invariance Techniques. IEEE Transactions on Communications, **50** (2002) 146–155
13. Zhang, Q., Wong, K.M., Yip, P.C., Reilly, J.P.: Statistical Analysis of the Performance of Information Theoretic Criteria in the Detection of the Number of Signals in Array Processing. IEEE Transactions on Acoustics, Speech, and Signal Processing, **37** (1989) 1557–1567

CRAM: An Energy Efficient Routing Algorithm for Wireless Sensor Networks

Zeng-wei Zheng[1,2], Zhao-hui Wu[1], Huai-zhong Lin[1], and Kou-gen Zheng[1]

[1] College of Computer Science, Zhejiang University
310027 Hangzhou, China
{Zhengzw,Wzh,Linhz,Zhengkg}@cs.zju.edu.cn
[2] City College, Zhejiang University
310015 Hangzhou, China
Zhengzw@zucc.edu.cn

Abstract. Wireless sensor networks (WSNs) can be used widely in the future. One disadvantage of the existing WSNs is the limited supply of energy. In order to postpone system lifetime and enhance energy efficiency, an energy-efficient routing algorithm for WSNs, termed as Clustering Routing Algorithm using Multi-CHs-One-Cluster method (CRAM), is presented in this paper. This algorithm selects Multi-Cluster-Heads (Multi-CHs) in every cluster together as one cluster head to perform data fusion and data transmission to improve energy efficiency and enhance data transmission reliability, since one cluster-head in a cluster may be unreliable and cause energy losing in case of node failure. Detailed simulations of sensor network environments indicate that CRAM algorithm improves energy efficiency, balances energy consumption of all sensor nodes, enhances data transmission reliability of cluster-head and postpones network system lifetime in comparison to clustering routing algorithm using one-CH-one cluster method.

1 Introduction

As a new technique of implementing ubiquitous computing [1,2], wireless sensor networks (WSNs) can be used in many aspects in the coming future, such as environmental monitoring [3]. However, there are some limitations in using WSNs:

Firstly, main limitation of WSNs is that network energy is dependent on each node's limited energy. Sensor nodes may use up their limited energy quickly during computing or transmitting information in a wireless environment.

Secondly, conventional Ad Hoc network protocols [4–6], such as many end-to-end routing protocols proposed for MANETs in recent years, are not well suitable for WSNs. Conventional Ad Hoc network protocols pay more attention to quality of service (QoS) instead of energy efficiency, but WSNs require their network protocols focusing on system lifetime and energy efficiency. Therefore, energy-efficient routing protocols for WSNs are desirable.

LEACH [7] is one of the most representative protocols using clustering-based algorithm in sensor network. This protocol utilizes energy consumption characteristic of sensor nodes, i.e. a sensor node expends maximum energy in data communication among sensing, communication and data processing [8], to add computations like data aggregation so as to steeply reduce the amount of data transfer and effectively saves energy.

To better understand the LEACH [7], it is described briefly here. Operation of LEACH [7] is divided into two phases, i.e. the setup phase and the steady-state phase. The summation of both phases is called a round. Each round begins with a setup phase when the clusters are organized, followed by a steady-state phase where several frames of data are transferred from the non-cluster-head (non-CH) nodes to the cluster-head (CH) node and on to the base station (BS). In the former phase, randomized rotation selection method is used to choose CH nodes, and then each CH node broadcasts its cluster-head node message (ADV packet) to its all non-CH nodes. In the latter phase, operation is broken into some frames (shown in Figure 1.), each CH node utilizes TDMA/DS-SS approach to collect data sensed by its non-CH nodes which send their data to the CH node at most once per frame during their allocated transmission slot. After aggregating data, each CH node sends data packet to the BS using a fixed spreading code and a CSMA approach. To minimize the setup phase overhead and improve energy efficiency, the steady-state phase must be longer than the setup phase (See Figure 1.).

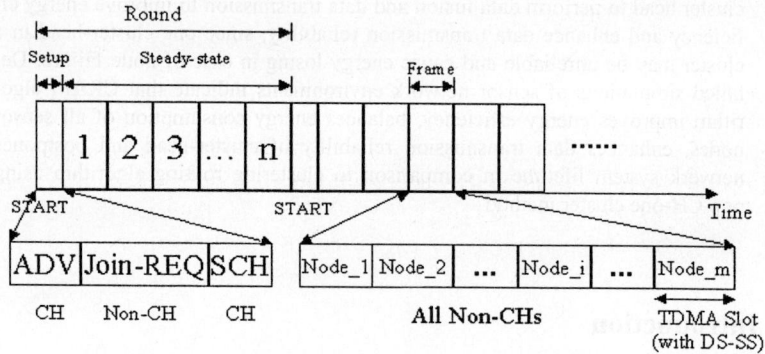

Fig. 1. Time-line showing LEACH operation

However, in sensor network environments, because energy-constrained sensor nodes are prone to failure, algorithm performance is significantly influenced by whether CH nodes aggregate data from non-CH nodes and transmit data packets successfully to the BS in each round. Therefore, this paper proposes an energy-efficient CRAM algorithm (Clustering Routing Algorithm using Multi-CHs-One-Cluster method). This algorithm selects Multi-CH nodes in every cluster together as one CH node to perform data fusion and data transmission to the BS so as to improve energy efficiency and enhance data transmission reliability, since one CH node in a cluster may be unreliable and cause energy losing in case of node failure or communication error.

The remainder of this paper is organized as follows: In section 2, limitations of clustering routing algorithm using one-CH-one-cluster like LEACH [7] are firstly analyzed, and this is followed by the corresponding solutions and the details of CRAM algorithm. The simulation results of analyses are illustrated in section 3. Finally, conclusions are made and some suggestions for future work are proposed.

2 Algorithm Analysis

2.1 One CH Method

Generally, errors of sensor nodes may occur in sensor network environments due to several reasons below:

Firstly, because sensor nodes' energy is limited, P_e can be defined as CH node failure rate, shown as follows:

$$P_e = f(E_r) = \begin{cases} 0, & if\ E_r \geq E_t + E_c + \sum E_p \\ 1, & if\ E_r < E_t + E_c + \sum E_p \end{cases} \quad (1)$$

Where E_r is the residual energy of CH node, E_t is the energy value of CH node sending a data packet to the BS, E_c is the energy value of CH node aggregating data one time, and $\sum E_p$ is the energy value of CH node collecting data sensed by its non-CH nodes.

Secondly, hardware malfunction of sensor nodes may occur; thirdly, communication channel error also may occur.

Therefore, WSNs are subject to node failure rate P_e, hardware malfunction rate P_f and channel error rate P_c, once one CH node loses the function of collecting data, aggregating data and sending data to the BS in the steady-state phase of one round, energy of all subsequent non-CH nodes used to sense and transfer data to the CH node in the cluster will be wasted.

Result 1. *The longer time of the steady-state phase, the lower rate of CH node sending data to the BS successfully and successively in the clustering routing algorithm using one-CH-one-cluster method (CRAO algorithm).*

Proof: Given n is the frame number of the steady-state phase, the rate of CH node sending data successfully to the BS is $(1-P_e)(1-P_f)(1-P_c)$ in the 1st time, the rate of CH node sending data to the BS successfully and successively is $[(1-P_e)(1-P_f)(1-P_c)]^2$ in the 2nd time, ..., therefore, the rate of CH node sending data to the BS successfully and successively is $[(1-P_e)(1-P_f)(1-P_c)]^n$ in the nth time.

Therefore, if $0<P_f<1$, $0<P_c<1$,

$$\lim_{n \to +\infty} [(1 - p_e)(1 - p_f)(1 - p_c)]^n = 0.$$

Corollary 1. *The more its non-CH node number of one cluster, the higher rate of non-CH node sending data to the CH node successfully and successively during one frame in the CRAO algorithm.*

Proof: During one frame, the rate of non-CH node sending data to the CH node successfully and successively is $1-(P_{ne}P_fP_c)^m$, where m is the slot number of one frame, P_{ne} is defined as non-CH node failure rate because of energy deficiency.

Hence, if $0<P_f<1$, $0<P_c<1$,

$$\lim_{m \to +\infty} [1 - (p_{ne} p_f p_c)^m] = 1.$$

According to the corollary 1, the algorithm can guarantee CH node to collect data successfully sensed by its non-CH nodes. And in terms of the result 1, it cannot ensure good performance of CRAO algorithm if the steady-state phase is longer. However, it is indispensable to minimize the setup phase overhead that duration of steady-state phase is long. Therefore, to improve the performance of CRAO algorithm, a new method is desirable.

2.2 Improved Method

CH Node Initiative Abdication. Assuming that P_f, P_c are not considered, in order to enhance reliability of CH nodes sending data to the BS, randomized rotation selection method is also used to choose CH nodes like LEACH [7] during the setup phase. When residual energy E_r of one CH node is met the conditions of: $E_r \geq E_t + E_c + \sum E_p + x_1$, $E_r \leq E_t + E_c + \sum E_p + x_2$ and $x_1 \leq x_2$ (the meanings of E_t and E_p are shown as above, x_1 and x_2 are in turn defined as lower threshold value and upper threshold value by the users.), the CH node will broadcast its abdication information to its all non-CH nodes, and the setup phase of next round will start up to avoid energy consumption of its non-CH nodes.

CH Node Passive Quit. Contrarily, if P_f and P_c are considered, CH node may lose the function of cluster head at any moment. Therefore, a good method is suggested to avoid energy waste as follows:

Firstly, during the setup phase, CH node in each cluster is selected; Then, CH nodes broadcast their cluster head message (ADV packet) and each non-CH node having received signals send an acknowledgement packet (i.e., Join-REQ packet, shown in Figure 1.) to its CH node which includes its residual energy value E_r; Next, the CH node selects one "lusty" non-CH node to inherit some control information from the CH node such as all non-CH nodes info in the cluster (When residual energy of one node is more than average energy of all nodes in the cluster, it can be called a "lusty" node.) and the "lusty" node intercepts the CH node's activity at intervals;

Finally, the CH node broadcasts a schedule (SCH packet, shown in Figure 1.) of collecting data to its all non-CH nodes. In the steady-state phase, the "lusty" node is only responsible for the CH node's activity and it is not concerned with data sensing and data transmission. Once it finds that the CH node loses its function, it will broadcasts this information to all non-CH nodes in the cluster, and the clustering process of next round will start up.

Multi-CHs Method. Actually, P_f, P_c and P_e should be all considered. In such a case, randomized rotation selection method is firstly used to select one CH node in each cluster during the setup phase. Then, each CH node broadcasts its cluster head information (ADV packet) to all nodes and every non-CH node selects to affiliate itself with one cluster based on the principle of minimum communication energy and sends an acknowledgement packet (Join-REQ packet) that includes its residual energy value E_r, to the cluster's CH node. If one non-CH node receives multi-signals from the CH nodes, the non-CH node will select a CH node whose signal strength is the highest to join the cluster. At the same time, several (L-1) "lusty" nodes among the all non-CH nodes in the cluster are selected to assist the CH node to finish data collection, data fusion and data transmission during the steady-state phase. For instance, the CH node in the cluster is chosen as the 1st CH, other (L-1) "lusty" nodes are in turn authorized by the 1st CH node as the 2nd CH, ..., the Lth CH.

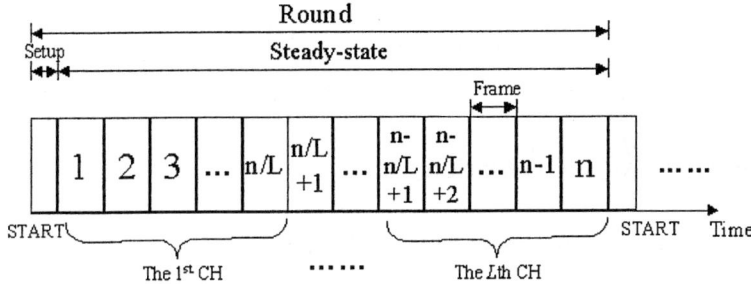

Fig. 2. Clustering routing algorithm using multi-CH-one-cluster

Finally, the 1st CH node broadcasts the information about L CH nodes and schedule (SCH packet) of receiving data to all non-CH nodes in the cluster. In the steady-state phase, duration of the steady-state phase is divided averagely into L time quanta which are used in turn by the 1st CH, the 2nd CH, ..., the Lth CH to act together as the cluster head to finish data collection, data fusion and data transmission to the BS (See Figure 2.).

Result 2. *A rate of CH node sending data to the BS successfully and successively of CRAM algorithm is higher than that of CRAO algorithm during one round.*

Proof: Given n is the frame number of the steady-state phase, time quanta of one CH node in a cluster are averagely equal to n/L frames in the CRAM algorithm. If m is defined as the integer portion of n/L and n is divided exactly by L, a rate of one CH node sending data to the BS successfully and successively will be $[(1-P_e)(1-P_f)(1-P_c)]^m$. Otherwise, it will be at least equal to $[(1-P_e)(1-P_f)(1-P_c)]^{m+1}$.

Therefore, no matter what n can be divided by L, the rate of one CH node sending data to the BS successfully and successively of CRAM algorithm is not less than:

$$MIN\left\{\underbrace{p_{success}^{a(1)}, p_{success}^{a(2)}, \bullet\bullet\bullet, p_{success}^{a(i)}, \bullet\bullet\bullet, p_{success}^{a(L)}}_{L}\right\}$$

$$= p_{success}^{m+1}$$

Where $\forall i \in [1, L]$, $a(i)$ is equal to m or m+1, $\sum_{i=1}^{L} a(i) = n$, and $p_{success}$ is equal to $(1-P_e)(1-P_f)(1-P_c)$.

And the rate of CH node sending data to the BS successfully and successively of CRAO algorithm is $[(1-P_e)(1-P_f)(1-P_c)]^n$.

Hence, if $0<P_f<1$, $0<P_c<1$, $0\leq P_e<1$, $1<L<n$,

$$\left[(1-p_e)(1-p_f)(1-p_c)\right]^{m+1} > \left[(1-p_e)(1-p_f)(1-p_c)\right]^n.$$

3 Performance Evaluation

3.1 Simulation Environment and Testing Criterion

A square region of $100 \times 100m^2$ has been generated and 200 sensor nodes are placed in the network randomly. All nodes start with an initial energy of 10J. Other network parameters involved are listed as follows:
- Data packet size: 525bytes
- Control packet size: 256bytes
- Bandwidth: 1Mbps
- Error rate: 20% (including all factors causing node errors such as communication jamming and hardware malfunction, etc.)
- The time ratio of the setup phase to the steady-state phase in one round: 1:30

Error nodes can resume their function after one round (except they are dead due to energy exhaustion, other factors causing node death are not considered here). Five nodes in each cluster of CRAM algorithm are selected as CH nodes in one round. In order to analyze and test CRAM algorithm performance, CRAO algorithm is utilized to compare with CRAM algorithm, and the following performance metrics are used:

(A) Network energy quadratic mean deviation (EQMD): This metric indicates evenness of network energy dissipated and reflects the ability of algorithm postponing system lifetime. A method of calculating this metric is shown as follows:

$$EQMD = \sqrt{\sum_j (\sum_i nodes(i).E_r / All\_nodes\_Num - nodes(j).E_r)^2} \qquad (2)$$

Where All_nodes_Num is the total number of sensor nodes in the network; nodes(i).E_r is defined as residual energy value of one node at the time.

(B) Success ratio of CH node sending data packet to the BS (p%): None but data packets of CH node sending successfully to the BS are useful for the users. Therefore, this metric shows the ability of algorithm enhancing data transmission reliability and a method of computing the metric is listed as follows:

$$p(\%) = \frac{Data\_Success\_Num}{Data\_All\_Num} \times 100\% \qquad (3)$$

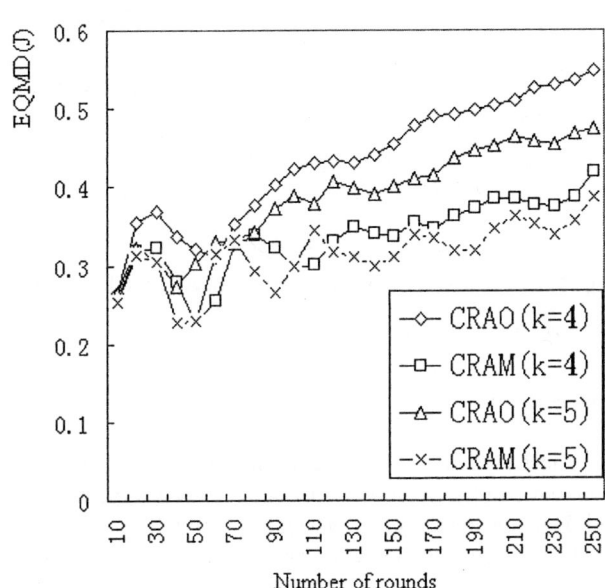

Fig. 3. Comparison of evenness of energy dissipated between CRAM and CRAO

Where Data_Success_Num is the total data packets of CH nodes sending data successfully to the BS during a period of time; Data_All_Num is the total data packets of CH nodes transmitting data to the BS during the same time without regard to any factors causing node errors such as node failure, etc..

(C) Energy cost per data packet of CH node sending successfully to the BS (E_P_D): This metric explains the ability of algorithm improving energy efficiency since it is valuable for an algorithm spending energy on data packets that CH nodes send successfully to the BS. A means of computing this metric is shown as follows:

$$E\_P\_D = \frac{\sum_i nodes(i).E_0 - \sum_i nodes(i).E_r}{Data\_Success\_Num} \quad (4)$$

Where nodes(i).E_0 is defined as an initial energy of one node, the meanings of Data_Success_Num and nodes(i).E_r are shown as above.

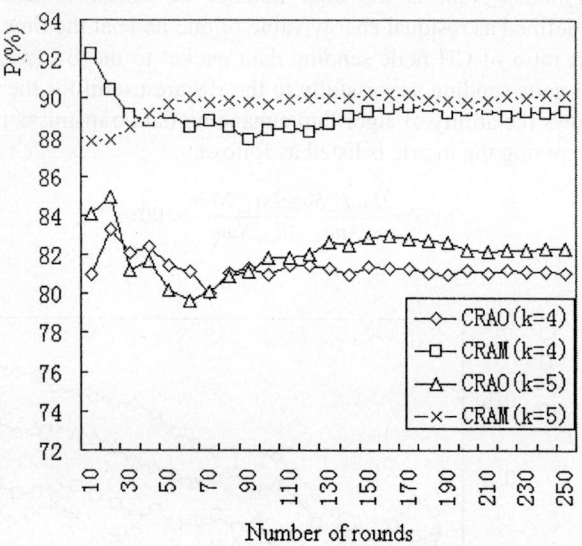

Fig. 4. Comparison of success ratio p between CRAM and CRAO

3.2 Result Discussion

First, in order to test evenness of dissipated network energy, simulation is performed with metric (A) and results are shown in Figure 3. When cluster number k is in turn equal to 4 and 5, better evenness of dissipated network energy of CRAM algorithm can be achieved. It indicates that this algorithm can effectively postpone system lifetime.

Then, data transmission reliability of algorithm is also tested with metric (B), as shown in Figure 4. When cluster number k is in turn equal to 4 and 5, CRAM algorithm can always achieve better data transmission than CRAO algorithm. The success ratio p% of CRAM algorithm is around 90%.

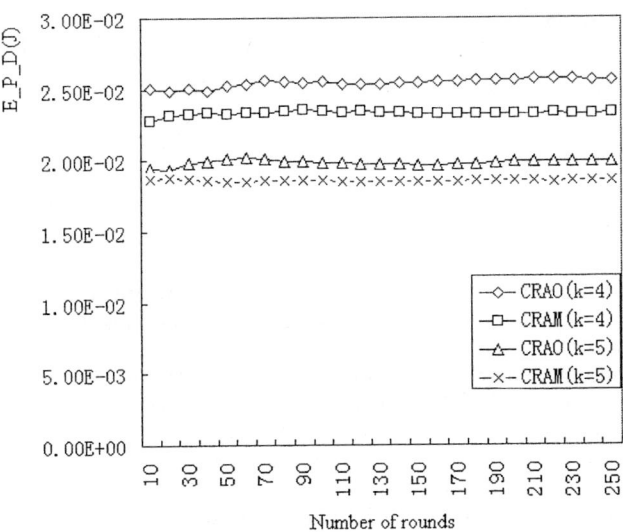

Fig. 5. Comparison of parameter E_P_D between CRAM and CRAO

Finally, comparison is made between CRAM algorithm and CRAO algorithm with metric (C) to test energy efficiency, and results are shown in Figure 5. When cluster number k is equal to different value, it is found that CRAM algorithm can gain better energy efficiency at all time.

Hence, based on the analyses with three metrics, it is found that CRAM algorithm can gain higher data transmission reliability, better evenness of dissipated network energy and energy efficiency as well as effectively postpone network lifetime.

4 Conclusions

In this paper, effects of CH nodes on the performance of clustering routing algorithm, such as data transmission reliability and energy efficiency are analyzed. CRAM algorithm, which is an energy-efficient clustering algorithm, is proposed and described. The results of a series of simulations of sensor network environments indicate that CRAM algorithm can work better on balancing network energy consumption, improving energy efficiency, enhancing data transmission reliability, and postponing network lifetime. This algorithm is well suitable for the static distributed WSNs. In the future topological transformation for several nodes mobility will be conducted so as to improve the algorithm to suit for dynamic WSNs.

Acknowledgments

This work is supported by the National High-Tech Research and Development Plan of China under Grant No. 2003AA1Z2080.

References

1. Weiser, M.: The Computer for the 21st Century. Scientific American (1991)
2. Zengwei Z., Zhaohui, W.: A Survey on Pervasive Computing. Computer Science **30**(4) (2003) 18–22
3. Mainwaring, A., Polastre, J., Szewczyk, R., Culler, D.: Wireless Sensor Networks for Habitat Monitoring. In: ACM WSNA'02, Atlanta, Georgia. (2002)
4. Johnson, D.B., Maltz, D.A.: Dynamic Source Routing in Ad Hoc Wireless Networking. In: Imielinski T., Korth, H.(eds.): Mobile Computing. Kluwer Academic Publishing (1996)
5. Perkins, C.: Ad Hoc Networking. Addison-Wesley (2000)
6. Perkins, C.: Ad Hoc On-Demand Distance Vector (AODV) Routing. IETF MANET, Internet-Draft, Dec. (1997)
7. Heinzelman, W., Chandrakasan, A., Balakrishnan, H.: An Application-Specific Protocol Architecture for Wireless Microsensor Networks. IEEE Transactions on Wireless Communications **1**(4) (2002) 660–670
8. Akyildiz, I. F., Su, W., Sankarasubramaniam, Y., Cayirci, E.: A Survey on Sensor Networks. IEEE Communications Magazine **40**(8) (2002) 102–114

An Approach for Spam E-mail Detection with Support Vector Machine and n-Gram Indexing*

Jongsub Moon[1], Taeshik Shon[1], Jungtaek Seo[2], Jongho Kim[1], and Jungwoo Seo[3]

[1] Center for Information Security Technologies, Korea University, Seoul, Korea
{jsmoon,743zh2k,sky45k}@korea.ac.kr
[2] National Security Research Institute, ETRI, Daejeon, Korea
seojt@etri.re.kr
[3] Samsung Electronics Co., Suwon, Korea
korea002@korea.ac.kr

Abstract. Many solutions have been deployed to prevent harmful effects from spam mail. Typical methods are either pattern matching using the keyword or method using the probability such as naive Bayesian method. In this paper, we proposed a classification method of spam mail from normal mail using support vector machine, which has excellent performance in binary pattern classification problems. Especially, the proposed method efficiently practices a learning procedure with a word dictionary by the n-gram. In the conclusion, we showed our proposed method being superior to others in the aspect of comparing performance.

1 Introduction

E-mail users have greatly increased as the internet became more wide-spread. Unlike the telephone, the e-mail system allows people to send mail whenever they wish, regardless of the recipients absence or intention. Due to such convenience, spam mail causes immense cost and time loss for both individuals and enterprises removing spam mail [16].

The efficient way of removing spam mail is to develop a tool, known as spam filter, that automatically screen spam mail. In content-based filtering, the spam filter searches for certain key word patterns or compares the senders' address with a prior generated blacklist of spammers. In case of naive Bayesian classification [8], it classifies the words of the text with a conditional probability method into spam mail or not, so it is successful in filtering out spam mail that follow the particular patterns [1,3].

This paper uses the support vector machine(SVM) to decide whether a received e-mail judges a spam mail or not. Specially, we use the n-gram indexing [11] and generate the word dictionary for feature processing [6,8].

The remainder of this paper is organized as follow: Section 2 overviews support vector machine; Section 3 explains a n-gram indexing method; Section 4

---

* This work was supported (in part) by the Ministry of Information&Communications, Korea, under the Information Technology Research Center (ITRC) Support program.

explains the proposed method for filtering spam mail; Section 5 discusses our experimental results; and Section 6 concludes.

2 Support Vector Machine

2.1 Background

Support vector machine(SVM) [3, 4, 6, 10, 7, 13] is a learning machine that plots the training vectors in high-dimensional feature space, and labels each vector by its class. SVM views the classification problem as a quadratic optimization problem. It combines generalization control with a technique to avoid the "curse of dimensionality" by placing an upper bound on a margin between the different classes, making it a practical tool for large and dynamic data set. SVM classifies data by determining a set of support vectors, which are members of the set of training inputs that outline a hyper plane in feature space.

The SVM is based on the idea of structural risk minimization, which minimizes the generalization error, i.e. true error on unseen examples. The number of free parameters used in the SVM depends on the margin that separates the data points to classes but not on the number of input features. Thus SVM does not require a reduction in the number of features in order to avoid overfitting. SVM provides a generic mechanism to fit the data within a surface of a hyper-plane of a class through the use of a kernel function. The user may provide a kernel function, such as a linear, polynomial, or sigmoid curve, to the SVM during the training process, which selects support vectors along the surface of the function. This capability allows classifying a broader range of problems. The primary advantage of SVM is binary classification and regression that it provides to a classifier with a minimal Vapnik Chervonenkis(VC) - dimension, which implies low expected probability of generalization errors [2, 15].

2.2 SVM for Categorization

In this section, we review some basic ideas of SVM [2, 6, 7, 13].

Given the training data set $\{(x_i, d_i)\}_{i=1}^{N}$, with input data $x_i \in R^N$ and corresponding binary class labels $d_i \in \{-1, 1\}$, the SVM classifier formulation starts from the following assumption. The classes represent by subset $d_i = 1$ and $d_i = -1$ are linearly separable, where $\exists w \in R^N$, $b \in R$ such that

$$\exists w, b \quad s.t. \begin{cases} w^T x_i + b > 0 \text{ for } d_i = +1 \\ w^T x_i + b < 0 \text{ for } d_i = -1 \end{cases}. \tag{1}$$

The goal of SVM is to find an optimal hyperplane for which the margin of separation ,ρ, is maximized. ρ is defined by the separation between the separating hyperplane and the closest data point. If the optimal hyperplane is defined by $(w^T \cdot x) + b_0 = 0$, then the function $g(x) = w^T x + b_0$ gives a measure of the distance from x to the optimal hyperplane.

Support vectors are defined by data points $x^{(s)}$ that lie the closest to the decision surface. For a support vector $x^{(s)}$ and the canonical optimal hyperplane g, we have

$$r = \frac{g(x^s)}{||w_0||} = \begin{cases} +1/||w_0|| \text{ for } d^{(s)} = +1 \\ -1/||w_0|| \text{ for } d^{(s)} = -1 \end{cases}. \qquad (2)$$

Since, the margin of separation $\rho \propto \frac{1}{||w_0||}$. Thus, $||w_0||$ should be minimal to achieve the maximal separation margin. Mathematical formulation for finding the canonical optimal separation hyperplane given the training data set $\{(x_i, d_i)\}_{i=1}^N$, solve the following quadratic problem

$$\begin{cases} \text{minimize } \tau(w, \xi) = \frac{1}{2}||w||^2 + C\sum_{i=1}^l \xi_i \\ \text{s.t. } d_i(w^T x_i + b) \geq 1 - \xi_i \text{ for } \xi_i \geq 0, i = 1, \ldots, l \end{cases}. \qquad (3)$$

Note that the global minimum of above problem must exist, because $\phi(w) = \frac{1}{2}||w_0||^2$ is convex in w and the constrains are linear in w and b. This constrained optimization problem is dealt with by introducing Lagrange multipliers $\alpha_i \geq 0$ and a Lagrangian function given by

$$L(w, b, \xi; \alpha, \nu) = \tau(w, \xi) - \sum_{i=1}^l \alpha_i [d_i(w_i^T x_i + b) - 1 + \xi_k] - \sum_{i=1}^l \nu_i \xi_i \qquad (4)$$

leads to

$$\frac{\partial L}{\partial w} = 0 \iff w - \sum_{i=1}^l \alpha_i d_i x_i \quad (\therefore w = \sum_{i=1}^l \alpha_i d_i x_i) \qquad (5)$$

$$\frac{\partial L}{\partial b} = 0 \iff \sum_{i=1}^l \alpha_i d_i = 0 \qquad (6)$$

$$\frac{\partial L}{\partial \xi_k} = 0, \text{ for } 0 \leq \alpha_i \leq c, k = 1, \ldots, l. \qquad (7)$$

The solution vector thus has an expansion in terms of a subset of the training patterns, namely those patterns whose α_i is non-zero, called *support vectors*. By the Karush-Kuhn-Tucker complementarity conditions, we have,

$$\alpha_i [d_i(w^T x_i + b) - 1] = 0 \text{ for } i = 1, \ldots, N \qquad (8)$$

by substituting (5), (6) and (7) into equation (4), find multipliers α_i which

$$\text{maximize } \Theta(\alpha) = \sum_{i=1}^l \alpha_i - \frac{1}{2} \sum_{i=1}^l \sum_{j=1}^l \alpha_i \alpha_j d_i d_j < x_i \cdot x_j > \qquad (9)$$

s.t. $0 \leq \alpha_i \leq c$, $i = 1, \ldots, l$ and $\sum_{i=1}^{l} \alpha_i y_i = 0$. (10)

The hyperplane decision function can thus be written as

$$f(x) = sgn\left(\sum_{i=1}^{l} y_i \alpha_i \cdot (x \cdot x_i) + b\right),$$ (11)

where b is computed using (8).

To construct the SVM, the optimal hyperplane algorithm has to be argumented by a method for computing dot products in feature spaces nonlinearly related to input space. The basic idea is to map the data into some other dot product space (called the feature space) F via a nonlinear map ϕ, and to perform the above linear algorithm in F, i.e nonseparable data $\{(x_i, d_i)\}_{i=1}^{N}$, where $x_i \in R^N$, $d_i \in \{+1, -1\}$, preprocess the data with

$$\phi : R^N \rightarrow \phi(x) \text{ where } l \ll \text{dimension}(F).$$ (12)

Here w and x_i are not calculated. According to Mercer's theorem,

$$\langle \phi(x_i), \phi(x_j) \rangle = K(x_i, x_j)$$ (13)

and $K(x, y)$ can be computed easily on the input space. Finally the nonlinear SVM classifier becomes

$$f(x) = sgn\left(\sum_{i=1}^{N} \alpha_i d_i K(x_i, x) + b\right).$$ (14)

Several choices for the kernel $K(\cdot, \cdot)$ are possible :

$K(x, y) = y^T x$: Linear SVM (dot product)
$K(x, y) = (y^T x + 1)^d$: Polynomial SVM of degree d
$K(x, y) = \exp\{-\|x - x_k\|^2 / \sigma^2\}$: RBF SVM
$K(x, y) = \tanh(k y_k^T x + \theta)$: MLP SVM

3 n-Gram Based Index

An n-gram based index method can solve a spacing words problem about a compositeness noun and not to request complex sentence analysis rule or the development of a language information like a morpheme analysis. We explain an indexing process which uses the n-gram method in Table 1 [11].

An indexing method using an n-gram has the advantage at the side of the retrieval effectiveness. The first, an n-gram based index eases a spreading effectiveness from the cutting error of the time which uses the word. The second, we ease the problem on a spacing words of a compositeness noun. The third, we can ease a spelling error or a foreign language problem.

Consequently, the n-gram based index method uses to find words in an e-mail title section in which the title in an e-mail is sometimes reconfigured due to deleting or adding special characters or blanks.

Table 1. An indexing process using n-gram

step 1 : Recognize all words of the sentence
step 2 : Remove the stopword
step 3 : Useless word removes in the sentence
step 4 : Generate index term using the n-gram

4 The Proposed Method for Filtering Spam Mails

To solve spam mail filtering, this paper proposes using n-gram method and the SVM classifier. The spam mail filtering method which uses n-gram indexing and SVM performs the following procedures.

4.1 Overall Composition of Spam Mail Filtering

Since spam mail such as porn usually contains figures only in body section of mail, our method uses only title of mail instead of body of mail for filtering target. Overall system consists of two steps. First, n-gram indexing method applied to title(subject) of mail. The SVM uses indices from word dictionary generated by the n-gram indexing method. The index is automatically formed by applying n-gram to the subject of the e-mails. The data set to train SVM requires both normal mails and spam mail in order to find boundary between normal mail and spam mail. Therefore, before training the SVM, we should collect both legitimate mail and spam mail from the various e-mail accounts. The learning data set and the test data set are indices which are in word dictionary, also these indices are composed through learning data.

The learning data set, which are indices, generated from subject of mails used to tune the parameter of SVM classifier at learning process. The test data set is submitted as an input to examine whether the given e-mail is legitimate or not.

The constitution module of the spam mail filtering used n-gram indexing(pre-processing step) and SVM is shown in Figure 1.

4.2 The Preprocessing Steps in Spam Mail Filtering

The Generation of a Term Dictionary. The word dictionary of size m is produced with examining the frequency of the words used in the titles of the e-mails, and then picking out m numbers of words among frequently used in

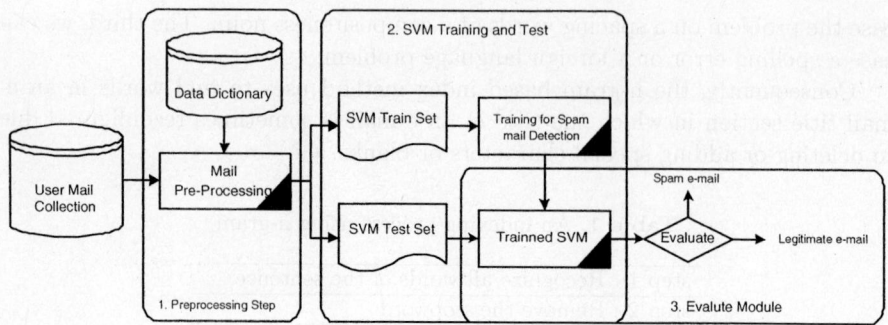

Fig. 1. Overall composition of spam mail filtering using n-gram indexing and SVM

mail. The word in the word dictionary should be derived from both spam mail and normal mail. The index of the word dictionary goes from 1 to m, so that the index corresponds to the number of SVM input nodes. Table 2 shows an example of the produced word dictionary.

Table 2. The generation example of a term dictionary

index	1	2	3	4	5	...	m-n
word dictionary	adult ad	spy cam	videos	porn	xxxmovies	...	sample
index	101	102	103	104	105	...	m
word dictionary	card debt	Free Money	arrears	bankruptcy	big money	...	loans

The Generation of an n-Gram Index Term. n-gram is first applied to the collected subject of e-mail in order to create the index term, and also produces the learning data set and the test data set for SVM. The index term formed by using the collected e-mail and applying it from 2-gram(spell) to 4-gram, as shown in Table 3. The learning data set and test data set are constructed by extracting the index term produced and the word dictionary produced in Table 2.

Table 3. An indexing process using n-gram

e-mail subject = {##you Reduce your Debt, and help you Avoid Bankruptcy!!!}
2-gram index term = yo, ou, ur, re, ed, du, uc, ce, ey, yo, ou, ur, ..., cy
3-gram index term = you, our, ure, red, edu, duc, uce, cey, eyo, ..., tcy
4-gram index term = your, oure, ured, redu, educ, duce, ucey, ..., ptcy

4.3 SVM Data Set Creation

Figure 2 illustrates the process of applying the index term formed by appling n-gram to the word dictionary. If the word from the index term turns out to be identical to the one of word dictionary, it attains value 1(matching) as in the example shown in table 4. If not, it gets the value 0(mismatching). Table 4 demonstrates an example of the result value obtained by matching the n-gram indexing and the word dictionary. When making one input datum for SVM, the target value for the mail also should be given with 1 (for spam mail) or 0 (for normal mail). Therefore, one input datum for SVM consists of indices term of word dictionary and target value.

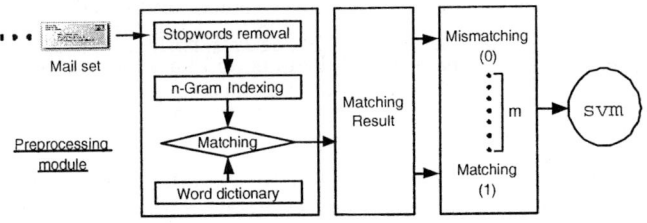

Fig. 2. Preprocessing step for SVM Apply.

Table 4. Example of matching results of a term dictionary with index term

index	1	2	3	4	5	6	...	m-1	m
mail set(1)	1	0	0	1	1	1	...	1	0
mail set(2)	1	0	0	0	1	1	...	0	0
mail set(n-1)					......				
mail set(n)	0	0	1	1	1	0	...	1	1

After constructing the learning data set and test data set by the attained matching value as in Table 4, for constructing SVM, the learning process should be made. Test process is done after tuning the parameter of SVM in learning process using input generated by the same n-gram indexing with each test mail from test mail set.

5 Experiment of Spam Mail Filtering through SVM

5.1 Experiment Method of Spam Mail Filtering

Preparation of Experimental Data. We collect data from various users' e-mail accounts (outlook and commercial e-mail) to test spam mail filtering. The collected subject of e-mail, through the preprocessing explained in Section 4, was converted to the learning data set and test data set for the SVM. Each set of data was constituted of legitimate and spam mail. Of the collected e-mail data, we concerned with money-loan advertise and porn site advertise for spam, and the rest were classified as legitimate mail. Table 5 explains the SVM learning data set for spam mail filtering. 500 legitimate mail and 500 spam mail constitutes 1000 learning data set.

Table 5. Training set for SVM learning

Data set Category	Training set (1000 messages)
Legitimate mail	legitimate mail(Except a loaning and an adult site e-mail) (500 messages)
Spam mail	spam mail(A loaning and an adult site e-mail) (500 messages)

The test data set must be constructed to examine whether the established filter system using SVM can accurately separate spam mail or not. Test data were constructed by the value attained by matching the collected e-mails to the word dictionary as described in Section 4. The test data set consists of 500 legitimate mails and 500 spam mails.

Table 6. Test set for SVM learning

Data set Category	Test set (1000 messages)
Legitimate mail	legitimate mail(Except a loaning and an adult site e-mail) (500 messages)
Spam mail	spam mail(A loaning and an adult site e-mail) (500 messages)

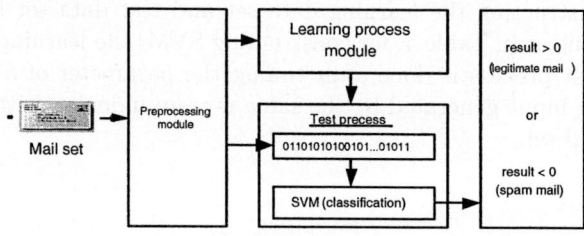

Fig. 3. Spam mail filtering process through SVM learning

Experimental Process. The general constitution of the spam mail filtering suggested in this paper is presented in Figure 3. The experiment was run by using the public library [9, 14] of mySVM for spam mail filtering. Section 5 compares the test results due to the parameters of mySVM.

5.2 Result of Spam Mail Filtering Experiment

Three different kinds of kernel functions were used for SVM; dot kernel, polynomial kernel and radial kernel. The spam mail filtering ratio using dot kernel is displayed in Figure 4.

In cases of polynomial kernel, tests can be run through adjusting the parameter value. Although the test using the polynomial kernel showed similar rate of false positive and false negative as the dot kernel, a comparative better result of higher rate of spam mail filtering was confirmed. The complete test result using the polynomial kernel is displayed in Figure 5. As it is shown in Figure 5, setting the parameters degree, d, as 1 has better performance than that of 3.

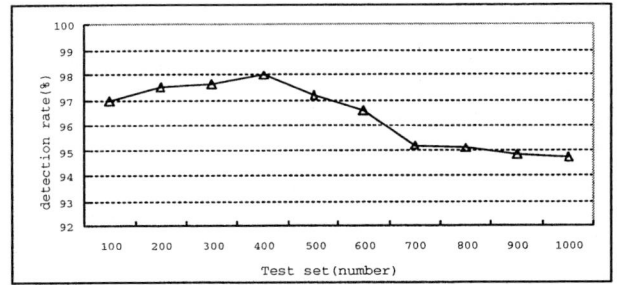

Fig. 4. Result of the test using a dot kernel

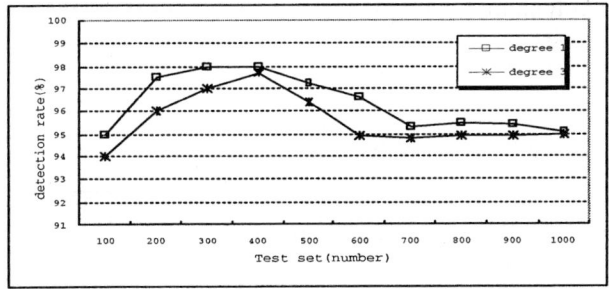

Fig. 5. Result of the test using a polynomial kernel

Finally, the radial kernel was applied last as the kernel function. The parameter attains a real number value, and the test was run by adjusting the variance(σ) value of the parameter.

Although the test using the radial kernel showed similar rate of false positive and false negative as both the dot kernel and the polynomial kernel, it showed the most superior results in overall spam mail filtering. The result using the radial kernel is illustrated in Figure 6. Three different parameter for variance were set for the test; 0.01, 0.1 and 0.5.

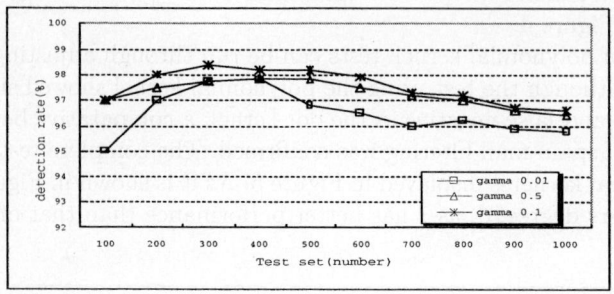

Fig. 6. Result of the test using a radial kernel

An important aspect using radial kernel was that when the variance value was set to 0.5, the rate of false negative was most excellent, whereas the increased rate of false positive proved to be a problem. Also, when the variance value was set to 0.001, the rate of detecting spam mail was similar to the ones using dot or polynomial kernel, yet fell in proficiency when compared to other variance value instances. The tests to each kernel function and parameter are presented in Table 7.

The evaluation of spam mail categorization ability was proven through spam precision and spam recall. As a result, as it is shown in Table 7, the method applying the radial kernel confirmed to be higher in proficiency than applying the dot or the polynomial method. The application of the radial kernel with the parameter value set to variance 0.1 especially showed the best results in spam mail filtering.

Table 7. Result of the test using SVM kernel function

Kernel definition	Feature (dimension)	Parameter	Test set (1000 messages)			
			FP	FN	spam racall	spam precision
dot kernel	201	-	1.5	3.8	94.7	96.8
polynomial kernel	201	degree 1	1.5	3.4	95.1	96.8
		degree 3	1.4	3.6	95.0	97.0
radial kernel	201	gamma 0.5	2.3	1.1	96.6	97.9
		gamma 0.1	2.0	1.1	96.9	97.9
		gamma 0.01	2.0	2.1	95.9	95.8

* spam precision(%) = #actual spammail / #classified spammail
  spam recall(%) = #actual spammail / #total spammail
  FP(%) = false positive, FN(%) = false negative.

5.3 Comparing the Performance of Spam Mail Filtering

The Naive Bayesian method and k-nearest neighbor method were used as filters for spam mail filtering [5, 8] for comparing with my system.

Table 8. Result of the categorization for a spam mail filtering performance comparison

Filter used	λ	gamma	spam recall(%)	spam precision(%)
Naive Bayesian	1	-	82.3	96.6
k-nearest neghbor method(1)	1	-	85.2	95.6
SVM	-	0.1	96.9	97.9

Both the proposed method and the existing methods were compared to spam precision and spam recall. The proposed method revealed higher performance than that of the k-nearest neighbor method and similar results to that of the Naive Bayesian method in view of spam precision. Also, in view of spam recall, it confirmed better results than both the Naive Bayesian method and the k-nearest neighbor method. As elucidated above, the spam mail filtering method using n-gram indexing and SVM showed the improved results in both spam precision and spam recall.

6 Conclusion

In this paper, we focused on spam mail filtering which has recently been a big issue. Also we proposed a spam mail filtering method with n-gram indexing and support vector machine(SVM). For the experiment of proposed methods, we practiced with e-mails collected from various users and performed the filtering procedure with SVM classifier which uses index term generated by n-gram indexing and data set generated by word dictionary.

We used dot, polynomial, and radial functions as SVM kernel functions. Each result is described in Table 8. In case of radial basis kernel function, we can see that it has the greatest performance. Compared with existing works such as a method of naive Bayesian classification and memory-based classification, our methods are more efficient than any others as illustrated in Table 8.

In this paper, we performed spam mail filtering in the limited source of adult and loan related advertisement. In future work, more variety field for spam mail may be in need to tune our system finely.

References

1. Androutsopoulos, I., Koutsias, J., Konstantinos, V.C., Constantine, D.S.: An Experimental Comparison of Naive Bayesian and Keyword-Based Anti-Spam Filtering with Personal E-mail Messages. In: 23rd ACM International Conference on Research and Development in Information Retrieval. (2000) 160–167
2. Burges, C.: A Tutorial on Support Vector Machines for Pattern Recognition. Data Mining and Knowledge Discovery **2** (1998) 121–167
3. Campbell, C., Cristianini, N.: Simple Learning Algorithms for Training Support Vector Machines. Technical report, University of Bristol (1998)
4. Cortes, C., Vapnik, V.: Support Vector Networks. Machine Learning **20** (1995) 273–297
5. Cover, T.M., Hart, P.E.: Nearest Neighbor Pattern Classification. IEEE Trans. on Information Theory **13** (1967) 21–27
6. Cristianini N., Shawe-Taylor, J.: An Introduction to Support Vector Machines. Cambridge University (2000)
7. Cristianini, N., Shawe-Taylor, J.: Support Vector Machine and other kernel-based learning machine. Cambridge (2000) 33–38
8. Ion, A., Georgios, P., Vangelis, K., Georgios S., Constantine, D.: Learning to Filter Spam E-Mail: A Comparison of a Naive Bayesian and a Memory-Based Approach. In: PKDD 2000. (2000) 1–13
9. Joachims, T.: mySVM - A Support Vector Machine. University of Dortmund.
10. Joachims, T.: Text Categorization with Support Vector Machine: Learning with Many Relevant Features. In: European Conference on Machine Learning. (1998) 137–142
11. Joonho, L., Jeongsoo, A., Hyunjoo, P., Myoungho, K.: An n-Gram-Based Indexing Method for Effective Retrieval of Hangul Tests. Korean Society for Information Management **7** (1996) 47–63
12. Mehran, S., Susan, D., David H., Eric, H.: A Bayesian Approach to Filtering Junk E-mail. In: AAAI-98 Workshop on Learning for Text Categorization. (1998)
13. Pontil, M., Verri, A.: Properties of Support Vector Machines. A.I. Memo No. 1612; CBCL paper No. 152, Massachusetts Institute of Technology, Cambridge (1997)
14. Ruping S.: mySVM-Manual. University of Dortmund, Lehrstuhl Informatik VIII (2000)
15. Vapnik, V.: The Nature of Statistical Learning Theory. Springer-Verlag (1995)
16. http://kr.fujitsu.com/webzine/dream/special_report/ 20030708_specialreport/special_030 7.html

Finding Breach Paths Using the Watershed Segmentation Algorithm in Surveillance Wireless Sensor Networks *

Ertan Onur[1,2], Cem Ersoy[2], Hakan Deliç[3], and Lale Akarun[4]

[1] ARGELA Technologies, Istanbul, Turkey
[2] NETLAB, Department of Computer Engineering
[3] BUSIM Laboratory, Department of Electrical and Electronics Engineering
[4] πLAB, Department of Computer Engineering
Boğaziçi University, Bebek 34342 Istanbul, Turkey

Abstract. Considering wireless sensor networks for border surveillance, one of the major concerns is sensing coverage. Breach probability can be used as a measure to analyze the tradeoffs and to determine the required number of sensors to be deployed to obtain a certain security level. In this paper, the sensing coverage of surveillance wireless sensor networks is studied by utilizing a well-known image processing technique. By applying the watershed segmentation algorithm to the sensing coverage graph, the contour points, which are followed by the breach paths, are found. To determine the weakest breach path by utilizing the contour points, Dijkstra's shortest path algorithm is used. Under uniformly distributed random deployment, the breach probability is evaluated against the sensor model parameters, field width and the number of sensors deployed.

1 Introduction

Recent research and development on wireless sensor networks (WSN) has progressed along with the rapid development in sensor technology. The easily deployable, self-organizing and self-healing WSNs suit well to surveillance applications. Specifically, surveillance wireless sensor networks (SWSN) are designed to secure a region against unauthorized traversals. A SWSN's task is to detect and track unauthorized access or crossing along a border or through a perimeter. Surveillance with wireless sensor networks may be employed in different areas such as country borders, wildlife parks, buildings. Intrusion detection through country borders is a significant military application where breach prevention challenges co-exists along with the WSN challenges.

One of the vital concerns of the surveillance application of WSNs is determining the sensing coverage and analyzing its effect on target detection [2, 12, 6].

---
* This work was supported by the State Planning Organization of Turkey underthe grant number 03K120250, and by the Boğaziçi University Research Projects under the grant number 04A105.

A running energy-efficient SWSN application is presented in [4]. During the deployment phase of the WSN applications, considering the sensing coverage, the most effective parameters are the sensing and communication ranges of the sensors. Carle and Simplot-Ryl assume that the communication and sensing range of a sensor node are equal [1]. For a set of sensor nodes that provide at least one-degree of coverage on a convex region (if the least number of sensor nodes that cover a region is K, then the coverage is said to be of K degrees), the communication graph is connected if the communication range of the sensor nodes is greater than or equal to twice the sensing range [8, 10].

In this paper, we study the sensing coverage provided by the sensor nodes in terms of the detection probability. We propose two schemes to calculate the sensing coverage by utilizing the sensor detection model presented in [11]. After deploying the sensor nodes, assuming that the positions are known, the sensing coverage is determined. Considering the calculated sensing coverage probability surface as an image, we apply the watershed algorithm to determine the contours. The contour pixels, which correspond to the grid points, provide the weak breach paths. To find the weakest one, we apply Dijkstra's shortest path algorithm [9].

In the next section, by revisiting the weakest breach path problem, we define the sensor detection and field models, and present how the watershed segmentation algorithm is used to find the breach paths in a SWSN. In Section 3, the scenarios used in the simulations, effects of the sensor detection model parameters on the breach probability, and the effect of number of sensors on breach probability are analyzed. The conclusions are drawn in Section 4.

2 The Weakest Breach Path Problem

The weakest breach path (WBP) problem is to determine the breach probability of the weakest path that a target traverses the region from the insecure side to the secure side [5]. As shown in Fig. 1.a, we model the field as a two-dimensional grid. In this grid-based field model along the y-axis, we add boundary regions to the two sides of the field. The lack of boundary regions misleads breach path calculations since the breach path follows either the leftmost or rightmost line along the y-axis when the boundaries are not provided. In order to find the sensing coverage, we utilize the sensor detection model that is defined by Elfes [3] and Zou & Chakrabarty [11]. The probability that sensor k detects a target on grid point (i, j) is represented by

$$P_{ijk} = \begin{cases} 0 & \text{if } r + r_e \leq d_{ijk}, \\ e^{-\lambda a^\beta} & \text{if } r_e > |r - d_{ijk}|, \\ 1 & \text{if } r - r_e \geq d_{ijk}, \end{cases} \quad (1)$$

where r_e ($r_e < r$) is a measure of uncertainty in sensor detection, λ and β are parameters that model different sensor characteristics, d_{ijk} is the sensor-to-target distance and $a = d_{ijk} - r + r_e$. With r, r_e, λ and β, the sensor detection model can be adjusted according to the physical properties of the sensor. In particular,

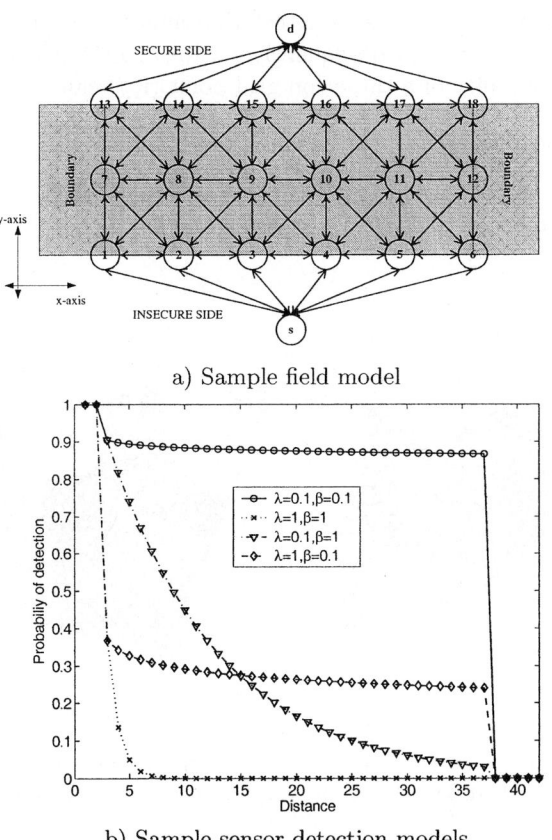

Fig. 1. Sample field and detection models where $r = 20$ m. and $r_e = 18$ m

r and r_e affect the threshold distances of target detection. When the sensor-to-target distance is smaller than $r - r_e$, the target is absolutely detected. When the sensor-to-target distance is larger than $r + r_e$, the target can not be detected. Sample sensor detection models are depicted in Fig. 1.b. If it is assumed that the measurements of individual sensors are statistically independent, then the detection probability of a target on grid point (i,j) is

$$P_{ij}^I = 1 - \prod_{k=1}^{R} (1 - P_{ijk}) \qquad (2)$$

where R is the total number of sensors deployed in the region. Thus, equation (2) represents the so-called uncorrelated coverage model.

When a decision whether a target exists is to be made, the individual decisions of a subset of sensors may be highly correlated. That is, if a sensor detects a target, it is highly probable that another sensor which is located in similar proximity as the first one will also detect the same target, assuming homogeneous environmental factors. Consequently, for the "correlated coverage model", the detection probability of a target on grid point (i,j) can be written as

$$P_{ij}^D = \max_{\{k:k=1,2,\ldots,R\}} P_{ijk}. \qquad (3)$$

The two probabilities P^I and P^D act as upper and lower bounds on the detection probability, respectively.

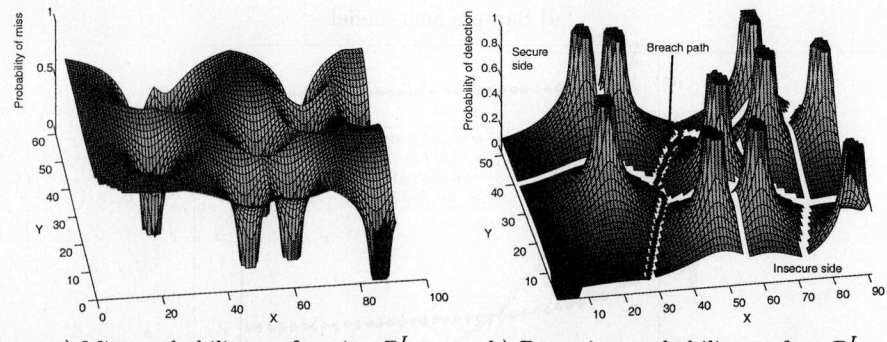

a) Miss probability surface $1 - P^I$ b) Detection probability surface P^I

Fig. 2. Miss probability surface and watershed segmentation shown on the detection probability surface where length=50 m, width=50 m, boundary=20 m., grid size=1 m., $R = 10, r = 15$ m., $r_e = 12$ m., $\lambda = 0.5$ and $\beta = 0.5$

The weakest breach path problem can now be defined as finding the permutation of a subset of grid points $V = [s, (x_0, y_0), (x_1, y_1), \ldots, (x_k, y_k), d]$ with which a target traverses from the starting point s to the destination d with the least probability of being detected. The nodes (x_{j-1}, y_{j-1}) and (x_j, y_j), $j = 0, 1, \ldots, k$, must be connected to each other, the starting node must be connected to (x_0, y_0), and the grid point (x_k, y_k) must be connected to the destination node. Here we can define the *breach probability* P_B of the weakest breach path V as

$$P_B = \prod_{(x_j, y_j) \in V} (1 - P_{x_j y_j}) \qquad (4)$$

where $P_{x_j y_j}$ is the detection probability associated with the grid point $(x_j, y_j) \in V$, and $P_{x_j y_j} = P^I_{x_j y_j}$ for the uncorrelated coverage model and $P_{x_j y_j} = P^D_{x_j y_j}$ for the correlated coverage model. The detection probability associated with the starting and destination dummy nodes is zero since they are not monitored.

Using the two-dimensional field model and adding the detection probability as the third axis, we obtain hills and valleys of detection probabilities (see Fig. 2.b). The weakest breach path problem can be informally defined as finding the path which follows the valleys and through which the target does not have to climb hills so much. Because, the valleys denote the lowest detection probabilities. Furthermore, regarding the two-dimensional field model as an image, where the detection probabilities of the grid points can be mapped to the gray levels of the pixels, suggests that image processing techniques can be employed.

One of the well-known image segmentation algorithms is the watershed algorithm [7]. The watershed algorithm is best-understood with an analogy to water flooding from the minimal points of a three dimensional topographic surface where the third dimension is the altitude. As the water increases, dams are built where the floods would merge. After the completion of immersion, only the dams emerge and separate the valleys. This algorithm can be easily applied to the coverage area of wireless sensor networks in order to find the possible breach paths. After deploying the sensors to the field and calculating the coverage area of the sensor network, utilizing the miss probabilities on the grid points produces hills and valleys where the altitude is mapped to the miss probability as shown in Fig. 2.a. The minimal points of this surface is the sensor node positions. Thus, analogously, it can be considered that the water starts flooding from the sensor nodes. After applying the watershed algorithm, the contour points (dams) correspond to possible breach paths as shown in Fig. 2.b.

Among these breach paths we still need to find the weakest one. For this reason, a graph is constructed using only the contour points and Dijkstra's shortest path algorithm is applied. A similar approach to the one explained in [5] is used. To identify the insecure side of the region the starting node is added which is connected to all of the points on the closest line of the grid on x-axis. Similarly, the secure side is identified with the destination node and all of the contour points of the farthest line of the grid are connected to the destination point. The aim of the target is to traverse the region from the starting node till the destination node by proceeding on the contour points where the detection probabilities are the smallest among all. The boundary regions are not taken into consideration while constructing this graph, because we want the breach path pass through the field, not through the boundaries.

Table 1. Surveillance field parameters

Parameter	Length	Width	Grid size	Boundary
EPS	200 m.	50 m.	1 m.	20 m.
CBS	1000 m.	100 m.	1 m.	50 m.

3 Analysis of the WBP Problem

The sensor detection model defined in the previous section reflects the infrared or ultrasound sensor characteristics [11]. In this work, we utilize an infrared sensor model where the sensor detection parameters are $r = 20$ m., $r_e = 18$

m., $\lambda = 0.3$ and $\beta = 0.8$. In order to analyze the watershed algorithm to find the breach paths, we use two scenarios where the fields differ in dimension. These are the *Embassy Perimeter Security* (EPS) scenario where the sensors are deployed in the perimeter to detect unauthorized access, and the *Country Border Surveillance* (CBS) scenario where a portion of the country border is monitored by a wireless sensor network to detect possible terrorist infiltration across a segment of the border. For these two scenarios, the field parameters are shown in Table 1. The grid size is taken to be 1 m. in the simulations. It is assumed that similar sensor types are used in both scenarios so that the sensor detection model parameters are taken to be the same.

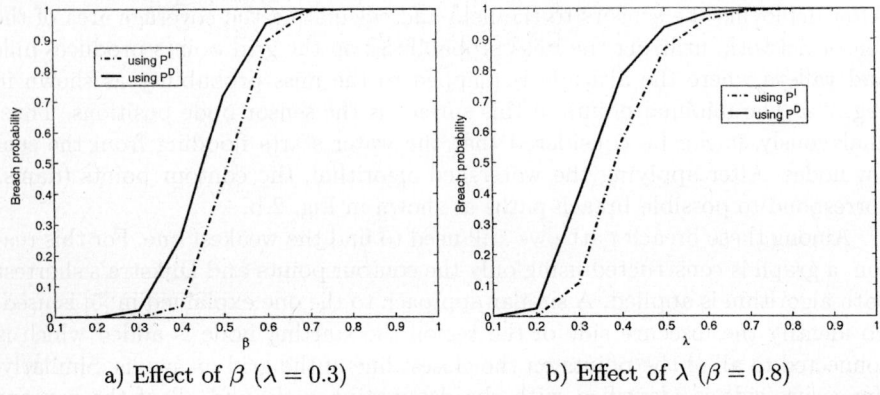

a) Effect of β ($\lambda = 0.3$) b) Effect of λ ($\beta = 0.8$)

Fig. 3. Effect of λ and β on breach probability for the EPS scenario where $r = 20$ m., $r_e = 18$ m

Upon analyzing the effect of β on the breach probability for the EPS scenario, it is seen that selecting a sensor with a larger value for β will increase the breach probability. Holding λ constant and increasing β decreases the detection probability (see Fig. 1.b). Thus, the breach probability shown in Fig. 3.a increases in β. The same conclusion can be drawn for λ on interpreting Fig. 3.b and Fig. 1.b. The increase in the breach probability is delayed in terms of parameter increase when the sensing coverage is calculated using Eq. 2. Furthermore, when compared to β, increasing λ causes a quicker rise in the breach probability.

In Fig. 4, the required number of sensors for a breach probability less than 0.01 is shown for different sensor characteristic parameters λ and β. Extreme values of λ and β provide special detection models. For example, when $\lambda = 1, \beta = 1$ or $\lambda = 0, \beta = 0$ the sensor detection model turns out to act as a binary detection model, where the threshold value becomes $r - r_e$ and $r + r_e$, respectively. Considering this, when Fig. 4 is analyzed, it can be concluded that the sensing range is very critical in determining the required number of sensors. Thus, while designing a SWSN, selection of sensors significantly affects the breach probability. The required number of sensors is 9 when $\lambda = 0, \beta = 0$. However, when λ

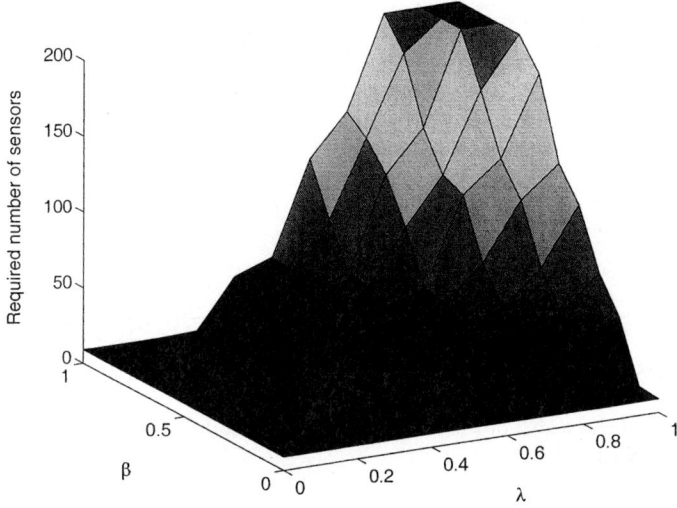

Fig. 4. Effect of λ and β on the required number of sensors for a breach probability less than 0.01

and β are set to one, the requirement becomes 200. As λ and/or β increase, the breach probability grows exponentially.

Holding the required number of sensors constant, when a large field in width is analyzed, larger breach probabilities are observed (see Fig. 5). Widening the field allows a target more space with smaller detection probabilities to traverse. When the EPS scenario is compared to the CBS scenario, the increase in breach probabilities for the two sensing coverage calculation schemes is larger in CBS. Similar trends are observed for the two sensing coverage calculations in EPS, whereas for the CBS, the two breach probability curves tend to converge to one. This is because, when the width is increased in the CBS scenario, the target is able to find a path which is distant enough from most of the sensor nodes such that the minimum distance between the sensors and the path is $r+r_e$. Therefore, when the width is greater than $r + r_e$, the breach probability increases more.

To determine the required number of sensor nodes for a given breach probability level, it is crucial to analyze the effect of the number of sensors on the breach probability. Since a truncated sensor detection model is used, the breach probability remains at a constant level as long as the deployed number of sensors are not sufficient to cover the region fully. Thus, for the EPS scenario, on analyzing Fig. 6.a, at about 15 to 40 sensors the breach probability is around 0.4. When 40 sensors are deployed to the field, the saturation or, in other words, full-coverage is achieved. Thus, at first a sharp decrease is observed when more than 40 sensors are deployed. Afterwards, the breach probability does not seem to be affected with additional sensor deployment. The reason behind the lack of further improvement is the value chosen for the field width. Since the field width is less in the EPS scenario compared to the CBS scenario, most of the

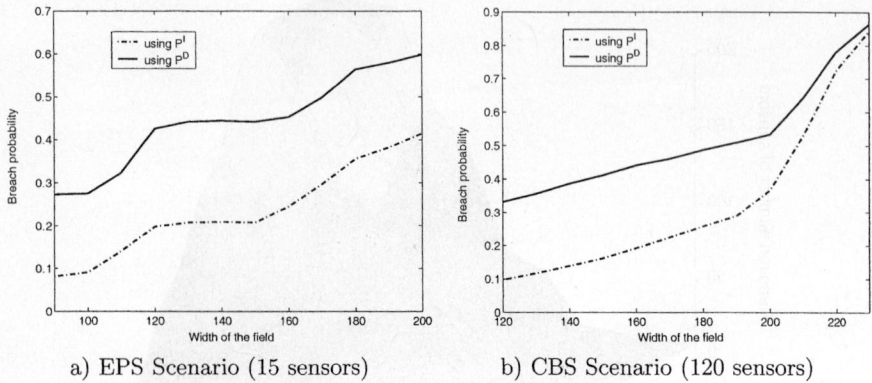

a) EPS Scenario (15 sensors)   b) CBS Scenario (120 sensors)

Fig. 5. Effect of the width of the field on breach probability for the EPS scenario where 15 sensors are utilized

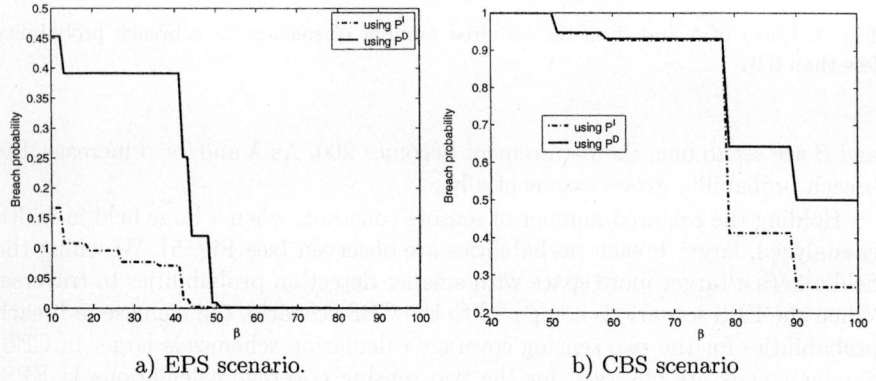

a) EPS scenario.   b) CBS scenario

Fig. 6. Effect of the number of sensor nodes on the breach probability

time the path does not curl in the region and flow along the x-axis. However, in the CBS scenario when Fig. 6.b is analyzed, considering that the same type of sensors are deployed (the detection probability is truncated to zero at a distance of $r + r_e = 38$ m.), the width of the field is twice the width of the EPS scenario. In this scenario, the path may curl and flow along the x-axis depending on the fact that smaller detection probabilities may exist. Consequently, there exist more steps in the curve of the breach probabilities in Fig. 6.b. More clearly, the additionally deployed sensor does not have an impact on the path, because the sensor-to-path distance is larger than $r + r_e$. The steps of the curves are more straight for P^D compared to P^I. This is due to the fact that the additional sensor deployment has no effect on the detection probability of the target-on-the-path if it is not closer than the closest sensor when the sensing coverage is calculated with P^D. However, when the sensing coverage is calculated with P^I, if the distance between the additionally deployed sensor and the path is less than $r + r_e$, the deployment affects the detection probability of the target-on-the-path.

4 Conclusions

In this paper, we applied the watershed segmentation algorithm on the sensing coverage to find the weakest breach path in surveillance wireless sensor networks. The sensor detection model proposed by Elfes is utilized to calculate the sensing coverage. This model has two significant properties: the detection model is a truncated one and it acts as a binary detection model when $\lambda = 1$, $\beta = 1$ or $\lambda = 0$, $\beta = 0$. Utilizing two scenarios, namely the embassy perimeter security and country border surveillance scenarios, we analyzed the effects of detection model parameters, sensor requirement and field width. The breach probability increases in λ and/or β. With constant number of sensor nodes, the breach probability also increases if the field is widened, especially when the width is larger than $r + r_e$. Furthermore, increasing the number of sensors does not affect the breach probability until a sensor is deployed close to the weakest path. As a future work, we are planning to analyze the breach probability for the three-dimensional terrains.

References

1. Carle J., Simplot-Ryl, D.: Energy-Efficient Area Monitoring for Sensor Networks. IEEE Computer **37** (2004) 40–46
2. Clouqueur, T., Phipatanasuphorn, V., Ramanathan, P., Saluja, K.K.: Sensor Deployment Strategy for Target Detection. In: Proceedings of the First ACM International Workshop on Wireless Sensor Networks and Applications, Atlanta, USA. (2002) 42–48
3. Elfes, A.: Occupancy Grids: A Stochastic Spatial Representation for Active Robot Perception. In: Proceedings of the Sixth Conference on Uncertainty in AI. (1990) 60–70
4. He, T., Krishnamurthy, S., Stankovic, J.A., Abdelzaher, T., Luo, L., Stoleru, R., Yan, T., Gu, L.: Energy-Efficient Surveillance System Using Wireless Sensor Networks. In: The Second International Conference on Mobile Systems, Applications, and Services, Boston, USA. (2004)
5. Onur, E., Ersoy, C., Deliç, H.: Finding Sensing Coverage and Breach Paths in Surveillance Wireless Sensor Networks. In: Proceedings of the 15th IEEE International Symposium on Personal, Indoor and Mobile Radio Communications, Barcelona, Spain. (2004)
6. Veltri, G., Qu, G., Huang, Q., Potkonjak, M.: Minimal and Maximal Exposure Path Algorithms for Wireless Embedded Sensor Networks. In: Proceedings of the First International ACM Conference on Embedded Networked Sensor Systems, Los Angeles, USA. (2003) 40–50
7. Vincent, L., Soile, P.: Watersheds in Digital Spaces: An Efficient Algorithm Based on Immersion Simulations. IEEE Transactions on Pattern Analysis and Machine Intelligence **13** (1991) 583–598

8. Wang, X., Xing, G., Zhang, Y., Lu, C., Pless, R., Gill, C.: Integrated Coverage and Connectivity Configuration in Wireless Sensor Networks. In: Proceedings of the First International ACM Conference on Embedded Networked Sensor Systems, Los Angeles, USA. (2003) 28–39
9. Weiss, M. A.: Data Structures and Algorithm Analysis in C++. Second Edition, Addison-Wesley, (1999)
10. Zhang, H., Hou, C.J.: Maintaining Sensing Coverage and Connectivity in Large Sensor Networks. In: Proceedings of the NSF International Workshop on Theoretical and Algorithmic Aspects of Sensor, Ad Hoc Wireless, and Peer-to-Peer Networks, Fort Lauderdale, USA. (2004)
11. Zou, Y., Chakrabarty, K.: Energy-Aware Target Localization in Wireless Sensor Networks. In: Proceedings of the First IEEE International Conference on Pervasive Computing and Communications, Fort Worth, USA. (2003) 60–67
12. Zou, Y., Chakrabarty, K.: Sensor Deployment and Target Localization Based on Virtual Forces. In: Proceedings of the IEEE INFOCOM, San Francisco, USA. (2003) 1293–1303

Biometric Authentication Using Online Signatures

Alisher Kholmatov and Berrin Yanikoglu

Sabanci University, Tuzla, Istanbul, Turkey 34956
alisher@su.sabanciuniv.edu, berrin@sabanciuniv.edu

Abstract. We overview biometric authentication and present a system for on-line signature verification, approaching the problem as a two-class pattern recognition problem. During enrollment, reference signatures are collected from each registered user and cross aligned to extract statistics about that user's signature. A test signature's authenticity is established by first aligning it with each reference signature for the claimed user. The signature is then classified as genuine or forgery, according to the alignment scores which are normalized by reference statistics, using standard pattern classification techniques. We experimented with the Bayes classifier on the original data, as well as a linear classifier used in conjunction with Principal Component Analysis (PCA). The classifier using PCA resulted in a 1.4% error rate for a data set of 94 people and 495 signatures (genuine signatures and skilled forgeries).

1 Introduction

Biometrics is the general term to refer to the utilization of physiological characteristics (e.g. face, iris, fingerprint) or behavioral traits (e.g. signature, keystroke dynamics) for verifying the identity of an individual. Authentication actually refers to two separate problems: identification and verification. In identification, Biometric authentication is gaining increasing popularity as a more trustable alternative to password or key based security systems. Signature is a behavioral biometric: it is not based on the physical properties, such as fingerprint or face, of the individual, but behavioral ones.

Signature verification is split into two according to the available data in the input. Offline (static) signature verification takes as input the image of a signature and is useful in automatic verification of signatures found on bank checks and documents. Online (dynamic) signature verification uses signatures that are captured by pressure-sensitive tablets that extract dynamic properties of a signature in addition to its shape. Dynamic features include the number and order of the strokes, the overall speed of the signature, the pen pressure at each point etc. and make the signature more unique and more difficult to forge. As a result, online signature verification is more reliable than offline signature verification. Application areas of online signature verification include protection of small personal devices (e.g. PDA, laptop); authorization of computer users for accessing sensitive data or programs; and authentication of individuals for access to physical devices or buildings.

As a behavioral biometric, signature is not as unique or difficult to forge as iris patterns or fingerprints, however signature's widespread acceptance by the public, make it more suitable for certain lower-security authentication applications, as well as certain applications where online signatures can be the most suitable biometric (e.g. online banking and in credit card purchases). Furhermore, one's signature may change over time; yet, a person signs his/her signature rather uniquely at any given time period and forgeries can be identified by human experts quite well.

In an online or offline signature verification system, users are first enrolled by providing signature samples (reference signatures). Then, when a user presents a signature (test signature) claiming to be a particular individual, this test signature is compared with the reference signatures for that individual. If the dissimilarity is above a certain threshold, the user is rejected, otherwise authenticated.

In evaluating the performance of a signature verification system, there are two important factors: the false rejection rate (FRR) and the false acceptance rate (FAR). As these are inversely related, decreasing the FRR results in an increase in the FAR. When a single figure is needed, the Equal Error Rate (EER), where FAR equals FRR, is often reported.

Since obtaining actual forgeries is difficult, two forgery types have been defined in signature verification papers: A *skilled* forgery is signed by a person who has had access to a genuine signature for practice. A *random* or *zero-effort forgery* is signed without having any information about the signature, or even the name, of the person whose signature is forged.

In the verification process, the test signature is compared to all the signatures in the reference set, resulting in several dissimilarity/distance values. One then has to choose a method to combine these distance values so as to represent the dissimilarity of the test signature to the reference set in a single number, and compare it to a threshold to make a decision. The single dissimilarity value can be obtained from the minimum, maximum or the average of all the distance values. Typically, a verification system chooses one of these approaches and discards the other ones. For instance, Jain et al. report the lowest error rates with the minimum distance criterion, among the other three [1]. We use all three in deciding whether the signature is genuine or not, instead of choosing which distance is most useful for the task.

These distance values, normalized by the corresponding average values of the reference set, are used as the features of a signature in its classification as genuine or forgery, as explained in Section 3.

2 Previous Work

A comprehensive survey of signature verification can be found in [2, 3]. Most commonly used on-line signature acquisition devices are pressure sensitive tablets with or without LCD screens, together with smart pens capable of measuring forces at the pen-tip exerted in three directions. More than 40 different feature types have been used for signature verification [1, 4, 5]. Features can be classified in two types: global and local. Global features are features related to the signature as a whole, for instance the signing speed, signature bounding box, and Fourier descriptors of the signature's trajectory. Local features correspond to a specific sample point along the trajectory of the signature. Examples of local features include distance and curvature change between successive points on the signature trajectory. In Jain et al. [1], some of these features are compared in order to find the more robust ones for signature verification purposes. Other systems have used Genetic Algorithms to find the most useful features [6].

Due to the variability in signing speed, two signatures belonging to the same person may have different trajectory lengths (hence feature vectors of differing lengths). Therefore, the dynamic time warping algorithm with some variant of the Euclidian distance [1, 5, 7, 8] and Hidden Markov models [9] are commonly used in aligning two signatures.

Number of signatures taken during the user enrollment also varies: between 3 and 20 samples are used in previous signature verification systems. The distance of the test signature to the closest reference signature has been found as most useful (giving the lowest error rates) in [1], however other criteria, such as the average distance to the reference signatures or the distance to a template signature are also used. Template generation is generally accomplished by simply selecting one or more of the sample signatures as templates [5, 10].

Various thresholds can be used in deciding whether the distance between the test signature and the reference and/or template signatures are acceptable. Two types of threshold selections are reported: writer dependent and writer independent thresholds [1]. In writer dependent scenario, thresholds are calculated for each user individually, whereas in writer independent one, a global threshold for all the writers is set empirically during the training phase of the system.

State of the art performance of the available on-line signature verification algorithms lies between 1% and 10% equal error rate.

3 Proposed Method

During the enrollment phase, the user supplies a set of reference signatures which are used to determine user dependent parameters characterizing the variance within the reference signatures. The reference set of signatures, together with these parameters, are stored with a unique user identifier in the system's database.

When a test signature is input to the system for verification, it is compared to each of the reference signatures of the claimed person. The person is authenticated if the resulting dissimilarity measure is low, rejected otherwise. The details of the system is described in the following sections.

3.1 Data Acquisition

We have used Wacom's Graphire2 pressure sensitive tablet and pen. The tablet is capable of sampling data at 100 samples per second: at each sample point, the x,y coordinates of the signature's trajectory and the time stamp are recorded. Unlike some other tablets, Wacom's pen capture samples only during the interaction of the pen tip with the tablet.

3.2 Feature Extraction

It is important to find features that are invariant with respect to small changes in genuine signatures, yet can be used to discriminate forgeries. We have experimented with the following local features of the points on the signature trajectory: x-y coordinates relative to the first point of signature trajectory, the x and y coordinate differences between two consecutive points(Δ_x, Δ_y), and the curvature differences between consecutive points. The results shown in Section 4 are for the Δ_x, Δ_y features which gave the lowest error rates.

A signature is considered a ballistic movement, and as such, the timing of someone's signature carries important information. For that reason, we have chosen not to do any preprocessing steps (e.g. resampling) in order to preserve the timing information of the signer. During the alignment of the two signatures, a significant difference in the speed and timing of two signatures, even if they have the same shape, results in a high dissimilarity score. This is desired, because the shape information can be easily copied if the forger gets a sample, whereas the timing information is more difficult to imitate (and to observe).

3.3 Signature Alignment

In order to compare two signatures of differing lengths, we use the dynamic time warping algorithm which is a well-known and widely used method for aligning vectors of different lengths. Dynamic time warping algorithm finds the best nonlinear alignment of two vectors such that the overall distance between them are minimized.

There are three parameters that needs to be set in the dynamic time warping algorithm. The missing point and spurious point costs, penalizing a missing or extraneous point in one of the signatures, are taken to be equal in our system. The actual value of this parameter is set so that small extra strokes do not cause a large dissimilarity score. When two points are aligned, we use the Euclidian distance between the features of the two points as the alignment cost. However, a threshold is added to this metric to allow for insignificant variation between two signatures, without adding to the cost.

Note that even though the dynamic time warping aligns signatures in differing lengths, the timing information that we intended to keep by not resampling is not lost: the speed difference between two signatures causes spurious points, adding to the total matching cost.

3.4 Enrollment

During enrollment to the system, the user supplies a number of signatures (eight in our system). Supplied signatures are pairwise aligned to find the distance between each pair, as described in Section 3.3.

From these alignment scores, the following reference set statistics are calculated: (i) average distance to nearest neighbor, $\overline{d}_{min}$ (ii) average distance to farthest signature, $\overline{d}_{max}$ (iv) average distance to the *template signature*, X_T, which is the signature with minimum average distance to all other supplied signatures, $\overline{d}_{tmp}$. These are illustrated in Figure 1.

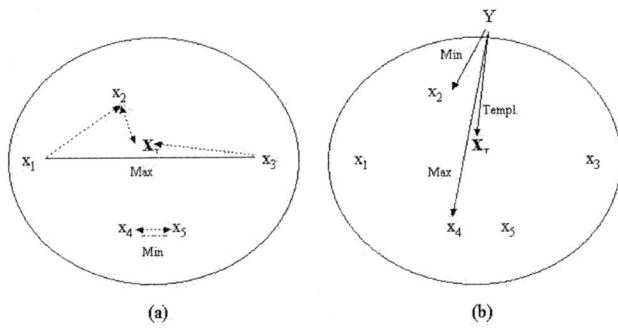

Fig. 1. a) Calculation of the reference set statistics b) Calculation of the test signature Y's distances to the reference set.

3.5 Training

A training data set consisting of 76 genuine signatures and 54 forgery signatures is collected in order to learn the threshold parameter separating the forgery and genuine classes. These signatures are separate from the signatures collected as reference signatures.

First, each training signature is compared to the reference set of signatures it claimed to belong, using the Dynamic Time Warping algorithm described in Section 3.3, giving a 3-dimensional feature vector $(d_{min}, d_{max}, d_{tmp})$. The feature values are then normalized by the corresponding averages of the reference set $(\overline{d}_{min}, \overline{d}_{max}, \overline{d}_{tmp})$ to give the distribution of the feature set shown in Figure 2. The distribution of this normalized data supports that genuine and forgery samples in the training set are well separated with these normalized features. Note that by normalizing the measured distance vectors by the corresponding reference set averages, we eliminate the need for user-dependent thresholds commonly used in deciding whether a signature is similar enough to the reference set.

Finally, we train a classifier to separate the genuine and forgery samples in this normalized feature space. For this work, we trained two classifiers: the Bayes classifier using the 3-dimensional feature vectors assuming independent covariance matrices and a linear classifier used in conjunction with the Principal Component Analysis (PCA). As the three features are highly correlated, we could reduce the dimensionality from three to one while keeping most of the variance, using Principal Component Analysis (PCA). Then, a linear classification is made by picking a threshold value separating the two classes within the training set. This threshold is fixed and later used in the verification process. The results are summarized in Section 4.

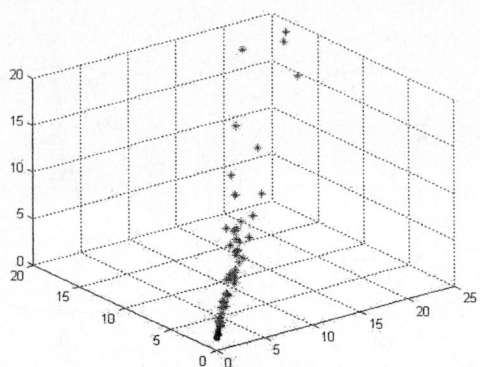

Fig. 2. Plot of genuine (dots) and forgery signatures (stars) with respect to the 3-dimensional normalized distance vector

3.6 Verification

In order to verify a test signature Y, we first proceed as in the training stage: the signature is compared to all the reference signatures belonging to the claimed ID using the Dynamic Time Warping algorithm described in Section 3.3. Then, the resulting distance values $((d_{min}, d_{max}, d_{tmp})$, normalized by the averages of the claimed reference set $(\bar{d}_{min}, \bar{d}_{max}, \bar{d}_{tmp})$, are used in classifying the signature as genuine or forgery, by the trained recognizer.

4 Performance Evaluation

The system performance was evaluated using the sample signatures supplied by 94 subjects enrolled to our system. Each subject supplied 10 to 15 genuine signatures in total. Eight of the signatures were used for profile creation (reference set) for that user and the rest was used in the evaluation of the system(DS1 of 182 genuine signatures). There were no constraints on how to sign, nor was any information given about the working of the system, so that the subjects signed in their most natural way.

To collect skilled forgeries we added a signing simulation module to our system. Simulation module animates the signing process of a given signature so that the forger could see not only the signature trajectory's points sequence but also the signing dynamics (speed and acceleration). Forgers had a chance of watching the signature's animation several times and practice tracing over the signature image a few times before forging it. Our forgery data set (DS2) consists of 313 skilled forgeries obtained in this way. Note that training data is separate from both the reference set of genuine signatures and the test data used to in performance evaluation.

The results shown in Tables 1 and 2 are with the Δ_x and Δ_y features, using the Bayes classifier and the PCA approach, respectively. Best results were obtained using PCA, with approximately a 1.4% total error rate (which is also roughly the equal error rate). The results of the experiments with the Bayes classifier using the 3-dimensional feature vector were inferior; this may be due to a poor fit to the assumed Gaussian distribution or the relatively small number of training data used to estimate the model parameters.

Table 1. Verification results obtained using the Bayes' classifier using the 3-dimensional data

Data Set	Type	Size	FRR	FAR
DS1	Genuine	182	2.19%	-
DS2	Skilled	313	-	3.51%

Table 2. Verification results obtained using the linear classifier used with PCA, with a 1.4% total error rate

Data Set	Type	Size	FRR	FAR
DS1	Genuine	182	1.65%	-
DS2	Skilled	313	-	1.28%

5 Summary and Conclusion

We have presented an online signature verification system that approaches the problem as a two-class pattern recognition problem. The distance values of a test signature to the reference set, normalized by the respective averages of the reference set, are used as features.

We experimented with two different classifiers and obtained a 1.4% overall error rate for a data set of 94 people and 495 signatures (genuine signatures and skilled forgeries). These results are quite good, given the fact that the forgeries used on the experiments were not random forgeries, as it is typically done, but relatively skilled forgeries. Even though these results are on our relatively small database, the proposed system received first place at the First International Signature Verification Competition [11], with the lowest average equal error rate ($< 2.9\%$) when tested with skilled forgeries with or without pressure information.

References

1. Jain, A., Griess, F., Connell, S.: On-line signature verification. Pattern Recognition **35** (2002) 2963–2972
2. Plamondon, R., Lorette, G.: Automatic signature verification and writer identification—state of the art. Pattern Recognition **22** (1989) 107–131
3. Leclerc, F., Plamondon, R.: Automatic signature verification: The state of the art. International Journal of Pattern Recognition and Artificial Intelligence **8** (1994) 643–660
4. Vielhauer, C., Steinmetz, R., Mayerhofer, A.: Biometric hash based on statistical features of on-line signatures. 16'th International Conference on Pattern Recognition (2002)
5. Ohishi, T., Komiya, Y., Matsumoto, T.: On-line signature verification using pen-position, pen-pressure and pen-inclination trajectories. In: ICPR. (2000) 547–550
6. Yang, X., Furuhashi, T., Obata, K., Uchikawa, Y.: Constructing a high performance signature verification system using a ga method. In: 2nd New Zealand Two-Stream International Conference on Artificial Neural Networks and Expert Systems. (1995)
7. Martens, R., Claesen, L.: Dynamic programming optimisation for on-line signature verification. In: ICDAR'97. (1997)
8. Parizeau, M., Plamondon, R.: A comparative analysis of regional correlation, dynamic time warping and skeletal tree matching for signatures. IEEE Trans. Pattern Analysis and Machine Intelligence **12** (1990) 710–717
9. Van Oosterhout, J.J., Dolfing, H., Aarts, E.: On-line signature verification with hidden markov models. In: ICPR. (1998)
10. Connell, S., Jain, A.: Template-based online character recognition. Pattern Recognition **34** (2001) 1–14
11. Yeung, D., Chang, H., Xiong, Y., George, S., Kashi, R., Matsumoto, T., Rigoll, G.: SV C2004: First international signature verification competition. In: Proceedings of the Int. Conf. on Biometric Authentication. (2004)

Moving Region Detection in Compressed Video

B. Uğur Töreyin[1], A. Enis Cetin[1], Anil Aksay[1], and M. Bilgay Akhan[2]

[1] Department of Electrical and Electronics Engineering
Bilkent University 06800 Bilkent, Ankara, Turkey
{ugur,cetin,anil}@ee.bilkent.edu.tr
[2] Visioprime 30 St. Johns Rd., St. Johns, Woking, Surrey, GU21 7SA, UK
bilgay.akhan@visioprime.com

Abstract. In this paper, an algorithm for moving region detection in compressed video is developed. It is assumed that the video can be compressed either using the Discrete Cosine Transform (DCT) or the Wavelet Transform (WT). The method estimates the WT of the background scene from the WTs of the past image frames of the video. The WT of the current image is compared with the WT of the background and the moving objects are determined from the difference. The algorithm does not perform inverse WT to obtain the actual pixels of the current image nor the estimated background. In the case of DCT compressed video, the DC values of 8 by 8 image blocks of Y, U and V channels are used for estimating the background scene. This leads to a computationally efficient method and a system compared to the existing motion detection methods.

1 Introduction

Video based surveillance systems are widely used in security applications. A typical system may be required to handle many cameras recording various locations. Some digital cameras have built-in data compression systems and provide only compressed video. In order to realize a computationally efficient automatic video processing system, it is required to process video in the compressed domain.

In this paper, it is assumed that the video is compressed either using the Discrete Cosine Transform (DCT) or the Wavelet Transform (WT). In the case of wavelet compressed video, the proposed moving object detection algorithm compares the WT of the current image with the WTs of the past image frames to detect motion and moving regions in the current image without performing an inverse wavelet transform operation. Moving regions and objects can be detected by comparing the wavelet transforms of the current image with the wavelet transform of the background scene which can be estimated from the wavelet transforms of the past image frames. If there is a significant difference between the two wavelet transforms then this means that there is motion in the video. If there is no motion then the wavelet transforms of the current image and the background image ideally should be equal to each other or very close to each other due to quantization process during compression. Stationary wavelet coefficients belong to the wavelet transform of the background. This is because the background of the scene is temporally stationary [1–5]. If the viewing range of the camera is observed for some time, then the wavelet transform of the entire background can be estimated as moving regions and objects occupy only some parts of the scene in a typical image of a video and they disappear over time. On the other hand, pixels of foreground objects and their wavelet coefficients change in time. Non-stationary wavelet coefficients over time correspond to the foreground of the scene and they contain motion information. A simple approach to estimate the wavelet transform of the background is to average the observed wavelet transforms of the image frames. Since moving objects and regions occupy only a part of the image they can conceal a part of the background scene and their effect in the wavelet domain is canceled over time by averaging.

A similar argument is also valid for DCT compressed video. DCT of the background scene can be estimated from the DCTs of the past image frames [3]. Both AC and DC coefficients are used in [3]. In this paper only the DC values of 8 by 8 DCT blocks are used for motion detection. In [3], only the luminance information is used whereas in this paper both luminance and chrominance channels are used for motion detection. A significant change in the DC values of 8 by 8 image blocks of Y, U and V channels of the estimated background image and the DCT of the current image indicates a motion in video. Since only the DC values are used, a computationally efficient system is achieved.

Any one of the space domain approaches [2–8] for background estimation can be implemented in compressed domain providing real-time performance. For example, the background estimation method in [2] can be implemented by simply computing the wavelet or discrete cosine transforms of both sides of their background estimation equations.

2 Hybrid Algorithm for Moving Object Detection

Background subtraction is commonly used for segmenting out objects of interest in a scene for applications such as surveillance. There are numerous methods in the literature [1–5]. The background estimation algorithm described in [2] uses a simple IIR filter applied to each pixel independently to update the background and use adaptively updated thresholds to classify pixels into foreground and background. This is followed by some post processing to correct classification failures. Stationary pixels in the video are the pixels of the background scene because the background can be defined as temporally stationary part of the video. If the scene is observed for some time, then pixels forming the entire background scene can be estimated because moving regions and objects occupy only some parts of the scene in a typical image of a video. A simple approach to estimate the background is to average the observed image frames of the video. Since moving objects and regions occupy only a part of the image, they conceal a part of the background scene and their effect is canceled over time by averaging. Our main concern is real-time performance of the system. In Video Surveillance and Monitoring (VSAM) Project at Carnegie Mellon University [2] a recursive background estimation method was developed from the actual image data. Let $I_n(x,y)$ represent the intensity (brightness) value at pixel position (x,y) in the nth image frame I_n. Estimated background intensity value at the same pixel position, $B_{n+1}(x,y)$, is calculated as follows:

$$B_{n+1}(x,y) = \begin{cases} aB_n(x,y) + (1-a)I_n(x,y) & \text{if } (x,y) \text{ is non-moving} \\ B_n(x,y) & \text{if } (x,y) \text{ is moving} \end{cases} \quad (1)$$

where $B_n(x,y)$ is the previous estimate of the background intensity value at the same pixel position. The update parameter a is a positive real number close to one. Initially, $B_0(x,y)$ is set to the first image frame $I_0(x,y)$. A pixel positioned at (x,y) is assumed to be moving if the brightness values corresponding to it in image frame I_n and image frame I_{n-1}, satisfy the following inequality:

$$|I_n(x,y) - I_{n-1}(x,y)| > T_n(x,y) \quad (2)$$

where $I_{n-1}(x,y)$ is the brightness value at pixel position (x,y) in the $(n-1)^{st}$ image frame I_{n-1}. $T_n(x,y)$ is a threshold describing a statistically significant brightness change at pixel position (x,y). This threshold is recursively updated for each pixel as follows:

$$T_{n+1}(x,y) = \begin{cases} aT_n(x,y) + (1-a)(c|I_n(x,y) - B_n(x,y)|) & \text{if } (x,y) \text{ is non-moving} \\ T_n(x,y) & \text{if } (x,y) \text{ is moving} \end{cases} \quad (3)$$

where c is a real number greater than one and the update parameter a is a positive number close to one. Initial threshold values are set to an experimentally determined value. As it can be seen from (3), the higher the parameter c, higher the threshold or lower the sensitivity of detection scheme. It is assumed that regions significantly different from the background are moving regions. Estimated background image is subtracted from the current image to detect moving regions. In other words all of the pixels satisfying:

$$|I_n(x,y) - B_n(x,y)| > T_n(x,y) \; . \quad (4)$$

are determined. These pixels at (x,y) locations are classified as the pixels of moving objects.

3 Moving Region Detection in Compressed Domain

Above arguments and the methods proposed in [6] and [7] are valid in compressed data domain as well, [3]. In [3], DCT domain data is used for motion detection in video. Our paper covers both wavelet and DCT based compressed video. The wavelet transform of the background scene can be estimated from the wavelet coefficients of past image frames, which do not change in time, whereas foreground objects and their wavelet coefficients change in time. Such wavelet coefficients belong to the background because the background of the scene is temporally stationary. Non-stationary wavelet coefficients over time correspond to the foreground of the scene and they contain motion information. If the viewing range of the camera is observed for some time, then the wavelet transform of the entire background can be estimated because moving regions and objects occupy only some parts of the scene in a typical image of a video and they disappear over time. Similarly, DC-DCT coefficients of the background scene can be estimated from the corresponding coefficients of the past image frames. Stationary coefficients correspond to background whereas non-stationary ones over time belong to the foreground of the scene.

Let B be an arbitrary image. This image is processed by a single stage separable Daubechies 9/7 filterbank and four quarter size subband images are obtained. Let us denote these images as $LL(1), HL(1), LH(1), HH(1)$ [9]. In a Mallat wavelet tree, $LL(1)$ is processed by the filterbank once again and $LL(2), HL(2), LH(2), HH(2)$ are obtained. Second scale subband images are the quarter size versions of $LL(1)$. This process is repeated several times in a typical wavelet image coder. DCT compressed images used in this paper encode a 2-D image using the DCT coefficients of 8 by 8 image regions. Only the DC-DCT coefficients are used for motion detection. DC-DCT coefficients of 8 by 8 image blocks of an image and a three scale wavelet decomposition of the same image are shown in Fig. 1.

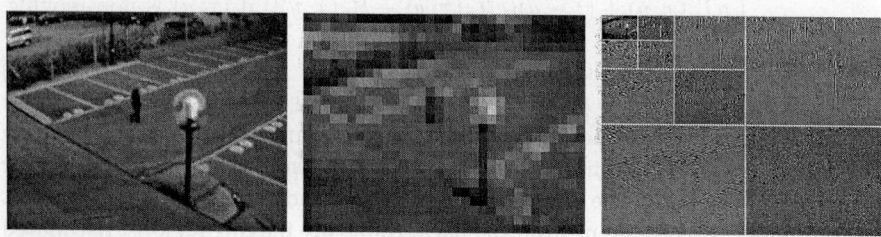

Fig. 1. Original image(left), the DC-DCT coefficients of 8 by 8 image blocks of the image(middle) and its corresponding three levels of the wavelet tree consisting of subband images (luminance data is shown)

Let D_n represent any one of the subband images of the background image B_n at time instant n. The subband image of the background D_{n+1} at time instant $n+1$ is estimated from D_n as follows:

$$D_{n+1}(i,j) = \begin{cases} aD_n(i,j) + (1-a)J_n(i,j) & \text{if } (i,j) \text{ is non-moving} \\ D_n(i,j) & \text{if } (i,j) \text{ is moving} \end{cases} \quad (5)$$

where J_n is the corresponding subband image of the current observed image frame I_n. The update parameter a is a positive real number close to one. Initial subband image of the background, D_0, is assigned to be the corresponding subband image of the first image of the video I_0. In Equations (1)-(4), (x,y)'s correspond to the pixel locations in the original image, whereas in (5) and in all the equations in this section, (i,j)'s correspond to locations of subband images' wavelet coefficients. In DCT compressed video, $D_n(i,j)$ and $J_n(i,j)$ represent the DC value of the $(i,j)^{th}$ block of the corresponding images at time instant n.

A wavelet coefficient at the position (i,j) in a subband image or a DC-DCT coefficient of the $(i,j)^{th}$ block is assumed to be moving if

$$|J_n(i,j) - J_{n-1}(i,j)| > T_n(i,j) \qquad (6)$$

where $T_n(i,j)$ is a threshold recursively updated for each wavelet or DC-DCT coefficient as follows:

$$T_{n+1}(i,j) = \begin{cases} aT_n(i,j) + (1-a)(b|J_n(i,j) - D_n(i,j)|) & \text{if } (i,j) \text{ is non-moving} \\ T_n(i,j) & \text{if } (i,j) \text{ is moving} \end{cases} \qquad (7)$$

where b is a real number greater than one and the update parameter a is a positive real number close to one. Initial threshold values can be experimentally determined. As it can be seen from the above equation, the higher the parameter b, higher the threshold or lower the sensitivity of detection scheme. Estimated compressed image of the background is subtracted from the corresponding compressed image of the current image to detect the moving coefficients and consequently moving objects as it is assumed that the regions different from the background are the moving regions. In other words, all of the coefficients satisfying the inequality

$$|J_n(i,j) - D_n(i,j)| > T_n(i,j) \qquad (8)$$

are determined.

It should be pointed out that there is no fixed threshold in this method. A specific threshold is assigned to each coefficient and it is adaptively updated according to (7).

Once all the coefficients satisfying the above inequalities are determined, locations of corresponding regions on the original image are determined. For the wavelet compressed video, if a single stage Haar wavelet transform is used in data compression then a wavelet coefficient satisfying (8) corresponds to a two by two block in the original image frame I_n. For example, if $(i,j)^{th}$ coefficient of the subband image $HH_n(1)$ (or other subband images $HL_n(1), LH_n(1), LL_n(1)$) of I_n satisfies (8), then this means that there exists motion in a two pixel by two pixel region in the original image, $I_n(k,m)$, $k = 2i, 2i-1, m = 2j, 2j-1$, because of the subsampling operation in the discrete wavelet transform computation. Similarly, if the $(i,j)^{th}$ coefficient of the subband image $HH_n(2)$ (or other second scale subband images $HL_n(2), LH_n(2), LL_n(2)$) satisfies (8) then this means that there exists motion in a four pixel by four pixel region in the original image, $I_n(k,m), k = 4i, 4i-1, 4i-2, 4i-3$ and $m = 4j, 4j-1, 4j-2, 4j-3$. In general, a change in the lth level wavelet coefficient corresponds to a 2^l by 2^l region in the original image. In DCT compressed video, if DC-DCT coefficient of $(i,j)^{th}$ block is found to be moving, then this means that there exists motion in an 8 by 8 region in the original image, $I_n(k,m), k = 8i, 8i-1, 8i-2, .., 8i-7$ and $m = 8j, 8j-1, 8j-2, .., 8j-7$.

In this paper, the wavelet compressed video is obtained using Daubechies' 9/7 biorthogonal wavelet. In this biorthogonal transform, the number of pixels forming a wavelet coefficient is larger than four but most of the contribution comes from the immediate neighborhood of the pixel $I_n(k,m) = (2i, 2j)$ in the first level wavelet decomposition, and $(k,m) = (2^l i, 2^l j)$ in the lth level wavelet decomposition, respectively. Therefore, in this paper, we classify the immediate neighborhood of $(2i, 2j)$ in a single stage wavelet decomposition or in general $(2^l i, 2^l j)$ in the lth level wavelet decomposition as a moving region in the current image frame, respectively.

Determining the moving pixels of the corresponding regions as explained separately for wavelet and DCT based compressed video above, the union of these regions on the original image is formed to locate the moving region(s) in the video. These pixels are processed by a region growing algorithm to include the pixels located at immediate neighborhood of them. This region growing algorithm checks whether the following condition is met for these pixels:

$$|J_n(i+m, j+m) - D_n(i+m, j+m)| > K \, T_n(i+m, j+m) \qquad (9)$$

where $m = \pm 1$, and $0.8 < K < 1$, $K \in \mathbf{R}^+$. If this condition is satisfied, then that particular pixel is also classified as moving. After this classification of pixels, moving regions are formed and encapsulated by their minimum bounding boxes.

4 Experimental Results

The above algorithm is implemented using C++ 6.0, running on a 1500 MHz Pentium 4 processor. The PC based system can handle 16 video channels captured at 5 frames per second in real-time. Each image fed by the channels has the frame size of PAL composite video format, which is 720 pixel by 576 pixel.

The video data is available in compressed form. For the wavelet compressed video, only the lowest resolution part of the compressed video bit-stream is decoded to obtain the low-low, low-high, high-low, and high-high coefficients which are used in moving object detection. Higher resolution wavelet sub-images are not decoded.

The performance of our algorithm is tested using different video sequences and real-time data. 76 of the test sequences are reported in this paper. These sequences have different scenarios, covering both indoor and outdoor videos under various lighting conditions containing different video objects with various sizes. Some example snapshots of wavelet and DCT compressed domain methods are shown in Fig. 2.

The moving regions are also detected over 180 by 144 size images by using the hybrid method of VSAM [2]. Another widely used background estimation method is based on Gaussian Mixture Modelling [8]. However, this method is computationally more expensive than other methods.

Moving objects of various sizes are successfully detected by these methods as summarized in Tables 1 and 2. The numbers listed in these tables are the frame numbers of frames in which detection took place. For example, MAN1 object in VIDEO-3 sequence in Table 1 is detected at the 15th frame in all

Fig. 2. Some detection results of DCT(left) and wavelet compressed domain methods

three methods, namely our methods utilizing the compressed data only and the method of VSAM [2].

Motion detection results in videos containing objects with sizes ranging from 20 by 20 to 100 by 100 objects are presented in Table 1. Such large moving objects are detected about at the same time by all methods. In Table 2, motion detection results of the algorithms with videos containing objects having sizes comparable to 8 by 8 are presented. In these videos, there is not much difference in terms of time delay between the methods, as well.

Time performance analysis of the methods are also carried out. The method of VSAM is implemented using videos with frame-size of 180 by 144. This image

Table 1. Comparison of motion detection methods with videos having large moving objects. All videos are captured at 10 fps except for VIDEO-4 which is captured at 5fps

Large Object Videos	Object	Compressed Domain Method		VSAM
		Wavelet	DCT	
VIDEO-1	MAN1	28	29	28
	MAN2	41	42	41
VIDEO-2	MAN1	19	19	19
	MAN2	75	75	75
VIDEO-3	MAN1	15	15	15
	MAN2	38	38	38
	MAN3	44	44	44
	MAN4	75	75	74
VIDEO-4	TRUCK1	6	6	4

Table 2. Comparison of motion detection methods with videos having small moving objects. VIDEO-5 is captured at 5 fps whereas the other videos are captured at 25 fps

Small Object Videos	Object	Compressed Domain Method		VSAM
		Wavelet	DCT	
VIDEO-5	MAN1	21	21	21
	MAN2	32	32	32
VIDEO-6	CAR1	55	55	55
	CAR2	62	62	62
	CAR3	63	64	63
	CAR4	98	100	98
VIDEO-7	CAR1	88	89	88

data is extracted from the low-low image of the 2nd level wavelet transform. Our method uses all the coefficients in the 4th level subband image, including low-low, high-low, low-high and high-high subimages. For the DCT based method, 360 by 288 image frames are fed to our system. Macro image blocks of 8 by 8 are formed to obtain the DC-DCT coefficients. Hence, the data handled by the system are equal in amount for both of the compressed domain methods. Performance results show that compressed domain method is significantly faster than the method of VSAM. Our method processes an image in $1.1 msec$, whereas ordinary VSAM method processes an image in $3.1 msec$, on the average. It is impossible to process 16 video channels consisting of 180 by 144 size images simultaneously using the VSAM and GMM based motion detection methods in a typical surveillance system implemented in a PC.

In indoor surveillance applications, the methods does not produce false alarms. On the other hand, in outdoor applications, false alarms occur in both of the methods due to leaves and tree branches moving in the wind, etc., as shown in Table 3.

Table 3. Frame numbers of some outdoor videos at which false alarms occur when leaves of the surrounding trees move with the wind. Indoor videos yield no false alarms

Videos	Compressed Domain Method		VSAM
	Wavelet	DCT	
OUTDOOR-1	126, 163	126, 163	87, 126, 163
OUTDOOR-2	No false alarms	No false alarms	No false alarms
INDOOR-1	No false alarms	No false alarms	No false alarms
INDOOR-2	No false alarms	No false alarms	No false alarms

Motion sensitivity of our compressed domain method can be adjusted to detect any kind of motion in the scene, by going up or down in the wavelet pyramid for the wavelet compressed video and playing with the parameter b in equation (7) for both of the compression types. However, by going up to higher resolution levels in the pyramid, the processing time per frame of the compressed domain method approaches to that of the ordinary background subtraction method of VSAM. Similarly, false alarms may be reduced by increasing b in (7) at the expense of delays in actual alarms.

5 Conclusion

A method for detecting motion in compressed video using only compressed domain data without performing the inverse transform is developed. The main advantage of the proposed method compared to regular methods is that it is not only computationally efficient but also it solves the bandwidth problem associated with video processing systems. It is impossible to feed the pixel data of 16 video channels into the PCI bus of an ordinary PC in real-time. However, compressed video data of 16 channels can be handled by an ordinary PC and its buses, hence real-time motion detection can be implemented by the proposed algorithm.

References

1. Foresti, G.L., Mahonen, P., Regazzoni, C.S.: Multimedia video-based surveillance systems: Requirements, issues, and solutions. Kluwer (2000)
2. Collins, R.T., Lipton, A.J., Kanade, T., Fujiyoshi, H., Duggins, D., Tsin, Y., Tolliver, D., Enomoto, N., Hasegawa, O., Burt, P., Wixson, L.: A system for video surveillance and monitoring: VSAM final report. Tech. Rept., CMU-RI-TR-00- 12, Carnegie Mellon University (1998)
3. Ozer, I.B., Wolf, W.: A hierarchical human detection system in (un)compressed domains. IEEE Transactions on Multimedia (2002) 283–300

4. Haritaoglu, I., Harwood, D., Davis, L.: W4: Who, when, where, what: A real time system for detecting and tracking people. In: Third Face and Gesture Recognition Conference. (1998) 222–227
5. Bagci, M., Yardimci, Y., Cetin, A.E.: Moving object detection using adaptive subband decomposition and fractional lower order statistics in video sequences. Signal Processing, Elsevier (2002) 1941–1947
6. Naoi, S., Egawa, H., Shiohara, M.: Image processing apparatus. U.S. Patent 6,141,435 (2000)
7. Taniguchi, Y.: Moving object detection apparatus and method. U.S Patent 5,991,428 (1999)
8. Stauffer, C., Grimson, W.E.L.: Adaptive background mixture models for real-time tracking. In: Proceedings of IEEE Computer Society Conference on Computer Vision and Pattern Recognition. (1999) 246–252
9. Antonini, M., Barlaud, M., Mathieu, P., Daubechies, I.: Image coding using wavelet transform. IEEE Transactions on Image Processing $1(2)$ (1992) 205–220

Shape Recognition with Generalized Beam Angle Statistics

Ömer Önder Tola, Nafiz Arıca, and Fatoş Yarman-Vural

Department of Computer Engineering
Middle East Technical University, Ankara
{onder,nafiz,vural}@ceng.metu.edu.tr

Abstract. In this study, we develop a new shape descriptor and a matching algorithm in order to find a given template shape in an edge detected image without extracting the boundary. The shape descriptor based on Generalized Beam Angle Statistics (GBAS) defines the angles between the lines connecting each boundary point with the rest of the points, as random variable. Then, it assigns a feature vector to each point using the moments of beam angles. The proposed matching algorithm performs shape recognition by matching the feature vectors of boundary points on the template shape and the edge pixels on the image. The matching process also considers the spatial distance of the edge pixels. The experiments performed on MPEG-7 data set show that the template shapes are found successfully on the noisy images.

1 Introduction

In many computer vision applications, it is required to detect and recognize objects in a given image. Shape detection is also considered as an out product of the segmentation process, which is one of the most difficult tasks in computer vision. However, the result of the segmentation techniques using low level image processing, does not always give satisfactory results for various reasons, including the existence of noise, shape complexity, variations within and across objects in the image, etc. Consequently, shape recognition process cannot be completed successfully. In order to improve the quality of segmentation, one should constrain the problem by exploiting the prior knowledge, which partly eliminates the ambiguities in detecting shapes. This task is generally performed by model-based approaches, which use deformable shape templates. These techniques combine the segmentation and recognition process in order to use the information about the objects that are to be located in the image [1,2].

In this study, a new method is developed for shape recognition in an edge-detected image without extracting the shape boundary. The method proposes a new shape descriptor and matching algorithm in order to detect a given template shape. The generalization of Beam Angle Statistics (BAS), which is previously developed by the authors of this study, forms the shape descriptor. Beam Angle Statistics is used to describe shape boundary as a series of 1-D functions independent of rotation, translation and scale [3]. But, like many other shape descriptors found in the literature [4,5], the shape descriptor based on BAS, assumes that the shape boundary pixels are extracted and ordered prior to the representation. This study generalizes the BAS function method in order to describe shapes, independent of the ordering of the boundary pixels. The proposed descriptor is called Generalized Beam Angle Statistics (GBAS). The input of GBAS is the edge-detected image that is the output of one of the existing edge detection algorithms. In this edge image, the boundary of the template shape cannot be defined by connected and closed boundary pixels, instead, boundary pixels are found in the set of unordered, missing and excessive edge pixels. The proposed shape descriptor identifies the required GBAS feature vector of each boundary pixel, performing a computation that is independent from the ordering of the edge pixels of the shape being described.

The matching algorithm is used to search a given template shape in an edge detected image. The algorithm provides matching of the GBAS features extracted from the boundary pixels of the template shape and the edge pixels of the given image. It also considers the spatial distance of edge pixels by using a dynamic programming approach.

GBAS Shape Descriptor and matching algorithm is described in Sections 2 and 3, respectively. The experiments performed on the proposed method are given in Section 4. Finally, the conclusions are discussed in Section 5.

2 Generalized Beam Angle Statistics

Let $P = \{p_1, p_2, \ldots, p_N\}$, be a set of edge pixels that are extracted using an edge detection algorithm from an image. The indices of the elements of the set P are assigned randomly. The *Beam Vector*, $V(p_i, p_j)$, is defined as a vector from an edge pixel, p_i, to another edge pixel, p_j (Figure 1).

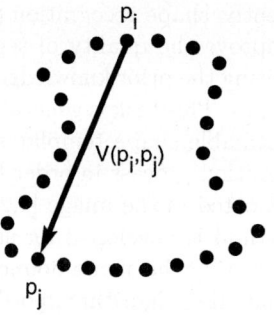

Fig. 1. Beam Vector

In order to compute the GBAS feature vector of an edge pixel, p_i, we first partition the set of edge pixels P into two disjoint sets of edge pixels relative to p_i. For this purpose, the *Mean Beam Vector*, $OK(p_i)$, of an edge pixel, p_i, is found (Figure 2). $OK(p_i)$ is the mean vector of all beam vectors originating at p_i and directed to all other edge pixels in P. Thus; in mathematical terms;

$$OK(p_i) = \sum_{j=1}^{N} V(p_i, p_j) \qquad (1)$$

where $\sum$ denotes vector addition operation.

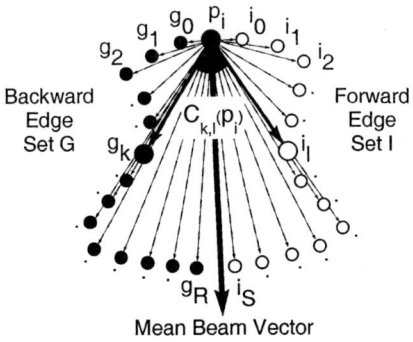

Fig. 2. Forward, I and backward, G edge pixels, mean beam vector, $OK(p_i)$ and generalized beam angle, $C_{k,l}(p_i)$

The Mean Beam Vector, partitions the edge pixels set P into two disjoint sets namely the *forward* I and backward G, edge pixel sets (Figure 2). The forward edge pixel set, $I = \{i_1, i_2, \ldots, i_S\}$ is the union of the edge pixels, whose beam vectors have less than π degrees with the mean beam vector in the counter clockwise direction. Similarly, the backward edge pixels set, $G = \{g_1, g_2, \ldots, g_R\}$ is the union of the edge pixels whose beam vectors have more than π degrees with the mean beam vector in the clockwise direction (Figure 2).

Next, we define the *beam angles matrix*, $K(p_i)$, of the edge pixel p_i. $K(p_i)$, denotes all beam angles formed by the forward and backward beam vectors that are created by the sets of forward I and backward G edge pixels, respectively. In mathematical terms, beam angles matrix is defined as;

$$K(p_i) = \lfloor C_{k,l}(p_i) \rfloor \quad k = 1, 2, \ldots, S \quad l = 1, 2, \ldots, R \qquad (2)$$

In the above equation, $C_{k,l}(p_i)$, denotes the angle that is formed by the forward $V(p_i, i_k)$ and backward $V(p_i, g_l)$ beam vectors that originate at p_i and are directed to i_k forward and g_l backward edge pixels, respectively (Figure 2). This angle is named as *generalized beam angle*. Since $K(p_i)$ incorporates all beam angles formed by the beam vectors that are created by the forward and backward edge pixel sets I and G respectively, it has $S * R$ elements. Generalized beam angle statistics are computed using all of these beam angles determined by $K(p_i)$ and GBAS feature vector is extracted independent of the ordering of the edge pixels.

In this study, for each edge pixel p_i, the beam angle $C_{k,l}(p_i)$ is taken as a random variable with the probability density function $P_i(C_{k,l}(p_i))$ and considered as an outcome of the stochastic process which generates the shape being described at different scales. Probability density function P_i is assumed to be uniform. As a result, moments of the beam angle random variable, $C_{k,l}(p_i)$, are defined as follows:

$$\Xi\left[C(p_i)^m\right] = \sum_{k=1}^{S}\sum_{l=1}^{R} C_{k,l}(p_i)^m P_i(C_{k,l}(p_i)) \quad m = 1, 2, \ldots, d \qquad (3)$$

In the above formula Ξ indicates the expected value operator. The moments describe the statistical behavior of the beam angles, that form the beam angles matrix $K(p_i)$, of the edge pixel p_i. Each edge pixel is then represented by the following *GBAS feature vector*;

$$\Gamma(p_i) = \left[\Gamma^1(p_i), \Gamma^2(p_i), \ldots, \Gamma^d(p_i)\right] \qquad (4)$$

whose components are the moments of the generalized beam angles;

$$\Gamma^m(p_i) = \Xi\left[C(p_i)^m\right] \quad m = 1, 2, \ldots, d \qquad (5)$$

3   Matching Algorithm

The *matching algorithm* is developed to detect a template shape given as a set of ordered boundary pixels;

$$S = \{s_1(x_1, y_1), s_2(x_2, y_2), \ldots, s_L(x_L, y_L)\} \qquad (6)$$

in a set of unordered edge pixels;

$$P = \{p_1(x_1, y_1), p_2(x_2, y_2), \ldots, p_N(x_N, y_N)\}. \qquad (7)$$

For this purpose, the algorithm finds a correspondence between two sets by comparing each boundary pixel with all edge pixels. As a result, a matching set is constructed;

$$M = \{(s_1, p(s_1)), (s_2, p(s_2)), \ldots, (s_L, p(s_L))\} \qquad (8)$$

where $p(s_i)$ denotes the edge pixel that is matched with the boundary pixel s_i.

The algorithm performs the matching by using the GBAS feature vectors and the Euclidean distances (spatial information) of the edge pixels (Figure 3). The algorithm constructs a matching graph, which represents all the matching alternatives between the template shape boundary pixels and the edge pixels. In the graph, every match of the elements of the boundary pixels set S and edge pixels set P are denoted by a matching node. It, then finds an optimum matching using dynamic programming method.

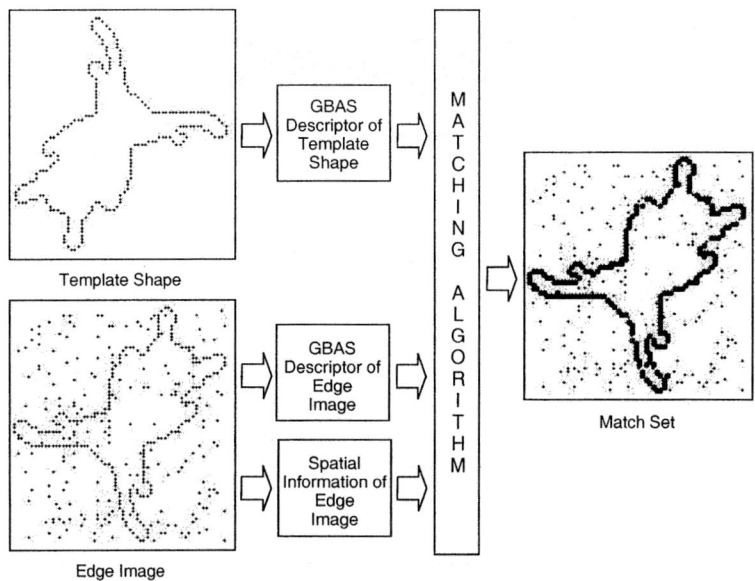

Fig. 3. Matching problem

Formally speaking, given a template shape S and an edge image P, let $Z(E, F)$ (Figure 4) be a multistage di-graph (matching graph), where the nodes $E(i, j) \in E$ represent the matching between s_i in the boundary pixels set S and p_j in the edge pixels set P.

In the *matching graph*, each row, $SE_i = \{E(i,j) | j = 1, 2, \ldots, N\}$ correspond to the set of all matching nodes of the boundary pixel s_i. The arcs in F are of the form $< E_{(i,j)}, E_{(i+1,k)} >$ for all $1 \leq k \leq N$ and $k \neq j$. Note that, in the matching graph, there exists an arc from the node $E(i,j)$ to the rest of the nodes in SE_{i+1}. The exception of this rule is the case where the matching nodes $E(i,j)$ and $E(i+1,k)$ are matched with the same edge pixel; $j = k$. Then, a matching graph can be represented by a multi-stage di-graph, as shown in Figure 4.

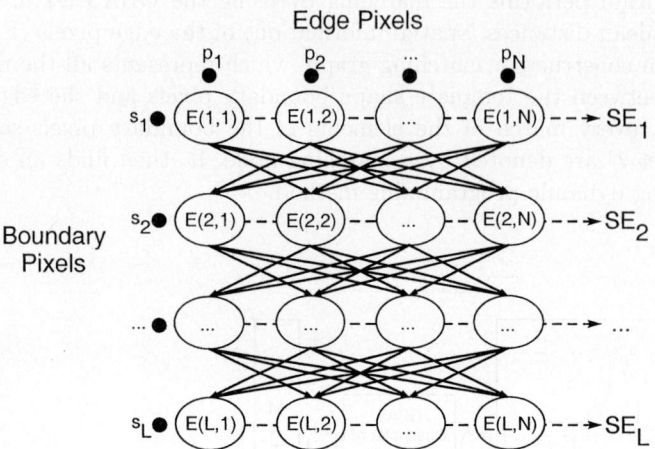

Fig. 4. Matching graph

In the matching graph, the cost of an arc $< E_{(i,j)}, E_{(i+1,k)} >$ is defined as follows;

$$F_{(i,j)(i+1,k)} = D(i,j) + \alpha U(p_j, p_k) \qquad (9)$$

where $D(i,j)$ is the distance of the s_i and p_j pixels GBAS feature vectors;

$$D(i,j) = \sum_{b=1}^{d} |\Gamma^b(s_i) - \Gamma^b(p_j)| \qquad (10)$$

and $U(p_j, p_k)$ is Euclidean distance of the p_j and p_k edge pixels.

$$U(p_j, p_k) = \sqrt{(x_k - x_j)^2 + (y_k - y_j)^2} \qquad (11)$$

The parameter α is the normalization factor that is used to normalize the Euclid distance between the edge pixels in order to make the algorithm independent of the image size. In other words, the matching path is a path that starts from SE_1 of the first boundary pixel s_i, ending in SE_L of the last boundary pixel s_L, forming a matching set such that each boundary pixel is matched with a unique edge pixel in the set of edge pixels, P. Let, $f_i(j)$ be the minimum accumulated cost at node $E(i,j)$ in row i and $Q_i(j)$ be the column of the node in SE_{i-1} on the shortest path to the node $E(i,j)$ in SE_i. We define the path with the minimum accumulated cost as the optimum matching, searched by the following algorithm:

In the algorithm, $Path(E(i,j))$ denotes the sub path that starts from the $E(i,j)$ matching node of the matching graph that is constructed by following $Q_i(j)$. Optimum matching path Y, is constructed by following $Q_L(t_{min})$ that is in the field SE_L of the last boundary pixel s_L and has the minimum cost.

Initialization:
  for $1 \leq j \leq N$
    $f_1(j) = D(1, j)$
Recursion:
  for $2 \leq i \leq L$
    for $1 \leq j \leq N$
      $t_{min} = min_{\{1 \leq t \leq N\}} \{F_{(t-1,t)(i,j)} + f_{(i-1)}(t)\}$, $p_j \notin Path(E(t-1, t_{min}))$
      $f_i(j) = F_{(t-1,t_{min})(i,j)} + f_{i-1}(t_{min})$
      $Q_i(j) = E(i-1, t_{min})$
Termination:
  $t_{min} = min_{\{1 \leq j \leq N\}} \{f_L(j)\}$
  $Y = Path(E(L, t_{min}))$

4 Experiments

The proposed generalized beam angle statistics and matching algorithm are tested with the MPEG-7 Core Experiments Shape-1 Part-B data set, which consists of 70 classes of shape images. In the experiments, our aim is to detect template shapes in noisy edge detected images.

An object shape in each class is used as a template for the representative of that class of shapes. For this purpose, the boundary of each template shape is extracted and represented by GBAS feature vector.

In order to construct the noisy edge images, Gaussian noise having zero mean and different values of variance (0.8, 1.4) is added to the shape images in the first step. The Canny edge detection algorithm is, then applied on these noisy images. Additionally, random noise is added to 50% of the number of edge pixels in the edge detected images. As a result, two types of noisy edge images are obtained for each template shape (see Figure 5). For each pixel of the edge images, GBAS feature vector is computed using all other edge pixels in the edge image.

In the matching process, template shapes boundary pixels are matched with the edge pixels of images. The detection of template shape in a given image is achieved by using the proposed matching algorithm. The examples from the experiments are presented in Figure 5.

5 Conclusion

The GBAS shape descriptor with the proposed matching algorithm can successfully extract a shape from an edge-detected image, provided that the noise in the image does not exceed a certain value. The amount and character of allowable noise depend on the size and the curvature of the template shape. Experiments are performed on the MPEG-7 Core Experiments Shape-1 Part B data set. Gaussian noise with various variances is added to the images.

It is observed that up to variance 1.4 and 50% of additive noise give satisfactory results in localizing the boundary shape in the edge detected image.

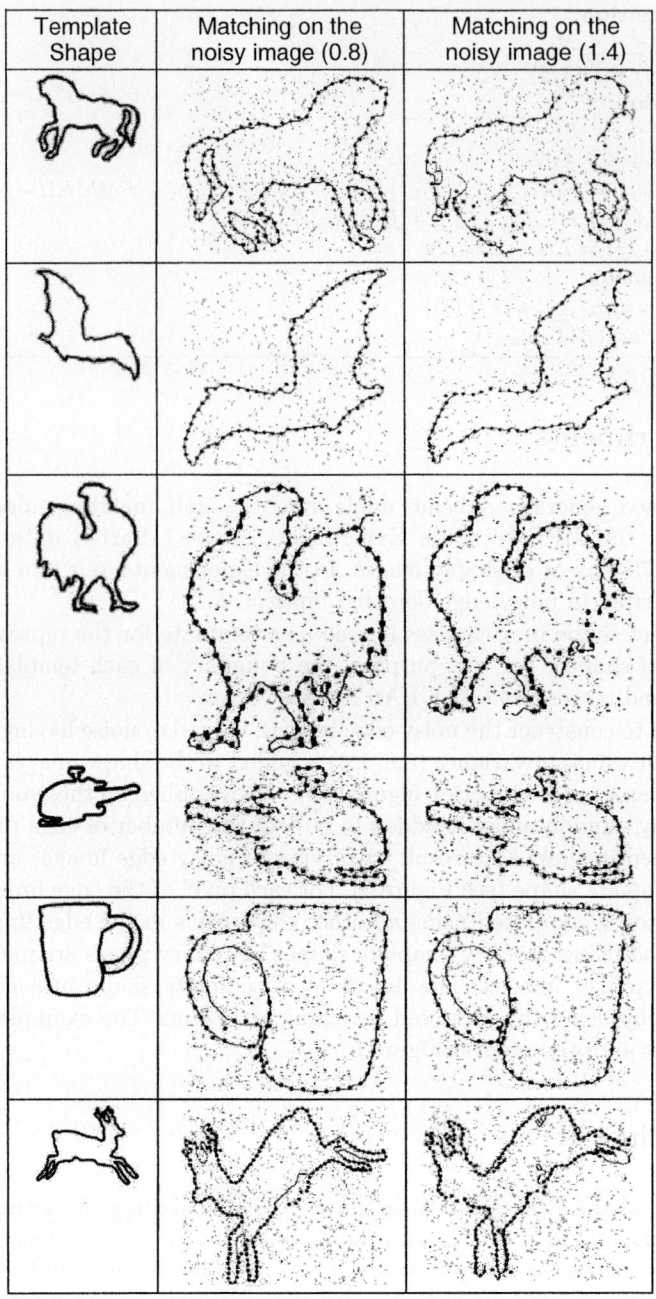

Fig. 5. Experimental results. Leftmost column shows template shapes. Other columns show the results of experiments performed. In these images, highlighted points indicate the matching points

The proposed matching algorithm yields very satisfactory results provided that the normalization factor α is adjusted carefully. The experiments indicate that the matching algorithm is sensitive to the shape symmetry and size. The dynamic programming algorithm allows half of the symmetric shape twice, leaving the other half untouched. Therefore, the matching algorithm extracts only half of the shape for fully symmetric objects. Also, the matching algorithm is not size invariant, which can only match the exact shape in the edge-detected image.

The weaknesses mentioned above will be attacked by improving the matching algorithm which is the subject of future studies.

References

1. Jain, A.K., Zhong, Y., Lakshmanan, S.: Object matching using deformable templates. IEEE Trans. On Pattern Analysis and Machine Intelligence **18** (1996) 267–278
2. Ratan, A.L., Grimson, W.E.L., Wells, W.M.: Object detection and localization by dynamic template warping. In: CVPR'98, Santa Barbara, CA. (1998) 634–640
3. Arıca, N., Yarman-Vural, F.: BAS: A perceptual shape descriptor based on the beam angle statistics. Pattern Recognition Letters **24** (2003) 1627–1639
4. Loncaric, S.: A survey of shape analysis techniques. Pattern Recognition **31** (1998) 983–1001
5. Veltkamp, R.C., Hagedoorn, M.: State of the art in shape matching. Principals of Visual Information Retrieval. Springer-Verlag (2001) 87–119

3D Cognitive Map Construction by Active Stereo Vision in a Virtual World

Ilkay Ulusoy, Ugur Halici, and Kemal Leblebicioglu

Department of Electrical and Electronics Engineering
Middle East Technical University, Ankara, Turkey
{ilkay,halici,kleb}@metu.edu.tr

Abstract. In this study, a multi-scale phase based disparity algorithm is developed. This algorithm is then applied in a simulated world. In this world there is a virtual robot which has a stereo camera system simulated with the properties similar to human eyes and there are 3D virtual objects having predefined simple shapes. The virtual robot explores its environment intelligently based on some heuristics. Only stereo images rendered from the virtual world are supplied to the robot. The robot extracts depth information from the stereo images and when an object is seen, it investigates the object in detail and classifies the object from the estimated shapes of the object parts.

1 Introduction

Navigation cannot be achieved unless distance information is obtained. In many robotics applications depth is usually extracted by cameras. For depth extraction, at least a stereo camera system is necessary. In a standard setting of stereo imaging used on a robot, two cameras are bound together with a certain displacement. Vision, especially stereo vision, provides different kinds of information altogether. Information related to obstacle detection, object recognition, 3D reconstruction, 3D map construction can also be extracted from the images besides depth information. There is evidence that higher vertebrates do learn the spatial layout of their environments enabling them to generate and follow more efficient paths to distant targets [10]. This requires the embedding of all known places and of their spatial relations into a common frame of reference. This goal independent memory is called cognitive map and stored in the hippocampal area of the brain. Based on neurophysiological investigations on rat hippocampus, many robotics researchers look for mapping models that can be implemented on an autonomous mobile robot [5].

In this study we develop a multi-scale phase based disparity algorithm for the purpose of depth estimation. We apply our stereo vision algorithm in a simulated world. The main goal is to construct a 3D map of the environment using the stereo images only. We also achieved a side goal which is to recognize 3D objects seen in this environment. The schema of the complete system is given in Figure 1. Our system is composed of two main modules: 1) Simulation module (SM) where the virtual environment exists, 2) Processor module (PM) where all kinds of control activities are achieved. Also, processor module is composed of two sub modules: a) Map formation and object recognition sub-module (MFOR), b) Navigation and camera controller sub-module (NACC). SM is a computer simulation of a very simple 3D environment. In this environment there are 3D virtual objects and a virtual robot (agent) that has a stereo imaging system modeled with the properties of human eye. The system works as follows: First, 2D stereo images are rendered from SM and passed to PM. Then, using our multi-scale phase based disparity algorithm, depth map is extracted for the current view and environmental map is updated by MFOR sub-module. From the environmental map formed up to date, navigation destination is decided and cameras are controlled by the NACC sub-module based on the exploration strategy. Finally, new camera locations and parameters are passed to the SM. All these steps are recursively processed until the environment is fully explored.

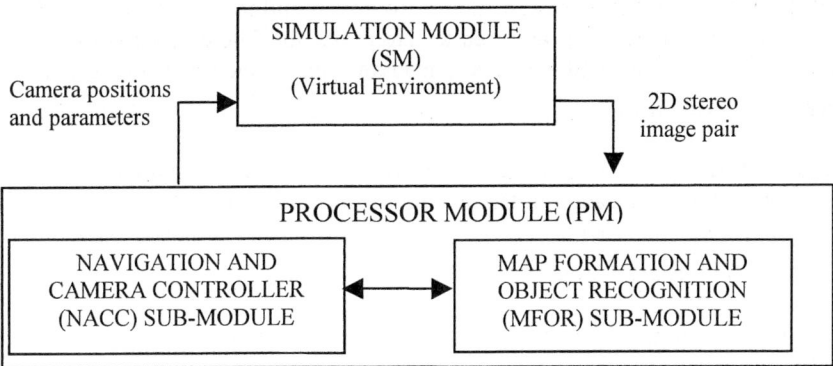

Fig. 1. Modules of the whole system

The disparity algorithm and stereo vision system will be explained in Section 2 in detail. Virtual world details and cognitive map formation are explained in Section 3. In Section 4 object recognition algorithm is introduced. Results are provided after algorithms have been explained. In the last section a conclusion is given.

2 Stereo Vision System

In our multi-scale phase based disparity algorithm, first of all, features which are oriented edges at various scales are extracted by using steerable filters. Then, corresponding pairs are matched based on multi-scale phase similarity. Finally, 3D world-centric location of each feature point is computed using the camera parameters.

To be successful for stereo applications, local features must be robust to typical image deformations such as noise, rotation, scale and brightness changes. Recently, Carneiro and Jepson build on their previous work in which it was shown that the phase information provided by steerable filters is often locally stable with respect to noise and brightness changes, and they showed that it is also possible to achieve stability under rotation by selecting steerable filters [1].

Feature points used in our study are extracted by using steerable filters as been done in [2]. The analytic filter $h(\mathbf{x})$, where $\mathbf{x} = (x,y)$ is the pixel location in the image I, to be used as the template filter is constructed from the filters provided in [3] as follows:

$$h(\mathbf{x}) = g(\mathbf{x}) + jq(\mathbf{x})$$

$$g(x,y) = \left(0.934 - 3.738x^2 + 1.246x^4\right) e^{-(x^2+y^2)} \quad (1)$$

$$q(x,y) = \left(2.858x - 2.982x^3 + 0.3975x^5\right) e^{-(x^2+y^2)}$$

For the multi-scale framework used in this study, $g(\mathbf{x})$ is chosen to be 4th derivative of a Gaussian, which is a steerable filter and $q(\mathbf{x})$ is chosen to be a steerable approximation to the Hilbert Transform of $g(\mathbf{x})$.

First of all, the stereo images are filtered with basis filters at three different scales where the width of the narrowest filter is six pixels and the largest filter is 18 pixels. Then, these filter responses are used to interpolate the filtered images of orientation between 0° to 180° with 10° degrees of interval. Finally, the orientation estimation for each pixel location $\tilde{\theta}(\mathbf{x}) = \arg\max_{\theta}\left\{\sum_{n=1}^{S} r_{n,\theta}(\mathbf{x})\right\}$ is done where $r_{n,\theta}(\mathbf{x})$ is the response of steerable filtering for scale n and orientation θ and S is the total number of scales. Then, at each pixel location, filters having that pixel's estimated orientation are used and that pixel is selected as a feature point if the sum of response magnitudes over different scales is greater than a threshold, i.e. $i = \left\{i \Big| \left|\sum_{n=1}^{S} r_{n,\tilde{\theta}}(\mathbf{x}_i)\right| > r_{thr}\right\}$. The main attributes used in this study for the corresponding pair matching of feature points are multi-scale phase and amplitude. We calculate phase and amplitude at each feature point as follows:

$$\phi_i = \arctan\left[\frac{real(r_{n,\theta}(\mathbf{x}_i))}{imag(r_{n,\theta}(\mathbf{x}_i))}\right] \quad (2)$$

$$r_i = |r_{n,\theta}(\mathbf{x}_i)| = \sqrt{real(r_{n,\theta}(\mathbf{x}_i))^2 + imag(r_{n,\theta}(\mathbf{x}_i))^2} \quad (3)$$

Here, the quantities ϕ_i and r_i are estimated phase and magnitude at feature point i, $real(r_{n,\theta}(\mathbf{x}_i))$ and $imag(r_{n,\theta}(\mathbf{x}_i))$ are real and imaginary parts of the filtered image respectively. We use the weighted phase measurements for filters of different width, i.e. different scales, to locate correspondences. Let $\mathbf{\Phi}_i = [\phi_1 \; \phi_2 \; \phi_3]^T$ be a vector of phase estimates obtained using three filters. For each feature point at the left image, we search over a window for feature points of similar phase vector in the right image. We measure the similarity of phase vectors with $\hat{j} = \arg\max_{j}\left\{\mathbf{\Phi}_i^T \mathbf{\Phi}_j C_{ij}\right\}$.

Weighting vector C_{ij} is constructed by using the method described in [12]. Each element $c_{ij}^n = \min\left(\frac{|r_{n,\theta}(\mathbf{x}_i)|}{|r_{n,\theta}(\mathbf{x}_j)|}, \frac{|r_{n,\theta}(\mathbf{x}_j)|}{|r_{n,\theta}(\mathbf{x}_i)|}\right)$ shows the similarity in the magnitudes of feature points i and j at scale n. The matching algorithm is cross checked for left to right correspondences and right to left correspondences. In this way, we discard occluded feature points and unsafe matches. The success of this algorithm has been tested on real stereo pairs and found to be around % 95 [15].

In this study, we work on stereo image pairs where parallel cameras are used. This means that the disparity is the horizontal pixel distance between corresponding feature point locations, i.e. $\delta = x_i - x_j$. This agent centered location information is converted to world centered location information by $z_W = \mathbf{R}z_C$ where R is the rotation and translation matrix which converts the camera coordinates $z_C = (x_c, y_c, z_c)$ to world coordinates $z_W = (x_w, y_w, z_w)$.

3 Virtual World

Real robotic applications are very complicated because besides the problems of finding how the robot should behave to complete the task at hand, the problems faced while controlling the robot's internal parameters bring high computational load. Thus, first working in a simulated environment in order to find the exploration strategy to be followed by the robot and then applying this on a real robot is preferable. In Terzopoulos and Rabie [13] biologically inspired active vision system is implemented on artificial fishes in a virtual environment. A simulation of a corridor world is constructed in [7]. In [8] 3D environment and a humanoid robot which has stereo vision system are simulated as a computer program. In this study, we also applied our stereo vision algorithm in a virtual world on an agent which has stereo cameras modeled based on human eye properties. There are 3D objects in this world and these can be placed anywhere on the ground and the agent can move anywhere around them. The cameras are positioned at a height above the ground level with a predefined distance between each other. Given a target location, both eyes look at the same target point with similar parameters such as focal length.

The simulation software is developed using C++ programming language and OpenGL graphics library on the Microsoft Windows operating system [14]. As the user interface of the software is depicted in Figure 2, it is composed of four panes showing the scene from different view points. The two panes above are views from the left camera (eye) and the right camera respectively. Only these stereo images are supplied to the agent. The bottom panes render the scene from the top viewpoint and front viewpoint. The software is designed such that there is a plug-in mechanism to load a camera controller by using dynamic-link libraries (DLL). Rendering stereo images is done via this plug-in automatically. This DLL also controls the agent through the virtual world in an intelligent way in order to extract environmental cognitive map and recognize objects. Specifying geometric shapes, i.e. 3D objects in the virtual world, is done via loading the shape and texture data from a disk file. The assumptions about the virtual world are as follows: 1. 3D objects in the virtual world are made up of two parts and each has one of the following basic shapes: {sphere, ellipsoid, cylinder, cone}. 2. The objects constructed from these basic shapes can be located anywhere in the world. 3. The objects are clearly separable. 4. The agent is aware of its initial position in the world and initial orientation with respect to global north. 5. The agent is aware of its internal and external camera parameters. 6. The cameras can see up to a predefined distance. 8. There is no error in agent movement, i.e. agent goes to its target with success.

4 Map Construction and Object Recognition

4.1 Exploration and Map Construction

The task of generating robot motion in the pursuit of building a map is commonly referred to as robotic exploration. While optimal robot motion is relatively well-understood in fully modeled environments, exploring robots have to cope with partial and incomplete models. Hence, any viable exploration strategy has to be able to accommodate contingencies and surprises that might arise during map acquisition. For this reason, exploration is a challenging planning problem, which is often solved sub-optimally via simple heuristics. In this study, our heuristic exploration strategy is based on stereo vision. The agent is supplied only the stereo images rendered from the virtual world. The agent extracts depth and builds 3D grid based map while it explores its environment. If the agent sees something new then it goes around and gets 3D point claud of the object. The details of map construction can be found in [16,17]. In the end the grid points which have high numbers, i.e. high belief of being full, are selected to be full. As an example, 3D cognitive map constructed for the environment given in Fig. 2 is shown in Figure 3.

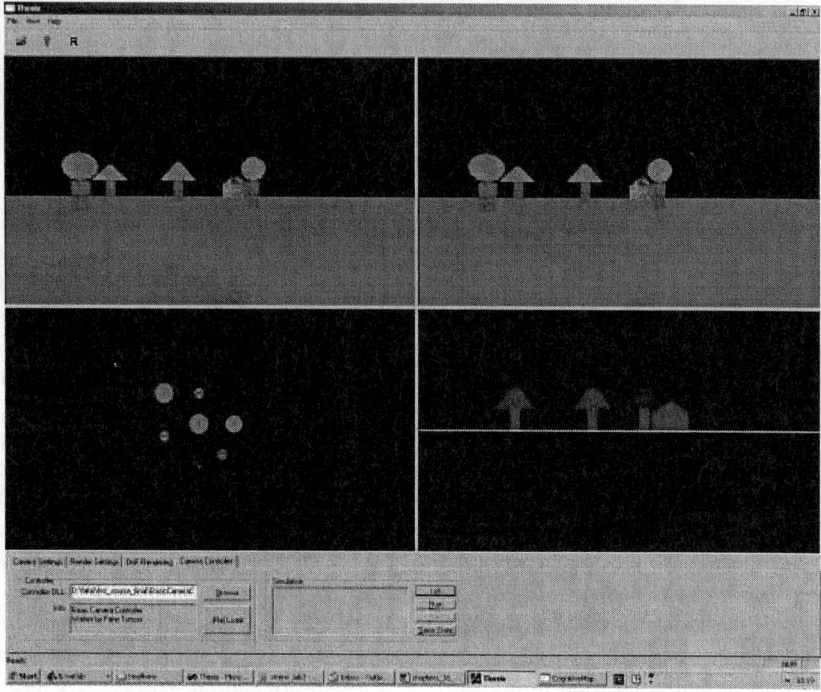

Fig. 2. A screen shot from the virtual environment

4.2 Active Vision and Object Recognition

There are different approaches for object recognition and classification. A popular framework is based on representing 2D object views as points in a high dimensional feature space and then performing some partitioning of the space into regions corresponding to the different classes [9]. However these methods fail for different postures of the same object. Other approaches attempt to describe all object views belonging to the same class using a collection of some basic building blocks and their configuration. For example in [6] generalized shapes such as cylinders are used as building blocks. Other part based schemes use 2D local image features such as local image patches, corners, simple line or edge configurations or small texture patches as the underlying building blocks. Although detection of such building blocks might be simple, combination of these in order to make a decision is hard, especially when occlusion of some parts occurs [18].

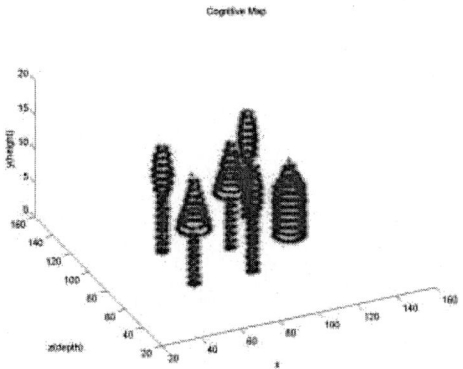

Fig. 3. 3D cognitive map

In this study, it is better to recognize the objects based on their 3D structure since we already obtain a point cloud for the location and shape of the objects while constructing the 3D map of the environment. These point claud consists of 3D world coordinates. While filling the cognitive map, the RGB color information is also saved for each grid. This is done by following these steps: First RGB value for each feature point is calculated. This is done by averaging the RGB values of the pixels falling into a window centered at the feature point location in the right image. Then RGB value for each grid is computed. This is done by computing averages of RGB values of feature points falling on the same grid of the map. Finally the RGB averages for each grid are calculated through time. This means that each time the cognitive map is updated, the color average stored at each grid is also updated since the content of the cognitive map changes. As a result, after completing a full turn around the object, the 3D location information in terms of grid locations and RGB color information for each grid are obtained.

The following steps are followed in order to recognize an object: First, the RGB color information is converted to HSV. Second, assuming that the top and body parts of the objects have different color content, the 3D object is segmented into two parts.

In doing this, the following basic ideas are used: 1. Color content of all the grids belonging to a segment of the object should be similar. 2. Grids containing similar color information should be connected. In this study, only the hue channel is found to be enough for segmentation and the neighboring grid points which have similar Hue values are clustered together. In the top image of Figure 4 hue value for an apple tree is given. In the bottom images of the same figure the segmented object parts are seen. In the third step of object classification algorithm, the shapes of the segmented parts are estimated by fitting the quadratic surface equation of three parameters. This is done as follows: First, triples (x,y,z) belonging to the part for which a shape will be estimated are used in the general quadratic equation in three variables (4) [9]. In this study, we assume that the parameter A in (4) is non-zero, since the shapes in our environment is either sphere, cylinder or cone. Reorganizing (4) we obtain (5) and the nine unknown equation parameters P={B',C',D',E',F',G',H',K',L'} are solved.

$$Ax^2 + By^2 + Cz^2 + 2Dxy + 2Exz + 2Fyz + 2Gx + 2Hy + 2Kz + L = 0 \qquad (4)$$

$$B'y^2 + C'z^2 + 2D'xy + 2E'xz + 2F'yz + 2G'x + 2H'y + 2K'z + L' = -x^2 \qquad (5)$$

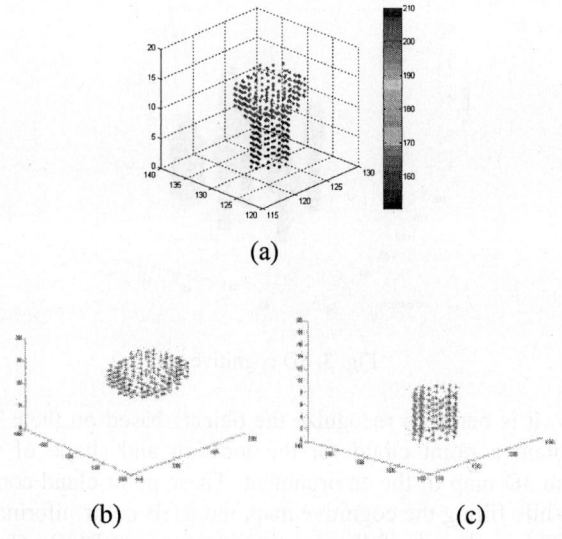

Fig. 4. (a) Location and color information (hue channel) stored in each grid for an apple tree in the cognitive map, (b) The top, (c) The body

In order to comment on the shape, first of all an S matrix and Q vector (6) are formed from the parameters [4]. This S matrix is a non-zero real symmetric matrix [11] and has real characteristic values, i.e. real eigenvalues $\lambda_1, \lambda_2, \lambda_3$, where at least one of them is different than zero. Since we deal with 3 basic shapes of sphere, cone and cylinder, we can say that all three are different than zero. Thus, there exists an orthogonal matrix R such that (7) holds. Considering the change of coordinates $\bar{x} = R^T x$ where $x = (x, y, z)$, equation becomes as in (8) where $\bar{G}', \bar{H}', \bar{K}'$ are calculated as in (9). Here, u_1, u_2, u_3 are the eigenvectors of S. Knowing that all three of the eigenvalues are non-zero, we can translate $\bar{x}$ system to $\tilde{x}$ system by $\tilde{x} = \bar{x} + \frac{\overline{G'}}{\lambda_1}$, $\tilde{y} = \bar{y} + \frac{\overline{H'}}{\lambda_2}$, $\tilde{z} = \bar{z} + \frac{\overline{K'}}{\lambda_3}$. Then the equation can be rewritten as in (10) where k is calculated as in (11).

$$S = \begin{bmatrix} 1 & D' & E' \\ D' & B' & F' \\ E' & F' & C' \end{bmatrix} \quad Q = \begin{bmatrix} G' \\ H' \\ K' \end{bmatrix} \tag{6}$$

$$R^T S R = \begin{bmatrix} \lambda_1 & 0 & 0 \\ 0 & \lambda_2 & 0 \\ 0 & 0 & \lambda_3 \end{bmatrix} \tag{7}$$

$$\lambda_1 \bar{x}^2 + \lambda_2 \bar{y}^2 + \lambda_3 \bar{z}^2 + 2\overline{G}'\bar{x} + 2\overline{H}'\bar{y} + 2\overline{K}'\bar{z} + L' = 0 \tag{8}$$

$$\overline{G}' = Q^T \mathbf{u}_1, \quad \overline{H}' = Q^T \mathbf{u}_2, \quad \overline{K}' = Q^T \mathbf{u}_3 \tag{9}$$

$$\lambda_1 \tilde{x}^2 + \lambda_2 \tilde{y}^2 + \lambda_3 \tilde{z}^2 = k \tag{10}$$

$$k = \frac{\overline{G}'^2}{\lambda_1} + \frac{\overline{H}'^2}{\lambda_2} + \frac{\overline{K}'^2}{\lambda_3} - L' \tag{11}$$

In order to comment about the shape of the object part, (10) can be transformed into (12) using the relations $a = \sqrt{\frac{k}{\lambda_1}}$, $b = \sqrt{\frac{k}{\lambda_2}}$, $c = \sqrt{\frac{k}{\lambda_3}}$ where a, b, c are nonzero.

$$\frac{x^2}{a^2} + \frac{y^2}{b^2} + \frac{z^2}{c^2} = 1 \tag{12}$$

If the shape is a sphere (for example the top of an apple tree) then these numbers are equal or very close to each other, i.e. a=b=c, and the average could give us the radius of the sphere. If the shape is a cylinder (for example the body of all tree types) then two of these numbers are equal or similar and the other one is very different and bigger than the other two. The similar ones give the radius of the cylinder. If the shape is a cone (for example the roof of a cottage) then one of these numbers is imaginary (i.e. square of the number is less than zero) and the other two are greater than zero.

After estimating shape for each part of an object, the object is recognized according to the following rules:

1. If there is a sphere on a small radius cylinder, this is an apple tree.
2. If there is a cone on a small radius cylinder, this is a pine tree.
3. If there is a cone on a big cylinder, this is a cottage.

After going around the environment and recognizing all the objects as explained above, we finally have the location information for all of the objects and label for each of them. In Figure 5 top view of the 3D map constructed for the virtual environment in Figure 2 is shown. Also, labels estimated for the objects are printed near the objects.

5 Conclusion

We have presented a complete vision system which extracts features, finds disparities and finally constructs 3D cognitive maps by exploring around objects and recognizing objects from their shapes. In our stereo correspondence method we used multi scale steerable filters. Thus, instead of calculating disparities using oriented filters and pooling the results over different orientations, a single orientation for each feature is obtained prior to disparity computation. Also, by using multi-scale filtering highly informative feature points are extracted even they are at different scales. As a result, although feature points extracted from image pairs are sparse, since they are the points of high contrast edges that define the bounding contours of objects, they still prove to be informative.

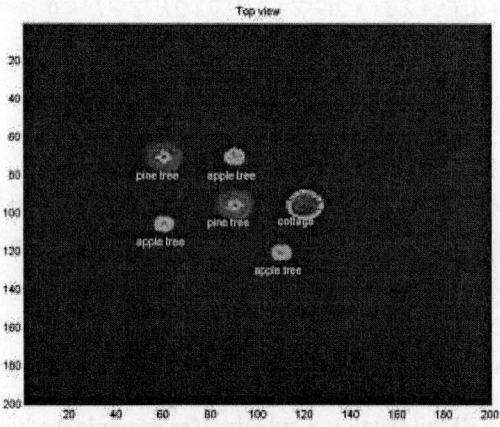

Fig. 5. 2D occupancy map with labeled objects

Correspondences between feature points are located using multi-scale phase information. Phase is sensitive to spatial differences, and hence it provides fine image detail which is helpful in discriminating neighboring image regions. Phase is also robust to small scale differences. Unfortunately, there are image locations where phase is singular and cannot be reliably used. In this study, by performing phase comparisons at multiple scales we overcome these difficulties. Also, the confidence weighting is used to augment phase information with information concerning the magnitude of the steerable filtered image to improve the correspondence method.

The complexity of our disparity algorithm is $O(N^2 SRn^2)$ where n is assumed to be the width of the widest filter, S is the total number of scales used and N is the image is assumed to be square. Using multi scale steerable filters takes time but matching and depth extraction is real time. However, with the recent development in hardware and software and with some parallel processing we are hoping to obtain our features in real time in the very near future.

Our stereo vision system is applied in a simulated world to recognize 3D object seen in the environment. The agent explores its environment based on some heuristics and simultaneously builds a 3D map. When an object is seen, the agent turns around it and obtains 3D locations of feature points extracted from the same object from different view angles. Then object is segmented into parts and quadratic surface equation of three parameters is fitted to each part in order to get the shape of the part. Finally, the object is recognized from the shapes and mutual configuration of its parts.

In very near future, our exploration strategy will be expanded and our complete system will be applied on real robots. In this case, camera calibration, robot control and localization will be the additional problems. Also, we only used world-centric coordinate system. However, human can prefer ego-centric or world-centric coordinate system with respect to the task performed. Thus, another future study is to use ego-centric and world-centric coordinates interchangeably.

References

1. Carneiro, G., Jepson, A.D.: Multi-scale phase-based local features. In: CVPR, Madison, WI, USA. (2003) 736–743
2. Erol, A.: Automatic fingerprint recognition. PhD. Thesis, Middle East Technical University, Electrical and Electronics Department, Ankara, Turkey (2001)
3. Freeman, W.T.: The design and use of steerable filters. IEEE Trans. Pattern Analysis and Machine Intelligence **13**(9) (1991)
4. Karakaş, H.I.: Analytic Geometry
5. Li, G., Svensson, B.: Navigation with a focus directed mapping network. Autonomous Robots **7** (1999) 9–30
6. Marr, D.: Vision. W. H. Freeman, San Francisco (1982)
7. Matsumoto, Y., Inaba, M., Inoue, H.: Visual navigation using view-sequenced route representation. In: Proc. IEEE Int'l Conf. Robotics and Automation 1. (1996) 83–88
8. Okada, K., Kino, Y., Kanehino, F., Kuniyoshi, Y., Inaba, M., Inoue, H.: Rapid development system for humanoid vision-based behaviours with real-virtual common interface. In: Proceedings of the International Conference on Intelligent Robotics and Systems, Laussanne, Switzerland. (2002)
9. Poggio, T., Sung, K.: Finding human faces with a Gaussian mixture distribution base face model. Computer Analysis of Image and Patterns (1995) 432–439
10. Prescott, T.J.: Spatial representation for navigation in animats. Adaptive Behaviour **4**(2) (1996) 85–123
11. Rogers, D.F., Adams, J.A.: Mathematical elements for computer graphics. 2nd edition. McGraw-Hill International Editions (1990)
12. Sanger, T. D.: Stereo disparity computation using Gabor filters. Biol. Cybern., **59** (1988) 405–418
13. Terzopoulos, D., Rabie, T.F.: Animat vision: Active vision in artificial animals. Journal of Computer Vision Research (1997) 2–19
14. Tunçer, F.: Image Synthesis for depth estimation using stereo and focus analysis. M.Sc. Thesis, Department of Electrical and Electronics Engineering, Middle East Technical University, Ankara, Turkey (2002)
15. Ulusoy, I., Hancock, E.R., Halici, U.: Disparity using multi-scale phase. In: SSPR. (2002)
16. Ulusoy, I.: Active stereo vision for object recognition and cognitive map formation in a virtual world. CVPR (2003)
17. Ulusoy, I.: Active stereo vision: Depth perception for navigation, environmental map formation and object recognition. Ph.D. Thesis, Middle East Technical University, Ankara, Turkey (2003)
18. Weber, M, Welling, M., Perona P.: Towards automatic discovery of object categories. In: CVPR 2 101–108

3D Real Object Recognition on the Basis of Moment Invariants and Neural Networks

Muharrem Mercimek and Kayhan Gulez

Yildiz Technical University,
Electrical-Electronics Faculty
Electrical Engineering Department
34349 Besiktas, Istanbul, Turkey
mercimek@yildiz.edu.tr, gulez@yildiz.edu.tr

Abstract: In this study, recognition system of the completely visible 3D solid objects of the real life is presented. The synthesis of analyzing two-dimensional images that are taken from different angle of views of the objects is the main process that leads us to achieve our objective. The selection of "Good" features those satisfying two requirements (small intraclass invariance, large interclass separation) is a crucial step. A flexible recognition system that can compute the good features for a high classification is investigated. For object recognition regardless of its orientation, size and position feature vectors are computed with the assistance of nonlinear moment invariant functions. After an efficient feature extraction, the main focus of this study, recognition performance of artificial classifiers in conjunction with moment–based feature sets, is introduced.

1 Introduction

Watanabe defines a pattern "as opposite of chaos; it is an entity, vaguely defined, that could be given a name." For example a pattern could be a fingerprint image, a handwritten cursive word, a human face, or a speech signal [1,2].

Pattern recognition is an essential part of any high-level image analysis systems. Most of these systems share a general structure of four building blocks [3]. Image acquisition, preprocessing of the images, feature extraction, classification.

The structure of recognition problem dictates the choice of sensor(s), preprocessing technique, representing scheme and decision-making model. It is generally agreed; well-defined and sufficiently constrained recognition problem will lead to a compact pattern representation and a simple decision–making strategy.

One of the widely used shape descriptors is a set of moment invariants derived by Hu [4]. These geometrical moment invariants have been then extended to larger sets by Wong and Siu [5], and other forms [6,7]. An image-processing algorithm developed in [8] for discrimination between images of three fish species in use of freshwater fish farm. Zernike velocity moments were developed in [9] to describe an object using not only its shape, but also its motion throughout an image sequence.

Hu's moment invariants and extended Zernike moments were used as feature extractors in [10]. NN based classifiers were compared with conventional classifiers on hand-written English character recognition problem. Complex-log conformal mapping combined with a distributed associative memory was used to create a system, recognizing objects regardless of changes in rotation or scale in [11]. Object simulations were created using computer. These were represented with geometrical moment feature vectors and classified with neural networks in [12].

The main focuses of this study are on the feature extraction and classifications and recognize the completely visible 3D solid objects of the real life. Using the scenes computer vision system, which determines which object exists in the captured image, is established. Considering, sensor can be located in different distances and angles according to objects; a vision system insensitive to changes in point of view is investigated. The organization of paper is as follows; Section 2 discusses moment invariant features. In Section 3, neural classifier basis and utilized structures are described. Section 4 reports experimental results. Section 5 gives conclusions and discussions of our study.

2 Moment Invariants

The ultimate aim in numerous pattern recognition applications is to extract the important features from the image data, such that a reasonable description, interpretation, or understanding of the scene can be achieved.

The idea of using moments in shape recognition gained prominence when Hu [4] derived a set of invariants using the algebraic invariants. Image or shape feature invariants remain unchanged if that image or shape undergoes any combination of the following changes; change of size, change of position, change of orientation.

Two-dimensional moments of a digitally sampled MxM image that have a gray function $f(x, y)$ $(x, y = 0,..M-1)$ is given as,

$$m_{pq} = \sum_{x=0}^{x=M-1} \sum_{y=0}^{y=M-1} (x)^p . (y)^q f(x,y) \quad p,q = ,0, 1, 2, 3, \cdot, \cdot. \qquad (1)$$

The moments of $f(x,y)$ translated by an amount (a,b), are defined as,

$$\mu_{pq} = \sum_x \sum_y (x+a)^p . (y+b)^q f(x,y) \qquad (2)$$

Thus the central moments m'_{pq} or μ_{pq} can be computed from the Eq. (2) substituting $a = -\bar{x}$ and $b = -\bar{y}$ as;

$$\bar{x} = \frac{m_{10}}{m_{00}} \text{ and } \bar{y} = \frac{m_{01}}{m_{00}}$$

$$\mu_{pq} = \sum_x \sum_y (x-\bar{x})^p . (y-\bar{y})^q f(x,y) \qquad (3)$$

The central moments when a scaling normalization is applied change as,

$$\eta_{pq} = \frac{\mu_{pq}}{\mu^\gamma{}_{00}}, \quad \gamma = \frac{p+q}{2}+1 \qquad (4)$$

In special case Hu [4] defines seven values computed from central moments through order three, that are invariant to object scale, position, and orientation. In terms of the central moments, the seven moments are given as,

$$\begin{aligned}
M_1 &= (\eta_{20} + \eta_{02}) \\
M_2 &= (\eta_{20} - \eta_{02})^2 + 4\eta_{11}^2 \\
M_3 &= (\eta_{30} - 3\eta_{12})^2 + (3\eta_{21} - \eta_{03})^2 \\
M_4 &= (\eta_{30} + \eta_{12})^2 + (\eta_{21} + \eta_{03})^2 \\
M_5 &= (\eta_{30} - 3\eta_{12})(\eta_{30} + \eta_{12})\left[(\eta_{30} + \eta_{12})^2 - 3(\eta_{21} + \eta_{03})^2\right] + \\
&\quad (3\eta_{21} - \eta_{03})(\eta_{21} + \eta_{03})\left[3(\eta_{30} + \eta_{12})^2 - (\eta_{21} + \eta_{03})^2\right] \\
M_6 &= (\eta_{20} - \eta_{02})\left[(\eta_{30} + \eta_{12})^2 - (\eta_{21} + \eta_{03})^2\right] + \\
&\quad 4\eta_{11}(\eta_{30} + \eta_{12})(\eta_{21} + \eta_{03}) \\
M_7 &= (3\eta_{21} - \eta_{03})(\eta_{30} + \eta_{12})\left[(\eta_{30} + \eta_{12})^2 - 3(\eta_{21} - \eta_{03})^2\right] - \\
&\quad (\eta_{30} + 3\eta_{12})(\eta_{21} + \eta_{03})\left[3(\eta_{30} + \eta_{12})^2 - (\eta_{21} + \eta_{03})^2\right]
\end{aligned} \qquad (5)$$

3 Neural Classifiers

In this study we use some neural network topologies such as Multilayer Perceptron (MLP), Radial Basis Function Network (RBF), Generalized Regression Neural Network (GRNN), Gaining Algorithm Learning Network (GAL). General descriptions about these structures will be given in experimental study section.

An artificial neural network is a network of simple processing units that are interconnected through weighted connections. There are number of advantages using neural network-type classifiers for pattern recognition,

- They can learn i.e., given a sufficiently large labeled training set, the parameters can be computed to optimize a given error criterion.
- There is no need for strong assumptions about the statistical distributions of the input features.
- They can generate any kind of nonlinear function of the input.
- Artificial neural networks are highly parallel and regular structures that make them especially amenable to high performance parallel architectures and hardware implementation [13].

Choice of the nonlinear functions, in order to obtain network classifiers that have appropriate decision boundaries, is a crucial step. Guided by analysis of networks and their function we can be informed choices of the scaling of inputs and outputs, types of the activation functions [14].

4 Experimental Study

The major building blocks of the pattern recognition system that we use in this paper were briefly given in moment invariants section. In this section these blocks will be extracted using the basis of our 3D object recognition problem.

4.1 Image Acquisition

An image display/recording system is a conceptually a scanning system. As a sensor, a camera that can transfer taken digital images via USB (Universal Serial Bus) is used in this paper. Three 3D objects used in this study are given in Figure 1. The information about the objects' original colors in RGB (Red-Green-Blue) norm is not used.

Fig. 1. Used 3D objects

4.2 Representation of 3D Objects Using 2D Images

Synthesis of 2D images is used practically in such applications, while transferring 3D objects of real life to computer, creating spatial object simulations.

Normally, the objects can be rotated in three different directions. In this study objects are rotated along z-axis only and the projection images on the yz plane are taken (Figure 2). Camera is stated along x-axis. With the 5° rotations from 0° to 360° around the z-axis 72 images for every object, totally 216 images are obtained.

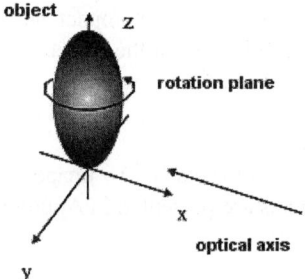

Fig. 2. Imaging system

4.3 Preprocessing of the Images

The brief descriptions about image preprocessing steps and the images changed after these steps are given as follows (Figure 3),

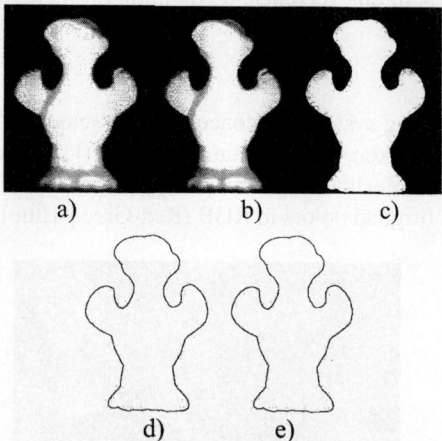

Fig. 3. The image preprocessing steps

a) The images are minimized to 300x340 pixel dimensions in order to ease computational burden.
b) The minimized images in the RGB norm are converted to the gray level coded images.
c) Secondly, thresholding process is applied and the gray level of the pixels between 0-255 changed to either 0 or 255. Threshold value is determined as the gray level of 90. The gray levels under 90 are changed to gray level of 0, and the gray levels over 90 are changed to 255. This process is necessary for the next step, edge detection.
d) The edge of an object is one of the most meaningful parts used for image recognition. In order to obtain compact feature vectors for every image, the pixels of the edge images of the target objects are used.
e) The last step is the converting gray level coded images to binary images, in order to use pixels with values of 1 and 0.

All these processes are applied to totally 216 images of three objects. A number of the edges images of three objects are presented in Appendix A.

4.4 Feature Vector Extraction

In this paper, the idea of representing the images with a set of moment invariant functions is applied. In order to normalize the different power of coefficients in Eq.5, one more enhancement is done using the distance, d between objects and camera. Finally coefficients of moment invariant functions according to [13] are,

$$M_1' = (\mu_{20} + \mu_{02})^{1/2} d = r.d$$
$$M_2' = M_2 / r^4$$
$$M_3' = M_3 / r^6$$
$$M_4' = M_4 / r^6 \qquad (6)$$
$$M_5' = M_5 / r^{12}$$
$$M_6' = M_6 / r^8$$
$$M_7' = M_7 / r^{12}$$

4.5 Training and Test Data

The patterns of the $\Re^7$ input space are divided into two parts. Totally 216 images and feature vectors representing these images with 7 coefficients of moment invariant functions were obtained previously. 108 feature vectors obtained from the images of every object, taken from the angles of $(10n)^o$ (n=0,1,2,.....,35), are included into training data set. 108 feature vectors obtained from the angles of $(10n+5)^o$, are included into test data set.

4.6 Classification

These processed data are presented to neural classifiers for classification problem. A flexible recognition system that can attain the best classification is investigated in this study. Using the Matlab 6.5 software MLP, RBF, GRNN, and GAL neural classifiers are created. The multidimensional input vectors $x \in \Re^7$ are assigned to one of the classes, $\{C_1, C_2, C_3\}$. $y_1(i)$, $y_2(i)$, $y_3(i)$ outputs obtained from the classifier are presented to a classification criterion algorithm,

```
c1=0; c2=0; c3=0
if (0.9 <= y₁(i) < 1) & (0 < (y₂(i), y₃(i)) < 0.1)
c1=c1+1;
if (0.9 <= y₂(i) < 1) & (0 < (y₁(i), y₃(i)) < 0.1)
c2=c2+1;
if (0.9 <= y₃(i) < 1) & (0 < (y₁(i), y₂(i)) < 0.1)
c3=c3+1;
```

Considering the separation of the pattern in the input space, using simple classifiers (perceptron etc.) that can implement linear decision boundaries will be inadequate. MLP, which is termed a universal function approximator, is selected as one of the classifiers. A structure of MLP with an input layer consists of 7 neuron units; a hidden layer consists of 12 neuron units; an output layer consists of 3 neuron units, is used. The activation functions of the output layer neurons are selected logsig function. The activation function of the hidden layers are selected either tansig or logsig. For different types of learning algorithms based on backpropagation the network iteratively changed its parameters to bring the actual outputs closer to desired target values.

Secondly, RBF is used. A RBF is a two-layer network, which performs a local mapping; meaning only inputs near a receptive field produce activation [14]. Receptive field center on areas of the input space where input vectors lie, and serve to cluster similar input vectors. The input layer of the RBF contains radial basis function neurons, which mostly used gaussian activation functions. Using two different RBF models newrb and newrbe, for different spread values of these activation functions, network is trained

GRNN is used as one other classifier. A GRNN is composed of three layers. The second layer is the pattern layer and has one neuron for each input pattern. This layer performs the same function as the first layer neurons of RBF; its output is a measure of distance the input is from the stored patterns. For different spread values of these activation functions, network is trained.

GAL is used as the last classifier. GAL determines the class boundaries in the feature vector space by mean of minimum distance criterion. In the training phase, the distance from input vector to initial nodes is computed. If the class of the input vector is same with the class of the node that is nearest to the vector, nothing is done. If not so, this vector is added as one of the nodes that represent the network. Since there is only one training data, there exists just only one network configuration. For all configurations testing performances are presented in Appendix B.

5 Conclusions and Discussions

Neural networks provide a new suite of nonlinear algorithms for pattern recognition. Non-linear function approximation ability, making no assumptions about the statistical distributions, adapting themselves to different input data makes neural networks challenging field of study.

In this paper we mainly focused on feature extraction and classification. An appropriate subspace of dimensionality in the original space is investigated with moment invariant functions set. Optimum network parameters are found empirically and the performances of the classifiers are compared (Appendix B). In all of the experiments, the MLP neural networks performed better than the three neural networks (Table 1).

The initial assumptions about the rotation direct of the objects make the recognition problem easier. It was possible to rotate objects around three dimensions. Besides, the recognition system is working offline. In the future study an online pattern recognition system can be developed.

Table 1. Overall performances of the classifiers

Classifier	Performance
MLP	%100
RBF	%94.44
GRNN	%91.67
GAL	%90.74

References

1. Watanabe, S., Pattern Recognition: Human and Mechanical. Wiley, New York (1985)
2. Jain, A.K., Duin, R.P.W., Mao J.: Statistical Pattern Recognition: A Review. IEEE Transactions on Pattern Analysis and Machine Learning 22(1) (2000)
3. Khotanzad, A., Lu, J.-H.: Classification of Invariant Image Representations Using a Neural Network. IEEE Transactions on Acoustics, Speech and Signal Processing 38(6) (1990)
4. Hu, M.: Visual Pattern Recognition by Moment Invariants. IRE Trans. Information Theory 8 (1962) 179–187
5. Wong, W.H., Siu, W.C.: Improved Digital Filter Structure for Fast Moment Computation. In: IEE Proceedings in Vision, Image, and Signal Processing. (1999) 73–79
6. Dudani, S.A., Breeding, K.J., Mcghee, R.B.: Aircraft Identification by Moment Invariants. IEEE Trans. on Computers 26(1) (1997) 39–46
7. Liao, S.X., Pawlak, M.: On the Accuracy of Zernike Moments for Image Analysis. IEEE Transactions on Pattern Analysis and Machine Intelligence 20(12) 1998
8. Zion, B., Shklyar A., Karplus, I.: Sorting Fish by Computer Vision. Computers and Electronics in Agriculture 8 (1999) 93–104
9. Shutler, J.D., Nixon, M.S., Harris, C.J.: Zernike Velocity Moments for Description and Recognition of Moving Objects. In: BMVC. (2001) 705–714
10. Khotanzad, A., Lu, J.-H.: Classification of Invariant Image Representations Using a Neural Network. IEEE Transactions on Acoustics, Speech and Signal Processing 38(6) (1990)
11. Wechsler, H., Zimmerman, G.L.: 2D Invariant Object Recognition Using Distributed Associative Memory. IEEE Transactions on Pattern Analysis and Machine Intelligence 10(6) (1998)
12. Üstün, A.: Cisim Tanıma Problemine Yapay Sinir Ağlarının Uygulanması, Yüksek Lisans Tezi, İ.T.Ü Fen Bilimleri Enstitüsü (1999)
13. Alpaydın, E., Gürgen, F.: Comparison of Statistical and Neural Classifiers and Their Applications to Optical Character Recognition and Speech Classification. In: Londes, C.T. (ed.): Image Processing and Pattern Recognition Academic Press, California (1998) 61–88
14. Duda, R.O., Hart, P.E., Stork D.G.: Pattern Classification. Second edition. John Wiley & Sons, New York (2000)

Appendix A: A Number of Edge Images for Objects

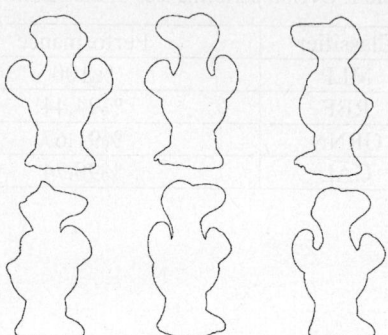

Fig A.1a. Edge images for Object 1

Fig A.1b. Edge images for Object 2

Fig A.1c. Edge images for Object 3

Appendix B: Classification Performances Using Test Data

	Learn. Rate	Class 1	Class 2	Class 3		Learn. Rate	Class 1	Class 2	Class 3
MLP trainoss	0.1	36	34	35	MLP trainlm	0.1*	30	32	32
	0.2	36	33	35		0.2	29	29	34
	0.3	36	35	34		0.3	25	33	30
	0.4	36	33	34		0.4	20	31	32
	0.5	36	35	35		0.5	26	31	30
	0.6	36	35	34		0.6	25	32	32
	0.7*	36	35	36		0.7	24	29	29
	0.8	36	33	35		0.8	27	29	31
	0.9	35	35	34		0.9	26	33	29
	1	35	36	34		1	27	31	32

	Learn. Rate	Class 1	Class 2	Class 3		Learn. Rate	Class 1	Class 2	Class 3
MLP trainrp	0.1**	36	36	36	MLP trainbfg	0.1	36	34	35
	0.2	34	34	34		0.2	35	33	35
	0.3	36	35	35		0.3	31	32	33
	0.4	36	34	34		0.4*	36	35	36
	0.5	36	35	34		0.5	34	28	31
	0.6	36	35	35		0.6	36	35	34
	0.7	35	34	35		0.7	35	35	36
	0.8	36	36	35		0.8	35	33	34
	0.9	36	36	35		0.9	33	35	36
	1	36	36	35		1	32	32	31

	Spread	Class 1	Class 2	Class 3		Spread	Class 1	Class 2	Class 3
RBF newrb	0.1	29	30	31	RBF newrbe	0.1	21	28	26
	0.2	29	32	32		0.2	21	22	28
	0.3	28	31	33		0.3	21	25	34
	0.4	24	32	32		0.4*	23	25	35
	0.5	28	34	33		0.5	17	22	34
	0.6	32	35	32		0.6	15	21	32
	0.7	33	35	32		0.7	20	22	32
	0.8	33	34	33		0.8	20	22	31
	0.9*	33	35	34		0.9	19	22	31
	1	33	35	33		1	20	20	33

	Spread	Class 1	Class 2	Class 3
GRNN	0.01	34	34	30
	0.02*	35	34	30
	0.03	35	33	28
	0.04	31	34	26
	0.05	30	34	25
	0.06	30	34	23
	0.07	28	34	23
	0.08	27	34	22
	0.09	29	34	22
	0.1	23	34	20

	Class 1	Class 2	Class 3
GAL	34	33	31

*Shows the appropriate Neural Network configurations.

** Shows the best MLP configuration.

A Novel Watermarking for Image Security

Jun Zhang and Feng Xiong

School of Information Science, Guangdong Commercial College
Guangzhou 510320, P.R.China
zhangjundan@263.net

Abstract. This paper proposes a novel robust image watermarking in which a logo watermark is embedded into the discrete multi-wavelet transform domain (DMWT) of an image. It is found that there are two characters in the low frequency band of the multi-wavelet domain. One is that the mean of corresponding coefficients in four subblocks is more stable than a single coefficient, and the other is that it is easily recognized whether a coefficient point is a smooth point or not by the difference between two corresponding coefficients in two subblocks. According to these unique characters, the watermark is embedded into the multiwaelet doman by quantizing the mean of corresponding coefficients in four subblocks. The quantization interval is decided by the character of the HVS based on the second character. Experimental results show that the proposed method is superior to the traditional wavelet-based quantization method.

1 Introduction

In the digital world of Internet, it is a challenging problem to protect the copyright of digital images and other multimedia products since the reproduction and distribution of them are very easy and fast. A watermarking, which embeds some owner information (mark) into host images, is regarded as a possible resolution to this problem[1].

Watermarking methods can be classified by different strategies. According to the embedding domain, they can be divided into two groups. One group is to modify the intensity value of the luminance in the spatial domain [2,3]. The other is to change the image coefficient in a transform domain such as DCT, DWT [4-6]. In general, spatial domain methods have good computing performance and transform domain methods have high robustness. According to the embedding scheme, watermarking methods can be divided into two types, too. One type is based on spread spectrum communication principle [7,8], and the other is based on quantization method [9-11]. A spread spectrum watermarking directly adds a watermark, usually in the form of a PN sequence, to the amplitude of the original image. Since the original image isn't taken into account in the embedding process, it will act as strong interference at the watermark extraction, which limits the performance in the absence of attacks, and also lim-

---

*This work is supported by the Guangdong Nature Science Foundation (No. 020199) and the Nature Science Foundation of Department of Education of Guangdong Province(No. Z02042).

its the embedded data capacity. The quantization watermarking quantises image samples to represent the embedded watermark bit. The watermark bit is recovered by checking which bin the sample falls into. So the original image no longer acts as interference. In general, the quantization watermarking can hide more data and has less robustness than the spread spectrum watermarking. According to the extracting scheme, watermarking techniques can also be split into two distinct categories: non-blind watermarking [7] and blind watermarking (public watermarking) [9]. In a non-blind watermarking, the original image is necessary for the watermark extraction. Although the existence of the original image facilitates to a great extent watermark extraction, such a requirement raises two problems: (i) owner of the original image is compelled unsecurely to share his work with anyone who wants to check the existence of the watermark , (ii) on the other hand, the searching within the database for the original image that corresponds to a given watermarked image would be very time consuming. Thus, blind watermarking, which does not need original images for the watermark extraction, would be preferable.

Robustness is a challenging problem in a blind wakermarking. For improving robustness, it is a very effective strategy to explore stable characters of an image and take into account of the characters of the human visual system (HVS). Liu et al. [12] argue that the low frequency coefficients are more stable than other coefficients in DWT domain, which is based on the following reasons: First, Cox et al. argued that the watermark should be embedded in those perceptually significant components. In DWT domain, the significant components are the low frequency coefficients. Second, the low frequency coefficients have larger perceptual capacity, which allows strong watermarks to be embedded without perceptual distortion. Third, according to the theory of signal, common image processing procedures, such as data compression and low-pass filter, tend to change the low frequency coefficients less than high frequency coefficients. Thus, they embed a watermark bit by replacing some least significant bits of a low frequency coefficient. Chen et al. [11] propose a mean quantization technique that embeds each watermark bit into n wavelet coefficients. This technique is based on the statistical principle: Given a set of samples, the population mean has a smaller variance than that of a single sample. It is expected that watermark embedded by modulating the mean of a set of wavelet coefficients is more robust than by modulating a single coefficient. Moreover, the technique also incorporates the human visual system (HVS) model to provide a maximum transparent watermark.

Based on above strategies, this paper proposes a novel robust watermarking method, which embeds a logo watermark into a new transform domain—discrete multi-wavelet transform domain (DMWT). It is found that there are two characters in the low frequency band of the multi-wavelet domain. One is that the mean of corresponding coefficients in four subblocks is more stable than a single coefficient, and the other is that it is easily recognized whether a coefficient point is a smooth point or not by the difference between two corresponding coefficients in two subblocks. According to these unique characters, the watermark is embedded into the multi-wavelet domain by quantizing the mean of corresponding coefficients in four subblocks. The quantization interval is decided by the characters of the HVS based on the second character of the multi-wavelet domain. The rest of this paper is organized as follows: Section 2 is to introduce multi-wavelet transform and its characters. Section 3 is to describe the watermark embedding and extracting method. Section 4 is to show the experimental results. Finally, Section 5 is to conclude this paper.

2 Multi-wavelet Transform and Its Characters

As in the scalar wavelet case, the theory of multi-wavelet is based on the idea of multiresolution analysis (MRA)[13]. The difference is that multi-wavelet system has several scaling functions and wavelet functions. It is defined as follows:

The translates of scaling functions $\varphi_1(t-k), \varphi_2(t-k), \cdots, \varphi_N(t-k)$ produce a basis of the subspace V_0.

The dilates $\varphi_1(2^j t-k), \varphi_2(2^j t-k), \ldots, \varphi_N(2^j t-k)$ generate subspace $V_j, j \in Z$, such that $\cdots \subset V_{-1} \subset V_0 \subset V_1 \subset \cdots \subset V_j \subset \cdots$

$$\bigcup_{j=-\infty}^{j=\infty} V_j = L^2(R), \quad \bigcap_{j=-\infty}^{\infty} V_j = \{0\}.$$

There are N wavelet functions and their translates $w_1(t-k), w_2(t-k), \cdots, w_N(t-k)$ produce a basis of the "detail" subspace W_0 to give $V_1: V_1 = V_0 \oplus W_0$.

Like the scalar wavelet case, the multi-wavelet decomposition of a 1-dimensional signal is performed by Mallat algorithm. However, because the lowpass filterbank and highpass filterbank are $N \times N$ matrices, the signal must be preprocessed to be a vector before decomposition. As for the decomposition of a 2-dimensional image, it can be performed by the 1-dimensional algorithm in each dimension. After one cascade step, the result can be realized as the following matrix:

$$\begin{bmatrix} L_1L_1 & L_2L_1 & H_1L_1 & H_2L_1 \\ L_1L_2 & L_2L_2 & H_1L_2 & H_2L_2 \\ L_1H_1 & L_2H_1 & H_1H_1 & H_2H_1 \\ L_1H_2 & L_2H_2 & H_1H_2 & H_2H_2 \end{bmatrix}$$

Note that a typical block H_2L_1 contains lowpass coefficients corresponding to the first scaling function in the horizontal direction and highpass coefficients corresponding to the second wavelet in the vertical direction. The next step of the cascade will decompose the low-lowpass submatrix

$$\begin{bmatrix} L_1L_1 & L_2L_1 \\ L_1L_2 & L_2L_2 \end{bmatrix}$$

(the coarsest level) in a similar manner. An example using multi-wavelet decomposition is shown in Figure.1(a). Compared with the scalar wavelet decomposition shown in Figure.1(b), there are four subblocks in the coarsest level of the multi-wavelet domain, while there is only one in that of the scalar wavelet domain. Furthermore, it is found that there are following characters in the coarsest level of the DMWT domain.

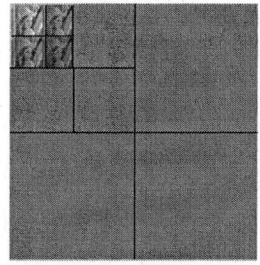
(a) Decomposition by the multi-wavelet

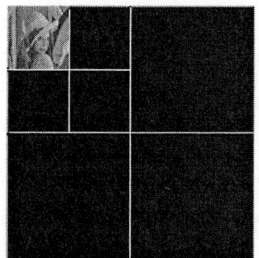
(b) Decomposition by the scalar wavelet

Fig. 1. The difference between the multi-wavelet domain and scalar wavelet domain

First, the mean of four corresponding coefficients in four subblocks is more stable than a single coefficient in the coarsest level after some attacks. (i) Conducted from theory: The subblock is respectively denoted as X_1, X_2, X_3, X_4. Their mean block $\overline{X}$ is computed as:

$$\overline{X} = \{\overline{x}(i,j) | \overline{x}(i,j) = (x_1(i,j) + x_2(i,j) + x_3(i,j) + x_4(i,j))/4, \ x_n(i,j) \in X_n\}$$

Fig.2. The texture point set P_1 with t=60

Table 1. Variance of the noise added to subblock and mean block after common processing operators

	X_1	X_2	X_3	X_4	$\overline{X}$
blurring	3.98	3.86	3.72	3.23	1.17
sharpening	5.62	5.32	5.21	5.18	1.55
noise-adding	0.47	0.50	0.47	0.35	0.22
JPEG compression	0.52	0.53	0.52	0.66	0.26

After some attacks, according to statistical principle, if the noise, which is added to $x_n, n = 1,2,3,4$, is modeled as a Gaussian distribution with zero mean and variance σ, than the variance of the mean $\overline{x}$ will be $\sigma/4$. (ii) Conducted from experiments: We calculate variance of the noise added to each subblock and mean block after common image process operators such as blurring, sharpening, noise-adding and JPEG compression. The results are listed in Table 1. According to this table, we can see the variance of the mean block is smallest. It means the mean coefficient is more stable than a single coefficient in a subblock after attacks.

Second, it is easily recognized whether a coefficient point is a smooth point by the difference between two corresponding coefficients in two subblocks. We compute the difference block $\hat{X}$ between the two of four subblocks as: $\hat{X} = \{\hat{x}(i,j) | \hat{x}(i,j) = x_1(i,j) - x_2(i,j), \ x_1(i,j) \in X_1, x_2(i,j) \in X_2\}$. Giving a threshold t, we compute two point sets P_1 and P_2 as: $P_1 = \{(i,j) | \hat{x}(i,j) \geq t\}$, $P_2 = \{(i,j) | \hat{x}(i,j) < t\}$. Fig.2 shows the set P_1 with $t = 60$. According to Fig.2, it is clear that if a point (i,j) belongs to P_1, then it is a texture point, otherwise it is a smooth point.

3 Watermark Embedding and Extraction Method

We quantize the mean of four corresponding coefficients in four subblocks in coarsest level into intervals and assign watermark bit (0,1) to each interval periodically. Since the mean is more stable than a single coefficient under some attacks, it will be difficult to move beyond the quantization interval where it is originally located. As a result, we can achieve high robustness. Moreover, according to characters of the HVS: eyes are more sensitive to the noise added to smooth areas than to texture areas, we use a large interval size to quantize the mean which locates at texture areas and a small interval size at smooth areas.

Let I be the original image of size $N \times N$, and the digital watermarking W be a binary image of size $M \times M$. The watermark embedding and extracting processes are described as follows.

3.1 The Steps of the Watermark Embedding

Step 1. Watermark Permutation
For the security of the watermark, the watermark must be permuted to a random pattern before embedding. Let W and W_p be the original and permuted watermark images, that is, $W_p = P(W,k)$,
$W_p = \{w_p(i,j) = w(i',j') | 1 \leq i, i' \leq M \text{ and } 1 \leq j, j' \leq M\}$, where pixel (i',j') is permuted to pixel (i,j) in a secret order. The secret order is generated by a linear feedback shift register. First, number each pixel from one to $M \times M$. Second, work out an pseudorandom sequence number using linear feedback shift register with a

screat seed k. Finally, work out the coordinate pairs by mapping the random sequence number into a 2-D sequence.

Step 2. Multi-wavelet Transformation of the Image

The transform of the image is implemented by a multi-wavelet system, denoted as $Y = FDMWT(I,l)$, where $FDMWT$ denotes the operator of forward discrete multi-wavelet transformation and l is the number of decomposition level.

Step 3. Quantization of the Mean

The four subblocks in the coarsest level are respectively denoted as X_1, X_2, X_3, X_4. Their mean block is denoted as $\overline{X}$. The quantization function Q is denoted as follows,

$$Q(\overline{x}(i,j),q) = \begin{cases} 1 & \text{if } kq \leq \overline{x}(i,j) < (k+1)q \text{ for } k=0,\pm2,\pm4,\cdots \\ 0 & \text{if } kq \leq \overline{x}(i,j) < (k+1)q \text{ for } k=\pm1,\pm3,\cdots \end{cases} \quad \overline{x}(i,j) \in \overline{X} \quad (1)$$

where q is the size of the quantization interval,

$$q = \begin{cases} q_1 & \text{if } (i,j) \in P_1 \text{ ie. } x_1(i,j) - x_2(i,j) \geq t \\ q_2 & \text{if } (i,j) \in P_2 \text{ ie. } x_1(i,j) - x_2(i,j) < t \end{cases}, \text{ here } P_1 \text{ is texture point set}$$

and P_2 is smooth point set.

Step 4. Embedding of the Permuted Watermark

Let the $w(i, j)$ be permuted watermark bit to be embeded. Let $r(i, j)$ be the quantization noise defined as

$$r(i,j) := \overline{x}(i,j) - floor\left(\frac{\overline{x}(i,j)}{q}\right) \bullet q . \quad (2)$$

To embed $w(i, j)$, we update the four coefficients $x_n(i, j)$ $n = 1,2,3,4$ in subblock X_i as follows,

$$x_n(i,j) := \begin{cases} floor\left(\frac{x_n(i,j)}{q}\right) \bullet q + 0.5q, & \text{if } Q(x_n(i,j),q) = w(i,j) \\ floor\left(\frac{x_n(i,j)}{q}\right) \bullet q + 1.5q, & \text{if } Q(x_n(i,j),q) \neq w(i,j) \text{ and } r(i,j) > 0.5q \quad x_n \in X_n \\ floor\left(\frac{x_n(i,j)}{q}\right) \bullet q - 0.5q, & \text{if } Q(x_n(i,j),q) \neq w(i,j) \text{ and } r(i,j) \leq 0.5q \end{cases} \quad (3)$$

These modifications will make the updated $x_n(i, j)$ shift to the middle of corresponding quantization interval or to the middle of its preceding interval or to the middle of its succedent interval according to the embeded bit. As a result the mean is relatively difficult to move away from the shifted interval.

Step 5. Inverse Multi-wavelet Transformation

After step 4, we get the modified coefficient image Y', and then inverse multi-wavelet transform of Y' to get the watermarked image, denoted as $I' = IMDWT(Y',l)$. The embedding process is complete.

3.2 The Steps of the Watermark Extracting

The extracting process of the watermark is similar to the embedding process. However, the extracting process of the watermark does not require the original image.

Step 1. The tested image I' is transformed by multi-wavelet transform: $\tilde{Y} = FMDWT(I',l)$.

Step 2. The mean of four corresponding coefficients in subblocks of corasest level of the $\tilde{Y}$ is calculated:

$$\tilde{X}' = \{\bar{x}'(i,j) | \bar{x}'(i,j) = (x'_1(i,j) + x'_2(i,j) + x'_3(i,j) + x'_4(i,j))/4, \; x'_n(i,j) \in X'_n\} \quad (4)$$

Step 3. The permuted watermark $\tilde{W}_p$ is extraced as follows:

$$\tilde{W}_p = \left\{\tilde{w}(i,j) | \tilde{w}(i,j) = \begin{cases} 1 & \text{if } Q(\bar{x}'(i,j),q) \text{ is even} \\ 0 & \text{if } Q(\bar{x}'(i,j),q) \text{ is odd} \end{cases}\right., \; 1 \leq i,j \leq M \quad (5)$$

Here, $q = \begin{cases} q_1 & \text{if } (i,j) \in P_1 \text{ ie. } x'_1(i,j) - x'_2(i,j) \geq t \\ q_2 & \text{if } (i,j) \in P_2 \text{ ie. } x'_1(i,j) - x'_2(i,j) < t \end{cases}$, and t is a threshold value.

Step 4. The watermark $\tilde{W}$ is obtained by inversing the permutation of $\tilde{W}_p$. The correctness of the extracted watermark $\tilde{W}$ is quantitatively measured by the bit corecct ratio (BCR), defined as follows:

$$BCR = \frac{\sum_{i=1}^{M}\sum_{j=1}^{M} \overline{w(i,j) \oplus \tilde{w}(i,j)}}{M \times M}, \quad (6)$$

where $\oplus$ denotes the exclusive-OR operator.

4 Experimental Results

In our experiment, the number of decomposition level of the discrete multi-wavelet transform l is 2, and the size of the quantization interval q_1 and q_1 are 12 and 10 respectively, and the threshold value t is 60. The Lena image with size 512*512 is used as test image, and the binary image with size 64*64 is used as watermark. The experimental result show that the PSNR of the watermarked image is 42db, which means the watermarking method has good imperceptibility. By this watermarked version, we test the robustness of the watermarking as follows:

Table 2. Robustness to some attacks

Blurring	Median filter	Sharpening	Noise-adding	Rescaling	Rotating
0.87	0.95	0.82	0.96	0.99	0.75

Table 3. Robustness to JPEG Compression

70/8.5	60/10.3	50/11.9	40/13.8	30/16.7	20/21.9
1	1	0.99	0.97	0.87	0.68

We test the robustness by common image processing and geometric transform operators. The experimental results are listed in Table 2. Column 1 of this table shows the extracted watermark with BCR=0.87, when the watermarked image is blurred by the Gaussian blur operator with a mask of size 3*3. The PSNR of the watermarked image is down to 32.1db. Column 2 of this table shows the extracted watermark with BCR=0.95, when the watermarked is attacked by median filter operator with a mask of size 3*3. Column 3 of this table shows the extracted watermark with BCR=0.82, when the watermarked image is sharpen with PSNR=26.7db. Although the quality of the watermarked image is severely damaged, the extracted watermark is still recognizable. Column 4 of this table shows the extracted watermark with BCR=0.96, when the Gaussian noise is added to the watermarked image, the PSNR of which is 33.51db. Column 5 of this table shows the extracted watermark with BCR=0.99, when the watermarked image is first scaled to be 1/2 of its original size, then the subsampled image is interpolated to the size of the original, the PSNR of which is 33.8db. Column 6 of this table shows the extracted watermark with BCR=0.75, when the watermarked image is first rotated at 10^0, then it is reverse, the PSNR of which is 29.4db. According to these experimental results, we can see that the watermarking is robust to common image processing and geometric transform operators.

Then, we test the robustness by JPEG compression operator. Table 3 shows the extracted watermarks from the JPEG compressed version of the watermarked images with various compression ratios. According to this table, we can see that the BCR value is 1 before the compression ratio is up to 11, and when the compression ratio is up to 21.9, the extracted watermark is still recognizable. So the watermark is highly robust to JPEG compression.

Table 4. Performance comparison between our method and Chen's method in [11]

	Lower Pass Filter	High Pass Filter	Histogram Equalization	Brightness Adjustment	Additive Guassian Noise	Rescaling	JPEG Comp. (50%)
Our method	0.99	0.99	1	1	0.96	0.98	0.99
Chen's method	0.84	1	1	1	0.53	0.61	0.98

Finally, we compare our scheme with Chen's method [11], which is based on mean quantization approach in the traditional DWT domain. Table 4 summarizes the performance comparison using the similarity measure (SM). In all cases, the results of our approach are better than those of the Chen's approach. In addition to, Chen encodes each watermark bit into eight wavelet coefficients while we only use four multi-wavelet coefficients to encode each watermark bit. Thus, our scheme can hide more data than Chen's method.

5 Conclusions

This paper proposes a novel robust blind watermarking method, which incorporates stable characters of an image and characters of the HVS. The main contributions made are as follows:

1) The embedding strategy makes use of the stable character of an image to embed a logo watermark. It embeds each watermark bit into multi-wavelet domain by quantizing the mean of corresponding coefficients in four subblocks in the coarsest level (low frequency band).

2) The embedding strategy takes into account the characters of the HVS. The HVS is more sensitive to the noise added to smooth areas than texture areas. In multi-wavelet domain, it is easily recognized whether a coefficient point is a smooth point or not by the difference between two corresponding coefficients in two subblocks. According to this character, the proposed method selects difference quantization interval size to embed a watermark bit.

Experimental results show that the proposed method has good imperceptibility and high robustness, and also is superior to the DWT-based quantization method in terms of robustness and data capacity.

References

1. Hartung, F., Kutter, M.: Multimedia watermarking techniques. In: Proceedings of the IEEE'87. (1999) 1079–1094
2. van Schyndel, R.G., Tirkel, A.Z., Osborne, C. F.: A digital watermark. In: Proceedings of the International Conference on Image Processing. Austin: IEEE Press. (1994) 86–90
3. Kutter, M., Jordan, F., Bossen, F.: Digital watermarking of color images using amplitude modulation. Journal of Electronic Imaging **7**(2) (1998) 326–332
4. Barni, M., Bartolini, F., Cappellini, Piva, A.: A doc-domain system for robust image watermarking. Signal Processing **66** (1998) 357–372
5. Lin, S.D., Chen, C.-F.: A robust DCT-based watermarking for copyright protection. IEEE Trans. On Consumer Electronics **46**(3) (2000) 415–420
6. Hsu, C.-T., Wu, J.-L.: Multiresolution watermarking for digital images. IEEE Trans. On Circutits Syst. II **45** (1998) 1097–1101
7. Cox, I.J., Killian, J., Leighton, F.L.Y., Shamoon, T.: Secure spread spectrum watermarking for multimedia. IEEE Trans. On Image Processing **6** (1997) 1673–1686
8. Joseph, J.K., Ruanaidh, O., Pun, T.: Rotation, scale and translation invariant spread spectrum digital image watermarking. Signal Processing **66** (1998) 303–317
9. Kundur, D., Hatzinakos D.: Digital watermarking for telltale tamper proofing and authentication. In: Proceeding of the IEEE 87. (1999) 116–1180
10. Yu, G.-J., Lu, C.-S., Liao, H-Y.M.: Mean quantization-based fragile watermarking for image authentication. Optical Engineering **40**(7) (2001)
11. Chen, L.H., Lin, J.J.: Mean quantization based image watermarking. Image and Vision Computing **21** (2003) 717–727
12. Liu, H., Liu, J., Huang, J.: A robust DWT-based blind data hiding algorithm. In: Proc. IEEE Int. Symp. Circuits and Systems, Arizona, IEEE Press. (2002) 672–675
13. Strela, V., Heller, P.N., Strang, G., Topiwala, P., Heil, C.: The application of multiwavelet filterbanks to image processing. IEEE Trans. On Image Processing **8** (1999) 548–563

Boosting Face Recognition Speed with a Novel Divide-and-Conquer Approach

Önsen Toygar and Adnan Acan

Computer Engineering Department, Eastern Mediterranean University
Gazimağusa, T.R.N.C., Mersin 10, Turkey
{onsen.toygar,adnan.acan}@emu.edu.tr

Abstract. Computational and storage space efficiencies of a novel approach based on appearance-based statistical methods for face recognition are studied. The new approach is a low-complexity divide-and-conquer method implemented as a multiple-classifier system. Appearance-based statistical algorithms are used for dimensionality reduction followed by distance-based classifiers. An appropriate classifier combination method is used to determine the resulting face recognized. FERET database and FERET Evaluation Methodology are used in all experimental evaluations. Time and space complexities of the proposed approach indicate that it outperforms the holistic Principal Component Analysis, Linear Discriminant Analysis and Independent Component Analysis in computational and storage space efficiencies. The experimental results show that the proposed approach also provides better recognition performance on frontal images.

1 Introduction

Appearance-based statistical methods are well-known dimensionality reduction methods among which Principal Component Analysis (PCA), Linear Discriminant Analysis (LDA) and Independent Component Analysis (ICA) are the most widely used algorithms for the solution of face recognition problem. PCA, also known as Eigenspace Projection, is used mainly for dimensionality reduction in compression and recognition problems [1,2]. It tries to find the eigenvectors of the covariance matrix in order to find the basis of the representation space. The eigenvectors correspond to the directions of the principal components of the original data, their statistical significance is given by their corresponding eigenvalues. Linear Discriminant Analysis (LDA), also known as Fisher's Discriminant Analysis, searches for those vectors in the underlying space that best discriminate among classes[1,2]. The basic idea of LDA is to find a linear transformation such that feature clusters are most separable after the transformation which can be achieved through scatter matrix analysis. The aim is to maximize the Between-class scatter matrix measure while minimizing the Within-class scatter matrix measure [1]. Another powerful method is Independent Component Analysis (ICA) which is a special case of redundancy reduction techniques and represents the data in terms of statistically independent variables [2,3]. ICA of a random vector consists of searching for a linear transformation that minimizes the statistical dependence between its components [1-3].

Face recognition is one of the well-known problems in the field of image analysis and understanding. An unknown person is recognized from his/her face image by comparing the unknown face with the known faces from a face database. The interest of researchers and engineers to develop efficient methods for the solution of the face recognition problem has grown rapidly in the recent years since there is a wide range of commercial and law enforcement applications in this field [4].

In this study, a face is partitioned into a number of equal-width horizontal segments where each segment is processed by an associated dimensionality reduction method. Each segment is classified by a simple distance-based classifier and a multiple-classifier combination method is used to combine individual classifier outputs to determine the resulting face recognized. To compare the performance of the proposed approach with the above mentioned holistic methods, the standard FERET (FacE REcognition Technology) database and the FERET Evaluation Methodology [5,6] are used in all experimental evaluations.

This paper is organized as follows: The proposed approach is described in the following section. Analysis of computational and storage space efficiencies are presented in Section 3. Experimental results are given in Section 4. Finally, Section 5 concludes this paper.

2 The Proposed Approach

A novel divide-and-conquer approach, implemented as a multiple-classifier system is introduced. Appearance-based statistical algorithms PCA, LDA, and ICA and simple distance-based classifiers are used for dimensionality reduction and classification. The aim is to improve the computational and storage space efficiencies and recognition performance of the holistic appearance-based methods. The main difficulties of applying appearance-based statistical face recognition algorithms, such as high computation time and memory requirements, are due to their holistic approach for feature extraction. Holistic approaches aim to find a reduced dimensional representation for a facial image using features extracted from the image as a whole. However, the most important characteristic features for face recognition are those extracted from the facial image between eyebrows and chin. Hence, extraction of these features from more localized portions of a facial image may provide better representations for the improvement of the recognition performance. Consequently, one can partition an input image into a number of smaller parts for the extraction of locally important features more efficiently and for the improvement of computational speed and storage space requirements. This way, face recognition using holistic face images and one classifier method is reduced to feature extraction over a number of smaller facial segments and recognition using multiple classifiers with one or more classifier methods and dedicated output combination approaches. Hence, instead of having a single holistic classifier, a number of lower-complexity classifiers, employing locally important features for classification, are obtained. The final decision for face recognition requires a multiple-classifier combination method [7,8] to combine individual classifier outputs into one decision for classification. It is well known that the classifier performance obtained by combining the outputs of several individual classifiers, can be better than the performance of a more powerful single classifier [7,8]. These are the main inspirations behind the proposed approach, the success of which is demonstrated by theoretical analysis and experimental evaluations using benchmark face databases.

In the implementation of the proposed approach, a face image is divided into a number of equal-width horizontal segments where each segment is processed by an associated dimensionality reduction method. Each segment is classified by a simple distance-based classifier and a multiple-classifier combination method is used to combine individual classifier outputs to determine the resulting face recognized. In this paper, a multiple classifier system (MCS) with five individual classifiers is used for experimental evaluations. Also, Borda Count method is considered as the classifier combination method due to its better performance over the other tested combination procedures. The reason why a multiple-classifier with five individuals is selected can be explained by the fact that when a normalized facial image is subdivided into five equal-width horizontal segments, distinctive features of the face such as the forehead, eyes, nose, mouth and the chin are placed into individual horizontal segments, from which locally important features are extracted in a better way than when they are extracted by holistic counterparts.

In this study, an input face image is cropped into a normalized size with predetermined number of rows and columns. Then the facial image is divided into equal-width horizontal segments as shown in Figure 1. Eventually, each horizontal segment is associated with an individual classifier which uses a particular dimensionality reduction method for feature extraction and a simple distance-based classifier for recognition. The same horizontal partitioning is applied to training and test images. The proposed approach can also be very suitable for partial face recognition; even one part of a facial image is damaged, obscured, or blurred, other parts may provide quite useful features for recognition.

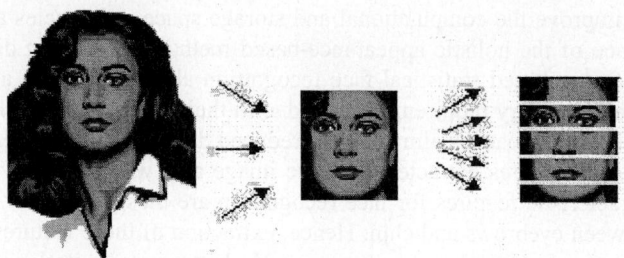

Fig. 1. The original face image, cropped image, and 5 horizontal segments of the divided face

3   Analysis of Computational and Storage Space Efficiencies

Considering a set of MxN holistic face images, with K images in the training set, computational and storage space efficiencies of holistic PCA, LDA and ICA approaches and the proposed multiple-classifier approach, in which individual classifiers use a particular appearance-based statistical algorithm, are evaluated in the following subsections.

3.1 Computational and Storage Space Efficiencies of Holistic Appearance-Based Statistical Approaches

Computational Efficiency of the PCA Algorithm. First of all, face images in the training set are centered by calculating the mean of each image in O(KMN) and a data matrix of the centered face images is created with a computational complexity of O(KMN). Computational complexity of constructing the covariance matrix is $O(K(MN)^2)$. The next step of the PCA algorithm is the computation of eigenvalues and the corresponding eigenvectors of the covariance matrix, for which the computational complexity is $O(K(MN)^3)$. Consequently, eigenvectors are sorted in decreasing order of their eigenvalues using the Merge Sort algorithm in $O(K((MN)\log_2(MN)))$. Since the first largest (K-1) eigenvalues and the associated eigenvectors are considered in the construction of the reduced eigenspace, computation of the reduced eigenspace is carried out in O((K-1)MN) whereas the projection of the images into this eigenspace requires a computational complexity of O(K(K-1)MN). If these computational complexity expressions are written in order, as they appear in the text, one gets the following sum and the overall computational efficiency as:

$$\begin{aligned}\textit{Computational efficiency of PCA} &= O(KMN) + O(KMN) + O(K(MN)^2) + \\ &\quad O(K(MN)^3) + O(K((MN)\log_2(MN))) + O((K-1)MN) + O(K(K-1)MN) \\ &= O(K(MN)^3)\end{aligned} \quad (1)$$

Computational Efficiency of the LDA Algorithm. LDA algorithm starts with the construction of a data matrix of the training faces, which is followed by the construction of covariance matrices. The computational complexities of these two procedures are O(KMN) and $O(K(MN)^2)$, respectively. The next step of the LDA approach deals with the computation of scatter matrices by the addition of covariance matrices. In this respect, Within-class scatter matrix is computed for each sample in each image class and Between-class scatter matrix is computed for each image class. Computational complexities of the two scatter matrix calculations are both O(KMN). Consequently, the inverse of Within-class scatter matrix is calculated in $O(K(MN)^{\log_2 7})$ using the Strassen's algorithm [9]. The inverses of Within-class scatter matrix and the Between-class scatter matrix are multiplied in $O((MN)^{\log_2 7})$ and its eigenvalues and the associated eigenvectors are found in $O(K(MN)^3)$. Sorting the eigenvalues, and their eigenvectors, in decreasing order using the Merge Sort algorithm, brings a computational complexity of $O(K(MN)\log_2(MN))$. The first largest (K-1) eigenvalues and the associated eigenvectors are considered in the construction of the reduced eigenspace. Its construction and the projection of face images into this space take O((K-1)MN) and O(K(K-1)MN), respectively. Summing up the above mentioned computational complexities in order, as they appear in the text, results in the following expression:

$$\begin{aligned}\textit{Computational efficiency of LDA} &= O(KMN) + O(K(MN)^2) + O(KMN) + \\ &\quad O(KMN) + O(K(MN)^{\log_2 7}) + O((MN)^{\log_2 7}) + O(K(MN)^3) + \\ &\quad O(K(MN)\log_2(MN)) + O((K-1)MN) + O(K(K-1)MN) \\ &= O(K(MN)^3)\end{aligned} \quad (2)$$

Computational Efficiency of the ICA Algorithm. ICA algorithm works similar to that of PCA. Calculation of the means for each image, construction of the data matrix for the centered training faces, computation of the covariance matrix together with its eigenvalues and the associated eigenvectors, and sorting the eigenvalues and their eigenvectors have computational complexities $O(KMN)$, $O(KMN)$, $O(K(MN)^2)$, $O(K(MN)^3)$, and $O(K(MN)\log_2(MN))$, respectively, exactly as in the case of the PCA complexity analysis. After sorting the eigenvalues, ICA proceeds with the whitening process, in which the diagonal matrix using the sorted eigenvalues, is computed first. This is followed by taking the square root of the diagonal matrix, which is also followed by matrix inversion. Since matrix inversion is the dominant operation within the whitening process, its overall complexity can be written as $O(K(MN)^{\log_2 7})$. The results of the whitening process are two matrices named whitening and dewhitening matrices, respectively. Using these two matrices, the mixing matrix A and its inverse W are estimated in $O((K-1)^2 MN)$. Finally, to find the independent components, W is multiplied with the face images and added with the product of W and the mean of face images. Since matrix multiplication is the dominant operation of this procedure, its computational complexity is $O(K(K-1)MN)$. The addition of all these computational complexity expressions, in the order they appear in the text, results in the overall complexity of $O(K(MN)^3)$:

$$\begin{aligned}
\text{Computational efficiency of ICA} &= O(KMN) + O(KMN) + O(K(MN)^2) + \\
&\quad O(K(MN)^3) + O(K(MN)\log_2(MN)) + O(K(MN)^{\log_2 7}) + \\
&\quad O((K-1)^2 MN) + O(K(K-1)MN) \\
&= O(K(MN)^3)
\end{aligned} \quad (3)$$

As a result of evaluations in the above three subsections, computational efficiencies of PCA, LDA and ICA are found to be equal to $O(K(MN)^3)$, where K is the number of training facial images, and M,N are the number of rows and number of columns of each facial image, respectively.

Considering the data structures used in the implementations of PCA, LDA and ICA approaches, it can easily be seen that in all of these methods, the covariance matrix is the largest size data item in use and its size is $O((MN)^2)$. Consequently, the storage space efficiencies of the three appearance-based statistical approaches, PCA, LDA, and ICA, are set equal to $O((MN)^2)$.

These computational and storage space complexities of PCA, LDA and ICA approaches result in long training times and large storage space requirements, particularly when dealing with large databases which is the case in most of the practical applications. These drawbacks also make the holistic PCA, LDA and ICA approaches quite inefficient for dynamic environments in which new faces are frequently added to databases.

3.2 Computational and Storage Space Efficiencies of the Proposed Approach

Considering a face image divided into P equal-width horizontal segments, our approach applies a particular appearance-based statistical method on each horizontal segment independent of each other. Consequently, a selected appearance-based method is applied P times with the use of smaller-size data items. Then, for a particular horizontal segment, a data matrix of the training faces, centered or not, is formed in $O(K((MN)/P))$. Construction of the covariance matrix has the computational complexity of $O(K((MN)/P)^2)$ and computational complexity of finding its eigenvalues and the associated eigenvectors is $O(K((MN)/P)^3)$. Computational complexity of sorting eigenvalues and their associated eigenvectors is $O(K(((MN)/P) \log_2 ((MN)/P)))$.

It can easily be seen that the items in the complexity expressions of holistic appearance-based statistical methods are divided by P in their size, and the resulting complexity terms are multiplied by P since the corresponding operation is performed P times on each horizontal segment. As a result, the computational complexity expressions for our MCS approach with three different appearance-based statistical dimensionality reduction methods are evaluated as:

Computational efficiency of MCS with PCA = $O(P.K((MN)/P))$ +
$O(P.K((MN)/P)) + O(P.K((MN)/P)^2) + O(P.K((MN)/P)^3)$ +
$O(P.K(((MN)/P) \log_2 ((MN)/P))) + O(P.(K-1)((MN)/P))$ +
$O(P.K(K-1)((MN)/P)) = O(K((MN)^3/P^2))$ (4)

Computational efficiency of MCS with LDA = $O(P.K((MN)/P))$ +
$O(P.K((MN)/P)^2) + O(P.K((MN)/P)) + O(P.K((MN)/P))$ +
$O(P.K((MN)/P)^{\log_2 7}) + O(P((MN)/P)^{\log_2 7}) + O(P.K((MN)/P)^3)$ +
$O(P.K((MN)/P) \log_2 ((MN)/P)) + O(P.(K-1)((MN)/P))$ +
$O(P.K.(K-1)((MN)/P)) = O(K((MN)^3/P^2))$ (5)

Computational efficiency of MCS with ICA = $O(P.K((MN)/P))$ +
$O(P.K((MN)/P)) + O(P.K((MN)/P)^2) + O(P.K((MN)/P)^3)$ +
$O(P.K(((MN)/P) \log_2 ((MN)/P))) + O(P.K.((MN)/P)^{\log_2 7})$ + (6)
$O(P.(K-1)^2((MN)/P)) + O(P.K.(K-1).((MN)/P)) = O(K((MN)^3/P^2))$

The time efficiencies of the holistic PCA, LDA and ICA approaches are found to be $O(K(MN)^3)$. The proposed approach improves the time efficiencies to $O(K((MN)^3/P^2))$. Therefore, the theoretical speedup of the proposed approach is evaluated as P^2 in Equation 7.

$$(O(K(MN)^3) / O(K((MN)^3/P^2))) = P^2 \qquad (7)$$

Additionally, storage space complexities of the holistic PCA, LDA and ICA approaches are $O((MN)^2)$ and the proposed approach improves storage space efficiencies to $O((MN)^2/P)$. According to this, the theoretical improvement achieved by the proposed approach for storage space efficiency is evaluated as P as illustrated in Equation 8.

$$(O((MN)^2) / O((MN)^2/P)) = P \qquad (8)$$

4 Experimental Results

Recognition performance of the new approach is measured using the FERET database and the FERET Evaluation Methodology. FERET Large gallery test, which measures an algorithm's performance against large databases, is followed in all of the experimental evaluations. Large gallery test results are represented by a performance statistics known as 'Cumulative Matched versus Rank' or 'Cumulative match' score. In this representation, the tested algorithm reports the top Q matches for each probe in a gallery of R images, in a rank-ordered list. From this list, one can determine if the correct answer for a particular probe is in the top Q matches, and if so, how far down the list is the correct match. In our experiments, the test case for which Q=20 and R=50 is followed.

The set of facial images used in this study, consists of male and female images of different racial origins. Some of the individuals have glasses and some of the male individuals have beards. Eight-bit gray-scale images are used which are cropped so that they only include the head of the individuals. These images are scaled down, without affecting the recognition performance, to speedup the computations and reduce the memory requirements.

As the first step of experimental evaluations, all faces in the database are cropped into a standard size of 45 rows and 35 columns, from the original size of 384x256. Then, each facial image is divided into P equal-width horizontal segments. Recognition performance of the proposed approach is tested with various number of horizontal segments. Multiple classifier systems with two to nine individual classifiers are built and tested for their face recognition performance. From these experiments, the best recognition rates are obtained with five individual classifiers and the details of these experimental evaluations can be found in [10]. Accordingly, five individual classifiers are used in this study and this selection achieves reasonably higher performance for low-rank values while demonstrating close to the best performance for high-rank cases.

Following the first step, a particular appearance-based approach is considered and a multiple classifier system with five individual classifiers, where each individual classifier uses the selected appearance-based approach, is constructed. In this way, a MCS with five classifiers and 50 classes is established. The five different classifier outputs, one for each horizontal segment, are combined using a particular classifier combination method. Combination of classifier outputs is obtained with Borda Count classifier combination method [7,8].

In the experimental studies, the probe set consists of different samples of all the individuals in the gallery. The gallery consists of 50 frontal images with two samples per person, whereas the probe set includes 50 different samples of the same individuals' images. The large gallery test results, shown as Cumulative match score, are presented in Figures 2, 3 and 4. Results on the recognition performance are for frontal images. Table 1 presents the CPU time and memory space used by different holistic algorithms and the proposed approach using a personal computer with a 400 MHz clock speed and 128 MB memory.

Table 1. Computation time and space requirements of the holistic and proposed PCA, LDA and ICA approaches

Algorithm	Holistic appearance-based statistical approach		The proposed MCS approach (with five classifiers)		
	CPU Time (seconds)	Memory Space used (MB)	Classifier Method	CPU Time (seconds)	Memory Space used (MB)
PCA	691	99	PCA	20	26
LDA	782	586	LDA	41	121
ICA	329	27.2	ICA	21	6.65

Results presented in Table 1 indicate that the presented approach reduces the overall CPU time ~35 times for PCA, ~19 times for LDA, and ~16 times for ICA. On the other hand, the reduction in the required memory space is ~4 times for PCA, ~5 times for LDA, and ~4 times for ICA. These results demonstrate that the proposed method outperforms the holistic appearance-based statistical approaches in both computational and storage space efficiencies. Compared to the theoretical values in computation time improvement and storage space reduction for five individual classifiers, which are 25 and 5 respectively, the obtained experimental results are compatible with the theoretical expected values.

The recognition performance of the proposed approach, compared to the performance of holistic appearance-based statistical methods, is illustrated on Figures 2, 3, and 4. Experiments demonstrate that the proposed approach achieves almost the same performance with PCA, and outperforms LDA and ICA. Particularly, when compared to ICA, our approach achieves an incomparable success level. Our approach also shows much better performance than LDA, especially for ranks below 12.

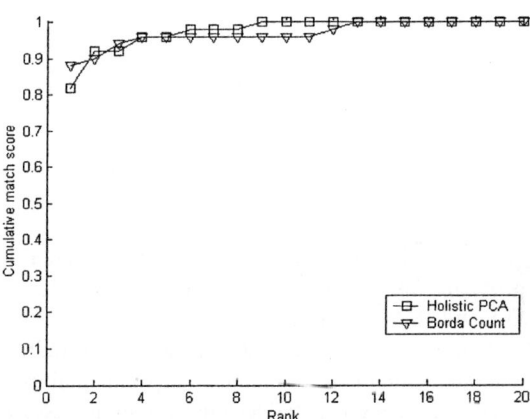

Fig. 2. PCA large gallery test: FA versus FB scores

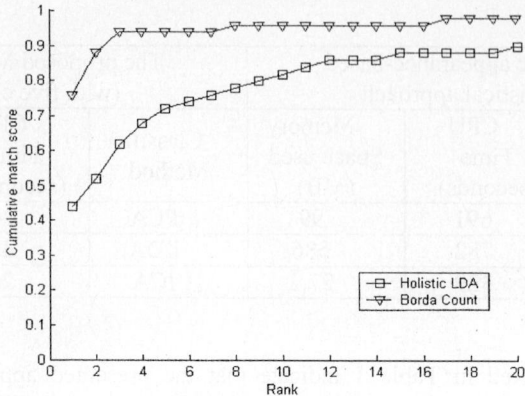

Fig. 3. LDA large gallery test: FA versus FB scores

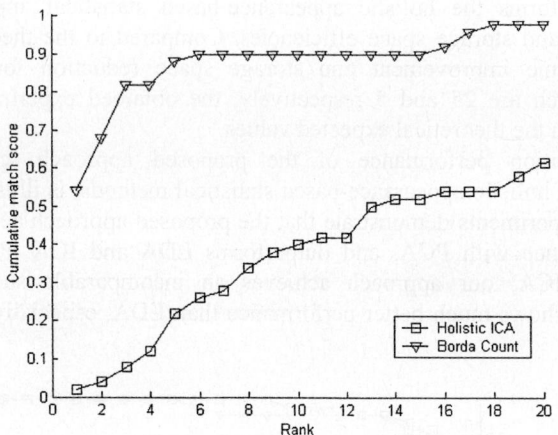

Fig. 4. ICA large gallery test: FA versus FB scores

5 Conclusions

A new, low-complexity and fast divide-and-conquer approach is presented for the face recognition problem. The proposed approach combines dimensionality reduction methods PCA, LDA and ICA and multiple classifier systems for the achievement of its objectives. The experiments were carried out using five individual classifiers and the Borda Count classifier combination method. Experimental evaluations are carried out on the FERET database using FERET Evaluation Methodology.

The proposed approach significantly improves computational efficiency, memory requirements and the recognition performance of the holistic methods. Theoretical evaluations indicate that the proposed approach improves the computational efficiency of PCA, LDA and ICA methods by P^2 where P is the number of classifiers. In addition to this, the theoretical reduction in memory space in all appearance-based statistical approaches is P. On the one hand, experimental results show that the proposed approach reduces the computation time ~35 times for PCA, ~19 times for LDA and ~16 times for ICA. On the other hand, the reduction in the required memory space is ~4 times for PCA, ~5 times for LDA and ~4 times for ICA. These results demonstrate that the proposed approach significantly outperforms the holistic methods in both the computation time and memory requirements. Compared to the theoretical values in computation time improvement and storage space reduction for five individual classifiers, the obtained experimental results are also compatible with the theoretical expected values. Tests performed on frontal images demonstrate that the proposed approach achieves almost the same performance with PCA, and outperforms LDA and ICA. As a further study, this work will be investigated by using unequal horizontal facial segments.

References

1. Martinez, A.M., Kak, A.C.: PCA versus LDA. IEEE Transactions on Pattern Analysis and Machine Intelligence **23**(2) (2001) 228–233
2. Toygar, Ö., Acan, A.: An Analysis of Appearance-Based Statistical Methods and Autoassociative Neural Networks on Face Recognition. In: The 2003 International Conference on Artificial Intelligence (IC-AI 2003), Las Vegas, Nevada, USA. (2003)
3. Hyvärinen, A.: Fast and Robust Fixed-Point Algorithms for Independent Component Analysis. IEEE Transactions on Neural Networks **10**(3) (1999) 626–634
4. Zhao, W., Chellappa, R., Rosenfeld, A., Phillips, P.J.: Face recognition: A literature survey. Technical Report CAR-TR-948, CS-TR-4167, N00014-95-1-0521 (2000)
5. Phillips, P.J., Wechsler, H., Huang, J., Rauss, P.: The FERET Database and Evaluation Procedure for Face Recognition Algorithms. Image and Vision Computing Journal **16**(5) (1998) 295–306
6. Phillips, P.J., Rauss, P.J., Der, S.Z.: FERET (Face Recognition Technology) Recognition Algorithm Development and Test Results. Technical Report, AR-TR-995, Army Research Laboratory (1996)
7. Achermann, B., Bunke, H.: Combination of Face Recognition Classifiers for Person Identification. In: Proceedings of 13th IAPR International Conference in Pattern Recognition (ICPR'96), Vienna, Austria. (1996) 416–420
8. Ho, T., Hull, J., Srihari, S.: Decision Combination in Multiple Classifier Systems. IEEE Transactions on Pattern Analysis and Machine Intelligence **16**(1) (1994) 66–75
9. Cormen, T.H., Leiserson, C.E., Rivest, R.L.: Introduction to Algorithms. The MIT Electrical Engineering and Computer Science Series (1990)
10. Toygar, Ö., Acan, A.: Multiple Classifier Implementation of a Divide-and-Conquer Approach Using Appearance-Based Statistical Methods for Face Recognition. Pattern Recognition Letters (accepted for publication) (2004)

A New Document Watermarking Algorithm Based on Hybrid Multi-scale Ant Colony System

Shiyan Hu

Department of Computer and Information Science
Polytechnic University
Brooklyn, NY 11201, USA
shu@cis.poly.edu

Abstract. This paper proposes and tests an improved method for a document image watermarking system. We first introduce a novel robust document image watermarking algorithm based on the concept of the weight-invariant partition in the spatial domain. The improvement of the proposed technique lies in reduction of the involved image partition problem to a combinatorial optimization problem. To solve this optimization problem, we propose a new hybrid multi-scale ant colony algorithm. The experimental results demonstrate the effectiveness of the improved method, especially that the resulting partitions are more secure and can lead to higher capacity.

1 Introduction

Digital image watermarking is a promising technique for intellectual property protection for the image information. Since last decade, a lot of progress has been made in this area such as [12, 14, 15, 20]. As a special case, security concern about document images is important, since document images are distributed in large amount both electronically and physically. They are easily copied and the copyright information is difficult to identify. Most watermarking algorithms for gray-scale images are based on "transform-domain" techniques and are less useful for document images because their modifications tend to be visible and are easily removed by binarization [16], which contribute the difficulties in designing algorithms for document watermarking. Some algorithms specific for document watermarking have been proposed in the literature such as [1, 4, 5, 11, 17].

This paper proposes and tests an improved method for a document image watermarking system. We first introduce a novel robust document image watermarking algorithm originally proposed in [11], which is based on the concept of the weight-invariant partition in the spatial domain. The improvement of the proposed technique lies in reduction of the involved image partition problem to a combinatorial optimization problem, which is then solved by a hybrid multi-scale ant colony algorithm. The experimental results demonstrate the effectiveness of the improved method.

The rest of this paper is organized as follows. Section 2 describes the watermarking method proposed in [11]. Section 3 describes the partition algorithm based on an enhanced ant colony algorithm. Section 4 shows the experimental results. Finally, concluding remarks are given in Section 5.

2 Embedding Watermark into Weight-Invariant Partitions

Suppose we want to embed the binary sequence τ to a document. To *partition* a document is to divide the whole document into pair-wise disjoint parts. In the following, we abuse the term "partition" a little: we also let partition mean the disjoint part in the above definition. Let $S(P)$ of cardinality n, i.e., $|S(P)| = n$, denote the set of all text lines in a partition P. The *weight* $w(l_i)$ of a text line l_i is the number of total pixels in l_i. The *sum weight* of P is the sum of the weight of all text lines in $S(P)$. The *average weight* $A(P)$ equals to the sum weight of P divided by n. We also call $A(P)$ the *weight of the partition* P. Let S_{in} of P denote the set of text lines with weight between $A(P) \pm \delta$, δ being a positive integer to be discussed later. Let $S_{out} = S - S_{in}$. The key observation of our method is that $A(P)$ of a partition P is not likely to be significantly changed due to noise. Therefore, $A(P)$ is a *partition modification invariant*.

First assume that we have eliminated the text lines which are too short, however, it is not necessary if we can partition the document in a nice way (refer to Section 3). Informally, a partition P is a *uniform partition* if half of lines in $S(P)$ have the weight very close to $A(P)$. From this, we expect that the median and the mean of weights of lines in $S(P)$ are roughly equivalent. Therefore, if δ is appropriately chosen, $|S_{in}|$ will not be too small and we can embed enough bits into a partition as follows. We first modify the partition so that all lines in S_{in} have weights of exactly $A + \delta$ or $A - \delta$. We call it *standardization process*. This process will not lead to significant modifications if δ is small enough. Suppose that we have added r pixels in a total (note that r can be negative) through the process. In order to maintain $A(P)$ of the partition, we must accordingly remove r pixels from lines in S_{out}, which is called *flushing*. We use *late flushing* strategy, that is, the flushing is delayed till the end of the embedding process. After the standardization process, τ is sequentially embedded to each line in S_{in}. We will further modify the partition only for embedding 0: we add or remove $\delta/2$ pixels to l_i such that after modification, l_i has a weight of exactly $A+\delta/2$ or $A-\delta/2$. To determine whether to add or remove pixels needs keeping track of the standardization process. Of course, we should also compensate it for maintaining $A(P)$: r is accordingly updated during the process and flush when the embedding process finishes.

We now show how to determine δ. Since half of lines have weights close to $A(P)$, we first increasingly sort all the lines in the partition according to their weights and select the middle $n/2$ lines starting with l_i ending with l_j. Set $\delta = \min\{A - |l_i|, |l_j| - A\}$. Then we have reasonable number $(n/4)$ of lines for flushing for either sign of r. On the other hand, due to the important fact that δ can be easily computed by extractor (see below), it need not be fixed. Therefore, by varying δ, we may select other lines (e.g., the middle $2n/3$ lines) to form S_{in}.

In the process of flushing, if $r < 0$, we add r pixels to S_{out} to maintain $A(P)$. Since $n/4$ lines have weights larger than $A + \delta$ in S_{out}, we can uniformly flush the pixels to these lines, i.e., each of $n/4$ lines will be added $4r/n$ pixels. Clearly after flushing, the weights of these $n/4$ lines will become even larger than $A + \delta$.

We similarly treat the case for $r > 0$. Finally note that we will embed 01 before τ to ensure that at least one 0 and 1 are embedded, which is useful for extracting.

The process of extracting watermarks from the embedded document is simple. Since the weight of a partition is not changed by the embedding process, we can simply search in the embedded partition, compute $A(P)$, and then compute δ as follows: find the line l_i such that $|A - w(l_i)| = \min_k |A - w(l_k)|$, then $\delta = 2|A - w(l_i)|$. With δ, the extraction is straightforward. Since there is always small noise, we have to set an error-tolerant constant ξ for practical purpose, i.e., we treat $\delta \approx \delta \pm \xi$.

The following principle is applied when we add (or remove) pixels to a text line. We first try to add (or remove) pixels to large-weight characters, and then uniformly modify the remaining characters in the text line. For a single character, the principle is to modify its boundary. These strategies usually lead to subtle modification indicated by our experiments.

A natural question now arises: how can we partition the whole document into smaller uniform partitions? The simplest way is that we first group a fixed number of consecutive pages as a partition and then check for the uniform condition. If the partition is not uniform, we divide it into smaller ones. This process is repeated until certain partitions are uniform. The main assumption of the above strategy is that a reasonable number of physically consecutive lines can form a uniform partition, however, this is not always true. Even if it is the case, partitions formed in this way are usually small (while there are not many uniform partitions), which greatly limits the capacity for embedding bits. Therefore, we propose an improved partition method in Section 3, eliminating the assumption.

We are now to discuss the robustness issue related to the watermarking method which is not thoroughly addressed in [11]. First note that although each text line is vulnerable to be attacked by noise, the average weight of all lines is unlikely to be changed due to noise, assuming that the partition itself is large enough. For the gap δ we maintains, we have set up an error-tolerant constant ξ to withstand the small noise. Furthermore, we can scale up δ to achieve good robustness, however, it cannot be raised too much, otherwise the modification would be visible. For better robustness, we can incorporate the idea of fault tolerance, i.e., τ is modified by using proper *error correcting code* or simply the *repetition code* before the embedding process. Refer to [11] for an improved repetition code whose embedding capacity is 33% larger than the naive repetition code in best case. In the following, we discuss the robustness of the method against different kinds of attempting geometrical attacks, namely translation, rotation and scaling.

For scaling attack, assume that the width and height of the document image will be uniformly changed. Suppose the document is scaled down by the corresponding factors H and W. For a text line l_i in P whose weight is $w(l_i)$, the weight is $w'(l_i) = \frac{w(l_i)}{H \cdot W}$ after scaling. Originally, $A(P) = \frac{w(l_1) + w(l_2) + ... + w(l_n)}{n}$, now $A'(P) = \frac{w(l_1) + w(l_2) + ... + w(l_n)}{n \cdot H \cdot W}$. That is, $A'(P) = \frac{A(P)}{H \cdot W}$. Similarly, one can see that the gap δ is now changed to $\frac{\delta}{H \cdot W}$. Clearly, the gap still exists and all lines are changed uniformly so our scheme is robust to this attack.

For translation and rotation attacks, since we always find the text line (through compensation for geometrical distortion) before embedding or extracting the watermark, these attacks will not hurt the marks. In addition, thanks to the simple structure of document images, compensations for rotations and translations are much easier than those in general images. There are a number of such techniques in the document image literature.

3 Partition Using Bottleneck Hamiltonian Path Algorithm

3.1 Reduction to Bottleneck Hamiltonian Path Algorithm

If the document are not partitioned in a regular way, the watermark will be more secure, since one must know the partition before extracting bits from it. In addition, we expect that most lines in a partition are similar to each other in order to embed enough bits. However, it is not easy to achieve so in general if we always select consecutive lines. Therefore, we would like to compute the partition composed of logically close lines, which are not necessarily physically close. For this, we first reduce the watermarking problem to a combinatorial problem and then an enhanced ant colony algorithm is applied to solve it.

Consider a (undirected) weighted complete graph $G = (V, E)$ where every line l_i in the document is mapped to a node v_i and the weight of the edge linking v_i, v_j is the absolute value of the difference between the weights of two corresponding lines l_i, l_j. Since we embed at most one bit to a line, imagine that we denote embedding a line by visiting its corresponding node in G. Then we want to compute a path visiting every node exactly once, and select some consecutive lines along the path to form partitions and embed bits to them. Since we expect that the lines within a partition are similar to each other, each edge along the path should be short. Therefore, the problem is reduced to the *Bottleneck Hamiltonian Path Problem* (or *BHP* in short), where one is interested in finding a Hamiltonian path that minimizes the length of the longest traveled edge. Formally, for a given $n \times n$ distance matrix $C = (c_{ij})$, we are to compute an acyclic permutation π of the set $\{1, 2, \ldots, n\}$ that minimizes

$$\max_{1 \leq i \leq n} \{c_{i\pi(i)}\}. \tag{1}$$

3.2 Brief Introduction to Ant Colony System

The problem is NP-hard and we compute an approximation by applying an ant colony algorithm, which is very effective in solving hard combinatorial optimization problems. Ant colony algorithms are a class of metaheuristics which are inspired from the behavior of real ants. The essential trait of ant colony algorithms is the combination of a prior information about the structure of a promising solution with a posterior information about the structure of previously obtained good solutions [19]. The ant colony algorithms have been successfully applied to solve some tough problems, such as [3, 6–9, 18, 21]. In this paper, we will focus on *Ant Colony System* (ACS) [8], which is also the base of many ant colony algorithms.

For an instance of bottleneck Hamiltonian path problem, in addition to the edge weight, each edge has also a desirability measure $\tau(r,s)$, called *pheromone*. ACS works as follows. In the initialization step, m ants are randomly positioned on nodes of the graph. Each ant generates a complete Hamiltonian path by choosing nodes according to a *probabilistic state transition rule*. While constructing its path, an ant also modifies the amount of pheromone on the visited edges by applying the *local updating rule*. Once all ants have completed their paths, a *global updating rule* is applied to modify the pheromone on edges. This process is iterated until certain condition is met. Generally, in ACS, ants are guided in building their paths by both heuristic information (preference of short edges) and by pheromone information (preference of high amount of pheromone). In the following, we elaborate some details of ACS.

The state transition rule is as follows: an ant positioned on node r chooses node s to move to by

$$s = \begin{cases} \arg\max_{u \in J_k(r)}\{[\tau(r,u)] \cdot [\eta(r,u)]^\beta\} & : q \leq q_0 \\ S & : \text{otherwise} \end{cases}, \quad (2)$$

where τ is the pheromone, η is the inverse of the distance between r and u, $J_k(r)$ is the set of nodes that remain to be visited by ant k positioned on the node r, β is the parameter controlling the relative importance of pheromone versus distance, q is a random uniform deviate, q_0 is a parameter controlling the relative importance of exploitation and exploration, and S is a random variable distributed according to

$$p_k(r,s) = \begin{cases} \dfrac{[\tau(r,s)] \cdot [\eta(r,s)]^\beta}{\sum_{u \in J_k(r)} [\tau(r,u)] \cdot [\eta(r,u)]^\beta} & : s \in J_k(r) \\ 0 & : \text{otherwise} \end{cases}. \quad (3)$$

For global updating rule, only the best ant is allowed to deposit pheromone to edges. The pheromone level is updated by

$$\tau(r,s) \leftarrow (1-\alpha)\tau(r,s) + \alpha \Delta\tau(r,s), \quad (4)$$

where

$$\Delta\tau(r,s) = \begin{cases} (L_{gb})^{-1} & : (r,s) \in l_{gb} \\ 0 & : \text{otherwise} \end{cases}, \quad (5)$$

and α is the pheromone decay parameter and L_{gb} is the length of longest edge of the current best bottleneck Hamiltonian path l_{gb}.

As regard to local updating rule, the pheromone level is updated by

$$\tau(r,s) \leftarrow (1-\rho)\tau(r,s) + \rho\Delta\tau(r,s), \quad (6)$$

where ρ is a controlling parameter and $\Delta\tau(r,s) = \tau_0$, τ_0 being the initial pheromone level.

3.3 Farthest-Point Heuristic

We occasionally carry out the following heuristic to further globally increase pheromone on some high-pheromone edges, and thus accelerate the ACS. Based on the assumption that ants can find good solution in the way that they prefer high-pheromone edge (and note that the ant needs to complete a Hamiltonian path), it is natural to increase pheromone along the *longest Hamiltonian path* (that is, the longest one over all Hamiltonian paths) of a corresponding graph with pheromone as edge weight to speed up ACS. Since longest Hamiltonian path (or the *MAX TSP*) problem is another NP-hard problem, we therefore introduce a *farthest-point heuristic* to approximate it. A new graph G' is computed from G by assigning the pheromone for each edge in G to the weight for the corresponding edge in G'. We first find the farthest pair of vertices in G' and then add one vertex v_i to the path each time, where v_i is farthest to any two adjacent vertices v_j, v_k along the path. Then we cut the edge $v_j v_k$ and insert edges $v_i v_j$ and $v_i v_k$ to the path. The process is repeated until every vertex has been added. We finally add a small amount of pheromone to edges along the path in G, which corresponds to the computed path in G'.

3.4 Multi-scale Approach for Improving ACS

The multi-scale strategy is motivated by [13]. Actually, such an idea can be traced back to [2] which proposes a method to speed up the spectral bisection and is later improved by [10] in the parallel computing literature. For large instance of bottleneck Hamiltonian path problem, ACS is not efficient enough, even if the farthest-point heuristic is combined. To further speed up ACS, we incorporate a multi-scale strategy to it as follows. The basic idea is to group some vertices together to form clusters using a *K-Nearest Neighbor* (KNN) algorithm. A new graph is obtained by shrinking each cluster to a single point. We recursively iterate this procedure until graph size is small. We then carry out the hybrid ACS from the coarsest graph to the finest (original) graph. A note-worthy detail is that when scaling the graph, pheromone for each smaller-scale edge equals to the average pheromone of all the incident larger-scale edges, i.e., for a node r expanded to $r_1, \ldots, r_n$, pheromone of each edge on the clique induced from $r_1, \ldots, r_n$ is the average pheromone of the edges incident to r in the coarser graph.

4 Experimental Results

We first test the algorithm on embedding the sequence "10011100101" to a single partition (recall that we also need to embed a "01" before the sequence). The original partition and the embedded partition are shown in Figure 1. The modification is not noticeable. The average text line weight and its standard deviation are shown in Table 1. From it, we see that after embedding the sequence, the average line weight remains, while the standard deviation moderately changes. The standard deviation does not change very large due to the principle for pixel addition and removal and the uniform flushing process.

smooth maintenance with approximate extents. Note that a covering approximates a set of points, but smooth maintenance *exactly* maintains an approximate covering. If we allow the extrema of each set to be inaccurate by some small amount, it is possible that we could maintain a covering that would be nearly as good, but with fewer KDS events. Agarwal and Har-Peled showed that one-dimensional approximate extrema can be maintained more cheaply than exact extrema [2]. It may be possible to use approximate extrema to improve the performance of the smooth maintenance scheme, at least in practice. (The smooth maintenance scheme is optimal in the worst case, because n points in linear motion can force $\Theta(n^2)$ cluster changes, even if approximate extrema are used; nevertheless, approximate extrema may still be of practical use.)

An intriguing direction for future work is smooth maintenance without dimensional reduction. For example, we would like to have a smooth maintenance scheme for two-dimensional clusters that does not project the points to the x and y axes separately. Given the complexity of our one-dimensional solution, a two-dimensional scheme would re-

Fig. 1. Original partition (left) and embedded partition (right)

Table 1. Average line weight and its standard deviation before/after the embedding phase in a single partition

Measure	Original document	Embedded document
Average text line weight	439890	439891
Standard deviation	23548	27759

We next apply the method to embed a 128-bit sequence τ into a twenty-six-page single-column paper, where the improved repetition code in [11] is used for high robustness. We first preprocess the document such that it contains only text by the standard block extraction method. We then apply the enhanced ACS to compute the approximation of bottleneck Hamiltonian path. In our ACS, we set $\beta = 2, q_0 = 0.8, \alpha = \rho = 0.1, \tau_0 = \frac{1}{nL_{nn}}$, where L_{nn} is the longest edge in the graph. In the experiment, we select every consecutive 100 lines along the bottleneck Hamiltonian path to form a partition (except the last one) and we have 9 partitions in a total. The average line weight and the standard deviation of the original document and the embedded document are summarized in Table 2. As before, the average line weight remains, while the standard deviation differs. Figure 2 shows which partition the incrementally indexed lines of the document are classified into. From Figure 2 and Table 2, one sees that within each partition, the lines are not always physically close but the weights of them are close. Therefore, we can embed enough number of bits into the partitions. Finally, the extractor is applied and τ is successfully extracted from the scanned embedded document.

5 Conclusion

The main contribution of this paper is two-fold. Firstly, for higher watermarking capacity, we improve the method proposed in [11] by reducing the partition problem involved in the embedding process to a combinatorial optimization problem,

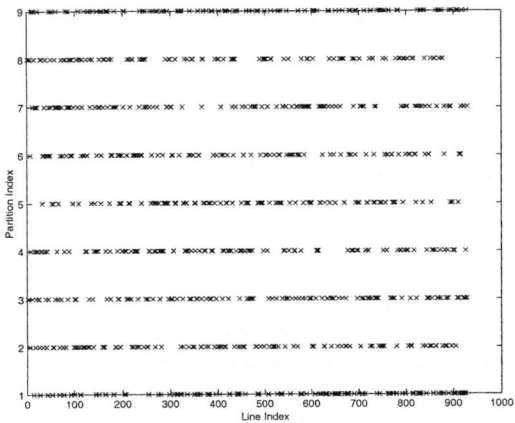

Fig. 2. Distribution of lines in partitions

Table 2. Average line weight and its standard deviation before/after the embedding phase

Original Document		Embedded Document	
Line Avg.	Standard Dev.	Line Avg.	Standard Dev.
48893	90843	48891	128920
46091	89043	46092	119453
50231	91062	50231	138067
50982	72075	50981	113801
49810	88943	49809	135925
47932	80438	47933	108932
49580	91854	49581	140382
45325	74390	45325	121748
47941	101478	47943	153930

which is then solved by a probabilistic metaheuristic. Applying such an algorithm leads to higher security than using conventional deterministic algorithms. Secondly, we propose a new hybrid multi-scale ant colony algorithm in this paper. The algorithm has its own interest as well and might be useful for related optimization problems.

References

1. Amano, T., Misaki, D.: A feature calibration method for watermarking of document images. In: Proc. 5th Int. Conf. Document Analysis and Recognition. (1999) 91–94
2. Barnard, S.T., Simon, H.D.: A fast multilevel implementation of recursive spectral bisection for partitioning unstructured problems. Concurrency: Practice and Experience **6**(2) (1994) 101–117

3. Bianchi, L., Gambardella, L.M., Dorigo, M.: Solving the homogeneous probabilistic traveling salesman problem by the aco metaheuristic. In: Ant Algorithms, Third International Workshop. (2002) 176–187
4. Brassil, J., Low, S., Maxemchuk, N.: Copyright protection for the electronic distribution of text documents. In: Proc. IEEE. **87** (1999) 1181–1196
5. Brassil, J., O'Gorman, L.: Watermarking document images with bounding box expansion. In: Proc. Info Hiding'96. (1996) 227–235
6. Bui, T.N., Rizzo, J.R.: Finding maximum cliques with distributed ants. In: GECCO. (2004) 24–35
7. Chitty, D.M., Hernandez, M.L.: A hybrid ant colony optimisation technique for dynamic vehicle routing. In: GECCO (2004) 48–59
8. Dorigo, M., Gambardella, L.M.: Ant colony system: A cooperative learning approach to the traveling salesman problem. IEEE Transactions on Evolutionary Computation **1**(1) (1997) 53–66
9. Gambardella, L.M., Taillard, E., Agazzi, G.: Ant colonies for vehicle routing problems. In: New Ideas in Optimization. McGraw-Hill (1999)
10. Hendrickson, B., Leland, R.: A multilevel algorithm for partitioning graphs. In: Proc. Supercomputing'95. (1995)
11. Hu, S.: Document image watermarking based on weight-invariant partition using support vector machine. In: International Workshop on Document Analyis Systems (DAS). (2004)
12. Jiang, G., Yu, M., Shi, S., Liu, X., Kim, Y.: New blind image watermarking in dct domain. In: Proc. 6th Int. Conf. Signal Processing. (2002) 1580–1583
13. Korosec, P., Silc, J., Robic, B.: Mesh partitioning: A multilevel ant-colony-optimization algorithm. In: IPDPS-NIDISC. (2003) 146
14. Kundur, D., Hatzinakos, D.: A robust digital image watermarking method using wavelet-based fusion. In: Proc. IEEE Int. Conf. Image Processing. (1997) 544–547
15. Lin, C.-Y., Wu, M., Bloom, J.A., Miller, M.L., Cox, I.J., Lui, Y.-M.: Rotation, scale, and translation resilient public watermarking for images. IEEE Transactions on Image Processing **10**(5) (2001) 767–782
16. Low, S., Maxemchuk, N.: Capacity of text marking channel. IEEE Signal Processing Letters **7**(12) (2000) 345–347
17. Low, S., Maxemchuk, N., Lapone, A,: Document identification for copyright protection using centroid detection. IEEE Transactions on Communications **46** (1998) 372–383
18. Maniezzo, V., Colorni, A.: The ant system applied to the quadratic assignment problem. IEEE Transactions on Knowledge and Data Engineering **11**(5) (1999) 769–778
19. Maniezzo, V., Gambardella, L.M., de Luigi, F.: Ant colony optimization. In: Onwubolu, G.C., Babu, B.V. (eds.): New Optimization Techniques in Engineering, Springer-Verlag, Berlin, Heidelberg (2004) 101–117
20. Moulin, R., Mihcak, M., Lin, G.: An information-theoretic model for image watermarking and data hiding. In: Proc. Int. Conf. Image Processing. (2000) 667–670
21. Shmygelska, A., Hernández, R.A., Hoos, H.H.: An ant colony optimization algorithm for the 2d hp protein folding problem. In: Ant Algorithms, Third International Workshop. (2002) 40–53

An Image Retrieval System Based on Region Classification

Özge Can Özcanlı and Fatoş Yarman-Vural

Middle East Technical University, Ankara, Turkey
vural@ceng.metu.edu.tr

Abstract. In this study, a content based image retrieval (CBIR) system to query the objects in an image database is proposed. Images are represented as collections of regions after being segmented with Normalized Cuts algorithm. MPEG-7 content descriptors are used to encode regions in a 239-dimensional feature space. User of the proposed CBIR system decides which objects to query and labels exemplar regions to train the system using a graphical interface. Fuzzy ARTMAP algorithm is used to learn the mapping between feature vectors and binary coded class identification numbers. Preliminary recognition experiments prove the power of fuzzy ARTMAP as a region classifier. After training, features of all regions in the database are extracted and classified. Simple index files enabling fast access to all regions from a given class are prepared to be used in the querying phase. To retrieve images containing a particular object, user opens an image and selects a query region together with a label in the graphical interface of our system. Then the system ranks all regions in the indexed set of the query class with respect to their L_2 (Euclidean) distance to the query region and displays resulting images. During retrieval experiments, comparable class precisions with respect to exhaustive searching of the database are maintained which demonstrates effectiveness of the classifier in narrowing down the search space.

1 Introduction

Content-based image retrieval research has been popular for over 3 decades. Several systems have been developed for commercial applications (see [9, 10] for good reviews). However, despite the apparent success of the querying systems, they are still far from retrieving images containing particular objects. Studies [7, 8] reveal the need to query in the "things" domain, which suggests integration of object recognition techniques with current retrieval architectures. However, object recognition is possible via the utilization of certain representation schemes which usually require clean segmentation of the object from the rest of the image. In this regard, segmentation of images into coherent regions and representing them as collections of regions is a strong candidate as an intermediate level representation [6, 12]. Current automatic image segmentation methods are far from extracting the objects. However, the regions coarsely correspond to objects or parts of objects in a natural image. A learning system that can query objects in an inexactly segmented database is highly desirable.

In this paper, such a system is proposed. It is well-known that conventional indexing schemes are not feasible for high dimensional feature vectors. Our system enables efficient indexing via classification of regions. Mpeg-7 content descriptors are used to encode various features of the regions forming a very high dimensional feature vector. Fuzzy ARTMAP supervised learning algorithm, which can rapidly self-organize stable categorical mappings between input and output vectors [4,5], is then utilized to classify image regions. Once all the regions in a database are classified, objects are queried effectively.

In Section 2, architectural details of our retrieval system will be summarized, in Section 3, fuzzy ARTMAP algorithm will be briefly introduced and results of our preliminary experiments for region classification will be given. Lastly, in Section 4 results of our experiments on an image database will be presented.

2 System

Our system works on presegmented image databases. The image data is generated by Normalized Cuts [11] automatic segmentation algorithm (Figures 2 and 3). Figure 1 gives an overview of the stages in our retrieval architecture which will be described next. Assuming that the aim of the user is to query certain objects in the database, the first stage is manually forming a training set. We developed a GUI, which enables the user to select images and label its regions according to the querying needs. Our system encodes certain features of regions and works in this feature domain. The next stage is feature extraction of the training set. These features constitute the input vectors to our fuzzy ARTMAP classifier and the class label ids are binary encoded output vectors. After training, in the database importing stage, all of the feature vectors are classified and their class labels are indexed. In the querying phase, user selects a region and a label whose index is used for fast access. The regions with this label are ranked and displayed to the user. An image is displayed only once if it has more than one regions with the same label. L_2 (Euclidean) distance between feature vectors is used to rank the regions.

2.1 Feature Extraction

In this study, we used all the descriptors designed for still image content description in MPEG-7 set, as follows: edge histogram (80 features); color layout (12 features); dominant color (4 features); region shape (35 features); scalable color (16 features); color structure (32 features) and homogeneous texture (60 features) [2]. The feature extraction schemes of each descriptor are explained in detail in [3]. All the features are mapped to analog [0-1] scale and concatenated to form the final feature vector of size 239 to represent each region.

3 Fuzzy ARTMAP Algorithm

ARTMAP is a class of Neural Network architectures that perform incremental supervised learning. ARTMAP was initially proposed to classify input patterns

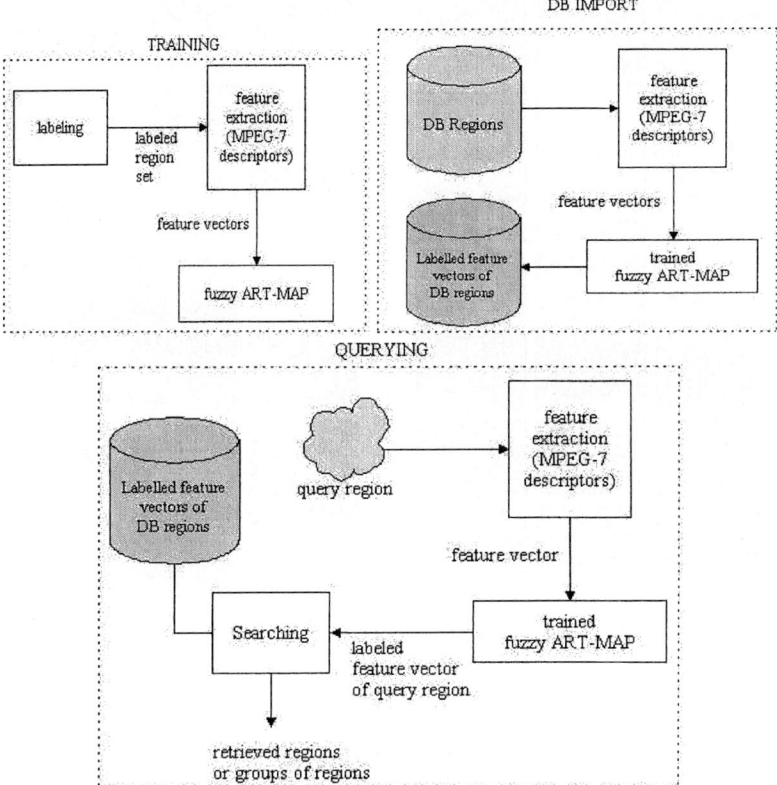

Fig. 1. Overview of the proposed CBIR system

represented as binary values. Carpenter et al. [5] refined the system to a general one by redefining ART dynamics in terms of fuzzy set theory operations. Fuzzy ARTMAP learns to classify inputs represented with a fuzzy set of features where each feature is a value in [0-1] scale indicating the extent to which that feature is present. The details of the algorithm can be found in [5].

In this study, fuzzy ARTMAP is chosen as a classifier because of the following reasons. First of all, more than one regions can be mapped to the same class. For example, the black and white regions of a penguin which are labeled with the same keyword "penguin" can be categorized differently while being associated to the same class. This is a rather fascinating property of fuzzy ARTMAP; since the regions can be grouped under proper classes even if their feature vectors are dissimilar. Such a property cannot be achieved by classical distance-based similarity measuring CBIR systems.

Another key characteristic of fuzzy ARTMAP is that it learns top-down expectations that can bias the system to ignore masses of irrelevant data. The system selectively searches for recognition categories whose top-down expectations provide an acceptable match to bottom-up data. Each top-down expecta-

Fig. 2. Sample images from the Corel data set

Fig. 3. Sample outputs of Normalized Cuts segmentation

tion focuses the attention upon, and bind, that cluster of input features that are part of the prototype which it has already learned, while suppressing features that are not. In the recall phase, only the group of features that are attended by the expectation of each class determine the classification. This process can be regarded as a salient feature detection in the form of expectations for each class. For instance, the system can learn to suppress color features and attend to Gabor filter responses at certain scales to categorize "flowers". In this way, a large variety of features extracted with different computational methods can be used in combination and their relative importance to discriminate different classes can be detected.

To demonstrate effectiveness of fuzzy ARTMAP in region classification, 5 training sets are formed via labeling of randomly chosen exemplars of 6 distinctive object classes from total of 13 classes. The sets and the number of regions they contain are given in Table 1. Some background regions are also labeled for completeness, however 5 test sets are formed from only object regions, i.e. by eliminating background regions from training sets.

During labeling operation training sets are prepared such that exemplars of each class are nearly ordered. Initial experiments are performed by presenting patterns to the network in their original order during training. After training, 5 classifiers trained with 5 training sets are tested using each of the test sets. The percentage of regions classified correctly in each test set are given in Figure 4 (Left) and as expected, performance increase with the increasing number of training patterns. Performances start to be satisfactory for sets 4 and 5. So from

Table 1. Hand-labeled region counts from different classes in each training set

class	set1	set2	set3	set4	set5
tiger	2	5	10	23	33
bear	2	5	10	20	30
plane	2	5	10	20	30
elephant	2	5	10	21	31
penguin	2	5	10	22	32
cheetah	2	5	10	20	30
grass	2	5	10	6	16
river	0	0	0	6	9
sky	2	5	10	7	15
tree	2	5	10	6	16
snow	2	5	10	6	16
rocks	0	0	0	6	6
water	2	5	10	5	12
total	22	55	110	168	276

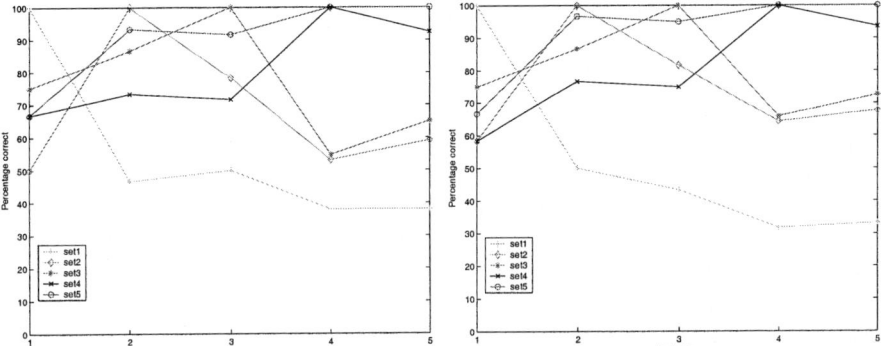

Fig. 4. Percentage of correctly labeled regions in the test sets after training with 5 different sets. With one voter, patterns presented in original order during training (Left). With 10 voters, patterns presented in random orders (Right)

Table 1, we see that 15-30 regions should be labeled for each class, since there are more than one class regions in each image, this means that 10-15 images should be chosen and labeled. Clearly, labeling only two regions from each class is not enough for the system to learn the correct classification of vectors with 239 dimensions. Actually, even training with 30 regions gives about 90% accuracy on average. But the number of regions that users can label in CBIR systems is limited and low which requires the ability of well generalization with less training and tolerance for errors. Our system uses the advantage that images contain more than one object regions to tolerate classification errors, correct classification of one of the regions is enough for the image to be considered for retrieval as explained in Section 4, reducing the chance of missing relevant images of a class due to classification errors.

During our preliminary experiments, we discovered that there are no other parameters that effect the performance of the system significantly. However, it is well-known that fuzzy-ARTMAP is vulnerable to the order of pattern presentation during training. In [5], authors point at this property and propose a voting scheme to overcome the vulnerability. Figure 4 (Right) shows the new performance rates of the system when a system with 10 voters is used. Each of the voters is trained with randomly ordered versions of the same pattern sets and a category of an unknown pattern in the test set is taken to be the majority vote. If left and right plots in Figure 4 are compared, it can be observed that there is a slight performance increase for each training set except set 1 which actually demonstrates one more time, the insufficiency of this set for classification purposes. During the experiments, we also observed that increasing number of voters do not affect the results significantly.

4 Retrieval Experiments

Our database contains 938 images from Corel data set [1] with 10 classes: "zebra" with 38 images, "tiger", "bear", "plane", "penguin", "cheetah", "elephant", "horse", "fox" and "flower" with 100 images each (see Figure 2 for examples from each class). The number of regions in the database is 6661. (After segmentation, images contain 2-20 regions and largest 8 are chosen when there are more.) To index the database with class labels, all the regions in the database are classified using the fuzzy ARTMAP modules trained with sets 4 and 5 which are extended to contain zebra, horse, fox and flower regions. 20 random regions from each of these classes are labeled and added to set 4 and 30 random regions from each are labeled and added to set 5. The performance of the proposed system is tested by

---

Algorithm 1 Find the average recall and precision for a given class

t = total number of relevant images of this class in the database
m = match threshold
find **SLR** = set of regions labeled with the label of this class
for each image **i** of the class
    for each region **r** of **i**
        for each region **rr** in **SLR**
            find the L_2 (Euclidean) distance between **r** and **rr**
        sort **SLR** according to the distance values
        take 1 region per image and find the sorted image list **LSI**
        correct = the relevant images of this class in top **m** images in **LSI**
        recall_region = **correct** / **t**
        precision_region = **correct** / **m**
    recall_image = best of all **recall_region** values
    precision_image = best of all **precision_region** values
recall_class = average of all **recall_image** values
precision_class = average of all **precision_image** values

Table 2. The CPU time in seconds for sample querying sessions

class	base	set8	set9
tiger	215.87	32.11	12.44
bear	207.24	4.91	9.42
plane	143.3	24.27	29.9

Algorithm 1. This algorithm computes the average recall and precision for each class by automatically querying with all regions of each image in the class. The recall and precision for an image is set to be the values of the region giving best recall and precision values. Since one of these regions is assured to belong to the distinctive object of the class, it is assumed that no other region can give better recall and precision values for that class. The motivation is that if a user was to query with this image, he/she would select one of the distinctive object regions and at best get the precision and recall found with this automatic method. In this way, the burden of preparing query for each class image manually is avoided. The algorithm initially finds the set of regions labeled with the label of this class after classification of all the database regions. This set is used for querying and the search space is reduced for each class depending on the number of regions labeled from that class after classification. (Tables 3 and 4 show these numbers for each training set.)

To determine the effectiveness of the system, a baseline method is needed for comparison. This method is obtained by querying the database without using the Fuzzy ARTMAP classification. An automatic method similar to Algorithm 1 is used which simply finds the Euclidean distance of each region in the database to all other regions instead of to the labeled set of the class (**SLR** in Algorithm 1). This method gives reasonable results, since the database size is not large (6661 regions). However, the complexity is $O(n^2)$ where n is the number of regions in

Table 3. The number of labeled database regions from each class after classification with 1 voter systems

class	set4	set5
tiger	1016	392
bear	162	319
plane	1134	1401
elephant	267	230
penguin	1687	392
cheetah	393	404
horse	365	1901
fox	275	185
zebra	211	233
flower	865	516

Table 4. The number of labeled database regions from each class after classification with 10 voter systems

class	set4	set5
tiger	586	365
bear	146	357
plane	1166	1512
elephant	111	211
penguin	1000	467
cheetah	410	393
horse	415	907
fox	1260	298
zebra	643	257
flower	829	663

the database. Indeed our system reduces the size of the search space by labeling the regions in the database, and it does not only speed up the querying process, but also enables larger databases to be searched effectively. Table 2 shows the CPU times for sample querying sessions, where the speed up is clearly observed.

Algorithm 1 and exhaustive searching algorithm are run for 5 different match threshold values: 10, 20, 30, 40 and 50. The performance of our systems are shown in Figures 5 and 6. Figures are the recall/precision plots of the class averages. Both baseline values and 1 voter and 10 voter systems' values are plotted for comparison. For most of the classes, precision rates are comparable to the base-

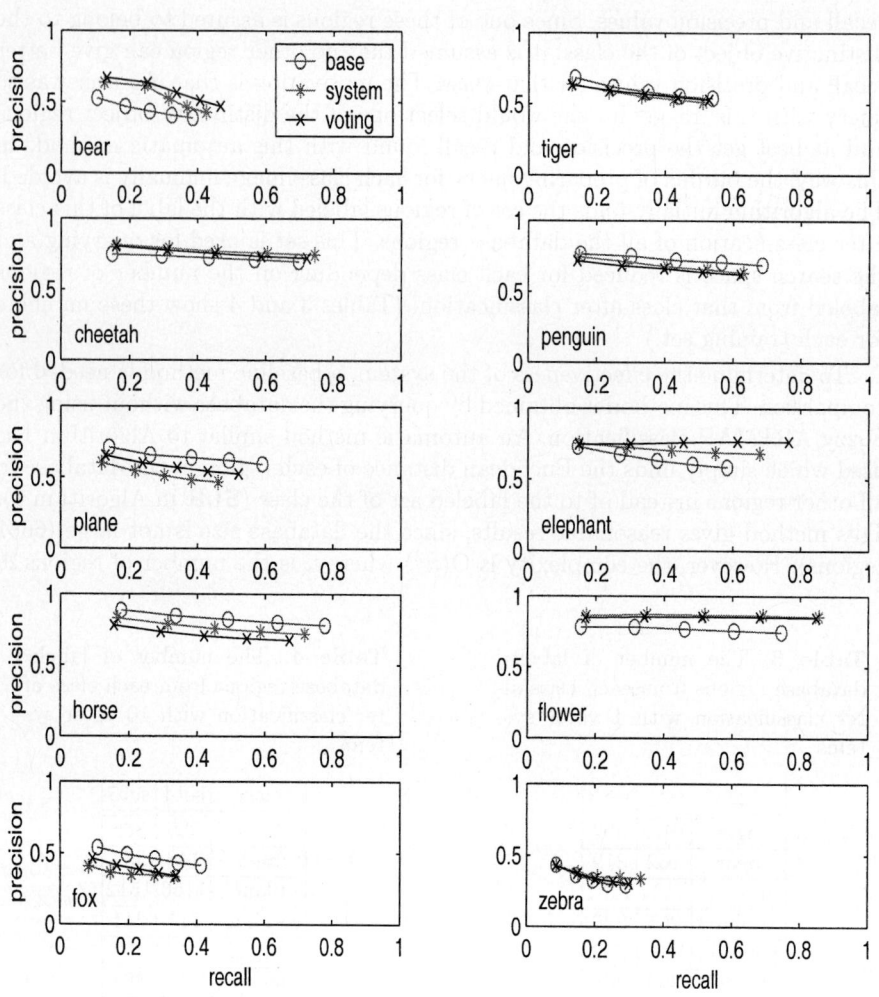

Fig. 5. Average recall and precision values for each class with training set 4

line values, which demonstrates the effectiveness of our system in narrowing the

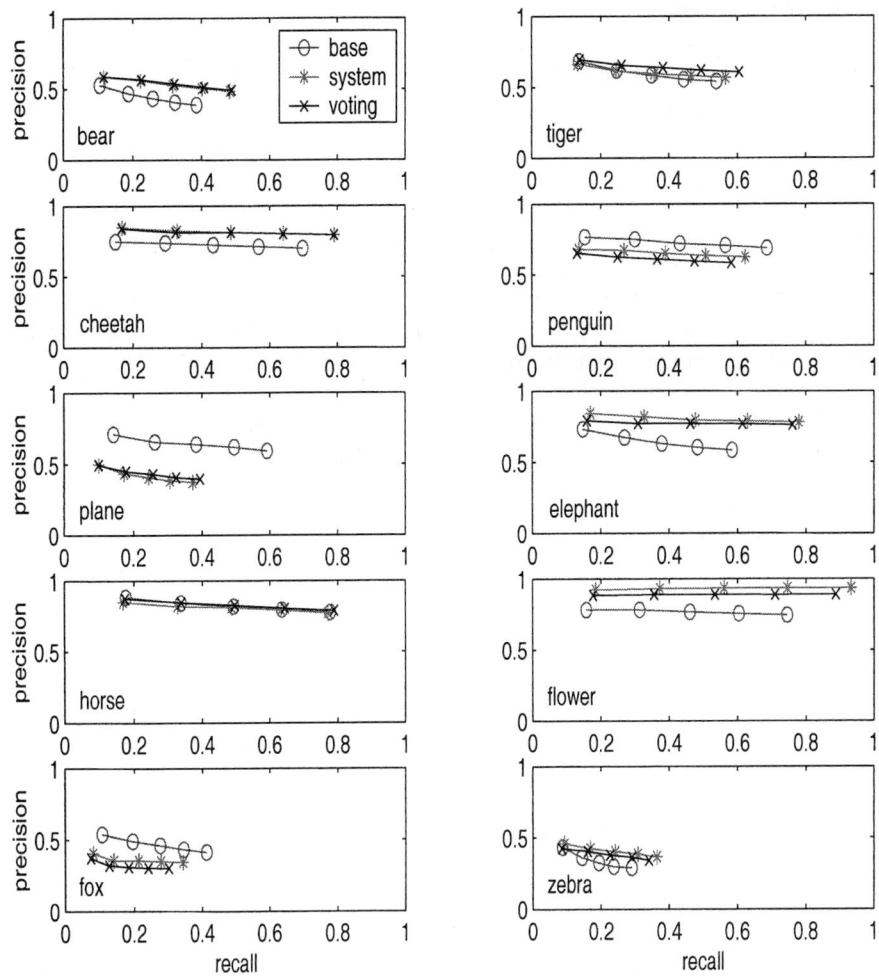

Fig. 6. Average recall and precision values for each class with training set 5

search space. Also, for certain classes like "flowers" precision is highly improved as exhaustive searching of the database creates many false alarms. On the other hand, "plane" class seems to suffer a lot from our method, which might be due to the high variability within the members of this class and fuzzy ARTMAP's being unable to group input patterns and find salient features to attend to for each group. Although a large number of database regions are labeled as "plane", most of these are false alarms regarding low precision values. Also it should be noted that voting mechanism is not effective in increasing precision values proving the relative unimportance of the presentation of the patterns during training for this task.

5 Conclusion

In this paper, it has been shown that Fuzzy ARTMAP classification of image regions is a promising step towards object based querying of large databases. ARTMAP is effective at assigning different salient features for each class and giving satisfactory classification rates despite the very high dimension of the feature vector and the limited amount of training as the comparably high precision values show. Correct classification of difficult classes, like planes due to their high within class variation remains as a challenge. This difficulty might be overcome in a retrieval system by the use of certain background regions to support the query. As a future study, we plan to improve our system in this direction to allow querying via combinations of different regions to increase precision.

References

1. Corel data set. http://www.corel.com/products/clipartandphotos
2. Mpeg-7 context, objectives and technical roadmap. Technical Report, ISO/IEC JTC1/SC29/WG11/N2861, International Organization for Standardisation, Coding of Moving Pictures and Audio (1999)
3. Multimedia content description interface, part 3 visual. Technical Report, ISO/IEC JTC1/SC29/WG11/N4062, International Organization for Standardisation, Coding of Moving Pictures and Audio (2001)
4. Carpenter, G.A.: Art neural networks: Distributed coding and artmap applications. Technical Report, CAS/CNS TR-2000-005, MA: Boston University (2000)
5. Carpenter, G.A., Grossberg, S., Markuzon, N., Reynolds, J.H., Rosen, D.B.: Fuzzy artmap: A neural network architecture for incremental supervised learning of analog multidimensional maps. IEEE Transactions on Neural Networks **3**(5) (1992) 698–713
6. Carson, C., Belongie, S., Greenspan, H., Malik, J.: Blobworld: Color and texture based image segmentation using em and its application to image querying and classification. IEEE Transactions on Pattern Analysis and Machine Intelligence **24**(8) (2002) 1026–1038
7. Enser, P.: Query analysis in a visual information retrieval context. J. Doc. and Text Management **1**(1) (1993) 25–52
8. Forsyth, D., Malik, J., Wilensky, R.: Searching for digital pictures. Scientific American **276**(6) (1997) 72–77
9. Forsyth, D.A., Ponce, J.: Computer vision: A modern approach. Prentice-Hall (2001)
10. Rui, Y., Huang, T.S., Chang, S.: Image retrieval: Current techniques, promising directions, and open issues. Journal of Visual Communication and Image Representation **10**(4) (1999) 39–62
11. Shi, J., Malik, J.: Normalized cuts and image segmentation. IEEE Transactions on Pattern Analysis and Machine Intelligence **22**(8) (2000) 888–905
12. Wang, J.Z., Li, J., Wiederhold, G.: Simplicity: Semantics-sensitive integrated matching for picture libraries. IEEE Transactions on Pattern Analysis and Machine Intelligence **23**(9) (2001) 947–963

Temporal Data Modeling and Integrity Constraints in Relational Databases[*]

Abdullah Uz Tansel[†]

Department of Statistics and Computer Information Systems
Baruch College - CUNY
55 Lexington Avenue, Box 11-220; NY, NY 10010
tansel@baruch.cuny.edu

Abstract. We address the key issues of temporal data modeling and temporal integrity constraints in the temporal extensions to the relational data model in attribute and tuple time stamping. These issues include representation of temporal data, temporal grouping identifiers, primary keys of temporal relations and other forms of temporal integrity constraints. We extend the traditional integrity constraints to the temporal domain. In tackling subtle issues temporality creates, we conceptualize that a temporal integrity constraint has a data and a temporal (time) component. The time component of a temporal integrity constraint limits the attribute values to the lifespan of an object (tuple). We also generalize single state integrity constraints to multi-state temporal integrity constraints and apply them to existential and referential integrity. We provide algorithms for enforcing the two types of temporal integrity constraints.

1 Introduction

The capability to maintain temporal data is a crucial requirement for any database management system. A **temporal database** has a time dimension and maintains time-varying data in contrast to a conventional database that carries only the current data. [1,15,23]. In handling temporal data there are many issues such as comparing the database states at two different time points, capturing the periods for concurrent events, handling multi-valued attributes, temporal grouping and coalescing [2,13] and restructuring temporal data, etc, [9,22]. We limit our attention to the relational data model since it is widely used in practice.

We focus on the temporal extensions to the relational data model and address the subtle issues in temporal integrity constraints. We generalize the traditional, single state integrity constraints as the multi-state temporal integrity constraints that apply on multiple states of data stored in a temporal database. There are two forms of multi-state integrity constraints: synchronous and asynchronous. The former is a generalization of the traditional integrity constraints whereas the latter is peculiar to the temporal data only. Moreover, a temporal integrity constraint has a data

---
[*] An extended abstract of this article appears in the proceedings of ITCC'04, April 2004, Las Vegas, NV.
[†] On leave from Baruch College – CUNY, 55 Lexington Avenue, Box 11-220; NY, NY 10010.

component and a time component that requires that all data pertaining to an object may only exist during the lifespan of that object.

Single state and multi-state integrity constraints are also called as static and dynamic (temporal) integrity constraints, respectively [3]. Chomicki uses Past Temporal Logic to formulate temporal integrity constraints and gives an efficient implementation method for them. Unlike our approach of keeping the entire history intact in the database, he extends every database state with auxiliary relations that contain the historical information necessary for checking the integrity constraints [3].

In Section 2, we discuss representation of temporal data and we elaborate on the temporal grouping identifiers and the primary keys of temporal relations. Temporal integrity constraints are the topic of Section 3. Section 4 is the conclusion.

2 Representing Temporal Data

In this section we review the previous work and provide the basic definitions. Atoms take their values from some fixed universe U of reals, integers, character strings and the value null. Some values in U represent time and T denotes the set of these values. We call (T, $\leq$) the time domain and T is a total order under '$\leq$' relationship. We assume for the sake of simplicity that time values range over the integers *0, 1, ... now*. *Now* is a special symbol, at any particular moment, it represents the current time. The value of *now* changes accordingly as the time advances. The symbol *0* represents the relative origin of time. In the context of time, a subset of T is called a **temporal set**. A temporal set that contains consecutive time points $\{t_i, t_{i+1}, ... t_{i+n}\}$ is represented either as a closed interval $[t_i, t_{i+n}]$ or as a half open interval $[t_i, t_{i+n+1})$. A **temporal element** [9] is a temporal set that is represented by the maximal intervals corresponding to its subsets having consecutive time points. Temporal sets, intervals, and temporal elements can be used as time stamps for modeling temporal data.

SALARY	SALARY	SALARY	SALARY
1, 20K	[1, 5), 20K	$\{[1,5) \cup [10,16)\}$, 20K	$\{1,2,3,4,10,11,..., 15\}$, 20K
10, 20K	[10, 16), 20K	$\{[16, now]\}$, 30K	$\{16,17,..., now\}$, 30K
16, 30K	[16, now], 30K		
(a)Time points	(b) Intervals	(c) Temporal element	(d) Temporal set

Fig. 1. Different timestamps

SALARY	START	END		SALARY	TIME
20K	1	5		20K	[1,5)
20K	10	16		20K	[10,16)
30K	16	now		30K	[16,*now*]
(a) With two time columns				(b) With an interval data type	

Fig. 2. Salary in tuple time-stamping

Time-varying data is commonly represented by time-stamping values. The timestamps in any time granularity can be time points [4,21], time intervals [5,10],

[11,13,14,16], temporal sets [18] and temporal elements [9]. Furthermore, these timestamps can be added to tuples or attributes that leads to two different approaches for handling temporal data in the relational data model. Figure 1 gives an example where time points, intervals, temporal elements, and temporal sets are used as attribute timestamps. Each value in Figure 1 is a temporal atom that consists of a salary value and its time reference that can be in any time granularity. We use the same example to illustrate the tuple time stamping, i.e., the timestamps are attached to tuples. Generally, the end points of an interval are added as two separate attributes to a relation. Figure 2(a) depicts Figure 1(b) in tuple time stamping. Figure 2(b) represents the same data by adding a time column whose values are intervals. There are also many other possible representations.

There are various aspects of temporal data such as the time at which the data becomes effective (i.e., **valid time**), or the time the data is recorded in the database (i.e., **transaction time**) etc [14]. In this article we will focus our discussion on the valid time aspect of temporal data. However, our discussion can easily be extended to databases that support transaction time as well.

2.1   Temporal Grouping Identifiers and Primary Keys

Temporal data belonging to an object forms a natural group. We discuss temporal grouping in both attribute time stamping and tuple time stamping. In the following we use same data to illustrate both approaches. In Figure 3, we show some sample employee data for the EMP relation over the scheme E# (Employee number), ENAME (Employee name), DNAME (Department name) and SALARY. E# and ENAME are constant attributes, i.e., they do not change over time whereas DNAME and SALARY are time-varying attributes. In EMP relation, temporal sets are attached to attributes to represent temporal data. Note that EMP is a nested [NINF] relation [19]. Figure 4 gives three 1NF relations in tuple time stamping, EMP_N, EMP_D, and EMP_S for the EMP relation. EMP_D and EMP_S have two additional attributes, START and END that represent the end points of the interval over which a tuple is valid.

Let $R(A_x, A_y)$ be a relation and A_x be the attributes corresponding to an object identifier for the objects R keeps data about. A_y are the remaining attributes. A_x may consist of one or more attributes. If no time is considered, A_x serves as a primary key for the relation R. In other words A_x functionally determines A_y provided that there are no multi-valued attributes in A_y.

In the case of tuple time stamping, each time dependent attribute in A_y requires a separate relation with the scheme (A_x, Z, Start, End) where Z is an attribute in A_y. The attribute combination (A_x, Start) is the primary key of that relation. In fact, A_x is **a temporal grouping identifier** since data that belong to an object are represented by tuples whose A_x values are the same [7]. Tuples with the same E# value represent the data that belong to the same employee.

E#	ENAME	DNAME	SALARY
<[10,now], 121>	Tom	<[10,12), Sales> <[14,18), Mktg>	<[10,15), 20K> <[15,17), 25K> <[17,now], 30K>
<[23,30), 133>	Ann	<[23,30), Sales>	<[23,30), 35K>
<[18,now], 147>	John	<[18,now], Toys>	<[18,now], 42K>

Fig. 3. The EMP relation in attribute time stamping

E#	ENAME
121	Tom
133	Ann
147	John

(a) EMP_N relation

E#	DNAME	START	END
121	Sales	10	12
121	Makt.	14	18
133	Sales	23	30
147	Toys	18	Now

(b) EMP_D relation

E#	SALARY	START	END
121	20K	10	15
121	25K	15	17
121	30K	17	Now
133	35K	23	30
147	42K	18	Now

(c) EMP_S relation

Fig. 4. The EMP relation in tuple time stamping

Essentially, a nested relation allows grouping of an object's entire data into one single tuple and it includes both functionally determined and multi-determined attributes [12]. Taking time into consideration and using attribute time stamping, we would still consider A_x as a primary key for the relation R since in the context of time functional dependencies turn into multi-valued dependencies [20].

3 Temporal Integrity Constraints

Each object, such as an employee, exists in a certain period of time, which is a subset of [0,*now*]. We call this period the object's *life*, denoted as $l(o)$ for the object o. Part or all of an object's life is stored in a database and we call it its *lifespan, ls(o)*. Hence, $ls(o) \subseteq l(o)$. Constant attributes of an object o do not change during $l(o)$ and hence $ls(o)$, whereas time-dependent attributes assume different values during this period of time. Some attributes may not even exist in part or all of these periods. Thus, a constant attribute, such as an employee number, can be represented with no timestamp where its time reference is implied as $ls(o)$. It can also be represented with an explicit time reference in the form of a temporal atom, $<(ls(o), o.E\#>$, where E# is the identifier of the object o. Naturally, $ls(o)$ would be the time reference of the tuple representing the object o in tuple time stamping.

A traditional database contains the current snapshot of the reality. The integrity constraints are enforced in this state of the database. We call them **single state** integrity constraints (also called static integrity constraints [3]) since they apply to the data valid at an instance of time, i.e. the current state of the database. Single state integrity constraints are directly applicable to any snapshot of a temporal database. On the other hand **multi-state integrity constraints** (also called dynamic or temporal integrity constraints [3]) apply on several snapshots (states) of a temporal database. There are two types of multi-state integrity constraints. A **synchronous multi-state integrity constraint** applies to several database states (snapshots) in sequence. In other words, it is a single state integrity constraint that applies to each of the several database states separately. This is the same as the **sequenced** interpretation of [15]. An **asynchronous multi-state integrity constraint** applies to several states of the database at the same time, i.e. limits the data values valid at different time instants. In other words, given the time instants t_1, t_2 and $t_1 \neq t_2$ an asynchronous multi-state integrity constraint involves the data values valid at t_1 and t_2.

A temporal integrity constraint has two components: a data component and a time (temporal) component. In most of the cases the data component of a temporal integrity constraint is a synchronous multi-state integrity constraint that is analogous to a traditional (single state) integrity constraint. The data component can also be an asynchronous multi-state integrity constraint that does not have a traditional (non-temporal) counterpart. The temporal component of a multi-state integrity constraint is peculiar only to the temporal databases. It is a direct consequence of the fact that the attributes of an object can assume values during any subset of that object's lifespan. In other words, an attribute of an object may not have any values outside of the lifespan of that object.

Two fundamental constraints in the relational data model are existential and referential integrity constraints. The former specifies that a primary key attribute may not have nulls, and the latter specifies that a relationship can exist only if the participating objects (entities) exist. We extend these constraints to the temporal databases.

3.1 Temporal Existential Integrity

Temporal existential integrity requires that attributes representing an object's identity (primary key) may not have null values in any part of the object's life ($l(o)$) or lifespan ($ls(o)$). In this respect, a traditional existential integrity constraint directly applies to temporal relations as a synchronous multi-state temporal integrity constraint. The time component of an existential integrity constraint requires that an object's attributes can only assume values during the lifespan of that object. Table 1 gives the rules for the temporal existential integrity constraint and Table 2 outlines the steps for enforcing the time component of an existential integrity constraint.

The lifespan of tuples (objects) need to be stored in the database since they are essential data in a temporal database. If we use N1NF temporal relations we can add it to the primary key (temporal grouping identifier) as its time references, the E# attribute of EMP relation of Figure 3. In case of tuple time stamping, the lifespan of objects should be stored in a separate relation. For instance, to represent EMP relations of Figure 4 (hence Figure 3), a separate relation EMP_LS(E#, Start, End) is needed to represent the lifespan of each employee (Figure 5). This data cannot be added to (or deduced from) the EMP_D or EMP_S relations in Figure 4 since they contain data about department and salary attributes and their time reference can only be a subset of an employee's lifespan, i.e., for the employee e $ls(e[\text{DNAME}]) \subseteq ls(e[\text{E\#}])$ and $ls(e[\text{SALARY}]) \subseteq ls(e[\text{E\#}])$.

E#	START	END
121	10	12
121	14	Now
133	23	30
147	18	Now

DNAME	BUDGETX
	BUDGET
<[0,30), Sales>	<[0,10), 10K>
	<[10,30), 20K>
<[14,*now*, Mkt>	<[14,*now*), 20K>
<[18,*now*, Toys>	<[18,*now*, 30K>

Fig. 5. EMP_LS relation in tuple time stamping

Fig. 6. DEPARTMENT relation in attribute time stamping

Therefore, in tuple time stamping a relation like EMP_LS (Figure 5) is required. Table 2 gives the procedures to enforce the time component of a temporal existential integrity constraint. To accommodate different time granularities a slight change is needed. A granularity conversion is added to step 2 and step 5 of the procedures for attribute and tuple time stamping, respectively. Certainly the respective granularities should be compatible and granularity of the primary key should be finer than the granularity of time-dependent attribute.

Table 1. Temporal existential integrity constraint

1. At any time instant the primary key and the temporal grouping identifier of a temporal relation may not have null values. 2. The primary key values and the temporal grouping identifier values are constant, i.e., the same for all the time instants in an object's lifespan. 3. Time reference of a primary key and the temporal grouping identifier in a tuple may not be null. 4. Any attribute of a temporal relation in a tuple t may not assume values outside of the lifespan of tuple t, i.e., the object tuple t represents.

Requirement 2 in Table 1 (the primary key values are constant) manifests itself differently between traditional and temporal databases as well as between tuple and attribute time stamping. In a traditional database if the primary key values are not allowed to change; this is enforced as a business rule outside of the database system. If the primary key values are allowed to change the database system does not track it. On the other hand, requirement 2 can be enforced in a temporal database as the data component of an existential integrity constraint. It is an asynchronous multi-state integrity constraint since it requires that the primary key attribute values at different time instants in object's lifespan should be the same. However, in tuple time stamping the temporal grouping identifier (for instance E#) looses its capability to group temporal data whereas no such loss occurs in attribute time stamping as we have discussed the details in Section 2. Reader is referred to [17] for further details.

Table 2. Enforcing time component of a temporal existential integrity constraint

1. Get the time reference of an attribute, i.e. salary. 2. Test to verify that attribute's time reference is a subset of the time reference of the primary key (temporal grouping identifier). 3. Repeat steps 1 and 2 for the remaining time dependent attribute. (Since the entire history of an attribute is in the same tuple the time reference of an attribute can easily be calculated).	1. Consider the lifespan relation, i.e., EMP_LS in Figure 7. 2. Consider a temporal relation, i.e., EMP_S in Fig. 4. 3. Join the relations of steps 1 and 2 on the equality of the temporal grouping identifier i.e. E#. 4. Group by (partition) the result of step 3 by the temporal grouping identifier i.e. E#. 5. Combine the time reference of the temporal grouping identifier and the time reference of the time dependent attribute for each partition. Then, verify that the latter is a subset of the former. 6. Repeat steps 1-5 for the remaining temporal relations
a) Attribute time stamping	b) Tuple time stamping

3.2 Temporal Referential Integrity

Referential Integrity requires that values in the referencing relation should exist in the referenced relation. Data maintenance operations violating referential integrity are not allowed or cascaded to enforce referential integrity. Table 3 lists the temporal referential integrity constraint. As in the case of temporal existential integrity there are two components of temporal referential integrity, the data and time components. Data component refers to the traditional referential integrity that can be intuitively applied at every time instant stored in the database that is a synchronous multi-state integrity constraint. This can be accomplished by synchronizing the times of attributes in the referenced and the referencing tables. Then the values are compared to verify that the referential integrity holds. This is the same as the notion of sequenced integrity constraint in [15]. Table 4 gives a sketch of the procedures to enforce the data component of a temporal referential integrity constraint for attribute and tuple time stamping, respectively. The time component is similar to the case of temporal existential integrity. Time of the foreign key attribute in the referencing table should be a subset of the time of the attribute (temporal grouping identifier) in the referenced temporal relation.

Table 3. Temporal referential integrity constraint

1. At any time instant a foreign key value in a tuple (referencing table) should be null or appears among the values of the temporal grouping identifier that is the part of the primary key in the referenced table. 2. Time reference of a forcign key value in a tuple should be a subset of the time reference of the temporal grouping identifier that is the part of the primary key in the referenced table.

To illustrate temporal referential integrity we will consider two examples. The first one involves to a 1:m relationship between employees and departments whereas the second one involves to a m:n relationship between employees and projects.

Consider the EMP relation of Figure 3 and the DEPARTMENT relations of Figure 6, respectively. There is a 1:m relationship between these relations. DNAME in EMP is a foreign key since DNAME in DEPARTMENT is the temporal grouping identifier (part of the primary key). Procedure (a) in Table 4 enforces the data part of a synchronous multi-state integrity constraint, that is, every DNAME value in EMP synchronously appears in some tuple of DEPARTMENT_LS relation. For the case of tuple time stamping consider the EMP_D relation of Figure 4 and DEPARTMENT_LS relation of Figure 7. Note that the DNAME is a temporal grouping identifier for DEPART-MENT relation. We follow the procedure (b) in Table 4 to enforce that the DNAME value in a tuple of EMP_D relation appears in some tuple of DEPARTMENT_LS relation.

Table 2 can slightly be modified to obtain the rules in Table 4 for enforcing the time component of a temporal referential integrity constraint, that is, for a tuple e of EMP relation and a tuple d of DEPARTMENT relation $ls(e[DNAME]) \subseteq ls(d[DNAME])$. The same requirement holds for the tuple time stamping too.

The second example involves a relationship between employees and the projects they work for. Consider a relation, EP(E#, P#, TOOLS) where an employee (E#) works for many projects (P#) and uses TOOLS. Also in a project many employees work. Due to space limitations we do not depict the EP relation. Let ep, e and p be tuples of EP, EMP and PROJECT relations respectively. E# attribute in EP is a foreign key attribute therefore, $ls(ep[E\#]) \subseteq ls(e[E\#])$. So is the case for P#, i.e., $ls(ep[P\#]) \subseteq ls(p[P\#])$. Moreover, the relationship, EP, can only exist during a common time period between the existence of an employee and a project that is $ls(ep[E\#, P\#]) \subseteq ls(e[E\#]) \cap ls(p[P\#])$.

Table 4. Enforcing temporal referential integrity

1. Consider a foreign key attribute, i.e., DNAME in EMP 2. Unnest the foreign key attribute, i.e., DNAME 3. Verify that time reference of foreign key attribute (i.e., DNAME) is a subset of the time reference of the primary key in the referenced relation, i.e., DNAME in the DEPARTMENT relation	1. Consider a temporal relation that has a foreign key attribute, i.e., EMP_D relation 2. Consider the lifespan relation where foreign key attribute appears as the primary key, i.e., DEPARTMENT_LS 3. Verify that time EMP_D is a subset of the time of DEPARTMENT_LS
a) Attribute time stamping	b) Tuple time stamping

In the temporal context, there is a possible interplay between the referential integrity and the domain constraints. The data component of a temporal referential integrity constraint may also be combined with domain constraints on the data valid at different times, i.e., an asynchronous multi-state temporal integrity constraint. For instance, the constraint that an employee could only work for the Toy department after working in the Sales department is an example of such a constraint. Thus, if the foreign key attribute in EMP relation has the values, toys at time instant t_i and sales at t_j then $t_i > t_j$ and there is no other time instant between t_i and t_j with a different data value. The constraint that an employee cannot work in the same department without working in all the other departments is another example for an asynchronous multi-state temporal integrity constraint. To be precise, these constraints can be visualized as a combination of temporal referential integrity and domain (attribute) integrity constraints. This combination is peculiar to the temporal databases. In a traditional database additional data is required to enforce such constraints.

DNAME	START	END
Sales	0	30
Mkt.	14	Now
Toys	18	Now

Fig. 7. DEPARTMENT_LS relation in tuple time stamping

DNAME	BUDGET	START	END
Sales	10K	0	10
Sales	20K	10	30
Mkt	20K	14	now
Toys	30K	18	now

Fig. 8. DEPARTMENT_BUDGET relation in tuple time stamping

Naturally, temporal referential integrity holds in relations in which relationships are embedded. In this case, temporal referential integrity has to be enforced within the same relation. If the EMP relation in Figure 3 includes the EP relation as well, then temporal referential integrity has to be enforced in EMP relation. Each tuple of EMP relation would contain a set of P# values or a sub-relation to represent the relationship. The time reference of keys in sub-relations (P#) should be within the time reference of the keys of outer relations i.e., E#. Let e be a tuple of the EMP relation augmented with EP relationship, then $ls(P\#$ in $e(\text{sub-relation}[P\#])) \subseteq ls(e[E\#])$.

The referencing attribute and the referenced attribute may have different time granularities. If these time granularities are compatible a slight modification in the procedure given in Table 4 would be sufficient. Step 3 of procedures (a) and (b) would be expended with a granularity conversion from the coarse one to the finer to accommodate the comparison operation.

4 Conclusion

We have discussed the representation of temporal data and temporal integrity constraints. Temporal grouping identifiers and primary keys in temporal relations are two essential and related constraints for temporal data. Most temporal extensions to the relational data model do not separate the primary keys and temporal grouping identifiers and load both functions the primary keys. Temporal grouping identifiers function differently in attribute time stamping and tuple time stamping. Temporal integrity constraints have two components: data component and time component. The former is a generalization of traditional integrity constraints whereas the time component is peculiar to temporal databases only. Moreover, traditional integrity constraints are single state constraints whereas temporal integrity constraints are multi state constraints and they can be synchronous or asynchronous. We did not address the issue of homogeneity [9] in this paper. It can also be considered as a form of integrity constraint and it has to be explicitly enforced in both attribute time stamping and tuple time stamping.

In our future work we plan to formally define temporal integrity constraints and explore efficient implementation methods for enforcing them and evaluate the performance of these methods. Considering the large volume of temporal data efficient implementation methods for temporal integrity constraints are especially important. We expect that our work will be useful for the researchers and the practitioners in modeling and managing temporal data.

Acknowledgements

Research is supported by the grant ##65406-00-34 from the PSC-CUNY Research Award Program.

References

1. Betteni, C., Jajodia, S., Wang, S.: Time Granularities in Databases. Data Mining and Temporal Reasoning, Springer-Verlag (1998)
2. Bohlen, M. H., Snodgrass, R. T., Soo, M. D.: Coalescing in Temporal Databases. In: Proceedings of International Conference on Very Large Databases. (1996)
3. Chomicki, J.: Efficient Checking of Temporal Integrity Constraints Using Bounded History Encoding. ACM Transactions on Database Systems 20(2) (1995) 149–186
4. Clifford, J., Croker, A.: The Historical Relational Data Model (HRDM) and Algebra Based on Lifespans. In: Tansel, A.U. et al. (eds.): Temporal Database Theory, Design and Implementation. Benjamin/Cummings (1993)
5. Clifford, J., Tansel, A. U.: On an Algebra for Historical Relational Databases: Two Views. In: Proceedings of ACM SIGMOD International Conference on Management of Data. (1985) 247–265
6. Clifford, J., Croker, A., Tuzhilin, A.: On Completeness of Historical Data Models. ACM Transactions on Database Systems (1993)
7. Clifford, J., Croker, A., Grandi, F., Tuzhilin, A.: On Temporal Grouping. In: Clifford, J., Tuzhilin, A. (eds.): Recent Advances in Temporal Databases. Springer-Verlag (1995)
8. Date, C. J., Darwen, H., Lorentzos, N.: Temporal Data and the Relational Data Model. Morgan Kaufmann Publishers, (2003)
9. Gadia, S.K.: A Homogeneous Relational Model and Query Languages for Temporal Databases. ACM Transactions on Database Systems 13(4) (1988) 418–448
10. Lorentzos, N., Johnson, R.G.: Extending Relational Algebra to Manipulate Temporal Data. Information Systems 13(3) (1988) 289–296
11. Navathe, S. B., Ahmed, R.: TSQL-A Language Interface for History Databases. In: Rolland, C., Bodart, F., Leonard, M. (eds.): Proceedings of the Conference on Temporal Aspects in Information Systems. (1987) 113–128
12. Ozsoyoglu, Z.M., Yuan, L.-Y.: A New Normal Form for Nested Relations. ACM Transactions on Database Systems 12(1) (1987)
13. Sarda, N.L.; Extensions to SQL for Historical Databases. IEEE Transactions on Systems 12 (2) (1987) 247–298
14. Snodgrass, R.: The Temporal Query Language Tquel. ACM Transactions on Database Systems 12(1) (1987) 247–298

15. Snodgrass, R.: Developing Time Oriented Applications in SQL. Morgan Kaufmann Publishers (2000)
16. Tansel, A.U.: Adding Time Dimension to Relational Model and Extending Relational Algebra. Information Systems **11**(4) (1986) 343–355
17. Tansel, A.U.: Temporal Data Modeling and Integrity Constraints in Relational Databases. Technical report, Baruch College, CUNY (2003)
18. Tansel, A.U.: Temporal Relational Data Model. IEEE Transactions on Knowledge and Database Engineering **9**(3) (1997) 464–479
19. Tansel, A.U.: On Handling Time-Varying Data in the Relational Databases. Journal of Information and Software Technology **46**(2) (2004) 119–126
20. Tansel, A.U., Garnett, L.: Nested Temporal Relations. In: Proceedings of ACM SIGMOD International Conference on Management of Data. (1989) 284–293
21. Toman, D., Point-Based Temporal Extension of SQL and Their Efficient Implementation. In: Etzion, O., et al. (eds.): Temporal databases: Research and practice. Springer-Verlag (1998)
22. Tansel, A.U., Tin E.: Expressive Power of Temporal Relational Query Languages. IEEE Transactions on Knowledge and Database Engineering **9**(1) (1997)
23. Tansel, A.U., Clifford, J., Gadia, S. K., Jajodia, S., Segev, A., Snodgrass, R.T. (eds): Temporal Databases: Theory, Design and Implementation. Benjamin/Cummings (1993)

Query Builder: A Natural Language Interface for Structured Databases

Jim Little, Michael de Ga, Tansel Özyer, and Reda Alhajj

Computer Science Dept., University of Calgary, Calgary, AB, Canada
{littlej,dega,ozyer,alhajj}@cpsc.ucalgary.ca

Abstract. In this paper, we describe a novel natural language interface (NLI) called Query Builder (QB). We simply identified some of the limitations that are generally encountered in existing NLIs, and hence implemented the presented NLI system that would address some of these issues. Namely, we developed our own parsing algorithms in order to provide a robust feedback system; a feature that we found lacking in other NLIs. Further, QB has been developed as an intelligent system because it addresses naïve users. This requires QB to be able to interactively guide the user by suggesting modified versions of the raised question.

1 Introduction

Designers of NLI generally face the problem of mapping from the linguistic complexity of natural languages to the structure and rigidity of structured query languages. Natural language questions have the freedom to be much more verbose and ambiguous than database queries [1]. It is up to the developer to be able to sift through these complexities to extract the intended meaning of the question, and properly translate it to an equivalent and syntactically valid database query.

When a valid query cannot be produced by the NLI, it would be useful to report to the user the reason his/her question failed. In some cases, the system is simply unable to handle the concepts or words given by the user (for example, a question asking for customer information directed to a database that stores employee information); this is known as *conceptual failure*. In other cases, the concepts in the question can be recognized by the system, but the question is phrased in a way that the system does not understand. This is known as *linguistic failure* [1]. These linguistic failures suggest that the question can be rephrased into a form such that it can be properly interpreted by the NLI. This process becomes easier if the user is given the appropriate feedback to help rephrase the question, i.e., the NLI should suggest possible alternatives which may guide the user in phrasing the question.

As described in the literature, there are different approaches of NLIs to databases, e.g., [1-10]; and by now their main advantages and disadvantages are well understood. PRECISE is one of the more recent NLI implementations [9]. After trying some of the sample questions provided, and entering some of our own, it was noted that the feedback system provided by PRECISE in the case of conceptual failures is minimal, and the feedback for linguistic failures is virtually non-existent. This is the main motivation to carry out the study described in this paper, which is a more detailed, helpful and informative feedback system.

We developed a novel NLI called Query Builder (QB), which addresses some of the limitations generally encountered in existing NLIs. Namely, we implemented our own parsing algorithms in order to provide a robust feedback system; a feature lacking in other NLIs. QB has been developed as an intelligent system because it addresses naïve users. This requires QB to be able to interactively guide the user by suggesting modified versions of the raised question. We tested QB on a Hockey database. The results are encouraging; demonstrate its applicability and effectiveness. The rest of the paper is organized as follows. Section 2 is an overview of QB. The basic architecture and functionality of QB are described in Section 3. Section 4 is conclusions and future work.

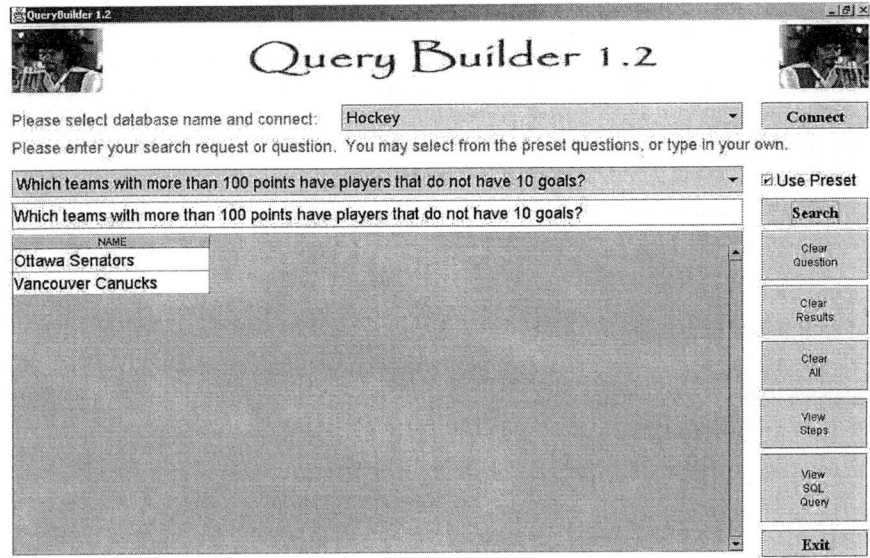

Fig. 1. Sample screen: main interface of our system

2 An Overview of Query Builder

QB is a modest, yet moderately successful contribution to the realm of NLI research. The first prototype has been developed using the Eclipse IDE and can connect to different DBMSs including MySQL, ORACLE, DB2 and ACCESS. QB has been primarily developed on a Dell Inspiron 8000, Pentium III, 256 MB RAM, running Windows 2000. The main interface of QB is shown in Figure 1.

We tested our prototype on a Hockey database, its schema is shown in Figure 2. Note that in certain questions it is important to be able to distinguish the table to select from, and attributes pertain to specific conditions in the question. For example, the question, *"Which players have at least 20 points in teams with at most 60 points?"* would have the following corresponding SQL query:

```
SELECT players.name
FROM players, teams
WHERE players.team=teams.name AND players.points>=20 AND teams.points<60
```

Next, we look further into the types of questions that can be handled by QB, as well as the linguistic limitations it faces.

TEAMS	NAME	WINS	LOSSES	TIES	POINTS

PLAYERS	NAME	TEAM	GOALS	ASSISTS	POINTS

F.K. "TEAM" references TEAMS.NAME

COACHES	NAME	TEAM	WINS

Fig. 2. Hockey database relational schema

The current implementation of QB can handle numeric-based questions involving comparison operators in number-centric databases. For instance, some example questions that QB can handle include: *What players have more than 10 goals? Which teams have players with 20 assists? What teams have fewer than 60 points?*

Each of these questions contains at least one condition that has an operator, an associated value, and an associated attribute. QB can also handle aggregate functions, such as: *How many players have over 10 points? How many teams have players with more than 20 goals?*

One of the limitations placed on the linguistic range of questions handled by QB is that it will not handle contractions. For instance, users should type, "do not" rather than "don't", "who have" instead of "who've", and so on. Examples of other questions that QB can handle include: *What team does Jarome Iginla play for? Which player has the most assists? What teams have more wins than losses?*

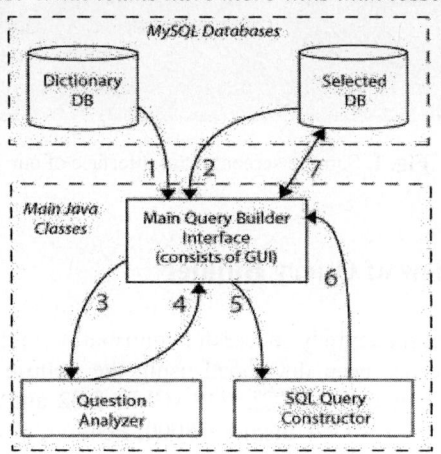

Fig. 3. Query builder architecture

3 Query Builder's Approach

The architecture of QB is shown in Figure 3. QB does the following: 1) loads all of the data from the dictionary database; 2) loads the metadata of the selected database; 3) the data from steps 1 and 2 (along with the question entered) is passed to the Question Analyzer; 4) the Question Analyzer processes this data, and returns the information needed for constructing the SQL query; 5) the information from step 4 is passed to the SQL Query Constructor class; 6) the SQL Query Constructor returns the SQL query to the interface; 7) the interface executes the query on the selected database, and the results are returned to the interface for viewing. Each of these steps will be further clarified in the subsequent sections.

3.1 Loading the Necessary Information

When QB starts, data contained in a *dictionary* database is loaded into its memory space. The dictionary database consists of several tables, each table containing a list of synonymous words that apply to any type of question, regardless of the database being queried. These tables are: *excludedWords*—words to be removed from the question because they do not contribute to the meaning of the question (e.g., "the", "that", "a", etc); *selectWords*—words that denote the SELECT action (e.g., "get", "find", "what", "which", "retrieve", etc...); *ownershipWords* – words that denote a possessive relationship (e.g., "has", "have", "having", "with", "on", "in", etc); *negationWords* – words that denote an operator should be inverted (e.g., "not", "no", etc); *equalWords* – words that map to "=" operator (e.g., "equal", "equals", "exactly", etc); *greaterWords* – words that map to ">" operator (e.g., "more", "over", "greater", etc); *lessWords* – words that map to "<" operator (e.g., "less", "under", "fewer", etc); *maxWords* – words that map to "<=" operator (e.g., "maximum", "at most", etc); *minWords* – words that map to ">=" operator (e.g., "minimum", "at least", etc). The last five tables are combined into a master list called *allOperators*, since these tables consist of the main mathematical operators involved in numeric conditions.

Once the dictionary data has been loaded, users are required to select the database that they would like to query because QB has not been designed for a specific database application. Then, QB will read and make use of database-specific information (database catalog) related to the selected database. This information includes: names of tables and attributes, primary keys, and foreign keys. QB makes use of the primary and foreign keys data to build an adjacency matrix. The importance of this step will become clear when we describe our method for constructing *join* conditions, a process that involves the use of a shortest-path graph-theory approach.

3.2 Preparing and Modifying the Question

The remaining steps will be explained first in general terms and then demonstrated with an example. In order to make the process easier to follow, the same example will be used for the entire process. For this example, the following question will be used: *Which of the players do not have 10 goals on teams with more than 60 points?*

Stripping the Question: This step is common to many NLIs. But for QB, the idea was inspired by PRECISE [9]. The strategy is to remove all of the words that do not contribute to the meaning of the question. First, all words are converted to lowercase, and all punctuations are removed. QB scans each word in the question, and it is stripped out if it is in *excludedWords* table. As a result, the example question becomes: "which players not have 10 goals on teams with more 60 points".

Inserting Implied Meaning: There are some cases where the question is conceptually and linguistically correct, but it is still unclear what data the user is requesting. QB is able to remove some of this ambiguity and even to suggest alternatives in a step to guide the user in the process.

After simplifying the question, QB scans through the remaining words looking for numeric values in the question. When it finds a value, it searches for an attribute and operator combination associated with this value. If an operator is not found, it is likely that there was an implied operator for this condition. In our example, "10" is the first value found. The attribute "goals" is found as an associated attribute, but there is no obvious operator for this condition. In this case, the implied meaning may have been "at least 10 goals", or "exactly 10 goals". QB will initiate a dialog with the user asking to clarify the intended operator by prompting if the operator was meant to be "at least", "more than", or "exactly". If the user specifies "at least", then a "minimum" operator word is inserted into the question. Note that with the second value "60", an attribute "points" and an associated operator "more" are found; the clarification and guidance procedure is not required. The example question then becomes: *"which players not have minimum 10 goals on teams with more 60 points"*.

In some cases involving numeric questions, users will ask a question such as *"Which players have no goals?"* QB has the ability to recognize that a quantity of zero is implied in this case, and would transform the "no" into "0".

Finding Meaning within the Question. With the unnecessary words removed, and implied meanings inserted, the question becomes more manageable to start the process of interpreting its meaning. To be a successful NLI, QB can handle simple SQL queries with the following format:

SELECT	*<information>*
FROM	*<table(s)>*
WHERE	*<conditions to be met>*

Therefore, our approach is to determine the combination of tables and attributes, operators, and values to complete the SELECT, FROM and WHERE clauses.

Here, it is worth mentioning a feature of QB called *pluralization*. Whenever a potential table or attribute is identified, several plural and singular forms of the word will be considered for matching purposes. For example, if a question contains the word "point," then a direct match can be made to the attribute "points" in either the Players or Teams table because the context of the singular form of the word should be mapped to the plural form of the attribute name. It is also important to note that in case tables and attributes do not have meaningful names, QB keeps a one to one mapping between the actual names and the corresponding meaningful ones.

The First Few Words: The first step QB takes is to determine which table to SELECT from. This step is taken with some important assumptions about the structure most questions will have: a) a question will start with an inquisitive word such as "what", "where", or "which" (i.e., those loaded from the *selectWord* table in the dictionary); b) a question will start with the intention of retrieving a specific number (i.e., it will begin by asking "how many..."); c) the name of the table of interest will typically follow immediately after the first instance of either of the above cases.

In our example, QB detects that the question begins with a *selectWord* ("which"), and checks to ensure that the next word (in this case "players") is in fact a table name. Hereafter, this table will be referred to as the *select table*. However, if the question had begun by asking "how many", the approach would have been slightly modified. In such case, the word following "many" could be either a table name, or an attribute name. In the former case, this table name is clearly the select table, and QB notes the need for a COUNT operator in the SELECT portion of the SQL query.

In the case of finding an attribute name after the word "many", determining the select table is not as obvious. To help demonstrate this, consider the following question: *"How many points does Jarome Iginla have?"* QB examines the database metadata to find any candidate tables that the attribute "points" could belong to: both the Players and Teams tables contain this attribute. In order to determine which of these tables to use, QB executes an internal SQL query on each table designed to search for an entry that matches the word "Jarome". The queries executed in these cases would be:

    SELECT * FROM teams WHERE teams.name LIKE "%Jarome%"
    SELECT * FROM players WHERE players.name LIKE "%Jarome%"

The Teams table does not contain an entry that matches the string "Jarome", and the query will therefore fail. The second query, however, will be successful, and QB will note both the name of the table, in this case Players, and the full string value of the entry found, in this case "Jarome Iginla". If this internal query fails for all candidate tables, QB will advise the user that it was unable to find the string entered, and stop processing the question; QB moves towards guiding the user to phrase the question. Also, if QB was unable to determine a select table, the user is notified of the error, and could be guided by given the suggestion that they begin their question with one of the words in the *selectWords* list.

Finding Tables with Conditions. The next step involves identifying tables that are used in the FROM and WHERE clauses of the SQL statement. To come up with an approach to solve this problem, we found it useful to compare a given question against its corresponding SQL query. Again, our processed question is: *"which players not have minimum 10 goals on teams with more 60 points"*. In this case, the SQL query would be:

```
SELECT   players.name
FROM     players, teams
WHERE    players.team = teams.name AND players.goals<10 AND teams.points>60
```

From this comparison, we observed that the two tables involved in the conditional statements of the SQL query were both followed by what we call an *ownership* word; "players" is followed by the ownership word "have" and "teams" is followed by the ownership word "with". Several other comparisons using different questions yield to the same observation. Therefore, we concluded that potential table names followed by an ownership word are likely to be tables that are used in a conditional statement.

Based on the above knowledge, QB's strategy is as follows: 1) Compare every word in the question against the list of table names that QB extracted from our data set's database. 2) If a match is identified, there is still a possibility that the potential table name is an attribute because some tables and attributes share the same name (note that "Teams" is a table name, but "Team" is also an attribute name in the other two tables). However, if an ownership word follows the potential table name, then we know it is indeed a table name. In our example, "players" is immediately followed by "not," which is a *negation* word, so we check the following word and it is the ownership word "have". The same comparison is done for "teams," except there is no negation word to worry about. At this point, QB has successfully identified "players" and "teams" as the tables we use in our conditional statements, and it is known that these tables belong in the FROM clause.

Table-Specific Ranges. By comparing a given question against its corresponding SQL query, we were able to make a second important distinction: the conditions associated with a given table can be determined by examining the words between the table name itself and the next table name. These words make up what we call a *table-specific range*. So for our example, there are table-specific ranges for each of the "players" and "teams" tables. Conceptually, the question can be broken down like this: Range 1: *players not have minimum 10 goals on*. Range 2: *teams with more 60 points*.

Forming the Condition Statements. *Identifying operators, values, and attributes*: Conditional statements in SQL are typically of the form: <table name>.<attribute> <operator> <value>. It is the job of QB to identify these tables, attributes, operators and values so that condition statements can be formed. The process for doing this is described below:
a) Determining conditional statements continues by identifying *operator* tokens in each table-specific range. Each token in the range is compared against the words in the operator tables, and if a match is found its location and equivalent operator value (>, <, =, <=, >=, <>) is recorded. A check is also done to see if either of the two previous tokens is a negation word, in which case the operator value is inverted (e.g. > to <=). In our example, "minimum," which is the >= operator is found in Range 1. However, a negation word occurs in the previous two tokens so the operator is inverted to <. In Range 2, "more," which is the > operator, is identified. So, we are given: Range 1: <; Range 2: >.
b) Identify the *value* associated with a given operator: If the question is linguistically correct, then it is likely that the token immediately after the operator token is the value. For our example we are given: Range 1: <10; Range 2: >60
c) Next, QB is faced with the task of identifying the *attribute* associated with a given operator. It is likely that the attribute token will appear immediately after the value token or immediately before the operator token. QB checks if either of these conditions is met, by checking to see if the potential attribute matches any of the valid table-attribute combinations extracted from the dataset database. So in our example, QB finds a valid attribute after both value tokens in each range and we are given: Range 1: *goals* < 10; Range 2: *points*>60.

d) Assembling the necessary conditional statements: In our example, QB constructs the following statements: *Players.goals<10; Teams.points>60.*

Table 1. Adjacency matrix for hockey database

	Players	Teams	Coaches
Players		players.team=teams.name	
Teams	players.team=teams.name		coaches.team=teams.name
Coaches		coaches.team=teams.name	

Constructing JOIN Conditions. QB assembles an adjacency matrix based on the primary and foreign keys of the database. To save QB the trouble of constructing joins in the future, the actual JOIN statements (e.g. *players.team=teams.name*) are stored as nodes in the matrix. To demonstrate how QB constructs JOIN conditions, the adjacency matrix for the Hockey database is shown in Table 1.

Dijkstra's Algorithm, makes use of this adjacency matrix to determine the shortest path (i.e. the joins) between two tables as demonstrated by the following example: Suppose we are given the question: *"What players have coaches with more than 50 wins?"* A connection needs to be formed between Players and Coaches, yet there is no direct relationship. Dijkstra's algorithm will determine that the shortest-path is to go from Players to Teams, and then to Coaches. Therefore, the resulting JOIN conditions will be: *players.team=teams.name, coaches.team=teams.name*. In this case, QB would also add the Teams table to the FROM clause of the SQL statement.

3.3 Building the SQL Statement

The information for our sample question that will be used in constructing the query can be summarized as follows: Select Table: Players; Tables to use: Players, Teams; Joins: Players.Team=Teams.Name; Conditions: Players.goals<10, Teams.points>60. It is a relatively simple task to build each of the SELECT, FROM, and WHERE clauses with this information.

The SELECT clause of the SQL statement is designed to select only on the primary key of the select table identified. By default, and to avoid redundant results, the DISTINCT operator is inserted. Therefore, using the primary key metadata from our example, QB will construct the string: SELECT DISTINCT players.name.

Note that if an aggregate function was needed, QB would have stored the required information, and would insert it into the query in the appropriate location of the SELECT clause. For the COUNT aggregate function, the SELECT statement would have the form: SELECT COUNT(DISTINCT(<table>.<primary key attribute>)).

The FROM clause of the SQL statement is the simplest to construct. It simply makes use of the identified tables to use in constructing the string: FROM players, teams.

Building WHERE: The WHERE clause of an SQL statement is where the majority of the detail is contained. QB begins by first adding the join conditions. If multiple joins are required, the AND operator is inserted between each. For our query, the WHERE string will therefore begin with form: WHERE players.team = teams.name.

Once each join condition has been added, QB then inserts the remaining conditions, separating each with the needed operator. The WHERE clause is finalized with form:
WHERE players.team=teams.name AND players.goals<10 AND teams.points>60.

Putting It All Together: The final step in constructing the SQL query is to concatenate the three clauses. In our example, the natural language question: *"Which of the players do not have 10 goals on teams with more than 60 points?"* is successfully translated to the SQL query:

| SELECT players.name |
| FROM   players, teams |
| WHERE players.team = teams.name AND players.goals < 10 AND teams.points > 60 |

Table 2. Summary of major QB's feedback system

Missing select word	Linguistic	Displays list of *selectWords*, and suggests the user place one at the start of the question
No attribute or table name for COUNT ("how many" case)	Linguistic	Indicates the word found that is not a table or attribute name
LIKE string not found in any primary key entries ("how many" case)	Conceptual	Indicates the word that could not be found
Missing *ownershipWord* for a table	Linguistic	Displays list of *ownershipWords*, and suggests the user place one with each table name that is missing one
Missing condition value	Linguistic	Indicates the attribute that was found to be missing a value
Missing operator	Linguistic	Indicates the attribute that was found to be missing an operator
Missing or invalid attribute	Linguistic	Indicates the value that was found to be missing an associated attribute name
Impossible table join	Conceptual	Advises the user that it does not understand how to link, or relate, the tables in question
SQL syntax error	Linguistic or Conceptual	General error message provided to user explaining that the question was misunderstood

3.4 Feedback

QB has been designed to be able to give more informative feedback about the type of error found before it reaches the step of constructing the SQL query. For all these cases, it is capable of suggesting alternatives to guide users in phrasing the question.

If no select word is found, the feedback does not simply give the user a general error message, but rather indicates that it could not determine the type of data to be retrieved. It also provides the suggestion to include one of the *selectWords* at the beginning of the question, since it is likely that one is missing. This is an example of QB detecting a linguistic error, and providing the users with detailed and informative feedback to aid them in rephrasing the question. Table 2 summarizes some of the major errors that can be detected by QB. The suggested alternatives are omitted here for lack of space. Finally, QB keeps a record of the most commonly raised questions and gives users the opportunity to ask a previous question as well.

4 Summary and Conclusions

The usefulness of NLI for a naïve database user is obvious. However, if a question cannot be properly translated to an equivalent SQL query, the user may feel as helpless as they did try to construct an SQL query without receiving feedback as to where and how the failure occurred. If informative and detailed feedback is provided in these cases, the user will at best be able to rephrase their question into a format understood by NLI, or at worst be informed about why their question was not understood. In either case, the user should gain in their understanding of the style and type of questions that can be managed by NLI. This understanding would hopefully help in reducing future translation failures that are due to both linguistic and conceptual errors.

QB is NLI designed with a detailed and informative feedback system in mind. It is able to detect both linguistic and conceptual errors, and provides useful feedback and guidance to the user in either case. By halting the translation process immediately upon encountering an error, QB's feedback is detailed and specific to the error found. This minimizes situations where, despite an error occurring, the translation process continues onto create and execute a syntactically invalid SQL statement.

We are working on expanding QB to handle more text-based queries. This is a much more complex style of questions to manage since the queries have to match strings on actual database data, rather than just make use of the database metadata. In order to handle these types of questions, the overall architecture and design of QB may need to be re-factored. Further, the feedback system will continue to evolve so that it can handle more conceptual and linguistic errors.

References

1. Androutsopoulos, G., Ritchie, D., Thanisch, P.: Natural language interfaces to databases - an introduction. Natural language Engineering **1**(1) (1995) 29–81
2. Barwise, J., Cooper, R.: Generalized quantifiers and natural language. Linguistics and Philosophy **4** (1981) 159–219
3. Clifford, J.: Formal semantics and pragmatics for natural language querying. Cambridge University Press, Cambridge (1990)
4. Copestake. K., Jones, S.: Natural language interfaces to databases. Knowledge Engineering Review **5**(4) (1990) 225–249
5. Crouch, R.S., Pulman, S.G.: Time and modality in a natural language interface to a planning system, Artificial Intelligence **63** (1993) 265–304
6. Jarke, M., et al.: A Field evaluation of natural-language for data retrieval. IEEE TSE **11** (1985) 97–114
7. Perrault, C.R., Grosz, B.J.: Natural language interfaces. In: Shrobe, H. E. (ed.): Exploring Artificial Intelligence. Morgan Kaufmann Publishers (1988) 133–172
8. Price, D., Rilofff, E., Zachary, J.L., Harvey, B.: NaturalJava: A natural language interface for programming in Java. In: Proc. of IUI. (2000) 207–211
9. Popescu, A.M., Etzioni, O., Kautz, H.: Towards a theory of natural language interfaces to databases. In: Proc. of IUI. (2003)
10. Shneiderman, B.: Improving the human factors aspect of database interactions. ACM TODS **3** (1978) 417–439

Situation-Aware Coordination in Multi-agent Filtering Framework

Sahin Albayrak and Dragan Milosevic

DAI-Labor, Technical University Berlin
Salzufer 12, 10587 Berlin, Germany
{sahin,dragan}@dai-lab.de

Abstract. In order to obtain an acceptable quality of filtering services under real time conditions, a trade-off between result relevance and response time has to be taken into consideration. Ignoring resource availability is a major drawback for many existed systems, which try to boost quality by making different synergies between filtering strategies. The essence of the proposed solution for combining filtering strategies is in a comprehensive situation-aware coordination mechanism which takes care about current resource usability. The applicability of the presented coordination between filtering strategies is illustrated in a system serving as intelligent personal information assistant (PIA). Experimental results show that long lasting filtering jobs with duration over 1000 seconds are eliminated with an acceptable decrease in a received feedback value, being within 3%.

1 Introduction

With an abundance of available filtering strategies [4,6,8,12,14,15,16,17], finding the most appropriate one in a particular situation can amount to a real challenge. Each and every strategy has its strengths and weaknesses and deciding how to combine them is something of an art, being addressed by many researchers. While even-based and content-based filtering are combined in Letizia [10] and Amalthaea [13] to better deduce the user model, by tracking its behaviour during Web browsing, whereas WebWatcher [19] and WAIR [2][20] additionally use reinforcement learning for adapting to constant changes in information needs. The same adaptation to user's interests is realised in PEA [20] and Newt [18] through the integration of evolution strategies, and in PIAgent [9] through neural network classification with content-based filtering. In order to utilise aspects being invisible to pure content-based analysis but being captured by humans, collaborative and content-based filtering are combined in FAB [1], Let's Browse [11], P-Tango [3], TripMatcher [5], and many others.

Up to the authors' best knowledge, the most of the mentioned systems are tested in highly protected environments, where usually resource availability has not been taken into consideration. Under real time conditions, the resource situation is unpredictable, being with no doubt one of the main difficulties for these systems in presenting successful deployments. Because filtering strategies differ not only in the quality of the produced results but also in the degree of resource consumption, the idea is to take care about resources when doing coordination between different strategies.

To support scalability in a multi-agent filtering framework, a resource situation-aware coordination mechanism will be essential, as it is going to be shown in the rest of this paper. In the next section a need for such coordination is presented through one scenario, illustrating coordination problems. The core contribution of this paper is then described in the section, which gives principles, being in the basis of the used coordination approach that is naturally separated to strategy evaluation, selection and hopefully in the future versions additionally to adaptation. A paper is finished with sections where implementation and experimental results are presented.

2 Problem Description

A fruitful history of information filtering technologies has produced many more or less successful filtering strategies, which makes each filtering problem solvable in many different ways (Fig. 1a). In order to be able to choose in a long run for as many filtering jobs as possible the most applicable solution, one obviously needs a sophisticated reasoning that tries to learn about strengths and weaknesses of the each available strategy. In today's real-time environments one should additionally estimate the applicability of a filtering strategy by taking into account both its behaviour in similar past situations and a level of the current system resource availability. The mentioned learning aspects and strategy applicability evaluation are going to be illustrated in the following scenario, being naturally separated into evaluation, selection and adaptation steps.

[Evaluation] After receiving a filtering job and before making a decision about which filtering strategy is going to be selected, the current runtime situation in the system will be determined. In a particular case this might actually mean measuring parameters such as system CPU and DB server load, and determining the amount of available free memory. In order not to ignore the quality of the found article, the successfulness in finding accurate results of each filtering strategy is also taken into consideration. The later actually means that instead of insisting on high article relevance, somebody can specify that a quick response is more important. On the other side for each and every available filtering strategy it is known how much computation power is required, to which extent it loads a database and the amount of needed free memory (Fig. 1b).

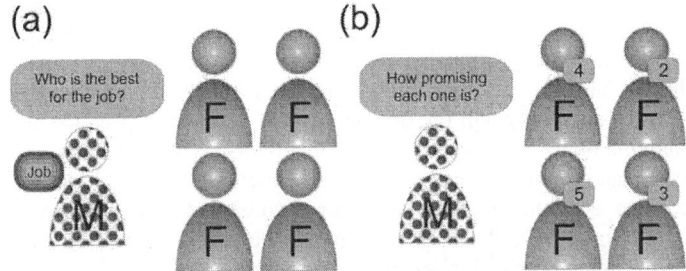

Fig. 1. (a) Manager should decide which filtering strategy is the most promising for a given job. (b) It then determines how each strategy can be successful in the current runtime situation, being illustrated on a figure by assigning larger number to the more promising strategy

[Selection] By using both determined environmental and filtering job relevance properties together with the characteristics of different strategies, the idea about which filtering strategy is the most suitable in the current situation should be obtained. In order to better explore characteristics of all available strategies, instead of giving a job always to the most promising one, sometimes another strategy is going to be chosen, being the way of giving a chance to that strategy to improve its qualifications (Fig. 2a).

[**Adaptation**] While runtime strategy characteristics can be adapted as soon as the filtering results become available, the measure of successfulness in finding accurate results cannot be changed before a feedback is not received. The ultimate goal of these adaptations is establishing a more realistic picture about potentials of available strategies. The expected final effect is that a system is hopefully going to learn to even better coordinate activities for future filtering jobs (Fig. 2b).

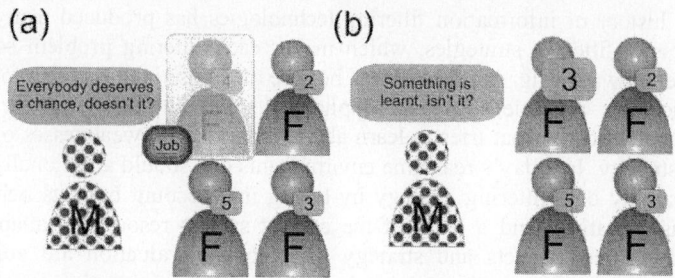

Fig. 2. (**a**) Manager chooses a filtering strategy that is going to perform actual filtering. (**b**) It then learns how good the chosen strategy is, based on the response time and feedback values

The given scenario should serve only as an illustration of the challenges which unfortunately exist when trying to do successful large scale coordination between many different filtering strategies. While the possible ways of addressing evaluation and selection problems will be the main topic in the following section, adaptation challenges are left for the future work.

3 Approach

The authors' thoughts about the coordination, being naturally separated in the previous section into evaluation, selection and adaptation (Fig. 3), are not only concerned with the ability of a filtering strategy to produce accurate results, but also with the demands of a particular strategy towards different system resources. A strategy, whose efficiency crucially depends on a resource that is currently highly loaded, should have a very low probability to be selected in coordination. The selection of such a strategy will not only have weak chances to produce usable results in a reasonable amount of time, but will probably also have a negative influence on many other already running filtering processes, which use that highly loaded resource. While the term accurate results stands for results that are as close to the user preferences as possible, the term usable results should be understood as sufficiently accurate results being obtained in acceptable response time.

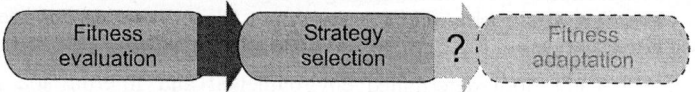

Fig. 3. Situation-aware coordination has evaluation, selection and hopefully adaptation steps

A natural way to realise such runtime-aware coordination is to first describe each and every filtering strategy through a set of fitness values which illustrate strategy runtime properties. Because central processor, database server and operational memory are, according to authors' assumptions, found to be the most important filtering resources, central processor (F_{CPU}), database (F_{DB}) and memory (F_m) fitness values are introduced and defined as follows:

Definition 1. *Central processor fitness* F_{CPU} describes filtering strategy behaviour with respect to a CPU load.

A general principle, which should be followed while assigning values to F_{CPU}, is that a higher F_{CPU} value means that less computing power is needed for the application of a filtering strategy being described by that F_{CPU} value. In practice, a high F_{CPU} value should be assigned to a filtering strategy which is able to successfully work even in the case where central processor is highly loaded. It is reasonable for example to assign high F_{CPU} value to a strategy which does not make complex and CPU expensive computations or applies many useful approximations which saves CPU power.

Definition 2. *Database fitness* F_{DB} corresponds to filtering strategy behaviour with respect to a database server load.

The assumed rule is that a high F_{DB} should be used for expressing the fact that a particular filtering strategy loads the database server only to a small extent. This further means that such strategy will probably have acceptable performances even in the case of a high database server load. The strategy which for example stores in a operational memory a lot of data used for guiding a search and retrieving from a database only really relevant data, will usually have acceptable performances in the case of high database server load and according to that should have a high F_{DB} value.

Definition 3. *Memory fitness* F_m relates to filtering strategy memory requirements.

The F_m value assigning principle is that a higher F_m means that less memory is needed for performing filtering which makes a particular strategy less dependant on the amount of available free memory. In the case where physical memory resources are not available in the needed quantity for a particular strategy, it is not only possible that a given strategy will have runtime difficulties, but also that maybe a whole filtering system will become un-operational. A natural guideline in such memory lacking situations is giving a priority to strategies with higher F_m values, because they need less memory for filtering.

In order not to obtain a coordination mechanism that is highly biased to system runtime properties, a filtering strategy ability to find accurate results, which will result in high user satisfaction, is modelled by quality fitness (F_q) value as follows:

Definition 4. *Quality fitness* F_q represents the level of user satisfaction with that strategy in the past.

A higher F_q value corresponds to a filtering strategy that has been more successful in satisfying a user in the past, and according to this, has received better user feedback values.

A concrete solution, showing how the presented F_q, F_{CPU}, F_{DB} and F_m values are going to be applied in the evaluation and selection steps of coordination mechanism, will be described in the following sub-sections.

3.1 Evaluation

The ultimate evaluation goal is to estimate the applicability of each available filtering strategy for a current filtering job processing, by first determining actual system runtime properties and then combining them with in the previous section introduced strategy fitness values (Fig. 4). System runtime properties, which are inside the evaluation interest scope, are CPU (ω_{CPU}), database server (ω_{DB}) and memory system (ω_m) load. These runtime properties correspond to the authors' assumptions about the most important filtering resources for which filtering strategy behaviour is already described through F_{CPU}, F_{DB} and F_m values. While a computation of a memory system load is based on determining the amount of used memory for which integrated system functions [1] can be used, both CPU and database server load computation are more sophisticated and require both the execution and response time measuring of specially designed expressions.

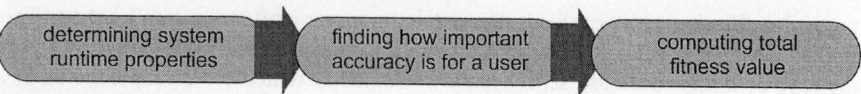

Fig. 4. Evaluation of filtering strategy total fitness value requires both the estimation of a system runtime situation and determining how important is result accuracy for a particular request

A CPU load is computed as $\omega_{CPU} = \beta_{CPU} t_{CPU}$, where β_{CPU} is a tuning parameter and t_{CPU} is the time being needed for a computation of an algebraic expression, being formed only in order to estimate current CPU load. A higher CPU load naturally implies longer computation time t_{CPU} and consequently larger ω_{CPU} value.

As expression for CPU load estimation, sum $\sum_{i=1}^{n_{SL}} f(i)$ is used, where function $f(i) = \frac{1}{\sigma\sqrt{2\pi}} e^{-(i-m)^2/(2\sigma^2)}$ is a Gaussian random variable [12] with a standard deviation $\sigma = 1 + ran(0,1)$ and a mean $m = ran(0,1)$. Value $ran(0,1)$, being a randomly generated real number from $[0,1]$, is added on both standard deviation and mean to make each execution different from others, and to insure that no internal CPU optimisations can use something that has been already computed and therefore make unfair future executions. The summation length n_{SL} should be chosen in the way that

---

[1] In java in Runtime class methods *freeMemory*, *maxMemory* and *totalMemory* are provided.

expression execution does not load CPU significantly and at the same time last long enough to provide accurate CPU load computation (Table 1, columns n_{SL} and t_{CPU}).

A database server load ω_{DB} is computed as $\omega_{DB} = \beta_{DB} t_{DB}$, where again β_{DB} is a suitable tuning parameter and t_{DB} is a time being needed for the execution of a SQL query that is specially designed to estimate database server load. As a consequence of further loading database server, t_{DB} will increase, which results in bigger ω_{DB} value.

The aggregate SQL query

SELECT sum(Salary) FROM Employers

WHERE Id > ran AND Id < n_{CS} + ran GROUP BY Department

should be executed on a very large table *Employers*(*Id*, *Departement*, *Salary*), storing data about employers' salaries and departments where they work. In a given query, *ran* is randomly generated number from [0,*rowcount*], which insures that always a summation is executed on a different cluster of employers, and consequently eliminates unwanted potential database server optimisations with already processed similar queries.

Table 1. CPU (Pentium IV on 2.5 GHz) is additionally loaded by $n_{Loaders}$ threads that repeatedly ask CPU to estimate its load while measuring t_{CPU}. DB server (Pentium IV on 1.6 GHz) is loaded by $n_{Loaders}$ threads that repeatedly demands load estimation while determining t_{DB}.

$n_{Loaders}$	n_{CS} [in thousands]	t_{CPU} [s]	n_{CS} [in thousands]	t_{DB} [s]
0	10	0.016	1	0.045
	20	0.031	2	0.096
	50	0.078	5	0.216
	100	0.125	10	0.499
	500	0.657	50	2.206
1	10	0.078	1	0.061
	20	0.109	2	0.118
	50	0.281	5	0.403
	100	0.563	10	0.803
	500	2.766	50	4.134
5	10	0.187	1	0.179
	20	0.328	2	0.419
	50	0.844	5	1.065
	100	1.688	10	2.070
	500	8.765	50	10.955
10	10	0.328	1	0.292
	20	0.625	2	0.620
	50	1.547	5	1.587
	100	3.078	10	3.523
	500	15.578	50	16.244

Cluster size is defined by n_{CS} and it should be small enough in order not to load database server significantly and at the same time big enough to provide accurate enough database server load computation (Table 1, columns n_{CS} and t_{DB}).

A memory load ω_m reflects the amount of used memory and it is computed as $\omega_m = \beta_m s_m$, where β_m is a tuning parameter and s_m is the size of the currently used memory in bytes. It is obvious from a given expression that more used memory s_m results in a larger memory load ω_m value. Because a system function for determining the amount of used memory usually exists, the problem of computing s_m is going to be assumed as a trivial one and will not be discussed in the rest of this paper.

After computing ω_{CPU}, ω_{DB} and ω_m values and under assumption that ω_q, showing how important it is to find accurate results, is obtained directly from the user, the so-called total fitness (F_t) can be computed as follows:

$$F_t = \frac{\omega_q F_q + \omega_{CPU} F_{CPU} + \omega_{DB} F_{DB} + \omega_m F_m}{\omega_q + \omega_{CPU} + \omega_{DB} + \omega_m}. \tag{1}$$

The inclusion of $\omega_q F_q$ in the (1), models the user willingness to accept longer response time in order to get more accurate results. Each and every ω_x parameter, $x \in \{q, CPU, DB, m\}$, plays a standard weighting role in a well known way that larger ω_x implies greater influence of the corresponding $\omega_x F_x$ on overall F_t value. In the case where for example only a database server is highly loaded, ω_{DB} will have a large value and $\omega_{DB} F_{DB}$ will dominate in the F_t computation. This further means that filtering strategy with the highest F_{DB} value will probably have the highest overall F_t value.

3.2 Selection

Selection simulates the evolutionary process of competition among available filtering strategies which are fighting for getting as many filtering jobs as possible. A probability of being selected $P^{(i)}$ for the filtering strategy i is computed as

$$P^{(i)} = \frac{e^{-\frac{\beta_t}{F_t^{(i)}}}}{\sum_{j=1}^{n} e^{-\frac{\beta_t}{F_t^{(j)}}}}. \tag{2}$$

In (2), a tuning parameter β_t controls the influence of a total fitness $F_t^{(i)}$ on $P^{(i)}$ in the way that larger β_t results in smaller $P^{(i)}$ for the same fitness $F_t^{(i)}$. Exponential function is used in order to both bound and control the influence of any strategy to $[0,1]$. Such defined probability $P^{(i)}$ is a growing function of $F_t^{(i)}$, and it holds $(F_t^{(i)} \to 0) \Rightarrow (P^{(i)} \to e^{-\infty} = 0)$ and $(F_t^{(i)} \to \infty) \Rightarrow (P^{(i)} \to e^0 = 1)$. Under assumption that n candidate strategies participate in a selection, a denominator $\sum_{j=1}^{n} e^{-\frac{\beta_t}{F_t^{(j)}}}$ sums all the probabilities and therefore insures $\sum_{j=1}^{n} P^{(j)} = 1$.

Because the probability $P^{(i)}$ of being selected is proportional to the $F_t^{(i)}$ fitness value of a filtering strategy, the used selection is nothing else than a well known proportional or roulette wheel selection [12]. Those filtering strategies with above average total fitness will, on average, receive more attention than those with below average total fitness. Even the one with the worst total fitness value will have a chance to be selected and to improve its fitness values, being the topic of the future analyses.

Example 1. Fig. 5 represents one example of the selection, being based on filtering strategy fitness values F_q, F_{CPU}, F_{DB} and F_m, and current system runtime situation ω_q, ω_{CPU}, ω_{DB} and ω_m.

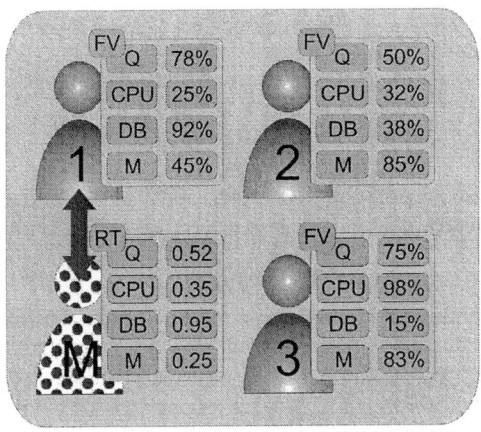

Fig. 5. Strategy is described only by quality (Q), central processor (CPU), database server (DB) and memory system (M) fitness values (FV) in a runtime (RT) situation

In the runtime situation ($\omega_q = 0.52$, $\omega_{CPU} = 0.35$, $\omega_{DB} = 0.95$, $\omega_m = 0.25$) shown on Fig. 5, total strategy fitness values are $F_t^{(1)} = 71.48$, $F_t^{(2)} = 45.67$ and $F_t^{(3)} = 52.31$, and consequently for $\beta_t = 100$ the corresponding selection probabilities are $P^{(1)} = 0.49$, $P^{(2)} = 0.22$ and $P^{(3)} = 0.29$. One should notice that the filtering strategy ($i = 1$), having the greatest database server fitness $F_{DB}^{(1)} = 92\%$, has the best chances to be selected because of a very high database server load, being currently $\omega_{DB} = 0.95$.

3.3 Adaptation

After completing a filtering job and receiving a user feedback about the found result relevance, learning through fitness value adaptation should take place in order to ensure that the assigned fitness values reflect as accurately as possible corresponding filtering strategy abilities. Even though the adaptation component is not yet implemented, evaluation and selection mechanisms have already shown excellent behaviour (see section 5). They demonstrated their applicability in large communities and at the same time significantly improved system runtime characteristics. These results encouraged the authors to present what has been already done together with adaptation ideas, which will complete a whole vision about situation-aware coordination.

4 Implementation

A playing ground for coordination between different filtering strategies is the so-called filtering community, which contains agents being tailored to do specific filtering and managing tasks in an efficient way. Instead of having only filtering agents, a community has also one so called filter manager agent that is mainly responsible for doing the coordination of filtering jobs.

Filtering communities are implemented in JIAC IV [2] (Java Intelligent Agent Component-ware, Version IV) being a comprehensive service-ware framework for developing and deploying agent systems covering design methodology and tools, agent languages and architecture, a FIPA compliant infrastructure, management and security functionality, and a generic scheme for user access [7]. The agent system JIAC IV is based on CASA (Component Architecture for Service Agents) having a modular internal structure consisting of an open set of components that can be adjusted to different requirements at design-time as well at run-time. This flexibility facilitates not only the easy integration of new filtering strategies, but also enables experiments with different coordination mechanisms.

In order to estimate under real time conditions both the flexibility of JIAC IV service framework and the applicability of filtering communities with a situation-aware coordination, personal information assistant (PIA) has been developed[3]. A typical user is guided by PIA starting from a collection of both information interests and delivery preferences to a relevant article presentation and feedback gathering. The authors' belief is that PIA is going to demonstrate under real conditions the applicability of both agent-based filtering systems and situation-aware coordination mechanisms.

5 Experimental Results

The expected benefit of the presented coordination approach should be found both in its applicability inside very large filtering communities and in its ability to eliminate long lasting filtering jobs. These aspects are going to be practically examined in following subsections, where the results of performed experiments are given.

---

[2] JIAC IV is developed at the DAI laboratory of the Technical University Berlin through projects funded by the Deutsche Telekom Berkom GmbH
[3] PIA can be accessed at http://www.pia-services.de .

5.1 Coordination Scaling Abilities

The situation-aware coordination is designed to address challenges that arise when the size of a filtering community is scaled to the hundreds or thousands of members. That is mainly achieved by establishing evaluation and selection coordination mechanisms in a way that the most time consuming activities should be the ones that compute CPU and DB server load, and that, at the same time, do not depend on the number of filtering agents.

In order to check the last assumption, communities with different numbers of filtering agents (n_{FA}) are created and each one are sent 100 jobs. It is measured how much time is needed to compute CPU load ($t_{\omega CPU}$), to estimate DB server load ($t_{\omega DB}$), and to performed all other coordination activities (t_C).

The obtained average values for $t_{\omega CPU}$, $t_{\omega DB}$ and t_C are given in Table 2. While $t_{\omega CPU}$ and $t_{\omega DB}$ slightly fluctuate regarding n_{FA}, because of being measured in real time conditions, t_C heavily depends on n_{FA}, mostly because it is concerned with the evaluation of a total fitness F_t, which has to be done for each filtering agent. Furthermore, t_C additionally assumes the application of a proportional selection, which also depends on n_{FA}. The last column t_C [%] in Table 2 gives in percents the contribution of t_C in the overall time that is needed for performing coordination. As it can be seen, for communities, having less than 200 agents, that t_C contribution is below 1%, which is a quite encouraging observation. Even in a case of very large community with 5000 agents, t_C contribution is only around 10%, being also acceptable.

Table 2. Computation of t_C, including neither $t_{\omega CPU}$ nor $t_{\omega DB}$, for different n_{FA} sizes

n_{FA}	$t_{\omega CPU}$ [ms]	$t_{\omega DB}$ [ms]	t_C [ms]	t_C [%]
10	32.97	83.75	0.15	0.12834774
20	32.74	107.27	0.46	0.32747206
50	33.39	87.39	0.6	0.49431537
100	32.79	81.26	0.66	0.57536396
200	32.29	82.85	0.83	0.71570234
500	32.53	81.23	1.24	1.07826087
1000	32.49	84.7	1.87	1.57063665
2000	32.58	87.74	3.43	2.77171717
5000	33.03	82.61	14.2	10.9365373
10000	32.81	83.74	33.91	22.5375515
20000	32.35	82.82	61.24	34.7145853

Results presented in Table 2 prove that in this paper described situation-aware coordination mechanisms are scaling well, and that they can be applied even inside very large filtering communities, having thousands of agents.

5.2 Long Lasting Filtering Job Elimination

A trial to escape long lasting filtering jobs, being usually a consequence of the important resource unavailability, was a main motivation for the realisation of the presented situation-aware coordination. Even though these long lasting jobs will probably produce perfect results in next few hours, to obtain nearly perfect results within few minutes is usually much more appropriate. Because a final judgement, concerning such trade-off statements, is always given by the user, this subsection gives comparisons between PIA system with and without resource aware coordination in both user feedback and response time domains.

Before the 14th of January 2004, PIA was working without a resource aware coordination and in that period of time it was actively used by 13 users, and 157 filtering jobs were processed. Fig. 6a and Fig. 6b respectively present 32 received feedback and corresponding response time values.

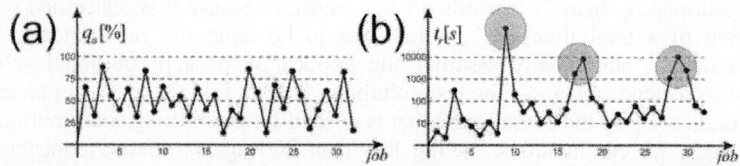

Fig. 6. (a) Received feedback and (b) response time without situation-aware coordination

After the 14th of January 2004, PIA is working with a resource aware coordination and in the first two weeks it was used by 21 users, and 218 filtering jobs were processed. Fig. 7a and Fig. 7b respectively present first 32 received feedback and corresponding response time values.

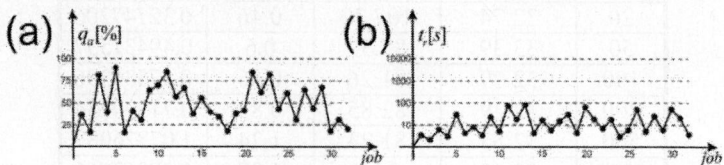

Fig. 7. (a) Received feedback and (b) response time with situation-aware coordination

The given figures clearly show that while the integration of a resource aware coordination does not significantly affect user feedback (Fig. 6a and Fig. 7a show only a slight feedback value decrease that is hopefully within 3%), it successfully eliminates long lasting filtering jobs (6 problematic long lasting jobs marked with circles on Fig. 6b, having a response time that is longer than 1000 seconds, do not occur anymore on Fig. 7b). While an even bigger decrease in quality was not detected by users probably because they were satisfied with a shorter waiting time, what is more important, by optimising a resource usage through a presented situation-aware coordination, PIA can provide filtering services to a significantly larger user community.

6 Conclusion

The goal of this paper was to provide solutions to the challenges in filtering strategy coordination being created by unpredictable environmental conditions. This was achieved through methods being able both to determine a degree of resource availability and to integrate obtained results in a strategy coordination process. The realised coordination is not based on activities, such as negotiation, having a complexity that dramatically increases with the number of participants, and according to that in this paper presented situation-aware coordination is particularly suitable for very large filtering communities.

Even though the first solutions for checking resources are given, future work will be concentrated on finding more accurate ways not only for estimating but also for predicting resource usability. As soon as more experimental results become available, the learning component, being responsible for the adaptation of filtering strategy properties, will become a main topic for future analysis. Even though presented results are just the initial step towards scalable multi-agent recommendation systems, authors' hope is that the deployed situation-aware coordination lays the foundation for one comprehensive framework that provides sophisticated filtering services.

References

1. Balabanovic, M., Shoham, Y.: Fab: Content-Based Collaborative Recommendation. Communication of the ACM **40**(3) (1997) 66–72
2. Byoung-Tak, Z., Y.-W., S.: Personalized Web-Document Filtering Using Reinforcement Learning. Applied Artificial Intelligence **15**(7) (2001) 665–685
3. Claypool, M., Gokhale, A., Miranda, T., Murnikov, P., Netes, D., Sartin, N.: Combining Content-Based and Collaborative Filters in an Online Newspaper. In: ACM SIGIR Workshop on Recommender Systems, Berkeley, CA. (1999)
4. Delgado, J.: Agent Based Information Filtering and Recommender Systems. Ph.D. Thesis. Nagoya Institute of Technology. Japan (2000)
5. Delgado, J., Davidson, R.: Knowledge Bases and User Profiling in Travel and Hospitality Recommender Systems, ENTER 2002. Springer-Verlag, Innsbruck Austria, (2002) 1–16.
6. Faloutsos, C., Oard, D.: A Survey of Information Retrieval and Filtering Methods. University of Maryland, Technical Report CS-TR-3514 (1995)
7. Fricke, S., Bsufka, K., Keiser, J., Schmidt, T., Sesseler, R., Albayrak, S.: Agent-Based Telematic Services and Telecom Applications. Communications of ACM (2001) 43–48
8. Han, J., Kamber, M.: Data Mining: Concepts and Techniques. MK Publishers, (2001)
9. Kuropka, D., Serries, T.: Personal Information Agent. Informatik (2001) 940–946
10. Lieberman, H.: Letizia: An Agent That Assists Web Browsing. In: International Joint Conference on Artificial Intelligence, Montreal. (1995)
11. Lieberman, H., Neil V.D., Vivacqua A.: Let's Browse: A Collaborative Browsing Agent. Knowledge-Based Systems **12**(8) (1999) 427–431
12. Michalewicz, Z., Fogel, D.: How to Solve It: Modern Heuristics. Springer-Verlag New York (2000)
13. Moukas, A.: Amalthaea: Information Discovery and Filtering using a Multi Agent Evolving Ecosystem. Practical Application of Intelligent Agents & MA Technology. London (1998)
14. Oard, D., Marchionini, G.: A Conceptual Framework for Text Filtering. University of Maryland, College Park, (1996)

15. Resnick, P., Iacovou, N., Suchak, M., Bergstrom, P., Riedl, J.: GroupLens: An Open Architecture for Collaborative Filtering of Net News. In: Proceedings ACM Conference on Computer-Supported Cooperative Work. (1994) 175–186
16. Sarwar, B., Karypis, G., Konstan, J., Riedl, J.: Analysis of Recommendation Algorithms for E-Commerce. In: Proceedings of the 2nd ACM Conference on Electronic Commerce (EC-00), Minneapolis, USA. (2000) 158–167
17. Schafer, B., Konstan, J., Riedl, J.: E-Commerce Recommendation Applications. Journal of Data Mining and Knowledge Discovery (2001) 115–153
18. Sheth, B. D.: A Learning Approach to Personalized Information Filtering. M.Sc. Thesis, MIT- EECS Dept, USA (1994)
19. Thorsten, J., Dayne, F., Tom, M.: WebWatcher: A Tour Guide for the World Wide Web. In IJCAI. **1** (1997) 770–777
20. Winiwarter W.: PEA - A Personal Email Assistant with Evolutionary Adaptation. International Journal of Information Technology **5**(1) (1999)
21. Young-Woo, S., Byoung-Tak, Z.: A Reinforcement Learning Agent for Personalized Information Filtering. In: Proceedings of the 5th International Conference on Intelligent User Interfaces, New Orleans, Louisiana, United States. (2000) 248–251

A Study on Answering a Data Mining Query Using a Materialized View[*]

Maciej Zakrzewicz, Mikolaj Morzy, and Marek Wojciechowski

Poznan University of Technology
Institute of Computing Science
ul. Piotrowo 3a, 60-965 Poznan, Poland
{mzakrz,mmorzy,marek}@cs.put.poznan.pl

Abstract. One of the classic data mining problems is discovery of frequent itemsets. This problem particularly attracts database community as it resembles traditional database querying. In this paper we consider a data mining system which supports storing of previous query results in the form of materialized data mining views. While numerous works have shown that reusing results of previous frequent itemset queries can significantly improve performance of data mining query processing, a thorough study of possible differences between the current query and a materialized view has not been presented yet. In this paper we classify possible differences into six classes, provide I/O cost analysis for all the classes, and experimentally evaluate the most promising ones.

1 Introduction

Data mining aims at discovery of useful patterns from large databases or warehouses. Nowadays we are witnessing the evolution of data mining environments from specialized tools to multi-purpose data mining systems offering some level of integration with existing database management systems. Data mining can be seen as advanced querying, where a user specifies the source dataset and the requested pattern constraints, then the system chooses the appropriate data mining algorithm and returns the discovered patterns to the user. Data mining query processing has recently become an important research area focusing mainly on constraint handling and reusing results of previous queries.

In our previous work we introduced the concept of materialized data mining views, providing a general discussion on their possible usage in mining various classes of frequent patterns [8][9]. In this paper we focus on the most prominent class of patterns – frequent itemsets. We present a thorough study of possible differences between the current frequent itemset query and a materialized view. We identify six classes of possible differences, providing I/O cost analysis for each of them. For the most promising classes we report results of conducted experiments.

---

[*] This work was partially supported by the grant no. 4T11C01923 from the State Committee for Scientific Research (KBN), Poland.

1.1 Background

Frequent Itemsets. Let $L=\{l_1, l_2, ..., l_m\}$ be a set of literals, called items. Let a non-empty set of items T be called an *itemset*. Let D be a set of variable length itemsets, where each itemset $T \subseteq L$. We say that an itemset T *supports* an item $x \in L$ if x is in T. We say that an itemset T *supports* an itemset $X \subseteq L$ if T supports every item in the set X. The *support* of the itemset X is the percentage of itemsets in D that support X. The problem of mining frequent itemsets in D consists in discovering all itemsets whose support is above a user-defined support threshold *minsup*.

Apriori Algorithm. *Apriori* is an example of a level-wise algorithm for frequent itemset discovery. It makes multiple passes over the input data to determine all frequent itemsets. Let L_k denote the set of frequent itemsets of size k and let C_k denote the set of candidate itemsets of size k. Before making the k-th pass, *Apriori* generates C_k using L_{k-1}. Its candidate generation process ensures that all subsets of size $k-1$ of C_k are all members of the set L_{k-1}. In the k-th pass, it then counts the support for all the itemsets in C_k. At the end of the pass all itemsets in C_k with a support greater than or equal to the minimum support form the set of frequent itemsets L_k. Figure 1 provides the pseudocode for the general level-wise algorithm, and its *Apriori* implementation. The *subset(t, k)* function gives all the subsets of size k in the set t.

C_1 = {all 1-itemsets from D}
for (k=1; $C_k \neq \emptyset$; k++)
    count(C_k, D);
    L_k = {$c \in C_k$ | $c.count \geq minsup$};
    C_{k+1} = generate_candidates(L_k);
Answer = $\bigcup_k L_k$;

L_1 = {frequent 1-itemsets}
for (k = 2; $L_{k-1} \neq \emptyset$; k++)
    C_k = generate_candidates(L_{k-1});
    forall tuples $t \in D$
        C_t=$C_k \cap$ subset(t, k);
        forall candidates $c \in C_t$
            $c.count$++;
    L_k = {$c \in C_k$ | $c.count \geq minsup$}
Answer = $\bigcup_k L_k$;

Fig. 1. A general level-wise algorithm for association discovery (left) and it's Apriori implementation (right)

1.2 Related Work

The problem of association rule discovery was introduced in [1]. In the paper, discovery of frequent itemsets was identified as the key step in association rule mining. In [3], the authors proposed an efficient frequent itemset mining algorithm called *Apriori*. Since it has been observed that generation of association rules from frequent itemsets is a straightforward task, further research focused mainly on efficient methods for frequent itemset discovery.

Incremental mining in the context of frequent itemsets and association rules was first discussed in [5]. A novel algorithm called *FUP* was proposed to efficiently discover frequent itemsets in an incremented dataset, exploiting previously discovered frequent itemsets.

The notion of data mining queries (or *KDD* queries) was introduced in [7]. The need for Knowledge and Data Management Systems (KDDMS) as second generation data mining tools was expressed. The ideas of application programming interfaces and data mining query optimizers were also mentioned.

In [10] the authors postulated to create a knowledge cache that would keep recently discovered frequent itemsets along with their support value, in order to facilitate interactive and iterative mining. Besides presenting the notion of knowledge cache the authors introduced several maintenance techniques for such cache, and discussed using the cache contents when answering new frequent set queries.

In [4] three relationships which occur between two association rule queries were identified. The relationships represented cases when results on one query can be used to efficiently answer the other. However, the relationships concerned association rules – not frequent itemsets.

The work on materialized views started in the 80s. The basic concept was to use materialized views as a tool to speed up queries and serve older copies of data. Materialized views have become a key element of data warehousing technology (see [11] for an overview).

2 Basic Definitions and Problem Formulation

Definition 1 (Data Mining Query). A *data mining query for frequent itemset discovery is a tuple dmq=($\mathcal{R}, a, \Sigma, \Phi, \beta$), where $\mathcal{R}$ is a database relation, a is a set-valued attribute of $\mathcal{R}, \Sigma$ is a data selection predicate on $\mathcal{R}, \Phi$ is a selection predicate on frequent itemsets, β is the minimum support for the frequent itemsets. The data mining query dmq returns all frequent itemsets discovered in $\pi_a \sigma_\Sigma \mathcal{R}$ having support greater than β and satisfying the constraints Φ*.

Example. *Given is the database relation $\mathcal{R}_1(attr_1, attr_2)$. The data mining query dmq_1 = ($\mathcal{R}_1$, "attr$_2$", "attr$_1$>5", "|itemset|<4", 3) describes the problem of discovering frequent itemsets in the set-valued attribute attr$_2$ of the relation $\mathcal{R}_1$. The frequent itemsets with support above 3 and length less than 4 are discovered in records having attr$_1$>5*.

Definition 2 (Materialized Data Mining View). *A materialized data mining view dmv=($\mathcal{R}, a, \Sigma, \Phi, \beta$) is a data mining query, whose both the definition and the result are permanently stored (materialized) in a database. All frequent itemsets being a result of the data mining query are called materialized data mining view contents.*

Definition 3 (Restricted Frequent Itemset Selection Predicate). *Given two data mining queries: dmq_1=($\mathcal{R}, a, \Sigma_1, \Phi_1, \beta_1$) and dmq_2=($\mathcal{R}, a, \Sigma_2, \Phi_2, \beta_2$). We say that the frequent itemset selection predicate Φ_1 is restricted with respect to the frequent itemset selection predicate Φ_2 (or Φ_2 is relaxed with respect to Φ_1), written as $\Phi_2 \subset \Phi_1$, if and* only if for each frequent itemset, satisfying Φ_1 implies also satisfying Φ_2. We say that the frequent itemset selection predicates are independent if $\Phi_1 \not\subset \Phi_2 \wedge \Phi_2 \not\subset \Phi_1 \wedge \Phi_1 \neq \Phi_2$.

Definition 4 (Stronger Frequent Itemset Selection Predicate). *Given two selection predicates on frequent itemsets: p_1 and p_2. We say that p_1 is stronger than p_2 if any of the conditions shown in Table 1 holds. We assume that items are integers. S represents a frequent itemset, min()/max() returns the highest/lowest item, count() returns the size of an itemset, sum() returns the sum of all items, range() returns the difference between the highest and the lowest item, V_1 and V_2 are sets of items, v_1 and v_2 are integers.*

Table 1. Conditions for p_1 being stronger than p_2

p_1	p_2	condition
$S \supseteq V_1$	$S \supseteq V_2$	$V_1 \supset V_2$
$S \subseteq V_1$	$S \subseteq V_2$	$V_1 \subset V_2$
$Min(S) \leq v_1$	$min(S) \leq v_2$	$V_1 < v_2$
$Min(S) \geq v_1$	$min(S) \geq v_2$	$v_1 > v_2$
$max(S) \leq v_1$	$max(S) \leq v_2$	$v_1 < v_2$
$max(S) \geq v_1$	$max(S) \geq v_2$	$v_1 > v_2$
$count(S) \leq v_1$	$count(S) \leq v_2$	$v_1 < v_2$
$count(S) \geq v_2$	$count(S) \geq v_2$	$v_1 > v_2$
$Sum(S) \leq v_1 \ (\forall x \in S, x \geq 0)$	$sum(S) \leq v_2 \ (\forall x \in S, x \geq 0)$	$v_1 < v_2$
$Sum(S) \geq v_1 \ (\forall x \in S, x \geq 0)$	$sum(S) \geq v_2 \ (\forall x \in S, x \geq 0)$	$v_1 > v_2$
$range(S) \leq v_1$	$range(S) \leq v_2$	$v_1 < v_2$
$range(S) \geq v_1$	$range(S) \geq v_2$	$v_1 > v_2$

Theorem 1. *Given two data mining queries: $dmq_1 = (\mathcal{R}, a, \Sigma_1, \Phi_1, \beta_1)$ and $dmq_2 = (\mathcal{R}, a, \Sigma_2, \Phi_2, \beta_2)$. The frequent itemset selection predicate Φ_1 is restricted with respect to the frequent itemset selection predicate Φ_2 if any of the following holds:*

(1) *The selection predicate Φ_2 is a conjunction of n predicates $p_1^2 \wedge p_2^2 \wedge ... \wedge p_n^2$, the selection predicate Φ_1 is a conjunction of $n+1$ predicates $p_1^1 \wedge p_2^1 \wedge ... \wedge p_n^1 \wedge p_{n+1}^1$, and for each $1 \leq i \leq n$ we have $p_i^1 = p_i^2$.*
(2) *The selection predicate Φ_1 is a conjunction of n predicates $p_1^1 \wedge p_2^1 \wedge ... \wedge p_{n-1}^1 \wedge p_n^1$, the selection predicate Φ_2 is a conjunction of n predicates $p_1^2 \wedge p_2^2 \wedge ... \wedge p_{n-1}^2 \wedge p_n^2$, for each $1 \leq i \leq (n-1)$ we have $p_i^1 = p_i^2$, and the predicate p_n^1 is stronger than p_n^2.*
(3) *There exists a frequent itemset selection predicate Φ_3, such that $\Phi_3 \subset \Phi_1 \wedge \Phi_2 \subset \Phi_3$.*

Proof. The proof is straightforward, based on definitions 3 and 4.

Definition 5 (Restricted Data Selection Predicate). *Given two data mining queries: $dmq_1 = (\mathcal{R}, a, \Sigma_1, \Phi_1, \beta_1)$ and $dmq_2 = (\mathcal{R}, a, \Sigma_2, \Phi_2, \beta_2)$. We say that the data selection predicate Σ_1 is restricted with respect to Σ_2 (or Σ_2 is relaxed with respect to Σ_2), written as $\Sigma_2 \subset \Sigma_1$, if and only if for each record of $\mathcal{R}$ satisfying Σ_1 implies also satisfying Σ_2. We say that the data selection predicates are independent if $\Sigma_1 \not\subset \Sigma_2 \wedge \Sigma_2 \not\subset \Sigma_1 \wedge \Sigma_1 \neq \Sigma_2$.*

3 Data Mining Query Execution Using a Materialized Data Mining View

Let us consider the problem of executing a data mining query using a materialized data mining view. Let $dmq=(\mathcal{R}, a, \Sigma_{dmq}, \Phi_{dmq}, \beta_{dmq})$, $dmv_1=(\mathcal{R}, a, \Sigma_1, \Phi_1, \beta_1)$. We will discuss different methods of employing dmv_1 in the process of executing dmq. We enumerate six query-view configuration classes, that enable us to use the materialized data mining view: (1) Class I – identical data selection predicates, identical frequent itemset selection predicates, identical minimum supports, (2) Class II – identical data selection predicates, frequent itemset selection predicate relaxed or independent in dmq or minimum support lowered in dmq, (3) Class III – identical data selection predicates, frequent itemset selection predicate restricted or equal in dmq, minimum support not lowered in dmq, (4) Class IV – data selection predicate restricted in dmv_1, identical frequent itemset selection predicates, identical minimum supports, (5) Class V – data selection predicates restricted in dmv_1, frequent itemset selection predicate relaxed or independent in dmq or minimum support lowered in dmq, (6) Class VI – data selection predicate restricted in dmv_1, frequent itemset selection predicate restricted or equal in dmq, minimum support not lowered in dmq. Classes I and IV are subclasses of classes III and VI respectively, offering more efficient query answering algorithms. In all other cases (data selection predicates independent or data selection predicate relaxed in dmq), dmv_1 is not usable in executing dmq (itemsets contained in dmv_1 were counted in parts of database that are not relevant to dmq).

Class I ($\Sigma_1=\Sigma_{dmq} \wedge \beta_1=\beta_{dmq} \wedge \Phi_1=\Phi_{dmq}$). Since the materialized data mining view dmv_1 contains the exact result of the data mining query dmq, then the execution of dmq only takes to read the contents of dmv_1. We will refer to this method as to *View Ready (VR)*. The I/O cost $cost_{VR}$ for *View Ready* involves only the retrieval of dmv_1 contents:

$$cost_{VR} = \|dmv_1\|, \qquad (1)$$

where $\|dmv_1\|$ is the size of dmv_1 contents (disk pages).

In order to estimate the benefits of using *View Ready*, let us consider the I/O cost $cost_{FULL}$ of executing a complete frequent itemset discovery algorithm (eg., *Apriori*) on $\sigma_{\Sigma dmq}\mathcal{R}$. The cost involves k scans of $\sigma_{\Sigma dmq}\mathcal{R}$ (k depends on the particular algorithm used):

$$cost_{FULL} = k \cdot \|\sigma_{\Sigma dmq}\mathcal{R}\|, \qquad (2)$$

where $\|\sigma_{\Sigma dmq}\mathcal{R}\|$ is the I/O cost of retrieving all records of $\mathcal{R}$ satisfying Σ_{dmq}. Notice that *View Ready* is useful if $\|dmv_1\| < k \cdot \|\sigma_{\Sigma dmq}\mathcal{R}\|$. Since in practical application of frequent itemset discovery, we usually have $\|dmv_1\| \ll \|\sigma_{\Sigma dmq}\mathcal{R}\|$, then it is highly beneficial to use the described method in order to execute a data mining query.

Class II ($\Sigma_1 = \Sigma_{dmq} \wedge (\beta_1 > \beta_{dmq} \vee \Phi_1 \not\subset \Phi_{dmq})$). Since the materialized data mining view is not guaranteed to contain all itemsets to be returned by *dmq*, the execution of *dmq* takes to perform a simplified frequent itemset discovery algorithm, eg., *Apriori*, in which we count only those candidates, that do not belong to dmv_1. If a candidate belongs to dmv_1, then we do not need to count it, because we already know its support. We will refer to this method as to *Complementary Mining (CM)*. The I/O cost $cost_{CM}$ for *Complementary Mining* involves k scans of $\sigma_{\Sigma dmq}\mathcal{R}$ (k depends on the particular algorithm used) and a single scan of dmv_1:

$$cost_{CM} = k \cdot \|\sigma_{\Sigma dmq}\mathcal{R}\| + \|dmv_1\|. \tag{3}$$

When we compare the I/O cost of *Complementary Mining* with the I/O cost of executing a complete frequent itemset discovery algorithm (eg., *Apriori*) on $\sigma_{\Sigma dmq}\mathcal{R}$, then we notice that *Complementary Mining* is more costly compared to not using a materialized data mining view at all. This fact actually eliminates *Complementary Mining* from practical applications. However, since the I/O cost is only a part of a total cost of executing a data mining query, then in a very specific case it might happen that the I/O overhead gets compensated by an improvement of CPU time. Such effects may occur e.g., in CPU-bound computer systems.

Class III ($\Sigma_1 = \Sigma_{dmq} \wedge \beta_1 \leq \beta_{dmq} \wedge \Phi_1 \subseteq \Phi_{dmq}$). Since the materialized data mining view dmv_1 contains a superset of the result of *dmq*, then the execution of *dmq* takes to read the contents of dmv_1 and filter the frequent itemsets with respect to β_{dmq} and Φ_{dmq}. We will refer to this method as to *Verifying Mining (VM)*. The I/O cost $cost_{VM}$ for *Verifying Mining* involves only the scan of dmv_1:

$$cost_{VR} = \|dmv_1\|. \tag{4}$$

When we compare the I/O cost of *Verifying Mining* with the I/O cost of executing a complete frequent itemset discovery algorithm (e.g., *Apriori*) on $\sigma_{\Sigma dmq}\mathcal{R}$, then we notice that *Verifying Mining* is useful if $\|dmv_1\| < k \cdot \|\sigma_{\Sigma dmq}\mathcal{R}\|$. According to our discussion above, we conclude that *Verifying Mining* is highly beneficial.

Class IV ($\Sigma_1 \subset \Sigma_{dmq} \wedge \beta_1 = \beta_{dmq} \wedge \Phi_1 = \Phi_{dmq}$). The database has been logically divided into two partitions (1) the records covered by the materialized data mining view dmv_1, (2) the records covered by the data mining query *dmq*, and not covered by the materialized data mining view. Since dmv_1 contains frequent itemsets discovered only in the first partition, therefore the executing of *dmq* takes to discover all frequent itemsets in the second partition (eg. using *Apriori*), to merge the discovered frequent itemsets with the frequent itemsets from dmv_1, and finally to scan the database in order to count and filter frequent itemsets. We will refer to this method as to *Incremental Mining (IM)* since it is similar to incremental update algorithms. The I/O cost $cost_{IM}$ for *Incremental Mining* involves k scans of $\sigma_{(\Sigma dmq - \Sigma dmq \cap \Sigma I)}\mathcal{R}$ (k depends on the particular algorithm used), a sigle scan of dmv_1, and a single scan of $\sigma_{\Sigma dmq}\mathcal{R}$:

$$cost_{CM} = k \cdot \|\sigma_{(\Sigma dmq - \Sigma dmq \cap \Sigma I)}\mathcal{R}\| + \|dmv_1\| + \|\sigma_{\Sigma dmq}\mathcal{R}\|. \tag{5}$$

When we compare the I/O cost of *Incremental Mining* with the I/O cost of executing a complete frequent itemset discovery algorithm (e.g., *Apriori*) on $\sigma_{\Sigma dmq}\mathcal{R}$, then we notice that *Incremental Mining* is useful if: $k \cdot \|\sigma_{(\Sigma dmq-(\Sigma dmq \cap \Sigma 1))}\mathcal{R}\| + \|dmv_1\| < (k-1)\cdot\|\sigma_{\Sigma dmq}\mathcal{R}\|$. Assuming that in practical applications we usually have: $\|dmv_1\| << \|\sigma_{(\Sigma dmq-(\Sigma dmq \cap \Sigma 1))}\mathcal{R}\| < \|\sigma_{\Sigma dmq}\mathcal{R}\|$, it means that *Incremental Mining* is beneficial (in terms of I/O costs) when $\|\sigma_{(\Sigma dmq-(\Sigma dmq \cap \Sigma 1))}\mathcal{R}\| < (k-1)/k \cdot \|\sigma_{\Sigma dmq}\mathcal{R}\|$, which means that e.g., for $k=10$ the materialized data mining view should cover at least 10% of the dataset covered by the data mining query.

Class V ($\Sigma_1 \subset \Sigma_{dmq} \wedge (\beta_1 > \beta_{dmq} \vee \Phi_1 \not\subset \Phi_{dmq})$). The database has been logically divided into two partitions (1) the records covered by the materialized data mining view dmv_1, (2) the records covered by the data mining query dmq, and not covered by the materialized data mining view. The materialized data mining view dmv_1 is not guaranteed to contain all the frequent itemsets that would be discovered in the first partition (using β_{dmq} and Φ_{dmq}). The execution of dmq is a two-step procedure. In the first step, we execute a simplified frequent itemset discovery algorithm, e.g. *Apriori*, in which we count only those candidates that do not belong to dmv_1. If a candidate belongs to dmv_1, then we do not need to count it, because we already know its support. In the second step, we discover all frequent itemsets in the second partition, we merge the discovered frequent itemsets with those from the first step, and finally we scan the database to count and filter them. Formally, this method is a combination of *Complementary Mining* and *Incremental Mining*, therefore its I/O cost is the following:

$$cost_{CM} + cost_{IM} = k \cdot \|\sigma_{\Sigma 1}\mathcal{R}\| + \|dmv_1\| + k \cdot \|\sigma_{(\Sigma dmq-(\Sigma dmq \cap \Sigma 1))}\mathcal{R}\| + \|\sigma_{\Sigma dmq}\mathcal{R}\| = (k+1) \|\sigma_{\Sigma dmq}\mathcal{R}\| + \|dmv_1\|. \quad (6)$$

When we compare the above I/O cost with the I/O cost of executing a complete frequent itemset discovery algorithm on $\sigma_{\Sigma dmq}\mathcal{R}$, then we notice that in most practical applications the above method is more costly compared to not using a materialized data mining view at all. However, since the I/O cost is only a part of a total cost of executing a data mining query, then in a very specific case it might happen that the I/O overhead gets compensated by an improvement of CPU time. Such effects may occur e.g., in CPU-bound computer systems.

Class VI ($\Sigma_1 \subset \Sigma_{dmq} \wedge \beta_1 \leq \beta_{dmq} \wedge \Phi_1 \subseteq \Phi_{dmq}$). The database has been logically divided into two partitions (1) the records covered by the materialized data mining view dmv_1, (2) the records covered by the data mining query dmq, and not covered by the materialized data mining view. The materialized data mining view dmv_1 contains a superset of all frequent itemsets that would be discovered in the first partition (using β_{dmq} and Φ_{dmq}). The execution of dmq is a two-step procedure. In the first step we scan dmv_1 and we filter its frequent itemsets with respect to β_{dmq} and Φ_{dmq}. In the second step, we discover all frequent itemsets in the second partition, we merge the discovered frequent itemsets with those from the first step, and finally we scan the database to count and filter them. Formally, this method is a combination of *Verifying Mining* and *Incremental Mining*, therefore its I/O cost is the following:

$$cost_{VR} + cost_{IM} = \|dmv_1\| + k \cdot \|\sigma_{(\Sigma dmq - (\Sigma dmq \cap \Sigma 1))}\mathcal{R}\| + \|\sigma_{\Sigma dmq}\mathcal{R}\|. \quad (7)$$

When we compare the above I/O cost with the cost of executing a complete frequent itemset discovery algorithm on $\sigma_{\Sigma dmq}\mathcal{R}$, then we notice that the discussed method is useful if: $\|dmv_1\| + k \cdot \|\sigma_{(\Sigma dmq - (\Sigma dmq \cap \Sigma 1))}\mathcal{R}\| < (k-1) \cdot \|\sigma_{\Sigma dmq}\mathcal{R}\|$. Assuming that in most practical applications we have: $\|dmv_1\| \ll \|\sigma_{(\Sigma dmq - (\Sigma dmq \cap \Sigma 1))}\mathcal{R}\| < \|\sigma_{\Sigma dmq}\mathcal{R}\|$, *Verifying Mining + Incremental Mining* is beneficial (in terms of I/O costs) if $\|\sigma_{(\Sigma dmq - (\Sigma dmq \cap \Sigma 1))}\mathcal{R}\| < (k-1)/k \cdot \|\sigma_{\Sigma dmq}\mathcal{R}\|$. For instance, for $k=10$ it means that the materialized data mining view should cover at leas 10% of the dataset covered by the data mining query.

Our above discussion has been summarized in the Table 2.

Table 2. Methods of executing a data mining query using a materialized data mining view

	$\Sigma_1 = \Sigma_{dmq}$	$\Sigma_1 \subset \Sigma_{dmq}$
$\beta_1 = \beta_{dmq} \wedge \Phi_1 = \Phi_{dmq}$	VR	IM
$\beta_1 > \beta_{dmq} \vee \Phi_1 \not\subset \Phi_{dmq}$	CM	CM, IM
$\beta_1 \leq \beta_{dmq} \wedge \Phi_1 \subseteq \Phi_{dmq}$	VM	VM, IM

4 Experimental Results

In order to evaluate performance gains stemming from using a materialized view, we performed several experiments on a Pentium II 433MHz PC with 128 MB of RAM. We experimented with synthetic and real datasets. The synthetic datasets were generated using the *GEN* generator from the *Quest* project [2]. The real datasets that we used came from the UCI KDD Archive [6]. Here we report results on the MSWeb[1] (Microsoft Anonymous Web Data) dataset and a synthetic dataset containing 148000 transactions built from 100 different items, with the average transaction size of 30.

In the tests we did not consider Class I (trivial, in practice always beneficial) and classes involving *Complementary Mining*, i.e., II and V (theoretically proven as inefficient). Thus, we focused on practical verification of *Verifying Mining* and *Incremental Mining*. As a complete data mining algorithm we used our implementation of *Apriori*. To simulate constraints of a multi-user environment, we limited the amount of main memory available to algorithms to 10-50kB. Each chart presents average results from a series of 20 experiments.

In the first series of experiments we varied the level of coverage of the query's dataset by materialized view's dataset. The minimum support of the query was by 10% higher than in case of the materialized view. Figure 2 presents the results for real and synthetic datasets.

---

[1] http://kdd.ics.uci.edu/databases/msweb/msweb.html .

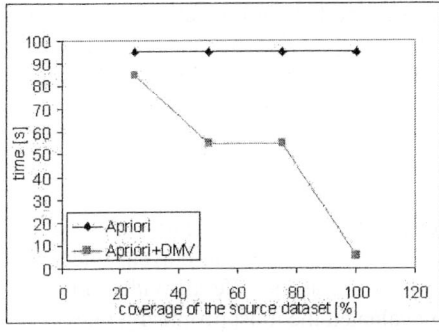 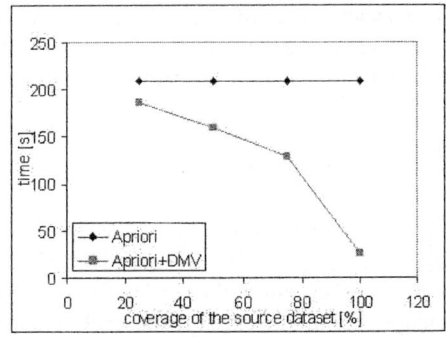

Fig. 2. Execution times for various levels of coverage of the query's dataset by materialized view's dataset for real (left) and synthetic (right) datasets

The experiments show that even for a materialized view based on the dataset covering 20% of the query's dataset, exploiting the results stored in the view reduces processing time. In general, more significant coverage results in better performance of the method using a materialized view. However, the exact performance improvement depends also on data distribution and the support threshold.

In the second series of experiments we tested the impact of difference between the support thresholds of the query to be answered and the materialized data mining view. The results for both considered datasets are presented in Fig. 3. The difference between the thresholds is expressed as the percentage of the support threshold of the query to be answered (the support threshold used for the materialized view was lower than the support threshold used in the query). For both datasets the source dataset for the view covered 75% of the dataset of the query.

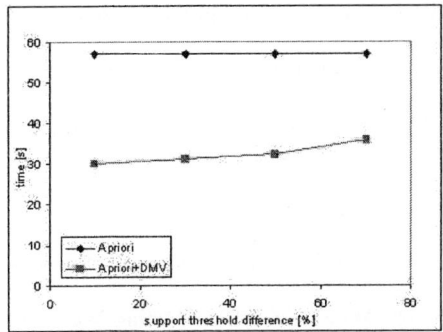 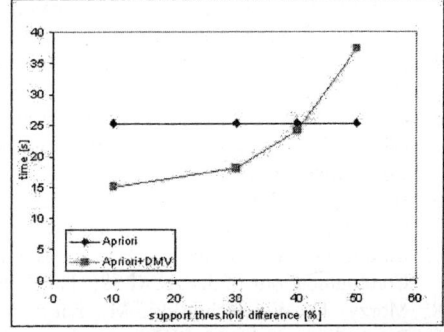

Fig. 3. Execution times for various relative differences in support thresholds for real (left) and synthetic (right) datasets

The experiments show that using a materialized view is more efficient when the difference between the support thresholds is small. For big differences it is even possible that using a materialized view is a worse solution than running the complete frequent itemset mining algorithm. This can happen since for a very low support threshold the size of a materialized view can be very big, introducing high I/O costs. The exact value of the difference between support thresholds for which using a materialized view is not beneficial depends on the actual threshold values, the nature of the dataset, and the coverage of the query's dataset by materialized view's dataset.

5 Conclusions

In this paper we discussed answering a frequent itemset query using a materialized data mining view. We classified possible differences between the current query and the query defining the materialized view into six classes. We provided I/O cost analysis for all the classes, and experimentally evaluated the most promising ones.

Theoretical analysis and experiments show that using a materialized view is an efficient solution in cases for which *View Ready*, *Verifying Mining*, and *Incremental Mining* techniques are applicable. The latter two methods perform particularly well when the support threshold of the view is close to the support threshold of the query and/or the source dataset of the view covers significant part of the query's dataset.

In the future we plan to consider situations in which a given query can be answered using a collection of materialized data mining views.

References

1. Agrawal, R., Imielinski, T., Swami, A.: Mining Association Rules Between Sets of Items in Large Databases. In: Proc. of the 1993 ACM SIGMOD Conf. on Management of Data. (1993)
2. Agrawal, R., Mehta, M., Shafer, J., Srikant, R., Arning, A., Bollinger, T.: The Quest Data Mining System. In: Proc. of the 2nd Int'l Conference on Knowledge Discovery in Databases and Data Mining, Portland, Oregon. (1996)
3. Agrawal, R., Srikant, R.: Fast Algorithms for Mining Association Rules. In: Proc. of the 20th Int'l Conf. on Very Large Data Bases. (1994)
4. Baralis E., Psaila, G.: Incremental Refinement of Mining Queries. In: Proceedings of the 1st DaWaK Conference. (1999)
5. Cheung, D.W.-L., Han, J., Ng, V., Wong, C.Y.: Maintenance of discovered association rules in large databases: An incremental updating technique. In: Proc. of the 12th ICDE Conference. (1996)
6. Hettich, S., Bay, S. D.: The UCI KDD Archive [http://kdd.ics.uci.edu]. University of California, Department of Information and Computer Science (1999)
7. Imielinski, T., Mannila, H.: A Database Perspective on Knowledge Discovery. Communications of the ACM **39**(11) (1996)
8. Morzy, T., Wojciechowski, M., Zakrzewicz, M.: Materialized Data Mining Views. In: Proceedings of the 4th PKDD Conference. (2000)
9. Morzy, T., Wojciechowski, M., Zakrzewicz, M.: Fast Discovery of Sequential Patterns Using Materialized Data Mining Views. In: Proceedings of the 15th ISCIS Conference. (2000)
10. Nag, B., Deshpande, P.M., DeWitt, D.J.: Using a Knowledge Cache for Interactive Discovery of Association Rules. In: Proceedings of the 5th KDD Conference. (1999)
11. Roussopoulos, N.: Materialized Views and Data Warehouses. SIGMOD Record **27**(1) (1998)

Efficient Methods for Database Storage and Retrieval Using Space-Filling Curves

Srinivas Aluru[1] and Fatih Erdogan Sevilgen[2]

[1] Iowa State University, Ames, IA 50011, USA
aluru@iastate.edu
[2] Gebze Institute of Technology, Gebze, Turkey
sevilgen@bilmuh.gyte.edu.tr

Abstract. Efficient storage and retrieval of records involving multiple keys is a difficult and well-studied problem. A popular solution employed is to visualize the records as points in multidimensional space and use a mapping from this multidimensional space to the one-dimensional space of block addresses in secondary storage. There is significant interest in performing such a mapping using space-filling curves. Unfortunately, space-filling curves are defined for points that lie on a uniform grid of a particular resolution. As a result, both storage and retrieval algorithms based on space-filling curves depend upon the size of the grid. This makes the run time of such algorithms dependent on the distribution of the points and in fact, unbounded for arbitrary distributions. There are two main contributions in this paper: First, we present a distribution-independent algorithm for storing records with multiple keys using space-filling curves. Our algorithm runs in $O(kn \log n)$ time for storing n records containing k key fields. We then present an algorithm for answering range queries with a bounded running time independent of the distribution.

1 Introduction

Efficient storage and retrieval algorithms are essential for ensuring the performance of database applications. Efficiency of querying a database depends on the storage organization and data structures used. Methods for storing and retrieving records using a single key have been extensively studied by many researchers and a large number of good data structures developed. For records involving multiple keys, the solutions devised are not as satisfactory. Some of the techniques developed are a natural extension of the single-key based data structures and do not necessarily perform well for queries involving multiple keys. Some data structures make querying efficient when using some subset of the keys, at the expense of slowing down queries when other keys are involved.

The problem of storing database records with multiple keys is equivalent to the problem of organizing points in a multidimensional space. A file (or a relation) in a database is a collection of records with each record containing k key fields (or key attributes) and other fields (attributes) that are never used to access data. We can represent each such record by a point in k-dimensional space by assigning a dimension to each key field and specifying a mapping from key values to coordinates. The records have to be stored on a secondary storage medium such as a disk. This requires mapping the k-dimensional points to the one-dimensional range of addresses on the disk.

Most database queries can be abstracted into the class of *range queries*, in which ranges are given for all or a subset of the key attributes with the objective of retrieving all records that satisfy the range criteria. The cost of a database query is dominated by the disk access time. It is also more economical to retrieve consecutive blocks on a disk instead of scattered blocks (reduces seek time overhead). To reduce the number of block accesses and to keep the block accesses consecutive, points that are proximate in the multidimensional space should be proximate in the one-dimensional ordering, i.e. the mapping should preserve the "proximity information" present in the multidimensional space. Of course, it is impossible to design a mapping function that strictly preserves the proximity information. For example, a point may have several nearest-neighbors in multidimensional space but can have only two nearest-neighbors in a one-dimensional ordering. Hence, the goal is to design mappings that preserve the "proximity information" to the extent possible.

Space-filling curves are mappings from a multidimensional grid to a linear ordering. The path implied in the multidimensional space by the linear ordering, i.e. the sequence in which the multidimensional grid cells are visited according to the linear ordering, forms a non-intersecting curve. By continually increasing the resolution of the grid, the curve can come arbitrarily close to any point in space. Hence the name, space-filling curve. The "proximity information" preserving properties of space-filling curves are studied experimentally by Abel et. al. [1] and Jagadish [6]. Some analytical results are given by Moon et. al. [7]. Further general discussion about space-filling curves can be found in [10].

Storing of database records using space-filling curves is first suggested by Orenstein et. al. [9]. The basic idea is to map the multidimensional data to one dimension using a space-filling curve and to employ any one dimensional storage structure (e.g. B-tree and its variants [3]) afterwards. Since the storage structures are efficient in one dimensional space, it is supposed that the resulting multidimensional storage structures are also efficient. However, space-filling curves are defined for uniform grids of a particular resolution. Keys that result in non-uniform distributions require a fine resolution, and the run-times of algorithms using space-filling curves are dependent on the resolution. Thus, the running times are dependent on the distribution and are in fact unbounded for arbitrary distributions.

In this paper, we present a simple, distribution-independent (i.e. the run time is a function of the number of records and independent of the distribution of the keys) and efficient technique for storing database records with multiple keys using space-filling curves. Our algorithm runs in $O(kn \log n)$ time for storing n records with k keys. It is based on a comparison routine we devised, which takes two k-dimensional points as input and decides in $O(k)$ time which of these

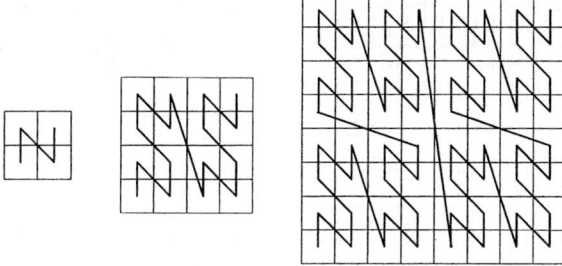

Fig. 1. Z-curve for grids of size 2×2, 4×4 and 8×8

two points is first visited by the space-filling curve. This not only makes the application of space-filling curves to arbitrary records efficient but also makes it easy to apply these strategies in the presence of insertions and deletions. Thus, our technique allows for keeping track of a dynamic database efficiently. We also present a distribution-independent algorithm for answering range queries. Orenstein et. al. [9] present some heuristics for reducing the run-time for range queries. While these heuristics may be useful in practice, they do little to remove the distribution-dependent nature of the algorithm. To the best of our knowledge, all the algorithms using space-filling curves that are reported in the literature are distribution-dependent.

2 Space-Filling Curves

In this section, we describe the notion of space-filling curves and describe some of the popularly used curves. We first restrict our attention to square two-dimensional case and describe space-filling curves recursively, i.e., the curve for a $2^k \times 2^k$ grid is composed of four $2^{k-1} \times 2^{k-1}$ grid curves.

Z-Curve. The Z-curve [8] for 2×2 grid (see Figure 1) look like the letter 'Z' rotated counterclockwise by 90°, hence the name Z-curve. Space-filling curves have a beginning called the *head* and the end is called the *tail*. The head of a Z-curve is in the lower left corner and the tail is in the upper right corner. The curve for a $2^k \times 2^k$ grid is composed of four $2^{k-1} \times 2^{k-1}$ grid curves one in each quadrant of the $2^k \times 2^k$ grid and the tail of one curve is connected to the head of the next as shown in the figure. The order in which the curves are connected is the same as the order of traversal of the 2×2 curve, and this holds true for all space-filling curves.

Graycode Curve. The graycode curve [4] can be described recursively as: Place four curves of the previous resolution in the four quadrants. Flip the upper quadrant curves once around one of the coordinate axes and then around the other axis. The four curves are then connected in the order of traversal of the 2×2 curve (Figure 2). The head of the curve is in the lower left hand corner.

Hilbert Curve. The Hilbert curve [5] is a smooth curve that avoids the sudden jumps present in the Z and the Graycode curves (Figure 2). The curve is

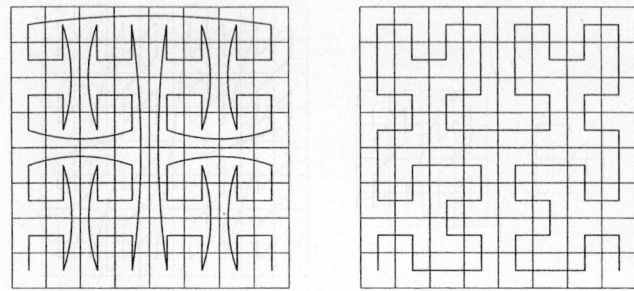

Fig. 2. Graycode curve and Hilbert curve for a grid of size 8 × 8

composed of four curves of the previous resolution placed in the four quadrants. The curve in the lower left quadrant is rotated clockwise by 90°. The curve in the lower right quadrant is rotated counterclockwise by 90°. The curves are connected in the order prescribed by the 2 × 2 curve.

The curves can be easily extended for cases when the dimension spans are uneven and for higher dimensional grids. Consider a $2^k \times 2^m$ grid ($k > m$). One can use 2^{k-m} curves each for a $2^m \times 2^m$ grid and place them next to each other. If needed, the curves can be tilted upside down as appropriate, to avoid sudden jumps. Alternatively, one can define a $2^{k-m+1} \times 2$ template and use it to construct the curve for a $2^k \times 2^m$ grid. The two strategies can also be combined: use a $2^{l+1} \times 2$ ($0 \leq l \leq k - m$) template to construct a curve for a $2^{m+l} \times 2^m$ grid and use 2^{k-m-l} copies of it placed next to each other. A higher dimensional curve can be obtained by using a template of the same dimension (such as a 2 × 2 × 2 grid for three dimensions). For a detailed description of space-filling curves for uneven dimension spans and higher dimensions can be found in [6].

3 Storing Database Records Using Space-Filling Curves

Consider the problem of storing n database records with k key fields. We first map each key field to a coordinate and view the records as points in k-dimensional space. We then order these points in the order in which a particular space-filling curve visits them and store the records according to this order. This order is equivalent to one-dimensional sorted data and a data structure such as a B-tree can be used to store the resulting data.

For convenience of presentation we focus on records with two keys, resulting in points in two dimensions. The same techniques can be easily extended to the case of multiple keys (points in multidimensions) in a straightforward manner.

Before we proceed, it is necessary to introduce some terminology: Let us call a square of length l containing all of the given n points as the *root cell*. We can imagine a sequence of $2^k \times 2^k$ grids ($0 \leq k < \infty$) imposed on the root cell. We will use the term *cell* to describe each grid cell of any of these hypothetical grids. Assume the lower left corner of the root cell to be the origin. Each cell can

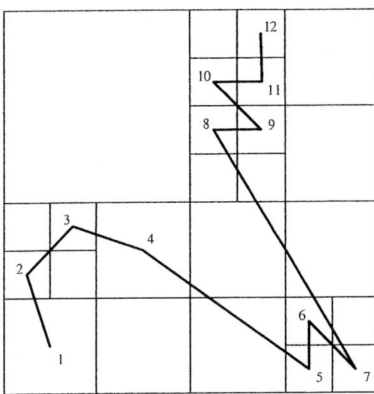

Fig. 3. Z-curve for a collection of 12 points using the hierarchical subdivision approach

be described by the position of the lower left corner of the cell and the length of an edge of the cell. The root cell contains 2^{2k} cells of length $\frac{l}{2^k}$. The cells are positioned at $(i\frac{l}{2^k}, j\frac{l}{2^k})$ $(0 \leq i,j < 2^k)$. A line is called a k-*boundary* if it contains an edge of a cell of length $\frac{l}{2^k}$. Each cell in the $2^k \times 2^k$ grid can be subdivided into four subcells of equal size in the $2^{k+1} \times 2^{k+1}$ grid. We can label the upper right subcell as subcell I, upper left subcell as subcell II, lower left subcell as subcell III and lower right subcell as subcell IV (following the usual quadrant I notation).

To order two dimensional points, we can continuously subdivide the root cell into grids of resolution $2^k \times 2^k$ (starting with $k = 0$ and increasing k) until no grid cell contains more than one point. As each grid cell contains only one point, the order in which the curve visits the grid cells also determines the order in which the curve visits the points. The problem with this approach is that the size of the grid required is dependent upon the distribution of the points and the resulting method does not have a bounded running time.

An easy improvement can be made to decrease the run-time of the above algorithm. Start with the root cell and subdivide the root cell into four subcells. Note that once the space-filling curve enters a grid cell, it will leave the grid cell only after traversing all the points in the cell (if we imagine a space-filling curve for infinite resolution) and will never reenter the cell again. Therefore, the relative order of points in different subcells determined by the order space-filling curve visits the subcells. For example, the Z-curve visits the subcells in the order subcell III, subcell II, subcell IV and subcell I. If a subcell is empty or contains only one point, nothing further needs to be done. If a subcell contains more than one point, recursively subdivide it using the same method. This hierarchical subdivision is identical to the adaptive region quadtree [11]. An example of this procedure is shown in Figure 3. This modification may significantly improve the run-time in practice but it does not change the distribution-dependent nature of the algorithm.

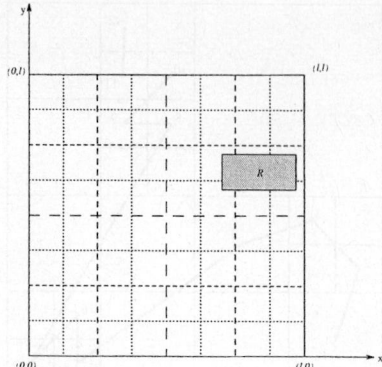

Fig. 4. A *root cell* of length l and a rectangle R. The big dashed lines are 1-*boundaries*, the small dashed lines are 2-*boundaries* and the dotted lines are 3-*boundaries*. 2-*boundaries* are also 3-*boundaries* and 1-*boundaries* are also 2-*boundaries* and 3-*boundaries*

Note that the order in which the space-filling curve visits two points is independent of the position and the presence of other points. Suppose that we are given two points with the goal of determining which of the two is first visited by the space-filling curve. We first determine the smallest subcell of the root cell that contains these two points. If we subdivide this subcell further into four subcells, the two points will lie in different subcells. Therefore, the order in which the space-filling curve visits the two points is determined by the order in which the four subcells are visited by the curve.

The problem of ordering points, therefore, reduces to finding the smallest subcell that can contain the given two points. Consider a rectangle R that has the given two points at the opposite ends of a diagonal. The smallest subcell of the root cell enclosing the two points is also the smallest subcell that encloses the rectangle R, which we will determine. We use the technique proposed by Aluru et al. [2] for this purpose. The smallest subcell of the root cell enclosing R is of size $\frac{l}{2^{k-1}}$, where k is the smallest number such that a k-*boundary* crosses the rectangle R (see figure 4). To determine this, we examine boundaries parallel to each coordinate axis in turn.

Consider boundaries parallel to the y-axis. These can be specified by their distance from the y-axis. The family of k-*boundaries* is specified by $i\frac{l}{2^k}$, $0 \leq i \leq 2^k$. We need to find the smallest integer k such that a k-*boundary* parallel to y-axis passes through R, i.e. the smallest k such that $x_{min} < i\frac{l}{2^k} < x_{max}$ for some i. By minimality of k, only one k-*boundary* passes through R. Let j be the smallest integer such that $\frac{l}{2^j} < (x_{max} - x_{min})$. $j = \lceil \log_2 \frac{l}{x_{max}-x_{min}} \rceil$. There is at least 1 and at most 2 j-*boundaries* passing through R. These boundaries are given by $h_1 = \lceil \frac{2^j x_{min}}{l} \rceil \frac{l}{2^j}$ and $h_2 = \lfloor \frac{2^j x_{max}}{l} \rfloor \frac{l}{2^j}$. Since $k \leq j$, any k-*boundary* is also a j-*boundary*, forcing the k-*boundary* passing through R to coincide with h_1 or h_2. Let a be $\lceil \frac{2^j x_{min}}{l} \rceil$. $h_1 = a\frac{l}{2^j}$ and $h_2 = h_1$ or $(a+1)\frac{l}{2^j}$. If $h_2 \neq h_1$, let

a' be the even integer among a and $a + 1$. Otherwise, let a' be equal to a. It is clear that $j - k$ is equal to the highest power of 2 that divides a'. One way to find this is $j - k = \log_2(1 + \{a' \oplus (a' - 1)\}) - 1$. Since all the above operations take constant time, we can determine in constant time the smallest numbered boundary parallel to a given axis and crossing the rectangle R. In general, we can find the smallest hypercube enclosing the hyperrectangle R in k-dimensional space in $O(k)$ time.

The procedure we adopt to order n points according to a given space-filling curve is as follows: We devise a comparison routine that takes two points as input and determines which of the two is first visited by the space-filling curve. This is done by first determining the smallest subcell of the root cell that encloses the two points, followed by determining the order in which the curve visits the four subcells of this subcell. Once we design such a comparison routine, we can use any sorting algorithm to order the points. In the following, we describe such a technique for some space-filling curves.

Z-Curve. The Z-curve visits the subcells of a cell in the order subcell III, subcell II, subcell IV and subcell I (see Figure 1). This is independent of the size and location of the cell. So, once we have the smallest subcell and the position of two points in that subcell, we can immediately find the order of these points on the resulting Z-curve.

Graycode Curve. For the graycode curve, the order is not so trivial. The order in which the graycode curve visits the subcells depends on the location of the cell in the grid it belongs. Fortunately, there are only two different orders possible: subcell III, subcell II, subcell I, and subcell IV and subcell I, subcell IV, subcell III, and subcell II. We refer to the former as ∩-order and the latter as ∪-order, respectively. Moreover, each row of cells in a grid has a unique order. If we number the rows in a grid bottom-up, the ∩-order can only be found at the odd numbered rows and even numbered rows have ∪-order. To compare two points in graycode order, we check the location of the smallest cell.

The same type of comparison routine for Hilbert curve seems to be more complicated and may be impossible in $O(k)$ time. As in the graycode curve, the visiting order of the subcells of a cell in the Hilbert curve depends on the location of the cell. However, this dependence is not as simple. While in the graycode curve the order depends on only the last bit of the location of the subcell in y-direction, all the bits of the location of the subcell in both directions is necessary to find the order for the Hilbert curve. This is because the rotations in the generation of graycode curve are only of one kind and the effect cancels out for every two rotations. On the other hand, there are two types of rotations in the Hilbert curve and the cancellations are not so trivial.

4 Range Queries Using Space-Filling Curves

Range queries are the most commonly encountered queries in database applications. In a range query, ranges are specified for all or a subset of the keys with the objective of retrieving all the records that satisfy the range criteria. In our mapping of records to multidimensional space, the ranges correspond to a (possibly open-ended) hyperrectangle. The objective is to retrieve all the points that lie in this hyperrectangular region (i.e. query region).

A simple algorithm to evaluate a range query based on a storage structure employing space-filling curves is to check the cells and their subcells recursively for the query region starting with the whole domain. For each subcell of a cell, a new query region is calculated by intersecting the query region with the subcell. There are three possibilities: the new query region could be empty, the whole subcell or a part of the subcell. If the query region is the whole subcell, we report all the points in the subcell. Note that a space-filling curve enters a subcell once and exits it only after visiting all the points in it. Therefore, all the points within a subcell are stored consecutively, making it easy to access them. If the subcell does not intersect with the query region, nothing further needs to be done for this subcell. Otherwise, we generate separate range queries with the subcells as search regions and associated new query regions.

To report the data points in a cell, we search the entrance point of the space-filling curve into the cell in the database. This point depends on the order in which the subcells of a cell are visited by the space-filling curve. For example, the first subcell of a cell visited by the Z-curve is the lower left subcell of the cell. Therefore, the entrance point of the Z-curve in a cell is its lower left corner. Once we find the first point in the cell, we report all the consecutive points until the point is out of the boundary of the cell.

The simple range query algorithm described above has two major drawbacks: Firstly, the query region is often a very small part of the whole domain. Consider the case where the smallest boundary passing through the query region is a j-boundary, for some j. Since each recursive call divides a cell along the next boundary, the recursion should continue from 1 to j to get the first hit on the query region. The effort spent until this point is wasted. This may occur not only at the initiation of a range query but also during any recursive call. Secondly, if there are points very close to the boundaries of the query region, it may be very expensive to check whether these points are in the query region or not with this algorithm. We divide the cell containing this point at the boundary into finer and finer granularities to find subcells that do not intersect but are completely inside or outside of the query region.

While the first problem is the result of the position and size of the query region, the second problem depends on the distribution of the data surrounding the query region. However, the effect is the same in both cases – unbounded running time. We now present an algorithm that eliminates large portions of the search region and at the same time guarantees bounded running time. The following terminology is to be used in understanding the algorithm: A *search cell* is a cell that contains the query region. For each search cell we keep track of a *search segment*, which is a continuous segment of the space-filling curve that contains points within this search cell. The search segment may not contain all the points in the search cell, but the algorithm ensures that it contains all the unreported points in the query region associated with the search cell.

Algorithm 1 Range_Search (query_region, search_cell, search_segment)

```
for each subcell of the search_cell
    search_cell = subcell
    query_region = query_region ∩ search_cell
    if query_region ≠ ∅
        search_cell = smallest subcell of search_cell containing query_region
        search_segment = segment of search_segment containing the search_cell
        while the first point in the search_segment is in the query_region
            report the point
        if search_segment ≠ ∅
            drop the subsegment included in the largest cell that contains the
            first point in the search_segment but does not intersect query_region
            from the search_segment
            adjust search_cell and query_region to conform with the
            search_segment
            Range_Search ( query_region, search_cell, search_segment )
```

Fig. 5. A distribution-independent algorithm for range queries.

We solve the first problem by directly finding the smallest subcell of a search cell that contains the query region of interest ($O(k)$ time for k-dimensional data), each time before dividing a search cell into subcells. Since we divide the smallest cell that contains the query region, at least two subcells should contain some part of the query region. This guarantees that each call divides the query region.

The number of search cells generated in this process need not be bounded because of the second problem. To solve this problem, we ensure that at least one point that is in the search region but not in the query region is eliminated (if such a point exists) before a search cell is subdivided into smaller search cells. We do this by examining the search segment sequentially and reporting all the points that are in the query region until we find the first point that is not in the query region. We then find the largest cell that contains this point but does not intersect the query region. All the points in this cell can be skipped without any loss of information. The largest cell can be found as follows: Draw the straight line that gives the shortest distance from the point to the query region. Since the query region is hyperrectangular, this straight line is parallel to one of the axes. Calculate the smallest numbered boundary that crosses this line. The cell can be inferred from this boundary information and the point.

The pseudo code of **Range_Search** using the techniques explained above is given in Figure 5. As in the simple algorithm, we break the search cell into four search subcells and split the query region into four query regions, one for each subcell as in the simple algorithm. However, before recursive calls we try to eliminate as much of each search subcell and the associated search segment as possible. First, we reduce each search subcell by finding the smallest subcell of it that still contains its query region. The search segment for each search subcell is the part of the search segment that lies in the search subcell. We then traverse the points in the search segment and report them until the first point not in the query region is found. We reduce the search segment by eliminating the largest cell that is outside of the query region, contained in the search subcell, and containing this point.

5 Conclusions and Open Problems

Proximity preserving mappings from multidimensions to one-dimension are of importance in storing database records. Space-filling curves can be used as an efficient tool to perform such a mapping with reasonable quality. In this paper, we presented practically efficient techniques for storing records with multiple keys in secondary storage using space-filling curves, without making any assumptions on the distribution of the keys. We also presented a distribution-independent algorithm for answering range queries. It would be of much interest to find if such algorithms can be designed for the Hilbert curve as well.

Space-filling curves are used when a "proximity preserving" mapping of multidimensional space to a one-dimensional space is needed. However, the clustering properties of space-filling curves have only been studied experimentally. Analytical studies are usually limited to cases where points occupy every cell in a fixed grid. It is important to study the clustering properties of space-filling curves vs. traditional data structures for arbitrary point sets.

References

1. Abel, D.J., Mark, D.M.: A comparative analysis of some two-dimensional orderings. International Journal of Geographical Information Systems **4**(1) (1990) 21–31
2. Aluru, S., Prabhu, G.M., Gustafson, J., Sevilgen, F.: Distribution-independent hierarchical algorithm for the n-body problem. Journal of Supercomputing **12** (1998) 303–323
3. Comer, D.: The ubiquitous B-tree. ACM Computing Surveys**11**(2) (1979) 121–137
4. Faloutsos, C.: Gray codes for partial match and range queries. IEEE Transactions on Software Engineering **14**(10) (1988) 1381–1393
5. Hilbert, D.: Über die stetige Abbildung einer Linie auf einem Flachenstück. Math. Ann. **38** (1891) 459–460
6. Jagadish, H.V.: Linear clustering of objects with multiple attributes. In: Proc. ACM SIGMOD International Conference on the Management of Data. (1990) 332–342
7. Moon, B., Jagadish, H.V., Faloutsos, C., Saltz, J.H.: Analysis of clustering properties of Hilbert space-filling curve. Technical Report, CS-TR-3590, University of Maryland Department of Computer Science (1996)
8. Morton, G.M.: A computer oriented geodetic data base and a new technique in file sequencing. IBM, Ottawa, Canada (1966)
9. Orenstein, J.A., Merrett, T.H.: A class of data structures for associative searching. In: Proc. ACM SIGACT/SIGMOD Symposium on Principles of Database Systems. (1984) 181–190
10. Sagan, H.: Space-filling curves. Springer-Verlag (1994)
11. Samet, H.: The design and analysis of spatial data structures. Addison-Wesley (1990)

Modelling Mobility with PEPA Nets

Jane Hillston[1]* and Marina Ribaudo[2]**

[1] Laboratory for Foundations of Computer Science, The University of Edinburgh
jeh@inf.ed.ac.uk
[2] Dipartimento di Informatica e Scienze dell'Informazione, Università di Genova
ribaudo@disi.unige.it

Abstract. We explain the use of PEPA nets in documenting high-level designs of mobile code and mobile computing systems. This modelling language (which allows the modeller to differentiate between location-changing and state-changing operations in the system, and to quantify their computational expense for use in predictive performance analysis) is applied to the problem of modelling the canonical mobile code design paradigms which are in practical application today, as described in [2].

1 Introduction

Mobile code design paradigms have received heightened attention with the advent of secure and portable programming languages such as Java. A mobile code infrastructure allows application designers to distribute computational effort across networked hosts which can have many benefits. For example it may be possible to reduce the workload on central server components by moving computation from the server to its clients.

Selecting the optimum design from a suite of alternative designs for a distributed mobile code system may involve ranking the alternatives on the basis of key performance metrics such as response time, throughput and utilisation. Statements of required performance measures such as these are increasingly being used in service-level agreements meaning that the efficient and reliable computation of performance measures from a high-level model of a mobile code system is becoming a critical part of state-of-the-art application development.

It is imperative that the modelling formalism used to express these high-level performance models should reliably capture notions of *location*, *context* and *evaluation environment*. Additionally, it should clearly distinguish local computation at one of the locations from the movement of code-containing objects from one location to another. The latter brings about a change in the communication topology of the system, allowing patterns of communication which had previously not been possible because the partners in the communication were separated by being on different hosts in different address spaces, or behind firewalls or other administrative domain boundaries.

---

* Jane Hillston is supported by the DEGAS (Design Environments for Global ApplicationS) IST-2001-32072 project in the FET Proactive Initiative on Global Computing.
** Marina Ribaudo is supported by the FIRB project WEBMINDS (Wide-scalE, Broadband, MIddleware for Network Distributed Services).

To this end we have developed a high-level Petri net formalism which we believe naturally captures performance models of mobile code systems meeting the requirements suggested above. The *PEPA nets* formalism uses Hillston's Performance Evaluation Process Algebra [6] as the inscription language for coloured stochastic Petri nets. We have implemented software tools to facilitate the processing and performance analysis of PEPA nets [5] and created a hierarchical drawing tool for representing them graphically on screen [3].

In Section 2 we present the description and formal definitions of the PEPA nets modelling language. The definitions are illustrated by simple examples. Section 3 discusses the key design paradigms for code mobility, presenting PEPA net models of each, and some conclusions and directions for future work are presented in Section 4.

2 PEPA Nets

In this section we provide a brief overview of PEPA nets and the PEPA stochastic process algebra. A fuller description is available in [4] and [6].

The tokens of a PEPA net are terms of the PEPA stochastic process algebra which define the behaviour of components via the activities they undertake and their interactions. One example of a PEPA component would be a *File* object which can be opened for reading or writing, have data read (or written) and closed. Such an object would understand the methods *openRead*(), *openWrite*(), *read*(), *write*() and *close*().

$$File \stackrel{def}{=} (openRead, r_o).InStream + (openWrite, r_o).OutStream$$

$$InStream \stackrel{def}{=} (read, r_r).InStream + (close, r_c).File$$

$$OutStream \stackrel{def}{=} (write, r_w).OutStream + (close, r_c).File$$

This PEPA model documents a high-level protocol for using *File* objects, from which it is possible to derive properties such as "it is not possible to write to a closed file" and "read and write operations cannot be interleaved: the file must be closed and re-opened first".

Every activity incurs an execution cost which is quantified by an estimate of the (exponentially-distributed) rate at which it can occur (r_o, r_r, r_w, r_c). Activities may be *passive*, i.e., they can be executed only in cooperation with corresponding active ones. The rate of a passive activity is denoted by ⊤.

A PEPA net is made up of PEPA *contexts*, one at each place in the net. A context consists of a number of *static* components (possibly zero) and a number of *cells* (at least one). Like a memory location in an imperative program, a cell is a storage area to be filled by a datum of a particular type. In particular in a PEPA net, a cell is a storage area dedicated to storing a PEPA component, such as the *File* object described above. The components which fill cells can circulate as the tokens of the net. In contrast, the static components cannot move. A typical place might be the following:

$$File[\_] \bowtie_L FileReader$$

where the *synchronisation set* L in this case is $\mathcal{A}(\textit{File})$, the *complete action type set* of the component, (*openRead, openWrite, ...*). This place has a *File*-type cell and a static component, *FileReader*, which can process the file when it arrives.

A PEPA net differentiates between two types of change of state. We refer to these as *firings* of the net and *transitions* of PEPA components. Each are special cases of PEPA activities. Transitions of PEPA components will typically be used to model small-scale (or *local*) changes of state as components undertake activities. Firings of the net will typically be used to model macro-step (or *global*) changes of state such as context switches, breakdowns and repairs, one thread yielding to another, or a mobile software agent moving from one network host to another. The set of all firings is denoted by $\mathcal{A}_f$, the set of all transitions by $\mathcal{A}_t$. We distinguish firings syntactically by printing their names in boldface.

Continuing our example, we introduce an instant message as a type of transmissible file.

$$InstantMessage \stackrel{def}{=} (\textbf{transmit}, r_t).File$$

Part of a definition of a PEPA net which models the passage of instant messages is shown below. An instant message *IM* can be moved from the input place on the left to the output place on the right by the **transmit** firing. In doing so it changes state to evolve to a *File* derivative, which can be read by the *FileReader*.

$$\boxed{InstantMessage[IM]} \xrightarrow{(\textbf{transmit}, r_t)} \boxed{File[\_] \underset{L}{\bowtie} FileReader}$$

The syntax of PEPA nets is given in Figure 1. S denotes a *sequential component* and P a *concurrent component* which executes in parallel. I stands for a constant denoting either a sequential or a concurrent component, as bound by a definition.

Definition 1 (PEPA Net). *A PEPA net* $\mathcal{N}$ *is a tuple* $\mathcal{N} = (\mathcal{P}, \mathcal{T}, I, O, \ell, \pi, \mathcal{C}, D, M_0)$ *such that*

- $\mathcal{P}$ *is a finite set of places;*
- $\mathcal{T}$ *is a finite set of net transitions;*
- $I : \mathcal{T} \to \mathcal{P}$ *is the input function;*
- $O : \mathcal{T} \to \mathcal{P}$ *is the output function;*
- $\ell : \mathcal{T} \to (\mathcal{A}_f, \mathbb{R}^+ \cup \{\top\})$ *is the labelling function, which assigns a PEPA activity ((type, rate) pair) to each transition. The rate determines the negative exponential distribution governing the delay associated with the transition;*
- $\pi : \mathcal{A}_f \to \mathbb{N}$ *is the priority function which assigns priorities (represented by natural numbers) to firing action types;*
- $\mathcal{C} : \mathcal{P} \to P$ *is the place definition function which assigns a PEPA context, containing at least one cell, to each place;*
- D *is the set of token component definitions;*
- M_0 *is the initial marking of the net.*

The structured operational semantics, defined in [4], give a precise definition of the possible evolution of a PEPA net, and shows how a CTMC can be derived, treating each marking as a distinct state.

$$
\begin{aligned}
N &::= D^+ M & &\text{(net)}\\
M &::= (M_{\mathbf{P}},\ldots) & &\text{(marking)}\\
M_{\mathbf{P}} &::= \mathbf{P}[C,\ldots] & &\text{(place marking)}\\
D &::= I \stackrel{def}{=} S & &\text{(component defn)}\\
&\mid \mathbf{P}[C] \stackrel{def}{=} P[C] & &\text{(place defn)}\\
&\mid \mathbf{P}[C,\ldots] \stackrel{def}{=} P[C] \underset{L}{\bowtie} P & &\text{(place defn)}
\end{aligned}
$$

$$
\begin{aligned}
P &::= P \underset{L}{\bowtie} P & &\text{(cooperation)}\\
&\mid P/L & &\text{(hiding)}\\
&\mid P[C] & &\text{(cell)}\\
&\mid I & &\text{(identifier)}\\
\\
C &::= \text{`\_'} & &\text{(empty)}\\
&\mid S & &\text{(full)}\\
\\
S &::= (\alpha, r).S & &\text{(prefix)}\\
&\mid S + S & &\text{(choice)}\\
&\mid I & &\text{(identifier)}
\end{aligned}
$$

Fig. 1. The syntax of PEPA nets

We define the firing rule of PEPA nets to respect the net structure in the usual way (one token from each input place, one token to each output place) but also to take into consideration the ability of tokens to participate in the firing (can they perform an activity of the correct type?), and the availability of vacant cells of the appropriate type in the output places. Note that we require that the net is *balanced* in the sense that, for each transition, the number of input places is equal to the number of output places. In classical Petri nets tokens are identitiless, and can be viewed as being consumed from input places and created into output places for each firing. In contrast, in PEPA nets our tokens have state and identity, and we view them as *passing through* net-level transitions. For each firing there must be as many output tokens as there were input tokens.

Definition 2 (Enabling). *An enabling is a mapping of places to tokens. A net level transition t has an enabling of firing type α, $\mathrm{E}(t,\alpha)$, if for each input place $\mathbf{P}_i$ of t there is a token T in the current marking of $\mathbf{P}_i$, which has a one-step α-derivative, T'.*

Note that there may be several enablings for a given transition firing in any particular marking, as the enabling selects one token to fire from each input place, and there may be more than one eligible token at each input place.

Since it is important that each fired token has a vacant cell to go into after the firing, we define a corresponding notion of *output*. A transition has an output if, in the current marking, there is at least one vacant cell in each output place.

Definition 3 (Output). *For any net level transition t, an output, denoted $O(t)$, is a mapping from the output places of t to vacant cells in the current marking.*

Since each token passes through a net level transition when it fires, such a transition is enabled only when there is a bijective function between the chosen enabling and an output.

Definition 4 (Concession). *A net level transition t has concession for a firing of type α if there is an enabling $\mathrm{E}(t,\alpha)$ such that there is a bijective mapping ϕ from $\mathrm{E}(t,\alpha)$ to an output $O(t)$, which preserves the types of tokens.*

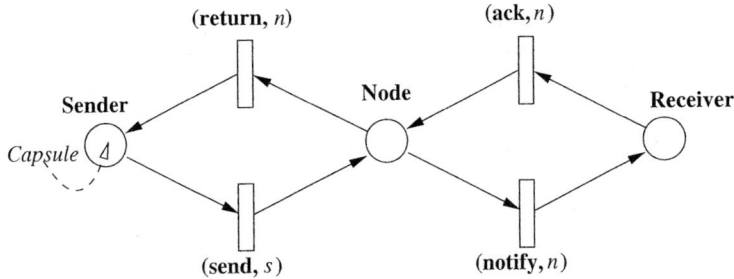

Fig. 2. PEPA net of the simple active network

As with classical Petri nets with priority, having concession identifies those transitions which could legally fire according to the net structure and the current marking. The set of transitions which *can* fire is determined by the priorities.

Definition 5 (Enabling Rule). *A net level transition t will be enabled for a firing of type α if there is no other net transition of higher priority with concession in the current marking.*

Definition 6 (Firing Rule). *When a net level transition t fires with type α on the basis of the enabling $E(t, \alpha)$, and concession ϕ then for each $(P_j, T,)$ in $E(t, \alpha)$, $T[T]$ is replaced by $T[\_]$ in the marking of P_j, and the current marking of each output place is updated according to ϕ.*

We assume that when there is more than one mapping ϕ from an enabling to an output, then they have equal probability and one is selected randomly. The rate of the enabled firing is determined using apparent rates, and the notion of bounded capacity, as usual for PEPA. We refer the reader to [5] for more details.

2.1 Small Example

We present a small example PEPA net in Figure 2 considering an *active switch* within an *active network*. In an active network, in addition to straightforward routing, a switch may carry out some computational task, processing the packets of a message as they pass through the node. Several approaches to active networking have been suggested, one of which is the use of *capsules*, i.e., special packets which activate the active network with respect to the following message, or stream of packets. Our model represents a sender and receiver communicating through an active intermediate node. We assume that the sender supplies a continuous stream of packets which are processed by the switch (not explicitly represented). When the sender wants to take advantage of the processing capabilities of the switch for some message, it sends a capsule to activate the switch. The capsule also notifies the receiver, and then resides in the switch until processing the message is complete, at which point it returns to the sender.

There is one token type in the PEPA net (*Capsule*), representing the capsule which is sent to activate an active switch, with respect to the following packets. We assume that after this (activity *activate*), a notification is sent to the *Receiver* that the following packets will have been processed in transit. This is acknowledged by the *Receiver*, returning the *Capsule* to the switch. After a random delay, approximating the length of the message to be processed, the *Capsule* reverts the *Switch* to normal processing via the activity *deactivate*. A final report is sent back to the *Sender*, represented by the firing **return**.

$$Capsule \stackrel{def}{=} (generate, \gamma).(\textbf{send}, \top).(activate, \alpha).(\textbf{notify}, \top).Capsule'$$
$$Capsule' \stackrel{def}{=} (\textbf{ack}, \top).(deactivate, \alpha).(\textbf{return}, \top).Capsule$$

In this model the places *Sender* and *Receiver* do not represent any functionality beyond the processing of the *Capsule*. Therefore each place simply contains a cell of type *Capsule*. We assume that in the initial marking the *Capsule* is with the *Sender* and that the *Receiver* has just an empty cell.

$$Sender \stackrel{def}{=} Capsule[Capsule] \qquad\qquad Receiver \stackrel{def}{=} Capsule[\_]$$

The remaining place, *Node*, representing the node hosting the switch, contains a static component. This component represents the functionality of the switch. Before activation it will repeatedly *route* packets arriving on the input stream. The activity *activate* must be carried out in cooperation with a *Capsule* component, and has the effect of introducing an additional step to packet processing: computation (activity *compute*) is done before routing. The switch continues in this mode until the *deactivate* activity is performed, again in cooperation with the *Capsule*. The place *Node* and the *Switch* component are defined as follows:

$$Node \stackrel{def}{=} Switch \underset{\{activate, deactivate\}}{\bowtie} Capsule[\_]$$
$$Switch \stackrel{def}{=} (route, \rho).Switch + (activate, \top).Active\_Switch$$
$$Active\_Switch \stackrel{def}{=} (compute, c).(route, \rho).Active\_Switch + (deactivate, \alpha).Switch$$

3 Design Paradigms for Code Mobility

In this section we assess the expressiveness of PEPA nets for modelling mobility. We consider a classification of types of mobility found in [2], where Fuggetta *et al.* identify four key design paradigms for code mobility: *Client-Server*, *Remote Evaluation*, *Code-on-Demand* and *Mobile Agent*. Each is exemplified by a simple scenario involving a chocolate cake and two friends, Louise and Christine. Here we present the PEPA net model of each scenario. The infrastructure of our model, representing the locations in the scenario, is as shown in Figure 3. The two places **LH** and **CH** represent Louise's house and Christine's house respectively. The labelling function for the transitions depends on the design paradigm. At the end of the section we also create and model an additional scenario, depicting the increasingly popular *Web Service* paradigm.

Client-Server. *Louise would like to have a chocolate cake, but she doesn't know the recipe, and she does not have the ingredients or an oven. Fortunately, she*

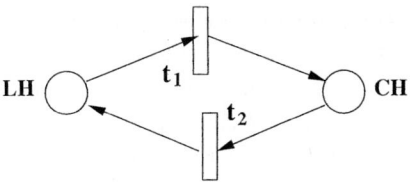

Fig. 3. Net structure for PEPA net models of all original chocolate cake scenarios

knows that Christine knows how to make a chocolate cake, and that she has a well supplied kitchen at her place. Since Christine is usually quite happy to prepare cakes on request, Louise phones her asking: "Can you make me a chocolate cake, please?" Christine makes the chocolate cake and delivers it back to Louise.

$Louise \stackrel{def}{=} (want, w).(eat, e).Louise$

$Recipe \stackrel{def}{=} (mix, m).Recipe \qquad Oven \stackrel{def}{=} (bake, b).Oven$

$Cake \stackrel{def}{=} (want, \top).(\mathbf{phone}, p).(mix, \top).(bake, \top).(\mathbf{deliver}, d).(eat, \top).Cake$

$\mathbf{LH} \stackrel{def}{=} Louise \underset{\{want, eat\}}{\bowtie} Cake[Cake] \qquad \mathbf{CH} \stackrel{def}{=} Cake[\_] \underset{\{mix, bake\}}{\bowtie} (Recipe \parallel Oven)$

$\ell(t_1) = \mathbf{phone}, \quad \ell(t_2) = \mathbf{deliver}$

This PEPA net has a single token which represents the cake, as it evolves from Louise's desire to an actual cake when Louise eats. There are three static components, representing Louise, the recipe and the oven respectively. The recipe is needed for the cake to be mixed and the oven for the cake to be baked: both are located, in this case, at Christine's house. Thus the cake moves from Louise's house to Christine's house for these stages of its evolution.

Remote Evaluation. Louise wants to prepare a chocolate cake. She knows the recipe but she has at home neither the required ingredients nor an oven. Christine has both at her place, yet she doesn't know how to make a chocolate cake. Louise knows that Christine is happy to try new recipes, therefore she phones Christine asking: "Can you make me a chocolate cake? Here is the recipe: take three eggs..." Christine prepares the cake following Louise's recipe and delivers it back to her.

$Louise \stackrel{def}{=} (want, w).(eat, e).Louise$

$Oven \stackrel{def}{=} (bake, b).Oven \qquad Recipe \stackrel{def}{=} (want, \top).(\mathbf{phone}, p).(mix, m).Recipe'$

$Cake \stackrel{def}{=} (mix, \top).(bake, \top).(\mathbf{deliver}, d).(eat, \top).Cake'$

$\mathbf{LH} \stackrel{def}{=} Louise \underset{\{want, eat\}}{\bowtie} (Recipe[Recipe] \parallel Cake[\_])$

$\mathbf{CH} \stackrel{def}{=} Cake[Cake] \underset{\{mix, bake\}}{\bowtie} (Recipe[\_] \parallel Oven)$

$\ell(t_1) = \mathbf{phone}, \quad \ell(t_2) = \mathbf{deliver}$

In this case there are two tokens: one for the cake and one for the recipe. When Louise decides that she wants a cake she changes the state of the *Recipe* component so that it may be moved to Christine's house where it contributes to the evolution of the cake. Once ready the cake is delivered to Louise's house. As previously the oven is represented by a static component, resident at Christine's house and contributing to the baking of the cake at the appropriate time.

Code-on-Demand. *Louise wants to prepare a chocolate cake. She has at home both the ingredients and an oven, but she lacks the proper recipe. However, Louise knows that Christine has the recipe and she has already lent it to many friends. So, she phones Christine asking "Can you tell me your chocolate cake recipe?" Christine tells her the recipe and Louise prepares the chocolate cake at home.*

$Louise \stackrel{def}{=} (want, w).(eat, e).Louise$

$Oven \stackrel{def}{=} (bake, b).Oven \qquad Recipe \stackrel{def}{=} (recipe, \top).(\mathbf{relate}, s).(mix, m).Recipe'$

$Cake \stackrel{def}{=} (want, \top).(mix, \top).(bake, \top).(eat, \top).Cake$

$Request \stackrel{def}{=} (want, \top).(\mathbf{request}, q).(recipe, c).Request'$

$\mathbf{LH} \stackrel{def}{=} Louise \underset{\{want, eat\}}{\bowtie} \left((Oven \parallel Recipe\,[\_]) \underset{\{mix, bake\}}{\bowtie} Cake \right) \underset{\{want\}}{\bowtie} Request\,[Request]$

$\mathbf{CH} \stackrel{def}{=} Request[\_] \underset{\{recipe\}}{\bowtie} Recipe[Recipe]$

$\ell(t_1) = \mathbf{request}, \quad \ell(t_2) = \mathbf{relate}$

Here the recipe is a token as it must be communicated from one location (**CH**) to another (**LH**). First, however this movement must be triggered. This is achieved by having another token, of type *Request*, which is sent from Louise's house to Christine's house. The static component representing the resource, the oven, is located at Louise's house and the chocolate cake is also a static component here.

Mobile Agent. *Louise wants to prepare a chocolate cake. She has the right recipe and ingredients, but she does not have an oven. However, she knows that Christine has an oven, and that she is happy to lend it. So, she prepares the cake batter and then goes to Christine's home, where she bakes the cake.*

$Louise \stackrel{def}{=} (want, w).(eat, e).Louise$

$Recipe \stackrel{def}{=} (mix, m).Recipe \qquad\qquad Oven \stackrel{def}{=} (bake, b).Oven$

$Cake \stackrel{def}{=} (want, \top).(mix, \top).(\mathbf{take}, t).(bake, \top).(\mathbf{return}, u).(eat, \top).Cake$

$\mathbf{LH} \stackrel{def}{=} (Louise \parallel Recipe) \underset{\{want, mix, eat\}}{\bowtie} Cake[Cake] \qquad \mathbf{CH} \stackrel{def}{=} Cake[\_] \underset{\{bake\}}{\bowtie} Oven$

$\ell(t_1) = \mathbf{take}, \quad \ell(t_2) = \mathbf{return}$

In this PEPA net, as in the first, the cake is the only token; the placement of the static components representing resources, however, differs. In this case the *Recipe* component is in the place representing Louise's house, while the *Oven* is located at Christine's house. As previously the *Cake* moves to fulfil its evolution. The difference is simply the locations in which the different stages are now exhibited.

We define a fresh scenario corresponding to the emerging paradigm of *Web services*, in which a service must first be located via a discovery service such as UDDI before invocations are made.

Web Service. *Louise would like to have a chocolate cake, but she doesn't know the recipe, and she does not have at home either the required ingredients or an*

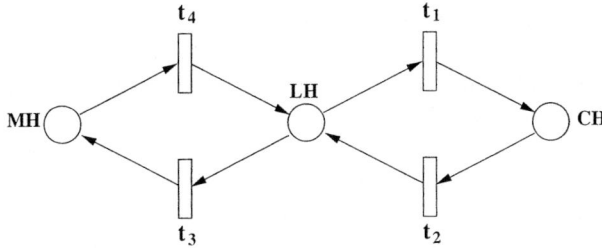

Fig. 4. Net structure for PEPA net model in the Web service chocolate cake scenario

oven, nor does she know anyone to ask. She asks her friend Marian, who knows everyone's capabilities. Marian tells her that Christine knows how to make a chocolate cake, and that she has a well-supplied kitchen at her place. Marian also gives Louise Christine's phone number and Louise phones Christine asking: "Can you make me a chocolate cake, please?" Christine makes the chocolate cake and delivers it back to Louise.

$Louise \stackrel{def}{=} (want, w).(eat, e).Louise$

$Marian \stackrel{def}{=} (cake\_query, q).Marian$

$Recipe \stackrel{def}{=} (mix, m).Recipe \qquad\qquad Oven \stackrel{def}{=} (bake, b).Oven$

$Query \stackrel{def}{=} (want, \top).(\mathbf{ask}, a).(cake\_query, \top).(\mathbf{reply}, r).(who, w).Query$

$Cake \stackrel{def}{=} (who, \top).(\mathbf{phone}, p).(mix, \top).(bake, \top).(\mathbf{deliver}, d).(eat, \top).Cake$

$\mathbf{MH} \stackrel{def}{=} Marian \bowtie_{\{cake\_query\}} Query[\_] \qquad \mathbf{CH} \stackrel{def}{=} Cake[\_] \bowtie_{\{mix, bake\}} (Recipe \parallel Oven)$

$\mathbf{LH} \stackrel{def}{=} Louise \bowtie_{\{want, eat\}} \left(Query[Query] \bowtie_{\{who\}} Cake[Cake] \right)$

$\ell(t_1) = \mathbf{phone}, \ \ell(t_2) = \mathbf{deliver}, \ \ell(t_3) = \mathbf{ask}, \ \ell(t_4) = \mathbf{reply}$

The scenario now involves three locations, as shown in Figure 4. In addition to the places for Louise's house and Christine's house, we have an additional place for the resource represented by the static component *Marian*. There are two tokens in the system: the *Cake* which follows a similar evolution to in the client-server scenario; and *Query* which carries out the discovery, initiated by Louise and satisfied by Marian. Once the query has been resolved, the two tokens synchronise (in the place **LH**) to pass on the information, which the cake can then use to determine its next move.

Whilst these scenarios are simple in terms of the number of components and locations involved, they do capture five key paradigms and we have shown that each can be readily modelled using PEPA nets. More realistic systems might be expected to entail a greater number of components and locations but the patterns of interaction, communication and movement would be the same, meaning that they could also be captured by PEPA nets.

4 Conclusions

Mobility and mobile agents pose interesting problems for modellers. New formalisms are emerging for modelling them. In this paper we have presented an introduction to one such formalism, PEPA nets. We have introduced PEPA nets in some detail and considered their expressiveness with respect to a published classification of mobile code design paradigms.

Several process calculi for modelling mobile computation, primarily for the purpose of functional verification, e.g., the π-calculus [8] (and its stochastic version [9]) and the calculus of mobile ambients [1] have appeared in the literature. There have also been extensions of Petri nets based on the use of "nets within nets", e.g., *Elementary Object Systems* [10] and *Reference nets* [7]. It is an area for future work to study the differences and similarities between these formalisms and PEPA nets.

References

1. Cardelli, L., Gordon, A.D.: Mobile Ambients. In: Nivat, M. (ed.): Foundations of Software Science and Computational Structures. Lecture Notes in Computer Science, Vol. 1378. Springer, Berlin Heidelberg New York (1998) 140–155
2. Fuggetta, A., Picco, G.P., Vigna, G.: Understanding Code Mobility. IEEE Transactions on Software Engineering **24** (1998) 342–361
3. Gilmore, S., Gribaudo, M.: Graphical Modelling of Process Algebras with DrawNET. In: Bause, F. (ed.): The Tools of the 2003 Illinois Multiconference on Measurement, Modelling, and Evaluation of Computer-Communication Systems. Research Report 781, Universität Dortmund, Informatik IV. (2003) 1–4
4. Gilmore, S., Hillston, J., Kloul, L., Ribaudo, M.: PEPA Nets: A Structured Performance Modelling Formalism. Performance Evaluation **54** (2003) 79–104
5. Gilmore, S., Hillston, J., Kloul, L., Ribaudo, M.: Software Performance Modelling using PEPA Nets. In: Proceedings of the 4th International Workshop on Software and Performance, California. (2004) 13–23
6. Hillston, J.: A Compositional Approach to Performance Modelling. Cambridge University Press (1996)
7. Köhler, M., Moldt, D., Rölke, H.: Modelling the Structure and Behaviour of Petri Nets Agents. In: Proceedings of the International Conference on Applications and Theory of Petri Nets. Lecture Notes in Computer Science, Vol. 2075. Springer, Berlin Heidelberg New York (2001) 224–241
8. Milner, R.: Communicating and Mobile Systems: The π Calculus. Cambridge University Press (1999)
9. Priami, C.: Stochastic π Calculus. In: Gilmore, S., Hillston, J. (eds.): Proceedings of the Third International Workshop on Process Algebras and Performance Modelling. Special Issue of The Computer Journal **38** (1995) 578–589
10. Valk, R.: Petri Nets as Token Objects—An Introduction to Elementary Object Nets. In: Desel, J., Silva, M. (eds.): Proceedings of the 19th International Conference on Application and Theory of Petri Nets, Portugal. Lecture Notes in Computer Science, Vol. 1420. Springer, Berlin Heidelberg New York (1998) 1–25

Modelling Role-Playing Games Using PEPA Nets

Stephen Gilmore[1], Leila Kloul[1]*, and Davide Piazza[2]

[1] LFCS, The University of Edinburgh, Edinburgh EH9 3JZ, Scotland
{stg,leila}@inf.ed.ac.uk
[2] OMNYS Wireless Technology, via Frassini, 35, 36100 Vicenza, Italy
davide.piazza@omnys.it

Abstract. We present a performance modelling case study of a distributed multi-player game expressed in the PEPA nets modelling language. The case study provides a modern complex distributed application programming problem which has many inherent communication and synchronisation complexities which are subtle to model accurately. We put forward the position that a high-level performance modelling language is well-suited to such a task. The structure of the model and the performance index which is most significant for the problem match well a solution method which has previously been applied in Petri net modelling. We apply this method to a PEPA net model for the first time in this paper.

1 Introduction

Performance models of computer and telecommunication systems are used to gain insights into the behaviour of the system under expected workload on the available hardware. The state-of-the-art in the design of computer systems grows ever more sophisticated as programming languages become more complex; application programs increasingly use additional layers of middleware and infrastructure; and software developers deploy complex patterns and idioms to structure their application code. Similarly, the computing platform on which these applications execute becomes more complex. A wide range of computing devices may be deployed, from high-end servers to battery-powered handheld devices. Other layers of interpretation may also be used: virtual machines such as the JVM or hardware emulators as in the Transmeta Crusoe processor. Each such layer adds complexity and degrades performance.

Complex software necessitates the use of a sophisticated modelling language which provides direct support for high-level configuration and re-configuration in addition to offering a behavioural specification language to be used to capture the application logic. The PEPA nets modelling language [5] is one such language, a high-level coloured stochastic Petri net formalism where the tokens of the net

---

* On leave from PRiSM, Université de Versailles, 45, Av. des Etats-Unis 78000 Versailles, France.

are themselves programmable stochastically-timed components. The modelling language which is used for the tokens of a PEPA net is Jane Hillston's Markovian process algebra PEPA (Performance Evaluation Process Algebra) [6]. The PEPA nets formalism is a recent research development and we are currently exploring its possibilities in tandem with developing its underlying theory [5]. To this end we have undertaken a number of case studies including the Jini discovery service and a mobile telephony scenario [5]; and the Mobile IP protocol [3]. The PEPA nets formalism is not described in this paper, all details of the PEPA nets and PEPA languages are found in [5] and [6].

In this paper we apply the PEPA nets language to the problem of modelling a complex distributed application, a multi-player online role-playing game. The game is one of the case studies from one of our industrial partners on the EC-funded DEGAS project (Design Environments for Global ApplicationS). The game is a characteristic "global computing" example, encompassing distribution, mobility and performance aspects. The representational challenges in modelling the game accurately include capturing location-dependent collaboration, multi-way synchronisation, and place-bounded locations holding up to a fixed number of tokens only. All of these are directly represented in the PEPA nets formalism.

In Section 2 we provide a high-level description of our modelling study, a role-playing game. In Section 3 we present the PEPA net model of the system. In Section 4 we make an analysis of the model, discuss solution methods for PEPA net models, and present results from our study. Conclusions follow at the end of the paper.

2 A High-Level Description of the Game

The Massive Multi-Player Online Role-playing Game (MMPORG) consists of a succession of game levels of increasing complexity. Each level is composed of a starting point and a certain number of rooms among which is a secret room.

In the game, a player is seen as an active entity who may interact with objects, locations (rooms), playing and non-playing characters of the virtual environment. Objects (weapons, medicine, food, ...) are one of the basic elements of the game environment that a player can collect and reuse later. The player has to explore the rooms to collect as many experience points as possible to improve character features such as strength, skill, luck, etc. Each obstacle or test successfully passed increases the number of experience points. Conversely, each failure decreases the number of points. If this number reaches zero, the player vanishes from the current room and is transferred back to the starting point of the current level. To progress to the next level, a player must find the secret room and pass the tests of this room. If they fail, they are once again transferred to the starting point of the level. The secret room can hold one player only, that is, at most one player can be inside at a time. A player may be in competition with one or several other players in the same room to acquire objects. The winner of a fight between two players earns experience points from the defeated player.

The MMPORG also features non-playing characters. Like the players, non-playing characters are active entities that may move from one room to another but they are confined to a single level and cannot access the secret room. These characters are generated by the rooms themselves. Non-playing characters like monsters are obstacles which a player will have to pass. Fighting is a direct interaction between characters within a room. These interactions are based on system of "cards" which can cause or neutralise some damage. The effect depends on the card features and on the features of the characters involved. Defeating a non-playing character allows the player to increase their current features. The player may acquire new cards and therefore increase their offensive or defensive skills.

All the computations resulting from the different interactions are performed by the rooms. Moreover, when a player selects the next room to visit, this room clones itself and sends its image to the player.

3 The PEPA Net Model

Assuming that L is the number of levels in the game and N_j is the number of rooms at level j, the PEPA net model consists mainly of three types of places: $ROOM_{ji}$, $SECRET\_R_j$ and $INIT\_R_j$ where $j = 1 \ldots L$ and $i = 1 \ldots N$. Respectively, these model room i, the secret room and the starting point at level j (see Figure 1). We use place OUT to stand for the environment outside the game.

Moreover we consider components *Player*, *NPlayer* and *Room* to model the behaviour of respectively the playing character, the non-playing character and the room.

3.1 The Components

- **Component Player.** Once connected (firing action **connect**), the player starts by choosing one of the rooms of the current level. This is modelled using firing action **select**$_i$ with rate $p_i \times r_0$, i being the room number at the current level and p_i the probability to select this room number.
  Once the player receives an image of the room, they may do different things: observe, walk, talk to another character (playing or non-playing). They may also try to use one of the objects they have with action type use_{obj} or to take a new one ($take_{obj}$) from the room. In this last case, the system, through the room character, may accept or refuse to let the player take the object using action type $accept_{obj}$ or $refuse_{obj}$. Here the rate of these actions is not specified by the player because the decision is made by the room.
  When the player is in the room, they may be attacked by another player ($fightP$) or a non-playing character ($fightNP$). The result of the fight may be either a defeat of the player ($PlossP$ or $PlossNP$) or its victory ($PwinP$ or $PwinNP$). In the former case, it loses points ($less_{pts}$) if the fight is against another player. If it has no more points ($zero_{pts}$), it is transferred to the starting point of the current level. This is modelled using firing action **failure**.

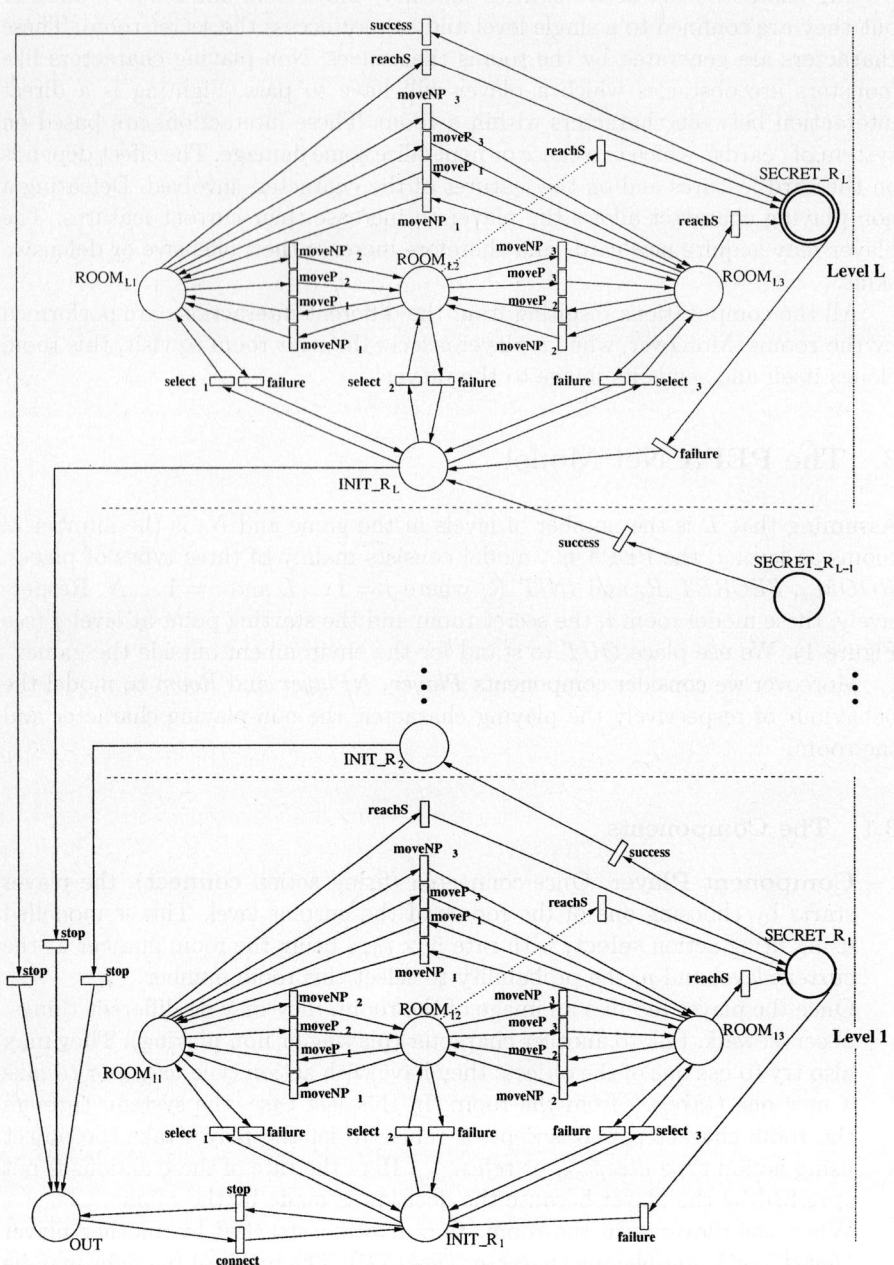

Fig. 1. PEPA net model for $N_j = 3$, $j = 1 \ldots L$

In the latter case, the player gets cards (new_{crd}) if it defeated a non-playing character.

The player may decide to move to another room i with action type **moveP$_i$** and probability q_i, or **reachS** if it finds the secret room. The player may also decide to stop the game at any moment as long as it is in the stating point $INIT\_R_j$ of a level. This is modelled using activity (**stop**, s).

$Player \stackrel{def}{=} (\mathbf{connect}, r).Player_0$

$Player_0 \stackrel{def}{=} \sum_{i=1}^{N_j}(\mathbf{select_i}, p_i \times r_0).(RImage, \top).Player_1 + (\mathbf{stop}, s).Player$

$Player_1 \stackrel{def}{=} (observe, \alpha_1).Player_1 + (walk, \alpha_2).Player_1 + (talk, \alpha_3).Player_1$
$\quad + (fightNP, \beta_1).Player_{21} + (fightP, \beta_2).Player_{31}$
$\quad + (use_{obj}, \delta_1).Player_4 + (take_{obj}, \delta_2).Player_5$
$\quad + \sum_{i=1}^{N_j-1}(\mathbf{moveP_i}, q_i \times r_1).Player_1 + (\mathbf{reachS}, r_2).Player_{70}$

$Player_{21} \stackrel{def}{=} (PlossNP, \top).Player_{22} + (PwinNP, \top).Player_{23}$
$Player_{22} \stackrel{def}{=} (less_{pts}, \gamma_1).Player_1 + (zero_{pts}, \gamma_2).Player_6$
$Player_{23} \stackrel{def}{=} (new_{crd}, \gamma_3).Player_1$

$Player_{31} \stackrel{def}{=} (PlossP, \top).Player_{32} + (PwinP, \top).Player_{33}$
$Player_{32} \stackrel{def}{=} (less_{pts}, \gamma_1).Player_1 + (zero_{pts}, \gamma_2).Player_6$
$Player_{33} \stackrel{def}{=} (get_{pts}, \gamma_4).Player_1$

$Player_4 \stackrel{def}{=} (less_{pts}, \gamma_1).Player_1 + (get_{pts}, \gamma_4).Player_1 + (zero_{pts}, \gamma_2).Player_6$
$Player_5 \stackrel{def}{=} (accept_{obj}, \top).Player_1 + (refuse_{obj}, \top).Player_1$
$Player_6 \stackrel{def}{=} (\mathbf{failure}, f).Player_0$

$Player_{70} \stackrel{def}{=} (RImage, \top).(test, \beta_3).Player_7$
$Player_7 \stackrel{def}{=} (win, \top).Player_8 + (lose, \top).Player_6$
$Player_8 \stackrel{def}{=} (get_{pts}, \gamma_4).(\mathbf{success}, c).Player_0$

- **Component NPlayer.** Once a non-playing character has been created by a room ($generateNP$), it may walk, use its own objects and meet a playing character. A fight may then follow and as explained before, if the non-playing character is defeated ($PwinNP$), it vanishes from the system (the room), via action type $destroyNP$. If it wins, it just continues its progression in the rooms of the current game level.

$NPlayer \stackrel{def}{=} (generateNP, \top).NPlayer_1$
$NPlayer_1 \stackrel{def}{=} (walk, \delta_1).NPlayer_1 + (talk, \top).NPlayer_1 + (fightNP, \delta_2).NPlayer_2$
$\quad + \sum_{i=1}^{N-1}(\mathbf{moveNP_i}, q_i \times v_1).NPlayer_1$
$NPlayer_2 \stackrel{def}{=} (PlossNP, \top).NPlayer_1 + (PwinNP, \top).NPlayer_3$
$NPlayer_3 \stackrel{def}{=} (destroyNP, \top).NPlayer$

- **Component Room.** The room creates and makes vanish the non-playing characters using respectively *generateNP* and *destroyNP*. When it is chosen by a player, the room clones itself and sends an image to them (*RImage*). The room makes also the acceptance ($accept_{obj}$) or the rejection ($refuse_{obj}$) of any attempt of a player to take an object from the location. Moreover it makes all computations related to the fights and sends the results to the characters using action types *PlossP* or *PwinP* and also *PlossNP* and *PwinNP*.

$$Room \stackrel{def}{=} (generateNP, \sigma_1).Room + (RImage, \sigma).Room + (fightP, \top).Room_2$$
$$+ (fightNP, \top).Room_3 + (take_{obj}, \top).Room_1 + (use_{obj}, \top).Room$$
$$Room_1 \stackrel{def}{=} (accept_{obj}, \rho_1).Room + (refuse_{obj}, \rho_2).Room$$
$$Room_2 \stackrel{def}{=} (PlossP, \phi_1).(PwinP, \phi_2).Room$$
$$Room_3 \stackrel{def}{=} (PlossNP, \phi_3).Room + (PwinNP, \phi_4).Room_4$$
$$Room_4 \stackrel{def}{=} (destroyNP, \sigma_2).Room$$

- **Component SRoom** models the secret room. It is similar to the other rooms except that at most one player can be inside and non-playing characters are not allowed to get in. Once inside, the player has to pass a different test to get to the higher level.

$$SRoom \stackrel{def}{=} (RImage, \sigma).(test, \top).SRoom_1$$
$$SRoom_1 \stackrel{def}{=} (lose, \phi_3).SRoom + (win, \phi_4).SRoom$$

3.2 The Places

The places of the PEPA net are defined as follows:

$$ROOM_{ji}\,[\_,\ldots,\_] \stackrel{def}{=} \left(Room \bowtie_{\mathcal{K}_1} \left(Player\,[\_] \bowtie_{\mathcal{K}_2} \ldots \bowtie_{\mathcal{K}_2} Player\,[\_] \right) \right) \bowtie_{\mathcal{K}_3}$$
$$\left(NPlayer\,[\_] \parallel \ldots \parallel NPlayer\,[\_] \right)$$

$$SECRET\_R_j\,[\_,\ldots,\_] \stackrel{def}{=} SRoom \bowtie_{\mathcal{K}_4} Player\,[\_]$$

$$INIT\_R_j\,[\_,\ldots,\_] \stackrel{def}{=} Player\,[\_] \parallel \ldots \parallel Player\,[\_]$$

$$OUT\,[\_,\ldots,\_] \stackrel{def}{=} Player\,[Player] \parallel \ldots \parallel Player\,[Player]$$

where $i = 1\ldots N$ is the room number and $j = 1\ldots L$ is the game level number. The synchronising sets are defined as follows

$\mathcal{K}_1 = \{take_{obj}, use_{obj}, accept_{obj}, refuse_{obj}, RImage, fightP, PlossP, PwinP,$
$\quad fightNP, PlossNP, PwinNP\}$
$\mathcal{K}_2 = \{fightP\}$
$\mathcal{K}_3 = \{generateNP, fightNP, PlossNP, PwinNP, destroyNP, talk\}$
$\mathcal{K}_4 = \{RImage, test, lose, win\}$

4 The Model Analysis

One of the stated aims of the PEPA nets modelling language is to allow analysis techniques and solution methods developed for Petri nets to be used either directly or in adaptation for PEPA nets. The structure of the present model allows us to do exactly this by deploying *flow-equivalent replacement* to bring about a dramatic reduction in the state-space of the model to be solved. The method works in the following fashion for this example. The purpose of the application logic encoded in the PEPA nets model of the MMPORG is to specify in detail the necessary steps to take in order to succeed at each level of the game (and thereby progress to the next level). Once this model has been solved to find the rate at which players progress from one level to the next then the application logic has served its purpose and the sub-model can be replaced by a suitably exponentially-distributed delay, eliding all of the (now) unnecessary detail.

We consider the abstraction of the PEPA net model of Figure 2 where each level j has one input and two output parameters. The input parameter denoted by λ_j represents the arrival rate of the players to the level. The first output parameter denoted by λ_{j+1} is nothing other than the input to the next level $j+1$. This represents the rate of successful players of level j. The second output parameter, noted μ_j, represents the rate of the players leaving the game.

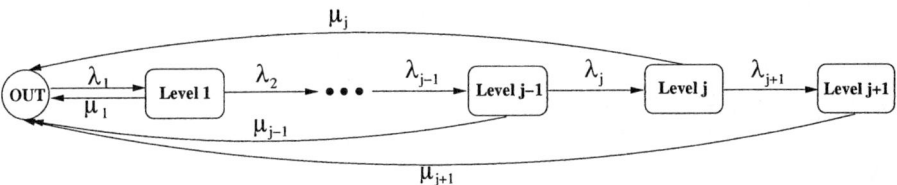

Fig. 2. Abstraction of the PEPA net model

This technique is very well suited to this application because it allows us to evaluate one of the key performance indices of a game application: *difficulty of completion*. If it is possible to progress too quickly from commencing playing to completing the final level of the game then the application may be considered unchallenging. Conversely, if it is very arduous to make progress in the game then the developers risk losing their target audience and finding their game consigned to being suited to hardcore game enthusiasts only.

4.1 Model Solution

We compiled the PEPA net model to an equivalent PEPA model [4]. When processed, this PEPA model will generate the same CTMC as the given PEPA net.

Solution procedures are accessed via the Imperial PEPA Compiler (IPC) [2]. IPC is a functional program written in the Haskell lazy functional programming language [8]. Its function is to compile a PEPA model into the input language of Knottenbelt's DNAmaca analyser [7].

The use of a chain of tools in this way might give the reader concern that this process is laborious or time-consuming and delays progress towards the computation of the performance results which are the real content of the analysis process. This is not the case as the entire end-to-end time of the analysis is itself small (60.41 *sec* for the MMPORG model), making the method suitable for productive interactive performance model development. All measurements were made on a 1.60GHz Intel Pentium IV processor machine with 256 KB of memory, running Red Hat Linux 9.0.

4.2 Model Results

The average activity times associated with the activities of the MMPORG model are shown in Table 1. The rate of each activity is the reciprocal of the average time. A scaling factor, k, initially 0.2, is used to vary the number of repetitions of some of the activities. These distinguished activities double in difficulty in moving from one level to the level above it.

Figure 3 shows the results generated for a game with four levels ($L = 4$). Each graph depicts the cumulative passage-time distribution function for a level of the game. This function is the probability of playing a level, from its starting state to the point where the player succeeds the test of the secret room and reaches the next level, in a certain interval of time.

We used the method of *stochastic probes* [1] to mark the start and end times of the path through the system which we wished to observe. From the graph we can read off high-level performance results such as "50% of the players of the first level will be able to reach the next level in six (6) minutes" and "nearly all players will be able to reach the next level in twenty (20) minutes". Figure 3 shows that things start to become more complicated for the players when they reach the upper levels. It shows that it may take more than ten (10) minutes for 50% of the players of the second level to reach the third one, and less than 35% will be able to finish the last level in less than twenty (20) minutes.

Table 1. Average activity times in the four levels of the MMPORG model

Activity	Level 1	Level 2	Level 3	Level 4
α_i	$k \times 5$ mins.	$2k \times 5$ mins.	$4k \times 5$ mins.	$8k \times 5$ mins.
b_i	6 secs.	6 secs.	6 secs.	6 secs.
β_i	$k \times 2$ mins.	$2k \times 2$ mins.	$4k \times 2$ mins.	$8k \times 2$ mins.
c	1 min.	1 min.	1 min.	1 min.
δ_1	$k \times 2$ mins.	$2k \times 2$ mins.	$4k \times 2$ mins.	$8k \times 2$ mins.
δ_2	$k \times 6$ secs.	$2k \times 6$ secs.	$4k \times 6$ secs.	$8k \times 6$ secs.
f	1 min.	1 min.	1 min.	1 min.
γ_i	6 secs.	6 secs.	6 secs.	6 secs.
h	k mins.	$2k$ mins.	$4k$ mins.	$8k$ min.
$p_i \times r$	3 secs.	3 secs.	3 secs.	3 secs.
$q_i \times r_1$	$k \times 4$ secs.	$2k \times 4$ secs.	$4k \times 4$ secs.	$8k \times 4$ secs.
r_0	1 min.	1 min.	1 min.	1 min.
ρ_i	6 secs.	6 secs.	6 secs.	6 secs.
σ	30 secs.	30 secs.	30 secs.	30 secs.
s	1 min.	1 min.	1 min.	1 min.
φ_i	2 mins.	2 mins.	2 mins.	2 mins.

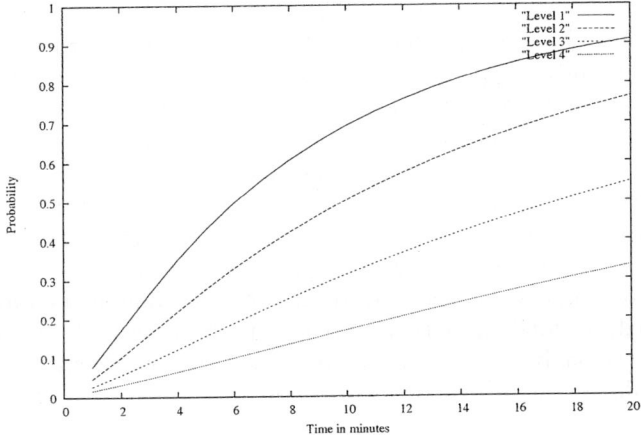

Fig. 3. Cumulative passage-time distribution function for completing each level

Figure 4 depicts the cumulative passage-time distribution function for the complete game, from the first level to the last one. It shows that, considering the parameters values used, less than 14% of the players will be able to go through the game tests in less than 1 hour and 20 minutes.

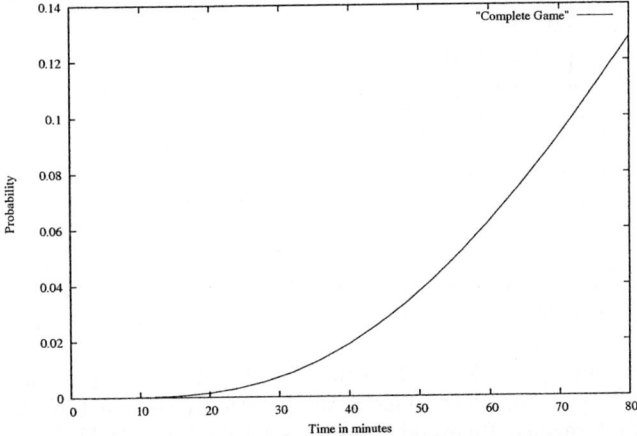

Fig. 4. Cumulative passage-time distribution function for the complete game

The degree of difficulty of completing tasks within the game (fighting other players, collecting objects, and similar tasks) may be changed using different parameters values. Moreover, other graphs of passage-time percentiles for different start and end points in the computation can be obtained by probing different starting points and end points similarly.

5 Conclusions

In this paper we have shown that complex, structured performance models of real-world computing applications can be efficiently solved to give insightful information about their performance behaviour at run-time. The application which we investigated was a mobile multi-player networked game for a handheld device with limited processing power and memory. There are many places for the performance of such an application to fall below the minimum standard expected by a customer who buys such a device. Repairing performance faults in software and firmware after the device has shipped may be cripplingly expensive. For this reason, developers who are concerned with developing marketable, popular products need to address performance-related problems as early as possible. Our methodology strongly supports this by bringing performance analysis capability back to the design phase of product development.

Acknowledgements

The authors are supported by the DEGAS (Design Environments for Global ApplicationS) IST-2001-32072 project funded by the FET Proactive Initiative on Global Computing.

References

1. Bradley, J.T., Dingle, N.J., Argent-Katwala, A.: Expressing Performance Requirements Using Regular Expressions to Specify Stochastic Probes over Process Algebra Models. In: Proceedings of the Fourth International Workshop on Software and Performance, Redwood Shores, California, USA. ACM Press (2004) 49–58
2. Dingle, N.J., Gilmore, S.T., Knottenbelt, W.J., Bradley, J.T.: Derivation of Passage-Time Densities in PEPA Models Using IPC: The Imperial PEPA Compiler. In: Kotsis, G. (ed.): Proceedings of the 11th IEEE/ACM International Symposium on Modeling, Analysis and Simulation of Computer and Telecommunications Systems, University of Central Florida. IEEE Computer Society Press (2003) 344-351
3. Gilmore, S., Hillston, J., Kloul, L.: PEPA Nets. In: Calzarossa, M.C., Gelenbe, E. (eds.): Performance Tools and Applications to Networked Systems: Revised Tutorial Lectures. Lecture Notes in Computer Science, Vol. 2965. Springer, Berlin Heidelberg New York (2004) 311–335
4. Gilmore, S., Hillston, J, Kloul, L., Ribaudo, M.: Software Performance Modelling Using PEPA Nets. In: Proceedings of the Fourth International Workshop on Software and Performance, Redwood Shores, California, USA. ACM Press (2004) 13–24
5. Gilmore, S., Hillston, J., Ribaudo, M., Kloul, L.: PEPA Nets: A Structured Performance Modelling Formalism. Performance Evaluation **54** (2003) 79–104
6. Hillston, J.: A Compositional Approach to Performance Modelling. Cambridge University Press (1996)
7. Knottenbelt, W.J.: Generalised Markovian Analysis of Timed Transition Systems. Master's thesis, University of Cape Town (1996)
8. Jones, S.P. (ed.): Haskell 98 Language and Libraries: The Revised Report. Cambridge University Press (2003)

Fault-Tolerant and Scalable Communication Mechanism for Mobile Agents*

JinHo Ahn

Dept. of Computer Science, College of Information Science, Kyonggi University
San 94-6 Yiuidong, Yeongtonggu, Suwon Kyonggido 443-760, Republic of Korea
jhahn@kyonggi.ac.kr

Abstract. This paper proposes a new fault-tolerant and scalable mobile agent communication mechanism to address both agent mobility and directory service node failures. The mechanism enables each mobile agent to keep its forwarding pointer only on a small number of its visiting nodes in an autonomous manner. As this desirable feature has every mobile agent's migration route be very considerably shortened, the time for forwarding each message to the agent becomes much smaller. Also, this feature causes each node to maintain much fewer forwarding pointers of mobile agents on its storage than in the traditional approach. Moreover, the mechanism allows each movement path of a mobile agent to be replicated in an effective way to preserve scalability of our proposed mechanism. This replication may require a little more agent location updating costs, but much more accelerate delivery of each message to the corresponding mobile agent.

1 Introduction

As wireless devices such as PDAs and cellular phones and new Internet based technologies, for example, grid, ubiquitous computing and active networks, has been rapidly emerged, modern computing environments are becoming very complex[1,5]. Also, mobility of users and devices leads to their softwares being executed on dynamically changing environments that support different capabilities and types of available local resources respectively. In terms of software development, these issues make it difficult to design the application programs because it is impossible to obtain completely accurate information about their dynamically changing runtime environments in advance. Thus, it is essential to develop a new middleware platform allowing software components to adapt to their local execution environments at runtime.

Mobile agent technology is gaining significant popularity as a potential vehicle for considering the complexity and variety[1,5,6]. Mobile agent is an autonomously running program, including both code and state, that travels from one node to another over a network carrying out a task on user's behalf. However, as the size of mobile agent systems rapidly increases, scalability is becoming the

---

* This work was supported by Kyonggi University Research Grant(2003-009).

most important issue and forces some components of the systems, e.g., agent communication, deployment, monitoring and security, to be redesigned. Among the components, designing reliable inter-agent communication facility in a scalable manner is essential for the systems.

Generally, this facility consists of two components, directory service and message delivery. First of all, to address the scalability issue, the centralized dependency on the home node of each mobile agent, which is the critical drawback of home-based approach[6], should be avoided in case of its location updating and message delivery. In terms of this overhead, forwarding-pointer based approach[4, 7, 10] is more preferable than the home-based one. However, the forwarding-pointer based approach has three problems in case that it is applied to a large-scale mobile agent system. First, it may lead to a very high message delivery cost whenever each message is sent to a mobile agent. The approach has this undesirable feature because as mobile agents frequently migrate, the length of their forwarding paths becomes rapidly increasing. Second, this approach requires a large size of storage where each directory service node maintains agent location information. The second problem results from greatly raising the number of forwarding pointers the node should keep on its storage because the system generally serves a large number of mobile agents running concurrently. To attempt to consider this problem, a previous mechanism[7] introduces a type of update message, inform message, to include an agent's current location for shortening the length of trails of forwarding pointers. It enables a node receiving the message to update its agent location information if the received information is more recent than the one it had. However, it presents no concrete and efficient solutions for this purpose, for example, when update messages should be sent, and which node they should be sent to. The third drawback is that even if among all service nodes on a forwarding path of a mobile agent, only one fails, any message destined to the agent cannot be delivered to it. This feature may significantly degrade reliability of the inter-agent communication facility, which becomes impractical. To consider this third issue, a fault-tolerant directory service for mobile agents using redundancy of forwarding pointers [8] was proposed, but doesn't address the first and the second problems stated previously.

In this paper, we present a new fault-tolerant and efficient mobile agent communication mechanism based on forwarding pointers to solve the three problems as follows. For the first and the second problems, each mobile agent enables its forwarding pointer to be saved only on the small number of its visiting nodes in an autonomous manner. As this desirable feature has every mobile agent's migration route be very considerably shortened, the time for forwarding each message to the agent is much smaller. Additionally, this feature causes each node to maintain much fewer number of forwarding pointers of mobile agents than in the traditional approach. For the third problem, each movement path of a mobile agent is replicated in an effective way to preserve the previously stated scalability of our proposed mechanism. Also, this replication much more accelerates delivering each message to the corresponding mobile agent whereas resulting in a little more agent location updating costs.

2 The Proposed Communication Mechanism

2.1 Fault-Tolerant Directory Service

First of all, let us define two important terms, *forwarding node* and *locator*. Forwarding node of an agent is a directory service node that maintains a forwarding pointer of the agent on its storage. Thus, there may be the various number of forwarding nodes of each agent in the system according to which agent communication mechanism is used. Locator of an agent is a special forwarding node managing the identifier of the service node that the agent is currently running on. Assuming every node is failure-free, our mechanism requires only one locator for each mobile agent to address agent mobility. But, if the mechanism intends to tolerate up to $F(F \geq 1)$ node failures, $(F+1)$ locators of each mobile agent should exist. Thus, every service node N_i needs to keep the following data structures to enable our fault-tolerant directory service algorithm to satisfy the goal mentioned in the previous section.

- $R\text{-}Agents_i$: It is a vector which records the location information of every agent currently executing on N_i. Its element consists of three fields, *agent_id*, *l_fwdrs* and *agent_t*. *l_fwdrs* is a set of identifiers of agent *agent_id*'s forwarding nodes which N_i guesses are alive. *agent_t* is the timestamp associated with agent *agent_id* when the agent is running on N_i. Its value is incremented by one whenever the agent moves to a new node. Thus, when agent *agent_id* migrates to N_i, N_i should inform only locators of the agent in *l_fwdrs* of both its identifier and *agent_t* so that the locaters can locate the agent.
- $AgentFPs_i$: It is a vector which maintains the location information of every mobile agent which is not currently running on N_i, but which N_i is a forwarding node of. Its element consists of five fields, *agent_id*, *next_n*, *agent_t*, *manage_f* and *migrate_f*. *next_n* is a set of identifier(s) of the node(s) which N_i thinks agent *agent_id* is currently running on or are the locators of the agent. *agent_t* is the timestamp associated with the agent when being located at the latest among the node(s). It is used for avoiding updating recent location information by older information[7]. *manage_f* is a bit flag indicating if N_i is a locator of agent *agent_id* or not. In the first case, its value is set to *true* and otherwise, *false*. *migrate_f* is a bit flag designating if the agent is currently moving to another node(=*true*) or not(=*false*).

Then, we assume that the value of F is 1 in all examples shown later for explaining. First, let us see how to perform failure-free operations of the algorithm using Figure 1. This figure illustrates basic agent migration procedures in order and their corresponding state changes in mobile agent location information maintained by each node when agent a moves from N_4 to N_6 via N_5 in case no node fails. In Figure 1(a), agent a was running on N_4 and its locators were N_{home} and N_1 before its migration procedure initiated. On attempting to move to N_5, agent a first should send its two locators each a message $migr\_init(Id_a)$, which indicates a's migration procedure starts from now. If N_{home} and N_1 receive this message, they change the value of field $migrate\_f$ of a's record in their $AgentFPss$ from $false$ to $true$, and then acknowledge the message to N_4. This invalidation procedure must be executed to prohibit wrong message forwarding from being performed during the agent migration operation. Otherwise, the following problem might occur. If N_{home} or N_1 receives any message destined to a, it forwards the message to N_4 as it cannot recognize whether the migration procedure for a is currently being executed. Unfortunately, in this case, a may be gone from N_4 while N_4 isn't a forwarding node and so has no location information of a in $AgentFPs_4$ in our algorithm. If so, agent a cannot receive the message. Therefore, after having completed the invalidation procedure, N_4 should push agent a to N_5 and then remove the element of a from R-$Agents_4$. Then, agent a increments a's timestamp, whose value becomes 5. In this case, it has N_5 become the latest locator of a, creates and inserts a's record into R-$Agents_5$, and changes the value of field l_fwdrs of the record from $\{1\}$ to $\{5,1\}$. Afterwards, N_5 transmits two different messages to its previous locators, N_{home} and N_1, respectively. First, it sends N_{home} a message $changelm(Id_a,\{5,1\},5)$ to inform N_{home} that N_{home} is a's locator no longer and N_1 and N_5 become two locators of a from now. Thus, N_{home} updates the values of fields $next\_n$ and $agent\_t$ of a's record in $AgentFPs_{home}$ to $\{5,1\}$ and 5 using the message, and resets both fields, $manage\_f$ and $migrate\_f$, to $false$. Second, as N_1 still continues to play the role of a's locator, agent a sends a message $update(Id_a,5)$ to N_1. When receiving the message, N_1 updates the state of a's record in $AgentFPs_1$ to $(Id_a, \{5\}, 5, true, false)$ using the message. Finally, in both cases, if the messages destined to a have been buffered in their message queues during the agent migration, the messages are forwarded to N_5.

Figure 1(b) shows an example that a attempts to migrate from the latest locator N_5 to N_6 after a has finished its partial task at N_5. In this case, the invalidation procedure is first executed like in Figure 1(a). Then, as N_5 is a's locator, it creates and inserts a's record $(Id_a, \{6\}, 5, true, true)$ into $AgentFPs_5$ and then dispatchs agent a to N_6. After that, N_6 increments a's timestamp and then saves a's record $(Id_a, \{5,1\}, 6)$ into R-$Agents_6$ like in the right-hand side of this figure because a wants N_6 to be just a visiting node. Then, N_6 sends a message $update(Id_a,6)$ to a's locators, N_1 and N_5 to notify them that a's agent migration procedure has terminated. After updating a's location information, the locators forward each all the messages in their message buffers, which should be sent to the agent, to N_6.

Next, we attempt to informally describe our fault-tolerant directory service algorithm in case some nodes fail using Figure 2. This figure shows an example that an FN N_5 crashes while agent a migrates from N_7 to N_8. In Figure 2(a), N_5 has failed before N_7 informs two locators of a, N_5 and N_1, that a attempts to move to N_8 by sending message $migr\_init(Id_a)$ to them. In this case, to keep the number of a's locators being $F+1$, N_7 sends message $migr\_init(Id_a)$ to N_{home}, which is currently a forwarding node of a, not its locator, to allow N_{home} to play a role of a's locator from now. On receiving the message, N_{home} changes the values of two fields $manage\_f$ and $migrate\_f$ of a's record in $AgentFPs_{home}$ to

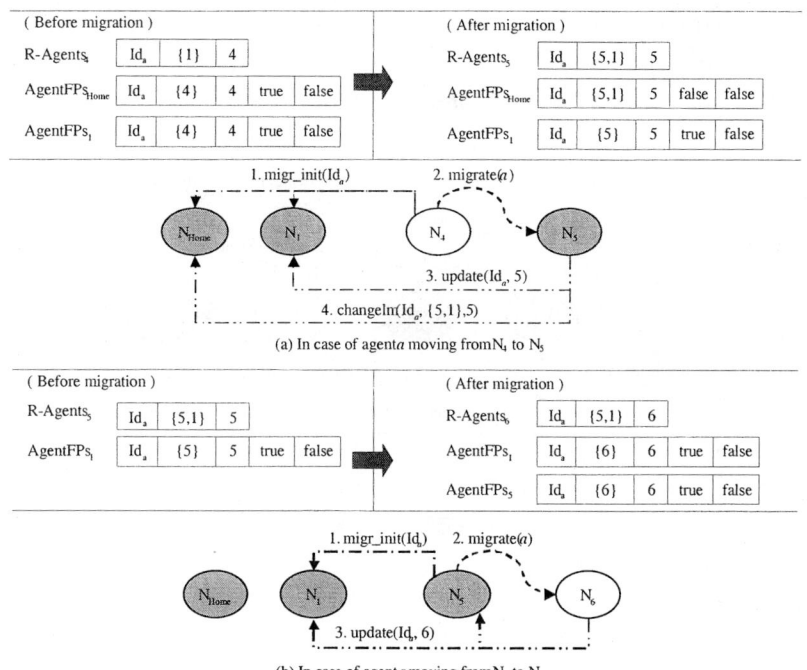

Fig. 1. In case agent a moves from N_4 to N_6 on its movement path without any node failures

$true$ and $false$. Then, it sends an acknowledgment message to N_7. After finishing all the invalidation procedures, N_7 enables agent a to migrate to N_8, and then N_8 sends each a message $update(Id_a, 8)$ to a's current locators, N_1 and N_{home}, to inform them of the termination of a's agent migration procedure. In this case, the two locators update the state of a's record in their $AgentFPs$s to $(Id_a, \{8\}, 8, true, false)$ respectively.

Figure 2(b) indicates an example that N_5 has failed after agent a migrates to N_8 and before N_8 sends message $update(Id_a, 8)$ to the current locators of a, N_5 and N_1, for notifying them of the completion of a's movement process. In this case, N_8 sends message $update(Id_a, 8)$ to N_{home} to force the number of a's locators to be still $F+1$. When it receives the message, N_{home} has the state of a's record in $AgentFPs_{home}$ become $(Id_a, \{8\}, 8, true, false)$ and then plays a role of a's locator from now on.

2.2 Message Delivery

To support reliable message delivery despite forwarding node failures, our mechanism requires the following agent location cache of every node N_i.

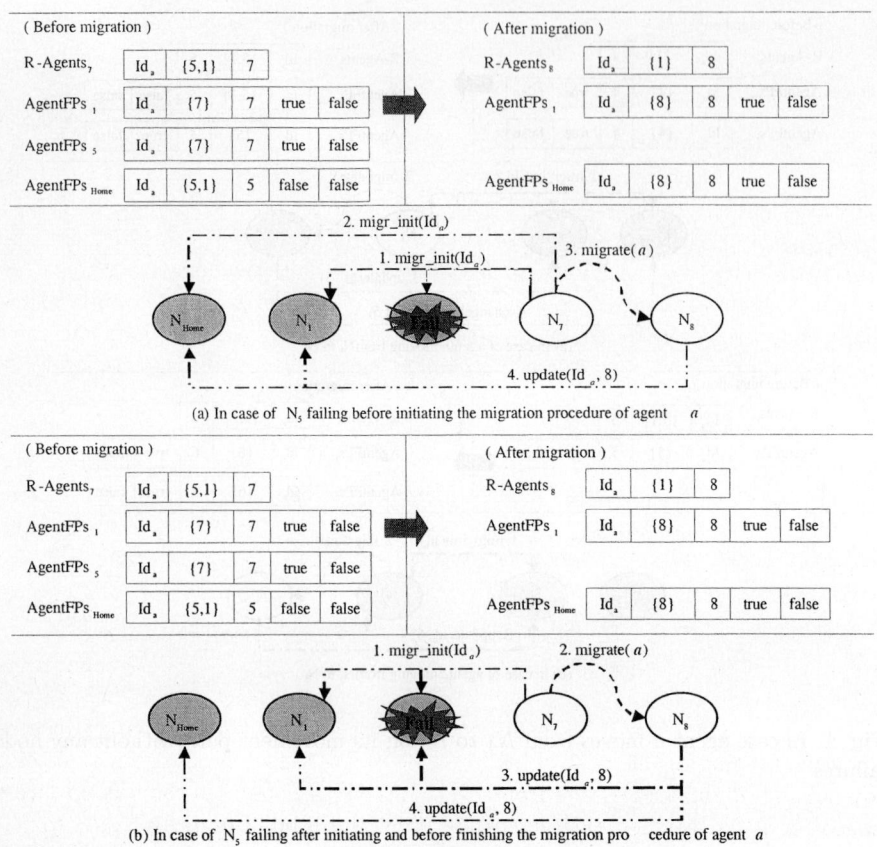

Fig. 2. In case an FN N_5 fails while a moving from N_7 to N_8

- $L\text{-}Cache_i$: It is a vector which temporarily keeps location information of each mobile agent which agents running on N_i communicate with. Its element consists of three fields, $agent\_id$, $fwdrs$ and $agent\_t$. $fwdrs$ is a set of identifiers of the nodes which N_i guesses are locators of agent $agent\_id$. Thus, to send messages to agent $agent\_id$, an agent on N_i forwards them to the latest among live locaters in $fwdrs$. If there is no live locater in $fwdrs$, the messages are sent to the home node of agent $agent\_id$. $agent\_t$ is the timestamp assigned to agent $agent\_id$ when the agent registered with the latest among all locators in $fwdrs$.

To illustrate how our message delivery algorithm based on the fault-tolerant directory service achieves the goal, Figure 3 shows an example that agent b sends two messages, m_1 and m_2, to agent a in this order while a is moving from N_7 to N_9 according to its itinerary. In Figure 3(a), agent b at N_{sender} attempts to deliver a message m_1 to agent a with no node failure after a has migrated from

N_7 to N_8. In this case, as N_{sender} maintains no location information for a in its agent location cache $L\text{-}Cache_{sender}$, it creates and inserts a's element (Id_a, {}, 0) into $L\text{-}Cache_{sender}$. After that, it sends the message m_1 to N_{home}. On receiving the message, N_{home} retrieves a's element from $AgentFPs_{home}$. In this case, as the value of the bit flag $manage\_f$ in the element is $false$, N_{home} isn't a's locator. Thus, it consults the element and forwards the message m_1 to the next forwarder N_5 that N_{home} guesses agent a is currently running on or that is the latest locator of a. On the receipt of the message, N_5 obtains a's element from $AgentFPs_5$ and then checks the flag $manage\_f$ in the element. In this case, N_5 is a's locator because the value of the flag is $true$. Also, as the value of the second flag $migrate\_f$ is $false$, it directly forwards the message to a's currently running node N_8 by consulting the element. After receiving the message, N_8 sends N_{sender} a message $updateLocs(Id_a, \{5,1\}, 8)$ containing the identifiers of a's current locators($=N_5,N_1$) and timestamp($=8$) because N_{sender} doesn't correctly know which nodes are a's current locators. Receiving the message, N_{sender} updates a's element in $L\text{-}Cache_{sender}$ using the message like in this figure. Thus, when agent b communicates with agent a from now, N_{sender} can directly send messages to the latest locator of a, N_5, with the assumption of N_5 never failing.

Unlike Figure 3(a), Figure 3(b) shows the case that the latest locator of a, N_5, fails after a has moved from N_7 to N_8. In this case, N_{sender} creates and keeps a's element on $L\text{-}Cache_{sender}$, and then forwards the message m_1 to N_{home}. Then, N_{home} attempts to transmit the message m_1 to the first latest locator N_5 by consulting a's element. However, as N_5 has failed, N_{home} cannot receive any acknowledgment message from N_5. Thus, N_{home} chooses the second latest locator of a, N_1, as the next forwarding node and sends the message m_1 to N_1. On receiving the message, N_1 finds a's element from $AgentFPs_1$ and then is able to know it is the locator of a. Thus, it sends the message to N_8 where a is currently running by looking up the second field of the element. When receiving the message, N_8 delivers it to agent a. Simultaneously, as N_8 becomes aware of N_5's failure, it forces N_{home} to play a role of a's locator by sending message $update(Id_a,8)$ to N_{home} like in Figure 2(b). In this case, N_{home} changes the state of a's record in $AgentFPs_{home}$ to (Id_a, {8}, 8, $true$, $false$) like in Figure 3(b). Then, N_8 updates the second field of a's element in $R\text{-}Agents_8$ from {5,1} to {1} and then informs N_{sender} of this update by sending a message $updateLocs(Id_a, \{1\}, 8)$. Receiving the message, N_{sender} updates a's element in $L\text{-}Cache_{sender}$ using the message like in this figure.

Figure 3(c) illustrates a different failure case that a's latest locator, N_5, crashes after a has migrated to N_9 from Figure 3(a). In this case, N_{sender} first finds a's element (Id_a, {5,1}, 8) from $L\text{-}Cache_{sender}$, and then attempts to transmit the second message m_2 to the latest locator N_5. But, N_{sender} recognizes N_5's failure because of receiving no acknowledgment message from it. Thus, N_{home} forwards message m_2 to the second latest locator of a, N_1, by looking up a's element in $L\text{-}Cache_{sender}$. On receiving the message, N_1 consults the second field of a's element in $AgentFPs_1$ and then sends the message m_2 to a's currently running service node, N_9. After having received the message, N_9 can recognize N_5 has crashed. Thus, it allows N_{home} to be a locator for a by sending message $update(Id_a,9)$ in the same manner as in Figure 3(b). In this case, values of all the fields of a's element in $AgentFPs_{home}$ becomes $(Id_a, \{9\}, 9, true, false)$ like in Figure 3(c). Then, N_9 changes the state of the corresponding element in $R\text{-}Agents_9$ to $(Id_a, \{1\}, 9)$ and sends a message $updateLocs(Id_a, \{1\}, 9)$ to N_{sender}.

3 Related Work

A broadcast-based mobile agent communication protocol was proposed by Murphy and Picco[9]. The protocol guarantees transparent and reliable inter-agent communication and can also provide multicast communication to a set of agents. But, to locate the message destination, it has to contact every visiting host in the network. Thus, its large traffic overhead makes broadcasts impractical in large-scale mobile agent systems.

Belle[2] proposed a hierarchical structure-based mechanism to form a location directory consisting of a hierarchy of servers. The location server at each level keeps lower-level object location information. For each object, the information is either a pointer to an entry at a lower-level location server or the agent's actual current location. However, this hierarchy cannot always be easily formed, especially in the Internet environment. Moreover, this mechanism may cause useless hops to be taken along the hierarchy.

Feng[3] introduced a mailbox-based mechanism to provide location-independent reliable message delivery. It allows messages to be forwarded at most once before they are delivered to their receiving agents. Also, the movement of agents can be separated from that of their mailboxes by determining autonomously whether each mailbox is migrated to its owner agent. However, uncertainty of message delivery to mailboxes may result in useless early pollings. On the other hand, even if urgent messages are forwarded to a mailbox on time, they can be delivered to its corresponding agent very late depending on the agent's polling time. Moreover, whenever each mailbox moves, its new location information should be broadcasted to every node where the mailbox has visited. This may incur high traffic overhead if assuming most agents are highly mobile.

All the works stated above doesn't consider failures of forwarding nodes for mobile agents.

4 Conclusion

In this paper, we presented a new fault-tolerant and scalable mobile agent communication mechanism based on forwarding pointers to address both agent mobility and directory service node failures. The mechanism enables each mobile agent to keep its forwarding pointer only on a small number of its visiting nodes in an autonomous manner. This feature can significantly shorten the path for

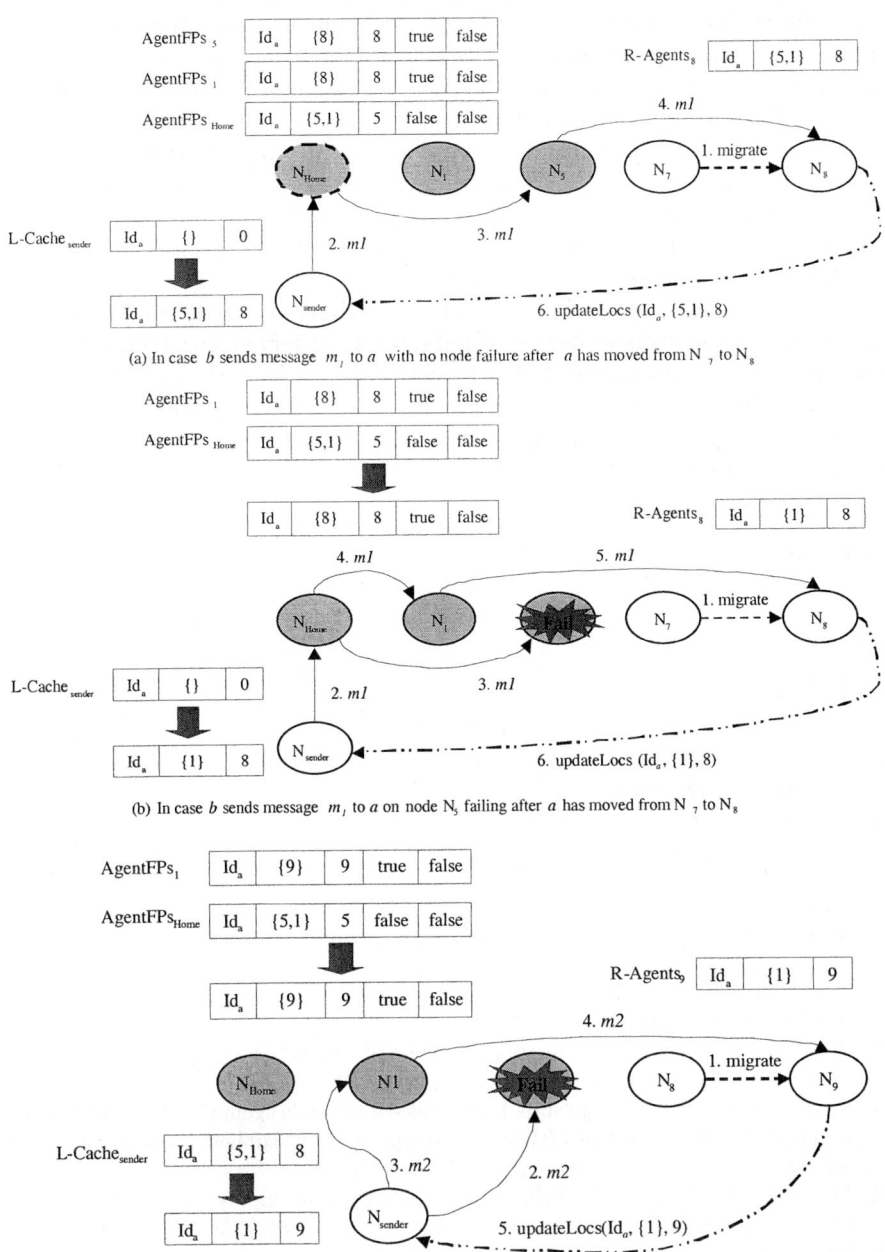

Fig. 3. An example agent b at N_{sender} sends two messages m_1 and then m_2 to agent a

routing each message to the corresponding mobile agent. Thus, the average message delivery time is much more reduced. Also, our mechanism requires a very small size of storage per each directory service node compared with the previous ones because the amount of agent location information the node keeps significantly decreases in the mechanism. Moreover, the mechanism allows $F+1$ locators of each agent to know its current location for tolerating a maximum of F failures of forwarding nodes. This behavior enables the inherent scalability of the proposed mechanism to be reasonably preserved. Also, our effective agent location cache much more speeds up the delivery of each message to the final destination even in case of node failures.

Choosing the proper forwarding nodes of each mobile agent among its visiting nodes and the optimal degree of redundancy of forwarding pointers is very important for our mechanism to work effectively. For this, we are currently implementing the mechanism in a lightweight mobile agent platform named μCode [11] and will perform various experiments to evaluate its scalability with respect to the two performance factors.

References

1. Bellavista, P., Corradi, A., Stefanelli, C.: The ubiquitous provisioning of internet services to portable devices. *IEEE Pervasive Computing* **1**(3) (2002) 81–87
2. Belle, W., Verelst, K., D'Hondt, T.: Location transparent routing in mobile agent systems merging name lookups with routing. In: Proc. of the 7th IEEE Workshop on Future Trends of Distributed Computing Systems. (1999) 207–212
3. Cao, J., Feng, X., Lu, J., Das, S.: Mailbox-based scheme for mobile agent communications. IEEE Computer **35**(9) (2002) 54–60
4. Desbiens, J., Lavoie, M., Renaud, F.: Communication and tracking infrastructure of a mobile agent system. In: Proc. of the 31st Hawaii International Conference on System Sciences. (1998) 54–63
5. Fukuda, M., Tanaka, Y., Suzuki, N., Bic, L.F., Kobayashi, S.: A mobile-agent-based PC grid. In: Proc. of the Fifth Annual International Workshop on Active Middleware Services. (2003) 142–150
6. Lange, D., Oshima, M.: Programming and deploying mobile agents with aglets. Addison-Wesley (1998)
7. Moreau, L.: Distributed directory service and message router for mobile agents. Science of Computer Programming **39**(2-3) (2001) 249–272
8. Moreau, L.: A fault-tolerant directory service for mobile agents based on forwarding pointers. In: Proc. of The 17th ACM Symposium on Applied Computing. (2002) 93–100
9. Murphy, A.L., Picco, G.P.: Reliable communication for highly mobile agents. Journal of Autonomous Agents and Multi-Agent Systems **5**(1) (2002) 81–100
10. ObjectSpace. Voyager. http://www.objectspace.com/
11. Picco, G.P.: μCode: A lightweight and flexible mobile code toolkit. In: Proc. of the 2nd Int. Workshop on Mobile Agents. (1998) 160–171

CSL Model Checking for the GreatSPN Tool*

Davide D'Aprile, Susanna Donatelli, and Jeremy Sproston

Dipartimento di Informatica, Università di Torino, Torino, Italy
{daprile,susi,sproston}@di.unito.it

Abstract. CSL is a stochastic temporal logic that has been defined for continuous time Markov chains, and that allows the checking of whether a single state, or a set of states, satisfies a given probabilistic condition defined over states or over a path of states. In this paper we consider the problem of CSL model checking in the context of Generalized Stochastic Petri Nets. We present a translation from Generalized Stochastic Petri Nets to the input formats of two well-known CSL model checkers, namely ETMCC and PRISM. The transformation to ETMCC is realized at the Markov Chain level, while that to PRISM is defined, as much as possible, at the net level. The translations are applied to a multiserver polling model taken from the literature.

1 Introduction

Generalized Stochastic Petri Nets (GSPN) [1] and their coloured counterpart Stochastic Well-formed Nets (SWN) [1,6] are widespread formalisms for the modelling of complex systems. They have been designed for performance evaluation, but they can, and have been, used also to validate qualitative properties of the system under study, either using *structural* properties, checkable on the net itself without building the state space, or using *reachability* analysis.

Recently a stochastic logic for Continuous Time Markov Chains (CTMC) has been defined [4,5], named Continuous Stochastic Logic (CSL), which collapses in a single logic the ability to specify qualitative and quantitative properties. CSL properties are verified at the state-space level using the model checking paradigm [8].

The ability to verify GSPN and SWN against CSL properties would increase the qualitative and quantitative verification capability of GSPN (and SWN) tools: in particular we think that this feature is particularly significant for SWN models, because of the limited availability of algorithms and tools to check structural properties on SWN (and in general on coloured nets). Moreover SWN is a very useful formalism for two main motivations: its ability to represent compactly complex models thanks to the ability of identifying tokens in a net using colours, and the possibility of computing the state space and the underlying CTMC in an efficient manner through the exploitation of symmetries [6]. Last, but definitely not least, we concentrate on this specific class of coloured nets for pragmatic reasons, because we have full access to a tool for the definition and analysis of GSPN and SWN, named GREATSPN [10], which has been developed over the last 20 years at our department. We add that there is not a wide

---
* Supported in part by the MIUR-FIRB project PERF.

choice of alternative tools for *stochastic* coloured nets: a simple form of colours is implemented in the APNN tool [3] of the University of Dortmund, and a notion of colours based on replication is implemented in UltraSAN [16] of the University of Illinois.

Our mid-term goal is indeed to have CSL facilities for SWN nets, and in this paper we report on the first step we have undertaken in this direction: to add to GREATSPN a CSL model-checking facility for GSPNs. Instead of building a new model checker we have linked GREATSPN to two well known CSL-model checkers: ETMCC [12], a joint effort of the Universities of Erlangen and Twente, and PRISM [15], of the University of Birmingham. We have not considered for the moment the CSL model checker built-in in APNN [3], instead preferring to use two "stand-alone" model checkers, the motivation being that we hope they can be not too difficult to connect with the GREATSPN modules for SWN, and because there is already some reported experience in interfacing other tools (ETMCC has been interfaced with the Petri net tool DaNAMiCS [9], and the process algebra tool TIPP [11], while PRISM has been interfaced with the PEPA process algebra [13]).

The paper is organized as follows. Section 2 provides the necessary background on CSL and on the tools used in this work (ETMCC, PRISM, and GREATSPN), Section 3 introduces the translations from GREATSPN to ETMCC and PRISM, translations which are used in Section 4 to show examples of CSL model checking for a GSPN model taken from the literature. Section 5 concludes the paper.

2 Preparing the Ground: CSL, ETMCC, PRISM, and GREATSPN

In this section we provide a brief, informal introduction of CSL followed by a presentation of the three tools involved in this work: ETMCC, PRISM, and GREATSPN. Due to space limitations, the presentation of the tools is only partial, centered on the main features used for our goals.

2.1 Model Checking CSL Properties

The syntax of CSL [4, 5] is defined as follows:

$$\Phi ::= a \mid \Phi \wedge \Phi \mid \neg \Phi \mid \mathcal{P}_{\bowtie \lambda}[X^I \Phi] \mid \mathcal{P}_{\bowtie \lambda}[\Phi U^I \Phi] \mid \mathcal{S}_{\bowtie \lambda}[\Phi]$$

where $a \in AP$ is an atomic proposition, $I \subseteq \mathbb{R}_{\geq 0}$ is a nonempty interval, interpreted as a time interval, where $\mathbb{R}_{\geq 0}$ denotes the non-negative reals, $\bowtie \in \{<, \leq, \geq, >\}$ is a comparison operator, and $\lambda \in [0, 1]$ is interpreted as a probability. CSL formulae are evaluated over CTMCs whose states are labelled with the subset of atomic propositions AP that hold true in that state. Atomic propositions represent elementary assertions that are either true or false in a state (such as *inCriticalSection*, *faultDetected*). As usual, $\Phi_1 \vee \Phi_2$ abbreviates $\neg(\neg\Phi_1 \wedge \neg\Phi_2)$, $\Phi_1 \Rightarrow \Phi_2$ abbreviates $\neg\Phi_1 \vee \Phi_2$, and X and U abbreviate $X^{[0,\infty)}$ and $U^{[0,\infty)}$ respectively.

The interpretation of the formulae of CSL is as follows: a state s satisfies the atomic proposition a if state s is labelled with a, $\wedge$ and $\neg$ have the usual interpretation, while s satisfies $\mathcal{S}_{\bowtie \lambda}[\Phi]$ if the sum of the steady state probabilities, obtained by letting the

CTMC evolve from state s, of the states that satisfy Φ is $\bowtie \lambda$. A state s satisfies the "bounded next" formula $\mathcal{P}_{\bowtie \lambda}[X^I \Phi]$ if the probability that the transition taken from s leads to a state satisfying Φ, and that the duration of the transition lies in I, is $\bowtie \lambda$. Finally, a state s satisfies the "bounded until" formula $\mathcal{P}_{\bowtie \lambda}[\Phi_1 U^I \Phi_2]$ if the probability of Φ_2 being true in a future execution from s after d time units have elapsed, where $d \in I$, and where the execution remains in states satisfying Φ_1 until Φ_2 is reached, is $\bowtie \lambda$. Examples of CSL formulae, taken from [5], are the following. The formula $\mathcal{S}_{\leq 10^{-5}}[a]$ is true if the probability of being in a state labelled by the atomic proposition a in steady-state is not greater than 0.00001. The formula $\mathcal{P}_{\leq 0.01}[aU^{[10,20]}b]$ is true if the probability of being in a b-labelled state after between 10 and 20 time units have elapsed, while remaining in a-labelled states before that point, is not greater than 0.01. Finally, the formula $\mathcal{P}_{\geq 0.5}[\neg a U^{[10,20]} \mathcal{S}_{\geq 0.8}[b \vee c]]$ is true if, with probability at least 0.5, we will reach a state between 10 and 20 time units (while avoiding a-states) in which the probability of being in a b- or c-labelled state in equilibrium is at least 0.8. The formal semantics of CSL can be found in [5].

Model checking a CTMC against a CSL formula Φ amounts to computing the set of states $Sat(\Phi)$ such that $s \in Sat(\Phi)$ if and only if Φ is true in state s. Model checking a formula Φ consists of computing the set $Sat(\Phi)$ of states which satisfy Φ by computing the sets of states which satisfy the subformulae of Φ; first, the sets of states satisfying the "shortest" subformulae of Φ (that is, the atomic propositions) are computed, then these sets are used to compute the sets of states satisfying progressively "longer" subformulae. When probability bounds are present in the formula (in the cases of $\mathcal{P}_{\bowtie \lambda}$ or $\mathcal{S}_{\bowtie \lambda}$) the model-checking algorithm requires the computation of transient or steady state probabilities of the original CTMC as well as, possibly, a number of additional CTMCs built through manipulation of the original one [5].

2.2 Three Tools: ETMCC, PRISM, and GREATSPN

The ETMCC Tool. ETMCC is a prototype tool supporting the verification of CSL-properties over CTMCs [12]. Once the rate matrix R and the labelling L (which can be regarded as a function from the set of states to the power set of atomic propositions, so that $L(s) \subseteq AP$ represents the set of atomic propositions true in state s) of a CTMC have been determined, model checking of CSL formulae can take place.

ETMCC has been written in JAVA and provides a simple graphical user interface. The input models for ETMCC are CTMCs, that can be provided in two different, ASCII-based formats. The set AP of atomic propositions and the labelling L is also specified in an input file (in the publicly available version the cardinality of AP is limited to 67). It is obvious that, for large CTMCs, the two input files should be automatically produced by some higher-level formalism: two tools supporting a high-level formalism that are already interfaced with ETMCC are the process algebra tool TIPP [11] and the SPN tool DaNAMiCS [9].

In terms of solution algorithms ETMCC supports the usual set of choices for Markov chains: Power method, Gauss-Seidel, Jacobi, JOR and SOR, as well as a solution for bounded until U^I and bounded next X^I based on numerical solution of a set of Volterra integral equations [12]. The CTMC is stored in sparse format.

The PRISM Tool. PRISM supports analysis of Discrete Time Markov Chains, Markov Decision Processes, and CSL model checking of CTMCs. An important characteristic of PRISM is its ability to work with symbolic data structures like BDDs and MTB-DDs [7], which can store the state space of the model efficiently. Three verification options are possible: fully symbolic (infinitesimal generator and probability vector as MTBDDs), fully sparse (infinitesimal generator as sparse matrix and the full probability vector) and hybrid (infinitesimal generator as MTBDDs and the full probability vector). In terms of solution algorithms PRISM supports the usual set of choices for Markov chains, including the Power method, Gauss-Seidel, Jacobi, JOR and SOR. The PRISM input language is based on the Reactive Modules language [2].

Model checkers only allow to check whether a certain formula is satisfied in a state, or to determine all the states that satisfy a formula. CSL formulae may include a probability bound, which has to be specified by the user. An interesting feature of PRISM is its ability to determine the value of this probability if it is left unspecified (by substituting the value with a "?") in the formula.

PRISM has a graphical interface for the management of modules and properties and for the visualization of results of multiple experiments. Model-checking analyses can be executed from the graphical user interface or from the command line.

The GREATSPN Tool. GREATSPN [10] is a tool for the definition and analysis of GSPN and SWN. Analysis in GreatSPN is supported by structural analysis of the net (computation of P- and T- invariants, deadlocks and traps), reachability analysis (liveness of transitions, ergodicity of the CTMC) and computation of performance indices through CTMC solutions or simulation. GreatSPN has a graphical interface for the definition and analysis, but all solution algorithms can also be launched from the command line thanks to a number of pre-defined scripts. The portion of GreatSPN that we shall use in this work relates to the computation of the state space and of the underlying CTMC.

3 Using PRISM and ETMCC with GREATSPN

As described in Section 2, CSL model checking of CTMCs requires three main ingredients: (1) a model, the underlying semantics of which is a CTMC, (2) a set AP of atomic propositions (simple strings) and a labelling function L from states of the Markov chain to subsets to AP, and (3) a CSL model checker.

CSL model checking of GSPNs requires a slightly modified set of ingredients: (1) a GSPN model, (2) a set of atomic propositions expressed in terms of net elements like the number of tokens in a place, comparison between marking of different places, and enabling degree of transitions, and (3) a CSL model checker.

In the following we illustrate two different approaches to GSPN model checking using preexisting tools: the first one is the interface with PRISM, which is realized at the net level, the second one is the interface with ETMCC, which is realized at the CTMC level.

3.1 GREATSPN and PRISM

The PRISM input language is a state-based language that is built upon modules and variables. The state of the system is a valuation of the variables of each of the system's modules. A module is a set of declarations and commands: each command is of the form GUARD ⟶ RATE : UPDATE, where GUARD specifies a logical condition on the system variables, RATE is the rate of the exponentially distributed delay associated to the command, and UPDATE is a set of assignments which specify the new values of the variables in terms of old ones (and a prime is used to distinguish the new value from the old one).

We define a translation to PRISM modules only for SPNs; that is, for GSPNs without immediate transitions (the classical SPN formalism defined by Molloy in [14]). An SPN is defined as (P, T, I, O, W, m_0), where P is the set of places, T is the set of transitions, $I, O : P \times T \to 2^\mathbb{N}$ is the set of input and output arcs with associated multiplicity, $W : T \to \mathbb{R}_{\geq 0}$ defines the rate of the exponential distributions associated to transitions, and $m_0 : P \to \mathbb{N}$ describes the initial marking. Due to space reasons we assume the reader is familiar with the SPN semantics.

For a bounded SPN, a unique PRISM module is created using the following rules:

1. For each place $p \in P$ a variable of name P is declared. Letting the bound for place p be denoted by b_p, we can let the range of the variable P be $[0, b_p]$. The variable P is initialized to the value of $m_0(p)$.
2. For each transition $t \in T$ a new command of the form GUARD ⟶ RATE: UPDATE is added to the module, where GUARD represents the enabling condition of t, expressed as the logical conjunction of as many predicates as there are input places to t. Each predicate is of the form $P \geq I(p,t)$, where P is the name of the PRISM variable for place p. We set RATE to $W(t)$. Finally, UPDATE represents the modification to the marking due to the firing of t, built as the conjunction of $|P|$ assignments, one for each place $p \in P$. The conjunct for place $p \in P$, with associated PRISM variable P, is defined by

$$P' = \begin{cases} P + O(p,t) - I(p,t) & \text{if } I(p,t) > 0 \wedge O(p,t) > 0 \\ P - I(p,t) & \text{if } I(p,t) > 0 \wedge O(p,t) = 0 \\ P + O(p,t) & \text{if } I(p,t) = 0 \wedge O(p,t) > 0. \end{cases}$$

Note that similar translations have been used to obtain PRISM modules of SPN models on the PRISM website [15].

With regard to the atomic propositions, in PRISM the set AP is implicitly defined, by allowing the user to include in a CSL formula any logical condition on the values of the variables. In the proposed translation place names are mapped one-to-one to variable names, and therefore any logical expression on place marking is allowed and is realized trivially.

The formalism of SPN can also be extended with *inhibitor arcs*, for which the presence of a given number of tokens in a place may preclude the firing of an otherwise-enabled transition. For example, inhibitor arcs of degree 1 can be incorporated in our translation in the following manner: for each transition $t \in T$, the enabling condition GUARD is defined as above, but is extended with an additional conjunct of the form

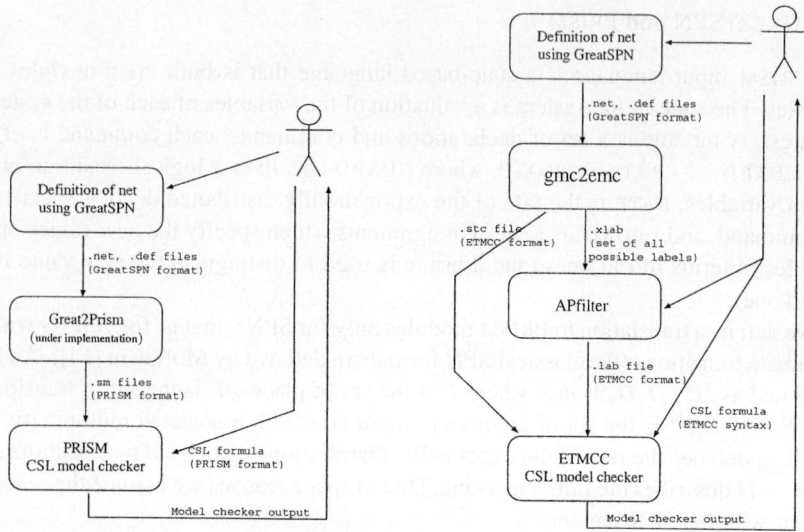

Fig. 1. Using PRISM and ETMCC to model check GreatSPN models

P= 0 for each inhibitor arc which points at t, where P is the variable associated with the source place of the inhibitor arc.

Figure 1 (left) describes the user point of view of the proposed approach: the GSPN model is defined using the graphical interface of GREATSPN, and structural analysis can be performed for a quick check of model correctness. The output of the GREATSPN interface (two files in ASCII that describe the GSPN) are passed to the translator (that is still under construction), that produces a PRISM module. CSL formulae are specified by the user through the graphical interface of PRISM using logical expressions on place names.

3.2 GREATSPN and ETMCC

The generation of the ETMCC input model from GREATSPN is simple, thanks to the use of two off-line solvers of GREATSPN: NEWRG for the generation of the reachability graph of the GSPN, NEWMT for the generation of the CTMC underlying the GSPN model, and SEEMTX for the visualization in ASCII of the CTMC itself. The output of SEEMTX is very similar to the .stc input file format of ETMCC, and the translation poses no particular problems.

More delicate is instead the definition of the .lab input file to ETMCC, which lists the set of atomic propositions and, for each CTMC state, the atomic propositions satisfied in that state. An atomic proposition in ETMCC is simply a string (with some syntactical limitations): we have chosen to define the atomic propositions by considering all possible numbers of tokens in places in all the reachable markings of the net, and defining properties for equality, greater than, etc. For example if p is a place in the net with 0, 1, or 2 tokens, then the set *AP* will include the strings: peq0, peq1, peq2, pgt0, pgt1, and pgt2. For $i \in \{0,1,2\}$, a state is labelled with peq$i$ (pgt$i$, respectively) if the corresponding marking has i tokens in place p (more than i tokens in place p, respectively). However, this approach tends to generate a (usually needlessly) large AP set, because only some of the atomic propositions defined are referred to in a given CSL formula. Also recall that the publicly-released version ETMCC version only allows for a maximum cardinality of 67. Therefore we have built a filter that selects only the atomic propositions used in the formula being checked.

The perspective of the user with regard to the translator is depicted in Figure 1 (right). As in Section 3.1, the user commences by defining the GSPN using GREATSPN. The gmc2emc converter is then used to produce the CTMC file (with extension .stc), and an intermediate file in .lab format (called .xlab) that contains the list of atomic propositions and the association with the states. The converter gmc2emc makes use of the off-line GREATSPN solvers mentioned above. The user then specifies the atomic propositions of interest and the APfilter module eliminates unnecessary elements from AP.

4 Example of CSL Model Checking

The translators defined in the previous section are now applied to an example taken from the literature: a cyclic multiserver polling system, as for example in [1]-chapter 9. Polling systems comprise a set of stations and a number of servers shared among the stations and that move from station to station. The servers follow a given order and a precise policy determining when and for how long the server should serve a given station before moving to the next one. Figure 2 depicts an SPN model of a polling system consisting of $N = 4$ stations and S servers. In each station i there are K clients that execute the cycle composed by places Pa_i, Pq_i, and Ps_i. A client in Pa_i is doing some local work (transition $arrive_i$ which has single server policy), it then goes to a queue place (Pq_i) where it waits for a server. When a server arrives, one client in the queue is selected and receives service (place Ps_i and transition $serve_i$ which has infinite server policy). A server which has provided service to queue i "walks" to the next queue (queue $(i+1)$ mod 4 since we are assuming a circular ordering), represented by a token in place Pw_i. When the server arrives at station (transition $walk_ia$) it provides service if some client is waiting in the queue; if not it moves on to the next queue (transition $walk_ib$). In Figure 3 we show the fragment of the PRISM code in which the variables and commands of one station are defined. A different translation of the system to a PRISM model can be found at the PRISM webpage.

Our experiments have considered three models. Model A has one client in each station, a single server and all transitions of rate 1. Model B has ten clients in station 0, two clients in the remaining stations, and two servers. All rates in model B are set to 1, apart from the rate of arrival of clients in station 0, which is 0.25, and the rate of arrival for all other stations is set to 0.5. Model C has thirty clients in station 0, four clients in the remaining stations, and three servers. All rates in model C are set to 1, apart from the rate of arrival of clients in station 0, which is 0.4, and the rate of arrival for all other stations is set to 0.25. All transitions in each model have a single server policy. Models A, B and C have 96, 7902 and 360104 states respectively.

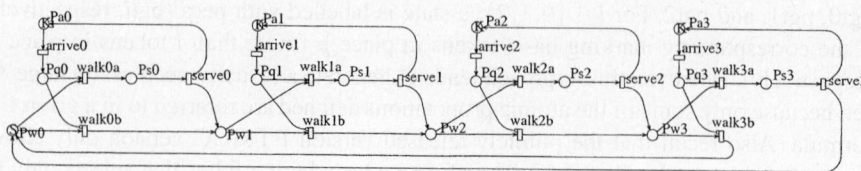

Fig. 2. SPN of a four-stations multiple server polling system

```
// variables: station1
Ps1 : [0..K];
Pw1 : [0..S];
Pa1 : [0..K] init K;
Pq1 : [0..K];

// commands: station1
// of transition walk1a
[] (Pq1>0) & (Pw1>0) -> 1 : (Pq1'=Pq1-1) & (Pw1'=Pw1-1) & (Ps1'=Ps1+1);
// of transition walk1b
[] (Pq1=0) & (Pw1>0) -> 1 : (Pw1'=Pw1-1) & (Pw2'=Pw2+1);
// of transition serve1
[] (Ps1>0) -> 1 : (Ps1'=Ps1-1) & (Pw2'=Pw2+1) & (Pa1'=Pa1+1);
// of transition arrive1
[] (Pa1>0) -> 1 : (Pa1'=Pa1-1) & (Pq1'=Pq1+1);
```

Fig. 3. Fragment of PRISM code for one station

We have verified the following properties using PRISM and ETMCC. Note that our atomic propositions are written as comparisons of the number of tokens in a place with natural numbers: such comparisons can be written in terms of variables in the case of PRISM (for example, P> 0), or as the strings introduced in Section 3.2 in the case of ETMCC (for example, pgt0).

Property (1) - Steady state probability of at least one client in queue 0:

$$S_{=?} \, [Pq_0 > 0] \, .$$

We are using here the PRISM notation $S_{=?}$ to indicate that we do not want to check a value, but we ask the tool to compute the steady state probability for all states that verify $Pq_0 > 0$. In ETMCC we have checked instead $S_{>0} \, [Pq_0 > 0]$; as expected, this property is satisfied in all states in all models, because the models are ergodic. During the computation ETMCC outputs also the aggregated probability for states satisfying $Pq_0 > 0$. This aggregated probability was computed also using GreatSPN, to increase our confidence in the translations.

Property (2) - Absence of starvation (clients waiting in a queue will be served):

$$(Pq_0 > 0 \Rightarrow \mathcal{P}_{\geq 1} \, [true \, U \, Pq_0 = 0]) \, .$$

In all models, the property is true in all states reachable from the initial state (including those in which $Pq_0 = 0$, since the second operand of the implication is satisfied in all states of each model). This property that does not require the CTMC solution, and instead relies on reachability analysis of the model's underlying graph.

Property (3) - Probability of service within a deadline: Since all transitions have infinite support and the CTMC is ergodic, then all states will have a non-null probability of service within a deadline, while only the states in which the service is being provided will have a 1 probability. The CSL formula that we have checked is

$$\mathcal{P}_{=?}\left[(Pq_0 > 0 \wedge Ps_0 = 0)\, U^{[0,5]}\, Ps_0 > 0\right].$$

The output of PRISM and ETMCC lists the probability of satisfying the until formula from each state.

Property (4) - Reproducibility of the initial marking: Since we are working only with reachable states, we can check the simple property

$$\mathcal{P}_{\geq 1}\left[true\, U\, \text{"init"}\right],$$

where "init" is a logical condition that fully characterizes the initial marking (and it is therefore different for the various systems that we have verified). This property is satisfied by all states in all models.

Property (5) - Reproducibility of the initial marking with a deadline:

$$\mathcal{P}_{=?}\left[true\, U^{[0,10]}\, \text{"init"}\right].$$

This property is similar to property (3); it is satisfied by all states and the same comments as above apply.

The tools produce the probability of reaching the "init" state from any of the states of the model. This probability is 1 from the "init" state itself and is instead very low for all other states: for model A, these probabilities for all states are less than 0.01, whereas, after changing the interval to [0,1000], the probabilities of all states are less than 0.25.

Property (6) - Circularity of a server: We wish to check whether a server will present itself more than once at station 0.

$$\mathcal{P}_{\geq 1}\left[G\,(Pw_0 = 1 \Rightarrow \mathcal{P}_{\geq 1}\left[X\,(Pw_0 = 0 \Rightarrow \mathcal{P}_{\geq 1}[true\, U\, Pw_0 = 1])\right])\right],$$

where $\mathcal{P}_{\geq 1}\left[G\Phi\right]$ (read "globally Φ with probability 1") abbreviates the CSL formula $\neg \mathcal{P}_{\leq 0}\left[true\, U\, \neg\Phi\right]$. The property is satisfied by all states in all models.

Comment. We observed that the speed of the two tools ETMCC and PRISM in obtaining results for our polling system models was comparable. Note that we chose the fully sparse verification engine of PRISM in order to be able to make this comparison; instead, PRISM also supports MTBDD and hybrid verification engines, which can facilitate verification of larger systems. We experimented with the Jacobi and Gauss-Seidel options, and generally found that verification using Gauss-Seidel was more efficient for our models (we terminated the experiments using Jacobi on model C after one hour). Finally, we observed that for models B and C (which both have thousands of states) methods for "filtering" the results of model checking were required, in order to output the probabilities for a small number of states of interest.

5 Conclusions

In this paper we have reported on our investigation to add CSL model checking capabilities to GREATSPN. For the time being the work has concentrated on GSPN models for which two CSL model checkers have been considered: ETMCC and PRISM. For the first one the implementation has been completed and it is available through the first author of this paper: indeed in this case, since the interfacing takes place at the CTMC level, an implementation was necessary to be able to experiment with GSPN of non trivial size. For PRISM instead the implementation is still under definition, although a syntactic translation from SPN to PRISM modules, upon which the implementation can be based, has been defined. The translation can be used to manually transform a SPN into a PRISM module relatively easily.

References

1. Ajmone Marsan, M., Balbo, G., Conte, G., Donatelli, S., Franceschinis, G.: Modelling with Generalized Stochastic Petri Nets. John Wiley (1995)
2. Alur, R., Henzinger, T.A.: Reactive Modules. Formal Methods in System Design **15** (1999) 7–48
3. APNN Web Page. http://ls4-www.cs.uni-dortmund.de/APNN-TOOLBOX/toolbox_en.html
4. Aziz, A., Sanwal, K., Singhal, V., Brayton, R.: Model-Checking Continuous Time Markov Chains. ACM Transactions on Computational Logic **1** (2000) 162–170
5. Baier, C., Haverkort, B., Hermanns, H., Katoen, J.-P.: Model-Checking Algorithms for Continuous-Time Markov Chains. IEEE Transactions on Software Engineering **29** (2003) 524–541
6. Chiola, G., Dutheillet, C., Franceschinis, G., Haddad, S.: Stochastic Well-Formed Coloured Nets for Symmetric Modelling Applications. IEEE Transaction on Computers **42** (1993) 1343–1360
7. Clarke, E.M., Fujita, M., McGeer, P., McMillan, K., Yang, J., Zhao, X.: Multi-Terminal Binary Decision Diagrams: An Efficient Data Structure for Matrix Representation. In: Proceedings of the International Workshop on Logic Synthesis (IWLS'93). (1993) 6a:1–15 Also available in Formal Methods in System Design **10** (1997) 149–169
8. Clarke, E.M., Grumberg, O., Peled, D.A.: Model Checking. MIT Press (1999)
9. DANAMiCS Web Page. http://www.cs.uct.ac.za/Research/DNA/DaNAMiCS/DaNAMiCS.html
10. The GreatSPN Tool. http://www.di.unito.it/~greatspn
11. Hermanns, H., Herzog, U., Klehmet, U., Mertsiotakis, V., Siegle, M.: Compositional Performance Modelling with the TIPPtool. Performance Evaluation **39** (2000) 5–35
12. Hermanns, H., Katoen, J.-P., Meyer-Kayser, J., Siegle, M.: A Tool for Model-Checking Markov Chains. International Journal on Software Tools for Technology Transfer **4** (2003) 153–172
13. Hillston, J.: A Compositional Approach to Performance Modelling. Cambridge University Press (1996)
14. Molloy, M.K.: Performance Analysis Using Stochastic Petri Nets. IEEE Transaction on Computers **31** (1982) 913–917
15. PRISM Web Site. http://www.cs.bham.ac.uk/~dxp/prism
16. UltraSAN Web Site. http://www.crhc.uiuc.edu/UltraSAN/index.html

Performance and Dependability Analysis of Fault-Tolerant Memory Mechanisms Using Stochastic Well-Formed Nets

Paolo Ballarini[1], Lorenzo Capra[2], and Guiliana Franceschinis[3]

[1] C.S. Dept., University of Liverpool, UK
paolo@csc.liv.ac.uk
[2] Di.C.O., Università di Milano, Italy
capra@dsi.unimi.it
[3] D.I., Università del Piemonte Orientale, Alessandria, Italy
giuliana@mfn.unipmn.it

Abstract. This paper presents a performance and dependability study of a software fault-tolerant memory mechanism, namely the Distributed Memory (DM), which has been developed within a R&D European project. Relying on the UML specification (produced within the project), Stochastic Well-Formed Nets models of the DM are developed and analysed. Combinatorial methods are used in conjunction with state space based methods to study the impact of the mechanism configuration on its reliability and performance.

1 Introduction

The design of fault tolerant systems based on distributed computer architectures raises interesting problems that call for adequate methodologies. In the specific case of safety/mission critical systems, the timing and dependability requirements are particularly stringent, and must be dealt with since the early stages of the design. Software solutions to fault tolerance (FT) requirements of critical systems, (e.g., plant control embedded systems) have been studied and proposed by several projects worldwide. In the TIRAN (TaIlorable fault toleRANce frameworks for embedded applications) and DepAuDE (Dependability of Automation Systems in Dynamic Environments) European projects [4, 1], involving both academic and industrial partners, one such solution has been proposed. The *TIRAN framework* is a middleware designed to be easily ported on any operating system (with basic real time functionalities), comprising a library of *mechanisms* (e.g., watchdog, voter, stable memory, etc.) to be used for error detection, fault containment, fault masking and recovery. Those mechanisms are implemented by tasks which are coordinated by a control layer called *backbone* (BB). The framework refers to a distributed architecture consisting of computing nodes connected through a standard communication network like an Ethernet LAN.

The TIRAN framework relies on a quite strong assumption: the underlying communication system is supposed to be reliable (how this could be achieved was out of the scope of TIRAN, and has been instead a central issue in DepAuDE). Modeling has been a fundamental part of both TIRAN and DepAuDE, with a twofold motivation: (1) supporting the framework designer in choosing between different alternatives; (2) helping the final user in the configuration of the framework with respect to the application requiring the FT services. From the specification documents (essentially UML diagrams provided by other project's partners), models of the framework have been developed, in terms of Stochastic Well-formed Nets (SWN), a coloured flavour of Stochastic Petri Nets by means of which both qualitative and quantitative analysis is achieved. Different level of abstraction have been considered for the models, depending on their use: for documentation purposes a more detailed model might be preferred, while when performing analysis a higher abstraction may be chosen to avoid state space explosion. In [2] it has been shown how, relying on the *behaviour inheritance* relation, (behaviourally) equivalent models of the TIRAN memory mechanisms can be built at different level of abstraction. In this paper, instead, the focus is posed on a combined performance/dependability study of the Distributed Memory (DM) mechanism. We shall adopt a blended analysis techniques: combinatorial methods can be used to evaluate the protection level with a given configuration, while the performance overhead introduced by the DM services is measured through state space methods.

The use of blended combinatorial and state space models in dependability analysis has been proposed in the dependability literature (e.g., a hierarchy of combinatorial and state space dependability models has been proposed in [8], and both type of models for analysing software fault tolerance are proposed in [7]), however our approach is more oriented towards performability evaluation [6], rather than towards modelling complex dependencies or fault correlations in dependability analysis.

The DM is strictly coupled with another mechanism, the Stable Memory (SM) which is the actual provider of the FT memory services to external applications. Because of the space limit, in this work only the DM models are treated. The paper is organised as follows: Section 2 contains a brief description of the memory mechanisms behaviour, with particular attention to the DM; in Section 3 a discussion on the impact of the DM configuration on the achievable dependability of the DM services is presented, based on purely combinatorial arguments; in Section 4 a SWN model of the DM is introduced, so to give a flavour of the model's complexity and of the chosen abstraction level. In Section 5 the performance of the DM mechanism is evaluated in terms of the completion time of the DMread service. Some curves are reported showing the incidence of the mechanism configuration on the read completion, for both the "normal" implementation and for an "optimised" one (by means of which concurrent DMread requests are served in parallel). Finally in Section 6 a summarise is presented together with some directions for future work.

2 Software Fault-Tolerant Memory Mechanisms

In the TIRAN framework the memory FT services are realized by means of two mechanisms: the SM and the DM, designed to deal with two different types of fault. The SM is meant to protect against (transient) faults affecting the user's application. This is achieved through time replication (i.e., the input value of a write request is actually stored in the memory only after the SMwrite service is consecutively executed a number of time on it). On the other hand the DM provides masking against (transient/permanent) faults corrupting the value stored in memory cells. This is achieved through spatial replication (i.e., memory cells are replicated). The SM and DM are, in general, independent mechanisms, but in the TIRAN framework they have been used in a strictly related way. The user application (i.e., a plant control system) requires the SM services while the SM services are implemented by means of the DM (i.e., each SM's variable is replicated a number of times in the DM).

Tasks' Replication and Coordination. In order to further improve protection, both the SM and the DM are replicated in a number of tasks, distributed over the nodes of the underlying architecture and grouped into "task-groups" (i.e., SM tasks, DM tasks). To each memory variable (either SM or DM variable) corresponds one "master" task of a "task-group", whose role is to coordinate the other tasks of the group when a Read or Write service is requested for that variable. Essentially the "master" task for a variable V, collects, from the other tasks in the group, the results of Read/Write operations on V, before replying to the client. The number of tasks in a task-group, their mapping onto the architecture's nodes and the association DM variable - master task, are all relevant configuration parameters of the framework.

The DMread (Double-Voting) and DMwrite (Synchronisation). The DM implements an abstraction of "fault tolerant variable", that can be read and written by a client using the operations $DM\_rd()$ and $DM\_wr()$. Each DM variable dmv_i is replicated a number of time on each DM task. As a result of the bi-dimensional replication (DMtask-DMvariable), a two-level voting is performed whenever a $DM\_rd()$ operation is executed: each DM task votes on its local-replicas (first-level voting) returning the majority value (if it exists) to the master which then votes again (second-level voting) on the first-voting result of all DM tasks, finally returning the majority (if it exists) of the second-voting to the client. Conversely, when a $DM\_wr(dmv_i)$ message is broadcast, each DM task locks and writes its local replicas of dmv_i, then waits to synchronise with all other DM tasks on the end-write event, before unlocking the local replicas of dmv_i. The behaviour of the DM and SM mechanisms[4] are formally described in the TIRAN specification documents by means of UML state diagrams (an example of which can be found in [2]): the models of the DM presented in this paper have been derived from such diagrams.

---

[4] For the sake of brevity we omit the detailed description of the SM behaviour in here; the interested reader can refer to [2].

3 Combinatorial Dependability Assessment

We are interested in two type of figures to characterise the mechanisms: the reliability as a function of the DM and SM configuration, and the performance of the mechanisms (mainly its average response time) as a function of the configuration and of a given fault model (so both the normal mode and degraded mode operation can be evaluated). In this section we present a study of the DM mechanism reliability as a function of its configuration parameters, based on combinatorial arguments. Once a configuration which guarantees the desired reliability has been selected, the corresponding overhead can be evaluated by solving a performance model, for which we have used the SWN formalism (see Section 4 and Section 5).

DM Reliability Analysis. The probability of a failure of a $DM\_rd()$ operation, essentially depends on two factors: (1) r, the number of DM tasks, and (2) l, the number of replicas in each task (we assume that DM variables are uniformly replicated over DMtasks, i.e., l is equal on each dmt_i). Then, if p is the probability of the occurrence of a fault corrupting the value of a single replica (equal and independent for each replica on each task), the probability of not being able to reconstruct the correct value for a given variable dmv is governed by a binomial distribution and it is given by

$$Pr(\text{Failure in } DM\_rd()\ ) = \sum_{i=\hat{r}}^{r} \binom{r}{i} stf^i (1-stf)^{r-i}$$

with $\hat{r} = r/2$ if r is even and $\hat{r} = \lceil r/2 \rceil + 1$ if r is odd, where stf is defined as

$$stf = Pr(\text{Failure in single } DM) = \sum_{i=\hat{l}}^{l} \binom{l}{i} p^i (1-p)^{l-i}$$

with $\hat{l} = l/2$ if l is even and $\hat{l} = \lceil l/2 \rceil + 1$ if l is odd.

The graph in Figure 1 illustrates the variation of the failure probability for the DM read operation with respect to both the number of replicas and the number of DM tasks (each line in the graph corresponds to a different number of DM tasks, from 3 to 7) when a fault affecting a single replica is supposed to have a 0.1% chance (i.e., $p = 0.001$). From the graph we can conclude that an *odd* configuration (i.e., one with an odd number of replicas and tasks) is always to be preferred to an *even* one as it guarantees a better protection against Read's failure[5]: the protection increment being approximatively of 5, 8 and 10 orders of magnitude respectively for configurations with 3, 5 and 7 tasks.

---

[5] This is a consequence of the majority voting.

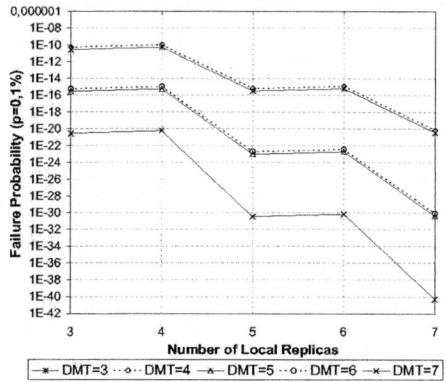

Fig. 1. Pr(Failure in $DM\_rd()$) wrt different combinations and with $p = 0.001$

4 SWN Models of the Mechanisms

Although combinatorial methods can be used for configuring the mechanisms with the desired dependability level, they do not allow one to assess the efficiency of such configurations. For that purpose SWN models of the mechanisms have been developed (by means of the *GreatSPN* tool [5]) relying on the following guidelines: (1) a model is (recursively) defined as a collection of submodels composed through suitable operators, so that the overall model will be a multi-level hierarchy of submodels; (2) a submodel represents a (part of a) component in the modelled system; (3) the submodels can be parametric, and parameters in different submodels may be related. Throughout our work several (sub)models have been developed corresponding to different levels of abstraction and tailored to the verification of the memory mechanisms under different circumstances . In this paper we focus on the analysis of the DM mechanism's behaviour under specific conditions, which are: a read service workload only (no write requests are considered) and in absence of faults (the mechanism is supposed not to be affected by any fault[6]). Concerning the abstraction level of models, we observe that very detailed models, although useful for documentation purposes (UML specifications can be enriched with an unambiguous and executable description of the intended behaviour, a problem faced, for example, in [3]), are hardly treatable for performance analysis because of the state-space explosion they trigger. Several criteria can be considered, when aiming to a version of the DM model suitable for performance analysis, like: (1) whether to explicitly represent replicas of each variable, (2) whether interleaving of broadcast messages has to be represented or can be abstracted away by assuming a "grouped" communication, (3) whether to explicitly represent resource contention (for CPU usage and

---

[6] Models for verification of both the DM and SM under different conditions, including the presence of faults, can be found in [2].

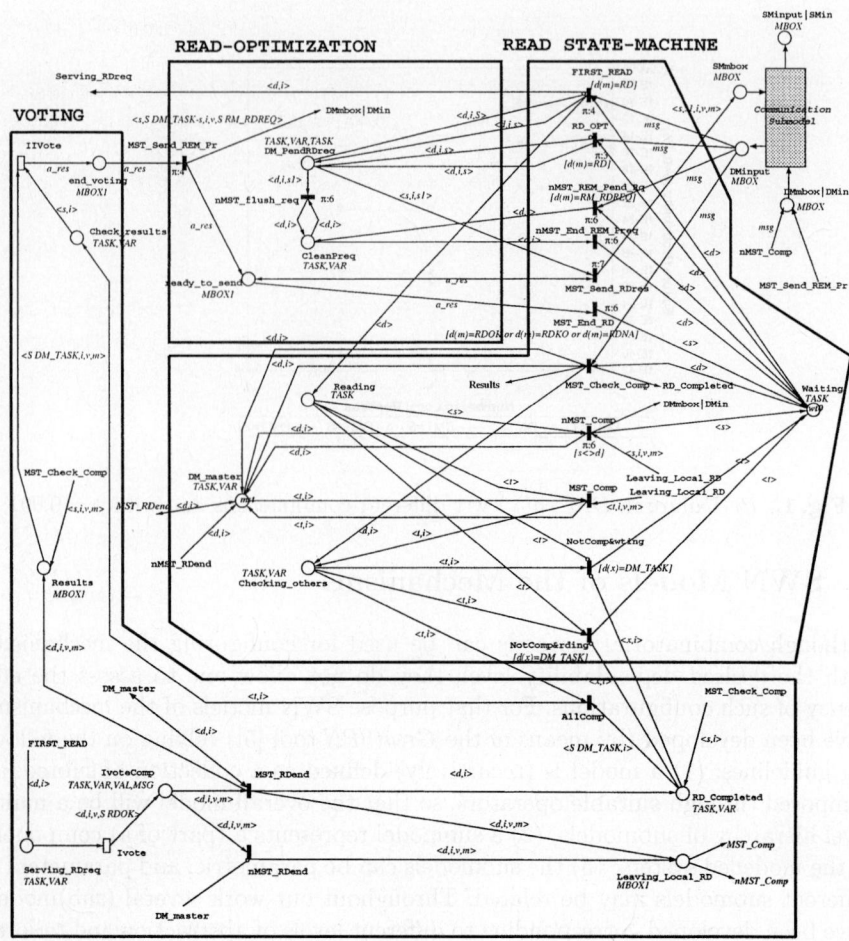

Fig. 2. The DM model for a read-only workload in absence of faults

communication links), (4) whether the model has to be used for a behaviour analysis both in presence and absence of faults. By means of those criteria a model tailored to the type of performance analysis one is interested in, can be obtained.

The DM Model (Read Workload/No-Faults). Figure 2 shows the SWN model of the DM mechanism suitable for performance evaluation under a read workload only and in absence of faults (this is a simplified evolution of the DM's model presented in [2]). The simplification is due to the following reasons: (1) in absence of fault an explicit representation of the DM variable replicas is not needed (variable replication becoming a stochastic parameter of the model, i.e., the exponential firing rate of transition Ivote); (2) the absence of write-requests results in no need for checking the *locked/unlocked* state of variable replicas. The model in Figure 2 consists of three main parts: i) a very abstract representation of the voting operations: the first-voting (local) (timed transition Ivote), and the second-voting (timed transition IIvote); ii) the precise representation of the DM state-machine for the READ protocol (places belonging to this part correspond to states characterising the DM behaviour as described by the UML specifications, e.g., places Waiting, Reading, RD_Completed...); iii) a communication sub-model (embedding a simple representation of a read-only workload) depicted as the shadowed box in the upper-right corner of Figure 2. In order to limit the state-space dimension, an hybrid solution has been adopted for the communication sub-model: broadcast of external messages to the DM task-group (i.e., read requests from the SM) are represented as atomic actions, while broadcast of internal messages (i.e., messages sent by a DM task to the others DM tasks) are modelled as sequential action (for the sake of space we omit here the detail of the Communication sub-model, it can be found in [2]).

An exhaustive description of the model depicted in Figure 2 is out of the scope of this work, however some relevant aspects may be pointed out. The model is completely parametric with respect to the following values: the number of tasks, their distribution over the nodes, the number of DM variables, the mastership association between DM variables and DM tasks. Parameters are instantiated by properly defining the model *color classes*, the color domain[7] and the initial marking. Timing information is also among the model's parameters. Essentially, in absence of faults, the time consuming activities, with respect to a read service are: the communication between tasks (timed transitions of the Communication sub-model) and the two voting phases (i.e., timed transitions Ivote and IIvote in Figure 2). The firing rates for those transitions have been defined as functions of few basic parameters such as the average time for reading a memory location, average time for comparing two values (for transitions Ivote and IIvote), and average time for local/remote message transmission (for the timed transition of the Communication sub-model). All those values have been derived from estimates found in the literature.

4.1 Optimized DM Read Protocol

Throughout the mechanisms design phase, an optimised protocol for the DM read service has been developed, so to reduce the completion time in case of concurrent read requests. The optimisation is achieved by keeping track of the concurrent $DM\_rd()$ requests
so that the the resulting value of a read service is actually returned to all *client* tasks whose request has been *registered* before service completion. The model in

---

[7] The SWN formalism is a High-Level Petri Net formalism, where information can be associated with tokens. Hence in this formalism tokens are no more indistinguishable, and this might be graphically represented by having tokens of different colours. The colour domain of a place (a Cartesian product of basic colour classes) is a set of colours the token in that place may have. The expressions labelling an arc connecting a given place and transition, represent the set of coloured tokens that a given transition firing must withdraw from/add into the place.

Figure 2 is designed so to cope with the optimised protocol (see the READ-OPT box in the upper part of Figure 2) and can be used for a compared optimised vs non-optimised performance analysis (i.e., the non-optimised behaviour can straightforwardly be reproduced by removing the untimed transition RD_OPT). A qualitative analysis of the *optimised* DM model has proved that the optimised protocol is not deadlock-free. This is a consequence of the order with which the broadcast messages are delivered to recipients (i.e., since no assumption can be made on the order with which concurrent read-request messages are received by each DM task, then, in principle, a concurrent read request could reach the master task after all the other tasks have received it and after the read service has completed, leading to an inconsistency in *Pending_Req* distributed table, which then results in a deadlock). Although theoretical unsafe, the choice adopted by the TIRAN designers to actually use the optimised DM read protocol may be justified by quantitative analysis considerations: the probability of reaching a deadlock state, that may be computed in terms of Mean Time To Absorption (MTTA) of the stochastic process underlying the SWN model, is indeed negligible. In order for a performance analysis of the optimised DM model, we used a communication submodel in which message broadcasting is represented as an atomic action (i.e., broadcast messages are delivered at the same time). That way the deadlock is overcome.

5 Performance Evaluation of the Mechanisms

Generally speaking, performance analysis of models can be used at different stage and for different purposes. In the modelling phase, it may be used to compare the performance of models at different levels of abstraction, aiming to estimate the approximation introduced by abstraction; in the design phase, it can help to establish which amongst different design alternatives/configuration results in the best performance; finally for verifying that the modelled system is performing as expected, i.e., it is able to react within given time constraints (in this case a validation of the model against actual measure on prototypes should be performed). In this section we present a performance analysis of the DM through which the mean time to completion for a Read service is evaluated for different configurations of the mechanism. These results have been obtained by solution of the SWN model given by composition of the DM model (see Figure 2) with a very abstracted representation of a workload in which the SM tasks iteratively issue a read request for a set of DM's variables (this cyclic behaviour corresponds to the TIRAN project demonstrator). The analysis we present here is not used for a precise verification of the DM service's response time (i.e., no model validation has been carried out), but yet provides useful indications concerning both the mechanism configuration (how much task's/variable's replication affects performance) and design (optimisation vs. non-optimisation).

The graphs in Figure 3 show the average $DM\_rd()$ time as a function of the DM configuration. The graph on the left (See Figure 3(a)) depicts the overhead introduced by increasing the task replication (for a fixed number of replicas,

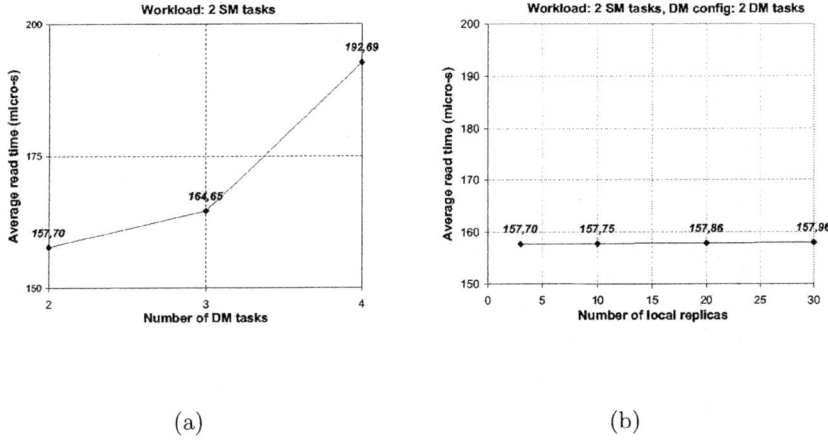

Fig. 3. Average $DM\_rd()$ completion time as a function (a) of the number of DM tasks, (b) of the number of local replicas

equal to 3), while that one the right (see Figure 3(b)) refers to the overhead resulting by increasing the number of local replicas (for a fixed number of DM tasks, equal to 2). By comparison we can conclude that the incidence of the variable-replication on the $DM\_rd()$ time is almost irrelevant when compared to task-replication (for an order of magnitude gradient of variable-replication, ie from 3 to 30, the increment of the read response-time, ie $0.26\mu sec$, is less than the 4% of that corresponding to a 1 task gradient, i.e., from 2 to 3, with constant variable-replication). As a result, once an appropriate upper bound for the failure probability has been chosen, then, amongst the set of configurations which matches it (determinable by means of formulae in Sec. 3), the one which minimises the number of task's replicas (maximising consequently the variable's replicas) is to be preferred, from a performance point of view. The communication model used for computing the curves in Figure 3, refers to atomic broadcast and no explicit representation of communication links contention. Turning to a communication model with sequential communication actions for each broadcast and explicit resource contention, led to significantly higher values for the read response time, but similar curves shape: this indicates that the approximation introduced by the model with atomic broadcast and no-contention should be compensated by tuning the timing parameters accordingly.

Finally the curves in Figure 4 refer to the mean-time to completion of concurrent Read requests (i.e., a workload of 4 concurrent requests are considered) for both the *non-optimised* protocol and the *optimised* one, as a function of the number of DM tasks. They show a significant improvement of performance when the *optimised* approach is used (i.e., the average improvement of the response time being 44.5% for configurations with 2 SM tasks and 59.2% for configurations with 3 SM tasks).

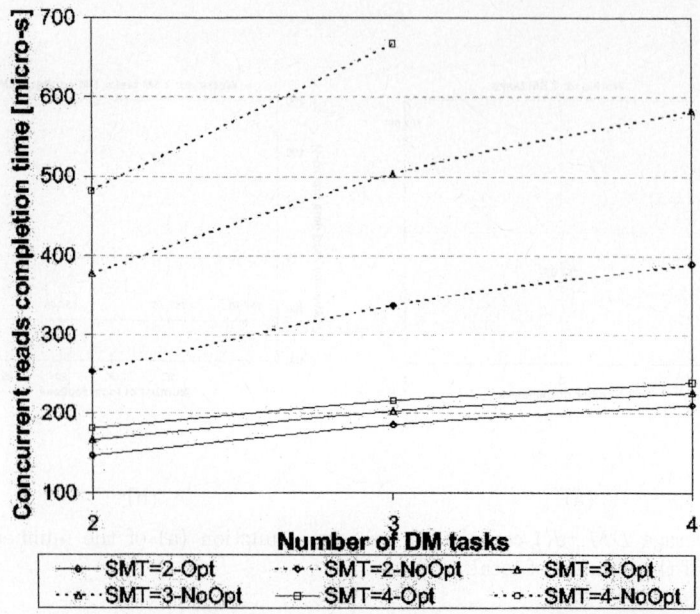

Fig. 4. Average completion time for a set of (4) concurrent reads on the same variable, as a function of the number of DM tasks

6 Conclusions

In this paper we have reported an experience of modelling activity concerning one of the mechanism (the DM) of a software fault tolerance framework. The relevance of modelling has been shown to be twofold: as a means for integrating the framework documentation and as a supporting tool for the framework design and configuration. An incremental and compositional modelling approach has been adopted. Two types of analysis have been combined in order to study the model: by means of combinatorial techniques the reliability corresponding to different configurations has been assessed and with that respect configurations with an odd number of replicas for both the tasks and the variables, have been proved to guarantee a better protection (i.e. a lower Failure probability). By solving the SWN model of the whole framework (DM composed with SM) the mean-time to completion of the DM Read service has been calculated, showing that the incidence of variables' replication on performance is much lower than tasks' replication and also that the *optimised* Read protocol actually performs better than the *non-optimised* one. The qualitative analysis of the SWN model has also been useful to prove that the proposed *optimised* protocol is not *deadlock-free*, the deadlock being a consequence of possible, but rather unlikely, significant delays in the client-to-server communication. Since the timing information we have used for the models' setup (i.e. the transition's exponential firing rates) has been derived from the literature, it would be of interest, as a further future development of this work, to address the issue of model's validation. This would require some testing of the actual TIRAN framework implementation on a benchmark (the so-called TIRAN demonstrator) so to derive measurements of the real mean-time to completion for the mechanism's services (i.e. DM Read, DM write) under different configurations.

The models' performance analysis has been referred only to a subset of fault scenarios, moreover for each study, we have tried to apply the highest possible abstraction in model's construction while maintaining a sufficient level of precision so to understand pros/cons of different design alternatives Finally the performance improvement introduced by an optimization of the DM read function has been assessed.

Acknowledgements

The work of Giuliana Franceschinis has been partially funded by the Italian MIUR FIRB project PERF; the work of Paolo Ballarini was done when he was at the University of Torino, and was partially funded by the MIUR FIRB project PERF.

References

1. DepAuDE Project Home Page. http://www.depaude.org
2. Ballarini, P., Capra, L., De Pierro, M., Franceschinis, G.: Memory Fault Tolerance Mechanisms: Design and Configuration Support through SWN Models. In: Proceedings of the 3rd International Conference on Application of Concurrency to System Design, Guimaraes, Portugal. (2003)
3. Bernardi, S., Donatelli, S., Merseguer, J.: From UML Sequence Diagrams and Statecharts to Analysable Petri Net Models. In: ACM Proceedings of the 3rd International Workshop on Software and Performance (WOSP 2002), Rome, Italy. (2002) 35–45
4. Botti, O., Florio, V.D., Deconinck, D., Cassinari, F., Donatelli, S., et al.: TIRAN: Flexible and Portable Fault Tolerance Solutions for Cost Effective Dependable Applications. In: Proceedings of 5th International Euro-Par Conference on Parallel Processing (Europar'99). Lecture Notes in Computer Science, Vol. 1685. Springer, Berlin Heidelberg New York (1999) 1166–1180
5. Chiola, G., Franceschinis, G., Gaeta, R., Ribaudo, M.: GreatSPN 1.7: Graphical Editor and Analyzer for Timed and Stochastic Petri Nets. Performance Evaluation (special issue on Performance Modeling Tools) **24** (1995) 47–68
6. Haverkort, B.R., Marie, R., Rubino, G., Trivedi, K.S. (eds.): Performability Modelling: Techniques and Tools. John Wiley & Sons (2001)
7. Lyu, M.R. (ed.): Software Fault Tolerance. John Wiley and Sons, New York (1995)
8. Malhotra, M., Trivedi, K.S.: Power-Hierarchy of Dependability-Model Types. IEEE Trans. on Reliability **43** (1994)

UML Design and Software Performance Modeling*

Salvatore Distefano, Daniele Paci, Antonio Puliafito, and Marco Scarpa

Dipartimento di Matematica, Università di Messina, 98166 Messina, Italy
{salvatdi,dpaci,apulia,mscarpa}@ingegneria.unime.it

Abstract. The importance of integrating performance evaluation into the software development process from the very early stages has been widely recognized during last years. The goal is to individuate performance behavior before the system is actually implemented reducing costs and time, and permitting to compare different design choices. The main drawback of this approach is the time and the background knowledge required to transform the specifications of a software system into a performance model. In this paper, we present a model for setting performance requirements collected from a UML [9] project. This represents the first step towards an automatic process for computing performance measures starting from an UML specified model. The approach proposed is based on open and well-known standards: UML for the software modeling, the *Profile for Schedulability, Performance, and Time Specification* for the performance annotations and XMI for the interchange of metadata.

1 Introduction

Performance is an important but often overlooked aspect of the software design. Indeed, the consideration on performance issues is in many cases left until late in the Software Development Process (SDP), when problems have already manifested themselves at system test or actually within the deployed system. Nevertheless, the importance of integrating performance evaluation into the whole SDP from the early stages has been recognized during last years in the Software Engineering community. This kind of approach realizes the so called *Software Performance Engineering* (SPE) [14] which allows to build performances into systems rather than add them later.

The birth of *UML* (Unified Modeling Language) [9] and its sudden spread on wide scale from 1996, favored the developing of SPE. An increasing number of researchers, encouraged by the standardization of this modeling language, began to be interested in such topic: King and Pooley in [11] evidenced as UML, considering both static and dynamic aspects of a system, lends particularly to the analysis of the performances, when annotations for timing and branching probabilities are added.

---
* This work is supported by Italian national project "FIRB - Performance Evaluation of Complex System: Techniques, Methodologies and Tools".

Since UML has been conceived as a general purpose modeling language, it has equipped with an open ended semantic, that can be extended and merged with various application domains. These extensions can be obtained through the UML profiles, a specialized subset of the UML that permits to extend the model using the lightweight extension mechanisms (*stereotypes, tagged values* and *constraints*). In particular the *UML Profile for Schedulability, Performance and Time Specification* (UML-RT) [8], is an OMG standard for the representation of performances and real-time properties, adopted here for the annotations of performance requirements in the UML model.

Insertion of performance requirements into UML models convinced many researchers to develop algorithms for automatic generation of Performance Models starting from UML diagrams, like in [2,7], where the authors formalize a structured methodology which sets a relation between an UML model defined through a Use Case Diagram (UC), a set of Sequence Diagrams (SDs) and State Chart Diagrams (SCs), with *Labeled General Stochastic PNs* (LGSPNs). These are subsequently linked together obtaining the PN describing the whole system.

Similarly, the synthesis of PN from UML diagrams is treated in [12]. Even in this case, SCs are used for the specification of the dynamic behaviors of an object, using Collaboration Diagrams (CoDs) to express the interaction between them.

Other approaches use target performance models different from PNs like *Generalized Semi-Markov Process* (GSMP) [6], *Stochastic Reward Nets* (SRN) [5], *Queuing Network Models* (QNM) [16], *Layered Queueing Networks* (LQN) [10]. In these cases, generation of performance model is obtained from an UML model based on SCs, ADs, or Deployment Diagram (DD).

A different approach has been presented in [1], where a simulation model is developed from a hierarchic UML model represented by UCs, DDs and ADs. This approach is highly integrated with the OMG's performance profile, indeed the performance model is based on the one defined in [8] (see Figure 1).

The work presented in [3] is particularly interesting: it defines an *Intermediate Model* (IM) as an hypergraph. Two steps permit to realize the mapping: in the first step, remarkable data on dependability are extracted projecting the UML entities into IM nodes and structural UML relations into IM arcs; then the IM is mapped to a PN model examining the hypergraph and generating a set of subnets for each IM element.

In order to realize the integration between SDP and performance analysis, we also introduce an intermediate model, called *Performance Context Model* (PCM). The idea of an intermediate model offers the advantage of being independent both from the particular UML representation and from the adopted analysis formalism.

The rest of this paper is organized as follows. Section 2 introduces the PCM. Section 3 presents the rules for mapping the UML model towards the PCM. Section 4 reports a simple case study. Conclusions and ideas concerning future work close the paper.

2 The Performance Context Model

Most of the proposals available in literature provide a limited integration of the performance aspects into UML models. In this paper, we intend to pursue such goal focusing on the *Performance Analysis Domain Model* (*PAD*), as defined in the UML-RT [8] and depicted in Figure 1.

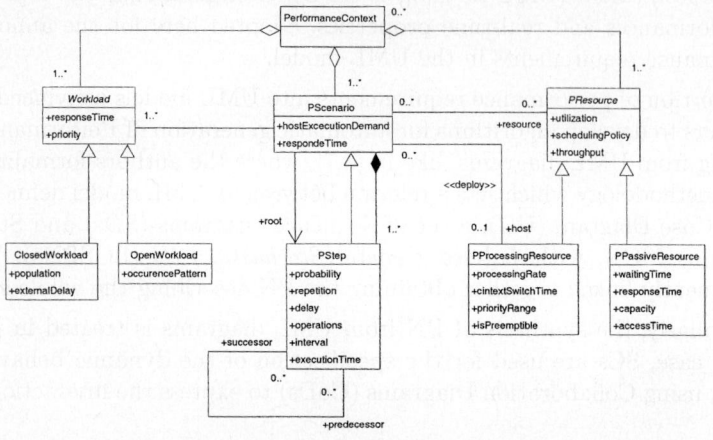

Fig. 1. UML-RT performances model

The PAD is constituted of many entities: a `PerformanceContext` specifies one or more *Scenarios* that are used to explore various dynamic situations involving a specific set of resources. The class `PScenarios` is used for modeling a response path whose end points are externally visible. Each *Scenario* is executed by a job or user class with an applied load intensity, represented by a (Open or Closed) *Workload*. The *Steps* are the elements of the Scenario, joined in a sequence of `predecessor-successor` relationship which may include forks, joins and loops. *Resources* are modeled as servers. *Active Resources* are the usual servers in performance models and have service time. *Passive Resources* are acquired and released and have holding time.

Like suggested from OMG in [8], we refined the PAD into a *Performance Context Model* (PCM), to take into account the properties of a generic performance model. The PCM we defined is depicted in Figure 2, and we propose to use it as an intermediate model between an UML project and the final performance model, whatever formalism is used to analyze the latter.

The structure of PCM (see Figure 2) is similar to that depicted in Figure 1, where the abstract classes have been specialized to contain performance informations.

- The PCM implements the generic concept of step, formally described from the abstract class *VertexStep*, by introducing the classes *DeciderStep*, *ForkStep*, *MergerStep*, *JoinStep*, and *TimedStep*.

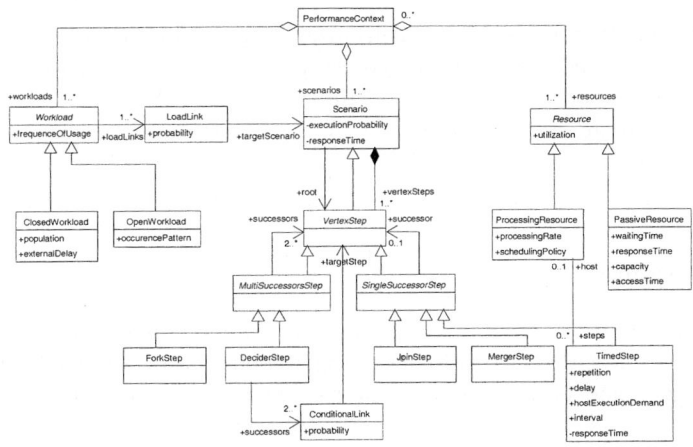

Fig. 2. The Performance Context Model

- The UML-RT associates the stereotype PAcontext to AD, restricting to use only one Scenario into a PerformanceContext. The PCM overrides this limit associating the PAcontext to the overall UML model.
- The UML-RT allies one Workload to each Scenario. Instead the PCM admits the definition of Workloads in the UCs, and it is able to compose them in different way and to link more Scenarios to the same Workload.

In the following, we give a more detailed description of the classes included in the PCM with their roles.

2.1 Performance Context

The role played from this class is to group all the elements necessary to describe the software from the performance analysis point of view.

2.2 Scenario

The role of this class is the same as in the PDA; the only difference is the attribute executionProbability used to model how much a *Scenario* is run. It depends on frequencyOfUsage of Workloads and probability of LoadLink.

Each *Scenario* represents some kind of computation, so that it is constituted of a sequence of elementary steps (the class VertexStep), where the first is located by the association root. We defined two kind of elementary steps to be able to model every kind of computation: MultiSuccessorsStep for modeling branching in computation (eventually parallel) and SingleSuccessorStep for modeling sequential computation.

The ForkStep is used to generate parallel threads. The DeciderStep is useful for representing a choice among different threads like the if-then construct. The choice is probabilistically done by ConditionalLink that pairs a DeciderStep with a VertexStep.

The `JoinStep` is used as synchronization point of concurrent threads, and it has a single successor; the `MergerStep` has a single successor too, but it is executed when just one of the concurrent threads completes. The `ForkStep`, `DeciderStep`, `JoinStep`, and `MergerStep` all express logical conditions on the software evolution so that no time delay is associated with them. The time is taken into account by the `TimedStep` associated to a resource (see section 2.3).

2.3 Resource

The abstract class *Resource* represents some resource used to produce computation. It can be either a real `Processing Resources` or a `Passive Resources`. The former models a computation units offering a service according to a fixed policy (e.g, a CPU, a communication network); the latter models the resources protected by an access mechanism. It may represent either a physical device or a logical protected-access entity.

The common attribute `utilization` returns a measure of the time during which the resource is active, and it must be computed by the performance model.

2.4 Workload

The abstract class *Workload* models how the requests of computation are submitted. When a finite population of user is supposed, the class `ClosedWorkload` has to be used by specifying the number of users (`population`) and their interarrival time (`externalDelay`); otherwise `OpenWorkload` is appropriate by specifying the interarrival time distribution only.

The class `LoadLink` is used to create a correspondence between *Workloads* and *Scenarios*. Since a *Workload* could be associated to more *Scenarios* each one is probabilistic selected by means of the attribute `probability`.

2.5 How to Use the PCM

Following the specifications of UML-RT, the software analyst will be able to use DDs for specifying the resources and UC for describing the workloads; the scenarios described in the UCs will be detailed by using SDs, ADs, and CoDs with the only restriction that each scenario can be specified by means of a single kind of diagram. According to this kind of project specification two levels of description are located (see Figure 3): the *Specification Level* including all the DDs and UCs, and the *Base Level* containing the SDs, ADs, and CoDs. Since all the scenarios are specified from the diagrams contained into the *Base Level*, these are used to translate performance specifications into a PCM, then employed for defining the final performance model. This approach differs from those presented up to now, where a particular mapping for each kind of UML diagram is required towards the performance model.

The overall process, is synthesized into two steps: 1) UML Source Model → PCM , 2) PCM → Performance Model During step 1) all the information about the software project will be specified in a UML model in a formal way, including the performance annotations; a solvable performance model will be produced by step 2).

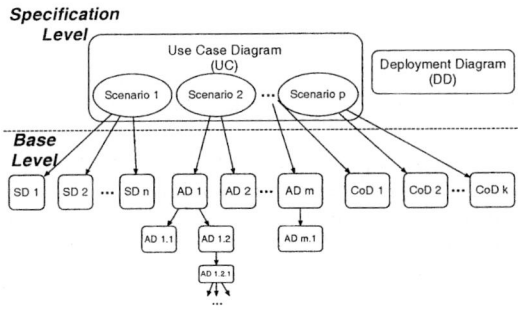

Fig. 3. Schematic view of *UMLBLM* (UML Bi-Level Methodology)

3 Mapping from UML to PCM

The previous section describes the classes that constitute the PCM and the relations existing among them. What we want now to establish is the correspondence between the UML domain and these classes, specifying indirectly the semantics of the subset of UML elements through which it is possible to model a PVM Software Analysis.

Consider the whole UML model represented by the *Performance Context*:

	Model
PCM	Performance Context
Stp	«PAContext»

Action State, Message, Stimulus, SubactivityState of AD, SD or CoD are associated to a PCM *TimedStep*, implemented by a *PAstep* stereotype (Stp), as described in the following table:

	Action State, Message, Stimulus, SubactivityState			
PCM	TimedStep			
Stp	«PAstep»			
Tag	Tag Name PCM Attribute		Type	Mult
	PAdemand ↔ TimedStep::hostExecutionDemand		PAperfValue	[0..*]
	PArep ↔ TimedStep::repetition		Integer	[0..1]
	PAinterval ↔ TimedStep::interval		PAperfValue	[0..1]
	PAdelay ↔ TimedStep::delay		PAperfValue	[0..*]
	PArespTime ↔ TimedStep::responseTime		PAperfValue	[0..1]
	PAexecHost ↔ TimedStep::host		String	[0..1]

The lower part of this table shows the set of tags related to the stereotype, which permits to specify the associated PCM attributes, the type of tag and its multiplicity (see [8] for details).

PCM *MergerStep* and *DeciderStep* represent a Branch Pseudostate UML, according to the constraints specified in tables:

Branch Pseudostate	
PCM element	MergerStep, DeciderStep
Constraints	*MergerStep*: Input Transition has to be greater than one and the output Transition has to be unique. *DeciderStep*: Input Transition has to be unique and the output Transition has to be greater than one. The outgoing Transition is a *Conditional Links*.

Strictly related to the previous tables is the following one regarding the *Conditional Link*:

Transition				
PCM element	ConditionalLink			
Tag	Tag Name	PCM Attribute	Type	Mult.
	PAprob ↔ ConditionalLink::probability		Real	[0..1]
Constraints	The Transition has to be an outgoing one from a Branch pseudostate representing a *DeciderStep*. The sum of all PAprob outgoing from the same *DeciderStep* has to be equal to one.			

In the same manner the following tables describe the rules which allow to execute the mapping from the UML domain toward the remaining PCM elements:

Join Pseudostate	
PCM element	JoinStep

Fork Pseudostate	
PCM element	ForkStep

Node				
PCM	Processing Resource			
Stp	≪PAhost≫			
Tag	Tag Name	PCM Attribute	Type	Mult.
	PAutilization ↔ Resource::utilization		Real	[0..1]
	PArate ↔ ProcessingResource::processingRate		Real	[0..1]
	PAschdPolicy ↔ ProcessingResource::schedulingPolicy		Enumeration	[0..1]

Actor				
PCM	Closed and Open Workload			
Stp	≪PAclosedLoad≫, ≪PAopenLoad≫			
Tag	Tag Name PCM Attribute		Type	Mult.
	PAfreqOfUsage ↔ Workload::frequencyOfUsage		Real	[0..1]
	PApopulation ↔ ClosedWorkload::population		Integer	[0..1]
	PAextDelay ↔ ClosedWorkload::externalDelay		PAperfValue	[0..1]
	PAoccurrence ↔ OpenWorkload::occurencePattern		RTarrivalPattern	[0..1]

Association				
PCM element	LoadLink			
Tag	Tag Name PCM Attribute		Type	Mult.
	PAprob ↔ LoadLink::probability		Real	[0..1]
Constraints	The Association has to be an outgoing one from an Actor representing a Workload. The sum of all PAprobs outgoing from the same Workload have to be equal to one.			

4 A Case Study: Web Video Application

To better clarify the proposed approach, in this section we present a case study delivered from the example reported in the OMG specifics: the video Web application described in [1]. It regards a *video streaming* application on the Web, where a user selects a movie by connecting to the *Web server*.

The DD of Figure 4 (b) represents the resources dislocation. The performance parameters are included into the diagrams by UML-RT annotations. The UC (see Figure 4 (a)) shows the workload applied to the system, characterized by a fixed number of users and an exponentially distributed interarrival time.

The scenario contained in the UC is detailed in the AD of Figure 4 (c), where a client requests a video to a remote *Web server*; the Web server selects the opportune *video server* that initializes the client's video player and starts the video streaming. At the same time, the Web server sends the client a confirmation message. Once the streaming is over the video server closes the application. From this UML model, by applying the rules described in section 3, it is possible to obtain the PCM of Figure 5.

5 Conclusions and Future Work

In this paper, we proposed a methodology that splits translation from UML to performances domains into two phases, interposing an intermediate step through a Performance Context Model (PCM). Such translation represents the strength of the proposed methodology.

The proposed approach represents the starting point of an intense research work based on SPE and UML design. We have already started the implementation of a submapping from PCM toward a *Petri Net* model. This also includes

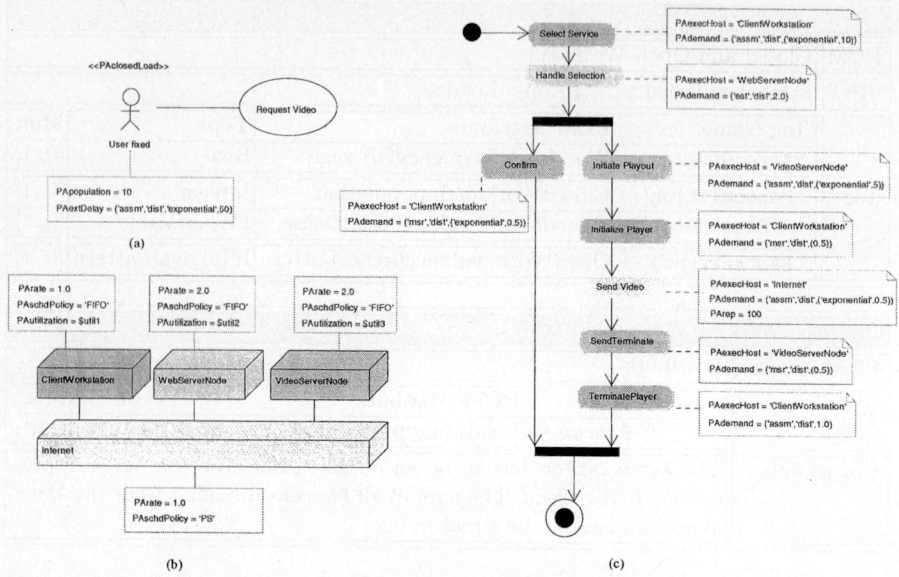

Fig. 4. (a) Use Case Diagram, (b) Deployment Diagram, and (c) Activity Diagram describing the Web-based video application

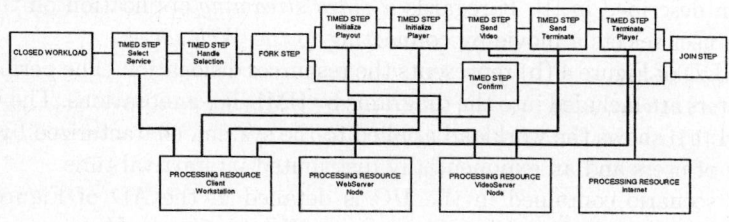

Fig. 5. PCM rappresenting the Web-based video application

the construction of a software performance design toolkit based on the WebSPN Petri Nets tool [4,13] and the UML CASE tool ArgoUML [15], through a specific plug-in. Another development concerns the formalization of a mapping among the behavioral diagrams used in UML-RT: SDs, ADs and CoD.

References

1. Balsamo, S., Marzolla, M.: A Simulation-Based Approach to Software Performance Modeling. In: European Software Engineering Conference and ACM SIGSOFT Symposium on the Foundations of Software Engineering (ESEC/FSE 2003), Helsinki, Finland. ACM SIGSOFT Software Engineering Notes **28** (2003) 363–366
2. Bernardi, S.: Building Stochastic Petri Net Models for the Verification of Complex Software Systems. Ph.D. thesis, Universitá di Torino, Italy. (2003)
3. Bondavalli, A., Majzik, I., Mura, I.: Automatic Dependability Analysis for Supporting Design Decisions in UML. In: Proceedings of the 4th IEEE International Symposium on High-Assurance Systems Engineering, Washington, D.C. IEEE (1999) 64–71
4. Horváth, A., Puliafito, A., Scarpa, M., Telek, M., Tomarchio, O.: Design and Evaluation of a Web-Based Non-Markovian Stochastic Petri Net Tool. In: Proceedings of the 13th International Symposium on Computer and Information Sciences (ISCIS'98), Antalya, Turkey. IOS/Ohmsha (1998) 101–109
5. Huszerl, G., Mjzik, I., Pataricza, A., Kosmidis, K., Chin, M.D.: Quantitative Analysis of UML Statechart Models of Dependable Systems. The Computer Journal **45** (2002) 260–277
6. Lindemann, C., Thümmler, A., Klemm, A., Lohmann, M., Waldhorst, O.P.: Performance Analysis of Time-Enhanced UML Diagrams Based on Stochastic Processes. In: Proceedings of the 3rd International Workshop on Software and Performance (WOSP 2002), Rome, Italy. ACM (2002) 25–34
7. Merseguer, J.: Software Performance Engineering Based on UML and Petri Nets. PhD thesis, University of Zaragoza, Spain. (2003)
8. Object Management Group. UML Profile for Schedulability, Performance, and Time Specification. OMG, Final Adopted Specification edn. (2002)
9. Object Management Group. UML Specification v. 1.5. OMG, 1.5 edn. (2003)
10. Petriu, D.C., Shen, H.: Applying the UML Performance Profile: Graph Grammar-Based Derivation of LQN Models from UML Specifications. In: Proceedings of the 12th International Conference on Computer Performance Evaluation, Modelling Techniques and Tools (TOOLS 2002), London, UK. Lecture Notes in Computer Science, Vol. 2324. Springer (2002) 159–177
11. Pooley, R., King, P.J.B.: The Unified Modeling Language and Performance Engineering. In: Proceedings of IEE - Software, Vol. 146. (1999) 2–10
12. Saldhana, J.A., Shatz, S.M., Hu, Z.: Formalization of Object Behavior and Interactions from UML Models. International Journal of Software Engineering and Knowledge Engineering **11** (2001) 643–673
13. Scarpa, M., Distefano, S., Puliafito, A.: A Parallel Approach for the Solution of Non-Markovian Petri Nets. In: Dongarra, J., Laforenza, D., Orlando, S. (eds.): Proceedings of the 10th European PVM/MPI Users' Group Meeting (Euro PVM/MPI 2003), Venice, Italy. Lecture Notes in Computer Science, Vol. 2840. Springer (2003) 196–203
14. Smith, C.U.: Performance Engineering of Software Systems. Addison-Wesley Longman, Boston (1990)
15. Tigris. ArgoUML. http://argouml.tigris.org/
16. Xu, Z., Lehmann, A.: Automated Generation of Queuing Network Model from UML-Based Software Models with Performance Annotations. Technical report 2002-06, Universität der Bundeswehr München. (2002)

Stubborn Sets for Priority Nets

Kimmo Varpaaniemi

Helsinki University of Technology
Laboratory for Theoretical Computer Science
P.O. Box 5400, FIN-02015 HUT, Espoo, Finland
kimmo.varpaaniemi@hut.fi

Abstract. Partial order methods, such as the stubborn set method and the priority method, reduce verification effort by exploiting irrelevant orders of events. We show how the stubborn set method can be applied to priority nets. By applicability we mean that for a given priority net, the stubborn set method constructs a reduced reachability graph that sufficiently represents the full reachability graph of the priority net. This work can also be considered as a combination of the stubborn set method and the priority method, to be used in "complete or moderated incomplete" verification when the original models are unprioritised nets.

1 Introduction

Partial order methods reduce verification effort by exploiting irrelevant orders of events. We consider *RGPOR* (*reachability graph partial order reduction*) methods, i.e. those partial order methods that proceed by constructing or traversing a *reduced reachability graph* at least until an observation of some fulfilled termination condition. RGPOR methods have been designed e.g. for PROMELA [15], SDL [18, 28, 32], CFSMs [16, 19, 22], multi-threaded software [7, 10, 30], process algebras [12, 25, 37], real-time formalisms [2, 3, 6, 20, 21, 23, 29, 40, 41], and for various classes of Petri nets [1, 9, 17, 20, 26, 29, 33, 36, 38, 40, 41]. Combinatorial explosion in model checking has been alleviated by RGPOR methods tailored e.g. for LTL [11, 24, 35, 39], CTL [8, 27], and for CTL* [8].

The *stubborn set method* [26, 27, 29, 33–37, 39] and the *priority method* [1, 38] are examples of RGPOR methods. We show how the stubborn set method can be applied to *priority nets* [4, 13]. By applicability we mean that for a given priority net, the stubborn set method constructs a reduced reachability graph that sufficiently represents the full reachability graph of the priority net.

If, as usual (though not necessary [31]) in the priority method, the original model is an unprioritised net, the question remains how well the full reachability graph of the priority net represents the full reachability graph of the original net. There are priority definition schemes [1] that ensure sufficient representation in that respect, but we do not consider such schemes in this paper. Instead, we promote the idea of error detection by "moderated incomplete" verification: the role of the stubborn set method is exactly as said above, but the user is allowed to define intentionally restrictive priorities.

2   Priority Nets

We use the notation "iff" for "if and only if", $\emptyset$ for the empty set, Z for the set of integer numbers, and N for $\{i \in Z \mid i \geq 0\}$. For any $a \in N$, $N_{<a} = \{i \in N \mid i < a\}$. For any real number x, $\lceil x \rceil$ is the least integer number that is greater than or equal to x. For any sets X and Y, for any $R \subseteq X \times Y$ and for any $x \in X$, $|X|$ is the cardinality of X, 2^X is the set of subsets of X, $[X \to Y]$ is the set of (total) functions from X to Y, $R^{-1} = \{\langle y, x\rangle \mid \langle x, y\rangle \in R\}$, and $R(x) = \{y \in Y \mid \langle x, y\rangle \in R\}$. For any alphabet X, ε is the empty word, and X^* is the set of finite words over X. For any finite word σ, $|\sigma|$ is the length of σ, whereas for any $i \in N_{<|\sigma|}$, $\sigma(i)$ is the $(i+1)^{\text{th}}$ letter in σ. A finite word δ is a permutation of a finite word σ iff every letter of σ occurs in δ exactly as many times as in σ, and every letter of δ occurs in σ exactly as many times as in δ.

Definition 1. *A priority net is a quintuple $\langle S, T, W, \rho, M_0\rangle$ such that S is the set of places, T is the set of transitions, $S \cap T = \emptyset$, $W \in [((S \times T) \cup (T \times S)) \to N]$ is the flow, $\rho \subseteq T \times T$ is the set of priorities, and $M_0 \in [S \to N]$ is the initial marking. (The condition "$\rho \subseteq T \times T$" is the only "constraint" on ρ in this paper.) We use the term finite transition sequences for the elements of T^* and the term markings for the elements of $[S \to N]$. The net is a finite net iff $S \cup T$ is finite. If $t \in T$, then the set of input places of t is $^\bullet t = \{s \in S \mid W(s,t) > 0\}$, and the set of output places of t is $t^\bullet = \{s \in S \mid W(t,s) > 0\}$. If $s \in S$, then the set of input transitions of s is $^\bullet s = \{t \in T \mid W(t,s) > 0\}$, and the set of output transitions of s is $s^\bullet = \{t \in T \mid W(s,t) > 0\}$.* □

In our figures, places are ovals, transitions are rectangles, and the number of black dots inside the oval of s is equal to $M_0(s)$. An *ordinary arc*, i.e. an arrow, is drawn from an element x to an element y iff x is an input element of y. Then $W(x, y)$ is called the *weight* of the arc. The weight is shown iff it is not 1. A definitely weightless *priority arc*, i.e. a variant of an arrow where a small circle denotes the head, is drawn from a transition u to a transition t iff $u \in \rho(t)$.

Definition 2. *Let $\langle S, T, W, \rho, M_0\rangle$ be a priority net. A transition t is semienabled at a marking M iff $\forall s \in S : M(s) \geq W(s,t)$. The set of transitions semienabled at a marking M is denoted by $\alpha(M)$. A transition t is enabled at a marking M iff $t \in \alpha(M)$ and $\alpha(M) \cap \rho(t) = \emptyset$. The set of transitions enabled at a marking M is denoted by $\beta(M)$. A marking M is terminal iff $\beta(M) = \emptyset$. (It is possible to construct examples where $\beta(M) = \emptyset \neq \alpha(M)$.) Let $f \in [[S \to N] \to (2^T)]$. A finite transition sequence, σ, f-leads from a marking M_1 to a marking M_2 iff $M_1 [\sigma\rangle_f M_2$, according to the recursive definition*
$\forall M \in [S \to N] : \forall M' \in [S \to N] : \forall t \in T : \forall \delta \in T^* :$
$(M [\varepsilon\rangle_f M' \Leftrightarrow M' = M) \wedge$
$(M [t\rangle_f M' \Leftrightarrow (t \in \beta(M) \cap f(M) \wedge \forall s \in S : M'(s) = M(s) + W(t,s) - W(s,t))) \wedge$
$(M [t\delta\rangle_f M' \Leftrightarrow (\exists M'' \in [S \to N] : M [t\rangle_f M'' \wedge M'' [\delta\rangle_f M'))$.
A finite transition sequence σ is f-enabled at a marking M ($M [\sigma\rangle_f$ for short) iff $\exists M' \in [S \to N] : M [\sigma\rangle_f M'$. A marking M' is f-reachable from a marking M iff some finite transition sequence f-leads from M to M'. A marking M' is

an f-reachable marking *iff* M' *is f-reachable from* M_0. *The f-reachability graph is* $\langle V, A \rangle$ *such that the set V of vertices is the set of f-reachable markings, and the set A of edges is* $\{\langle M, t, M' \rangle \mid M \in V \wedge t \in T \wedge M' \in V \wedge M\,[t\rangle_f\,M'\}$. *For any marking M and for any* $\sigma \in T^*$, $\gamma(M, \sigma)$ *denotes the function from S to Z such that* $\forall s \in S : \gamma(M, \sigma)(s) = M(s) + \sum_{i=0}^{|\sigma|-1} (W(\sigma(i), s) - W(s, \sigma(i)))$. □

From now on, we use a plain ")" instead of "$\rangle_\beta$", and as far as the notions of Definition 2 are concerned, we replace "β-xxx" by "xxx" (where xxx is any word), with the exception that the β-reachability graph of the net is called the *full reachability graph* of the net. When f is clear from the context or is implicitly assumed to exist and be of a kind that is clear from the context, then the f-reachability graph of the net is called the *reduced reachability graph* of the net.

Lemma 1. *Let* $\langle S, T, W, \rho, M_0 \rangle$ *be a priority net. Let* $M \in [S \to N]$, $M' \in [S \to N]$ *and* $\sigma \in T^*$ *be such that* $M\,[\sigma\rangle\,M'$. *Then* $M' = \gamma(M, \sigma)$.

Proof. The result is essentially built in Definition 2. □

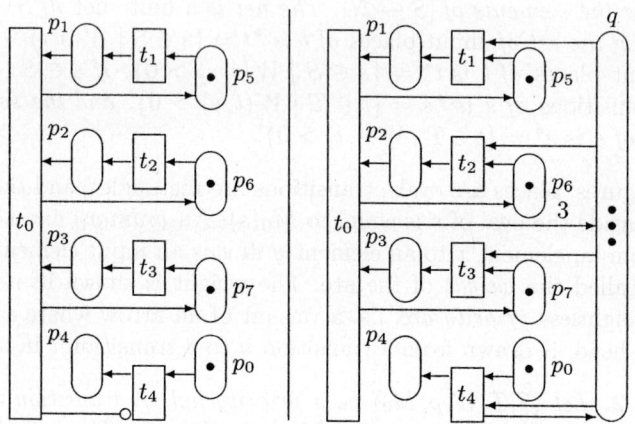

Fig. 1. The full reachability graphs of these two nets are "perfectly isomorphic"

The considerations in [4, 5, 13] can be used for designing algorithms that for a given finite priority net construct a "behaviourally close enough" *inhibitor net* or, when bounds are known for the multiplicities in the places, a *place/transition net*. It is actually quite tempting to use the recognisably low-degree polynomial time "known bounds" transformations in [4] as an excuse for not directly supporting priorities in an analysis algorithm. Let us look at Figure 1 that displays two priority nets and demonstrates the technique presented by [4]. The rightmost net simulates the leftmost net by using a complement counter, the place q, for the input places of t_0, and is effectively a place/transition net by not having any "special arc". Let $J_\ell = \langle S_\ell, T, W_\ell, \rho, M_\ell \rangle$ be the leftmost net with the full reachability graph $G_\ell = \langle V_\ell, A_\ell \rangle$, and let $J_r = \langle S_\ell \cup \{q\}, T, W_r, \emptyset, M_r \rangle$ be the rightmost net with the full reachability graph $G_r = \langle V_r, A_r \rangle$. It is straightforward to show that G_ℓ and G_r are "perfectly isomorphic", i.e. there is a bijection g from V_ℓ to V_r such that $\{\langle g(M), t, g(M') \rangle \mid \langle M, t, M' \rangle \in A_\ell\} = A_r$ and $g(M_\ell) = M_r$.

3 Stubborn Sets

Since the introduction of the term "stubborn set" [33], dynamic stubbornness has at least implicitly been used as an interface between requirements and implementations.

Definition 3. *Let $\langle S, T, W, \rho, M_0 \rangle$ be a priority net. Let M be a marking and $L \subseteq T$. L fulfils the principle D1 at M iff*
$\forall t \in L : \forall \sigma \in (T \setminus L)^* : M [\sigma t\rangle \Rightarrow M [t\sigma\rangle$. *$L$ fulfils the principle D2 at M iff*
$\exists \tau \in L \cap \beta(M) : \forall \sigma \in (T \setminus L)^* : M [\sigma\rangle \Rightarrow M [\sigma\tau\rangle$. *$L$ is dynamically stubborn at M iff L fulfils both D1 and D2 at M. A function $f \in [[S \to N] \to (2^T)]$ is a dynamically stubborn function iff for each nonterminal marking M', $f(M')$ is dynamically stubborn at M'.* □

Let us look at the nets in Figure 1 again. The sets fulfilling Dn ($n \in \{1, 2\}$) at M_ℓ in the context of J_ℓ are the same as at M_r in the context of J_r because, as explained above, the full reachability graphs are "perfectly isomorphic". In the following, M_0 means either M_ℓ in the context of J_ℓ or M_r in the context of J_r. The set $\{t_1\}$ does not fulfil D1 at M_0 since $t_2 t_3 t_4 t_1$ is enabled but $t_1 t_2 t_3 t_4$ is not enabled. The disabledness of $t_1 t_2 t_3 t_4$ also implies that $\{t_4\}$ does not fulfil D2 at M_0. The smallest dynamically stubborn sets at M_0 are $\{t_1, t_2\}$, $\{t_1, t_3\}$, $\{t_1, t_4\}$, $\{t_2, t_3\}$, $\{t_2, t_4\}$, and $\{t_3, t_4\}$. Let us then consider the net $J_u = \langle S_\ell, T, W_\ell, \emptyset, M_\ell \rangle$, i.e. the net obtained simply by removing the only priority arc of J_ℓ. The net J_u allows more behaviours but also smaller dynamically stubborn sets than J_ℓ: the smallest dynamically stubborn sets at M_ℓ in the context of J_u are $\{t_1\}$, $\{t_2\}$, $\{t_3\}$, and $\{t_4\}$. This example suggests that "blind" application of the stubborn set method to priority nets is not necessarily the most efficient way to combine the stubborn set method with the priority method.

Proposition 1. *Let $\langle S, T, W, \rho, M_0 \rangle$ be a priority net. Let f be a dynamically stubborn function of the net. Let M be a marking, M_d a terminal marking and σ a finite transition sequence such that $M [\sigma\rangle M_d$. Then there is some finite transition sequence δ such that $M [\delta\rangle_f M_d$ and δ is a permutation of σ.*

Proof. We use induction on the length of the sequence. If $\sigma = \varepsilon$, the claim holds with $\delta = \varepsilon$. We assume inductively that the claim holds when restricted to sequences of length n. Let σ be of length $n + 1$. If no member of $f(M)$ occurs in σ, then D2 forces $\sigma\tau$ to be enabled for some $\tau \in f(M)$, which is contradictory to the fact that M_d is terminal. So, some member of $f(M)$ must occur in σ. Let $M' \in [S \to N]$, $t \in f(M)$, $\sigma' \in (T \setminus f(M))^*$, and $\sigma'' \in T^*$ be such that $\sigma = \sigma' t \sigma''$ and $M [\sigma' t\rangle M'$. D1 and Lemma 1 now imply that $M [t\sigma'\rangle M'$, and consequently,

$M\,[t\sigma'\sigma''\rangle\,M_d$. Let $M'' \in [S \to N]$ be such that $M\,[t\rangle\,M''$. Then $M''\,[\sigma'\sigma''\rangle\,M_d$. By the induction hypothesis, there is some $\delta' \in T^*$ such that $M'\,[\delta'\rangle_f\,M_d$ and δ' is a permutation of $\sigma'\sigma''$. It immediately follows that $M\,[t\delta'\rangle_f\,M_d$ and $t\delta'$ is a permutation of σ. □

The proof of Proposition 1 resembles the proof of Theorem 2.4 of [33]. As a matter of fact, for any "sufficiently abstract" result concerning dynamically stubborn sets in place/transition nets, Lemma 1 ensures that an analogous result holds in the case of priority nets. So, a quick look at e.g. [39] reveals that Proposition 1 is just "the top of the iceberg".

Definition 4. Let $\langle S, T, W, \rho, M_0 \rangle$ be a priority net. The function E_1 from $[S \to N] \times S$ to 2^T, the functions E_2 and E_3 from $[S \to N] \times T \times S$ to 2^T, and the function E_4 from S to 2^T are defined as follows. Let $M \in [S \to N]$, $t \in T$, and $s \in S$. Then
$E_1(M,s) = \{u \in {}^\bullet s \mid M(s) \geq W(s,u) \wedge W(u,s) > W(s,u)\}$,
$E_2(M,t,s) = E_4(s) \cup \{u \in s^\bullet \mid W(s,t) > W(t,s) \wedge \gamma(M,t)(s) < W(s,u)\}$,
$E_3(M,t,s) = E_1(M,s) \cup \{u \in {}^\bullet s \mid M(s) \geq W(s,u) \wedge W(u,s) > W(t,s)\}$, and
$E_4(s) = \{u \in s^\bullet \mid W(s,u) > W(u,s)\}$. □

We use the functions E_1, E_2, E_3 and E_4 (cf. [39]) for defining "algorithmically feasible" stubbornness. Every hypothetical execution of a transition of $E_1(M,s)$ increases the contents of s, whereas every hypothetical execution a transition of $E_4(s)$ decreases the contents of s. Every transition in $E_3(M,t,s) \setminus E_1(M,s)$ has a greater output flow to s than t has. None of the transitions in $E_3(M,t,s)$ (or in its subset $E_1(M,s)$) is disabled by s at M. For each $u \in E_2(M,t,s) \setminus E_4(s)$, an execution of t at M either makes or keeps u disabled by s. (The condition "$W(s,t) > W(t,s)$" in the expression of E_2 ensures that if $W(s,t) \leq W(t,s)$, then $E_2(M,t,s) = E_4(s)$.)

Definition 5. Let $\langle S,T,W,\rho,M_0 \rangle$ be a priority net. Let M be a marking and $L \subseteq T$. A transition d is E_1-activation-closed by L at M iff
$\exists s \in {}^\bullet d:\ M(s) < W(s,d) \wedge E_1(M,s) \subseteq L$.
A transition d is E_4-activation-closed by L at M iff
$\exists v \in \alpha(M) \cap \rho(d): \forall q \in {}^\bullet v:\ E_4(q) \subseteq L$.
The set L is feasibly semistubborn at M iff each t in $L \cap \beta(M)$ satisfies
$(\forall s \in {}^\bullet t: W(s,t) \leq W(t,s) \vee E_2(M,t,s) \subseteq L \vee E_3(M,t,s) \subseteq L) \wedge$
$(\forall x \in t^\bullet: W(x,t) \geq W(t,x) \vee$
$\quad (\forall v \in x^\bullet: \rho^{-1}(v) \subseteq L \vee$
$\quad\quad (\exists q \in {}^\bullet v: \gamma(M,t)(q) < W(q,v) \wedge E_1(\gamma(M,t),q) \subseteq L)))$
and each d in $L \setminus \beta(M)$ is E_1-activation-closed by L at M or E_4-activation-closed by L at M. A transition τ is a key transition of L at M iff
$\tau \in L \cap \beta(M) \wedge (\forall s \in {}^\bullet \tau: E_4(s) \subseteq L) \wedge$
$(\forall v \in \rho(\tau): \exists q \in {}^\bullet v: M(q) < W(q,v) \wedge E_1(M,q) \subseteq L)$.
The set L is feasibly stubborn at M iff L is feasibly semistubborn at M and some transition is a key transition of L at M. □

Proposition 2. *For any priority net and for any nonterminal marking, the set of all transitions is feasibly stubborn at the marking.*

Proof. The result can be shown by mechanically referring to the definitions. □

In the case $\rho = \emptyset$, feasible stubbornness coincides with the stubbornness defined for place/transition nets in [39]. A feasibly stubborn set L at a marking M is *inclusion minimal w.r.t. enabled transitions* iff for each feasibly stubborn set L' at M, $L' \cap \beta(M) \subseteq L \cap \beta(M) \Rightarrow L' \cap \beta(M) = L \cap \beta(M)$. It is straightforward to adapt the *and/or-graph-based deletion algorithm* [34, 39] to Definition 5 in such a way that for a given finite priority net and for a given nonterminal marking M, the algorithm computes a set that is feasibly stubborn at M and inclusion minimal w.r.t. enabled transitions, in low-degree polynomial time w.r.t. $|S| + |T| + \lceil \log_2 \max(\{1\} \cup \{W(i,j) \mid \langle i,j \rangle \in (S \times T) \cup (T \times S)\} \cup \{M(s) \mid s \in S\}) \rceil$.

Let us have yet another look at the nets in Figure 1. In the context of J_ℓ, every dynamically stubborn set at M_ℓ happens to be feasibly stubborn at M_ℓ. In the context of J_r, the feasibly stubborn sets at M_r are $\{t_1, t_2, t_3\}$, $\{t_0, t_1, t_2, t_3\}$, $\{t_1, t_2, t_3, t_4\}$, and $\{t_0, t_1, t_2, t_3, t_4\}$. So, despite of being equivalent w.r.t. dynamically stubborn sets at the initial markings, J_ℓ and J_r effectively differ from each other w.r.t. feasibly stubborn sets at the initial markings. This example suggests that it may be better to tailor stubborn set computation algorithms for priority nets than to operate on unprioritised nets that simulate priority nets. We devote the rest of this section to showing that feasibly stubborn sets are dynamically stubborn. Without such a result, it would not necessarily make much sense to compute feasibly stubborn sets.

Lemma 2. *Let $\langle S, T, W, \rho, M_0 \rangle$ be a priority net. Let M and M' be markings, $L \subseteq T$ and $u \in T \setminus L$ in such a way that $M[u\rangle M'$. Let τ be a key transition of L at M. Then τ is a key transition of L at M'.*

Proof. (i) Let $s \in {}^\bullet\tau$. From the definition of key transitions it follows that u is not in $E_4(s)$. Consequently, $M'(s) \geq M(s)$. (ii) Let $v \in \rho(\tau)$ and $q \in {}^\bullet v$ be such that $M(q) < W(q,v)$ and $E_1(M,q) \subseteq L$. Clearly, u is not in $E_1(M,q)$. Consequently, $M'(q) \leq M(q)$. The definition of E_1 now implies that $E_1(M',q) \subseteq E_1(M,q)$. So, we have $M'(q) < W(q,v)$ and $E_1(M',q) \subseteq L$. (iii) Since $\tau \in L \cap \beta(M)$ and the above considerations hold regardless of s and v, we conclude that τ is in $L \cap \beta(M')$ and also satisfies the other criteria of a key transition of L at M'. □

Lemma 3. *Let $\langle S, T, W, \rho, M_0 \rangle$ be a priority net. Let M be a marking and $L \subseteq T$ such that some transition is a key transition of L at M. Then L fulfils D2 at M.*

Proof. The result follows from Lemma 2 by naive induction. □

Lemma 4. *Let $\langle S, T, W, \rho, M_0 \rangle$ be a priority net. Let M and M' be markings, $L \subseteq T$ and $u \in T \setminus L$ in such a way that $M[u\rangle M'$. Let $k \in \{1,4\}$ and $d \in T$ be such that d is E_k-activation-closed by L at M. Then d is E_k-activation-closed by L at M'.*

Proof. Case $k = 1$: Let $s \in {}^\bullet d$ be such that $M(s) < W(s,d)$ and $E_1(M,s) \subseteq L$. We observe that u is not in $E_1(M,s)$. Consequently, $M'(s) \leq M(s)$. The definition of E_1 now implies that $E_1(M',s) \subseteq E_1(M,s)$. So, we have $M'(s) < W(s,d)$ and $E_1(M',s) \subseteq L$.

Case $k = 4$: Let $v \in \alpha(M) \cap \rho(d)$ and $q \in {}^\bullet v$. We observe that u is not in $E_4(q)$. Consequently, $M'(q) \geq M(q)$. Since this holds regardless of q, we conclude that $v \in \alpha(M')$. □

Lemma 5. *Let $\langle S, T, W, \rho, M_0 \rangle$ be a priority net. Let M be a marking and $L \subseteq T$ such that L is feasibly semistubborn at M. Then L fulfils D1 at M.*

Proof. For any $\delta \in T^*$ and for any $i \in N_{<|\delta|+1}$, let $\psi_{\delta,i}$ denote the prefix of δ that has the length i.

Let $t \in L$ and σ in $(T \setminus L)^*$ be such that $M[\sigma t\rangle$. If t were disabled at M, then Lemma 4 and naive induction suffice for showing that t is disabled at $\gamma(M, \sigma)$. So, t must be enabled at M. Our goal is to show that for each $i \in N_{<|\sigma|+1}$, $M[t\psi_{\sigma,i}\rangle$. We use induction on i. (This induction is strictly separate from the above mentioned "naive induction".) The case $i = 0$ has already been handled. Our induction hypothesis is that for $j \in N_{<|\sigma|}$, $M[t\psi_{\sigma,j}\rangle$. Let us proceed to the case $i = j + 1$. Let $M_1 = \gamma(M, \psi_{\sigma,j})$ and $M_2 = \gamma(M, t\psi_{\sigma,j})$. By the definition of γ, we know that $\forall s \in S : M_2(s) = M_1(s) + W(t,s) - W(s,t)$. On the other hand, $\sigma(j) \in (T \setminus L) \cap \beta(M_1)$ and $\psi_{\sigma,j+1} = \psi_{\sigma,j}\sigma(j)$.

Let $v \in \rho(\sigma(j))$. Let us first consider the case $\exists x \in {}^\bullet v : W(x,t) < W(t,x)$. The definition of feasible semistubbornness now implies that v is E_1-activation-closed by L at $\gamma(M,t)$. Lemma 4 and (yet another strictly separate) naive induction then suffice for showing that v is E_1-activation-closed by L at M_2. Consequently, $\alpha(M_2) \cap \{v\} = \emptyset$.

Let us then consider the case $\forall x \in {}^\bullet v : W(x,t) \geq W(t,x)$. Then $\forall x \in {}^\bullet v : M_2(x) \leq M_1(x)$. Consequently, $\alpha(M_2) \cap \{v\} \subseteq \alpha(M_1) \cap \{v\}$. Since $\sigma(j) \in \beta(M_1)$ and $v \in \rho(\sigma(j))$, we must have $\alpha(M_1) \cap \{v\} = \emptyset$. Consequently, $\alpha(M_2) \cap \{v\} = \emptyset$.

Let $z \in {}^\bullet\sigma(j)$. If $W(z,t) \leq W(t,z)$, then $M_2(z) \geq M_1(z) \geq W(z,\sigma(j))$. So, let $W(z,t) > W(t,z)$. Let us first consider the case $E_2(M,t,z) \subseteq L$. Now $\sigma(j) \in T \setminus E_2(M,t,z)$, and the definition of E_2 ensures that $\gamma(M,t)(z) \geq W(z,\sigma(j))$. Since $E_4(z) \subseteq E_2(M,t,z)$, we know that for each $h \in N_{<|\sigma|}$, $\kappa(\sigma,h) \in T \setminus E_4(z)$. The definition of E_4 now ensures that for each $h \in N_{<|\sigma|}$, $\gamma(M, t\psi_{\sigma,h+1})(z) \geq \gamma(M, t\psi_{\sigma,h})(z)$. This implies that $M_2(z) \geq \gamma(M,t)(z)$. Consequently, $M_2(z) \geq W(z,\sigma(j))$.

Let us then consider the case $E_3(M,t,z) \subseteq L$. Since $E_1(M,z) \subseteq E_3(M,t,z)$, we know that for each $h \in N_{<|\sigma|}$, $\sigma(h) \in T \setminus E_1(M,z)$. Let m be the least number in $N_{<|\sigma|}$ for which $M(z) < W(z, \sigma(m))$. The definition of E_1 ensures that for each $h \in N_{<m}$, $\gamma(M, \psi_{\sigma,h+1})(z) \leq \gamma(M, \psi_{\sigma,h})(z)$. Consequently, $\gamma(M, \psi_{\sigma,m})(z) < W(z,\sigma(m))$, which implies that $\psi_{\sigma,m+1}$ is not enabled at M which in turn is a contradiction with the enabledness of σ at M. So, it must be the case that for each $h \in N_{<|\sigma|}$, $M(z) \geq W(z, \sigma(h))$. Using the definition of E_1 again, we see that for each $h \in N_{<|\sigma|}$, $\gamma(M, \psi_{\sigma,h+1})(z) \leq \gamma(M, \psi_{\sigma,h})(z)$. Since $M[\sigma t\rangle$, we conclude that $\gamma(M_1, \sigma(j))(z) \geq \gamma(M, \sigma)(z) \geq W(z,t)$. Since $\sigma(j) \in T \setminus E_3(M,t,z)$ and $M(z) \geq W(z, \sigma(j))$, the definition of E_3 ensures that $W(t,z) \geq W(\sigma(j), z)$. So, $M_2(z) = M_1(z) + W(t,z) - W(z,t) = \gamma(M_1, \sigma(j))(z) + W(z, \sigma(j)) - W(\sigma(j), z) + W(t,z) - W(z,t) \geq W(z, \sigma(j)) - W(\sigma(j), z) + W(t,z) \geq W(z, \sigma(j))$.

Since the above considerations hold regardless of v and z, we conclude that $\alpha(M_2) \cap \rho(\sigma(j)) = \emptyset$ and $\sigma(j) \in \alpha(M_2)$. So, $\sigma(j) \in \beta(M_2)$, which means completion of the induction step. □

The considerations on z in the proof of Lemma 5 are similar to the proof of Theorem 2.2 of [33].

Proposition 3. *Let $\langle S, T, W, \rho, M_0 \rangle$ be a priority net. Let M be a nonterminal marking and $L \subseteq T$ such that L is feasibly stubborn at M. Then L is dynamically stubborn at M.*

Proof. The result is an immediate consequence of Lemmas 3 and 5. □

4 Conclusions

Definition 5 and Proposition 3 form the theoretical contribution of this paper. As expressed in the discussion after Proposition 2, it is straightforward to adapt the and/or-graph-based deletion algorithm [34, 39] to Definition 5 in such a way that the algorithm computes in low-degree polynomial time a feasibly stubborn set that is inclusion minimal w.r.t. enabled transitions. Since the end of June 2004, the reachability analysis tool PROD [14, 39] has had such an algorithm, in an extended form that can be used for all those verification tasks that were in the scope of the stubborn set method for unprioritised nets in the earlier versions of PROD.

As expressed in the discussion after Definition 3, "blind" application of the stubborn set method to priority nets is not necessarily the most efficient way to combine the stubborn set method with the priority method. (Consequently, a user of PROD is unfortunately likely to encounter a case where the reduced reachability graph constructed by the stubborn set method for a priority net is larger than the reduced reachability graph constructed by the stubborn set method for the "underlying unprioritised net".) A more efficient combination might be something where easily recognisable "stubborn set simulation" priorities are treated in some special way.

References

1. Bause F.: Analysis of Petri Nets with a Dynamic Priority Method. In: ICATPN'97. LNCS, Vol. 1248, Springer-Verlag (1997) 215–234
2. Belluomini, W., Myers, C.J.: Efficient Timing Analysis Algorithms for Timed State Space Exploration. In: 3rd International Symposium on Advanced Research in Asynchronous Circuits and Systems, IEEE Computer Society Press. (1997) 88–100

3. Bengtsson, J., Jonsson, B., Lilius, J., Yi, W.: Partial Order Reductions for Timed Systems. In: CONCUR'98. LNCS, Vol. 1466, Springer-Verlag (1998) 485–500
4. Best, E., Koutny, M.: Petri Net Semantics of Priority Systems. Theoretical Computer Science **96**(1) (1992) 175–215
5. Chiola, G., Donatelli, S., Franceschinis, G.: Priorities, Inhibitor Arcs and Concurrency in P/T Nets. In: 12th International Conference on Application and Theory of Petri Nets, Gjern, Denmark. (1991) 182–205
6. Dams, D., Gerth, R., Knaack, B., Kuiper, R.: Partial-Order Reduction Techniques for Real-Time Model Checking. Formal Aspects of Computing **10**(5-6) (1998) 469–482
7. Flanagan, C., Qadeer, S.: Transactions for Software Model Checking. In: SoftMC 2003: Workshop on Software Model Checking. Electronic Notes in Theoretical Computer Science, Elsevier **89**(3) (2003)
8. Gerth, R., Kuiper, R., Peled, D., Penczek, W.: A Partial Order Approach to Branching Time Logic Model Checking. In: 3rd Israel Symposium on the Theory of Computing and Systems, IEEE Computer Society Press. (1995) 130–139
9. Godefroid, P.: Using Partial Orders to Improve Automatic Verification Methods. In: CAV'90. LNCS, Vol. 531, Springer-Verlag (1991) 176–185
10. Godefroid, P.: Model Checking for Programming Languages Using VeriSoft. In: 24th ACM SIGPLAN-SIGACT Symposium on Principles of Programming Languages, ACM Press. (1997) 174–186
11. Godefroid, P., Wolper, P.: A Partial Approach to Model Checking. In: 6th Annual IEEE Symposium on Logic in Computer Science, IEEE Computer Society Press. (1991) 406–415
12. Groote, J.F., Sellink, M.P.A.: Confluence for Process Verification. In: CONCUR'95. LNCS, Vol. 962, Springer-Verlag (1995) 204–218
13. Hack, M.: Petri Net Languages. Computation Structures Group Memo 124, Project MAC, Massachusetts Institute of Technology, Cambridge, MA, USA (1975)
14. Helsinki University of Technology: PROD (Reachability Analysis Tool). Espoo, Finland, http://www.tcs.hut.fi/Software/prod/
15. Holzmann, G.J., Peled, D.: An Improvement in Formal Verification. In: Formal Description Techniques VII (FORTE'94), Chapman & Hall (1995) 197–211
16. Itoh, M., Ichikawa, H.: Protocol Verification Algorithm Using Reduced Reachability Analysis. The Transactions of the IECE of Japan **66**(2) (1983) 88–93
17. Janicki, R., Koutny, M.: Using Optimal Simulations to Reduce Reachability Graphs. In: CAV'90. LNCS, Vol. 531, Springer-Verlag (1991) 166–175
18. Kurshan, R., Levin, V., Minea, M., Peled, D., Yenigün, H.: Verifying Hardware in Its Software Context. In: 1997 IEEE/ACM International Conference on Computer-Aided Design, IEEE Computer Society Press. (1997) 742–749
19. Liu, H., Miller, R.E.: Generalized Fair Reachability Analysis for Cyclic Protocols: Part 1. In: Protocol Specification, Testing and Verification XIV (PSTV'94), Chapman & Hall (1995) 271–286
20. Mercer, E.G., Myers, C.J., Yoneda, T., Zheng, H.: Modular Synthesis of Timed Circuits using Partial Orders on LPNs. In: Theory and Practice of Timed Systems. Electronic Notes in Theoretical Computer Science, Elsevier **65**(6) (2002)
21. Minea, M.: Partial Order Reduction for Verification of Timed Systems. Doctoral Dissertation, Report CMU-CS-00-102, School of Computer Science, Carnegie Mellon University, Pittsburgh, PA, USA (1999)
22. Özdemir, K., Ural, H.: Deadlock Detection in CFSM Models via Simultaneously Executable Sets. In: 6th International Conference on Communication and Information, Peterborough, Ontario, Canada. (1994) 673–688

23. Pagani, F.: Partial Orders and Verification of Real-Time Systems. In: Formal Techniques in Real-Time and Fault-Tolerant Systems (FTRTFTS'96). LNCS, Vol. 1135, Springer-Verlag (1996) 327–346
24. Peled, D.: All from One, One for All: on Model Checking Using Representatives. In: CAV'93. LNCS, Vol. 697, Springer-Verlag (1993) 409–423
25. Quemada, J.: Compressed State Space Representation in LOTOS with the Interleaved Expansion. In: Protocol Specification, Testing and Verification XI (PSTV'91), North-Holland. (1991) 19–35
26. Roch, S.: Stubborn Sets of Signal-Event Nets. In: Workshop on Concurrency, Specification and Programming, Informatik-Bericht 110, Institut für Informatik, Humboldt-Universität zu Berlin, Germany. (1998) 197–203
27. Schmidt, K.: Stubborn Sets for Model Checking the EF/AG Fragment of CTL. Fundamenta Informaticae **43**(1–4) (2000) 331–341
28. Şen, M.A.: Verification of SDL Systems with Partial Order Methods. Master's Thesis, Department of Electrical and Electronics Engineering, Middle East Technical University, Ankara, Turkey (1997)
29. Sloan, R.H., Buy, U.: Stubborn Sets for Real-Time Petri Nets. Formal Methods in System Design **11**(1) (1997) 23–40
30. Stoller, S.D.: Model-Checking Multi-threaded Distributed Java Programs. In: SPIN 2000. LNCS, Vol. 1885, Springer-Verlag (2000) 224–244
31. Teruel, E., Franceschinis, G., De Pierro, M.: Well-Defined Generalized Stochastic Petri Nets: A Net-Level Method to Specify Priorities. IEEE Transactions on Software Engineering **29**(11) (2003) 962–973
32. Toggweiler, D., Grabowski, J., Hogrefe, D.: Partial Order Simulation of SDL Specifications. In: SDL'95: With MSC in CASE, North-Holland. (1995) 293–306
33. Valmari, A.: Error Detection by Reduced Reachability Graph Generation. In: 9th European Workshop on Application and Theory of Petri Nets, Venice, Italy. (1988) 95–112
34. Valmari, A.: Heuristics for Lazy State Space Generation Speeds up Analysis of Concurrent Systems. In: STeP-88, Finnish Artificial Intelligence Symposium, Helsinki, Finland. (1998) 640–650
35. Valmari, A.: A Stubborn Attack on State Explosion. In: CAV'90. LNCS, Vol. 531, Springer-Verlag (1991) 156–165
36. Valmari, A.: Stubborn Sets of Coloured Petri Nets. In: 12th International Conference on Application and Theory of Petri Nets, Gjern, Denmark. (1991) 102–121
37. Valmari, A., Clegg, M.: Reduced Labelled Transition Systems Save Verification Effort. In: CONCUR'91. LNCS, Vol. 527, Springer-Verlag (1991) 526–540
38. Valmari, A., Tiusanen, M.: A Graph Model for Efficient Reachability Analysis of Description Languages. In: 8th European Workshop on Application and Theory of Petri Nets, Zaragoza, Spain. (1987) 349–366
39. Varpaaniemi, K.: On the Stubborn Set Method in Reduced State Space Generation. Doctoral Dissertation, Report A 51, Digital Systems Laboratory, Helsinki University of Technology, Espoo, Finland (1998)
40. Yoneda, T., Nakade, K., Tohma, Y.: A Fast Timing Verification Method Based on The Independence of Units. In: 19th International Symposium on Fault-Tolerant Computing, IEEE Computer Society Press. (1989) 134–141
41. Yoneda, T., Shibayama, A., Schlingloff, B.H., Clarke, E.M.: Efficient Verification of Parallel Real-Time Systems. In: CAV'93. LNCS, Vol. 697, Springer-Verlag (1993) 321–332

Model-Driven Maintenance of QoS Characteristics in Heterogeneous Networks*

Andrea D'Ambrogio, Vittoria de Nitto Personé, and Giuseppe Iazeolla

Dept. of Computer Science
University of Roma TorVergata
1 Via del Politecnico, I-00133 Roma, Italy
{dambro,denitto,iazeolla}@info.uniroma2.it

Abstract. System QoS maintenance is the activity intended to maintain the system QoS at acceptable levels. The activity consists of continuously measuring the system QoS characteristics and adjusting the system parameters that affect them. This paper introduces a model-driven approach to the maintenance of QoS characteristics in heterogeneous networks that support geographically distributed processing services. The model is used as an on-line tool that enables network managers to rapidly adjust the network parameters to maintain the network QoS characteristics at required levels. The on-line use of the model requires short model evaluation times, which are obtained by use of a multi-level hierarchical hybrid technique. The application to the maintenance of time-related and capacity-related network QoS characteristics is illustrated.

1 Introduction

In recent times a structured collection of concepts, called QoS framework, has been developed to describe the Quality of Service (QoS) of IT systems and its use in providing open distributed processing services [5]. The framework is intended to assist those that produce specification and design of IT systems and those that define the communication services.

In this paper we deal with the framework concepts applied to a heterogeneous network, simply called *network*, that supports geographically distributed processing services. In particular the paper deals with concepts related to *network* QoS *characteristics* and QoS *requirements*, *network* QoS *management*, *operational phase* of the network QoS management, *network* QoS *maintenance* and *tuning activity* of the QoS maintenance [5].

A QoS characteristic of the network is a quantified aspect of QoS, for example time delay, capacity, accuracy etc.

A QoS requirement is the user expectation of the QoS, for example expectation that the time for a specific service (e.g. downloading a stream of data) must not exceed a specified value.

The network QoS management refers to all the activities designed to assist in satisfying one or more QoS requirements.

---

* Work partially supported by funds from the FIRB project on "Performance Evaluation of Complex Systems" and from the University of Roma TorVergata CERTIA Research Center.

The operational phase of the network QoS management denotes management activities intended to honor the agreements on the QoS to be delivered.

The network QoS maintenance is the activity intended to maintain QoS to acceptable levels. This is performed by the tuning activity of the network consisting of a compensatory adjustment of the network operation.

In this paper we assume that the network QoS tuning activity is directed by an efficient performance model to support the management decision process. Performance modeling has been in many cases used as an off-line approach to system evaluation [1,7]. This paper, on the contrary, deals with the on-line use of the model. In other words, the performance model is part of the compensatory adjustment loop of the network operation.

The time-efficiency of the model is in this case essential to conduct the decision process in due time. Indeed, the model-based tuning mechanism requires the network manager to identify in a short time the network parameters to reset. The integration of similar performance models into commercially available network management tools is part of the advancement in the maintenance of the network QoS characteristics to effectively support geographically distributed services.

2 The Considered Network

Figure 1 gives a description of the network we consider, with a view of two communicating hosts, Host A and Host B, each one residing on an independent local area network (LAN), separated by a wide area network (WAN). By looking at the communication between two hosts residing on two separated LANs, we do not neglect the fact that there may exist hundreds of hosts, on thousands of LANs that compete for the use of the common WAN. The considered interaction, that can regard e.g. a two-host web communication, involves the following subset of elements of the network:

(1) Host A (HA), playing the role of client host with an operating user;
(2) Host B (HB), playing the role of server host;
(3) the heterogeneous network N, composed of:
   (a) two separate LANs, the first (LAN1) a Token Ring for HA, and the second (LAN2) an Ethernet for HB
   (b) two gateways GW1 and GW2, that connect LAN1 and LAN2 to the WAN, respectively
   (c) the WAN, X.25 packet switched network, with its PS1, ..., PSn packet switching nodes.

It is assumed the user residing in HA runs its client/server web application WP, consisting of two parts, WPA and WPB, running on HA and HB, respectively [3]. The WPA part is accessed by use of a web browser running on HA, and communicates with its peer part WPB, managed by the web server running on HB. It is assumed the interaction between WPA and WPB is based on the use of the application layer protocol HTTP [4]. This interaction takes place over the various components of the heterogeneous network N involving several technologies (Token Ring, X.25, Ethernet) and thus several mechanisms to deal with heterogeneity, in particular:

(m1) protocol conversion, from the application layer protocol HTTP to the transport layer protocol TCP, to the network layer protocol IP, to the data-link layer and physical layer protocols (and viceversa), in either direction from HA to HB, with the IP to X.25 (and viceversa) protocol conversion at the gateway level;

(m2) packet fragmentation and re-assembly at many protocol conversion interfaces;

(m3) window-type flow control procedure operated at transport layer by protocol TCP for a fixed window size of value C (for the sake of simplicity neither variable window sizes, nor the use of congestion-avoidance algorithms are considered).

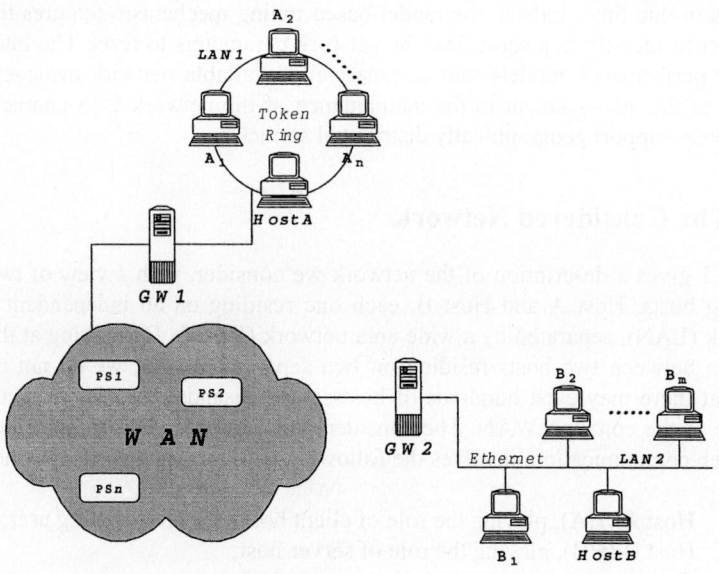

Fig. 1. General view of the considered network

The more detailed view of the packet flow in the system platform is given in the network model illustrated later on in Figure 3. The model puts into evidence the work performed by hosts HA and HB and by the remaining components of the network in order to deal with mechanisms m1, m2 and m3, when transferring data from HA to HB (a symmetrical flow holds when transferring data from HB to HA).

Packets in the IP form enter LAN1, from where they exit in LLC/MAC802.5 form to enter GW1, that first converts them into IP form and then fragments the IP packets into X.25 form to be accepted by the WAN. Vice versa for the GW2, where X.25 packets are first re-assembled into IP packets and then converted into LLC/MAC802.3 form for the LAN2, which in turn converts LLC/MAC802.3 packets into IP form.

3 The Network Performance Model

The considered network consists of various subsystems each of different complexity, and in turn consisting of various subsystems of various complexities. Each one of the LANs, for example, is in itself a complex network (see Figure 2), and similarly the WAN, and each of its PS1, ..., PSn packed switching nodes, and so on.

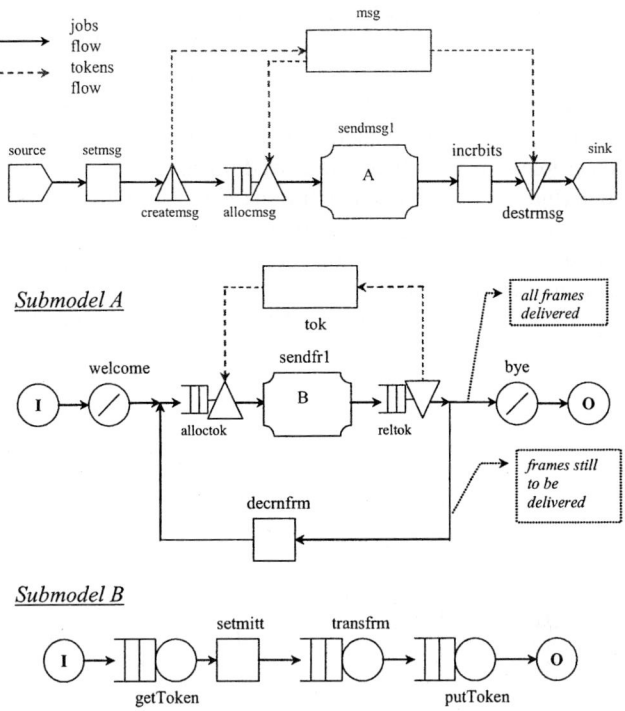

Fig. 2. Part of Level-1 model (Token Ring part)

Figure 2 gives a hierarchical illustration of the LAN model further detailed into submodels A and B, with additional symbols (createmsg, allocmsg, destrmsg, etc.) which are standard symbols of the extended queueing network notation [8].

Producing a model of the network with a unique abstraction-level could yield so many components and details to make the model very difficult to handle, and its evaluation so time-consuming (only simulation modeling would be possible) to make the model useless for its on-line use in the tuning activity of QoS network maintenance.

In order to obtain model efficiency this paper thus introduces a hierarchical hybrid approach [6] basing on decomposition and aggregation [2].

To this scope, three abstraction levels are introduced:

Level-1 Abstraction. At this level the separable subsystems are first identified according to decomposability theory [2], and then studied in isolation. Assume the LAN1 is a separable subsystem. In this case it can be preliminarily studied separately from the rest of the network, then evaluated to obtain its end-to-end delay, and finally substituted in the network N by an equivalent service center whose service time is the end-to-end delay obtained above. The decomposition and aggregation theory [2] tells us under which circumstances such a substitution can be done without a large error. If this is possible, the LAN1 model, that normally consists of a very large number of service centers (see Figure 2), where the extended queueing network notation [8] is used), is collapsed into a single equivalent center. The decomposability conditions for the LAN1, which can be formally verified, are respected in the considered model. The same reasoning applies to the LAN2, and to the WAN.

In conclusion, at this level subsystems LAN1, LAN2 and WAN can be separately evaluated off-line to obtain their equivalent end-to-end delay and can then be replaced each by a single equivalent center. The off-line evaluation is made either numerically (Markov chain modeling) or by simulation since each independent model of such subsystems is too complex to be evaluated in closed form.

Level-2 Abstraction. At this level the entire network N is modeled as in Figure3, in a simplified way, since its LAN1, LAN2, and WAN subsystems have been each aggregated into a single equivalent center, with service time (mean, variance, distribution) being the end-to-end delay obtained at Level-1.

The aggregated service time of each LAN takes into consideration that fact that there may exist hundreds of hosts on the same LAN. In a similar way, the aggregated service time of the WAN takes into consideration the fact that there may be thousands of LANs that compete for the use of the WAN.

The host HA is modeled as being divided into two sections to indicate a division of work between the application WPA & HTTP work (performed by the first section) and the TCP-IP conversion work performed by the second section. For similar reasons the host HB is divided into two sections.

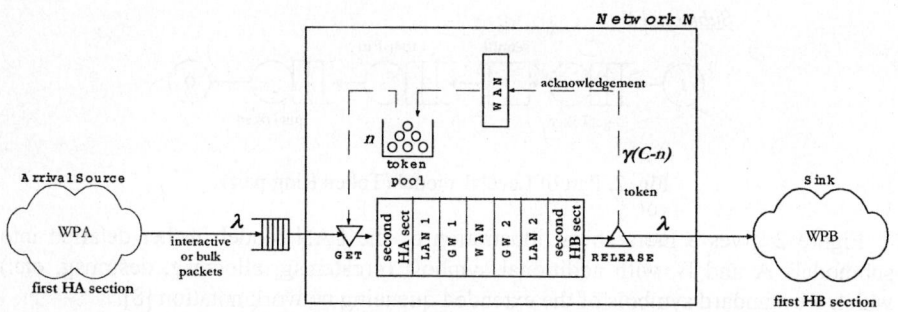

Fig. 3. Level-2 model

The token pool with the GET and RELEASE nodes is used to model the so-called passive queue [8] to represent the window-type flow control procedure implemented by TCP between the exit of the first HA section and the entrance of the first HB section. For a window size C, up to C consecutive TCP packets can GET a token from the pool and enter the second HA section. Non-admitted packets are enqueued in front of this section. On the other hand, admitted packets exit the second HB section and RELEASE their token before entering the first HB section, thus allowing another packet to enter. When data transfer takes place in the opposite direction (from HB to

HA), the GET node with its queue takes the place of the RELEASE node, and vice versa.

The Level-2 model is however still too complex to be evaluated in closed form, and thus we assume its evaluation is also made off-line, numerically or by simulation. The evaluation will yield the acknowledgement throughput (or number of returned acks per time unit, in the figure), denoted as $\gamma(C-n)$, where C is the chosen window size, n the number of acknowledged packets and $C-n$ the number of still unacknowledged ones in the network. The evaluation is very time-intensive, being done for each C and n, and makes it imperative to execute it off-line.

Level-3 Abstraction. At this level the entire network N is replaced by a single equivalent center (see Figure 4) whose service rate is the ack throughput $\gamma(C-n)$ calculated at abstraction level 2. In other words, the entire network N is now seen as a single server

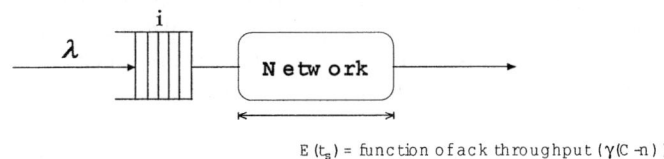

Fig. 4. Level-3 model

system with arrival rate λ (the packets arrival rate from the user application in HA) and mean service time of value $E(t_s)$ depending on the $\gamma(C-n)$ throughput, namely:

$E(t_s)\quad = 1/\gamma(i) \quad$ for $\ 0 \leq i \leq C$
$\quad = 1/\gamma(C) \quad$ for $\ i > C$

with i the number of packets in the queue, including server. Such a model is a model of the M/M/1 type [7] with state-dependent service time (i.e. dependent on the number n of packets in the center). Its response time gives the network end-to-end time delay, and its throughput the network capacity we are looking for. The evaluation can be done by a markovian approach [6] in a sufficiently short time.

The poisson assumption (M) for the arrival process of mean λ is a reasonable assumption for the packets flow from the client user application. The exponential assumption (M) for the network service time is a pessimistic assumption that introduces a security factor on the QoS maintenance, which can however be replaced by a general service time assumption (G) by introducing the coxian approximation without a large impact on the model processing time.

This final model is thus the one to be used on-line in the tuning activity of the network QoS maintenance.

3.1 Model Effectiveness

By use of the proposed multi-level approach that combines, in a hybrid way, simulation evaluations (Level-1 and Level-2) and analytical evaluation (Level-3), the model evaluation time is drastically reduced with respect to the brute-force single-level approach in which the entire network is simulated with all the details of the LANs, the WAN, etc. Indeed, the evaluation time in the multi-level approach is of just a few seconds of Pentium4, against the about 30 hours of the brute force single-level approach.

In more detail, the 30 hours reduce themselves to just 40 minutes if the Level-2 model is simulated, and to just a few seconds if the Level-3 model is analytically evaluated instead.

4 The Model-Driven QoS Maintenance Process

The QoS characteristics we address are time-related and capacity-related characteristics. The time-related one is the network *end-to-end delay*, or the time for a packet (generated by the user application) to get across network N. The capacity related one is instead the network *throughput* or number of packets per time unit that can be delivered from source (HA) to sink (HB) through the network. Such two characteristics are of interest to the QoS maintenance tuning activity since they directly affect the ability of network N to meet the QoS requirements, as seen below.

The window size C is an important factor for both such QoS characteristics, together with the arrival rate λ of packets generated by the user application and characterized by a given proportion α of so-called bulk packets with respect to interactive packets. Bulk packets are packets whose average length is much larger than that of interactive ones (e.g. 8000 bytes against 100) and the proportion α depends on the type of user application. Interactive packets are the dominant part in applications where command sending and short reply dominate, while bulk packets prevail in applications with many upload and download operations.

As stated above, our model can address time- and capacity-related characteristics. An example of QoS requirement with capacity-related characteristic is:

E1: the time to download a stream of data of x KByte of length from sending host A to receiving host B should not exceed y sec.

An example of QoS requirement with time-related characteristic is:

E2: the time to receive at host B a command of one packet length sent from host A should not exceed z sec.

In order to maintain QoS to the levels specified by QoS requirements like E1 or E2, in this Section we focus on the QoS tuning activity (see Sect.1) of the network throughput or else end-to-end delay.

To this purpose a control system is foreseen which takes account of the difference between the required and the measured QoS and yields a tuning feedback to the system. Figure5 illustrates the tuning mechanism. The mechanism includes the following operations [5]:

    a) measurement of the system performance (SP) characteristics, e.g. mean network throughput or mean end-to-end delay;
    b) translation to QoS values;
    c) calculation of QoS difference;
    d) identification of QoS related system components;
    e) modification of parameters of identified components and system reset.

The system performance characteristics to be measured are related to each considered QoS requirement. In case E1 the system performance characteristic to monitor is the mean network throughput, measured in packets per second. In case E2 the system performance characteristic is the mean end-to-end delay, or the time to send a packet from host A to host B, measured in seconds.

Assume the agreed QoS requirement is e.g. E1. Being E1 a capacity-related QoS requirement the network throughput should be continuously monitored. This can be done by use of a measurement probe of the SP (see Figure 5) and then translating it into QoS values, i.e. in terms of the time to download the stream of data. In such a way it is possible to verify if the negotiated QoS requirement E1 is satisfied. To this purpose the difference (ΔQoS) between the measured QoS and the negotiated QoS is calculated and in case an established threshold is exceeded the necessary adjustment of system parameters is performed and the system is reset to obtain the required QoS.

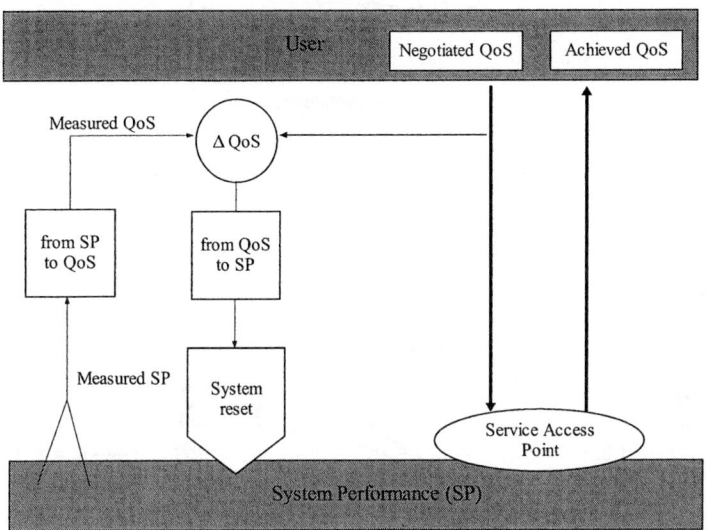

Fig. 5. Network tuning mechanism [5]

By incorporating the performance model into the decision process of the tuning operations *d)* and *e)*, the QoS related system components can be identified and directions can be obtained on the reset of system parameters to obtain performance improvements.

The efficiency of the proposed model (see Sect.4) is an essential means to conduct the decision process in due time. Indeed the tuning mechanism requires that by use of such model the network manager make model evaluation in a way to identify in a short time the system parameters to reset to new values. According to the illustrated model, main parameters to reset are:
• arrival rate λ of user application packets
• network window size C

and decisions are to be taken on the effects on end-to-end delay and network throughput of such parameters reset.

Figure 6 gives the mean end-to-end delay as a function of the packets arrival rate λ, for various values of the window size C and for a fixed percentage of interactive/bulk packets $\alpha = 0.9$.

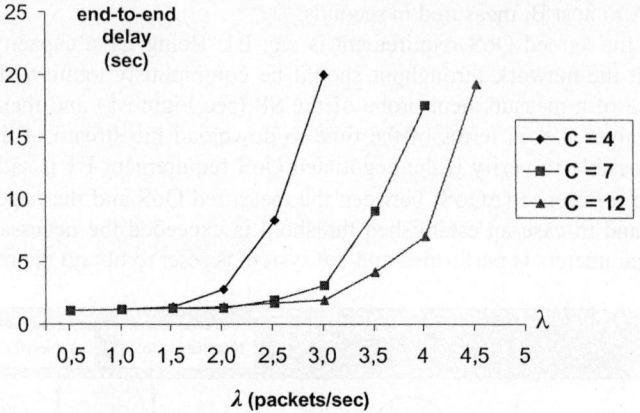

Fig. 6. Mean end-to-end delay versus λ, for $\alpha=0.9$

Figure 7 gives the network throughput as a function of the packets arrival rate λ, for various values of the window size C and for a fixed percentage of interactive/bulk packets $\alpha = 0.4$.

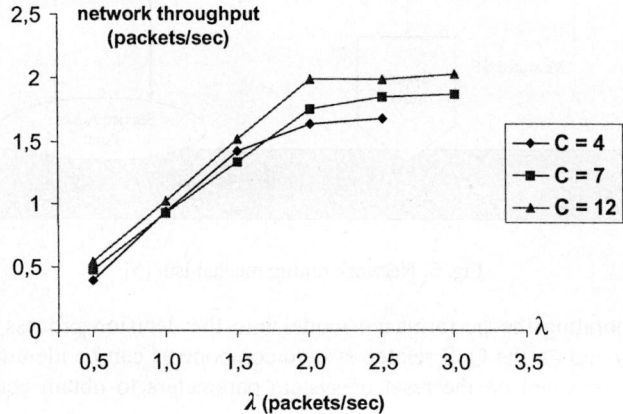

Fig. 7. Network throughput versus λ, for $\alpha=0.4$

As an example application of the network tuning decision process, assume to be in the case of the QoS requirement E1, and that the negotiated QoS is a time of no more than 10 seconds to download a stream of data of 140 Kbytes. In other words, a throughput of no less than 14 Kbytes/sec, or 1,75 packets/sec for packets of 8 Kbytes length, is required.

By use of the model it is possible to find the values of the parameters λ or C that guarantee a mean network throughput greater than or equal to 1,75 packets per second. By looking at Figure 7 it is easily seen that for $1,75 \leq \lambda \leq 2$ only a window size C=12 can be chosen, while for $\lambda > 2$ C=7 can be chosen as well.

In a similar way, assume to be in the case of the QoS requirement E2, and that the negotiated QoS is a time of no more than 15 seconds to deliver a command of one packet length to B.

By use of the model it is possible to find the values of the parameters λ or C that guarantee a mean end-to-end delay lower than or equal to 15 seconds. By looking at Figure 6 it is easily seen that:
- for $\lambda \leq 2,8$ all values of the window size C (4, 7 or 12) can be chosen,
- for $2,8 < \lambda \leq 3,8$ C=7 or C=12 can be chosen,
- for $3,8 < \lambda \leq 4,3$ only C=12 can be chosen,

while no values of C can guarantee the considered requirement if $\lambda > 4,3$.

5 Conclusions

A performance model-driven approach to network QoS maintenance has been introduced.

The considered network is a heterogeneous network that supports geographically distributed processing services.

The performance model allows to effectively implement tuning activities by enabling network managers to identify in a short time how to adjust the network parameters in order to continuously maintain at the required levels the network QoS characteristics.

The necessary model efficiency has been obtained by use of a multi-level hierarchical hybrid technique.

The model-driven approach has been applied to the maintenance of time-related and capacity-related network QoS characteristics.

References

1. Bolch, G., Greiner, S., de Meer, H., Trivedi, K.S.: Queueing Networks and Markov Chains. Wiley, New York (1998)
2. Courtois, P.J.: Decomposability: Queueing and Computer System Applications. Academic Press (1997)
3. D'Ambrogio, A., Iazeolla, G.: Steps Towards the Automatic Production of Performance Models of Web Applications. Computer Networks 41(2003) 29–39
4. Fielding, R., Irvine, U.C., Gettys, J., Mogul, J.C., Frystyk, H., Masinter, L., Leach, P., Berners-Lee, T.: Hypertext Transfer Protocol – HTTP/1.1, Internet Request for Comments RFC *616* (1999)
5. ISO/IEC 13236-1998 International Standard. Information Technology–Quality of Service: Framework
6. Korner, U., Fdida, S., Perros, H., Shapiro, G.: End-to-End Delays in a Catenet Environment. Performance Evaluation Review **15** (1988)
7. Lavenberg, S.S.: Computer Performance Modeling Handbook. Academic Press, New York (1983)
8. Sauer, C., Mac Nair, G.A.: Simulation of Computer Communication Systems. Prentice Hall (1983)

A Performance Study of Context Transfer Protocol for QoS Support

Novella Bartolini[1], Paolo Campegiani[2],
Emiliano Casalicchio[2], and Salvatore Tucci[2]

[1] Universitá di Roma "La Sapienza", Via Salaria 113 - 00198 Roma, Italy
novella@dsi.uniroma1.it
[2] Universitá di Roma "Tor Vergata", Via del Politecnico, 1 - 00133 Roma, Italy
{campegiani,casalicchio,tucci}@ing.uniroma2.it

Abstract. In nowadays wireless networks, mobile users frequently access context dependent Internet services. During handover procedures, the management of context related information introduces additional overheads to transfer context-aware service sessions. The overhead due to context transfer procedures may affect the quality of service perceived by mobile users making more difficult to realize seamless handover procedures. Context Transfer Protocol can improve the QoS perceived by mobile nodes that access context dependent services. In this paper we extend motivations for context transfer, and we introduce three different scenarios for Context Transfer Protocol. We propose a performance model to compare these scenarios when context transfer protocol run on top of IPv6 with fast handover mechanisms.

1 Introduction

Nowadays internet services are often session oriented, delay bounded (or realtime) and context sensitive. Just to mention some, VoIP, multimedia streaming, on-line games, on-line transactions and many Content Delivery Networks related services are often session oriented, delay bounded and context sensitive.

In wired networks, the use of broadband technologies has a significant impact on the user perceived Quality of Service (QoS) making it possible to fulfill Service Level Agreements (SLA). On the contrary, in wireless networks the introduction of broadband wireless connectivity is not sufficient to guarantee the fulfillment of QoS requirements mostly due to users movement across network coverage areas managed by different Access Routers (AR). Handover requests may be issued during critical service phases for which the avoidance of service disruption is mandatory, and the connection must be seamlessly handed off from a point of access to another.

The fast handover mechanism, introduced to reduce the packet losses during handovers, needs to be enhanced with proper mechanisms to preserve the session continuity. In context-aware services, handover is not only a matter of keeping a connection alive during users movements, but also of transferring the necessary information to avoid the re-establishment of a service session every time the user reaches a new point of access. The re-establishment of a service session causes the repetition of the service initiation message flow from scratch and, most of all, the unavailability of the necessary information to keep the service alive without the need of a restart. Thence session continuity and context transfer during handover procedures are very critical for delay sensitive and context dependent application. We extend the general motivation for context transfer identified by the IETF SeaMoby working group [5]. Exchanged informations could relate to:

- authentication, authorization, and accounting information [5] needed to permit the re-authentication of the mobile host and the mobile host's authorization to access the network service from a new subnet;
- header compression [5] information that is necessary to avoid the repetition of messages between the last hop router and the mobile host with full or partially compressed headers before full compression is available;
- network QoS information to avoid the re-negotiation and re-establishment of QoS agreements between the mobile node and routers;
- application level QoS parameters, e.g. maximum end-to-end perceived latency, level of image resolution (e.g. high-level resolution for laptop and low-level resolution for enlarged mobile phone/palmtop), maximum/minimum bit-rate for streaming sessions, security specification (e.g. which suite of encryption algorithms is allowed/used) service authentication (e.g. certificate, list of certification authorities, list of trusted servers);
- session state information, e.g. the number of items in the basket or the phase that most likely will be entered next, for an e-commerce session or the next chunk of data needed in a streaming session, the next game phase for an on-line game session, the mailbox state or the file system information of an e-storage account.

In all these scenarios, if procedures were conducted without transferring any context related information, descriptive parameters should be re-defined from scratch whenever the mobile host reaches a new access point. The re-negotiation of these parameters is too complex and may require longer time than the one that is needed to perform the handover. The best solution is to transfer context from the access router of the region from which the mobile node is coming (pAR) to the access router of the area targeted by the mobile node (nAR).

In section 2, we show the interaction between Context Transfer Protocol (CTP) [7] and Mobile IPv6 protocol, with fast handover mechanisms to reduce packet losses. In section 3 we describe the CTP message flow in some relevant cases. Section 4 shows a performance model of CTP using different metrics. Section 5 concludes the paper.

2 Mobility Management Mechanisms

To evaluate the impact of CTP on performance, its interaction with the underlying mobility management protocol must be considered and evaluated. Although an efficient and transparent mobility management mechanism affects every level of the TCP/IP protocol stack, we consider only handovers that need to be managed at the network level (e.g. not analyzing handover occurring only at Data Link level) focusing on some relevant aspects of IPv6 and its fast handover mechanism.

Mobile IPv6 [4] defines the protocol operations and messages to achieve intra and inter-domain mobility within IPv6.

Auto-configuration [8][9] is an essential part of IPv6, and it's also used by a mobile node to obtain a new Care Of Address (nCOA) when it handovers to a new AR: the mobile node sends a Router Solicitation message (RtSol), and the AR responds with a Router Advertisement message (RtAdv) which contains the information needed by the mobile node to construct its nCOA as a global unicast address [2][3]. RtAdv messages are also broadcasted periodically. When the mobile node obtains its nCOA, it performs the return routability procedure, then it sends a Binding Update (BU) message to inform the CN of its nCOA. Only after these steps are concluded the CN and the mobile node can communicate directly, without routing triangularly via the Home Agent.

The time needed to complete this procedure is called handoff latency, and it is worth trying to reduce it as much as possible. This goal is pursued by the fast handover extension for IPv6 [6]. If this mechanism is put in place, the current AR not only broadcast its advertisement but also relays advertisements from confining ARs, by a Proxy Router Advertisement message (PrRtAdv), periodically broadcasted or sent out as an answer for a Proxy Router Solicitation message (PrRtSol), issued by a MN when it detects, by some layer two indicator, that a handoff is likely to occur.

Fast handover optimization also allows the MN to communicate its nCOA to the current AR (via a Fast Binding Update (FBU) message), so a layer 3 tunnel between the current AR (pAR, as the current AR is about to be the previous AR) and the new AR (nAR) could be established. This bidirectional tunnel is used to route packets from the nAR to the pAR.

It is worth pointing out that the whole fast handover mechanism can be applied only if the wireless interface is provided with an indicator of link layer level events such as discovering of a new AR or degradation of signal quality to the current AR.

3 The Context Transfer Protocol

When the mobile node moves to a new AR all context related data must be transferred from the previous AR and not obtained by an additional message exchange between the new AR and the mobile node, in order to avoid unnecessary bursts of data packets as the node gets connected to the new AR and to minimize the number of application data packets which cannot be processed properly due the lack of context-oriented information.

Context Transfer Protocol is composed of few messages: the Context Transfer Activate Request message (**CTAR**); the Context Transfer Request message

(**CTR**); the Context Transfer Data message (**CTD**); the Context Transfer Activate Acknowledge message (**CTAA**); the Context Transfer Data Reply message (**CTDR**); the Context Transfer Cancel message (**CTC**). For a complete description see [7].

The Context Transfer Protocol could be initiated by one of the ARs or by the mobile node, as a trigger (a Context Transfer Trigger) arises.

The pAR may initiate the CTP if it someway detects that the MN is about to handoff to another AR: in such a case it predictively sends the CTD message to the nAR.

The same could be done by the nAR when it detects that a mobile node is about to get connected to it: the nAR sends a CTR message to the pAR before the mobile node sends the CTAR message, so the CTD message (in reply to the CTR message) is received by the nAR before the time it would have been received if the nAR had waited for the CTAR message from the mobile node.

These first two scenarios are predictive, that is the context data transfer is initiated more or less before the actual handoff, and handoff latency is reduced.

The context transfer procedure can also be performed reactively: when the mobile node starts the handover at the data link layer, a CT Trigger arises so that the mobile node sends the CTAR message to the nAR, which in turn issues a CTR message to the pAR and receives from it the CTD message. This is a worst case scenario, showing the longest time to transfer the context.

3.1 Interactions between Fast Handover and Context Transfer Protocol

The context transfer is always triggered by means of a Context Transfer Trigger. The current version of the draft [7] doesn't define exactly what a CT Trigger is, although it seems to envision that the CT Trigger is a level two (data link) trigger. We believe that the CT Trigger could be better defined as a network level trigger. By doing so, we have a trigger which could be managed by the mobile node operating system, without requiring a hook provided by the wireless interface firmware.

The main idea is to use the Fast Handover messages as CT Trigger. As an example, if a pAR sends a PrRtAdv message to a nAR, it should also send a CTD to the nAR it is proxying advertisements for, because after the reception of a PrRtAdv message (or RtAdv) the MN is capable of performing an actual handover.

We can have these different scenarios:

Dummy Context Transfer Protocol. This is the completely reactive case when the fast handover mechanism doesn't take place, so the context transfer is initiated after the handoff of the mobile node from pAR to nAR: the nAR sends a RtAdv message to the mobile node which constructs its nCOA and sends a CTAR message to the nAR, which in turn sends a CTR message to the pAR. Figure 1(a) depicts this scenario, where no tunnelling is performed.

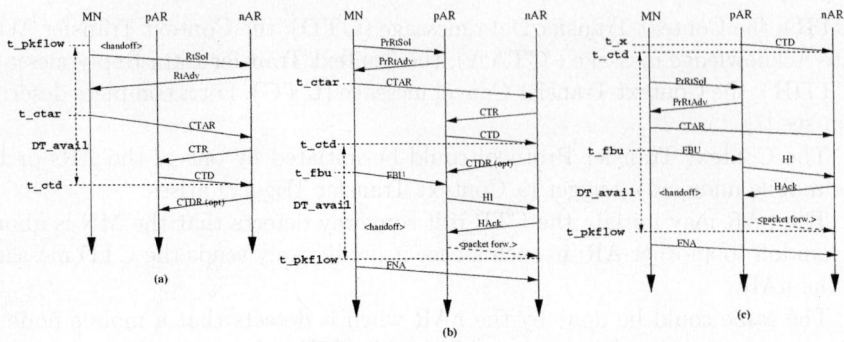

Fig. 1. Context Transfer Protocol scenarios: Dummy (a), Mobile Initiated (b) and Access Router initiated (c). The Definition of ΔT_{avail} in the three scenarios will be discussed in the performance analysis section

Mobile Node Initiated Context Transfer Protocol. The mobile node receives a PrRtAdv message from the pAR, and sends a CTAR to the nAR because it realizes that a handoff to the nAR is about to begin. It's worth noting that the mobile node could receive more than one PrRtAdv Message on behalf of different nARs, because the pAR could advertise (and usually do advertise) for all the confining nARs, and the mobile node could send the CTAR to one or more of advertised nAR, without knowing in advance which one it will handoff to (or *if* an handoff will take place): as the mobile node is still connected to the pAR, the pAR will receive all the CTAR messages and route them to the different ARs; if a targeted ARs respects the Context Transfer Protocol it will, after the reception of the CTAR, send a CTR to the current AR. Figure 1(b) shows the most favorable message flows for this scenario, when the actual handoff takes place after the context data have been transferred. The mobile node initiated case is designed to allow the new access router to use the context information to decide whether to manage or deny service to the new mobile node.

Access Router Initiated Context Transfer Protocol. The most predictive option is when the pAR (when it still is the current Access Router) sends a CTD describing a mobile node's context to one or more of its confining ARs. This can be done periodically or as a consequence of a CT Trigger. The receiving ARs cache this context, to be able to use it immediately after an handoff takes place. The context data are considered valid for a short period of time (possibly depending on the context type), after which they are removed; this soft-state approach is envisioned both for scalability and because the context data could (although slowly) change. Frequency of the CTD messages and cache duration must be defined accordingly to handoff frequency, available bandwidth for inter-AR communication and context data semantics.

A Performance Study of Context Transfer Protocol for QoS Support   599

Figure 1(c) shows the flow of messages when the pAR sends a CTD before the mobile node sends a PrRtSol message. Alternatively the pAR can trigger a PrRtSol message and send the CTD to the candidate nARs.

4 Performance Analysis of CTP

We introduce a performance model to evaluate the cost of CTP in terms of: consumed bandwidth and number of packets that have been lost or erroneously processed according to the default method, without considering the necessary context information.

At least three entities are involved in CTP: the mobile node, the previous access router and one or more new access routers. Thus we distinguish among the bandwidth consumed by the mobile node, B^{MN}; the bandwidth consumed by the previous access router B^{pAR}; and the bandwidth consumed by the new access router B^{nAR}.

When a mobile node handovers to a new mobile access router, N_{lost} packets could be lost, and $N_{default}$ packets could be erroneously served by default, without considering context related information. If an access router receives a packet before being able to consider the context related information, it processes the packet according to the default procedure, until the necessary information becomes available. When the AR receives context information and re-establishes the proper QoS level, packets will be properly prioritized.

4.1 Bandwidth Consumption Analysis

The Context Transfer Protocol works on an UDP-based transport layer. Our model is based on the assumption that CTP messages must fit the Maximum Segment Size (MSS) of a data link frame (and obviously must be contained in one UDP/IP packet), to reduce the packet fragmentation and reassembly overhead. For synchronization messages it is easy to fit the MSS, nevertheless context data could need a proper encoding and/or compression.

Each CTP message travels over an UDP segment, therefore the total overhead that is needed to send a CTP message is $O = O_{udp} + O_{ip} + O_{frame}$, where $O_{udp} = 8$ bytes, $O_{ip} = 20$ bytes and $O_{frame} = 18$ bytes (for ethernet frames).

In our analysis we give a formulation of upper bounds on the total amount of bandwidth consumed by each participant to perform the context transfer procedure. We use the following notation: $B^{participant}_{scenario}$ is the upper bound on the bandwidth consumed by participant, where $participant \in \{MN, pAR, nAR\}$ and the triggering mechanism is $scenario \in \{dummy, MN_{init}, AR_{init}\}$.

In the following expressions S is the maximum size of the messages that are exchanged to perform the context transfer in the different scenarios. s_{ctd} is the size of the message containing context data and k is the number of new candidate access routers.

In the worst case, the pAR will complete the context transfer with all k candidates nARs. In a well designed architecture the nAR or pAR should abort the context transfer when it is sufficiently clear that the mobile node will not enter the service area of the nAR.

We now formulate $B_{\text{scenario}}^{\text{participant}}$ for the different entities and different scenarios.

$$B_{\text{dummy}}^{\text{MN}} = 3(S+O), \tag{1}$$

$$B_{\text{dummy}}^{\text{pAR}} = [2(S+O)+(s_{\text{ctd}}+O)], \tag{2}$$

$$B_{\text{dummy}}^{\text{nAR}} = 3(S+O)+[2(S+O)+(s_{\text{ctd}}+O)], \tag{3}$$

$$B_{\text{MNinit}}^{\text{MN}} = (4+k)(S+O), \tag{4}$$

$$B_{\text{MNinit}}^{\text{pAR}} = 3(S+O)+\{k[2(S+O)+(s_{\text{ctd}}+O)]+2(S+O)\}, \tag{5}$$

$$B_{\text{MNinit}}^{\text{nAR}} = 2(S+O)+[4(S+O)+(s_{\text{ctd}}+O)], \tag{6}$$

$$B_{\text{ARinit}}^{\text{MN}} = (4+k)(S+O), \tag{7}$$

$$B_{\text{ARinit}}^{\text{pAR}} = 3(S+O)+[k(s_{\text{ctd}}+O)+2(S+O)], \tag{8}$$

$$B_{\text{ARinit}}^{\text{nAR}} = 2(S+O)+[2(S+O)+(s_{\text{ctd}}+O)]. \tag{9}$$

The first observation is that the bandwidth consumed at the MN (equations 1, 4 and 7) is directly proportional to the size of synchronization messages S in all scenarios, and also proportional to the number of k candidate nARs, in the mobile node initiated and access router initiated scenarios. In mobile initiate and access router initiated scenario it's important to operate a correct prediction of feasible next access router thus to reduce the bandwidth consumed at the MN that typically have no much bandwidth available.

The second characteristics of $B_{\text{scenario}}^{\text{nAR}}$ is that the bandwidth consumed at the nAR (equations 3, 6 and 9) is directly proportional to the size of context data s_{ctd}. The first term of equations 3, 6 and 9 gives a measure of the bandwidth consumed on the nAR-MN communication channel on the contrary, the second term, measures the bandwidth consumed on the pAR-nAR communication channels.

The third observation is that the bandwidth consumed by the pAR, in the last two scenarios, is a function of the number k of candidate nARs and of the size of context data s_{ctd}. The first terms of equations 5 and 8 give a measure of the bandwidth consumed on the pAR-MN communication channel, while equation 2 and the second terms of equations 5 and 8 measure the bandwidth consumed on the pAR-nARs communication channels, that is a function of s_{ctd} in the dummy scenario and a function of s_{ctd} and k in the mobile node initiated and access router initiated scenarios.

As a numerical example to give a quantitative idea of $B_{\text{scenario}}^{\text{participant}}$ we consider $S = 300$ bytes, $K = 4$ candidate access routers. This numerical example is shown in figures 2 and 3.

The mobile node initiate scenario is more bandwidth consuming than the access router initiated scenario because in the worst case the MN sends a CTAR message to each candidate nARs. In an analogous way, the pAR is the most stressed entity in terms of bandwidth because in the worst case the context will be broadcast to all the nARs that reply to the CTAR message or that are candidates. For the MN the dummy triggering mechanism consume less bandwidth that the other mechanisms, at the price of a degraded QoS. Figure 3 shows the trend of $B^{participant}_{scenario}$ when the number of candidate nARs increases (from 1 to 10) and the context data size has a fixed value 1020 bytes.

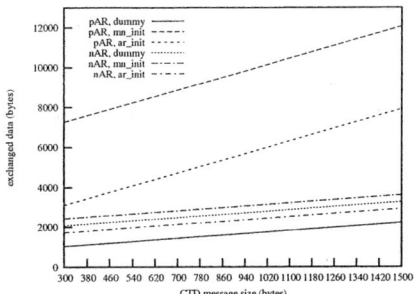

Fig. 2. Bandwidth consumed at the ARs by the CTP in function of the context data size

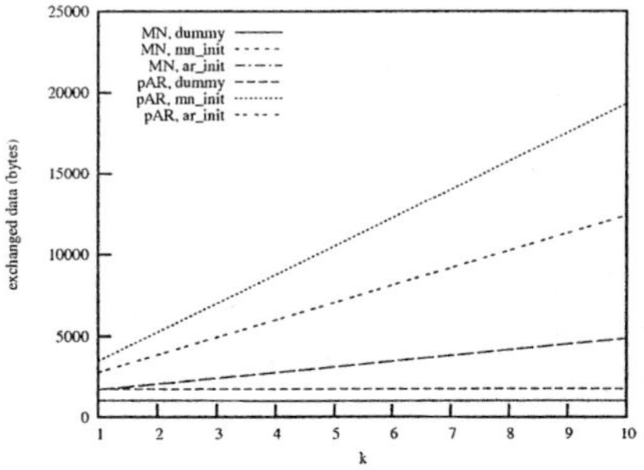

Fig. 3. Bandwidth consumed by the CTP in function of the number of candidate nARs and $s_{ctd} = 1020$ byte

4.2 Packet Loss and Bad Prioritization Analysis

Let r be the cumulative rate at which the mobile node and its related correspondent node inject packets into the network, and D the latency in the communication path between the mobile node and the correspondent node, through the pAR.

When a handoff occurs the MN registers itself in the new network and reestablishes the connection with the CN in D_{conn} time units. In absence of a buffering mechanism between the pAR and the nAR, N_{lost} packets are lost during handovers, where $N_{lost} = (t - t_{hoff}) \cdot r = D_{conn} \cdot r$, t_{hoff} is the handover start time and t the instant of handover completion. On the contrary, if we use Fast Handover, packets are buffered by the pAR until a tunnel between the pAR and the nAR is established, therefore $N_{lost} = 0$.

In QoS sensitive applications, even a short sequence of packet loss could result in a SLA violation. For example a random packet loss can be tolerated in a low quality audio/video streaming session but it is prohibited in a secure transaction data flow.

In this paper we only focus on QoS sensitive application, where the condition $N_{lost} = 0$ is required, therefore the attention is restricted to the mobile initiated or access router initiated scenario. We refer to t_{ctd} as to the instant in which the context is available to the nAR, and we refer to t_{pkflow} as to the time the nAR starts processing packets directed from the CN to the MN. The elapsed time between the actual availability of the context data and the moment the first packets directed to the mobile node arrive to the nAR, can be expressed as $\Delta T_{avail} \leq (t_{pkflow} - t_{ctd})$.

As shown in figure 1 the context transfer begins at the instant t_{ctar} in the mobile node initiated scenario and at time t_x in AR initiated scenario the nAR receives the context at time t_{ctd}, the handoff procedure starts at time t_{fbu} and the nAR starts receiving packets addressed to the MN at time t_{pkflow}. When the context transfer procedure suffers from excessive delays and $\Delta T_{avail} < 0$, there is a period of time, that is $t_{ctd} - t_{pkflow}$, during which a certain number of packets belonging to an ongoing service, are erroneously treated by a default procedure, without considering context related information, thus causing a violation of the agreements on quality. The average number of packets erroneously treated by default is $N_{default} = -\Delta T_{avail} \cdot r = -(t_{pkflow} - t_{ctd}) \cdot r$. On the other side, if the handover procedure is completed on time, that is, if $\Delta T_{avail} \geq 0$, the SLA will be satisfied and $N_{default} = 0$.

We can conclude that a sufficient condition for the fulfillment of the SLA is $\Delta T_{avail} \geq 0$.

For lack of space we do not show the ΔT_{avail} model. A detailed dissertation is given in [1]. In the dummy scenario, the context transfer procedures are activated after the completion of the handover at the lower levels of the protocol stack, therefore by definition $N_{lost} > 0$ and $\Delta T_{avail} < 0$. Such a message flow scenario, definitely cannot be used to improve QoS.

In the Mobile Initiated scenario (figure 1(b)), in order for the context to be timely available at the nAR, the CTAR message must be sent as soon as possible, and the context transfer must be completed before the tunnel is established between the two access routers. In case of high mobility, the Mobile Initiated scenario shows a high $N_{default}$ value. It is worth noting that the tunnel setup is faster than the context transfer procedure and that the necessary time to establish a tunnel between the ARs could be saved by means of persistent connections.

The access router initiated scenario guarantee that $\Delta T_{avail} > 0$. The anticipation of the context transfer procedure can be delayed to reduce the waste of bandwidth due to the necessity to send the context related information to all the candidate nARs, thus giving the possibility to the pAR to based the procedure on a more refined choice of candidates. A high delay in the context transfer procedure brings to a scenario that is very similar to the mobile initiated one, showing that tradeoff solutions could be considered between a high bandwidth waste for many anticipated context transfers that guarantee high handover performances, and a low bandwidth waste of a delayed context transfer scenario that could lead to handover performance degradation.

5 Conclusions and Remarks

A considerable number of network services characterized by long lived sessions show a strong need for transparent procedures to transfer context information between network access points. The context transfer must be efficient to support low-latency and real-time application.

In this paper we made a performance analysis of context transfer protocols, comparing three scenarios differentiated on the basis of the trigger mechanism in use to activate the context transfer procedures. Our analysis points out that for small context data a mobile initiated procedure guarantees a good performance also for clients showing high mobility. We also explain how predictive mechanisms, reduce the cost of handovers (in terms of number of lost packets and of packets processed as default), though requiring more bandwidth than dummy or mobile initiated solutions. Protocols optimizations can be introduced to reduce the number of CTD messages sent to candidate nARs.

Acknowledgements

The work of Novella Bartolini has been partially funded by the WEB-MINDS project supported by the Italian MIUR under the FIRB program. The work of Emiliano Casalicchio and Salvatore Tucci has been partially funded by the PERF project supported by the Italian MIUR under the FIRB program.

References

1. Bartolini, N., Campegiani, P., Casalicchio, E.: A Performance Model Of Context Transfer Protocol. Dipartimento di Informatica Sistemi e Produzione, University of Tor Vergata, Roma. (2004)
2. Hinden, R., Deering, S.L.: IPv6 Addressing Architecture. RFC 2373, (1998)
3. Hinder, R., Deering, S.: IP version 6 Addressing Architecture. IETF Internet Draft, (2003)
4. Johnson, D., Perkins, C., Arkko, J.: Mobility Support in IPv6. IETF Mobile IP Working Group RFC 3775, (2004)
5. Kempf, J. Ed.: Problem Description: Reasons For Performing Context Transfers Between Nodes in an IP Access Network. Network Working Group, RFC3374, (2002)
6. Koodli R.: Fast Handovers for Mobile IPv6. IETF Mobile IP Working Group Internet-Draft, (2004)
7. Loughney J. et al. Context Transfer Protocol. IETF Seamoby WG Internet-Draft, (2004)
8. Nartel T. et al.: Neighbor Discovery for IP Version 6 (IPv6). RFC 2461, (1998)
9. Thomson, S., Narten, T.: IPv6 Stateless Address Autoconfiguration. RFC 2462, (1998)

A Methodology for Deriving Per-Flow End-to-End Delay Bounds in Sink-Tree DiffServ Domains with FIFO Multiplexing[*]

Luciano Lenzini, Linda Martorini, Enzo Mingozzi, and Giovanni Stea

Dipartimento di Ingegneria dell'Informazione, University of Pisa
Via Diotisalvi 2, I-56122 Pisa, Italy
{l.lenzini,l.martorini,e.mingozzi,g.stea}@iet.unipi.it

Abstract. In a DiffServ architecture, packets with the same marking are treated as an aggregate at core routers, independently of the flow they belong to. Nevertheless, for the purpose of QoS provisioning, derivation of upper bounds on the delay of individual flows is required. In this paper, we consider the derivation of per-flow end-to-end delay bounds in DiffServ domains where per-egress (or *sink-tree*) FIFO aggregation is in place. We expose a general methodology to derive delay bounds, and we instantiate it on a case study. We show that the methodology yields a tighter bound than those available from the literature, and we express a worst-case scenario for the case study network, in which the bound is actually achieved.

1 Introduction

The Differentiated Services (DiffServ) architecture [5] addresses the problem of providing scalable QoS in the Internet. Scalability is achieved by aggregating flows that traverse network domains into a small number of QoS classes, named Behavior Aggregates (BAs). The forwarding treatment offered to a BA at a router is called Per-Hop Behavior (PHB). In DiffServ, the Expedited Forwarding PHB [6] offers per node delay guarantees; as such, it can be employed to support real-time, bounded delay services, often referred to as *Virtual Wire* or *Premium* services, and this requires computing tight end-to-end delay bounds for *single flows* within BAs. To present date, few results relating per-aggregate provisioning to per-flow delay bounds have been derived. A closed form per-flow delay bound has been derived in [3] for a generic network configuration. However, the bound holds provided that the network utilization is smaller than a factor which is inversely proportional to the number of traversed nodes, which severely constrains its applicability to practical cases. It is also shown therein that better bounds can be derived by exploiting knowledge of the network topology. For

---

[*] This work has been carried out within the framework of the FIRB-PERF project, funded by the Italian Ministry for Education and Scientific Research (MIUR).

instance, *feed forward* (i.e., loop free) networks are known to be stable, which implies that delay bounds can be computed for any utilization value below 100% [1].

In this paper we consider a specific type of feed forward networks, namely *sink-trees*, which have recently been considered in the context of devising efficient resource management policies in DiffServ domains [7]. In a sink-tree network flows are aggregated according to their egress node, which allows admission control to be performed directly at the ingress node. Furthermore, sink-tree aggregation can be implemented by using Multi Protocol Label Switching (MPLS), whose application in the context of DiffServ has been documented in [9]. In this paper, a methodology for deriving a delay bound in sink-tree networks, based on Network Calculus [1], is described. Such methodology generalizes and puts in the proper theoretical framework the analysis reported in [11]. We instantiate the methodology on a 3-node sink-tree, and we show that the bound obtained is tighter than those reported in the previous work, and that it is in fact *tight*, i.e. actually achievable, under the hypotheses that we formulate.

2 Network Calculus Fundamentals

Network calculus is a theory for deterministic network analysis [1]. The concept of *service curve (SC)*, on which it is based, allows one to model a network node (or a tandem of network nodes) in terms of worst-case relationships between the input and output of a flow traversing that node. Moreover, the worst-case traffic arrivals for a flow in any time interval is represented by means of its *arrival curve (AC)*. By measuring the maximum horizontal distance between a flow's AC $\alpha(t)$ and a node's SC $\beta(t)$, it is possible to compute the delay bound $h(\alpha,\beta)$ for the flow at that node. Regarding FIFO multiplexing, a fundamental result is given in [1]. Assume that flows 1 and 2 are FIFO-multiplexed into the same node, characterized by aggregate SC $\beta(t)$. Assume $\alpha_2(t)$ is an AC for flow 2. Then, the service received by flow 1 can be described in terms of an *equivalent* SC $\beta^1(t,\tau)$, as follows.

Theorem 1. *Let us define the family of functions* $\beta^1(t,\tau) = \left[\beta(t) - \alpha_2(t-\tau)\right]^+ 1_{\{t>\tau\}}$. $\forall \ \tau \geq 0$, *if* $\beta^1(t,\tau)$ *is wide-sense increasing, then flow 1 has* $\beta^1(t,\tau)$ *as a SC.*

Notation $[x]^+$ denotes $\max\{0,x\}$. The indicator function $1_{\{expr\}}$ is equal to 1 if *expr* is true, and 0 otherwise. For ease of notation, we write $A(\beta,\alpha,\tau)$ to denote that Theorem 1 is applied to a SC $\beta(t)$, by subtracting from it the AC $\alpha(t-\tau)$. Note that Theorem 1 describes an *infinity* of equivalent SC $\beta^1(t,\tau)$, each instance of which is obtained by selecting a nonnegative value for τ.

3 System Model

We focus on a DiffServ domain, represented by a set of *nodes*, each one of which models the output links of a router (see Fig. 1a). A flow's *path* through the domain is thus a sequence of nodes, from an ingress node (represented in gray in Fig. 1) to an egress node. We assume that flows are aggregated on a *per-egress basis* (*sink-tree aggregation*): in order for flows to be part of the *same* aggregate, they must exit the domain at the *same* egress node (i.e., the sink-tree root). This implies that *at least* one aggregate exists for each egress node within the domain (nothing forbids defining more, e.g. one per QoS class at each egress node).

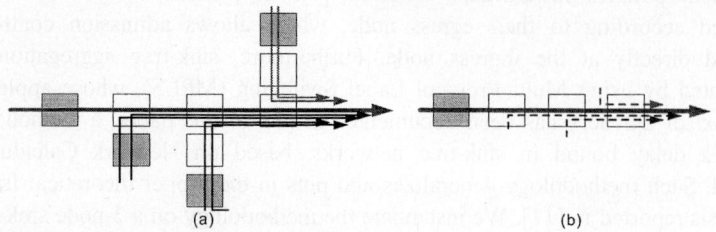

Fig. 1. A sample sink-tree domain (a) and its equivalent representation (b)

At the output link of node i, the service offered to the flows belonging to the sink-tree can be modeled by a *rate–latency* SC $\beta_i = \beta_{R_i,\theta_i}(t) = R_i \cdot (t - \theta_i)^+$ [1]. The EF PHB definition actually requires a stricter form of guarantee, namely the *Packet Scale Rate Guarantee* (PSRG) [4, 6]. However, it has been shown in [4] that PSRG is offered by many common rate-latency schedulers. Thus, the analysis reported in this paper can be applied to EF flows as well. Moreover, we assume that traffic from different flows of an aggregate is served at a node in a FCFS way, which we denote as *FIFO multiplexing* for short. We model a flow as a stream of *fluid*, i.e. we assume that it is feasible to inject and service an arbitrarily small amount of traffic. We assume that flows are *leaky bucket constrained* at their ingress node, i.e. their AC is $\alpha(t) = \gamma_{\sigma,\rho}(t) = \sigma + \rho \cdot t$. We assume that the rate provisioned for the aggregate at a node is no less than the sum of the sustainable rates of the flows traversing that node, i.e. $\sum_{i, i \mapsto h} \rho_i \leq R_h$, for every node h, where $i \mapsto h$ means that flow i has node h along its path. We focus on a tagged flow traversing the domain as part of an aggregate (e.g. the one represented with a thicker line in Fig. 1a), whose delay bound we want to compute. Hereafter, we omit repeating that curves are functions of time whenever doing so does not generate ambiguity.

4 Analysis

We describe below the three-step methodology which we design for computing the end-to-end delay bound for a tagged flow. The first step consists in deriving a single-path model (such as that shown in Fig. 1b) for the tagged flow. The second step consists in deriving an infinity of end-to-end SCs for the tagged flow. The third step consists in actually computing the lowest upper delay bound, which is achieved by selecting one specific SC out of that infinity.

As far as the first step is concerned, we start with observing that a set of n flows spanning the *same* path can be considered as a *single flow*, whose AC is the sum of the n flow ACs (see [8]). Therefore, we can assume that a given sink-tree is traversed by *one* flow per ingress node. Let us focus on a tagged flow, and let us number the nodes that it traverses from 1 to K. At each node j, $2 \le j \le K$, a set of n_j flows may join the aggregate, with $n_j \ge 0$. According to the system model, all flows have a leaky-bucket AC *at an ingress node*. However, flows can join the path of the tagged flow at an arbitrary (e.g., core) node. Therefore we need a method for computing the AC of an *aggregate* of flows at the exit of an N-node sink-tree. To this purpose, we report the following result, whose proof is shown in [8].

Theorem 2. *Consider an N-node sink-tree, in which flow i, $1 \le i \le N$, joins the aggregate at node i and has an AC $\alpha_i = \gamma_{\sigma_i, \rho_i}$. Let $\beta_i = \beta_{\theta_i, R_i}$ be the aggregate SC at node i. Then, the aggregate AC at the exit of node N is $\alpha^* = \gamma_{\sigma^*, \rho^*}$, where:*

$$\sigma^* = \sum_{i=1}^{N} \sigma_i + \sum_{i=1}^{N} \theta_i \cdot \sum_{j=1}^{i} \rho_j, \quad \rho^* = \sum_{i=1}^{N} \rho_i$$

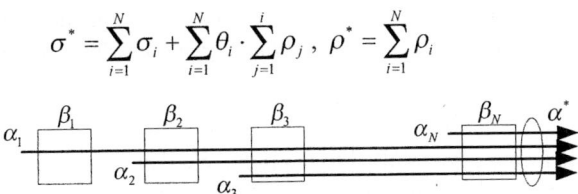

Fig. 2. AC for an N-node sink-tree

We can therefore compute the AC of the set of flows n_j by considering node j as the root of a sink-tree and recursively applying Theorem 2 up to the domain ingress nodes. On the basis of the above theorem, each aggregate of n_j flows joining the aggregate at node j can be modeled as a *single* leaky-bucket constrained flow. Suppose now that *no* flow joins the aggregate at node j. Then the traffic entering node j is the same leaving node $j-1$. In that case, nodes $j-1$ and j can be represented as a single SC, obtained by convolving β_{j-1} and β_j (see [1]). Thus, without any loss of generality, we can restrict our analysis to considering a tandem of N nodes, at each one of which *one* leaky-bucket constrained flow joins the aggregate (as in Fig. 2). Accordingly, we number both nodes and flows from 1 to N, denoting as flow j the flow that joins the aggregate at node j, and denoting as flow 1 the tagged flow. Consequently, the rate provisioning inequalities expressed in the previous section can be reformulated as $\sum_{i=1}^{h} \rho_i \le R_h$, $1 \le h \le N$.

The *second step* consists in obtaining an end-to-end equivalent SC for flow 1, which can be done as follows. Start from the rightmost node; apply Theorem 1 to obtain an equivalent SC for the aggregate of flows 1 to $N-1$, say β_N^{eq}. Now, β_{N-1} and β_N^{eq} are SCs offered to the same aggregate of flows, so they can be convolved into a single SC, with which we have transformed the original N-node sink-tree into an equivalent $(N-1)$-node one. After $N-1$ iterations, we obtain the end-to-end SC for flow 1. The algorithm can be formalized as follows:

1) Set $j = N$, $\beta = \beta_N$
2) If $j = 1$, exit
3) Compute $\beta_j^{eq} = A(\beta, \alpha_j, \tau_j)$ by applying Theorem 1.
4) Set $\beta := \beta_{j-1} \otimes \beta_j^{eq}$
5) Set $j := j-1$.
6) Go back to 2).

Call $\beta_{1,N}^{eq}$ the SC obtained at the end of the algorithm. Now, $\beta_{1,N}^{eq}$ depends on $N-1$ parameters τ_i, $2 \le i \le N$. Thus, it is in fact a family of SCs, each instance of which is obtained by assigning each of the τ_i's a specific value. For any possible choice of the τ_i's, a delay bound $v(\tau_2,...,\tau_N)$ can then be computed which is – by definition – an upper bound on the delay experienced by flow 1. Therefore, the *third step* of the methodology consists in computing:

$$V = \min_{\tau_i \ge 0, 2 \le i \le N} \{v(\tau_2,...,\tau_N)\} \tag{1}$$

which is the lowest upper delay bound obtainable with this methodology. As far as the second step is concerned, we show a formulation that considerably speeds up the computation of $\beta_{1,N}^{eq}$. We define a *pseudoaffine* curve one which can be described as:

$$\beta = \delta_D \otimes \bigwedge_{1 \le x \le n} \gamma_{\sigma_x,\rho_x} \tag{2}$$

i.e., as a multiple affine curve shifted to the right. We denote as *offset* the term D, and as *leaky-bucket stages* the affine curves. We denote with ρ_β^* the smallest rate among the leaky-bucket stages of the pseudoaffine curve β, i.e. $\rho_\beta^* = \min_{x=1,...,n}(\rho_x)$. A rate-latency curve is a pseudoaffine curve, since it can be expressed as $\beta_{R,\theta} = \delta_\theta \otimes \gamma_{0,R}$. Pseudoaffine curves enjoy some interesting properties, which we now enumerate (proofs can be found in [8]). Let us denote with T the family of pseudoaffine curves.

Property 1. $\beta_1, \beta_2 \in T \Rightarrow \beta_1 \otimes \beta_2 \in T$, i.e. T *is closed with respect to convolution.*

Property 2. Let $\beta \in T$ *and* $\alpha = \gamma_{\sigma,\rho}$. *If* $\rho_\beta^* \ge \rho$, *then:* $\forall \tau \ge 0$, $A(\beta,\alpha,\tau) \in T$ *and it is wide sense increasing. Furthermore, it is* $\rho_{A(\beta,\alpha,\tau)}^* = \rho_\beta^* - \rho$.

Therefore, by Property 1 and 2, the end-to-end SC for flow 1 is a pseudoaffine curve.

Property 3. Let $\beta \in T$ *and* $\alpha = \gamma_{\sigma,\rho}$. *If* $\rho_\beta^* \ge \rho$, *then:* $h(\alpha,\beta) = \beta^{-1}(\sigma)$, *where* $\beta^{-1}( )$ *denotes the pseudo-inverse of* $\beta( )$. *Moreover, it can be shown that:*

$$h(\alpha,\beta) = \beta^{-1}(\sigma) = D + [\max_i(\sigma - \sigma_i)/\rho_i]^+ \tag{3}$$

Property 4. *Let* $\beta_1, \beta_2 \in T$ *with* $\beta_1 \le \beta_2$, *and let* $\alpha_1 \ge \alpha_2$. *Then* $A(\beta_1,\alpha_1,\tau) \le A(\beta_2,\alpha_2,\tau)$. *Moreover, if* $0 \le \tau_1 \le \tau_2 \le h(\alpha,\beta)$, $A(\beta,\alpha,\tau_1) \le A(\beta,\alpha,\tau_2)$.

Properties 3 and 4 have an important implication. In fact, they show that, for the purpose of computing (1), every time we apply Theorem 1 in step 3), we can enforce the constraint $\tau_j \ge h(\alpha_j,\beta)$. Not only this reduces the region in which the min is to be searched for in (1), but – more interestingly – it allows us to specialize Theorem 1 as follows:

Corollary 1. *Let* $\beta \in T$ *as in (2), and let* $\alpha = \gamma_{\sigma,\rho}$, *with* $\rho_\beta^* \ge \rho$. *Then the family of SCs obtained by computing* $A(\beta,\alpha,\tau)$ *with* $\tau \ge h(\alpha,\beta)$ *is the following:*

$$\beta^{eq} = \left[\delta_{D + \left[\max_{i=1,...,n} \frac{\sigma - \sigma_i}{\rho_i}\right]^+ + s}\right] \otimes \left[\bigwedge_{1 \le x \le n} \gamma_{\rho_x, \left\{s + \left[\max_{i=1,...,n} \frac{\sigma - \sigma_i}{\rho_i}\right]^+ - \frac{\sigma - \sigma_x}{\rho_x}\right\} \cdot \rho_x - \rho}\right], \quad s \ge 0 \tag{4}$$

Thus, though by applying Corollary 1 we do *not* consider all the equivalent SCs given by Theorem 1, we only neglect those that would yield looser delay bounds, i.e.:

$$\min_{\tau_i \geq 0, 2 \leq i \leq N} \{v(\tau_2,...,\tau_N)\} = \min_{s_i \geq 0, 2 \leq i \leq N} \{v(s_2,...,s_N)\}$$

Thus, we can substitute Corollary 1 to Theorem 1 in step 3) of the above algorithm. This drastically simplifies performing the second step of the methodology, although it does not reduce the number of degrees of freedom when searching for the min.

As an example, we perform step 2 of the methodology on a 3-node sink-tree. We start with $j = 3$, $\beta = \beta_3$, and we apply Corollary 1, obtaining the following SC:

$$\beta_3^{eq} = \delta_{\theta_3 + \frac{\sigma_3}{R_3} + s_3} \otimes \gamma_{R_3 s_3, R_3 - \rho_3}, \quad s_3 \geq 0$$

We convolve β_2 with β_3^{eq}, thus obtaining:

$$\beta = \delta_{\theta_2 + \theta_3 + \frac{\sigma_3}{R_3} + s_3} \otimes \left[\gamma_{R_3 s_3, R_3 - \rho_3} \wedge \gamma_{0, R_2} \right] \quad (5)$$

We decrease j and step back to 2). Again, we apply Corollary 1 to (5).

$$\beta_2^{eq} = \delta_{\theta_2 + \theta_3 + \frac{\sigma_2}{R_2} + \frac{\sigma_3}{R_3} + \left[\frac{\sigma_2 - R_3 s_3}{R_3 - \rho_3} - \frac{\sigma_2}{R_2}\right]^+ + s_2 + s_3} \otimes \begin{bmatrix} \gamma_{(R_3 - \rho_3)\left(s_2 + \left[\frac{\sigma_2}{R_2} - \frac{\sigma_2 - R_3 s_3}{R_3 - \rho_3}\right]^+\right), R_3 - \rho_3 - \rho_2} \wedge \\ \gamma_{R_2\left(s_2 + \left[\frac{\sigma_2 - R_3 s_3}{R_3 - \rho_3} - \frac{\sigma_2}{R_2}\right]^+\right), R_2 - \rho_2} \end{bmatrix}, \quad s_2, s_3 \geq 0$$

And we convolve β_1 with β_2^{eq}, thus obtaining the end-to-end SC for flow 1.

$$\beta = \delta_{\sum_{x=1..3} \theta_x + \frac{\sigma_2}{R_2} + \frac{\sigma_3}{R_3} + \left[\frac{\sigma_2 - R_3 s_3}{R_3 - \rho_3} - \frac{\sigma_2}{R_2}\right]^+ + s_2 + s_3} \otimes \wedge \begin{bmatrix} \gamma_{(R_3 - \rho_3)\left(s_2 + \left[\frac{\sigma_2}{R_2} - \frac{\sigma_2 - R_3 s_3}{R_3 - \rho_3}\right]^+\right), R_3 - \rho_3 - \rho_2} \\ \gamma_{0, R_1} \\ \gamma_{R_2\left(s_2 + \left[\frac{\sigma_2 - R_3 s_3}{R_3 - \rho_3} - \frac{\sigma_2}{R_2}\right]^+\right), R_2 - \rho_2} \end{bmatrix} \quad (6)$$

From (1), and keeping into account Property 3, we obtain:

$$V = \min_{\substack{s_2 \geq 0 \\ s_3 \geq 0}} \left\{ \sum_{x=1..3} \theta_x + \frac{\sigma_3}{R_3} + \frac{\sigma_2}{R_2} + \left[\frac{\sigma_2 - R_3 \cdot s_3}{R_3 - \rho_3} - \frac{\sigma_2}{R_2}\right]^+ + s_2 + s_3 + \max \begin{bmatrix} \left\{\sigma_1 - (R_3 - \rho_3)\left[s_2 + \left(\frac{\sigma_2}{R_2} - \frac{\sigma_2 - R_3 \cdot s_3}{R_3 - \rho_3}\right)^+\right]\right\} \Big/ (R_3 - \rho_3 - \rho_2) \\ \sigma_1 / R_1 \\ \left\{\sigma_1 - R_2\left[s_2 + \left(\frac{\sigma_2 - R_3 \cdot s_3}{R_3 - \rho_3} - \frac{\sigma_2}{R_2}\right)^+\right]\right\} \Big/ (R_2 - \rho_2) \end{bmatrix} \right\} \quad (7)$$

Now, (7) is an optimization problem with linear constraints and a piecewise linear objective function. Although standard techniques exist for solving such kind of problems, in a 2-dimensional setting we can obtain a solution more straightforwardly by considering each linear piece separately. Accordingly, we obtain:

$$V = \sum_{x=1,3} \theta_x + \frac{\sigma_3}{R_3} + \frac{\sigma_2}{\wedge\left(R_2, R_3 \cdot \frac{R_2}{R_2 + \rho_3}\right)} + \frac{\sigma_1}{\wedge\left(R_1, R_3 \cdot \frac{R_1}{R_1 + \rho_2 + \rho_3}, R_2 \cdot \frac{R_1}{R_1 + \rho_2}, R_3 \cdot \frac{R_2}{R_2 + \rho_3} \cdot \frac{R_1}{R_1 + \rho_2}\right)} \quad (8)$$

Expression (8) is *a* delay bound for flow 1, specifically, it is the lowest upper delay bound that can be obtained by applying the methodology. However, this does not necessarily imply that it is *tight* (i.e. actually achievable). We prove the tightness by setting up a scenario in which a bit of flow 1's traffic actually experiences a delay V. Let us assume that flow 1 sends its burst σ_1 at time $t = 0$ and then stops. The scenario is based on the following two assumptions:

Assumption 1. *Nodes are "as lazy as possible"*. For each node j, $1 \leq j \leq 3$, $D_j(t) = [A_j \otimes \beta_j](t)$, where $A_j(t)$ $(D_j(t))$ is the aggregate input (output) at node j.

Assumption 1 implies that the output at node j is *non-bursty*, even if arrivals are bursty. In fact, a burst in $A_j(t)$ is cleared at a rate R_j.

Assumption 2. *Call a_j (x_j) the arrival time of bit 0 (bit σ_1) of flow 1's burst at node j, $1 \leq j \leq 3$. Flows 2 and 3 have the following input $F_j(t)$ in $[0, x_j]$:*

$$F_j(t) = \begin{cases} \rho_j \cdot (t - a_j)^+ & t < x_j \\ \rho_j \cdot (x_j - a_j) + \sigma_j & t = x_j \end{cases}$$

That is, flow j sends its traffic at its sustainable rate starting from the time instant at which the *first* bit of traffic coming from an upstream node arrives at node j; furthermore, *just before* the σ_1-th bit from flow 1's burst arrives at node j, flow j sends out its whole burst σ_j. Since we are computing the delay of the σ_1-th bit from flow 1's burst, and since nodes are FIFO, we are not interested in describing $F_j(t)$ for $t > x_j$. Due to FIFO multiplexing, the last bit of flow 1's burst leaves node 3 *right after* the last bit of flow 3's burst. Let us show that, under assumptions 1 and 2, the delay achieved by the last bit of flow 1's burst is exactly (8).

Flow 1 sends a burst σ_1 at time $t = 0$, which is cleared at node 1 at a rate R_1, i.e. within $[\theta_1, \theta_1 + \sigma_1/R_1] \equiv [a_2, x_2]$. By summing up the arrivals at flow 2, we obtain that $A_2(t)$ has a slope $R_1 + \rho_2$ up to x_2 and a burst σ_2 at time x_2. Two cases are given:

Case 1: $R_1 + \rho_2 \geq R_2$: $A_2(t)$ has a larger slope than the SC's rate, and therefore by Assumption 1 we obtain that the output at node 2 has a slope R_2. In this case, the output at node 2 consists of a linear piece of slope R_2, which leaves the node within $[\theta_{1,2}, \theta_{1,2} + \sigma_1/R_1 \cdot (R_1 + \rho_2)/R_2 + \sigma_2/R_2] \equiv [a_3, x_3]$, with $\theta_{1,2} \triangleq \theta_1 + \theta_2$.

Case 2: $R_1 + \rho_2 \leq R_2$: the slope of the first linear piece of the aggregate input is smaller than the SC's rate. Therefore, the output at node 2 consists of two linear pieces, one of slope $R_1 + \rho_2$, which leaves the node within $[\theta_{1,2}, \theta_{1,2} + \sigma_1/R_1]$, and the other of slope R_2, which leaves the node within $[\theta_{1,2} + \sigma_1/R_1, \theta_{1,2} + \sigma_1/R_1 + \sigma_2/R_2]$. Thus, $[a_3, x_3] \equiv [\theta_{1,2}, \theta_{1,2} + \sigma_1/R_1 + \sigma_2/R_2]$.

At node 3, we compute $A_3(t)$ by taking into account the contribution of flow 3. We compare again the slope of each linear piece of the aggregate with the SC's rate, and distinguish 5 cases. Starting from Case 1 ($R_1 + \rho_2 \geq R_2$), $A_3(t)$ has a slope $R_2 + \rho_3$ and then a burst σ_3 at time x_3. Thus we distinguish Case 1.1: $R_2 + \rho_3 \geq R_3$, and Case 1.2: $R_2 + \rho_3 \leq R_3$. Starting from Case 2 ($R_1 + \rho_2 \leq R_2$), $A_3(t)$ has two linear pieces of increasing slope $R_1 + \rho_2 + \rho_3$ and $R_2 + \rho_3$, and then a burst σ_3 at time x_3. Thus we distinguish Case 2.1: $R_2 + \rho_3 \leq R_3$, Case 2.2: $R_1 + \rho_2 + \rho_3 \leq R_3 \leq R_2 + \rho_3$, and Case 2.3: $R_3 \leq R_1 + \rho_2 + \rho_3$. By repeating the same reasoning as for node 2, we obtain that the σ_1-th bit from flow 1 leaves node 3 at the time reported in the table below. It can be observed that each instance of (8), obtained by considering a given set of rate inequalities, is equal to the corresponding delay reported in Table 1 computed under the same inequalities. Thus, (8) is a tight bound.

Table 1. Delay computed according to Assumptions 1 and 2

Case	Inequalities	Delay
1.1	$R_1 + \rho_2 \geq R_2$, $R_2 + \rho_3 \geq R_3$	$\sum_{x=1..3} \theta_x + \frac{\sigma_3}{R_3} + \frac{\sigma_2}{R_3 \cdot \frac{R_2}{R_2 + \rho_3}} + \frac{\sigma_1}{R_3 \cdot \frac{R_2}{R_2 + \rho_3} \cdot \frac{R_1}{R_1 + \rho_2}}$
1.2	$R_1 + \rho_2 \geq R_2$, $R_2 + \rho_3 \leq R_3$	$\sum_{x=1..3} \theta_x + \frac{\sigma_3}{R_3} + \frac{\sigma_2}{R_2} + \frac{\sigma_1}{R_2 \cdot \frac{R_1}{R_1 + \rho_2}}$
2.1	$R_1 + \rho_2 \leq R_2$, $R_2 + \rho_3 \leq R_3$	$\sum_{x=1..3} \theta_x + \frac{\sigma_3}{R_3} + \frac{\sigma_2}{R_2} + \frac{\sigma_1}{R_1}$
2.2	$R_1 + \rho_2 \leq R_2$, $R_1 + \rho_2 + \rho_3 \leq R_3 \leq R_2 + \rho_3$	$\sum_{x=1..3} \theta_x + \frac{\sigma_3}{R_3} + \frac{\sigma_2}{R_3 \cdot \frac{R_2}{R_2 + \rho_3}} + \frac{\sigma_1}{R_1}$
2.3	$R_1 + \rho_2 \leq R_2$, $R_3 \leq R_1 + \rho_2 + \rho_3$	$\sum_{x=1..3} \theta_x + \frac{\sigma_3}{R_3} + \frac{\sigma_2}{R_3 \cdot \frac{R_2}{R_2 + \rho_3}} + \frac{\sigma_1}{R_3 \cdot \frac{R_1}{R_1 + \rho_2 + \rho_3}}$

4.1 Discussion

We analyze the sensitivity of (8) with respect to the flows' and nodes' rate. In doing this, we also compare it to the delay bound of a σ, ρ-constrained flow in a tandem of N rate-latency nodes, in which per-flow scheduling is in place (as in IntServ, [10]). First of all, it is immediate to show that $\partial V / \partial \rho_1 = 0$, i.e. the delay bound of flow 1 does not depend on its sustainable rate, as long as the network is correctly provisioned. The same occurs in per-flow scheduling, where, if $\bigwedge_{1 \leq i \leq N}(R_i) \geq \rho$, then $V = \sigma / \bigwedge_{1 \leq i \leq N}(R_i) + \sum_{i=1}^{N} \theta_i$ and $\partial V / \partial \rho = 0$.

In per-flow scheduling, the delay bound does not depend on the presence of competing flows (save, possibly, for a dependency in the flow's own latency).

Instead, the sustainable rate of flows 2 and 3 might appear in (8). However, it is not always so. Whenever $\partial V/\partial \rho_j = 0$, it is thus possible to alter ρ_j without altering flow 1's delay bound, as long as the aggregate rate provisioning is adequate and case inequalities are not modified. Furthermore, we observe that $\partial V/\partial \sigma_j > 0$. Finally, we observe that $\partial V/\partial R_j < 0$ (except for the trivial case $\sigma_j = 0$), i.e. increasing *any* node's rate actually decreases the delay bound. However, it is not possible to determine R_j such that $|\partial V/\partial R_j| = \max_{1 \leq i \leq N}|\partial V/\partial R_i|$, i.e. the rate whose increment warrants the sharpest decrease in the delay bound, without taking into account the actual value of the flows' and nodes' parameters. Note that, in per-flow scheduling, it is $\partial V/\partial R_j < 0$ only if $R_j = \wedge_{1 \leq i \leq N}(R_i)$. Thus, in order to decrease the delay bound for a flow, the only possibility is to increase the rate of the *bottleneck* node (or, in case all nodes have the same rate, of *all* nodes).

5   Comparison with Previous Work

Despite the research efforts, the amount of results related to deriving end-to-end delay bounds for FIFO multiplexing are quite poor. A survey on the subject can be found in [4]. A similar approach as ours has been proposed in [2]. It consists in applying Theorem 1 iteratively in order to obtain an end-to-end SC for a tagged flow. However, each time Theorem 1 is applied, a specific value of τ is selected, namely $\tau = h(\alpha, \beta)$. The following Corollary can be easily proved:

Corollary 2. Let $\beta = \beta_{\theta,R}$, $\alpha = \gamma_{\sigma,\rho}$. If $R \geq \rho$, then $A(\beta, \alpha, h(\alpha,\beta)) = \beta_{\theta+\sigma/R, R-\rho}$.

Therefore, the result in [2] can be obtained by applying the same methodology shown in this paper, with Corollary 2 to replace Corollary 1. According this methodology, computation of a delay bound is more straightforward, since at iteration j, a *single* rate-latency SC (rather than a j-dimensional infinity of pseudoaffine SCs) is considered. However, it is possible to show that i) the delay bounds thus obtained are always no better than ours, and that ii) they can be arbitrarily loose, e.g. they can go to infinite when the rate provided for the aggregate is sufficient, and all the aggregate rates are finite.

Regarding i), we observe that the methodology in [2] consists in always choosing the equivalent SC obtained from Corollary 1 for $s = 0$, which might or might not be the one with which the min is achieved. Our bound is computed as the min of a set of bounds which include the one found by iteratively applying Corollary 2. Therefore, it is always no worse. Regarding ii), consider a 3-node sink-tree. By applying the methodology described in [2] we obtain the following delay bound:

$$V^* = \sum_{x=1..3} \theta_x + \frac{\sigma_3}{R_3} + \frac{\sigma_2}{\wedge(R_2, R_3 - \rho_3)} + \frac{\sigma_1}{\wedge(R_1, R_2 - \rho_2, R_3 - \rho_2 - \rho_3)} \qquad (9)$$

Suppose now that $\rho_1 = 0$, which implies that the tagged flow can send up to σ_1 bits and then must stop. Suppose then that $R_2 = \rho_2$, $R_3 > \rho_2 + \rho_3$, $R_1 > R_3$. According to (9), the traffic of the tagged flow might experience an arbitrarily large delay. Instead, according to (8), a tight delay bound is the one reported in the table, Case 1.2. Furthermore, consider a 3-node sink-tree with $\rho_2 = \rho_3 = \rho = 10$, $\rho_1 = \rho/1000$,

$\sigma_i = 1000$, $1 \le i \le 3$, $R_1 = R_2 = 110$, $R_3 = 2\rho + \rho_1 + R$, with $R \ge 0$. Fig. 3, left, shows the ratio V^*/V against R. As expected, the ratio is always above 1, and it grows indefinitely as the overprovisioning on node 3 is reduced. Consider then the following scenario: $\rho_2 = \rho_3 = \rho = 10$, $\rho_1 = a \cdot \rho$, $\sigma_i = 1000$, $1 \le i \le 3$, $R_1 = a \cdot \rho + 3R$, $R_2 = (1+a) \cdot \rho + 2R$, $R_3 = (2+a) \cdot \rho + R$, with $a \ge 0$, $R \ge 0$. Fig. 3, right, shows the ratio V^*/V against R, which is always above 1, and grows arbitrarily large as $a \to 0$, i.e. as flow 1's rate grows smaller with respect to the other flows' rate.

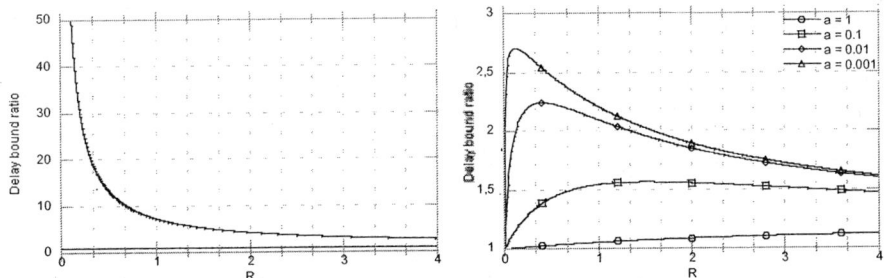

Fig. 3. Ratios V^*/V in two different scenarios

6 Conclusions and Future Work

In this paper we have presented a methodology for deriving per-flow end-to-end delay bounds in sink-tree DiffServ domains. We have instantiated it on a case study network, and we have shown that the delay bound is actually achievable, and better than any other result available from the literature. The work reported in this paper can be extended in two directions: First, deriving a closed form delay bound for an N-node sink-tree. Second, generalizing the methodology derived for sink-trees to other topologies (e.g., source-trees). Research on both issues is well underway at the time of writing.

References

1. Le Boudec, J.-Y., Thiran, P.: Network Calculus. LNCS, Vol. 2050. Springer-Verlag (2001)
2. Fidler, M., Sander, V.: A Parameter Based Admission Control for Differentiated Services Networks: Elsevier Computer Networks **44** (2004) 463–479
3. Charny, A., Le Boudec, J.-Y.: Delay Bounds in a Network with Aggregate Scheduling. In: First Int. Work. QoFIS 2000, Berlin, Germany. (2000)
4. Bennett, J.C.R. et al.: Delay Jitter Bounds and Packet Scale Rate Guarantee for Expedited Forwarding. IEEE/ACM Trans. Networking **10**(4) (2002) 529–540
5. Blake, S., Black, D., Carlson, M., Davies, E., Wang, Z., Weiss, W.: An Architecture for Differentiated Services. IETF RFC 2475 (1998)
6. Davie, B., et al.: An Expedited Forwarding PHB. IETF RFC 3246 (2002)

7. Choi, B., Bettati, R.: Endpoint Admission Control: Network Based Approach. In: Proc. IEEE Int. Conf. Distributed Computing Systems (ICDCS), Phoenix, Az. (2001) 227–235
8. Lenzini, L., Martorini, L., Mingozzi, E., Stea, G.: End-to-End Per-Flow Delay Bounds in Sink-Tree DiffServ Domains with FIFO Multiplexing. Tech. Rep., Univ. of Pisa (2004)
9. Le Faucher, F., Davie, B., Davari, S., Krishnan, R., Cheval, P., Heinanen, J.: Multi Protocol Label Switching (MPLS) Support of Differentiated Services. IETF RFC 3270 (2002)
10. Braden, R., Clark, D., Shenker, S.: Integrated Services in the Internet Architecture: An Overview. IETF RFC 1633 (1994)
11. Lenzini, L., Mingozzi, E., Stea, G.: Delay Bounds for FIFO Aggregates: A Case Study. In: Proc. of QoFIS 2003, Stockholm, Sweden. LNCS, Vol. 2811. Springer-Verlag (2003) 31-40

Performance Analysis of a Predictive and Adaptive Algorithm in Cluster-Based Network Servers with Resource Allocation

Katja Gilly[1], Carlos Juiz[2], Ramon Puigjaner[2], and Salvador Alcaraz[1]

[1] Universidad Miguel Hernández
Departamento de Física y Arquitectura de Computadores
Avda. del Ferrocarril, 03202 Elche, Spain
{katya,salcaraz}@umh.es
[2] Universitat de les Illes Balears
Departament de Ciències Matemàtiques i Informàtica
Carretera de Valldemossa, km 7.5, 07071 Palma de Mallorca, Spain
{cjuiz,putxi}@uib.es

Abstract. Our paper proposes an algorithm for a web switch that manages a cluster of web servers, evaluated through discrete event simulation as the first step in the construction of a new web switch. The web switch model is based on the estimation of the throughput that the servers would have in the next future to dynamically balance the workload according to a pre-established quality of service for different types of users. In order to reduce the checking time, estimations are only computed in a variable slot scheduling. Simulation results show that a commitment between overhead and performance should be established to obtain good results in a stressed web cluster of servers.

1 Introduction

The main focus of this research is the design of an algorithm for a Web switch that manages a cluster of Web servers that implement a Quality of Service (QoS). We have developed an algorithm that resides in a Web switch and controls all incoming traffic of the whole web system. The web switch not only controls the status of the Web servers but also balances the workload according to the values of selected performance magnitudes. This paper presents a simulation model for an adaptive solution of a web switch, based on the estimation of servers' throughput in the next future to reserve resources in servers and balance the load among them. Estimation is obtained from previous servers' throughput, peak characteristics of incoming traffic and servers' current utilization. The dispatching algorithm also takes into account the burstiness factor of the web servers to control the duration of the slots. Thus, this research represents the first step in the construction of a new web switch; the performance evaluation of a model through discrete event simulation.

There are several studies on this subject. Unlike our work, Aron et al. [2] cluster reserve's requires significant changes in the operating system kernel of all nodes of the system for customizing resource scheduling. In addition, Aron proposes an optimization algorithm to determine the cluster reserve during execution that implies a high computational cost for the front end node. Li et al. [10] implement a thin layer between Ethernet driver and IP layer. We propose a modification of code just in the web switch, leaving the server's operating system untouched. Other works ([11],[17]) based their study in M/M/1 model for servers so no bursty arrivals are considered . Lu et al. [11] combine a queuing – theoretic predictor with feedback control architecture to achieve relative delay guarantees in high performance server.

The remainder of this paper is organized as follows: Section 2 includes a short description of our Web cluster architecture. The dispatching algorithm is described completely in Section 3. Workload conditions and simulation results are depicted on Section 4 and 5 respectively. Finally, Section 6 presents some concluding remarks.

2 System Architecture

A set of servers plus a switch housed together in the same physical location compose a Web cluster. The switch, considered as a layer-7 web switch, is the first device belonging to the web system that users' requests meet. The web switch could be considered a content-aware switch [5] that means that it can examine the content of HTTP incoming requests, and balance them according to the type of page requested by the user. The architecture of the web cluster is shown in Figure 1. The switch takes over incoming requests, selects a server inside the cluster and routes the requests to the server.

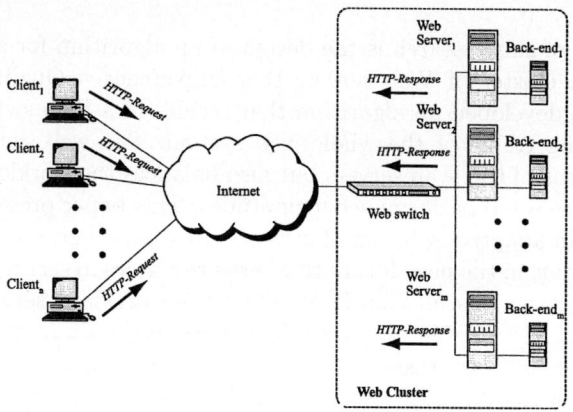

Fig. 1. Web cluster architecture

3 Dispatching Algorithm

Given a web cluster that provides demanding web services, a pre-defined Service Level Agreement (SLA) has to be set. Thus, two types of users have been defined depending on two different web service profiles: *first class* users and *second class* users. We will name their respective incoming requests as *class 1* and *class 2* in the rest of this paper. The switch should guarantee this level of agreement for first class users; therefore it has to transmit their requests to best performing servers while the corresponding service level for the rest of users is lower and may not be guaranteed.

Two throughput estimators of performance have been considered for each server during each slot. Each of the servers attends both types of user requests according to the proposed resource allocation strategy.

3.1 Burstiness and Performance

It is critical to understand the nature of network traffic in order to design a good dispatching algorithm for the Web switch. Several studies have revealed that workload in Internet traffic has self-similar characteristics ([7],[14],[9]). This implies that significant traffic variance or burstiness is present in a wide range of time scales. Therefore burstiness needs to be controlled in a web site to procure a good performance of the whole system, especially when demand is high enough. Burstiness control has been included in the form of a burstiness factor defined as a coefficient, which enables the switch to restrain an eventual saturation of web servers. Given a measurement interval T and a number of slots n, the duration of each fixed slot k is obtained as

$$D_k = \frac{T}{n} = t_k - t_{k-1}. \qquad (1)$$

The mean arrival rate for each server i during the whole measurement interval is noted as λ_i. For each slot k and each server i, $\lambda_{i,k}$ is the corresponding arrival rate. If $\lambda_{i,k} > \lambda_i$ then the slot is considered as a "bursty" slot. Given n slots, *burstiness factor* is defined as the relation between the cumulative number of slots that satisfy $\lambda_{i,k} > \lambda_i$, called n_i^+ [12]:

$$b_{k,i} = \frac{n_i^+}{n}. \qquad (2)$$

In this paper we consider a variable duration slot schedule. The value of the burstiness factor on the current slot is the magnitude that will define the duration of the next slot. Thus, if burst is detected in the servers during current slot, the following testing time is reduced to check earlier the incoming traffic. If no burst appears, the duration of the following slot is enlarged in order to reduce the overhead. By controlling the duration of testing slots, the reduction on future performance of web servers may be forecasted. Let's consider the observation time, T, divided into several slots of variable duration. Due to the fact that the duration of the slots is variable, the number of them during running time is also variable. Let us define e_k as the current number of slots in the time t_k (beginning of slot $k + 1$) being $D_k = t_k - t_{k-1}$, the duration of the last slot in t_k, as is illustrated in Figure 2.

$$D_k = \frac{T}{e_k}. \qquad (3)$$

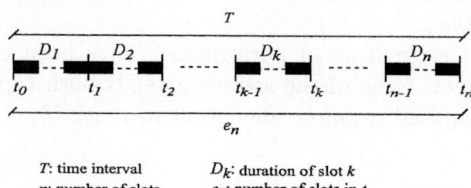

T: time interval D_k: duration of slot k
n: number of slots e_k: number of slots in t_k

Fig. 2. Variable-adaptive slotted time

Several rules have been defined to control the duration of the slots in the variable slotted time schedule. At the end of the slot k, the proposed algorithm recalculates the number of slots e_{k+1}, to use in the following slot, based on the maximum burstiness detected among the set of servers, denoted as $\hat{b}_k$, the minimum burstiness, denoted as $\check{b}_k$, and the number of slots previously defined e_k.

$$\begin{aligned} e_{k+1} &= e_k + \check{b}_k \cdot e_k & if\ \hat{b}_k - \hat{b}_{k-1} &> 0, \\ e_{k+1} &= e_k - \hat{b}_k \cdot e_k & if\ &\begin{cases} \hat{b}_k - \hat{b}_{k-1} \leq 0 \\ and\ \hat{b}_k \neq 0, \end{cases} \\ e_{k+1} &= e_k/n & if\ \hat{b}_k &= \check{b}_k = 0. \end{aligned} \qquad (4)$$

Once e_{k+1} is calculated, the duration of the following slot $k + 1$, D_{k+1}, is obtained by applying the expression 3. The duration of the first slot must be long enough to avoid the first transient period resulting of the initialization of the system.

3.2 Throughput Forecasting

This paper considers the need of approximately calculating next future performance behavior of web servers. These forecasting tasks avoid the use of delayed load information, also called "*herd-effect*" [8]. This effect implies that machines that appear to be underutilized quickly become overloaded because all requests are sent to those machines until new load information is propagated. Using forecasting information, we try to predict the behaviors of the web servers in a close future time to prevent from "herd-effect". However, to avoid the overhead produced by testing continuously the performance of servers, both estimations are done according to an adaptive slotted testing period.

Filter Prediction. Filter prediction is based on previous estimation of throughput and real throughput measured from the servers for each client requests type. For a slot k, the filter includes the throughput measurement of current and previous slot for each server i, and traffic class j, namely $X_{k,i,j}$ and $X_{k-1,i,j}$. Thus, let's define $\tilde{X}^I_{k,i,j}$, the mean estimated throughput at slot k for the server i and traffic class j,

$$\tilde{X}^I_{k,i,j} = A_k \cdot \tilde{X}^I_{k-1,i,j} + (1 - A_k) \cdot \frac{X_{k,i,j} + X_{k-1,i,j}}{2}. \qquad (5)$$

Thus, this estimated throughput depends on two terms: the last computed prediction and the average of the actual and previous measurements. The result of this computation is filtering throughput values based on the probability A_k [6]. This exponential smoothing places more weight on recent historical prediction. Therefore, the *Adaptive Estimated Probability*, A_k, is defined as follows:

$$A_k = \frac{2 \cdot e_k - 1}{2 \cdot e_k + 1}. \qquad (6)$$

Since the average number of slots computed at slot k, known as e_k, is inversely proportional to the duration of the slot, D_k, the weight of A_k probability indirectly depends on burstiness (see 4). If the current slot is "long", then estimation places even more weight to previous throughput estimation. On contrast, if current slot is "short", the prediction stresses throughput measured in servers during slots k and $k-1$.

This filtering provides two throughput estimations for each server in the cluster for the corresponding slot. The main effect of this estimation is smoothing traffic peaks to hold an accurate performance estimation of the servers in a long run.

Burst Prediction. The difference of burstiness in two consecutive slots averaged by the difference of their respective measured throughputs, for each server i and traffic class j, is represented by a *Locking Indicator* in each slot k.

$$\beta_{k,i,j} = (b_{k,i} - b_{k-1,i}) \cdot (X_{k,i,j} - X_{k-1,i,j}). \qquad (7)$$

This locking indicator computes the throughput variation during the last two periods. Thus, the locking indicator measures the difference between the current and the previous burstiness factors and if it is greater than zero, then multiplies it by the difference between measured throughputs at k and k-1 slots. The resulting product of the locking indicator expresses the amount of variation of servers' performance due to the burstiness on client transactions arrivals. If the burstiness detected in the slot is lower than the burstiness detected in the previous slot, then the locking factor is annulled. Therefore, the locking indicator is averaged dividing the utilization of the server i attending requests of type j, $U_{k-1,i,j}$, by the burstiness factor of the server detected at the previous slot $k-1$ [4].

$$\tilde{X}^{II}_{k,i,j} = \tilde{X}^{II}_{k-1,i,j} - \left(\beta_{k,i,j} \cdot \frac{U_{k-1,i,j}}{b_{k-1,i,j}}\right). \tag{8}$$

The role of this second estimator is to prevent the servers' performance computation degeneration caused by incoming traffic that show bursty behavior.

3.3 Resource Allocation

It is necessary to specify a resource allocation strategy in servers among the two types of client requests that can reach the system. We have elaborated a policy in basis of the utilization of servers and backend servers. So each class of incoming traffic has a fraction of server's utilization level guaranteed for each slot. Let's define a constant *weighting index* of class j as c_j, representing the user's relative utilization specifications. This index is recalculated in each slot for each server and for each traffic class depending on best and worst performing tactics, that consist on computing the Euclidean distance from the throughput estimation of server candidates to the origin (0, 0). The selected "best" server for traffic class j is the one that maximizes this distance among the m servers belonging to the current set at slot k for traffic class j. The more distance from the origin to the two-dimension estimation point, the faster is the considered web server. The "worst" server minimizes this distance.

$$q_{k,i,j} = \sqrt{\left(\tilde{X}^{I}_{k,i,j}\right)^2 + \left(\tilde{X}^{II}_{k,i,j}\right)^2}. \tag{9}$$

So, recalculation of the weighting indexes for "best" and "worst" servers of traffic class 1 and 2 is done as follows, being N the total number of pair (server, backend server) of the system. The rest of the servers maintain the value of the weighting index in previous slot.

$$
\begin{array}{lll}
c'_{k,i,1} = c'_{k-1,i,1} + A \cdot N \cdot c_1; & c'_{k,i,2} = c'_{k-1,i,2} - A \cdot N \cdot c_2 & if \ \max\{q_{k,i,1}\}, i \in N \\
c'_{k,i,1} = c'_{k-1,i,1} - A \cdot N \cdot c_1; & c'_{k,i,2} = c'_{k-1,i,2} + A \cdot N \cdot c_2 & if \ \max\{q_{k,i,2}\}, i \in N \\
c'_{k,i,1} = c'_{k-1,i,1} - A \cdot N \cdot c_1; & c'_{k,i,2} = c'_{k-1,i,2} + A \cdot N \cdot c_2 & if \ \min\{q_{k,i,1}\}, i \in N \\
c'_{k,i,1} = c'_{k-1,i,1} + A \cdot N \cdot c_1; & c'_{k,i,2} = c'_{k-1,i,2} - A \cdot N \cdot c_2 & if \ \min\{q_{k,i,2}\}, i \in N \\
c'_{k,i,1} = c'_{k-1,i,1} & & otherwise.
\end{array}
\tag{10}
$$

We have introduced a new factor A in expression 10, that is obtained from the number of servers, N divided by a reducing factor, ε.

These values will determine the use of servers during execution time. The web switch sums up the weighting indexes for each server for the following slot and divides the total available resource proportionally among both traffic classes.

Servers are selected by a RR policy for each class of traffic. When a traffic class' weighting index is reached in a server, it is removed from that traffic class' RR queue until the following slot. So requests will be discarded only if all servers have reached their weighting indexes for a traffic class.

3.4 Switching Algorithm Design

The general structure of the switch algorithm is basically comprised in two parts, the *computing* phase and the *transient* phase. During testing time of each slot, the web switch is running on the *transient* phase. At the end of each slot, the *computing* phase prepares the system for the following slot.

Transient and *computing* phases is detailed in Figure 3.

```
TRANSIENT PHASE:                        COMPUTATION PHASE:
//    INCOMING REQUESTS                 for all class
while TRUE {                               for all serv {
   get_next_request(req);                    compute(X^I_k,serv,class);
   serv=RR(req.class);                       compute(X^II_k,serv,class);
   if serv=0 then transit(OUT);              euc_distance(sever,class)
   else transit(serv);                       compute(c'_k,serv,class);
//    OUTGOING RESPONSES
while TRUE {
   get_next_response(res, serv);
   modify_throughput(serv);  }
```

Fig. 3. Transient and Computation phase.

4 Workload Conditions

The expected workload model considered in this paper includes general features of web sites. Web content is mainly composed by two classes of web pages: *static* and *dynamic* content. The content size requested by each request ranges between 5-13 Kbytes [2]. Experimental measures have been taken to obtain service times and arrival rates, by running several benchmarks in a client and a server connected through a 10/100 Mpbs local area network. Workload has been generated by three different benchmarks: *Webstone* [16], *Httperf* [13] and *Apache Benchmark* [1].

WebStone benchmark measures the throughput and latency of each HTTP transfer and reports a useful metric derived from Little's Law. Results obtained by *Webstone* benchmark have been confronted with *Apache* benchmark and *Httperf* reports. Thus, saturation frequencies of HTTP requests (maximum throughput) per class (static and dynamic) of each server have been supplied by the tests performed with these three benchmarks. This set of saturation frequencies represents the 100% of simulated servers' utilization.

Several distributions could be considered but a clear picture of this is revealed in [3]. Since the nature of the Internet traffic is self-similar, we have defined the arrival rate of incoming requests as Pareto-distributed:

$$P(x) = \frac{\alpha \cdot b^\alpha}{x^{\alpha+1}}, \tag{11}$$

with $\alpha = 1.4$ and b obtained form saturation rate for each request type. On the other hand, service times for static and dynamic requests at servers are modeled according to different hyperexponential distributions where average values were obtained from benchmarking.

5 Simulation Results

A simulation model of complete web cluster system has been constructed using QNAP2 [15]. The experimental model includes six servers and six back-end servers that perform client transactions. The weighting index of class 1 has been defined as $c_1 = 0.5$ and $c_2 = 0.3$ for class 2, that means al least 50% of the utilization level of pairs (server, back-end server) should belong to requests of class 1 and 30% to class 2. Three different switch algorithms have been implemented, namely, *pure static*, *pure dynamic* and *adaptive*. They have been simulated until confidence intervals arrive to the 95%. We perform several simulations of 60 seconds each, where arrival rate is being increased in order to raise the utilization level of the system, until it is equal to the maximum. Figures shown in this section present the results of these simulations.

In order to confront the different performance behavior of switch algorithms, all of them have been tested under the same workload conditions. Overhead has also been computed to examine the goodness of the estimations.

5.1 Pure Static Algorithm

The term *static* means that the weighting indexes do not change during execution time. In this case, there is neither need of throughput prediction nor need of taking measures of server throughputs. This implies a perfect situation in terms of overhead, because the algorithm runs in the switch and no additional measurements of server throughput should be taken to control the performance of the system. Slots duration are calculated as expressed in formulas 3 and 4 to control when weighting indexes are reached and then to remove the server from the corresponding RR queue.

5.2 Pure Dynamic Algorithm

This version of the algorithm executes *computing* and *transient phase* for each incoming request, so it is not necessary to divide simulation time under a slotted schedule. This means that the pure dynamic algorithm achieves the best performance until servers' saturation because switch chooses "best" and "worst" servers at each transaction. When servers are overloaded, RR queues are quickly emptied of servers so requests' refusal begins in a quite short period of time. The overhead of the system can be calculated on basis of arrival rate level of requests because each time a request arrives to the system, the switch computes off server's throughput predictors and checks if resource allocation has to be modified.

5.3 Predictive and Adaptive Algorithm

This last version of the algorithm includes throughput predictors introduced in Section 3.2, and *transient* and *computing phases* described in Figure 3. The duration of the slots varies depending on *burstiness factor*, so that, in the worst case, the overhead will be as high as pure dynamic algorithm. Our intention is to find a balanced solution able to maintain system stability by guaranteeing SLA constraints and reducing the overhead level of the pure dynamic algorithm.

Simulation results of adaptive algorithm show that the mean value of computing phase executions is 141 for a total of 487383 arriving requests. Thus, the comparison of overhead level is less than 0.28% of the pure dynamic algorithm.

Figure 4 shows in horizontal axis the relation between the mean number of class 1 requests attended , and the mean number of queued requests during several simulations of 60 seconds. It can be observed that adaptive algorithm serves more requests than dynamic and static, and that it has less queued requests than static. Requests refusal is quite meaningful to understand the benefits of adaptive algorithm, we will analyze it below. If we contrast these results to Figure 5, we can conclude that back-end servers are less overloaded when system utilization level is near to 100% in adaptive algorithm than in static and dynamic algorithms, even serving more requests. We have chosen back-end servers because they are easily overloaded attending dynamic requests.

Finally, we compare throughput and rejected requests of algorithms. Figure 6 shows in vertical axis the result of subtracting rejected requests per second to throughput of adaptive and static algorithms and Figure 7 includes also dynamic algorithm. Adaptive algorithm does not reject any class 1 request, while static begins the rejection of class 1 when system is at 95% of level utilization and dynamic begins when utilization level is near 75%. Dynamic algorithm rejects lots of requests because is continuously testing servers' weighting indexes that show in real time how quickly servers are becoming congested.

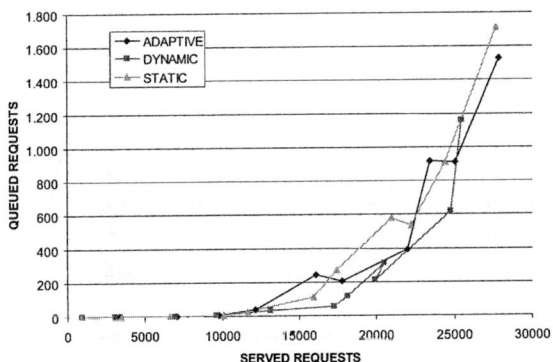

Fig. 4. Served requests versus queued requests of traffic class 1

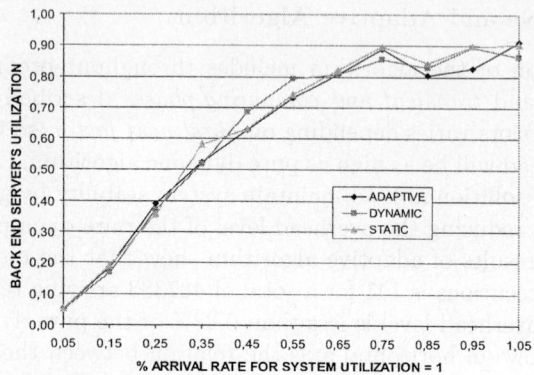

Fig. 5. Back-end servers' utilization

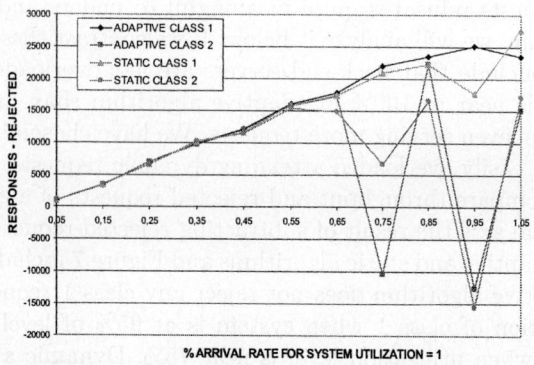

Fig. 6. Served requests minus rejected requests for adaptive and static algorithm

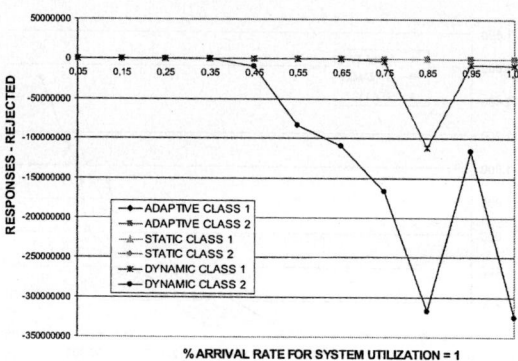

Fig. 7. Served requests minus rejected requests for three versions of algorithm

6 Conclusions

This paper has presented a new proposal of adaptive switching algorithms for web clusters. The algorithm relies on throughput estimations scheduled on slotted time periods, including a burst predictor that detects the burstiness of traffic and the variation on future servers' throughput. The filter predictor reduces the impact of typical traffic peaks due to the Internet nature. Both are combined to select the best performance server in the cluster to guarantee the SLA. Thus, the switching algorithm is three times adaptive: in the transient phase when the slot time of testing period is variable depending on the traffic conditions, in the computing phase when resource allocation for the "best" and "worst" servers for each traffic class is recalculated to improve efficiency and when utilization level of each server is compared to weighting indexes to know when to stop sending requests to it. All these procedures are done controlling the overhead produced. The proposal has been confronted by simulation with pure static and pure dynamic scheduling. This paper tries to establish new ways of implementing non-functional requirements on web switching algorithms. Therefore, the continuous refinement on the web switching design including not only performability but also availability, security, etc. estimations will improve the perceived service for users.

References

1. Apache Benchmark. http://www.apache.org
2. Aron, M.: Differentiated and Predictable Quality of Service in Web Server Systems. PhD thesis, Department of Computer Science, Rice University. (2000)
3. Barford, P., Bestavros, A, Bradley, A. and Crovella, M. E.: Changes in Web Client Access Patterns: Characteristics and Caching Implications. World Wide Web 2(1-2) (1999) 15–28
4. Buzen, J. P.: Operational Analysis: an Alternative to Stochastic Modelling. In: Performance of Computer Installations, North Holland. (1978) 175–194
5. Casalicchio, E., Colajanni, M.: Scalable Web Cluster with Static and Dynamic Contents. In: Proc. IEEE Int'l Conf. on Cluster Computing, Chemnitz, Germany. (2000)
6. Casetti, C., Gerla, M., Mascolo, S., Sanadidi, M., Wang, R.: TCP Westwood: Bandwidth Estimation for Enhanced Transport over Wireless Links. In: Proceedings of ACM MOBICOM. (2001)
7. Crovella, M., Bestavros, A.: Self-Similarity in World Wide Web Traffic: Evidence and Possible Causes. In: Proceedings of SIGMETRICS'96: The ACM International Conference on Measurement and Modeling of Computer Systems, Philadelphia, Pennsylvania. (1996)
8. Dahlin, M.: Interpreting Stale Load Information. In: Proceedings of the 19th International Conference on Distributed Computing Systems. (1999)
9. Kant, K.: On Aggregate Traffic Generation with Multifractal Properties. In: Proceedings of GLOBECOM, Rio de Janeiro, Brazil. (2000)
10. Li, C., Peng, G., Golapan, K., Chiueh, T.-C.: Performance Guarantee for Cluster-Based Internet Services. In: 9th International Conference on Parallel and Distributed Systems, Taiwan. (2002)

11. Lu, Y., Abdelzaher, T., Lu, Ch., Sha, L., Liu, X.: Feedback Control with Queueing-Theoretic Prediction for Relative Delay. In: Real-Time and Embedded Technology and Applications Symposium, Toronto, Canada. (2003)
12. Menascé, D.A., Almeida, V.A.F.: Scaling for E-Business. Prentice Hall. (2000)
13. Mosberger, D., Jin, T.: Httperf: A Tool for Measuring Web Server Performance. In: First Workshop on Internet Server Performance. (1998) 59–67
14. Pitkow, J.E.: Summary of WWW Characterizations. Computer Networks and ISDN Systems **30**(1-7) (1998) 551–558
15. Simulog Corp. The QNAP Reference Manual. V.4.
16. Webstone Benchmark. http://www.mindcraft.com/webstone/
17. Zhang, A., Santos,P., Beyer, D., Tang, H.-K.: Optimal Server Resource Allocation Using an Open Queueing Network Model of Response Time. Technical Report, Hewlett Packard Laboratories, Number HPL-2002-301, p. 16. (2002)

ARTÌS: A Parallel and Distributed Simulation Middleware for Performance Evaluation*

Luciano Bononi, Michele Bracuto, Gabriele D'Angelo, and Lorenzo Donatiello

Dipartimento di Scienze dell'Informazione, Università degli Studi di Bologna
Via Mura Anteo Zamboni 7, 40126, Bologna, Italy
{bononi,bracuto,gdangelo,donat}@cs.unibo.it

Abstract. This paper illustrates the motivation, the preliminary design and implementation issues, of a new distributed simulation middleware named Advanced RTI System (ARTÌS). The aim of the ARTÌS middleware is to support parallel and distributed simulations of complex systems characterized by heterogeneous and distributed model components. The ARTÌS design is oriented to support the model components heterogeneity, distribution and reuse, and to increase the simulation performances, scalability and speedup, in parallel and distributed simulation scenarios. Another design issue of the ARTÌS framework is the dynamic adaptation of the interprocess communication layer to the heterogeneous communication support of different simulation scenarios. In this paper we illustrate the guidelines and architecture that we considered in the design and implementation of the ARTÌS middleware, and we sketch some case studies that demonstrated the ARTÌS utility and motivation, e.g., a distributed simulation of massively populated wireless ad hoc and sensor networks.

1 Introduction

The design of complex systems composed by many heterogeneous components requires appropriate analysis methodologies and tools to test and to validate the system architectures, the integration and interoperability of components, and the overall system performances [18]. The performance evaluation of complex systems may rely on simulation techniques because the model complexity obtained with alternative analytical and numerical techniques often results in unpractical or unaffordable methods and computation [18, 8, 1, 2, 9, 25]. Well known sequential and monolithic event-based simulation tools have been created for analyzing general purpose system models (e.g., computation architectures, systems on chip, database systems) [15, 16] and more targeted system models (e.g., computer networks) [14, 17]. The problem with a sequential monolithic simulator is that it must rely on the assumption of being implemented on a single execution unit, whose resources may be limited, and it cannot exploit any degree of

---

* This work is supported by MIUR FIRB funds under the project "Performance Evaluation of Complex Systems: Techniques, Methodologies, and Tools".

computation parallelism. To obtain a significant insight of a complex system, detailed and fine-grained simulation models must be designed, implemented and executed as a simulation process, often resulting in high computation and high memory allocation needs.

This fact translates in computation and memory bottlenecks that may limit the complexity and the number of model components (i.e., the simulated system scalability) that can be supported by the simulation process. One solution to overcome these limitations can be found in parallel and distributed simulation techniques, in which many simulation processes can be distributed over multiple execution units. The simulation semantics, the event ordering and event causality can be maintained and guaranteed with different approaches (e.g., optimistic vs. conservative), by relying on distributed model-components' communication and synchronization services.

Parallel and distributed simulation platforms and tools have been demonstrated to be effective in reducing the simulation execution time, i.e., in increasing the simulation speedup. Moreover, parallel and distributed platforms could exploit wide and aggregate memory architectures realized by a set of autonomous and interconnected execution units, by implementing the required communication and synchronization services. Examples of the Parallel and Distributed Discrete Event Simulation (PDES) approach can be found in [8,9], e.g., Glomosim [25] based on PARSEC [1], Maisie [22], parallel and distributed implementations based on Network Simulator (ns-2) [14,20] based on RTI-Kit [20], on ANSE/WARPED [19], Wippet [12], SWiMNET [3], and many others [13,22]. More recently, the distributed simulation world agreed on the need for standards, and converged in the definition of a new standard, named IEEE 1516 Standard for parallel and distributed modeling and simulation [11]. The High level Architecture (HLA) has currently become a synonymous for the middleware implementation of distributed simulation services and a RunTime (RTI) simulation kernel, based on the IEEE 1516 Standard definition [11,4,5].

Unfortunately, the need for distributed model-components communication and synchronization services may require massive interprocess communication to make the distributed simulation to evolve in correct way. Complex systems with detailed and fine-grained simulation models can be considered communication-intensive under the distributed simulation approach. As a result, interprocess communication may become the bottleneck of the distributed simulation paradigm, and solutions to reduce the cost of communication must be addressed by the research in this field [8,2,9,24]. Additional research studies, aiming to exploit the maximum level of computation parallelism, dealt with dynamic balancing of logical processes' executions (both cpu-loads and virtual time-advancing speeds) by trading-off communication, synchronization and speedup, both in optimistic and conservative approaches [7,10,23,24].

The efficient implementation of interprocess communication is required as a primary background issue, to overcome the possible communication bottleneck of parallel and distributed simulations. The way interprocess communication can be sustained in distributed systems would depend mainly on the execution units' architectures and on the simulation system scenario. Recently proposed and implemented middleware solutions based on the IEEE 1516 Standard for distributed simulation and the High level Architecture (HLA) [11, 5, 4] have shown that the parallel and distributed simulation of massive and complex systems can suffer the distributed communication bottlenecks, due to suboptimal implementation of the interprocess communication services, over the simulation execution platform.

In this paper we propose an overview of the design, preliminary implementation results and guidelines, for a new, parallel and distributed simulation middleware named Advanced RTI System (ARTÌS). The design of the ARTÌS middleware architecture is based on the guidelines provided by the analysis and evaluation of existing HLA-based RTI implementations, and on the observations about the sub-optimal design and management of distributed interprocess communication. Specifically, we oriented the ARTÌS design towards the adaptive evaluation of the communication bottlenecks and interchangeable support for multiple communication infrastructures, from shared memory to Internet-based communication services.

This paper is organized as follows. In Section 2 we sketch the motivations for our study, and some comments on existing implementations. In Section 3 we present the design and architecture of the ARTÌS middleware, with some emphasis on the implementation guidelines. Section 4 sketches some simulation testbeds and case studies we defined to test the ARTÌS implementation. Section 5 presents conclusions and future work.

2 Motivation and Preliminary Discussion

In the following we give a short description of the motivations for this study, and the comments that have been originated by the analysis of existing middleware implementations of the HLA-based distributed simulation middleware.

Model components' reuse is considered a relevant issue to be supported in designing a new simulation system. On the other hand, model components may be confidential information on behalf of the companies that designed them. The owner companies could be interested, under a commercial viewpoint, in allowing their models to be embedded as "black box" components for evaluating the integration analysis and compliance with other solutions. The open model-component source code could introduce the risk to reveal the confidential know-how in the component design solutions. A way to overcome this problem would be given by supporting the model component simulation in distributed way, and more specifically, over execution units local to the owner company domain. Distributed model components would simply export their interfaces and interactions (i.e., messages) with the simulation middleware and runtime infrastructure (RTI) implementing a distributed simulation. This scenario would require that a general network communication infrastructure (e.g., the Internet) would support the message passing communication between distributed model components of a parallel or distributed simulation. This is the reason why we conceptualized a distributed simulation that could be performed over TCP/IP or Reliable-UDP/IP network protocol stacks, like in web-based simulations. Under the latter assumption, the distributed simulation platform is intended as a way to interconnect protected objects, instead of a way to improve the simulation speedup. Other possible killer applications for such a distributed simulation middleware design would be the distributed Internet Gaming applications, gaining an even growing interest nowadays. The opportune design of the simulation framework, based on the exploitation of the communication scenario heterogeneities and characteristics, could improve the overall simulation performance of distributed and remotely executed processes.

The most natural and efficient execution scenarios for parallel and distributed simulations often involve shared memory (SHM) and/or local area networks (LAN) as the infrastructures supporting inter-process communication and synchronization services. Nowadays, it is even more frequent the adoption of networked cluster of PCs, in the place of shared-memory or tightly-coupled multiprocessors, as the execution units of the distributed simulation, primarily for cost reasons. The aforementioned motivations for model reuse and wide distribution of the model component execution is demanding for a generalized support for inter-process communication, up to the Internet-based services. It is self-evident how the increase of the communication cost (i.e., the communication latency of local and wide area network-based communication) would result in a reduction of the simulation speed. In other words, any reduction of the communication-time cost would translate in more efficiency of the simulation processes. The communication-time reduction could play a fundamental role in determining the communication and synchronization overheads between the distributed model components.

As remarked in [2], a distributed simulation approach is not always guaranteed to gain in performance with respect to a sequential simulation. The problem with the distributed simulation arises when a high degree of interactions is required in dynamic environments, mapping on distributed synchronization and inter-process communication. The basic solution to distribute the events information among interacting distributed components was the information flooding (broadcast) solution. This solution is quite immediate to implement over a generalized communication platform, but it was also originating the communication bottleneck effect for the distributed simulation. It was immediately clear that a reduction of communication would have been needed, by following two possible approaches: model aggregation and communication filtering. Model aggregation incarnates the idea to cluster interacting objects, by exploiting a degree of locality of communications that translates in a lower communication load than the one obtained in flat broadcast (that is, communication flooding) systems. Model aggregation can be performed by simplifying the model, or by maintaining the model detail. Solutions based on model simplification have been proposed, based on relaxation and overhead elimination, by dynamically introducing higher levels of abstraction and merging in system sub-models [2, 19, 23]. These solutions allow a reduction of communication since the messages are filtered on the basis of the level of abstraction considered. Solutions preserving full model-detail have been proposed by dynamically filtering the event- and state-information dissemination. Examples can be found [2], based on interest management groups [23], responsibility domains, spheres of influence, multicast group allocation, data distribution management [21,5], grid distribution and routing spaces [21,5,7], model and management partitioning [3]. These approaches rely on the reduction of communication obtained when the update of an event- or state-information (e.g., event and/or anti-message) does not need to be flooded to the whole system, but is simply propagated to all the causally-dependent components. This is the basis of publishing/subscribing mechanisms for sharing state-information and event-notifications between causally dependent components [21,5,20]. The solution provided in order to dynamically filter the communication among distributed objects was the ancestor of the Data Distribution Management (DDM) concept realized and implemented in HLA-based solutions [11].

The High Level Architecture (HLA) is a middleware implementation based on recently approved standard (IEEE 1516) dealing with component-oriented distributed simulation [11]. The HLA defines rules and interfaces allowing for heterogeneous components' interoperability in distributed simulation. The definition of distributed model components (formally known as federates) with standard management APIs brings to a high degree of model re-usability. The HLA standard defines APIs for the communication and synchronization tasks among federates. The distributed simulation is supported by a runtime middleware (RTI). The RTI is mainly responsible for providing a general support for time management, distributed objects' interaction, attributes' ownership and many other optimistic and conservative event-management policies. The IEEE 1516 standard has gained a good popularity but still has not reached the planned diffusion. The main reasons are the complex definitions and design work required to modelers. On the other hand, the preliminary implementations of distributed simulation middleware solutions and architectures were too complex, too slow and required a great startup time to achieve the expected results. Specifically, since its definition, the IEEE 1516 Standard has been criticized about its structure and its effective ability to manage really complex and dynamic models [6]. By analyzing the existing RTI implementations, to the best of our knowledge, few currently available middleware solutions have been designed with some emphasis on the adaptive exploitation of the communication infrastructure heterogeneity which may be characterizing the distributed simulation-execution scenario. More specifically, the Georgia-tech RTI-kit [21] implementation has been realized by introducing some elasticity and optimization in the exploitation of the shared memory execution-system architecture, whereas many other implementations still rely on UDP or TCP socket-based interprocess communication even on a single execution unit. It is worth noting that rare implementations provided the source code to users, allowing them to configure the middleware on the basis of the user needs and execution-system architecture.

The support for heterogeneous communication services and architectures should be considered as a design principle in the implementation of a distributed simulation middleware. Moreover, the adaptive optimization and management of the middleware communication layer realized over heterogeneous network architectures, technologies and services should be considered both in the initialization phase, and at runtime, in a distributed simulation process. Our ARTÌS implementation aims to be Open Source, and to provide an elastic, easy to configure adaptation of the communication layer to the execution system.

3 The ARTÌS Middleware

The HLA implementation criticisms and the lack of Open Source implementations are the main motivations behind the design and implementation of ARTÌS (Advanced RTI System). The main purpose of ARTÌS is the efficient support of complex simulations in a parallel or distributed environment.

The ARTÌS implementation follows a component-based design, that should result in a quite extendible middleware. The solutions proposed for time management and synchronization in distributed simulations have been widely analyzed and discussed. Currently, ARTÌS supports the conservative time management based on both the time-stepped approach, and the Chandy-Misra-Bryant algorithm. In the near future we have planned to extend ARTÌS to support optimistic time management algorithms. The initial choice to support the conservative approach was a speculation on the highly unpredictable characteristics of our target models of interest [2], which would have led to frequent rollbacks. Anyway, we plan to investigate this assumption, and compare the optimistic and conservative approaches as a future work.

In ARTÌS, design optimizations have been applied to adapt adequate protocols for synchronization and communication in Local Area Network (LAN) or Shared Memory (SHM) multiprocessor architectures. In our vision the communication and synchronization middleware should be adaptive and user-transparent about all optimizations required to improve performances. The presence of a shared memory for the communication among parallel or distributed Logical Processes (LPs) offers the advantage of low latency, and reliable communication mechanism. Interactions are modeled as read and write operations performed in shared memory, within the address space of logical processes. A memory access is faster than a network communication, but the shared memory itself is not sufficient to alleviate the distributed communication problem. To take advantage of the shared memory architecture, concurrent accesses to memory require strict synchronization and mutual exclusion, together with deadlock avoidance and distributed control.

Figure 1 shows the structure of the ARTÌS middleware. ARTÌS is composed by a set of logical modules organized in a stack-based architecture. The communication layer is located at the bottom of the middleware architecture, and it is composed by a set of different communication modules. The ARTÌS middleware is able of adaptively select the best interaction module with respect to the dynamic allocation of Logical Processes (LPs) in the execution environment. The current scheme adopts an incremental straightforward policy: given a set of LPs

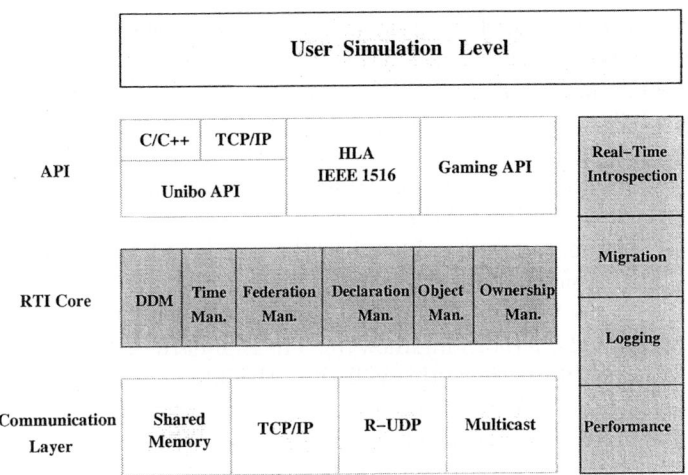

Fig. 1. The ARTÌS modules' structure and layered architecture

on the same physical host, such processes always communicate and synchronize via shared memory. To implement these services we have designed, implemented and tested many different solutions. The first implementation was based on Inter Process Communication (IPC) semaphores and locks. This solution was immediately rejected both for performance reasons (semaphore and locks introduce not negligible latency), and for scalability reasons (since the number of semaphores that could be instantiated in a system is limited and statically controlled in the operating system kernel). Among other possible solutions (e.g., we also considered busy-waiting) the current ARTÌS synchronization module works with "wait on signals" and a limited set of temporized spin-locks. This solution has demonstrated very low latency and limited CPU overhead, and it is really noteworthy for good performances obtained in multi-CPU systems, good scalability and also because it does not require any reconfiguration at the operating system kernel level.

In ARTÌS, two or more LPs located on different hosts (i.e., no shared memory available), on the same local area network segment, communicate by using a light Reliable-UDP (R-UDP) transport protocol over the IP protocol. Ongoing activity is evaluating the use of raw sockets for R-UDP data segments directly encapsulated in MAC Ethernet frames (i.e., bypassing the IP layer). The drawback of this solution is that it could be adopted only within a common LAN segment technology. Two or more LPs located on Internet hosts rely on standard TCP/IP connections. Ongoing activity at this level is performed by considering the exploitation of reliable multicast-IP solutions.

The ARTÌS runtime (RTI) core is on the top of the communication layer. It is composed by a set of management modules, whose structure and roles have been inherited by a typical HLA-based simulation middleware, compliant with the IEEE 1516 Standard. The modules currently being under the implementation phase are: the Data Distribution Management (DDM) in charge of managing the dynamic subscription/distribution of event and data update messages, the Time Management module currently implementing the conservative, time-stepped distributed time management, the Federation Management, Declaration Management, Object Management and Ownership Management modules in charge of administrating all the remaining management issues accordingly with the standard rules and APIs.

The ARTÌS runtime core is bound to the user simulation layer by modular sets of application programming interfaces (APIs). Each API group was included in order to allow a full integration and compliance of many distributed model components with the ARTÌS middleware. The Standard API is implemented as the HLA IEEE 1516 interface: this will allow the integration of IEEE 1516 compliant models to the ARTÌS framework. Only a subset of the full Standard API is currently implemented in ARTÌS. The new set of APIs of ARTÌS is called the *University of Bologna APIs* (Unibo APIs). These APIs are currently designed and implemented to offer a simpler access to distributed simulation services than the Standard APIs. This would make easier and simpler for the modelers to create and instantiate a distributed simulation with ARTÌS, than with the Standard APIs. The programming handles of the Unibo APIs are currently provided for C/C++ language code. We planned also to include in ARTÌS an API set specific for Internet Gaming applications, whose design is still in preliminary phase.

Additional orthogonal modules are planned to be dedicated to other specific features, oriented to the adaptive runtime management of synchronization and communication overheads. As an example, a real-time introspection mechanism would be devoted to offer an internal representation of the middleware state while the simulation is running. Logging and Performance modules would support the user simulation with online traces, statistics and runtime data analysis. Previous research works shown that more efficient simulation of dynamic models can be obtained by introducing additional software components implementing distributed model entities migration [2]. The Migration module should be orthogonal in the middleware, with the target to reduce runtime communication overheads accordingly with the coordination supported with other peer modules. To this end, future work is planned to include in ARTÌS a dynamic model-entity migration support that we conceived and illustrated, as a prototype, for the HLA-based middleware on [2]. By defining a dynamic allocation of simulated model entities over different physical execution units we obtained speed-up improvements (and communication overheads reduction) that could be further optimized in ARTÌS, when supported by opportune coordination of the migration modules.

4 ARTÌS Test and Validation

The verification and validation test of the preliminary implementation of the ARTÌS framework has been executed over a set of distributed and heterogeneous model components implemented in C code. The tests performed were based on models of wireless networks' components. The wireless ad hoc networks models were mobile hosts with IEEE 802.11 network interfaces, and static sensor networks based on small-communication-range components. We are also realizing models and experiments to test distributed protocols over large, scale-free networks. All the simulation experiments performed were realized with several thousands model components, and with many logical processes distributed over local (i.e., shared memory) and distributed physical execution units connected by a Fast-Ethernet (100 Mbps) LAN segment. The set of execution units we used in the tests is composed by: several dual Xeon 2.8 GhZ with 2GB RAM, and one Quadral Xeon 1.4 GhZ with 2 GB RAM, all with Debian GNU/Linux OS with kernel version 2.6. All the tests performed shown the ARTÌS framework was correctly implemented, by supporting a scalable number of model components in a conservative distributed simulation. The tests of TCP/IP (i.e., Internet-like) communication scenario were executed over our department's LAN network. The performance comparison of the shared memory, R-UDP and TCP/IP implementation is beyond the scope of this paper and will be done as a future work. Anyway, it was clearly indicated by preliminary results that orders of magnitude differences in simulation performances can be obtained under the different approaches, and this would confirm that adaptive and runtime management realized by the ARTÌS framework to exploit models' and system dynamics, would result in relevant simulation performance gain and overheads reduction.

5 Conclusions and Future Work

In this paper we illustrated the motivation and preliminary design and implementation issues of a new distributed simulation middleware named Advanced RTI System (ARTÌS). The aim of the ARTÌS middleware is to support parallel and distributed simulations of complex systems characterized by heterogeneous and distributed model components. The ARTÌS design is oriented to support the model components heterogeneity, distribution and reuse, and to reduce the communication overheads, by increasing the simulation performances, scalability and speedup, in parallel and distributed simulation scenarios. The ARTÌS design and architecture was presented to illustrate how the reduction of the communication cost and the exploitation of heterogeneous execution platforms could be considered in the design and implementation of parallel and distributed simulation middlewares based on the IEEE 1516 (HLA) Standard. Future work includes the complete implementation of the ARTÌS APIs and management modules, the full investigation of the ARTÌS performance and scalability, the implementation of model component migration and dynamic adaptation primitives, the design of new model components libraries and the distributed Gaming APIs.

References

1. Bagrodia, R., Meyer, R., Takai, M, Chen, Y., Zeng, Z., Martin, J., Song, H.Y.: Parsec: A Parallel Simulation Environment for Complex Systems. Computer **31** (1998) 77-85
2. Bononi, L., D'Angelo, G., Donatiello, L.: HLA-Based Adaptive Distributed Simulation of Wireless Mobile Systems. In: Proceedings of the 17th Workshop on Parallel and Distributed Simulation (PADS 2003), San Diego, California. IEEE Computer Society (2003) 40-49
3. Boukerche, A., Fabbri, A.: Partitioning Parallel Simulation of Wireless Networks. In: Joines, J.A., Barton, R.R., Kang, K., Fishwick, P.A. (eds.): Proceedings of the 32nd Conference on Winter Simulation (WSC 2000), Orlando, Florida. Society for Computer Simulation International (2000) 1449-1457
4. Dahmann J.S., Fujimoto R.M., Weatherly, R.M.: The Department of Defense High Level Architecture. In: Andradóttir, S., Healy, K.J., Withers, D.H., Nelson, B.L. (eds.): Proceedings of the 29th Conference on Winter Simulation (WSC'97), Atlanta, Georgia. ACM (1997) 142-149
5. Dahmann, J.S., Fujimoto, R.M., Weatherly R. M.: The DoD High Level Architecture: An Update. In: Medeiros, D.J., Watson, E.F., Carson, J.S., Manivannan, M.S. (eds.): Proceedings of the 30th Conference on Winter Simulation (WSC'98), Washington, D.C. IEEE Computer Society (1998) 797-804
6. Davis, W.J., Moeller, G.L.: The High Level Architecture: Is There a Better Way? In: Farrington, P.A., Nembhard, H.B., Sturrock, D.T., Evans, G.W. (eds.): Proceedings of the 31st Conference on Winter Simulation (WSC'99), Phoenix, Arizona, Vol. 2. ACM (1999) 1595-1601
7. Deelman, E., Szymanski, B.K.: Dynamic Load Balancing in Parallel Discrete Event Simulation for Spatially Explicit Problems. In: Proceedings of the 12th Workshop on Parallel and Distributed Simulation (PADS'98), Banff, Alberta. IEEE Computer Society (1998) 46-53
8. Ferscha, A.: Parallel and Distributed Simulation of Discrete Event Systems. In: Zomaya, A.Y.H. (ed.): Handbook of Parallel and Distributed Computing. McGraw-Hill, New York (1996)
9. Fujimoto, R.M.: Parallel and Distributed Simulation Systems. John Wiley & Sons, New York (2000)
10. Gan, B.P., Low, Y.H., Jain, S., Turner, S.J., Cai, W., Hsu, W.J., Huang, S.Y.: Load Balancing for Conservative Simulation on Shared Memory Multiprocessor Systems. In: Proceedings of the 14th Workshop on Parallel and Distributed Simulation (PADS 2000), Bologna, Italy. IEEE Computer Society (2000) 139-146
11. IEEE Std 1516-2000: IEEE Standard for Modeling and Simulation (M&S) High Level architecture (HLA) - Framework and Rules, - Federate Interface Specification, - Object Model Template (OMT) Specification, - IEEE Recommended Practice for High Level Architecture (HLA) Federation Development and Execution Process (FEDEP). (2000)
12. Kelly, O.E., Lai, J., Mandayam, N.B., Ogielski, A.T., Panchal, J., Yates, R.D.: Scalable Parallel Simulations of Wireless Networks with WiPPET: Modeling of Radio Propagation, Mobility and Protocols. Mobile Networks and Applications **5** (2000) 199-208
13. Liu, W.W., Chiang, C.-C., Wu, H.-K., Jha, V., Gerla, M., Bagrodia, R.L.: Parallel Simulation Environment for Mobile Wireless Networks. In: Proceedings of the 28th Conference on Winter Simulation (WSC'96), Coronado, California. ACM (1996) 605-612

14. NS-2: The Network Simulator. (2004) http://www.isi.edu/nsman/ns/
15. OMNeT++: Discrete Event Simulation Environment. (2004) http://www.omnetpp.org
16. Open SystemC Initiative. (2004) http://www.systemc.org
17. OpNet Simulation Platform. (2004) http://www.opnet.com
18. PERF Project. Performance Evaluation of Complex Systems: Techniques, Methodologies and Tools, Italian MIUR-FIRB. (2002) http://www.perf.it
19. Rao, D.M., Wilsey, P.A.: Parallel Co-simulation of Conventional and Active Networks. In: Proceedings of the 8th International Symposium on Modeling, Analysis and Simulation of Computer and Telecommunication Systems (MASCOTS 2000), San Francisco, California. IEEE Computer Society (2000) 291–298
20. Riley, G.F., Fujimoto, R.M., Ammar, M.H.: A Generic Framework for Parallelization of Network Simulations. In: Proceedings of the 7th International Symposium on Modeling, Analysis and Simulation of Computer and Telecommunication Systems (MASCOTS'99), College Park, Maryland. IEEE Computer Society (1999) 128–137
21. RTI-Kit. Parallel and Distributed Simulation, Georgia Institute of Technology Research. (2003) http://www.cc.gatech.edu/computing/pads/software.html
22. Short, J., Bagrodia, R., Kleinrock, L.: Mobile Wireless Network System Simulation. Wireless Networks **1** (1995) 451–467
23. Som, T.K., Sargent, R.G.: Model Structure and Load Balancing in Optimistic Parallel Discrete Event Simulation. In: Proceedings of the 14th Workshop on Parallel and Distributed Simulation (PADS 2000), Bologna, Italy. IEEE Computer Society (2000) 147–154
24. Vee, V.-Y., Hsu, W.-J.: Locality-Preserving Load-Balancing Mechanisms for Synchronous Simulations on Shared-Memory Multiprocessors. In: Proceedings of the 14th Workshop on Parallel and Distributed Simulation (PADS 2000), Bologna, Italy. IEEE Computer Society (2000) 131–138
25. Zeng, X., Bagrodia, R., Gerla, M.: GloMoSim: A Library for Parallel Simulation of Large-Scale Wireless Networks. In: Proceedings of the 12th Workshop on Parallel and Distributed Simulation (PADS'98), Banff, Canada. IEEE Computer Society (1998) 154–161

Comparison of Web Server Architectures: A Measurement Study*

Davide Pagnin[1], Marina Buzzi[2], Marco Conti[2], and Enrico Gregori[2]

[1] SSSA, ReTiS Lab, piazza Martini 12, 56100, Pisa, Italy
pagnin@sssup.it
[2] CNR-IIT, via Moruzzi 1, 56124 Pisa, Italy
{marina.buzzi,marco.conti,enrico.gregori}@iit.cnr.it

Abstract. The Quality of Service (QoS) perceived by users is the dominant factor for the success of an Internet-based Web service. Thus, capacity planning has become essential for deploying Web servers. The aim of this study is to understand the key elements in Web server performance. We created a controlled test-bed environment, which allows one to analyze Web server performance in a simple and effective way. In this paper we present an analysis of two different Web server architectures and their performance, with particular focus on discovering bottlenecks.

1 Introduction

Since the mid-1990s, Web Services have been the dominant source of traffic on the Internet. Web server performance has great impact on the popularity of Web sites; thus studies concerning Web performances have become an important research topic in recent years [2, 9, 11, 13, 16]. The key factor is that HTTP-request traffic presents observable burstiness [10, 4, 7] with peak rates exceeding the average rate by an order magnitude [20], thus easily exceeding the capacity of the server. This is a potential source of problems: i.e., difficulties in planning for needed resources, or unacceptable degradation of user perceived QoS. A known issue is that many Web servers suffer from poor overload behavior. For example, under heavy network load, interrupt-driven systems can enter a receiver-livelock state [17]. Therefore it is important to evaluate Web server performance under overload in order to eliminate possible bottlenecks and to allow proper capacity planning [5, 6, 14].

In this study we describe the methodology we adopted and the necessary steps for setting up an effective environment for observing Web server performance. This environment allows fine-tuning of Web server components as well as bottleneck discovery. This methodology for measuring and comparing Web server performances has many other interesting applications. It is possible to tune a Web server against the expected workload, thus achieving improved performance and better user-perceived

---

* Work carried out under the financial support of the FIRB-PERF Project and Roberto del Moretto Memorial Fund.

QoS with an optimized configuration. In addition, it is also possible to compare the efficiency of different operating systems and reveal any error in the implementation of the Web server or operating system.

By applying our methodology to comparison of Web server architectures we observed that:
- o The single-process architecture (i.e., Boa) has better performances than the multi-thread architecture if disk access is limited
- o The multi-thread architecture (i.e., Apache2) is CPU-intensive but is less penalized by disk access
- o Disk-access is the most limiting factor for the server throughput
- o User-perceived QoS degrades greatly when the server is overloaded

This paper is divided into four sections. Section 2 contains a description of the test-bed environment, section 3 presents the indexes adopted for analyzing performances and in section 4 several experiments are fully described and discussed.

2 Test-Bed Characteristics

The approach of directly evaluating the performance of a Web server suffers from difficulties related to the irreproducibility of real workloads together with the highly unpredictable behavior of the Internet and the need for non-intrusive measurement of a live system [1, 21]. The alternative is evaluation through generation of synthetic HTTP client traffic in a controlled environment. However this must be done with great care since generating heavy and realistic traffic with a small number of client machines is difficult [5, 7].

In the following we briefly describe our test-bed environment; the reasons for our choices are discussed in [15]. For introducing WAN delays in the router machine we chose dummynet [19], a system facility that allows control over traffic going through the various network interfaces by applying bandwidth and queue size limitations and simulating delays and losses. With dummynet it is possible to configure many parameters for each connection that crosses the router. The most important are: Link Bandwidth; Buffer Dimensions; Transmission Delay; and Packet Loss Rate.

For workload generation we chose HTTPERF [18] which is capable of sustaining server overload and leaves nearly total freedom as to the kind of workload and measurements to be performed. At the end of each experiment, HTTPERF summarizes the information gathered and generates some statistics related to HTTP connections. Important parameters to be considered for each experiment are:
- o The *request rate*, i.e., the number of HTTP requests/sec;
- o The total number of requests to perform;

Other useful optional parameters are the users' think time for simulating human responsiveness during Web navigation, and the possibility of using traces of requests to drive the workload generation. In addition, a critical parameter for tuning is the *request timeout*, which sets a time limit for the HTTP connection to be completed.

We are interested in observing how servers react to different workloads and how hardware components influence the overall results. In our study we focused our comparison on multi-threaded and single-process architectures, which are the most popular. As a representative of multi-threaded architecture we deployed Apache 2.0, the newest implementation of the most popular general-purpose Web server [3]. As a sample of single-process architecture we used Boa 0.94.13, which has a very efficient and lightweight implementation with very low memory requirements [12]. Other possible choices such as THTTPD [1] and Mathopd [8] were discarded because during preliminary testing, Boa was faster and more reliable. All experiments were carried out using HTTP version 1.0.

Our goal was to investigate bottlenecks in the Web server, caused by either hardware or software. To accomplish this, we decided to run the Web server on an old Pentium class machine, based upon an ASUS TX97E motherboard with Intel 430TX chipset and with 256Mb of memory. This choice was made in order to load the server quite easily at full capacity, without saturating the available Fast-Ethernet LAN bandwidth; using a machine at the top configuration would make this very difficult. The operating system was a Linux Redhat 7.3 with 2.4.18-19.7.x kernel rpm version. During the experiments, we evaluated the influence of the processor, switching from a Pentium 133Mhz to a Pentium MMX 200Mhz.

The pool of client machines (from 5 to 10) running HTTPERF was Linux Redhat 7.3, with 2.4.18-19.7.x kernel rpm version and no active firewall. Hardware ranged from K6 III at 450Mhz to Athlon XP 2000+. All systems were equipped with full duplex Fast-Ethernet network card and system memory between 256Mb and 512Mb.

A switch with a 2.4Gbps back-panel formed the LAN. The WAN simulator gateway was a dual Pentium III at 1GHz with 1Gb of memory and 2 Fast-Ethernet network adapters, with FreeBSD 4.7 release and dummynet option enabled. The whole test-bed is logically represented in Figure 1. Dummynet was configured to simulate a population of 20% ADSL (128/256Kbit/sec) and 80% MODEM (56Kbit) connections with a RTT delay of 200msec.

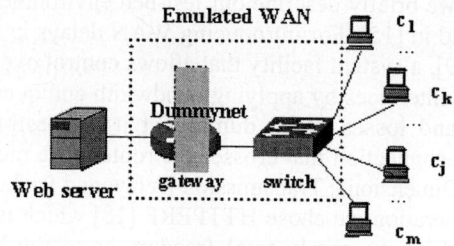

Fig. 1. LAN environment with dummynet

3 Performance Figures

In order to understand how performance indexes can be extracted, in Table 1 we present a snapshot of an HTTPERF output summary. It should be noted that in order to have some additional information in the experiment summary, we slightly modified the original code.

The average connection setup time, the average response time and the average transfer time are calculated, averaging the time spent in the corresponding phase. In the summary we see the average connection setup time [connect] in line 4, average response time [response] and average transfer time [transfer] in line 9. In line 1 [requests] indicates the number of request attempts (and corresponds to the number of connections that completed the connection setup phase), and analogously [replies] corresponds to the number of connections that completed the response phase. In line 14 [number of connections completed] is the number of connections that completed transfer phase.

Table 1. HTTPERF summary example

1	For Total: connections 3000 requests 3000 replies 3000 test-duration 300.705 s
2	Connection rate: 10.0 conn/s (100.2 ms/conn, <=9 concurrent connections)
3	Connection time [ms]: min 757.4 avg 803.8 max 807.9 median 804.5 stddev 6.8
4	Connection time [ms]: connect 205.5
5	Connection length [replies/conn]: 1.000
6	Request rate: 10.0 req/s (100.2 ms/req)
7	Request size [B]: 64.0
8	Reply rate [replies/s]: min 8.4 avg 10.0 max 10.2 stddev 0.2 (60 samples)
9	Reply time [ms]: response 257.3 transfer 341.0
10	Reply size [B]: header 189.0 content 7054.0 footer 0.0 (total 7243.0)
11	Reply status: 1xx=0 2xx=3000 3xx=0 4xx=0 5xx=0
12	CPU time [s]: user 32.19 system 268.52 (user 10.7% system 89.3% total 100.0%)
13	Net I/O: 71.2 KB/s (0.6*10^6 bps)
14	Number of connections completed: 3000
15	Average Connection throughput: 8.8 KB/s (70.4 Kbps)
16	Average Reply throughput: 11.8 KB/s (94.6 Kbps)
17	Average Transfer throughput: 20.8 KB/s (166.0 Kbps)
18	Errors: total 0 client-timo 0 socket-timo 0 connrefused 0 connreset 0
19	Errors: fd-unavail 0 addrunavail 0 ftab-full 0 other 0

In line 1 we find the number of request [requests] and reply [replies] attempted and thus the number of connections that completed the previous phase (i.e., connection setup and response, respectively). In the computed averages, only connections that successfully complete the corresponding phase are considered. By observing how many connections completed the relative phase we have a clue to the possible cause of timeout. For example, timeouts in the connection setup phase mean high congestion in the listen queue of the server, while timeouts in the transfer phase are often due to an improper setting with respect to the dimension of the file to be transferred.

[Net I/O] in line 13 is calculated by summing up all the bytes transferred by a connection (request size plus reply size) divided by the duration of the experiment; this index (summed up for all the HTTPERF instances) is the server throughput. The number of completed requests per second can be found in line 8 as [avg].

To summarize, the performance indexes used are:
Average connection setup time;
Average response time;
Average transfer time;
Server throughput;
Completed requests per second.

At the end of each experiment some error fields must be checked in order to verify that the client's resource constraints have not influenced the measures; in particular the unavailable file descriptors error [fd_unavail] in line 19 must be zero, to indicate that the client's sockets were always available during the experiment. Another meaningful index is [client-timo] in line 18, which counts how many connections have timed out before completion.

4 Experimental Results

This section presents the most interesting experiments carried out in this study. Numerous variables affect performance. Thus, it is appropriate to change one parameter at a time to identify its influence on overall performance. In the following experiments, the effects of retrieving files from cache/memory/disk are highlighted in both single-process and multi-threaded Web server architectures, in order to learn how different conditions influence performance.

It is important to notice that each experiment is composed of a set of measurements, repeated under the same conditions except for the request rate. Each measurement is carried out with constant request rate and file size. For example, Figure 2 shows the throughput of the Boa server, Pentium MMX 200Mhz, for a single file of 7Kbytes. In this graph the first point represents the average server throughput at 100 req/sec, the second one at a rate of 150 req/sec and so on. Each measurement presents an initial a warm-up period (about 100 sec) during which the measured throughput is less than the steady state one. For this reason each measurement period was much longer than this warm up period (from 33 to 90 min) to render the impact of the warm-up period negligible.

4.1 Maximum Server Throughput: Cached Files

As an initial experiment, we observed the server in a near-optimal condition: all clients request the same file, in order to maximize the probability of retrieving the requested data from the system cache.

Although we carried out a set of experiments with both Boa and Apache2 and with files of different sizes (from 1KB to 72KB), the behavior was similar in all cases. Thus, due to limited space, hereafter we discuss only the case of Boa with a 7KB file, as shown in Figure 2. Details of the experiments can be found in [15].

At first, we can see that until maximum server capacity is reached, throughput increases linearly with the request load (this linear phase is bounded by server resources). When server saturation starts (after 550 requests/sec) there is a sudden decrease in throughput. In this experiment, after saturation we observe a throughput fall of 520KB/sec, i.e., 12% less than maximum throughput achieved. We observe that before resource saturation, the server's accept queue is not full, and apart from a queuing delay effect, no SYN packet losses are experienced; after saturation the listen queue is full and some SYN packets are dropped. This leads to the clients' retransmissions, which further increases SYN packets received by the server, thus causing even more drops. Thus, the saturated server operates in a less efficient way. However, to fully explain the sudden fall in throughput, we must consider that the server needs to execute portions of code that were not present in the system cache. After this fall, the server reaches a new equilibrium. During this saturated phase, throughput has a slight linear decrease. This behavior can be explained by the increase in SYN packets received and then dropped and by the parallel increase in network interrupts handled. As request load increases we expect that the equilibrium will not change until the number of received packets overwhelms the server and trashing starts.

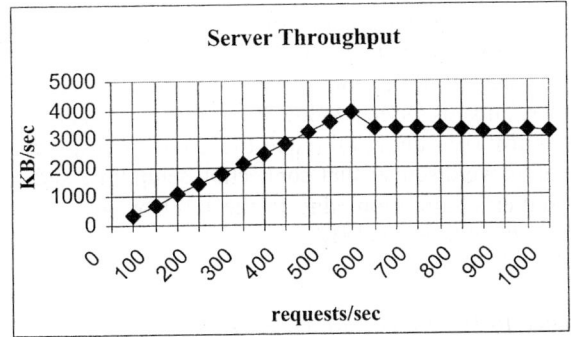

Fig. 2. Boa 0.94.13 server, Pentium MMX 200Mhz, single file of 7Kbytes, 5 sec timeout

Although the throughput of a saturated server is still high, clients perceive a highly degraded QoS. Server responsiveness is probably the most important parameter for measuring the QoS provided by a Web server. After requesting the main page of a Web site, the user expects a reply from the server within a few seconds. If he/she receives a "connection refused" message, perhaps he/she will reload the page, but a negative impression of unreliability remains. The QoS is represented in Figure 3 where we report the time needed to complete the file downloads.

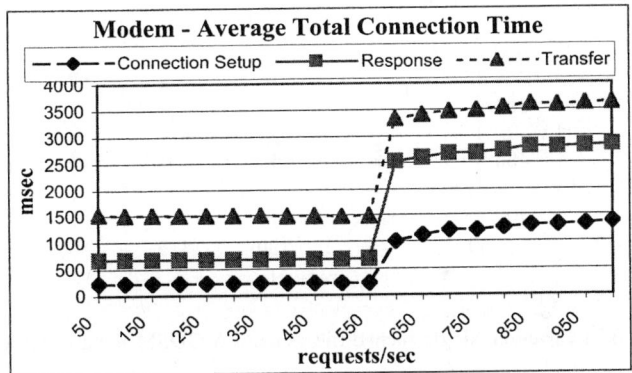

Fig. 3. Boa 0.94.13 server, Pentium MMX 200Mhz, single file of 7Kbytes, 5 sec timeout

Although we carried out experiments with MODEM and ADSL emulated connections, we report only the MODEM case (download: 56Kbit/sec, upload: 33.6Kbit/sec) as they show a similar behavior. When the server is in the linear phase (from 0 to 550 requests/sec) the duration of modem connections is around 1.5 sec; varying the request loads in that range does not influence this time. This simply means that the server should work as much as possible in this ideal situation so that users do not perceive any particular delay. When the saturation phase is reached, things change drastically. The average total connection time becomes 3.3 seconds (a more than 100% increase), and it continues to increase at higher loads. Furthermore, it must be considered that since a 5-second request timeout was used within HTTPERF, this limited possible SYN packet retransmissions to one for each connection setup attempt; i.e., we cut the tail of the connection distribution hence the total connection time reported underestimates the real value. It must be noted that the time spent in the transfer phase is almost constant in all request load conditions. Indeed, observing the total connection time, we discover that connection setup time and response time are affected by the server's saturation (due to the limit on the maximum number of backlogged packets in the listen socket).

4.2 From Cached to Memory-Mapped Files

Working with cached files is an optimal condition but it cannot always be achieved. Therefore, it is interesting to evaluate a less optimal situation, where all requested files (a set of 2500 files of 28KB) are already mapped in memory and no disk access is needed. As expected, at light loads the throughput is similar; but in the memory-mapped case the server saturation is reached earlier. However, for this experiment (see Figure 4) it is more interesting to observe the average response time experienced in the linear phase.

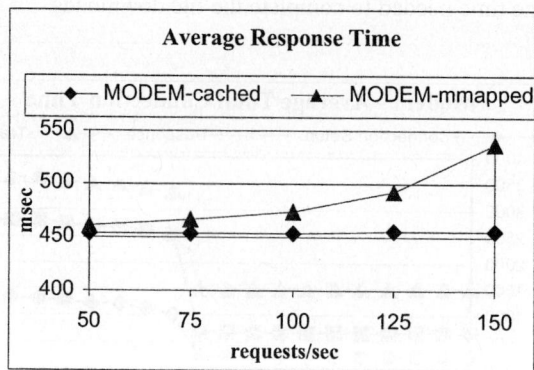

Fig. 4. Boa 0.94.13 server, single cached file vs many MODEM-mmapped files, file size 28K

The average response time can be considered in a first approximation constant when the server works with a cached file; instead, when same-sized files are retrieved from memory, it presents a more than linear increase. Of course this depends on the complexity of the file retrieval algorithm, although the key factor is the memory latency.

Server Architectures: Single-Process versus Multi-threaded. In this set of experiments the behavior of the two server architectures (single-process and multi-threaded) is compared (see Figure 5 and Figure 6). We can see the comparison of server throughput for different file sizes (4KB, 12KB, 28KB). In all the experiments we ensured that all the files in the working set were mapped in memory.

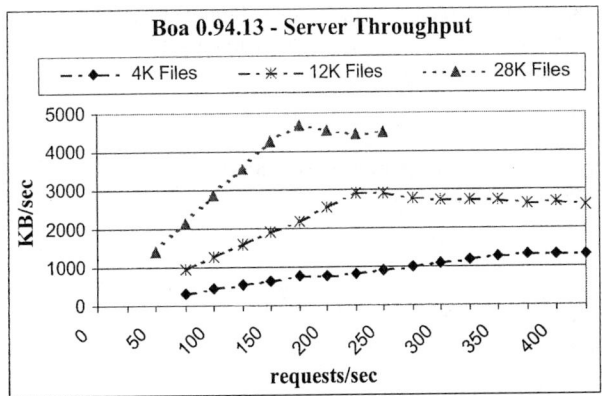

Fig. 5. Pentium 133Mhz, 2500 different memory-mapped files

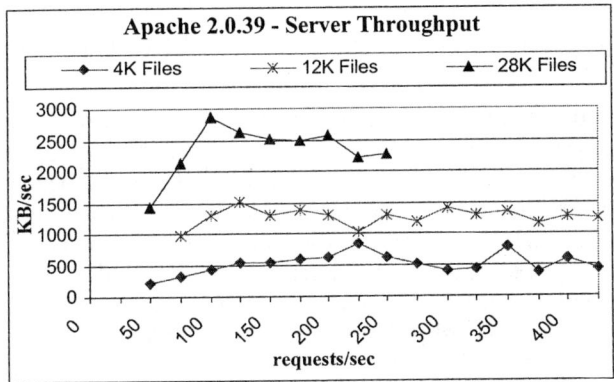

Fig. 6. Pentium 133Mhz, 2500 different memory-mapped files

Each experiment presents an initial linear phase and a subsequent saturation phase. It is remarkable that Boa is far more efficient than Apache2. The fact that all requested files are memory mapped (thus eliminating the potential bottleneck of disk access) is a substantial advantage for single-process architecture. In contrast, the limited amount of system memory (256 MB) and a great number of context switches for each thread, do hit multi-threaded architecture heavily. The Apache2 maximum throughput varies from 40% to 60% of Boa maximum throughput. However, it must be considered that Apache2 is a general-purpose server with full implementation of HTTP 1.1 options; instead Boa implements only the most common ones. Focusing on server behavior for different file dimensions, we immediately observe that, at light loads, throughput is linearly dependent on file size.

4.3 From Memory-Mapped to Disk-Accessed Files

Files are not always mapped in memory; when the server needs to retrieve data from the disk this greatly influences performance. This last experiment compares the efficiency of the analyzed server architectures, when a set of 100,000 different files of 12KB is retrieved from the disk (see Figure 7).

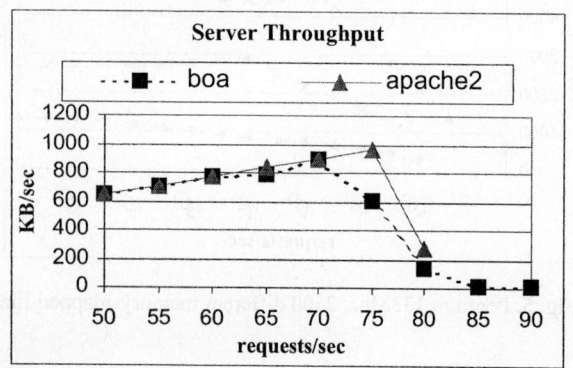

Fig. 7. Boa and Apache2 server throughput when 12K files are retrieved from the disk

The single-process Boa server performance decreases greatly when it needs to access the disk; in fact Boa reaches saturation before Apache2, in contrast with previous experiments where its efficient implementation led to better performance. These results are influenced by file dimension. The difference between Boa and Apache2 increases with the increase in file size because this makes the disk access more and more relevant. Anyway it is clear that accessing files from the hard disk leads to a huge performance penalty due to higher access time and narrow bandwidth between memory and disk. Maximum throughput achieved is reduced to 19% for Boa, and 33% for Apache2. This demonstrates that it is essential for performance to work with memory-mapped files. Thus, the amount of system memory should be carefully determined with respect to the size of the working set of the Web site.

References

1. ACME Laboratories Freeware Library: THTTPD Web Server. http://www.acme.com/software/thttpd
2. Almeida, J., Almeida, V., Yates, D.: Measuring the Behavior of a World-Wide Web Server. Technical report TR-96-025, Boston University, CS Dept. (1996)
3. Apache Software Foundation: Apache HTTP Server Project. http://httpd.apache.org

4. Arlitt, M.E., Williamson, C.L.: Internet Web Servers: Workload Characterization and Performance Implications. IEEE/ACM Transactions on Networking **5** (1997) 631–645
5. Banga, G., Druschel, P.: Measuring the Capacity of a Web Server Under Realistic Loads. World Wide Web, Vol. 2. Kluwer, Dordrecht (1999) 69–83
6. Banga, G., Mogul, J.C.: Scalable Kernel Performance for Internet Servers Under Realistic Loads. In: Proceedings of the 1998 USENIX Technical Conference. (1998) 1–13
7. Barford, P., Crovella, M.: Generating Representative Web Workloads for Network and Server Performance Evaluation. In: Proceedings of the ACM Sigmetrics. (1998) 151–160
8. Boland, M.: Mathopd Web Server. http://www.mathopd.org
9. Braun, H.W., Claffy, K.C.: Web Traffic Characterization: An Assessment of the Impact of Caching Documents from NCSA's Web Server. Computer Networks and ISDN Systems **28** (1995) 37–51
10. Crovella, M., Bestavros, A.: Self-Similarity in World Wide Web Traffic: Evidence and Causes. In: Proceedings of the ACM Sigmetrics. (1996) 160–169
11. Fox, A., Gribble, S.D., Chawathe, Y., Brewer, E.A., Gauthier, P.: Cluster-Based Scalable Network Services. In: Proceedings of the ACM Symposium on Operating System Principles. (1997) 78–91
12. Doolittle, L., Nelson, J.: Boa Web Server. http://www.boa.org
13. Maltzahn, C., Richardson, K.J., Grunwald, D.: Performance Issues of Enterprise Level Web Proxies. In: Proceedings of the ACM Sigmetrics. (1997) 13–23
14. Nahum, E., Rosu, M., Seshan, S., Almeida, J.: The Effects of Wide-Area Conditions on WWW Server Performance. In: Proceedings of the ACM Sigmetrics. (2001) 257–267
15. Pagnin, D., Buzzi, M., Conti, M., Gregori, E.: A measurement of Web Server Performance. Technical report IIT TR-007/2004, Institute for Informatics and Telematics, CNR (2004)
16. Pai, V., Druschel, P., Zwaenepoel, W.: Flash: An Efficient and Portable Web Server. In: Proceedings of the USENIX Technical Conference. (1999) 199–212
17. Mogul, J.C., Ramakrishnan, K.K.: Eliminating Receive Livelock in an Interrupt-Driven Kernel. ACM Transactions on Computer Systems **15** (1997) 217–252
18. Mosberger, D., Jin, T.: HTTPERF: A Tool for Measuring Web Server Performance. ACM SIGMETRICS Performance Evaluation Review **26** (1998) 31–37
19. Rizzo, L.: Dummynet: A Simple Approach to the Evaluation of Network Protocols. ACM SIGCOMM Computer Communication Review **27** (1997) 31–42
20. Stevens, W.R.: TCP/IP Illustrated, Vols. 1,2,3. Addison-Wesley (1996)
21. The Standard Performance Evaluation Corporation (SPEC): SPECWeb99 Benchmark. http://www.spec.org/web99/

Modeling Dynamic Web Content*

Antonio Barili[1], Maria Carla Calzarossa[1], and Daniele Tessera[2]

[1] Dipartimento di Informatica e Sistemistica
Università di Pavia, I-27100 Pavia, Italy
{abarili,mcc}@unipv.it
[2] Dipartimento di Matematica e Fisica
Università Cattolica del Sacro Cuore, I-25121 Brescia, Italy
d.tessera@dmf.unicatt.it

Abstract. Web sites have become increasingly complex and offer a large variety of services and contents. The proliferation of dynamic Web contents opens up new challenging performance and scalability issues. This paper addresses the characterization of dynamic Web contents by studying their update process. We identify parameters and metrics that describe the properties of Web pages and we derive an analytical model that captures their behavior. The model is then validated against simulation experiments.

1 Introduction

Web sites have become increasingly complex and offer a large variety of services and contents. Static pages, that is, pages whose contents seldom change, have been largely replaced by dynamic pages whose contents change with high rates and can be customized according to the user's preferences. Many sites rely on dynamic pages to provide users with dynamic, interactive and personalized contents. A dynamic page is typically generated by a combination of servers, that is, a front-end Web server, an application server and a database server, and involves computation and bandwidth requirements.

The proliferation of dynamic Web contents opens major performance and scalability issues and new challenges for efficient content delivery. In [1] and [2], the performance of different dynamic Web technologies is compared. The study presented in [2] shows that the overheads of dynamic contents generation significantly reduce the request peak rate supported by a Web server.

Caching at the server side can reduce server resource demands required to build the page, thus reducing the server side delays to make information available to the users. Proxy caching and content replication can reduce the latency to retrieve Web pages at the expense of very complex consistency and update management policies. These issues have been largely addressed in the literature and various caching and replication schemes have been proposed (see e.g., [3–9]).

An accurate characterization of Web pages is very beneficial for developing efficient caching policies. In spite of its importance, few studies focus on the

---

* This work has been supported by the Italian Ministry of Education, Universities and Research (MIUR) under the FIRB-Perf project.

behavior of Web pages. In [10] the dynamics of server content are studied by considering the process of creation and modification of HTML files of a large commercial news site. This study shows that the server content is highly dynamic. In particular, the files tend to change little when they are modified and modification events tend to concentrate on a small number of files. The stochastic properties of the dynamic page update patterns and their interactions with the corresponding request patterns are studied in [11]. This study shows that the pages of highly dynamic sport sites are characterized by a large burst of updates and by a periodic behavior. Moreover, the stochastic properties can differ significantly from page to page and vary over time. In [12], the object change characteristics are used to classify the objects at the server side. The four identified categories take into account how frequently objects change and whether their changes are predictable. In [13], the workload of a personalized Web site is studied by analyzing the document composition, the personalization behavior and the server side overheads. A methodological approach to evaluate the characteristics of dynamic Web contents is presented in [14]. As a result of this methodology, models for independent and derived parameters are obtained. These models rely on the analysis of measurements collected at six representative news and e-commerce sites. The analysis shows that the sizes of the objects can be captured by exponential or Weibull distributions, whereas the freshness times are distributed according to a Weibull or a bimodal distribution.

In this paper, we study the characteristics and properties of Web pages and we propose an analytical model that captures their update process. This model helps in better understanding the behavior of the workload of Web servers and can be used to optimize the generation and the delivery of dynamic pages and to develop consistency management policies that take into account the page characteristics.

Our study is more general than the studies described in [11] and [14] in that we predict the behavior of Web pages as a function of the behavior of their constituting objects rather than deriving the models from the observed behavior of the pages.

In what follows we assume that a Web page consists of a collection of static and dynamic objects (or fragments) whose number does not vary over time. Each object corresponds to a portion of the page and can be treated independently of the other objects. A Web page can then be seen as consisting of two components: contents and layout. The contents are associated with the objects. The layout can be seen as a special object that specifies how the contents have to be displayed. A page changes whenever its contents change, that is, the contents of one or more of its objects change. Note that our study focuses on the properties and behavior of the Web pages and it is out of the scope of this paper to model how the users access the pages.

The paper is organized as follows. Section 2 introduces the parameters that characterize dynamic Web contents and describes the analytical model that captures their update process. Section 3 presents a few simulation experiments aimed at validating the model. Finally, Section 4 summarizes the paper and outlines future research directions.

2 Analytical Model

The characterization of dynamic Web content is based on the analysis of the properties of the Web pages which are in turn derived by studying the properties of their constituting objects.

Let us model a Web site as a set $\mathcal{P}$ of N different pages $\{P_i,\ i=1,\ \ldots, N\}$. Each page is a set of n_i distinct objects drawn from the set $\mathcal{O}$ of all possible objects $\{o_j,\ j=1,\ldots, M\}$, where M denotes the number of different objects. An object o_j may belong to one or more pages and, in general, there is a many-to-many correspondence between $\mathcal{P}$ and $\mathcal{O}$. Note that the set $\mathcal{P}$ can be seen as a subset of $\mathcal{P}(\mathcal{O})$, where $\mathcal{P}(\mathcal{O})$ is the power set of $\mathcal{O}$.

Objects are associated with different content types and exhibit different characteristics in terms of how often and to what extent their content changes. Our study focuses on the update process of the objects, that is the sequence of their update events.

Even though objects may exhibit predictable or unpredictable update patterns, we focus on unpredictable updates as their study is more challenging. To model the update process of object o_j we consider the sequence $\{u_{o_j,k},\ k \geq 0\}$ of its update events and we denote with $t_{o_j,k}$ the instant of time of occurrence of the event $u_{o_j,k}$. In what follows we refer to the k-th update event of object o_j as the k-th generation of the object. The time-to-live of the k-th generation of object o_j, that is, the time between two successive updates, is defined as

$$ttl_{o_j}(k) = t_{o_j,k+1} - t_{o_j,k}.$$

We then introduce the counting process $\{X_{o_j}(t),\ t \geq 0\},\ j=1,\ldots, M$ that models the number of update events occurred to object o_j up to time t. If the $\{ttl_{o_j}(k),\ k \geq 0\}$ are independent and identically distributed random variables, then $X_{o_j}(t)$ is a renewal process.

Once we have characterized the update process of the objects, we study the update process of page P_i as the superposition of the update processes of its constituting objects. For this purpose, we introduce a counting process $\{Y_i(t),\ t \geq 0\},\ i=1,\ldots, N$ that models the number of updates of page P_i up to time t due to the updates of its objects as

$$Y_i(t) = \sum_{o_j \in P_i} X_{o_j}(t).$$

Let $\tau_{i,s}$ denote the instant of time of the s-th update event of page P_i, that is, its s-th generation. As the contents of a page change whenever the contents of any of its constituent objects change, we obtain that $\{\tau_{i,s},\ s \geq 0\}$ is equal to $\bigcup_{o_j \in P_i} \{t_{o_j,k},\ k \geq 0\}$, with $\tau_{i,s+1} > \tau_{i,s}$. Even if the update processes of the constituent objects of page P_i are modeled by renewal processes, the page update process is not necessarily a renewal process.

The time-to-live of s-th generation of page P_i is then given by

$$TTL_i(s) = \tau_{i,s+1} - \tau_{i,s}.$$

We can predict the time–to–live of page P_i, provided that the expectations of the time–to–live of its constituent objects are known. Indeed, it is known (see [15]) that the superposition of n mutually independent renewal processes approximates a Poisson process as n goes to infinity.

An interesting metric that can be easily derived is the rate–of–change $R_i(t,T)$ of page P_i over the interval $[t, t+T]$, defined as the ratio between the number of update events occurred in the interval and its length. As the updates of page P_i are the superposition of the updates of its constituent objects, the rate–of–change $R_i(t,T)$ is obtained from the rate–of–change $r_{o_j}(t,T)$ of the objects as

$$R_i(t,T) = \sum_{o_j \in P_i} r_{o_j}(t,T).$$

This metric describes how fast the contents of a page change. Note that static objects are characterized by a rate–of–change equal to zero over any interval of length T.

As a refinement, we study the probability that page P_i sampled at time t will be up–to–date at time $t+T$:

$$D_i(t,T) = Prob \left[(Y_i(t+T) - Y_i(t)) = 0 \right].$$

This metric allows us to compute the expected time–to–live of a page, an information very useful to implement efficient page and object caching strategies. Note that under the assumptions of independent and stationary increments of the update process of page P_i and of mutually independent update processes of its constituting objects, we obtain that $D_i(t,T)$ is independent of t and we can write it as

$$D_i(t,T) = D_i(T) = Prob \left[Y_i(T) = 0 \right] = \prod_{o_j \in P_i} Prob \left[X_{o_j}(T) = 0 \right].$$

A closed form of $D_i(T)$ can be obtained, provided that the probability distributions of the $X_{o_j}(T)$ are known. For example, if each $X_{o_j}(T)$ is a Poisson process with rate λ_{o_j}, then $D_i(T) = e^{-\Lambda_i T}$, where $\Lambda_i = \sum_{o_j \in P_i} \lambda_{o_j}$.

Moreover, under the same assumptions of independent and stationary increments of the update process of page P_i and of mutually independent update processes of its constituting objects, the rate-of-change $R_i(t,T)$ of page P_i does not depend on t and is then equal to $R_i(T)$.

For each page P_i, we can also compute the average number of updates per object in the interval $[t, t+T]$. This metric is obtained as the ratio between the number of update events occurred in the interval and the number of objects n_i of page P_i. Under the assumption that none of the objects has been updated more than once in the considered time interval, this metric measures the fraction of the objects of page P_i that are out–of–date after T time units.

Once we have modeled the update process of the pages, we can focus on the page size. Let $s_{o_j,k}$, $k \geq 0$ denote the size in bytes of the k-th generation of object o_j. As we assume that the size of an object varies only in correspondence to an update event, we obtain that $s_{o_j}(t) = s_{o_j,k}$ for $t_{o_j,k} \leq t < t_{o_j,k+1}$.

Page size at time t is then given by

$$S_i(t) = \sum_{o_j \in P_i} s_{o_j}(t).$$

Since an object can belong to more than one page, we can study the degree of object sharing, that is the fraction of objects shared across pages. This metric provides a measure of content reusability across pages. Let M be the total number of objects belonging to the N pages:

$$\tilde{M} = \sum_{i=1}^{N} n_i.$$

As M counts the number of distinct objects, we obtain that $\tilde{M} \geq M$. The ratio between $\tilde{M}$ and M measures the degree of object sharing. This ratio is equal to one for Web sites with no sharing at all across pages. The larger the degree of sharing the larger the probability of multiple page updates due to a single object update.

Similarly, we introduce a metric that measures the content sharing, that is the fraction of bytes shared across pages. Note that the degree of object sharing is a property of the Web site and depends on the page composition, whereas the content sharing varies with time as a consequence of the object updates. The content sharing is defined as

$$cs(t) = \frac{\sum_{i=1}^{N} S_i(t)}{\sum_{j=1}^{M} s_{o_j}(t)}.$$

This metric can be used to assess the benefits of caching at the object level. When no content is shared across pages, the value of $cs(t)$ is equal to one, hence, the benefit of caching at the object level is rather limited. As the values of $cs(t)$ become larger, caching at the object level become more and more beneficial.

3 Simulation Experiments

To validate the analytical model introduced in Section 2, we have performed a few simulation experiments. These experiments are aimed at assessing whether the time–to–live of the pages obtained by simulation probabilistically supports the theoretical model, that is, the goodness–of–fit between the empirical distribution function of the time–to–live $TTL_i(s)$ of page P_i and the exponential distribution. For this purpose, we have applied the Anderson–Darling (A^2) test [16]. Note that the hypothesis of an underlying exponential distribution is tested at 0.05 significance level. Since it is known that this test applied to large data sets fails, we based our analysis on random samples of the update events occurred to each page during the simulation interval. Moreover, to assess the sensitivity of the results, we have analyzed the time–to–live of the pages as a function of their composition, namely, varying the number of objects constituting each page and the distribution of their time–to–live.

An obvious result obtained is that, whenever we compose in a page any number of objects, each with update events modeled by a Poisson process, the time–to–live of the page is exponentially distributed. We have further investigated the behavior of $TTL_i(s)$ when the time–to–live of the constituting objects is characterized by distributions other than the exponential. We have performed various experiments with $ttl_{o_j}(k)$ characterized by a uniform distribution. In particular, we focused on a uniform distribution over the time interval $(90, 110)$, that is, a distribution characterized by a mean and a standard deviation equal to 100 and 5.77 time units, respectively. Figure 1 shows the empirical distribution function of the time–to–live of a page consisting of 5 objects and its corresponding exponential model.

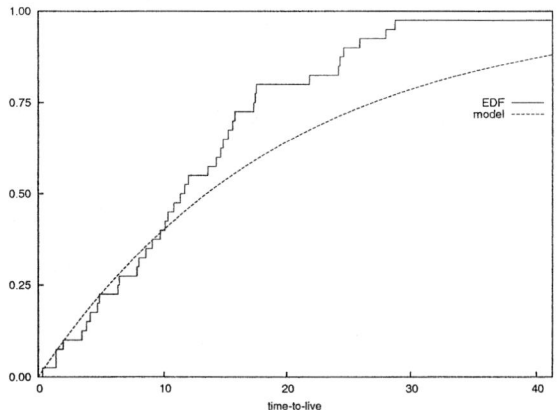

Fig. 1. Empirical distribution function (EDF) and distribution of the exponential model of time–to–live of a page consisting of 5 objects

The mean value of the empirical distribution is equal to 13.085 time units and its standard deviation is equal to 8.980 time units. Even though the distribution is slightly right skewed and its median (equal to 11.321 time units) is smaller than the mean, the A^2 test applied to this distribution does not indicate a good fit to the exponential model. The value of A^2 is equal to 1.596 and is larger than the corresponding critical value at 0.05 significance level, that is 1.323. This could be due to the small number of objects in the page. For this experiment, we have computed $Prob\ [\ Y_i(T) = 0\ ]$ for $T = 5$, 10 and 15 time units. The values obtained are equal to 0.757, 0.544 and 0.375, respectively. As expected, the probability of having no update events in an interval of length T steadily decreases as T increases.

Table 1 summarizes the statistical values of the experiments with time–to–live of the objects uniformly distributed over the time interval $(90, 110)$. As can be seen, as the number of objects per page increases, the empirical distribution function accurately reflects the analytical model of $TTL_i(s)$. For pages with 10 objects or more, the A^2 test at 0.05 significance level indicates a good fit to the exponential model.

Table 1. Statistical summary of the experiments with time–to–live of the objects uniformly distributed over the interval $(90, 110)$

# objects	mean	st. dev.	A^2	critical value
2	56.988	26.002	4.992	1.323
5	13.085	8.980	1.596	1.323
10	10.275	8.733	0.405	1.323
20	4.680	4.135	0.415	1.323
50	1.541	1.402	0.312	1.323
100	0.826	0.868	0.167	1.323

Similar conclusions can be drawn in the case of pages constituted by objects whose time–to–live is described by a uniform distribution with a standard deviation of an order of magnitude larger. There is a significant goodness–of–fit of the empirical distribution functions and the corresponding exponential models even with pages consisting of as few as 5 objects, where the value of A^2 is equal to 0.413, that is much smaller than the corresponding critical value (equal to 1.323). The same conclusions hold for pages with objects characterized by a time–to–live distributed according to a Weibull distribution. The A^2 test applied to pages with 5 objects indicates a good fit to the exponential model, whereas the test applied to pages with 2 objects rejects the exponential model. The values of A^2 are equal to 0.510 and 1.486, respectively.

To assess how these conclusions are influenced by the type or parameters of the distributions, we simulated the case of objects exhibiting a "quasi–deterministic" behavior, that is ttl_{o_j} distributed according to a uniform distribution over the time interval $(99, 101)$. In this case, the A^2 test, even at 0.01 significance level, rejects the exponential assumption for pages with a number of objects as large as 100. The value of A^2 is equal to 4.758, whereas the critical value at 0.01 significance level is equal to 1.945.

Finally, we have studied the behavior of pages consisting of a mix of objects. These pages are composed by "slow" varying and "fast" varying objects with different distributions of their time–to–live. Figure 2 shows an example of the empirical distribution function and of the corresponding exponential model for an experiment with pages consisting of 10 objects. The time–to–live of the objects are distributed according to either Weibull, exponential or uniform distributions.

The good fit that can be visually perceived is confirmed by the A^2 test whose value is equal to 0.623. In general, we have noticed that when the fraction of "fast" objects is dominant in a page, the time–to–live of the pages best fits an exponential distribution even when the number of objects per page is small, whereas the same conclusions cannot be drawn for pages where the fraction of "slow" varying objects is prevalent.

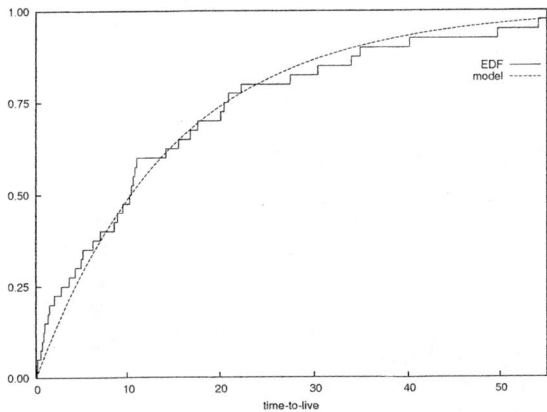

Fig. 2. Empirical distribution function (EDF) and distribution of the exponential model of time–to–live of a page consisting of 10 objects with time–to–live characterized by "mixed" distributions

4 Conclusions

Performance and scalability issues have become crucial due to the large increase and popularity of dynamic Web contents. Hence, the development of efficient consistency management policies and the delivery of dynamic contents play a key role. Within this framework, an accurate description of the behavior and of the properties of dynamic Web pages is very beneficial. The characterization proposed in this paper focuses on the analysis of the properties of Web pages as a function of the properties of their constituting objects. We model the update process of the pages and we introduce metrics that describe the degree of sharing of the contents across pages. These metrics are very useful to assess the benefit of caching at the object level other than at the page level. Simulations performed by varying the composition of the pages and the distribution of the time–to–live of the objects have shown that, as the number of objects per page increases, the distribution of the time–to–live of the page best fits the exponential model. However, there are cases where these results do not hold. These cases correspond to pages consisting of a mix of "slow" varying and "fast" varying objects and of objects exhibiting a "quasi–deterministic" behavior. All these results provide very good insights to understand the behavior of dynamic content and to develop efficient caching and consistency policies.

As a future work, we plan to extend our models to take into account correlations among object update processes and time-varying change rates. Moreover, experimental data will be used for validation purposes.

Acknowledgments

The authors wish to thank the anonymous referee for the valuable comments.

References

1. Apte, V., Hansen, T., Reeser, P.: Performance Comparison of Dynamic Web Platforms. Computer Communications **26** (2003) 888–898
2. Titchkosky, L., Arlitt, M., Williamson, C.: A Performance Comparison of Dynamic Web Technologies. ACM SIGMETRICS Performance Evaluation Review **31** (2003) 2–11
3. Zhu, H., Yang, T.: Class-based Cache Management for Dynamic Web Content. In: Proc. of the Twentieth Annual Joint Conference of the IEEE Computer and Communications Societies, Vol. 3. (2001) 1215–1224
4. Bhide, M., Deolasee, P., Katkar, A., Panchbudhe, A., Ramamritham, K., Shenoy, P.: Adaptive Push-Pull: Disseminating Dynamic Web Data. IEEE Transactions on Computers **51** (2002) 652–668
5. Cohen, E., Kaplan, H.: Refreshment Policies for Web Content Caches. Computer Networks **38** (2002) 795–808
6. Yin, J., Alvisi, L., Dahlin, M., Iyengar, A.: Engineering Web Cache Consistency. ACM Transactions on Internet Technology **2** (2002) 224–259
7. Fei, Z.: A New Consistency Algorithm for Dynamic Documents in Content Distribution Networks. Journal of Parallel and Distributed Computing **63** (2003) 916–926
8. Mikhailov, M., Wills, C.E.: Evaluating a New Approach to Strong Web Cache Consistency with Snapshots of Collected Content. In: Proc. of the Twelfth ACM International Conference on World Wide Web (WWW'03). (2003) 599–608
9. Datta, A., Dutta, K., Thomas, H., VanderMeer, D., Ramamritham, K.: Proxy-Based Acceleration of Dynamically Generated Content on the World Wide Web: An Approach and Implementation. ACM Transactions on Database Systems **29** (2004) 403–443
10. Padmanabhan, V.N., Qiu, L.: The Content and Access Dynamics of a Busy Web Site: Findings and Implications. In: Proc. of the ACM SIGCOMM Conference on Applications, Technologies, Architectures, and Protocols for Computer Communication. (2000) 111–123
11. Challenger, J.R., Dantzig, P., Iyengar, A., Squillante, M.S., Zhang, L.: Efficiently Serving Dynamic Data at Highly Accessed Web Sites. IEEE/ACM Transactions on Networking **12** (2004) 233–246
12. Mikhailov, M., Wills, C.E.: Exploiting Object Relationships for Deterministic Web Object Management. In: Proc. of the Seventh International Workshop on Web Content Caching and Distribution. (2002) 164–179
13. Shi, W., Wright, R., Collins, E., Karamcheti, V.: Workload Characterization of a Personalized Web Site and Its Implications for Dynamic Content Caching. In: Proc. of the Seventh International Workshop on Web Content Caching and Distribution. (2002) 73–88
14. Shi, W., Collins, E., Karamcheti, V.: Modeling Object Characteristics of Dynamic Web Content. Journal of Parallel and Distributed Computing **63** (2003) 963–980
15. Feller, W.: An Introduction to Probability Theory and Its Applications, Vol. II. Wiley, New York (1971)
16. D'Agostino, R.B., Stephens, M.A. (eds.): Goodness–of–Fit Techniques. Marcel Dekker, New York (1986)

Behavioral Intrusion Detection*

Stefano Zanero

Dipartimento di Elettronica e Informazione, Politecnico di Milano
Via Ponzio 34/5, 20133 Milano, Italy
stefano.zanero@polimi.it

Abstract. In this paper we describe anomaly-based intrusion detection as a specialized case of the more general behavior detection problem. We draw concepts from the field of ethology to help us describe and characterize behavior and interactions. We briefly introduce a general framework for behavior detection and an algorithm for building a Markov-based model of behavior. We then apply the framework creating a proof-of-concept intrusion detection system (IDS) that can detect normal and intrusive behavior.

1 Introduction

The landscape of the threats to the security of computer systems is continuously evolving. Attacks and viruses are constantly on the rise. For this reason, it is important to design better systems for detecting infections and intrusions, making the reaction to security incidents quicker and more efficient.

In particular, we are realizing the limits of the misuse-based approach to intrusion detection. A misuse detection system tries to define what an attack is, in order to detect it. While this kind of approach has been widely successful and is implemented in almost all the modern antivirus and intrusion detection tools, its main drawback is that it is unable to properly detect previously unknown attacks (i.e., it is *reactive* and not *proactive*).

Antivirus vendors have responded with state of the art research facilities, round-the-clock response teams, and fast signature distribution methodologies. However, the diffusion of flash malware [1] is a hard to meet challenge. In the intrusion detection field maintaining a knowledge base of attack is impossible, both for the high number of new vulnerabilities that are discovered every day and for the even higher number of unexposed vulnerabilities that may not be immediately available to the experts for analysis and inclusion in the knowledge base (which, in general, does not happen for viral code).

Additionally, since there usually exist a number of ways to exploit the same vulnerability (polymorphism), it is difficult to develop compact signatures that detect all the variations of the attack and at the same time do not incur in false positives. Finally, many intrusions are performed by insiders who are abusing their privileges. In this case, since no attack against known vulnerabilities is performed, a misuse-based IDS is useless.

---
* Work partially supported by the FIRB-Perf Italian project.

An obvious solution to all these problems would be to implement an anomaly detection approach, modeling what is *normal* instead of what is *anomalous*, going back to the earliest conceptions of what an IDS should do [2].

Anomaly detection systems have their own problems and show an alarming tendency to generate huge volumes of false positives. In addition, it has always been a difficult task for researchers to understand what to monitor in a computer system, and how to describe and model it. Even if not really successful in commercial systems anomaly detection has been implemented in a number of academic projects with various degrees of success.

In this paper, we will try to explore a behavioral approach to anomaly based intrusion detection. We will leverage an ongoing trend in knowledge engineering, which is called *behavior engineering* [3]. We draw concepts from the field of ethology to help us describe and characterize behavior and interactions. We briefly introduce a general framework for behavior detection and an algorithm for building a Markov-based model of multiple classes of behavior. We then apply the framework creating a proof-of-concept system that can detect normal and intrusive behavior.

The remainder of the paper is organized as follows. In Section 2 we introduce the problem of behavior detection, and we examine insights coming from ethology and behavioral sciences. In Section 3 we introduce a general framework for behavior detection problems, and we describe an algorithm for building a model of behavior based on Markov chains. In Section 4 we apply the model to the problem of intrusion detection and give proof-of-concept results. Finally, in Section 5 we will draw our conclusions and plan for future work.

2 The Problem of Behavior Detection

2.1 Introduction to Behavior Detection Problems

We propose to consider anomaly based intrusion detection in the more general frame of *behavior detection* problems. This type of problems has been approached in many different fields: psychology, ethology, sociology. Most of the techniques applied in these areas are of no immediate use to us, since they are not prone to be translated into algorithms. However, some useful hints can be drawn forth, in particular by analyzing the quantitative methods of ethology and behavioral sciences [4].

In order to understand the problem and to transfer knowledge between these different fields, we must analyze parallel definitions of concepts we will be dealing with. The first term is "behavior", which ethology describes as the stable, coordinated and observable set of reactions an animal shows to some kinds of stimulations, either inner stimulations (or motivations) or outer stimulations (or stimuli). The distinction between "stimuli" and "motivations" is as old as ethology itself, being already present in Lorenz's work [5].

Our definition of "user behavior" is quite different. We could define it as the "coordinated, observable set of actions a user takes on a computer system in order to accomplish some task". Depending on the observation point we assume, we can give different definition of actions, but for the scope of this paper we will define them as the commands, the data communications and the inputs that the user exchanges with the system. We wish to make clear that our effort is not focused on the behavior of the computer system (which is by definition entirely predictable) but on the behavior of the user, which has relevant intentional components.

We will also make use of the concept of "typical behavior", which quantitative ethology would describe as the "most likely" one. In our definition, this behavior is the "normal" user behavior, as opposed to an "atypical" behavior which is not, however, always devious or dangerous.

2.2 Motivations for Action and Action Selection

This consideration brings us to the point of analyzing the motivations of behavior. We are interested in detecting any anomalous behavior which is motivated by the desire to break the security policy of the system. Anomalous behavior with no devious motivation is not a problem by itself; on the other hand perfectly normal, inconspicuous network traffic, motivated by a devious goal, should in some way be detected by a perfect intrusion detection system.

Even if terminology varies from school to school in behavioral sciences, we can recognize three broad levels of increasing complexity in the analysis of behavior: reflex behavior (sensorial stimuli and innate reactions), instinctual behavior (genetically evolved, innate behavior of a species), and finally intentional behavior, with actions that an animal begins autonomously to reach its own goals.

Clearly, when dealing with computer misuse, we are mostly dealing with intentional behavior, and we need to define what *motivates* an action. The concept of motivation is crucial to ethology, and it has been a theme of a number of philosophical researches as well. Without getting deeply into the philosophical debate, we can define motivations as the dynamic factors of behaviors, which trigger actions from an organism and direct it towards a goal. We will try to recognize which motivations are behind a particular behavior of a user.

2.3 Fixed Action Patterns, Modal Action Patterns, and Ethograms

Closely associated with these concepts are *patterns*, elements shared by many slightly different behaviors, which are used to classify them. The concept of "behavioral pattern" is widely used in ethology.

Ethologists typically define as *Fixed Action Patterns* (FAP) the atomic units of instinctual behavior. FAPs have some well defined characteristics: they are mechanic; they are self-similar (stereotyped) in the same individual and across a species, and they are extensively present; they usually accomplish some objective. More importantly, they are atomic: once they begin, they are usually completed by the animal, and if the animal is interrupted, they are aborted.

A FAP must also be independent from (not correlated with) other behaviors or situations, except at most one, called a "releaser", which activates the FAP through a filter-trigger mechanism, called Innate Release Mechanism (IRM). The IRM can be purely interior, with no external observable input (emitted behavior), or it can be external (elicited behavior). In the latter case, sometimes the strength of the stimulus results in a stronger or weaker performance of the FAP (response to supernormal stimulus). In other cases, there is no such relation.

In [6], the whole concept of FAPs and IRMs is examined in detail. The author criticizes the rigid set of criteria defining a FAP, in particular the fact that the IRM must be different for each FAP; the fact that the IRM has no further effect on the FAP once it has been activated; and the fact that components of the FAP must fall into a strict order. Many behaviors do not fall into such criteria. Barlow proposes then to introduce MAPs, or *Modal Action Patterns*, action patterns with both fixed and variable parts, which can occur in a different order and can be modulated during their execution. Barlow suggests that the environment can modulate even the most stereotyped behavior. His definition of MAP is a "spatio temporal pattern of coordinated movement that clusters around some mode making it recognizable as a distinct behavior pattern". Unfortunately, the flexibility of a MAP is difficult to implement in a computer-based model of behavior.

A subset of FAPs, called "displays", are actually communication mechanisms. In an interesting chain of relations, a display can be the releasor of an answer, creating a communication sequence. An interesting characteristic of displays is the principle of *antithesis*, stating that two displays with opposite meanings tend to be as different as they can be. This is not necessarily true in behavior detection problems: for example, malicious computer users will try to hide behind a series of innocent-like activities.

We must also introduce the concept of an *ethogram*, which is an attempt to enumerate and describe correctly and completely the possible behavioral patterns of a species. On the field, an ethologist would observe the behavior of animals and list the different observed behavioral patterns in a list, annotated with possible interpretations of their meaning. Afterwards, s/he would observe at fixed interval the animals and "tick" the appropriate squares in an ethogram, generating a sequence data on the behavior of the observed animals. A similar discretization will be used also in our framework.

3 A Framework for Behavioral Detection

3.1 A Methodology for Behavioral Detection

We will try to exploit the similarities we have found, in order to propose a framework for studying behavior detection and classification problems.

First of all, we need to specify which kind of displays of behavior we can detect and build appropriate sensors for detecting them. It is not difficult to collect and analyze the logs of a workstation, but detecting the behaviors of users in a virtual classroom environment could be difficult. For our example architecture we choose to use the interactions with a terminal. Other likely displays that could be analyzed are the logs of the interactions between a user and a web application, the sequence of system calls generated by user processes [7], or the generation of audit data (using for instance the syslog facilities of UNIX and similar systems). We refer the reader to one of our previous works [8] for considerations on network based anomaly detection systems. In this paper we will focus instead on host based anomaly detection.

As a second step, we must choose an appropriate model for representing the behavior. We could approach the problem at different levels of abstraction, making hypotheses on the action selection problem (as seen in 2.2) and analyzing the actual process which generates the behavior. However, we will use a traditional approach in quantitative behavior study, trying to model just the sequence of the displays of behavior, in order to infer various properties about the subject. In order to choose an appropriate model, we must understand if we want a binary classification, or a more complex one with several disjunct classes, or even one with overlapping categories.

Upon this model we must build an inference metamodel, which can help us learn actual parameters from observed data in order to tune the model. This is a classical instance of machine learning problem. Finally, we must set thresholds and logics that help us extract useful information from the observed behavior. Due to space constraints, we will now focus our discussion on how to build an appropriate model for representing the behavior. As a future work we will deal with the other steps required for building a complete behavior detection system.

3.2 Representing Behavior: Markov Models

Markov models are widely used in quantitative behavioral sciences to classify and report observed behaviors. In particular, in ethology simple Markov Models are built on field observation results. A time domain process demonstrates a Markov property if the conditional probability density of the current event, given all present and past events, depends only on the K most recent events. K is known as the *order* of the underlying model. Usually, models of order $K = 1$ are considered, because they are simpler to analyze mathematically. Higher-order models can usually be approximated with first order models, but approaches for using high-order Markov models in an efficient manner have also been proposed, even in the intrusion detection field [9].

A first order Markov Model is a finite set of N states $S = \{s_1, s_2, \ldots s_n\}$, each of which is associated with a (generally multidimensional) probability distribution. Transitions among the states are governed by a set of probabilities called transition probabilities $a_{i,j} = P\{t = k+1, s_j \,|\, t = k, s_i\}$ (whereas in order K models the probability depends on the states in the K previous steps, generating a $K+1$-dimensional array of probabilities). We consider a time-homogeneous model, in which $A = a_{i,j}$ is time-independent.

In a Hidden Markov Model, in any particular state, an outcome or observation o_k can be generated according to a probability distribution associated to the state ($b_{j,k} = P\{o_k \,|\, s_j\}$), in an alphabet of M possible observations. These probabilities obviously form a matrix $B = b_{j,k}$ which we also suppose to be time independent. Only the outcome, and not the state, is visible to an external observer; therefore states are "hidden" from the outside. The definition also implies an assumption which is probably not true: the output is assumed to be statistically independent from the previous outputs. If the observations are continuous, then a continuous probability density function is used, approximated by a mixture of Gaussians. However, ethologists discretize animal behavior using FAPs and MAPs and ethograms, in order to simplify the model. In our case, user-computer interactions are mostly discrete sequences of events. Obviously, non hidden Markov models are special, simple cases.

In order to use HMMs in behavior detection, we need to solve two common problems associated with HMMs [10]. The first is the *evaluation problem*, which means, given a sequence of observations and a model, what is the probability that the observed sequence was generated by the model. The second is the *learning problem*: building from data a model, or a set of models, that properly describe the observed behavior. A third problem, the so called *decoding problem*, is not of particular interest to us.

3.3 An Algorithm for Building Markovian Models of Behavior

The *evaluation problem* is trivial to solve in the case of a normal model, more complex to solve in the case of an HMM: in this case, the naive approach yields a complexity of N^T, where T is the length of the sequence of observations. The so-called forward algorithm [11] can be used, which has a complexity of $N^2 T$.

The *learning problem* is more complex, in particular if we do not know the structure of the model. First of all, we need to choose the order of the model we will use. Often a first-order approximation is used for simplicity, but more complex models can be considered. A good estimate for an HMM can be extracted from data using the criteria defined in [12]; for normal Markov models, a χ^2-test for first against second order dependency can be used [13], but also an information criterion such as BIC or MDL can be used.

In order to estimate the correct number of states for an HMM, in [14] an interesting approach is proposed, by eliminating the time dependency and constructing a classification by means of clustering of the observations, considering each state as a generation mechanism.

Once we have chosen the model structure, learning a sequence of T observations means to find the matrices $\{A, B\}$ that maximize the probability of the sequence: $\max P[o_1 o_2 \ldots o_T | A, B]$. This is computationally unfeasible, however the Baum-Welch algorithm [15] can give a local maximum for that function. Another approach to the parameter estimation problem is proposed in [16]. If the model is not hidden, however, the calculations become simple.

In many earlier proposals for the use of Markovian models in intrusion detection [17] the authors either build a Markov model for each user and then try to find out masquerading users (users accessing illicitly the account of another user); or they build a Markov model for the generic user and flag as anomalous any user who behaves differently. The first approach brings an explosion of models, lacking generalization or support for users who are not identified uniquely to the system, while the second approach ignores the existence of different classes of users on the system.

In order to account for the existence of different *classes* of user behaviors, we propose the following algorithm, based on a Bayesian approach. Denoting with M a generic model and with O a sequence of observations, $P(M|O) \propto P(O|M)P(M)$. This means that, if we have a set of I models $M_1, M_2 \ldots M_I$, the most likely model for the sequence of observations O is given by: $\max_i P(M_i|O) = \max_i P(O|M_i) P(M_i)$

We need now to choose an appropriate prior $P(M_i)$ for the models. Let us suppose that this procedure is iterative, which means that we have built the existing I models out of K observation sequences $O_1 \ldots O_K$, iteratively associating each sequence with the best-fitting model and retraining the model with the new observations. This also means that we need to define a criterion for choosing whether it is appropriate to associate the new observations O_k with an existing model, or to create a new model for representing them.

A common decomposition for studying the prior of the model would be $P(M_i) = P(\theta_i|M_s)P(M_s)$, denoting with $P(\theta_i)$ the probability of the particular parameter set of M_i given a basic structure M_s and with $P(M_s)$ the probability of the structure itself. However, this type of approach leads to very complex calculations.

Using a simpler approach, we could proceed as follows. Let us call O_i the union of the observation sequences that have generated model M_i. We can build a non-informative prior criterion such as

$$P(M_i) = \left(\frac{|O_i| + |O_k|}{(\sum |O_i|) + |O_k|} \right)^{log(|O_k|)}.$$

which penalizes more particular models, favoring more general ones. Inserting the exponent $log(|O_k|)$ is necessary in order to account for the fact that different length of observation strings will generate different orders of magnitude in posterior probability. This generates also a simple criterion for the creation of new models. In fact, denoting with M_{I+1} a new model built on the new observations O_k, we would choose $\max_i P(M_i|O_k) = \max_i P(O|M_i)P(M_i)$ with $1 \leq i \leq I+1$, defining

$$P(M_{I+1}) = \frac{|O_k|}{(\sum |O_i|) + |O_k|}.$$

In this way, the prior biases the probability towards more general models instead of more fitting but less general ones, averaging out the fact that less general models tend to have a higher posterior probability $P(M_i|O_k)$. Once we have selected which model the k-th sequence O_k will be associated with, we re-train the model including in training data the new sequence.

Afterwards, we may optionally include a *merging* step, which means we will try to find couples of models M_i, M_j such that, denoting with $M_{i,j}$ the "merged" model and with O_i and O_j the observations associated with M_i and M_J:

$$P(O_i \cup O_j|M_{i,j})P(M_{i,j}) > P(O_i|M_i)P(M_i),$$
$$P(O_i \cup O_j|M_{i,j})P(M_{i,j}) > P(O_j|M_j)P(M_j).$$

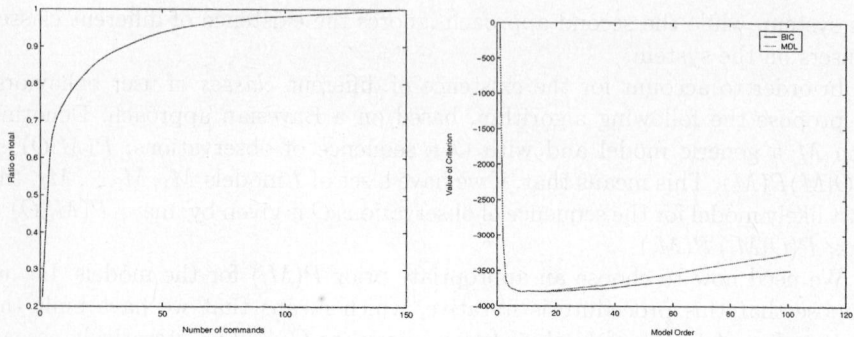

Fig. 1. Cum. distribution of commands   **Fig. 2.** Inf. Criterion: MDL and BIC

In this case, a suitable criterion for selecting models to merge and for merging them must be also researched. There are some examples in literature of criteria for measuring a distance between two Markov models, for instance in [18] the following (asymmetric) distance is proposed: $D(M_i, M_j) = 1/T[logP(O^{(i)}|M_i) - logP(O^{(i)}|M_j)]$, where $O^{(i)}$ is a sequence of observations generated by model M_i. Criteria for merging HMM models can be found in [19] [20], where they are proposed as a suitable way to induce the models by aggregation.

If we wish to incorporate the insights from section 2.3 on the presence of FAPs and MAPs in behavior, we will need to use higher order models, because we need to express the probability on the base of a history. A suggestion that we may borrow from Barlow's studies on modal components of behavior, however, is that we may also want to detect clusters of states in the Markov chain that exhibit the following properties: they have "similar" outgoing transition probabilities and "similar" symbol emission probabilities (if we are dealing with an HMM). These states can be collapsed together in a single state, with simple probability calculations that we omit. This method is also applied in quantitative behavioral science, see [21].

4 Case Study: Behavioral Intrusion Detection

We acquired test data from a limited number of users of two different terminal systems, with about 10 users for each system and some months of data. We prepared the data by discarding command options and encoding each different command with a number. In one of these systems, for example, on 2717 interactions, 150 unique commands were used. However, as we can see in Figure 1, a significant fraction of the interactions consists of a limited subset of frequently used commands, so we can set a minimum threshold below which we will group all the commands together as "other".

In order to estimate the optimal order for the model, we used both the BIC and MDL criteria, and both agree on order $k = 4$ as being the optimal value. However, as a first approximation we will use a first-order model to fit the observations (approximation supported by the steep descent in criteria curves,

Table 1. Performance of our algorithm vs. naive application of Markov models

Commands	Our algorithm		Naive Markov
	Fitting	Detection	Detection
60	90.0	95.9	90.0
40	89.2	95.6	87.8
30	87.8	94.8	86.3
20	84.8	92.9	78.9
10	67.4	81.1	65.6
8	61.1	78.5	59.3
6	38.1	63.3	51.5
4	20.4	55.9	50.7

which can be observed in Figure 2). Also, since the observations are finite in number, we use a normal Markov chain and not an HMM, to fit it.

We trained a set of Markov models following the basic algorithm outlined above. We experimented with various combinations of thresholds and parameters: we show the results in Table 1, compared with a naive application of Markov models (by pre-labeling the traces and building a transition matrix for each user, or class of user). For our models, we show also a measure of the overfitting of the model classes on the training sequences (the higher the fitting, the lower the generalization capacity of the algorithm). Creating Markov models with a high number of nodes increases both detection rate (because users are identified by relatively uncommon commands they perform) and overfitting. Using only 6 types of commands, we obtain a much better generalization and still a 63.3% detection rate. The rate may seem overall low, but it is still much higher than the detection rate of a naive application of Markov models. The computation time for building the model is quite higher than the naive one (about 6 times higher), but still in the order of seconds. At runtime, there is no difference in complexity between our model and a naive one.

5 Conclusions

In this paper, we have described a behavioral approach to anomaly detection. By analyzing and leveraging concepts from the field of ethology, we have presented a general framework to build behavior detection systems. We have also introduced a simple algorithm to build a Markov-based model of multiple classes of behavior. We have shown that a behavior classifier built with this algorithm is capable of detecting intrusion attempts on computer systems. Future extensions of this work could include a deeper analysis of the prior for the Bayesian choice between different models and applications to other problems in the area of behavior detections.

References

1. Serazzi, G., Zanero, S.: Computer Virus Propagation Models. In: Calzarossa, M.C., Gelenbe, E. (eds.): Performance Tools and Applications to Networked Systems:

Revised Tutorial Lectures. Lecture Notes in Computer Science, Vol. 2965. Springer (2004)
2. Anderson, J.P.: Computer Security Threat Monitoring and Surveillance. Technical report, James P. Anderson Company, Fort Washington, Pennsylvania. (1980)
3. Colombetti, M., Dorigo, M., Borghi, G.: Behavior Analysis and Training: A Methodology for Behavior Engineering. IEEE Transactions on Systems, Man and Cybernetics **26** (1996) 365–380
4. Martin, P., Bateson, P.: Measuring Behaviour: An Introductory Guide. 2 edn. Cambridge University Press, Cambridge, UK (1993)
5. Lorenz, K.Z.: The Comparative Method in Studying Innate Behaviour Patterns. In: Symposia of the Society for Experimental Biology. (1950) 226
6. Barlow, G.W. In: Ethological Units of Behavior. Chicago University Press, Chicago (1968) 217–237
7. Jha, S., Tan, K., Maxion, R.A.: Markov Chains, Classifiers, and Intrusion Detection. In: 14th IEEE Computer Security Foundations Workshop. (2001) 0206
8. Zanero, S., Savaresi, S.M.: Unsupervised Learning Techniques for an Intrusion Detection System. In: Proceedings of the 2004 ACM Symposium on Applied Computing. ACM Press (2004) 412–419
9. Ju, W.H., Vardi, Y.: A Hybrid High-Order Markov Chain Model for Computer Intrusion Detection. Journal of Computational and Graphical Statistics **10** (2001) 277–295
10. Rabiner, L.R.: A Tutorial on Hidden Markov Models and Selected Applications in Speech Recognition. In: Proceedings of the IEEE, Vol. 77. (1989) 257–286
11. Baum, L.E., Eagon, J.A.: An Inequality with Applications to Statistical Prediction for Functions of Markov Process and to a Model of Ecology. Bulletin of the American Mathematical Society (1967) 360–363
12. Merhav, N., Gutman, M., Ziv, J.: On the Estimation of the Order of a Markov Chain and Universal Data Compression. IEEE Transactions on Information Theory **35** (1989) 1014–1019
13. Haccou, P., Meelis, E.: Statistical Analysis of Behavioural Data. An Approach Based on Time-Structured Models. Oxford University Press (1992)
14. Cheung, Y.M., Xu, L.: An RPCL-Based Approach for Markov Model Identification with Unknown State Number. IEEE Signal Processing Letters **7** (2000) 284–287
15. Baum, L.: An Inequality and Associated Maximization Technique in Statistical Estimation for Probabilistic Functions of Markov Processes. Inequalities (1972) 1–8
16. Moore, J.B., Krishnamurthy, V.: On-line Estimation of Hidden Markov Model Based on the Kullback-Leibler Information Measure. IEEE Transactions on Signal Processing (1993) 2557–2573
17. Yeung, D.Y., Ding, Y.: Host-Based Intrusion Detection Using Dynamic and Static Behavioral Models. Pattern Recognition **36** (2003) 229–243
18. Juang, B.H., Rabiner, L.: A Probabilistic Distance Measure for Hidden Markov Models. AT&T Technical Journal **64** (1985) 391–408
19. Stolcke, A., Omohundro, S.: Hidden Markov Model Induction by Bayesian Model Merging. In: Advances in Neural Information Processing Systems, Vol. 5. Morgan Kaufmann (1993) 11–18
20. Stolcke, A., Omohundro, S.M.: Best-First Model Merging for Hidden Markov Model Induction. Technical Report TR-94-003, Berkeley, CA (1994)
21. te Boekhorst, I.R.J.: Freeing Machines from Cartesian Chains. In: Proceedings of the 4th International Conference on Cognitive Technology. Lecture Notes in Computer Science, Vol. 2117. Springer (2001) 95–108

Biological Metaphors for Agent Behavior*

Erol Gelenbe, Varol Kaptan, and Yu Wang

Deptartment of Electrical and Electronic Engineering
Imperial College, London, SW7 2BT, UK
{e.gelenbe,v.kaptan,yu.wang3}@imperial.ac.uk

Abstract. A wide variety of practical problems related to the interaction of agents can be examined using biological metaphors. This paper applies the theory of G-networks to agent systems by considering a biological metaphor based on three types of entities: normal cells C, cancerous or bad cells B, and immune defense agents A which are used to destroy the bad cells B, but which sometimes have the effect of being able to destroy the good cells C as well (autoimmune response). Cells of type C can mutate into cells of Type B, and vice-versa. In the presence of probabilities of correct detection and false alarm on the part of agents of Type A, we examine how the dose of agent A will influence the desired outcome which is that most bad cells B are destroyed while the damage to cells C is limited to an acceptable level. In a second part of the paper we illustrate how a similar model can be used to represent a mixture of agents with the ability to cooperate as well as to compete.

1 Introduction

A wide variety of practical problems related to the interaction of agents, or to the operations research of competition among different adversarial teams, can be examined using biological metaphors [10,16]. The purpose of this paper is to investigate such biological metaphors so as to determine how overall levels of system protection can be achieved in a meta-model which is presented in biological terms. Specifically, we consider two examples. In the first one, we model the interaction between cancerous cells B, normal cells C (in a network this would be the bona fide traffic), and the immune system cells A (the spam or virus filtering software agents) which are used to eliminate the cancerous cells. In the second model we again consider three populations, but in this case, the agents A are able to enhance the level of protection of a family of cells B which are being attacked by a set of cells C. The systems we consider are modeled mathematically using the theory of G-networks developed in [1–9, 11–15].

2 A Mathematical Model for a Set of Competing Agents

Undesirable or malicious network traffic of various forms, such as spam, viruses, worms, and denial of service attacks, have become very common in the Internet. As users of the Internet, we are all familiar with spam which arrives to us despite the

---

* This work is supported by the UK MoD Defense Technology Centre for Data and Information Fusion.

presence of a spam blocker. Thus inevitably, the software which detects and eliminates nuisance traffic will have some probability of detection, say d, which is less than one: thus with probability d, an item of nuisance traffic is identified, while with probability (1-d) it is not. Similarly, we know that some bona fide traffic may be mistakenly taken to be spam and it will be blocked or destroyed. This is also true about attachments which may be interpreted to be viruses, when they are just bona fide programs. These events correspond to false alarms. Thus with probability f, a bona fide traffic item in the network will be taken to be a nuisance item and will be destroyed, while with probability (1-f) it will be correctly recognize. Clearly, if our filtering functions are carried out very well, we would ideally expect to have d=1 and f=0, but that of course will never be the case and we can expect that any system will have some level of errors of both kinds.

In the first model that we consider, an A-type agent (the immune system cell) will examine both B-cells (the bad cancerous cells) and C-cells (the normal cells); with probability d it will correctly recognize a B-cell and it will destroy it, and with probability f it will mistake a C-cell for a B-cell and also destroy it. In both cases, we assume that the A-type agent is expended in the process and that it cannot be used again. However, going beyond the requirements of the Internet related model, we also assume that C-cells can mutate into B-cells with probability π_{CB} and that the opposite is also possible with probability π_{BC}. The state of the system under consideration will be the vector $k(t) = (k_A(t), k_B(t), k_C(t))$, where the elements of the vector are the number of autoimmune agents (expressed as an integer), of cancer cells, and of normal cells, respectively, at time t, respectively. Note that these (discrete) numbers may also refer to concentrations of the cells. The immunity defense agents into the system in a Poisson process of rate λ_A, while the cancerous and normal cells are generated in Poisson processes of rate λ_B and λ_C, respectively. All of the Poisson processes are independent of each other.

The immune cells will bind into other cells at rate R_A, and will select the type of target (normal or cancerous cell) based on the relative number of cells of each type present in the system. Thus an immune system cell will select a normal cell (Type C) with probability c, or it will attempt to bind to a cancer cell with probability b:

$$c = \frac{n_C}{n_B + n_C} \text{ and } b = \frac{n_B}{n_B + n_C},$$

where n_B and n_C are the average numbers of bad B (cancerous) and normal C cells, respectively. If the cell which is targeted is cancerous (B), the immune system cell will bind to it and destroy it with probability d (i.e. it has correctly identified the nature of the cell) or it will be ineffective with probability (1-d) and the bad cell will survive. If it targets a normal cell, with probability f it will mistakenly bind to it and destroy it (the probability of a false alarm), or with probability (1-f) it will not destroy the cell. In both cases, the immune cell is expended and cannot be re-used. Concurrently, provided cancer cells exist, they take action at rate R_B either by killing an immune cell with probability π_{BA}, or they mutate into normal cells with probability π_{BC}. If a cancer cell attacks an immune cell, both cells will be destroyed. At the mean time, provided normal cells exist, they take action at rate R_C by transforming into cancer cells with probability π_{CB}. In a "normal" environment, we would have: $n_C \gg n_B$ (i.e. the number of cancerous cells B is much smaller than the number of normal cells C in the system), and $d > f$, i.e. the immune agent A recognizes cancerous cells more accurately than it mistakenly identifies normal cells as being cancerous. The interaction of these different types of agents is illustrated schematically in Figure 1.

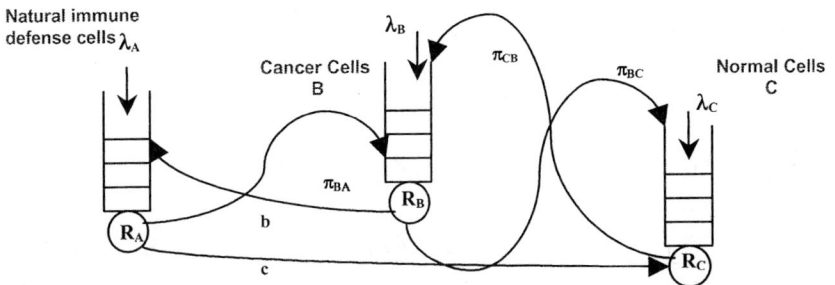

Fig.1. A biological model with immune system cells and cancer and normal cells

2.1 System Equations

In the sequel we assume that all the rates defined above are parameters of exponential distributions for independent random variables, so that the system we have described is reduced to an infinite and discrete state space, and continuous time, Markov chain. We will not detail the derivation of the following equation (1), but simply indicate that the process {k(t): t ≥0} can be studied by writing the Chapman-Kolmogorov equations for p(k,t) = Prob[k(t) = k], where k = (k_A,k_B,k_C) is a 3-vector of non-negative integers representing the number or density of immune cells (expressed as an integer), the of cancer and of normal cells in the system, respectively.

Proposition 1. *The Chapman-Kolmogorov equations for the system we have described are:*

$$\frac{d}{dt}p(k,t) = \lambda_A p(k - z_A, t)1[k_A > 0] + \lambda_B p(k - z_B, t)1[k_B > 0]$$

$$+ \lambda_C p(k - z_C, t)1[k_C > 0] + R_B \pi_{BA} p(k + z_B + z_A, t)$$

$$+ R_A bdp(k + z_B + z_A, t) + R_A cfp(k + z_C + z_A, t) \quad (1)$$

$$+ R_A cp(k + z_A, t)(1[k_C = 0] + (1 - f)1[k_C > 0])$$

$$+ R_A bp(k + z_A, t)(1[k_B = 0] + (1 - d)1[k_B > 0])$$

$$+ R_C \pi_{CB} p(k + z_C - z_B, t)1[k_B > 0]$$

$$+ R_B \pi_{BC} p(k + z_B - z_C, t)1[k_C > 0]$$

$$- (\lambda_C + \lambda_B + \lambda_A) p(k,t)$$

$$- (R_C 1[k_C > 0] + R_A 1[k_A > 0] + R_B 1[k_B > 0]) p(k,t)$$

where on the right hand side we show the transition rates from neighboring states into state k, and $z_A = (1,0,0)$, $z_B = (0,1,0)$ and $z_C = (0,0,1)$.

Theorem 1. *When the stationary solution of these equations exists, it has the following form* (see references [1-9]):

$$p(k) = (1-\rho_A)(1-\rho_B)(1-\rho_C)\, \rho_A^{k_A} \rho_B^{k_B} \rho_C^{k_C}$$

where $k_A \geq 0$, $k_B \geq 0$, $k_C \geq 0$, *and the* $0 \leq \rho_A, \rho_B, \rho_C < 1$ *satisfy the following system of algebraic non-linear equations:*

$$\rho_A = \frac{\lambda_A}{R_A + \pi_{BA}\rho_B R_B}, \quad \rho_B = \frac{\lambda_B + \pi_{CB}\rho_C R_C}{R_B + db\rho_A R_A}, \quad \rho_C = \frac{\lambda_C + \pi_{BC}\rho_B R_B}{R_C + fc\rho_A R_A}$$

Corollary 1. *Let* $n_B = \lim_{t \to \infty} E[x_B] = \frac{\rho_B}{1-\rho_B}$ *and* $n_C = \lim_{t \to \infty} E[x_C] = \frac{\rho_C}{1-\rho_C}$. *Then the proportion of cancerous cells in the system is given by*

$$N = \frac{n_B}{n_C + n_B}.$$

2.2 Numerical Examples

In this section we present some of the numerical results obtained from the model under different parameter settings. To simplify the matter, we start with $R_A = R_B = R_C = 1$. We use the percentage of the cancer cells in the system, N, as the objective function and vary the parameter values. Using the value of d and f, we first examine the impact of the accuracy of the immune system in identifying the other cells affects N. Starting with a simple case, we set $\lambda_B = 0.062$, $\lambda_C = 0.882$, $\lambda_A = 0.990$. Both π_{BA} and π_{BC} are set to 0 to indicate the cancer cells neither attack the immune defense cells nor transform to normal cells. π_{CB} are set to be 0.1 to reflect that, with probability 0.1, the normal cells are mutated to cancer cells. Under these circumstances, we observe that as d and f vary, the cancer cells are within the range of 0 to 10 percent of the cell population.

In Figure 2, each horizontal line represents d over the range 0 to 1 in steps of 0.1. The color variation from green to red reflects the value of f changing from 0 to 1. Figure 2 shows that compared to f, d has a smaller effect on the ratio of the cancer to normal cells. When the probability that immune defense cells correctly identify the cancer cells increases, N decreases, i.e. the percentage of the bad cells decreases. When the immune defense cells are falsely identifying the victim cell, N increases when more false alarms occur.

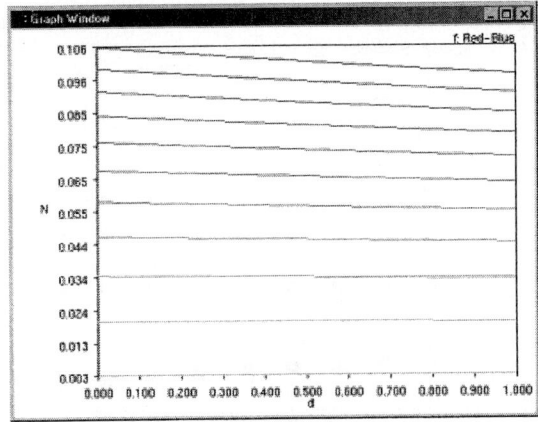

Fig.2. N varying as a function of d and f

We then set $\lambda_B = 0.007$, $\lambda_C = 0.882$ and $\lambda_A = 0.990$ to indicate that the cancer cells are generated at a rather low rate compared with the normal cells and the immune defense cells. π_{BA} is set to be 0.8, π_{BC} and π_{CB} are set to be 0.2 and 0.382 respectively. With this set of parameter settings, we model the situation where the normal cells have a higher probability of mutating to cancerous cells than the opposite. We examine the effect of d and f. Obviously, the higher the value of d and the smaller the value of f, the better the immune agent is performing.

Keeping all the variables the same, and increasing λ_B to 0.367, we see that the model still converges but we start obtaining invalid solutions, as illustrated by the black squares in Fig. 4. As mentioned earlier, the stationary solution of the non-linear equations exists if $0 \leq \rho_A, \rho_B, \rho_C < 1$ are satisfied. When any one of the ρ's reaches 1, the condition is not satisfied and invalid solutions are obtained.

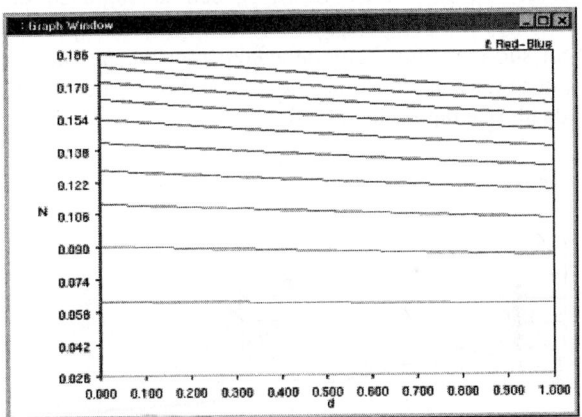

Fig.3. N varying as a function of d and f

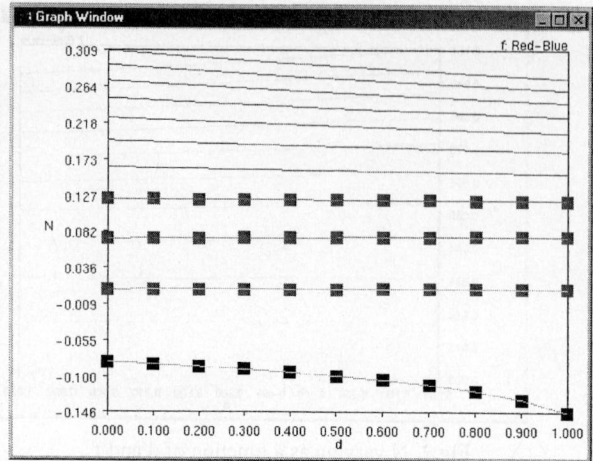

Fig.4. N as a function of the probability that immune reaction cells correctly target cancer cells

3 A Scenario with Collaborating and Competing Agents

The previous scenario represents a system in which only competition is taking place; in other words agents only tend to destroy each other if they can. Of course, there are numerous practical instances where agents can both enhance and hinder each others' behavior and in the sequel we will briefly discuss such a case. Consider the system which is schematically represented below, where agents of type A or B are being attacked by type E agents. Type A agents on the other hand will act upon the B cells in the following manner: any B-cell encountered by an A-cell will be "upgraded" so that it becomes more resistant to attack by E cells. Thus B-cells will in fact belong to one of the classes B_1, B_2, ... so that a B_i cell is upgraded to a B_{i+1} cell after encountering an A-type cell. The upgrading will result in a probability $p_{i+1} > p_i$ that the B-type agent survives after being attacked by a E-type agent. Agents of type A and E have intrinsic rates at which they act denoted by B_i and R_E, while B-type agents have a natural death rate represented by R_B.

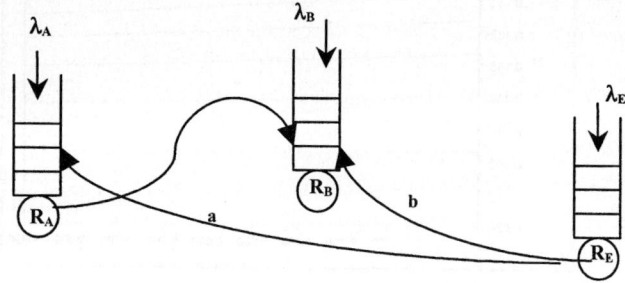

Fig. 5. Interaction between type A, B, and E agents

We will not dwell upon the Chapman-Kolmogorov equations for the system, but just give the characteristic parameters for each class of agents which will satisfy the following approximate relations:

$$\rho_A = \frac{\lambda_A}{R_A + a\rho_E R_E}, \quad \rho_E = \frac{\lambda_E}{R_E}, \quad c_i = \frac{\rho_{B(i)}}{\rho_B}, \quad p_{i+1} = dp_i$$

$$\rho_{B(1)} = \frac{\lambda_B}{R_B + (1-a)c_1(1-p_1)\rho_E R_E + \rho_A R_A c_1}$$

$$\rho_{B(i+1)} = \frac{\rho_{B(i)}\rho_A R_A c_i}{R_B + (1-a)c_{i+1}(1-p_{i+1})\rho_E R_E + \rho_A R_A c_{i+1}}, \quad \rho_B = \sum_{i=1}^{\infty} \rho_{B(i)}$$

where d <1 allows a B-agent of class (i+1) to be better protected than one of class i, while c_i is the probability that a B-agent of class i is selected by either an E-agent or an A-agent.

Let us consider a special case with $R_B=0$. After some transformations, the above equations yield:

$$\rho_{B(i+1)} = \rho_{B(i)}[\delta_{i+1}], \quad \text{where} \quad \delta_i = \sqrt{\frac{\lambda_A}{\lambda_A + \lambda_E(1-p_i)}}, \quad i>1,$$

and

$$\rho_B = \frac{\lambda_B}{\lambda_A + \lambda_E(1-p_1)}[1 + \sum_{i=2}^{\infty} \prod_{j=2}^{i} \delta_j], \quad \rho_{B(1)} = \rho_B \sqrt{\frac{\lambda_B}{\lambda_A + \lambda_E(1-p_1)}}$$

so that, in principle, the system can be solved analytically. The probability p_i should tend to some maximum value, such as 1, as i increases, to represent the fact that the class of agents B(i+1) is more resilient than agents of type B(i), for instance $p_{i+1} = [p_i + (M - p_i).d]$ for $i \geq 1$, where d<1 and $M \leq 1$.

It is interesting to consider how λ_A impacts the population of "normal" agents B. This is schematically presented in the following figure where we see the impact of d, which modulates the resilience, as well as of the arrival rate of the "enhancing" agents A. We have taken $p_1=0.1$, M = 0.9, and $\lambda_B = \lambda_E =1$. Although the total average number of A type agents is not shown, from the curves below we see that they will increase very rapidly with λ_A.

Modeling HIV. Consider now the following simple model. We consider three types of agents: viruses (V), uninfected "good" cells (G) and infected or bad cells (B). Uninfected cells become infected under the influence of viruses. In turn, viruses are further generated by infected cells. Viruses and uninfected cells both are replenished at some "external arrival" or birth rate λ_v and λ_G, respectively, and they die at rates $(1-q)\mu_v$ and μ_G, respectively where $0 \leq q \leq 1$. A cell is infected by an encounter with a virus. This encounter occurs at rate $q\mu_v$ provided that a virus exists, and with probability r it will result in the normal cell becoming infected. With probability (1-r), despite the encounter between a normal cell and the virus, the normal cell does not become infected. Normal cells die at rate μ while infected cells die at rate $\beta\mu$.

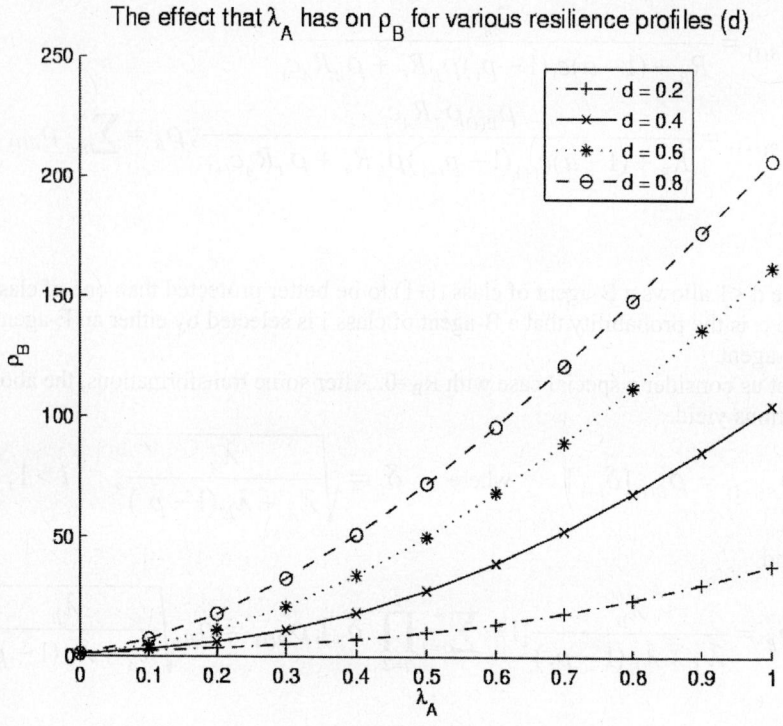

We now introduce an anti-viral agent E that acts on the viruses by rendering them harmless. E arrives into the system via an external arrival rate λ_E; as a result of the encounter of an element of E with a virus, with probability h the virus will be destroyed, while with probability (1-h) the virus encountering an agent E survives. If the virus survives its first encounter with the agent E it joins the class of viruses v(1). More generally, a virus of class v(i) that encounters agent E will be destroyed with probability h_i, or it will survive and become a member of class v(i+1) with probability (1- h_i). For notational convenience we treat the base class v as v=v(0). This change of class by viral agents can model a mutation of the viruses that encounter the anti-viral agent E into a more resistant strain, or it may represent the fact that a virus which encounters the anti-viral agent and survives in fact belongs to a more resistant sub-strain.

Using the Chapman-Kolmogorov equations, we end up with the G-network model parameters with all the populations as follows:

$$\rho_v = \frac{\lambda_v + \rho_I \beta \mu p}{\mu_v}, \qquad \rho_G = \frac{\lambda_G}{\mu + \rho_v \mu_v qr}, \qquad \rho_I = \frac{\rho_G \rho_v \mu_v qr}{\beta \mu}$$

which results in the equation

$$\rho_G^2 \mu qrp - \rho_G(\mu + q\lambda_v + \lambda_G qrp) + \lambda_G = 0, \qquad \text{yielding}$$

$$\rho_G = \frac{(\mu + q\lambda_v + \lambda_G qrp) \pm \sqrt{(\mu + q\lambda_v + \lambda_G qrp)^2 - 4\lambda_G \mu qrp}}{2\mu qrp}$$

References

1. Gelenbe, E.: Réseaux stochastiques ouverts avec clients négatifs et positifs, et réseaux neuronaux. Comptes-Rendus Acad. Sciences de Paris, t. 309, Série II, (1989) 979–982
2. Gelenbe, E.: Random neural networks with positive and negative signals and product form solution. Neural Computation **1**(4) (1989) 502–510
3. Gelenbe, E., Schassberger, M.: Stability of product form G-networks. Probability in the Engineering and Informational Sciences **6** (1992) 271–276
4. Gelenbe, E.: G-networks with triggered customer movement. Journal of Applied Probability **30**(3) (1993) 742–748
5. Gelenbe, E.: G-networks with signals and batch removal. Probability in the Engineering and Informational Sciences **7** (1993) 335–342
6. Gelenbe, E.: Learning in the recurrent random neural network. Neural Computation **5** (1993) 154–164
7. Gelenbe, E.: G-networks: A unifying model for queuing networks and neural networks. Annals of Operations Research **48**(1–4) (1994) 433–461
8. Gelenbe, E.: G-networks with triggered customer movement. J. Applied Probability **30** (1993) 742–748
9. Fourneau, J.-M., Gelenbe, E., Suros, R.: G-networks with multiple classes of negative and positive customers. Theoretical Computer Science **155** (1996) 141–156
10. Gelenbe, E.: A class of genetic algorithms with analytical solution. Robotics and Autonomous Systems **22** (1997) 59–64
11. Gelenbe, E., Labed, A.: G-networks with multiple classes of signals and positive customers. European Journal of Operations Research **108**(2) (1998) 293–305
12. Gelenbe, E., Hussain, K.: Learning in the multiple class random neural network. IEEE Trans. on Neural Networks **13**(6) (2002) 1257–1267
13. Gelenbe, E.: G-networks: Multiple classes of positive customers, signals, and product form results. Performance (2002) 1–16
14. Gelenbe, E., Fourneau, J.-M.: G-networks with resets. Performance Evaluation **49** (2002) 179–191
15. Fourneau, J.-M., Gelenbe, E.: Flow equivalence and stochastic equivalence in G-networks. Computational Management Science **1**(2) (2004) 179–192
16. Nowak, M.A., Sigmund, K.: Evolutionary dynamics of biological games. Science **303** (5659) (2004) 793–799

The Effects of Web Logs and the Semantic Web on Autonomous Web Agents

Michael P. Evans[1], Richard Newman[1], Timothy A. Millea[1],
Timothy Putnam[1], and Andrew Walker[2]

[1] Applied Software Engineering Group, School of Systems Engineering
The University of Reading, Reading, UK
{michael.evans,r.newman,t.a.millea,t.putnam}@reading.ac.uk
[2] School of Mathematics, Kingston University
Kingston-upon-Thames, Surrey, UK
andrew.walker@altoncollege.ac.uk

Abstract. Search engines exploit the Web's hyperlink structure to help infer information content. The new phenomenon of personal Web logs, or 'blogs', encourage more extensive annotation of Web content. If their resulting link structures bias the Web crawling applications that search engines depend upon, there are implications for another form of annotation rapidly on the rise, the Semantic Web. We conducted a Web crawl of 160 000 pages in which the link structure of the Web is compared with that of several thousand blogs. Results show that the two link structures are significantly different. We analyse the differences and infer the likely effect upon the performance of existing and future Web agents. The Semantic Web offers new opportunities to navigate the Web, but Web agents should be designed to take advantage of the emerging link structures, or their effectiveness will diminish.

1 Introduction

The World Wide Web is an open and distributed system. With content published at the rate of 1.5 million pages per day, expected mean persistence of just 18 days [1], and an architecture that can be freely extended according to need, the Web may also be regarded as an evolving system.

This evolution is reflected in the Web's hyperlink structure, the set of all Web pages and their hyperlinks known as the *Web Graph*, which is fuzzy in nature, and constantly changing over several different time scales [2]. Despite this, several empirical studies have identified many stable properties, which are exploited by search engines in order to classify and rank Web pages, and by navigational agents in order to find information of behalf of users.

Recently, however, two new trends have emerged that may impact upon the performance of these applications:

– The growing use of Web logs, or *blogs* (online journals published by individuals), which foster a different style of Web usage that could change the Web Graph

- The development of the Semantic Web, which aims to enrich the Web with machine-understandable metadata, enabling a new generation of intelligent Web applications.

To determine the effect these technologies will have on Web crawling applications, we performed the following:

- An analysis of the Web Graph for the Web as a whole and for the sub-set comprising blogs, using our own stochastic heuristic-based Web crawler over some 160,000 Web pages
- Based on this analysis, an assessment of the impact the Semantic Web is likely to have on such applications, given the way the technology is currently developing and the challenges facing it.

The paper is organized as follows: Section 2 provides a background discussion on these technologies together with an overview of related work. Section 3 presents the design of our Web crawler and compares its results with similar Web crawls to validate its accuracy. Section 4 presents an analysis of the impact of annotation technologies upon the evolution of the Web. Section 5 looks ahead to the new Semantic Web technologies, and assesses the effect that semantically-rich metadata will have upon existing Web crawling applications. The paper concludes by envisaging the capabilities of the next generation of Web crawlers.

2 Background and Related Work

Since the Web was first created, there has been a need to search it. As the Web has grown, manual browsing has been assisted through increasingly sophisticated automated search engines, which help identify and locate relevant material. Search engines rely upon Web crawlers that systematically navigate and index the Web, and infer meaning from the information content of individual pages and their link structure. As such, any changes to this content or to the link structure, such as those introduced by the use of blogs or the Semantic Web, may therefore have a dramatic impact on the effectiveness of a crawler in producing balanced and pertinent results.

2.1 Current Structure of the Web Graph

The structure of the Web Graph has been well documented with many studies identifying its key properties. For example, Broder *et al.* performed a Web crawl [3] on 200 million nodes and identified what was termed a 'Bow Tie' structure, containing four separate, well-defined components:

- A core, forming a Strongly Connected Component (SCC), in which pages can reach others via directed paths
- An IN component, in which pages contain hyperlinks that link to the SCC, but which are not themselves linked to by pages from the SCC

– An OUT component, in which pages contain hyperlinks are linked to by pages from the SCC, but which do not themselves link to any pages in the SCC
– Tendrils, which can be reached by a path from a page in the IN component, or link to a page in the OUT component, but which have no connection to the SCC.

Other studies have discovered that the Web Graph exhibits 'Small World' features [4], and a range of properties that follow Power Laws have been identified, such as the distribution of site sizes [5], and the distribution of the number of hyperlinks per Web page [4].

Web crawlers and navigational agents rely on these findings to:

– Search for content across the Web [6, 7]
– Identify authoritative pages [8]
– Identify communities of related Web pages [9–11]
– Rank pages according to the number of links connecting to them [12].

A significant change in the Web Graph will therefore affect the performance of the Web crawlers that the search engines rely upon. Although existing studies into the Web Graph have provided revealing insights into its structure, none has yet dealt with the changing use of the Web caused by blogs and the Semantic Web. They may therefore have missed a new evolutionary trend in the Web's underlying link structure.

2.2 The Impact of Blogging on the Web Graph

'Blogging' has become something of a new social phenomenon of an increasingly large subset of the Web's population. Estimates put the number of active blogs at around 1,880,000 [13], with a growth rate of 105% per year [14]. However, blogs increase the degree of Web interactivity, with content being more easily authored, linked to and commented upon (using software such as MoveableType (http://www.moveabletype.org) and Blogger (http://www.blogger.com)). This leads to a different style of web content: more richly linked than traditional web pages. As such, the combination of the dramatic growth in blogs, coupled with the change in content they introduce, may be changing the structure of the Web Graph.

2.3 The Impact of the Semantic Web

In 1989, Tim Berners-Lee proposed a hypertext system for CERN to manage their documents and information in the face of staff changes [15]. This hypertext system, named the 'Mesh', would consist of typed nodes (*e.g.* people or software modules) connected by typed links (*e.g.* 'refers to', 'made') representing relationships between the nodes.

This proposal evolved into the Web as we know it: display-oriented pages containing simple hyperlinks to other pages. The Semantic Web is closer to Berners-Lee's original vision of the Web: a machine-understandable Web of *meaning* [16], which attempts to address the issues of context, querying, provenance and trust.

The Semantic Web is navigated by software agents, rather than directly by humans. As an example of the likely impact the Semantic Web will have, consider the search for information. Currently, web crawlers must index the blind search of millions of pages to enable a search engine to give some potentially relevant results. Languages of the Semantic Web, such as RDF [17] and OWL [18, 19], enable Web resources to be meaningfully annotated in a machine-readable form, with rich meta-data embedded within links. Semantic Web agents are being developed to perform inference upon this data [20, 21] and generate, respond to and refine queries [22]. Centralised Web search engines with their huge cached repositories would therefore be replaced by lightweight directory services and local agents able to navigate the Web directly by meaning.

The Semantic Web has enormous implications for users of the Web in the way in which they store, interrogate, share and interact with information. The richer meta-data of its links, and emphasis on autonomous navigation, will also impact the structure of the Web Graph and the operation of crawlers and other agents that exploit it.

2.4 Assessing the Impact on Web Crawlers

Both blogs and the Semantic Web have the potential to transform the structure of the Web Graph, and thus the performance of Web Crawlers. To assess the impact these technologies may have, we designed a Web crawler with random heuristics to sample a random subset of the Web. The data was validated by comparing it with other large-scale crawls, and analysed for any change in the Web Graph caused by blogs. The results are presented in Section 4. To estimate the impact of the Semantic Web, we used existing information on its current state of development, and present our analysis in Section 5.

3 Designing a Web Crawler to Sample the Web

3.1 Crawler Design

For our Web crawler, we represent the Web Graph as the directed graph $G = (V, E)$, where $V = \{v_1, v_2, \ldots v_n\}$, the set of vertices representing Web pages, and E the collection of edges representing hyperlinks ('links') that connect the Web pages. Thus, G represents the structure of the Web in terms of its pages and links. When sampling Web pages, a random walk across G is required, using a stochastic process that iteratively visits the vertices of the graph G [23].

A random walk across G should generate a finite-state discrete-time Markov chain, in which each variable v_n (where $v_n \in V$) in the chain is independent of all other variables in the chain. Thus, the probability of reaching the next

Web page should be independent of the previous Web page, given the current state [2].

The following represents an overview of the crawling algorithm:

1. Crawling:
   (a) Download the page referenced by the URL submitted to the crawler
   (b) Search the page for links and other information about the page
   (c) Resolve local addresses used in links to absolute URLs through a *URL Resolver*, which converts links into the form
   `http://subdomain.hostname.tld/path/file.ex`
   (d) Remove links deemed to be of no use (*e.g.* undesired file type, such as executables)
   (e) Check the database to see if the page has already been crawled.
2. Record in the database all URLs found on the page.
3. Randomly select a resolved URL from the database and repeat the process by submitting the URL to the crawler.

3.2 Validating the Results of the Web Crawl

We ran the crawler between 2003-04-28 and 2003-07-29 with 31 users blindly interacting with it. Some 160,000 URLs were collected. Once the crawl was complete, we analyzed the Web pages referenced by these URLs, and used the statistics obtained to compare the results with those of other Web crawlers from other studies in order to validate the results. Note that the number of Web pages indexed by Google stands at 4,285,199,774, as of April 2004. Of these it is estimated that only 1.88 million are blog pages [13]. Although we suspect that the hyperlink structure of blog pages will be different from that of general Web pages, the number of blogs should not have a noticeable effect on the Web Graph as a whole. Consequently, comparing the structure of the Web Graph from that determined by other crawls is still valid.

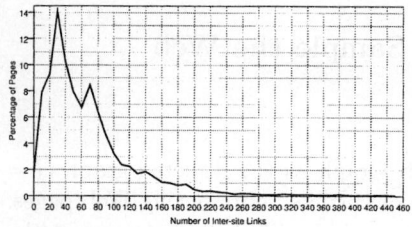

Fig. 1. Distribution of inter-site links

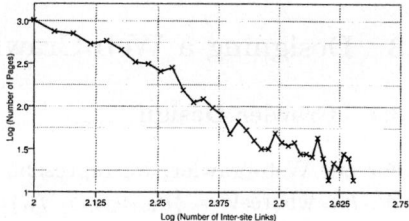

Fig. 2. Log-Log plot of inter-site links, revealing Power Law

Figures 1 and 2 show the distribution of *inter-site links* (*i.e.* those on a Web page that reference another Web page in a different domain) across the different

Web pages crawled by our crawler and give a good indication of the underlying structure of the Web Graph. The mean number of links was found to be 48, and the median 77.8. Both Figures 1 and 2 clearly show the power law that exists in the Web Graph and compare well with similar results by Broder et al. [3], Henzinger et al. [24], Barabasi and Bonabeau [25], and Huberman and Adamic [5]. In particular, the line of best fit for Figure 2 reveals an exponent of 3.28, which compares well with Kumar et al.'s value of 2.72 [26], obtained with a crawl of some 200 million Web pages. Thus, the similarity of the structure revealed by our results to that identified by other, more extensive studies, validates the effectiveness of our Web crawling heuristics in revealing the structure of the Web Graph to a good approximation.

4 Determining the Impact of Blogs

In order to determine the impact of blogs on the performance of Web agents, we separated the Web pages we found into two different categories: general Web pages and those Web pages we determined to be blog pages. For each category we also separated the pages into those we classified as *homepages* (*i.e.* entry pages into the site) and *non-homepages* (*i.e.* all others). We analysed each category to determine the hyperlink structure for each.

4.1 Distribution of Inter-Site Links for Ordinary Homepages and Blog Homepages

Our first analysis focused on the link structure of homepages. Homepages are the front pages of a Web site, and are usually the page through which most visitors to the site will arrive. As such the homepage could be thought of as serving a slightly different purpose to pages on the rest of the site, and so it is possible pages categorised as homepages may exhibit different traits to other pages. For the purposes of our analysis, we classified a homepage as a URL with no query string and one of the following potential file paths:

– /
– /index *(with any file extension)*
– /default *(with any file extension)*

Once we had identified the homepages, we then separated those homepages belonging to traditional Web sites from those belonging to blogs, identifying a blog as a Web page with the word 'blog' in either its URL, or page title. Once complete, we charted the Inter-Site Link distribution of each. We found the results to be quite striking.

Although the asymptotic trend evident in Figure 3 still exists in Figure 4, it is significantly less smooth. Charting a Log-Log plot on each graph reveals that the Power Law that was evident in Figure 2 (Log-Log plot of the Inter-Site Link distribution for all Web pages) is less pronounced for all homepages (Figure 5), and has broken down completely for blog homepages (Figure 6).

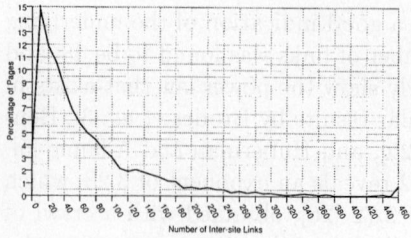
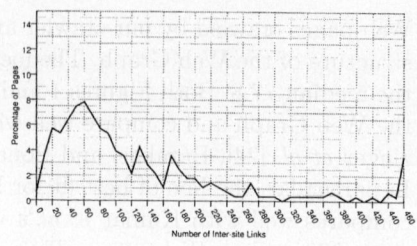

Fig. 3. Inter-site link distribution for homepages.

Fig. 4. Inter-site link distribution for blog homepages

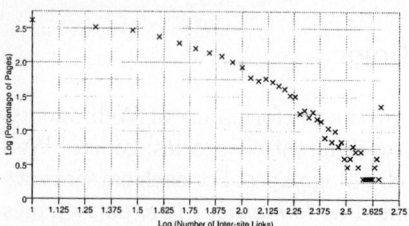
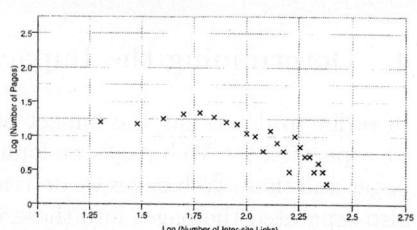

Fig. 5. Log-Log plot of inter-site link distribution for all homepages.

Fig. 6. Log-Log plot of inter-site link distribution for blog homepages

The reason for this becomes clear when we examine the distribution of the percentage of *Inter*-Site Links and *Intra*-Site Links (*i.e.* those links to other pages within the same site), as shown in Figures 7 and 8.

As is clearly evident, the pattern of links between a standard Web homepage and a blog homepage are significantly different. In particular, we found that it was most common (34.5%) for traditional Web homepages to have up to 10% of the total Inter-Site Links. In contrast, blog homepages most commonly (18.996% of pages) seem to have between 61% and 70% Inter-Site Links.

The more richly connected nature of the blog homepage becomes even more evident when we chart the distribution of all Inter-Site Links for standard homepages and blog homepages (Figures 9 and 10). We conjecture that the use of blogrolling (a constantly changing list of blogs included on the blog homepage [27]) is a major factor in this disproportionate number of links in a blog homepage.

4.2 Distribution of Inter-Links for Ordinary Non-homepages

When analysing pages other than homepages, the difference in link structure is less pronounced, as Figures 11 and 13 show. However, although the link structures for non-homepages differ less than for the homepage comparisons, there is still a marked difference between the link structure of a blog non-homepage and that of an general Web page, as the log-log plots show (Figures 12 and 14).

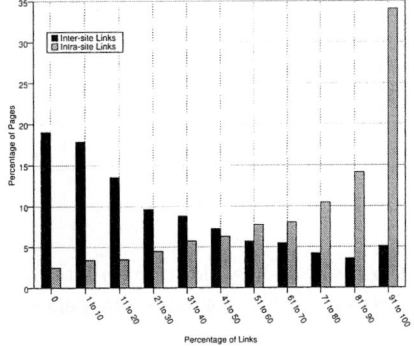
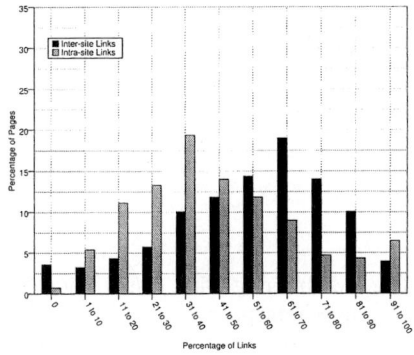

Fig. 7. Distribution of the percentage of links on homepages, split into inter-site and intra-site links

Fig. 8. Distribution of the percentage of links on blog homepages, split into inter-site and intra-site links

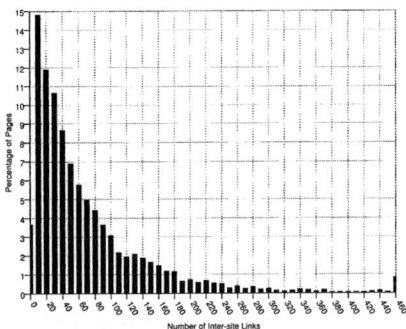
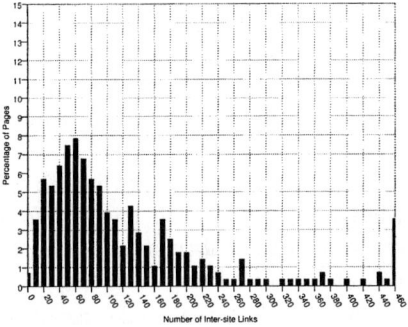

Fig. 9. Distribution of total inter-site links for all homepages

Fig. 10. Distribution of total inter-site links for blog homepages

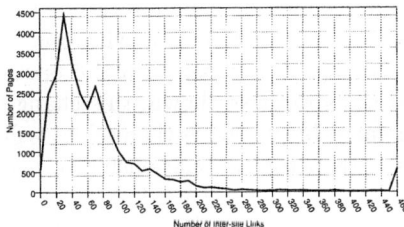
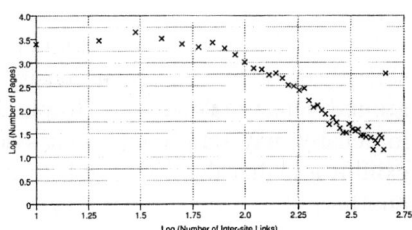

Fig. 11. Inter-site link distribution for all non-homepages.

Fig. 12. Log-Log plot of inter-site link distribution for all non-homepages

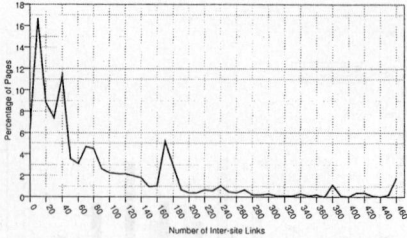 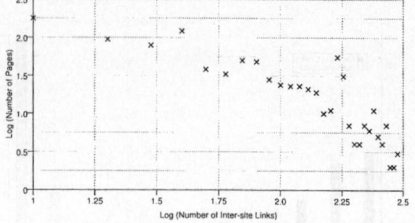

Fig. 13. Inter-site link distribution for blog non-homepages

Fig. 14. Log-Log plot of inter-site link distribution for blog non-homepages

4.3 Assessing the Impact of Blogs on Current Web Crawler Technology

The difference in link structure between blogs and general Web pages currently has no significant impact on the overall Web Graph due to the relatively low proportion of blog pages. However, if blog pages rise as a proportion of the Web as expected, the change in link structure will become readily apparent. Indeed, anecdotal evidence suggests that blogs are already having an impact on various search engines' ranking algorithms due to the distribution of Inter-Site Links within their pages [27].

Our results show that the link structure for blog pages is significantly different than for general Web pages. We suggest that the richness of the blogs' link structure can be attributed to the fact that blogs tend to cluster into communities as authors link from their blog to other blogs they find of interest.

Applications that make use of the Web Graph, such as Web crawlers, ranking algorithms and generative models of the Web, must take care to ensure that the sample of Web pages crawled is sufficiently random to be representative of the Web as a whole. Even today, the degree of cross linking between blogs can bias the sample set of pages of a Web crawler considerably.

The rich linking and community-oriented nature of the blogs presents a real problem to Web crawling heuristics that attempt to identify communities by the nature of their links. Such heuristics infer that topics are related whenever a statistically-significant high density of links is found compared with the background density of the Web Graph [2]. However, as we have shown, this change in density may simply represent a set of unrelated blogs, which themselves will exhibit a higher density of links, irrespective of their topical relationship to one another.

More positively, the significant difference between the link structures of blogs and of the general Web could be exploited by Web crawling applications to identify blogs and make adequate compensation for them in returned results. Furthermore, the relative confidence in which they may be identified enables their inclusion, or exclusivity, to be further search parameters.

5 Estimating the Impact of the Semantic Web

Blog posts typically take the form of an annotation: the thoughts of the author on a link, film, person, book, or another post. The richness of linking is as a consequence of the inevitable cross-referencing to the subject of the post, and to related commentaries.

This has clear parallels with the emerging Semantic Web. Consider a blog post discussing a film. That post may link heavily — to a DVD trader, to reviews, to the official site — and will make a number of statements in natural language. The same content could be presented on the Semantic Web through statements expressing formally-specified relationships between the author, the film, and other Web entities[3].

These statements act as links on the Semantic Web — for instance, allowing navigation to the film's official site. Here an agent may find further useful statements about the film.

The Semantic Web is founded on annotation and recombination, with reuse of ontologies and combination of information from different sources being key aspects. In this way, all Semantic Web documents will tend towards the 'blog model' — most documents will refer heavily to resources and ontologies on other sites, rather than taking the 'Web model' by relying on self-contained content. The Web Graph will change as a result, and the assumptions that crawlers use (e.g. that a link to a page has value, and asserts a positive relationship) will become increasingly flawed. However, the assumptions will no longer be necessary to achieve current goals, because the semantics of the 'links' will be explicitly provided in the document, as Berners-Lee intended.

Instead, we may look forward to more intelligent crawlers, exploiting the rich link structures to retrieve statements, and performing sophisticated reasoning to satisfy requests.

A possible future of this kind of annotation is shown by the W3C's Annotea project [28]. Annotea allows comments and other remarks to be attached to Web resources, with these annotations being stored on annotation servers around the Web. On visiting a Website, attached statements can be retrieved from these servers. Useful applications are annotation with bookmarks ('see also'), comments and reviews, and corrections. Furthermore, these Semantic Web annotations can be used to directly shape the Web Graph; providing direct links for common paths, for example.

Annotations are described in RDF, which means they are extensible and machine-understandable. Annotea is one way in which the Semantic Web could be applied directly to enrich Web agents — the meta-data attached to or comprising pages may provide 'hints' or 'short-cuts' to crawlers, transmitting additional information beyond the simple link structure of the document.

---

[3] There are real initiatives to develop ontologies for this kind of purpose: e.g. the RVW ontology for reviews
(http://www.pmbrowser.info/hublog/archives/000307.html).

The Semantic Web will not only alter the Web Graph in a similar way to blogs, by providing a higher density of categorised links, but will also provide new directions for improving the performance of Web agents that can capitalise on the *semantics* of this new Web.

6 Conclusion

We have assessed the impact that blogs and the Semantic Web could have on Web crawling applications, and the subsequent effect on autonomous navigational agents that are used to index, classify, and find information on behalf of human users. We have shown how blogs have a different structure from traditional Web pages, one that could confuse current Web crawling applications, but which ultimately could be harnessed to provide such applications with a greater understanding of the content they index. Further, we have also suggested that the Semantic Web, by emphasising and formalising annotation, description, and information combination, will similarly reshape the Web. Its potential for semantically-rich annotation and description of resources will reduce reliance on simplistic measures of relevance, opening the door to both better indexing and intelligent browsing, with all of the inherent performance implications.

References

1. Brewington, B.E., Cybenko, G.: How dynamic is the Web? In: Proc. 9th Int. World Wide Web Conf. on Computer Networks: The Int. Journal of Computer and Telecommunications Networking, North-Holland Publishing (2000) 257–276
2. Baldi, P., Frasconi, P., Smyth, P.: Modeling the Internet and the Web. John Wiley and Sons, England (2003)
3. Broder, A., Kumar, R., Maghoul, F., Raghavan, P., Rajagopalan, S., Stata, R., Tomkins, A., Wiener, J.: Graph structure in the Web. In: Proc. 9th Int. World Wide Web Conf. on Computer Networks: The Int. Journal of Computer and Telecommunications Networking, North-Holland Publishing (2000) 309–320
4. Albert, R., Jeong, H., Barabási, A.L.: The diameter of the World Wide Web. Nature **401** (1999)
5. Huberman, B.A., Adamic, L.A.: Growth dynamics of the World Wide Web. Nature **401** (1999) 131
6. Adamic, L.A., Lukose, R.M., Puniyani, A.R., Huberman, B.A.: Search in power-law networks. Physical Rev. E **64** (2001)
7. Kleinberg, J.M., Lawrence, S.: The structure of the Web. Science **294** (2001) 1849–1850
8. Kleinberg, J.M.: Authoritative sources in a hyperlinked environment. In: Proceedings of the 9th ACM-SIAM Symposium on Discrete Algorithms (SODA), ACM Press. (1998) 668–677
9. Chakrabarti, S., Joshi, M.M., Punera, K., Pennock, D.M.: The structure of broad topics on the Web. In: Proceedings of the 11th International World Wide Web Conference, ACM Press. (2002) 251–262
10. Flake, G.W., Lawrence, S., Giles, C.L.: Efficient identification of Web communities. In: Proceedings of the 6th ACM SIGKDD International Conference on Knowledge Discovery and Data Mining, ACM Press. (2000) 150–160

11. Kleinberg, J.M.: Hubs, authorities, and communities. ACM Computing Surveys **31**(5) (1999)
12. Brin, S., Page, L.: The anatomy of a large-scale hypertextual Web search engine. Computer Networks and ISDN Systems **30** (1998) 107–117
13. NITLE: National Institute for Technology and Liberal Education Weblog Census, http://www.blogcensus.net (2004)
14. Henning, J.: The blogging iceberg. Technical report, http://www.perseus.com/blogsurvey/thebloggingiceberg.html (2004)
15. Berners-Lee, T.: Information management: A proposal. http://www.w3.org/History/1989/proposal.html (1989)
16. Berners-Lee, T., Hendler, J., Lassila, O.: The Semantic Web. Scientific American **284** (2001) 34–43
17. W3C Recommendation: RDF concepts and abstract syntax. http://www.w3.org/TR/rdf-concepts (2004)
18. Antoniou, G., van Harmelen, F.: Web Ontology Language: OWL. In: Staab, S., Studer, R. (eds.): Handbook on Ontologies in Information Systems. Springer-Verlag (2003)
19. Horrocks, I., Patel-Schneider, P.F., van Harmelen, F.: From SHIQ and RDF to OWL: The making of a Web Ontology Language. Web Semantics **1** (2003) 7–26
20. Berners-Lee, T., Connolly, D., Palmer, S., Nottingham, M.: cwm — A general-purpose data processor for the semantic web http://www.w3.org/2000/10/swap/doc/cwm (2004)
21. Haarslev, V., Möller, R.: Racer: A core inference engine for the Semantic Web. In: Sure, Y., Corcho, O. (eds.): Proceedings of the 2nd International Workshop on Evaluation of Ontology-based Tools. Vol. **87** CEUR Workshop Proceedings, Montreal, Canada. (2003)
22. Fikes, R., Hayes, P., Horrocks, I.: OWL-QL — A language for deductive query answering on the Semantic Web. Technical Report, Knowledge Systems Laboratory, Stanford University, Stanford, CA, 94305–9020, USA (2003)
23. Bar-Yossef, Z., Berg, A., Chien, S., Fakcharoenphol, J., Weitz, D.: Approximating aggregate queries about Web pages via random walks. In: Proceedings of the 26th International Conference on Very Large Data Bases, Morgan Kaufmann Publishers Inc. (2000) 535–544
24. Henzinger, M.R., Heydon, A., Mitzenmacher, M., Najork, M.: On near-uniform URL sampling. (2000) 295–308
25. Barabási, A.L., Bonabeau, E.: Scale-free networks. Scientific American **288** (2003)
26. Kumar, R., Raghavan, P., Rajagopalan, S., Sivakumar, D., Tomkins, A., Upfal, E.: The Web as a graph. In: Proc. 19th ACM SIGACT-SIGMOD-AIGART Symposium on Principles of Database Systems, (PODS), ACM Press. (2000) 1–10
27. Starr, S.: Google hogged by blogs. http://www.spiked-online.co.uk/Articles/00000006DE60.htm (2003)
28. WWW Consortium: Annotea project. http://www.w3.org/2001/Annotea

Social Network of Co-occurrence in News Articles

Arzucan Özgür and Haluk Bingol

Department of Computer Engineering, Boğaziçi University
34342, Bebek, Istanbul, Turkey
{ozgurarz,bingol}@boun.edu.tr

Abstract. Networks describe various complex natural systems including social systems. Recent studies have shown that these networks share some common properties. While studying complex systems, data collection phase is difficult for social networks compared to other networks such as the WWW, Internet, protein or linguistic networks. Many interesting social networks such as movie actors' collaboration, scientific collaboration and sexual contacts have been studied in the literature. It has been shown that they have small-world and power-law degree distribution properties. In this paper, we investigate an interesting social network of co-occurrence in news articles with respect to small-world and power-law degree distribution properties. 3000 news articles selected from Reuters-21578 corpus, which consists of news articles that appeared in the Reuters newswire in 1987 are used as the data set. Results reveal that like the previously studied social networks the social network of co-occurrence in news articles also possesses the small-world and power-law degree distribution properties.

1 Introduction

Networks with complex topology describe various complex real world systems such as neural network of a worm (C.Elegans), power grid of the Western United States, phone-call networks, networks of linguistics, protein-folding, World Wide Web, Internet and social systems. Recent studies have shown that these networks possess some common properties such as being small-world and scale-free. Social networks describe human societies whose nodes are individual people and links represent a social interaction among these people [1]. Although obtaining data about social networks is difficult, many interesting social networks such as social network of scientific collaboration [2], movie actors' collaboration [3], sexual contacts [4], and email lists [5] have been studied in the literature. It has been shown that they share the small world concept and power law degree distribution property of scale-free networks. In this paper we investigate the small-world and scale-free properties of an interesting and previously unstudied social network of co-occurrence in news articles. In Section 2, we discuss how we have constructed this social network. In Section 3, we examine the small-world properties such as network diameter, clustering coefficient and average path length and scale-free properties such as degree distribution of the network. We conclude in Section 4.

2 Construction of the Social Network

Reuters-21578 corpus [6] consists of 21578 news articles that appeared in the Reuters newswire in 1987. This is a standard data set used extensively in research in automatic document categorization, information retrieval, machine learning and other corpus-based research. The news articles in the corpus are mostly about economics and politics.

Undirected graph of social network of co-occurrence in news articles is constructed as follows:

(i) 3000 news articles in the Reuters-21578 corpus [6] are read and person names are identified;
(ii) Nodes of the network are defined as distinct people;
(iii) A link is constructed between two people if their names appear in the same news article.

The social network constructed consists of 459 nodes and 1422 edges. To analyze and visualize the network Pajek Network Analysis and Visualization Program [7] is used. The graph of the constructed network is presented in Figure 1. It can be seen from the graph that there are many vertices that have 1 or 2 connections such as Gerhard de Kock, who was the Governor of the Central Bank of South Africa in 1987, Ferdinand Lacina, who was the Finance Minister of Austria in 1987, and Subroto, who was the Mining and Energy Minister of Indonesia in 1987. We can also observe that there are vertices which are very highly connected such as Ronald Reagan, the President of the USA in 1987 and James Baker, the Treasury Secretary of the USA in 1987.

3 Characteristics of the Social Network of Co-occurrence in News Articles

In this section, diameter, clustering coefficient, average path length and degree distribution properties of the network will be discussed. An early model for complex graphs is the Random-Graph model, which is due to the work of Erdos and Renyi [8]. In Random Graphs, a large number of nodes are randomly connected and the properties of the graph as the number of nodes goes to infinity are studied. Properties observed in real world complex networks are compared with respect to that of random graphs since they constitute a measure.

3.1 Small-World Property

Small-world concept describes the fact that despite their large size, most real world networks have a relatively short distance between any two nodes. *Distance* between two nodes is defined as the number of edges along the shortest path between them. *Diameter* of a network is the longest of the shortest distances between all pairs of nodes in the network. The property of small-world

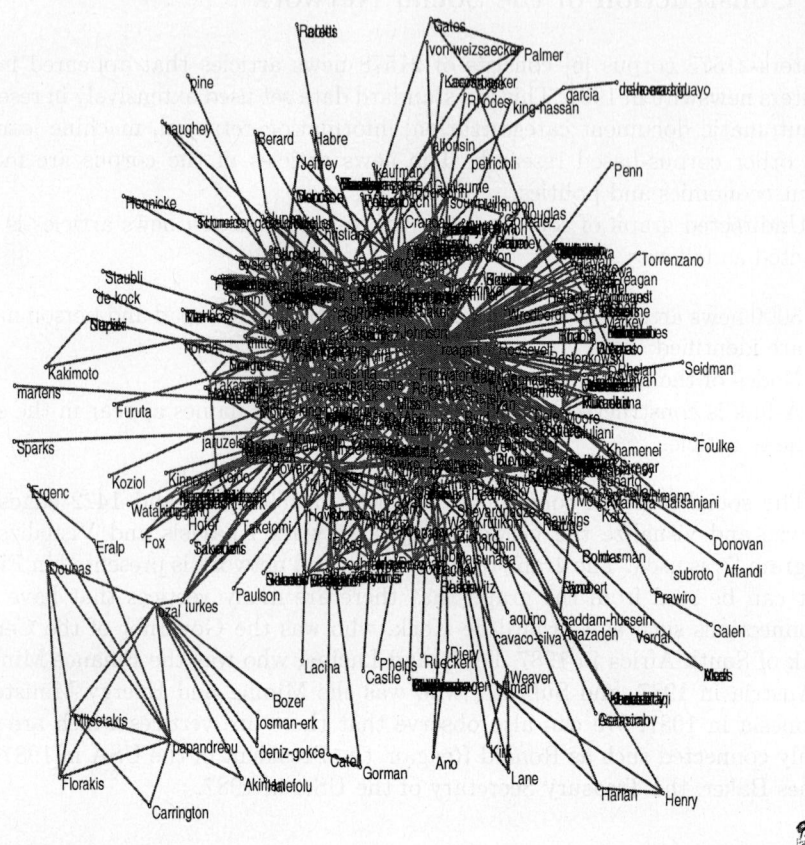

Fig. 1. Visualization of the social network of co-occurrence in news articles

networks is that they have small diameter and small average path length between vertices. The most popular example of small world networks is the "six-degree-of-separation" concept uncovered by the social psychologist Stanley Milgram in 1967 [9]. Stanley Milgram concluded that there is a path of acquaintances with a typical length of six between most pairs of people in the United States [9]. Other small-world network examples are actor-movie network and chemicals in a cell network [9]. Actors in Hollywood are on average three co-stars apart from each other, when generalized to the actors all over the world this distance increases to six. Likewise, chemicals in a cell are separated typically by three reactions.

In order to observe whether the small-world concept is valid for our social network of co-occurrence in news articles, we have calculated its diameter and average path length. The diameter of the network is calculated to be 8 due to the path from Oil, Mines and Parastatal Industry Minister of Mexico in 1987 Alfredo Del Mazo to the Turkish Foreign Ministry spokesman Yalim Eralp in 1987.

The average path length of the network is calculated to be 2,98. The diameter and average path length of the network are relatively small compared to the size of the network. Thus, we can conclude that this is a small world network.

3.2 Clustering Coefficient

A property of social networks is that cliques exist, where there are circles of individuals that all know each other. This property is quantified by the clustering coefficient. *Clustering coefficient of a node i* is defined as [9]:

$$C_i = \frac{2E_i}{k_i(k_i-1)}. \tag{1}$$

Here, k_i is the degree of node i and E_i is the number of links between the k_i neighbors of node i. *Clustering coefficient of the whole network* is the average of all C_i's. We have calculated the clustering coefficient of the network as 0,02. The clustering coefficient of a random network with the same size and average degree generated according to the Erdos-Renyi Model [8] is calculated to be 0.003, which is an order of magnitude smaller than our social network. This is another indicator that our network has small-world property.

3.3 Degree Distribution

Degree of a node is the number of edges the node has. The spread of the degrees of nodes in a network is characterized by a distribution function $P(k)$. $P(k)$ is the probability that a randomly selected node has k edges. In random graphs, $P(k)$ follows a Poisson distribution which has a peak at the average degree of the network $\langle k \rangle$. Therefore majority of the nodes have the same degree around $\langle k \rangle$ and extremely few nodes have very small or very large degrees. In the recent years, studies have shown that most real world networks such as World Wide Web [10], Internet [11], metabolic networks [12] and social networks such as movie actors [3], coauthor networks [2], sexual contacts network [4] follow power law degree distribution characterized as:

$$P(k) \sim k^{-\gamma}. \tag{2}$$

Here γ is called the scaling factor and such networks are called scale-free [9]. Power law distribution implies that nodes with few links are numerous, while very few nodes have very large number of links. In this study, we observed the degree distribution of the social network of co-occurrence in news articles. In Table 1, the degree distribution is given. Since in social networks persons are important, a representative person for each frequency is also given. Average degree of the network is calculated to be $\langle k \rangle = 6.02$. It is observed that most of the nodes have degrees less that 10. Very few nodes have large degree values. The most connected node is the node representing Ronald Reagan, with degree 209. This node acts as the hub of the network since 45% of the nodes are connected directly to it.

Table 1. Frequency of the degrees of nodes and a representative node for each degree

Degree	Frequency	Representative (Position)
1	74	Von-Weizsaecker (President of West Germany)
2	80	Haughey (Prime Minister of Ireland)
3	72	Ongpin (Finance Minister of the Philippines)
4	28	Alfonsin (President of Argentina)
5	52	Brodersohn (Finance Secretary of Argentina)
6	29	Wilson (Finance Minister of Canada)
7	35	Conable (World Bank President)
8	21	de-Larosiere (Central Bank of France Governor)
9	13	Camdessus (International Monetary Fund Managing Director)
10	10	Leigh-Pemberton (Central Bank of England Governor)
11	10	Sprinkel (Chairman of Council of Economic Advisers)
12	5	Reid (Reid-Ashman Inc Company Founder)
13	2	Schlesinger (Vice-President of Central Bank of West Germany)
14	2	Carter (Former President of USA)
15	4	Sumita (Central Bank of Japan Governor)
16	4	Lawson (Finance Minister of UK)
18	1	Gorbachev (President of USSR)
19	1	Balladur (Minister of State for Economy, Finance and Privatization of France)
20	1	Shultz (U.S. Secretary of State)
25	1	Kohl (Chancellor of West Germany)
26	1	Poehl (President of Central Bank of West Germany)
28	1	Miyazawa (Finance Minister of Japan)
29	1	Gephardt (Representative, Missouri Democrat, USA)
30	1	Yeutter (Representative for Trade Negotiations of USA)
31	2	Greenspan (Chairman of Federal Reserve Board of USA)
32	1	Howard-Baker (White House Chief of Staff)
35	1	Lyng (Agriculture Secretary of USA)
37	1	Volcker (Federal Reserve Board Chairman of USA)
42	1	Stoltenberg (Finance Minister of West Germany)
43	1	Thatcher (Prime Minister of UK)
58	1	Nakasone (Prime Minister of Japan)
77	1	James-Baker (Treasury Secretary of USA)
209	1	Reagan (President of USA)

Graph of the degree distribution of the network is drawn in the logarithmic scale as in Figure 2. We can see that this degree distribution does not follow Poisson distribution, but follows power-law distribution. Scaling factor γ is calculated to be 1,7.

3.4 Summary of General Characteristics of the Network together with Other Real World Social Networks

In Table 2, summary of the properties of the social network of co-occurrence in news articles is given together with some other previously studied social networks. $Size$, is the number of nodes in the network, $\langle k \rangle$ is average degree of the

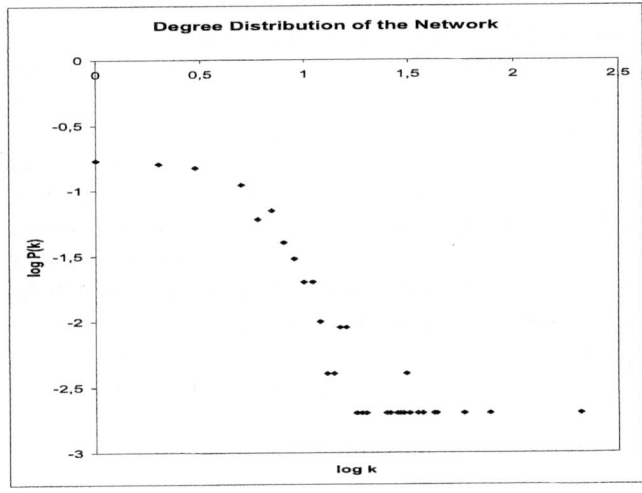

Fig. 2. Degree distribution of the social network of co-occurrence in news articles

nodes of the network, $\langle l \rangle$ is average path length between a pair of nodes in the network, C is the clustering coefficient of the network, $C(rand)$ is the clustering coefficient of a random network with same size and same number of edges, and γ is the scaling factor of the network.

Table 2. General properties of some social networks

Network	Size	$\langle k \rangle$	$\langle l \rangle$	C	$C(rand)$	γ
Coauthors, SPIRES [9]	56 627	173,0	4,0	0,726	0,003	1,2
Social network of co-occurrence in news articles	459	6,02	2,98	0,02	0,003	1,7
Coauthors, neuroscience [9]	209 293	11,5	6,0	0,76	0,000055	2,1
Movie Actors [3]	225 226	61,0	3,65	0,79	0,00027	2,3
Coauthors, Math. [9]	70 975	3,9	9,5	0,59	0,000054	2,5
Sexual Contacts [4]	2 810	-,-	-,-	-,-	-,-	3,4

Common properties of all the networks listed in Table 2 are that they have relatively small average path length and diameter compared to their sizes; they follow the power-law degree distribution and have relatively high clustering coefficient compared to the random networks with same sizes and same average degrees.

4 Conclusion

In this paper we investigated the small-world and scale-free properties of an interesting social network not studied previously. 3000 news stories mostly related to economics and politics that appeared in the Reuters newswire in 1987 are read and people names are extracted. The Reuters-21578 corpus from where the news stories are read is a standard data set used widely in information retrieval, machine learning and document categorization. A social network is constructed from this data. Nodes of the network are distinct people. There is a link between two people if they have appeared in the same news story. The resulting network is an undirected network composed of 459 nodes and 1422 links.

We have observed that this network has a relatively small diameter and average path length compared to its size. It has also relatively large clustering coefficient compared to the clustering coefficient of random network of the same size and average degree. The degree distribution of the network is also studied and it has been shown that it follows a power law distribution. There are numerous nodes with small degrees and very few nodes with high degrees. The most connected node is the node representing Ronald Reagan, the President of USA in 1987. 45% of the nodes are directly connected to that node and it plays the role of a hub in this network. It is concluded that like the previously studied social networks such as movie-actor collaboration network, co-authorship network and the sexual contact network the co-appearance in news article social network possesses the small world property and power low degree distribution property of the scale-free networks. As feature work, we will extend our network to cover more articles from the Reuters-21578 data set and observe the properties of this extended network. We expect to use our approach as a function of search engines to find related people. This needs further study.

Acknowledgments

This work has been partially supported by Boğaziçi University Research Fund under the grant number 33HA101.

References

1. Barabasi, A.L., Deszo Z., Ravasz E., Yook S.H., Oltvai Z.: Scale-free and hierarchical structures in complex networks. In: Sitges Proceedings on Complex Networks (to appear)
2. Barabasi, A.L., Jeong, H., Neda, Z., Ravasz, E., Schubert A., Vicsek, T.: Evaluation of the social network of scientific collaborations. Physica A (2002) 590–614
3. Watts, J.D., Strogatz, S.H.: Collective dynamics of small-world networks. Nature **393** (1998) 440–442
4. Liljeros, F., Edling, C.R., Amaral, L.A.N. , Stanley, H.E., Aberg, Y.: The web of human sexual contacts. Nature **411** (2001) 907–908
5. Kirlidog, M., Bingol, H.: The shaping of an electronic list by its active members. In: 5th International IT in Regional Areas Conference. (2003) 40–48

6. Lewis, D.D.: Reuters-21578 corpus. Available at
   http://kdd.ics.uci.edu/databases/reuters21578/reuters21578.html
7. Pajek. Package for large network analysis. Available at
   http://vlado.fmf.uni-lj.si/pub/networks/pajek/
8. Erdos, P., Renyi, A.: On Random Graphs I. Publ. Math. Debrecen **6** (1959) 290–297
9. Albert, R., Barabasi, A.L.: Statistical mechanics of complex networks. In Reviews of Modern Physics **73** (2002) 47–97
10. Adamic, A.L., Huberman, B.A.: Growth dynamics of the World Wide Web. Nature **401** (1999) 131
11. Yook, S., Jeong, H., Barabasi, A.L.: Modeling the Internet's large-scale topology. PNAS **99** (2002) 13382–13386
12. Jeong, H., Tombor, B., Albert, R., Oltvai, Z.N., Barabasi, A.L.: The large-scale organization of metabolic networks. Nature **407** (2000) 651

Using CORBA to Enhance HLA Interoperability in Distributed and Web-Based Simulation*

Andrea D'Ambrogio and Daniele Gianni

Department of Computer Science, System and Production
University of Rome TorVergata
1 Via del Politecnico, I-00133 Rome, Italy
{dambro,gianni}@info.uniroma2.it

Abstract. In distributed simulation, various simulation programs, or else components of a given simulation program, interact as elements of a simulation-oriented distributed computation. The High Level Architecture (HLA) is a standardization effort that provides a general framework for promoting interoperability and reusability in the simulation field. When applied to distributed simulation HLA shows some drawbacks that limit the desired degree of interoperability and reusability. This paper proposes a CORBA-based approach to overcome such drawbacks and improve HLA capabilities. The paper also illustrates how to combine the use of HLA and CORBA for Web-based simulation, which is the extension of distributed simulation to Web-based network infrastructures.

1 Introduction

In *distributed simulation*, complex simulation scenarios are built through the interconnection of a number of simulation programs in which simulated entities interact and cooperate among themselves. Such simulation programs may be executed on distributed, heterogeneous hardware/software platforms connected by a LAN/WAN infrastructure.

The term distributed is to be interpreted in the sense of traditional distributed computing, based on the client/server paradigm. Although distributed simulation has been originally developed for military applications, here the term is used to mean a broader range of applications in the simulation field.

HLA is a widely accepted standard that provides a general framework to promote interoperability and reusability in the simulation field. Nevertheless, when applied to distributed simulation, HLA shows some drawbacks that reduce its expected capabilities. This is mainly due to the fact that HLA has been

---

* Work partially supported by funds from the FIRB project "Software frameworks and technologies for the development and maintenance of open-source distributed simulation code, oriented to the manufacturing field" and by the University of Rome TorVergata CERTIA Research Center.

designed to be simulation-specific and not as a general framework for distributed computing. On the other hand, CORBA is a well-known standard designed to provide high levels of interoperability for distributed object computing, but it is not simulation-specific.

This paper proposes a CORBA-based approach to increase the degree of interoperability in HLA-based distributed simulation applications.

The paper also illustrates how to combine the use of CORBA and HLA for Web-based simulation, which is the extension of distributed simulation to Web platforms.

The paper is organized as follows. Section 1 gives a short overview about HLA and CORBA. Section 2 describes the proposed CORBA-based approach to improve interoperability and reusability of distributed simulation HLA applications. Section 3 extends the proposed approach to Web-based simulation by illustrating how CORBA can be used to implement Web-based HLA applications. Finally, Section 4 outlines the related work.

2 Background

This section briefly reviews the basic features of HLA and CORBA, illustrated in Section 2.1 and 2.2 respectively.

2.1 High Level Architecture (HLA)

The HLA provides a general framework within which simulation developers can structure and describe their simulation applications. HLA promotes *interoperability* between simulation applications and *reusability* of simulation components in different contexts [1]. Although it has been originally introduced by the Defense Modeling and Simulation Office (DMSO) of the U.S. DoD in 1995, HLA has been published as IEEE standard number 1516 in 2000 and is currently used by many organizations working both in the industry and in the research field. To certify its wide acceptance, HLA has also been recognized as a facility for distributed simulation by the OMG (Object Management Group).

A HLA simulation consists of [2]:

- a set of *Federates*, each representing a unit of simulation which can be of three types:
  - a remote simulation program;
  - an interface to control the behavior of live participants (human in the loop);
  - a simulation utility (e.g., data collector, passive viewer, etc.);
- a *Federation*, that identifies the overall simulation consisting of the set of federates;
- a *RTI* (*Run Time Infrastructure*), which is a simulation oriented middleware that provides services for communication and coordination among federates, time synchronization and simulation management. Federates interact through the RTI by use of either data sharing (*HLA Objects*) or messages exchange (*HLA Interactions*).

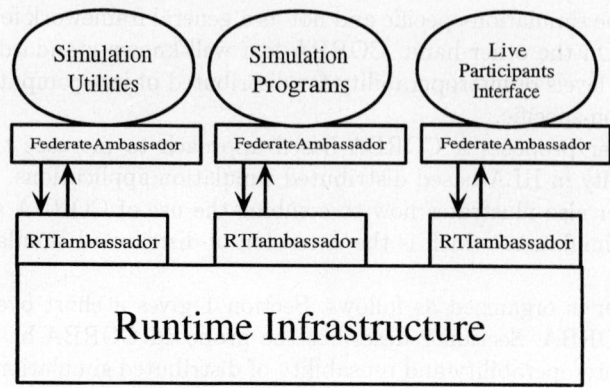

Fig. 1. Main components of a HLA simulation

Figure 1 shows a typical HLA simulation and highlights how the interaction between federates and RTI is carried out. On the federate side the RTIambassador is used as a local interface to access the RTI services, while on the RTI side the FederateAmbassador is used as a local reference to the federate. A complete RTI implementation provides both the RTIambassador library to be used by federates and the FederateAmbassador library to be used by the RTI.

The *IEEE Standard 1516* consists of four parts:

- *1516 HLA Rules*, which govern the behavior of both the federation and the federates [1];
- *1516.1 Object Model Template*, which defines the formats for documenting HLA simulations [3];
- *1516.2 Interface Specification*, which defines both the RTI – federate and the federate – RTI interfaces [4];
- *1516.3 Federate Execution and DEvelopment Process*, which provides a reference process for the development of HLA simulations [5].

2.2 Common Object Request Broker Architecture (CORBA)

CORBA is an OMG's standard for *distributed object computing*. The main feature of CORBA is that client objects may invoke services of other objects on a distributed system without knowledge of their locations and implementations [6].

The object interface is defined by the use of *IDL (Interface Definition Language)*, a declarative language which is independent of the implementation language, the location, the hardware and software architecture and the network technology. IDL provides both basic and constructed data types and operations to define services offered by the objects. The interface declaration defines the construct that holds data types and operations. An IDL compiler is available to map IDL into any programming language (e.g., C, C++, Java), thus achieving a high degree of interoperability and reusability.

A CORBA-based distributed application consists of *clients* that request services offered by remote servers (or *object implementations*).

The *Object Request Broker* (*ORB*) provides communication transparency by operating control and data transfers between clients and servers. A CORBA ORB supports two kinds of client/server invocations: static and dynamic. In the static approach, the client uses *IDL stubs* to send a request to the object implementation on the server side. These IDL client stubs, as well as the associated IDL server stubs (called *IDL skeletons*), are automatically generated by compiling the IDL code that defines the interface to the services. In the dynamic approach, the *Dynamic Invocation Interface* (*DII*) allows clients to construct and issue a request by discovering the method to be invoked at run time.

On the server side, an *Object Adapter* resides between the object implementations and the ORB. It provides the run time environment for instantiating object implementations, passing requests to them and assigning them an object reference, that is the mechanism used by the ORB to identify, locate, activate and manage object implementations.

CORBA is part of the Object Management Architecture (OMA), which defines additional services for CORBA-based distributed applications. Example services are the *Naming Service*, for registering object implementations and obtaining object references, and the *Security Service*, which provides a security infrastructure for object authentication and authorization [6].

3 The HLA/CORBA Combined Approach for Distributed Simulation

As already mentioned in Section 1.1, HLA is widely accepted as a general framework for promoting interoperability and reusability in the simulation field. Nevertheless HLA shows some drawbacks that reduce its expected capabilities when used for the development of distributed simulation applications.

This is mainly due to the fact that HLA has been designed to be *simulation-specific* and not as a general framework for distributed computing. As an example, HLA only defines interfaces for simulation datatypes without specifying how to convert them into basic datatypes. Moreover, HLA does not define the format of protocol data units that allow to establish the communication between remote federates through the RTI. For such reasons, the following shortcomings can be identified:

1. the federates are tied to a specific implementation of the RTI;
2. different RTI implementations do not interoperate.

One more limitation of currently available RTI implementations is the lack of widely used open source implementations, that could be easily adopted to broaden the HLA usage and obtain an increased level of reusability. Even though this weakness cannot be directly ascribed to HLA, which only defines the API without specifying implementation details, it has to be taken into consideration when evaluating the reusability properties of current distributed simulation applications.

Our proposal overcomes the aforementioned disadvantages by using a CORBA-based approach, that allows to obtain higher levels of interoperability and reusability, along with location and platform transparency. Moreover, several open source CORBA implementations are currently available.

The CORBA-based approach obtains such benefits by introducing an open source implementation of HLA interfaces on the CORBA client side, which makes use of a private RTI implementation executing on the CORBA server side, as better described in the following section.

3.1 HLA/CORBA Architecture

Figure 2 illustrates the proposed HLA/CORBA architecture for distributed simulation applications.

The application is started by a person or a software component (activation agent) that is responsible for the activation (dashed lines) of the set of federates (papyri) executed on the hosts *1* through *n* of the distributed platform (each host executes one or more federates). The architecture also includes a *RTI server*, that provides a complete RTI implementation (`RTIAmbassador` and `FederateAmbassador`) to the set of federates running on the remote hosts. HLA service requests and responses, as well as activation requests, are sent through the ORB to the RTI server. The main advantage of such a solution is that the federates do not need a local `RTIAmbassador` implementation because they make use of the one provided by the RTI server.

The proposed approach is based on the following assumptions:

1. the federates must be HLA compliant; in other words, they must be able to use HLA services specified by the IEEE standard 1516;
2. the implementation of the HLA interfaces are available by use of remote CORBA servers.

Such assumptions are reflected in the implementation of each federate, which is split into a *CORBA-HLA Proxy*, running on one of the available hosts (1 through *n*), and a *CORBA-HLA Server*, running on the RTI server. The full HLA compliance is guaranteed by the implementation schema illustrated by the class diagram in Figure 4. The CORBA-HLA Proxy class is a Java class that implements the HLA Java interface specified by the IEEE standard 1516 and uses the IDL stub to send HLA requests to the CORBA-HLA Server Class, that includes the complete RTI implementation. The IDL interfaces that are compiled to obtain the client stub and the server skeleton specify the set of services that vehicle HLA requests and responses.

An important feature of this approach is that CORBA, with its location and platform transparency, hides the complexity of the back-end infrastructure used

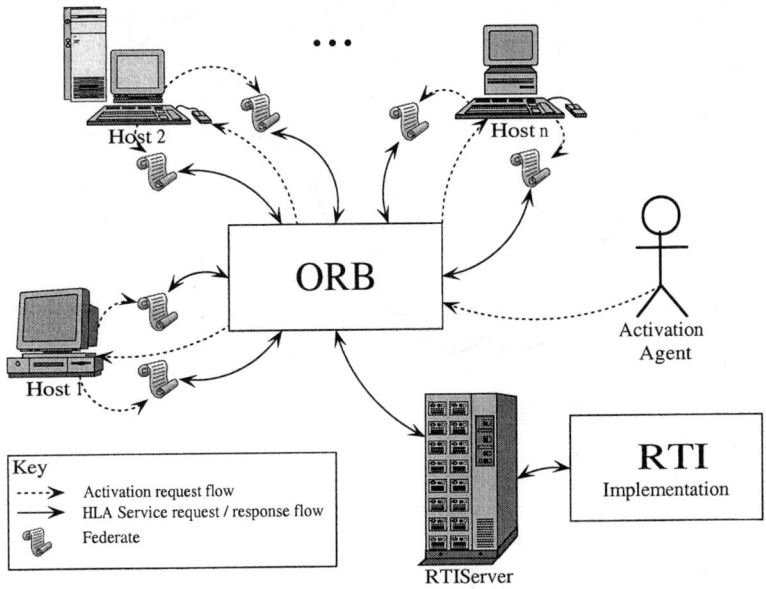

Fig. 2. Global view of the HLA/CORBA architecture

to elaborate HLA requests. Figure 3 describes the typical steps of a HLA service request. The CORBA-HLA Proxy Class uses the IDL stub (arrow 1) to send a HLA request to the ORB (arrow 2), making all conversions needed to transport data (e.g., objects serialization on byte array or string). The request is then transparently transferred from the client side to the server side (arrow 3), where the skeleton gathers the request and activates the CORBA-HLA Server Class (arrow 4), which in turn is responsible for elaborating the HLA request by use of the RTI implementation (arrow 5).

The CORBA-based approach allows to increase the degree of interoperability and reusability of HLA distributed applications, because of the following features:

- federates can be developed without the need of a specific RTI implementation; they are only required to send HLA requests by using CORBA, for which several open source implementations are available;
- federates implemented in a given programming language can use a RTI implementation available for a different language without requiring additional bridging libraries. Moreover, the federates can actually be implemented in programming language whose binding is not yet specified by the IEEE HLA standard (only C++, Java and Ada95 mappings are currently defined);
- federates can join federations implemented by use of different RTI implementations (wrapped by different CORBA-HLA Servers);

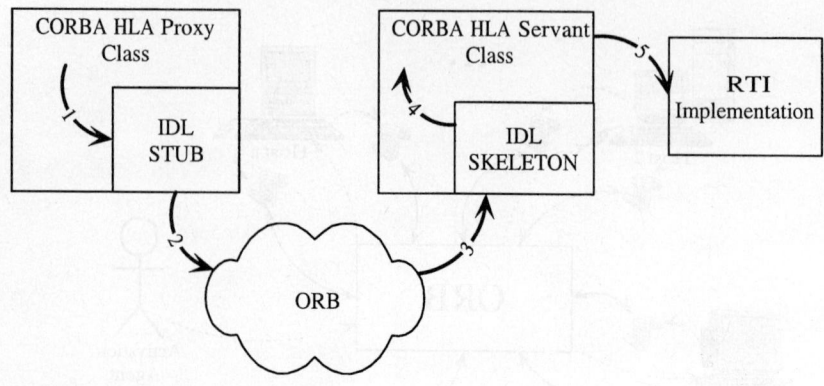

Fig. 3. Steps of a HLA service request

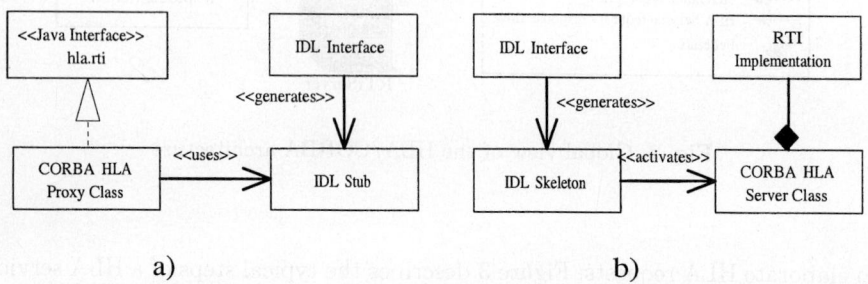

a)   b)

Fig. 4. a) Client side schema, b) Server side schema.

- CORBA Services can effectively be used to provide additional features to distributed simulation applications. As an example, the Security Service can be used to authenticate federates and verify if they are authorized to join a specific federation.

The main disadvantage of the proposed solution may be identified from the efficiency point of view. The use of the CORBA-based infrastructure to vehicle HLA requests and responses introduces additional overhead and precludes the use of multicasting communication and message caching. However, it must be noted that the CORBA-based transmission of requests and responses is not CPU intensive, and that by adopting solutions with a lower degree of interoperability the impact on the overall efficiency can be further reduced. As an example, HLA data structures could be directly implemented on the CORBA client side instead of accessing them on the server side, thus limiting the degree of interoperability but reducing the number of remote interactions.

4 Extension to Web-Based Simulation

Web-based simulation is a recently introduced term to denote the use of Web technology in the simulation field. As illustrated in [7], Web-based simulation applications can be classified in the areas of:

- *Web-enabled Simulation Environments (WSE)*, or environments that facilitate the reuse of simulation programs available on the Web [8];
- *Web-based Distributed Interactive Simulation (WDIS)*, or the extension of the distributed simulation approach to Web-based network infrastructures.

Figure 5 illustrates a WDIS-oriented extension to the HLA/CORBA approach illustrated in Section 3. The user interacts with the HLA/CORBA distributed simulation application by use of a common Web browser. On the Web server side a *Web Simulation Manager* component is executed to implement both the Web interface (run on the Web browser) and the necessary conversion work to transform HTTP requests into IIOP requests. The *IIOP (Internet Inter-Orb Protocol)* defines a set of message formats and common data representations for ORB-based communications over a TCP/IP network [6].

The Web Simulation Manager forwards user requests to the back-end HLA/CORBA distributed simulation application by using the following CORBA servers:

- the *Federates Server*, which is executed to select the set of federates from a list of available federates and then to activate the selected ones;
- the *Federation Controller*, which manages the execution of the federation;
- the *Federate Controllers*, which manage the execution of the federates (*1* through *n*) joining the federation;
- the *Simulation Results Server*, which records the simulation results for off-line detailed analysis or to get useful data for future simulation applications.

Figure 5 shows that the Web server is only used to interface common Web browsers to the back-end infrastructure, where CORBA-based protocols and servers are used to wrap the HLA/CORBA distributed simulation application. Unfortunately, neither HLA nor CORBA hold all the necessary characteristics to fully exploit the Web capabilities. As an example, the use of IIOP for ORB-based communication denies the transmission of requests and responses through network firewalls, that typically allows HTTP traffic only.

Work is in progress to combine HLA and Web Services technology in order to obtain a more effective and convenient solution for Web-based simulation.

5 Related Work

The need for increased interoperability between different HLA implementations is an issue that is gaining considerable attention. Research in this field is addressing the development of a standardized inter-RTI protocol, in analogy to the

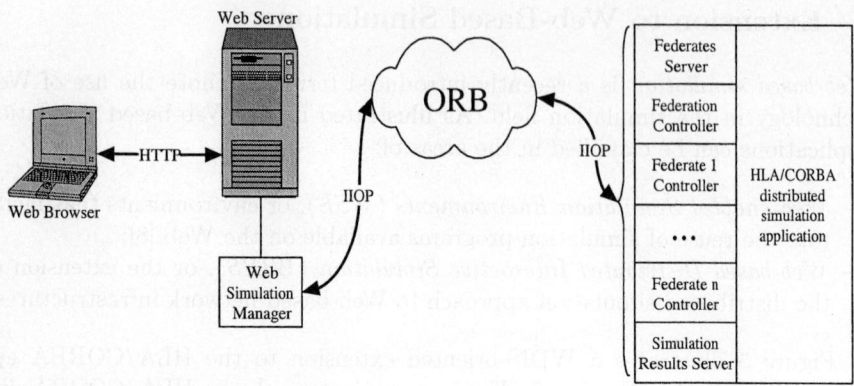

Fig. 5. HLA/CORBA architecture for Web-based simulation

inter-ORB protocol (IIOP) that has been developed in response to the lack of interoperability between different CORBA implementations. Work is in progress both at *SISO* (Simulation Interoperability Standards Organization) [9] and at research institutions leading the development of the *XMSF* (Extensible Modeling and Simulation Framework) [10].

The HLA/CORBA integrated architecture this paper proposes represents a short-term solution to the availability of a standard *inter-RTI protocol*, which is not expected to happen in the immediate future.

Previous efforts dealing with the use of IDL for the description of HLA interfaces, such as the one sponsored by the DMSO [11] and Bachmann's work [12], have not been successful nor adequately considered within the SISO community [13], due to the following main drawbacks that have instead been overcome by the approach illustrated in Section 3:

- the need for specific functions to convert HLA interfaces into their equivalent IDL interfaces;
- the explicit description of basic datatypes to be used for implementing HLA interfaces for simulation datatypes, which are instead left undefined by the IEEE HLA standard 1516, that enforces this choice by explicitly providing examples implementations of simulation datatypes that use different basic datatypes.

An alternative solution to the lack of interoperability between different HLA implementations is the development of appropriate *gateways* between two heterogeneous federations. A gateway should be placed at the boundary of each federation, executed by different HLA implementations, and be responsible for the necessary data conversion to guarantee the communication between heterogeneous federates. Unfortunately, the gateway-based approach has shown to introduce deadlocks [14], and it does not primarily address RTI interoperability aspects.

6 Conclusions

The characteristics of distributed simulation applications and the associated HLA limitations in terms of interoperability and reusability have been illustrated. A CORBA-based approach that overcomes such limitations has been introduced. The approach maintains a full HLA compliance by using a CORBA infrastructure that provides transparent and uniform access to the heterogeneous RTI implementations. A proposed extension to Web-based simulation has also been illustrated.

References

1. IEEE: Standard for Modeling and Simulation (M&S) High Level Architecture (HLA) - Frameworks and Rules. Technical report 1516. IEEE (2000)
2. Khul, F., Weatherly, R., Dahmann, J.: Creating Computer Simulation Systems: An Introduction to the High Level Architecture. Prentice Hall, Upper Saddle River, New Jersey (1999)
3. IEEE: Standard for Modeling and Simulation (M&S) High Level Architecture (HLA) - Federate Interface Specification. Technical report 1516.1. IEEE (2000)
4. IEEE: Standard for Modeling and Simulation (M&S) High Level Architecture (HLA) - Object Model Template (OMT) Specification. Technical report 1516.2. IEEE (2000)
5. IEEE: Recommended Practice for High Level Architecture (HLA) Federation Development and Execution Process (FEDEP). Technical report 1516.3. IEEE (2003)
6. Mowbray, T.J., Ruh, W.A.: Inside CORBA: Distributed Object Standards and Applications. Addison Wesley, Reading, Massachusetts (1997)
7. D'Ambrogio, A., Iazeolla, G.: Distributed Systems for Web-Based Simulation. In: Proceedings of the 13th International Symposium on Computer and Information Sciences (ISCIS'98), Antalya, Turkey. IOS/Ohmsha (1998) 1–8
8. Iazeolla, G., D'Ambrogio, A.: A Web-Based Environment for the Reuse of Simulation Models. In: Proceedings of the 1998 International Conference on Web-Based Modeling and Simulation (Part of the 1998 SCS Western MultiConference on Computer Simulation), San Diego, California. SCS (1998)
9. Stratton, D., Parr, S., Miller, J.: Developing an Open-Source RTI Community. In: Proceedings of the 2004 Spring Simulation Interoperability Workshop, Arlington, Virginia. SISO (2004)
10. eXtensible Modeling and Simulation Framework (XMFS) Project. http://www.MovesInstitute.org/xmsf
11. Kuhl, F.: Distributed Simulation Systems (DSS) Specification. Technical report 02-11-11. OMG (2002)
12. Bachmann, R: HLA und CORBA: Ansätze zur Verbesserten Integration. In: HLA-Forum der Tagung Simulation und Visualisierung, Magdeburg. (2001)
13. Tolk, A.: Avoiding Another Green Elephant - A Proposal for the Next Generation HLA Based on the Model Driven Architecture. In: Proceedings of the 2002 Fall Simulation Interoperability Workshop, Orlando, Florida. (2002)
14. Dingel, J., Garlan, D., Damon, C.: Bridging the HLA: Problems and Solutions. In: Proceedings of the 6th IEEE International Workshop on Distributed Simulation and Real Time Applications, Fort Worth, Texas. IEEE Computer (2002) 33–43

Designing and Enacting Simulations Using Distributed Components[*]

Alberto Coen-Porisini, Ignazio Gallo, and Antonella Zanzi

Dipartimento di Informatica e Comunicazione – Università degli Studi dell'Insubria
Via Mazzini, 5 – Varese 21100, Italy
{alberto.coenporisini,ignazio.gallo}@uninsubria.it
antonella.zanzi@uninsubria.it

Abstract. In the simulation field the demand for distributed architectures is increasing for several reasons, mainly to reuse existing simulators and to model complex systems that could be difficult to realize with a single application. In this paper the ASIA platform that aims at supporting the simulation design and simulators integration is presented. The paper focuses mainly on the comparison of the ASIA platform and the High Level Architecture standard. An example in the manufacturing field is presented as a basis for the comparison of the two approaches. Finally, some considerations are outlined in the perspective of the integration of the two environments.

1 Introduction

Simulation allows one to see the effect of the design, configuration or control choices without having to build or modify such systems, providing in this way a flexible and cost effective way to assess design, configuration or control choices.

Many simulation tools are available supporting approaches based on different mathematical models. Moreover, in recent years the issue of interoperability among such tools has been addressed by many people. One of the main efforts has led to the definition of the High Level Architecture (HLA) [1], which was initially developed by the US DoD and more recently has become an IEEE standard [2]. HLA defines a common architecture supporting reuse and interoperability of simulations and is intended to have a wide applicability to many different areas. However, its practical use requires highly skilled people because of its inherent complexity. Moreover, HLA does not fully address the problem of providing an integrated design environment that one can use to design simulations while designing systems.

Another approach was introduced by the ESPRIT Project ASIA, which aimed at defining and implementing an open platform for supporting design and simulation activities and allowing the integration of simulation tools. The definition of such an environment required to identify all activities that occur when designing/simulating a system. The initial results led to the implementation of a CORBA based platform allowing interoperability among simulators.

---

[*] Work supported by the Italian MIUR-FIRB – Tecnologie abilitanti per la Società della conoscenza ICT.

This paper reports on the results of a long term research, aimed at defining an open-source platform for supporting design and simulation activities and allowing integration of simulation tools. The paper reviews the main results of the ASIA project and discusses the relationship among the ASIA approach and HLA by providing an evaluation of both approaches and by discussing how they can be actually integrated. One of the advantages we expect from such integration is in term of usability since users can carry out the activities related to designing and simulating systems within a single framework.

The paper is organized in the following way: Section 2 presents the ASIA approach; Section 3 provides a short description of HLA; Section 4 introduces an example in the domain of Flexible Manufacturing Systems and shows how it can be dealt with using both ASIA and HLA; Section 5 discusses the main differences and similarities between the two approaches; Section 6 discusses how ASIA and HLA can be integrated, while Section 7 reviews the related works. Finally, Section 8 draws some conclusions.

2 The ASIA Approach

The Esprit ASIA (1998-2001) project aimed at defining and implementing an open platform for supporting both design and simulation activities and allowing an effective integration of simulation tools. Two different application domains were taken into account: space communication and traffic management. Starting from the requirements expressed by end users of the above mentioned domains ASIA defined an environment in which all the different activities related to the design and simulation of systems were supported. However, many issues that were initially identified were not investigated during the project. Thus, the research on simulation integration has continued and is still ongoing. In what follows we summarize the ASIA approach referring to its actual status, which has significantly evolved since the end of the original project.

2.1 Simulation Design Process

In what follows we briefly discuss a process lifecycle, which is referred to as the *simulation design process*, even if what is taken into account is a simulation based system design. The design process guides system engineers through the enactment of their systems and can be modeled by a set of "macro" activities, which are general enough to be applied to almost any domain. The simulation design process, shown in Figure 1, comprises three main activities.
1. Defining the *Information Model* means to define the elements that belong to an application domain, which represent either the logical components of a system or the simulators. In the latter case it is referred to as a Simulation Information Model.
2. Designing the *System/Simulation Architecture* means to build a system by instantiating the elements of the information model. Depending on whether the information model provides the logical components of the system or the simulators, the architecture is referred to as System or Simulation Architecture.

3. Executing the simulation architecture means defining how it has to be simulated, that is, to define which simulations will be performed, what simulation models are used, and how they are grouped and organized to carry out the simulation.

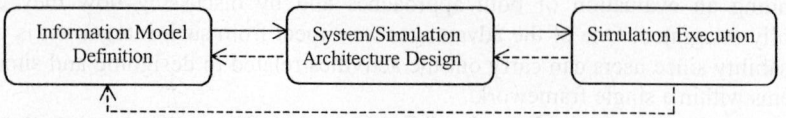

Fig. 1. Simulation process lifecycle (dashed arrows indicate feedback actions)

The first phase of the simulation design process is devoted to activities carried out before designing the integrated simulation. The simulation architecture, instead, provides a logical view of how the different simulation models cooperate. Such view provides both a data flow description, that is, which data are exchanged, and the control flow description, that is, the way in which the simulators interact.

In order to describe all artifacts (Information Model, Simulation Architecture, etc) produced during the design phases, ASIA defined a Simulation Architecture Description Language (SADL). SADL is based on a double language approach [3] that provides a domain independent abstract notation along with specific concrete notations, one for each domain. The abstract notation is defined as a simulation-oriented reuse of UML, domain-specific notations are obtained by means of the customization facilities of UML. In this way, one can define a specific notation for each domain as a transformation from the core notation. Once these transformations are defined, users can work using their own notations. Interested readers can refer to [4] for a thorough discussion of the ASIA meta-model and the associated SADL.

2.2 The ASIA Functionalities and Tools

The ASIA environment supports the following logical activities:
Modeling. Each entity involved in the previous mentioned phases is modeled using SADL. The core notation is used internally and is not viewed by users (except for the information model). Users rely on the domain-specific representation to define their models (system/simulation architecture).
Consistency Check. Each phase of the design process is based on the results obtained during the previous phases. Thus, it is necessary to check whether each phase is consistent with respect to the previous ones (e.g., the objects are connected according to their declared connectivity, when designing a system architecture).
Executing an Integrated Simulation. In order to execute an integrated simulation it is necessary to specify the actual data the simulators must use. Moreover, it may be also necessary to define where the output data will be stored, to set up some parameters for some simulators (e.g., time step) and so on. Providing all this information is referred to as *Setting up an experiment*. Once an experiment is set up one can run the experiment.

The ASIA approach is supported by three tools. The first one (IME) allows users to define an information model; the second one (SysAde) allows users to develop system-simulation architectures. Finally the third tool (DSC) allows one to define and execute an integrated simulation starting from a simulation architecture. All the tools are under development using Java and XML and are open-source.

In the next sub-sections we will focus on the main features of simulation architectures and on the way in which simulators can be integrated.

2.3 Simulation Architectures

A simulation architecture is designed by instantiating the elements of the Simulation Information Model (SIM). Such elements are instances of the following types:
SimulationComponent, representing a simulator or a simulation model. A SIM can contain SimulationComponents representing different tools (simulators) and/or simulation models that will be executed using some software tool.
Filter, representing a component that can perform some syntactic transformation on data. Its role is to transform data from one format to another so that two simulators can actually exchange information even if they use different data representation.
Activator, representing a component that can control the flow of execution within a simulation architecture.
Input/Output, representing a component providing (user-defined) input/output data used/produced by one or more SimulationComponent.

Each component comprises input and output *Gates*, which are in turn linked by means of *SimulationLinks*. In particular, an input gate is a gate through which a component receives data, while an output gate is a gate through which a component sends data.

2.4 Semantics of Simulation Architectures

The semantics of the simulation architecture is given in term of High Level Petri Nets (HLPN) [5] in which one can associate values with tokens and actions with transitions. Each component is associated with a HLPN and thus the simulation architecture results in a HLPN obtained by composing the different HLPN associated with the components therein. For instance a stand-alone simulator[†] having n input gates and m output gates is modeled by a single transition having n input places and m output places, as shown in Figure 2. The marking of each input place represents the availability of the data on the corresponding input gate of the simulator. The value associated with each token represents the data needed by the simulator. Thus, the firing of the transition represents the execution of the simulator that will mark the output places to represent that the result of the simulation has been produced. As a second example Figure 2 shows an activator named two-way selector, which can receive inputs from two different sources and provides as output one of the two inputs depending on the selection condition.

[†] A stand-alone simulator requires all input data to be available before starting the simulation. Once started, no data exchange occurs until the simulation ends. When the simulation ends the output data is available.

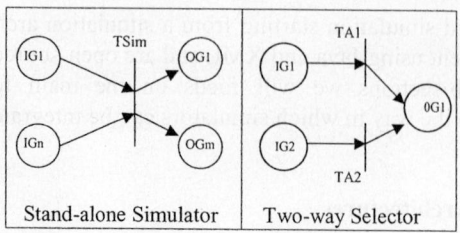

Fig. 2. The HLPN representation of two elements

2.5 Executing Distributed Simulations

In order to run a simulation one has to set up an experiment, that is to define the input data needed by the different simulators. Once the experiment has been set up, the execution is carried out by a tool named Distributed Simulation Controller (DSC), which is in charge of determining the control flow by executing the HLPN associated with the simulation architecture and managing data exchange among simulators. When a simulator produces a new data it notifies DSC, which, in turn, determines which simulators should receive it.

Communication between DSC and the simulators is implemented using CORBA[6]. The motivations behind such choice are: (1) CORBA is a standard middleware defined by the OMG and many implementations are available (Some of them are freeware or even open-source); (2) CORBA supports many programming languages and operating systems and thus it is very effective when one needs to integrate components written in different programming languages and/or working with different operating systems.

The CORBA Interface Definition Language (IDL) is used to describe the interfaces of the objects connected to the CORBA Object Request Broker. Thus ASIA requires each simulator to support two IDL interfaces, which we refer to as the *simulation control interface*, allowing DSC to drive a simulator by calling the methods to initialize, activate, suspend, restart and terminate the execution, and the *data exchange interface*, allowing DSC to handle data exchange among simulators.

Thus, the integration of a simulator requires the development of an *ad hoc* adaptor supporting on one side the two IDL interfaces and on the other side the simulator API. Also DSC has an IDL interface, in order to allow simulators to notify that they have produced new data and/or they have ended a simulation. The interested reader can refer to [7].

3 An Overview of the High Level Architecture

The High Level Architecture (HLA) [1,8] provides a framework to describe simulation applications, to facilitate interoperability among simulations and to promote reuse of simulations and their components. HLA describes simulations in terms of federations of federates, where a federation is a simulation system composed of two or more simulator federates communicating through the Run-Time Infrastructure (RTI).

HLA requires federations and federates to be described by an object model that identifies the data exchanged at runtime. This is accomplished by the HLA Object Model Template (OMT), which defines the object classes (objects) and the interaction classes (interactions). Objects represent the data structures shared by more than one federate, while interactions represent data sent from one federate to others. The OMT defines the format of the following key models:

Federation Object Model (FOM), providing the specification for data exchange among federates. It describes the objects, attributes, and interactions used across a federation.

Simulation Object Model (SOM), describing the federate in terms of objects, attributes, and interactions that it can offer to a federation. The SOM describes the capabilities of a federate to exchange information as part of a federation.

Management Object Model (MOM), identifying the objects and the interactions used by the RTI to manage the federation state.

In order to ensure proper interaction of federates in a federation and to describe the responsibilities of federates and federations, HLA defines a set of rules, which are divided into two groups one for federations and the other for federates.

The functional interfaces between federates and the RTI is defined by means of the Interface Specification. Federates do not talk to each other directly; the communication between federates is managed by the RTI and is based on the publish/subscribe mechanism. The RTI takes care of communication between the simulators and provides the required services to the simulation systems. It let federates join/leave the federation, declare their intent to publish/subscribe information, etc. In order to allow each federate to implement the described functionalities the RTI provides to every federate a set of API (Application Programming Interfaces) [1]. There are two main interfaces: *RTIambassador* and *FederateAmbassador*. Communication between federates and the RTI is based on RTIambassador and FederateAmbassador interfaces. RTIambassador is used by every federate to communicate with the RTI, while FederateAmbassador is used by the RTI to communicate with federates. Finally, RTI supports federations through services such as the time management service [9] (to correctly reproduce the temporal aspects of the modeled world).

4 An Example of Use: Flexible Manufacturing System

A *Flexible Manufacturing System* (FMS) is composed of several machines connected by means of a transport system. The transport system carries the raw parts to the machines on pallets where they are processed. Once the machines have finished their job the parts are moved back to the load station where they are unloaded. Moreover the machines use a tool-room as a repository for the tools they actually need in order to properly work the raw parts. A computer controls the machines and the transport system [10].

Using a distributed simulation in the FMS field provides some advantages. It is possible, for example, to solve the problem of confidentiality in the context of a supply-chain with external supplier. Moreover, a distributed simulation provides the possibility of simulating multiple levels of manufacturing systems at different degrees of resolution, creating an array of low-cost simulation models that can be integrated into larger models [11].

We used a simplified FMS to compare ASIA and HLA. The system consists of two machines working the parts on the pallet; a load/unload station that loads (unload) the pallets onto (from) the buffer; a tool room that stores all the tools used by the machines; and a buffer that can hold worked pallets and pallets that need to be worked.

4.1 FMS Simulation Using ASIA

According to the ASIA development process one has to create the (Simulation) Information Model (IM), design the System/Simulation Architecture and implement or adapt the simulators. The IM defines the components needed to model the FMS, which are Load/Unload, Buffer, Machine A, Machine B, Tool Room (see Figure 3) and the standard components such as Activator, Input and Output. The System/Simulation Architecture allows one to instantiate and compose the elements of the IM.

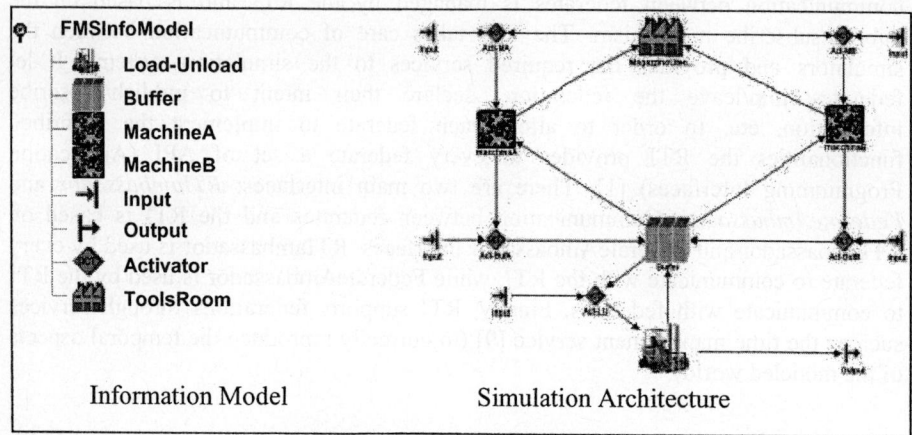

Information Model   Simulation Architecture

Fig. 3. The FMS and ASIA description

Each simulator sends and receives messages to other simulators according to the Simulation Architecture. Messages represent requests for loading/unloading a pallet or for getting/putting back a specific tool from/to the tool room and so on. Ten different messages are required to properly model the behavior of the whole system. Activators (two-way selectors) are used to provide either the initial user-defined input data or the messages coming from other simulation components.

The simulators have been written in Java and have been extended to support the required IDL interfaces. Each simulator is composed of three different parts: the actual simulator, the CORBA server and the adaptor, which implements the IDL interfaces, as shown in Figure 4a. The CORBA server is a Java program that initializes and registers the adaptor in the CORBA Naming service (used to identify the objects plugged onto the ORB). The adaptor receives/sends messages from/to ASIA DSC according to the IDL interfaces and takes care of receiving/sending the appropriate messages to the actual Simulator. All components have been hand written but in principle both the CORBA Server and the skeleton of the adapter can be automatically generated.

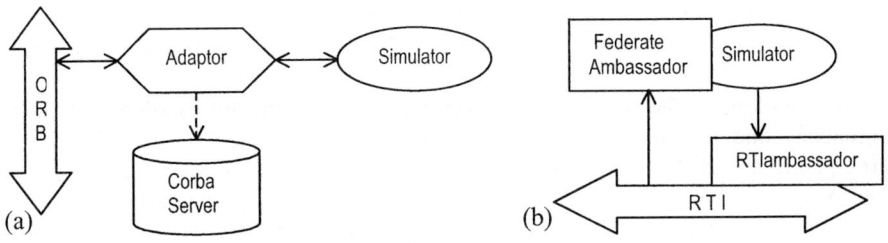

Fig. 4. The ASIA and the HLA run time structures

4.2 FMS Using HLA

In what follows we describe how the FMS has been simulated with HLA, using the same simulators of the previous example and an IEEE 1516 compliant RTI.

HLA requires to define a federation in which each simulator represents a federate. Moreover, it is necessary to define the FOM for the whole federation, describing the classes used by the federates and one SOM for each federate, describing its capabilities. The communication between the simulators has been defined using interaction classes only, and more specifically one class for each message identified in the previous sub-section. As a result the FOM contains ten different interaction classes.

Every simulator has been extended in order to become a federate. This required writing code for implementing both the initialization of the distributed simulation (federation creation, simulators joining the federation, simulators publishing/subscribing interactions) and the handling of data for each simulator (sending/receiving interaction to/from RTI). In particular, one has to implement the FederateAmbassador in order to create (if not already existent) and to join the federation and to publish/subscribe to the interaction classes of interest. This is done using the methods provided by the RTIAmbassador, which comes with the RTI implementation. Moreover the user has to implement the method receiveInteraction() in the FederateAmbassador to let the RTI notify the federate of any interaction to which it has subscribed, while for sending an interaction the federate has to call the method sendInteraction() of the RTIAmbassador. Figure 4b shows the data exchange of the HLA-based implementation.

5 Comparison Between ASIA and HLA

Both ASIA and HLA address the problem of integrating simulators to allow one to execute distributed simulations. However, there are many differences and complementarities between the two approaches. First of all ASIA provides an integrated environment in which one can design systems and simulations beside providing support for executing a distributed simulation, while HLA focuses mainly on the latter problem. Thus, ASIA provides an approach having a higher level of abstraction with respect to HLA. In fact HLA can be integrated in ASIA in order to allow execution of simulation architectures. This point is discussed in the next section.

When looking at the way in which distributed simulations are handled in the two approaches one can notice that ASIA provides a static view of the simulators participating at a distributed simulation, while HLA is based on a dynamic view. In other words in ASIA one has to know before starting the distributed simulation how many simulators will cooperate and how they are interconnected, while HLA allows simulators to join and leave a federation during the execution of a distributed simulation. However, in many domains the static approach provided by ASIA is sufficient to model even complex systems. For example, a FMS is usually designed in a static way, that is it is necessary to determine how many (and what kind of) machines will compose the system.

The dynamic approach used by HLA reflects the particular application domain for which HLA was initially developed that is military simulations, where a dynamic view of the system is necessary. However, in many non-military domains a dynamic approach is not required and sometimes may also be counterproductive being more difficult to handle.

Another difference between ASIA and HLA is in the way in which communication among simulators is handled. In ASIA, when designing the simulation architecture one has to statically determine how simulators are interconnected, while in HLA simulators are implicitly connected by using a publish/subscribe mechanism. Such difference is a consequence of the different ways in which systems are described. In other words since HLA allows simulators to join and leave a federation at run-time, the only way to handle communication is by using the publish/subscribe mechanism, while ASIA can make use of point-to-point communication since the different simulators and their role are known before starting the simulation. Moreover, HLA provides two different ways for simulators to exchange data: shared objects and interactions, while ASIA provides only message passing. It is well known that inter-process communication can be based either on shared memory or on message passing. These two mechanisms are "computationally equivalent" although the shared memory paradigm is easier to use for programmers but requires a more complex infrastructure (e.g., CORBA, RMI) while message passing is more complex to use but it is simpler to support. Thus, HLA choice to support both of them does not provide any functionality that could not be obtained by using message passing.

In conclusion, we claim that the ASIA approach is more abstract than HLA and that ASIA and HLA can be integrated by using HLA as the communication infrastructure used to make simulators communicate.

6 Integration Between ASIA and HLA

We are currently working to integrate HLA within ASIA. In fact, as stated before, HLA can be used as the communication infrastructure of ASIA instead of CORBA. Notice that the first phases of the development process are not affected by the choice of using HLA, that is both the information model and the system/simulation architecture do not depend on which technology is used for integrating simulators. The integration requires to modify the role of ASIA Distributed Simulation Controller. When using HLA it behaves like a monitor allowing users to keep track of the status of the simulation.

It must be noticed that the integration does not modify the way in which a distributed simulation is designed, that is by statically defining the simulators and their interactions. Thus, the main limitation to the integration is represented by the fact that it is not possible to use ASIA whenever the system to be simulated requires that simulators (federates) can be added/removed at run-time. However, many application domains, for which simulation is very important, do not require such possibility. In the sequel we sketch the main problems and solutions for integrating ASIA and HLA.

HLA requires the user to provide a FOM for the whole federation and a SOM for each federate. The FOM declares the interaction classes and the object classes, which describe the way in which the different simulators interact. The former mechanism is similar to the ASIA approach in which interactions among simulators are expressed in terms of data flowing from one simulator to another. Thus, a system architecture provides the information necessary to derive the corresponding FOM in which only interaction classes are used. Also the SOM can be derived starting from the information provided by the system architecture. However, it must be noticed that both the FOM and the SOM are "conceptual entities", that is what is actually implemented is an XML file containing the information represented by the FOM and the SOM. Then the FederateAmbassador needs to be implemented (see Sec. 4) to allow a simulator to be integrated using HLA. This step is similar to the development of the ASIA adaptor and can be carried out in the same way: we can automatically derive its skeleton, while the part representing the "business logics" needs to be written "by hand".

When executing a distributed simulation using HLA, the ASIA DSC plays a different role with respect to the one it has when using CORBA. In fact, HLA takes care of all the communication aspects that are handled by DSC. However, DSC can still be used to monitor the interactions among simulators. This is done by introducing a component called DSC Monitor that is viewed by HLA as another simulator. The difference between a real simulator and the DSC Monitor is that the former is expected to receive and to send data, while the latter will only receive data. This is done by having the DSC Monitor subscribe to all interactions (objects updates) that occur during a distributed simulation.

There are some open points that are currently investigated. More specifically we still have to address the possibility of deriving from a system architecture a FOM (and SOMs) in which object classes are used. Secondly, we need to investigate how already existing HLA compliant simulators (i.e., the simulators coming with an already developed SOM and FederateAmbassador) can be represented within the ASIA framework.

7 Related Works

The notations defined in ASIA are used to define the architecture of a system or of an integrated simulation and therefore can be viewed as an Architecture Description Language (ADL). Many ADLs have been defined [12–14] but none of them takes into account the specific needs required when dealing with simulation.

Several works have been done on the problem of integrating simulators. Some of them were domain-specific such as the CIM Framework architecture [15], in the context of semi-conductor environment, or [16, 17], which concern the introduction of data standard or language definition to describe simulation models.

Finally, several works concerning different aspects of HLA are worth to be mentioned. First of all there are several tools that support the development of HLA-based distributed simulation such as Visual OMT [18] or OMDT Pro [19] that can be used to develop the Federate Object Model. Some other tools claim to support the entire development process such as STAGE [20], which is devoted mainly to military applications, or FedDirector [19], which allows one to monitor and control a distributed simulation at run-time. Finally, Calytrix Symplicity [21] provides support for designing and implementing an HLA-based distributed simulation. However, all these tools either do not support the "more abstract" phases of simulation design or are very tied to HLA technology, that is they require a deep knowledge of HLA. Instead, our approach tries to hide as much as possible the technical aspects of the technology used to make simulators interact allowing users to focus on the modeling aspects of their systems.

8 Conclusions

This paper presented an approach for designing and executing distributed simulations referred to as the ASIA approach, which is the result of an on-going effort started within the ASIA ESPRIT project. Currently the approach is supported by a set of tools, some of which are not yet fully implemented, allowing users to define the components needed in their own domain, to instantiate them and to execute them in an integrated way. The approach was initially meant to be based on CORBA and is now extended in order to allow users to choose between CORBA and HLA. The future work will mainly be devoted to automatize as much as possible the development process and to enrich the existing tools in order to provide full support for the automatized process.

References

1. Kuhl, F., Weatherly, R., Dahmann, J.: Creating computer simulation systems – An introduction to the high level architecture. Prentice Hall PTR (2000)
2. http://www.ieee.org
3. Baresi, L.: Formal customization of graphical notations. PhD. Thesis, Dipartimento di Elettronica e Informazione – Politecnico di Milano (1997)
4. Baresi, L., Coen-Porisini, A.: An approach for designing and enacting distributed simulation environments. In: International Conference on Software: Theory and Practice, Beijing, China. (2000) 25–28
5. Jensen, K.: Coloured petri nets: Basic concepts, analysis methods and practical use. Analysis Methods, Monographs in Theoretical Computer Science, Springer-Verlag (1997)
6. http://www.omg.org/
7. Coen-Porisini, A.: Using CORBA for integrating heterogeneous simulators. In: 14th International Conference on Software and Systems Engineering and their Applications, Paris. (2001)
8. IEEE 1516.1: Standard for modeling and simulation (M&S) high level architecture (2000)
9. Fujimoto, R.M.: Time management in the high level architecture. Simulation **71**(6) (1998)
10. Upton, D.M.: A flexible structure for computer-controlled manufacturing systems. Manufacturing Review **5**(1) (1992) 58–74
11. McLean, C., Riddick, F.: The IMS mission architecture for distributed manufacturing simulation. In: Proceedings of the 2000 Winter Simulation Conference. 1538–1548
12. Allen, R.: A formal approach to software architecture. PhD. Thesis, School of Computer Science, Carnegie Mellon University (1997)
13. Magee, J., Dulay, N., Eisenbach, S., Kramer, J.: Specifying distributed software architectures. In: Proceedings the 5th European Software Engineering Conference. LNCS Vol. 989. Springer-Verlag (1995) 137—153
14. Luckham, D.: Rapide: A language and toolset for causal event modeling of distributed system architectures. In: Proceedings of the 2nd International Conference on Worldwide Computing and Its Applications. LNCS, Vol. 1368. Springer-Verlag (1998) 88–103
15. The CIM framework architecture guide 1.0. http://www.sematech.org/
16. ISO (International Organisation for Standardization): Industrial automation systems and integration – Product data representation and exchange (1994)
17. IEEE standard for distributed interactive simulation – application protocols. IEEE standard, 1278.1 (1995)
18. http://www.pitch.se/visualomt1516
19. http://www.aegistg.com/labcut/Labworkscut.html
20. http://www.engenuitytech.com/products/STAGE/index.shtml
21. http://simplicity.calytrix.com/calytrix/simplicity_pages/index.html

Semi-formal and Formal Models Applied to Flexible Manufacturing Systems[*]

Andrea Matta[1], Carlo A. Furia[2], and Matteo Rossi[2]

[1] Dipartimento di Meccanica, Politecnico di Milano
9, Via Bonardi, 20133 Milano, Italy
andrea.matta@polimi.it

[2] Dipartimento di Elettronica e Informazione, Politecnico di Milano
32, Piazza Leonardo da Vinci, 20133 Milano, Italy
{furia,rossi}@elet.polimi.it

Abstract. Flexible Manufacturing Systems (FMSs) are adopted to process different goods in different mix ratios allowing firms to react quickly and efficiently to changes in products and production targets (e.g. volumes, etc.). Due to their high costs, FMSs require careful design, and their performance must be precisely evaluated before final deployment. To support and guide the design phase, this paper presents a UML semi-formal model for FMSs that captures the most prominent aspects of these systems. For a deeper analysis, two refinements could then be derived from the UML intermediate description: simulation components for "empirical" analysis, and an abstract formal model that is suitable for formal verification. In this paper we focus on the latter, based on the TRIO temporal logic. In particular, we hint at a methodology to derive TRIO representations from the corresponding UML descriptions, and apply it to the case of FMSs. A subset of the resulting formal model is then used to verify, through logic deduction, a simple property of the FMS.

1 Introduction

Flexible Manufacturing Systems (FMSs) are widely used in shop floors to produce a large set of product families in small/medium volumes. In FMSs, the high flexibility of machines allows manufacturing different products in different mix ratios, thus providing firms the ability to react quickly and efficiently to changes in products, volumes and mix ratios. However flexibility has a cost, and the capital investment sustained by firms to acquire such types of manufacturing systems is generally very high. Therefore, in the development of a FMS, particular attention must be paid to the design phase, where the performance of the system has to be accurately evaluated so that the most appropriate resources

---

[*] Work supported by the FIRB project: "Software frameworks and technologies for the development and maintenance of open-source distributed simulation code, oriented to the manufacturing field." Contract code: RBNE013SWE.

(those that optimize the processes of the FMS) are selected since the early stages of the development process [1].

Discrete event simulation is generally used to estimate in detail the performance of FMSs. Starting from a description of the FMS, which can consist of a simple natural-language representation of the system or a more formal description, a simulation model is built, validated and run to numerically obtain the system performance. The development phase of a simulation model is time-consuming and depends on the complexity of the system and the (mostly informal) way in which it is described. In addition, simulation experiments need long computations to obtain a deep knowledge of the system and of its structural properties. Current FMS design techniques rely heavily on simulation models [1], and the specifications from which these models are built are still mostly written in natural language. This practice requires that the implementors of the simulator are also domain experts who can precisely understand the initial description.

In this paper we address these limitations in two ways. As a first contribution, a semi-formal UML [2] model for describing FMSs is developed. The UML description is used as the conceptual model of the system during the building of the simulator, thus improving the development phase. In addition, the UML representation can be used as a *lingua franca* between the specifiers of the FMS and the implementors of the simulation model, who now need not be domain experts in order to build the simulator (although a certain understanding of the application cannot be entirely eliminated).

Despite its popularity in the software-development world, standard UML is inadequate to carry out precise analysis of systems for its lack of a well-defined semantics. To fill this gap, two approaches can be followed: one could try to give formal semantics to the various UML diagrams, or UML diagrams could be translated in an existing formal notation. Here we follow the latter approach: as a second contribution, this paper hints at a simple methodology to derive formal descriptions expressed in the TRIO temporal logic [3] from semi-formal UML diagrams. TRIO is a powerful formal language that supports a variety of verification techniques (test case generation, model checking, theorem proving). In this work, the aforementioned methodological steps are applied to the UML-based FMS representation to derive a TRIO-based formal description. This TRIO model supports and eases the design phase of FMSs through formal verification. In particular, it allows one to perform theorem-proving-based analysis on manufacturing systems, which can spare FMS developers running expensive simulations.

The paper is structured as follows: Section 2 introduces FMSs; Section 3 presents the UML model; Section 4 sketches the methodological steps to derive TRIO descriptions from UML ones; Section 5 shows an example of formal analysis; the TRIO model can support formal finally, Section 6 draws conclusions and outlines possible future work.

2 Flexible Manufacturing Systems

FMSs are production systems composed of computer numerically controlled (CNC) machining centers that process prismatic metal components. A process cycle defining all the technological information (e.g. type of operations, tools, feed movements, working speeds, etc.) is available for each product so that the system has the whole knowledge for transforming *raw parts*, the state in which a piece enters into the system, into *finished parts*, the state in which a piece has completed the process cycle. The main components of FMS are described below.

CNC machines perform the operations on raw parts. A machining operation consists in the removal of material from the raw parts with a tool, fixed in the machine. The machines are CNC in that their movements during the machining operations are locally controlled by a computer. Machines can differ in size, power, speed and number of controlled axes.

Pallets are the hardware standard physical interfaces between the system components and the parts. Parts are clamped on pallets by means of automated fixtures that provide stability during the machining operation. Generally, but not always, fixtures are dedicated to products.

Load/unload stations clamp raw parts onto pallets before they enter the system and remove finished parts after their process cycle has been completed by the machines of the system. Stations can be manned, i.e. an operator accomplishes the task, or unmanned, i.e. a gantry robot accomplishes the task.

Part handling sub-system is the set of devices that move parts through the system. Different mechanical devices are adopted in reality: automated guided vehicles, carriers, conveyors, etc.

Tools perform the cutting operations on raw parts. Since tools are expensive resources their number is limited and as a consequence they are moved through the system when requested by machines.

Tool handling sub-system is the set of devices that move tools through the system. The most frequently adopted solution is a carrier moving on tracks.

Central part buffer is the place where pallets wait for the availability of system resources (i.e. machines, carriers, load/unload stations).

Central tool buffer is the place where tools can be stored when they are not used.

Supervisor is the software that controls resources at the system level by assigning pallets to machines and load/unload stations and by scheduling tool/pallet transports.

Tool room is the place where tools are reconditioned after the end of their life.

Let us now describe the flow of parts in the system. Generally more than one part is loaded on pallets at the load/unload station of the system. The type and the number of parts on the same pallet depend on products and system components. In detail, the number of parts depends on the physical dimensions of parts and machines, while the types of products depend on the technical feasibility of clamping different products with the same fixture. Most times the parts loaded on the same pallet are of the same type, however it is increasing the number of cases in which different part types are loaded on the same pallet. If the loading operation is executed manually by operators, then the corresponding time can be considered a random variable according to some estimated distribution; otherwise, if automated devices (e.g. a gantry robot) perform the operations and no source of uncertainty is present in the task, the assumption of deterministic loading/unloading times holds.

After parts are loaded on pallets, they are managed by the supervisor which decides the path each pallet has to follow to complete the process cycle of all its parts. In order to complete the process cycle, pallets must visit at least one machine; if machines are busy, pallets wait in the central buffer. Each machine has at least two pallet positions: the first one is the *pallet working position*, when the pallet is machined by the tool, while the other positions, known as *pallet waiting positions*, are used to decouple the machine from the part handling sub-system. Indeed, the pallet in the waiting position waits for the availability of the machine, or of the carrier if the pallet has already been worked. The machine is equipped with a pallet changer to move a pallet from a waiting position to the working position and vice versa; this movement is executed by automated devices and can be considered deterministic since there is no source of variability in the operation. After the pallet has been blocked in the working position and the tools necessary for the operations are available to the machine, the processing operations can be executed. Processing times of machines can reasonably be assumed deterministic. In fact, the trajectory of the tool during the cutting of material is computer numerically controlled and therefore the sources of variability are eventually negligible.

3 UML Description of a FMS

The UML model of a generic FMS is now briefly described. Following the usual structure of UML [2], the proposed model is divided into three areas of major interest: model management area, structural area and dynamic area. Each area represents a particular point of view of the modelled system and is presented in the remainder of this section.

3.1 Model Management Area

The only diagram belonging to this area is the package diagram. It represents how the model is organized by grouping the objects of the system into three main packages and by specifying the dependencies among them. The three main packages of a FMS system are: working sub-system, material handling sub-system and supervision sub-system. Each package represents the homonymic sub-system of real FMSs. The supervision sub-system is divided into two sub-packages: system supervisor and operation manager. The former contains the elements dealing with part and tool management policies of the FMS at the system level. The latter includes all system components providing production management and planning tools. All packages depend on the supervisor, which coordinates and schedules all the activities of machines, transporters and load/unload stations.

3.2 Structural Area

In this area both the physical elements and the abstract concepts belonging to a FMS are described using common object-oriented modeling tools such as classes, associations, generalization, aggregation, composition, etc. The supervisor class

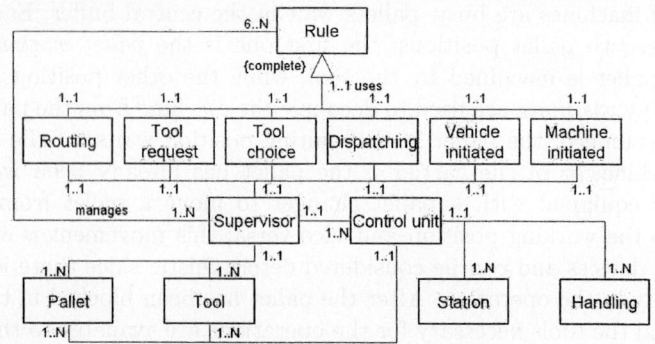

Fig. 1. UML model: supervisor class diagram

diagram, shown in Figure 1, defines the management aspects of the system. The Supervisor is a singleton, i.e. only an instance can be defined, and controls at the system level all the macro resources: machining centers, load/unload stations and part/tool handling sub-systems. A Control unit controls locally a Station (i.e. a machining center, or a load/unload station) or a Handling sub-system (i.e. a part or tool handling sub-system). There are as many Control unit instances as the number of workstations and material handling sub-systems in the real system. The Supervisor controls the overall system, by scheduling Pallet operations and Pallet/Tools transport by means of the management rules defined in the class Rule, which in turn is made up of six different types of rules.

In the Routing rule class there are rules to select the Pallet path in the system. In practice, different machines can often perform the same types of operations and, therefore, a decision concerning the best machines visiting sequence has to be taken on the basis of the system state. In order to simplify the system management, in most real cases the routing of pallets is decided statically off-line. This is a system level rule used by the Supervisor to schedule the pallet flow. In the Tool request rule class there are rules to select the first tool request to satisfy. Notice that tool requests can be emitted only by machining centers, when they need the tool to process a part, or by the tool room when the tool has finished its life. This is a system level rule used by the Supervisor to schedule the tool flow. In the Tool choice rule class there are rules to select the copy of a tool used to satisfy requests. Typically more than one copy of the same tool is present in real FMSs. This is a system level rule used by the Supervisor to schedule the tool flow. In the Dispatching rule class there are rules to select the first pallet to work (or to load) in the next period. This is a local level rule used by the Control unit of a Station. In the Vehicle and Tool initiated rule classes there are rules to assign a pallet or a tool to a vehicle (only for transport networks with vehicles). The Control unit of a part handling sub-system uses this rule at the local level.

The remainder of the FMS class diagram is not described in this paper for the sake of space. The interested reader may refer to [4] for more details.

3.3 Dynamic Area

This area describes the dynamic behavior of FMSs. Only the dynamics of pallets is presented in this section and the reader can refer to [4] for more details on the tool flow. The most interesting aspects of the pallet flow are the loading/unloading on/from the system, the transport, and the processing at machining centers.

In the loading task of a pallet with raw workpieces, the parts are fixed on a pallet in order to be handled by any device in the FMS. The fixing of raw parts on pallets is executed in the load/unload station which is modelled as any other station of the system. The selection of which parts to load on pallets is managed by the Control unit of the load/unload Station using a rule in the Dispatching rule class. When the Pallet has been assembled, it is sent to the output Secondary buffer of the loading Station and a transport request is sent to the Supervisor. The unloading task is the dual of the loading: finished parts are removed from the pallet and can leave the FMS.

The task of transporting a pallet from a station to another is managed by the Supervisor, which receives the requests, decides which request has to be satisfied first, and assigns tasks to the part handling sub-system controlled at the local level by its Control unit. The path of pallets (i.e. the sequence of stations each pallet has to visit) is decided at the system level by the Supervisor on the basis of the Routing rule.

A necessary condition for the starting of the Pallet processing is that the pallet is available in the waiting position modelled by the Secondary buffer of a Station. Once the Machine of that Station is idle, the Control unit of the Station selects a Pallet among those that are waiting in the Secondary buffer. The rule selection is taken from the Dispatching rule class. When the selected Pallet is in the working position and the necessary Tools are available to the Machine, the processing of the Pallet can start; now, the Pallet is under working and the Machine is no more idle. When the Machine finishes all the operations, assigned by the Supervisor, on the Pallet, the Supervisor selects the next destination of the Pallet by applying a Routing rule and allows the Machine to unload the pallet into the output Secondary buffer of the Station. Then, a pallet transport request is sent to the Supervisor.

4 From UML to TRIO

The UML model, partially described in the previous section, gives us a semi-formal representation of a FMS. However, if we want to carry out a quantitative analysis on the system performance it is necessary to translate the UML model in a formal model. The common practice in manufacturing is to build a simulation model to study numerically the system; instead, in this section we show how to use the TRIO language as a modeling tool, different than simulation, to analyze the main FMS properties. Notice that the shown formal approach is complementary, rather than alternative, to simulation: it does permit a deeper analysis of certain aspects of the system, and gives *certain* (i.e. formally proved), rather than *probable*, results.

TRIO [3] is a general-purpose specification language that is suitable for modeling systems with significant temporal constraints; it is a temporal logic that supports a metric notion of time. In addition to the usual propositional operators and quantifiers, it has a single basic modal operator, called *Dist*, that relates the *current time*, which is left implicit in the formula, to another time instant: given a formula F and a term t indicating a time distance, the formula $Dist(F,t)$ specifies that F holds at a time instant at t time units (with $t \gtreqless 0$) from the current instant. A number of *derived temporal operators* can be defined from the basic *Dist* operator through propositional composition and first order quantification on variables representing a time distance. For example operators *Lasted*, *WithinP*, *Alw* and *Since* are defined, respectively, as $Lasted(F,t) \triangleq \forall d \ (0 < d < t \Rightarrow Dist(F,-d))$, $WithinP(F,t) \triangleq \exists d \ (0 < d < t \wedge Dist(F,-d))$, $Alw(F) \triangleq \forall d \ (Dist(F,d))$, and $Since(F,G) \triangleq \exists d \ (d > 0 \wedge Lasted(F,d) \wedge Dist(G,-d))$. TRIO is well-suited to deal with both continuous and discrete time, with only minor changes in the definition of some operators. In addition, TRIO has the usual object-oriented concepts and constructs such as classes, inheritance and genericity, which are suitable for specifying large and complex systems.

Figure 2 shows the graphical representation of a subset of the TRIO specification that corresponds to the FMS semi-formal model presented in Section 3. It depicts the TRIO classes representing, respectively, the supervisor (box SV), the transport network (box TN), and the set of stations that perform operations on the raw parts (boxes ST). Figure 2 shows that the supervisor class SV can send the stations (array ST) a process_pallet event, and that it contains an internal (i.e. not visible outside the class) state processing[3].

The behavior of the components of the system is defined by the *axioms* belonging to the corresponding TRIO classes. In our example, let us assume that the pallets are identified by a positive integer in the range $PID = [1..N_p]$, while stations are identified by a positive integer in the range $SID = [1..N_s]$ (which is the domain of the indexes of array ST of Figure 2). The following axiom (where $pid \in PID$ and $src, dst \in SID \cup \{0\}$, with 0 representing the central part buffer)

---

[3] Informally speaking, an event is a predicate that holds only in isolated time instants, while a state is a predicate that holds in intervals of non-null duration (see [5]).

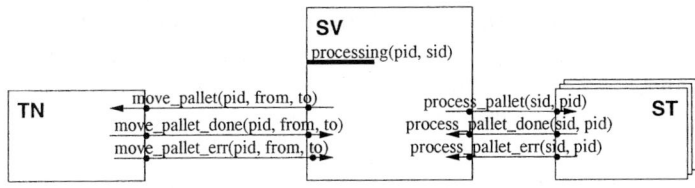

Fig. 2. TRIO classes corresponding to a subset of the FMS model

of class SV states that, if a pallet completes a move (i.e. event move_pallet_done occurs), or if there is a move error (move_pallet_err), a move_pallet command was issued in the past Δ time units.

Axiom 1. move_pallet_done(pid, src, dst) ∨ move_pallet_err(pid, src, dst) ⇒ $WithinP$(move_pallet$(pid, src, dst), \Delta)^4$.

Furthermore, let us assume that the pallets are partitioned into three subgroups A, B, C and the stations are partitioned into two subgroups D, E. Then if $pid \in$ PID, $isA(pid)$ (respectively $isB(pid)$, $isC(pid)$) is true if and only if pid is the identifier of a pallet belonging to subgroup A (resp. B, C). In a similar way, if $sid \in$ SID, $isD(sid)$ (resp. $isE(sid)$) is true if and only if sid is the identifier of a station belonging to subgroup D (resp. E). Axiom 2 of class SV states that when a pallet is moved from a source to a station, some compatibility constraints are enforced; more precisely, pallets of type A can only be moved to machines of subgroup D, while pallets of type C can only be moved to stations of subgroup E (pallets of type B, instead, can be moved anywhere).

Axiom 2. move_pallet(pid, src, dst) ⇒ $(isA(pid)$ ⇒ $isD(dst)) \wedge (isC(pid)$ ⇒ $isE(dst))$.

The structure of the TRIO description (i.e. the division in classes and corresponding items, events, and states) can be derived from the UML class diagram through (rather loose) methodological considerations. TRIO axioms (that is, the behavior contained in the classes) can then be written by taking into consideration, among other things, UML behavioral diagrams (sequence diagrams, etc.). Obviously, UML diagrams do not contain all the required information to build a completely formal model; therefore, the translation process cannot be completely automated. Nonetheless, suitable tools can manage most low-level details, thus restricting the amount of required interaction to a minimum (namely comparable to that required in building a simulation model).

The basic idea when passing from UML to TRIO is to transform UML classes into TRIO classes. Then, from the UML diagram of Figure 1 we determine that there must be a TRIO class to model the supervisor and a TRIO class to model the machining centers (other classes could be introduced, but are not included in the current description for the sake of brevity and simplicity).

---

[4] TRIO formulae are implicitly temporally closed with the Alw operator.

The methods of the UML classes, instead, are modeled in TRIO through combinations of states and events. For example, UML class Transport Network has a method move_pallet (not shown here for the sake of brevity), which is translated into events move_pallet and move_pallet_done, representing, respectively, the invocation and successful response of the method. Event move_pallet_err, instead, represents an incorrect termination of (i.e. an exception being raised by) method move_pallet. The basic semantics of UML methods is then captured by TRIO axioms on the corresponding events. For example, Axiom 1 shown above describes a most natural property of method move_pallet and, more precisely, that a method terminates (successfully or not) only if it was previously invoked.

In addition, the TRIO counterpart of a UML method might also include a state that models when a method is executing. For example, state processing of class SV is true when method process_pallet is computing. This is represented by the following axiom of class SV, which defines that state processing is true only if neither event process_pallet_done nor event process_pallet_err has occurred since event process_pallet occurred.

Axiom 3. $processing(pid, sid) \Rightarrow Since(\neg(process\_pallet\_done(sid, pid) \vee process\_pallet\_err(sid, pid)), process\_pallet(sid, pid))$.

Other axioms are not related to the basic behavior of single methods, but, rather, to how classes combine methods to achieve the desired results. This kind of information can be extracted from UML sequence diagrams and statecharts, following certain methodological guidelines. For example, a sequence diagram, not shown here for the sake of brevity, says that a pallet starts being processed when it completes a successful move into a station. This is modeled by the following axiom of class SV:

Axiom 4. $process\_pallet(sid, pid) \Rightarrow$
$\exists src \in SID : move\_pallet\_done(pid, src, sid)$.

Armed with the formal model presented above, it is possible to formally prove properties of the modeled system, as the next section will show.

5 Verification of the Formal Model

Let us consider a very simple property verification for the TRIO model of the FMS system. Fragments of the formal specification of the model have been introduced in Sections 3 and 4. From those axioms, we are able to prove a simple property by deducing its validity via theorem-proving. Obviously, other approaches to formal verification could be chosen (e.g. model-checking). Moreover, it is likely that in the overall verification of a complex description of a FMS different techniques are combined to compose local properties into a complete global verification. Notice that this kind of analysis is not possible with a simulation model (which only gives statistical results) or with the UML model alone (which lacks a non-ambiguous semantics).

The property we consider in this simple example is stated informally as following: whenever a pallet pid is being processed in a station sid, the compatibility constraint that every pallet of type A (resp. C) is processed in stations of type D (resp. E) is respected for the pair pid, sid. This means that the constraint enforced on the moving of pallets (as in Axiom 2) is also guaranteed during the processing of pallets.

The following theorem formally states the above (partial) correctness requirement.

Theorem 1 (partial correctness). processing$(pid, sid) \Rightarrow$
$(isA(pid) \Rightarrow isD(sid)) \land (isC(pid) \Rightarrow isE(sid))$.

Proof (sketch). Consider a generic $pid \in PID$ such that $isA(pid)$. Assuming processing(sid, pid) holds at the current time t, we must show that $isD(sid)$. We deduce that $Since(\neg(\text{process\_pallet\_done}(sid, pid) \lor \text{process\_pallet\_err}(sid, pid))$, process_pallet$(sid, pid))$ holds at t, by considering Axiom 3. If we consider the definition of the *Since* operator, this means that $\exists u < t$ such that $Lasted(\neg(\text{process\_pallet\_done}(sid, pid) \lor \text{process\_pallet\_err}(sid, pid)), t-u)$ holds at t and process_pallet(sid, pid) holds at u. Let us focus on the latter term: process_pallet(sid, pid) is true at u. Therefore, we can use Axiom 4 to infer that move_pallet_done(pid, src, sid) is also true at u, for some $src \in SID$. This also makes true the antecedent of the implication in Axiom 1, so that we deduce that $WithinP(\text{move\_pallet}(pid, src, sid), \Delta)$ holds at u. By the definition of the $WithinP$ operator, we immediately infer that there exists an instant $v \in (u - \Delta, u)$ such that move_pallet(pid, src, sid) holds at v. Now, we consider Axiom 2, which relates move_pallet events to the type of its arguments. We conclude that $isD(sid)$, since $isA(pid)$. This means that the theorem holds for all $pid \in A \subseteq PID$. The cases for $pid \in B$ and for $pid \in C$ are very similar and are omitted. □

6 Conclusions and Future Works

In this paper we applied modeling techniques typical of the software development domain to flexible manufacturing systems. Our goal was twofold: on the one hand we developed a UML-based description of FMSs, which is an intermediate representation between informal specifications written in natural language and simulation models written in some object-oriented simulation language; on the other hand, from this UML description we derived a formal model expressed in the TRIO temporal logic, which was used to formally analyze a part of the system with deductive verification techniques.

This paper is a just a preliminary result of a large project, and a variety of future developments will follow in the next future. First, a complete methodology to derive simulation models from UML and TRIO descriptions would greatly enhance the design of a FMS. This would both simplify the development process of simulation models, and provide users with two complementary descriptions, which would allow a more comprehensive and thorough analysis of the properties of the analyzed FMS. Armed with this methodology, the user could map TRIO concepts to simulation elements (and vice versa), thus improving the interactions between the two models.

A natural extension of our approach would be to prove more complex properties of the system and to validate the implemented FMS using the TRIO model. This can be done in different ways. For example, test cases (that is, execution traces) could be (semi)automatically derived from the TRIO description [6], and then compared with the behavior of the actual FMS. Vice versa, one could capture both the most common and least common behaviors of the implemented system and check if they are compatible with the TRIO model (in TRIO terms, this is called *history checking*).

While in this paper we focused on simple properties of single parts of a FMS, TRIO is a flexible formalism that can be used to verify a number of different (local and global) types of properties. For example, one could formally compare different management policies (scheduling, loading of parts, tool dispatching, etc.) to determine which ones should be adopted in a specific FMS. Another interesting application would be to verify, with respect to a certain overall goal, the consistency of the several management rules introduced in the simulation model by the developer.

Finally, in a sort of "automatic design" approach [3], we plan on using the TRIO model to prove that, for some property to hold (e.g. the pallet flowtime being lower than a specified value, etc.), FMS configuration parameters must be in some precise range.

Acknowledgements

The authors would like to thank Dino Mandrioli, Pierluigi San Pietro, Quirico Semeraro and Tullio Tolio for their useful suggestions and comments, and the anonymous reviewers for their suggestions for improvements.

References

1. Matta, A., Tolio, T., Karaesmen, F., Dallery, Y.: An integrated approach for the configuration of automated manufacturing systems. Robotics and CIM **17** (2001) 19–26
2. OMG: UML specification, 2003-03-01. Technical report, OMG (2003)
3. Ciapessoni, E., Coen-Porisini, A., Crivelli, E., Mandrioli, D., Mirandola, P., Morzenti, A.: From formal models to formally-based methods: An industrial experience. ACM TOSEM **8** (1999) 79–113
4. A. Matta: D1.1: UML description of FMS. Technical report, FIRB Project, Contract code: RBNE013SWE (2004)
5. Gargantini, A., Morzenti, A.: Automated deductive requirement analysis of critical systems. ACM TOSEM **10** (2001) 255–307
6. Pietro, P.S., Morzenti, A., Morasca, S.: Generation of execution sequences for modular time critical systems. IEEE Transactions on Software Engineering **26** (2000) 128–149

New Computer Model of a Dipolar System with Hexagonal Geometry in Presence of an External Electric Field

Rafaella Turri, M. Buscaglia, Giovanni Danese, Ivo De Lotto, and Francesco Leporati

Dip. di Informatica e Sistemistica, Università di Pavia, Via Ferrata 1, Pavia, Italy
INFM – UdR Pavia via Bassi 6, 27100 Pavia Italy
{rafaella.turri,gianni.danese,ivo.delotto}@unipv.it
francesco.leporati@unipv.it

Abstract. We present a Monte Carlo – Metropolis computer simulation study of the equilibrium configurations in an hexagonal lattice model of anisotropically polarisable particles. In the presence of an external field the spins polarize and couple via dipolar interactions. We found that the dipolar interactions induce a new and unexpected orientational order, characterized by a depressed value of the orientational order parameter $\langle P_2 \rangle$ so confirming the results already identified in similar analyses carried, however, on a more elementary cubic lattice organization.

1 Introduction

In this paper, we present a study of the effect of interactions among induced dipoles on the order of an anisotropic particle ensemble, using Monte Carlo - Metropolis (MM) computer simulations [1].

Diluted polarisable particle systems in presence of an electric field tend to align their axis of maximum polarisability with the applied field direction. At increasing densities, however, this is not always true: in particular, in concentrated colloidal suspensions of rod-like polyelectrolytes (polymers, DNA, virus etc.), particles oriented perpendicularly to the electric field were observed (Fig. 1).

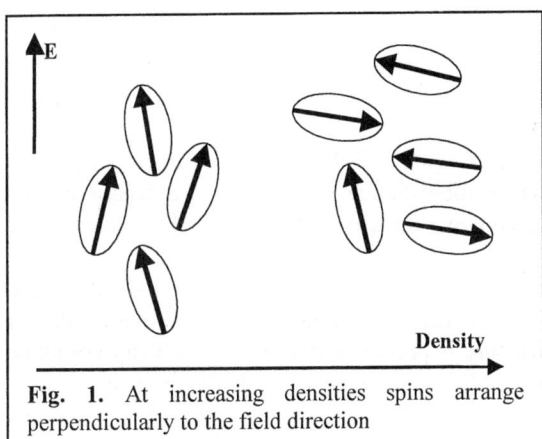

Fig. 1. At increasing densities spins arrange perpendicularly to the field direction

This anomalous behaviour could also be revealed by measuring the system's electric bi-refringence, whose sign changes since particles lay perpendicularly to the external field, from a particular concentration on: this phenomenon is known as "anomalous Kerr effect" [2, 3].

An interesting hypothesis assumes presence of induced dipole – induced dipole (ID-ID) interactions among the particles, each one with a strongly anisotropic polarisability. These interactions play a fundamental role only when other usually stronger interactions (Van der Waals, H bond) are negligible, like in anisotropic polarisable particles and particularly in rod-like polyelectrolytes, where polarisability is high. These systems are object for experimental observation and computer simulation: flexible chains with polarized clusters at the tips (ionomers) [4] and ordered phases of particles without axial symmetry [5] are examples of studies into which both the approaches are exploited. We studied the order in such systems considering particles (spins) with null permanent moment, but easily polarisable along their axis. Previous papers analysed the behaviour of these spins with ID-ID interactions located on a cubic lattice [6], finding a decrease in the orientational order along the direction of the applied electric field. In particular, when interactions among the spins increase, new orientational orders have been found forming a complex phase diagram, into which a tri-critical point and a re-entrant phase were identified [7].

The present work originates from the need of generalising results obtained with a cubic symmetry, for other topologies closer to effective experimental situations. In this case a *hexagonal close packed* structure was simulated, a well known structure, experimentally reproducible in situations where spins are tightly packed, like in concentrated colloidal systems or liquid crystals watered emulsions. The implemented model features short range interactions among the spins (i.e. with 12 first neighbours) whose local electric field is the sum of the external applied one, plus that induced from the neighbour spins and is calculated recursively on each spin (as it will be described below). This elaboration represents the computational core of the simulation and is very heavy, requiring more computing power for large size system simulations (a small 14-cube system takes 3 days running on a 2 GHz PC with 512 MB Ram, and up to 50-cube systems could be required for significant simulations where the processing load grows up proportionally to the particle number). In the implemented model all the relevant physical parameters are combined in two dimensionless parameters, the former (ρ) proportional to the system density and the latter (τ) given by the ratio between the thermal energy and the energy due to the external electric field.

Results can be summarised as follows:
- as in the case of cubic lattice simulations, a decrease in the spin orientational order takes place along the direction of the applied field, when ρ increases and τ drops down;
- a new orientational order appears, featuring a periodic sequence of planes parallel to the field direction into which spins alternate perpendicular and aligned with the field. This structure is present whatever are boundary conditions and system size considered;

- to characterise this new phase, an order parameter was proposed, i.e. the amplitude of the oscillation of the orientational order on planes perpendicular to a characteristic direction in the lattice;
- this parameter features a typical 1st order phase transition, when the density changes;
- this phase has been revealed in different size lattices and with different boundary conditions. The typical period in oscillations is comprised within 1.6 and 1.8 lattice steps and so is a non integer multiple of the lattice step.

This activity was carried on by the Complex Fluid Physics Laboratory at the University of Milan and the Microcomputer Laboratory at the University of Pavia, Italy.

2 Simulation Model

We implemented a MM simulation of a system of spins interacting with an external applied field (due to their tensorial polarisability) and among themselves (through ID-ID interactions), spatially located on a *hexagonal close packed* lattice free of rotating but not of translating in the space. This kind of geometry is well studied since it has been often observed in highly packed systems. Moreover, the face centered cubic structure is the preferred one in case of charged colloidal particles system, where spins arrange in such a way to maximise their distance due to the effect of electrostatic repulsion. To this family belong those systems with anomalous behaviour in presence of electric field for which the *hexagonal close packed* structure seems to be the closest one to the reality. For example in watered liquid crystal emulsions, particles, when settled, arrange themselves like drops located with triangular symmetry on planes randomly overlapping. The simulation aims to identify new phase transitions compatible with the new lattice topology and to compare this behaviour with the cubic lattice previously achieved. This will allow exploring common features due to ID-ID interactions and independent on the chosen geometry.

We considered a system of N spins characterized by a finite polarisability $\alpha_\parallel$ along their axis and by a negligible perpendicular polarisability, i.e. $\alpha_\perp = 0$. An external field $\mathbf{E}_0$ in the z direction polarizes the system. The induced dipolar moment $\mathbf{p}_i$ on the i-th spin whose orientation is defined by the unit vector $\mathbf{s}_i$ can be expressed through the tensorial polarisability α_i,

$$\mathbf{p}_i = \alpha_i \cdot \mathbf{E}_{i,loc} \tag{1}$$

The local field $\mathbf{E}_{i,loc}$ is

$$\mathbf{E}_{i,loc} = \mathbf{E}_0 + \sum_{j \neq i} \mathbf{E}_{j \to i} \tag{2}$$

where $\mathbf{E}_{j \to i}$ is the field in i due to the dipole $\mathbf{p}_j$. The resulting Hamiltonian of the system is:

$$H = -\frac{1}{2} \sum_{i=1}^{N} (\alpha_i \mathbf{E}_{i,loc}) \cdot \mathbf{E}_{i,loc} \tag{3}$$

Within the limit of extreme dilution, the contributions from $\mathbf{E}_{j \to i}$ become negligible and we simply obtain

$$\mathbf{p}_i = \alpha_\parallel E_0 \cos \vartheta_i \mathbf{s}_i \tag{4}$$

Within this limit, the system energy is exclusively due to the external electric field, so that

$$H_0 = -\frac{1}{2}\alpha_\| E_0^2 \sum_{i=1}^N \cos^2 \vartheta_i \qquad (5)$$

When the density of spins is not negligible, the effect of $\mathbf{E}_{j \to i}$ should be considered. Calculating $\mathbf{E}_{j \to i}$ from the dipolar field of $\mathbf{p}_j$, we obtain

$$\mathbf{E}_{j \to i} = \frac{\alpha_\|}{4\pi\varepsilon r^3}\left(\mathbf{s}_j \cdot \mathbf{E}_{j,loc}\right)\left[3\left(\mathbf{s}_j \cdot \mathbf{u}_{ij}\right) \cdot \mathbf{u}_{ij} - \mathbf{s}_j\right] \qquad (6)$$

where ε is the dielectric constant of the medium the particles are in, r is the distance between the ith and the jth spin, $\mathbf{u}_{ij}$ is a unit vector along the direction of the vector joining site i with site j. If we limit our attention to 12 nearest neighbour effects, r corresponds to the simulated lattice unit.

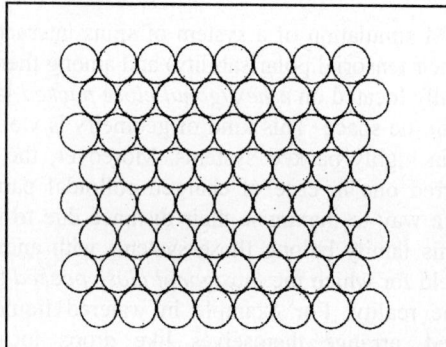

Fig. 2. A planar hexagonal close packed lattice

Physical quantities appear in the simulation through two independent dimensionless quantities.

$$\rho = \frac{\alpha_\|}{4\pi\varepsilon r^3} \qquad (7)$$

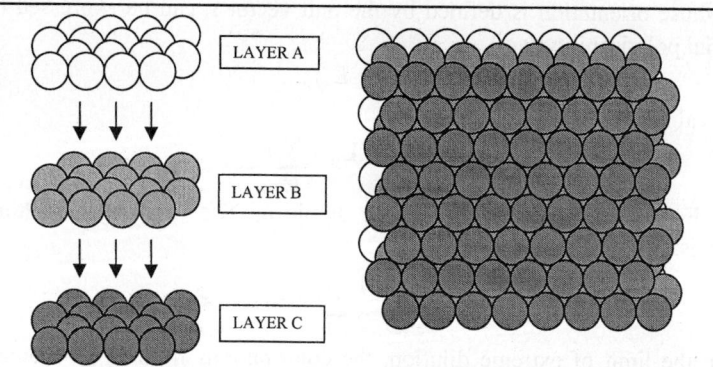

Fig. 3. The 3D layer obtained by overlapping three hexagonal closed packed lattices

ρ is a dimensionless parameter proportional to the spin density and to its polarisability.

$$\tau = \frac{k_B T}{\alpha_\| E_0^2} \tag{8}$$

τ is a dimensionless parameter proportional to the temperature and inversely proportional to the squared amplitude of the electric field. In the following we will refer to τ and ρ respectively as "reduced temperature" and "reduced density".

Spins are located on a *hexagonal close packed* 2D-lattice (layer A) as shown in Fig. 2, where each one is surrounded by six others. A 3D-structure (Fig. 3) can be then obtained by overlapping another similar layer, with each spin located in the interstitial spaces formed by three spins of the lattice below (Fig. 3, layer B). The final lattice, really used in the simulations, is obtained by overlapping a further layer on the second one: this can be done in two ways. The spins can occupy those holes of the first layer not filled in the second layer (layer C) or they can be aligned with the spins of the first layer so reproducing the A configuration. This way, the spatial distribution of the planes is a ABCABC... sequence or ABABAB... sequence and without similar adjacent planes. In any case, however, the number of neighbours for each spin is 12.

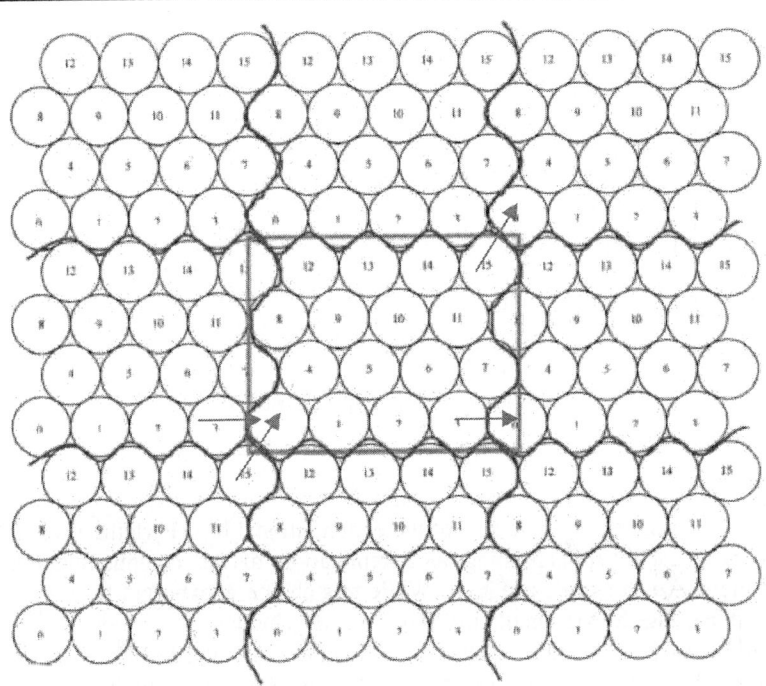

Fig. 4. Simulation box with periodic boundary conditions applied: arrows show the particles considered for interactions as neighbours of those on the edge of the computational box

The total system energy can be expressed through the Hamiltonian operator

$$H = \frac{1}{2} \sum_{i=1}^{N} (\vec{E}_{Loc_i} \cdot \vec{s}_i)^2 \qquad (9)$$

which can be rewritten as

$$\vec{E}_{Loc_i} \cdot \vec{s}_i = \sum_{j \neq i} \vec{E}_{Loc_{j \to i}} \cdot \vec{s}_i + \vec{E}_0 \cdot \vec{s}_i = \sum_{j \neq i} \rho (\vec{E}_{Loc_{j \to i}} \cdot \vec{s}_j)[(3\vec{s}_j \cdot \vec{u}_{ji}) \vec{u}_{ji} - \vec{s}_j] \cdot \vec{s}_i + E_0 \cdot \vec{s}_i \qquad (10)$$

which is an implicit expression into which the local field is recursively evaluated: in fact, when the ith spin is moved, it modifies the local field of its neighbours and these, in turn, influence the local field on the moved spin itself. Several methods exist to evaluate this local field (Ewald potentials, Reaction Field method, … [8]), but in our case we chose to re-calculate the term $\vec{E}_{Loc_i} \cdot \vec{s}_i$ until the local field becomes stable. This, however, represents the most onerous portion of the calculation.

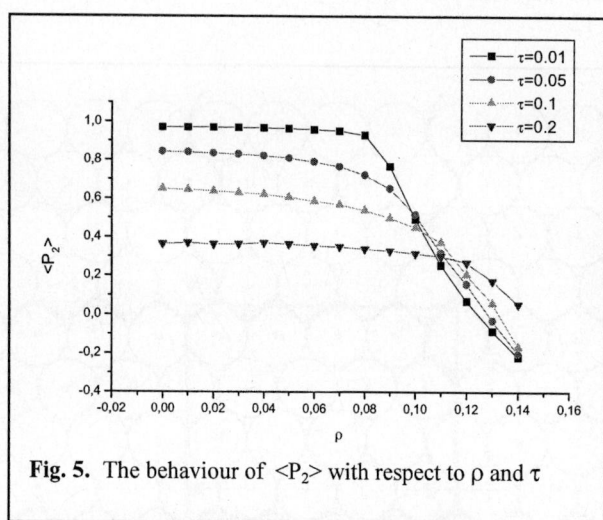

Fig. 5. The behaviour of $<P_2>$ with respect to ρ and τ

To minimise the effect of the finite size of the computational box, Periodic Boundary Conditions were used [9], consisting in a replication of the computational box throughout the space as shown in Fig. 4. While this choice is expected to overcome finite size effects due to the simulation box, the introduction of periodicity in the system could affect the generality of the result. We have simulated systems to which Free Boundary Conditions (FBC, i.e. no replication of the computational box is applied and peripheral particles feature less interactions than those in the bulk of the box) and Random Boundary Conditions (RBC) (i.e. spins on the faces of the cube are arranged in a random 'frozen' way) were applied, achieving nearly the same results.

3 Results

All MM simulations executed 10.000 macrosteps (i.e. a tentative move was tried for each spin) which is a well dimensioned length to calculate all relevant physical quantities, since after 1000-2000 macrosteps the system yet reaches equilibrium.
In particular the program evaluates the second rank Legendre polynomial

$$\langle P_2 \rangle = \frac{1}{2}\langle (3\cos^2 \theta - 1) \rangle \qquad (11)$$

which acts as the nematic order parameter [8] and will be frequently used in the following as a measure of the orientational order in the simulated system.
Simulations were made considering several lattices with different dimensions and boundary conditions. During the simulations we calculated interesting physical parameters like energy at different macrosteps, the order parameter <P_2> and the spin's angular values of vertical elevation θ and horizontal rotation φ respect the direction of the electric field.

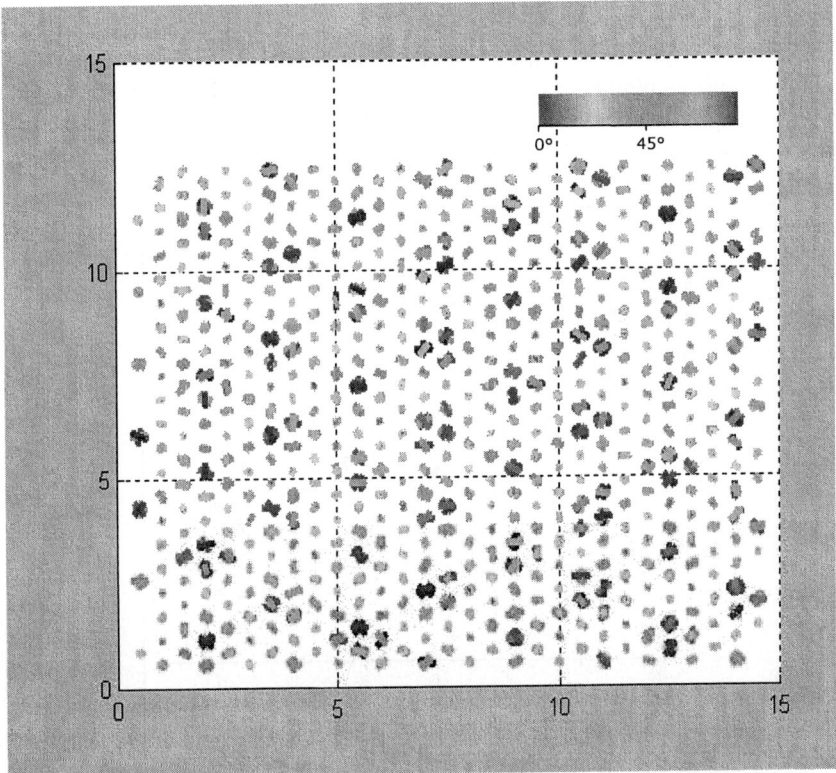

Fig. 6. The alternate disposition of spins, parallel (red-yellow) and perpendicular (green-blue) to the electric field

The analysis of a few preliminary results leads us to the following considerations

1. the interaction among spins brings the system to a new order having a lower degree of orientational order along the field. To quantify this behavior, we calculated the order parameter $<P_2>$ for different values of ρ and τ, finding that it decreases when ρ grows up and τ drops down (Fig. 5). The spins interaction seems to be the reason of the new order taking place whatever lattice, boundary conditions and number of first neighbors are considered.

2. This new order features a periodic sequence of planes parallel to the field direction, into which spins are alternatively perpendicular and parallel to the field arranging themselves in a typical hexagonal structure (Fig. 6). To quantify the new phase, we choose a new order parameter defined as the amplitude of the oscillations of the orientational order on planes perpendicular to a characteristic direction of the lattice

$$P_2(x) = <P_2> + A\cos(Wx+\varphi), \qquad (12)$$

where A is the amplitude, φ is the phase and W is the period of the oscillations.

In Fig. 7 the amplitude of the oscillations with respect the side in a 12 cube lattice is portrayed: the figure shows that the periodicity of the oscillations is not an integer multiple of the lattice step, comprised between 1.6 and 1.8 lattice steps.

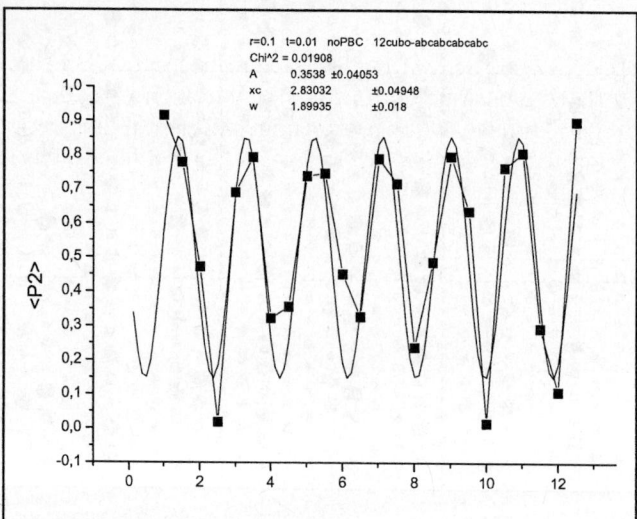

Fig. 7. Periodicity of the oscillations in the oriental order parameter P_2

For this reason we concentrated our simulations on 14^3 lattices. This topology is of particular interest, because the new structures present a possible period of 1.75 lattice steps (which is a sub-multiple of 14) and this means that it could be a good model for illustrating the new obtained structures. Another evidence of this could be found in the fact that the amplitude of the oscillations changes when the size of the lattice does not correspond to 14, as Table 1 demonstrates: the amplitude is different when the size is in the range 10^3-12^3 and varies even when simulations with same size are repeated. This means that spins are not "well packed" in this kind of lattices and they tend to be trapped in a configuration with local minimum energy without evolving to configurations with lower energies. They are know as "frustrated" system and their behavior is called "non-ergodic". The effect seems to diminish when sizes closer to the preferred one are considered: this is not the case, when lattices 14^3 are considered (Fig. 8 (a-b))

Table 1. The oscillation amplitude is not constant when the lattice size varies

Lattice size	Oscillation amplitude
10^3	0,1789
11^3	0.14322
12^3	0,19255
14^3	0,17647

The simulations were made by applying PBCs on the plane xy and FBCs in the z direction. Figure 9 shows a snapshot obtained by a simulation with these boundary conditions where spins assume the typical configuration strip-like toward every characteristic direction achievable in an hexagon. The period of this periodic arrangement is around 1.75 which is nearly the same obtained, on the other hand, by the interpolation with (12), 1.749.

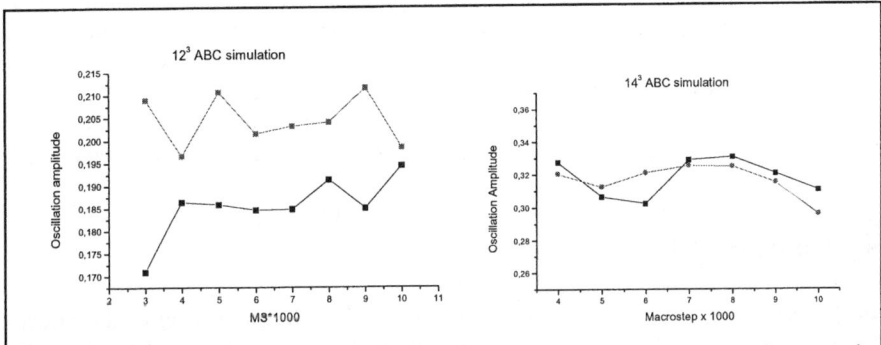

Fig. 8. The comparison (a)(b) between the amplitude oscillations in 12^3 and 14^3 simulations indicates that the last one is ergodic

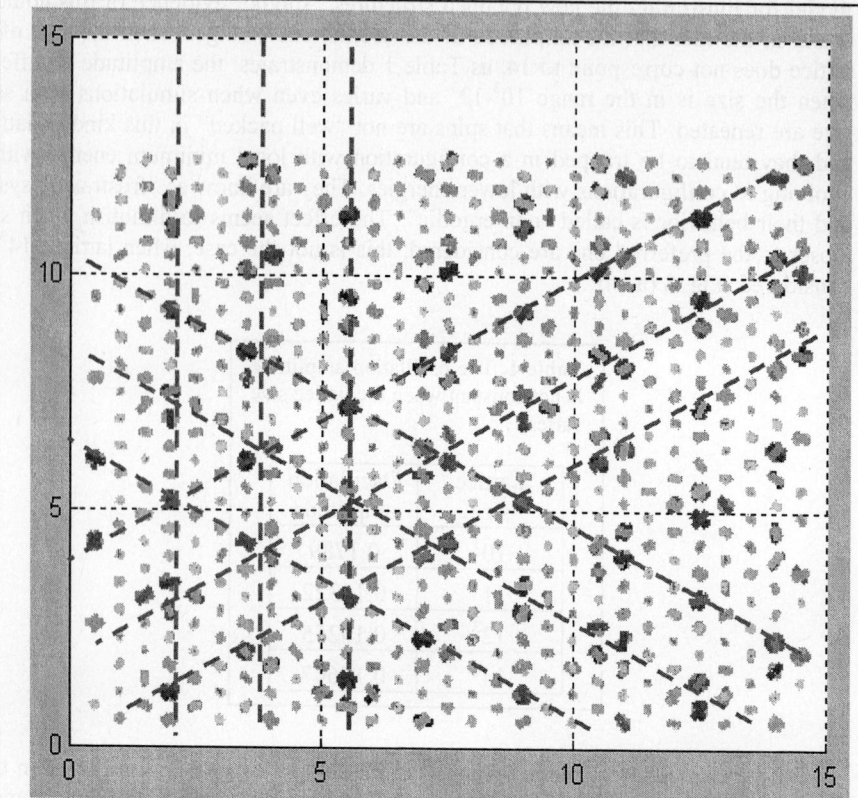

Fig. 9. The structure into which spin arrange shows a periodic strip configuration in all the characteristic direction of an hexagon

3. the parameter proposed to characterize this structure features a typical 1st order phase transition, when density changes. In Fig. 10, the abrupt change in the slope of P_2 (typical in 1st order phase transitions) is portrayed [11,12]. This corresponds very closely to what happened considering cubic lattices. The same evidence may be found concerning the temperature: simulations are in progress to verify if a 1st or a 2nd order transition (as in the cubic lattice case) takes place.

4 Conclusions

In this paper we have shown a Monte Carlo -Metropolis simulation of the effect of Induced Dipole - Induced Dipole interactions on the order of an anisotropic particle ensemble. The particles (spins) have been located on an hexagonal closed packed lattice, to verify the generality of the results previously achieved on a cubic lattice.

A model has been designed and implemented for the simulation on the computer, where all the relevant physical quantities were incorporated in the two dimensionless parameters ρ (reduced density) and τ (reduced temperature).

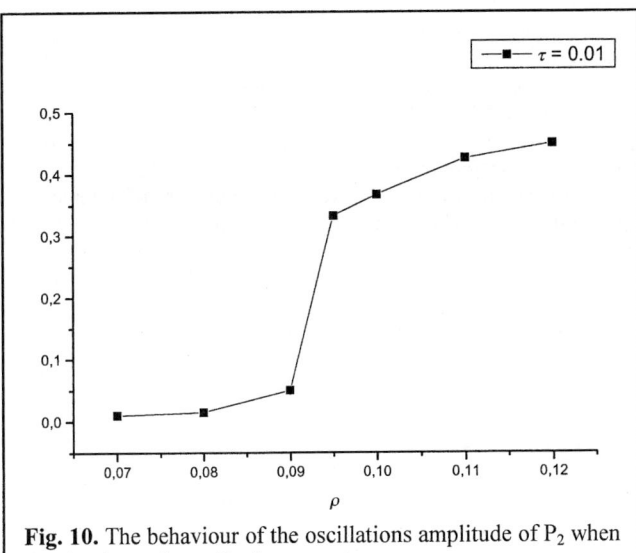

Fig. 10. The behaviour of the oscillations amplitude of P_2 when the density varies at fixed temperature

The main result consists in the confirmation of what we already found, by doing simulations on the cubic lattice, but considering a structure closer to the real way into which particles tend to organise themselves: although numerical response is strongly affected by the geometrical topology chosen, the orientational order diminishes along the electric applied field direction also in this case. As a consequence, a new spin order seems to take origin, with a periodical sequence of planes (parallel to the field) on which spins aligned and perpendicular to the field alternate: the period of this repetitive sequence is a non integer multiple of the lattice step.

Simulations, moreover, show evidence of a order transitions when density and temperature rise. These transitions have been verified for different sizes and periodic boundary conditions applied and are thoroughly compatible with the phase diagram found for the cubic lattice. The main direction to which this activity will be oriented consists in simulations into which spins are free of translating or into which long range interactions are considered. These developments will contribute to significantly refine the model used until now.

References

1. Metropolis, N., et al.: Equation of state calculations by fast computing methods. The Journal of Chemical Physics **21** (1953) 11–16
2. Cates, M.E.: The anomalous Kerr effect: Implications for structure. J. Polyelectrolyte, Phys. **2** (1992) 1109–1119
3. Zannoni, C.: Molecular design and computer simulations of novel mesophases. J. Mater. Chem. **11** (2001) 2637–2646
4. Banaszak, M., Clarke, J.H.R.: Computer simulation of microphase separation in ionic copolymers. Phys. Rev. **E 60** (1999) 5753–5756
5. Elliott, J.A., et al.: Atomistic simulation and molecular dynamics of model systems for perfluorinated ionomer membranes. Phys. Chem **1** (1999) 48–55
6. Danese, G., et al.: Monte Carlo - Metropolis simulation of interacting anisotropic polarizable spins on a lattice. Computer Physics Commun., Elsevier Science B. V. **134**(1) (2001) 47–57
7. Bellini, T., et al.: Field induced anti-nematic ordering in assemblies of anisotropically polarizable spins. Europhysics Letters **55**(3) (2001) 362–368
8. Allen, M.P., Tildesley, D.J.: Computer simulation of liquids. Oxford Science Publ. (1987)
9. Frenkel, D., Smit, B.: Understanding molecular simulation. Academic Press (1996)
10. Pasini, P., Zannoni, C.: Advances in the computer simulations of liquid crystals. Kluwer Academic Publishers (1998)
11. Binder, K., Heermann, D.W.: Monte Carlo simulation in statistical physics – An Introduction. Springer-Verlag (1988)
12. Stanley, H.E.: Introduction to phase transitions and critical phenomena. Oxford University Press (1971)

A Linguistically Motivated Information Retrieval System for Turkish

F. Canan Pembe and Ahmet Celal Cem Say

Dept. of Computer Engineering, Boğaziçi University
80815 Bebek, İstanbul, Turkey
{canan.pembe,say}@boun.edu.tr

Abstract. Information retrieval (IR) has become an important application in today's computer world because of the great increase in the amount of web-based documents and the widespread use of the Internet. However, the classical "bag of words" approach no longer meets user expectations adequately. In this context, natural language processing (NLP) techniques come into mind. In this paper, we investigate the question of whether NLP techniques can improve the effectiveness of information retrieval in Turkish. We implemented and tested a linguistically motivated information retrieval system, which uses knowledge of the morphological, lexico-semantical and syntactical levels of Turkish.

1 Introduction

1.1 Information Retrieval

Information retrieval (IR) [1] is the task of finding relevant documents in a large collection in order to satisfy user requests (queries) for particular items of information. Although IR is a relatively old field with more than four decades of research, its importance has grown tremendously in the last years. The reason is the big increase in the number of documents in digital form and the widespread use of the World Wide Web. However, information retrieval techniques have not developed with the same speed. Usually, the users of current information retrieval systems, such as Google [2] and Yahoo [3], face two important problems. One problem is having to go through hundreds and thousands of irrelevant hits even for a simple search. Another problem is that in such a search, some of the documents will be missing in the results although they are relevant to the user's information need.

There are two metrics commonly used for evaluating the effectiveness of an IR system: precision and recall. *Precision* is defined as the ratio of the number of relevant retrieved documents to the total number of retrieved documents. *Recall* is defined as the ratio of the number of relevant retrieved documents to the total number of relevant documents in the whole document collection. Degraded precision causes a lot of garbage hits, whereas degraded recall corresponds to useful documents missing in the results, both of which are undesirable.

The ultimate goal of every IR system is to increase both precision and recall. The challenge is to understand and represent the documents in the corpus and the user queries in such a way that relevance decisions can be made efficiently.

1.2 Motivation for Natural Language Processing in IR

Traditional IR systems are based on the simple assumption that if a query and a document have a (key)word in common, then the document is to some extent about the query [4]. This is the well-known "bag of words" approach. That is, each document in the corpus is simply represented as a "bag" of words and tried to be matched with the "bag" of words representation of the user's query. This simple approach does not take the linguistic properties and variation of the text enough into consideration. In [4], linguistic variation is categorized into four groups:
- Morphological variation: For example, *kitap* (book), *kitabım* (my book) and *kitaplar* (books) are three different variations of the same word in Turkish.
- Lexical variation: Different words can represent the same meaning (synonyms). For example, *hikaye* and *öykü* (story) are used interchangeably for the same meaning in Turkish.
- Semantical variation: A single word may have different meanings in different contexts. For example, someone searching for *site* in Turkish, can find documents in both web design and real estate contexts.
- Syntactical variation: The phrases *nehir yakınındaki hava kirliliği* (air pollution near the river) and *nehir kirliliği* (river pollution) have two words in common, but they have different meanings.

Traditional IR systems usually do not consider these kinds of linguistic variation. As a result, they have degraded precision and recall rates. However, the corpus to be searched is essentially a natural language text. Moreover, when using a search engine, we try to formulate queries in an intelligent way by selecting the right words and the right logical and proximity operators (e.g AND, OR, NEAR etc) in order to have effective results. The motivation for Natural Language Processing (NLP) in IR is to build some of this knowledge and understanding into the system for better search results [5].

Information retrieval systems can incorporate different levels of NLP. As an example, IRENA [6] is a system which makes use of morphological, lexico-semantical and syntactical analyses of the English language. Çiftçi's work [7] is an information retrieval system which uses only morphological analyses of the Turkish language. The work reported in this paper also involves higher levels of NLP, namely the lexico-semantical and syntactical levels, as well as the morphological level.

1.3 Our Approach

In the morphological level, the *stemming* technique is performed. The words are stripped of their suffixes to find their *stems*. As an example, all the different variations of *okul* (school) found in the documents, such as *okulda* (in the school), *okula* (to the school), *okulum* (my school), will be indexed as *okul* (school). Similarly, the query terms are also stemmed. In this way, documents containing different morphological forms of the same word can be retrieved, improving the recall. This approach may be especially beneficial for languages like Turkish, which is highly rich in suffix usage.

In the lexico-semantical level, we implement the *query expansion* technique. That is, a given word is expanded to all of its synonyms. For example, when the user enters a query containing the word *hayat* (life), the query is expanded in order to include also its synonym *yaşam*. With this approach, the documents containing the synonym but not the actual word can also be retrieved, increasing the recall.

In the syntactical level, we considered the "Phrase Retrieval Hypothesis" stated in [4], in order to overcome the shortcomings of the traditional "bag of words" approach. The Phrase Retrieval Hypothesis states that, if a query and a document have a phrase in common, then the document is to some extent about the query. This approach encourages the use of phrases instead of just single words as indexing terms. There are several NLP-based IR systems based on the idea of analyzing the text syntactically in order to extract phrases (especially noun phrases) for indexing purposes [8, 9, 10]. The reason for using noun phrases in these systems is that they are important content carriers in almost every natural language [4]. Therefore, we concentrated on Turkish noun phrases in the syntactical part of this work.

The use of noun phrases as indexing terms promises an increase in precision. However, recall would decrease if the problem of syntactical variation is not considered. For example, *nehir kirliliği*, *nehirdeki kirlilik*, and *nehrin yoğun kirliliği* are different syntactical formulations about almost the same meaning (pollution of the river). Therefore, some form of regularization is necessary for phrases. In [4], this kind of regularization is called *syntactical normalization*. The aim is to map alternative formulations of the same meaning to a single *normalized form*, such as *nehir+kirlilik*. The normalization technique we use is the extraction of word pairs with *head-modifer relation* from noun phrases [8, 9, 10]. For example, given the phrase *aile şirketlerinin kurumsallaşması* (institutionalization of family firms), the head-modifier pairs are *aile* (modifier) + *şirket* (head) and *şirket* (modifier) + *kurumsallaşma* (head), which can be easily found because Turkish is a head-final language, i.e., modifiers always precede the head [11]. Using such subcompounds in indexing and retrieval instead of whole noun phrases is a widely used solution to the normalization problem.

The rest of this paper is organized as follows: In Section 2, a brief overview of the system architecture is presented. A detailed description of the syntactical analyzer is given in Section 3. The indexing and retrieval strategy is described in Section 4. This is followed by a performance evaluation in Section 5, and a conclusion in Section 6.

2 System Architecture

The proposed system (Figure 1) consists of six different modules: crawler, morphological parser, syntactical parser, indexer, lexico-semantical expander and retrieval engine.

The *crawler* is related to the web programming part of the system and is common to almost every web-based information retrieval system. Given the URL (Uniform Resource Locator) of a web site, the crawler retrieves the HTML document residing at this URL and the documents linked by it recursively up to a certain level. The documents retrieved by the crawler are processed in morphological and syntactical levels, and sent to the indexer.

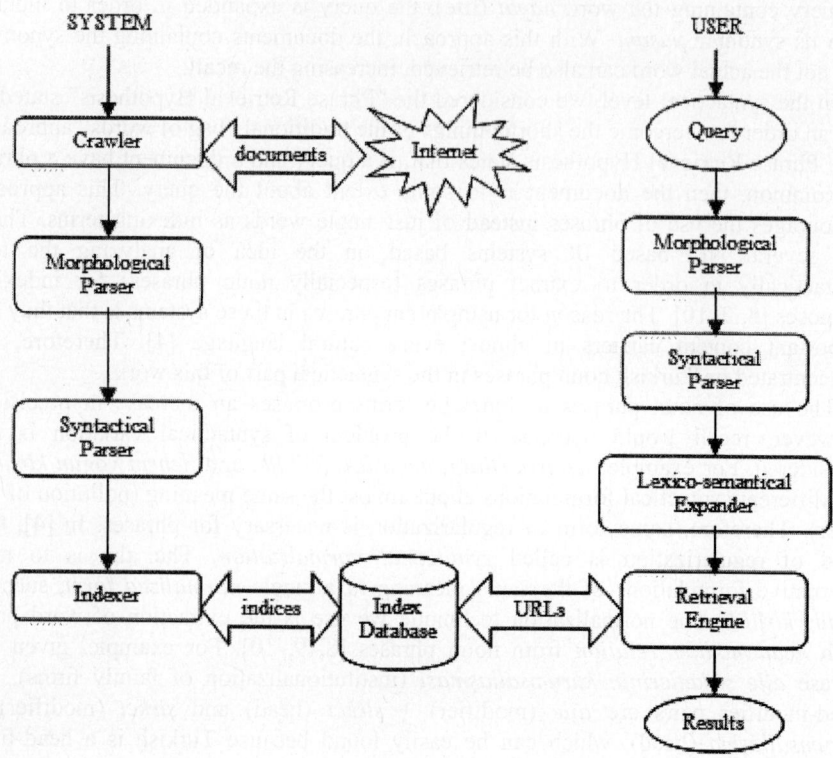

Fig. 1. Overview of the system architecture

The *morphological parser* used in this work is the Turkish morphological analyzer, developed by Oflazer [12] based on the PC-KIMMO environment [13], and a lexicon of about 23000 root words. The input to the morphological parser is a file containing the words of a given document. The output is the corresponding computed morphological and lexical forms of each word where each word may have more than one different morphological and lexical parses. The morphological parser serves two different purposes. First, its output is sent to the syntactical parser for a higher level analysis. Second, the roots obtained from morphological parsing are also used as indexing terms by the indexer, as will be explained later.

The *syntactical parser* accepts the output of the morphological parser as input, that is, the sentences of a document whose words are morphologically parsed. The task of the syntactical parser is to extract noun phrases, which will be used in the indexing part.

The noun phrases obtained by the syntactical parser are processed, and head-modifier pairs are extracted from them in order to be used as indexing terms. The *indexer* stores all of the indexing terms in a vector space model.

The *lexico-semantical expander* is the module which is responsible for expanding words in a given user query to all of its synonyms. It is also possible to expand a word to its *hyponyms* and *hypernyms* (the *is-a* relation), *meronyms* and *holonyms* (the *part-*

of relation). For lexico-semantical expansion, we make use of Turkish WordNet, which is being constructed as a part of BalkaNet Project [14, 15].

The *retrieval engine* takes the user queries which are entered as natural language text, and processed morphologically and syntactically in the same way as the documents of the corpus. One difference is that the terms in the queries can also be lexico-semantically expanded depending on the choice of the user. Using the indexing information, the query is tried to be matched with the documents in the collection. The list of documents returned by the retrieval system are ranked and displayed to the user.

3 Syntactical Analyzer

When designing a syntactical analyzer for an information retrieval application, three requirements should be considered [8]. First, the system should be able to process large amounts of text (usually gigabytes) in a reasonable time. Second, the system should be able to process unrestricted text. That is, the system should be robust to the problems of unrestricted natural language corpora, such as unknown words and unrecognized structures. Finally, only a shallow understanding may be sufficient for an IR application because the goal of an IR system is essentially to classify documents as relevant or irrelevant with respect to a user query. This makes an NLP-based IR application easier to realize than some other NLP applications such as machine translation [8].

Keeping these requirements in mind, we considered different formalisms for the syntactical processing. Context-Free Grammars (CFGs) are the most commonly used systems for modeling constituency structure in natural languages. There are several methods for parsing with context-free grammars, such as top-down, bottom-up and a combination of these methods [16]. However, the problem with context-free grammar parsing is the lack of efficiency and robustness necessary for an IR application.

Another idea is to use finite-state methods in syntactical parsing. It is stated that finite-state methods are sufficient for applications which do not require complete parses [16]. Finite-state methods are more efficient than other methods when an unrestricted text corpus is to be parsed, because they rely on simple finite-state automata rather than full parsing [16]. Information retrieval can be considered as such an application.

A finite-state cascade [17] consists of a sequence of finite-state automata. A given sentence is parsed going through this sequence of levels. At each level, certain kinds of phrases are built upon the phrases found in previous levels. In this method, there is no recursion; i.e., phrases do not contain same or higher level phrases. This is the point where finite-state methods are distinguished from context-free grammars, which can contain recursive rules [16]. Thus, it can be argued that it is not possible to model all of the syntax of a natural language with a finite-state method. However, finite-state methods can approximate the syntax adequately for our purposes.

After considering previous work done on Turkish grammar [11, 18] and on finite-state modeling of Turkish noun compounds [19], we built a simple finite-state cascade (see Figure 2) which can recognize a subset of noun phrases in Turkish. The application of this finite-state cascade on an example sentence is given in Figure 3.

T_1 :

    NP1 → noun
    NP1 → noun* con noun
    AP → adj* (con adj)

T_2 :

    NP2 → NP1$_{nom}$ NP1$_{poss}$

T_3 :

    NP3 → (AP) NP1
    NP3 → (AP) NP2

T_4 :

    NP4 → NP3$_{gen}$ (NP3$_{gen+poss}$)* NP3$_{poss}$

Fig. 2. A finite-state cascade approximating Turkish noun phrase structure

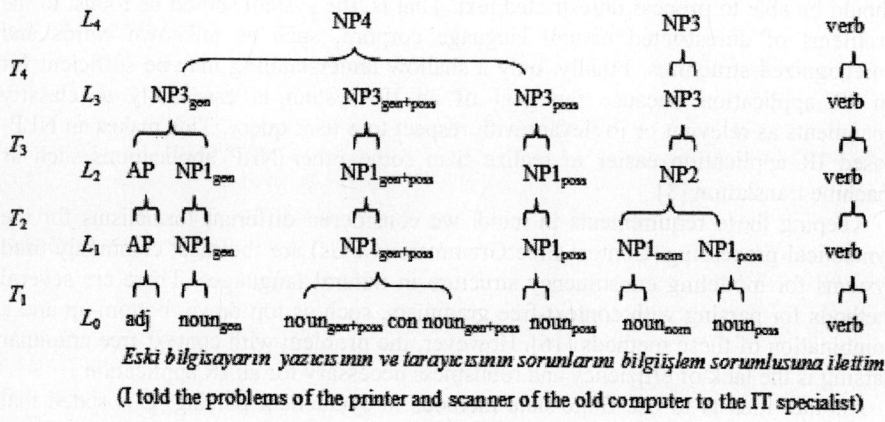

Eski bilgisayarın yazıcısının ve tarayıcısının sorunlarını bilgiişlem sorumlusuna ilettim
(I told the problems of the printer and scanner of the old computer to the IT specialist)

Fig. 3. Application of the finite-state cascade to an example Turkish sentence

The syntactical processing starts at level 0 (L_0), given the part-of-speech tags and features of each word in the sentence as input (see Fig. 3). At each level, L_{i-1} is taken as input and L_i is produced as output, using only the T_i rules corresponding to that level. With each rule application, a sequence of elements is reduced to a single element. If no rule applies at a level, the element is passed to the higher level wihout change. At the end of this four-level processing, the noun phrases in the sentence, and their inner structure are obtained.

There is ambiguity both in morphological and syntactical level processing, a well-known problem in natural languages. According to our approach, the syntactical analyzer considers all the different morphological parses and produces all the possible different syntactical parses according to the rules.

4 Indexing and Retrieval Strategy

The structural information obtained from the syntactical analysis is used in extracting the head-modifier pairs from the identified phrases. In the above sentence, the head-modifier pairs *eski+bilgisayar, bilgisayar+yazıcı, bilgisayar+tarayıcı, yazıcı+sorun* and *tarayıcı+sorun* can be obtained from the noun phrase *eski bilgisayarın yazıcısının ve tarayıcısının sorunlarını* (the problems of the printer and the scanner of the old computer) using an *unnesting* process [4] according to the inner structure of the compound. The head-modifier pairs obtained in this way are used as indexing terms in addition to words and stems obtained from the documents. The precision of the syntactical parser is 0.70; out of 1357 head-modifier pairs obtained, 954 were correct in a test set of 46 documents.

The retrieval system is based on the Vector Space Model [20] where each document i and query t is represented as vectors of weights where N is total number of distinct indexing terms in the document collection:

$$D_i = <w_{i1}, w_{i2}, \ldots, w_{iN}>, \quad Q_t = <w_{t1}, w_{t2}, \ldots, w_{tN}> \quad (1)$$

The weights are computed using the well-known weighting scheme $tf \times idf$ where tf (term frequency) refers to the number of times a particular term occurs in a given document or query, and idf (inverse document frequency) is a measure of how rarely a particular term appears across all of the documents in the collection. With this scheme, frequently used terms in a document will have higher weights, whereas terms common to most of the documents in the collection will receive lower weights. The similarity between a query Q_t and a document D_i is computed using the dot product formula normalized with document length in order not to favor longer documents [20].

5 Performance Evaluation

5.1 Experiment Setup

TREC [21] is a well-known organization which provides standard document collections, queries, and relevance decisions to be used in IR research experiments for languages such as English and Spanish. However, currently there is no such standard document collection and queries for Turkish. Therefore, for this experiment, we have collected approximately 615 Turkish documents about different topics from the Internet. Although the size of the corpus is small with respect to TREC Databases, which contain tens of thousands of documents, it is a reasonable size to start the tests. We also formed five different long, natural language queries as in TREC corpus and determined the documents which are relevant with respect to the queries.

In order to see the comparative performance of different indexing and retrieval approaches, we used the different experiment runs given in Table 1. The simplest approach is using only single words as indexing terms. This is followed by approaches using different combinations of stems and head-modifier pairs. Another option is the use of lexical expansion in the query terms.

Table 1. Different combinations of indexing and retrieval approaches used in the experiments

Run	Indexing and retrieval approach
0	Single words only (baseline)
1	Stemmed words only
2	Stemmed words + query expansion
3	Stemmed words + head-modifier pairs
4	Stemmed words + query expansion + head-modifier pairs
5	Stemmed words + head-modifier pairs heavily weighted
6	Stemmed words + head-modifier pairs heavily weighted + query expansion

5.2 Results

Run 0 represents the traditional approach in which only single words are indexed without the use of morphological, lexico-semantical and syntactical analyses. As seen in Table 2, the incorporation of morphological information in Run 1, by means of stemming, improves the effectiveness significantly.

Table 2. Interpolated precision results of different runs together with the relative improvement of Run 5 with respect to the baseline

Recall	Run 0	Run 1 (base)	Run 2	Run 3	Run 4	Run 5	Run 6	Imp. of Run 5
0.0	0.32	0.83	0.70	0.80	0.81	0.93	0.87	33%
0.1	0.32	0.83	0.70	0.80	0.81	0.93	0.87	33%
0.2	0.35	0.73	0.67	0.78	0.67	0.78	0.76	16%
0.3	0.37	0.74	0.67	0.76	0.67	0.76	0.71	13%
0.4	0.38	0.68	0.58	0.71	0.62	0.72	0.64	24%
0.5	0.38	0.66	0.57	0.66	0.58	0.72	0.58	26%
0.6	0.32	0.64	0.57	0.66	0.58	0.67	0.58	18%
0.7	0.30	0.56	0.55	0.58	0.54	0.61	0.54	11%
0.8	0.25	0.53	0.41	0.52	0.41	0.52	0.44	7%
0.9	0.20	0.39	0.32	0.38	0.33	0.39	0.33	22%
1.0	0.12	0.25	0.17	0.24	0.16	0.26	0.17	53%

In a previous work on the effect of stemming for Turkish text retrieval [22], precision and recall are computed for the first 10 and 20 documents retrieved, and the number of relevant documents is less than this number for some of the queries, which can result in small and misleading numbers for precision. In our experiment, we show precision values at different recall levels which is more precise.

The introduction of lexico-semantical expansion generally resulted in a decrease in precision, whereas the introduction of syntactical information, with head-modifier pairs as indexing terms, in runs 3, 4, 5 and 6, generally gives improved results. Also, the runs in which head-modifier pairs are more heavily weighted than single words, give better results. In Table 3, the recall values at different document levels are given.

Table 3. Recall results for different runs

Document level	Run 0	Run 1	Run 2 (base)	Run 3	Run 4	Run 5	Run 6
10	0,10	0,24	0,21	0,25	0,20	0,25	0,23
20	0,22	0,38	0,32	0,39	0,32	0,40	0,33

6 Conclusion

This paper presented the design and implementation of a linguistically motivated information retrieval system for Turkish, as an attempt to break out of the traditional "bag of words" approach. The system uses morphological, lexico-semantical, and syntactical levels of NLP in document and query processing with a robust and efficient approach suitable to IR purposes. Keeping the phrase retrieval approach in mind, the syntactical head-modifier pairs in the noun phrases are used to improve the retrieval effectiveness. Although the finite-state cascade we designed is very limited currently, the results are promising. As a future work, the grammar will be improved. Moreover, the tests will also be extended to investigate the effects of expanding the query terms with semantically related words other than the synonyms, e.g. the words with the part-of relation, with a larger corpus.

Acknowledgements

We would like to thank Kemal Oflazer and Özlem Çetinoğlu for providing Turkish WordNet, which is under development as a part of BalkaNet Project, to be used in our experiments. We thank Kemal Oflazer also for developing the Turkish Morphological Analyzer used in the morphological part of this work. We thank Istanbul Kultur University for their support. This work was partially supported by the Boğaziçi University Research Fund (Grant no: 03A102).

References

1. Salton G., McGill, M.J.: Introduction to modern information retrieval. McGraw-Hill, New York (1983)
2. Google. http://www.google.com
3. Yahoo!. http://www.yahoo.com
4. Arampatzis, A., Weide, T., Koster, C., Bommel, P.: Linguistically motivated information retrieval. Encyclopedia of Library and Information Science, Marcel Dekker, Inc., New York **69** (2000) 201–222
5. Feldman, S.: NLP meets the Jabberwocky: Natural Language Processing in Information Retrieval. Online (1999)
6. Arampatzis, A.T., Tsoris, T., Koster, C.H.A.: IRENA: Information retrieval engine based on natural language analysis. In: Proceedings of RIAO'97, Computer-Assisted Information Searching on Internet, McGill University, Montreal, Canada. (1997) 159–175

7. Çiftçi, T.: Multimedia search engine for content based retrieval of images and text. M.Sc. Thesis, Boğaziçi University, İstanbul, Turkey (2002)
8. Evans, D.A., Zhai, C.: Noun-phrase analysis in unrestricted text for information retrieval. In: 34th Annual Meeting of the Association for Computational Linguistics. (1996) 17–24
9. Zhai, C., Tong, X., Milic-Frayling, N., Evans D.A.: Evaluation of syntactic phrase indexing, CLARIT NLP track report. In: Harman, D.K. (ed.): The Fifth Text Retrieval Conference (TREC-5), NIST Special Publication. (1997)
10. Strzalkowski, T., Carballo, J.P.: Recent developments in natural language text retrieval. In: TREC. (1993) 123–136
11. Göçmen, E., Şehitoglu, O., Bozşahin, C.: An outline of Turkish syntax. Technical Report 95-2, METU Department of Computer Engineering, Ankara, Turkey (1995)
12. Oflazer, K.: Two-level description of Turkish morphology. Literary and Linguistic Computing 9(2) (1994)
13. Antworth, E. L.: PC-KIMMO: A two-level processor for morphological analysis. Summer Institute of Linguistics, Dallas, Texas (1990)
14. Stamou, S., Oflazer, K., Pala, K., Christoudoulakis, D., Cristea, D., Tufis, D., Koeva, S., Totkov, G., Dutoit, D., Grigoriadou, M.: Balkanet: A multilingual semantic network for Balkan languages. In: Proceedings of the First International WordNet Conference, Mysore India. (2002)
15. Bilgin, O., Çetinoğlu, Ö., Oflazer, K.: Morphosemantic relations in and across wordnets: A preliminary study based on Turkish. In: Proceedings of the Global WordNet Conference, Masaryk, Czech Republic. (2004)
16. Jurafsky, D.S., Martin, J.H.: Speech and language processing. Prentice Hall, Inc. (2000)
17. Abney S.: Partial parsing via finite-state cascades. Natural Language Engineering, Cambridge University Press (1995)
18. Darcan, O.N.: An intelligent database interface for Turkish. M.Sc. Thesis, Boğaziçi University, İstanbul, Turkey (1991)
19. Birtürk, A.A., Fong, S.: A modular approach to Turkish noun compounding: The integration of a finite-state model. In: Proceedings of the 6th Natural Language Processing Pacific Rim Symposium (NLPRS2001), Tokyo, Japan (2001)
20. Lee, D.L., Chuang, H., Seamons, K.: Document ranking and the vector-space model. IEEE Computer, Theme Issues on Assessing Measurement (1997) 67–75
21. Text REtrieval Conference (TREC). http://trec.nist.gov/
22. Solak, A., Can, F.: Effects of stemming on Turkish text retrieval. Technical Report, BU-CEIS-94-20, Computer Engineering and Information Science Dept., Bilkent University, Ankara, Turkey (1994)

SmartReader: An NLP-Based Interactive Reading Application for Language Learning

Kemal Oflazer[1] and Meryem Pınar Dönmez[2]*

[1] Faculty of Engineering and Natural Sciences
Sabancı University, Tuzla, Istanbul, Turkey 34956
oflazer@sabanciuniv.edu
[2] Language Technologies Institute, School of Computer Science
Carnegie Mellon University, Pittsburgh, PA, 15213, USA
pinar@su.sabanciuniv.edu

Abstract. This paper describes an interactive language learning application employing natural language processing (NLP) technology to make reading an active and an interactive process. The application called SMARTREADER is envisioned to run on tablet-PC or future e-book hardware platforms. By using NLP technology, SMARTREADER provides access to extra-textual information to help the reader with the comprehension of the text. The current application of SMARTREADER is for improving the learning experience of advanced learners of English, who, with a working knowledge of the grammar of the language, can read an advanced text, with the SMARTREADER providing access to lexical resources, extracting additional useful information like summaries and concordances.

1 Introduction

The SMARTREADER project aims to develop a tablet-PC based general purpose "reading appliance" for the learning applications of the future in order to make reading textual material, an "active" and "interactive" process and experience. Using the SMARTREADER, a user can interact with the text in a variety of ways using *anytime-anywhere contextually guided access to information* with the functionality provided. The SMARTREADER platform employs advanced natural language processing technologies on which sophisticated intermediate-to-advanced level language learning and general reading applications can be built.

In the following sections, we provide a vision of the SMARTREADER application and describe the current functionality and implementation.

2 The Vision of SmartReader

The SMARTREADER project is motivated by the observation that *text is still the predominant medium for learning especially at the advanced level regardless of the*

---

* This work was conducted as a senior thesis while the second author was at Sabancı University.

subject. For example, intermediate and advanced learning of a foreign language still relies on reading and understanding of textual material. *On the other hand, text, being "bland", is hardly a conducive and motivating medium for learning, especially when the reader does not have access to aids that would enable her to get over minor and not-so-minor roadblocks ranging from unknown vocabulary to unrecognized and forgotten names or events, to complicated hard-to-understand sentences, and to external knowledge that would help her understand the textual content better.* SMARTREADER empowers the reader to access the content by helping her overcome any language and possibly content-related hindrances.

A very important impact of SMARTREADER in the future may be that it can make accessible textbooks in highly-technical fields to students in higher learning. Typically such technical (text)books may not be available in the native languages of students, but students with some working knowledge of the language the textbook is written in (e.g., English, German, French) may be able to use the textbook, with the SMARTREADER enabling the student overcome language-related hindrances. This is a crucially different approach in making content in a foreign-language accessible: *it empowers the consumer of the content* with all kinds of aids to overcome the language barrier. This is in contrast to machine translation which is still not available in an acceptable way except for a very few language pairs.

In order to motivate an understanding of the potential that SMARTREADER can provide, we list below some interesting ways a user of SMARTREADER can interact with the text she is reading, in various scenarios employing a *future* version of SMARTREADER:

- While reading some text, an advanced learner of a language can select a word and inquire about its meaning *in-context*, synonyms, antonyms; investigate usage examples in other parts of the text or similar text by looking at *concordances*; navigate a Wordnet conceptual hierarchy to perhaps better situate the meaning; understand the morphology, etc. This can be thought as a "pervasive semantic tooltip" that is everywhere accessible, even within the information provided in the "tooltip", in case the information provided to the user is not clear enough.
- A reader reading a multi-chapter book with SMARTREADER may ask the SMARTREADER to extract a summary of the last chapter, so that she remembers the relevant aspects of the content at the point she left off, before continuing reading the book. A reader may also ask the SMARTREADER to summarize an upcoming section or chapter, so that she has some idea about what is coming up as she is reading.
- A reader reading a book may select a person's name, say one of the heroes in the story, and then SMARTREADER can provide immediate "flashback" to the first (or the last) time the person was encountered, so she can re-read about the details of the person, and perhaps remember more about the person. This kind of flashback functionality can, in the future, be used on any named-entity, such as places, named events, etc.

- An intermediate learner of a language may encounter a sentence that she may not be able to understand fully for a number of reasons. She can select the sentence and ask the SMARTREADER to simplify the sentence so that she can comprehend it better.
- A teacher in a classroom of students each using the SMARTREADER may set up the students' environments so that the their comprehension can be automatically checked with random factual quizzes, as students proceed with reading a text. A student "turning" the page over, may be asked to answer a simple factual question constructed automatically by the SMARTREADER, and perhaps be asked to reread the relevant content when the student is not successful.
- A teacher may access the logs of an individual student's SMARTREADER, and *evaluate* a student's progress by checking her behaviour during the reading process, in terms of queries she posed to the SMARTREADER and her responses to the queries SMARTREADER poses to the student (see above). The *aggregate behaviour* of a group of students can also be quantified and evaluated by using *data mining techniques* on the logs of all the students so the teacher can evaluate how the class is "doing."

2.1 Related Work

Although there has been much prior work in the use of computers in language learning, dubbed *Computer Assisted Language Learning* (CALL), many CALL systems have made very little use of advanced language technology with the possible exception of some recent *intelligent* CALL systems which have used sentence analysis functionality in the form parsers to aid learners. Borin, in a recent paper reviewing the relationship between natural language processing and CALL [1], essentially concludes that, even though there should be very close interaction between the disciplines of CALL and NLP, " ... in the eye of the casual beholder – the two disciplines seem to live in completely different worlds." Borin states from the vantage point of NLP, CALL does not seem to have a place in natural language processing, despite some fledging applications, though there have been applications of AI in the broader field of *intelligent tutoring systems*. Similarly, practitioners of CALL do not make use substantial and broad use of NLP (for a survey of NLP in CALL, see Nerbonne [2].)

There have been a number recent of projects that have made use of language engineering technology to varying extents in language learning. The GLOSSER Project [3] has developed a system that aids readers of foreign language text, by providing access to a dictionary, after performing a morphological analysis and part-of-speech disambiguation of a word selected by the reader. The project has concluded that, based on user-feedback, such an aid has benefited and improved the reading process. The FreeText Project [4], aims to develop a computer assisted language learning system for intermediate to advanced learners of French. It relies on various natural language processing tools. The LISTEN project at CMU on the other hand, aims to tutor elementary school students in reading English text by using speech technology [5].

2.2 The Use of Natural Language Technologies in SmartReader

As alluded to above, SMARTREADER makes extensive use of natural language processing technologies and resources. Some of the technologies that SMARTREADER uses, such as part-of-speech taggers (e.g., Schmid [6] and Brill [7], and morphological analyzers (e.g., Daniel el al. [8]), are fairly mature and can be used off-the-shelf. The same can also be said of certain machine-readable resources such as dictionaries, and other lexical databases such as Wordnet [9]. Certain technologies such as information extraction for recognition of named-entities are also fairly well developed [10, 11], but may need further development depending on the application. On the other hand, technologies such as general purpose word sense disambiguation are not mature enough to be used in general applications despite the substantial amount of research effort [12]. The same goes for summarization technology; although there are many systems that have come out of research efforts, e.g. Mead by Radev et al. [13], the quality of the resulting summaries still have a lot to be desired. Nevertheless, such technologies will mature enough in the coming years to be usable in SMARTREADER-like applications.

The current initial implementation of SMARTREADER makes use of mature NLP technologies to demonstrate a system that is functionally and performance-wise usable, and plans to experiment with maturing technologies in near-future versions.

3 The Current Implementation of SmartReader

We have started the first prototype implementation of SMARTREADER as a test-bed of ideas to pursue, and for a pilot deployment for use in advanced language learning at Sabancı University. Figure 1 shows the main screen of the SMARTREADER when it starts up, with the functions available under the lexical lookup-menu visible. This prototype SMARTREADER provides the functionality summarized in the following sections:

3.1 Access to Lexical Information

SMARTREADER provides, anywhere-anytime ubiquitous access to lexical information such as *word meaning, synonyms, antonyms, usage examples in other parts of the text, sentence examples including the inquired word*. In this version, we do not attempt to do word-sense disambiguation, but make use of morphological analysis and part-of-speech tagging [6], with which we determine with great precision, the syntactic category of the word, and then do a look-up of the word with the extracted root word, filtering the dictionary output with the part-of-speech predicted for the word. Figures 2 and 3 shows such a lookup where a small pop-up window appears with the meaning(s) of the selected word. In Figure 2, the part-of-speech disambiguator predicts that *caring* is used as an adjective and provides the meaning of the adjectival use of the word, while in Figure 3, *caring* is used as a gerund verb and we see the meaning of the root verb *care*.

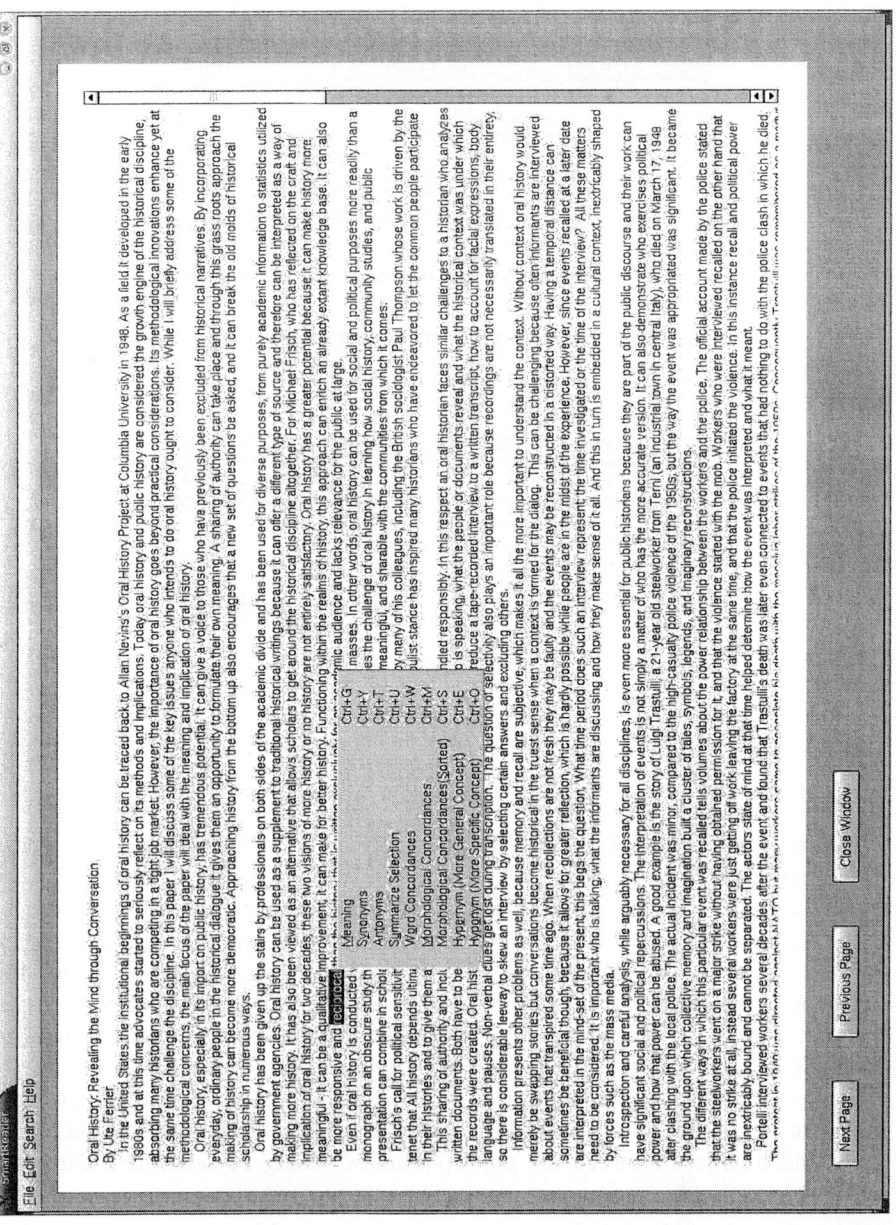

Fig. 1. The SMARTREADER user interface

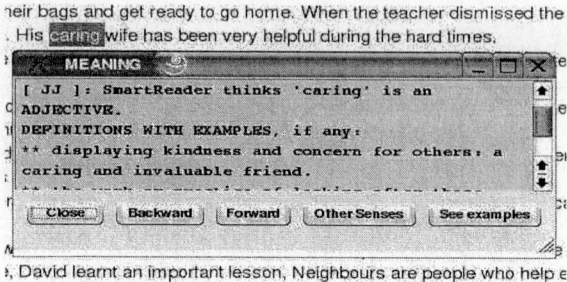

Fig. 2. Look-up of *caring* as an adjective

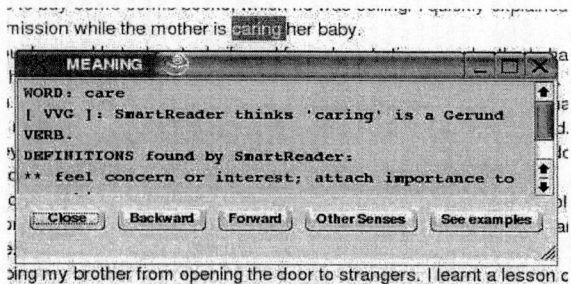

Fig. 3. Look-up of *caring* as a verb

Since this version of SMARTREADER does not attempt to do word sense disambiguation, if the reader feels that the meaning presented is not actually right, she may scroll down the pop-up window to see any other sense associated with this part-of-speech. Also, although over 95% of the time the part-of-speech predictions of the tagger used by SMARTREADER are correct, sometimes the tagger may make an error. In such cases, the *Other Senses* functionality helps the user access the meanings of the word with other parts-of-speech whenever available. The user can also use the *See examples* functionality, to see usage examples provided by the dictionary. Further, the look-up functionality is also available in the pop-up window so the user can (recursively) inquire about words there and navigate between the pop-up windows using *Forward* and *Backward* buttons.

Another capability worth mentioning is that we enable the user to select more than one word at a time. It is really important for intermediate or advanced language learners to deal with phrases, collocations, etc. Phrases are usually embedded within the context of single words in most dictionaries. For instance, if someone wants to look up the meaning of the phrase *looking forward to*, she has to find the word *look* first, and then within it, she can find what she inquires about. SMARTREADER simplifies this process by allowing multi-word selections. A depiction of such a use shown presented in Figure 4.

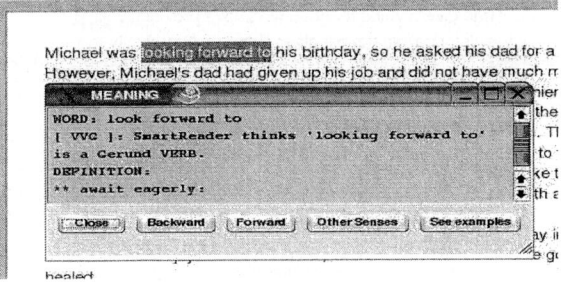

Fig. 4. Look-up of the *looking forward to*

Double clicking on a word is the easiest and fastest way to access its meaning. But SMARTREADER also provides this functionality through a right-click menu. The right-click menu also provides a number of other functions such as summarization, finding the concordances, synonyms and antonyms of a selected word, and navigating the conceptual hierarchy in Wordnet; see Figure 1.

3.2 Text Summarization

SMARTREADER provides a summarization functionality using the Mead toolkit for English [13]. The reader can summarize the whole text or a selected portion of it by providing a compression percentage. The Mead summarizer performs extractive summarization which is a very robust method for text summarization. It involves assigning salience scores to units (e.g., sentences or paragraphs) in a document and then extracting those with the highest scores.

3.3 Intelligent Concordancing

SMARTREADER also provides a sophisticated concordancing facility that makes use of morphological analysis and part-of-speech tagging. A basic concordance essentially shows a small amount of context around all occurrences of a word, enabling a user to understand the syntactic and semantic context a word is typically used in. In addition to a basic concordance, where concordancing is made only using word-forms, we provide a more sophisticated concordance functionality. When the user selects a word, we use its part-of-speech and root, and root-part-of-speech from the morphological analysis, and then scan the text for all occurrences of words whose roots and root part-of-speech agree with the selected word. Once all such occurrences are identified, a window with those words and the context around them pops up as depicted in Figure 5. All SMARTREADER functionality is also available in this window.

3.4 Activity Logging

SMARTREADER also provides another useful feature for logging reader activities about the words that were queried together along with data presented in response

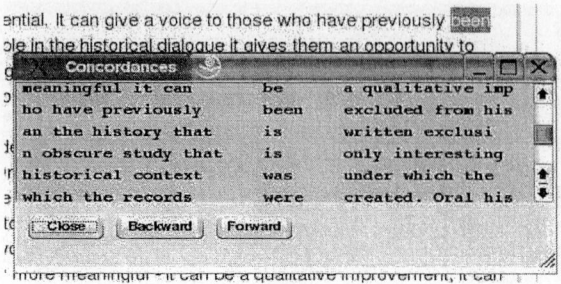

Fig. 5. Morphological concordance of *been*

to the queries. This log can be used as a vocabulary study guide. The reader can look at this log anytime she wants to go over the words she has had problems with.

4 Some Implementation Issues

The current version of SMARTREADER has been implemented under Linux/KDE environment. We have used the platform independent user interface development toolkit QT for developing the user interface component of the application.[3] QT provides an object-oriented framework for rapid application development.

SMARTREADER uses the freely available database package *mysql*.[4] *mysql* provides a sophisticated relational database engine that runs in the background as a separate process and responds to queries from client processes, expressed in the query language *sql*. We have used *mysql* to manage the full-size Oxford Dictionary of English with about 300,000 head-words, and the Wordnet database which provides the synonyms, antonyms, hyponyms and hypernyms of the selected words.

In order to provide instantaneous access to lexical information so that requests are not slowed down by any OS-related reasons such as database communication or paging delays, we use a speculative caching using multiple execution threads. Once the text is loaded into SMARTREADER, a concurrent tagger thread starts part-of-speech tagging of the text. Since the user is involved in reading the text, the CPU is essentially idle and the effect of the background tagging thread is not at all noticeable. Once the tagging thread is finished, a dictionary look-up thread is initiated. This thread uses the output of the tagging program and fills up a dictionary cache with the data about the words that the reader *may* inquire in the near future – say, in the next few paragraphs. This thread makes use of the stop words in English and ignores them while caching. When this thread completes a round, it goes into sleep waking up every so often, or when there

---

[3] See http://www.trolltech.com/ for details.
[4] See http://www.mysql.com/ for details.

is a substantial change in user's focus, most likely, after an unexpected paging through the text. The cache is managed in a first-in-first-out unless a word to be expunged actually happens to be in the set to be cached. In essentially all cases, a dictionary request is satisfied directly from the cache instantaneously, with no database and disk access. Since the lexical access functionality is available everywhere, this thread also kicks in when a dictionary entry is displayed.

5 Deployment and Evaluation

The prototype SMARTREADER for intermediate to advanced learners of the English language is planned for deployment at the *School of Languages Sabancı University*, where incoming freshmen without adequate language skills in English to follow undergraduate education, go through a very intensive *reading-based* advanced language skills education. The crucial feature in this application is that the language learning will *not* be on canned text but on arbitrary textual content used by the curriculum at the School of Languages. We expect to initially deploy SMARTREADER on the laptops of a small groups of students who are willing to evaluate it and provide feedback both to us as developers and to the faculty of the School of Languages.

6 Conclusions

We have presented the synopsis of the SMARTREADER project that aims to develop an active and interactive reading environment for intermediate-to-advanced language learning applications. SMARTREADER employs natural language processing technology coupled with a number of concurrent processing techniques for enhancing performance. SMARTREADER also uses wide-coverage resources (morphological analyzers, on-line dictionaries, Wordnet, etc.). We expect to deploy the first version of SMARTREADER at the Sabancı University School of Languages.

We are currently working on adding new functionalities to the SMART-READER. One important such functionality is the identification and tracking of named-entities in text such as persons, locations and, where possible, named or easily identifiable events, so that a reader can select a named-entity such as a person that she has encountered while reading, and immediately gain access to information about the named-entity in, say, prior sections of the text.

Acknowledgments

We thank Dr. Deniz Kurtoğlu Eken, Director of Sabancı University School of Languages, for her support in SMARTREADER development and pilot deployment. We also thank Oxford University Press for granting our project a license to use the machine-readable version of the Oxford English Dictionary.

References

1. Borin, L.: What have you done for me lately? The fickle alignment of NLP and CALL. Paper presented at the EuroCALL 2002 pre-conference workshop on NLP in CALL Jyväskylä, Finland (2002)
2. Nerbonne, J.: Computer-assisted language learning and natural language processing. In: Mitkov, R. (ed.): Handbook of Computational Linguistics. Oxford University Press (2002)
3. Nerbonne, J., Karttunen, L., Paskaleva, E., Proszeky, G., Roosmaa, T.: Reading more into foreign languages. In: Proceedings of the Conference on Applied Natural Language Processing. (1997) 135–138
4. Hamel, M.J., Girard, M.C.: FreeText—an advanced hypermedia CALL system featuring NLP tools for a smart treatment of authentic documents and free production exercises. In: Proceedings of EuroCALL-2000. (2000)
5. Mostow, J., Aist, G.: Evaluating tutors that listen: An overview of project LISTEN. In: Forbus, K.D., Feltovich, P.J.(eds.): Smart Machines in Education. MIT/AAAI Press (2001) 169–234
6. Schmid, H.: Probabilistic part-of-speech tagging using decision trees. In: Proceedings of International Conference on New Methods in Language Processing. (1994)
7. Brill, E.: Transformation-based error-driven learning and natural language processing: A case study in part-of-speech tagging. Computational Linguistics **21** (1995) 543–566
8. Daniel, K., Schabes, Y., Zaidel, M., Egedi, D.: A freely available wide coverage morphological analyzer for English. In: Proceedings of the 14th International Conference on Computational Linguistics. (1992)
9. Fellbaum, C.(ed.): WordNet, an electronic lexical database. MIT Press (1998)
10. Appelt, D.: Introduction to information extraction technology. Tutorial presented at IJCAI-99, available as
http://www.ai.sri.com/ appelt/ie-tutorial/icjcai99.pdf (1999)
11. Hobbs, J.R., Appelt, D., Bear, J., Israel, D., Kameyama, M., Stickel, M., Tyson, M.: FASTUS: A cascaded finite state transducer for extracting information from natural language text. In: Roche, E., Schabes, Y. (eds.): Finite State Language Processing. MIT Press (1997)
12. Ide, N., Veronis, J.: Introduction to the special issue on word sense disambiguation: The state of the art. Computational Linguistics **24** (1998) 1–40
13. Radev, D., Allison, T., Blair-Goldensohn, S., Blitzer, J., Çelebi, A., Dimitrov, S., Drabek, E., Hakim, A., Lam, W., Liu, D., Otterbacher, J., Qi, H., Saggion, H., Teufel, S., Topper, M., Winkel, A., Zhang, Z.: Mead—a platform for multidocument multilingual text summarization. In: Proceedings of LREC. (2004)

A Preprocessor for Turkish Text Analysis

Kemal Oflazer[1], Özlem Çetinoğlu[1], Orhan Bilgin[1], and Bilge Say[2]

[1] Faculty of Engineering and Natural Sciences
Sabancı University, Tuzla, Istanbul, Turkey, 34956
{oflazer,ozlemc,orhanb}@sabanciuniv.edu
[2] Informatics Institute, Middle East Technical University
Ankara, Turkey
bsay@ii.metu.edu.tr

Abstract. This paper describes a preprocessor for Turkish text that involves various stages of lexical, morphological and multi-word construct processor for preprocessing Turkish text for various language engineering applications. We present the architecture of the system with special emphasis on how various kinds of collocations and other similar multi-word constructs are handled and present an evaluation from a test corpus.

1 Introduction

All natural language processing applications require that the input text be annotated with morpho-lexical information at various levels of detail. The attachement of such annotations to elements of the text almost always involve ambiguities which have to be produced but then filtered so that only the contextually salient ambiguities are retained with the additional benefit of reducing computational costs of the further analysis processes. Another important task in this annotation process is the identification of sequences of text elements whose internal linguistic structure is of no importance to further structural analysis, that is, for the purpose of structural analysis such sequences of text elements can and should be treated as single-elements. Sequences of tokens making up time and date expressions, multi-token proper names of persons, companies and other organizations, locations, brand-names and linguistically non-compositional collocations are examples of such sequences.

This paper describes a comprehensive preprocessor for processing Turkish text for subsequent processes such as information extraction noun-phrase extraction and parsing. In the following sections, we describe the architecture of this preprocessor, putting special emphasis on how we handle various kinds of non-compositional collocations.

2 The Architecture of the Preprocessor

The architecture of the preprocessor is given in Figure 1. The first component is a standard tokenizer which splits input text into constituent tokens. The tokenizer consists of a normalizer which normalizes the input characters into a standard character set, and a segmenter that uses tens of regular expressions recognizing different token types found in real-life-text. It is very careful about uses of punctuation as parts of tokens e.g., in abbreviations, numbers and URLs. As tokenization is a very standard operation we do not present the details here.

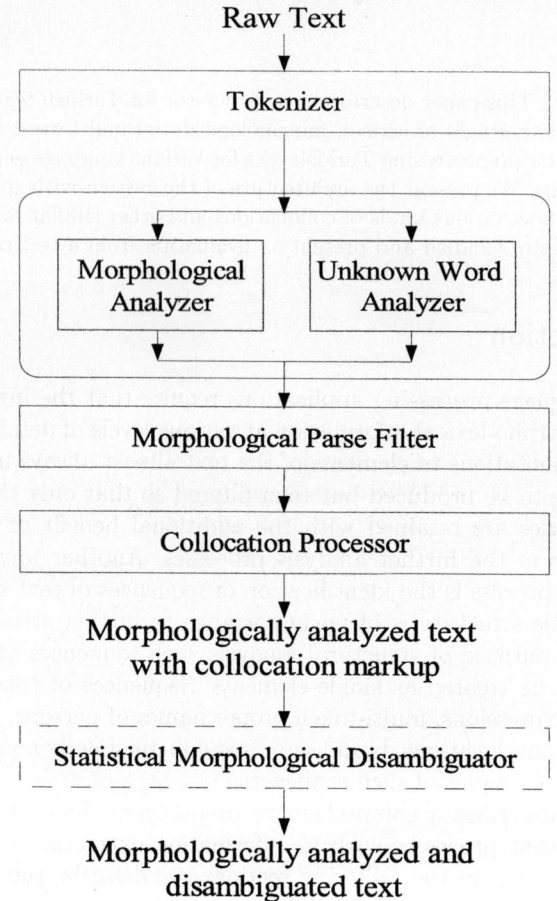

Fig. 1. The architecture of the text preprocessor

The outputs of the tokenizer then go into a wide-coverage *morphological analyzer* [1] implemented using XRCE finite state technology [2], which generates, for all tokens, all possible morphological analyses. Turkish word forms consist of morphemes concatenated to a root morpheme or to other morphemes. Except for a very few exceptional cases, the surface realizations of the morphemes are conditioned by various morphophonemic processes. The morphotactics of word forms can be quite complex when multiple derivations are involved. For instance, the derived modifier sağlamlaştırdığımızdaki[1] would be represented as: [2]

```
sağlam+Adj^DB+Verb+Become^DB+Verb+Caus+Pos^DB
    +Adj+PastPart+P1sg^DB+Noun+Zero+A3sg+Pnon+Loc^DB+Adj
```

This word starts out with an adjective root and after five derivations, ends up with the final part-of-speech adjective which determines its role in the sentence.

This morphological analyzer has a root lexicon of over 25K nouns and 4K verbs, and also knows about over 70K proper nouns, and implements all the morphographemic rules of Turkish. This analyzer is augmented with an unknown word analyzer. This second analyzer is based on the first one, but with only a single noun root lexicon which matches an arbitrary sequence of Turkish characters. This analyzer will hypothesize interpretations of unknown character sequences subject to Turkish morphographemic and morphotactic constraints. Our previous work with this approach has shown that it is very effective for unknown words in Turkish [3]. Thus all tokens coming out of the morphological analysis stage either are known and get one or more analyses, or are unknown and get one or more noun analyses based on the possible interpretation of the suffixes.

The next stage is the *morphological parse filter* which eliminates by using a collection of about few hundred regular expresssion patterns, quite a num-

---

[1] Literally, "(the thing existing) at the time we caused (something) to become strong". Obviously this is not a word that one would use everyday. Turkish words (excluding noninflecting frequent words such as conjunctions, clitics etc) found in typical text average about 10 letters in length.

[2] The morphosyntactic features and their semantics for the morphological representations used in the text are as follows. ^DB marks a derivation boundary.

- Parts-of-speech:+Noun, +Adjective, +Adverb, +Verb, +Dup (for onomatopoeic words which always appear in duplicate), +Question (yes/no question marker clitic), +Number, +Determiner
- Agreement: +A[1-3][sg-pl], e.g., +A3pl.
- Possessive agreement: +P[1-3][sg-pl] and +Pnon, e.g., +P1sg
- Case: +Nominative, +Accusative, +Locative, +Ablative, +Instrumental, +Genitive, +Dative.
- Miscellaneous Verbal Features: +Causative, +Passive, +Positive Polarity, +Negative Polarity, +Optative Mood, +Aorist Aspect, +Become, +Conditional Mood, +Imperative Mood, +Past tense
- Miscellaneous POS Subtypes: Adverbs: +By (as in "house by house"), +ByDoingSo, (as in "he came by running"), +Resemble (as in "he made sounds resembling .."), +Ly (as in "slowly") +AsSoonAs (as in "he came down as soon as he woke up"); Adjectives: +With (as in "the book with red cover"), +FutPart – future participle – as in ("the boy who will come"); Nouns:+Proper Noun, +Ness (as in "sick-ness"), +FutPart – future participle fact – as in ("I know that he will come"); Numbers: +Cardinal

ber of parses whose roots and/or feature combinations are either impossible or extremely improbable. For instance, a token like *bunda* gets two analyses – one with the pronoun root *bu* and the other with the noun root *bun* which is extremely improbable. One can safely remove the latter parse reducing the morphological ambiguity substantially since words involving the pronoun root *bu* are relatively frequent.

The next-to-last stage in the pipeline handles various kinds of collocations. Collocation extraction is an important component in language processing. It aims to identify segments of input text where the syntactic structure and the semantics of a sequence of words (possibly not contiguous) are usually not compositional. Idiomatic forms, support verbs, verbs with specific particle or pre/post-position uses, morphological derivations via partial or full word duplications are some examples of collocations. Further, expressions such as time-date expressions or proper nouns which can be described with simple grammars, and whose internal structure is of no real importance to the overall analysis of the sentence, can also be considered under this heading.

Turkish presents some interesting issues for collocation processing as it makes substantial use of support verbs with lexicalized direct or oblique objects subject to various morphological constraints. It also uses partial and full reduplication of forms of various parts-of-speech, across their whole domain to form what we call *non-lexicalized* collocations, where it is the duplication and contrast of certain morphological patterns that signal a collocation rather than the specific root words used. We discuss this stage in detail in the next section.

The last stage shown in Figure 1 with dashed lines which currently under (re)implementation, is a statistical morphological disambiguation stage that extracts with large precision and recall the contextually salient morphosyntactic interpretations of the remaining ambiguous tokens. It employs statistical techniques similar to Hakkani et al.'s approach [4] but is expected to have a much higher speed and slightly better precision.

3 Collocations in Turkish

Collocations and other multiword constructs in Turkish can be classfied into essentially five groups:

1. Lexicalized Collocations
2. Semi-lexicalized Collocations
3. Non-lexicalized Collocations
4. Multi-word Named-entities
5. Structured Sequences

3.1 Lexicalized Collocations

Under the notion of lexicalized collocations, we consider the usual fixed multiword expressions whose resulting syntactic function and semantics are not readily predictable from the structure and the morphological properties of the constituents. An example of the collocations that we consider under this grouping is the following:[3]

- *ipe sapa gelmez*
  - ip(rope)+Noun+A3sg+Pnon+Dat sap(handle)+Noun+A3sg+Pnon+Dat
    gel(come)+Verb+Neg+Aor+A3sg
  - ipe_sapa_gelmez+Adj
  "worthless" (literally "(he) does not come to rope and handle")

3.2 Semi-lexicalized Collocations

Collocations that are considered under this heading are compound and support verb formations where there are two or more lexical items the last of which is a verb or is a derivation involving a verb. These are formed by a lexically adjacent, direct or oblique object, and a verb, which for the purposes of syntactic analysis, may be considered as single lexical item: e.g., *kafayı ye-* (literally *to eat the head* – to get mentally deranged), etc.[4] Even though components other than the final verb can themselves be inflected, they can be assumed to be fixed for the purposes of the collocation, and the collocation assumes its morphosyntactic features from the last verb which itself may undergo any morphological derivation or inflection process. For instance in

- *kafayı ye-*
  - kafa(head)+Noun+A3sg+Pnon+Acc   ye(eat)+Verb...
  - kafayı_ye+Verb...
  "get mentally deranged" (literally "eat the head")

the first part of the collocation, the accusative marked noun *kafayı*, is the fixed part and the part starting with the verb *ye-* is the variable part which may be inflected and/or derived in myriads of ways: *kafayı yedim* "I got mentally deranged"; *kafayı yiyeceklerdi* "they were about to get mentally deranged"; *kafayı yiyenler* "those who got mentally deranged"; *kafayı yediği* "the fact that (s/he) got mentally deranged".

Under certain circumstances, the "fixed" part may actually vary in a rather controlled manner subject to certain morphosyntactic constraints.[5]

In their simplest forms, it is sufficient to recognize a sequence of tokens one of whose morphological analyses matches the corresponding pattern, and then coalesce these into a single collocation representation. However, some of these

---

[3] In every group we first list the morphological features of all the tokens, one on every line (with the glosses for the roots), and then provide the morphological features of the multi-word construct and then provide glosses and literal meanings.

[4] Here we just show the roots of the verb with - denoting the rest of the suffixes for any inflectional and derivational markers.

[5] Due to space restrictions we omit the details of such cases. *kafayı çekmek* (drink alcohol - literally "pull the head") and *kafaları çekmek* are examples where such a controlled variation is possible.

collocations present further complications brought about by the relative freeness of the constituent order in Turkish, and by the interaction of various clitics with such collocations.[6]

When such collocations are coalesced into a single morphological entity, the ambiguity in morphological interpretation is also reduced as we see in the following example:

– *yardým etti*
- yardým(help)+Noun+A3sg+Pnon+Nom   et(make)+Verb+Pos+Past+A3sg
  *yar(cleave)+Verb+Pos+Past+A1sg   *et(meat)+Noun+A3sg+Pnon+Nom
                                      ˆDB+Verb+Past+A3sg
- yardým_et+Verb+Pos+Past+A3sg
  "(he) helped" (literally "made help")

Here when this semi-lexicalized collocation is recognized, other morphological interpretations of the components (marked with a * above) can safely be removed, contributing to overall morphological ambiguity reduction.

3.3 Non-lexicalized Collocations

Turkish employs quite a number of non-lexicalized collocations where the sentential role of the collocation has (almost) nothing to do with the parts-of-speech and the morphological features of the individual forms involved. Almost all of these collocations involve partial or full duplications of the forms involved and can actually be viewed as morphological derivational processes mediated by reduplication across multiple tokens. The *morphological feature representations* of such collocations follow one of the patterns:

1) $\omega\ \omega$ 2) $\omega\ Z\ \omega$ 3) $\omega + X\ \omega + Y$ 4) $\omega_1 + X\ \omega_2 + X$

where ω (and ω_1, ω_2) is the duplicated string comprising the root, its part-of-speech and possibly some additional morphological features encoded by any suffixes. X and Y are further duplicated or contrasted morphological patterns and Z is a certain clitic token.

Below we present the more interesting non-lexicalized collocation patterns along with some examples and issues.

1. Nouns and adjectives appearing in duplicate following the first pattern above form collocations which behaves like a manner adverb – with semantics of "*noun* by *noun*" for nouns, and with the semantics of *-ly* adverbs in English, for adjectives. Such sequences have to be coalesced into a representation indicating these derivational processes as we see below:
   – *kapý kapý* ($\omega\ \omega$)
     - kapý(door)+Noun+A3sg+Pnon+Nom kapý+Noun+A3sg+Pnon+Nom
     - kapý+Noun+A3sg+Pnon+NomˆDB+Adverb+By
       "door by door" (literally "door door")

---

[6] The question and the emphasis clitics which are written as separate tokens, can occasionally intervene between the components of a semi-lexicalized collocation. We omit the details of these due to space restrictions.

- *yavaş yavaş* $(\omega\ \omega)$
    - yavaş(slow)+Adj   yavaş+Adj
    - yavaş+Adj^ DB+Adverb+Ly
  "slowly" (literally "slow slow")
  This kind of duplication can also occur when the adjective is a derived adjective as in *hızlı hızlı* "rapidly" (literally "with-speed with-speed")

2. Turkish has a fairly large set of onomatopoeic words which always appear in duplicate and and the collocation functions a as manner adverb. The individual words by themselves have no other usage and literal meaning, and mildly resemble sounds produced by natural or artificial objects. In these cases, both words should be of the part-of-speech category +Dup.
   - *akır ukur* $(\omega_1 + X\ \omega_2 + X\ )$
     - akır+Dup   ukur+Dup
     - akýr_ukur+Adverb+Resemble
   "making clacking noises" (no literal meaning)

3. Duplicated verbs with optative mood and third person singular agreement function as manner adverbs, indicating that another verb is executed in a manner indicated by the duplicated verb:
   - *koşa koşa* $(\omega\ \omega)$
     - koş(run)+Verb+Pos+Opt+A3sg   koş(run)+Verb+Pos+Opt+A3sg
     - koş+Verb+Pos+^ DB+Adverb+ByDoingSo
   "by running" (literally "let him run let him run")

4. Duplicated verbs in aorist mood with third person agreement and first positive then negative polarity, function as temporal adverbs with the semantics "as soon as one has *verbed*"
   - *gider gitmez* $(\omega + X\ \omega + Y)$
     - git(go)+Verb+Pos+Aor+A3sg   git+Verb+Neg+Aor+A3sg
     - git+Verb+Pos+^ DB+Adverb+AsSoonAs
   "as soon as (he) goes" (literally "(he) goes (he) does not go")
   An interesting point is that non-lexicalized collocations can interact with semi-lexicalized collocations since they both usually involve verbs as in cases 3 and 4 above. For instance, in the case of the collocation example *kafayý çeker çekmez* (as soon as (I/she/he/we/you/they) gets drunk) first the non-lexicalized collocation (the latter two tokens) has to be recognized into
   - çek+Verb+Pos^ DB+Adverb+AsSoonAs
   and then the semi-lexicalized collocation processor kicks in to package the whole collocation into
   - kafa_çek+Verb+Pos^ DB+Adverb+AsSoonAs
   ("as soon as (I/she/he/we/you/they) get drunk")

5. Finally, the following non-lexicalized collocation involving adjectival forms involving duplication and a question clitic is an example of the last type of non-lexicalized collocation.
   - *güzel mi güzel* $(\omega\ Z\ \omega)$
     - güzel+Adj   mi+Ques   güzel+Adj
     - güzel+Adj+Very
   "very beautiful" (literally "beautiful (is it?) beautiful")

3.4 Multi-word Named-Entities and Structured Sequences

Another class of constructs that our collocation processor handles is the class of multi-token named-entities denoting persons, organizations and locations, etc. We essentially treat these just like the semi-lexicalized collocation discussed earlier, in that, when such named-entities are used in text, all but the last component are fixed and the last component will usually undergo certain morphological processes demanded by the syntactic context as in *Türkiye Büyük Millet Meclisi'nde* .....[7] Here, the last component is case marked and this represents a case marking on the whole named-entity. We package this as

– Türkiye_Büyük_Millet_Meclisi+Noun+Prop+A3sg+Pnon+Loc

To recognize these named entities we use a rather simple approach employing a rather extensive database of person, organization and place names, instead of using a more sophisticated named-entity extraction scheme [5].

As structured sequences, our collocation processor currently handles datetime expressions. These are recognized by tens of patterns matching sequences such as *9 Temmuz 2004, Cuma* (9 July 2004, Friday), *19 Ocak 2004 saat 16:45*, *Haziran'ın 15'i* (15th of June)etc., and packaging into a representation with the appropriate tags, and reducing ambiguity at the same time.

3.5 Implementation

The tokenizer module and the morphological parse filter have been implemented in Perl, while the morphological analyzer and the unknown word analyzer have been implemented using XRCE finite state tools.

The collocation processor actually has three internal stages with the output of one stage feeding into the next stage:

1. The first stage handles lexicalized collocations and multi-word named-entities and other structured stages such as date and time patterns
2. the second stage handles non-lexicalized collocations,
3. The third stage handles semi-lexicalized collocations. The reason semi-lexicalized collocations are handled last, is that any duplicate verb formations have to be processed before compound verbs are combined with their lexicalized complements

The rule bases for the three stages of the collocation processor are maintained separately and then compiled offline into regular expressions which are then used by Perl at runtime.

Table 1 presents statistics on the current rule base of our collocation extraction processor. For named entity recognition, we use a list of about 60,000 first and last names, a list of about 16,000 multi-word organization and place names.

---

[7] In the Turkish Grand National Assembly.

Table 1. Rules base statistics

Rule Type	Rules
Lexicalized Colloc.	363
Semi-lexicalized Colloc.	731
Non-lexicalized Colloc.	16

4 Evaluation

The tokenizer module is highly accurate and segments the incoming text into tokens with almost 100% accuracy. The morphological analyzer and the accompanying unknown word analyzer are wide coverage. All incoming tokens get analyzed into one or more morphosyntactic analyses.

Since the gist of this paper in on collocation recognition we present a bit more detail on the accuracy of the collocation extraction stage. During the construction of our collocation processor, to improve and evaluate our collocation extraction processor, we used two corpora of news text. We used a corpus of about 730,000 tokens to incrementally test and improve our semi-lexicalized collocation rule base, by searching for compound verb formations, etc. Once such rules were extracted, we tested our processor on this corpus, and on a small corpus of about 4200 words to measure precision and recall.

Table 2 shows the result of collocation extraction on the large (training) and the small (test) corpus. It should be noted that we only mark multi-word named-entities, not all. Thus many references to persons by their last name are not marked, hence the low number of named-entities extracted.[8]

Table 2. Collocation extraction statistics on the training and test corpora

Training Corpus

MW Type	Extracted
Lexicalized Colloc.	3,883
Semi-lexicalized Colloc.	9,173
Non-lexicalized Colloc.	220
Named-Entities	4,480
Date-Time Expressions	60
Total	17,810

Test Corpus

MW Type	Extracted
Lexicalized Colloc.	15
Semi-lexicalized Colloc.	62
Non-lexicalized Colloc.	0
Named-Entities	99
Date-Time Expressions	3
Total	179

We manually marked up the small corpus into a gold-standard corpus to test precision and recall. The results on the right in Table 2 correspond to an overall

---

[8] Since the training corpus is very large corpus, we have no easy way of obtaining accurate precision and recall figures, except by sampling but since collocations are rather infrequent sampling may not be very meaningful either.

recall of 65.2% and a precision of 98.9%, over all classes of collocations. When we consider all classes except named-entities, we have a recall of 60.1% and a precision of 100%. An analysis of the errors and missed collocations indicates that the test set had a certain variant of a compound verb construction that we had failed to extract from the larger corpus we used for compiling rules. Failing to extract the collocations for that compound verb accounted for most of the drop in recall. Since we are currently using a rather naive named-entity extraction scheme, recall is rather low as there are quite a number of foreign multi-word named-entities (persons and organizations mostly) that do not exist in our database of named-entities.

5 Conclusions

We have described preprocessor for Turkish text with an emphasis on collocation extraction. Our proprocessor handles various types of collocations such as semi-lexicalized and non-lexicalized collocations which depend on the recognition of certain morphological patterns across tokens. Our results indicate that with about 1100 rules (most of which were semi-automatically extracted from a large "training corpus" searching for patterns involving a certain small set of support verbs), we were able get almost 100% precision and around 60% recall on a small "test" corpus. We expect that with additional rules from dictionaries and other sources we will improve recall significantly.

Acknowledgments

We thank Esra Karakaş for implementing the tokenizer and the date-time parser.

References

1. Oflazer, K.: Two-level description of Turkish morphology. Literary and Linguistic Computing **9** (1994) 137–148
2. Karttunen, L., Gaal, T., Kempe, A.: Xerox finite-state tool. Technical report, Xerox Research Centre Europe (1997)
3. Oflazer, K., Tür, G.: Combining hand-crafted rules and unsupervised learning in constraint-based morphological disambiguation. In: Brill, E., Church, K. (eds.): Proceedings of the ACL-SIGDAT Conference on Empirical Methods in Natural Language Processing. (1996)
4. Hakkani-Tür, D., Oflazer, K., Tür, G.: Statistical morphological disambiguation for agglutinative languages. Computers and the Humanities **36** (2002)
5. Tür, G., Hakkani-Tür, D.Z., Oflazer, K.: A statistical information extraction system for Turkish. Natural Language Engineering **9** (2003)

The Effect of Part-of-Speech Tagging on IR Performance for Turkish

B. Taner Dinçer and Bahar Karaoğlan

Ege Üniversitesi, Uluslararası Bilgisayar Enstitüsü,
35100 Bornova, İzmir, Türkiye
{dtaner,bahar}@ube.ege.edu.tr

Abstract. In this paper, we experimentally evaluate the effect of the Part-of-Speech (POS) tagging on Information Retrieval performance for Turkish. We used four term-weighting schemas to index SABANCI-METU Turkish Treebank corpus. The term weighting schemas are "*tf*", "*tf* x *idf*", "Ltu.ltu", and "Okapi". Each weighting scheme is factored over three POS tagging cases that are namely "No POS tagging", "POS tag with no history (i.e. 1-gram)", and "POS tag with one step history (i.e. 2-gram)". The Meta-scoring function is used to analyze the effect of these nine factors on IR performance. Results show that weighting schema are significantly different from each other with a p-value of 0.04 (Friedman Non-parametric Test), but there is not enough evidence in the corpus to reject the *null* hypothesis that the three weighting schemas, on the average, show equal performance over the three cases of POS tagging with a p-value of 0.36.

1 Introduction

Information Retrieval (IR) systems are used to search a large number of electronic documents for user information needs. Information on a document is composed of words' semantics. Hence, an IR system actually deals with those words, which are the representatives of semantics that are truly the building blocks of intended information. Index term selection is a task of finding manually or automatically the words or collocations that are the representatives of the potential information in a particular document. Those terms are then used to represent the document in an IR system for further processing purposes. The major task of IR systems, which use automatic indexing, is to find the most important terms to represent the documents. Term weighting or index term weighting is the task of assigning a quantitative value to a particular term according to its importance of being a representative for each document in the collection.

POS (Part-of Speech) Tagging is the process of assigning grammatical functions to terms in a written text. Tagging a term with a part-of-speech allows the use of this information in term weighting schemas. The natural language processing techniques such as POS tagging may improve retrieval performance, but the degree of improvement varies from minimal to moderately helpful [1].

In this study, we examine the effect of POS tagging on three different index term weighting schemas, consequently the retrieval performance. The standard "$tf \times idf$" [2], the "$Ltu.ltu$" [3] and the "$Okapi$" [4] are used as weighting schemas in our experiments. Term weighting without POS tagging, with POS tag of the target term, and with the POS tag of the target and previous term are taken as the treatment groups. The Meta-Scoring function [1] is used to evaluate a quantitative metric to compare the results obtained from constructed nine test beds without precision and recall. Jin et. al. [1] states that Meta-Scores are always consistent with the average precision for all their six test collections and four different term weighting schemas. The results reveal that there is a significant difference between weighting schemas with or without POS tag information for Turkish texts, free from any statistical fluctuations with a significance level of 0.04 percent (i.e. Friedman non-parametric test, p-value of 0.04). Although there seems no difference between "no tagging", "tag with target term POS" and "tag with target and previous term" for all weighting schemas, it is false to say that there is no tendency to favor POS tagging against "no tagging". The p-value of 0.36 may not mean a strong evidence of the complete randomness. However, it is also not enough to say that there exists a difference. This inconclusive situation may be due to the small size of the test collection and will be further discussed in Section 3.

The paper is organized as follows: In Section 2, we give our experimental design. In Section 3, we present the results and the discussions of our experiments. The conclusions are given in Section 4.

2 Experimental Design

2.1 The Test Corpus

We used the SABANCI-METU Turkish Treebank [5, 6] as our test corpus. It contains 7,262 sentences that are manually POS and syntactic function tagged and disambiguated. Some statistics and proportion of the genres of the corpus is given in Table 1. The corpus has been constructed from the parts of the METU Turkish Corpus [7] and has approximately the same proportion of genres. Intuitively, a corpus length of 63,916 token is not large enough for statistical test of hypothesis with a high level of confidence. However, it is not that small to conclude that it entails no information to test some linguistic methods. Besides, it is the only corpus, which is manually tagged and disambiguated for Turkish.

Table 1. Some descriptive statistics of SABANCI-METU Turkish Treebank

	Doc.	Parag.	Sent.	Token	
Topics	%	%	%	#	%
Memoirs	3.03	3.30	3.72	4519	7.07
Research	6.06	3.09	24.98	13135	20.55
Essay	9.09	15.55	5.08	2284	3.57
Travel	3.03	1.10	3.18	2908	4.55
News	27.27	16.04	4.79	4040	6.32
Paper	9.09	2.28	17.55	7659	11.98
Story	18.18	22.83	2.27	2142	3.35
Short Story	6.06	3.34	11.78	11919	18.65
Novel	18.18	32.48	26.66	15310	23.95
Total	100	100	100	63916	100

The vocabulary size of the corpus is 17,518 tokens. This value is approximately equal to the 30% of the corpus size, which causes the document-term matrixes for any weighting scheme to be sparse. This appalling situation of huge vocabulary size is a side affect of Turkish as an agglutinative language and brings the need for stemming as a major preparation step for Information Retrieval tasks. However, we did no stemming in our study, because our aim is to find the POS tagging effect on retrieval performance independent of any other factor. Another problem is in our evaluation metric, Meta-Scoring may be thought as a discriminant analysis of n-dimensional document space. In other words, the score increases while a weighting schema can discriminate the "document content" space into a number of orthogonal axes that fit the number of collection space dimensions. However, vocabulary of that size may readily discriminate the space into all possible orthogonal axes. In this case, the Meta-Scoring assessment is limited to a small room for discrimination that can be produced by the weighting schemas, which are meaningless with respect to the statistical significance of change.

2.2 Evaluation Metric: Meta-scoring

In Information retrieval, performance is evaluated with a widely accepted precision and recall metrics [2]. To evaluate these metrics for a corpus with given queries requires human judgments about relevance between the queries and the retrieved documents. There are two disadvantages of this method for performance evaluation: 1-) Relevance judgments of human subjects for every document for all queries is very expensive because of the large size of the collections used for IR purposes. 2-) Human judgment about relevance between documents and queries is not free from bias. Human judgments are subjective, thus to make an objective evaluation of IR performance more than one person are needed to judge the relevance. The most essential property of Meta-Scoring method is that it evaluates an objective relevance judgment for all possible queries that can be formulated from the considered collection against all documents.

Meta-scoring [1] is a way of bypassing the human effort for relevance judgment. It compares two different document-term matrixes generated by two different term weighting schemas and computes a "goodness" score for them. Jin et. al. state that this "goodness" score for different weighting schemas are correlated with their information retrieval performances evaluated by average precision metric. The Meta-score is based on the notion of Mutual Information between two random variables C and D, and is written as:

$$I(C;D) = H(C) - H(C|D) \qquad (1)$$

In other words, Mutual Information $I(C;D)$ is the difference between the entropy of the random variable C, $H(C)$ and the average entropy of the random variable C when the value of random variable D is given $H(C|D)$. In the Meta-Scoring formulation random variable, C represents the "document contents" and the random variable, D represents the content vectors. To model the "document contents" they used the idea of Latent Semantic Indexing (LSI) [8]. Therefore, the random variable C can take the values from the set of eigenvectors $\{\vec{v}_1, \vec{v}_2, \ldots, \vec{v}_n\}$ of the document matrix D. The probability of C is equal to any eigenvector $\vec{v}_i$ $i = 1,\ldots,n$ i.e. $P(C = \vec{v}_i)$ that can be calculated by the corresponding eigenvalues λ_i $i = 1,\ldots,n$ of document matrix D as:

$$P(C = \vec{v}_i) = \frac{\lambda_i}{\sum_{j=1}^{n} \lambda_j}, \quad 1 \le i \le n \qquad (2)$$

The document matrix D is a square and symmetric matrix, and evaluated from the document-term matrix M as:

$$D_{n \times n} = M_{n \times m} M_{m \times n}^{T} \qquad (3)$$

The random variable D can take values from the set of document vectors, i.e. documents in the collection $\{\vec{d}_1, \vec{d}_2, \ldots, \vec{d}_n\}$. Since, every document in the collection has equal importance, $P(D = \vec{d}_i)$ will be constant.

$$P(D = \vec{d}_i) = \frac{1}{n}, \quad 1 \le i \le n \qquad (4)$$

To compute intended mutual information, the last probability that must be evaluated is $P(C = \vec{v}_i | D = \vec{d}_j)$. In other words, the probability of the document content is equal to the eigenvector $\vec{v}_i$, given that the random variable D is equal to the document vector $\vec{d}_j$.

$$P(C = \vec{v}_i | D = \vec{d}_j) = \frac{|\vec{d}_j^T \vec{v}_i|}{\sum_{k=1}^{n} |\vec{d}_j^T \vec{v}_k|} \, , \, 1 \leq i, j \leq n \tag{5}$$

2.3 Weighting Schemas Used in Experiments

In our study, we used three different weighting schemas to evaluate the effect of POS tagging on IR performance shown in Table 2. They are namely the standard *tfxidf* [2], the *Ltu* [3] and the *Okapi* [4] weighting schemes. In addition to these three methods, *tf* (i.e. raw term frequencies) is used as a base line for the performance considerations. The *Ltu* and the *Okapi* are the two well-known term weighting schemas. They consider the document lengths, which is not a property of *tfxidf* scheme.

Table 2. Term-weighting schemas used in experiments. *tf* is the frequency of a term, *max_tf* is the maximum term frequency in a document. *N* is the total number of documents in the collection, *df* is the document frequency, *dl* is the document length and *avg_dl* is the average document length

Name	Term weighting schema
tf	Tf
tfxidf	$tf * \log(\frac{N}{df})$
Ltu	$\dfrac{(\log(tf)+1)\log(\frac{N}{df})}{0.8+0.2\dfrac{dl}{avg\_dl}}$
Okapi	$\dfrac{tf}{0.5+1.5\dfrac{dl}{avg\_dl}+tf} \log(\dfrac{N-df+0.5}{df+0.5})$

2.4 Description of the Experiments

We evaluated all of the four weighting schema for each POS tagging cases in the SABANCI-METU Turkish Treebank [5, 6]. This results in twelve document-term matrixes that have to be tested. Enumerations of the test treatments are shown in Table 3. Columns of the table show the POS tagging treatments: *Case0* represents no tagging where weighting scheme considers only the *terms* (i.e. words). *Case1* represents the case where the term ($term_i$) is tagged with its POS (tag_i). In *Case2*, the triple $(tag_1, tag_2, term_2)$ represents the target term ($term_i$), its POS tag (tag_i) and the POS tag of the previous term (tag_{i-1}). In other words, Cases may be thought as *n-grams* in POS sequence: *0-gram* for *Case0*, *1-gram* for *Case1* and *2-gram* for *Case2*.

Table 3. Enumeration of test cases

	Case0	*Case1*	*Case2*
tf	$term_i$	$(tag_i, term_i)$	$(tag_{i-1}, tag_i, term_i)$
tfxidf	$term_i$	$(tag_i, term_i)$	$(tag_{i-1}, tag_i, term_i)$
Ltu	$term_i$	$(tag_i, term_i)$	$(tag_{i-1}, tag_i, term_i)$
Okapi	$term_i$	$(tag_i, term_i)$	$(tag_{i-1}, tag_i, term_i)$

3 Results and Discussions

Figure 1, shows the over all results of the factors of the four weighting schemas and the three POS tagging treatments. The effect of all treatments and weighting schemas for index term weighting are tested by Friedman non-parametric test for statistical independence (Friedman test statistics is the non-parametric equivalence of 2-way ANOVA for the parametric case).

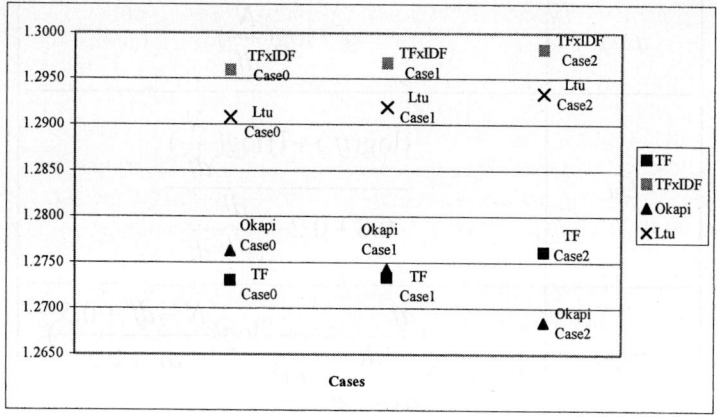

Fig. 1. Meta-scores of all test treatments

As seen in the figure, the standard *tfxidf*-weighting scheme outperforms the other two schemas for SABANCI-METU Turkish Treebank corpus. This is not an expected situation when an English corpus is under consideration. This may be due to the large size of vocabulary and the insufficient size of the corpus for IR purpose.

The *tfxidf* is significantly different with a significance level of 0.10 from both *Ltu* scheme with *p-value* of 0.08 and the *Okapi* scheme with p-value of again 0.08. In addition, the *Ltu* scheme is significantly different from *Okapi* scheme with a p-value of 0.08. The three weighting schemas are significantly different with a significance level of 0.05 from each other with a p-value of 0.04 without treatments effect (i.e. without POS tagging effect). It is worth to note that Jin et. al [1] states the close performance of *Ltu* and *Okapi* weighting schemas against six different test collections for English in their original work. However, *Ltu* weighting scheme performs much better than *Okapi* weighting scheme for Turkish.

Although there is no empirical result that any of these weighting schemas differ in their performance when the POS tag information is included, it will not be true to judge that all these weighting schemas are completely independent of POS tag information. It is statistically evident from the corpus that there is no significant difference between these three weighting schemes, but as can be seen in the Figure 1, *tfxidf*, *Ltu* and also *tf* weighting schemas tend to increase their performance while information gathered from POS tag context increase. These results with POS tag reveal clearly the fact that the corpus size is not sufficient to make confident decisions about the effect of POS information on retrieval performance. Nevertheless, there is an empirical tendency towards differentiation between considered weighting schemas with a p-value of 0.36.

4 Conclusion

In this paper, we examined the effect of POS tag information on the performance of Information Retrieval systems for Turkish by four different weighting schemas. We used a Meta-Scoring [1] function as the evaluation metric. This method enables to avoid the need for human relevance judgment of queries against retrieved documents. Our results reveal that there is a significant difference between weighting schemas, namely the standard *tfxidf* [2], the *Ltu* [3] and the *Okapi* [4], free from any statistical fluctuations with a significance level of 0.05 percent (i.e. Friedman non-parametric test, p-value of 0.04). On the other hand, statistically speaking, the test corpus does not carry enough evidence to judge whether POS tag information is helpful or not. However, it would be false to say that retrieval performance is completely independent of the POS tag information, because we have failed to reject the null hypothesis of the dependency with a relatively low value of p (i.e. 0.36).

References

1. Jin, R., Faloutsos, C., Hauptmann, A.G.: Meta-Scoring: Automatically Evaluating Term Weighting Schemes in IR without Precision-Recall. In: Proceedings of the 24th ACM SIGIR Conference on Research and Development in Information Retrieval, New Orleans, Louisiana. (2001)
2. Baeza-Yates, R., Ribeiro-Neto, B.: Modern Information Retrieval. 1st edition. Addison-Wesley, England (1999)
3. Buckley, C., Singhal, A., Mitra, M.: New Retrieval Approaches Using SMART. In: Harman, D.K. (ed.): Proceedings of the Fourth Text Retrieval Conference (TREC-4), Gaithersburg. (1996)
4. Robertson, S.E., Walker, S.: Okapi/Keenbow at TREC-8. In: Voorhees, E.M., Harman, D.K. (eds.): Proceedings of the Eighth Text Retrieval Conference (TREC-8), Gaithersburg. (2000)
5. Oflazer, K., Say, B., Hakkani-Tür, D.Z., Tür, G.: Building a Turkish Treebank. In: Abeille, A. (ed.): Building and Exploiting Syntactically-Annotated Corpora. Kluwer Academic Publishers (2003)
6. Atalay, N.B., Oflazer, K., Say, B.: The Annotation Process in the Turkish Treebank. In: Proceedings of the EACL Workshop on Linguistically Interpreted Corpora, Budapest, Hungary. (2003)
7. Say, B., Zeyrek, D., Oflazer, K., Özge, U.: Development of a Corpus and a Treebank for Present-Day Written Turkish In: Proceedings of the Eleventh International Conference of Turkish Linguistics. (2002)
8. Kwok, K.L., Grunfeld, L., Xu, J.H.: TREC-6 English and Chinese Retrieval Experiments Using PRICS. In: Voorhees, E.M., Harman, D.K. (eds.): Proceedings of Sixth Text Retrieval Conference (TREC-6), Gaithersburg. (1997)

A New Pareto-Based Algorithm for Multi-objective Graph Partitioning

Raul Baños[1], Concolación Gil[1], M. G. Montoya[1], and Julio Ortega[2]

[1] Dept. Arquitectura de Computadores y Electrónica, Universidad de Almería
La Cañada de San Urbano s/n, 04120 Almería, Spain
{rbanos,cgil,mari}@ace.ual.es
[2] Dept. Arquitectura y Tecnología de Computadores, Universidad de Granada
Campus de Fuentenueva, Granada, Spain
julio@atc.ugr.es

Abstract. One significant problem of optimization which occurs in many real applications is that of graph partitioning. It consist of obtaining a partition of the vertices of a graph into a given number of roughly equal parts, whilst ensuring that the number of edges connecting vertices of different sub-graphs is minimized. In the single-objective (traditional) graph partitioning model the imbalance is considered a constraint. However, in same applications it is necessary to extend this model to its multi-objective formulation, where the imbalance is also an objective to minimize. This paper try to solve this problem in the multi-objective way by using a population version of the SMOSA algorithm in combination with a diversity preservation method proposed in the SPEA2 algorithm.

1 Introduction

The Graph Partitioning Problem (GPP) occurs in many areas, such as scientific computation [1], load balancing [2], VLSI design [3], task scheduling [4], datamining [5], etc. As the problem is NP-complete [6], efficient procedures providing high quality solutions in reasonable execution times are very useful. Most of the proposed algorithms to solve the GPP are single-objective, i.e., the objective is to minimize the number of edges connecting vertices belonging to different sub-graphs, while the imbalance is considered a constraint. Thus far, there are few works reported for the multi-objective case.

In this paper, a new algorithm for multi-objective GPP is presented. This algorithm is a population version of SMOSA metaheuristic [7], which includes a diversity preservation strategy proposed in SPEA2 [8].

Section 2 provides a more precise definition of the GPP, and describes the current state of the art. Section 3 presents the new algorithm here proposed, while the results obtained are offered in Section 4. Finally, Section 5 provides the conclusions of this work and suggests areas for future research.

2 The Graph Partitioning Problem

Let $G = (V, E)$ be a undirected graph, where V is the set of vertices, $|V|=n$, and E the set of edges which determines the connectivity of V. The GPP consists of dividing V into K balanced sub-graphs, $V_1, V_2,..., V_K$, such that $V_i \cap V_j = \phi$, $\forall i \neq j$; and $\sum_{k=1}^{K} |V_k| = |V|$. The balance constraint is defined by the maximum sub-graph weight, $M = \max(|V_k|), \forall k \in [1, K]$.

In single-objective GPP, the objective is to minimize the number of edges that join vertices belonging to different sub-graphs (ncuts), while the imbalance defined by M is considered a constraint. Thus, if the maximum allowed imbalance is $x\%$, the partition must verify that $M \leq ((n/K)*((100+x)/100))$. There exist many algorithms [9] to solve the traditional GPP. The main weakness of this model is the dependency on the imbalance constraint. Figure 1 shows two partitions, s and s^*, and their representation in the solution space. Thus, if the maximum allowed imbalance is, for example, x=30%, the solution s would be selected as the best. However, if the maximum imbalance is x=20%, the best would be s^*, due to s has a forbidden imbalance, despite having less cuts.

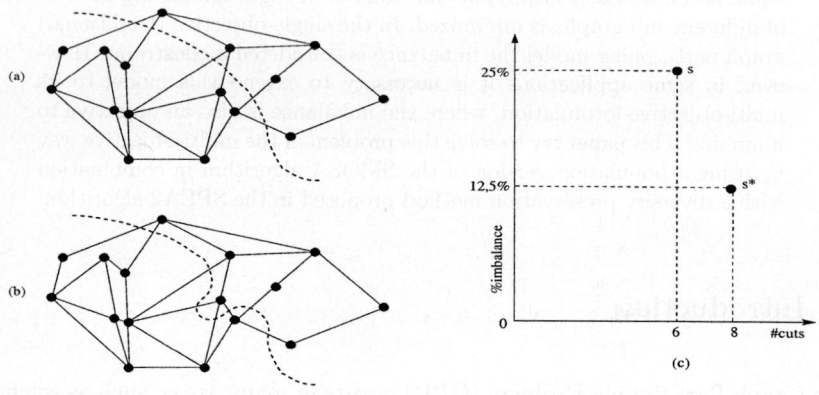

Fig. 1. Movement of s (a) to s^* (b), and their location in the solution space (c)

Traditional packages [10, 11] that solve the GPP often work very well with specific imbalance ratios. However, in some cases it is interesting to focus the problem in its multi-objective way, obtaining solutions with different imbalance degrees. Many authors have designed algorithms to treat general multi-objective optimization problems, but, thus far, the number of works deal with the GPP is very limited [12, 13]. As a result of these few works, two general approaches have been developed for combining multiple objectives in the GPP [12]. The first approach keeps the objectives separate and couples them by assigning different priorities to each one. Under this approach, a solution that optimizes the highest priority objective is always preferred, while the secondary objective is used to decide among equivalent solutions in terms of the higher priority objective. The second alternative is based on creating a mathematical multi-objective function as the weighted sum of the individual objective functions. Under this context, the choice of the weighting values is used to determine the relative importance of the objectives. Thus, a possible cost function could be the following:

$$c(s) = \alpha \cdot ncuts\ (s) + \beta \cdot \tfrac{M}{n/K}\ (s) \qquad (1)$$

The main trouble with these approaches is the difficulty of assigning adequate weight values to each objective. An interesting way to overcome this disadvantage is to use the Pareto-dominance concept [14]. Let P be a MOO problem, with $Z \geq 2$ objectives. Instead of giving a scalar value to each solution, a partial order is defined based on Pareto-dominance relations. A solution s^* is said to dominate another s ($s^* \prec s$) when it is better on at least one objective, and not worse on the others. Two solutions are indifferent ($s \sim s^*$) if neither s dominates s^*, nor s^* dominates s. A solution is said to be non-dominated if no solution can be found that dominates it. The set of non-dominated solutions is called Pareto optimal set. Since all the objectives are equally important, this set normally contains not one solution, but several. Thus, the aim of multi-objective optimization is to induce this entire set.

The Pareto-optimization has been successfully applied to many multi-objective optimization problems. However, in the context of the GPP it is still an open question. We can reference the work of Rummler and Apetrei [13], where an adaptation of the SPEA multi-objective algorithm [15] to the GPP was proposed. They tested the performance of this Multi-Objective Evolutionary Algorithm (MOEA) on several hyper-graphs, obtaining low quality partitions. They remark that the main cause of these disappointing results is the redundancy in the representation of the solutions for this problem, which causes the evolutionary operators not to work as well as in other problems. Their experimental results indicated that the use of a local search procedure allows for improvement in the quality of the solutions in comparison with the SPEA adaptation. This is the reason why we use local search Multi-Objective Meta-Heuristics (MOMHs), instead of using MOEAs.

3 The New Pareto-Based Algorithm: eSMOSA

3.1 The Multi-objective Meta-heuristic: SMOSA

One of the first proposed MOMHs was Serafini's Multi-Objective Simulated Annealing (SMOSA) [7]. In single-objective Simulated Annealing (SA) [16] better neighboring solutions are always accepted, whereas worsening solutions are accepted with a probability value. This probability is calculated by using the Metropolis function [17] according to the degree of deterioration in the quality of the solution, and a parameter, called *temperature*. In a multi-objective context, it can be seen as always accepting a new solution (s^*) if it dominates the current one (s), i.e. ($s^* \prec s$); and to accept s^* with a given probability if it is dominated by s, i.e. ($s \prec s^*$). However, there is a special case to consider when both solutions are indifferent, i.e., neither s dominates s^*, nor s^* dominates to s ($s \sim s^*$). Serafini suggested different transition probabilities for this case: one of these rules (P) is used for the strong acceptance case, in which only dominating neighbors should be accepted with probability one, while other rule (W) is used for the weak acceptance case, in which only dominated neighboring solutions should be accepted with a probability of less than one. Finally, Serafini combined P and W, obtaining a composite rule (M) (see Table 1) whose results [7] outperforms those obtained by P and W.

Table 1. Acceptance rules in SMOSA

Rule	Mathematical Definition
P	$p_{s,s*}(t) \leftarrow (\min\{1, e^{((cuts(s*)-cuts(s))/t)}\}) * (\min\{1, e^{((imb(s*)-imb(s))/t)}\})$
W	$p_{s,s*}(t) \leftarrow \min\{1, max\{e^{((cuts(s*)-cuts(s))/t)}, e^{((imb(s*)-imb(s))/t)}\}\}$
M	$p_{s,s*}(t) := \alpha P + (1-\alpha)W$; ($\alpha = 0.9$)

The initial solutions are obtained by using the Graph Growing Algorithm (GGA) [18]. The operator used to obtain a new solution s^*, from the current one s is based on moving vertices from a sub-graph to other in the neighborhood. Figure 1(a) shows a partition s. Figure 1(b) shows the movement of s to s^* by relocating a boundary vertex from a sub-graph to the neighboring one. This example clearly shows as the objectives are often in conflict, i.e., the improvement of one of them usually implies the deterioration of others.

3.2 Extending SMOSA by Using a Population of Solutions in Combination with an External Archive

In SMOSA a single solution is used during the search process. All the non-dominated solutions (ND) found after this optimization process are returned as the final solution. In order to improve the quality of the ND set, we propose extending SMOSA by using a population of individuals (S) which evolves in parallel. This population version of SMOSA, here called eSMOSA (extended-SMOSA) allows to explore more efficiently the search space. However, good solutions may be lost during the optimization process due the random effects. An interesting way to reduce the impact of this problem is to maintain a secondary population, ND (external set or archive), where promising solutions of S are copied at each generation. For this task, we have used the archiving strategy proposed in SPEA2 [8]. Starting with an initial population and an empty archive, the following steps are performed in each iteration of SPEA2. First, all non-dominated solutions of the population are copied to the archive. Any dominated solutions or duplicates are removed from the archive during this update operation. If the size of the update archive exceeds the established length, some archive solutions are deleted by a clustering technique which preserves the characteristics of the non-dominated set. After applying a variation to the population, by using in our case the SMOSA strategy (mutation and crossover in the case of SPEA2), a new set of solutions is obtained. Finally, the population of the next iteration is created by mating selection. This selection procedure consist of combining the new solutions of S, and the previously stored in ND to construct a diverse set of solutions to be used in the next iteration.

Algorithm 1 : Extended Serafini's Multi-Objective Simulated Annealing (eSMOSA)

1) **input**: G, K, —S—, RULE, $T_i, T_{factor}, T_{stop}$;
2) s←GGA(G); cuts[s]←calculate_cuts(s); imb[s]←calculate_imbalance(s); ($\forall s \in S$)
3) ND←Environmental_selection(ND, S); t←T_i;
4) **while** (t>T_{stop}) **do**
5)   S←Mating_selection(S, ND);
6)   **for** ($\forall s \in S$) **do**
7)   s*←neighbor(s);
8)   probability←Apply RULE(s,s*);
9)   **if** (Metropolis(probability,t)=1) **then** s←s*;
10)   t←t*T_{factor};
11)   ND←Environmental_selection(ND, S);
12) **return** ND;

Algorithm 1 provides the eSMOSA pseudo-code. In line 1, input parameters are shown: target graph, number of sub-graphs to divide G, population size, acceptance rule, annealing values, and temperature used in the stop criterion. In line 2, all the solutions of the population are created by using GGA before to be evaluated in each objective. The external archive, here called non-dominated set (ND) is updated by using the strategy proposed in SPEA2. Also in line 3, the current temperature is initialized. The main loop of eSMOSA is shown in line 4. The first action of the main loop (line 5) consist of applying the mating selection previously described to build the set of solutions to be used in this iteration. After that, line 6, the same process is repeated for all the solutions of S. First step of the inner loop is to obtain a neighboring solution to the current one. The acceptance probability of this new solution (line 8), and the current temperature are used as a input parameter in the Metropolis function (line 9). If it is accepted, the new solution substitutes the current one, and the non-dominated set is updated. The temperature is updated in line 10. Last step of the outer loop is to update the external archive by using the strategy proposed in SPEA2. When the stop condition is true, the set of non-dominated solutions is returned (line 12).

4 Experimental Results

The executions were performed by using a 2.4 GHz Intel processor with 512 MB of memory. The graphs used to compare the MOMHs belong to a public domain set frequently used to evaluate single-objective graph partitioning algorithms. Table 2 briefly describes them: number of vertices, number of edges, maximum connectivity *(max)* (number of neighbors to the vertex with the highest neighborhood), minimum connectivity *(min)*, and average connectivity *(avg)*. These test graphs, and the best known solutions for them in the single-objective way, can be found in Walshaw's Graph Partitioning Archive [19].

Table 2. A summary of the test graphs

graph	$|V|$	$|E|$	min	max	avg
add20	2395	7462	1	123	6.23
whitaker3	9800	28989	3	8	5.92
crack	10240	30380	3	9	5.93
memplus	17758	54196	1	573	6.1

4.1 Parameter Setting

In order to evaluate the quality of the solutions of the algorithm here proposed, we compare eSMOSA versus SMOSA. Further, we have adapted the Pareto Simulated Annealing (PSA) algorithm proposed by Czyzak and Jaszkiewicz [20]. This is also a SA-based MOMH, which uses a set of solutions, in the same way than eSMOSA. The population and external archive sizes have been set to $|S| = |ND| = 35$ in PSA and eSMOSA. In [21] we presented an algorithm to solve the single-objective GPP, which used $Ti=100$, and $Tfactor=0.995$ as annealing parameters (this annealing scheduling implies a number of 1500 iterations to fall bellow t=0.01). Thus, we have used again the same annealing values for the multi-objective case.

The results here shown correspond to the partitioning of the test graphs into 16 sub-graphs. All the best known solutions displayed in [19] have an imbalance $M \leq 1.05$. Thus, we have considered an additional constraint in order to discard those solutions with an imbalance ratio greater than 5%.

4.2 Metrics Used to Evaluate the Quality of the Solutions

In order to compare the quality of the non-dominated solutions, we have used the following metrics:

- Metric *M1*: This metric represents the number of non-dominated solutions obtained after the execution of the algorithm. Seeing Figure 2(a), ND2 is better than ND1, due to |ND2|=6, while |ND1|=4.

$$M1 := |ND|$$

- Metric *M2*: As the Pareto-optimal set is unknown, it is not possible calculate the distance of the non-dominated solutions to this set. We have adapted the metric proposed in [13]. Thus, M2 represents the average area under the non-dominated solutions. This area is calculated taking as reference the enclosed area by the maximum number of cuts of the initial solutions and the maximum allowed imbalance. Low values of M2 denote proximity to the (unknown) Pareto-optimal front. In Figure 2(b) we can observe that the average enclosed area is smaller in ND1 than in ND2.

$$M2 := \sum_{i=1}^{|ND|} \left(\frac{\#cuts[i]}{\#max\_cuts} * \frac{\#imbalance[i]}{\#max\_imbalance} \right) / |ND|; \quad \forall i \in ND$$

- Metric M3: M3 denotes the distance between the most distant non-dominated solutions. To calculate this distance, M3 uses as reference the maximum possible distance by considering the initial solution and maximum imbalance. In Figure 2(c), the dotted line d represents this reference. In this figure it is clearly shown as ND2 is more extensive than ND1.

$$M3 := \max\{distance(i,j)\}; \quad \forall \; i,j \in ND, \; i \neq j$$

- Metric M4: M4 indicates the penalty of the non-dominated solutions in function of their crowing degree. To calculate this distribution of each MOMH, M4 multiplies the distances of each solution in the non-dominated set to the nearest neighbor, using as reference again the maximum distance used in M3. High values reveal good distributions. In Figure 2(d) we can observe that ND1 is better distributed than ND2.

$$M4 := \sqrt{|ND| \prod_{i=1}^{|ND|} distance(i,j)}; \quad i, j \in ND, \; j = \text{nearest solution to } i.$$

Table 3. Comparing SMOSA, PSA and eSMOSA

graph	MOMH	M1	M2	M3	M4	run-time (secs.)
add20	SMOSA	8	0.364	0.707	0.054	29
	PSA	8	0.352	0.683	0.048	869
	eSMOSA	11	0.258	0.628	0.037	1171
whitaker3	SMOSA	2	0.033	0.023	0.023	96
	PSA	6	0.062	0.193	0.033	929
	eSMOSA	3	0.024	0.05	0.023	3077
crack	SMOSA	3	0.053	0.239	0.073	110
	PSA	10	0.063	0.281	0.028	1329
	eSMOSA	6	0.021	0.238	0.03	3459
memplus	SMOSA	4	0.05	0.266	0.028	186
	PSA	10	0.499	0.75	0.013	6090
	eSMOSA	16	0.11	0.639	0.012	6715
AVG	SMOSA	4.25	0.125	0.309	**0.045**	105
	PSA	8.5	0.244	**0.477**	0.031	2304
	eSMOSA	**9**	**0.103**	0.389	0.026	3606

Table 3 compares the results obtained by the three MOMHs for these test graphs. As we can see, the number of non-dominated solutions (M1) obtained by eSMOSA is higher than in PSA and SMOSA. Further, the average area under

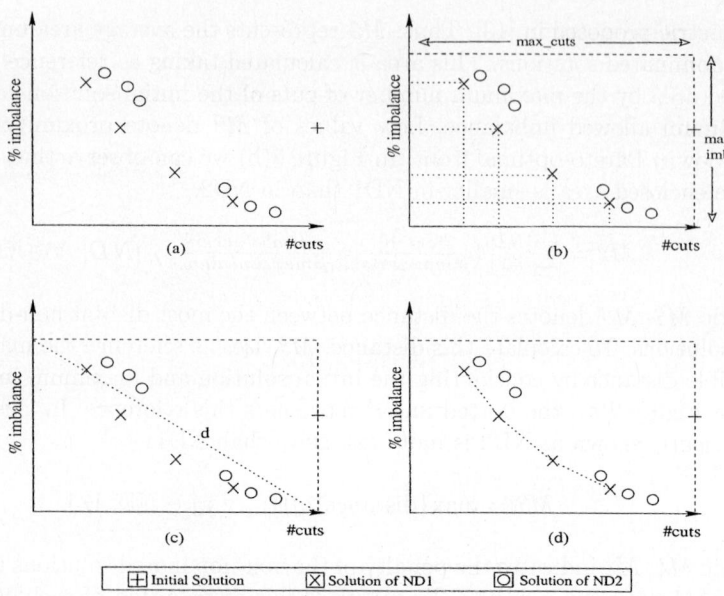

Fig. 2. Graphical explanation of the metrics used over two non-dominated sets

the ND (M2) is much smaller in eSMOSA than in SMOSA and PSA, which shows the good performance of eSMOSA. PSA obtains the maximum spread of the ND set (M3), although eSMOSA and SMOSA are very close. Finally, Metric M4 indicates that the dispersion of ND is very similar in all the cases, although in SMOSA it is a little better. Finally, in last column we can observe that SMOSA obtain the best runtimes. It is due to this version uses a single solution to perform the optimization process, reason why it is faster than the population-based MOMHs.

With the objective of clarifying these results, Figure 3 shows the ND sets obtained by all the MOMHs here compared, in the partitioning of *add20* into $K=16$ subgraphs. As we can see the non-dominated set obtained by eSMOSA has more solutions and has better solutions than the other MOMHs, reason why it obtains better results in M1 and M2 for this graph. The more spread non-dominated set is obtained by SMOSA, although PSA and eSMOSA also obtain a wide range of solutions in both objectives (M3, for this graph, is very similar in the tree MOMHs). Finally, we can observe as the non-dominated solutions obtained by PSA are better distributed than in eSMOSA and PSA.

In Figure 3 we have also included the partitions found by METIS [10], a public domain graph partitioning software, frequently used to compare single-objective graph partitioning algorithms. This package has two different implementations, *pMetis*, based on multilevel recursive bisection, and *kMetis*, based on a multilevel k-way partitioning. It is important to indicate the difficulty of this comparison, due to METIS implementations obtain a single-solution, while eSMOSA obtains

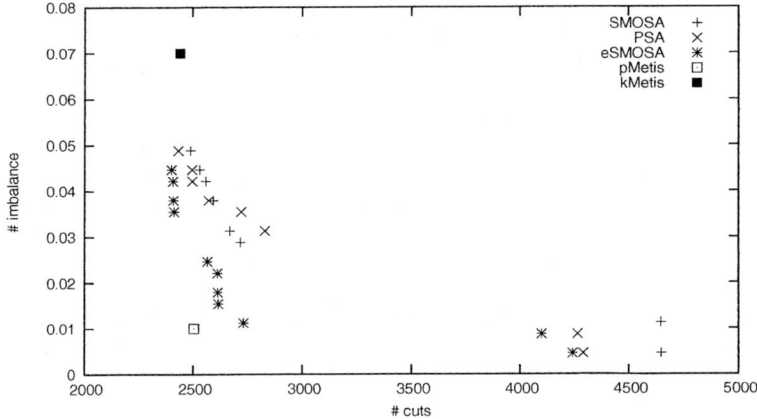

Fig. 3. Non-dominated sets obtained by SMOSA, PSA, eSMOSA, pMetis, and kMetis

a set of non-dominated solutions. As we can observe, results obtained are of high quality in comparison with METIS implementations, despite of eSMOSA solve the multi-objective case.

5 Conclusions and Future Work

In this paper, we have presented a new algorithm for multi-objective graph partitioning which uses a general purpose MOMH in combination with a powerful archiving technique. Results obtained for several test graphs indicate the good performance of this new algorithm in comparison with the adaptation to this problem of other MOMHs. In the future we plan to analyze the use of other MOMHs to solve this problem, including also different diversity preservation techniques. Other work area is the parallelization of the algorithm in order to improve the quality of the solutions, by using larger populations.

Acknowledges

This work was supported by the Spanish MCyT (project TIC2002-00228).

References

1. Teresco, J.D.: Hierarchical Partitioning and Dynamic Load Balancing for Scientific Computation. Tech. Report CS-04-04, Williams College, Dept. Comp. Science (2004)
2. Walshaw, C., Cross, M., Everett., M.G.: Mesh Partitioning and Load-Balancing for Distributed Memory Parallel Systems. In: Topping, B.H.V. (ed.): Parallel & Distributed Processing for Computational Mechanics: Systems and Tools 110–123

3. Gil, C., Ortega, J., Montoya, M.G.: Parallel VLSI Test in a Shared Memory Multiprocessors. Concurrency: Practice and Experience **12**(5) (2000) 311–326
4. Aleta, A., Codina, J.M., Sanchez, J., Gonzalez, A.: Graph-Partitioning Based Instruction Scheduling for Clustered Processors. In: Proc. of 34th Annual International Symposium on Microarchitecture. (2001) 150–159
5. Mobasher, B., Jain, N., Han, E.H., Srivastava J.: Web Mining: Pattern Discovery from World Wide Web Transactions. Tech. Report TR-96-050, Department of Computer Science, University of Minnesota, Minneapolis (1996)
6. Garey, M.R., Johnson, D.S: Computers and Intractability: A Guide to the Theory of NP-Completeness. W.H. Freeman & Company, San Francisco (1979)
7. Serafini P.: Simulated Annealing for Multi-objective Optimization Problems. In: Tzeng, G.H., Wen, U.P., Yu, P.L. (eds.): Multiple Criteria Decision Making: Expand and Enrich the Domains of Thinking and Application, Springer-Verlag (1993)
8. Zitzler, E., Laumanns, M., Thiele L.: SPEA2: Improving the Performance of the Strength Pareto Evolutionary Algorithm. Tech. Report 103, Computer Engineering and Communication Networks Lab (TIK), Zurich (2001)
9. Chamberlain, B.L.: Graph Partitioning Algorithms for Distributing Workloads of Parallel Computations. Tech. Report UW-CSE-98-10-03, Univ. of Washington (1998)
10. Karypis, G., Kumar, V.: METIS: A Software Package for Partitioning Unstructured Graphs, Partitioning Meshes, and Computing Fill-Reducing Orderings of Sparse Matrices. Version 4.0. Department of Computer Science Department, University of Minnesota (1998)
11. Walshaw, C.: JOSTLE–Graph Partitioning Software, http://staffweb.cms.gre.ac.uk/~c.walshaw/jostle/
12. Selvakkumaran, N., Karypis, G.: Multi-objective Hypergraph Partitioning Algorithms for Cut and Maximum Subdomain Degree Minimization. In: Proc. of International Conference on Computer Aided Design. (2003) 726–733
13. Rummler, A., Apetrei, A.: Graph Partitioning Revised–a Multiobjective Perspective. In: Proc. of 6th World MultiConference On Systemics, Cybernetics and Informatics. (2002)
14. Goldberg, D.E.: Genetic Algorithms in Search, Optimization and Machine Learning. Addison-Wesley Publisher (1989)
15. Zitzler, E., Thiele L.: Multiobjective Evolutionary Algorithms: A Comparative Case Study and the Strength Pareto Approach. IEEE Transactions on Evolutionary Computation **3**(4) (1999) 257–271
16. Kirkpatrick, S., Gelatt, C.D., Vecchi, M.P.: Optimization by Simulated Annealing. Science **220**(4598) (1983) 671–680
17. Metropolis, N., Rosenbluth, A., Rosenbluth, M., Teller, A., Teller, E.: Equation of State Calculations by Fast Computing Machines. Journal of Chemical Physics **21**(6) (1953) 1087–1092
18. Goehring, T., Saad, Y.: Heuristic Algorithms for Automatic Graph Partitioning. Tech. Report, Department of Computer Science, University of Minnesota (1995)
19. Graph Partitioning Archive, http://staffweb.cms.gre.ac.uk/c.walshaw/partition/
20. Czyzak, P., Jaszkiewicz, A.: Pareto Simulated Annealing–A Metaheuristic Technique For Multiple-Objective Combinatorial Optimization. Journal of Multi-Criteria Decision Analysis **7** (1998) 34–47
21. Baños R., Gil, C., Ortega, J., Montoya, F.G.: Multilevel Heuristic Algorithm for Graph Partitioning. In: Proc. 3rd European Workshop on Evolutionary Computation in Combinatorial Optimization. LNCS, Vol. 2611, Springer-Verlag (2003) 143–153

Par*k*way 2.0: A Parallel Multilevel Hypergraph Partitioning Tool

Aleksandar Trifunovic and William J. Knottenbelt

Department of Computing, Imperial College London
South Kensington Campus, London SW7 2AZ, UK
{at701,wjk}@doc.ic.ac.uk

Abstract. We recently proposed a coarse-grained parallel multilevel algorithm for the k-way hypergraph partitioning problem. This paper presents a formal analysis of the algorithm's scalability in terms of its isoefficiency function, describes its implementation in the Par*k*way 2.0 tool and provides a run-time and partition quality comparison with state-of-the-art serial hypergraph partitioners. The isoefficiency function (and thus scalability behaviour) of our algorithm is shown to be of a similar order as that for Kumar and Karypis' parallel multilevel graph partitioning algorithm. This good theoretical scalability is backed up by empirical results on hypergraphs taken from the VLSI and performance modelling application domains. Further, partition quality in terms of the k-1 metric is shown to be competitive with the best serial hypergraph partitioners and degrades only minimally as more processors are used.

1 Introduction

A hypergraph generalises a graph, such that hyperedges of a hypergraph connect arbitrary, non-empty, sets of vertices. Like graphs, hypergraphs can be used to represent the structure of sparse irregular problems such as data dependencies in distributed databases and component connectivity in VLSI circuits. Hypergraphs may also be partitioned such that a cut metric (a function of the interconnect in a partition) is minimised subject to a load balancing criterion. Hypergraph cut metrics provide a more accurate model than graph partitioning in many cases of practical interest such as the row-wise decomposition of a sparse matrix for parallel matrix–vector multiplication [4].

Algorithms for serial hypergraph partitioning have been studied extensively [9, 2, 14] and tool support exists (e.g. hMeTiS [13] and PaToH [4]). However, these are limited by the computing power and memory available on a single processor. Recently, we proposed the first parallel hypergraph partitioning algorithm [21]. However, while capacity was significantly improved, absolute run times and scalability were poor and partition quality was highly dependent on the structure of the input hypergraph. In [20] we proposed a new coarse-grained algorithm which improved processor utilisation and removed the structural dependency.

In this paper, we introduce an analytical performance model for the asymptotic run time complexity of the new parallel algorithm, derive its isoefficiency function and perform an empirical evaluation of the algorithm's implementation in the tool Parkway 2.0. We consider example hypergraphs from two application domains and compare the performance of Parkway 2.0 with that of two state-of-the-art serial partitioners in terms of run time and partition quality.

The remainder of this paper is organised as follows. Section 2 outlines serial multilevel hypergraph partitioning. Section 3 describes the parallel algorithm and its scalability analysis. Section 4 presents the experimental evaluation. Section 5 concludes and considers future work.

2 Serial Multilevel Hypergraph Partitioning

A hypergraph $H(V, E)$ is defined as follows. Let V be the set of vertices and E the set of hyperedges, where each hyperedge $e_i \in E$ is a non-empty subset of the vertex set V. The map $f_w : V \to \mathbf{Z}$ assigns an integer weight w_i to every vertex $v_i \in V$ and the map $f_c : E \to \mathbf{Z}$ assigns a cost c_i to each hyperedge $e_i \in E$. The *size* of a hyperedge is defined as its cardinality. The sum of the sizes of the hyperedges in a hypergraph, denoted here by m, is referred to as the number of *pins* in the hypergraph.

We formally define the k-way partitioning problem as follows. The goal is to find k disjoint subsets (or parts) V_i, $(i = 0, \ldots, k-1)$ of the vertex set V with corresponding part weights W_i (given by the sum of the constituent vertex weights), such that, given a prescribed balance criterion $0 < \epsilon < 1$,

$$W_i < (1 + \epsilon) W_{avg} \qquad (1)$$

holds $\forall i = 0, \ldots, k-1$ and an objective function over the hyperedges is minimized. Here W_{avg} denotes the average part weight. If the objective function is the *hyperedge cut* metric, then the partition cost (or cut-size) is given by the sum of the costs of hyperedges that span more than one part. Alternatively, when the objective function is the k-1 metric, the partition cost is given by

$$P_{cost} = \sum_{i=0}^{|E|-1} (\lambda_i - 1) c_i \qquad (2)$$

where λ_i is the number of parts spanned by hyperedge e_i. Computing the optimal bisection of a hypergraph under the hyperedge cut metric (and hence the k-1 metric since $k = 2$ for a bisection) is known to be NP-complete [10]. Thus, research has focused on developing polynomial-time heuristic algorithms resulting in good sub-optimal solutions. The k-way partition is typically computed either directly or by recursive bisection. As it scales well in terms of run time and solution quality with increasing problem size, the *multilevel* paradigm is preferred to solely *flat* approaches because the likelihood of flat heuristic algorithms converging to poor local minima rises significantly with increasing problem size. Flat heuristic algorithms such as spectral bisection and simulated annealing methods are reviewed in more detail in [2]. Note that flat approaches can also be used at the coarsest levels of the multilevel framework. The following subsections briefly describe the main phases of the multilevel paradigm.

2.1 The Coarsening Phase

The original hypergraph is approximated via a succession of smaller hypergraphs that maintain its structure as accurately as possible. A single coarsening step is performed by merging the vertices of the original hypergraph together to form vertices of the coarse hypergraph, denoted by a map $f_{merge} : V \to V_{coarse}$, where

$$\frac{|V|}{|V_{coarse}|} = r, r > 1 \qquad (3)$$

and r is the prescribed reduction ratio. The map f_{merge} is used to transform the hyperedges of the original hypergraph to the hyperedges of the coarse hypergraph. Single vertex hyperedges in the coarse hypergraph are discarded as they cannot contribute to the cut-size of a partition of the coarse hypergraph. When multiple hyperedges map onto the same hyperedge of the coarse hypergraph, only one of the hyperedges is retained, with its cost set to be the sum of the costs of the hyperedges that mapped onto it (thus preserving the cut-size properties of the original hypergraph). Coarsening algorithms are discussed in detail in both [2] and [12].

2.2 The Initial Partitioning Phase

The coarsest hypergraph is partitioned using a flat partitioning method such as an iterative improvement algorithm. As the coarsest hypergraph is significantly smaller than the original hypergraph, flat partitioning methods are computationally feasible and the time taken to compute the initial partition is usually considerably less than the time taken by the other phases of the multilevel pipeline. Since heuristic algorithms are typically used, the best solution out of a number of runs is chosen as the starting point for the uncoarsening phase.

2.3 The Uncoarsening Phase

The initial partition is propagated up through the successively finer hypergraphs and at each step the partition is further refined using heuristic refinement techniques. When the k-way partition is computed via recursive bisection, the refinement phase consists of bisection refinement, typically based on the Fiduccia-Mattheyses (FM) algorithm [9]. Conversely, when it is computed directly, the *greedy refinement* algorithm [14] has been shown to perform well, especially with increasing values of k. Both refinement algorithms typically converge within a few *passes*, during each of which each vertex is moved at most once. More sophisticated refinement algorithms have been developed, motivated by the idea of escaping from poor local minima [18, 6–8, 12, 3].

3 Parallel Algorithm and Performance Model

This section briefly reviews our parallel multilevel partitioning algorithm and then presents its analytical performance model. Since the algorithms that make up the multilevel pipeline are inherently serial in nature, we sought a coarse-grained formulation of the multilevel k-way partitioning algorithm [14]. This was chosen over the recursive bisection algorithm as the k-way refinement algorithm has better opportunities for concurrency than variants of the FM bisection refinement, where ways to perform the gain update calculations in parallel are not readily apparent.

Only the coarsening and refinement phases are parallelised since the coarsest hypergraph should be small enough for the initial partition to be rapidly computed serially. Multiple runs of the initial partitioning algorithm are carried out on the available processors in parallel with the best partition selected for further refinement. The initial partitioning phase commences when the coarsest hypergraph has approximately $100 \times k$ vertices.

3.1 Data Distribution

If p denotes the number of processors, we store the hypergraph across the processors by storing $|E|/p$ hyperedges and $|V|/p$ vertices on each processor. We assume that each processor initially stores a set of contiguous vertices (in terms of their indices), although a random initial allocation of vertices to processors can be supported via a reassignment of vertex indices. In addition, for each of these vertices the processor stores the index of the corresponding vertex in the coarse hypergraph and the part index of the vertex.

With each hyperedge we associate a b-bit hash-key, computed using a variant of the load balancing hash-function f_2 from [17]. It has the desirable property that $f_2(e) \bmod p$ is near-uniformly distributed, independent from the input hyperedge e. Consequently, to ensure an even spread of hyperedges across the processors, each hyperedge e resides on the processor given by $f_2(e) \bmod p$. To calculate the probability of collision, assume that f_2 distributes the keys independently and uniformly across the key space (i.e. that all $M = 2^b$ key values are equally likely) and let $C(N)$ be the number of hash-key collisions among N distinct hyperedges. Then,

$$\mathbb{P}(C(N) \geq 1) = 1 - \mathbb{P}(C(N) = 0) \tag{4}$$

$$= 1 - \frac{M!}{(M-N)! M^N} \tag{5}$$

$$\leq e^{\frac{-N^2}{2M}} \tag{6}$$

if $N^2 << M$, as shown in [17]. We have $b = 64$ and $N = |E|$. This ensures that the probability of collisions occurring is remote – for example, when $|E| = 10^8$, $\mathbb{P}(C(N) \geq 1) \leq 0.0003$ – and thus facilitates rapid hyperedge comparison.

At the beginning of every multilevel step, each processor assembles the set of hyperedges that are adjacent to its locally held vertices using an all-to-all personalised communication. A map from the local vertices to their adjacent hyperedges is then built. At the end of the multilevel step, the non-local assembled hyperedges are deleted together with the vertex-to-hyperedge map. Frontier hyperedges may be replicated on multiple processors, but only for the hypergraph used in the current multilevel step. Experience suggests that the memory overhead incurred by duplicating frontier hyperedges is modest (see Table 3).

3.2 Parallel Coarsening Phase

We parallelised the *First Choice* (FC) [14] serial coarsening algorithm. Briefly, the serial algorithm proceeds as follows. The vertices of the hypergraph are visited in a random order. For each vertex v_i, all vertices (both those already matched and those unmatched) that are connected via hyperedges incident on v_i are considered for matching with v_i. A connectedness metric is computed between pairs of vertices and the most strongly connected vertex to v_i is chosen for the matching, provided that the resulting cluster does not exceed a prescribed maximum weight. This condition is imposed to prevent a large imbalance in vertex weights in the coarsest hypergraph.

In parallel, each processor i traverses the local vertex set V_i in random order, computing the vertex matchings as prescribed by the FC algorithm. Each processor also maintains request sets to the $p-1$ remote processors. If the best match for a local vertex v becomes a vertex w stored on processor j, $i \neq j$, then the vertex v is placed into the request set $S_{i,j}$. If another local vertex subsequently chooses v or w as its best match then it is also added to the request set $S_{i,j}$. The local matching computation terminates when the ratio of the initial number of local vertices to the number of local coarse vertices exceeds a prescribed threshold (cf. Eq. 3). When computing the cardinality of the local coarse vertex set, we include the potential matches with vertices from other processors.

Each processor i then communicates its request sets to the other processors, including the weights of the vertices that are involved in the matching request. The processors concurrently decide to accept or reject matching requests from other processors. Denote by $M_{i,j}^w$ the set of vertices (possibly consisting of a single vertex) from the remote processor i that seeks to match with a local vertex w stored on processor j (thus, $S_{i,j} = \bigcup_x M_{i,j}^x$). Processor j considers these sets for each of its requested local vertices in turn, handling them as follows:

1. If w is unmatched, matched locally or already matched remotely, then a match with $M_{i,j}^w$ is granted to processor i if the weight of the combined cluster (including vertices already matched with w) does not exceed the maximum allowed coarse vertex weight.
2. If w has been sent to a processor l, $l \neq i$, as part of a request for another remote match, then processor j informs processor i that the match with $M_{i,j}^w$ has been rejected. This is necessary since granting this match may otherwise result in a coarse vertex that exceeds the maximum allowed coarse vertex weight, if the remote match of w with a vertex on processor l is granted. When informed of the rejection by processor j, processor i will locally match the set $M_{i,j}^w$ into a single coarse vertex.

In order to enable a match between two vertices on remote processors that make requests to each other, we communicate the request sets in two stages. In the first stage, processor i communicates request sets $S_{i,j}$ to processor j and receives replies to its requests from j if $i > j$, while in the second stage processor i communicates request sets $S_{i,j}$ to processor j and receives replies to its requests from j if $i < j$. Note that only the combined weight of the vertices in $M_{i,j}^w$ and the index of vertex w need to be communicated from processor i to processor j, further reducing the communication requirements. The sets $M_{i,j}^w$ are received as an array on processor j and are processed in random order.

The coarsening step is completed by contracting the hyperedges of the finer hypergraph onto the hyperedges of the coarse hypergraph. Each processor contracts the $|E|/p$ locally stored hyperedges. The matching vector values for vertices not stored locally are assembled using an all-to-all personalised communication. The removal of duplicate coarse hyperedges on remote processors and load balancing is done as follows. Processors communicate each hyperedge e and its cost to the destination processor given by $f_2(e) \bmod p$. Each processor retains distinct hyperedges, setting their cost to be the sum of the costs of their respective duplicates (if any). The parallel coarsening step concludes with a load-balancing communication of coarse vertices such that each processor has $|V_{coarse}|/p$ local vertices at the start of the subsequent coarsening step.

3.3 Parallel Uncoarsening Phase

Firstly, the partition of the coarse hypergraph is used to initialise the partition of the finer hypergraph. Processors scan the local vertex list of the finer hypergraph and if the part index value of the corresponding coarse vertex is not available, it is requested from the relevant processor. Our parallel refinement algorithm then proceeds in passes; however, instead of moving single vertices across a partition boundary as in the serial algorithm, the parallel algorithm moves sets of vertices. The processors traverse the local vertex set in random order and compute the best move for each vertex. The best moves resulting in positive gain are maintained in sets $U_{i,j}$, $i \neq j$, $i, j = 0, \ldots, k-1$, where i and j denote current and destination parts respectively. In order to prevent vertex thrashing, the refinement pass proceeds in two stages. During the first stage, only moves from parts of higher index to parts of lower index are permitted and vice versa during the second stage. Vertices moved during the first stage are locked with respect to their new part in order to prevent them moving back to their original part in the second stage of the current pass. The balance constraint on part weights (cf. Eq. 1) is maintained as follows. At the beginning of each of the two stages, the processors know the exact part weights and maintain the balance constraint during the local computation of the sets $U_{i,j}$. The associated weights and gains of all the non-empty sets $U_{i,j}$ are communicated to the root processor which then determines the actual partition balance that results from the moves of the vertices in the sets $U_{i,j}$. If the balance criterion is violated, the root processor determines which of the moves should be taken back to restore the balance and informs the processors containing the vertices to be moved back. Currently, this is implemented as a greedy scheme favouring taking back moves of sets with large weight and small gain. Finally, the root processor broadcasts the updated part weights before the processors proceed with the subsequent stage. As in the serial algorithm, the refinement procedure terminates when the overall gain of a pass is not positive. Note that vertices are not explicitly moved between processors; rather, their part index value is changed by the processor that stores the vertex.

3.4 Analytical Performance Model

Suppose that $|V| = n$ and $|E| = \Theta(n)$. Let h and d denote the average hyperedge size and the average vertex degree of the original hypergraph respectively. In our analysis, we assume that $h << n$, $d << n$ and that the numbers of vertices and hyperedges are respectively reduced by constant factors $1+v$ and $1+\omega$ ($\omega, v > 0$) at each coarsening step. We consider the computation and the communication requirements in turn, assuming $O(\log n)$ coarsening steps.

During each coarsening step, $O(dh)$ computation steps are performed for matching each vertex and $O(h \log h)$ computation steps in contracting each hyperedge. Once a coarse hyperedge is constructed, checking for local duplicate hyperedges is done using a hash table. It takes $O(h)$ steps to check for and resolve a possible collision if a duplicate key is found in the table. Thus, the computation requirement during each coarsening step is $O(n/p)$. At the initial partitioning phase, the hypergraph has size $O(k)$ and can be partitioned in $O(k^2)$ time. During each pass of a refinement step, we compute the vertex gains concurrently and then compute rebalancing moves on the root processor if required. In order to compute the gains for a vertex, we need to visit all the hyperedges incident on each vertex and determine the connectedness to the source and destination parts. These computations have complexity $O(n/p)$ per pass. The rebalancing computation has complexity $O(pk^2)$. As the number of passes during a refinement stage is a small constant, the overall asymptotic computational complexity is given by

$$T_{comp} = O(n/p) \left(\sum_{i=0}^{\log n} \frac{1}{(1+v)^i} + \sum_{i=0}^{\log n} \frac{1}{(1+\omega)^i} \right) + O(pk^2 \log n) \quad (7)$$

$$\leq O(n/p) \left(\sum_{i=0}^{\infty} \frac{1}{(1+v)^i} + \sum_{i=0}^{\infty} \frac{1}{(1+\omega)^i} \right) + O(pk^2 \log n) \quad (8)$$

$$\leq O(n/p) + O(pk^2 \log n) \quad (9)$$

In the following communication cost analysis, we assume the underlying parallel architecture to be a p-processor hypercube. During both the coarsening and refinement stages the hyperedges adjacent to the locally held vertices are assembled at each processor using an all-to-all personalised communication. The required matching vector entries during coarsening and the required entries of the partition vector during refinement are assembled in the same fashion. We will compute an average-case time for hyperedge communication. As each processor stores $O(n/p)$ vertices, it requires $O(n/p)$ adjacent hyperedges (since d is a small constant). Thus, each remote processor will on average contribute $O(n/p^2)$ of its hyperedges, resulting in message size of $O(n/p^2)$ in the all-to-all personalised communication. This is a reasonable assumption since the hash function scatters the hyperedges randomly across the processors with a near-uniform distribution. An all-to-all personalised communication with this message size can be performed in $O(n/p)$ time [11]. During coarsening, we also require the computation of prefix sums to determine the numbering of the vertices in the coarser hypergraph, which has complexity $O(\log p)$. During refinement, we require an additional broadcast of rebalancing moves and a reduction operation to compute the cut-size, which have complexities $O(k^2 \log p)$ and $O(\log p)$ respectively (since each processor may be required to take moves back in $O(k^2)$ directions). Arguing as for the overall computational complexity, we deduce that the overall asymptotic communication cost is

$$T_{comm} = O(n/p) + O(k^2 \log p \log n) \qquad (10)$$

Eliminating dominated terms from equations 9 and 10, the parallel run time of the multilevel partitioning algorithm is

$$T_p = O(n/p) + O(pk^2 \log n) \qquad (11)$$

As the complexity of the serial algorithm is $O(n)$, we deduce that the isoefficiency function is $W = O(k^2 p^2 (\log p + \log k))$. Thus, if the number of processors is doubled and the number of parts is kept constant, the input problem size must increase by a factor of just over 4 to maintain a given level of efficiency. This isoefficiency function is of the same order as that given in [15] for the parallel graph partitioning algorithm implemented in the ParMeTiS tool [16].

4 Experimental Results

4.1 Implementation and Test Environment

The three phases of our parallel multilevel k-way partitioning algorithm were implemented in C++ using the Message Passing interface (MPI) standard [19], thus forming the Par$k$way 2.0 tool. It is an optimised version of the first Par$k$way implementation [20]. Par$k$way 2.0 interfaces with the HMETIS_PartKway() routine from the hMeTiS [13] library for the initial partitioning phase when the coarsest hypergraph from the parallel coarsening phase has less than $100 \times k$ vertices. The best partition obtained by p serial runs of HMETIS_PartKway() in parallel is then passed to the parallel uncoarsening phase.

Base-case serial comparison was provided by the state-of-the-art hypergraph partitioning tools khMeTiS [13] and PaToH [5]. Like Par$k$way 2.0, khMeTiS is a direct k-way partitioner implementing the HMETIS_PartKway() routine and thus can be compared fairly with our tool. For comparison with the recursive bisection algorithm, PaToH was preferred to the recursive bisection variant hMeTiS [13] because it produced partitions of comparable quality at significantly faster run times.

Par*k*way 2.0: A Parallel Multilevel Hypergraph Partitioning Tool   797

Table 1. Characteristics of the test hypergraphs

Hypergraph	#vertices	#hyperedges	#pins	min	max	avg	variance
Voting 175	1 140 050	1 140 050	6 657 722	2	7	5.84	3.37
ibm 16	183 484	190 048	778 823	2	40	4.10	13.06
ibm 17	185 495	189 581	860 036	2	36	4.54	16.57
ibm 18	210 613	201 920	819 617	2	66	4.06	15.71

The architecture used in all the experiments consisted of a Beowulf Linux Cluster with 64 dual-processor nodes (although we only had access to a 32-processor partition due to configuration limitations and high machine utilisation). Each node has two Intel Xeon 2.0GHz processors and 2GB of RAM. The nodes are connected by a Myrinet network with a peak throughput of 250 MB/s.

4.2 Empirical Evaluation

We evaluated our parallel algorithm on hypergraphs from the domain of performance modelling and VLSI circuit design. **Voting 175** is the hypergraph representation of a transition matrix derived from a high-level semi-Markov model of a voting system with 175 voters. It has an almost lower-triangular structure typical of transition matrices from the domain of performance modelling [21, 17]. The three largest hypergraphs from the ISPD98 Circuit Benchmark Suite [1] (**ibm16–ibm18**) were also used in the evaluation. The main characteristics of the test hypergraphs are shown in Table 1, where **min** and **max** denote the minimum and maximum hyperedge length respectively while **avg** and **variance** denote the average and variance of hyperedge length. We sought partitions with a 5% imbalance according to Eq. 1. When computed by recursive bisection using the PaToH tool, this meant that the maximum imbalance factor on each bisection was set to $(1.05/k)^{1/\log_2 k} - 0.5$ in order to enforce the 5% balance criterion in the final partition. Since the k-1 metric was evaluated, we set the partitioning objective to SOED (sum of external degrees) in khMeTiS and HMETIS_PartKway() [14] while for PaToH we used settings for sparse matrices or VLSI hypergraphs as appropriate [5]. The V-Cycle feature was turned off for all experimental runs as it was observed to provide only a marginal increase in partition quality at a large run time cost. The coarsening reduction ratio from Eq. 3 was set to 2.0 in the Par*k*way 2.0 tool. The results were averaged over ten runs for each parameter configuration. Table 2 presents the results of our experiments. The parallel implementation achieves a ten-fold speedup over the fastest serial time on the larger Voting 175 hypergraph with 32 processors, as seen in Fig. 1. We observe absolute speedups over the PaToH base-case when four or more processors are used and a near-linear speedup trend as the number of processors increases. The latter supports the scalability behaviour predicted by our analytical performance model. On the VLSI hypergraphs, good speedups are harder to achieve because the communication overhead in the parallel algorithm is more significant given the small problem sizes. However, in general, absolute run times decrease as p increases. In terms of partition quality, we note that our parallel algorithm outperforms the serial partitioners on almost all the VLSI benchmark

Table 2. Partitioning results for four sample hypergraphs. Here p is the number of processors used and time is the average of ten serial/distributed run times

p	Tool	Partition Size					
		8		16		32	
	ibm16	time (s)	cut-size avg (best)	time (s)	cut-size avg (best)	time (s)	cut-size avg (best)
1	PaToH	8.20	10 036 (9 381)	9.67	15 565 (14 536)	10.77	22 906 (22 394)
1	khMeTiS	8.66	8 651 (7 696)	11.58	13 719 (13 214)	15.52	20 713 (20 216)
2	Parkway 2.0	10.17	8 472 (8 125)	12.23	13 882 (13 639)	17.52	21 605 (21 114)
4	Parkway 2.0	6.71	8 221 (7 931)	10.02	13 813 (13 305)	13.16	21 250 (20 979)
8	Parkway 2.0	4.96	8 357 (7 865)	7.70	13 615 (13 269)	13.50	20 961 (20 639)
16	Parkway 2.0	5.07	7 974 (7 713)	7.37	13 374 (13 245)	10.35	20 747 (20 388)
	ibm17	time (s)	cut-size avg (best)	time (s)	cut-size avg (best)	time (s)	cut-size avg (best)
1	PaToH	9.62	12 731 (11 715)	11.74	19 586 (18 774)	13.37	27 597 (26 959)
1	khMeTiS	11.02	13 181 (12 636)	14.99	19 797 (18 700)	20.57	28 476 (27 567)
2	Parkway 2.0	11.26	12 194 (11 767)	14.63	19 390 (19 059)	20.76	25 932 (25 448)
4	Parkway 2.0	7.40	12 173 (11 846)	11.71	18 669 (17 978)	15.82	26 164 (26 013)
8	Parkway 2.0	5.63	11 834 (11 489)	9.30	18 574 (18 188)	15.96	25 696 (25 453)
16	Parkway 2.0	6.11	11 477 (11 411)	8.88	18 661 (18 336)	13.20	25 649 (25 328)
	ibm18	time (s)	cut-size avg (best)	time (s)	cut-size avg (best)	time (s)	cut-size avg (best)
1	PaToH	8.76	12 169 (11 415)	10.34	17 340 (16 318)	11.79	23 252 (22 454)
1	khMeTiS	9.91	7 973 (7 465)	12.93	12 084 (11 190)	17.75	18 271 (17 510)
2	Parkway 2.0	11.15	8 440 (7 806)	13.64	13 544 (11 947)	20.05	18 307 (17 803)
4	Parkway 2.0	7.58	8 076 (7 677)	9.33	12 760 (12 213)	14.58	17 445 (17 078)
8	Parkway 2.0	5.36	8 376 (7 560)	7.90	11 806 (11 430)	10.99	17 845 (17 226)
16	Parkway 2.0	5.48	7 181 (6 837)	7.63	11 317 (11 096)	10.55	17 007 (16 858)
	Voting 175	time (s)	cut-size avg (best)	time (s)	cut-size avg (best)	time (s)	cut-size avg (best)
1	PaToH	41.40	22 863 (22 191)	54.30	46 496 (45 960)	67.13	93 045 (92 654)
1	khMeTiS	53.76	25 387 (24 600)	58.39	50 588 (49 246)	67.92	95 072 (94 352)
2	Parkway 2.0	66.30	26 227 (25 605)	74.60	52 876 (51 673)	90.57	97 715 (97 043)
4	Parkway 2.0	30.41	26 230 (25 785)	35.78	53 031 (52 313)	46.18	98 201 (97 819)
8	Parkway 2.0	14.66	26 406 (26 160)	17.37	53 207 (52 973)	30.81	97 534 (96 832)
16	Parkway 2.0	6.57	26 671 (26 548)	9.68	53 013 (52 160)	19.93	98 000 (97 078)
32	Parkway 2.0	4.10	26 570 (25 786)	5.55	53 411 (52 679)	11.18	98 082 (97 217)

Table 3. Maximum number of hypergraph pins on a processor after hyperedges adjacent to local vertices have been assembled

Hypergraph	Number of Processors					
	1	2	4	8	16	32
Voting 175	6 657 722	3 369 040	1 718 498	886 076	469 206	260 828
ibm 16	778 823	692 001	539 420	377 743	243 514	-
ibm 17	860 036	776 561	622 477	445 314	291 184	-
ibm 18	819 617	734 599	571 752	403 543	263 631	-

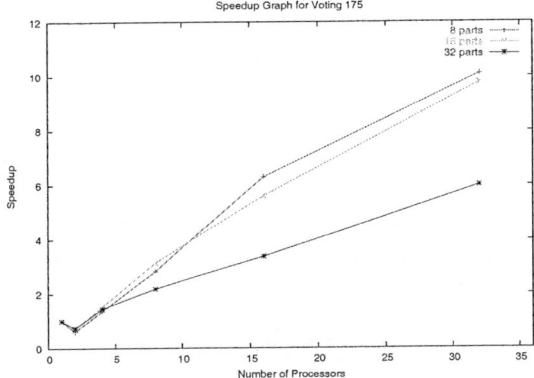

Fig. 1. Speedup results on Voting 175 hypergraph using PaToH as base-case

hypergraphs. This may be because Parkway 2.0 utilises all processors during the initial partitioning phase, enabling it to select the best quality partition from many more candidate runs than is possible on a single processor. In addition, this superior initial partition quality helps to maintain overall partition quality as the number of processors is increased. Hypergraphs arising from the performance modelling domain exhibit regularity and are more amenable to recursive bisection (divide and conquer) solution methods than the more irregular VLSI benchmark hypergraphs. This may explain the slightly higher partition quality achieved by PaToH over the direct k-way partitioners. We note that the partition quality of Parkway 2.0 is comparable to that produced by khMeTiS for the Voting 175 model. Finally, Table 3 shows the maximum number of hypergraph pins per processor after frontier hyperedges adjacent to local vertices have been assembled in the multilevel steps involving the original hypergraph.

5 Conclusion

This paper has presented an analytical performance model for our recently proposed parallel multilevel hypergraph partitioning algorithm. By deriving the isoefficiency function from the performance model we have shown that our algorithm is scalable in a technically correct sense. This has been empirically confirmed by running our parallel tool on hypergraphs taken from two different application domains.

In the future, we aim to apply our tool to an even wider range of application domains, for example bioinformatics and computational grids. We will also investigate parallel formulations of the recursive bisection algorithm.

References

1. Alpert, C.J.: The ISPD98 Circuit Benchmark Suite. In: Proc. International Symposium of Physical Design. (1998) 80–85
2. Alpert, C.J., Huang, J.H., Kahng, A.B.: Recent Directions in Netlist Partitioning. Integration, the VLSI Journal **19**(1–2) (1995) 1–81
3. Caldwell, A.E., Kahng, A.B., Markov, I.L.: Improved Algorithms for Hypergraph Bipartitioning. In: Proc. 2000 ACM/IEEE Conference on Asia South Pacific Design Automation. (2000) 661–666
4. Catalyurek. U.V., Aykanat. C.: Hypergraph-Partitioning-Based Decomposition for Parallel Sparse-Matrix Vector Multiplication. IEEE Transactions on Parallel and Distributed Systems **10**(7) (1999) 673–693
5. Catalyurek. U.V., Aykanat. C.: PaToH: Partitioning Tool for Hypergraphs, Version 3.0 (2001)
6. Dutt, S., Deng, W.: A Probability-based Approach to VLSI Circuit Partitioning. In: Proc. 33rd Annual Design Automation Conference. (1996) 100–105
7. Dutt, S., Deng, W.: VLSI Circuit Partitioning by Cluster-Removal Using Iterative Improvement Techniques. In: Proc. 1996 IEEE/ACM International Conference on Computer-Aided Design. (1996) 194–200
8. Dutt, S., Theny, H.: Partitioning Around Roadblocks: Tackling Constraints with Intermediate Relaxations. In: Proc. 1997 IEEE/ACM International Conference on Computer-Aided Design. (1997) 350–355
9. Fiduccia, C.M., Mattheyses, R.M.: A Linear Time Heuristic For Improving Network Partitions. In: Proc. 19th IEEE Design Automation Conference. (1982) 175–181
10. Garey, M.R., Johnson, D.S.: Computers and Intractability: A Guide to the Theory of NP-Completeness. W.H. Freeman and Co. (1979)
11. Grama, A., Gupta, A., Karypis, G., Kumar, V.: Introduction to Parallel Computing. 2nd edition. Addison-Wesley (2003)
12. Karypis, G.: Multilevel Hypergraph Partitioning. Technical Report, 02-25, University of Minnesota (2002)
13. Karypis, G., Kumar, V.: hMeTiS: A Hypergraph Partitioning Package, Version 1.5.3. University of Minnesota (1998)
14. Karypis, G., Kumar, V.: Multilevel k-way Hypergraph Partitioning. Technical Report, 98-036, University of Minnesota (1998)
15. Karypis, G., Kumar, V.: A Parallel Algorithm for Multilevel Graph Partitioning and Sparse Matrix Ordering. Journal of Parallel and Distributed Computing **48** (1998) 71–95
16. Karypis, G., Schloegel, K., Kumar, V.: ParMeTiS: Parallel Graph Partitioning and Sparse Matrix Ordering Library, Version 3.0. University of Minnesota (2002)
17. Knottenbelt, W.J.: Parallel Performance Analysis of Large Markov Models. PhD. Thesis, Imperial College, London, United Kingdom (2000)
18. Krishnamurthy, B.: An Improved min-cut Algorithm for Partitioning VLSI Networks. IEEE Transactions on Computers **33**(C) (1984) 438–446
19. Snir, M., Otto, S., Huss-Lederman, S., Walker, D., Dongarra, J.: MPI – The Complete Reference. 2nd edition. MIT Press, Cambridge, Massachussets (1998)
20. Trifunovic, A., Knottenbelt, W.J.: A Parallel Algorithm for Multilevel k-way Hypergraph Partitioning. In: Proc. 3rd International Symposium on Parallel and Distributed Computing, University College Cork, Ireland. (2004)
21. Trifunovic, A., Knottenbelt, W.J.: Towards a Parallel Disk-Based Algorithm for Multilevel k-way Hypergraph Partitioning. In: Proc. 5th Workshop on Parallel and Distributed Scientific and Engineering Computing, Santa Fe, NM, USA. (2004)

Data-Parallel Web Crawling Models*

Berkant Barla Cambazoglu, Ata Turk, and Cevdet Aykanat

Department of Computer Engineering, Bilkent University
06800, Ankara, Turkey
{berkant,atat,aykanat}@cs.bilkent.edu.tr

Abstract. The need to quickly locate, gather, and store the vast amount of material in the Web necessitates parallel computing. In this paper, we propose two models, based on multi-constraint graph-partitioning, for efficient data-parallel Web crawling. The models aim to balance the amount of data downloaded and stored by each processor as well as balancing the number of page requests made by the processors. The models also minimize the total volume of communication during the link exchange between the processors. To evaluate the performance of the models, experimental results are presented on a sample Web repository containing around 915,000 pages.

1 Introduction

During the last decade, an exponential increase has been observed in the amount of the textual material in the Web. Locating, fetching, and caching this constantly evolving content, in general, is known as the crawling problem. Currently, crawling the whole Web by means of sequential computing systems is infeasible due to the need for vast amounts of storage and high download rates. Furthermore, the recent trend in construction of cost-effective PC clusters makes the Web crawling problem an appropriate target for parallel computing.

In Web crawling, starting from some seed pages, new pages are located using the hyperlinks within the already discovered pages. In parallel crawling, each processor is responsible from downloading a subset of the pages. The processors can be coordinated in three different ways: *independent*, *master-slave*, and *data-parallel*. In the first approach, each processor independently traverses a portion of the Web and downloads a set of pages pointed by the links it discovered. Since some pages are fetched multiple times, in this approach, there is an overlap problem, and hence, both storage space and network bandwidth are wasted. In the second approach, each processor sends its links, extracted from the pages it downloaded, to a central coordinator. This coordinator, then assigns the collected URLs to the crawling processors. The weakness of this approach is that the coordinating processor becomes a bottleneck.

Our focus, in this work, is on the third approach. In this approach, pages are partitioned among the processors such that each processor is responsible from

---

* This work is partially supported by The Scientific and Technical Research Council of Turkey (TÜBİTAK) under project EEEAG-103E028.

fetching a non-overlapping subset of the pages. Since some pages downloaded by a processor may have links to the pages in other processors, these inter-processor links need to be communicated in order to obtain the maximum page coverage and to prevent the overlap of downloaded pages. In this approach, each processor freely exchanges its inter-processor links with the others.

The page-to-processor assignment can be hierarchical or hash-based. The hierarchical approach assigns pages to processors according to the domain of URLs. This approach suffers from the imbalance in processor workloads since some domains contain more pages than the others. In the hash-based approach, either single pages or sites as a whole are assigned to the processors. This approach solves the load balancing problem implicitly. However, in this approach, there is a significant communication overhead since inter-processor links, which must be communicated, are not considered while creating the page-to-processor assignment.

The page-to-processor assignment problem has been addressed by a number of authors. Cho and Garcia-Molina [3] used the site-hash-based assignment technique with the belief that it will reduce the number of inter-processor links when compared to the page-hash-based assignment technique. Boldi et al. [2] applied the consistent hashing technique, a method assigning more than one hash values for a site, in order to handle the failures among the crawling processors. Teng et al. [7] used a hierarchical, bin-packing-based page-to-processor assignment approach. In this work, we propose two models based on multi-constraint graph partitioning for load-balanced and communication-efficient parallel crawling.

The rest of the paper is organized as follows. In Section 2, the proposed parallel crawling models are presented. In Section 3, we provide some implementation details about our parallel Web crawler. In Section 4, experimental results are presented. Finally, we conclude in Section 5.

2 Web Graph Partitioning

2.1 Graph Partitioning Problem

An undirected graph $\mathcal{G} = (\mathcal{V}, \mathcal{E})$ [1] is defined as a set of vertices $\mathcal{V}$ and a set of edges $\mathcal{E}$. Every edge $e_{ij} \in \mathcal{E}$ connects a pair of distinct vertices v_i and v_j. Multiple weights $w_i^1, w_i^2, \ldots, w_i^M$ may be associated with a vertex $v_i \in \mathcal{V}$. A cost c_{ij} is assigned as the cost of an edge $e_{ij} \in \mathcal{E}$.

$\Pi = \{\mathcal{V}_1, \mathcal{V}_2, \ldots, \mathcal{V}_K\}$ is said to be a K-way partition of $\mathcal{G}$ if each part $\mathcal{V}_k$ is a nonempty subset of $\mathcal{V}$, parts are pairwise disjoint, and the union of the K parts is equal to $\mathcal{V}$. A partition Π is said to be balanced if each part $\mathcal{V}_k$ satisfies the balance criteria

$$W_k^m \leq W_{\text{avg}}^m (1 + \epsilon), \text{ for } k = 1, 2, \ldots, K \text{ and } m = 1, 2, \ldots, M. \quad (1)$$

In Eq. 1, each weight W_k^m of a part $\mathcal{V}_k$ is defined as the sum of the weights w_i^m of the vertices in that part. W_{avg}^m is the weight that each part should have in the case of perfect load balancing. ϵ is the maximum imbalance ratio allowed.

In a partition Π of $\mathcal{G}$, an edge is said to be cut if its pair of vertices fall into two different parts and uncut otherwise. The cutsize definition for representing the cost $\chi(\Pi)$ of a partition Π is

$$\chi(\Pi) = \sum_{e_{ij} \in \mathcal{E}} c_{ij} \ . \tag{2}$$

After these definitions, the K-way, multi-constraint graph partitioning problem [5, 6] can be stated as the problem of dividing a graph into two or more parts such that the cutsize is minimized (Eq. 2) while the balance criteria (Eq. 1) on the part weights is maintained. This problem is known to be NP-hard.

2.2 Page-Based Partitioning Model

A major assumption in our models is that the crawling system runs in sessions. Within a session, if a page is downloaded, it is not downloaded again, that is, each page can be downloaded just once in a session. The crawling system, after downloading enough number of pages, decides to start another download session and recrawls the Web. For efficient crawling, our models utilize the information (i.e., the Web graph) obtained in the previous crawling session and provide a better page-to-processor mapping for the following crawling session. We assume that between two consecutive sessions, there are no drastic changes in the Web graph (in terms of page sizes and the topology of the links).

We describe our parallel crawling models on the sample Web graph displayed in Figure 1. In this graph, which is assumed to be created in the previous crawling session, there are 7 sites. Each site contains several pages, which are represented by small squares. The directed lines between the squares represent the hyperlinks between the pages. There may be multi-links (e.g., (i_1, i_3)) and bidirectional links between the pages (e.g., (g_5, g_6)). In the figure, inter-site links are displayed as dashed lines. For simplicity, unit page sizes and URL lengths are assumed.

In our page-based partitioning model, we represent the link structure between the pages by a page graph $\mathcal{G}^\mathrm{p} = (\mathcal{V}^\mathrm{p}, \mathcal{E}^\mathrm{p})$. In this representation, each page p_i corresponds to a vertex v_i. There exists an undirected edge e_{ij} between vertices v_i and v_j if and only if page p_i has a link to page p_j or vice versa. Multi-links between the pages are collapsed into a single edge. Two weights w_i^1 and w_i^2 are associated with each vertex v_i. The weight w_i^1 of vertex v_i is equal to the size (in bytes) of page p_i, and represents the download and storage overhead for p_i. The weight w_i^2 of vertex v_i is equal to 1, and represents the overhead for requesting p_i. The cost c_{ij} of an edge $e_{ij} \in \mathcal{E}^\mathrm{p}$ is equal to the total string length of the links (p_i, p_j) and (p_j, p_i) (if any) between pages p_i and p_j. This cost corresponds to the volume of communication performed for exchanging the links between pages p_i and p_j in case p_i and p_j are mapped to different processors.

In a K-way partition $\Pi^\mathrm{p} = (\mathcal{V}_1^\mathrm{p}, \mathcal{V}_2^\mathrm{p}, \ldots, \mathcal{V}_K^\mathrm{p})$ of the page graph $\mathcal{G}^\mathrm{p}$, each vertex part $\mathcal{V}_k^\mathrm{p}$ corresponds to a subset $\mathcal{P}_k$ of pages to be downloaded by processor P_k. That is, every page $p_i \in \mathcal{P}_k$, represented by a vertex $v_i \in \mathcal{V}_k^\mathrm{p}$, is fetched and stored by processor P_k. In this model, maintaining the balance on part weights W_k^1 and

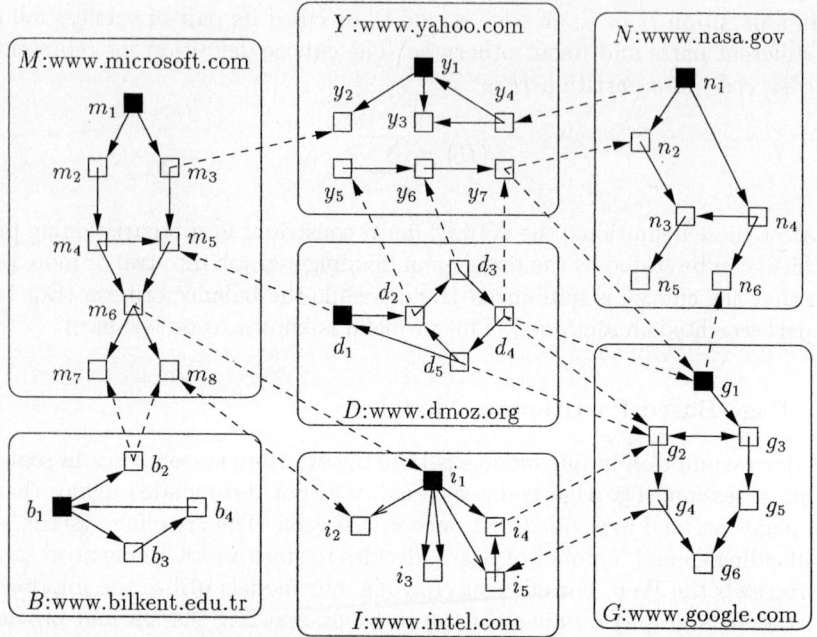

Fig. 1. An example to the graph structure in the Web

W_k^2 (Eq. 1) in partitioning the page graph $\mathcal{G}^{\mathrm{p}}$, effectively balances the download and storage overhead of processors as well as the number of page download requests issued by processors. Minimizing the cost $\chi(\Pi^{\mathrm{p}})$ (Eq. 2) corresponds to minimizing the total volume of inter-processor communication that will occur during the link exchange between processors.

Figure 2 shows a 3-way partition for the page graph corresponding to the sample Web graph in Figure 1. For simplicity, unit edge costs are not displayed. In this example, almost perfect load balance is obtained since weights (for both weight constraints) of the three vertex parts $\mathcal{V}_1^{\mathrm{p}}$, $\mathcal{V}_2^{\mathrm{p}}$, and $\mathcal{V}_3^{\mathrm{p}}$ are respectively 14, 13, and 14. Hence, according to this partitioning, each processor P_k, which is responsible from downloading all pages $p_i \in \mathcal{P}_k^{\mathrm{p}}$, is expected to fetch and store almost equal amounts of data in the next crawling session. In Figure 2, dotted lines represent the cut edges. These edges correspond to inter-processor links, which must be communicated. In our example, $\chi(\Pi^{\mathrm{p}}) = 8$, and hence, the total volume of link information that must be communicated is 8.

2.3 Site-Based Partitioning Model

Due to the enormous size of the Web, the constructed page graph may be huge, and hence it may be quite costly to partition it. For efficiency purposes, we also propose a site-based partitioning model, which considers sites instead of pages as the atomic tasks for assignment. We represent the link structure between

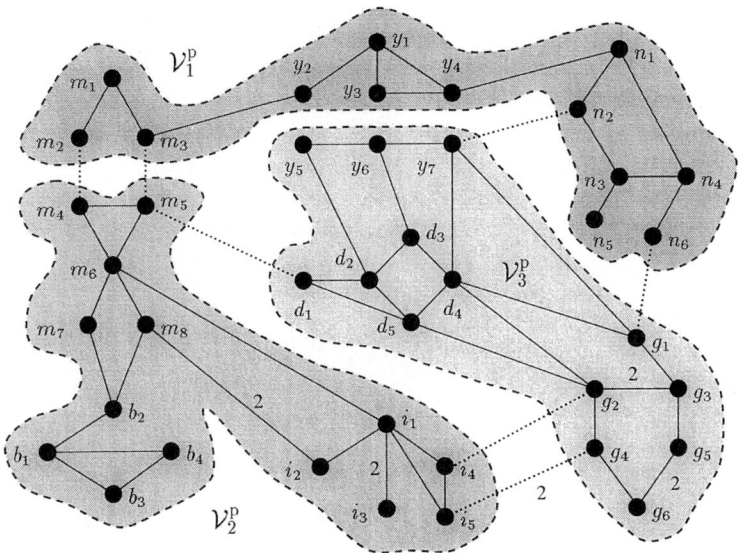

Fig. 2. A 3-way partition for the page graph of the sample Web graph in Figure 1

the pages by a site graph $\mathcal{G}^S = (\mathcal{V}^S, \mathcal{E}^S)$. All pages belonging to a site S_i are represented by a single vertex $v_i \in \mathcal{V}^S$. The weights w_i^1 and w_i^2 of each vertex v_i are respectively equal to the total size of the pages (in bytes) and the number of pages hosted by site S_i. There is an edge e_{ij} between two vertices v_i and v_j if and only if there is at least one link between any pages $p_x \in S_i$ and $p_y \in S_j$. The cost c_{ij} of an edge $e_{ij} \in \mathcal{E}^S$ is equal to the total string length of all links (p_x, p_y) and (p_y, p_x) between each pair of pages $p_x \in S_i$ and $p_y \in S_j$. All intra-site links, i.e., the links between the pages belonging to the same site, are ignored.

In a K-way partition $\Pi^S = (\mathcal{V}_1^S, \mathcal{V}_2^S, \ldots, \mathcal{V}_K^S)$ of graph $\mathcal{G}^S$, each vertex part $\mathcal{V}_k^S$ corresponds to a subset $\mathcal{S}_k$ of sites whose pages are to be downloaded by processor P_k. Balancing the part weights (Eq. 1) and minimizing the cost (Eq. 2) has the same effects with those in the page-based model.

Figure 3 shows a 2-way partition for the site graph corresponding to the sample Web graph in Figure 1. Vertex weights are displayed inside the circles, which represent the sites. Part weights are $W_1^1 = W_1^2 = 17$ and $W_2^1 = W_2^2 = 24$ for the two parts $\mathcal{V}_1^S$ and $\mathcal{V}_2^S$, respectively. The cut edges are displayed as dotted lines. The cut cost is $\chi(\Pi^P) = 1+1+3 = 5$. Hence, according to this partitioning, the total volume of communication for the next crawling session is expected to be 5.

3 Implementation Details

We developed a data-parallel crawling system, which utilizes the proposed models. The crawler is implemented in C using MPI libraries for message passing.

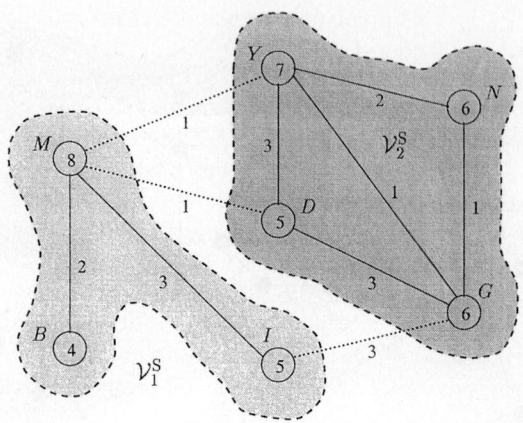

Fig. 3. A 2-way partition for the site graph of the sample Web graph in Figure 1

In our parallel crawling system, each crawling processor uses synchronous I/O and concurrently crawls the set of pages it is responsible from. Processors run several threads to fetch data from multiple servers simultaneously. Threads perform three different tasks: domain name resolution, page download, and URL extraction from downloaded pages. Intermediate data such as downloaded URLs, page-content hashes, and resolved DNS entries, which must be stored in memory, are kept in dynamic trie data structures. FIFO queues are used for coordinating the data flow between threads of a processor.

As explained in Section 2, the page-to-processor assignment is determined using page- or site-based partitioning models prior to the crawling process. The state-of-the-art graph partitioning tool MeTiS [4] is used for partitioning the constructed page and site graphs. The resulting part vectors are replicated at each processor. Whenever a URL which has not been crawled yet is discovered, the processor responsible from the URL is located by the part vector. If a newly found URL which is not listed in the part vector is discovered, the discovering processor becomes responsible from crawling that URL.

4 Experimental Results

In the experiments, the multi-constraint, multi-level k-way partitioning algorithm of MeTiS is used. The imbalance tolerance is set to 5% for both weight constraints. Due to the randomized nature of the algorithms, experiments are repeated 8 times, and the average values are reported. Results are provided for load imbalance values in storage and page request amounts of processors as well as the total volume of inter-processor communication in link exchange. We compared the proposed models with the hash-based assignment techniques. Experiments are conducted on the K values 8, 16, 24, 32, 40, 48, 56, and 64. As the test dataset, the sample (8 GB) Web collection provided by Google Inc. [8]

Table 1. The load imbalance values in storage amounts of processors

K	Page-based		Site-based	
	GP-based	Hash-based	GP-based	Hash-based
8	3.31	1.04	4.59	15.32
16	4.02	1.73	4.72	22.94
24	4.44	1.88	4.74	30.15
32	4.66	2.53	4.75	36.61
40	4.68	2.64	4.76	41.22
48	4.69	2.93	4.76	44.59
56	4.76	3.70	4.76	52.73
64	4.76	3.84	4.76	54.19

is used. This collection contains 913, 570 pages and 15, 820 sites. Average vertex degrees are respectively 4.9 and 10.5 for the page and site graphs created.

Table 1 displays the load imbalance values observed in storage amounts of processor for the graph-partitioning-based (GP-based) and hash-based techniques. Table 2 shows the imbalance values observed for the number of page download requests issued by processors. Experiments on page-based assignment show that the hash-based approach performs slightly better than our GP-based model in balancing both the storage overhead and the number of page download requests. In site-based assignment, the GP-based model outperforms the hash-based approach, whose imbalance rates deteriorate with increasing K values. This is basically due to the high variation in the sizes of the sites in the dataset used. Since solution space is more restricted in the site graph, the site-based GP model produces slightly inferior load imbalance rates compared to the page-based GP model.

Table 3 presents the total volume of link information that must be communicated among the processors for different techniques. As expected, an increasing

Table 2. The load imbalance values in page requests made by processors

K	Page-based		Site-based	
	GP-based	Hash-based	GP-based	Hash-based
8	3.44	0.78	4.57	3.84
16	4.01	1.15	4.75	6.17
24	4.50	1.40	4.75	7.03
32	4.68	1.56	4.75	8.89
40	4.74	1.66	4.76	10.78
48	4.74	1.95	4.76	12.16
56	4.76	2.09	4.76	13.49
64	4.76	2.34	4.76	13.73

Table 3. The total volume of communication (in bytes) during the link exchange

K	Page-based		Site-based	
	GP-based	Hash-based	GP-based	Hash-based
8	64,489	5,306,461	131,129	1,001,602
16	69,643	5,685,823	151,264	1,070,871
24	71,385	5,811,600	163,454	1,095,860
32	75,285	5,875,123	180,751	1,108,891
40	82,038	5,912,733	187,987	1,114,957
48	80,038	5,938,494	193,011	1,117,739
56	92,947	5,956,059	213,642	1,122,955
64	92,467	5,969,393	234,272	1,126,470

trend is observed in communication volumes as K increases. Site-based hashing results in around 5 times less communication than page-based hashing. This is due to the fact that many inter-processor links are eliminated since sites act as clusters of pages, and almost 4 out of 5 page links turn out to be an intra-processor link when site-based hashing is employed.

According to Table 3, the proposed GP-based models perform much better in minimizing the total communication volume. However, in contrast to the hash-based techniques, the site-based GP model causes an increase in the communication volume. This can be explained by the sparsity of our dataset and the simpler (relative to the page graph) site graph topology which causes a reduction in the solution space. Due to the sparsity of our dataset, there are many pages which do not link each other although they are associated with the same site. By working on the coarser site graph, the MeTiS graph partitioning tool fails to utilize the good edge cuts that cross across the sites (e.g., in Figure 2, pages y_1, y_2, y_3, and y_4 are mapped to $\mathcal{V}_1^p$ while y_5, y_6, and y_7 are mapped to $\mathcal{V}_3^p$). Consequently, the site-based GP model results in partitions with higher cut costs and hence communication volumes.

5 Conclusion

In this paper, we presented two models, based on multi-constraint graph partitioning, for data-parallel Web crawling. Compared to the hash-based assignment techniques, the proposed models produced similar load imbalance values for storage overheads and page download requests of processors while producing superior results in minimizing the total volume of communication in inter-processor link exchange. Currently, we are about to start a large crawl of the Web using the developed parallel Web crawler on a 48-node PC cluster. This will allow us to repeat the experiments presented in this paper on a larger collection of pages and verify the validity of our theoretical results in practice.

References

1. Berge, C.: Graphs and hypergraphs. North-Holland Publishing Company (1973)
2. Boldi, P., Codenotti, B., Santini, M., Vigna, S.: Ubicrawler: A scalable fully distributed Web crawler. In: Proceedings of AusWeb02, the Eighth Australian World Wide Web Conference. (2002)
3. Cho J., Garcia-Molina, H.: Parallel crawlers. In: Proceedings of the 11th World Wide Web conference (WWW11), Honolulu, Hawaii. (2002) 124–135
4. Karypis, G., Kumar, V.: MeTiS: A software package for partitioning unstructured graphs, partitioning meshes and computing fill-reducing orderings of sparse matrices. Technical Report, University of Minnesota (1998)
5. Karypis, G., Kumar, V.: Multilevel k-way partitioning scheme for irregular graphs. Journal of Parallel and Distributed Computing **48**(1) (1998) 96–129
6. Schloegel, K., Karypis, G., Kumar, V.: Parallel multilevel algorithms for multi-constraint graph partitioning. In: Proceedings of the 6th International Euro-Par Conference on Parallel Processing. (2000) 296–310
7. Teng, S., Lu, Q., Eichstaedt, M., Ford, D., Lehman, T.: Collaborative Web crawling: Information gathering/processing over Internet. In: 32nd Hawaii International Conference on System Sciences. (1999)
8. http://www.google.com/

Parallel Implementation of the Wave-Equation Finite-Difference Time-Domain Method Using the Message Passing Interface

Omar Ramadan[1], Oyku Akaydin[1],
Muhammed Salamah[1], and Abdullah Y. Oztoprak[2]

[1] Department of Computer Engineering
Eastern Mediterranean University, Gazimagusa, Mersin 10, Turkey
{omar.ramadan,oyku.akaydin,muhammed.salamah}@emu.edu.tr
[2] Department of Electrical and Electronic Engineering
Eastern Mediterranean University, Gazimagusa, Mersin 10, Turkey
abdullah.oztoprak@emu.edu.tr

Abstract. The parallel implementation of the Wave Equation Finite Difference Time Domain (WE-FDTD) method, using the Message Passing Interface system, is presented. The WE-FDTD computational domain is divided into subdomains using one-dimensional topology. Numerical simulations have been carried out for a line current source radiating in two-dimensional domains of different sizes and performed on a network of PCs interconnected with Ethernet. It has been observed that, for large computational domains, the parallel implementation of the WE-FDTD method provides a significant reduction in the computation time, when compared with the parallel implementation of the conventional FDTD algorithm.

1 Introduction

Nowadays, numerical methods play a major role in almost all branches of science and technology as they accelerate and facilitate research and industrial development. The Finite-Difference Time-Domain method (FDTD) [1] is one of the most widely used numerical time-domain techniques in electromagnetism, as it covers many applications [2], such as antennas, optics, high-speed electronic circuits, and semiconductors, etc. Furthermore, the FDTD method provides a wideband frequency response via a simple Fourier transform of the time domain solutions. The primary advantage of the FDTD method is that it is a straightforward solution of the six-coupled field components of the Maxwell's curl equations. This method, known as Yee's algorithm [1], computes the field components by discretizing the Maxwell's curl equations both in time and space, and then solving the discretized equations in a time marching sequence by alternatively calculating the electric and magnetic fields in the computational domain [1].

Recently, the FDTD method has been extended to solve the scalar Helmholtz wave equation in source-free domains [3]. Unlike the conventional FDTD approach, this new method, which is called the Wave Equation FDTD (WE-FDTD), allows computing any single field component without the necessity of computing other field components. Therefore, significant savings in the computational time and the memory storage can be achieved [3]. In addition, it has been shown that the WE-FDTD method is both mathematically and numerically equivalent to Yee's algorithm [3] in source free regions.

A major drawback of both the FDTD and the WE-FDTD schemes is that very large computational time and very large computer memory storage are required for analyzing large computational domains. Parallelizing these schemes is one way for overcoming these drawbacks. In order to do this, the computational domain is divided into subdomains, and each subdomain is processed by one processor. Recently, different techniques have been introduced for the parallel implementation of the conventional FDTD method [4], [5]. These techniques are based on the Single-Program-Multiple-Data (SPMD) architecture. In [4], a one-dimensional parallelism using the Parallel Virtual Machine (PVM) has been introduced. This approach is based on the TCP/IP protocol over the Ethernet for passing inter-processor messages. In [5], a new parallel FDTD algorithm based on the Message-Passing Interface (MPI) system has been introduced. This approach is becoming the new international standard for parallel programming and it is tending to replace the other parallel systems, such as the PVM [6], [7].

In this paper, the MPI is used in the parallel implementation of the WE-FDTD algorithm. The two-dimensional computational domain is divided into subdomains along one direction by using the one-dimensional topology introduced in [4]. Numerical simulations were carried out on a network of PCs interconnected with Ethernet and significant savings in the computational time were achieved.

The paper is organized as follows. In Section 2, the formulations of both the FDTD and the WE-FDTD algorithms are presented. In Section 3, the proposed parallelization techniques are described. Section 4 includes the results of several numerical tests which show the effectiveness of the proposed method. Finally, a summary and conclusions are included in Section 5.

2 Formulation

In a linear, homogeneous, isotropic lossless medium, the Maxwell's equations can be written as

$$\nabla \times \mathbf{H} = \varepsilon_0 \frac{\partial}{\partial t}\mathbf{E} \quad (1)$$

$$\nabla \times \mathbf{E} = -\mu_0 \frac{\partial}{\partial t}\mathbf{H}, \quad (2)$$

where $\mathbf{E}$ and $\mathbf{H}$ are the electric and the magnetic field vectors, respectively, ε_0 is the electric permittivity, and μ_0 is magnetic permeability of the medium. In the rectangular coordinate system, the above coupled curl equations can be decomposed into a system of six scalar differential equations in terms of the E_x, E_y, E_z, H_x, H_y, and H_z field components. For the sake of simplicity, a two dimensional transverse electromagnetic (TM) case is considered, where only the field components E_z, H_x, and H_y exist. In this case, (1) and (2) give the following:

$$\frac{\partial E_z}{\partial t} = \frac{1}{\varepsilon_0}\left(\frac{\partial H_y}{\partial x} - \frac{\partial H_x}{\partial y}\right) \tag{3}$$

$$\frac{\partial H_x}{\partial t} = -\frac{1}{\mu_0}\frac{\partial E_z}{\partial y} \tag{4}$$

$$\frac{\partial H_y}{\partial t} = \frac{1}{\mu_0}\frac{\partial E_z}{\partial x}. \tag{5}$$

By using the Yee's algorithm [1], the above equations can be discretized in space and time as

$$E_{z_{i,j}}^{n+1} = E_{z_{i,j}}^{n} + \frac{\Delta_t}{\varepsilon_0 \Delta}\left(H_{y_{i,j}}^{n+1/2} - H_{y_{i-1,j}}^{n+1/2} - H_{x_{i,j}}^{n+1/2} + H_{x_{i,j-1}}^{n+1/2}\right) \tag{6}$$

$$H_{x_{i,j}}^{n+1/2} = H_{x_{i,j}}^{n-1/2} - \frac{\Delta_t}{\mu_0 \Delta}\left(E_{z_{i,j+1}}^{n} - E_{z_{i,j}}^{n}\right) \tag{7}$$

$$H_{y_{i,j}}^{n+1/2} = H_{y_{i,j}}^{n-1/2} + \frac{\Delta_t}{\mu_0 \Delta}\left(E_{z_{i+1,j}}^{n} - E_{z_{i,j}}^{n}\right), \tag{8}$$

where Δ_t is the time step size and Δ is the space cell size in the x, and y directions, respectively. To reduce the computational requirements of the conventional FDTD algorithm described above, (3)-(5) can be combined in a source free two-dimensional domain [3] as

$$\frac{1}{c^2}\frac{\partial^2 E_z}{\partial t^2} = \frac{\partial^2 E_z}{\partial x^2} + \frac{\partial^2 E_z}{\partial y^2}, \tag{9}$$

where c is the speed of light in the domain medium. Equation (9) forms the basics of the WE-FDTD algorithm, which can be discretized as

$$E_{z_{i,j}}^{n+1} = 2E_{z_{i,j}}^{n} - E_{z_{i,j}}^{n-1} + \frac{c^2 \Delta_t^2}{\Delta^2}\left(E_{z_{i+1,j}}^{n} + E_{z_{i-1,j}}^{n} + E_{z_{i,j+1}}^{n} + E_{z_{i,j-1}}^{n} - 4E_{z_{i,j}}^{n}\right). \tag{10}$$

To truncate open region problems, Absorbing Boundary Conditions (ABCs) are needed. In this paper, Mur's first order ABCs are used [8]. As an example, the E_z field along the $x = 0$ boundary can be computed as

$$E_{z_{0,j}}^{n+1} = E_{z_{1,j}}^{n} + \frac{c\Delta_t - \Delta}{c\Delta_t + \Delta}\left(E_{z_{1,j}}^{n+1} - E_{z_{0,j}}^{n}\right). \tag{11}$$

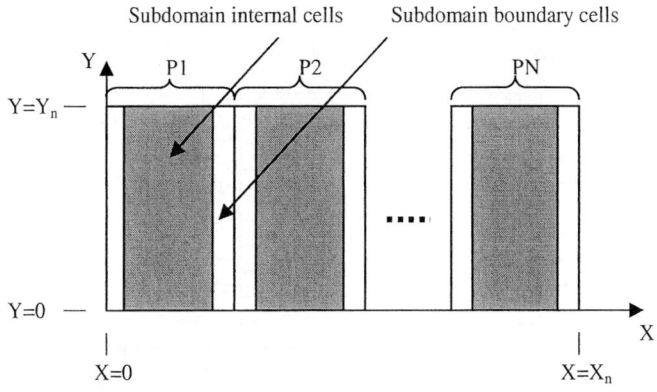

Fig. 1. Computational domain partitioning

3 Parallelizing the FDTD and the WE-FDTD Algorithms

In order to parallelize the FDTD and the WE-FDTD algorithms, the computational domain is divided into subdomains. Using the one-dimensional topology introduced in [4], the computational domain is divided into subdomains along the x−direction, where each subdomain is assigned to one processor, as shown in Figure 1. At the computational domain boundaries, i.e., $X = 0$, $X = X_n$, $Y = 0$ and $Y = Y_n$, the fields are computed by using ABCs [8]. At the internal cells of the subdomains, the fields are computed directly from (6)-(8) in the case of the FDTD method, and from (10) in the case of the WE-FDTD method. However, to calculate the fields at the subdomain boundaries, data from the neighboring subdomains are needed. In this paper, the MPI system is used to exchange data between processors. A complete detail of the MPI is provided in [6], [7].

Figure 2 shows the data to be exchanged between neighboring subdomains in order to parallelize the conventional FDTD method. As can be seen from Figure 2, to calculate the E_z using (6) at the cells located at the left boundary of a subdomain, the values of the H_y field from the subdomain on the left of the domain are needed. Similarly, this subdomain must send the values of H_y at cells located at the right boundary to the subdomain on its right. To calculate H_y using (8) at the cells located at the right boundary of the subdomain, the values of the E_z from the right subdomain are needed. Also, this subdomain should send the values of the E_z at the cells located at the left boundary to the left subdomain. Based on Figure 2, the parallel implementation of the FDTD algorithm can be summarized as:

1. MPI initialization.
2. Reading the simulation parameters.
3. Divide the computational domain into subdomains.

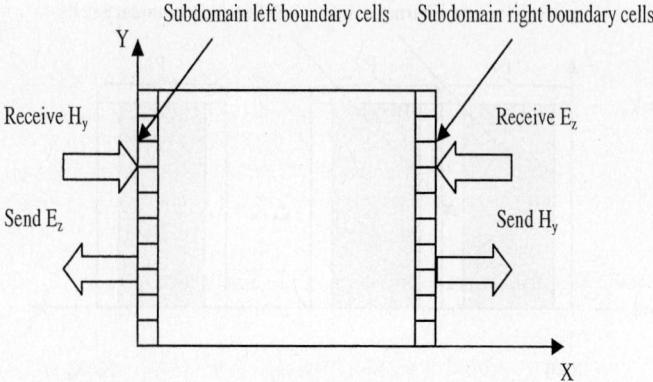

Fig. 2. Communications at the boundaries of a subdomain for the one-dimensional topology of the conventional FDTD method

4. At each time step:
   4.1 Calculate the H_y field component.
   4.2 Communicate the H_y field component at the subdomain boundaries.
   4.3 Calculate the E_z field component.
   4.4 Apply the ABCs at the computational domain boundaries.
   4.5 Communicate the E_z field component at the subdomain boundaries.
5. MPI finalization.

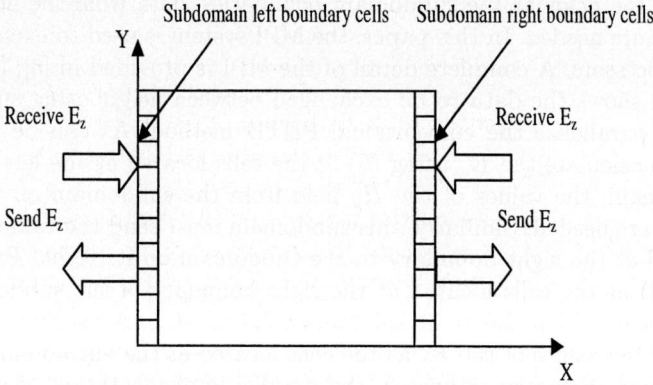

Fig. 3. Communications at the boundaries of a subdomain for the one-dimensional topology of the conventional WE-FDTD method

Similarly, Figure 3 shows the data to be exchanged between neighboring subdomains to implement the WE-FDTD algorithm described in (10). To calculate the E_z field component at the cells located at the left and the right boundaries of the subdomain, the values of E_z from the left and the right subdomains are needed. Similarly, this subdomain must also send the values of the E_z at the left and the right boundaries to the left and the right subdomains. Therefore, the steps for the parallel implementation of the WE-FDTD algorithm can be summarized as:

1. MPI initialization.
2. Reading the simulation parameters.
3. Divide the computational domain into subdomains.
4. At each time step:
   4.1 Calculate the E_z field component.
   4.2 Apply the ABCs at the computational domain boundaries.
   4.3 Communicate the E_z field component at the subdomain boundaries.
5. MPI finalization.

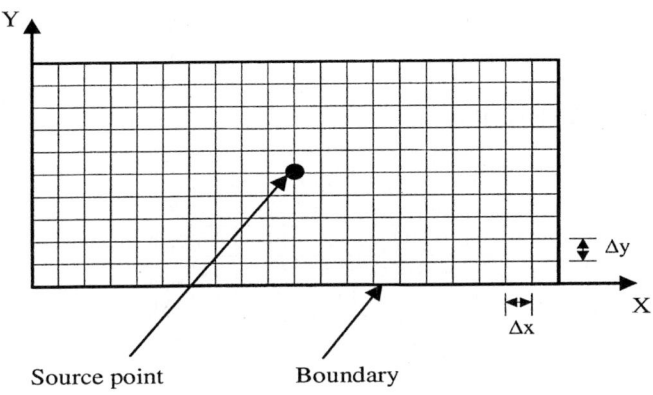

Fig. 4. Computational domain for the numerical study

4 Simulation Study

To demonstrate the performance of the proposed parallel algorithms, numerical simulations were carried out using a line current source at the center and perpendicular to the domain as shown in Figure 4. A line current source is a source which radiates equally in all directions in a two dimensional domain. The simulations were carried out for the Transverse Magnetic (TM) case [8]. The space cell size in the x and y directions was chosen as $\Delta = \Delta x = \Delta y = 0.015m$ [8]. The time step was $25ps$, and the simulation time was taken to be 500 time steps. The excitation used was a Gaussian pulse defined [8] as

$$E_{z_0,0}^n = \begin{cases} \alpha(10 - 15\cos\omega_1\xi + 6\cos\omega_2\xi - \cos\omega_3\xi) & \xi \leq \tau \\ 0 & \xi > \tau \end{cases}, \quad (12)$$

where $\alpha = \frac{1}{320}$, $\tau = 10^{-9}s$, $\xi = n\Delta t$, and $\omega_m = \frac{2\pi m}{\tau}$, $m = 1, 2, 3$. The tests were carried out for different number of processors and for different computational domain sizes, on a network of Celeron^{TM} 333 MHz PCs running with 64 MB of memory each. The PCs were interconnected with a 10 Mbit/s Ethernet. Tables 1 and 2 show the simulation time (in seconds) for the parallel FDTD and the parallel WE-FDTD algorithms obtained by using one, three, and five PCs for three different domain sizes.

Table 1. Simulation time for the parallel FDTD algorithm

Grid Size	Number of PCs		
(cells)	1 PCs	3 PCs	5 PCs
150 × 50	8.09 s	4.40 s	3.55 s
300 × 100	32.51 s	14.25 s	9.77 s
600 × 200	129.08 s	49.06 s	31.70 s

Table 2. Simulation time for the parallel WE-FDTD algorithm

Grid Size	Number of PCs		
(cells)	1 PCs	3 PCs	5 PCs
150 × 50	3.34 s	2.57 s	3.58 s
300 × 100	13.86 s	7.61 s	5.89 s
600 × 200	55.72 s	22.69 s	16.28 s

To measure the performance of the parallel algorithms, the speedup was calculated as

$$S(N) = T(1)/T(N), \qquad (13)$$

where $T(1)$ is the time needed to solve the problem using one PC and $T(N)$ is the time needed to solve the same problem using N PCs. Figures 5 and 6 show the speedup obtained with three and five PCs. For the purpose of comparison, the ideal speedup was also shown. From Figures 5 and 6, it can be observed that as the computational domain size increases, the efficiency of the parallel FDTD and the WE-FDTD algorithms increases. On the other hand, when the computational domains are partitioned for many processors, especially for the small domains, the efficiency of the parallelization will reach a limitation. This is because the communication time needed to perform the data exchange between the processors becomes larger than the computational time needed to update the field components. This explains the abnormal efficiency obtained with the parallel WE-FDTD algorithm for solving the 150 × 50 domain using five processors, as shown in Figure 6. This abnormal phenomenon is not as significant for the parallel FDTD algorithm. This is due to the fact that the computational

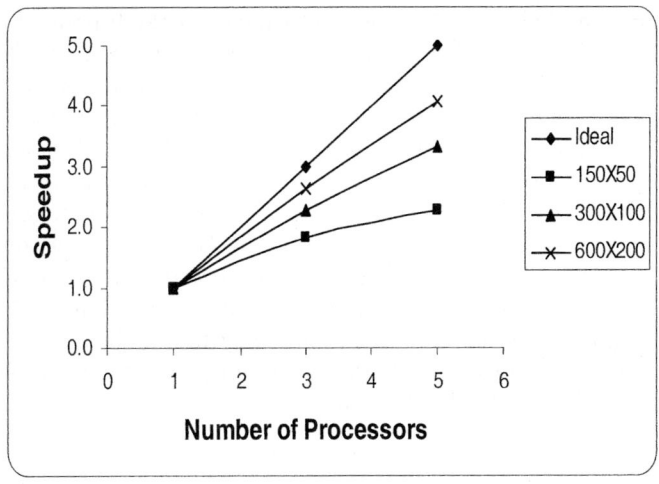

Fig. 5. Speed-up using the parallel FDTD algorithm

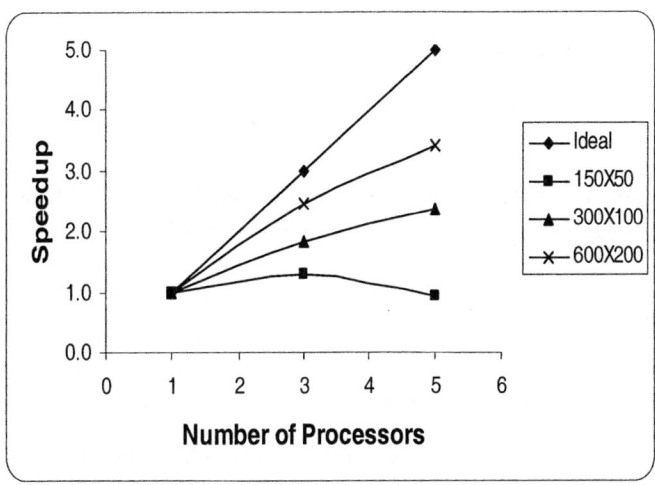

Fig. 6. Speed-up using the parallel WE-FDTD algorithm

time of the WE-FDTD method is much less than that of the FDTD algorithm as can be seen clearly from Tables 1 and 2.

5 Conclusion

In this paper, two parallel algorithms, based on the conventional FDTD and the new WE-FDTD algorithms have been implemented for solving the Maxwell's curl equations using the MPI system. The performance of these parallel algorithms has been studied by using a line current source radiating in a two-dimensional domain. It has been observed that the parallel implementations of these two methods provide a significant reduction in the simulation time as compared with the sequential solution. On the other hand, when partitioning the computational domains over many processors, especially for the small domains, the efficiency of the parallelization will reach a limitation. Finally, it has been observed that for large computational domains, the parallel WE-FDTD algorithm provides much more saving in the computational time compared with the parallel FDTD algorithm. The scheme can be generalized to two dimensional mesh of processors in the same manner. Finally, the new parallel algorithm can be improved by using better boundary conditions to truncate the computational domains such as the Perfectly Matched Layer (PML) [9], [10].

References

1. Yee, K.S.: Numerical solution of initial boundary value problems involving Maxwell's equations in isotropic media. IEEE Transaction on Antennas and Propagation **14** (1966) 302–307
2. Taflove, A.: Computational electrodynamics: The finite-difference time-domain method. Artech House, Boston, London (1995)
3. Aoyagi, P.H., Lee, J.-F., Mittra, R.: A hybrid Yee algorithm/scalar-wave equation approach. IEEE Transaction Microwave Theory and Techniques **41** (1993) 1593–1600
4. Varadarajan, V., Mittra, R.: Finite-difference time domain (FDTD) analysis using distributed computing. IEEE Microwave and Guided Wave Letters **4** (1994) 144–145
5. Guiffaut, C., Mahdjoubi, K.: A parallel FDTD algorithm using the MPI library. IEEE Antennas and Propagation Magazine **43** (2001) 94–103
6. Gropp, W., Lusk, E., Skjellum, A.: Using MPI: Portable parallel programming with the message-passing interface. MIT Press, Cambridge, Mass. (1994)
7. Pacheco, P.S.: Parallel programming with MPI. Morgan Kaufmann Publishers, San Francisco (1997)
8. Tirkas, P.A., Balanis, C.A., Renaut, R.A.: Higher order absorbing boundary conditions for the finite-difference time-domain method. IEEE Transaction on Antennas and Propagation **40** (1992) 1215–1222
9. Berenger, J.P.: A perfectly matched layer for the absorption of electromagnetic waves. Journal of Computational Physics **114** (1994) 185–200
10. Ramadan, O., Oztoprak, A.Y.: An efficient implementation of the PML for truncating FDTD domains. Microwave and Optical Technology Letters **36** (2003) 55–60

A Parallel Genetic Algorithm/Heuristic Based Hybrid Technique for Routing and Wavelength Assignment in WDM Networks

A. Cagatay Talay

Department of Computer Engineering, Istanbul Technical University
34469 Istanbul, Turkey
talay@cs.itu.edu.tr

Abstract. The routing and wavelength assignment problem which is known to be NP-hard, in all-optical transport networks is considered. The present literature on this topic contains a lot of heuristics. These heuristics, however, have limited applicability because they have a number of fundamental problems including high time complexity, and lack of scalability with respect to optimal solutions. We propose a parallel hybrid genetic algorithm/heuristic based algorithm. Parallel genetic algorithms represent a new kind of meta-heuristics of higher efficiency and efficacy thanks to their structured population and parallel execution. The hybrid algorithm presented uses an object-oriented representation of networks, and incorporates four operators: semi-adaptive path mutation, single-point crossover, reroute, and shift-out. Experimental results of the test networks make clear that, when the network cost depends on heavily wavelength assignment, the proposed parallel GA/Heuristic hybrid approach provides promising results.

1 Introduction

Recently, there has been considerable progress in the area of all-optical networks, in particular the networks based on wavelength division multiplexing (WDM). WDM technology has been shown to provide cost-effective transmission and switching. WDM based all optical networks offering multi-gigabit rate per wavelength may soon become economical as the underlying backbone in wide area networks.

When individual static traffic requirements are supposed to be routed independently on a single wavelength end-to-end, one aspect of the optical-path-layer design of all-optical transport networks is to determine the route, fibers, and wavelength each connection will use. This problem and its variants have attracted considerable interest, with a variety of solution approaches including heuristics, genetic algorithms (GAs), and integer linear programming (ILP) technique. Those heuristic algorithms have restricted applicability in a practical environment because they have a number of fundamental problems including high time complexity, lack of robustness and no performance guarantee with respect to the optimal solutions.

Our Parallel GA/Heuristic approach is to incorporate some advanced heuristics into an overall parallel genetic algorithm. It adopts a problem-specific encoding based on object-oriented manner, and then employs problem-specific operators that together combine the best existing heuristics for the problem with an overall parallel GA framework.

The paper is organized as follows: Section 2 contains introductory material about genetic algorithms. Section 3 summarizes the problem considered. Section 4 gives the detailed information about the GA/heuristic technique proposed here. Section 5 presents the simulation environment and results obtained. Finally, Section 6 concludes the paper.

2 Genetic Algorithms

A sequential GA (Fig. 1) proceeds in an iterative manner by generating new populations of strings from the old ones. Every string is the encoded (binary, real, ...) version of a tentative solution. An evaluation function associates a fitness measure to every string indicating its suitability to the problem. The algorithm applies stochastic operators such as selection, crossover, and mutation on an initially random population in order to compute a whole generation of new strings. Unlike most other optimization techniques, GAs maintain a population of tentative solutions that are competitively manipulated by applying some variation operators to find a global optimum. For nontrivial problems this process might require high computational resources (large memory and search times, for example), and thus a variety of algorithmic issues are being studied to design efficient GAs. With this goal, numerous advances are continuously being achieved by designing new operators, hybrid algorithms, termination criteria, and more [1]. We adopt one such improvement consisting in using parallel GAs (PGAs) and incorporating some advanced heuristics into an overall genetic algorithm.

```
Initialize population      //with randomly generated solutions
Repeat i=1,2,…             //reproductive loop
    Evaluate solutions in the population
    Perform competitive selection
    Apply variation operators
Until convergence criterion satisfied
```

Fig. 1. Pseudo-code of a sequential genetic algorithm

PGAs are not just parallel versions of sequential genetic algorithms. In fact, they reach the ideal goal of having a parallel algorithm whose behavior is better than the sum of the separate behaviors of its component sub-algorithms, and this is why we directly focus on them.

Several arguments justify our work. First of all, PGAs are naturally prone to parallelism since the operations on the representations are relatively independent from each other. Besides that, the whole population can be geographically structured [2,3] to localize competitive selection between subsets, often leading to better algorithms. The evidences of a higher efficiency [4,6], larger diversity maintenance [6], additional availability of memory and CPU, and multisolution capabilities [7] reinforce the importance of the research advances in the field of PGAs.

Using PGAs often leads to superior numerical performance (not only to faster algorithms) even when the algorithms run on a single processor [4,8]. However, the truly interesting observation is that the use of a structured population, either in the form of a set of islands [9] or a diffusion grid [3], is responsible for such numerical benefits. As a consequence, many authors do not use a parallel machine at all to run structured-population models and still get better results than with serial GAs [4,10,11]. Hardware parallelization is an additional way of speeding up the execution of the algorithm, and it can be attained in many ways on a given structured-population GA. Hence, once a structured-population model is defined, it could be implemented in any uniprocessor or parallel machine. There exist many examples of this modern vision of PGAs, namely, a ring of panmictic GAs on a MIMD computer, a grid of individuals on uniprocessor/MIMD/SIMD computers, and many hybrids.

A PGA has the same advantages as a serial GA, consisting of using representations of the problem parameters (and not the parameters themselves), robustness, easy customization for a new problem, and multiple-solution capabilities. These are the characteristics that led GAs and other EAs to be worth of study and use. In addition, a PGA is usually faster, less prone to finding only sub-optimal solutions, and able to cooperate with other search techniques in parallel. For an overview of the applications of PGAs, see [5,10,12,13]. Also, there is a lot of evidence of the higher efficacy and efficiency of PGAs over traditional sequential GAs (e.g., [13–15]).

2.1 Algorithmic Description of a PGA

In this section, we formalize and visualize the different types of PGAs from a unifying point of view. The outline of a general PGA is shown in Fig. 2. As a stochastic technique, we can distinguish three major steps, namely, *initial sampling*, *optimization*, and checking the *stopping criterion*.

Therefore, it begins ($t=0$) by randomly creating a population $P(t=0)$ of μ structures, each one encoding the p problem variables on some alphabet. An evaluation function Φ is needed each time a new structure is generated in the algorithm. This evaluation is used to associate a real value to the (decoded) structure indicating its quality as a solution to the problem. Some selected structure encodes tentative solutions to complex systems in a single genetic individual. This individual is used to simulate this complex system every time an evaluation is requested by the algorithm. Consequently, it can be inferred that considerable time is spent when complex and real-life applications are being tackled with GAs, thus supporting our claims about the need of using PGAs as more efficient search methods.

Afterward, the GA iteratively applies some set of variation operators on some selected structures from the current population. The goal is to create a new pool of λ tentative solutions and evaluate them to yield $P(t+1)$ from $P(t)$. This generates a sequence of populations $P(0), P(1), P(2), \ldots$ with increasingly fitter structures. The stopping criterion ι is to fulfill some condition like reaching a given number of function evaluations, finding an optimum (if known), or detecting stagnation in the algorithm after a given number of generations. The selection $S_{\Theta s}$ uses the relationship among the fitness of the structures to create a mating pool. Some parameters Θ_s might be required depending on the kind of selection. Typical variation operators are crossover ($\otimes$ binary operator) and mutation (m, unary operator). Crossover recombines two parents by exchanging string slices to yield two new offspring, while mutation randomly alters the contents of these new structures. They both are stochastic operators whose behavior is governed by a set of parameters like a probability of application: $\Theta_c = \{\rho_c\}$ -high- and $\Theta_m = \{\rho_m\}$ -low-.

```
t=0;
initialize:      P(0) = {ā₁(0),...,āμ(0)} ∈ I^μ;
evaluate:        P(0) = {Φ(ā₁(0)),...,Φ(āμ(0))}
while ι(P(t)) ≠ true do    //reproductive plan
    select:      P'(t) = s_Θₛ (P(t));
    recombine:   P''(t) = ⊗_Θc (P'(t));
    mutate:      P'''(t) = m_Θm (P''(t));
    evaluate:    P'''(t) : {Φ(ā₁'''(0)),...,Φ(āλ'''(0))};
    replace:     P(t+1) = r_Θr (P'''(t) ∪ Q);
    <communication>
    t=t+1;
end while
```

Fig. 2. Pseudo-code of a parallel genetic algorithm

Finally, each iteration ends by selecting the μ new individuals that will comprise the new population. For this purpose, the temporary pool $P'''(t)$ plus a set Q are considered. Q might be empty ($Q=\emptyset$) or contain part or all of the old population $Q=P(t)$. This step applies a replacement policy r that uses the temporary pool (and optionally the old pool) to compute the new population of μ individuals. The best structure in one population usually deterministically survives in the next generation, giving rise to the so-called elitist evolution (or R-elitism if $R>1$ -more than one string survives-). The best structure ever found is used as the PGA solution.

3 Problem Formulation

A unique feature of optical WDM networks is the tight coupling between routing and wavelength selection. A lightpath (Lightpaths, are clear optical paths between two edge nodes) is implemented by selecting a path of physical links between the source and destination edge nodes, and reserving a particular wavelength on each of these links for the lightpath. Thus, in establishing an optical connection we must deal with both routing and wavelength assignment. The resulting problem is referred to as the routing and wavelength assignment (RWA) problem [16], and is significantly more difficult than the routing problem in electronic networks. The problem of wavelength assignment and routing is proved to be NP-hard. Many researchers [17-21] have considered a low network wavelength requirement (NWR) as a design objective due to the technological limitations, and resulting cost implications, of carrying more than a small number of wavelengths over national or even international distances. However, an objective that consists of a simplified assessment of the cost of the

whole network including, at an appropriate level the cost of exceeding the minimum NWR, is arguably superior.
The original version of the cost model used in this study can be found in [21].

4 Hybrid Algorithm

The GA/heuristic hybrid algorithm described here represents networks as objects, composed not only of nodes, links and ordered sequences of paths, but also objects representing the network's adjacency matrix, connection matrix and the traffic requirements. Further more, networks include additional objects to represent the cable, fiber and wavelength-routed structure of an optical network. Consequently, the approach used in this paper, rather than using a binary representation, network objects are themselves the structures undergoing adaptation, a highly structured and very problem-specific representation that requires no decoding or interpretation.

Similarly, the PGA is also implemented using object technology, with a population of individuals (each simply consist of a single network object and some additional accounting information) and an operator pool of operators. As, in Davis [22], the probabilities of individual operators being applied to an individual adapt through the course of a run using a credit assignment algorithm (Fig. 3), rather than being chosen with a fixed probability throughput. Whenever an individual is created whose fitness exceeds that of the best individual up to the end of the previous generation, the improvement in fitness is credited to the responsible operator. In addition, a decreasing fraction of the credit is awarded to the parent operator and grandparent operator, to ensure that two and three operator sequences are rewarded appropriately. After a few generations, a small proportion of the operator probabilities are reassigned according to the average credit earned per child each operator has generated. In addition, operators are given a minimum probability to ensure they do not lose the opportunity to gain some credit if they, having decayed to the minimum level, are later found to be useful to further evolve the population.

A variety of operators have been incorporated PGA: Wavelength-allocation path mutation (WM), wavelength-allocation single-point crossover (WCO), wavelength-allocation path reroute operator (WRR) and wavelength-allocation path shift-out operator (WSO). For a random requirement, path mutation simply reroutes on a randomly chosen k-shortest path, using the lowest available wavelength on the path. Path single-point crossover operates on two networks. The first is modified such that up to a randomly selected individual requirement (considered in order of their end node ids), all the paths remain unchanged, but from then on the paths used are those in the second network, except that the lowest wavelength actually available is used in each case. (However, if any requirement was unsatisfied in the second network, then a random k-shortest path is used instead.) The second network undergoes the complementary recombination. The path reroute operator locates the first path in the network which has the highest wavelength number (found by searching the cables in order of their end node ids), and attempts to reroute it on a lower wavelength number using one of the k-shortest paths (where k is an operator parameter, and the shortest path selected if there is more than one at the lowest available wavelength number). It is based on Step 2a in Wauters and Demeester's HRWA algorithm [23]. The path shift-out operator locates the first path in the network, which has the highest wavelength number, attempts to shift it to a lower wavelength number by shifting out (rerouting) all the paths blocking that particular wavelength number. The wavelength chosen is the one that results in the smallest increase in overall path length, given the constraint that all rerouting must be to lower wavelength numbers than the original wavelength of the path being shifted down. It is based on Step 2b in Wauters and Demeester's HRWA algorithm [23].

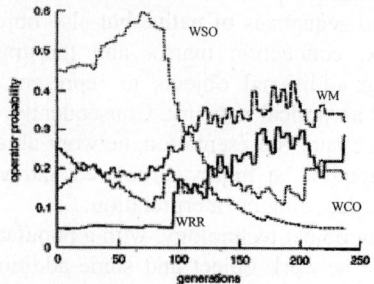

Fig. 3. Operator probability adaptation

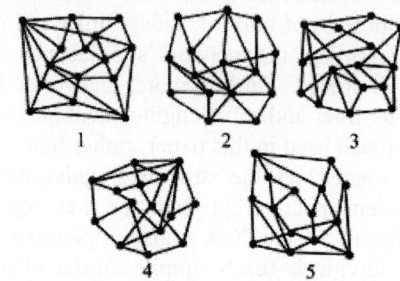

Fig. 4. Test network topologies

5 Experimental Results

The PGA/heuristic hybrid technique was implemented on a MIMD computer, the Parsytec CC system with 24 nodes. The proposed technique outperforms the other approaches with an efficiency of 92%. The results show that the fitness value increases quicker and more regularly by using our proposed technique. The results obtained from the PGA/heuristic hybrid approach are compared with a generational sequential GA and three of the recent wavelength allocation algorithms: Wuttisittikulkij and O'Mahony's heuristic [19] (W&O), Wauters and Demeester's [23] modified Dijkstra based heuristic (W&D), and their HRWA heuristic (W&D2). Five test network topologies adopted from [25] are employed in experiments. The initial node locations and traffic requirements for the networks (Fig. 4) are generated using the approach described by Griffith et al. [25], after being modified to ensure reasonable node separations. Each network with 15 nodes, covers a 1000km×1000km area and carries an overall traffic of 1500Gbit/s. The proposed parallel hybrid method generates the best results over the other compared algorithms. The simulations for the PGA/heuristic hybrid method have a population size of 500 networks. A maximum of 10000 generations, and tournament selection of size 4 are used. The operators' initial probabilities are 0.05 for WM, 0.25 for WCO, 0.15 for WRR, and 0.45 for WSO. The probabilities are selected after a few trial runs, aiming that would remain approximately constant for 50 or so generation. It could be argued that such starting values best promote high-quality solutions by approximately matching operator probabilities according to their effectiveness.

Each hybrid is run ten times with different initial random seeds. Simulations are repeated with different α and β values as shown in Tables 1-6. In addition, SGA,

W&O, W&D1 and W&D2 are also run for the test networks for each setting of α, β and γ and the best result is considered. When necessary in heuristics k value is taken as 8. The results are given in Tables 1-6, with the lowest cost in each table for a given network shown in bold. All values are in terms of 10^6. For all network topologies, the lowest cost values are obtained by the proposed parallel hybrid algorithm.

Table 1. Network cost for $\alpha=\beta=1$ and $\gamma=0.5$

Net.	SGA	W&O	W&D1	W&D2	Hybrid
1	4.57	5.90	6.01	6.36	**4.43**
2	3.88	5.15	5.24	5.28	**3.79**
3	3.97	5.15	5.71	5.64	**3.85**
4	4.12	5.41	5.53	5.76	**4.02**
5	4.11	5.42	5.78	5.66	**4.01**

Table 2. Network cost for $\alpha=\beta=1$ and $\gamma=1$

Net.	SGA	W&O	W&D1	W&D2	Hybrid
1	4.90	5.70	5.17	5.90	**4.80**
2	4.39	5.08	4.59	5.05	**4.38**
3	4.41	5.05	4.62	5.45	**4.32**
4	4.64	5.31	4.81	5.39	**4.51**
5	4.52	5.30	4.81	5.33	**4.40**

Table 3. Network cost for $\alpha=\beta=1$ and $\gamma=0$

Net.	SGA	W&O	W&D1	W&D2	Hybrid
1	5.61	6.04	6.84	6.82	**5.52**
2	5.01	5.21	5.90	5.51	**4.43**
3	4.49	5.23	6.79	5.83	**4.35**
4	4.76	5.50	6.25	6.14	**4.60**
5	4.62	5.54	6.74	5.99	**4.51**

Table 4. Network cost for $\alpha=\beta=0.8$ and $\gamma=0.5$

Net.	SGA	W&O	W&D1	W&D2	Hybrid
1	3.45	4.65	4.89	5.10	**3.34**
2	3.09	4.09	4.24	4.21	**3.00**
3	3.21	4.14	4.66	4.56	**3.14**
4	3.63	4.31	4.47	4.61	**3.53**
5	3.44	4.31	4.68	4.52	**3.34**

Table 5. Network cost for $\alpha=\beta=0.8$ and $\gamma=1$

Net.	SGA	W&O	W&D1	W&D2	Hybrid
1	3.76	4.49	4.23	4.76	**3.61**
2	3.06	4.04	3.73	4.04	**3.01**
3	3.11	4.06	3.80	4.41	**3.03**
4	3.59	4.23	3.91	4.32	**3.42**
5	3.40	4.22	3.91	3.27	**3.30**

Table 6. Network cost for $\alpha=\beta=0.8$ and $\gamma=0$

Net.	SGA	W&O	W&D1	W&D2	Hybrid
1	3.94	4.75	5.55	5.45	**3.81**
2	3.22	4.13	4.74	4.38	**3.16**
3	3.28	4.20	5.51	4.70	**3.19**
4	3.37	4.38	5.04	4.90	**3.29**
5	3.36	4.41	5.45	7.77	**3.27**

6 Conclusions

In this study, a PGA/heuristic based hybrid technique is proposed. Object oriented network representation is employed. Two metrics for network effectiveness assessment are used: one is based on NWR, and the other is based on a simplified model of network cost. The results obtained with the hybrid technique are compared with those obtained from the recent wavelength-allocation heuristics and the sequential GA. It is observed that the proposed parallel hybrid technique has very promising results under various parameter settings.

References

1. Holland, J.H.: Adaptation in Natural and Artificial Sys. U. of Michigan Pr., Ann Arbor, (1975)
2. Gorges-Schleuter, M.: ASPARAGOS: An Asynchronous Parallel Genetic Optimisation Strategy. In: Schaffer, J.D. (ed.): Proc. of the 3rd ICGA. Morgan Kaufmann, (1989)

3. Spiessens, P, Manderick, B.: A Massively Parallel Genetic Algorithm. In: Belew R.K. (ed.): Proceedings of the 4th Int. Conf. on Genetic Algorithms. Morgan Kaufmann, (1991)
4. Gordon, V.S., Whitley, D.: Serial and Parallel Genetic Algorithms as Function Optimizers. In: Forrest, S. (Ed.): Proc. of the 5th ICGA. Morgan Kaufmann, (1993)
5. Stender, J. (Ed.): Parallel Genetic Algorithms: Theory and Applications. IOS Press, (1993)
6. Lin, S., Punch, W.F., Goodman, E.D.: Coarse-grain Parallel Genetic Algorithms: Categorization and New approach. Parallel & Distributed Processing, (1994)
7. Belding, T.C: The Distributed Genetic Algorithm Revisited. In: Eshelman, L.J. (ed.): Proc. of the 6th ICGA. Morgan Kaufmann, (1995)
8. Herrera, F., Lozano, M.: Gradual Distributed Real-coded Genetic Algorithms. Technical Report #DECSAI-97-01-03, (1997) (Revised version 1998)
9. Tanese, R.: Distributed Genetic Algorithms. Schaffer, J.D. (ed.): Proc. of 3rd ICGA. (1989).
10. Alba, E., Aldana, J.F., Troya, J.M.: A Genetic Algorithm for Load Balancing in Parallel Query Evaluation for Deductive Relational Databases. In: Pearson, D.W., Steele, N.C., Albrecht, R.F. (eds.): Procs. of the I. C. on ANNs and GAs. Springer-Verlag, (1995)
11. Lozano, M.: Application of Fuzzy Logic Based Techniques for Improving the Behavior of GAs with Floating Point Encoding. Ph.D. Thesis. University of Granada, (1996)
12. Alba, E., Aldana, J.F., Troya, J.M.: Full Automatic ANN Design: A Genetic Approach. In: Mira, J., Cabestany, J., Prieto, A. (eds.): Lecture Notes in Computer Science, Vol. 686. Springer-Verlag, (1993)
13. Alba, E., Cotta, C.: Evolution of Complex Data Structures. Informatica y Automatica **30**(3) (1997) 42–60
14. Cantu-Paz, E.: A Summary of Research on Parallel Genetic Algorithms. R. 95007, (1995). Also revised version, IlliGAL R. 97003, (1997)
15. Ribeiro Filho, J.L., Alippi, C., Treleaven, P.: Genetic Algorithm Programming Environments. In: Stender, J. (ed.): Parallel Genetic Algorithms: Theory & Applications. IOS Press, (1993)
16. Zang, H., Jue, J.P., Mukherjee, B.: A Review of Routing and Wavelength Assignment Approaches for Wavelength-routed Optical WDM networks. Optical Networks **1**(1) (2000)
17. Nagatsu, N., Hamazumi, Y., Sato, K.I.: Number of Wavelengths Required for Constructing Large-scale Optical Path Networks. El. Com. Jpn. 1, Com. 78 (1995) 1–11
18. Nagatsu, N., Hamazumi, Y., Sato, K.I.: Optical Path Accommodation Designs Applicable to Large Scale Networks. IEICE Trans. Commun. E78-B, 4 (1995) 597–607
19. Wuttisittikulkij, L., O'Mahony, M.J.: A Simple Algorithm for Wavelength Assignment in Optical networks. In: Proc. 21st European conf. on Optical Commun, Brussels. (1995) 859–862
20. Tan, L.G., Sinclair, M.C.: Wavelength Assignment Between the Central Nodes of the COST239 European Optical Network. In: Proc. of 11th UK Perf. Eng., W. Liverpool, UK. (1995) 235–247
21. Talay, A.C., Oktug, S.: A GA/Heuristic Based Hybrid Technique for Routing and Wavelength Assignment in WDM Networks. Lecture Notes in Computer Science, Vol. 3005. Springer-Verlag, (2004) 150–159
22. Davis, L. (Ed.): Handbook of Genetic Algorithms. Van Nostrand Reinhold (1991)
23. Wauters, N., Demeester, P.: Design of the Optical Path Layer in Multiwavelength Cross-connected Networks. IEEE J. Sel. Areas Commun. **14**(5) (1996) 881–892
24. Mikac, B., Inkret, R.: Application of a Genetic Algorithm to the Availability-Cost Optimization of a Transmission Network Topology. In: Proc. 3rd Intl. Conf. on Artificial Neural Networks and GAs (ICANNGA'97), Univ.of East Anglia, Norwich, UK. (1997) 304–307
25. Griffith, P.S., Proestaki, A., Sinclair, M.C.: Heuristic Topological Design of Low-Cost Pptical Telecommunication Networks. In: Proc. of the 12th UK Perf. Eng. Workshop, Edinburgh, UK. (1996) 129–140

Static Mapping Heuristics for Tasks with Hard Deadlines in Real-Time Heterogeneous Systems

Kavitha S. Golconda[1], Atakan Doğan[2], and Füsun Özgüner[1]

[1] Department of Electrical Engineering, The Ohio State University
2015 Neil Avenue, Columbus, OH 43210-1272, USA
{golcondk,ozguner}@ece.osu.edu
[2] Department of Electrical and Electronics Engineering
Anadolu University, 26470 Eskişehir, Turkey
atdogan@anadolu.edu.tr

Abstract. Hard real-time tasks are associated with strict deadlines. Classical scheduling heuristics ensure fairness among tasks and prevent deadlock, but are not concerned with deadline compliance. Hence, there is a need for scheduling heuristics which prioritize tasks in a real-time system in a manner which guarantees timely completion of maximum number of tasks. In this paper, several static heuristics for mapping hard real-time tasks to machines in a heterogeneous distributed system have been described. These heuristics differ in their method of prioritizing tasks for scheduling, which results in varied performance. The heuristics have been outlined and simulated using a common set of assumptions. The performance parameter considered in this study is the number of user satisfied tasks.

1 Introduction

The problem of matching and scheduling tasks in a Heterogeneous Computing (HC) system is proven to be NP-hard [1]. This challenge is complicated further in real-time systems. Real-time systems require both functionally accurate results and timely completion of task execution [2]. Tasks in such systems have explicit deadlines associated with them. Classical scheduling theory uses metrics such as minimizing the sum of completion times, the number of processors required, or the maximum lateness [3]. These scheduling algorithms try to ensure fairness among tasks, and prevent starvation and deadlocks [2]. However, fairness is not an issue in real-time systems. The goal of scheduling in real-time systems is to find an optimal algorithm which is defined as follows: An optimal scheduling algorithm is one that may fail to meet a deadline only if no other scheduling algorithm can meet it [3]. This problem has been shown to be NP-complete. Hence, heuristic algorithms which attempt to find a feasible schedule, not necessarily optimal, which minimizes the deadline miss-rate of tasks is required.

Tasks in real-time systems can have several properties such as, arrival time, execution time, worst-case execution time, deadline, etc. These tasks can be labeled as either hard or soft, depending upon the laxity of deadlines [4], where laxity is defined as the amount of time by which a task can miss its deadline without facing severe consequences. Hard real-time systems have zero laxity and have to complete before their deadline, whereas soft real-time tasks can tolerate a certain amount of laxity. Each task must be guaranteed successful completion once it is scheduled.

In this paper, several heuristics for scheduling tasks in a real-time system have been outlined. All the tasks are assumed to be hard real-time and hence require strict deadline compliance. Static versions of the heuristics have been considered. Therefore, it is assumed that the execution time of the tasks on each machine is known in advance and is stored in the ETC (expected time to compute) matrix. The heuristics have been simulated to evaluate their performance in terms of number of satisfied user tasks.

The remainder of this paper is organized as follows. Section 2 describes the simulation model used to determine a feasible schedule for the hard real-time scheduling problem. Section 3 provides a description of eight static scheduling heuristics which have been considered in this study. The results of the simulations are presented in Section 4. Section 5 concludes.

2 Simulation Model

Consider a HC system composed of m heterogeneous machines, denoted by set $M = \{m_1, m_2, \ldots, m_m\}$. Let $T = \{t_1, t_2, \ldots, t_n\}$ denote the set of n hard real-time tasks. The tasks are assumed to be independent, i.e., the tasks comprise a meta-task. The execution time of task t_i on machine m_j is represented as $ETC(i, j)$ and is contained within the ETC matrix. The ETC matrix is generated using the method proposed in [5], where $\mu_{task} = \mu_{mach} = 100$, and $V_{task} = V_{mach} = 0.5$.

All the tasks must specify their worst-case execution time on each machine, which will be considered in place of their actual execution time during the scheduling, in order to guarantee completion of hard real-time tasks once they are scheduled. The worst-case execution time of task t_i on machine m_j is defined as: $WTC(i,j) = 2 \frac{\sum_{j=1}^{m} ETC(i,j)}{m} + ETC(i,j)$ [6]. Let V_S denote the schedule length of the task assignment resulting from assigning each task to a machine which minimizes its worst-case completion time. The hard deadline D_i, of task t_i is calculated as, $D_i = (V_D \times rand)V_S$, where $V_D \geq 0$ is a variable used to control the process of assigning deadlines to tasks and $rand$ is a function which generates a uniformly distributed random number between 0 and 1. As the value of V_D decreases, the tightness of task deadlines increases, making it more difficult for tasks to complete on time.

In this paper, a HC system with 10 to 25 machines is considered. The number of tasks ranges from 100 to 500. The simulations were performed for $V_D \in \{0.05, 0.10, 0.50\}$, where $V_D = 0.05$ results in the tightest value of task deadlines. The hard real-time scheduling heuristics attempt to determine a feasible schedule which maximizes the number of successful user tasks.

3 Heuristic Descriptions

A description of eight hard real-time scheduling heuristics is given below. These heuristics employ different methods of prioritizing tasks for allocating system resources. Some of the heuristics have been modified from their original version to adapt them for use in a real-time environment. Let U denote the set of all unmapped tasks.

3.1 Deadline-Based Heuristics

In the Deadline-based heuristics, tasks in set U are considered for scheduling in increasing order of task deadlines. This approach is based on the idea that assigning tasks with deadlines closest to the current time will increase their chances of completion, and in turn increase the total number of satisfied user tasks. The first phase in this class of heuristics sorts the tasks in ascending order of deadlines. The task are considered for scheduling in this order. The completion time c_{ij} of each task t_i is determined on every machine m_j in set M. The second phase of the heuristic is different for the individual deadline-based heuristics and is described as follows:

Minimum heuristic: Tasks in the sorted set are assigned in that order to a machine which minimizes their completion time, provided the deadline of the task is met on that machine. The time complexity of Minimum heuristic is $O(nlogn + nm)$.

Maximum heuristic: Tasks in the sorted set are assigned in that order to a machine which produces maximum completion time, less than or equal to the task deadline. The time complexity of Maximum heuristic is $O(nlogn + nm)$.

Median heuristic: For each task in the sorted set, the machines in set M are sorted in increasing order of completion times, and the machine closest to the mid-point of the list which meets the deadline of the task is chosen to execute the task. The time complexity of Median heuristic is $O(nlogn + nmlogm)$.

Random heuristic: In this heuristic each task in the sorted set is assigned to a random machine which meets its deadline, provided such a machine does exist for the task. Otherwise, the task is dropped. The time complexity of Random heuristic is $O(nlogn + nm)$.

3.2 QSMTS-IP Algorithm

The QSMTS-IP (QoS-based meta-task scheduling for time-invariant resource usage penalties) algorithm [6] with only the timeliness dimension and without the pricing strategy is shown in Figure 1. Step 1 of the algorithm sorts the tasks in set U in increasing order of deadlines, thereby scheduling urgent tasks first. Steps 3 to 7 determine a *feasible position* for each task in the sorted list on the machines in set M. A feasible position for task t_i on machine m_j is defined to be the position in machine m_j's FIFO task queue closest to the tail for which the hard deadline of t_i is met without violating the deadline requirements of the other tasks already in the queue beyond this position. The completion time

```
(1)  Sort tasks in set U in increasing order of deadlines;
(2)  for each task t_i ∈ U
(3)      for each machine m_j ∈ M
(4)          if a feasible position exists
(5)              Compute c(i, j);
(6)          endif.
(7)      endfor.
(8)      Find machine m_min which minimizes completion time for t_i;
(9)      if c(i, min) > D_i
(10)         Remove t_i from set U;
(11)     else
(12)         Assign task t_i to a feasible position on m_min;
(13)     endif.
(14) endfor.
```

Fig. 1. QSMTS-IP algorithm

$c(i,j)$ of task t_i on a feasible position on machine m_j is computed. Steps 8 to 13 are used to determine a possible machine assignment for each task in the sorted list. The machine m_{min} which yields minimum completion time for the task is determined. If this minimum completion time does not meet the deadline of the task, then it cannot be scheduled to complete on any machine. Hence the task is removed from set U. Otherwise, the task is assigned to machine m_{min}. This process is repeated for all the tasks in set U. The time complexity of QSMTS-IP algorithm is $O(n^2 + nm)$.

3.3 Min-min Heuristic

The Min-min heuristic [7] is shown in Figure 2. Steps 2 to 12 constitute the first phase of the Min-min heuristic. Steps 3 to 5 compute the completion time $c(i,j)$ of task t_i on every machine m_j in set M. The machine m_{min}, which gives minimum completion time for t_i is determined in step 6. Steps 7 and 8 check to see if this minimum completion time is greater than the deadline of t_i, and if true the task is dropped from the set U. Otherwise, the task-machine pair is stored in CT, which is the set of all candidate task-machine pairs (steps 9 and 10). This process is repeated for all the unmapped tasks in set U. The second phase of the heuristic consists of steps 13 to 15. The task-machine pair (t_i^*, m_j^*), with the overall minimum completion time in set CT is determined. Task t_i^* is assigned to the end of m_j^*'s FIFO queue and the task is removed from set U. The two phases of the heuristic are repeated until all the tasks are either scheduled or dropped because they cannot meet their deadline on any machine. The time complexity of Min-min heuristic is $O(n^2m)$.

```
(1)  repeat
(2)     for each task $t_i \in U$
(3)        for each machine $m_j \in M$
(4)           Compute $c(i,j)$;
(5)        endfor.
(6)        Find $m_{min}$ which gives minimum completion time for $t_i$;
(7)        if $c(i, min) > D_i$
(8)           Remove $t_i$ from set $U$;
(9)        else
(10)          Save task-machine pair is set $CT$;
(11)       endif.
(12)    endfor.
(13)    Find $(t_i^*, m_j^*)$ with minimum completion time in set $CT$;
(14)    Assign task $t_i^*$ to the end of machine $m_j^*$'s FIFO queue;
(15)    Remove $t_i^*$ from set $U$;
(16) until$(U = \emptyset)$.
```

Fig. 2. Min-min heuristic

3.4 Least Slack First Algorithm

As the name suggests, the Least Slack First algorithm schedules the task with minimum slack value first and is based on [8]. The slack value of task t_i is a measure of how farther away a task is from its deadline and is defined as:

$$Slack_i = D_i - \frac{\sum_{j=1}^{m} c(i,j)}{m}, \qquad (1)$$

where D_i is the deadline of task t_i and $c(i,j)$ is the completion time of task t_i on machine m_j. Figure 3 shows an outline of the algorithm. Steps 1 to 6 compute the completion time of all unmapped tasks. The slack value is computed using the average completion time of the task. The tasks are sorted in ascending order of their slack values in step 7. Step 9 determines machine m_{min} which gives minimum completion time for task t_i. Steps 10 and 11 check to determine if the deadline of the task is met, and drops the task otherwise. Task t_i is assigned to the end of machine m_{min}'s FIFO queue. This process is repeated for all the tasks in set U. The time complexity of Least Slack First is $O(n \log n + nm)$.

3.5 Sufferage Heuristic

Sufferage heuristic is based on the idea that better mappings can be generated by assigning a machine to a task that *suffers* most in terms of expected completion time, if that particular machine is not assigned to it [9]. Sufferage value of a task is defined as the difference between the earliest completion time (on machine m_{min}) and second minimum completion time (on machine $m_{next-min}$).

Steps 3 to 5 in Figure 4 compute the completion time $c(i,j)$, of task t_i on every machine m_j in set M, based on the execution time of t_i and the availability time

(1) for each task $t_i \in U$
(2)   for each machine $m_j \in M$
(3)   Compute $c(i,j)$;
(4)   endfor.
(5)   Compute $Slack_i = D_i - \frac{\sum_{j=1}^{m} c(i,j)}{m}$;
(6) endfor.
(7) Sort tasks in set U in ascending order of their $Slack$ values;
(8) for each task $t_i \in U$
(9)   Find machine m_{min} with minimum completion time;
(10)   if $c(i, min) > D_i$
(11)   Remove t_i from set U;
(12)   else
(13)   Assign t_i to the end of machine m_{min}'s FIFO queue;
(14)   endif.
(15) endfor.

Fig. 3. Least Slack First algorithm

of m_j. Steps 6 to 8 calculate the *Sufferage* of t_i as the difference in completion times on machine m_{min} and machine $m_{next-min}$. All the machines in set M are marked as available in step 10. For each unmapped task t_i in set U, steps 12 to 13 drop those tasks for which the minimum completion time does not meet the deadline. Otherwise, the availability of machine m_{min} is checked. If the machine is available (steps 15 to 18), task t_i is assigned to it and the machine is marked as unavailable. However, if the machine is not available (steps 19 to 26), the sufferage of task t_x already assigned to m_{min} is compared with the sufferage of t_i. If t_i has a higher value of sufferage, then task t_x is removed from m_{min}'s FIFO queue and t_i is assigned to it. Task t_x is added back to set U. Steps 2 to 28 constitute one pass through the heuristic, during which several tasks may be scheduled, but only one task may be assigned to a machine. This process is repeated until set U is empty. The time complexity of Sufferage heuristic is $O(n^2 m)$.

4 Results

The performance of the eight heuristics are compared in terms of number of satisfied user tasks (tasks which complete before their deadline). The HC system under consideration is over-subscribed, with the degree of over-subscription dependent on the value of V_D. The results of the study for a HC system with $m = \{10, 25\}$ machines, and $V_D = \{0.05, 0.10, 0.50\}$ averaged over 100 simulation runs are shown in Figure 5.

According to Figure 5, for $V_D = 0.05$ (tightest deadlines) and $m = 10$, QSMTS-IP algorithm and Minimum heuristic satisfy maximum number of users. QSMTS-IP produces maximum number of satisfied users since it assigns tasks

```
(1)  repeat
(2)      for each task $t_i \in U$
(3)          for each machine $m_j \in M$
(4)              Compute $c(i,j)$;
(5)          endfor.
(6)          Determine minimum completion time on machine $m_{min}$;
(7)          Determine second minimum completion time on $m_{next-min}$;
(8)          Compute Sufferage of task $t_i$ ;
(9)      endfor.
(10)     Mark all machines in set $M$ as available;
(11)     for each task $t_i$ in set $U$
(12)         if $c(i, min) > D_i$
(13)             Remove task $t_i$ from set $U$;
(14)         else
(15)             if machine $m_{min}$ is available
(16)                 Assign task $t_i$ to $m_{min}$;
(17)                 Remove $t_i$ from set $U$;
(18)                 Mark machine $m_{min}$ as unavailable;
(19)             else
(20)                 Let $t_x$ be the task already assigned to $m_{min}$;
(21)                 if $Sufferage(t_i) > Sufferage(t_x)$
(22)                     Remove $t_x$ from $m_{min}$'s FIFO queue and add it to set $U$;
(23)                     Assign task $t_i$ to machine $m_{min}$;
(24)                     Remove task $t_i$ from set $U$;
(25)                 endif.
(26)             endif.
(27)         endif.
(28)     endfor.
(29) until($U = \emptyset$).
```

Fig. 4. Sufferage heuristic

to a *feasible position* on a machine. This methodology enables task insertion between already scheduled tasks. Hence for any task, if a position exists in a machine's queue which satisfies its deadline requirement without altering the requirements of already scheduled tasks, then QSMTS-IP algorithm will find it. In the Minimum heuristic, tasks are assigned to the machine which gives minimum completion time. This reduces the time the task engages a machine, thereby increasing the time the machine is free for other unmapped tasks. In addition, tasks whose deadline is the nearest is scheduled first, thereby increasing their chance of completion.

Random, Median and Maximum heuristics perform well for the same reason as Minimum heuristic, i.e, tasks closest to their deadlines are scheduled first. However, the decrease in number of satisfied users when compared to Minimum heuristic can be explained as follows: Random heuristic assigns tasks to a random machine which meets the tasks' deadline. However, this machine may not be the

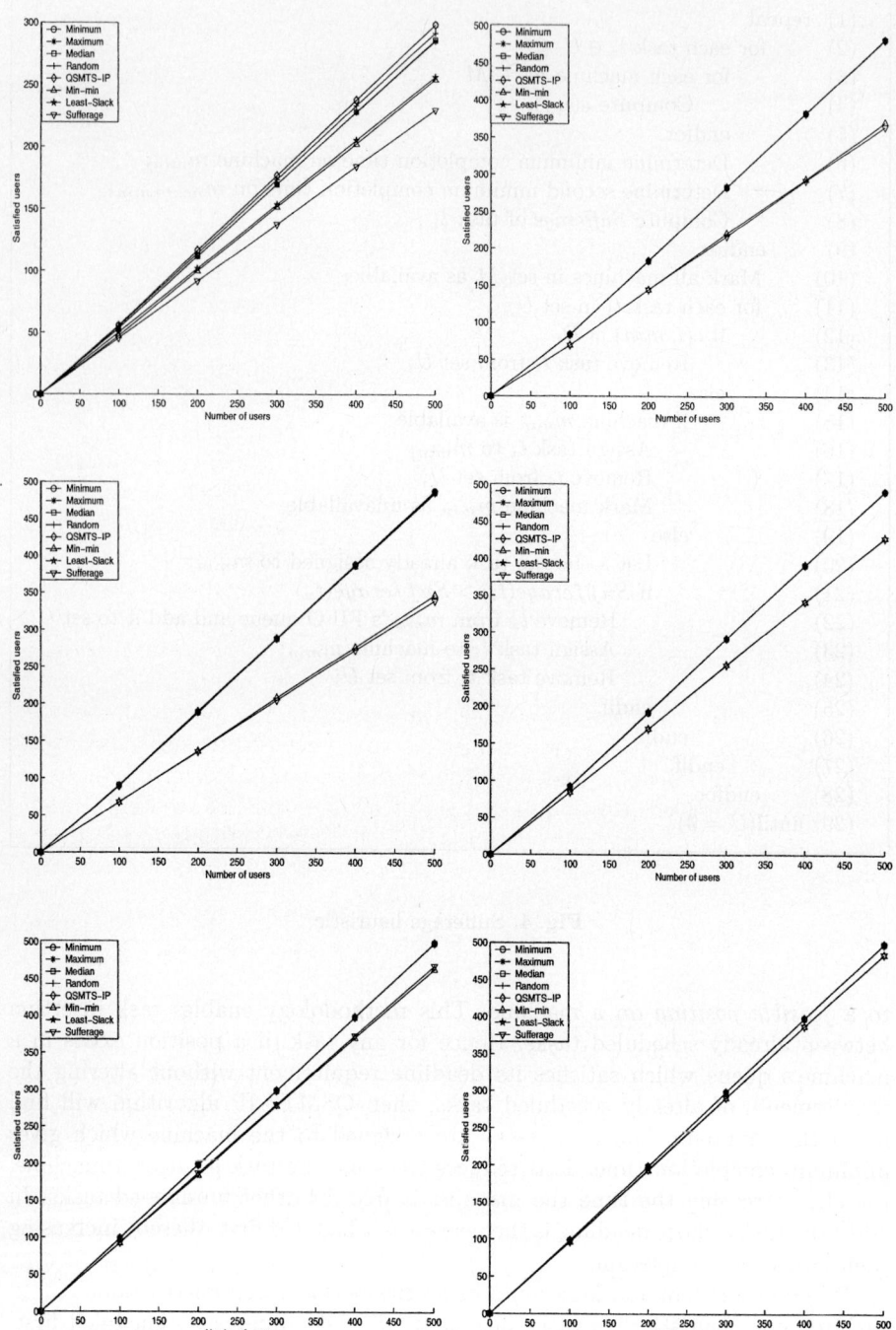

Fig. 5. Impact of increasing V_D on the performance of the eight heuristics in terms of number of satisfied users, for $m = 10$ (on the left) and $m = 25$ (on the right)

one with minimum completion time. Hence, the machines are busy for longer lengths of time thereby reducing the probability of completion of the remaining unmapped tasks. Median and Maximum heuristics satisfy even fewer number of users, since tasks are assigned to the machine with median and maximum completion time respectively. Such machines yield large execution times and hence reduce the number of tasks which complete before their deadlines.

Least Slack algorithm and Min-min heuristic produce significantly reduced performance in comparison. In the case of Least Slack algorithm, tasks are scheduled in ascending order of slack value. When the deadlines are tight, tasks with large execution times will produce larger slack values than tasks with smaller execution times but same or earlier deadlines. Hence, the former tasks are scheduled earlier than the latter. This in turn increases the time the machines are occupied, which causes the other tasks to miss their deadlines. Min-min heuristic aims only at minimizing makespan of the meta-task by assigning the task with minimum completion time at each iteration. However, this approach will cause most tasks to miss their deadlines, since tasks closer to their deadlines are given no preference in scheduling. Sufferage heuristic satisfies the least number of users among the eight heuristics. When two tasks produce minimum completion time on the same machine, the task with larger sufferage value is assigned to the machine. The task with smaller sufferage is not assigned to another machine in that iteration, but has to wait for the next iteration to be scheduled. In the meantime, all such tasks may miss their deadlines.

Decreasing the tightness of deadlines (increasing V_D) or increasing the number of machines in the HC system reduces the difference in performance between QSMTS-IP, Deadline-based heuristics and Least Slack algorithm in terms of number of satisfied users. This is a result of more relaxed deadlines, which enables most tasks to complete within time. Min-min and Sufferage heuristics continue to satisfy less number of users than the other heuristics.

5 Conclusions

This paper describes a heterogeneous real-time computing environment. Eight hard real-time scheduling heuristics have been described and their performance is compared in terms of the number of satisfied users. In the worst-case scenario where task deadlines are tight and the number of machines is small, QSMTS-IP and Minimum heuristic perform the best. Min-min and Sufferage heuristics satisfy the least number of user tasks. Least Slack, Median and Random heuristics perform well for the average case when the deadlines are more relaxed, but deteriorate in the worst-case situation. This paper aims at providing the reader with an understanding of a heterogeneous hard real-time scheduling environment and possible solutions to handle the hard real-time scheduling problem. This analysis can be used as a guideline to develop scheduling heuristics where task execution-time is not known *a priori* and inter-task communication exists.

References

1. Eshagian, M.M.: Heterogeneous computing. Artech House (1996)
2. Ramamritham, K., Stankovic, J.A., Shiah, P.F.: Efficient scheduling algorithms for real-time multiprocessor systems. IEEE Transactions on Parallel and Distributed Systems **1** (1990) 184–194
3. Stankovic, J.A., Spuri, M., Natale, M.D., Buttazzo, G.: Implications of classical scheduling results for real-time systems. IEEE Computer **28** (1995) 16–25
4. Gantman, A., Guo, P., Lewis, J., Rashid, F.: Scheduling real-time tasks in distributed systems: A survey (1998)
5. Ali, S., Siegel, H.J., Maheswaran, M., Hengsen, D.: Task execution time modelling for heterogeneous computing. In: IPDPS Workshop on Heterogeneous Computing, Cancun, Mexico. (2000) 185–199
6. Dogan, A., Ozguner, F.: On QoS-based scheduling of a meta-task with multiple QoS demands in heterogeneous computing. In: Int'l Parallel and Distributed Processing Symposium, Fort Lauderdale, FL. (2002)
7. Braun, T.D., Siegel, H.J., Beck, N., Boloni, L.L., Maheswaran, M., Reuther, A.L., Robertson, J.P., Theys, M.D., Yao, B., Hensgen, D., Freund, R.F.: A comparison study of static mapping heuristics for a class of meta-tasks on heterogeneous computing systems. In: 8th IEEE Workshop on Heterogeneous Computing Systems (HCW '99), San Juan, Puerto Rico. (1999) 15–29
8. Maheswaran, M.: Quality of service driven resource management algorithms for network computing. In: Int'l Conf. on Parallel and Distributed Processing Techniques and Applications, Las Vegas, NV. (1999) 1090–1096
9. Maheswaran, M., Ali, S., Siegel, H.J., Hengsen, D., Freund, R.F.: Dynamic matching and scheduling of a class of independent tasks onto heterogeneous computing systems. In: Heterogeneous Computing Workshop, San Juan, Puerto Rico. (1999) 30–44

An Advanced Server Ranking Algorithm for Distributed Retrieval Systems on the Internet

Byurhan Hyusein and Joe Carthy

Intelligent Information Retrieval Group (IIRG)
Department of Computer Science, University College Dublin
Belfield, Dublin 4, Ireland
{byurhan.hyusein,joe.carthy}@ucd.ie

Abstract. Database selection, also known as resource selection, server selection and query routing is an important topic in distributed information retrieval research. Several approaches to database selection use document frequency data to rank servers. Many researchers have shown that the effectiveness of these algorithms depends on database size and content. In this paper we propose a database selection algorithm which uses document frequency data and an extended database description in order to rank servers. The algorithm does not depend on the size and content of the databases in the system. We provide experimental evidence, based on actual data, that our algorithm outperforms the vGlOSS, CVV and CORI database selection algorithms in respect of the precision and recall evaluation measures.

1 Introduction

The explosive growth in the number of Web pages and users on the Internet has resulted in a significant degradation of the service quality provided by most of the existing centralised Web search engines (SEs). The current trend for Web SEs is towards distributed search engines (DSE) in order to increase not only the capacity of the SEs but also their delivery of reasonable and acceptable performance to end-users. In contrast to centralized search, distributed search includes two additional vital activities:

1. Selecting a subset of the SEs in the distributed system to which a query should be propagated.
2. Merging the results from the separate SEs into a single response.

Although there is considerable interest in both aspects, this research focuses specifically on the first activity.

We investigate techniques for database (DB) selection within a DSE. We propose a new DB selection algorithm that is based on existing DB selection algorithms such as vGlOSS, CVV, and CORI that use document frequency data in order to select an appropriate DB for a given query. The proposed algorithm uses an extended DB description called *Virtual Topic-Specific Database* (VTSDB).

The performance of the DB selection algorithm is evaluated using the WT10g document collection [1].

This work is a part of the Adaptive Distributed Search and Advertising (ADSA) project [7] that is developing a distributed document search system for the World Wide Web where document DBs are independently owned and controlled.

2 Database Selection

Database selection is the first step in a process that continues with search at the distributed sites and merging of result lists from the sites. The primary goal in the database selection step is to select as small a set of databases as possible to send a query to without sacrificing retrieval effectiveness. Several approaches to database selection use document frequency (df) data to rank servers [16, 5, 2]. In this research work we will call such algorithms df-based DB selection algorithms.

Yuwono and Lee [16] proposed a DB selection algorithm based on estimated suitability for answering a given query, called the Cue-Validity Variance (CVV) ranking method, developed as part of the Distributed WWW Index Servers and SE (D-WISE) research project [15]. The authors described a centralized Broker architecture in which the Broker maintains df tables for all servers. The variance of df values across servers is used to select terms from the user query which best discriminate between servers, and then servers with higher df values for those terms are selected to process the query. Servers must transmit changes in df values when they occur and therefore need to know the address of the Broker.

The GlOSS system of Gravano and Garca-Molina [5] allows for a hierarchical Broker structure in which first-level Brokers characterize servers according to term df's and aggregated term weights and where second-level Brokers characterize first-level Brokers in the same fashion. Servers need to know how to contact all first-level Brokers, and first-level Brokers need to know how to contact all second-level Brokers, in order to keep information up-to-date. The goal is to use the information held by the Brokers to estimate the number of relevant documents likely to be held by each server.

Callan et al. [2] use a probabilistic approach to database selection called Collection Retrieval Inference (CORI) Nets. The CORI algorithm uses a Bayesian inference network and an adaptation of the Okapi term frequency normalization formula to rank resources. The probabilities that flow exists along the arcs of the network are based upon statistics analogous to term frequency tf and inverse document frequency idf in document retrieval, document frequency df (the number of documents containing the term) and inverse collection frequency icf (calculated using the number of collections containing the term).

By contrast, a number of other approaches to the server selection problem are based on the use of server descriptions. Chakravarthy and Haase [3] proposed a method for locating the Internet server containing a known item. They manually characterize a large set of servers using semantic structures expressed in WordNet style [9]. For each new search specification, a semantic distance based on WordNet hyponymy trees is computed for each server, and the server with the smallest such distance is chosen. They also use the SMART retrieval system to select servers based on unstructured, manually generated server descriptions and compare performance of the two methods. Kirk et. al. [8] propose the use of Knowledge Representation technology to represent both queries and server content and have developed algorithms for choosing a necessary and sufficient subset of servers described in this way.

3 The Effect of Database Size and Content on Database Selection Algorithms

Prior research by several different researchers using different datasets has shown the df-based database selection algorithms to be the most effective. Although they perform better than the other methods mentioned in the previous section, their effectiveness heavily depends on database size and content [10, 11].

Si and Callan [10] found that in order to have good performance in different environments, it is very important to include a database size factor into a database selection algorithm. However many of these algorithms have weak database size normalization components. That is why it is important for DBs in a DSE to have the same size or relatively the same size.

If in the DSE, SEs contain only single-topic DBs, this would help the Broker direct the relevant DBs to the users queries. If the DBs contain multiple topics, this will increase the difficulty in the Broker selecting the most-appropriate DBs. This is because each DB could contain documents on all (or many) topics, therefore their descriptions become very similar and they are barely differentiated. So the ideal case for a DSE is when all DBs contain the same number of documents (or words) and DBs are topic oriented.

In a DSE where DBs are independently owned and controlled the ideal case is unlikely to be achieved. That is because SEs are usually interested in indexing many documents on different topics. A possible solution is to cluster documents in each DB and organize them in separate physical DBs where each one has its own SE. However firstly it will require maintaining many DBs, secondly there is no automatic classification algorithm that can 100% accurately classify documents, so misclassified documents can be omitted during the search. A better solution is to create an extended description of each DB (see Section 4) that we call *Virtual Topic-Specific Databases* (VTSDB) in this research work and use the algorithm described in Section 5.

4 Database Described by VTSDB

A VTSDB is a logical DB consisting of a subset of entries in a real DB. A VTSDB should be identified by a single topic (see the Example below). A real DB could host many VTSDBs. A VTSDB should appear from a Broker's point of view to be just the same as a real DB, i.e. a VTSDB is transparent to the

Broker. VTSDBs could however meet the contradictory requirements of a DB having just one and many topics simultaneously.

Example: Let us suppose that two databases DB_1 and DB_2 contain documents on topics $T_1, T_2, \ldots, T_n$. Then a table such as the one shown bellow can represent DB_1 and DB_2.

Table 1. Databases represented by VTSDBs

DB_1				DB_2			
DB_1^1	DB_1^2	DB_1^3	$\cdots$	DB_1^n	DB_2^1	DB_2^2	DB_2^3	$\cdots$	DB_2^n

In Table 1 DB_i^j represents all documents on topic T_j in database DB_i. In this paper we refer to DB_i^j as a VTSDB.

This DB representation is similar, but not the same as if DB_1 and DB_2 are divided into three topic-specific physical DB. Using this DB representation and DB selection algorithm described in Section 5 the Broker of a distributed search system can more precisely determine the appropriate DBs for users' queries.

5 Database Selection Using VTSDB

Let DB_i consist of the following VTSDBs: $DB_i^j \in DB_i$, $i = 1, \ldots, |DB|$, $|DB|$ is the number of physical databases in the system, $j = 1, \ldots, |DB_i|$, $|DB_i|$ is the number of VTSDBs in DB_i. Then the goodness of DB_i is defined as follows:

$$goodness(DB_i, Q) = \max_{j=1,\ldots,|DB_i|} goodness(DB_i^j, Q) \qquad (1)$$

where $goodness(DB_i^j, Q)$ is the goodness of VTSDB $DB_i^j \in DB_i$ calculated using any *df*-based database selection algorithm.

Once the Broker selects the proper DB_i, search continues at the DB side as all documents belonging to DB_i are evaluated against the query Q. Evaluation of all documents belonging to DB_i against Q is necessary because there is no automatic classification algorithm that can 100% accurately classify documents. Therefore if the search is performed only in $DB_i^p \in DB_i$ such that $goodness(DB_i^p, Q) = \max_{j=1,\ldots,|DB_i|} goodness(DB_i^j, Q)$, some relevant documents to the queries may be missed. This could lead to low precision as in the case of cluster-based document retrieval.

Creating VTSDBs can be expensive for large DBs. In this case some fast but less effective clustering algorithms can be employed. To compensate for this, the above database selection algorithm has to be slightly changed. Instead of taking only the best VTSDB in DB_i to query Q as a DB_i representative, the top b VTSDB have to be considered, i. e.:

$$goodness(DB_i, Q) = \sum_{p=1}^{b} \max_{j=1,\ldots,|DB_i|} goodness(DB_i^j, Q) \qquad (2)$$

where $\max_p$ denotes the pth highest value. The parameter b depends on the classification algorithm used for creation of VTSDBs and can be experimentally determined. If $b = 1$ both database selection algorithms are equivalent.

The second database selection algorithm assumes that the same classification algorithm is used in all physical databases. Otherwise determination of the best value of b would be very difficult.

6 Experiments

This section describes the experiments we performed in order to evaluate the effectiveness of the proposed DB selection algorithm.

6.1 Test Collection

The 10 GB collection of documents (WT10g) available for participants of the Web track main task in the TREC-9 [14] experiments was used in our experiments. This collection is a subset of 100 gigabyte VLC2 collection created by the Internet Archive in 1997 [6].

6.2 VTSDB

For the purpose of evaluating the performance of the DB selection algorithm, the WT10g document collection was divided into 50 DBs, which consequently are clustered using the *partitional* clustering method proposed by Cutting et al. in [4]. Then each VTSDB is represented by a cluster (not a cluster centroid), i.e. by the documents belonging to that cluster. The database sizes range from 3029 to 97130 documents per database and cluster (VTSDB) sizes range from 1 to 36512 documents per cluster. The number of clusters per database was 20.

6.3 Queries

The TREC data includes a number of topics (queries), each of which is a statement of information needed to be described in natural language [14]. Topics are given in a structured way, having a brief description in the *Title* field, a more detailed description in the *Description* field, and the rules of relevance judgment in the *Narrative* field. For our experiments the search queries were automatically generated from the *Title* field of the Web track topics 451-500.

6.4 Relevance Judgments

The accuracy of evaluation is performed against relevance judgments provided by organizers of the TREC-9 conference. Relevance judgments are given in 3-level forms: non-relevant documents, relevant documents, and highly relevant documents [13]. In the evaluation of the DB selection algorithms, the highly relevant document may be given different weights compared to other relevant documents.

6.5 Evaluation Criteria

Several metrics for measuring the performance of DB selection algorithms were developed recently, the most important being the recall and precision analogues discussed by Gravano et al. in [5]. The calculation of these metrics is based on comparison of baseline ranking B, that represents a desired goal of each query, and estimated ranking E, that is a result of the DB selection process.

Let B_i and E_i denote the merit associated with DB_i in the baseline and estimated ranking respectively. The baseline ranking for each query is constructed by ordering all the DBs in the descending order of their merit for that query.

Gravano et al. [5] defined the recall R metric as follows:

$$R_n = \frac{\sum_{i=1}^{n} E_i}{\sum_{i=1}^{n} B_i}. \quad (3)$$

This is a measure of how much of the available merit in the top n ranked databases of the baseline has been accumulated via the top n databases in the estimated ranking.

Gravano et al. [5] have also proposed a precision P metric:

$$P_n = \frac{|\{DB \in Top_n(E) | merit(Q, DB) > 0\}|}{n}. \quad (4)$$

This gives a fraction of top n ranked DBs in the estimated ranking that have non-zero merit. The bigger the values of recall and precision metrics achieved when evaluating a DB selection algorithm, the better the algorithm is.

7 Results

In this Section, we report the comparison of vGlOSS, vGlOSS-VTSDB, CVV, CVV-VTSDB, CORI and CORI-VTSDB database selection algorithms. X-VTSDB means that algorithm X is used to calculate the goodness of VTSDBs. The values of recall R_n and precision P_n for $n = 1, \ldots, 5$ are given in Tables 2 and 3. These values are obtained with parameter $b = 1$. VTSDB algorithms achieved generally better results for both R_n and P_n than vGlOSS, CVV and CORI. With parameter $b = 2$ similar results were obtained, however for $b > 2$ the results of the selection were affected by giving less precision and recall.

Table 2. Recall obtained for vGlOSS, vGlOSS-VTSDB, CVV, CVV-VTSDB, CORI and CORI-VTSDB using 50 DBs

Recall	vGlOSS	vGlOSS-VTSDB	CVV	CVV-VTSDB	CORI	CORI-VTSDB
R_1	0.111	0.114	0.115	0.141	0.120	0.142
R_2	0.127	0.130	0.147	0.154	0.146	0.157
R_3	0.157	0.160	0.180	0.203	0.183	0.201
R_4	0.185	0.204	0.191	0.208	0.191	0.211
R_5	0.203	0.229	0.215	0.230	0.215	0.233

Table 3. Precision obtained for vGlOSS, vGlOSS-VTSDB, CVV, CVV-VTSDB, CORI and CORI-VTSDB using 50 DBs

Precision	vGlOSS	vGlOSS-VTSDB	CVV	CVV-VTSDB	CORI	CORI-VTSDB
P_1	0.320	0.470	0.460	0.497	0.480	0.500
P_2	0.300	0.450	0.450	0.480	0.450	0.490
P_3	0.320	0.466	0.460	0.493	0.460	0.493
P_4	0.330	0.450	0.425	0.480	0.425	0.475
P_5	0.332	0.444	0.408	0.484	0.412	0.484

8 Conclusions and Future Work

In this research work we proposed a new technique for database representation and selection. We have also investigated vGlOSS, vGlOSS-VTSDB, CVV, CVV-VTSDB, CORI and CORI-VTSDB database selection algorithms and examined their performance using the WT10g document collection. Recall and precision analogues were used for evaluating the performance of database selection algorithms. In our experiments, the VTSDB algorithms performed generally better than vGlOSS, CVV and CORI. The performance of the proposed database selection algorithm depends on the quality of the VTSDBs. We have found that the *partitional* clustering method proposed by Cutting et. al. in [4] is a good algorithm for creating VTSDBs. This research also confirms the work carried out by Si and Callan [10] and Si et al. [11] that database selection algorithms do not work well in environments with a skewed distribution of database sizes.

Future work will be concentrated on the evaluation of the VTSDB algorithms using different clustering algorithms. This will allow the determination of the effect of the clustering algorithm on the effectiveness of database selection algorithms.

References

1. Bailey, P., Craswell, N. Hawking, D.: Engineering a Multi-Purpose Test Collection for Web Retrieval Experiments. Information Processing and Management, (2002).
2. Callan, J.P, Lu, Z., Croft, W.B.: Searching Distributed Collections with Inference Networks. In: Proceedings of the 18th Annual International ACM SIGIR Conference on Research and Development in Information Retrieval. ACM Press, (1995) 21–28
3. Chakravarthy, A.S., Haase, K.B.: NetSerf: Using Semantic Knowledge to Find Internet Information Archives. In: Proceedings of the Eighteenth Annual International ACM SIGIR Conference on Research and Development in Information Retrieval. (1995) 4–11
4. Cutting D.R., Karger, D.R., Pederson , J.O, Tukey, J.W.: Scatter/Gather: A Cluster-based Approach to Browsing Large Document Collections. In: Proceedings of the 15th Annual International ACM SIGIR Conference on Research and Development in Information Retrieval. (1992) (318–329)
5. Gravano, L., Garcia-Molina, H.: Generalizing GlOSS to Vector-Space Databases and Broker Hierarchies. In: Proceedings of the 21st International Conference on Very Large Data Bases (VLDB '95. (1995) 78–89
6. Internet Archive. Internet Archive: Building an Internet Library. http://www.archive.org. (1997)
7. Khoussainov, R., O'Meara, T, Patel, A.: Adaptive Distributed Search and Advertising for WWW. In: Callaos, N., Holmes, L. Osers, R. (eds.): Proceedings of the Fifth World Multiconference on Systemics, Cybernetics and Informatics (SCI 2001). 5 (2001) 73–78
8. Kirk, T., Levy, A.Y., Sagiv, Y., Srivastava, D.: The Information Manifold. In: Knoblock, C., Levy, A.(eds.): Information Gathering from Heterogeneous, Distributed Environments. (1995)
9. Miller, G. A.: WordNet: A Lexical Database for English. Communications of the ACM 38(11) (1995) 39–41
10. Si, L., Callan, J.: The Effect of Database Size Distribution on Resource Selection Algorithms. In: Callan, J., Crestani, F. Sanderson, M. (eds.): Proceedings of the SIGIR 2003 Workshop on Distributed Information Retrieval. (2003)
11. Si, L., Lu, J., Callan, J.: Distributed Information Retrieval With Skewed Database Size Distribution. In: Proceedings of the National Conference on Digital Government Research. (2003)
12. Van Rijsbergen, C.J.: Information Retrieval. Department of Computing Science, University of Glasgow, 2nd edn. Butterworths, (1979)
13. Voorhees, E.M.: Evaluation by Highly Relevant Documents. In: Croft, W.B., Harper, D.J, Kraft, D.H., Zobel, J. (eds.): Proceedings of the 24th Annual International ACM SIGIR Conference on Research and Development in Information Retrieval ACM Press, (2001) 74–82
14. Voorhees, E.M., Harman, D.K.: Overview of the Ninth Text Retrieval Conference (TREC-9). In: Proceedings of the Ninth Text REtrieval Conference (TREC-9). Department of Commerce, National Institute of Standards and Technology, (2001)
15. Yuwono, B., Lee, D.K.: WISE: A World Wide Web Resource Database System. Knowledge and Data Engineering 8(4) (1996) 548–554
16. Yuwono, B., Lee, D.L.: Server Ranking for Distributed Text Retrieval Systems on the Internet. In: Topor, R.W., Tanaka, K. (eds): Proceedings of the Fifth International Conference on Database Systems for Advanced Applications (DASFAA). World Scientific, (1997) 41–50

Energy-Aware Strategies in Real-Time Systems for Autonomous Robots[*]

Giorgio Buttazzo, Mauro Marinoni, and Giacomo Guidi

University of Pavia, Pavia, Italy
{buttazzo,mauro.marinoni,giacomo.guidi}@unipv.it

Abstract. Most battery operated robots have to work under timing constraints to exhibit a desired performance and must adopt suitable control strategies to minimize energy consumption to prolong their lifetime. Unfortunately, energy saving strategies tend to reduce resource availability and, hence, degrade robot performance. As a consequence, an integrated approach is needed for balancing energy consumption with real-time requirements. In this paper, we present an integrated approach to energy management in real-time robot systems to prolong battery lifetime and still guarantee timing constraints. The method is applied to a six-legged robot controlled by a PC104 microprocessor and equipped with a set of sensors for the interaction with the environment. Specific experiments are reported to evaluate the effectiveness of the proposed approach.

1 Introduction

With the progress of technology, cost and size of robot systems are reducing more than ever, not only for wheeled vehicles, but also for walking machines, which can be used to work in open environments on more irregular terrains. This enables the development of distributed systems consisting of teams of robots, which can cooperate to collect information from the environment and perform a common goal. Typical applications of this type are aimed at monitoring, surveillance, searching, or rescuing. In this type of activities, the use of a coordinated team of small robots has many advantages with respect to a single bigger robot, increasing the probability of success of the mission.

On the other hand, the use of small robot systems introduce a lot of new problems that need to be solved for fully exploiting the potential benefits coming from a collaborative work. Most of the problems are due to the limited resources that can be carried onboard by a small mobile robot. In fact, cost, space, weight, and energy constraints, impose the adoption of small microprocessors with limited memory and computational power. In particular, the computer architecture should be small enough to fit on the robot structure, but powerful enough to execute all the robot computational activities needed for achieving the desired

---

[*] This work has been partially supported by the European Union, under contract IST-2001-34820, and by the Italian Ministry of University Research, (MIUR) under contract 2003094275.

level of autonomy. Moreover, since such systems are operated by batteries, they have to limit energy consumption as much as possible to prolong their lifetime.

The tight interaction with the world causes the robot activities to be characterized by timing constraints, that must be met to achieve the expected robot behavior. In order to achieve stability and guarantee a desired performance, timing constraints need to be enforced by the operating system that supports the application. In particular, the operating system should guarantee that all periodic tasks are activated according to their specified periods and executed within their deadlines.

Some of the issues discussed above have been deeply addressed in the literature. For example, the feasibility of a set of periodic tasks with real-time constraints can be easily analyzed if tasks are scheduled with the Rate Monotonic (RM) algorithm (according to which priorities are inversely proportional to task periods), or with the Earliest Deadline First (EDF) algorithm (according to which priorities are inversely proportional to absolute deadlines). Liu and Layland [11] proved that, in the absence of blocking factors, a set of n periodic tasks is schedulable if the total processor utilization is less than or equal to a given bound U_{lub}, which depends on the adopted algorithm. This result has later been extended also in the presence of blocking factors due to the interaction with mutually exclusive resources [13].

In the context of real-time systems, different energy-aware algorithms have been proposed to minimize energy consumption. They basically exploit voltage variable processors to minimize the speed while guaranteeing real-time constraints [2, 3, 12, 14]. What is missing, however, is an integrated framework for energy-aware control, where different strategies can be applied at different levels of the architecture, from the hardware devices to the operating system, up to the application level.

In this paper, we present a system wide approach to energy management applied to all the architecture levels and integrated with the scheduling algorithm to guarantee real-time constraints. The method is applied to an autonomous walking robot controlled by a PC104 microprocessor and equipped with a set of sensors for the interaction with the environment.

2 System Architecture

The robot described in this work is a walking machine with six independent legs, each having three degrees of freedom. The mechanical structure of the robot is illustrated in Figure 1 and a view of the robot with sensors and processing units is shown Figure 2. The robot is actuated by 18 Hitec HS-645MG servomotors including an internal position control loop that allows the user to specify angular set points through a PWM input signal. The internal feedback loop imposes a maximum angular velocity of 250 degrees per second and each motor is able to generate a maximum torque of 9.6 kg·cm.

The robot is equipped with a color CMOS camera mounted on a micro servomotor that allows rotations around its vertical axis. Other sensors include a pair

Energy-Aware Strategies in Real-Time Systems for Autonomous Robots

Fig. 1. Mechanical structure of the robot

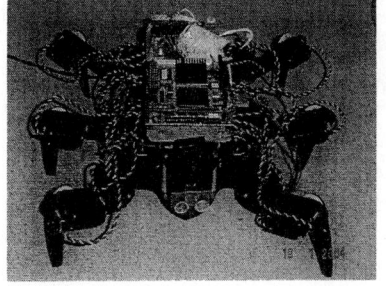

Fig. 2. A view of the robot

of ultrasound transducers for proximity sensing, two current sensors on each leg for measuring the torque during walking (so detecting possible obstacles in front of the legs) and a battery sensor for estimating the residual level of charge.

A block diagram of the hardware architecture is shown in Figure 3.

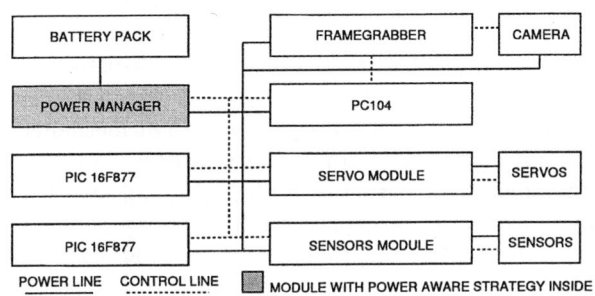

Fig. 3. Block diagram of the hardware architecture

All software activities carried out by the robot are partitioned in two hierarchical processing units. The high level unit consists of a PC104 Pentium-like computer with a Geode GX1 CPU at 266 MHz mounted on a Eurotech CPU-1432 motherboard. It includes a 128 MBytes RAM and a solid state hard disk of 640 KBytes. A CM7326 PC/104-Plus frame grabber is connected to the motherboard via PCI bus for image acquisition from the camera. The high level unit is responsible for walking control, image acquisition, sensory processing, and power management.

The low level unit consists of a pair of Microchip 16F877 Programmable Interrupt Controllers (PICs), which are dedicated to motor driving, sensory acquisition, and preprocessing. Input set points for the servomotors are received from the walking layer via a standard RS232 serial line, which allows a transfer rate up to 115 Kbaud.

The current consumed by each leg is converted to a voltage signal and is sampled by the PIC through its analog input lines upon a specific command coming from the serial line. The PWM signal generator is interrupt driven and can drive up to 16 motors, hence two PICs are used to drive all the servomotors.

Through the remaining I/O lines of the PIC, it is possible to control external sensors, like infrared or ultrasonic proximity sensors. If a sensor is not used, the PIC interface disables its power line by sending a signal to the Power Manager.

To enforce real-time constraints on critical control activities, the software on the PC104 runs under the SHARK operating system, which is briefly described in the following section.

2.1 The SHARK Kernel

SHARK is a real time operating system [9] developed for supporting predictable control applications consisting of tasks with different constraints and timing requirements (e.g., hard, soft, non real-time, periodic, aperiodic, etc.). The most peculiar features of this kernel include:

- **Modularity.** All kernel mechanisms are developed independently of other internal components and several options are available for each mechanism.
- **Dynamic Scheduling.** The kernel provides direct support for deadline-based scheduling, which guarantees predictable responsiveness and full processor utilization.
- **Resource Reservation.** A *temporal protection* mechanism based on the Constant Bandwidth Server [1] allows the user to reserve a fraction of the processor bandwidth to activities with highly variable computation time. This prevents execution overruns to create unpredictable interference and allows tasks to execute in isolation as they were executing alone on a slower dedicated processor.
- **Bounded Blocking.** Priority inversion caused by resource sharing can be avoided through specific concurrency control protocols, including Priority Inheritance, Priority Ceiling [13], or Stack Resource Policy [4]. In addition, a fully asynchronous (non blocking) mechanism is available for exchanging data among periodic tasks running at different rates.
- **Predictable Interrupt Handling.** A device driver does not fully interfere with application tasks, since can be split into a *fast handler* (executing in the context of the running task) and a *safe handler* (guaranteed by the system).

3 Power-Aware Management

Hardware and software components cooperate to reach the following main goals: low power consumption, onboard sensory processing, and real-time computation capabilities. In order to contain costs, the robot is built with generic mechanical and electrical components, making the low-power objective more difficult to be satisfied. Nevertheless, the adoption of power-aware strategies inside the robot hardware and software modules significantly increased the system lifetime. To achieve significant energy saving, power management is adopted at different architecture levels, from the hardware components to the operating system, up to and the application.

3.1 Hardware Level

The simultaneous activity of 18 servomotors creates sporadic high peak loads of current that must be handled by the power supply circuit. For this reason Lead-Acid batteries are chosen as a preliminary test-set, due also to low cost and fast recharge. A Lithium battery could also be a good alternative.

Without proper precautions, the current instability induced by servomotors can cause unpredictable resets and anomalies inside the microprocessor boards used in the system. To avoid such problems, these systems are typically designed with two different battery packs, one for the servomotors and non-critical electronics, and the other for the microprocessor board. Such a solution, however, is not efficient since does not exploit the full available energy.

The solution we adopted to optimize battery duration uses a single battery pack, with a specific control circuit (the Power Manager) for eliminating peak disturbances caused by servomotors that could reset the processor. The Power Manager is one of the most critical parts of the robotic system. The high current flow and the presence of inductances inside the batteries make the power voltage extremely unstable. If connecting the batteries directly to the servomotors, a simple robot movement would cause a temporary voltage breakdown that would disable all the other boards. In our solution, the voltage breakdown is avoided by a feedback circuit and a set of backup capacitors. When a high peak of current is requested by the actuation system and the power line inductance causes a voltage breakdown, a feedback circuit decreases the current flow and a set of backup capacitor, isolated by a fast Schotty diode, keeps the PC104 and other critical parts alive. The Power Manager can also disable specific subsystems of the robot, like sensors or servomotors, when the power-aware algorithm (running in the PC104) sends a specific control command.

3.2 Operating System Level

In a computer system, the power consumption is related to the voltage at which the circuits operate according to an increasing convex function, whose precise form depends on the specific technology [8]. Hence, the amount of energy consumed by the processor can be controlled through the speed and voltage at which the processor operates.

When processor speed is increased to improve performance, we would expect the application tasks to finish earlier. Unfortunately this is not always the case, because several anomalies [10] may occur in the schedule when tasks have time and resource constraints, making the performance discontinuous with the speed.

Conversely, when voltage is decreased to save energy consumption, all computation times increase, so the processor might experience an overload condition that could make the application behavior quite unpredictable.

In [7] it has been shown that, to prevent scheduling anomalies and achieve scalability of performance as a function of the speed, tasks should be fully preemptive and should use non blocking mechanisms to access shared resources. Under SHARK, non blocking communication is provided through the Cyclic Asynchronous Buffers (CABs) [9]. Moreover, to avoid the negative effects of overload caused by a speed reduction, periodic tasks should specify their period with some degree of flexibility, so that they can be resized to handle the overload. In our system, when an overload is detected, rate adaptation is performed using the elastic model [5, 6], according to which task utilizations are treated like springs that can adapt to a desired workload through period variations. Viceversa, if the load is less than one, the processor speed can be reduced to get a full processor utilization, thus meeting timing constraints while minimizing energy. The elastic task model is fully supported by the SHARK kernel as a new scheduling module.

One problem with the adopted architecture is that the PC104 is not a new generation power-aware CPU with voltage and frequency scaling. Nevertheless, it is possible to force the CPU in a sleep mode for a specific amount of time, during which the processor enters in standby. Switching the CPU on and off, as a PWM signal, the average processor speed can be continuously varied from the two extreme values. If Q_A is the interval of time the CPU is active at its maximum frequency f_M and Q_S is the interval in which it is in sleep mode, the average frequency is given by $\overline{f} = f_M Q_A/(Q_A + Q_S)$. If $\sigma = Q_A/(Q_A + Q_S)$ denotes the active fraction of the duty cycle in the PWM mode of the CPU, the average frequency of the processor becomes $\overline{f} = f_M \sigma$. Since $\overline{f} < f_M$, all tasks run with an increased computation time given by

$$C'_i = \frac{f_M}{\overline{f}} C_i = \frac{Q_A + Q_S}{Q_A} C_i = \frac{C_i}{\sigma}.$$

Finally, if P_M is the power consumption in the active mode and P_S the one in the sleep mode, then the average power consumption is linearly dependent from σ and is given by

$$\overline{P} = \frac{P_A Q_A + P_S Q_S}{Q_A + Q_S} = P_A \sigma + P_S(1 - \sigma) = P_S + (P_A - P_S)\sigma.$$

3.3 Application Level

To achieve a significant reduction in the power consumption, it is essential that appropriate strategies are adopted also at the application level. For some devices, like the camera and the frame grabber, the only strategy that can be adopted is to turn them off while they are not used. For other devices, like the ultrasonic sensor and the servomotors, more careful strategies can be adopted. The ultrasonic sensor, when turned on, can be in three different states: standby, working, and beam mode. The acquisition period is also important; in fact a short period causes too much energy consumption due to frequent beam generations, whereas a long period can lead to missing some obstacles. Table 1 shows the power consumption of the devices used on the robot.

Table 1. Power consumption of the robot devices

Device	Power (W)
Frame grabber	1
CCD camera	0.4
Servomotor	0.4 - 20
Ultrasonic sensor	0.15 - 0.75 - 2.5

To minimize energy consumption in the servomotors, it is important not only to move the hexapod with a given speed in a desired direction, but also to select a leg posture and a walking mode that drains less current. This is crucial when comparing walking robots with wheeled vehicles, which have a negligible consumption when they do not move.

The algorithms we propose to coordinate the legs modulate a reference walking step through a number of parameters. An important parameter is the maximum angle that each leg covers in the horizontal plane during its motion. A difference in such angles for the left and right legs causes the robot to turn. Another parameter that can be tuned is the raise that each leg performs in the vertical plane. This value depends on the type of surface on which the robot walks: small values are sufficient for walking on smooth surfaces, whereas higher values are needed in the presence of obstacles or protruding regions.

To guarantee the equilibrium of the robot during walking, the algorithm always keeps at least three legs in touch with the ground, so that the center of mass of the robot always falls in the polygon defined by the touching points. Two different walking modes are considered in this paper, depending on the number of legs that are moved at the same time: one or three. They will be referred to as 1-leg and 3-leg algorithms.

When adopting the 1-leg algorithm, it is necessary to evaluate the exact order in which legs are moved forward. Two very simple rules would be to maintain the support polygon made with the touching legs as large as possible, or to have a little phase difference between adjacent legs.

In the 3-leg algorithm, the specific position set points for the motors involved in the horizontal motion are generated by sampling two cosine functions with opposite phases. Similarly, a pair of sine functions with opposite phases was initially used for the vertical leg motion. However, this solution has been modified since it was causing the robot to have a significant roll while walking. The specific shape of the waveform depends on many actors, including equilibrium requirements, speed, and maximum allowed roll.

4 Experimental Results

This section presents some experimental results performed on the robot to evaluate the power consumption related to different postures and walking modes.

In a first experiment, we evaluated how the power consumption is affected by the robot posture. To do that, we measured the current drained by the motors as the angles, α and β, of the joints corresponding to the two horizontal axes of the legs were varied in a given range. The angles of the joints rotating around the vertical axes were set to keep the legs parallel to each other. The results are reported in Figure 4. A dash in the table means that the leg was not touching the floor, so consuming a negligible power. As intuitive, the minimum power consumption was reached when the legs were vertical (that is, $\alpha = 0$ and $\beta = -90$), however such a posture resulted to be quite critical for the stability of the robot. As shown in the table, the minimum current consumption in a stable configuration was obtained with $\alpha = 45$ and $\beta = -45$.

$\alpha \backslash \beta$	-45	-30	-15	0	15	30
0	0.62	0.86	-	-	-	-
15	0.43	0.72	0.73	-	-	-
30	0.13	0.55	0.78	-	-	-
45	0.09	0.26	0.55	0.77	-	-
60	0.18	0.14	0.30	0.58	-	-
75	0.19	0.13	0.15	0.35	0.25	-
90	0.28	0.20	0.20	0.19	0.55	0.20

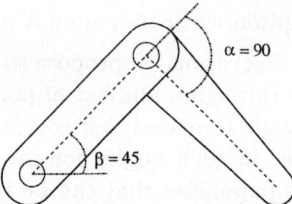

Fig. 4. Current values for different postures

A second experiment has been carried out to test the power consumption for different walking modes, namely the 1-leg and 3-leg modes. The 3-leg mode was tested for three different speeds, obtained by changing the period T_s of a basic leg step. To compare the two modes, we monitored a set of parameters while the robot was walking along a straight line path 1 meter long. In particular, we measured the time T_d to complete the path, the energy E consumed by the system in T_d, and the average current I_{avg} drained by all the motors. The results of this experiment are reported in Table 2.

Note that, when legs are moving at the same speed ($T_s = 0.9$), the 3-leg mode is faster than the 1-leg mode and consumes less current. This counterintuitive result can be explained by considering the non-linearity in the current/torque function, which makes the robot to consume more current when its weight is distributed on five legs rather than on three legs. Hence, the 3-leg mode resulted to be more efficient both in terms of energy and performance. We also observed that the energy consumed by the system to accomplish the task decreases as the leg speed gets higher. This happens because, in a fast walking, the reduction

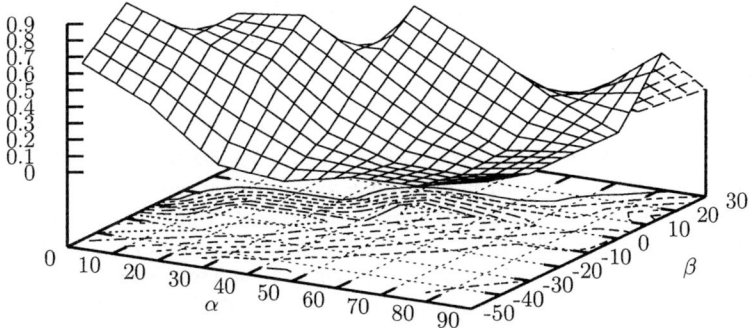

Fig. 5. Current drained in function of α and β

Table 2. Comparing different walking modes

	1-leg	3-leg	3-leg	3-leg
T_s (s)	0.9	1.8	0.9	0.23
T_d (s)	34.3	21.8	9.87	3.42
E (J)	512	273	140	73.6
I_{avg} (A)	1.86	1.56	1.77	2.69

of time T_d for completing the task is more significant than the increase of the average current drained by the motors, making fast walking more effective.

5 Conclusions

In this paper we presented an integrated approach for designing robot systems with real-time and energy-aware requirements. We showed that to achieve a predictable timing behavior and a significant saving in the energy consumption, a combined effort is required at different architecture levels. At the hardware level, the processor must provide different operational modes to balance speed versus power consumption. At the operating system level, a specific power management layer should set the appropriate operational mode to minimize energy consumption while guaranteeing the timing constraints. Finally, at the application level, the control strategies should be tunable to trade performance with energy consumption, so that the robot can switch to a different behavior to prolong its lifetime when the batteries are low, still performing useful tasks.

We showed how the techniques discussed above can be implemented in a small walking robot using commercial low-cost hardware components. As a future work, we plan to perform a more extensive experimentation on the robot, in order to derive a complete set of strategies to allow the power management unit to select the most appropriate operational mode based on the task to be performed and on the residual energy available in the batteries.

References

1. Abeni, L., Buttazzo, G.C.: Integrating Multimedia Applications in Hard Real-Time Systems. In: Proc. of the IEEE Real-Time Systems Symposium. (1998)
2. Aydin, H., Melhem, R., Mossé, D., Mejia Alvarez, P.: Determining Optimal Processor Speeds for Periodic Real-Time Tasks with Different Power Characteristics. In: Proceedings of the Euromicro Conference on Real-Time Systems. (2001)
3. Aydin, H., Melhem, R., Mossé, D., Mejia Alvarez, P.: Dynamic and Aggressive Scheduling Techniques for Power-Aware Real-Time Systems. In: Proceedings of the IEEE Real-Time Systems Symposium. (2001)
4. Baker, T.P.: Stack-Based Scheduling of Real-Time Processes. The Journal of Real-Time Systems **3**(1) (1991) 76–100
5. Buttazzo, G.C., Lipari, G., Abeni, L.: Elastic Task Model for Adaptive Rate Control. In: Proc. of the IEEE Real-Time Systems Symposium. (1998) 286–295
6. Buttazzo, G.C., Lipari, G., Caccamo, M., Abeni, L.: Elastic Scheduling for Flexible Workload Management. IEEE Transactions on Computers **51**(3) (2002) 289–302
7. Buttazzo, G.C.: Scalable applications for energy-aware processors. In: Proc. of the 2nd Int. Conf. on Embedded Software, Grenoble, France. LNCS, Vol. 2491, Springer-Verlag (2002) 153–165
8. Chan, E., Govil, K., Wasserman, H.: Comparing Algorithms for Dynamic Speedsetting of a Low-Power CPU. In: Proceedings of the First ACM International Conference on Mobile Computing and Networking. (1995)
9. Gai, P., Abeni, L., Giorgi, M., Buttazzo, G.C: A New Kernel Approach for Modular Real-Time System Development. In: Proc. 13th IEEE Euromicro Conf. on Real-Time Systems. (2001)
10. Graham, R.L.: Bounds on the Performance of Scheduling Algorithms. In: Computer and Job Scheduling Theory. John Wiley and Sons (1976) 165–227
11. Liu, C.L., Layland, J.W.: Scheduling Algorithms for Multiprogramming in a Hard Real-Time Environment. Journal of the ACM **20**(1) (1973) 40–61
12. Melhem, R., AbouGhazaleh, N., Aydin, H., Mosse, D.: Power Management Points in Power-Aware Real-Time Systems. In: Graybill, R., Melhem, R. (eds.): Power Aware Computing. Plenum/Kluwer Publishers (2002)
13. Sha, L., Rajkumar, L.R., Lehoczky, J.P.: Priority Inheritance Protocols: An Approach to Real-Time Synchronization. IEEE Transactions on Computers **39**(9) (1990)
14. Yao, F., Demers, A., Shenker, S.: A Scheduling Model for Reduced CPU Energy. In: IEEE Annual Foundations of Computer Science. (1995) 374–382

Multirate Feedback Control Using the TinyRealTime Kernel

Dan Henriksson and Anton Cervin

Department of Automatic Control
Lund Institute of Technology
Box 118, SE-221 00 Lund, Sweden
{dan,anton}@control.lth.se

Abstract. Embedded microcontrollers are often programmed in plain C and lack support for multithreading and real-time scheduling. This can make it very cumbersome to implement multirate feedback control applications. We have developed the TINYREALTIME kernel for the Atmel ATmega8L AVR to show that it is feasible to use high-precision, deadline-based scheduling even in a tiny 8-bit processor with 1 KB of RAM. The kernel is demonstrated in a multirate control application, where six periodic real-time tasks (four control tasks and two pulse width modulation tasks) are used to control two ball-and-beam processes.

1 Introduction

The growing complexity of embedded real-time control applications has increased the need for kernel support for multiprogramming and dynamic real-time scheduling even in tiny embedded systems. Traditionally, embedded systems have been programmed in plain C, using interrupt routines to handle the time-critical operations. This approach works fine as long as there is only one activity with strict timing requirements in the system. For multirate control applications, however, such an approach can quickly become very cumbersome. We argue that the convenient techniques of concurrent programming and real-time scheduling are feasible even for tiny embedded systems.

In this paper, we describe the architecture and application of TINYREALTIME [1], a tiny real-time kernel for the Atmel ATmega8L 8-bit AVR microcontroller. The ATmega8L features a RISC processor with up to 16 MIPS throughput at 16 MHz, 8 KB flash program memory, and 1 KB SRAM. For timing, the microcontroller features one 16-bit timer/counter and two 8-bit timers/counters with separate prescalars. The ATmega8L has a rich I/O interface, including a 6-channel 10-bit A/D converter, 23 programmable digital I/O ports, three PWM channels, and various serial communication interfaces. For a more detailed description of the ATmega8L AVR, see [2].

The TINYREALTIME kernel is event-triggered and implements fully preemptive earliest-deadline-first (EDF) task scheduling. Counting semaphores are provided to support task synchronization. The Stack Resource Protocol (SRP) [3] will be implemented as resource access policy.

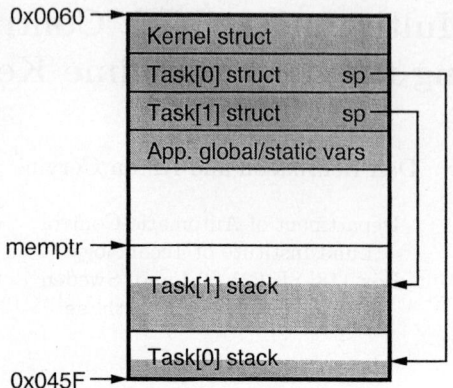

Fig. 1. Memory layout of the real-time kernel

The memory requirement of the kernel is small, with a flash memory footprint of approximately 1200 bytes. It further occupies 11 bytes of RAM for the kernel data structure plus an additional 11 bytes for each task and one byte for each semaphore.

2 Kernel Overview

2.1 Memory Layout and Data Structures

A multirate real-time control application has been developed to demonstrate the feasibility of the real-time kernel. The application involves two ball-and-beam laboratory processes which are concurrently controlled using six application tasks. Each controller is implemented using a cascaded structure with two tasks running at different rates. Two additional tasks are used to implement a simple pulse width modulation of the output signal. The experiments display satisfactory control performance, good timing behavior, and low CPU utilization of the target system.

Related Work

There exist dozens of commercial and non-commercial real-time kernels for small embedded systems that support either cooperative, round-robin, or priority-preemptive scheduling. These kernels do not, however, support explicit timing constraints in the form of deadlines and dynamic-priority scheduling. One noticeable exception is ERIKA Enterprise [4], a commercial variant of the open-source kernel ERIKA Educational kernel [5]. ERIKA Enterprise supports several scheduling algorithms and resource protocols, including fully preemptive EDF with the stack resource protocol. It has a small ROM footprint (about 1600 bytes), making it suitable for tiny embedded systems. Supported targets include the Hitachi H8 and the ARM 7.

The ATmega8L AVR has 1120 memory locations, of which the first 96 bytes are used for the register file and the I/O memory, and the following 1024 bytes represent the internal RAM. In the kernel implementation, the 1024 bytes of RAM are utilized according to the memory layout in Figure 1, which shows the location of the kernel and task data structures and the individual stack memories. The kernel data structure and the task data structure are given by Listings 1 and 2.

As seen in Figure 1, the kernel and task data structures are allocated statically from low addresses upwards followed by possible global and static variables for the particular application. Each task has an associated stack, and the stacks are allocated from the maximum address downwards. The stack sizes are specified by the user upon task creation, and it is the responsibility of the user not to exhaust the available memory.

Listing 1. The kernel data structure

```
#define MAXNBRTASKS ...
#define MAXNBRSEMAPHORES ...

struct kernel {
    uint8_t nbrOfTasks;                         // number of created tasks
    uint8_t running;                            // index of the running task
    struct task tasks[MAXNBRTASKS+1];           // task structures (+1 for idle task)
    uint8_t semaphores[MAXNBRSEMAPHORES];       // semaphore counters
    uint8_t *memptr;                            // pointer to free memory
    uint16_t cycles;                            // number of major timer cycles
    uint32_t nextHit;                           // next kernel wake-up time
};
```

Listing 2. The task data structure

```
struct task {
    uint16_t sp;          // stack pointer
    uint32_t release;     // current/next release time
    uint32_t deadline;    // current absolute deadline
    uint8_t state;        // 0=terminated, 1=readyQ, 2=timeQ, i=semQ[i-2]
};
```

A task occupies 11 bytes of memory, where 2 bytes are used to store the stack pointer of the task, 4 bytes each to represent the release time and absolute deadline of the task, and one byte to represent the state of the task. The kernel data structure occupies a total of 11 bytes of memory to represent; the number of tasks in the system, the currently running task, pointers to task and semaphore vectors, pointer to next available stack memory address (see Figure 1), number of major timer cycles (see Section 2.2), and the next wake-up time of the kernel.

In order to reduce the RAM memory requirement of the kernel, no queues or sorted list functionality is implemented for the time queue, ready queue, and semaphore waiting queues. Instead, each task has an associated state, and linear

Table 1. Trade-off between clock resolution and system life time

Prescalar	Clock resolution	System life time
1	68 ns	5 min
8	543 ns	39 min
64	4.3 µs	5 h
256	17.4 µs	21 h
1024	69.4 µs	83 h

search is performed in the task vector each time a task should be moved from the time queue to the ready queue, etc. The state will be any of: terminated (state==0), ready (state==1), sleeping (state==2), or waiting on semaphore i (state==2+i). Depending of the maximum number of tasks, n_1, and the maximum number of semaphores, n_2, the total RAM memory requirement of the kernel is $11 + 11n_1 + n_2$.

2.2 Timing

The output compare match mode of the 16-bit timer of the AVR is used to generate clock interrupts. Each time the timer value matches the compare match value, an interrupt is generated. The associated interrupt handler then contains the main functionality of the real-time kernel, such as releasing tasks, determining which ready task to run, and to perform context switches.

Each time the kernel has executed, i.e., at the end of the output compare match interrupt routine, the output compare value is updated to generate a new interrupt at the next time the kernel needs to run. If this next wake-up time is located in a later major cycle (each timer cycle corresponds to 2^{16} timer ticks), the output compare value is set to zero. This way we make sure to get an interrupt at timer overflow to increase the cycles variable of the kernel data structure.

The timer uses a 16-bit representation and, as seen in the kernel data structure in Listing 1, an additional 16 clock bits are used to store major cycles. The time associated with each timer tick depends on the chosen prescalar factor of the timer (1, 8, 64, 256, or 1024). The choice of prescalar factor of the timer determines both the clock resolution and the system life time. No cyclic time is implemented, and thus the system life time is limited by the time it takes to fill all 32 clock bits in the time representation. The higher clock resolution (i.e., the smaller time between each timer tick), the shorter time before all 32 clock bits are filled. The life time and resolution for the different prescalar factors of the AVR are shown in Table 1.

The problem with limited life time versus high timing resolution can be avoided by using a circular clock implementation [6]. The extra cost introduced by this approach is that the clock needs to be checked for overrun at each invocation of the kernel, whereas an added advantage is that a fewer number of bits can be used for the clock representation (thus giving less computational overhead in every timing operation).

2.3 Kernel Internal Workings

The kernel is implemented in the interrupt handler associated with the output compare match interrupt of the timer. When the interrupt handler is entered, the status register and the 32 working registers are stored on the stack of the currently running task.

Thereafter, the task vector is traversed in order to determine if any tasks should be released at the current time. In accordance with EDF, the ready task with the closest absolute deadline is then made the running task, which may trigger a context switch. In that case, the current address of the stack pointer is stored in the task struct associated with the preempted task, and the stack pointer is updated with the corresponding value of the new running task.

Finally, a new clock interrupt is set up, by updating the output compare match register. The clock interrupt is set to the closest release time among the sleeping tasks.

2.4 API and Real-Time Primitives

The API of the TINYREALTIME kernel is shown in Table 2. `trtInitKernel` is used to initialize the kernel and must be called first of all from the main program. Tasks are then created by the function `trtCreateTask`. Here the user specifies the code function to be executed, stack size, release offset, deadline, and an arbitrary data structure for the task. Tasks may be terminated using the function `trtTerminate`.

The implementation also provides a number of real-time primitives that may be called from the application programs. These include functions to retrieve the current global time, set and get the release and absolute deadline of a task, put a task to sleep until a certain time, and to wait for and signal semaphores.

The `trtSleepUntil` call involves both setting the new release time and the new absolute deadline the task will have when it is awakened. This needs to be done in a single function, since these calls would otherwise individually change the state of the task and possibly cause context switches.

Table 2. The API of the TINYREALTIME kernel

Command	Description
trtInitKernel	Initialize the kernel.
trtCreateTask	Create a task, specifying its release time and absolute deadline.
trtTerminate	Terminate the execution of the current task.
trtCurrentTime	Get the current system time.
trtSleepUntil	Put the running task to sleep, specifying new release and deadline.
trtGetRelease	Retrieve the release time of the running task.
trtGetDeadline	Retrieve the absolute deadline of the running task.
trtCreateSemaphore	Create a semaphore.
trtWait	Wait on a semaphore.
trtSignal	Signal a semaphore.

Fig. 2. The ball-and-beam laboratory process

Counting semaphores has also been implemented in order to support task synchronization and communication under mutual exclusion. A semaphore is represented by an 8-bit unsigned integer (see Listing 1), and the signal and wait operations basically correspond to incrementing and decrementing this counter. If a task does a wait on semaphore i with the counter being zero, the task is suspended and its state is set to $i + 1$, as described in Section 2.1. When a task does a signal on a semaphore, the task vector of the kernel is scanned for tasks waiting for this semaphore. Of these tasks, if any, the one with the shortest time to its deadline is made ready.

For a complete description and implementation details of the various real-time primitives and the kernel initialization and task creation functions, see [1].

3 Multirate Feedback Control

The TINYREALTIME kernel was used to implement concurrent control of two ball-and-beam laboratory processes. Three tasks were used to control each process, for a total of seven tasks (including the idle task). The controller was implemented using a cascaded structure with one task for the inner and one task for the outer loop of the cascade. Since the AVR only supports digital output, pulse width modulation (PWM) was necessary to generate the desired control signal. This was implemented in software as two separate tasks, one for each control loop.

3.1 The Process

The ball-and-beam laboratory process is shown in Figure 2. The horizontal beam is controlled by a motor, and the objective is to balance the ball along the beam. The measurement signals from the system are the beam angle, denoted by ϕ, and the ball position on the beam, denoted by x. A linearized model of the system is given by

$$G(s) = G_\phi(s)G_x(s), \tag{1}$$

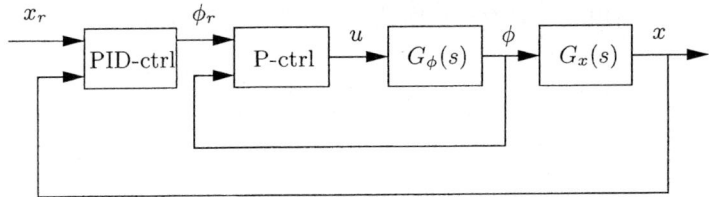

Fig. 3. The cascaded controller structure for the ball-and-beam process

where
$$G_\phi(s) = \frac{k_\phi}{s} \quad (2)$$
is the transfer function between the motor input and the beam angle, and
$$G_x(s) = -\frac{k_x}{s^2} \quad (3)$$
is the transfer function between the beam angle and the ball position. The gains of the systems are given by $k_\phi \approx 4.4$ and $k_x \approx 9$.

3.2 The Controller

The structure of the cascaded controller is shown in Figure 3. The outer controller is a PID-controller and the inner controller is a simple P-controller. The outer controller was implemented according to the equations

$$\begin{aligned} D(k) &= a_d D(k-1) - b_d \left(y(k) - y(k-1) \right) \\ u(k) &= K \left(y_r - y(k) \right) + I(k) + D(k) \\ I(k+1) &= I(k) + a_i \left(y_r - y(k) \right) \end{aligned} \quad (4)$$

with the input signal, y, being the measured ball position and the output, u, being the reference angle for the inner P-controller. The parameters a_d, b_d, and a_i are precomputed and are given by

$$a_d = \frac{T_d}{T_d + Nh}, \quad b_d = \frac{KT_D N}{T_d + Nh}, \quad a_i = \frac{Kh}{T_i}.$$

The controller was implemented as a multirate controller, where one task was used for the inner loop and another task for the outer loop. The inner controller was running with a 20 ms sampling interval, whereas the outer controller used a 40 ms sampling interval, see Figure 4.

The controller parameters were chosen to $K_{inner} = 2$, $K_{outer} = -0.25$, $T_i = 10$, $T_d = 0.9$, and $N = 10$, giving the lumped controller parameters $a_d = 0.692$, $b_d = 1.731$, $a_i = 0.004$. The relatively large difference in magnitude of the parameters affected the implementation, which was performed by fixed-point arithmetics with a representation using 5 integer bits and 11 fractional bits.

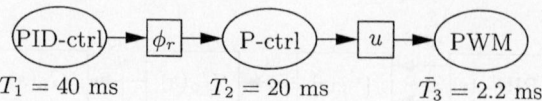

$T_1 = 40$ ms $\quad T_2 = 20$ ms $\quad \bar{T}_3 = 2.2$ ms

Fig. 4. Communicating tasks and shared variables in the multirate structure

The angle reference is communicated between the outer and inner controller tasks, and the control signal is communicated between the inner controller and the PWM task, as shown in Figure 4. Global variables were used for the communication and two semaphores were created for mutual exclusion when accessing the common variables.

3.3 Pulse Width Modulation

The control signal generated by the inner P-controller is an integer number in the interval $[-512, 511]$. This signal needs to be converted to an output in the interval $[-10, 10]$. However, the output channels can only generate $+10$ or -10 volt, depending on the value of the corresponding bit in the $PORTB$ register of the AVR.

To solve this problem, a pulse width modulation task was implemented for each control loop. The PWM task runs with a 128 tick cycle time (corresponding to 2.2 ms with the prescalar set to 256), outputting $+10$ volt in x ticks and -10 volt in $(128 - x)$ ticks. The x is determined from the desired control signal. E.g., to output 0 volt, x is chosen to 64.

3.4 Experiments

In the experiments six tasks were used to control two ball-and-beam processes concurrently. Results of the experiments are shown in Figures 5-7 for one of the processes.

Two things can be noted from the plots. First, the integral action is quite slow, which is mainly due to the quantization in the control signal relative the increments of the I-part. Because of the large relative round-off error in the a_i-parameter of Equation 4, it was not possible to increase the integral further without jeopardizing the stability of the system during the transients. Second, it can also be seen that the control signal is quite noisy. This is due to our implementation of the PWM, which is switching between $+10$ and -10 volts with a quite slow frequency. The software implementation of the PWM output was done only to include more tasks, for the purpose of stressing the real-time kernel. Otherwise, a far superior option would have been to use the PWM functionality of the AVR hardware.

The kernel was monitored using the serial communication to estimate the system load. The currently running task was written at a 115.2k Baud rate to sample the execution trace. The result is shown in Figure 8, and it can be seen that the load of the system is quite low. The approximate utilization was calculated to 10 percent.

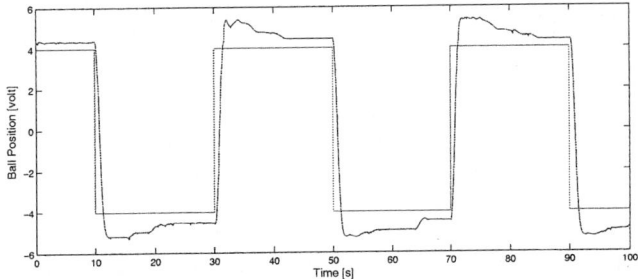

Fig. 5. Ball position and reference during the experiment

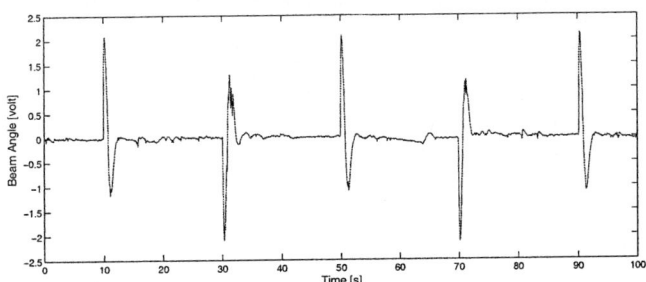

Fig. 6. Beam angle during the experiment

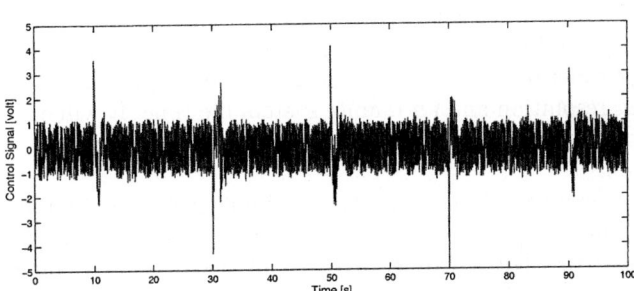

Fig. 7. Control signal during the experiment

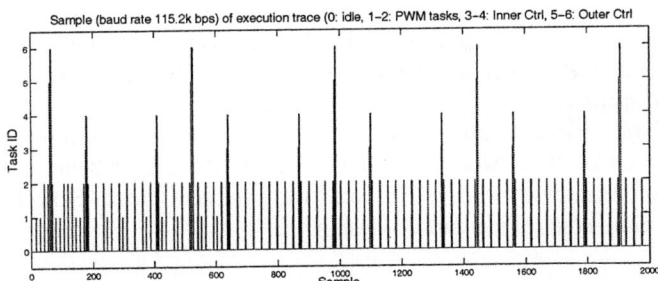

Fig. 8. Sample of the execution trace during the experiment

4 Conclusions

The paper has described the design and application of TINYREALTIME, an event-triggered real-time kernel for an Atmel AVR 8-bit micro-controller. The kernel supports multiprogramming by means of dynamic deadline-based scheduling of tasks and counting semaphores for synchronization. The kernel footprint is small ($\approx$ 1200 bytes).

The kernel was evaluated in a real-time control application involving six user tasks. The application demonstrated the feasibility of implementing event-based deadline-driven scheduling with high timing resolution on a tiny embedded system such as the Atmel AVR. The RAM memory requirement for the kernel and task data structures in the application was about 100 bytes.

Future Work

The TINYREALTIME kernel may be extended in many ways. The current implementation can be made more efficient, and because of the relatively low memory requirement of the current implementation a lot of additional functionality may be implemented. Some of the things that will be implemented in the future are summarized below.

The current version of the kernel was written specifically for the AVR 8-bit RISC platform. However, it is desirable to have a kernel architecture that supports other platforms as well. This would require the definition of a hardware abstraction layer for the hardware-dependent routines, such as interrupt and context switch handling.

The cyclic timer mentioned in Section 2.2 will be implemented. This will allow a high timing resolution and an infinite system life time. It will also increase the performance of the kernel by reducing the number of bits used in the timing representation.

Currently, no resource access protocol is implemented for the semaphores. To this end we intend to implement the Stack Resource Protocol (SRP) [3]. This is an extension to EDF-scheduled systems of the Priority Ceiling Protocol [7] that provides low worst-case blocking times. We will also implement higher-level synchronization mechanisms, such as monitors with condition variables.

An additional advantage of SRP is that it guarantees that once a task starts executing, it will not be blocked until completion. This means that a lower-priority task never will be executed before the task is completed. This allows for a more efficient implementation where all tasks in the system can share the same single stack.

Finally, we intend to implement kernel primitives to handle execution time budgets for tasks. This would facilitate EDF-based server scheduling, such as the Constant Bandwidth Server [8], and the related Control Server mechanism [9] for real-time control system co-design.

References

1. Henriksson, D., Cervin, A.: TinyRealTime—An EDF Kernel for the Atmel ATmega8L AVR. Technical report ISRN LUTFD2/TFRT--7608--SE, Department of Automatic Control, Lund Institute of Technology, Sweden (2004)
2. Atmel: AVR 8-Bit RISC. http://www.atmel.com/products/AVR (2004)
3. Baker, T.P.: Stack-Based Scheduling of Real-Time Processes. Journal of Real-time Systems **3** (1991) 67–99
4. Evidence: ERIKA Enterprise. http://www.evidence.eu.com/Erika.asp (2004)
5. Gai, P., Lipari, G., Di Natale, M.: A Flexible and Configurable Real-Time Kernel for Time Predictability and Minimal RAM Requirements. Technical report RETIS TR 2001-02, ReTiS Lab, Scuola Superiore S. Anna, Pisa, Italy (2001)
6. Carlini, A., Buttazzo, G.C.: An Efficient Time Representation for Real-Time Embedded Systems. In: Proceedings of the 2003 ACM Symposium on Applied Computing, Melbourne, Florida. ACM (2003) 705–712
7. Sha, L., Rajkumar, R., Lehoczy, J.P.: Priority Inheritance Protocols: An Approach to Real-Time Synchronization. IEEE Transactions on Computers **39** (1990) 1175–1185
8. Abeni, L., Buttazzo, G.: Integrating Multimedia Applications in Hard Real-Time Systems. In: Proc. 19th IEEE Real-Time Systems Symp., Madrid, Spain. IEEE Computer (1998) 4–13
9. Cervin, A., Eker, J.: Control-Scheduling Codesign of Real-Time Systems: The Control Server Approach. Journal of Embedded Computing (2004) to appear

An Educational Open Source Real-Time Kernel for Small Embedded Control Systems

Michele Cirinei, Antonio Mancina, Davide Cantini,
Paolo Gai, and Luigi Palopoli

ReTiS Lab, Scuola Superiore S. Anna - Pisa, Italy
{michele,antonio,davide,pj,luigi}@gandalf.sssup.it

Abstract. This paper describes ERIKA Educational, an open source, integrated real-time kernel architecture used for developing embedded real-time applications. This version of the kernel is especially targeted for an educational audience, that wants to experiment embedded system design, real-time scheduling and wireless communication on a simple inexpensive platform such as the LEGO Mindstorms RCX[1]. The kernel architecture provides support for advanced scheduling algorithms and primitives, and for the standard devices available on the LEGO Mindstorms. A radio frequency module that interact with the RCX IR sensor has also been developed to enable easy cooperation between different entities. A case study is finally presented showing how ERIKA Educational can be used to create small networked embedded control systems.

1 Introduction

Real-time computing is required in many application domains, ranging from embedded process control to multimedia streaming. Each application has peculiar characteristics in terms of timing constraints and computational requirements. A particular class of real-time applications is related to small embedded control systems, which are often implemented as system-on-chip (SoC), featuring low performance in terms of computing power and available memory. Typical examples are the CPUs used in the automotive field, and many other small-scale control devices.

The lack of computing power and memory typically raises a number of interesting problems related to an efficient application fitting on tiny requirements maintaining the needed predictability. These problems can be solved using small RTOS carefully designed to meet the constraints of SoC, and using an appropriate design methodology that guides the users to the specification and the verifications of the temporal constraints of the various applications.

Guidelines for the application development and for the services that have to be supported by small RTOSes have been incorporated in industrial standards, such as the OSEK/VDX [16] standard. These services usually include a

---
[1] LEGO, Mindstorms and RCX are trademarks of the LEGO Group of companies which does not sponsor, authorize or endorse this paper and the the ERIKA Educational Project. For more details, please read the LEGO Fair Play Message [12].

suitable real-time scheduling algorithms, such as fixed priority deadline monotonic [1] with a Non-Preemptive protocol for accessing mutually exclusive shared resources. From the educational point of view, all these methodologies are advanced topics that are difficult to teach because of the lack of low-cost testbeds that students can use to test different applications in a low-performance control environment.

For this reason, in this paper we present ERIKA Educational, a research kernel purposely designed to help students implementing small embedded systems similar in the architecture and footprint to those that are really used in industries. As the reference hardware architecture, we chose to use the LEGO Mindstorms RCX[1] platform, that allows an easy development of small robotic applications. ERIKA Educational provides a full fledged operating system similar in the performance to typical commercial kernels implementing the BCC1 conformance class of the OSEK OS standard [16].

ERIKA Educational supports many devices and sensors provided with the RCX platform, and also gives a set of primitives that implements an IR communication protocol, optionally using an RF interface that enables different robots to cooperate exchanging data. Such communication protocol has also been ported to the SHaRK Kernel [8] to enable communication between the robots and a common PC.

Finally, the paper presents a case study showing the usage of ERIKA Educational for building small embedded control applications made of different robots dynamically exchanging information through the wireless device.

The rest of the paper is organized as follows. Section 2 presents the related work. Section 3 introduces the overall architecture of the system. Sections 4 and 5 describe device drivers and network support. Section 6 briefly presents a case study, and finally Section 7 states our conclusions and future work.

2 Related Work

ERIKA Educational is a project started at the ReTiS Lab of the Scuola Superiore S. Anna in the context of the MADESS Research Project [18, 9]. In particular, ERIKA Educational implements the SRP Protocol [3, 4] with preemption threshold, first introduced by Express Logic in the ThreadX kernel [7], and then further analyzed in [6, 21, 22, 10, 20]. That scheduling methodology has also been incorporated in the OSEK/VDX automotive standard [17], allowing predictable response time in tiny systems such as the power-train microcontrollers.

The hardware we used for ERIKA Educational is the LEGO Mindstorms RCX platform[1][13]. The RCX platform hosts an Hitachi H8 microcontroller at 16 MHz with a 16 Kb ROM and 32 Kb RAM memory, three input ports for external sensors, three output ports for motors, an infrared port (at 1200 or 2400 baud), and some other interfaces.

There has been a lot of community driven work on the RCX Platform. This work was started by Kekoa Proudfoot [11] and then continued by other volunteers in the open source community (like for example BrickOS [15]), that differs from

ERIKA Educational in the architecture design approach: whereas BrickOS was born as a firmware replacement for the RCX, our project aims to producing a minimal kernel focused on the real-time aspects for small embedded systems; the usage of the RCX platform is a consequence of the ease of implementation of control applications on top of it.

Wireless data exchange is supported by many industrial standards, such as the IrDA Data, IrDA Control, Bluetooth and IEEE 802.11 with its supplements. The main problem to face adopting one of these standards is the minimum hardware requirements that is needed to support the protocol stack. The RCX only supports a 2400 baud connection, that makes impossible the implementation of these protocols. For that reason, we decided to design and implement a simple protocol that could serve as wireless gateway for the RCX IR communication.

3 System Architecture

The architecture of ERIKA Educational consists of two main layers: the Kernel Layer and the Hardware Abstraction Layer. The Kernel Layer contains a set of modules that implement task management and real-time scheduling policies (currently we support Fixed Priority[1, 14] with Stack Resource Policy [4] and preemption thresholds, similar in the performance to the OSEK OS BCC1 conformance class), interrupt processing and error treatment. The kernel modules offer a common interface which contains the basic kernel services to applications.

The Hardware Abstraction Layer (HAL) contains very basic architecture-specific services, like context-switch, interrupt handling, low-level timers and memory management initialization. This layered approach trades (very little) performance for the confinement of all hardware specific code in a very limited number of Hardware Abstraction Layer services. When porting the kernels on new architectures, only the HAL has to be rewritten. In general, different applications can require different level of services. For example, in the automotive industry, one of the constraints is the RAM footprint to be as small as possible. To do this, a mono-stack kernel solution should be preferred against a multi-stack one. In a mono-stack kernel all the tasks use the same stack; hence, the concurrency model used by the kernel must be constrained: it is not possible to interleave the execution of the tasks. Other types of applications, that have less constraints on the RAM usage, can be built on the multi-stack model. In our work, we provided two HALs for the target architecture, one suitable for mono-stack models, the other one for multi-stack models.

So far, ERIKA Educational provides only a HAL for the RCX Platform. The RCX Hal also supports two mathematic libraries, a floating point library derived from the newlib mathematic library for gcc 3.3 [19], and a fixed point library implemented in [5]. The following section shortly describes which device drivers are currently available for that HAL.

4 Device Drivers

The RCX Platform is a nice little device that supports up to three sensors and up to three actuators (typically motors). ERIKA Educational gives the possibility to write application defined interrupt handlers, that can be linked to the various interrupts on the RCX. These interrupts can be used to handle button, timer, watchdog, A/D and serial interrupts.

Based on this interrupt handling feature, ERIKA Educational offers a set of API that simplify the use of the following peripherals:

Button handling. The application is able to check whether the four buttons are pressed or not; an interrupt can be raised when some buttons are pressed.
LCD display. The application is able to display a number of 4 digits.
Sensors. The RCX input ports that can be sampled using the A/D interface.
Sound. The application can play single notes or melodies.
IR Communication. The RCX platform is able to communicate to other RCX or to an IR Tower using an infra-red (IR) transmitter/receiver, connected to the H8 serial interface. ERIKA Educational provides an Infrared Layer that supports IR transmission in a way similar to the ISO/OSI standard. More details on the IR communication layer can be found in Section 5.
Motors. The RCX platform provides three 2-pin output ports that can be programmed by the software to control DC motors. To obtain a more flexible control on these motors, we implemented a software Pulse Width Modulation (PWM) that allows PWM frequencies of 1-2 KHz with negligible overhead.

5 Infrared and Radio Frequency Support

The RCX platform hosts an Infrared (IR) LED attached to the serial interface of the Hitachi H8. That interface, initially thought for uploading RCX software, can be used to send and receive application data at a speed up to 2400 bps. ERIKA Educational uses the IR interface to implement a wireless transmission protocol between different robots. The protocol stack supported by ERIKA Educational has been divided into three layers. The **higher layer** is an *Interaction Layer*, that exports a small database of *variables*. A variable is a shared memory location (8/16 bit), that a node wants to share with other nodes (for example, a variable could be a sensor reading or a control parameter). Variables can be sent on the network periodically (e.g., for monitoring reasons) or upon explicit request (e.g., to implement application commands). The **middle layer** is the *Data Link Layer*, which implements message transmission providing a channel abstraction with error control. The **lower layer** is the *Physical Layer* represented by the IR serial channel, that allows the higher layers to send data frames composed by one or more bytes. These layers have also been ported to the SHaRK Kernel [8] to let standard PCs communicate to an RCX running ERIKA Educational using a LEGO IR Tower.

The format of an IR frame allows from 1 to 16 bytes of payload to be sent. Its shape strongly depends on the IR technology used, that imposes each node

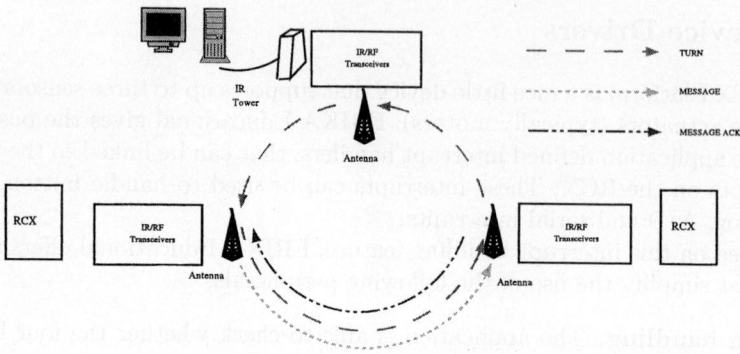

Fig. 1. Structure of the network used to test protocol functionality

to send each byte followed by its complement. Due to lack of space, we will not describe the IR frame format in detail.

Unfortunately, the physical layer suffers of two problems: the communication speed, that is limited to 2400 bps half duplex, and the components, that are highly directional. For these reasons, we decided to develop a simple Radio Frequency (RF) communication infrastructure that is able to guarantee higher performances when there are more than two nodes, and that does not suffer of the directionality problem of the RCX Infrared device.

5.1 Towards Radio Frequency Transmission

We implemented a RF gateway that reads IR frames and forwards RF frames. This approach solves the previous problems, because the RF transmission is independent of the physical orientation of the robots, and because its bandwidth is much higher than the IR transmission speed, mitigating transmission bandwidth loss when parallel transmissions take place.

The idea is that each node transmits its messages to the local wireless gateway. Then, the wireless gateway sends the message to the destination gateway, which in turns sends the data back to the destination RCX. Figure 1 shows a typical network topology, composed by a set of independent RCXs, and PCs connected using the wireless gateways.

The choice of the radio frequency transceivers have been guided by the need of enough bandwidth to support a few parallel transmission/reception between different groups of nodes, with negligible overhead compared against a single point-to-point transmission. We chose an AUREL XTR-434 [2], that is able to reach a 100 Kbps bandwidth, representing a good compromise between the cost/range of the transceiver, and its bandwidth.

The effect of the wireless gateway becomes important considering a topology with three or more nodes in which more than two nodes may need to communicate at the same time: in that case, a simple IR layer suffers IR conflicts and extremely severe delays in delivering messages. In that scenario, the wireless gateway plays the double role of buffering and delivering messages at a much higher rate than a simple point to point IR link.

5.2 Implementation of the Wireless Gateway

The wireless gateway has been implemented using the AUREL XTR-434, an IR receiver/transmitter, and a Microchip PIC 16F876, that is responsible for the translation of the data frames from RF to IR and vice versa. Once configured, the wireless gateways define a fully distributed structure in which every unit (formed by a RCX or a PC with a wireless gateway) has the same role, without any kind of master/slave approach. We implemented a Token Ring protocol where every unit have to receive the token to has the right to send an RF frame. The format of an RF frame allows a particular node from 1 to 15 bytes of payload to be sent. Due to lack of space, we will not describe the RF frame format in detail. The typical behavior of a wireless gateway is to wait for a transmission, that may arrive from both the sources of messages (IR and RF). If a gateway receives the token (that is a 3 byte RF frame) from the RF interface, it proceeds as follows: if the wireless gateway has a pending IR message (from 2 to 16 bytes) to transmit, it starts transmitting immediately (no collision can occur), then it waits for an ACK before transmitting again the token to another node; if the wireless gateway does not have a pending IR message, it passes the turn to the next node, sending again the token to the next node. Wireless gateways can store only one incoming IR message for the RCX in their internal memory.

5.3 Performance Analysis of the Wireless Protocol

This subsection presents a simple worst case analysis for the transmission timings of a wireless gateway. The temporal behavior of a wireless gateway is highly influenced by the physical characteristics of the HW components used. In particular, the XTR-434 requires about 1.5 ms to enable or disable the state of transmission/reception (the RF transceiver, as the IR, works half duplex), which causes a $\beta = 3\,ms$ dead time needed when a gateway wants to enable the transmission. The timings of the most important events in the system are shown in Table 1. Please note that, due to the difference of transmission speed of the two interfaces, the transmission of an IR frame is around 50 times slower than the transmission of an RF frame.

When there are no pending messages to be transmitted (that is, in idle mode), the token will do a complete round passing from all the nodes in about $(\tau+\beta)*N$ (where N is the number of nodes).

In the worst case, when all the nodes have an IR message in their buffer to send via RF, a token may need up to

$$W = [(\beta + \lambda) + (\beta + \gamma) + (\beta + \tau)] * N\,ms$$

to come back to the same node. In W, $\beta + \lambda$ is the time spent by a node to enable the transmission and then send an RF message; $\beta + \gamma$ is the time spent

Table 1. Timings measured from the wireless gateway

Event measured	time
Token transmission	$\tau = 1.108\,ms$
Message send from unit x to unit y	from $\lambda_{min} = 1.280\,ms$ up to $\lambda_{max} = 3.628\,ms$
ACK reception from unit y to unit x	$\gamma = 1.108\,ms$
IR message send/reception (2400 bps)	from 50.4 ms up to 178.7 ms

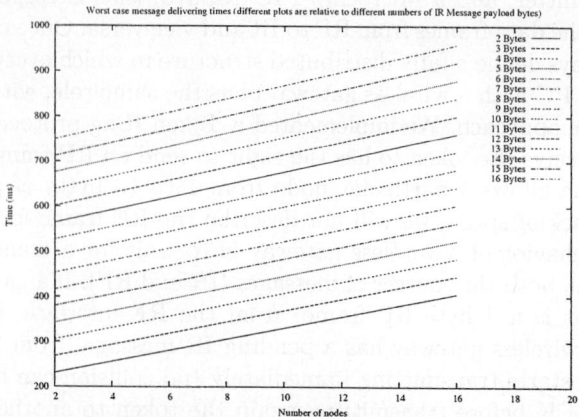

Fig. 2. Worst case message delivery time depending on the length of the frame being sent and on the number of nodes in the network.

to enable the reception and then receive the ACK; $\beta + \tau$ is the time needed to send the token to the next node.

To consider the worst case of the transmission of a frame from a RCX to another, we have to consider the following situation: the sending RCX wants to send a 15 bytes payload IR message, but it cannot start immediately because the gateway has just started sending an IR message. In the worst case, the gateway just forwarded the RF token, forcing itself to wait for the next token arrival. Besides, every unit of the round has got an IR message to transmit, so waiting for the RF token takes the maximum possible time. As the RF message reaches its destination, the same thing happens: the destination gateway cannot transmit its IR message to the RCX because the RCX starts in that moment an IR transmission towards the gateway. Figure 2 shows the worst case timings for different number of nodes and payload lengths.

Figure 3 plots the utilization of the wireless channel, depending on the percentage α of the number of nodes in the system that have to transmit messages. We suppose that not all the nodes have always to transmit messages, because some nodes (e.g., the robots) will usually send a continuous stream of data, whereas some other nodes (e.g., the PC running SHaRK) will usually receive the data. As it can be seen, the wireless channel can only be used up to around 42% because of the influence of the dead times β.

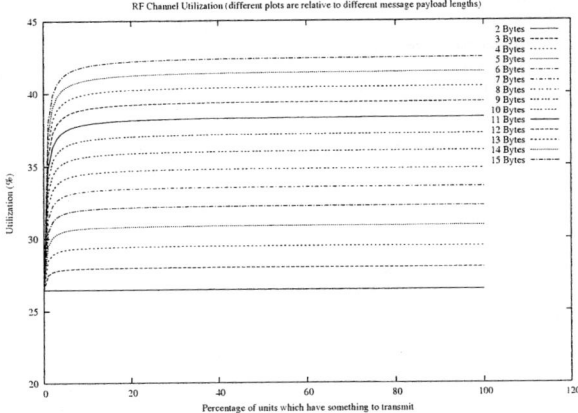

Fig. 3. RF channel utilization depending on the number of units which have something to transmit

6 A Case Study

This section presents a case study that shows a typical application that can be designed using ERIKA Educational and the wireless gateway presented in Section 5. The case study is composed by three nodes working together with wireless gateways. Two nodes are RCX robots hosting an embedded control system using ERIKA Educational, whereas the third node is a monitoring application running on a PC using the SHaRK Kernel.

The robots are vehicles following a shaded (from black to white) path painted on the floor. Two light sensors are used to estimate the trajectory and the position of the robot with respect to a given reference value. These values are then used to control the speed and the direction of the robot. The control algorithm is a differential steering algorithm: the relative speed of the two wheels gives information about the trajectory of the robot. The robot has also a rear wheel that is only used to maintain the system equilibrium (see Figure 4.a).

The control algorithm has a concept of a reference position (plotted in Figure 4.b as the X axis); when running, the system reads the value of the two light sensors, and computes two errors: y_{err}, which represents the distance of the vehicle from the X axis; and θ_{err}, which represents the angle between the longitudinal axis of the vehicle (tangent to the two sensors) and the X axis.

Since the path we used for the experiment is a shaded path between black and white, it is possible to transform the sensor readings in values on the X axis. If we consider Figure 4.b), we can define the values of y_{err} and θ_{err} as $y_{err} = \frac{y_A + y_B}{2}$ and $\theta_{err} = arcsin\left(\frac{y_A - y_B}{q}\right)$, where q is the distance in centimeters between the two sensors. The robot is in the reference position when the middle point between the two sensors is on the X axis, and when the reference angle θ_{err} is 0. To follow the ideal reference as much as possible, we adopted a control algorithm that minimizes both y_{err} and θ_{err}.

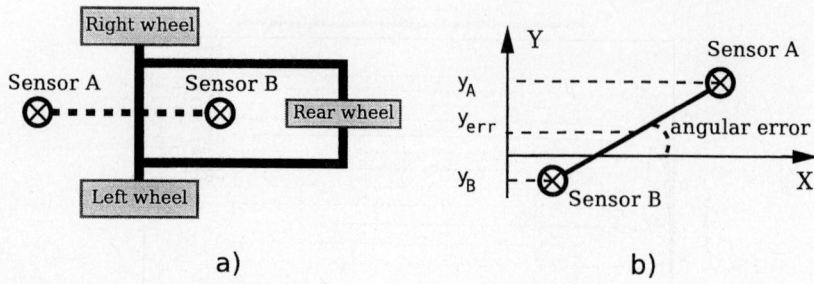

Fig. 4. This Figure shows: a) a simplified scheme of the robot, and b) the two errors computed by the control algorithm

The two robots composing the case study are also connected to the PC node using the wireless gateway described in Section 5. The wireless connection is used to enable the robots to pull out some control informations (like sensor readings, relative position in the path, ...) which are shown in a graphical way on the PC node, and commands, that are sent by the PC to the nodes to control the behavior of each robot and to tune the control algorithm parameters (e.g., speed references, gains, ...). Due to lack of space, we cannot describe the case study in further detail. More informations about this case study can be found in the ERIKA Educational website.

7 Conclusions and Future Work

This paper described the ERIKA Educational Project as a useful educational platform for implementing embedded real-time control systems. Thanks to the modularity of the architecture, and the availability of predictable scheduling algorithms the platform enables designers to develop small robotic applications ideal for teaching real-time control theory on small constrained systems. Moreover, the wireless support helps the realization of a network of robots, further extending the possibilities of the platform towards cooperative control algorithms. Finally, a case study showed the applicability of the architecture on real control application testbeds. As future work, we plan to implement better control algorithms for the robots, and we plan to explore different wireless mechanisms alternative to the Token Ring approach presented in this paper. We also plan to enable a better usage of the wireless channel and to address power consumption issues. ERIKA Educational and SHaRK are both free software projects distributed under the GPL license. Their source code can be downloaded from http://erika.sssup.it and http://shark.sssup.it.

References

1. Audsley, N.C., Burns, A., Davis, R., Tindell, K., Wellings, A.J.: Fixed Priority Pre-emptive Scheduling: A Historical Prespective. Journal of Real-Time Systems 8 (1995) 173–198
2. AUREL S.p.A. Wireless Tranceiver XTR-434. http://www.aurelwireless.com/
3. Baker, T.P.: A Stack-Based Allocation Policy for Realtime Processes. In: Proceedings of the 11th IEEE Real-Time Systems Symposium. (1990) 191–200
4. Baker, T.P.: Stack-Based Scheduling of Real-Time Processes. Journal of Real-Time Systems 3 (1991) 67–99
5. Cantini, D.: Progetto e Realizzazione di un Sistema Operativo Real-Time per Sistemi Embedded con Riferimento al Dispositivo RCX LEGO. Master thesis, Università degli Studi di Pisa, Italy (2002) http://feanor.sssup.it/~cantini/grad_thesis.shtml
6. Davis, R., Merriam, N., Tracey, N.: How Embedded Applications Using an RTOS Can Stay within On-chip Memory Limits. In: Proceedings of the Work in Progress and Industrial Experience Session, Euromicro Conference on Real-Time Systems. (2000)
7. Express Logic. Threadx Kernel. http://www.expresslogic.com/
8. Gai, P., Abeni, L., Giorgi, M., Buttazzo, G.: A New Kernel Approach for Modular Real-Time Systems Development. In: Proceedings of the 13th IEEE Euromicro Conference on Real-Time Systems. IEEE Computer (2001) 199–208
9. Gai, P., Lipari, G., Abeni, L., di Natale, M., Bini, E.: Architecture for a Portable Open Source Real-Time Kernel Environment. In: Proceedings of the Second Real-Time Linux Workshop and Hand's on Real-Time Linux Tutorial. (2000)
10. Gai, P., Lipari, G., Di Natale, M.: Stack Size Minimization for Embedded Real-Time Systems-on-a-Chip. Design Automation for Embedded Systems (2002) 53–87
11. Kekoa Proudfoot. http://graphics.stanford.edu/~kekoa/rcx/
12. LEGO Fair Play Message. http://www.lego.com/eng/info/fairplay.asp
13. LEGO Group. http://mindstorms.lego.com
14. Liu, C.L., Layland, J.W.: Scheduling Algorithms for Multiprogramming in a Hard-Real-Time Environment. Journal of the Association for Computing Machinery 20 (1973) 179–194
15. Noga, M.L.: Brickos. http://brickos.sourceforge.net
16. OSEK. OSEK/VDX: Open Systems and the Corresponding Interfaces for Automotive Electronics. http://www.osek-vdx.org/mirror/os21.pdf
17. OSEK Consortium. The OSEK/VDX Standard. http://www.osek-vdx.org
18. Progetto Finalizzato Madess II. http://www.madess.cnr.it/
19. RedHat Inc. Newlib. http://sources.redhat.com/newlib/
20. Regehr, J.: Scheduling Tasks with Mixed Preemption Relations for Robustness to Timing Faults. In: Proceedings of the 23rd IEEE Real-Time Systems Symposium (RTSS 2002), Austin, Texas. IEEE Computer (2002) 315–326
21. Saksena, M., Wang, Y.: Scalable Real-Time System Design Using Preemption Thresholds. In: Proceedings of the 21st IEEE Real Time Systems Symposium, (RTSS 2000) Orlando, Florida. IEEE Computer (2000) 25–36
22. Wang, Y., Saksena, M.: Fixed Priority Scheduling with Preemption Threshold. In: Proceedings of the 6th International Conference on Real-Time Computing Systems and Applications, Hong-Kong, China. IEEE Computer (1999) 328–337

Coordinating Distributed Autonomous Agents with a Real-Time Database: The CAMBADA Project[*]

Luis Almeida[1], Frederico Santos[2], Tullio Facchinetti[3],
Paulo Pedreiras[1], Valter Silva[4], and L. Seabra Lopes[1]

[1] LSE-IEETA/DET, University of Aveiro, Portugal
{lda,pedreiras,lsl}@det.ua.pt
[2] DEE-ISEC, Polytechnic Institute of Coimbra, Portugal
fred@mail.isec.pt
[3] DIS, University of Pavia, Italy
tullio.facchinetti@unipv.it
[4] ESTGA, University of Aveiro, Portugal
vfs@estga.ua.pt

Abstract. Interest on using mobile autonomous agents has been growing, recently, due to their capacity to cooperate for diverse purposes, from rescue to demining and security. However, such cooperation requires the exchange of state data that is time sensitive and thus, applications should be aware of data temporal coherency. In this paper we describe the architecture of the agents that constitute the CAMBADA (Cooperative Autonomous Mobile roBots with Advanced Distributed Architecture) robotic soccer team developed at the University of Aveiro, Portugal. This architecture is built around a real-time database that is partially replicated in all team members and contains both local and remote state variables. The temporal coherency of the data is enforced by an adequate management system that refreshes each database item transparently at a rate specified by the application. The application software accesses the state variables of all agents with local operations, only, delivering both value and temporal coherency.

1 Introduction

Coordinating several autonomous mobile robotic agents in order to achieve a common goal is currently a topic of intense research [15,7]. This problem can be found in many robotic applications, either for military or civil purposes, such as search and rescue in catastrophic situations, demining or maneuvers in contaminated areas.

The technical problem of building an infrastructure to support the perception integration for a team of robots and subsequent coordinated action is common to the above applications. One recent initiative to promote research in this field is RoboCup [7] where several autonomous robots have to play football together as a team, to beat the opponent. We believe that researching ways to solve the perception integration problem in RoboCup is also very relevant to real-world applications.

---

[*] This work was partially supported by the Portuguese Government – FCT, POSI/ROBO/ 43908/2002 (CAMBADA), and the European Comission – IST-2001-34820 (ARTIST).

Currently, the requirements posed on such teams of autonomous robotic agents have evolved in two directions. On one hand, robots must move faster and with accurate trajectories to close the gap with the dynamics of the processes they interact with, e.g., a ball can move very fast. On the other hand, robots must interact more in order to develop coordinated actions more efficiently, e.g., only the robot closer to the ball should try to get it while other robots should move to appropriate positions. The former requirement demands for tight closed-loop motion control while the latter demands for an appropriate communication system that allows building a global information base to support cooperation. Both cases are subject to time constraints that must be met for adequate performance.

In this paper we describe the architecture of the robotic agents that constitute the CAMBADA middle-size robotic soccer team of the University of Aveiro, Portugal, which is well suited to support the requirements expressed above. The hardware architecture follows the biomorphic paradigm while the software architecture is based on a real-time database, i.e., a structure containing the current values of relevant local state variables together with local images of (remote) state variables of other cooperating agents. The temporal coherency, i.e., degree of timeliness, of the data is enforced by an adequate management system that refreshes each database item at a rate specified by the application.

This architecture is innovative in what concerns the mix of using replicated databases together with temporal coherency information and a management system that uses real-time communication techniques to schedule the traffic and enforce timely updates of the database items, dynamically adapting to the conditions of the communication channel. This paper is structured as follows: The following section discusses the generic computing and communications architecture of CAMBADA. Section 3 describes the high-level coordination system, focusing on the real-time database (RTDB). Section 4 describes the communication protocol among agents. Section 5 describes the communication requirements of the current implementation and section 6 concludes the paper.

2 Computing and Communications Architecture

The computing architecture of the robotic agents follows the biomorphic paradigm [11], being centered on a main processing unit (*the brain*) that is responsible for higher-level behaviors coordination. This main processing unit handles external communication with other agents and has high bandwidth sensors, typically vision, directly attached to it. Finally, this unit receives low bandwidth sensing information and sends actuating commands to control the robot attitude by means of a distributed low-level sensing/actuating system (*the nervous system*). This biomorphic architecture is depicted in Fig. 1.

The main processing unit is currently implemented on a laptop that delivers sufficient computing power while offering standard interfaces to connect the other systems, namely USB. The wireless interface is either built-in or added as a PCMCIA card. The laptop runs the Linux operating system over the RTAI (Real-Time Applications Interface [12]) kernel, which provides timeliness support, namely for time-stamping, periodic transmissions and task temporal synchronization. This approach follows a similar paradigm as the Timely Computing Base proposed in [13]. The agents that constitute the team communicate with each other by means of an IEEE 802.11b wireless network as depicted in Fig. 2. The communication is managed, i.e., using a base station, and it is constrained to using a single channel, shared by both teams in each game. In order to improve the timeliness of the communications, our team uses a further transmission control protocol that minimizes collisions of transmissions within the team. An important feature is that the communication follows the producer-consumer co-operation model, according to which each robot regularly broadcasts, i.e. produces, its own data while the remaining ones receive, i.e. consume, such data and update their local structures. Beyond the robotic agents, there is also a coaching and monitoring station connected to the team that allows following the evolution of the robots status on-line and issuing high level team coordination commands.

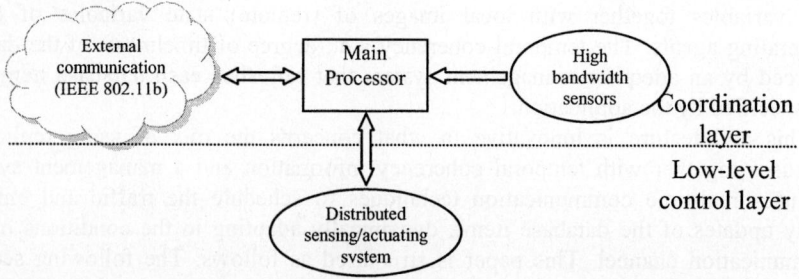

Fig.1. The biomorphic architecture of the CAMBADA robotic agents

The low-level sensing/actuating system follows the fine-grain distributed model [8] where most of the elementary functions, e.g. basic reactive behaviors and closed-loop control of complex actuators, are encapsulated in small microcontroller-based nodes, interconnected by means of a network. This architecture, which is typical for example in the automotive industry, favors important properties such as scalability, to allow the future addition of nodes with new functionalities, composability, to allow building a complex system by putting together well defined subsystems, and dependability, by using nodes to ease the definition of error-containment regions.

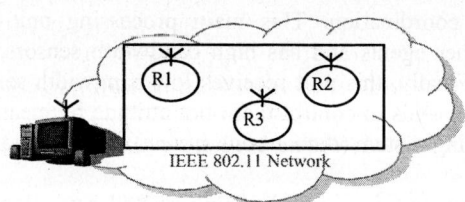

Fig. 2. Global team communications architecture, with the robotic agents and a monitoring station interconnected by means of an IEEE 802.11 wireless network

This architecture relies strongly on the network, which must support real-time communication. For this purpose, Controller Area Network (CAN) [2] has been chosen, which is a real-time fieldbus typical in distributed embedded systems. This network is complemented with a higher-level transmission control protocol to enhance its real-time performance, composability and fault-tolerance, namely the FTT-CAN protocol (Flexible Time-Triggered communication over CAN) [1]. The use of FTT-CAN has the advantage of combining time-triggered communication, which is adequate for closed-loop control functions, with operational flexibility supporting on-line reconfiguration and thus higher maintainability and capacity to cope with evolving requirements.

Currently, the interconnection between CAN and the laptop is carried out by means of a gateway, either through a serial port operating at 115Kbaud or through a serial-to-USB adapter. The nodes of the system are based on an 8-bit microcontroller from Microchip, namely the PIC 18F485 [9].

3 RTBD — The Real-Time Database

Similarly to other teams [4,6,14], our team software architecture emphasizes cooperative sensing as a key capability to support the behavioral and decision-making processes in the robotic players. A common technique to achieve cooperative sensing is by means of a *blackboard* [5], which is a database where each agent publishes the information that is generated internally and that maybe requested by others. However, typical implementations of this technique seldom account for the temporal validity (coherence) of the contained information with adequate accuracy, since the timing information delivered by general-purpose operating systems such as Linux is rather coarse. This is a problem when robots move fast (e.g. above 1m/s) because their state information degrades faster, too, and temporal validity of state data becomes of the same order of magnitude, or lower, than the operating system timing accuracy.

Another problem of typical implementations is that they are based on the client-server model and thus, when a robot needs a datum, it has to communicate with the server holding the blackboard, introducing an undesirable delay. To avoid this delay, we use two features: firstly, the dissemination of the local state data is carried out using broadcasts (Fig. 3), according to the producer-consumer cooperation model, as referred in the previous section; secondly, we replicate the blackboard according to the *distributed shared memory* model [10]. In this model, each node has local access to all the process state variables that it requires. Those variables that are remote have a local image that is updated automatically by an autonomous communication system.

We call this replicated blackboard the Real-time Data Base (RTDB), similarly to the concept presented in [8], which holds the state data of each agent together with local images of the relevant state data of the other team members. A specialized communication system triggers the required transactions at an adequate rate to guarantee the freshness of the data. This is carried out under control of the RTAI kernel, guaranteeing that the transmission instants are respected within small tolerances, contributing to achieve better close-loop control of the robots.

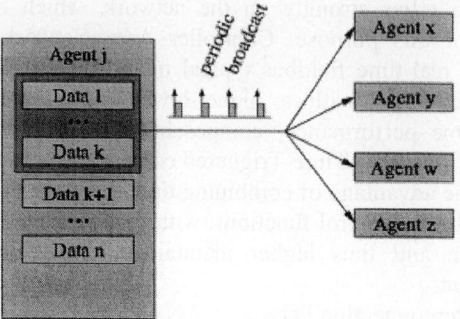

Fig. 3. Each agent broadcasts periodically its subset of state data that might be required by other agents

Generally, the information within the RTDB holds the absolute positions and postures of all players, as well as the position of the ball, goal areas and corners in global coordinates. This approach allows a robot to easily use the other robots sensing capabilities to complement its own. For example, if a robot temporarily loses track of the ball, it might use the position of the ball as detected by another robot.

3.1 RTDB Implementation

The RTDB is implemented over a block of shared memory, between Linux and RTAI. It contains two main areas: a private area for local information, only, i.e., which is not to be broadcast to other robots; and a shared area with global information. The shared area is further divided into a number of areas, one corresponding to each agent in the team. One of the areas is written by the agent itself and broadcast to the others while the remaining areas are used to store the information received from the other agents.

The allocation of shared memory is carried out by means of a specific function call, DB_init(), called once by every Linux process that needs access to the RTDB. The actual allocation is executed within RTAI by the first such call, only. Subsequent calls just return the shared memory block handler and increment a process count. Conversely, the memory space used by the RTDB is freed using the function call DB_free() that decreases the process count and, when zero, releases the shared memory block.

The RTDB is accessed concurrently from Linux processes that capture and process images and implement complex behaviors, and from RTAI tasks that manage the communication both with the lower-level control layer (through the CAN gateway) and with the other agents (through the wireless interface). The Linux processes access the RTDB with local non-blocking function calls, DB_put() and DB_get() that allow writing and reading records, respectively (Fig. 4 shows the prototypes of the RTDB related function calls). DB_get() further requires the specification of the agent from which the item to be read belongs to, in order to identify the respective area in the database.

```
int DB_init (void);
void DB_free (void);
void DB_put (int _id, void *_value);
int DB_get (int _agent, int _id, void *_value).
```

Fig. 4. The RTDB related function calls

3.2 Synchronization of Concurrent Accesses

A specific synchronization mechanism allows enforcing data consistency during concurrent accesses among Linux processes and between these and RTAI tasks. This mechanism uses two features. Firstly, the DB_put() primitive sends all RTDB update requests to RTAI where they are handled by only one real-time task, *DB_writer*, which actually writes in the database. This same task also handles the RTDB updates arriving from the lower-level control layer. This ensures atomic access during local write operations. Notice that remote write operations with the information received from other agents are carried out by another real-time task, *DB_IO*, which is not concurrent with *DB_writer* because they write in different areas.

Secondly, there is a control field in each record that allows knowing whether an item was updated since it was last read. This field is set by any write operation on that item and reset within DB_get() just before reading the information. DB_get() also checks the status of that control field after retrieving the data and thus, if the field changes status in between, then there was a write operation that corrupted the read operation and this one is repeated. This ensures consistent data retrieval.

The software architecture of the main processing unit that holds the RTDB is illustrated in Fig. 5. The actual wireless communication is handled within Linux by a high-priority task, with SCHED_FIFO scheduler, due to unavailability of RTAI device drivers for certain wireless cards.

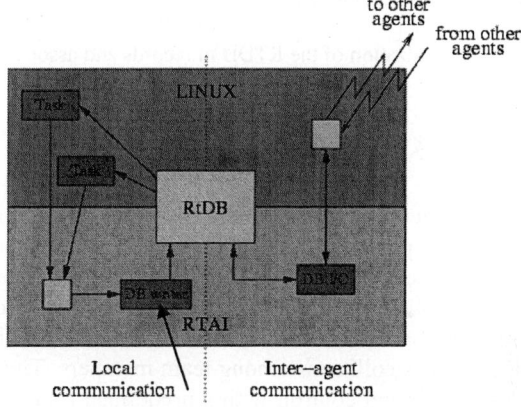

Fig. 5. The software architecture of the main processing unit, highlighting the RTDB, the Linux processes, and the related real-time tasks

3.3 Internal Structure of the RTDB

The RTDB is organized in a set of records plus a set of related data blocks. The records contain the fields referred in Fig. 6, i.e., an identifier, a pointer to the respective data block, the size of that block, a timestamp of the last update instant, the update period and a control field for synchronization purposes as referred previously.

```
typedef struct _TRec {
    int id;              // entity identification
    unsigned long int offset;
    unsigned long int size;
    unsigned long int time;
    int period;
    unsigned char write_control;
} Trec;
```

Fig. 6. The fields of the generic RTDB record

For the sake of regularity, all the records are stored sequentially in the initial part of the RTDB, followed by all the respective data blocks (Fig. 7).

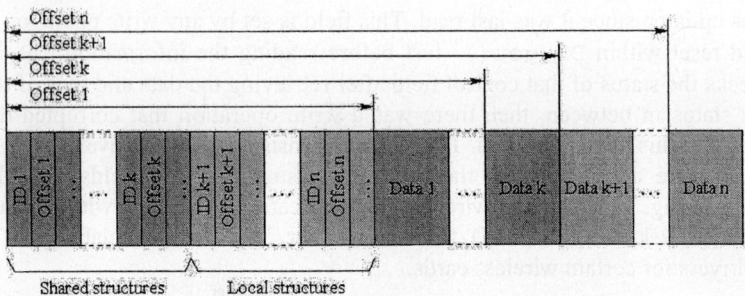

Fig. 7. The internal organization of the RTDB in records and associated data blocks

4 Communication Among Agents

As referred in section 2, agents communicate using an IEEE 802.11 network, sharing a single channel with the opposing team and using managed communication (through the access point). This raises several difficulties because the access to the channel cannot be controlled [3] and the available bandwidth is roughly divided by 2.

Therefore, the only alternative left for each team is to adapt to the current channel conditions and reduce access collisions among team members. This is achieved using an adaptive TDMA transmission control, with a predefined round period called *team update period (Ttup)* that sets the responsiveness of the global communication. Within such round, there is one single slot allocated to each team member so that all slots in the round are separated as much as possible.

The transmissions generated by each agent are scheduled within *DB_IO*, according to the production periods specified in the RTDB records. Currently a rate-monotonic scheduler is used. When the respective TDMA slot comes, all currently scheduled transmissions are piggybacked on one single 802.11 frame and sent to the channel. The required synchronization is based on the reception of the frames sent by the other robots during *Ttup*. With the reception instants of those frames, their lengths and the target inter-slot period *Txwin* it is possible to generate the next transmission instant. If no frame is received during a round, then the next frame is sent *Ttup* after the previous one. If these delays affect all TDMA frames in a round, then the whole round is delayed from then on, thus its adaptive nature. Fig. 8 depicts one TDMA round indicating the slots allocated to each robot.

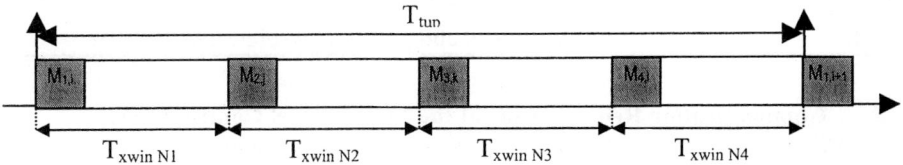

Fig. 8. TDMA transmission control of wireless communication within the team

Carrying out the bandwidth allocation in this way contributes to increase the protocol resilience since the messages are transmitted as far apart as possible and thus being more tolerant to deviations either caused by temporary loss of communication or by interference from other traffic.

5 Communication Requirements

In this section we present the effective communication requirements of the current CAMBADA robots implementation, both concerning the inter-robots communication and the intra-robots communication with the distributed sensing and actuation system.

5.1 Inter-Robots Communication Requirements

The inter-robots communication is directly deduced from the contents of the RTDB shared areas. Particularly, each robot has to transmit its own area which contents are show in Table 1. When all items are ready for transmission simultaneously, the total data to be transmitted amounts to 1420 bytes. At 11Mbps, this takes slightly less than 1.2ms, a time that is doubled because of the managed communication (requiring re-transmission by the access point). Therefore, the total time per-transaction is upper-bounded to 2.4ms.

Moreover, a value of 100ms for *Ttup*, the TDMA round period, seems adequate for refreshing the remote images of the state variables, since these are not used within high-speed closed-loop control. This value also establishes a good compromise in terms of used bandwidth. In fact, considering 4 team members, yields *Txwin*=25ms and thus, the bandwidth taken to broadcast the robots state data is less than 10%.

Table 1. State data of each robot, to be shared with the remaining team members

Object	Quantity	Size (Bytes)	Short description
Robot	4	157	Rotation, speed, position (absolute and relative)
Opponent	4	157	Rotation, speed, position (absolute and relative)
Self	1	20	Identifier, role and behavior, displacement since last odometry reset and flags indicating objects locally identified.
Team	1	2	Current field side
Ball	1	144	Speed and position (absolute and relative)

5.2 Communication Requirements of the Lower-Level Control Layer

The lower-level control layer is formed by the distributed sensing and actuating system interconnected to the main processing unit. This distributed system includes a set of nodes that are depicted in Fig. 9. The communication requirements at this level are shown in Table 2. As referred in section 2, this distributed system is based on a CAN network complemented with the FTT-CAN protocol. The former operates at 250Kbps and, according to this transmission rate and to the requirements in Table 2, the FTT-CAN protocol is configured with an Elementary Cycle (EC) 10ms long and a maximum Synchronous Window (LSW) of 28% the duration of the EC.

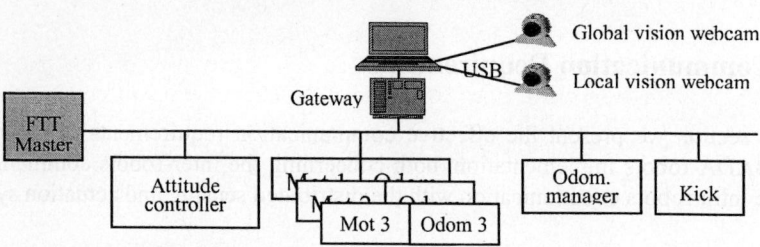

Fig. 9. The hardware architecture of the distributed sensing/actuating system

Moreover, an efficient use of the FTT-CAN protocol further requires the separation of the message streams in two sets, the synchronous set (SS) and the asynchronous set (AS). In this case, the SS is composed by messages {M1, M3.1-M3.3, M4.1, M4.2, M6.1, M6.2} while messages {M2, M5.1, M5.2, M7} belong to the AS.

Basically, M6 conveys movement vectors from the laptop to the node *Pic-base*. This node computes the individual set points for each motor (holonomic motion) and sends them to the motors via M1. These two messages, M6 and M1, support closed loop controlled motion of visually tracked items, e.g. the ball. Each motor sends its odometry readings to the Pic_Odom node, using M3. Finally, Pic_Odom estimates the robot position and reports it to the laptop using M4. M5 allows setting or resetting the robot position. Finally, M7 is used to actuate the ball kicker while M2 alerts the system that batteries charge is running low.

Table 2. Communication requirements of the lower-level control layer

ID	Source	Target	Type	Period/mit(ms)	Size (B)	Short description
M1	Pic_base	Motor[1:3]	Periodic	30	6	Aggregate motor set points
M2	Pic_base	Laptop	Sporadic	1000	2	Battery status
M3.1-M3.3	Motor[1:3]	Pic_odom	Periodic	10	3*3	Wheel encoder value
M4.1-M4.2	Pic_odom	Laptop	Periodic	50	7+4	Robot position (position + rotation)
M5.1-M5.2	Laptop	Pic_odom	Sporadic	500	7+4	Set/reset robot position (position + rotation)
M6.1-M6.2	Laptop	Pic_base	Periodic	30	7+4	Movement vector (rot+translational velocity)
M7	Laptop	Pic_base	Sporadic	1000	1	Kicker actuation

The analysis presented in [1] allows verifying that all time constraints are met, i.e., all the transmissions occur within the respective periods. The traffic scheduling policy followed by the FTT-Master is also rate-monotonic.

6 Conclusion

Cooperating robots is a field currently generating large interest in the research community. RoboCup is one example of an initiative developed to foster research in that area.

This paper described the computing and communication architecture of the CAMBADA middle-size robotic soccer team being developed at the University of Aveiro. This team has just participated in a few preliminary tournaments, with encouraging results, and it is expected to do participate at the next RoboCup event, in Lisbon, June/July of 2004. One of its distinguishing features is the smooth and effective motion control at relatively high speeds, e.g. when tracking and following the ball. This is achieved by means of a computing and communication architecture that includes real-time concerns from the bottom layers up to the coordination. In particular, the robots coordination is based on a replicated database, i.e., the Real-Time Data Base (RTDB) that includes local state variables together with images of remote ones. These images are updated transparently to the application software by means of an adequate real-time management system. Moreover, the RTDB is accessible to the application using a set of non-blocking primitives, thus yielding a fast data access.

The paper finishes with a brief analysis of the communication requirements of the current robots implementation.

References

1. Almeida, L., Pedreiras, P., Fonseca, J.: The FTT-CAN protocol: Why and How. IEEE Transactions on Industrial Electronics **49**(6) (2002) 1189–1201
2. CAN Specification - Version 2.0. Robert Bosch GmbH. Stuttgart, (1991)
3. Decotignie, J.-D., et al.: Architecture for the Interconnection of Wireless and Wireline Fieldbuses. FeT 2001 - IFAC Conf. on Fieldbus Technologies, Nancy. (2001)

4. Dietl, M., J.-S. Gutmann, B. Nebel.: Cooperative Sensing in Dynamic Environments. In: Proc. IROS. (2001)
5. Erman, L.D., F. Hayes-Roth, V.R. Lesser, D.R. Reddy: The HERSAY-II Speech Understanding System: Integrating Knowledge to Resolve Uncertainty. Computing Surveys **12**(2) 1980
6. Jamzad, M. et al.: Basic Requirements for a Teamwork in Middle Size RoboCup. Sharif-ARVAND team description. (2001)
7. Kitano, K., M. Asada, Y. Kuniyoshi, I. Noda, E. Osawa.: RoboCup: The Robot World Cup Initiative. In: Proc. of IJCAI-95 Workshop on Entertainment and AI/Alife, Montreal. (1995)
8. Kopetz, H.: Real-Time Systems Design Principles for Distributed Embedded Applications. Kluwer, (1997)
9. Microchip PIC18F458 datasheet. available at http://ww1.microchip.com/downloads/en/DeviceDoc/41159c.pdf .
10. Milutinovic, V., Stenström, P.: Special Issue on Distributed Shared Memory Models. In: Proceedings of the IEEE **87**(3) (1999)
11. In: Proc. of the NASA Workshop on Biomorphic Robotics, Jet Propulsion Laboratory, California Institute of Technology, USA. (2000) August 14–16
12. RTAI for Linux. available at http://www.aero.polimi.it/~rtai/ .
13. Veríssimo, P., Casimiro, A.: The Timely Computing Base Model and Architecture. IEEE Transactions on Computers **51**(8) (2002)
14. Weigel, T., et al.: CS Freiburg: Sophisticated Skills and Effective Cooperation. In: Proc. European Control Conference (ECC-01), Porto. (2001)
15. Weiss, G.: Multiagent Systems: A Modern Approach to Distributed Artificial Intelligence. MIT Press, (2000)

A Static Approach to Automated Test Data Generation in the Presence of Pointers

Insang Chung

School of Computer Engineering, Hansung University
389-2 Ga, SamsunDong, Sungbuk-Gu, Seoul 136-792, S. Korea
insang@hansung.ac.kr

Abstract. The shape problem in the context of program testing refers to the problem of figuring out a shape of the input data structure required to cause the traversal of a given path. In this paper, we introduce a static approach to the shape problem. The approach converts the selected path into Static Single Assignment (SSA) form without pointer dereferences. This allows us to consider each program point in the selected path as a constraint involving equality or inequality. A simple, but illustrative example is given to explain our approach.

1 Introduction

The shape problem arises when testing is conducted for programs with pointers. By the "shape problem" we mean the problem of finding a shape of the input data structure to cause the traversal of a selected path. Most work to date for automatic program testing has focused on search algorithms that come up with input values to traverse the selected path in the absence of pointers.

Korel [5] is a pioneer to attack the shape problem. His method requires actual execution of a program so that the program flow can be monitored to determine whether the intended path was taken. Because the exact locations that pointer variables point to are known during program execution, it is possible to identify a shape of the input data structure required to traverse a given path. However, many iterations may be required if the program execution flows in the wrong direction before a suitable input (pointer) value is found.

This paper introduces a new method to help identify automatically test data on which a selected path in the program is executed in the presence of pointers. The proposed method statically analyzes the selected path. If the analysis is completed successfully, then we yield:

- a shape of the input data structure and
- a set of constraints describing how to assign values for non-pointer input variables in order to cause the traversal of the selected path.

The main contribution of the paper is a static approach to automatic program testing for programs in the presence of pointers. The approach does not require any means for controlling execution of the target program unlike execution-based approaches which require the actual execution of the program [2, 4, 5].

The proposed method also generates a constraint system from the selected path by converting each program point in the path into Static Single Assignment(SSA) form [1] involving no pointer dereferences. One important feature of SSA form is that each variable has at most one definition. This feature allows us to deal with each program point as an equality or an inequality [3].

We do not have to develop a technique to solve the generated constraint system. We can use current constraint solving techniques such as [3, 6] to solve the generated constraint system which have been well studied relatively. Solving the constraint system provides the input values for the variables of non-pointer types needed to exercise the selected path.

In [7], Visvanathan and Gupta presented a two-phase approach that first generates the shape of the data structure for functions with pointer inputs and then generates the integer and real values in the data fields of the data structure. Since this approach does not produce any constraints for non-pointer input variables during the first phase, i.e., the shape identification phase, additional work is required in order to make advantage of current constraint solving techniques.

The rest of the paper is organized as follows. In Section 2, we will explain in detail SSA form, basic terminologies, and definitions which will be used in the subsequent sections. In Section 3, we define transfer functions associated with various types of expressions and assignments involving the pointer dereference operator '*'. We also illustrate our method through an example. Finally, we conclude with some comments on directions for future work.

2 Preliminaries

A key property of SSA form is that each variable has a unique static definition point [1]. In order to ensure this property, variable renaming is usually done as follows:

- every assignment to a variable v generates a new SSA variable v_i where i is a unique number,
- just after the assignment to v, v_i becomes the current name (the last version or the current instance) of v, and
- every subsequent use of v is replaced by its current name v_i.

We assume that the subscript number of each SSA variable starts with 0. For example, the sequence of code "x=10;x=x+3;" is converted into SSA form as follows: $x_1 = 10; x_2 = x_1 + 3$". As a result, we can regard the assignments as the constraints, i.e., the equalities.

However, the presence of pointers complicates conversion of the selected path into SSA form because aliases can occur and a variable can be defined indirectly via a pointer dereference. Our approach exploits the points-to information at each program point in the selected path and then replaces each pointer dereference with its points-to result. For example, the sequence of assignments given by "x=&a;*x=10;y=a" can be converted to the SSA form without the pointer

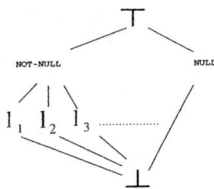

Fig. 1. The structure of locations

dereference "$x_1 = \&a_0; a_1 = 10; y_1 = a_1$" by using the points-to information that x points to a after evaluating the first assignment.

We represent points-to relations for each program point with σ mapping variables to memory locations:

$$\sigma \in \text{State} = \text{Var} \rightarrow \text{Loc}$$

Var is the (finite) set of variables occurring in the SSA form of the program path of interest. Loc is a set of locations (addresses) partially ordered as depicted in Figure 1.

States are assumed to be partially-ordered as follows:

$$\sigma_i \sqsubseteq \sigma_j \text{ if for all } x, \sigma_i(x) \sqsubseteq \sigma_j(x)$$

We also introduce $\bot_\sigma$ such that for all $\sigma \in \text{State}$, $\bot_\sigma \sqsubseteq \sigma$. We will use $\bot_\sigma$ to denote that a selected path is infeasible.

When we refer to a location, it is often convenient to use a symbolic name instead of its address. In this paper, we assume that the targets of pointers always possess a (symbolic) name. Under this assumption, the fact that variable x points to a location named y can be represented by $\sigma(x) = y$ without any confusion.

However, this assumption does not hold for the variables that are not in the scope of a function but might be accessible through indirect reference. For example, consider function fun with the formal parameter x of type int **: fun(int **x) {...}. The problem lies in the fact that the function fun can refer to memory locations through '*x' or '**x' which are not in the scope of fun. In order to capture points-to information accurately, we need to name such locations. To the end, we make use of the concept of invisible variables. Invisible variables are names used for the variables that are not in the scope of a function but accessible through indirect reference. For example, the invisible variables for the variable x with type int ** are 1_x with type int * and 2_x with type int **, respectively.

We also define the function "last_σ" which gives a last version of a variable with respect to σ. For example, suppose that σ is the state after executing the sequence of the assignments "x=10; y=x+1; x=y". Then, $\text{last}_\sigma(x)$ will give x_2. last_σ can also accept the SSA variable as input instead of the original variable. Thus, $\text{last}_\sigma(x)$, $\text{last}_\sigma(x_1)$, and $\text{last}_\sigma(x_n)$ ($n \leq 2$) will get the same result x_2. On the other hand, let σ be the state immediately after executing the first assignment. Then, $\text{last}_\sigma(x)$ will give x_1 because we assume that the SSA number starts with 0 and x is defined at the first assignment.

Finally, we will use $[x]_\sigma$ denote the collection of the pointer variables pointing to the location which is pointed to by $\text{last}_\sigma(x)$.

3 Shape Identification for Program Testing

This section defines the transfer functions for boolean expressions and assignments used in the shape identification. We then illustrate how our approach works through an example.

3.1 Transfer Functions for Boolean Expressions

$$\|x == \text{NULL}\|\sigma = \sigma \odot \{(k, \text{NULL}) | k \in [x]_\sigma\} \text{ if } \sigma(\text{last}_\sigma(x)) \sqsupseteq \text{NULL}$$
$$= \bot_\sigma \text{ otherwise}$$

$$\|x <> \text{NULL}\|\sigma = \sigma \odot \{(k, \text{new}-\text{name}(x, \sigma)) | k \in [x]_\sigma\} \text{ if } \sigma(\text{last}_\sigma(x)) = \top$$
$$= \sigma \text{ else if } \sigma(\text{last}_\sigma(x)) = \text{NOT-NULL or } \sigma(\text{last}_\sigma(x)) = l$$
$$= \bot_\sigma \text{ otherwise}$$

$$\|x == l\|\sigma = \sigma \odot \{(k, l) | k \in [x]_\sigma\} \text{ if } (\sigma(\text{last}_\sigma(x)) \sqcap l) \neq \bot$$
$$= \bot_\sigma \text{ otherwise}$$

$$\|x == y\|\sigma = \sigma \odot \{(k, \sigma(\text{last}_\sigma(x)) \sqcap \sigma(\text{last}_\sigma(y))) | k \in [x]_\sigma\}$$
$$\text{if } (\sigma(\text{last}_\sigma(x)) \sqcap \sigma(\text{last}_\sigma(y))) \neq \bot$$
$$= \bot_\sigma \text{ otherwise}$$

$$\|x <> y\|\sigma = \bot_\sigma \text{ if } \text{last}_\sigma(x) \in [y]_\sigma \text{ or } \text{last}_\sigma(y) \in [x]_\sigma$$
$$= \sigma \text{ otherwise}$$

Fig. 2. The transfer functions for boolean expressions. The operator $\odot$ is the function overriding operator. The function $f \odot g$ is defined on the union of the domains f and g. On the domain of g it agrees with g, and elsewhere on its domain it agrees with f. l denotes the address of a certain location

Figure 2 shows the transfer functions for boolean expressions involving pointers. For a given boolean expression and a given state, the main idea here is to derive the largest solution (state) from the given state which will evaluate the target boolean expression to true.

We only illustrate the transfer function associated with the boolean expression of the form "$x <> \text{NULL}$". What is interesting is when $\sigma(\text{last}_\sigma(x)) = \top$. This implies the points-to relation such that the pointer variable, say $\text{last}_\sigma(x)$, should point to a certain memory location, but its exact address may be unknown at the moment. Then, we face a problem of how to represent such a points-to relation.

In order to cope with the problem, we materialize a concrete location from ⊤. The address of the materialized location is given NOT-NULL rather than a specific address. We need to name the location. The naming is done by using the function "new-name(v, σ)" defined as follows:

$$\text{new} - \text{name}(v, \sigma) = \begin{cases} \text{k+1\_last}_\sigma(x), & \text{if k\_last}_\sigma(x) \in [v]_\sigma; \\ \text{1\_last}_\sigma(v), & \text{otherwise.} \end{cases}$$

The function "new-name(v,σ)" is based on the concept of invisible variables and associates a name with the location pointed to by $\text{last}_\sigma(v)$. It firstly checks whether an invisible variable is included in the collection $[v]_\sigma$. If there already exists an invisible variable of the form "k_last$_\sigma$(p)", then the anonymous location will be named "k + 1_last$_\sigma$(p)". We create a new invisible variable "1_last$_\sigma$(v)" to name the anonymous location, otherwise.

Once a name is associated with the materialized location, we introduce a new points-to relation by making the pointer variable x point to new-name(x,σ). Note that the address of the materialized location is regarded as NOT-NULL to reflect that it can represent any location. This is very important when there exists another pointer variable, say y, which points to a concrete location named m and at some point in the given program path, m is shown to refer to the materialized location. That is, (*x, *y) forms an alias pair. Then, the exact address of the materialized location is reduced to the address of m. If we assign a specific address to the materialized location, it would not possible to detect such an alias pair because inconsistency occurs, i.e., $\sigma(x) \sqcap \sigma(x) = \bot_\sigma$.

One important thing we need to mention is that our approach defers the evaluation of the boolean expression of the form x<>y until points-to information for the path is collected. The reason for the deferred evaluation is because pointer variables are assumed to point to distinct locations unless it can be shown that they point to the same location. Without having information about what pointer variables are pointing to, we could not accurately determine whether two pointer variables are pointing to.

3.2 Transfer Functions for Assignments

The forms of the assignments that we consider in this paper include "x=y", "x=*y", "*x=y", "x=&y", and "x=NULL". Complex statements can be treated in terms of the basic assignments. For example, the assignment "*x=*y" are broken into "temp=*y; *x=temp".

The effect of the assignments that has in common is to generate new SSA variables since they define variables directly or indirectly. If the variable x is defined at an assignment, then the transfer function associated with the assignment makes use of the function "GP(x,σ)" which handles the generation of a new SSA variable for the variable x with respect to the state σ and records the newly created SSA variable as the last version of x. The function GP(x,σ) also generates new SSA variables for all pointer variables that point to $\text{last}_\sigma(x)$ on σ.

$$\|x = \text{NULL}\|\sigma = \|x == \text{NULL}\|GP(x,\sigma)$$

$$\|x = \&a\|\sigma = \|x == l_a\|GP(x,\sigma)$$

$$\|x = y\|\sigma = \|x == y\|GP(x,\sigma)$$

$$\begin{aligned}\|x = *y\|\sigma &= \|x == \text{new}-\text{name}(y,\sigma)\|GP(x,\sigma_y) \text{ if } \sigma(\text{last}_\sigma(y)) = \mathsf{T}\\ &= \|x == m_y\|GP(x,\sigma) \text{ else if}\\ &\quad \sigma(\text{last}_\sigma(y)) = \text{NOT-NULL or } \sigma(\text{last}_\sigma(y)) = l_{m_y}\\ &= \bot_\sigma \text{ otherwise}\end{aligned}$$

$$\begin{aligned}\|*x = y\|\sigma &= \|\text{new}-\text{name}(x,\sigma) == y\|GP(x,\sigma_x) \text{ if } \sigma(\text{last}_\sigma(x)) = \mathsf{T}\\ &= \|m_x == y\|GP(m_x,\sigma) \text{ else if}\\ &\quad \sigma(\text{last}_\sigma(x)) = \text{NOT-NULL or } \sigma(\text{last}_\sigma(x)) = l_{m_x}\\ &= \bot_\sigma \text{ otherwise}\end{aligned}$$

Fig. 3. The transfer functions for the assignments. In the transfer functions, l_k denotes the address of k, m_p denotes the location pointed to by $\text{last}_\sigma(p)$, σ_p is the state computed by $\sigma_p = \sigma \odot \{(k, \text{new}-\text{name}(p,\sigma) | k \in [p]_\sigma \}$

Figure 3 defines the transfer functions for the assignments. Note that they are formulated in terms of those of the boolean expressions. The transfer functions associated with the last two assignments play an important role in determining a shape of the input data structure required to traverse the path of interest. The primary effect of these types of assignments is to introduce new points-to relations whenever necessary, then making concrete a shape of input data structure. We illustrate only the transfer function associated with the assignment of the form "x=*y" because the other can be easily understood.

The transfer function associated with the assignment of the form "x=*y" attempts to transform the assignment into the form without the pointer dereference operator. This can be done by using the points-to information for y. The first clause concerns the case where $\sigma(\text{last}_\sigma(y)) = \mathsf{T}$. In this case, we materialize a location from T whose name is given by new-name(y, σ). Once a name is associated with the materialized location, we introduce a new points-to relation by making the pointer variable y point to new-name(y,σ). Of course, this change should be made for all pointer variables belonging to the same collection as y is belonging to. The next step is simply to evaluate the transfer function associated with the equality "x==new-name(y,σ)".

The second clause of the transfer function takes case of the case where y point to a materialized location or a concrete location. In this case, we simply replace the right-hand side of the assignment with the location y is pointing to. For example, if y points to a certain location, say v, then the right-hand side of the assignment will be replaced by v and then the transfer function associated with the boolean expression "x==v" will be evaluated.

```
void Example(int **x, int **y, int v){
   int *p, *q, *r, z;

   1:        p = *x;
   2:        q = *y;
   3:        if (p == q) {
   4,5:         if (p == NULL) *q = v;
   6,7:         else if (q == NULL) *p = v;
                else {
   8:              r = &z;
   9:              *r = 10;
   10,11:          if (z == v) *q = v;
              }
           }
           else {
   12,13:     *p = v; *q = v;
           }
}
```

Fig. 4. An example program

The last clause concerns the case where y has the NULL value. Obviously, dereferencing y at the assignment causes a violation. Thus, the result will be $\bot_\sigma$, indicating that the path under consideration cannot be executed.

3.3 An Example

Suppose that we want to identify a shape of input data structure required to traverse the path <1,2,3,4,6,8,9,10,11> of the program in Figure 4.

For the sake of clarity, we will represent each state by a pictorial representation called a shape graph. In a shape graph, square nodes model concrete memory locations. Edges model pointer values. Suppose that $\sigma(x)$ gets y. Then, there exists a directed edge from the square node named x to the square node named y. But, we will not explicitly show $\bot$ in shape graphs.

First of all, we start with an initial state σ_0 such that $\sigma_0(x_0) = \sigma_0(y_0) = \top$, $\sigma_0(p_0)=\sigma_0(q_0)=\sigma_0(r_0)=\sigma_0(v_0)=\sigma_0(z_0)=\bot$. Note that initial versions of input variables of pointer type are initialized to $\top$ while local variables or variables of non-pointer type are initialized to $\bot$. We also assume that each pointer variable initially belongs to a distinct collection. Figure 5(a) depicts the shape graph corresponding to σ_0.

After evaluating the assignments 1 and 2, we get the following points-to information:

- x_0 points to 1_x_0 and
- y_0 points to 1_y_0.

That is to say, the effect of assignments 1 and 2 is to introduce new points-to relations by materializing the locations named 1_x_0 and 1_y_0 from $\top$ pointed

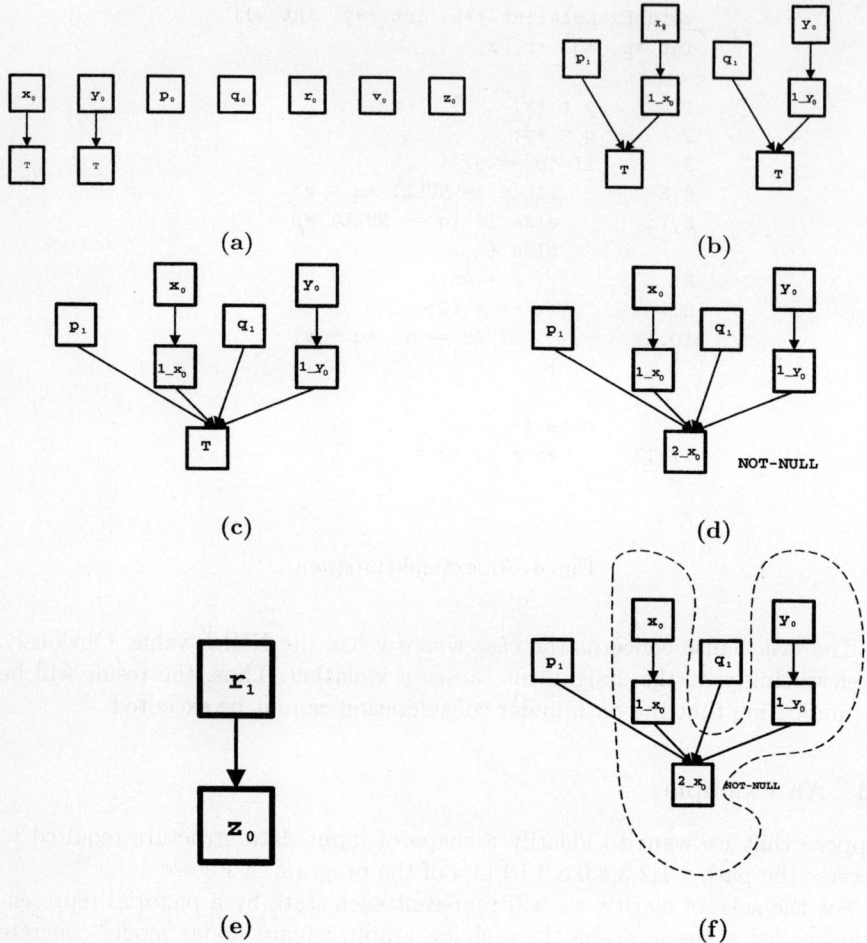

Fig. 5. The shape graphs that arise when the shape analysis algorithm is applied to the given path of the example program in Figure 4; (a) depicts the initial state σ_0, (b) depicts the shape graph after evaluating the sub-path <1,2>, (c) depicts the shape graph after evaluating the sub-path <1,2,3>, and (d) depicts the shape graph after evaluating the sub-path <1,2,3,4>. As a matter of fact, evaluation of the given path <1,2,3,4,6,8,9,10,11> does not affect the shape graph given in (d) any more. (e) shows the points-to relation arisen after evaluating the assignment 8. The part enclosed in the dotted line in (f) shows the shape of the input data structure that can cause the traversal of the target path <1,2,3,4,6,8,9,10,11>

to by x_0 and y_0, respectively. We also observe that since they define p and q, respectively, their last versions are changed to p_1 and q_1. As a result, we yield the shape graph shown in Figure 5(b).

Let us consider "p==q". Its effect is to make p_1 and q_1 belong to the same collection because they can possibly point to the same location. Consequently, the top nodes pointed by p_1 and q_1 are merged, so that it indicates that p_1 and q_1 should point to the same location as shown in Figure 5(c).

Now, we are in a position to evaluate "p==NULL". Since we want the boolean expression to evaluate to false, we can consider the form "p<>NULL" instead. It allows us to exclude the case where both p_1 and q_1 will be NULL. Thus, the top node pointed by both p_1 and q_1 (of course, also pointed by 1_x_0 and 1_y_0) is changed to the node labeled with NOT-NULL which we need to name. The candidates include 1_p_1, 2_x_0, 2_y_0, and 1_q_1. It does not matter which one is used. Figure 5(d) shows the situation where 2_x_0 is selected as its name. Similarly, we can evaluate "q<>NULL".

Figure 5(e) shows the points-to information that r_1 points to z_0 introduced immediately after evaluation of the assignment 8. Consequently, the variable z_0 will be defined at the assignment 9 indirectly. In addition, the function GP generates new versions of r and z: r_2 and z_1. As a result, the assignment is converted into SSA form without pointer dereference as follows: $z_1==10$. Conversion of the boolean expression "z==v" into SSA form is simple: "$z_1==v_0$".

The last statement we need to consider is "*q=v". Its evaluation is carried out in the same manner as that of the assignment 9 by using the points-to information of q. Since q_1 points to 2_x_0, it is converted into the SSA form as follows: $2\_x_0==v_0$.

We are interested in the portion of the final shape graph that is associated with initial input (pointer) variables because it gives a shape of the input data structure required to traverse the selected path. By initial input variables we mean the versions of input variables before any modification; they have 0 as their subscript number. The partial shape graph enclosed by dotted lines in Figure 5(f) shows the shape of the input data structure required to traverse the selected path.

Once we have found a shape of the input data structure required to traverse the selected path, we need to find values for input variables of non-pointer types. We can find such values by solving the constraints generated from the selected path. Having the constraints, we can apply various methods to come up with a solution [3, 6]. In the example, we have the constraints as follows: $z_1 == 10$, $z_1 == v_0$, and $2\_x_0 == v_0$. It is not difficult to see that the solution will be: z_1:10, v_0:10, 2_x_0:10.

The variable v_0 is only of concern to us since it gives the input value of v which should be supplied from outside. Consequently, we need to form the input data structure as the part enclosed by the dotted line shown Figure 5(f) and provide 10 for the value of the formal parameter v.

4 Concluding Remarks

While our research offers improvements over past work, there are some issues that are worthy further research. In particular, we are currently extending our work to pointer arithmetic. Pointers do not have to point to single variables. They can also point at the cells of an array. Once we have a pointer pointing into an array, we can start doing pointer arithmetic. The use of pointer arithmetic avoids the need to introduce an extra variable for the array indices. However, pointer arithmetic can complicate the identification of a suitable shape of the input data structure because of the presence of overlapping pointers which reference the same array at different offsets. For example, consider the pointer arithmetic "p=q+i" where p and q are pointer variables. In order to cope with such pointer arithmetic, our approach needs to be extended to infer that p points to the same physical array as q but but an offset of i bytes.

Acknowledgments

This research was financially supported by Hansung University in the year of 2003.

References

1. Cytron, R., Ferrante, J., Rosen, B.K., Wegman, M.N., Zadeck, F. K.: Efficiently Computing Static Single Assignment Form and the Control Dependence Graph. ACM Trans. on Programming Languages and Systems **13**(4) (1991) 451–490
2. Gallagher, M.J., Narasimhan, V.L.: ADTEST: A Test Data Generation Suite for Ada Software Systems. IEEE Trans. on Software Eng. **23**(8) (1997) 473–484
3. Gotlieb, A., Botella, B., Rueher, M.: Automatic Test Data Generation using Constraint Solving Techniques. In: Proc. ACM ISSTA. (1998) 53–62
4. Gupta, N., Mathur, A., Soffa, M.L.: Generating Test Data for Branch Coverage. In: Proceedings of 15th IEEE Int. Conf. on Automated Software Eng. (2000)
5. Korel, B.: Automated Software Test Data Generation. IEEE Trans. on Software Eng. **16**(8) (1990) 870–879
6. Meudec, C.: ATGen: Automatic Test Data Generation using Constraint Logic Programming and Symbolic Execution. In: Proc. IEEE/ACM Int. Workshop on Automated Program Analysis Testing and Verfication. (2000) 22–31
7. Visvanathan, S., Gupta, N.: Generating Test Data for Functions with Pointer Inputs. In: Proc. 17th IEEE International Conference on Automated Software Engineering. (2002) 149–160

A Use-Case Based Component Identification Approach for Migrating Legacy Code into Distributed Environment*

Hyeon Soo Kim[1], Heung Seok Chae[2], and Chul Hong Kim[3]

[1] Dept. of Computer Science and Engineering, Chungnam Nat'l Univ.
220 Gung-dong, Yuseong-gu, Daejeon 305-764, South Korea
hskim@ce.cnu.ac.kr
[2] Dept. of Computer Science and Engineering, Pusan Nat'l Univ.
30 Jangjeon-dong, Geumjeong-gu, Busan 609-735, South Korea
hschae@pusan.ac.kr
[3] Software Engineering Research Team
Electronics and Telecommunications Research Institute
161 Gajeong-dong, Yuseong-gu, Daejeon 305-350, South Korea
kch@etri.re.kr

Abstract. Due to not only proven stability and reliability but a significant investment and years of accumulated experience and knowledge, legacy systems have supported the core business applications of a number of organizations over many years. In this paper we suggest a systematic approach to identifying components that perform specific business services and that consists of the legacy system's assets to be leveraged on the modern platform such as J2EE/EJB.

1 Introduction

Due to not only their proven stability and reliability but a significant investment and years of accumulated experience and knowledge, legacy systems have supported the core business applications of a number of organizations such as banks, securities, insurance companies, and general companies over many years [2, 5, 10]. Since, however, these legacy applications developed a long time ago, it is required to invest much capital and time for their operation and maintenance. Besides it is becoming increasingly difficult to find qualified personnel to do the necessary system maintenance on older systems. This makes it difficult to add new functionality and keep up with business requirements [4].

While the Internet has converged with other forces to fundamentally reshape the face of various industries. Internet technologies make it possible to create a wealth of new opportunities for Web-based commerce [8]. Connectivity to the Internet environment has become essential for maintaining a competitive advantage in today's business arena. The most appropriate solution for the organizations seeking to maintain and improve their competitive edge is to integrate

---

* This research was partially supported by University IT Research Center Project.

Internet access with the existing legacy systems [6, 11]. The difficulty, however, is that the majority of corporate legacy systems were built on the monolithic, homogeneous platforms, and as a result do not readily lend themselves to modern technology systems possessing the new characteristics such as distributed, heterogeneous architectures; component-based encapsulation; compliance with modern industry standards [4].

This paper has been motivated by the need of legacy modernization that enables the legacy systems to be leveraged on the modern platform such as J2EE environment. In this paper, we propose an approach to identifying components from the legacy code in order to support its migration into modern distributed environment such as J2EE/EJB. With applying this approach, each large-scale business process becomes a set of self-contained units of manageable size, making it easier to deploy in a client-server or Web-based environment.

2 Component Identification Procedure

A typical legacy system is composed of hundreds or thousands of programs. These programs work together in a hard-wired web of business process flows. In order to migrate the legacy system into modernized distributed application, it is important to segregate these programs into clearly identified components that perform in-kind business functions. This section describes the steps needed to identify component for the migration of the legacy code into the distributed environment such as J2EE/EJB [1].

2.1 Step 1. Use Case Recovery

The component identification approach proposed in this paper is based on the use case concept. A use case is a unit of functionalities provided by a system and modern software development processes have been conducted around use cases; that is, during the requirement analysis, use cases are identified from the obscure and incomplete problem statements given by customers and, then, the identified use cases are designed by system elements such as classes and components and, finally, implemented in programming languages such as Java [3].

Our approach discovers use cases from the legacy code. It is based on screen flow graph that shows the transitions between the screens used for the user interface of a legacy system. First, we construct a screen flow graph for a legacy system and, then, define a set of use cases by analyzing the screen flow graph.

Step 1.1. Screen Flow Graph Construction. A screen flow graph shows the screens of an application and the transitions between them. The construction of a screen flow graph starts with the identification of the central(or main) screen opened firstly at the beginning of the application. Next, we trace the associated screens that are traversed from the main screen. For example, Figure 1 shows the screen flow graph for an ATM(Automated Teller Machine) system. The system provides users with account inquiry, withdrawal, and transfer services via cash cards or credit cards. The screen flow graph shows the seven screens that constitute the ATM system and the valid transitions between those screens.

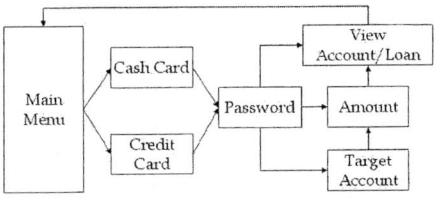

Fig. 1. The screen flow graph for an ATM system

Step 1.2. Use Case Identification from Screen Flow Graph. We can derive use cases from the screen flow graph. Because a use case is a dialogue between a user and the system via a series of screen, it is reasonable to define a use case for each transition path of the screen flow graph. For example, use case $CashInquiry$ is identified by the screen flow path of $CashCard \rightarrow Password \rightarrow ViewAccount/Loan$ and use case $CreditWithdrawal$ is identified by the screen flow path of $CreditCard \rightarrow Password \rightarrow Amount \rightarrow ViewAccount/Loan$.

For the clear description, UC is defined to denote a set of use cases identified from a screen flow graph.

Definition 1. *UC is a set of use cases identified from a screen flow graph.*

For example, in the ATM system, $UC = \{CashInquiry, CashWithdrawal, CashTransfer, CreditInquiry, CreditWithdrawal, CreditTransfer\}$.

2.2 Step 2. Design Recovery

After recovering use cases from the legacy code, we construct a design model for each use case. A design model shows the system elements that realize the functionalities of the corresponding use case and the relationships between them.

Definition 2. *A system element is a basic building block composing the legacy system and can be divided into five categories; Map set elements(ME), Entity elements(EE), User interface elements(UE), Data access elements(DE), and Business logic elements(BE).*

- ME is a set of the map sets. A map set is a collection of maps that define the screens that are going to be used by the program.
- EE denotes a set of entity elements that indicate some persistent information that are implemented by files and/or databases. From the legacy code, an entity element can be defined for each file and/or database table.
- UE is a set of user interface elements. User interface elements are paragraphs that write data into or read data from screens defined by map sets. For example, in CICS programs, a paragraph that contains SEND MAP command or RECEIVE MAP command can be considered an user interface element.

- DE is a set of data access elements. Data access elements are paragraphs that manipulate entity elements. For example, a paragraph is a data access element when it manipulates file or database by using READ command, WRITE command, EXEC SQL command, etc.
- BE is a set of business logic elements. Business logic element are paragraphs that perform the various operations and/or computations to fulfill business logics of the application. For example, the paragraphs which perform functions such as 'move account information to record-field' and/or 'compute monthly interest' correspond to the business logic elements.

In this paper, system elements are identified for each use case. In other words, system elements for a use case consists of all the map set elements, entity elements, user interface elements, data access elements, and business logic elements that contribute to realizing the use case. And, a design model is introduced to represent the design information of the legacy code on which component identification approach is based.

Definition 3. A design model for a use case $uc(uc \in UC)$, denoted by DM_{uc} is a representation of the relationships among the system elements that are needed to realize the use case uc. DM_{uc} is defined as an undirected graph $G = (N, E)$ with $N = ME_{uc} \cup EE_{uc} \cup UE_{uc} \cup DE_{uc} \cup BE_{uc}$, where ME_{uc}, EE_{uc}, UE_{uc}, DE_{uc}, BE_{uc} denote the ME, EE, UE, DE, BE that contribute to the implementation of the use case uc, respectively. And $E = \{(se_i, se_j) | se_i \text{ uses } se_j \text{ or } se_j \text{ uses } se_i\}$.

The meaning for 'use' varies with the type of the associated system elements. In the case of UE and ME, 'use' relation indicates that the user interface element manipulates a screen via the map set element. In the case of DE and EE, 'use' indicates that the data access element manipulates the file or database denoted by the entity element. Figure 2 illustrates the design model for use cases *CashInquiry* and *CreditInquiry*. In the figure, a rectangle represents a system element and its type is denoted by << and >> above its name.

2.3 Step 3. Component Identification

Based on the design model constructed in the previous step, components are identified by clustering the system elements associated with the use cases that have similar business functionalities. The detailed steps concerned with component identification are as follows.

Step 3.1. Preliminary Component Identification. Initially, we identify a component candidate by collecting the system elements of the related use cases with respect to the entity elements. Because the business functions provided by the legacy system mainly focus on the information management, it is not unusual that almost use cases are related with entity elements. In addition, two use cases that manipulate the same entity elements can be considered to conduct very similar functionalities. Therefore, we employ an entity centric approach for

A Use-Case Based Component Identification Approach   901

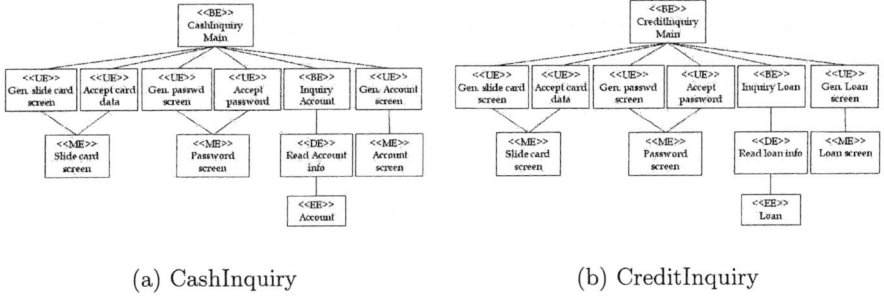

(a) CashInquiry   (b) CreditInquiry

Fig. 2. The design models for use cases $CashInquiry$ and $CreditInquiry$

clustering use cases; that is, all the system elements of the use cases sharing the same entity elements are combined into a single component candidate. The detailed steps for clustering use cases are as follows.

1. Identify key entity elements for each use case. An entity element is a key entity element if the entity element represent a meaningful information. Thus, in the ATM system, the entity elements $Account$, $Loan$, and $Customer$ are the key entity elements. Let us define KEE_{uc} be the set of key entity elements for use case uc. For example, $KEE_{CashInquiry} = KEE_{CashWithdrawal} = KEE_{CashTransfer} = \{Account\}$, $KEE_{CreditInquiry} = KEE_{CreditWithdrawal} = \{Loan\}$, and $KEE_{CreditTransfer} = \{Account, Loan\}$.
2. Initially, define a component for each use case. Let us define SC be the set of components that are identified from the set of use case UC and C_{uc} be the component identified from use case uc. Then, initially $SC = \{C_{uc}|uc \in UC\}$ and $C_{uc} = \{se|se \in N(DM_{uc})\}$, where $N(DM_{uc})$ denotes the system elements in the design model of use case uc.
3. Merge the components of the use cases commonly accessing key entity elements. We combine two components of the corresponding use cases if they have the same key entity elements. $KEE_{uc_i} = KEE_{uc_j} \Rightarrow SC = SC - \{C_{uc_i}, C_{uc_j}\} \cup \{C_{uc_i\_uc_j}\}$ where $C_{uc_i\_uc_j} = C_{uc_i} \cup C_{uc_j}$.

Following the described steps, we obtain three components from the design model of ATM system. For example, component $CashService$ consists of use cases $CashInquiry$, $CashWithdrawl$, and $CashTransfer$ all of which have common key entity element $Account$. Component $CreditService$ is defined for use cases $CreditInquiry$ and $CreditWithdrawal$ because $KEE_{CreditInquiry} = KEE_{CreditWithdrawl} = \{Loan\}$. Finally, component $CreditCashService$ is defined from use case $CreditTransfer$ because $KEE_{CreditTransfer} = \{Account, Loan\}$.

Step 3.2. Common Element Management. Two or more component candidates can have common system elements. To promote the reusability and prevent the duplicated code, the proper management of the common elements is needed. The common elements can be componentized, partitioned, or duplicated based on the measurement result of cohesion and coupling.

Definition 4. *Let us assume that DM_1 and DM_2 are two design models. Then, the common design model of them, CDM_{1_2}, is defined as the common part to DM_1 and DM_2. That is, CDM_{1_2} is an undirected graph $G = (N, E)$ with $N = N(DM_1) \cap N(DM_2)$, $E = \{(se_i, se_j) | (se_i, se_j) \in E(DM_1) \cap E(DM_2)\}$, where $E(DM_i)$ denotes the set of edges in the design model, DM_i.*

For example, in the case of ATM system, the common design model of two design models $DM_{CashInquiry}$ and $DM_{CreditInquiry}$ (see Figure 2) is denoted by $CDM_{CashInquiry\_CreditInquiry}$, and $N(CDM_{CashInquiry\_CreditInquiry}) = \{$ Gen.SlideCardScreen, AcceptCardData, SlideCardScreen, Gen.PasswordScreen, AcceptPassword, PasswordScreen $\}$.

In order to support the decision on common element management, cohesion and coupling metrics are defined as follows.

Definition 5. *Let CDM_{1_2} be the common design model of two design models DM_1 and DM_2.*

- *Cohesion of the CDM_{1_2}, $CH(CDM_{1\_2})$, represents the degree to which the elements in CDM_{1_2} are related.*
  $CH(CDM_{1\_2}) = \frac{1}{|connected\ components\ of\ CDM_{1\_2}|}$
- *Coupling of the CDM_{1_2}, $CP(CDM_{1\_2})$, represents the degree to which the elements in CDM_{1_2} depend on other elements not in CDM_{1_2}.*
  $CP(CDM_{1\_2}) = \frac{|\{se | \exists ce \in CDM_{1\_2} \cdot (se, ce) \in DM_1 \cup DM_2 \wedge se \notin N(CDM_{1\_2})\}|}{2}$

For example, $CH(CDM_{CashInquiry\_CreditInquiry}) = \frac{1}{2}$ because there is no connection between $\{$ Gen.SlideCardScreen, AcceptCardData, SlideCardScreen $\}$ and $\{$ Gen.PasswordScreen, AcceptPassword, PasswordScreen $\}$. $CP(CDM_{CashInquiry\_CreditInquiry}) = 1$ because the system elements accessed by $CDM_{CashInquiry\_CreditInquiry}$ are $\{$ CashInquiryMain, CreditInquiryMain $\}$.

After the measurement of cohesion and coupling for the common design model, there can be three choices according to the measurement results.

Componentization. In the case of high cohesion and low coupling, the common elements seem to provide some reusable function. Thus, the common elements are encapsulated into a separate component and are removed from the existing component that accesses the common elements.

Partition. In the case of low cohesion and low coupling, the common elements have several independent computational threads on the common elements. In this situation, we divide and regroup the common elements with respect to the independent computational threads.

For example, $CDM_{CashInquiry-CreditInquiry}$ has a disjoint pattern and the interaction with the system elements other than $CDM_{CashInquiry-CreditInquiry}$ is very low, so we can partition $CDM_{CashInquiry-CreditInquiry}$ into two components, $CardValidation$ and $PasswordValidation$.

Duplication. In the case of low cohesion and high coupling, the common elements seem not to be encapsulated into an independent component and they have strong interaction with the system elements in its original component. Therefore, it is desired that the common elements remain as duplicated.

In the case of high cohesion and high coupling, there are two choices; componentization or duplication. Because the common elements have strong cohesion, it can be encapsulated into a separate component. However, it also has many interaction with its original component. Strong interaction between components can increase the communication overhead. Therefore, if there is a weak requirement on performance, the common elements of high cohesion and high coupling is encapsulated into a separate component. Otherwise, the common elements are duplicated in order to reduce the communication overhead.

Step 3.3. Component Granularity Refinement. In 3-tier distributed environment such as J2EE/EJB, a component can be divided into more fine-grained components: user interface component, business logic component, and data handling component [1]. User interface component eventually is implemented by JSPs or Servlets. Business logic component corresponds to a session type EJB. Data handling component is realized by an entity type EJB.

Definition 6. *Let C be a component. Then, C can be divided into user interface component(UIC), business logic component(BLC), and data handling component(DHC).*
$UIC = \{se|se \in C \land T(se) = UE \text{ or } ME\}$
$BLC = \{se|se \in C \land T(se) = BE\}$
$DHC = \{se|se \in C \land T(se) = DE \text{ or } EE\}$, *where $T(se)$ denotes the type of system element se.*

Step 4. Component Interface Definition

Interface provides a gateway for a component client to access the functionalities of the component. A component provides two kinds of functionalities such as business logic and data access logic.

Definition 7. *Let I_C be the interface for a component C. Then, the operations of I_C consist of the business logic and data access logic implemented in the component C.*
$I_C = \{op|op \in BE(C) \cup DE(C)\}$, *where $BE(C)$ and $DE(C)$ denote the business logic elements and data access element contained in C, respectively.*

3 A Case Study

Our approach presented in this paper has been realized as a part of the project whose goal is to develop the legacy modernization processes. The project named **MaRMI-RE** (Magic and Robust Methodology Integrated-ReEngineering) is being progressed by ETRI (Electronics and Telecommunications Research Institute) and the consortium that consists of a number of companies and Universities in Korea.

We have applied our approach to pilot projects and now are applying it to real projects. In this section, we present the results of one case study applied to a pilot project. The goal of this project is to modernize the Cost Accounting System (CAS) which is a legacy system being operated by a textile company. CAS, which runs on an IBM mainframe, consists of approximately 60,000 lines of COBOL code distributed into 61 source code files. CAS is a monolithic system without adequate documentation.

Our approach converts the legacy system into a collection of components that publish their services in J2EE/EJB environment. Our method generates 14 business components, which are further divided into 33 JSPs, 14 session-type EJBs, and 10 entity-type EJBs. Figure 3 shows 14 identified session-type components from the CAS system.

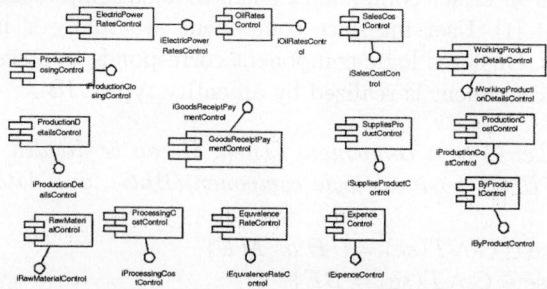

Fig. 3. The identified components from the legacy CAS

For example, consider the component *ByProductControl*. In order to understand the steps required to identify and construct it, let's trace out the processes that built it. First of all, we have constructed a screen flow graph that represents the sequences of screens in the CAS system. Figure 4 shows a part of the graph, which consists of the screens participating in the computation of the cost of byproduct. We have in turn identified two use cases from the graph as follows: *ProductCost* → *RegisterByproduct* → *ReplaceByproduct* and *ProductCost* → *InquiryByproduct*, named *CostingByproduct* and *ByproductCostInquiry*, respectively.

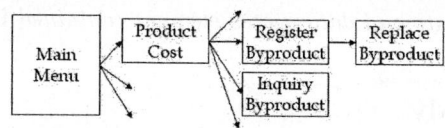

Fig. 4. The screen flow graph with respect to *ByProductControl* component

Secondly we have recovered design models for two use cases. Two design models are shown in Figure 5. The use case *CostingByproduct* performs the functions such as registering and replacing byproduct items, quantities, and unit costs, computing the costs of individual items and total sum of them, and finally storing all those information into the file *Byproduct*. Whereas the use case *ByproductCostInquiry* retrieves information such as the list of items and the costs of individual byproducts and total sum of them from the *Byproduct*. Since both use cases access the same entity element *Byproduct*, thus a business component *ByproductManagement* could be identified around it. The component in turn could be divided into more fine-grained components: 3 JSPs, 1 session-type EJB, and 1 entity-type EJB. *ByProductControl* is just the session-type component that consists of the system elements *ComputeByproductCost* and *InquireByproductCost*, whose interface named **iByProductControl** therefore has two operations such as *computeBPCost()*, *inquireBPCost()*. Other components were constructed with the very similar way.

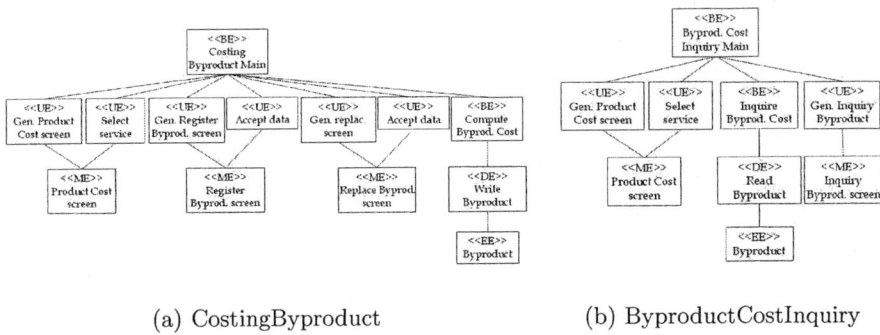

(a) CostingByproduct   (b) ByproductCostInquiry

Fig. 5. The design models for use cases *CostingByproduct* and *ByproductCostInquiry*

4 Concluding Remarks

There are a number of approaches to extracting components from a legacy system. Serrano, et al. try to recognize the new identified subsystem as a component [9]. They first construct a database view of the system which represents the program-uses-file relationships. And then they incorporate the related system elements over associations between programs and databases into a cluster and the cluster may be mapped to a component when the system is migrated to Web-based distributed environments.

Another is a feature-based approach [7]. This approach recognizes a cluster that includes system elements related to the specific functions as a component. The method has a code rating tool to evaluate how much the code is related to the specific functions. This approach has a benefit that the reusable components are identified easily, whereas it does not consider the point about migrating and/or reusing the whole system. It only focuses to identify reusable components at the local perspectives.

Another is a workflow based approach [5]. Once a user requests some service to the system, the system conducts their functions according to the predefined order. The workflow represents the sequence of business processes. In this approach, the captured workflows are used as a basis for creating components. That is, a component is composed of the elements involved in each captured workflow. It, however, creates too many fine-grained components for each captured workflow.

We believe that our use case based approach is unique in the works for identifying components from the legacy system and has advantages over the existing methods on identifying large-grained components. Because the use case is the basic unit of the functionalities in the object-oriented and component-based systems [3], it makes sense that components are defined by collecting some related use cases that are identified from the legacy code. In addition, the use case based approach supports the possibility that the identified components are more meaningful in the domain than the existing methods.

The work reported in this paper has been motivated by the need of legacy modernization that enables the various legacy systems to be leveraged on the modern platform such as J2EE environment. To do this, we have suggested a component identification method that identifies the components from the legacy systems. We believe that the technique will provide a basis for migrating the legacy systems into modern distributed environment such as J2EE/EJB.

References

1. Alur, D., Crupi, J., Malks, D.: Core J2EE Patterns: Best practices and design strategies. Prentice Hall PTR (2001)
2. Battaglia, M., Savoia, G., Favaro, J.: RENAISSANCE: A method to migrate from legacy to immortal software systems. In: Proc. of CSMR'98. IEEE Computer Society (1998) 197–200
3. Eeles, P., Houstion, K., Kozaczynski, W.: Building J2EE applications with the rational unified process. Addison-Wesley (2003)
4. Erlikh, L.: Leveraging legacy systems in modern architectures. White Paper from Relativity Technologies (2001)
5. Intercomp: MineIT: Automated extraction of business rules from legacy COBOL applications to Java applications and objects. White Paper from Intercomp (2001)
6. Intercomp: WebIT: Web-enabling of legacy applications. White Paper from Intercomp (2001)
7. Micro Focus: Componentization of legacy assets: A rapid, low-risk method of creating reusable components from legacy CICS applications. White Paper from Micro Focus (2002)
8. SEEC: A next-generation architecture for financial services on the internet. White Paper from SEEC (2000)
9. Serrano, M.A., Carver, D.L., Oca, C.M.: Reengineering legacy systems for distributed environments. The Journal of Systems and Software **64**(1) (2002) 37–55
10. Sneed, H.M.: Extracting business logic from existing COBOL programs as a basis for redevelopment. In: Proc. of the 9th Int'l Workshop on Program Comprehension. (2001) 167–175
11. Ulrich, W.M.: Legacy systems: transformation strategies. Prentice Hall PTR (2002)

Software Testing via Model Checking

Fevzi Belli and Barış Güldalı

University of Paderborn
Dept. of Computer Science, Electrical Engineering and Mathematics
{Fevzi.Belli,Baris.Gueldali}@upb.de

Abstract. Testing is a necessary, but costly process for user-centric quality control. Moreover, testing is not comprehensive enough to completely detect faults. Many formal methods have been proposed to avoid the drawbacks of testing, e.g., model checking that can be automatically carried out. This paper presents an approach that (i) generates test cases from the specification and (ii) transfers the specification-oriented testing process to model checking. Thus, the approach combines the advantages of testing and model checking assuming the availability of (i) a model that specifies the expected, desirable system behavior as required by the user and (ii) a second model that describes the system behavior as observed. The first model is complemented in also specifying the undesirable system properties. The approach analyzes both these specification models to generate test cases that are then converted into temporal logic formulae to be model checked on the second model.

1 Introduction, Background, and Related Work

Testing is the traditional and still most common validation method in the software industry [3, 5, 18]. It entails the execution of the software system in the real environment, under operational conditions; thus, testing is directly applied to software. It is user-centric, because the user can observe the system in operation and justify to what extent his/her requirements have been met. Nevertheless, testing is a cost-intensive process because it is mainly based on the intuition and experience of the tester that cannot always be supported by existing test tools. Apart from being costly, testing is not comprehensive in terms of the validated properties of the system under test (SUT).

Testing will be carried out by *test cases*, i.e., ordered pairs of *test inputs* and expected *test outputs*. A *test* represents the execution of the SUT using the previously constructed test cases. If the outcome of the execution complies with the expected output, the SUT *succeeds* the test, otherwise it *fails*. There is no justification, however, for any assessment on the correctness of the SUT based on the success (or failure) of a single test, because there can potentially be an infinite number of test cases, even for very simple programs. Therefore, many strategies exist to compensate these drawbacks.

Large software systems will be developed in several stages. The initial stage of the development is usually the requirements definition; its outcome is the specification of the system's behavior. It makes sense to construct the test cases and to define the test process (as a *test specification*) already in this early stage, long before the implementation begins, in compliance with the user's expectancy of how the system should behave. This test specification materializes "the rules of the game". Thus, tests can be run without any knowledge of the implementation (*specification-oriented testing*, or *black-box testing*). One can, of course, exploit the knowledge of the implementation—if available—to construct test cases in compliance with the structure of the code, based on its data or control flow (*implementation-oriented,* or *white-box testing*).

Regardless of whether the testing is specification-oriented or implementation-oriented, if applied to large programs in the practice, both methods need an *adequacy criterion,* which provides a measure of how effective a given set of test cases *(test suite)* is in terms of its potential to reveal faults [21]. During the last decades, many adequacy criteria have been introduced. Most of them are *coverage-oriented*, i.e., they rate the portion of the system specification or implementation that is covered by the given test suite in relation to the uncovered portion when this test suite is applied to the SUT. This ratio can then be used as a decisive factor in determining the point in time at which to stop testing, i.e., to release SUT or to improve it and/or extend the test set to continue testing.

The conceptual simplicity of this very briefly sketched test process is apparently the reason for its popularity. Motivated by this popularity, the combination of formal methods and test methods has been widely advocated [6, 17, 19]. Model checking belongs to the most promising candidates for this marriage because it exhaustively verifies the conformance of a specified system property (or a set of those properties) to the behavior of the SUT.

Model checking has been successfully applied for many years to a wide variety of practical problems, including hardware design, protocol analysis, operating systems, reactive system analysis, fault tolerance and security. This formal method primarily uses graph theory and automata theory to automatically verify properties of the SUT, more precisely by means of its state-based model that specifies the system behavior. A *model checker* visits all reachable states of the model and verifies whether the expected system properties, specified as temporal logic formulae, are satisfied over each possible path. If a property is not satisfied, the model checker attempts to generate a counterexample in the form of a trace as a sequence of states [2, 10].

The following question arises when model checking is applied: Who, or what guarantees that all of the relevant requirements have been verified? To overcome this problem, the existing approaches combine testing and model checking in order to automatically generate test cases which are then exercised on the real, target system [1, 8, 11, 12, 19].

The present paper modifies and extends the existing approaches in that, after the test case generation, a "model checking" step supports, even replaces the manual test process. This has evident advantages: The manual exercising of the vast amounts of test cases and observing and analyzing the test outcomes to decide when to stop testing, etc., is much more expensive and error-prone than model checking that is to automatically run.

Based on the *holistic* approach to specification-based construction of test suites and tests, introduced in [4], the approach proposes to generate test cases to cover both the specification model and its complement. The aim is the coverage of all possible properties of the system, regardless of whether they are desirable or undesirable. This helps also to clearly differentiate the correct system outputs from the faulty ones as the test cases based on the specification are to succeed the test, and the ones based on the complement of the specification are to fail. Thus, the approach handles a tough problem of testing (*oracle problem*) in an effective manner. This is another advantage of the approach.

There are many approaches to generate test cases from finite-state machines [3, 5, 9]. Some also attempt to extend and/or modify the underlying model, e.g., using mutation operations [1, 13, 16] which can be seen as special cases of the complementing. Thus, the method presented in this paper is different from the existing approaches in this aspect.

Section 2 summarizes the theoretical background and describes the approach, which is explained along with a trivial, widely known example. To validate the approach and demonstrate the tool support, Section 3 introduces a non-trivial example which is analyzed and automatically model checked. Section 4 concludes the paper and gives insight into prospective future work.

2 Approach

2.1 Preliminaries

A model is always helpful when the complexity of the system under consideration exceeds a certain level. It is then appropriate to focus on the relevant features of the system, i.e., to abstract unnecessary detail from it. There are several kinds of models.

During the development, a model prescribes the *desirable behavior* as it should be, i.e., the functionality of the system in compliance with the user requirements (*specification model*, M_{Spec}). For validation purposes, one needs another model that describes the *observed behavior* of the system (*system model*, M_{Syst}).

M_{Spec} is represented in this paper by a *finite state machine (FSM)* as a triple (S, R, s_0), where S is a (finite) set of states, $R \subseteq S \times S$ is a transition relation, and $s_0 \in S$ is an initial state. Any $(s_1, s_2) \in R$ is called an *edge* of the graphical representation of the FSM.

For model checking, a test case is represented as a *linear temporal logic (LTL) formula* φ which is either of the following [10, based on 20]:
- p, where p is an atomic proposition, or
- a composition $\neg \varphi$, $\varphi_1 \vee \varphi_2$, $\varphi_1 \wedge \varphi_2$, $X \varphi_1$, $F \varphi_1$, $G \varphi_1$, $\varphi_1 U \varphi_2$, $\varphi_1 R \varphi_2$,

where the *temporal operators* have the following meaning over an infinite sequence of states, called a *path*:
- X (*neXt*) requires that a property holds in the *next* state of the path.
- F (*Future*) is used to assert that a property will hold at *some* state on the path.
- G (*Global*) specifies that a property holds at *every* state on the path.
- U (*Until*) holds if there is a state on the path where the second property holds, and at every preceding state on the path, the first property holds.
- R (*Release*) is the logical dual of U. It requires that the second property holds along the path up to and including the first state where the first property holds. However, the first property is not required to hold eventually.

M_{Syst} is presented in this paper as a Kripke structure that will be defined as follows [10]: Let AP be a set of atomic propositions; a *Kripke structure* M over AP is a quadruple (S, S_0, R, L) where S is a finite set of states, $S_0 \subseteq S$ is the set of initial states, $R \subseteq S \times S$ is a transition relation such that for every state $s \in S$ there is a state $s' \in S$ in that $R(s, s')$ and $L:S \rightarrow 2^{AP}$ is a function that labels each state with the set of atomic propositions that are true in that state.

2.2 Test-Driven Model Checking

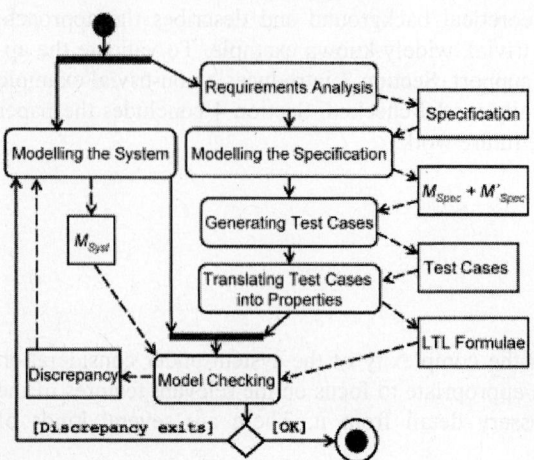

Fig. 1. Overall structure of the approach

Figure 1 depicts different aspects and the structure of the approach, which is illustrated as an UML-Activity diagram [15] including control-flow (solid lines) for activities and data-flow (dashed lines) for the in-puts/outputs of the activities. The main components of the data-flow are: SUT, its specification and the models M_{Spec}, its complement M'_{Spec}, and M_{Syst}.

M_{Spec} is constructed from the specification that has been produced prior to system development. M_{Syst} is constructed from the view of the (end) user in several steps, incrementally increasing his/her intuitive cognition of the SUT, usually by experimenting without any primary knowledge about its structure.

The approach tentatively assumes that the specification and M_{Spec} is correct. Thus, it also tentatively assumes that SUT might not be in compliance with M_{Spec}. As a result of the latter assumption, the correctness of the M_{Syst} is also questionable. This is the reason why model checking of M_{Syst} is invoked which is to be controlled by test cases that have been generated from M_{Spec} and its complement M'_{Spec}. Note that M'_{Spec} is also a FSM because the expressive power of FSM is given by type-3 grammars which are closed under complementing.

The selection of the test cases is carried out applying the *edge coverage* criterion introduced in [4] to M_{Spec}: The edges of the FSM represent test cases; the criterion requires all edges be covered by test cases.

The selected test cases, represented as LTL formulae, are viewed as properties to be model checked. Whenever model checking reveals an inconsistency, a fault is detected. This can, in turn, be caused by an error in SUT, M_{Syst}, M_{Spec}, or specification itself. Remember that the approach tentatively started with the checking of the SUT.

To put it in a nutshell, the approach assumes that the user has an, even rudimentary, understanding of the functionality of the SUT. This understanding leads to M_{Syst} which is compared with M_{Spec}. The model checking step is expected to reveal discrepancies. These discrepancies, if any, are the key factors of the fault localization that is now a straight-forward process: Check whether the inconsistency is caused by a fault in SUT. If not, check M_{Syst}. If the cause of the inconsistency is located in M_{Syst}, a fault in the user's understanding of the system is revealed that must be corrected, i.e., M_{Syst} is to be "repaired". Other sources of faults are the specification and M_{Spec} that are to be checked in the same way.

As a result, the approach makes testing as a separate process "leaner", even dispensable: Test cases, which are previously generated and selected by means of the specification, are represented as properties to be model checked on M_{Syst}. Each time an inconsistency is identified, a fault has been detected which is to be located in a well-determined way. The process terminates when the finite set of test cases is exhausted.

2.3 Example

A simple example, borrowed from [18], is used to illustrate the approach. A traffic light system is informally specified by the sequence of the colors, red as the initial state:

$$\text{red} \rightarrow \text{red/yellow} \rightarrow \text{green} \rightarrow \text{yellow} \rightarrow \text{red} \rightarrow \dots \quad (1)$$

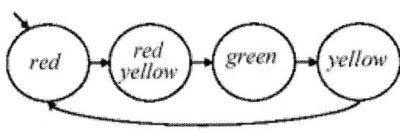

Fig. 2. Traffic light system as a FSM

Figure 2 transfers this specification to a model M_{Spec}. In this graphical representation, the nodes of M_{Spec} can be interpreted as states or events. They can also be viewed as inputs that trigger events to occur or cause states to take place. Any transition and any transition sequence of this graph, e.g.,

$$\text{red} \rightarrow \text{red/yellow} \quad (2)$$

is valid (legal) in the sense of the specification M_{Spec}. As a test input, these sequences should cause the system to succeed the test. The generation of the test cases is explained in [4]. For the sake of simplicity, any single transition is considered as a test sequence that plays the role of a test input coupled with an unambiguous test output "succeeded". This is the way the approach handles the oracle problem.

The sequence in (2) can be transferred in an LTL formula:

$$\text{red} \rightarrow \text{red/yellow}: \varphi = \mathbf{G}(red \rightarrow \mathbf{X}(red \wedge yellow)) \quad (3)$$

This transformation has been intuitively carried out, with the following meaning: Globally, it must be satisfied that if in the present state the property "red" holds, in the next state the property "red and yellow" holds.

Adding the missing edges to the FSM of Figure 2 makes the complementary view of the specification visible. In Figure 3, the dashed lines are transitions that are not included in the M_{Spec} (Note that loops starting and ending at the same node are not considered to keep the example simple).

Thus, these additional transitions are called *invalid* or *illegal*. Invalid transitions can be included in sequences starting at a valid one, e.g.,

$$\text{red} \rightarrow \text{red/yellow} \rightarrow \text{green} \rightarrow \text{red} \quad (4)$$

The invalid transitions transfer the system into faulty states; thus, the corresponding test reveals a fault. Therefore, the expected test output is "failed". Accordingly, (5) represents the LTL format of the test case given in (4):

$$\text{green} \to \text{red}: \varphi = F(green \to Xred) \tag{5}$$

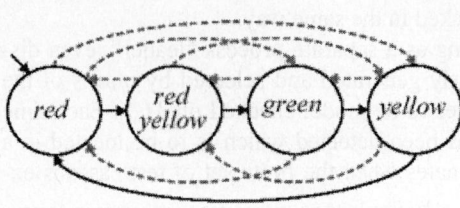

Fig. 3. Complementing (with dashed lines) of the M_{Spec} of Figure 2

This transformation has been intuitively carried out, with the following meaning: At some state, it must be satisfied that if in the present state the property "green" holds, in the next state the property "red" holds. This implies to the operation of the traffic light system that, if in some state the action "green" is enabled, then in the next state, the action "red" must be enabled. However, the property in (5) is expected not to be satisfied by model checking, because (4) is generated based on the M'_{Spec}.

The behavior-oriented model M_{Syst} of the system is given in Figure 4. Note the discrepancies to Figure 2: Some faults have deliberately been injected to check whether the model checking would reveal them.

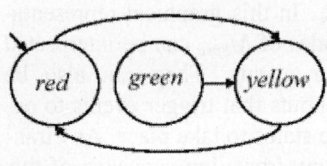

Fig. 4. Behavior-oriented system model M_{Syst}

Figure 5 transfers the FSM in Figure 4 into a Kripke structure. The transitions conserve the three states *red, green* and *yellow* of M_{Syst}, but rename them as s_1, s_2 and s_3. The atomic propositions *red, green*, and *yellow* are assigned to these states in combination of a negated and not-negated form, expressing the color of the traffic light in each state of M_{Syst}. The manual model checking of the Kripke structure of Figure 5 is sketched in Table 1

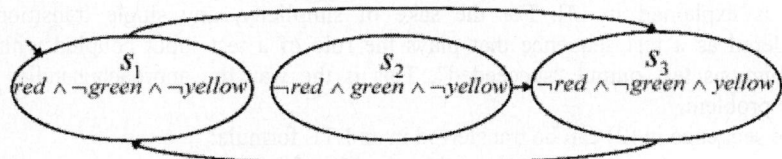

Fig. 5. Kripke structure for M_{Syst} of Figure 4

The results of the analysis of Table 1 are summarized as follows:
- 1 of 4 legal tests leads to inconsistencies in M_{Syst}.
- 1 of 8 illegal tests leads to inconsistencies in M_{Syst}.

Tabel 1. Manual model checking of the example

Valid Transitions		Invalid Transitions	
φ_1 = G(red →X(red ∧ yellow))	−	φ_5 = F(red →Xgreen)	−
φ_2 = G((red ∧ yellow) →Xgreen)	+	φ_6 = F(red →Xyellow)	+
φ_3 = G(green →Xyellow)	+	φ_7 = F((red ∧ yellow) →Xred)	−
φ_4 = G(yellow →Xred)	+	φ_8 = F((red ∧ yellow) →Xyellow)	−
Legend:		φ_9 = F(green →Xred)	−
+: the property is verified to be valid		φ_{10} = F(green →X(red ∧ yellow))	−
−: the property is verified to be invalid		φ_{11} = F(yellow →Xgreen)	−
		φ_{12} = F(yellow →X(red ∧ yellow))	−

Thus, the model checking detected all of the injected faults:
- The system does not conduct something that is desirable (φ_1), i.e. does not do something it is expected to do.
- The system conducts something that is undesirable (φ_6), i.e. does something it is expected not to do.

Any of the inconsistencies reveals a discrepancy between SUT, M_{Syst}, M_{Spec} and the specification. Each property that has been violated gives a hint to localize the fault.

3 A Non-trivial Example and Tool Support

To validate the approach, the user interface of a commercial system is analyzed. Figure 6 represents the utmost top menu as a graphical user interface (GUI) of the *Real Jukebox* (*RJB*) of the RealNetworks. RJB has been introduced as a personal music management system. The user can build, manage, and play his or her individual digital music library on a personal computer. At the top level, the GUI has a pull-down menu that invokes other window components.

As the code of the RJB is not available, black-box testing only is applicable to RJB. The on-line user manual of the system delivers an informal specification that will be used here to produce the specification model M_{Spec}.

As an example, the M_{Spec} in Figure 7(a) represents the top-level GUI to produce the desired interaction "Play and Record a CD or Track". The user can play/pause/re-cord/stop the track, fast forward (FF) and rewind. Figure 7(a) illustrates all sequences of user-system interactions to realize the operations the user might launch when using the system. As the bold dashed line indicates, a transition from "Pause" to "Record" is not allowed. In the following, this property will be used as an example for model checking.

As common in the practice, the user experiments with the system and finds out how it functions -- a process that leads to M_{Syst}. Figure 7(b) depicts M_{Syst} as a Kripke structure of the same abstraction level as Figure 7(a).

The analysis process of the RJB delivers a variety of M_{Spec} and M_{Syst} of different abstraction levels that are handled by the approach as described in Section 2.

Fig. 6. Top menu of the RealJukebox (RJB)

Because of the relatively large number of test cases and corresponding properties, an automated framework of tools is needed. This framework should explore the M_{Spec} and extract the test cases, convert them into properties and model check these properties. For the latter step, SPIN [14] is deployed which is a generic verification tool that supports the design and verification of asynchronous process systems. It accepts

- the system model described in PROMELA (a Process Meta Language) [14], and
- correctness claims specified in the syntax of standard LTL.

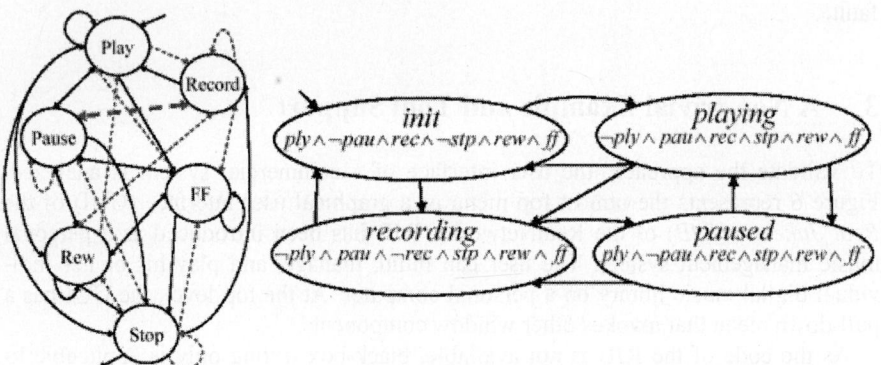

Fig. 7(a). M_{Spec} Fig. 7(b). M_{Syst} of the top GUI level of the RJB

Figures 8(a) and 8(b) contain screenshots of the user interface XSPIN of SPIN to demonstrate some steps of the tool deployment. Figure 8(a) shows the PROMELA representation of the Kripke structure in Fig 7b. A useful utility of XSPIN is the LTL property manager. It allows for the editing of LTL formulae and the conversion of them automatically into Büchi automata [7, 20], which is then used to verify the defined property. Figure 8(b) shows how LTL formula "F($pau \rightarrow Xrec$)" is model checked on M_{Syst} and verified as not valid. The command line SPIN *utilities* are used for a *batch processing* implemented by an additional script where several LTL properties are converted and verified. As an outcome, a protocol is produced including the verification result for each property. An excerpt of the faults the approach detected is given in Table 2.

Software Testing via Model Checking 915

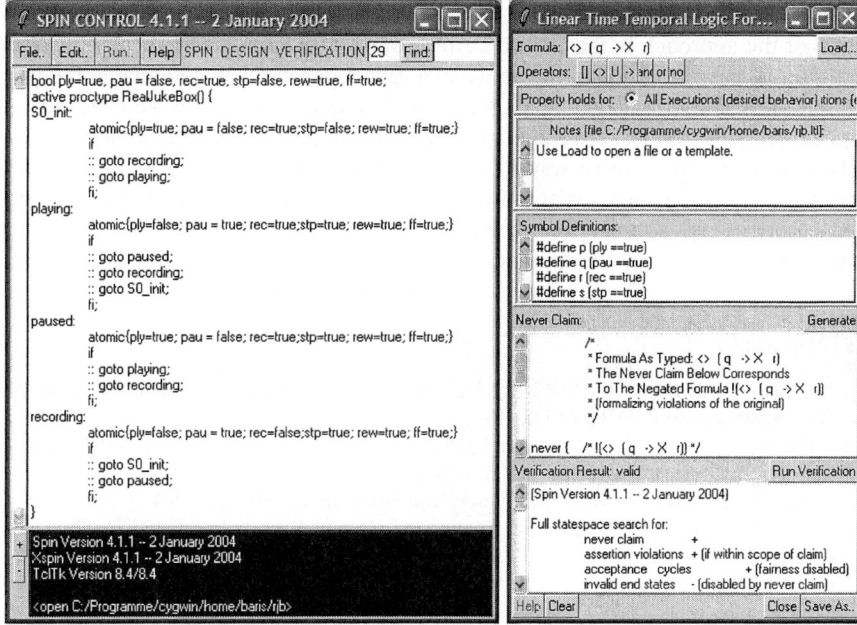

Fig. 8(a). PROMELA definition of Figure 7(b) Fig. 8(b). LTL formula for $F(pau \rightarrow Xrec)$

Table 2. Detected faults and their interpretation

No.	Fault Detected
1.	While recording, pushing the forward button or rewind button stops the recording process without a due warning.
2.	If a track is selected but the pointer refers to another track, pushing the play button invokes playing the selected track; the situation is ambiguous.
3.	During playing, pushing the pause button should exclude activation of record button. This is not ensured.
4.	Track position could not be set before starting the play of the file.

4 Conclusion and Future Work

An approach to combining specification-based testing with model checking has been introduced. Its novelty stems from (i) the holistic view that considers testing of not only the desirable system behavior, but also the undesirable one, and (ii) supporting and partly replacing the test process by model checking.

The approach has numerous advantages over traditional testing. First, model checking is automatically performed implying an enormous reduction of the costs and error-proneness that stemmed from manual work. Second, the test case and test generation are controlled by the coverage of the specification model and its complement. This enables an effective handling of the test termination and oracle problems.

To keep the examples simple, test sequences of relatively short length have been chosen; checking with longer sequences would increase the likeliness of revealing more sophisticated faults.

Apart from making use of tools, there is still potential for a more efficient application of the approach in the practice: Automatically or semi-automatically transferring the test cases to LTL formulae. Also a report generator would enable the production of meaningful and compact test reports in accordance with the needs of the test engineer, e.g., on test coverage, expected time point of test termination, etc.

In this paper, an intuitive way of the construction of the system model has been considered. Proposals also exist, however, for formalization of the model construction, e.g., in [19], applying learning theory. Taking these proposals into account would further rationalize the approach.

References

1. Ammann, P., Black, P.E., Majurski, W.: Using Model Checking to Generate Tests from Specifications. In: ICFEM. (1998) 46–54
2. Ammann, P., Black, P.E., Ding, W.: Model Checkers in Software Testing. NIST-IR 6777, National Institute of Standards and Technology. (2002)
3. Beizer, B.: Software Testing Techniques. Van Nostrand Reinhold (1990)
4. Belli, F.: Finite-State Testing and Analysis of Graphical User Interfaces. In: Proc. 12th ISSRE, IEEE Computer Society Press. (2001) 34–43
5. Binder, R.V.: Testing Object-Oriented Systems. Addison-Wesley (2000)
6. Bowen, J.P., et al.: FORTEST: Formal Methods and Testing. In: Proc. COMPSAC 02, IEEE Computer Society Press. (2002) 91–101
7. Büchi, J.R.: On a decision method in restricted second order arithmetic. In: Proc. Int. Cong. on Logic, Methodology, and Philosophy of Science, Stanford University Press. (1962) 1–11
8. Callahan, J., Schneider, F., Easterbrook, S.: Automated Software Testing Using Model-Checking. In: Proc. of the 1996 SPIN Workshop, Rutgers University, New Brunswick, NJ. (1996) 118–127
9. Chow, T.S.: Testing Software Designed Modeled by Finite-State Machines. IEEE Trans. Software Eng. (1978) 178–187
10. Clarke, E.M., Grumberg, O., Peled, D.: Model Checking. MIT Press (2000)
11. Engels, A., Feijs, L.M.G., Mauw, S.: Test Generation for Intelligent Networks Using Model Checking. In: Proc. TACAS (1997) 384–398
12. Gargantini, A., Heitmeyer, C.: Using Model Checking to Generate Tests from Requirements Specification. In: Proc. ESEC/FSE '99, ACM SIGSOFT. (1999) 146–162
13. Ghosh, S., Mathur, A.P.: Interface Mutation. In: Software Testing, Verif. and Reliability. (2001) 227-247
14. Holzmann, G.J.: The Model Checker SPIN. IEEE Trans. Software Eng. (1997) 279–295
15. Object Management Group. UML specification version 1.3 (1999)
16. Offutt, J., Liu, S., Abdurazik, A., Ammann, P.: Generating Test Data From State-Based Specifications. In: Software Testing, Verif.,and Reliability. (2003) 25–53
17. Okun, V., Black, P.E., Yesha, Y.: Testing with Model Checker: Insuring Fault Visibility. WSEAS Transactions on Systems (2003) 77–82
18. Peled, D.: Software Reliability Methods. Springer-Verlag (2001)
19. Peled, D., Vardi, M.Y., Yannakakis, M.: Black Box Checking. Journal of Automata, Languages and Combinatorics (2002) 225–246
20. Wolper, P.: Constructing Automata from Temporal Logic Formulas: A Tutorial. In: Proc. European Educational Forum: School on Formal Methods and Performance Analysis. (2000) 261–277
21. Zhu, H., Hall, P.A.V., May, J.H.R.: Unit Test Coverage and Adequacy. ACM Comp. Surveys (1997) 366–427

Mutation-Like Oriented Diversity for Dependability Improvement: A Distributed System Case Study*

Daniel O. Bortolas[1,3], Avelino F. Zorzo**[3],
Eduardo A. Bezerra[2,3], and Flavio M. de Oliveira[1,3]

[1] Hewlett-Packard/PUCRS, Research Centre on Software Testing (CPTS)
[2] Hewlett-Packard/PUCRS, Research Centre on Embedded Systems (CPSE)
[3] Faculdade de Informática (FACIN/PUCRS)
Pontifícia Universidade Católica do Rio Grande do Sul
Av. Ipiranga, 6681 – Prédio 30, 90619-900, Porto Alegre, RS, Brazil
{dbortolas,zorzo,eduardob,flavio}@inf.pucrs.br

Abstract. Achieving higher levels of dependability is a goal in any software project, therefore strategies for software reliability improvement are very attractive. This work introduces a new technique for reliability and maintainability improvement in object-oriented systems. The technique uses code mutation to generate diverse versions of a set of classes, and fault tolerance approaches to glue the versions together. The main advantages of the technique are the increase of reliability, and the proposed scheme for automatic generation of diverse classes. The technique is applied to a distributed application which uses CORBA and RMI. First results show promising conclusions.

1 Introduction

The use of computer systems is growing fast and becoming more pervasive in every day life. This is frequently called ubiquitous computing [1]. As a consequence, computers are each time more needed and it has become difficult to picture the modern world without them. Computers are so widespread that they are used even in places where responsibility is huge and failures may result in a tragedy, e.g. airplanes, trains or air traffic control systems. Computer high reliability is essential in these type of systems, and fault tolerance is a strategy used to minimize the effects of possible faults occurring in such systems.

Redundancy is the main mechanism employed in the construction of fault-tolerant systems at both, hardware and software levels. Replication of a hardware component ensures that when a failure happens, another component replaces the defective one [2].

The main problem in hardware components are the physical failures, e.g. broken wires or short cuts. Therefore, a failure in a hardware component does

---
* This work was developed in collaboration with HP Brazil R&D.
** Partially supported by CNPq Brazil (grant 350.277/2000-1).

not imply that another "copy" of the same component will produce the same failure. This same strategy cannot be applied directly to software components. If a software component is replicated, its faults (*bugs*) will also be replicated. This is true as faults in software components are classified as *design faults* [2], and each time a problem happens, the replaced component will have the same behaviour. Although hardware faults could be also the result of design mistakes, this is not common and therefore will not be considered in this work.

Design diversity is an approach used to overcome the replication problem in software [3]. Components conceived diversely have the same interface and functionality, but are designed and implemented using different techniques by separate groups of programmers, working independently. It is expected that groups working independently do not make the same mistakes. Thus, redundancy of software components might not present the same faults under the same environmental conditions.

Although design diversity has clear benefits to software dependability improvement, they do not come cheap. The high costs of this technique are mainly due to the need of several development teams working simultaneously. Therefore, this research is directed towards the automation of some steps of diversity programming, in order to minimize its cost.

The main objective of this work is dependability improvement of object-oriented systems using automatic code generation mechanisms. Dependability of a system is the ability to deliver services that can be trusted [4]. The concept includes several attributes [4], but this work targets mainly "reliability" and "maintainability". It will be shown also that automatic generation can help to ease the development and maintainability activities in software fault-tolerant systems, and can even decrease the total cost of these systems. Automatic generation can be used to reduce the amount of faults introduced during the implementation of diverse versions of a software.

In the proposed approach, traditional software fault tolerance mechanisms as, for instance, N-version programming (NVP) [5] and recovery block [6], are used to improve the reliability of software systems. The innovative aspect introduced in this paper is not the use of these fault tolerance mechanisms, but the whole process for automatic generation of new diverse classes of a system.

This approach is called Mutation-like Oriented Diversity (MOD). It uses a controlled sort of mutation, and not the one existing in nature and employed as a model in the traditional Mutant Analysis testing technique [7]. The approach's central idea is the modification of some specific parts of the source code of an application, targeting the generation of new diverse versions. Existing components are used as basic building blocks, and the generation of diverse versions is performed by applying *ad-hoc* mutant operators to the original code. The whole process was conceived to ease the automation process, and a tool aiming this objective is under development.

The remaining of this paper is organized as follows. Section 2 presents some related work. Section 3 describes the proposed approach. Section 4 discusses a distributed system used as a case study, presenting some interesting results. Section 5 presents the conclusions and future work.

2 Related Work

Mutation Analysis [7] is a testing technique that has as goal the evaluation of a set of test cases selected to a particular application. The technique uses a large number of modified programs, called mutants, that may be automatically generated by performing small modifications in the original code, producing new syntactically correct programs. The modifications are performed by mutant operators [8], which are specifically designed to certain constructions of a language and, consequently, each language has its own set of mutant operators. These operators have as objective to produce a wrong behaviour in resultant mutants, which are used to distinguish good from bad test cases. In this way, the set of test cases can be reduced and, as a consequence, the testing time is also shortened. However, this is not always true, as it is the case of the equivalent mutants [9].

MOD has some similarities to Demillo's Mutation Analysis, as the objective is to automatically create new diverse versions of some classes of an application, and these versions are generated by a set of mutant operators. Differently, however in MOD the new versions are produced to have a similar behaviour as the original part of the code from which they were generated. In MOD, mutant operators perform replacements in statements of the original application source code, by statements that are intended to have the same functionality as the original one.

Software fault tolerance applied to object-oriented systems is not a new research topic in Computer Science. For instance, [10] states that software fault tolerance cannot be achieved by just implementing traditional fault tolerance schemes in object-oriented systems. They propose a new system structure to deal with problems that arise from the fault tolerance applied to object-oriented software. Their framework to develop fault-tolerant software is based on diversely designed components that provide two types of redundancy: masking redundancy and dynamic redundancy. [11] proposes a new N-version programming strategy in which the diversity of the components is applied at the class level. The classes are developed separately and independently, and are encapsulated into a diversely designed object. This new NVP approach uses the general framework proposed in [10].

MOD tries to tolerate faults in a similar way to those approaches. It provides support for masking and dynamic redundancy, and it is also applied to the level of classes. The main difference in MOD is that the diverse classes are generated automatically. This feature reduces the complexity of incorporating new designed components to the system during its lifetime.

3 Mutation-Like Oriented Diversity (MOD)

The proposed approach has as a main objective to significantly enhance the reliability and maintainability figures of object-oriented (OO) systems. Figure 1 shows the design of a non-fault-tolerant OO software, which is divided in layers to better describe some particularities of the strategy. The *component classes layer* is where the basic building classes, or basic building components, of the system are located. The *intermediate classes layer* is composed of classes that will be diversely replicated. Finally, the *user classes layer* contains the remaining classes of the system. The starting point to understand MOD is to comprehend that it needs to be applied to an initial piece of software. This means that it is necessary to have, at least, the components shown in all of the three layers of Figure 1. The process is then carried out in two stages. First the mutants are generated, and next an extra layer, the *controller classes layer*, is added to the system, in order to attach the newly created mutant classes.

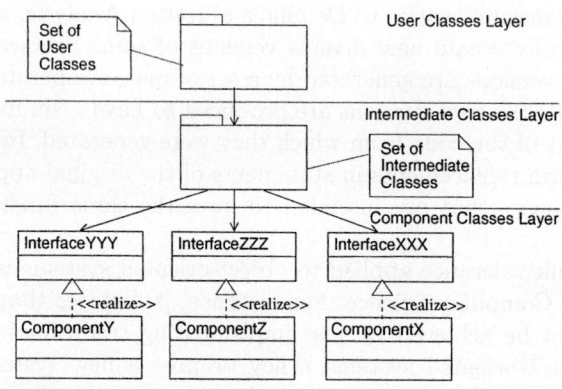

Fig. 1. Software design

3.1 Mutant Generation

In this phase the set of classes in the intermediate layer of the original software are replicated diversely, generating the intermediate layer of the new fault-tolerant system. Figure 2 shows the class diagram of a fault-tolerant system generated using MOD. The new *controller classes layer* shown in Figure 2 is discussed in the next section.

The generated classes in the intermediate layer are called *mutants*. They represent the new diverse versions obtained from the mutation of the intermediate classes layer. In the mutation process, *mutant operators* are used to replace constructions and instructions in the source code.

Changes in single instructions as, for instance, arithmetic or relational expressions, are not sufficient to introduce diversity to the newly generated mutated software versions. For this reason, a coarse grain mutation should be performed.

In MOD, the mutation takes place at the class level, which means that the mutated instruction is an entire class. These classes are represented by elementary components in the component classes layer (Figure 1).

The elementary components in the component layer are essential to the approach. They must implement the interfaces used by the intermediate layer classes, and they must be developed according to the design diversity methodology. In this work it is assumed that at the time of applying the proposed technique the diverse versions of components to be used are already available. An important point is that the source code of the components is not required, which means that commercial-off-the-shelf (COTS) components can be used.

An interesting point to be noticed is that since system diversity is provided by elementary components, the more components used the better the diversity of the new generated classes. Another point is that, since the process of generating mutants is automatic and therefore cheaper, new elementary components can be easily incorporated to the system during its lifetime, thus opening the possibility for new reliability improvements.

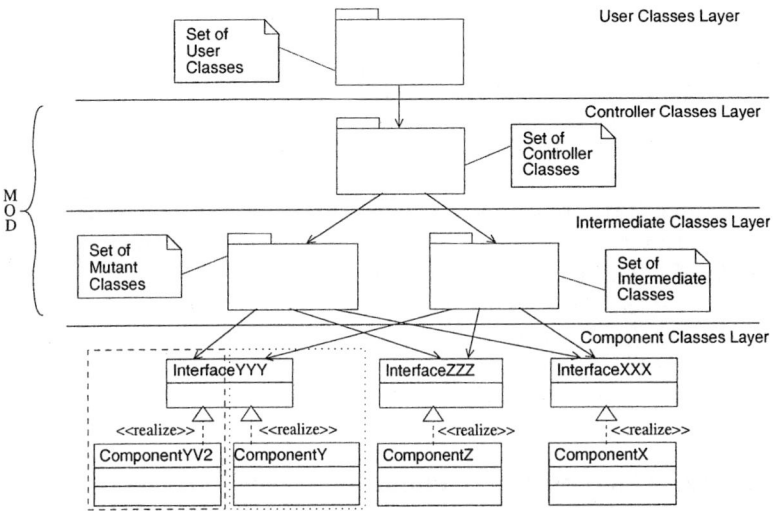

Fig. 2. Mutant generation

3.2 Controller Construction

Having the new intermediate classes layer, the next step is to join the several mutants and to use them in a software fault tolerance mechanism. The controller layer implements the software fault tolerance mechanism used to join the generated mutants. Any technique based on diversity can be used as, for instance, N-version programming or recovery block.

The controller layer must have exactly the same interface as the intermediate layer in the original system, since the user layer is not modified at all. The process can be better structured using, for example, reflection as in [12]. This will certainly reduce the modification that the approach has to perform in the original system. This may also improve the final result as it will allow the user interface to be any class that makes access to the intermediate classes. This alternative is under investigation and is the subject of a future work.

4 Using MOD in the Design of a Distributed Application

The selected case study to explain MOD's usage, and also for its initial evaluation, is a Reverse Polish Notation (RPN) calculator for a distributed environment. The motivations for choosing this case study are straightforward. First, the model of an RPN calculator matches perfectly with MOD. Second, an RPN calculator is not difficult to implement, as the basic building block is a stack. Finally, it has some facilities to test and make measurements from resulting data.

Although the case study is not complex, it can be seen as an ambitious implementation. Two types of distributed objects are used, RMI and CORBA. Specific mutant operators have been created in order to accomplish with the task of translating a user class of RMI objects into a user class of CORBA objects.

Considering the architecture shown in Figure 1, the original version of the case study has three main classes: the *MainProgram* class in the user layer; the *Calculator* class in the intermediate layer; and the *StackImpl* class, which is a component in the component layer.

The case study is implemented in Java and an obvious choice to distribute the application is the use of Java RMI. Thus, the *StackImpl* class is an implementation of an RMI object and the *Calculator* class is a user of this distributed RMI object. Having the first version of the calculator program, the next step is to get hold of additional diverse components (Stack programs) that implement the *Stack* interface. After that, the program mutation in the Calculator class is conducted aiming the generation of diverse Calculator classes. This mutation is performed based on the new elementary components. Finally, the controller classes (controller layer) are created.

4.1 Diverse Components (Component Layer)

Diverse components are required in the component layer in order to introduce diversity to the intermediate layer. As discussed in Section 3.1, COTS could be used in this layer. However, for this case study, a faster option was an inhouse implementation of extra versions for the Stack interface. In addition to the original RMI *StackImpl* class, five extra components have been built: two more RMI classes and three CORBA classes. A total of six diverse components are used in this case study.

A stack implementation is relatively simple and it is not likely to present a faulty behaviour. As it might be difficult to observe reliability improvements, it has been decided to inject faults in the source code of each implemented stack. The fault injection was designed aiming a failure rate of 2% in all method calls of the different stacks. A possible observed failure in a pop call is the situation in which instead of the correct value, a new integer is randomly generated and returned to the caller of the method. Another situation is when instead of the value, an exception is returned to the caller of the method. A problem in a push call could be when pushing the correct value, another number is randomly generated and pushed back into the stack.

4.2 Mutation Approach (Intermediate Layer)

The mutation happens in the classes belonging to the intermediate Layer, in order to generate new diverse replicated classes. Two mutant operators are very common and may take part in almost any system that uses MOD. They are the *Instantiation Operator (InOp)* and the *Import Operator (ImOp)*.

In general, the *InOp* operator creates a new mutant by replacing component instantiations in intermediate layer classes, by new diverse component instantiations. For example, if the Java code in the original program is *"Stack st = new StackImplA();"* the *InOp* operator will change this line into *"Stack st = new StackImplB();"*.

The *ImOp* operator is used to replace or to insert Java *import* instructions in intermediate layer classes. Each time a new package is requested by the application, an *import* instruction is inserted in the source code. When a package is not any longer needed, the mutant operator removes the respective *import* instruction from the code. This operator is usually applied right after an *InOp*. For example, an intermediate class that uses a package called *StackA* has the instruction *"import br.pucrs.cpts.StackA.*;"*. As a result of a mutation performed by an *InOp* operator, a new package *StackB* is needed, and the previous package has to be removed. The *ImOp* operator will make the change, replacing the original import instruction by *"import br.pucrs.cpts.StackB.*;"*.

In the distributed application, in this paper, the classes belonging to the intermediate layer do not create instances of objects, instead, they obtain instances of distributed objects from some sort of service directory. As a result, the *InOp* operator could not be used straight away and it had to be split into two operators, the RMI to RMI operator (*R2ROp*) and the RMI to CORBA operator (*R2COp*). *R2ROp* reads an intermediate layer class having RMI object references and creates a mutant intermediate layer class having other RMI object references. Basically, *R2ROp* performs the replacement of the URL of the original intermediate layer class by the URL of the new mutant class.

The *R2COp* operator reads an RMI intermediate layer class and produces a CORBA intermediate layer class. The translation of an RMI object reference into a CORBA object reference is not direct. In this case, the *R2COp* operator translates an RMI instruction into a set of CORBA instructions, in order to modify the calls to get the object references. The translation is not straightforward, but it is feasible to be accomplished. Another aspect to be observed is that an RMI object reference has a different type when comparing to a CORBA object reference. The original *InOp* operator is used here to solve the differences.

For the case study, the mutation process generates a total of six versions of the intermediate layer classes. These new classes are obtained after having applied the necessary mutant operators to the original intermediate layer classes of the distributed RPN calculator program.

4.3 Adding Fault Tolerance Mechanisms (Controller Layer)

The new diverse versions generated in the previous section are used by the controller layer to introduce fault tolerance capabilities to the system. The controller layer is created using the N-version programming model. This fault tolerance technique was chosen as a consequence of the case study distributed features. The controller layer classes are built in a way that they offer the same names for the user layer, and therefore the classes do not need to be modified.

There are some options to automate the generation process of the controller layer classes as, for instance, templates for some pre-defined fault tolerance mechanisms. However, in the present version this process is not completely automated, and the controller construction is the module of MOD that needs the larger amount of manual intervention.

4.4 Preliminary Results

First, in order to observe the behaviour of the original program, a total of 10^4 test sets were created to feed the distributed calculator. Each test set is an expression having 2, 3, 4, 5, 6 or 7 operands (expression "3 4 + 5 +", for instance, has three operands, which are underlined). The result of this experiment is represented by the dotted line in Figure 3.

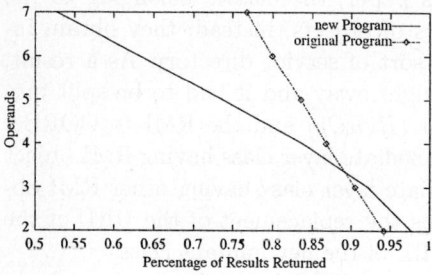 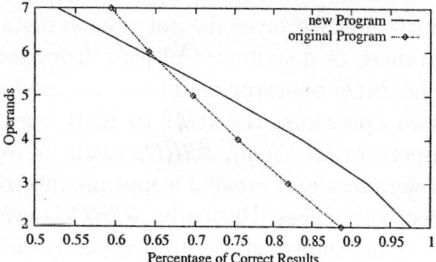

Fig. 3. All returned results vs. number of operands in an expression

Fig. 4. Correct results vs. number of operands in an expression

Considering the selected expressions, one could expect the stack to present a correct behaviour in 98% of the method calls. However, this figure is never observed when running the experiment, as it is necessary more than one method call to perform a calculation. It is observed also that as the number of method calls increases, so does the chance of getting erroneous output. As shown in

Figure 3, the percentage of responses, both correct and incorrect, in the original program (dotted line), decreases as the number of operands increases (the number of calculations and, therefore, the method calls increase).

The dotted line in Figure 3 represents all the results that do not raise exceptions during the evaluation of an expression. However, there is yet a chance that the returned result is erroneous. For this reason a gold calculator was designed and used to verify the returned results from the original calculator program. The dotted line in Figure 4 shows the percentage of only the correct results returned from the execution of the original calculator program, employing the same 10^4 test cases executed previously.

The same set of test cases was applied to the new program generated by MOD. Observing the solid lines in Figures 3 and 4, it is possible to conclude that the number of all returned results and the number of only correct outputs are identical.

The diagram shown in Figure 3, is the most significative one as it represents all the responses provided to the user, both the correct and the incorrect ones. Comparing the original program to the new generated one, it is possible to see that for the majority of the test cases (4, 5, 6 and 7 operands), the original program returns more results than the generated one. In the worst case, the 7 operands test cases, the new generated program could only return a result in a few more than 50% of all calculated expressions.

However, it is necessary to know if the returned results (Figure 3) can be trusted. When they are compared against the correct ones (Figure 4) it is possible to observe that the percentage of results in the original program vary too much and, therefore, they are not as reliable as the returned results of the new generated one.

5 Conclusions and Future Work

This work introduces a new strategy for developing systems having high reliability requirements. First results are still incipient, but the main idea could be verified through a case study. Several enhancements are under investigation and they will be discussed in a future work.

The results of applying the proposed methodology appear to be as reliable as traditional fault tolerance software approaches. However, the advantages of applying the methodology are not only related to the level of reliability reached, but also to the ease of maintainability of code and the level of automation of the strategy. The intermediate classes of the program are replicated through the mutation mechanism, in other words, the logic of the replicated code is the same, and no extra maintaining is needed for this code. The automation is an important feature, as it can accelerate the development phase and even decrease the chance of introducing hand made modification faults.

The approach also has some disadvantages. As the methodology uses traditional fault tolerance software strategies, the drawbacks are similar. For example, the problems related to the use of fault-tolerant software in object-oriented languages [10], or even the restrictions imposed by the nature of the application [2]. Another drawback concerns shared resources. As mutant versions are generated from a single set of classes, in case several mutants have access to the same resource (e.g. file, I/O), it may result in a system failure. Other problems are mainly related to the design of the software, which must follow strict rules (see Section 3). For instance, the system shall be designed aiming high cohesion and low coupling. The mutant generation task may become difficult or even impossible to be accomplished in highly coupled systems.

Finally, there is a large amount of future work to be done. It is necessary to implement tools to support the automatic generation of the mutant mechanism, and also to design/implement new case studies. Another research issue under investigation is the possibility of increasing the reliability of a system by combining parts of different components to build a new class.

References

1. Weiser, M.: Ubiquitous computing. IEEE Computer–Hot Topics **26** (1993) 71–72
2. Jalote, P.: Fault tolerance in distributed systems. Prentice Hall (1994)
3. Litlewood, B., Popov, P., Strigini, L.: Modeling software design diversity–A review. ACM Computing Surveys **33** (2001) 177–208
4. Laprie, J.C.: Dependable computing and fault tolerance: Concepts and terminology. In: Digest of FTCS-15. (1985) 2–11
5. Avizienis, A.: The n-version approach to fault-tolerant software. IEEE Transactions on Software Engineering **11** (1985) 1491–1501
6. Randell, B.: System structure for software fault tolerance. In: Proceedings of the International Conference on Reliable Software. (1975) 437–449
7. Demillo, R.A., Lipton, R.J., Sayward, F.G.: Hints on test data selection: Help for the practicing programmer. Computer **11** (1978) 34–41
8. Offutt, A.J., Lee, A., Rothermel, G., Untch, R., Zapf, C.: An experimental determination of sufficient mutant operators. ACM Transactions on Software Engineering and Methodology **5** (1996) 99–118
9. Offutt, A.J., Pan, J.: Automatically detecting equivalent mutants and infeasible paths. The Journal of Software Testing, Verification, and Reliability **7** (1997) 165–192
10. Xu, J., Randell, B., Rubira-Casavara, C.M.F., Stroud, R.J.: Toward an object-oriented approach to software fault tolerance. In: Pradhan, D.K., Avresky, D.R. (eds.): Recent Advances in Fault-Tolerant Parallel and Distributed Systems. IEEE Computer Society Press (1995) 226–233
11. Romanovsky, A.: Diversely designed classes for use by multiple tasks. ACM SIGAda Ada Letters **20** (2000) 25–37
12. Xu, J., Randell, B., Zorzo, A.F.: Implementing software fault tolerance in C++ and Openc++: An object-oriented and reflective approach. In: International Workshop on Computer Aided Design, Test and Evaluation for Dependability. (1996) 224–229

JAWIRO: Enhancing Java with Roles

Yunus Emre Selçuk and Nadia Erdoğan

Istanbul Technical University, Electrical – Electronics Faculty
Computer Eng. Dept., 34469 Ayazaga, Istanbul, Turkey
selcukyu@itu.edu.tr, erdogan@cs.itu.edu.tr

Abstract. This paper introduces a role model named JAWIRO, which enhances Java with role support. JAWIRO implements features expected of roles, allowing a role to be acquired, dropped, transferred, suspended, resumed, etc. The main contribution of the proposed model is the provision of multiple object-level inheritance together with class-level inheritance. JAWIRO provides a better means to model dynamically evolving systems and increases the performance of method calls when compared to class-level inheritance.

1 Introduction

Although the real world mainly consists of objects which constantly change and evolve, the relationship between an object and its respective class is persistent, static and exclusive in the class-based object-oriented programming (OOP) paradigm. This property of OOP makes it suitable for modeling real world objects that can be divided into distinct classes and never change their classes. The need of a better way for modeling dynamically evolving entities has led many researchers to come up with different paradigms such as prototype-based languages [1], dynamic reclassification [2], subject oriented programming [3], design patterns [4], etc.

OOP requires programmers to define classes that determine the behavior of each separate role in the modeled system. In a system where objects evolve in time by acquiring multiple roles, additional classes should be constructed for each possible combination of roles by using the previously defined classes. Such combination classes are called *intersection classes* and they are usually obtained via multiple inheritance. This approach leads to an exponentially growing tree of a class hierarchy, which is usually sparsely populated with the necessary objects. Moreover, multiple inheritance is not supported by all OOP languages where the work of embedding necessary functionality into the intersection classes will be hard.

This paper presents a role model implementation, JAWIRO, which enhances Java with role support for better modeling of dynamically evolving real world systems. JAWIRO provides all expected requirements of roles, as well as providing additional functionalities without a performance overhead when executing methods.

2 Role Based Programming and Role Models

The role concept comes from the theoretical definition where it is the part of a play that is played by an actor on stage. Roles are different types of behavior that different types of entities can perform. Kristensen [5] defines a role as follows: A role of an object is a set of properties which are important for an object to be able to behave in a certain way expected by a set of other objects. The term *role model* specifies a style of designing and implementing roles. Role based programming (RBP) is accepted as a way to overcome the previously mentioned drawbacks of OOP when modeling dynamic systems. RBP provides a direct and general way to separate internal and external behaviors of objects. Besides, RBP extends the concepts of OOP naturally and elegantly.

When modeling evolving entities, specialization at the instance level is a better approach than specialization at the class level. In this case, an entity is represented by multiple objects, each executing a different role that the real-world entity is required to perform. In role based programming, an object evolves by acquiring new roles and this type of specialization at the instance level is called *object level inheritance*. When multiple objects are involved, the fact that all these objects represent the same entity is lost in the regular OOP paradigm unless the programmer takes extra precaution to keep that information such as utilizing a member in each class for labeling purposes. Role models take this burden from the programmer and provide a mechanism for object level inheritance.

Object level inheritance successfully models the *IsPartOf* [6] relation where class level inheritance elegantly models the *IsA* [6] relation. As both types of relationship are required when modeling of real world systems, both types of inheritance should coexist in an object-oriented environment. Therefore, many role models are implemented by extending an object-oriented language of choice, such as INADA [7], DEC-JAVA [8], the works of Gottlob et al. [9] and Lee and Bae [10], etc.

3 JAWIRO: A Role Model for Java

The aim of this work is to design a role model and to extend the Java programming language with role support. Java has been chosen as the base language because even though it has advanced capabilities that help to its widespread use, it lacks features to design and implement roles in order to model dynamic object behaviors. The focus is to implement an extendible, simple yet powerful role model without the restrictions, which are elaborated in Section 4, imposed by previous work on role models.

3.1 Role Model of JAWIRO

A role model named JAWIRO is implemented to enhance Java with role support. JAWIRO lets roles to be acquired, suspended to be resumed later, abandoned or transferred to another owner without dropping its sub roles. JAWIRO supports all requirements of roles without any restrictions, including aggregate roles – the only restriction is imposed by the Java language itself, which does not support multiple class-level inheritance. The resulting model is a flexible one that enables coexistence of both regular class-level inheritance and multiple object-level inheritance.

Role model of JAWIRO uses a tree representation for modeling relational hierarchies of roles. A hierarchical representation enables better modeling of role ownership relations, as well as more elegant and robust implementation of roles' primary characteristics.

JAWIRO enables multiple object-level inheritance. A role object can be played by owners from different classes if it is required for better modeling of a real world system. This will not cause any ambiguities since a role instance can be played by only one owner at the same time. However, the mentioned owners should implement a common interface and the programmer is responsible from this task. This is not an elegant approach as owners need to implement methods that they do not use directly. A future enhancement will eliminate this necessity as mentioned in Section 5.

JAWIRO works with a consultation mechanism [8], shown in Figure 1, where the implicit this parameter points to the object the method call has been forwarded to.

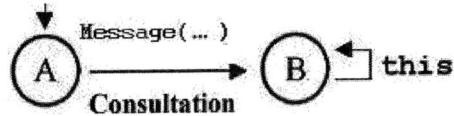

Fig. 1. Consultation mechanism

Basic features of roles defined by Kristensen [5] are implemented by JAWIRO:
- Visibility: The access to an object is restricted by its current view, e.g. current role.
- Dependency: Roles are meaningful only when attached to an owner.
- Identity: The notion that a real world object is defined by all its roles are preserved, e.g. each role object is aware of its owner and the root of the hierarchy.
- Dynamism: A role can be added to and removed from an object during its lifetime.
- Multiplicity: An entity can have more than one instance of the same role type. Such roles are called *aggregate roles*, which are distinguished from each other with an identifier.
- Abstraction: Roles can be organized in various hierarchical relationships.
- Roles of roles: A role can play other roles, too.

JAWIRO implements the following features as well:
- Class level inheritance can be used together with object level inheritance.
- Some roles of an object can share common structure and behavior. This is achieved by generating role classes via class level inheritance, e.g. previous feature.
- Multiple object level inheritance is supported.
- Roles can be suspended for a while and resumed later.
- A role can be transferred to another owner without dropping its sub roles.
- An entity could switch between its roles any time it wishes. This means that any of the roles of an object can be accessed from a reference to any other role.
- Different roles are allowed to have members with same names without conflicts.
- Entities can be queried whether they are currently playing a certain type of role or a particular role object.

Table 1. Application programming interface and important members of JAWIRO. All checking operations search the entire hierarchy

Methods of RoleInterface	
Name	Explanation
public boolean addRole(Role r)	Adds a new role to this object
public boolean canDelegate(Role r)	Checks whether r exists in the same role hierarchy with this object
public boolean canSwitch(String className)	Checks whether this object has the given role type (aggregate or normal)
public Object as(String className)	Role switching command.
public Object as(String className, String identifier)	Role switching command for aggregate roles.
public boolean canSwitch(String className, String identifier)	Checks whether this object has the given aggregate role type with a specific identifier.
Additional Member of the Actor class	
Name	Explanation
RoleHierarchy hierarchy	Maintains the role hierarchy where this Actor object is its root.
Additional Member and Methods of the Role class	
Name	Explanation
RoleInterface owner	The object which plays this role. Can be an instance of Actor, Role or AggregateRole
Actor root	Root of the role hierarcy.
public Object playedBy( )	Returns the object which plays this role.
public Object Actor()	Returns the root of the role hierarcy in which this object exists.
public boolean resign( )	Permanently loosing this role
public boolean suspend( )	Temporarily leaving this role for later resuming
public boolean resume( )	Resuming this suspended role.
public boolean transfer(RoleInterface newOwner)	Transfer this role and its sub roles to another owner.
Additional Member of the AggregateRole class	
Name	Explanation
String identifier	Used for distinction of aggregate roles

API of our role model and some important members are summarized in Table 1. Real world objects, which can be the root of a role hierarchy, are modeled with the Actor class. The role objects are modeled with the Role class. The aggregate roles are implemented by deriving a namesake class via class-level inheritance from Role class. The backbone of the role model is implemented in the RoleHierarchy class, where each Actor object has one member of this type. There are two more classes for representing the relational hierarchy of roles and their instances are member(s) of

Actor and Role classes in order to avoid redundant traversals of the role hierarchy. These classes are omitted in Table 1, as they are not parts of the user interface. Actor and role classes implement the same interface, the RoleInterface.

3.2 Using Roles with JAWIRO

To show role usage and the capabilities of JAWIRO, an example containing two hierarchies is given in Figure 2 is used by the partial code shown in Figure 3. The first hierarchy is introduced in [9] and the second hierarchy is added to illustrate object level multiple inheritance. Realization of Figure 2 is omitted due to space constraints; however, a complete listing can be accessed at [11].

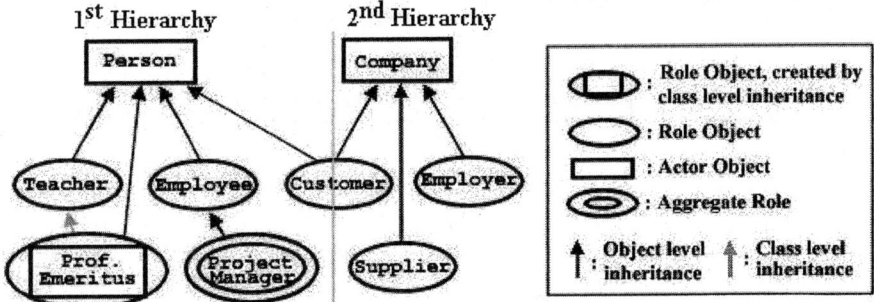

Fig. 2. A sample hierarchy in JAWIRO

```
Company co1,co2; Employer er;        t.resume(); //then continues teaching.
Supplier su; Customer cu1,cu2;       ee2=new Employee(er,"453-543");
Person p1,p2; Teacher t;             p2=new Person("Gordon Fast","637-252");
ProfEmeritus pe; Employee ee1,ee2;   p2.addRole(ee2); //Gordon enters MTCX
ProjectManager pm1,pm2;
                                     t.resign(); //Tom retires,but ...
co2=new Company("Black Mesa Lbs","BML"); pe=new ProfEmeritus(t);
su=new Supplier();                   p1.addRole(pe);//becomes prof.emeritus.
co2.addRole(su);
                                     ee1=new Employee(er,"628-749");
co1=new Company("Metacortex","MTCX"); p1.addRole(ee1); //Tom works in MTCX
er=new Employer();                   pm1=new ProjectManager("Vir.Rlt","VR");
co1.addRole(er); //MTCX ready to enlist. ee1.addRole(pm1);
cu1=new Customer(su);                //Tom becomes a project manager
co1.addRole(cu1);                    pm2=new ProjectManager("Art.Int","AI");
//MTCX becomes a customer of BML
                                     ee1.addRole(pm2);
if(co1.canSwitch("examples.Customer")) //Tom has another project to lead.
//Checking role ownership,1st way    pm2.transfer(p2);
 ((Customer)er.as("examples.Customer")) cu2=new Customer(su);
 .buy(3); //MTCX buys 4 goods        p1.addRole(cu2);
//Role switching : employer to customer. //Tom becomes personal customer of BML
                                     if(p1.canDelegate(cu2))
p1=new Person("Tom Anderson","843-663"); //Checking role ownership,2nd way
t=new Teacher("Physics");             cu2.buy(2); /*No need for role
p1.addRole(t); //Tom becomes a teacher, switching, we learned p1 plays cu2*/
t.suspend();//temporarily stops teaching
```

Fig. 3. An example of using roles in JAWIRO

3.3 Performance Evaluation

We have decided to measure and compare the cost of execution of programming in JAWIRO to that of an implementation using class level inheritance to provide evidence on the feasibility of the proposed model. The middle branch of the role hierarchy for Person in Figure 2 is implemented by class level inheritance, as in Figure 4 and then the time needed to execute the whoami method of ProjectManager when switched from Person is compared to the time it takes when the same method of AltProjMgr called directly. The whoami method prints two lines to the standard output, which contain the names of the person and the managed project.

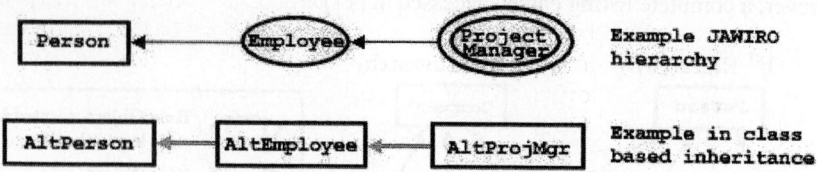

Fig. 4. Hierarchies used in performance evaluation

Table 2. Performance of JAWIRO compared to regular class-based inheritance. All results are in milliseconds and for 1000 operations

	JAWIRO Role Model			Class Level Inheritance Hierarchy		
	Construction	Execution	Total	Construction	Execution	Total
1st run	47	454	501	31	469	500
2nd run	31	454	485	16	469	485
3rd run	47	453	500	31	453	484
4th run	31	453	484	31	453	484
5th run	47	453	500	15	469	484
6th run	31	453	484	16	453	469
7th run	47	453	500	16	469	485
8th run	32	453	485	16	453	469
9th run	47	453	500	15	437	452
10th run	31	437	468	16	469	485
Average	39.1	451.6	490.7	20.3	459.4	479.4

Execution times are measured with System.currentTimeMillis method. Constructing the required hierarchy and executing the whoami method are timed separately and both are repeated 1000 times. The testing process is repeated ten times. The results obtained with a PC having 256MB RAM, 1.6GHz CPU and JDK1.4.1 are given in Table 2. Results reveal that although constructing a role hierarchy takes roughly about twice longer than constructing a class hierarchy, method execution time is 1.7% shorter when using roles. However, the results for the total times measured for JAWIRO is 2.3 percent slower than using class-based inheritance in the example. It should be kept in mind that method execution time is more significant than the time it takes for constructing a hierarchy because the construction is a one-time process in typical systems while method execution takes place constantly.

4 Related Work

Readers can refer to [12] for a review and comparison of proposed role models in programming languages other than Java. Recent works [8,10] with JAVA are compared with JAWIRO in this chapter, with the addition of the work in Smalltalk by Gottlob et al. [9] and INADA [7], which is implemented in C++.

INADA [7] is an extension of C++ with role support in a persistent environment where every type is equal to a role. Roles are presented in a set based fashion, which is a weaker representation than the relational hierarchy of roles. The limitations of INADA are its inability to support aggregate roles and the non-existence of methods for run-time type control. Other primary characteristics of roles are implemented.

The role model proposed by Gottlob et al. [9] is very flexible and supports all primary characteristics of roles. The only limitation is imposed on aggregate roles: Sub-roles of aggregate roles are also required to be aggregate roles. However, aggregate roles can play both regular roles and/or aggregate roles in JAWIRO.

DEC-JAVA [8] bears inspirations from the decorator design pattern [4]. The role model of DEC-JAVA is based on two kinds of objects: *Component* objects which represent a state are embedded in *decorator* objects. Current state of a real world object is projected to its behavior by decorator objects. A component object can be decorated by more than one decorator objects. Nested decorations are also supported where the outmost decorator can access both inner decorators and inner components. This property of DEC-JAVA makes it possible to use it as a RBP language that uses relational hierarchies of roles.

Although DEC-JAVA supports primary characteristics of roles, it limits the user to object-level inheritance only and does not support class-level inheritance. Moreover, it doesn't support methods returning a value and methods can only be evolved by adding additional code only to the end of them via decorators in DEC-JAVA.

Lee and Bae [10] propose a unique role model where the focus is not the dynamic evolution but preventing the violation of structural constraints and abnormal role bindings. The constraints and abnormalities are imposed by the system to be modeled. In contrast with other models, *core* objects (actors) are assigned to role object, instead of assigning roles to actors. When a core object has multiple roles, individual role objects are grouped into one big, composite role. This prevents a hierarchical relation between roles but we believe hierarchical representation is a more natural approach.

Lee and Bae's model [10] is implemented in such a way that supporting aggregate roles is impossible. The final drawback of Lee and Bae's model [10] is the missing *Select* composition rule. When there are name conflicts (a primary characteristic of roles) between two roles that form a composite role, this rule enables selection of the necessary attributes and methods according to the role state at run-time.

5 Conclusions and Future Work

As the use of reflection capabilities of Java is kept at minimum, JAWIRO does not introduce a performance penalty. On the contrary, it gives better performance than using class-level inheritance. Moreover, JAWIRO does not need further reflection capabilities of other third party tools. The only tool planned for the future is a simple preprocessor to eliminate the complex parenthesizing in role switching commands.

As a future work, persistence capabilities will be added to JAWIRO, so that users will be able to save entire role hierarchies to disk for later use. The final task for the future is to enable the use of a member or a method in the role hierarchy without explicitly mentioning the respective class. If any name conflicts occur, the most evolved role's member will be used. This functionality will also remove the necessity of implementing a common interface in multiple owners of a role that uses multiple object-level inheritance. However, multiple object-level inheritance will be more costly than single inheritance as the mentioned functionality needs to be implemented by using native reflection capabilities of Java.

The only unplanned functionality of JAWIRO is a means to enforce the structural and behavioral constraints of the real world system to be modeled. However, the authors believe that this task is up to the programmers, not up to the role model, and it can be achieved by careful design and proven software engineering methodologies.

References

1. Ungar, D., Smith, R.B.: Self: The Power of Simplicity. In: Proc. ACM Conf. on Object Oriented Programming Systems, Languages and Applications. (1987) 212–242
2. Drossopoulou, S., Damiani, F., Dezani, C.M.: More Dynamic Object Reclassification: Fickle. ACM Trans. Programming Languages and Systems **2** (2002) 153–191
3. Wong, R.K., et. al.: A Data Model and Semantics of Objects with Dynamic Roles. In: IEEE Int'l Conf. On Data Engineering. (1997) 402–411
4. Gamma, E., Helm, R., Johnson, R., Vlissides, V.: Design Patterns Elements of Reusable Object Oriented Software. Addison Wesley (1994)
5. Kristensen, B.B.: Conceptual Abstraction Theory and Practical Language Issues. Theory and Practice of Object Systems **2**(3) (1996)
6. Zendler, A.M.: Foundation of the Taxonomic Object System. Information and Software Technology **40** (1998) 475–492
7. Aritsugi, M., Makinouchi, A.: Multiple-Type Objects in an Enhanced C++ Persistent Programming Language. Software–Practice and Experience **30**(2) (2000) 151–174
8. Bettini, L., Capecchi, S., Venneri, B.: Extending Java to Dynamic Object Behaviours. Electronic Notes in Theoretical Computer Science **82**(8) (2003)
9. Gottlob, G., Schrefl, M., Röck, B.: Extending Object-Oriented Systems with Roles. ACM Trans. Information Systems **14**(3) (1996) 268–296
10. Lee, J.-S., Bae, D.-H.: An Enhanced Role Model For Alleviating the Role-Binding Anomaly. Software–Practice and Experience **32** (2002) 1317–1344
11. http://www.library.itu.edu.tr/~yeselcuk/iscis.html.
12. Selçuk, Y.E., Erdoğan, N.: How to Solve the Inefficiencies of Object Oriented Programming: A Survey Biased on Role-Based Programming. In: 7th World Multiconf. Systemics, Cybernetics and Informatics. (2003) 160–165

A Survey of Public-Key Cryptography on J2ME-Enabled Mobile Devices

Stefan Tillich and Johann Großschädl

Graz University of Technology
Institute for Applied Information Processing and Communications
Inffeldgasse 16a, A–8010 Graz, Austria
{Stefan.Tillich,Johann.Groszschaedl}@iaik.at

Abstract. The advent of hand-held devices which incorporate a Java Virtual Machine (JVM) has greatly facilitated the development of mobile and wireless applications. Many of the possible applications, e.g. for e-commerce or e-government, have an inherent need for security which can be satisfied by methods of public-key cryptography. This paper investigates the feasibility of public-key implementations on modern midrange to high-end devices, with the focus set on Elliptic Curve Cryptography (ECC). We have implemented the Elliptic Curve Digital Signature Algorithm (ECDSA) for both signature generation and verification and we show that both can be done on a J2ME-enabled cell phone—depending on the device—in times of a few seconds or even under a second. We also compare the performance of ECDSA with RSA signatures and provide some key issues for selecting one protocol type for implementation in a constrained device.

1 Introduction

Today the market for mobile communication and computing devices like cell phones and PDAs is growing rapidly. The issue of application development for such a great number of different devices has been addressed by the integration of Java Virtual Machines (JVMs). Most of today's devices conform to Sun Microsystems' Java 2 Platform, Micro Edition (J2ME). J2ME devices allow a fast deployment of mobile and wireless applications. Many possible applications have an inherent need for security, e.g. applications for mobile electronic payment, authentication to access secure networks, digitally signed mobile transactions, secure messaging and digital rights management. Cryptographic secret-key and public-key algorithms can be employed to satisfy this need for security.

It is noteworthy that public-key methods require the presence of a public-key infrastructure (PKI). A PKI allows public keys to be validated and connected to the respective owner. This is accomplished through the generation, provision and revocation of user certificates which is usually done by trusted parties called Certificate Authorities (CAs). Once established, PKI services can be provided to all network-enabled devices including hand-held devices.

It is a good practice to implement security systems as open systems. An open system complies with specified, publicly maintained, readily available standards and can therefore be connected to other systems that comply with the same standards. Such systems bear many advantages, e.g. interoperability, flexibility, and public acceptance. For example, an operator of an e-commerce portal may want to enable customers to buy via cell phones. Requirements for transactions are most likely secrecy, protection from data manipulation and non-repudiation. Additionally, the customers could require the e-commerce portal to authenticate itself. All these services can be provided by a set of secret-key and public-key cryptographic methods. If public standards like [1, 12–14] are used, then the portal can make use of already established PKIs, interact with already existing client application and may even be able to act as a intermediary for other portals.

The usefulness of public-key methods in mobile and wireless applications is evident, but they come at a price. All public-key algorithms require complex mathematical computations. Constrained devices may not be able to offer enough resources to allow an implementation of the required public-key protocols. The work described in this paper has been conducted to examine the current situation in this regard. With our implementations we show the feasibility of digital signature operations in modern-day cell phones. We provide performance timings which have been measured on four different cell phone types for implementations of ECDSA and RSA signatures. The results are subsequently used to derive some general recommendations for mobile and wireless applications.

The rest of the paper is organized as follows. Section 2 gives a short overview of public-key cryptography and highlights important properties of Java-enabled hand-held devices. Section 3 deals with optimizations for Java applications which incorporate public-key algorithms. In Section 4 we provide the results and conclusions from our performance measurements on four different cell phone models. Section 5 gives a short summary of the presented work and also some prospects on the integration of public-key algorithms into constrained computing devices.

2 Public-Key Cryptography in Constrained Devices

2.1 Public-Key Cryptography

Public-key cryptography is a relatively new topic in the long history of cryptography. It was first proposed in the 1970s by Diffie and Hellman with their key agreement protocol [2] and by Rivest, Shamir, and Adleman with the RSA algorithm [15].

Public-key methods are generally based upon so-called trapdoor one-way functions. These are mathematical functions which are easy to compute in one direction, but are hard to invert. However, the inversion can be facilitated if one is in the possession of some piece of additional information: the so-called trapdoor information. The main current public-key algorithms rely on the hardness of one of two mathematical problems: integer factorization (IF) or discrete logarithm problem (DLP). The equivalent of the DLP for elliptic curves—denoted as elliptic curve discrete logarithm problem (ECDLP)—is particularly interesting, as no subexponential-time algorithm for solving it has been discovered so far. This fact distinguishes Elliptic Curve (EC) algorithms from other cryptosystems which are based on IF or DLP like RSA [15] and Diffie-Hellman [2]. In contrast to the ECDLP, there are known subexponential-time algorithms for solving both the IF problem and the DLP in conventional number fields.

A general relation exists between the hardness of the underlying problem and the minimal length of the operands, i.e. keys and other parameters, of the public-key algorithm. For a given cryptographic algorithm and a desired level of security the operands must have a certain length. The operand length has a direct impact on the performance and memory requirements of an implementation of the algorithm. The assumed hardness of ECDLP results in shorter operands for EC methods in comparison to other algorithms. In [9], Lenstra et al. provide a thorough comparison of the security of public-key cryptosystems based on IF, DLP, and ECDLP. For instance, a key size of 190 bit for an EC algorithm is approximately equivalent to an RSA key size of 1937 bit under the condition that there will be some progress made towards more efficient solutions of the ECDLP in the future. If no such progress is made, then the required RSA key for equivalent security even grows to over 3137 bit.

2.2 Properties of Java-Enabled Devices

If public-key algorithms are to be implemented in constrained devices then EC methods appear to be an attractive option. But all public-key operations require substantial computing resources. Furthermore, despite the many advantages which are offered by Java it has a poor performance in comparison to native code. Therefore, achieving an adequate performance is the biggest challenge of implementing public-key algorithms in Java on constrained devices. In the following we will examine the current situation on Java-enabled devices regarding support for cryptographic algorithms.

The most widely supported mechanism for Java deployment on hand-held devices conforms to Sun Microsystems' Java 2 Platform, Micro Edition (J2ME). The base set of application programmer interfaces (APIs) is defined in the Connected Limited Device Profile (CLDC) which is currently available in version 1.0 and 1.1 [17,19]. The CLDC together with the Mobile Information Device Profile (MIDP) form the Java runtime environment for most of today's Java-enabled hand-held devices. The MIDP is available in version 1.0 [18] and version 2.0 [6]. Applications which conform to MIDP are commonly called MIDlets. MIDP 1.0 provides a thinned down variant of the standard Java API and is implemented today in many mobile devices. MIDP version 2.0 adds limited support for games, media control and public-key certificates. Moreover, secure connections over HTTPS and secure socket streams (based on either TLS version 1.0, SSL version 3.0 or WTLS) are provided. However, there is no access to the cryptographic algorithms which implement the secure connection. Therefore, tasks like data signing cannot be done with the MIDP 2.0 API.

The best solution for the provision of general public-key methods for the application programmer would be the inclusion of the required cryptographic algorithms into MIDP. In this scenario, the computational extensive methods could be implemented efficiently by the Java Runtime Environment (JRE) and could use all the features of the respective device. Unfortunately, so far neither version of MIDP offers support for cryptographic methods. Not even the highly useful BigInteger class from the standard Java API, which facilitates low-level arithmetic for many cryptographic algorithms, is included. However, the Java Specification Request (JSR) 177 [7], which is currently being prepared for first release, proposes the integration of a Security Element (SE) into J2ME devices. Such an SE provides support for secure storage of sensitive data, cryptographic operations and a secure execution environment for security features. The integration of these APIs into J2ME devices will be a big step towards mobile and wireless application security. But J2ME devices without such a support will nevertheless stay in broad use in the next years.

Device-specific APIs for cryptographic operations could be provided by the manufacturer. But the use of such APIs would necessitate different Java MIDlet versions for different devices. So this option is only applicable if there is a known and relatively small number of target devices.

Due to complications with code signing, MIDP 2.0 does not include the possibility for the installation of user libraries. Therefore it is not possible to install a cryptographic library shared by different MIDlets to reduce code size.

The current situation leaves only one practical option for applications which require access to cryptographic algorithms. This option is to bundle the required cryptographic classes with the actual application classes. A drawback of bundling is that it leads to relatively large code sizes. This can cause problems with devices which enforce a limit of the application size and therefore inhibit application deployment.

3 Implementation Issues

As outlined in Section 2, two important factors must be considered for MIDlets which include public-key algorithms: performance and code size. Based on our practical work, we provide some hints for optimization of both factors.

3.1 Performance

The effectiveness of different performance optimizations is dependent on the underlying machine and JRE. However, there is a number of useful general rules which should be regarded. Many articles are available which give hints for achieving better performance in Java. From our experience, some of these hints are more applicable to public-key implementations than others and we try to list the more effective ones in the following.

The most convenient way for optimization is to use the optimization switch of the java compiler (-O for Sun's javac). Such an compiler optimization can both increase performance and decrease code size.

An important step of optimization consists of application profiling. Profiling identifies methods, which are frequently called and are worth optimizing. Various tools are available for profiling of Java applications. For example, Sun's JRE has a non-documented switch -prof which turns on profiling. All general rules for optimization like object recycling, avoidance of String concatenation, inlining of short methods and replacement of short library methods (e.g. Math.max) by local methods should be considered.

Implementations of public-key algorithms often deal with multi-word values and look-up tables. Java arrays seem to be the natural choice, but it should be noted that array accesses introduce a certain overhead for index range checking. If array elements are statically indexed, i.e. the index is a constant value, then it can be favorable to break the array into a number of separate variables. Application wide constants should always be declared as static final, which allows for better performance and reduces code size.

Another problem can be posed by lengthy initialization code. Such initializations can be moved to a static initializer block of a class which is loaded at startup. This way the execution of the actual public-key algorithm can be shortened at the expense of a longer MIDlet load time. Another way is to do initialization in a separate background thread. This approach can be very favorable if the MIDlet has to wait for input, as the initialization can be done during this period. In the case of ECDSA signature generation, this strategy can lead to a dramatic performance gain, as outlined in Section 4.2.

3.2 Code Size

The first step to reduce code size is to get rid of unused classes. If all of the MIDlet classes are written by the developer, then he can handcraft them to his specific requirements. In this fashion, the code size can be kept small. When an existing cryptographic library is included, then there are often many unused classes. There are quite a few tools available which can analyze MIDlets and remove unnecessary classes.

Most J2ME devices require the class files and additional resources (e.g. picture files) to be put in a Java Archive (JAR) file. A JAR file conforms to the widely adopted ZIP format and features some additional meta data. Most importantly JAR files provide compression of the bundled files. Compression is optional, but should always be used for MIDlets.

Another possibility for code size reduction is obfuscation. Normally, obfuscation is used to prevent decompilation of Java class files. Obfuscator tools usually replace field, method and class names with shorter ones, remove debug information and compress constants. These measures can result in a substantially smaller bytecode. There are however some issues related to obfuscation which can affect the functionality of a program. Most importantly, class renaming can prevent the explicit dynamic loading of classes. Obfuscation tools can be configured to perform only certain code modifications and we recommend a careful selection of those modifications.

4 Practical Results

We have implemented the complete ECDSA signature generation as specified in ANSI X9.62 [1] in a Java MIDlet. We have used the parameters and vectors of Section J.2.1 of ANSI X9.62, which are based on an elliptic curve over the binary extension field $GF(2^{191})$. All our MIDlets bundle the application classes with the library classes which provide the cryptographic functionality. The MIDlets have been built with Sun's Wireless Toolkit version 2.1 and J2SDK 1.4.2.

Four different J2ME-enabled cell phone types have been used to measure execution times for EC point multiplication and ECDSA and RSA signature generation and verification. Timing results for the mid-range devices Siemens S55, Nokia 6610, Nokia 6600, and the high-end Ericsson P900 are provided.

All measurements have been done on the actual devices using their system time features available through the CLDC 1.0 API. Therefore the accuracy of the measured times is not very high. Nevertheless the measurements provide a solid basis for comparison of different algorithms and for estimates of response times of public-key enabled applications. The measurements of different algorithms are given as time for the first execution and—where sensible—as an average of 20 executions. Algorithms with running times of more than 30 seconds are clearly unsuited for that particular device and therefore no averaging was done (RSA signature generation on Nokia 6610 and Siemens S55, ECDSA signature generation on Siemens S55). Note that normally, but not always, the first execution takes longer than the average due to initializations like class loading.

4.1 EC Point Multiplication

The fundamental building block of virtually all EC cryptosystems is a computation of the form $Q = k \cdot P$, which is nothing else than adding a point $k - 1$ times to itself, i.e. $k \cdot P = P + P + \cdots + P$. This operation is called *point multiplication* or *scalar multiplication*, and dominates the execution time of EC cryptosystems. Scalar multiplication on an EC is analogous to exponentiation in a multiplicative group. The inverse operation, i.e. to recover the integer k when the points P and $Q = k \cdot P$ are given, is the elliptic curve discrete logarithm problem (ECDLP). The hardness of the ECDLP is fundamental to the security of ECC as outlined in Section 2.1.

The time which is required for a EC point multiplication determines the overall execution time of an ECC algorithm to a very high degree. Therefore we concentrated our effort on an efficient implementation of the point multiplication. We used Montgomery's method [11] in combination with the fast multiplication (projective version) as described by López et al. [10]. For the arithmetic operations in the underlying finite field $GF(2^{191})$ we implemented methods described in [4]. For field multiplication we used the left-to-right comb method (Algorithm 4 in [4]) with a window size of 4. Squaring was done with precomputed 8-bit polynomials (Algorithm 7) and inversion with the Extended Euclidean Algorithm for inversion in $GF(2^m)$ (Algorithm 8).

Table 1. EC point multiplication execution time (in ms)

Device	First execution	Average
Nokia 6610	2.183	2.150
Nokia 6600	984	720
Ericsson P900	578	428
Siemens S55	17.135	17.216

Table 2. ECDSA and RSA signature generation execution time (in ms)

	ECDSA		RSA	
Device	First execution	Average	First execution	Average
Nokia 6610	2.294	2.266	74.682	N/A
Nokia 6600	860	763	7.125	4.077
Ericsson P900	453	418	3.703	2.725
Siemens S55	18.963	18.117	883.602	N/A

Table 1 lists the measured execution times in milliseconds for a single point multiplication over the finite field $GF(2^{191})$ on the different tested devices. An EC point multiplication can be realized in under a second to a few seconds on three of the tested devices. However, it can be seen that the performance on the Siemens S55 is not high enough to allow an implementation of EC algorithms with a sensible response time.

4.2 ECDSA and RSA Signature Generation and Verification

The timings for ECDSA and RSA signature generation are given in Table 2, while the signature verification results are listed in Table 3. The key sizes of both implementations have been chosen according to [9] to provide the same level of security. Both algorithms use the hash method SHA-1 for message digesting.

The ECDSA implementation uses elliptic curves over the binary extension field $GF(2^{191})$ and a key size of 191 bit. For the test runs, the parameters and vectors of Section J.2.1 of ANSI X9.62 [1] have been used. The implementation uses the code of the previously described EC point multiplication. Modular multiplication and inversion in $GF(p)$ are done in the Montgomery domain. We have used Montgomery multiplication with the Separated Operand Scanning (SOS) as described in [8] by Koç et al. and the Modified Kaliski-Montgomery inverse as described in [3] by Savaş et al.

The RSA implementation uses a key size of 1937 bit. The implementation is based on the IAIK JCE micro edition [5], which uses the Chinese Remainder Theorem and Montgomery multiplication. The RSA implementation just serves as comparison for the ECDSA implementation and therefore no special algorithms like Multi-Prime RSA [16] have been examined.

The code sizes of our MIDlets were 53 kB for ECDSA and 60 kB for RSA. These figures refer to the size of the JAR file of the full implementations of signing and verifying including test code. No obfuscation has been used.

Table 3. ECDSA and RSA signature verification execution time (in ms)

Device	ECDSA		RSA	
	First execution	Average	First execution	Average
Nokia 6610	4.382	4.449	2.825	2.488
Nokia 6600	1.266	1.247	157	139
Ericsson P900	843	854	109	97
Siemens S55	35.277	N/A	30.094	30.661

ECDSA signature generation has the property that a great deal of precomputation can be done which does not involve the signed data. Most significantly, the EC point multiplication can be precomputed at runtime. If an application has some idle time (e.g. waiting for user input), then the precomputation can be done in the background in a low priority thread. In this way, the completion of the signing process upon availability of the data to sign becomes negligible. Our tests showed that signing can be done in a few milliseconds.

4.3 Analysis of the Measured Data

It can be seen from the listed timings that the EC point multiplication is indeed the dominating factor for the ECDSA operations. ECDSA signing requires one point multiplication while verifying requires two. Therefore verification takes approximately twice the time of signing. The difference between signing and verification is more dramatic for RSA signatures. RSA public-key pairs are normally selected so that the public key is relatively small while the private key is big. This is the reason that the RSA signature verification is up to 30 times as fast as signature generation (Nokia 6600).

A direct comparison of ECDSA and RSA signatures reveals that ECDSA signing is faster than RSA signing (33 times on the Nokia 6610) and RSA verifying is faster than ECDSA verifying (9 times on the Nokia 6600 and Ericsson P900). ECDSA signing and verifying performs in under 5 seconds on all devices (except Siemens S55). RSA verifying performs in under 3 seconds on all devices (except Siemens S55). RSA signing takes under 5 seconds on the Nokia 6600 and the Ericsson P900 but is very slow on the Nokia 6610, probably due to the lack of an efficient hardware multiplier. Unfortunately, there are rarely any details like microprocessor type, incorporated hardware accelerators (e.g. coprocessors), memory types and sizes, clock frequency etc. publicly available for the particular phone models. This hampers all attempts to interpret the measured results based on these data and to draw conclusions in this regard.

Decisions for a cryptosystem should be based on details of the particular application. Important factors can be the number and ratio of signature generations and verifications, the presence of waiting times for user input and compatibility with existing systems. For example, the full check of digital signed data requires the retrieval of the whole certificate chain and one verification for each certificate. In this case RSA should be chosen for its faster verification. On the other hand, applications which perform a signature of data which is entered by the user could perform precomputations for ECDSA during waiting times and do the actual signing in a few milliseconds.

The following general recommendations for implementation of public-key cryptosystems in J2ME devices can be derived from our measured performance results:

- If only the verification of digital signatures is to be performed, then RSA signatures should be implemented.
- If only signing of data is required, then ECDSA signatures should be chosen.
- If both signing and verification are required, then the choice should be dependent on the particular application.

5 Summary

In this paper we have outlined the current situation regarding the implementation of public-key algorithms in J2ME-enabled devices. We have presented some practical hints for the optimization of performance and code size. Furthermore we have shown the feasibility of Java implementations of public-key operations on constrained devices regarding both ECDSA and RSA signatures. Our timing results have shown that modern J2ME devices are capable of performing public-key algorithms which offer a high degree of security (191 bit ECDSA, 1937 bit RSA). High-end devices like the Ericsson P900 can even execute ECDSA signature generation and verification in under one second. Furthermore we have compared ECDSA and RSA signature algorithms which can serve as a basis for selecting particular public-key protocols for secure mobile applications.

It is only a matter of time until the growing processing power of mobile devices allows for an easy integration of public-key algorithms into mobile and wireless applications. The adoption of the Security and Trust Services API (JSR 177) [7] by device manufacturers will provide a good basis for application developers to produce secure MIDlets. And such secure applications are vital for building trust of end users and for opening whole new fields of application for mobile computing.

Acknowledgements

The research described in this paper was supported by the Austrian Science Fund (FWF) under grant number P16952N04 "Instruction Set Extensions for Public-Key Cryptography". The work described in this paper has been supported in part by the European Commission through the IST Programme under Contract IST-2002-507932 ECRYPT. The information in this document reflects only the author's views, is provided as is and no guarantee or warranty is given that the information is fit for any particular purpose. The user thereof uses the information at its sole risk and liability.

References

1. American National Standards Institute (ANSI). X9.62-1998, Public Key Cryptography for the Financial Services Industry: The Elliptic Curve Digital Signature Algorithm (ECDSA) (1999)
2. Diffie W., Hellman M. E.: New Directions in Cryptography. IEEE Transactions on Information Theory **22**(6) (1976) 644–654
3. Savas, E., Koç, Ç.K.: The Montgomery Modular Inverse—Revisited. IEEE Transactions on Computers **49**(7) (2000) 763–766
4. Hankerson, D.R., López Hernandez J.C., Menezes A.J.: Software Implementation of Elliptic Curve Cryptography over Binary Fields. In: Koç Ç. K., Paar C. (eds.): Cryptographic Hardware and Embedded Systems — CHES 2000. Lecture Notes in Computer Science, Vol. 1965. Springer Verlag, Berlin, Germany, (2000) 1–24
5. IAIK Java Security Group. IAIK Java Cryptography Extension Micro Edition (IAIK-JCE ME). Available at http://jce.iaik.tugraz.at/products/
6. JSR 118 Expert Group. Mobile Information Device Profile, Version 2.0. Available for download at http://java.sun.com. (2002)
7. JSR 177 Expert Group. Security and Trust Services API (SATSA), JSR 177. Available for download at http://java.sun.com, (2003)
8. Koç, Ç. K., Acar, T., Kaliski, B.S.: Analyzing and Comparing Montgomery Multiplication Algorithms. IEEE Micro **16**(3) (1996) 26–33
9. Lenstra A. K. and Verheul E. R.: Selecting Cryptographic Key Sizes. In: Imai, H., Zheng, Y. (eds.): Public Key Cryptography PKC 2000. Lecture Notes in Computer Science, Vol. 1751. Springer Verlag, Berlin Germany (2000) 446–465
10. López, J., Dahab, R.: Fast Multiplication on Elliptic Curves over $GF(2^m)$ Without Precomputation. In Koç, Ç. K., Paar, C. (eds.): Cryptographic Hardware and Embedded Systems — CHES '99. Lecture Notes in Computer Science, Vol. 1717. Springer Verlag, Berlin Germany (1999) 316–327
11. Montgomery, P.L.: Speeding the Pollard and Elliptic Curve Methods of Factorization. Mathematics of Computation **48**(177) (1987) 243–264
12. National Institute of Standards and Technology (NIST). Recommended Elliptic Curves for Federal Government Use, (1999)
13. National Institute of Standards and Technology (NIST).: Advanced Encryption Standard (AES). Federal Information Processing Standards (FIPS). Publication 197 (2001)
14. National Institute of Standards and Technology (NIST).: Secure Hash Standard (SHS). Federal Information Processing Standards(FIPS) Publication 180-2 (2002)
15. Rivest, R.L., Shamir, A., Adleman, L.M.: A Method for Obtaining Digital Signatures and Public Key Cryptosystems. Communications of the ACM **21**(2) (1978) 120–126
16. RSA Data Security, Inc.: PKCS #1 v2.1: RSA Cryptography Standard (2002)
17. Sun Microsystems. Connected Limited Device Configuration, Version 1.0a. Available for download at http://java.sun.com, (2000)
18. Sun Microsystems. Mobile Information Device Profile, Version 1.0a. Available for download at http://java.sun.com, (2000)
19. Sun Microsystems. Connected Limited Device Configuration, Version 1.1. Available for download at http://java.sun.com, (2003)

Thread-Sensitive Points-to Analysis for Multithreaded Java Programs*

Byeong-Mo Chang[1] and Jong-Deok Choi[2]

[1] Dept. of Computer Science
Sookmyung Women's University, Seoul 140-742, Korea
chang@sookmyung.ac.kr
[2] IBM T. J. Watson Research Center
P.O. Box 704 Yorktown Heights, NY 10598 USA
jdchoi@watson.ibm.com

Abstract. Every running thread has its own thread context that consists of values of the fields of the target thread object. To consider the thread context in understanding the behaviors of concurrently running threads, we propose a thread-sensitive interprocedural analysis for multithreaded Java applications. Our thread-sensitive analysis exploits thread-context information, instead of the conventional calling-context information, for computing dataflow facts holding at a statement. The thread-sensitive analysis is highly effective in distinguishing dataflow facts for different threads, producing more precise dataflow information than non-thread-sensitive analysis. The analysis is also generally much more efficient than conventional (calling) context-sensitive analysis. It uses the target thread objects at a thread start site to distinguish different thread contexts. We give a thread-sensitive points-to analysis as an instance of thread-sensitive analysis. We have implemented it and give some experimental results. We discuss several possible applications of the analysis.

1 Introduction

Multithreading in Java has become widely used in developing concurrent and reactive software. One of the most important analyses for Java is points-to analysis, which provides information about the objects, to which references point. Potential applications of points-to analysis for multithreaded programs include synchronization elimination, alias analysis, escape analysis, static datarace detection, software engineering tools and compiler optimizations [2–4, 12, 9]. Several points-to analyses was proposed for Java [8, 13]. However, they treat threads just like methods without paying special attention to threads, and do not provide experimental results for multithreaded Java programs.

In multithreaded programs, there are multiple concurrently running threads for one thread definition. Every running thread has its own thread context that

---
* This Research was supported by the Sookmyung Women's University Research Grants 2004.

consists of values of the fields of the target thread object. Moreover, it has its own instances for locals, newly created objects, and method invocations.

In this paper, we propose a thread-sensitive interprocedural analysis for multithreaded Java programs to consider the thread context in understanding the behaviors of concurrently running threads. Our thread-sensitive analysis exploits thread-context information, instead of the conventional calling-context information, for computing dataflow facts holding at a statement. It is highly effective in distinguishing dataflow facts for different threads, producing more precise dataflow information than non-thread-sensitive analysis. It is also generally much more efficient than conventional (calling) context-sensitive analysis. It uses the target thread objects at a thread start site to distinguish different thread contexts. We give a thread-sensitive points-to analysis as an instance of it.

For thread-sensitive points-to analysis, we first identify thread objects statically by making one (abstract) thread object for each thread object creation site. Then we do separate points-to analyses for possible target thread objects at each thread start site. Conceptually, every thread is replicated for each possible target thread object. A thread-sensitive analysis for each target thread object starts from its run() method and analyzes all methods reachable from it. For clear presentation, we present the thread-sensitive analysis based on constraint-based analysis [5]. While context-insensitive analysis makes one set-variable for every reference variable, the thread-sensitive analysis makes as many set-variables as the number of its target thread objects for every reference variable (not static) in a thread definition to model that every thread has its own instance. We construct a separate collection of set-constraints for each target thread.

We have implemented the thread-sensitive points-to analysis based on conventional iterative algorithm by extending the inclusion-based points-to analysis [13]. We first do context-insensitive points-to analysis of the main thread to extract abstract thread objects, and then identify the run() method of each abstract thread object. Then we do separate points-to analysis specific to each target thread. We have evaluated the impact of the analysis over nine benchmark programs along with the work in [13]. We also observed that codes for run() methods have to be connected with its start site in the analysis, because threads are started by native code. Otherwise, it will be missing as in [13] when analyzing multithreaded Java programs. We have implemented the functionality to connect and analyze the run() methods of started threads automatically.

The rest of the paper is organized as follow. We first give a motivation in Section 2. We present the thread-sensitive analysis in Section 3 and its implementation and experiments in Section 4. Section 5 discusses some applications of it such as synchronization removal, datarace detection, and software engineering tools. Section 6 discusses related works and Section 7 concludes this paper.

2 Motivation

We consider a multithreaded Java program in Figure 1 from the book [7]. This program divides a picture to be rendered into two parts, leftHalf and rightHalf, and then creates two threads, leftThread and rightThread, to

render left and right parts respectively. After rendering, it finally combines the
two images rendered by the two threads.

```
class RenderWaiter extends Thread {
  private PictureRenderer ren;   // service object
  private byte [] arg;           // arguments to its method
  private Picture rslt = null;   // results from its method
  RenderWaiter(PictureRenderer r, byte[] raw) {
    ren = r; arg = raw;
  }
  synchronized Picture result() { return rslt; }
  public void run() {
    rslt = ren.render(arg);
  }
}

class DumbPictureRenderer implements PictureRenderer {
  public Picture render(byte[] raw) {
    return new Picture(new String(raw, raw.length));
  }
}

public class SplitRenderer implements PictureRenderer {
  PictureRenderer renderer1;     // group member 1
  PictureRenderer renderer2;     // group member 2
  public SplitRenderer() {
    renderer1 = new DumbPictureRenderer();
    renderer2 = new DumbPictureRenderer();
  }
  public Picture render(byte[] rawPicture) {
    byte[] rawLeft = leftHalf(rawPicture);    // split
    byte[] rawRight = rightHalf(rawPicture);
    RenderWaiter leftThread = new RenderWaiter(renderer1, rawLeft);
    RenderWaiter rightThread = new RenderWaiter(renderer2, rawRight);
    leftThread.start();          // start threads
    rightThread.start();
    ...    // join both of them
    Picture leftImg = leftThread.result();    // use results
    Picture rightImg = rightThread.result();
    return combinePictures(leftImg, rightImg);
  }
  byte[] leftHalf(byte[] arr) { ... }
  byte[] rightHalf(byte[] arr) { ... }
  Picture combinePictures(Picture a, Picture b) {
    return new Picture(a.image() + b.image());
  }
}
```

Fig. 1. Example program

Conventional context-insensitive points-to analyses collect all the objects passed to a parameter, into one set-variable [8, 13]. Because they also collect target thread objects in the same way when analyzing run method, they cannot distinguish different thread contexts at a thread start site. However, each thread can have different thread contexts and can behave differently depending on its target thread object. For example, the method run in RenderWaiter accepts the two thread objects, leftThread and rightThread, passed to this parameter. So, in the context-insensitive analysis, the field this.ren points to the objects pointed by renderer1 and renderer2, and the field this.arg points to the objects pointed by rawLeft and rawRight. So, it cannot provide separate points-to analysis information specific to each target thread, because it does neither pay special attention to threads and nor distinguish different thread contexts.

In this paper, our thread-sensitive analysis will analyze `RenderWaiter` twice with `leftThread` and `rightThread` as its target thread object, respectively. The analysis now can provide separate analysis information specific to each thread. For example, we can determine from the analysis information that `this.ren` in each thread actually points to *only one* object. This information can be useful for such thread-related applications as synchronization removal or static datarace detection.

In this paper, the set of all reference variables in a program is denoted by Ref. The set of all abstract objects in a program is denoted by $AbsObj$. Each abstract object $O \in AbsObj$ is a mapping $O : Field \rightarrow \wp(AbsObj)$ where $Field$ is the set of fields of the object O. We denoted by O_{c_ℓ} an abstract object of a class c created at a label l. For simple presentation, we only discuss the statements: (1)Direct assignment: `p = q` (2) Instance field write: `p.f = q` (3) Static field write: `c.f = q` (4) Instance field read: `p = q.f` (5) Static field read: `p = c.f` (6) Object creation: `p = new c` (7)Virtual invocation: `p = a₀.m(a₁,...,aₖ)`.

Context-insensitive points-to analysis makes one set-variable $\mathcal{X}_v$ for every reference variable $v \in Ref$. A set variable $\mathcal{X}_v$ is for objects, which the reference v points-to. A set expression se is an expression to denote a set of objects, which is of this form:

$$se ::= O_{c_\ell}(\text{new object}) | \mathcal{X}_v(\text{set variable}) | se \cup se(\text{set union}) | se \cdot f(\text{object field}),$$

where a set-expression $se \cdot f$ represents the set of objects pointed by the field f of the objects represented by se.

A set-constraint is of this form: $\mathcal{X}_v \supseteq se$ or $\mathcal{X}_v \supseteq_f se$. The meaning of a set constraint $\mathcal{X} \supseteq se$ is intuitive: the set $\mathcal{X}_v$ contains the set of objects represented by the set expression se. A set constraint $\mathcal{X}_v \supseteq_f se$ means that the field f of the objects in the set $\mathcal{X}_v$ contains the set of objects represented by se. Multiple constraints are conjunctions. We write $\mathcal{C}$ for such conjunctive set of constraints. The semantics of the context-insensitive points-to analysis can be found in [8].

3 Thread-Sensitive Points-to Analysis

We describe a thread-sensitive interprocedural analysis for multithreaded Java applications in terms of points-to analysis. Our thread-sensitive analysis exploits thread-context information, instead of the conventional calling-context information, to distinguish dataflow facts for different threads. It uses the target thread objects at a thread start site to distinguish different thread contexts.

We define a thread-sensitive points-to analysis for multithreaded Java programs based on constraint-based analysis framework [5]. To distinguish different thread contexts, we analyze each thread definition separately for each target thread object, on which it may be started. Conceptually, every thread can be thought to be replicated for each possible target thread object.

We denote a thread definition (i.e. thread defining class) by T. We make its abstract thread objects for every thread creation site for T. We denote them by $O_{T_1}, ..., O_{T_n}$. An abstract thread represented by T_i is a replica of the thread definition with a possible thread object O_{T_i} as its target object. It actually includes the run method started with O_{T_i} as its target object and all methods that can be reachable from it.

Our thread-sensitive points-to analysis consists of three steps:
(1) *Identification of abstract thread objects*: We first identify abstract thread objects by examining thread creation sites. We can identify a number of abstract thread objects $O_{T_1}, ..., O_{T_n}$ for a thread defining class T.
(2) *Set-constraint construction*: We construct separate set-constraints for each abstract thread T_i with its target thread object O_{T_i}.
(3) *Solving the set-constraints*: Solve all the set-constraints constructed in the second step.

While conventional context-insensitive analysis makes one set-variable for every reference variable, our thread-sensitive analysis makes as many set-variables as the number of its abstract threads for every reference variable in a thread definition, which is not static. This can model that every thread has its own instances for every reference variable if it is not static.

$$\begin{aligned}
\langle p = \text{new } c_\ell \rangle &\Rightarrow \{\mathcal{X}_p^i \supseteq O_{c_\ell}^i\} \\
\langle p = q \rangle &\Rightarrow \{\mathcal{X}_p^i \supseteq \mathcal{X}_q^i\} \\
\langle p = c.f \rangle &\Rightarrow \{\mathcal{X}_p^i \supseteq \mathcal{X}_{c.f}\} \\
\langle c.f = q \rangle &\Rightarrow \{\mathcal{X}_{c.f} \supseteq \mathcal{X}_q^i\} \\
\langle p.f = q \rangle &\Rightarrow \{\mathcal{X}_p^i \supseteq_f \mathcal{X}_q^i\} \\
\langle p = q.f \rangle &\Rightarrow \{\mathcal{X}_p^i \supseteq \mathcal{X}_q^i \cdot f\} \\
\langle p = a_0.m(a_1, ..., a_k) \rangle &\Rightarrow \{\mathcal{X}_{f_0}^i \supseteq \mathcal{X}_{a_0}^i, ..., \mathcal{X}_{f_k}^i \supseteq \mathcal{X}_{a_k}^i, \mathcal{X}_p^i \supseteq \mathcal{X}_{ret}^i | \\
& \quad m(f_0, ..., f_k, ret) \in targets(\mathcal{X}_{a_0}^i, mc)\}
\end{aligned}$$

Fig. 2. Thread-sensitive set constraints for statements

$$\begin{aligned}
\langle p = \text{new } c_\ell \rangle &\Rightarrow \{\overrightarrow{\mathcal{X}_p} \supseteq \overrightarrow{O_{c_\ell}}\} \\
\langle p = q \rangle &\Rightarrow \{\overrightarrow{\mathcal{X}_p} \supseteq \overrightarrow{\mathcal{X}_q}\} \\
\langle p = c.f \rangle &\Rightarrow \{\overrightarrow{\mathcal{X}_p} \supseteq \mathcal{X}_{c.f}\} \\
\langle c.f = q \rangle &\Rightarrow \{\mathcal{X}_{c.f} \supseteq \bigcup_i \mathcal{X}_q^i | \mathcal{X}_q^i \in \overrightarrow{\mathcal{X}_q}\} \\
\langle p.f = q \rangle &\Rightarrow \{\overrightarrow{\mathcal{X}_p} \supseteq_f \overrightarrow{\mathcal{X}_q}\} \\
\langle p = q.f \rangle &\Rightarrow \{\overrightarrow{\mathcal{X}_p} \supseteq \overrightarrow{\mathcal{X}_q} \cdot f\} \\
\langle p = a_0.m(a_1, ..., a_k) \rangle &\Rightarrow \{\overrightarrow{\mathcal{X}_{f_0}} \supseteq \overrightarrow{\mathcal{X}_{a_0}}, ..., \overrightarrow{\mathcal{X}_{f_k}} \supseteq \overrightarrow{\mathcal{X}_{a_k}}, \overrightarrow{\mathcal{X}_p} \supseteq \overrightarrow{\mathcal{X}_{ret}} | \\
& \quad m(f_0, ..., f_k, ret) \in targets(\mathcal{X}_{a_0}^i, mc)\}
\end{aligned}$$

Fig. 3. A system of thread-sensitive set constraints

Specifically, for each abstract thread T_i of a thread class T, we make one set variable $\mathcal{X}_p^i$ for a reference variable p, if it is not static. As in Figure 2, we construct set-constraints for all statements in all instance methods of every abstract thread T_i. In case of static variables or static methods we make set variables or set-constraints as conventional context-insensitive analysis.

We first consider an object creation statement p = new c. Since each thread T_i has its own instance p^i for the local reference variable p and its own instance $O_{c_\ell}^i$ for the new object, we construct a set constraint $\mathcal{X}_p^i \supseteq O_{c_\ell}^i$. For a direct assignment p = q, we simply construct a set constraint $\mathcal{X}_p^i \supseteq \mathcal{X}_q^i$ to model that the variable instance p^i gets the objects of the variable instance q^i in each thread T_i. Consider an instance field read p = q.f. Each thread T_i has its own instances p^i and q^i and the instance p^i gets the field f of the instance q^i. So we construct a set constraint $\mathcal{X}_p^i \supseteq \mathcal{X}_q^i \cdot f$. In case of a static field write c.f = q, because every thread can share a static field $c.f$, we have only one instance for it and so construct a set-constraint $\mathcal{X}_{c.f} \supseteq \mathcal{X}_q^i$.

Consider a virtual method invocation $p = a_0.m(a_1, ..., a_k)$. We denote by mc the method call $a_0.m(a_1, ..., a_k)$. Each thread T_i has its own instance for formal parameters as local variables. To model parameter passing and return, we construct set-constraints as follows:

$$\{\mathcal{X}_{f_0}^i \supseteq \mathcal{X}_{a_0}^i, ..., \mathcal{X}_{f_k}^i \supseteq \mathcal{X}_{a_k}^i, \mathcal{X}_p^i \supseteq \mathcal{X}_{ret}^i | m(f_0, .., f_k, ret) \in targets(\mathcal{X}_{a_0}^i, mc)\},$$

where the function $targets$ returns the set of possible methods invoked by the method call mc for the target objects in $\mathcal{X}_{a_0}^i$.

In addition, if $O_{T_1}, ..., O_{T_n}$ are abstract thread objects for a thread class T such that $run(f_0) \in T$, we also make a set-constraint $\mathcal{X}_{f_0}^i \supseteq O_{T_i}$ for each abstract thread object O_{T_i} to simulate passing the target thread object to the run method. If there are n abstract threads for a thread class T, there are n instances of a reference variable p in abstract threads, if it is not static. So, we can make a vector of set variables for one reference variable p in T as follows: $\overrightarrow{\mathcal{X}_p} = \langle \mathcal{X}_p^1, ..., \mathcal{X}_p^n \rangle$. In the same way, we can make a vector of abstract objects created at an object creation site ℓ as follows: $\overrightarrow{O_{c_\ell}} = \langle O_{c_\ell}^1, ..., O_{c_\ell}^n \rangle$. Then, we can make a system of set constraints for all abstract threads $T_1, ..., T_n$ of a thread class T as in Figure 3.

Consider the main thread started from main method. We denote this abstract thread by T_{main}. Note that there is only one thread instance for the abstract thread T_{main}. We can construct a context-insensitive points-to analysis like [8] for every statement reachable from *main* by replacing the index i by *main* in Figure 2. So, $\mathcal{X}_v^{main}$ denotes the set of abstract objects pointed by a reference variable v in the main thread.

We construct set-constraints for each abstract thread (object) as in Figure 2, and collect all set-constraints including those for main thread. We can solve the collection of set-constraints as usual in [5]. The time complexity of the constraint-solving is $k \cdot n^3$ where k is the number of abstract thread objects and n is the number of reference variables.

4 Experimental Results

We have implemented the thread-sensitive points-to analysis by extending the inclusion-based points-to analysis, which is an iterative fixpoint algorithm based on method summaries [13]. It is implemented on an experimental Java virtual machine called joeq [14, 13]. We also observed that codes for run() methods have to be connected with its start site during analysis, because threads are started by native code. Otherwise, it will be missing, when analyzing multithreaded Java programs [13]. They missed codes for new threads and actually analyzed codes for main thread only in the analysis.

We have also implemented the functionality to connect and analyze the run() methods of started threads automatically. Our implementation consists of the following steps: (1) the context-insensitive points-to analysis of the main thread (2) extraction of abstract thread objects from that analysis (3) identification of the run() method of each abstract thread object, and (4) one thread-specific analysis of the run method for each target thread object

A thread-specific analysis starts from the run method of a thread class and analyzes all methods reachable from it. The algorithm iterates until there are no more newly called methods. We implement the analysis by creating one points-to analysis object and starting the iteration for each target thread object.

Table 1. Benchmarks and points-to analysis of main thread

Programs	Classes	Methods	Calls	Size	Points-to	Time	Iter.
SplitRenderer	308	2108	7295	12K	1.67(88.4%)	12.7	48
AssemblyLine	136	456	1423	21K	1.61(87.7%)	12.7	24
ATApplet	319	2093	7274	120K	1.73(88.5%)	243.4	48
EventQueue	107	394	1220	20K	1.55(86.4%)	12.2	23
Raytrace	108	402	1232	20K	1.55 (86.6%)	12.1	24
mtrt	108	402	1233	20K	1.55 (86.6%)	12.1	24
Timer	107	388	1176	19K	1.57(86.0%)	12.7	24
TLQ	310	2109	7309	120K	1.71(88.4%)	250.0	48
ToolTip	532	4206	18601	243K	1.86(89.8%)	292	37

All experiments were performed on a PC with 1.3 GHz Pentium 4 processor and 1 GB of memory running Redhat Linux 7.2. We have experimented over 9 multithreaded Java benchmarks programs. All programs are compiled with IBM Java 2.13 compiler, and their bytecodes are analyzed. SplitRenderer is the example program in this paper. mtrt and raytrace are two ray tracing programs from the standard SpecJVM98 benchmark suite. ToolTip is a class library to manage tool tips, which is from the javax.swing package. ATApplet is an applet for auto bank transfer from the book [7]. AssemblyLine is an applet for simulating assembly line from the book [7]. EventQueue is a library class from java.awt. It is a platform-independent class that queues events. Timer is a class library from java.util. It produces tasks, via its various schedule calls, and the timer thread consumes, executing timer tasks as appropriate, and removing them from the queue when they're obsolete. TLQApplet is an applet for two lock queue with TLQProducer and TLQConsumer.

Table 1 shows some characteristics of the benchmark programs. The first four columns show the numbers of classes, methods, call sites and the size of bytecode. This table also shows analysis results of the main thread for each benchmark program, which is actually analysis results of [13]. The next column

"Points-to" shows average number of targets per a call site and a ratio of a single target among all call sites in the parenthesis. The last two columns shows the computation time and the number of iterations to complete.

Table 2. Thread-sensitive analysis

Thread classes	Abs.	Classes	Methods	Calls	Size	Points-to	Time	Iter.
SplitRenderer:T1	2	239	1178	4383	71K	2.05(91.6%)	70	19
Assembly:T1	5	5	9	12	0.16K	1.09(91.6%)	0.2	6
ATApplet:T1	4	226	1050	3938	63K	2.12(92.0%)	87	15
ATApplet:T2	3	233	1064	3941	64K	2.12(92.0%)	108	21
ATApplet:T3	3	237	1172	4360	71K	2.06(91.6%)	102	18
EventApplet:T1	1	281	1940	6685	113K	1.74(87.4%)	76.3	39
Raytrace:T1	2	139	515	2429	33K	1.21(80.0%)	8.3	17
mtrt:T1	2	139	515	2429	33K	1.21(80.0%)	8.3	17
Timer:T1	1	4	9	15	0.5K	1.07(93.3%)	0.08	5
TLQApplet:T1	4	230	1050	3912	63K	2.13(92.9%)	156	23
TLQApplet:T2	4	228	1042	3897	63K	2.14(92.0%)	158	23
TLQApplet:T3	4	239	1178	4384	71K	2.05(91.6%)	141	18
ToolTip:T1	2	336	1530	5508	83K	3.06(88.8%)	197	19

In Table 2, the first column shows the number of thread classes in each benchmark program, and the second column shows the number of abstract threads, which is the same as the number of target thread objects passed to the run method of each thread class. In case of ATApplet, there are 3 thread classes denoted ATApplet:T1, ATApplet:T2 and ATApplet:T3. There are 4 target thread objects for the first thread class, which means 4 abstract threads. There are 3 target thread objects for the second and third thread classes, respectively. The next columns show the number of classes, methods and calls, and the bytecode size of each thread. This table shows analysis results of each thread. A thread is analyzed once for each target thread object, and their average values are listed in the table. The column "Points-to" shows average number of targets per a call site and a ratio of a single target among all call sites in the parenthesis. In case of the first thread class ATApplet:T1, average number of targets per a call site is 2.12 and single target ratio is 92%.

5 Applications

Since thread-sensitive analysis can provide analysis information specific to each thread, it can be applied to applications related with threads. Its potential applications include synchronization elimination, static datarace detection, software engineering tools, and alias analysis.

(1) *Synchronization elimination*: A simple synchronization elimination is to detect thread-local object, which do not escape its creating thread. Escape analyses have been used to identify thread-local objects and remove synchronization associated with such objects [2, 3, 12]. By the thread-sensitive analysis, we can

record all threads accessing a synchronization object, and get more precise information on use of synchronization objects from the thread-sensitive analysis. This information enables more precise synchronization elimination.

(2) *Static datarace detection*: A datarace analysis requires a points-to analysis of thread objects, synchronization objects and access objects. The thread-specific analysis can provide more precise points-to information by recording threads accessing objects. With this information, we can identify which threads access each object. With this thread-specific analysis, we cannot only detect static dataraces more precisely, but it also provide more specific datarace information such as which threads may be involved in a datarace.

(3) *Software engineering tools*: There are a few known researches on debugging multithreaded Java programs utilizing static analysis information [4]. The proposed thread-specific analysis can give information specific to a particular thread. Software engineering tools together with this thread-specific information helps programmers to understand the behavior of a particular thread more precisely and to debug multithreaded program more easily.

6 Related Works

Steensgaard pointer and alias analysis is a context-insensitive and flow-insensitive algorithm, which is fast but imprecise. It has almost linear time complexity. Andersen's constraint-based analysis is a more precise points-to analysis for C programs, which is also a context-insensitive and flow-insensitive algorithm [1]. It has cubic worst time complexity. Rountev et al. presented a points-to analysis for Java by extending Andersen points-to analysis for C programs [8]. They implement the analysis by using a constraint-based approach which employs annotated inclusion constraints and compare with a basic RTA analysis. Whaley and Lam also presented an inclusion-based points-to analysis for Java by adapting and extending CLA algorithm [6], which allows Andersen's algorithm to be scalable. They treat threads just like methods.

There have been several escape analyses connected with points-to analysis [2, 3, 12, 10]. They usually apply escape information to synchronization removal and/or stack allocation of objects. A combined pointer and escape analysis for multithreaded Java programs was presented based on parallel interaction graphs which model the interactions between threads [9]. The analysis information was applied to efficient region-based allocation.

Our thread-sensitive analysis is unique in that it is context-sensitive for target thread objects only and can provide separate analysis information for each thread. When k is the number of abstract thread objects and n is the number of reference variables, the time complexity of our thread-sensitive analysis is $k \cdot n^3$.

7 Conclusion

We have presented the idea of thread-sensitive analysis in terms of points-to analysis. The idea of thread-sensitive analysis can be applied to other analyses, and the analysis results can be applied to thread-related applications, since they can provide analysis information specific to each thread. There can be two research directions in future works. One direction of future works is to investigate the effectiveness of the thread-sensitive points-to analysis more by developing more applications. Another direction of future works is to extend the idea of thread-sensitive analysis to other static analyses such as escape analysis and exception analysis. This kind of analyses could provide more thread-specific information on escaping objects and exceptions.

References

1. Andersen, L.: A program analysis and specialization for the C programming language. PhD. Thesis, DIKU (1994)
2. Blanchet, B.: Escape analysis for object-oriented languages: Applications to Java. In: Proceedings of ACM Conference on Object-Oriented Programming Systems, Languages, and Applications. (1999) 20–34
3. Choi, J.-D., Gupta, M., Serrano, M., Sreedhar, V.C., Midkiff, S.: Escape analysis for Java. In: Proceedings of ACM Conference on Object-Oriented Programming Systems, Languages, and Applications. (1999)
4. Choi, J.-D., Lee, K., Loginov, A., O'Callahan, R., Sarkar, V., Sridharan, M.: Efficient and precise datarace detection for multithreaded object-oriented programs. In: Proceedings of ACM Conference on Programming Languages Design and Implementation. (2002) 258–269
5. Heintze, N.: Set-based program analysis. PhD. Thesis, Carnegie Mellon University (1992)
6. Heintze, N., Tardieu, O.: Ultra-fast aliasing analysis using CLA: A million lines of C code. In: Proceedings of ACM Conference on Programming Languages Design and Implementation. (1998) 85–96
7. Lea, D.: Concurrent programming in Java: Design principles and patterns. Addison-Wesley (2000)
8. Rountev, A., Milanova, A., Ryder, B.G.: Points-to analysis for Java using annotated constraints. In: Proceedings of ACM Conference on Object-Oriented Programming Systems, Languages, and Applications. (2001)
9. Salcianu, A., Rinard, M.: Pointer and escape analysis for multithreaded programs. In: Proceedings of ACM Symposium on Principles and Practice of Parallel Programming. (2001) 12–23
10. Ruf, E.: Effective synchronization removal for Java. In: Proceedings of ACM Conference on Programming Language Design and Implementation. (2000) 208–218
11. Steensgaard, B.: Points-to analysis in almost linear time. In: Proceedings of ACM Symposium on Principles of Programming Languages. (1996) 32–41
12. Whaley, J., Linard, M.: Compositional pointer and escape analysis for Java programs. In: Proceedings of ACM Conference on Object-Oriented Programming Systems, Languages, and Applications. (1999)
13. Whaley, J., Lam, M.S.: An efficient inclusion-based points-to analysis for strictly-typed languages. In: Proceedings of Static Analysis Symposium. (2002)
14. Whaley, J.: Joeq: A Virtual Machine and Compiler Infrastructure. In: Proceedings of ACM SIGPLAN Workshop on Interpreters, Virtual Machines and Emulators. (2003)

Correctness Requirements for Multiagent Commitment Protocols

Pınar Yolum

Department of Artificial Intelligence, Vrije Universiteit Amsterdam
De Boelelaan 1081a, 1081 HV Amsterdam, The Netherlands
pyolum@few.vu.nl

Abstract. Commitments are a powerful abstraction for representing the interactions between agents. Commitments capture the content of the interactions declaratively and allow agents to reason about their actions. Recent work on multiagent protocols define agent interactions as the creation and manipulation of commitments to one another. As a result, commitment protocols can be executed flexibly, enabling the agents to cope with exceptions that arise at run time. We study the correctness requirements of commitment protocols that are necessary to ensure correct specification and coherent execution. We analyze and formalize various requirements for commitment protocols and draw relations among them. The main contribution of this analysis is that it allows protocol designers to develop correct protocols by signaling possible errors and inconsistencies that can possibly arise at run time. Since the requirements are formal, they can be incorporated in a software tool to automate the design and specification of commitment protocols.

1 Introduction

Multiagent systems consist of autonomous, interacting agents. To operate effectively, the interactions of the agents should be appropriately regulated. Multiagent interaction protocols provide a formal ground for enabling this regulation. However, developing effective protocols that will be carried out by autonomous agents is challenging [8]. Similar to the protocols in traditional systems, multiagent protocols need to be specified rigorously so that the agents can interact successfully. Contrary to the protocols in traditional systems, multiagent protocols need to be specified flexibly so that the agents can exercise their autonomy to make choices as best suits them or to handle unexpected situations that arise at run time. This basic requirement rules out many traditional formalisms, such as finite state machines (FSMs) or Petri nets. These formalisms only specify sequences of actions and leave no room for the agents to act flexibly.

Recently, social constructs are being used to specify agent interactions. These approaches advocate declarative representations of protocols and give semantics to protocol messages in terms of social (and thus observable) concepts. Alberti et al. specify interaction protocols using social integrity constraints and reason about the expectations of agents [1]. Fornara and Colombetti base the semantics of agent communication on commitments, such that the meanings of messages are denoted by commitments [6]. Yolum and Singh develop a methodology for specifying protocols wherein protocols capture the possible interactions of the agents in terms of the commitments to one another [14].

In addition to providing flexibility, these approaches make it possible to verify compliance of agents to a given protocol. Put broadly, commitments of the agents can be stored publicly and agents that do not fulfill their commitments at the end of the protocol can be identified as non-compliant. In order for these approaches to make use of all these advantages, the protocols should be designed rigorously. For example, the protocol should guarantee that, if an agent does not fulfill its commitment, it is not because the protocol does not specify how the fulfillment can be carried out. The aforementioned approaches all start with a manually designed, correct protocol. However, designing a correct protocol in the first place requires important correctness properties to be established and applied to the protocol. A correct protocol should define the necessary actions (or transitions) to lead a computation to its desired state. Following a protocol should imply that progress is being made towards realizing desired end conditions of the protocol. The followed actions should not yield conflicting information and lead the protocol to unrecoverable errors. That is, the protocol should at least allow a safe execution.

This paper develops and formalizes design requirements for developing correct commitment protocols. These requirements detect inconsistencies as well as errors during design time. These requirements can easily be automated in a design tool to help protocol designers to develop protocols.

The rest of the paper is organized as follows. Section 2 gives a technical background on event calculus and commitments. Section 3 discusses commitment protocols. Section 4 develops correctness requirements for commitment protocols. Section 5 discusses the recent literature in relation to our work.

2 Technical Background

We use event calculus to study commitment protocols and their design requirements. Since event calculus can operate on actions well, it provides a useful way to manage the creation and manipulation of commitments through actions. Next, we give a brief overview of event calculus and then summarize our previous formalization of commitments and their operations in event calculus [13].

2.1 Event Calculus

The event calculus is a formalism based on many-sorted first order logic [9]. The three sorts of event calculus are *time points* (T), *events* (E) and *fluents* (F). Fluents are properties whose truth values can change over time. Initiating and termination of events allow manipulation of fluents. Table 1 supplies a list of predicates to help reason about the events in an easier form. Below, events are

Table 1. The event calculus predicates

$Initiates(a, f, t)$	f holds after event a at time t.
$Terminates(a, f, t)$	f does not hold after event a at time t.
$Initially_P(f)$	f holds from time 0.
$Initially_N(f)$	f does not hold from time 0.
$Happens(a, t_1, t_2)$	event a starts at time t_1 and ends at t_2.
$Happens(a, t)$	event a starts and ends at time t.
$HoldsAt(f, t)$	f holds at time t.
$Clipped(t_1, f, t_2)$	f is terminated between t_1 and t_2.
$Declipped(t_1, f, t_2)$	f is initiated between t_1 and t_2.

shown with $a, b, \ldots$; fluents are shown with $f, g, \ldots$; and time points are shown with $t, t_1,$ and t_2.

We introduce the subset of the EC axioms that are used here; the rest can be found elsewhere [10]. The variables that are not explicitly quantified are assumed to be universally quantified. The standard operators apply (i.e., $\leftarrow$ denotes implication and $\wedge$ denotes conjunction). The time points are ordered by the $<$ relation, which is defined to be transitive and asymmetric.

1. $HoldsAt(f, t_3) \leftarrow Happens(a, t_1, t_2) \wedge Initiates(a, f, t_1) \wedge (t_2 < t_3) \wedge$
   $\neg Clipped(t_1, f, t_3)$
2. $Clipped(t_1, f, t_4) \leftrightarrow \exists a, t_2, t_3 \; [Happens(a, t_2, t_3) \wedge (t_1 < t_2) \wedge (t_3 < t_4) \wedge$
   $Terminates(a, f, t_2)]$
3. $\neg HoldsAt(f, t) \leftarrow Initially_N(f) \wedge \neg Declipped(0, f, t)$
4. $\neg HoldsAt(f, t_3) \leftarrow Happens(a, t_1, t_2) \wedge Terminates(a, f, t_1) \wedge (t_2 < t_3) \wedge$
   $\neg Declipped(t_1, f, t_3)$

2.2 Commitments

Commitments are obligations from one party to another to bring about a certain condition [3]. However, compared to the traditional definitions of obligations, commitments can be carried out more flexibly [11]. By performing operations on an existing commitment, a commitment can be manipulated (e.g., delegated to a third-party).

Definition 1. *A unilateral commitment* C*(x, y, p) is an obligation of x to y to bring about a condition p* [11]. *x is the debtor and y is the creditor of the commitment.*

When a commitment of this form is created, x becomes responsible to y for satisfying p, i.e., p holds sometime in the future. Notice that we do not differentiate whether p is brought about deliberately or accidentally. The condition p does not involve other conditions or commitments.

Definition 2. *A bilateral commitment* CC*(x, y, p, q) denotes that if the condition p is satisfied, x will be committed to bring about condition q.*

Bilateral commitments are useful when a party wants to commit only if a certain condition holds or only if the other party is also willing to make a commitment. It is easy to see that a unilateral commitment is a special case of a bilateral commitment, where the condition p is set to true. That is, $C(x, y, q)$ is an abbreviation for $CC(x, y, true, q)$. Commitments are represented as fluents in the event calculus. Hence, the creation and the manipulation of the commitments are shown with the *Initiates* and *Terminates* predicates.

Operations. We summarize the operations to create and manipulate commitments [11, 12]. In the following discussion, x, y, z denote agents, c, c' denote commitments, and e denotes an event.

1. *Create(e, x, c):* When x performs the event e, the commitment c is created.
   $Create(e, x, C(x, y, p))$: $\{Happens(e, t) \land Initiates(e, C(x, y, p), t)\}$
2. *Discharge(e, x, c):* When x performs the event e, the commitment c is resolved.
   $Discharge(e, x, C(x, y, p))$: $\{Happens(e, t) \land Initiates(e, p, t)\}$
3. *Cancel(e, x, c):* When x performs the event e, the commitment c is canceled. Usually, the cancellation of a commitment is followed by the creation of another commitment to compensate for the former one.
   $Cancel(e, x, C(x, y, p))$: $\{Happens(e, t) \land Terminates(e, C(x, y, p), t)\}$
4. *Release(e, y, c):* When y performs the event e, x no longer need to carry out the commitment c.
   $Release(e, y, C(x, y, p))$: $\{Happens(e, t) \land Terminates(e, C(x, y, p), t)\}$
5. *Assign(e, y, z, c):* When y performs the event e, commitment c is eliminated, and a new commitment c' is created where z is appointed as the new creditor.
   $Assign(e, y, z, C(x, y, p))$: $\{Happens(e, t) \land Terminates(e, C(x, y, p), t) \land Initiates(e, C(x, z, p), t)\}$
6. *Delegate(e, x, z, c):* When x performs the event e, commitment c is eliminated but a new commitment c' is created where z is the new debtor.
   $Delegate(e, x, z, C(x, y, p))$: $\{Happens(e, t) \land Terminates(e, C(x, y, p), t) \land Initiates(e, C(z, y, p), t)\}$

The following rules operationalize the commitments. Axiom 1 states that a commitment is no longer in force if the condition committed to holds. In Axiom 1, when the event e occurs at time t, it initiates the fluent p, thereby discharging the commitment $C(x, y, p)$.

Commitment Axiom 1. *Discharge(e, x, C(x, y, p))* ← *HoldsAt(C(x, y, p), t)* $\land$ *Happens(e, t)* $\land$ *Initiates(e, p, t)*

The following two axioms capture how a bilateral commitment is resolved based on the temporal ordering of the commitments it refers to.

Commitment Axiom 2. *Initiates(e, C(x, y, q), t)* ← *HoldsAt(CC(x,y,p,q), t)* $\land$ *Happens(e, t)* $\land$ *Initiates(e, p, t) Terminates(e, CC(x, y, p, q), t)* ← *HoldsAt(CC(x, y, p, q), t)* $\land$ *Happens(e, t)* $\land$ *Initiates(e, p, t)*

When the bilateral commitment $CC(x, y, p, q)$ holds, if p becomes true, then the original commitment is terminated but a new commitment is created, since the debtor x is now committed to bring about q.

3 Commitment Protocols

A commitment protocol is a set of actions such that each action is either an operation on commitments or brings about a proposition.

Definition 3. *A commitment protocol $\mathcal{P}$ is a set of Initiates and Terminates clauses that define which fluents in the protocol are initiated and terminated by each action. A protocol run is a set of Happens clauses along with an ordering of the referred time points* [13].

Hence, following a protocol is executing actions which in return create or manipulate fluents. As said before, these fluents can be atomic propositions or commitments. An agent can start a protocol by performing any of the actions that suits itself. The transitions of the protocol are computed by applying the effect of the action on the current state. In most cases this corresponds to the application of commitment operations. Figure 1 gives an overview of the possible commitment transitions. Given a protocol specification, actions of the protocol can be executed from an arbitrary initial state to a desired final state. A protocol run can be viewed as a series of actions; each action happening at a distinct time point.

To ease the explanation, we introduce the following notation. Let F be the set of fluents referred to with *Initiates* and *Terminates* clauses in the protocol. F is $CS \cup CCS \cup PS$ such that CS is the set of unilateral commitments, CCS is the set of bilateral commitments and PS is the set of propositions in the protocol. Let c be a commitment such that $c \in CS$ then $O(c)$ is the set of operations allowed on the commitment c in the protocol. Since a commitment cannot be part of a protocol if it cannot be created, we omit the create operation from the set. Hence, $O(c)$ can at most contain five operations in Section 2.2, namely, discharge, cancel, release, delegate, and assign. We assume that all the propositions referred by the commitments in CS and CCS are in PS.

Example 1. *We consider the Contract Net Protocol (CNP) as our running example* [5]. *CNP starts with a manager requesting proposals for a particular task. Each participant either sends a proposal or a reject message. The manager accepts one proposal among the submitted proposals and (explicitly) rejects the rest. The participant with the accepted proposal informs the manager with the proposal result or the failure of the proposal.*

Specifying a protocol in terms of commitments is significantly different from specifying a protocol in terms of an FSM. One major advantage of the commitment-based approach is that the execution of the protocol becomes more flexible than the execution of an FSM. Whereas in an FSM the execution is restricted to the predefined sequences, with commitment protocols participants are free to execute actions as long as they fulfill their commitments.

Example 2. *By sending a proposal to the manager, a participant creates a bilateral commitment such that if the manager accepts the proposal, then the participant will deliver the result of the proposal (e.g.,* CC*(participant, manager,*

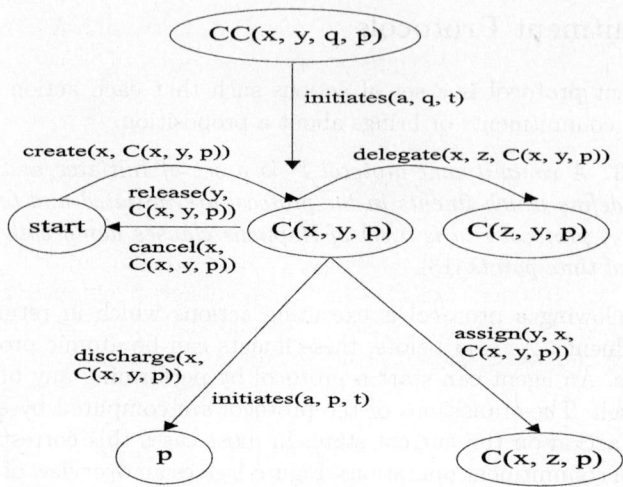

Fig. 1. Transitions in commitment protocols

*accepted, result). If the manager then sends an accept message, this bilateral commitment will cease to exist but the following unilateral commitment will hold: C(participant, manager, result). Since the commitments can be easily manipulated, the participant can manipulate its commitment in the following ways: (1) it can discharge its commitment by sending the result as in the original CNP (*discharge*), (2) it can delegate its commitment to another participant, who carries out the proposal (*delegate*), or (3) it can send a failure notice as in the original protocol (*cancel*). Meanwhile, if for some reason, the manager no longer has a need for the proposed task, (1) it can let go of the participant (*release*) or (2) let another agent benefit from the proposal (*assign*).*

4 Protocol Correctness

Analyzing a commitment protocol is significantly more difficult than analyzing an FSM. First, the states of a commitment protocol are not given *a priori* as is the case with FSMs. Two, the transitions are computed at run time to enable flexible execution. To study a commitment protocol, we study the possible protocol runs that can result. A protocol run specifies the actions that happen at certain time points. We base the definition of a protocol state on these time points. More specifically, a state of the protocol corresponds to the set of propositions and commitments that hold at a particular time point.

Definition 4. *A protocol state $s(t)$ captures the content of the protocol with respect to a particular time point t. A protocol state $s(t)$ is a conjunction of $HoldsAt(f, t)$ predicates with a fixed t but possibly varying f. Formally, $s(t) \equiv \bigwedge_{f \in F} HoldsAt(f, t)$.*

Two states are equivalent if the same fluents hold in both states. Although the two states are equivalent, they are not strictly the same state since they can come about at different time points.

Definition 5. *The $\equiv$ operator defines an equivalence relation between two states $s(t)$ and $s(t')$ such that $s(t) \equiv s(t')$ if and only if $\forall f \in F : (HoldsAt(f,t) \Rightarrow HoldsAt(f,t'))$ and $\forall f \in F : (HoldsAt(f,t') \Rightarrow HoldsAt(f,t))$.*

Protocol execution captures a series of making and fulfilling of commitments. Intuitively, if the protocol executes successfully, then there should not be any open unilateral commitments; i.e., no participant should still have commitments to others. This motivates the following definition of an end-state.

Definition 6. *A protocol state $s(t)$ is a proper end-state if no unilateral commitments exist. Formally, $\forall f \in F : HoldsAt(f,t) \Rightarrow f \notin CS$.*

Generally, if the protocol ends in an unexpected state, i.e., not a proper end-state, one of the participants is not conforming to the protocol. However, to claim this, the protocol has to ensure that participants have the choice to execute actions that will terminate their commitments. What are the requirements to establish this? The following analysis derives the requirements for correct commitment protocols.

Holzmann labels states of a protocol in terms of their capability of allowing progress [7]. Broadly put, a protocol state can be labeled as a progressing state if it is possible to move to another state. For a protocol to function correctly, all states excluding the proper end-states should be progressing states. Otherwise, the protocol can move to a state where no actions are possible, and hence the protocol will not progress and immaturely end.

Definition 7. *A protocol state $s(t)$ is progressing if*

- *$s(t)$ is not a proper end-state (e.g., $s(t) \Rightarrow \exists f \in CS : HoldsAt(f,t)$), and*
- *there exists an action that if executed creates a transition to a different state. (e.g., $s(t) \Rightarrow \exists t' : t < t' \land s(t) \not\equiv s(t')$).*

At every state in the protocol, either the execution should have successfully completed (i.e., proper end-state) or should be moving to a different state (i.e., progress state).

Definition 8. *A protocol $\mathcal{P}$ is progressive if and only if each possible state in the protocol is either a proper end-state or a progressing state.*

This follows intuitively from the explanation of making progress. A progressive protocol exhibits the liveness property of traditional network protocols. Lemma 1 formalizes a sufficient condition for ensuring that a commitment protocol is progressive.

Lemma 1. *Let $\mathcal{P}$ be a commitment protocol and c be a unilateral commitment. If $\forall c \in CS : O(c) \neq \emptyset$, then $\mathcal{P}$ is progressive.*

Proof. By Definition 8, every state in $\mathcal{P}$ should be a proper end-state or a progress state. If a state does not contain open commitments then it is a proper end-state (Definition 6). If the state does contain a unilateral commitment, then since at least one operation exists to manipulate it, the protocol will allow a transition to a new state. Thus, the state is a progressing state (Definition 7). □

Example 3. *If a participant has a commitment to the manager to deliver the result (C(participant, manager, result)), then there needs to be at least one operation on this commitment so that the commitment can be terminated.*

Ensuring a progressing protocol is the first step in ensuring correctness. If a protocol is not progressing, then the participants can get stuck in an unexpected state and not transition to another state. However, progress by itself does not guarantee that the interactions will always lead to a proper end-state. This is similar in principle to livelocks in network protocols, where the protocol can transition between states but never reach a final state [7, p.120].

Example 4. *Consider a participant x whose proposal has been accepted. Hence, $C(x, manager, result)$ holds (state 1). Next, the participant delegates its commitment to another participant z $C(z, manager, result)$ (state 2). Next, participant z delegates the commitment back to participant x and thus the protocol moves back to the previous state where $C(x, manager, result)$ holds. Participants x and z delegate the commitment back and forth infinitely.*

Obviously, the situation explained in Example 4 is is not desirable. It is necessary to ensure progress but this is not sufficient to conclude that the protocol is making *effective* progress.

Definition 9. *A cycle in a protocol refers to a non-empty sequence of states that start and end at equivalent states. A cycle can be formalized by the content of the beginning and ending states. That is, an execution path is a cycle if:*
$\exists t, t', t'' \in T : (s(t) \equiv s(t')) \wedge (t < t'' < t') \wedge (s(t) \not\equiv s(t''))$.

Definition 10. *An infinitely repeating cycle is a cycle with progressive states such that if the protocol gets on to one of the states then the only execution sequence is to move to a state in the cycle [7].*

In Example 4, the two delegate actions form an infinitely repeating cycle. Once the protocol gets into state 1 or state 2, it will always remain in one of these two states.

Lemma 2. *An infinitely repeating cycle does not contain any proper end-states.*
Proof. By Definition 10 an infinitely repeating cycle only contains progressing states and by Definition 7, a progressing state cannot be an end-state. □

Given a cycle, it is easy to check if it is infinitely repeating. Informally, for each state in the cycle, we need to check if there is a possible transition that can cause a state outside the cycle. This can be achieved by applying all allowed operations (by the proposition) to the commitments that exist in that state. As soon as applying a commitment operation to a state in the cycle yields a state not included in the cycle, the procedure stops, concluding that the cycle is not infinitely repeating.

Lemma 3. *Let l be a cycle. Let $c \in CS$ be a commitment that holds at a state $s(t)$ on this cycle at any time t. If* discharge, cancel *or* release $\in O(c)$ *then cycle l is not infinitely repeating.*

Proof. A cycle is not infinitely repeating if there is a path from a state in the cycle to a state outside the cycle. Discharging, canceling, or releasing a commitment will lead the protocol to go to a proper end-state. Since no proper end-state is on an infinitely repeating cycle, the cycle will not repeat (Lemma 2). □

Example 5. *In Example 4, if either participant could discharge the commitment or could have been released from the commitment, then there need not have been an infinitely repeating cycle.*

Definition 11. *A protocol $\mathcal{P}$ is effectively progressive if and only if and only if (1) $\mathcal{P}$ is progressive and (2) $\mathcal{P}$ does not have infinitely repeating cycles.*

Theorem 1. *Let $\mathcal{P}$ be commitment protocol such that for all the commitments $c \in CS$,* discharge$\in O(c)$ *or* cancel$\in O(c)$ *or* release$\in O(c)$. *Then, $\mathcal{P}$ is effectively progressive.*

Proof. By Lemma 1, any one of the commitment operations is sufficient to make the protocol progressive. By Lemma 3, any of the three operations will avoid infinite cycles. □

Note that we are not concerned about the choices of the agents in terms of which actions to take. Looking back at Example 4, assume that agent x could also execute an action that could discharge its commitment (to carry out the proposal), but choose instead to delegate it to agent z. The protocol then would still loop infinitely. However, our purpose here is to make sure that agent x has the choice of discharging and delegating. The protocol should allow an agent to terminate its commitment by providing at least one appropriate action. It is then up to the agent to either terminate it or delegate it as best suits it.

5 Discussion

We review the recent literature with respect to our work. Fornara and Colombetti develop a method for agent communication, where the meanings of messages denote commitments [6]. In addition to unilateral and bilateral commitments, Fornara and Colombetti use precommitments to represent a request for a commitment from a second party. They model the life cycle of commitments in the system through update rules. However, they do not provide design requirements on correctness as we have done here.

Artikis et al. develop a framework to specify and animate computational societies [2]. The specification of a society defines the social constraints, social roles, and social states. Social constraints define types of actions and the enforcement policies for these actions. A social state denotes the global state of a society based on the state of the environment, observable states of the involved agents, and states of the institutions. Our definition of a protocol state is similar to the global state of Artikis et al.. The framework of Artikis et al. does not specify any design rules.

Alberti et al. specify interaction protocols using social integrity constraints [1]. Given a partial set of events that have happened, each agent computes a set of expectations based on the social integrity constraints; e.g., events that are expected to happen based on the given constraints. If an agent executes an event that does not respect an expectation, then it is assumed to have violated one of the social integrity constraints. Alberti et al. does not provide any design rules to ensure the correctness of their interaction protocols.

Endriss et al. study protocol conformance for interaction protocols that are defined as deterministic finite automaton (DFA) [4]. The set of transitions of a DFA are known *a priori*. If an agent always follows the transitions of the protocol, then it is compliant to the given protocol. Hence, the compliance checking can be viewed as verifying that the transitions of the protocol are followed correctly. DFAs have been analyzed extensively and many correctness properties have been formalized. However, DFAs represent sequences of actions and thus does not allow the agents to flexibly execute a protocol.

In our future work, we plan to work on other design requirements for commitment protocols, such as those for avoiding deadlocks. Identifying and formalizing these requirements will facilitate correct commitment protocols to be designed.

Acknowledgments

I have benefited from discussions with Munindar Singh and Ashok Mallya on commitments. The reviewers' comments have greatly improved the paper.

References

1. Alberti, M., Daolio, D., Torroni, P.: Specification and verification of agent interaction protocols in a logic-based system. In: Proc. ACM Symp. on Applied Computing (SAC). (2004) (to appear)
2. Artikis, A., Pitt, J., Sergot, M.: Animated specifications of computational societies. In: Proc. Intl. Joint Conf. on Autonomous Agents and MultiAgent Syst. (2002) 1053–1061
3. Castelfranchi, C.: Commitments: From individual intentions to groups and organizations. In: Proc. Intl. Conf. on Multiagent Systems. (1995) 41–48
4. Endriss, U., Maudet, N., Sadri, F., Toni F.: Protocol conformance for logic-based agents. In: Proc. Intl. Joint Conf. on Artificial Intelligence. (2003) 679–684
5. Foundation for Intelligent Physical Agents. Contract net interaction protocol specification, Number 00029 (2002)

6. Fornara, N., Colombetti, M.: Operational specification of a commitment-based agent communication language. In: Proc. Intl. Joint Conf. on Autonomous Agents and MultiAgent Syst. (2002) 535–542
7. Holzmann, G.J.: Design and Validation of Computer Protocols. Prentice-Hall, NJ (1991)
8. Jennings, N.R.: On agent-based software engineering. Artificial Intelligence **177**(2) (2000) 277–296
9. Kowalski, R., Sergot, M.J.: A logic-based calculus of events. New Generation Computing 4(1) (1986) 67–95
10. Shanahan, M.: Solving the Frame Problem: A Mathematical Investigation of the Common Sense Law of Inertia. MIT Press, Cambridge (1997)
11. Singh, M.P.: An ontology for commitments in multiagent systems: Toward a unification of normative concepts. Artificial Intelligence and Law **7** (1999) 97–113
12. Venkatraman, M., Singh, M.P.: Verifying compliance with commitment protocols: Enabling open Web-based multiagent systems. Autonomous Agents and Multi-Agent Systems **2**(3) (1999) 217–236
13. Yolum, P., Singh, M.P.: Flexible protocol specification and execution: Applying event calculus planning using commitments. In: Proc. Intl. Joint Conf. on Autonomous Agents and MultiAgent Systems. (2002) 527–534
14. Yolum, P., Singh, M.P.: Reasoning about commitments in the event calculus: An approach for specifying and executing protocols. Annals of Math. and AI **42**(1–3) (2004)

Generating Equiprobable Superpositions of Arbitrary Sets for a New Generalization of the Deutsch-Jozsa Algorithm

Elton Ballhysa and Ahmet Celal Cem Say

Department of Computer Engineering
Boğaziçi University, Bebek 34342 İstanbul, Turkey
eballhysa@hititcs.com, say@boun.edu.tr

Abstract. We examine the problem of generating equal-probability superpositions of sets whose cardinalities are not necessarily powers of two. Alternative quantum circuits for this purpose are compared with respect to complexity and precision, and a variant based on the Grover iteration is shown to yield an algorithm with one-sided error for a generalization of the Deutsch-Jozsa problem, where the task is to decide whether a specified subset of the oracle function is constant or balanced.

1 Introduction

An examination of the remarkably short list of known fast quantum algorithms [7,8] shows that almost all of them start by setting a register to an equiprobable superposition of all classical values (basis states) that can exist in a register of that size, and make crucial use of the parallelism introduced in this step during the remainder of the procedure. In this paper, we consider the more general problem of generating equiprobable superpositions for a quantum register when the number of the states in superposition is not necessarily a power of two. We start with a brief introduction to the Deutsch-Jozsa algorithm, and an analysis and comparison of two alternative quantum circuits for our task. A new generalization of the Deutsch-Jozsa problem, where we seek to determine whether a subset of the oracle function is balanced or constant, is presented as evidence of the usefulness of the capability of generating equiprobable superpositions of arbitrary sets. One of the variants for generating equiprobable superpositions is shown to yield to an algorithm with one-sided error for this problem.

2 The Deutsch-Jozsa Algorithm

For an introduction to the concepts and notation used in the rest of this paper, see any introductory text on quantum computing, like [8].

Deutsch and Jozsa were the first to present a quantum algorithm which was exponentially faster than any exact classical algorithm for the same task [4,8]. The algorithm could solve the following promise problem:

We are promised that a function $f: \{0,1\}^n \to \{0,1\}$ is either constant or balanced. A *constant* function is one which returns the same value for all inputs. A *balanced* function is one which returns 0 for exactly half of the inputs and returns 1 for the other half. We are provided with an oracle which returns the value $f(x)$ for any input x. We are required to determine the class of function f with a minimum possible number of oracle queries.

The most efficient deterministic classical algorithm for this problem requires $2^{n-1}+1$ oracle queries at the worst case, whereas a probabilistic algorithm requires polynomially many queries.

The quantum Deutsch-Jozsa algorithm solves this problem exactly by making a single oracle query. The circuit for this algorithm is given in Figure 1. The first n qubits are initialized to $|0\rangle$, and the final qubit is initialized to $|1\rangle$.

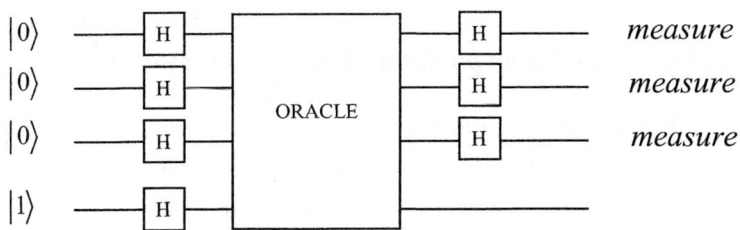

Fig. 1. Quantum circuit for the Deutsch-Jozsa algorithm

The oracle implements the transformation $|x,y\rangle \to |x, y \oplus f(x)\rangle$, where x is supposed to be entered in the first register of n qubits, and $f(x)$ is XORed by the initial value y of the $(n+1)$st qubit (the second register) as a result. A trace follows:

1. The initial state of the register set is

$$|0^n\rangle \otimes |1\rangle.$$

2. All $n+1$ qubits are passed through Hadamard gates:

$$\left[\frac{1}{\sqrt{2^n}} \sum_{x=0}^{2^n-1} |x\rangle\right] \otimes \left[\frac{|0\rangle - |1\rangle}{\sqrt{2}}\right]$$

3. Perform the oracle call:

$$\left[\frac{1}{\sqrt{2^n}} \sum_x (-1)^{f(x)} |x\rangle\right] \otimes \left[\frac{|0\rangle - |1\rangle}{\sqrt{2}}\right]$$

Note that the last qubit remains unchanged and unentangled with the top register.

4. Apply inverse Hadamard transform to the top register:

$$\frac{1}{2^n} \sum_{z=0}^{2^n-1} \sum_x (-1)^{f(x)+x \cdot z} |z\rangle \otimes \left[\frac{|0\rangle - |1\rangle}{\sqrt{2}}\right]$$

5. Measure the top register to observe the value r. If r is 0, then the algorithm outputs "constant"; otherwise, it outputs "balanced".

The algorithm works correctly, because the amplitude of state $|0\rangle$ in the first register just before the measurement is

$$\alpha_0 = \frac{1}{2^n}\sum_x (-1)^{f(x)}.$$

In case of a constant function, the sum above is 1 if the function evaluates to 0, and -1 if it evaluates to 1. Since the probability of observing state $|i\rangle$ upon measurement of a register is $|\alpha_i|^2$, we conclude that we observe $|0\rangle$ with certainty. If the function is balanced, there are exactly 2^{n-1} terms that evaluate to 1 and exactly 2^{n-1} terms that evaluate to -1 inside the summation, thus yielding 0 and implying the impossibility of observing $|0\rangle$ upon measurement.

3 Equiprobable Superposition of Arbitrary Subsets

As mentioned above, almost all useful quantum algorithms start by setting an n-qubit register which is initialized to $|0\rangle$ to an equiprobable superposition of all the 2^n basis states. As we saw in the Deutsch-Jozsa algorithm, this transformation can be done easily using n Hadamard gates with zero error, that is, all the amplitudes in the resulting superposition are *exactly* equal to each other. We will now consider a generalized version of this task, that of transforming the state of a quantum register from the initial all-zero state to the equiprobable superposition of a given arbitrary subset of the set of basis states. Our input then consists of a set containing q n-bit numbers; $S = \{s_0, s_1, \ldots s_{q-1}\}$. The state we want to generate is

$$|\varphi\rangle = \frac{1}{\sqrt{q}} \sum_{i=0}^{q-1} |s_i\rangle.$$

We will discuss in detail two algorithms for this task. The first one, Algorithm KSV, is based on a circuit described by Kitaev et al. [7] for a similar problem. The second alternative, Algorithm G, is based on Grover's quantum search algorithm [5].

3.1 Algorithm KSV

Kitaev et al. consider a problem similar to ours in [7]; that of generating the state $|\eta_{n,q}\rangle$, the equiprobable superposition of states in $Q=\{0, 1, \ldots q-1\}$. The input to this algorithm will just be the number q, rather than the entire set Q. The output of the algorithm is an approximation to $|\eta_{n,q}\rangle$,

$$\sum_{i=0}^{q-1} \delta_i |i\rangle.$$

The solution that Kitaev *et al.* propose for this problem involves a circuit that is allowed to be constructed using elements from the infinite set of all possible two-qubit gates. It is actually an approximate implementation of the recursive formula

$$|\eta_{n,q}\rangle = \cos v |0\rangle \otimes |\eta_{n-1,q'}\rangle + \sin v |1\rangle \otimes |\eta_{n-1,q''}\rangle, \text{ where}$$

$q' = 2^{n-1}$, $q'' = q - q'$, $v = \cos^{-1}\sqrt{q'/q}$ if $q > 2^{n-1}$,
$q' = q$, $q'' = 1$, $v = 0$ if $q \leq 2^{n-1}$.

Consider the first q n-bit nonnegative integers. We would list them as (00...0), (00...1) and so on until ($b_{n-1}b_{n-2}...b_0$), where $b_{n-1}b_{n-2}...b_0$ is the binary representation of q-1. Then q' and q'' denote the counts of numbers in Q whose first bits are respectively 0 and 1. The algorithm rotates the first qubit (which is initially $|0\rangle$) by angle v in the plane defined by the $|0\rangle$ and $|1\rangle$ axes, where v is calculated according to the ratio of q' and q. The rest of the register is set in the same way recursively until we reach the last qubit ($n=1$). Table 1 summarizes this algorithm.

Table 1. Algorithm KSV', described by Kitaev et al. for the generation of state $|\eta_{n,q}\rangle$

1. Compute q', q'' and v/π, with the latter number represented as an approximation by L binary digits.
2. Apply the rotation operator R(v) to the first qubit of the register in which we are computing $|\eta_{n,q}\rangle$

$$R(v) = \begin{pmatrix} \cos v & -\sin v \\ \sin v & \cos v \end{pmatrix}$$

3. In the remaining n-1 qubits, construct $|\eta_{n-1,q'}\rangle$ if the first qubit is zero, construct $|\eta_{n-1,q''}\rangle$ if it equals one.
4. Reverse the first stage to clear the supplementary memory

The operator $R(v)$ is implemented approximately by making use of the following observation. Let $T = 0.t_1 t_2 ... t_L$ be the L-bit binary expression of the approximated v/π value. It follows that

$$\frac{\vartheta}{\pi} = 0.t_1 t_2 ... t_L = \frac{t_1}{2} + \frac{t_2}{4} + ... + \frac{t_L}{2^L} \leftrightarrow v = \pi(t_1 2^{-1} + t_2 2^{-2} + ... + t_L 2^{-L}).$$

We conclude that we can approximate rotation by angle v as a series of rotations by angle $\pi/2^i$, where each rotation is controlled by the corresponding bit in T, t_i: For each i, if t_i is $|1\rangle$, the qubit under consideration gets rotated by $\pi/2^i$ radians.

This algorithm, which we will call KSV', generates an approximation to the equiprobable superposition of basis states $|0\rangle$, $|1\rangle$, ..., $|q-1\rangle$. We want to generate the equiprobable superposition of all states s_i in an *arbitrary* given set S. For this purpose, we reduce our more general problem to the problem of Kitaev et al. by applying an appropriately constructed permutation operator P_S to the result of algorithm KSV'. The permutation operator P_S has the task of mapping set Q to set S. While any of the $q!$ possible permutations may do, we can choose in general to perform the permutation $|i\rangle \to |s_i\rangle$. Stated as such, this is only a partial permutator, however, considering only the subset Q is enough for our purposes. It is straightforward to show that, given S, the construction of P_S can be realized in time polynomial in q. Algorithm KSV is summarized in Table 2.

Table 2. Algorithm KSV

On input $S = \{s_0, s_1, \ldots s_{q-1}\}$
1. Construct the permutation P_S corresponding to S
2. Obtain an approximation to the state $|\eta_{n,q}\rangle$ by applying algorithm KSV' with q as input.
3. Obtain an approximation to the desired state $|\varphi\rangle$ by applying permutation operator P_S to $|\eta_{n,q}\rangle$.

3.2 Algorithm G

The second algorithm that we discuss for the task of generating equiprobable superpositions is based on the fast search algorithm proposed by Grover [5]. Suppose we are given the oracle for a function $f: \{0..N-1\} \rightarrow \{0,1\}$. N is 2^n, where n is the number of bits in the input. Let $S = \{x \mid f(x)=1\}$ and $q=|S|$. This algorithm performs $\Theta(\sqrt{N/q})$ oracle queries, before outputting with high probability some i so that $f(i) = 1$. The best possible classical algorithm for this purpose needs $\Theta(N/q)$ queries. Grover's algorithm starts with a superposition of all the N possible basis states, and then applies a series of operations which are collectively called the Grover iteration $k = \lfloor (\pi/4)\sqrt{N/q} \rfloor$ times. Finally, the register is observed, and the measured value is outputted. The failure probability is at most q/N. In the case where $q > N/2$, we will need to add an extra qubit to the oracle's input register in order to increase the search space and reduce the failure probability. In general, if we allow for a corresponding increase in the running time, we can reduce the error probability to $q/2^cN$ by adding c extra qubits. A nice property of Grover's algorithm is that it can be implemented for any problem size using only gates from a finite standard set [8].

An analysis [2,5] of the algorithm shows that the resulting superposition (just before the measurement) is a sum of two different equiprobable superpositions of the form

$$a\sum_{i \in S}|i\rangle + b\sum_{i \notin S}|i\rangle.$$

The algorithm is said to succeed when a solution state is observed, otherwise it fails. Let the success probability be p, thus the failure probability is $1-p$. The algorithm equally distributes p among the solution states and $1-p$ among the non-solution ones. Amplitudes of individual solution and non-solution states, a and b, are expressed in terms of p as $a = \sqrt{p/q}$ and $b = \sqrt{(1-p)/(N-q)}$.

We can therefore use Grover's algorithm for the generation of an equiprobable superposition of elements of a given set S. First, we have to implement the "oracle" ourselves. The first implementation that comes to mind is to have $f(x) = 1$ iff $x \in S$, but this idea leads to an unnecessarily inefficient circuit. Instead, we build an oracle which returns 1 if its input x is less than q, and 0 otherwise. This single comparison can be implemented efficiently. If we run Grover's algorithm with this oracle and stop without a measurement, the state of the resulting register will be given as

$$|\varphi_Q\rangle = a \sum_{i \in Q} |i\rangle + b \sum_{i \notin Q} |i\rangle,$$

where Q is as defined in the previous subsection.
To get from this state to the superposition

$$a \sum_{i \in S} |i\rangle + b \sum_{i \notin S} |i\rangle,$$

we use the permutation P_S that maps i to s_i, as discussed in the previous subsection. After the end of the Grover iterations, we apply permutation P_S, and we are done. A summary of the algorithm is given in Table 3:

Table 3. Algorithm G

On input $S = \{s_0, s_1, \ldots s_{q-1}\}$
1. Construct the "oracle" corresponding to Q
2. Construct the permutation P_S corresponding to S
3. Perform Grover's algorithm up to the measurement to obtain $\|\varphi_Q\rangle$
4. Perform permutation P_S on $\|\varphi_Q\rangle$ to obtain an approximation to state $\|\varphi\rangle$

3.3 Comparison of the Algorithms

The general specification of Algorithm KSV (unrealistically) assumes that the infinite set of $R(\pi/2^i)$ gates, for any i, is available to us. In this respect, Algorithm G is superior as it uses a finite set of standard gates. When required to work with the same gate set as G, KSV would necessarily make some approximation errors in addition to those that will be analyzed below.

Algorithm KSV approximates arbitrary rotations by the (possibly irrational) angle v by a series of controlled rotations by angles of the form $\pi 2^{-i}$, introducing a discrepancy between the actual angle v and the implemented angle v'. Because of this discrepancy, the probabilities are not distributed perfectly equally among the solution states. For example, when preparing the state $|\eta_{3,6}\rangle$, the ideal rotation angle for the first qubit is approximately 0.1959π radians. With four bits of accuracy for storing the value v/π, the rotation is actually implemented by an angle of nearly 0.1875π radians. Using seven bits, the resulting rotation angle would be nearly 0.1953π radians. Assuming no discrepancy in the remaining two qubits, the resulting superpositions are respectively

$$|\varphi_1\rangle = [0.4157 \quad 0.4157 \quad 0.4157 \quad 0.4157 \quad 0.3928 \quad 0.3928 \quad 0 \quad 0]^T, \text{ and}$$

$$|\varphi_2\rangle = [0.4088 \quad 0.4088 \quad 0.4088 \quad 0.4088 \quad 0.4072 \quad 0.4072 \quad 0 \quad 0]^T.$$

(It is easy to come up with examples where this same problem causes some of the s_i to disappear altogether from the resulting superposition.) On the other hand, Algorithm G does not pose such problems, because it distributes the success probability perfectly equally among solution states, and also distributes failure probability perfectly equally among the non-solution states. The significance of this property will be exhibited in the next section.

Algorithm KSV', and therefore our algorithm KSV, do not produce any unwanted states (i.e. any numbers not in S) in the resulting superposition. In order to see this, note that at the basis step, when the algorithm arrives at the last qubit, the two possible states are $|\eta_{1,1}\rangle$ or $|\eta_{1,2}\rangle$, corresponding to respective rotation angles of 0 and $\pi/4$. The bit representation for v/π for these angles is finite, and therefore results in no approximation errors. On the other hand, Algorithm G is based on the Grover iteration, which increases the amplitude of the solution and decreases the amplitude of non-solutions. This goes on with each iteration until we pass a critical value. However, even with the optimal iteration count, if we do not have access to perfectly implemented gates of possibly irrational rotation angles, the total probability of solution states does not sum to one, and therefore the probability of non-solution states is not zero.

Note that the Quantum Fourier Transform [7,8] can also be used as a way of producing nearly equiprobable superpositions. It should be mentioned that the QFT has basically the same disadvantages as Algorithm KSV' when the number of states in the superposition is not a power of two.

4   A New Generalization of the Deutsch-Jozsa Algorithm

By making use of one of the algorithms presented in sections 3.1 and 3.2 as a subroutine, we can construct a probabilistic algorithm for the following generalized version of the Deutsch-Jozsa problem: As before, f is a function from $\{0,1\}^n$ to $\{0,1\}$. Let S be a given subset of q numbers in the interval $U_n = [0..2^n-1]$. The problem is subject to the following promises:
- q is even and is greater than 2^{n-1}
- f is balanced on S' $= \bar{U}_n S$
- f is either balanced or constant on S

We are required to find whether f is constant or balanced on S by making the minimum possible number of oracle calls. Note that by letting $S = U_n$, we obtain the original Deutsch-Jozsa problem as a special case. The algorithm we propose for this problem is similar to the one described in Section 2, with the single difference that instead of the n Hadamard gates that generate the equiprobable superposition of all numbers in U_n, we will use an algorithm for generating the equiprobable superposition of only the numbers in S. The overall simplified circuit is given in Figure 2.

Let us follow the algorithm step by step and inspect the state of the registers:

1. As in the original algorithm, the initial state of the registers is given as $|0\rangle \otimes |1\rangle$.

2. In the first stage, we apply an algorithm for generating the equiprobable superposition on input set S in the first register and an Hadamard gate to the final qubit. For the time being, let us assume that this algorithm produces a perfect superposition with no unwanted elements. The overall state of the registers is then

$$\left[\frac{1}{\sqrt{q}}\sum_{x\in S}|x\rangle\right]\otimes\left[\frac{|0\rangle-|1\rangle}{\sqrt{2}}\right].$$

3. In the next stage, we make the oracle call, which affects only the top register:

$$\left[\frac{1}{\sqrt{q}}\sum_{x\in S}(-1)^{f(x)}|x\rangle\right]\otimes\left[\frac{|0\rangle-|1\rangle}{\sqrt{2}}\right]$$

4. At the last stage, we apply the Hadamard transform to the top register to obtain

$$\frac{1}{\sqrt{2^n}}\sum_{z=0}^{2^n-1}\left[\frac{1}{\sqrt{q}}\sum_{x\in S}(-1)^{x\cdot z+f(x)}|z\rangle\right]\otimes\left[\frac{|0\rangle-|1\rangle}{\sqrt{2}}\right].$$

5. Measure the top register to observe the value r. If r is 0, then the algorithm outputs "constant"; otherwise, it outputs "balanced".

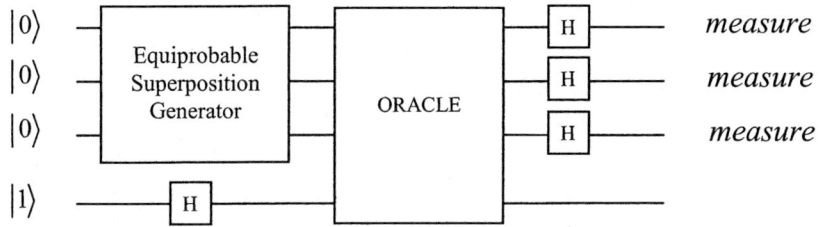

Fig. 2. Circuit for the new generalization of the Deutsch-Jozsa algorithm

Let $p(i)$ denote the probability that $|i\rangle$ is observed upon this final measurement. Note that the amplitude of state $|0\rangle$ is

$$\alpha_0 = \frac{1}{\sqrt{2^n q}}\sum_{x\in S}(-1)^{f(x)}.$$

If the function f is balanced on S, this summation will vanish, leaving, as expected, $\alpha_0 = 0$. So in the case of a balanced function, the probability of observing $|0\rangle$ in the top register is zero. In the case of a constant function f on S,

$$\alpha_0 = (-1)^{f_S}\sqrt{q/2^n},$$

where f_S denotes the constant value of the function. No matter whether f_S is 0 or 1,

$$p(0) = |\alpha_0|^2 = q/2^n.$$

So if we could obtain a perfectly equiprobable superposition of S in step 2, then the probability of correctly observing state $|0\rangle$ in the case of a constant function on S is $q/2^n$. The promise that $q > 2^{n-1}$ ensures that the correctness probability exceeds ½. This is not an exact algorithm, as was the case with the original Deutsch-Jozsa algorithm. However it has the nice "one-sided error" property than when the function is balanced, it is correctly classified with certainty. Note that the best (probabilistic) classical algorithm for this problem also has one-sided error, but requires polynomially many oracle calls at a minimum.

How would our generalized Deutsch-Jozsa circuit behave if we substituted the ideal superposition generator in the first stage with one of the actual circuits examined in this paper, none of which produce the desired perfect equiprobable superposition?

Let us consider the KSV algorithm first. The actual superposition produced by this module is, as already discussed,

$$\sum_{\forall s_i \in S} \delta_i |s_i\rangle,$$

where the δ_i's are, because of approximation problems, near, but not equal to, $1/\sqrt{q}$, and are therefore also not equal to each other. As a result, the amplitude of $|0\rangle$ just before the measurement will be

$$\alpha_0 = \frac{1}{\sqrt{2^n}} \left[\sum_{x \in S} (-1)^{f(x)} \delta_i \right].$$

For a balanced f, we expect the amplitude of $|0\rangle$ to be exactly zero after the oracle call. However, because the amplitudes of the desired states were not all equal to each other, we will not have a complete cancellation, and therefore the probability of observing the state $|0\rangle$ would be a (small) nonzero number. As a result, integrating KSV as the superposition generation module makes our generalized Deutsch-Jozsa algorithm lose its one-sided error property.

Interestingly, integrating Algorithm G as the superposition generation module solves this problem. We know that G produces the superposition

$$a \sum_{i \in S} |i\rangle + b \sum_{i \notin S} |i\rangle,$$

where a is possibly slightly less than $1/\sqrt{q}$, therefore allowing b to assume a (small) nonzero value. By a straightforward extension of the analysis at the beginning of this section, it is seen that the amplitude of $|0\rangle$ just before the measurement will be

$$\alpha_0 = \frac{1}{\sqrt{2^n}} \left[a \sum_{x \in S} (-1)^{f(x)} + b \sum_{x \notin S} (-1)^{f(x)} \right].$$

But since f is balanced on $S' = U_n\text{-}S$, the second summation vanishes, and the probability of measuring $|0\rangle$, given that function f is balanced over S, is zero. So the incorporation of Algorithm G preserves the one-sided error property of the generalized Deutsch-Jozsa algorithm.

When f is constant, the probability of measuring $|0\rangle$ will be $(qa)^2/2^n = qp/2^n$ rather than $q/2^n$, which would be the case with the ideal algorithm, but we can fix the number of Grover iterations and ancilla qubits in G to ensure that this probability never falls below ½, ensuring the correctness of our probabilistic algorithm.

5 Related Work and Conclusion

Several generalizations of the Deutsch-Jozsa algorithm in different "directions" exist in the literature: Cleve et al. [4] handle oracles with multiple-bit outputs. Chi et al. [3] show how to distinguish between constant and "evenly distributed" functions. Bergou et al. [1] distinguish between balanced functions and a subset of the class of "biased" functions. Holmes and Texier [6] determine whether f is constant or balanced on each coset of a subgroup of U_n. Our algorithm provides a different generalization, where the domain of the function that we are really interested in is not necessarily a power of two.

Of the two alternative equiprobable superposition generation subroutines that we considered, we concluded that, if one's primary concern is obtaining an algorithm with one-sided, rather that two-sided, error for our problem, the Grover-based Algorithm G should be preferred. Note that, if one is more concerned about the cost of implementing the superposition generator, things change considerably, since KSV' has only polynomial complexity, whereas the worst-case complexity of Grover's algorithm is exponential. (It should be noted that one can achieve much better performance with Grover if certain restrictions [2] on the relation between N and q are acceptable.)

The Deutsch-Jozsa problem is one of the hidden subgroup problems [7,8], which form one of the two classes for which quantum algorithms have been shown to lead to exponential speedup over classical ones. We are currently trying to apply the idea of working with perfectly equal distributions of arbitrary sets to other hidden subgroup problems, and to come up with similar generalizations for those algorithms as well.

Acknowledgements

We thank Peter Høyer and Mike Vyalyi for their helpful answers to our naïve questions, Cem Keskin for the useful discussions, and Nafiye Kıyak for providing most of our references.

References

1. Bergou, J.A., Herzog, U., Hillery, M.: Quantum State Filtering and Discrimination between Sets of Boolean Functions. Physical Review Letters **90** (2003) 257901
2. Boyer, M., Brassard, G., Høyer, P., Tapp, A.: Tight Bounds on Quantum Searching. Fortschritte Der Physik **46** (1998) 493–505
3. Chi, D.P., Kim, J., Lee, S.: Initialization-free Generalized Deutsch-Jozsa Algorithm. Journal of Physics A: Mathematical and General **34** (2001) 5251–5258
4. Cleve, R., Ekert, A., Macchiavello, C., Mosca, M.: Quantum Algorithms Revisited. In: Proc. R. Soc. London A. (1998) 339–354
5. Grover, L.: A Fast Quantum Mechanical Algorithm for Database Search. In: Proceedings of the Twenty-eighth Annual ACM Symposium on Theory of Computing, Philadelphia, Pennsylvania. (1996) 212–219
6. Holmes R.R., Texier F.: A Generalization of the Deutsch-Jozsa Quantum Algorithm. Far East J. Math Sci. **9** (2003) 319–326
7. Kitaev, A.Y., Shen, A.H., Vyalyi, M.N.: Classical and Quantum Computation. American Mathematical Society, Providence, Rhode Island (2002)
8. Nielsen, M.A., Chuang, I.L.: Quantum Computation and Quantum Information. Cambridge University Press (2000)

Proof of the Basic Theorem on Concept Lattices in Isabelle/HOL

Barış Sertkaya[1,2] and Halit Oğuztüzün[2]

[1] Institute of Theoretical Computer Science
Dresden University of Technology, Dresden, Germany
sertkaya@tcs.inf.tu-dresden.de
[2] Department of Computer Engineering
Middle East Technical University, Ankara, Turkey
oguztuzun@ceng.metu.edu.tr

Abstract. This paper presents a machine-checked proof of the Basic Theorem on Concept Lattices, which appears in the book "Formal Concept Analysis" by Ganter and Wille, in the Isabelle/HOL Proof Assistant. As a by-product, the underlying lattice theory by Kammueller has been extended.

1 Introduction

Formal concept analysis (FCA) [4] is an emerging field of applied mathematics based on a lattice-theoretic formalization of the notions of concept and conceptual hierarchy. It thereby facilitates mathematical reasoning for conceptual data analysis and knowledge processing. In FCA, a concept is constituted by two parts: its *extent*, which consists of all the objects belonging to the concept, and its *intent*, which contains the attributes common to all objects of the concept. This formalization allows the user to form all concepts of a context and introduce a subsumption hierarchy between the concepts, resulting in a complete lattice called the *concept lattice* of the context. Concept lattice is used to query the knowledge and to derive implicit information from the knowledge.

Isabelle [7,10], on the other hand, is a generic interactive theory development environment for implementing logical formalisms. It has been instantiated to support reasoning in several object-logics. Specialization of Isabelle for Higher Order Logic is called Isabelle/HOL.

The long term goal of this effort is to formalize the theory of FCA in Isabelle/HOL. This will provide a mechanized theory for researchers to prove their own theorems with utmost precision and to verify the knowledge representation systems based on FCA. Another potential utility of formalization is extracting programs from constructive proofs. See, for example, [1,12].

The specific accomplishment of this work is a machine-checked version of the proof of the Basic Theorem of Concept Lattices, which appears in the book "Formal Concept Analysis" by Ganter and Wille [4]. As a by-product, the underlying lattice theory developed by Kammueller [5] has been extended.

In an effort along the same direction, Schwarzweller presents a formalization of concept lattices in Mizar Proof Assistant [13, 14]. Some applications of FCA to knowledge engineering and software engineering have been reported [6, 9, 18].

2 Isabelle Proof Assistant

Isabelle is a *generic* interactive theorem prover, designed for reasoning in a variety of formal theories. It is generic in the sense that it provides proof procedures for Constructive Type Theory, various first-order logics, some systems of Modal Logics, Zermelo-Fraenkel Set Theory, and Higher-Order Logic, which are called *object-logics*. Object-logics are formalized within Isabelle's *meta-logic*, which is intuitionistic higher-order logic with implication, universal quantifiers, and equality. The specialization of Isabelle for Higher Order Logic is called Isabelle/HOL [8]. It is a widely used object-logic for proof-checking tasks.

2.1 Isabelle Theories

Working with Isabelle/HOL means creating theories. Roughly speaking, a *theory* is a named collection of types, functions, theorems and their proofs. The general format of a theory T is

```
theory T = B1 + ... + Bn:
  declarations, definitions, and proofs
end
```

where B1, ... , Bn are the names of existing (parent) theories that T is based on and declarations, definitions and proofs represent the newly introduced concepts (types, functions etc.) and proofs of theorems. Everything defined in the parent theories (and their parents recursively) is visible.

2.2 Theorem Proving with Isabelle

Proof trees are derived rules, and are built by joining rules together. This comprises both forwards and backwards proof. A backwards proof works by matching a goal with the conclusion of a rule; the premises become the subgoals. A forwards proof works by matching theorems to the premises of rules, making a new theorem.

A typical proof starts with first stating the goal using the Goal command, proceeds with applying tactics aiming to solve this goal using the by command, and ends with the qed command which names and stores the proved theorem. Tactics may lead to zero or more subgoals. The proof process continues until no subgoals are left.

Isabelle/HOL has a huge number of predefined tactics. Some of the most widely used groups of tactics are resolution, rewrite, induction, assumption, tableau, automatic and simplification tactics. Apart from them, the user can define her/his own tactics. A complete list of tactics can be found in [11].

2.3 Lattice Theory in Isabelle/HOL

Our formalization is based on the theory Tarski, which was developed by Florian Kammueller to prove Tarski's Fixpoint Theorem. At the time this work started, the theory was available in old style proof script. It contains a minimal version of lattice theory providing partial orders, complete lattices, least upper bound, greatest lower bound and fixed points of complete lattices. The type of a partially ordered set is defined by the record type 'a potype as:

```
record 'a potype =
  pset  :: "'a set"
  order :: "('a * 'a) set"
```

The field pset is the set of elements of the partial order and the field order is the set of pairs of elements with the meaning that the first element of the pair is less than or equal to the second one. Using syntactic translations, the field pset of a partial order V is accessed as V.<A> and the field order is accessed as V.<r>. The theory provides the least upper bound and the greatest lower bound operations on a partially ordered set with the lub and glb functions respectively. Apart from these, it provides the predicates islub to check if a given element is the least upper bound of a partial order, and the predicate isglb to check if a given element is the greatest lower bound of a partial order. Using these definitions and some auxiliary definitions, the theory introduces complete lattices. In addition to these definitions, it also provides the proofs of the uniqueness of the lub and the glb, the proof that lub and glb are elements of the lattice, properties about duality, and finally the Tarski's lemma on fixpoints.

We extended the theory with the formal definitions of supremum and infimum preserving maps on complete lattices, order preserving maps, order embeddings, supremum/infimum-dense sets, supremum/infimum-irreducible elements, complete lattice homomorphism and complete lattice isomorphism. (For the Isabelle symbols appearing in the following definitions, please refer to [8, 11] or Table 1 on page 984.) Since we are dealing with complete lattices, we defined supremum preserving maps on complete lattices as:

```
supremum_preserving :: "['a => 'b, 'a potype, 'b potype] => bool"
"supremum_preserving f V1 V2 == (V1 : CompleteLattice) &
 (V2 : CompleteLattice) & (f ' (V1.<A>) <= V2.<A>) &
 (! X <= V1.<A> . ! x : V1.<A> . (islub X V1 x) -->
 (islub (f ' X) V2 (f x)))"
```

Infimum preserving map infimum_preserving is defined in a similar way. Order preserving maps and order embeddings are defined as:

```
order_preserving :: "['a => 'b, 'a potype, 'b potype] => bool"
"order_preserving f V1 V2 ==  ! x : V1.<A> . ! y : V1.<A> .
  ((x,y) : V1.<r>) --> (((f x) , (f y)) : V2.<r>)"

order_embedding :: "['a => 'b, 'a potype, 'b potype] => bool"
"order_embedding f V1 V2 ==  ! x : V1.<A> . ! y : V1.<A> .
  ((x,y) : V1.<r>) = (((f x) , (f y)) : V2.<r>)"
```

Using the functions defined above, we defined a lattice homomorphism to be a supremum, infimum and order preserving map:

```
lattice_homomorphism :: "['a => 'b, 'a potype, 'b potype] => bool"
"lattice_homomorphism f V1 V2 == (supremum_preserving f V1 V2) &
 (infimum_preserving f V1 V2) & (order_preserving f V1 V2)"
```

And a lattice isomorphism to be an injective and surjective lattice homomorphism:

```
lattice_isomorphism :: "['a => 'b, 'a potype, 'b potype] => bool"
"lattice_isomorphism f V1 V2 == (lattice_homomorphism f V1 V2) &
 (inj f) & (my_surj f (V1.<A>) (V2.<A>))"
```

Since the Isabelle primitive surj for surjective maps does not take types into account, we defined our own typed surjective maps my_surj as:

```
my_surj :: "['a => 'b,'a set,'b set] => bool"
"my_surj f V1 V2 == ! y : V2 . ? x : V1 . y = (f x)"
```

And we defined supremum-dense sets as:

```
supremum_dense :: "['a set,'a potype] => bool"
"supremum_dense X V == (X <= V.<A>) & (! v : V.<A> .
 ? A <= X . islub A V v)"
```

Infimum-dense set infimum_dense is defined in a similar way.

In preparation for the proof of the Basic Theorem, we proved some theorems from Lattice Theory. We proved that the supremum/infimum dense property is preserved under an isomorphism. We also proved that the supremum of a subset of a set is less than or equal to the supremum of its superset. The formal proofs can be found in [15] as stand alone lemmata with names sup_dense_preserved, inf_dense_preserved and sup_lt_ss respectively.

3 Formalization

In this section, we present the basic notions of Formal Concept Analysis and their formalizations in Isabelle/HOL in an interleaved manner. First we give the mathematical notions as in [4], then we give the corresponding Isabelle/HOL proof script and related commentary. Due to space limitations, we can not give the proofs in full details, the interested reader may see [4] for the mathematical notions and proofs, and [15] for the corresponding Isabelle/HOL proof script and a detailed commentary of it.

We start with basic definitions, and datatypes defined for them in Isabelle/HOL.

3.1 Definitions and Datatypes

Definition 1. *A* **Formal Context** $\mathbb{K} := (G, M, I)$ *consists of two sets G and M and a relation I between G and M. The elements of G are called the* **objects** *and the elements of M are called the* **attributes** *of the context. The I relation between an object g and an attribute m is written as gIm or $(g, m) \in I$ and read as "the object g has the attribute m". The relation I is also called the* **incidence relation** *of the context.*

Using the definition, formal context type is formalized as a record type with fields object_set, attribute_set and incidence_rel as:

```
record ('a,'b) formal_context_type =
    object_set      :: "'a set"
    attribute_set   :: "'b set"
    incidence_rel   :: "('a * 'b) set"
```

Through syntactic translations, the object set of a formal context K is accessed as K.<OS>, attribute set as K.<AS> and the incidence relation as K.<IR>.

Definition 2. *For a set $A \subseteq G$ of objects, the set of attributes common to the objects in A is defined as: $A' = \{m \in M \mid (g, m) \in I \text{ for all } g \in A\}$. Correspondingly, for a set $B \subseteq M$, the set of objects which have all attributes in B is defined as: $B' = \{g \in G \mid (g, m) \in I \text{ for all } m \in B\}$*

The polymorphic prime operator is formalized as two separate functions namely common_attributes and common_objects, in the following manner:

```
common_attributes :: "'a set => ('a,'b) formal_context_type =>
    'b set"
"common_attributes os fc == {
    m . m : fc.<AS> & (! g : os . (g,m) : fc.<IR>) & os <= fc.<OS>
}"
```

common_attributes is the formal definition of a function taking a set of objects os of type 'a set and a formal context fc of type ('a,'b) formal_context_type and returns the set of attributes (of type 'b set) common to all objects in os.

```
common_objects :: "'b set => ('a,'b) formal_context_type =>
    'a set"
"common_objects as fc == {
    g . g : fc.<OS> & (! m : as . (g,m) : fc.<IR>) & as <= fc.<AS>
}"
```

Correspondingly, common_objects is the formal definition of a function which takes a set of attributes as of type 'b set and a formal context fc of type ('a,'b) formal_context_type and returns the set of objects (of type 'a set) which have all attributes in as.

Definition 3. *A* **Formal Concept** *of the context* $\mathbb{K} := (G, M, I)$ *is a pair* (A, B) *with* $A \subseteq G$, $B \subseteq M$, $A' = B$ *and* $B' = A$. *A is called the* **extent** *and B is called the* **intent** *of the formal concept* (A, B).

From the definition, formal concept type is formalized as a record type with fields extent and intent as:

```
record ('a,'b) formal_concept_type =
    extent          :: "'a set"
    intent          :: "'b set"
```

Similarly, through syntactic translations, the extent of a formal concept C is accessed as C.<E>, and the intent as C.<I>. The relation between the extent and the intent of a formal concept is checked with the boolean function FormalConcept. Given a tuple C of type formal_concept_type and a triple K which is of type formal_context_type, it checks if C is a formal concept of K. It is formalized as:

```
FormalConcept :: "('a,'b) formal_concept_type =>
    ('a,'b) formal_context_type => bool"
"FormalConcept C K == C.<E> <= K.<OS> & C.<I> <= K.<AS> &
    C.<E> = common_objects (C.<I>) K &
    common_attributes (C.<E>) K = C.<I>"
```

Proposition 1. *If T is an index set and, for every $t \in T$, $A_t \subseteq G$ is a set of objects, then*

$$\left(\bigcup_{t \in T} A_t \right)' = \bigcap_{t \in T} A'_t$$

The same holds for the sets of attributes.

The proposition is formalized as:

```
Goal "[| ! t : T . (F t) <= K.<OS> |] ==> (common_attributes (
UN t : T . (F t)) K) = (INT t : T . (common_attributes (F t) K))";
```

We are not going to give the proof here, the interested reader may see [4] and [15]. But we would like to draw attention to the following point: In the proof in [4], the case where the index set T can be empty is not worked out explicitly. But in the formalization we need to do a case analysis for T being empty or not, since the set theory does not have the convention about empty index sets. This case is handled with an axiom which states that common attributes of an empty object set is equal to the attribute set of the context. Similarly, an axiom is added which states that common objects of an empty attribute set is equal to the object set of the context.

Definition 4. *If (A_1, B_1) and (A_2, B_2) are concepts of a context, (A_1, B_1) is called a* **subconcept** *of (A_2, B_2), provided that $A_1 \subseteq A_2$ (which is equivalent to $B_2 \subseteq B_1$). In this case, (A_2, B_2) is a* **superconcept** *of (A_1, B_1) and the ordering is written as $(A_1, B_1) \leq (A_2, B_2)$. The relation $\leq$ is called the* **hierarchical**

order *(or simply* **order***) of the concepts. The set of all concepts of* (G, M, I) *ordered in this way is denoted by* $\mathfrak{B}(G, M, I)$ *and is called the* **Concept Lattice** *of the context* (G, M, I).

The concept lattice of a context K is formalized with the function ConceptLattice which takes a context K and returns the concept lattice of it as a partial order type:

```
ConceptLattice :: "('a,'b) formal_context_type =>
    ((('a,'b) formal_concept_type) potype)"
"ConceptLattice K == (|
    pset = {C . (FormalConcept C K)},
    order = { (C1,C2) . FormalConcept C1 K & FormalConcept C2 K &
        C1.<E> <= C2.<E> & C2.<I> <= C1.<I> } |)"
```

3.2 The Basic Theorem on Concept Lattices

Theorem 1 (The Basic Theorem on Concept Lattices). *The concept lattice* $\mathfrak{B}(G, M, I)$ *is a complete lattice in which infimum and supremum are given by:*

$$\bigwedge_{t \in T} (A_t, B_t) = \left(\bigcap_{t \in T} A_t, \left(\bigcup_{t \in T} B_t \right)'' \right)$$

$$\bigvee_{t \in T} (A_t, B_t) = \left(\left(\bigcup_{t \in T} A_t \right)'', \bigcap_{t \in T} B_t \right)$$

A complete lattice **V** *is isomorphic to* $\mathfrak{B}(G, M, I)$ *if and only if there are mappings* $\tilde{\gamma} : G \to V$ *and* $\tilde{\mu} : M \to V$ *such that* $\tilde{\gamma}(G)$ *is supremum-dense in* **V**, $\tilde{\mu}(M)$ *is infimum-dense in* **V** *and* gIm *is equivalent to* $\tilde{\gamma}g \leq \tilde{\mu}m$ *for all* $g \in G$ *and all* $m \in M$. *In particular,* $\mathbf{V} \cong \mathfrak{B}(V, V, \leq)$.

We prove the theorem in four major parts, as four lemmas. First we prove the claims about the infimum and supremum of a concept lattice, and then both directions of the double implication about the isomorphism.

The argument about the infimum is formalized as:

```
Goal "[| S <= (ConceptLattice K).<A> |] ==>
    isglb S (ConceptLattice K) (| extent = (INT C : S . C.<E>) ,
    intent = (common_attributes (common_objects
    (UN C : S . C.<I>) K) K) |)";
```

The `isglb` is a predicate from the underlying lattice theory. It checks if the third argument is the infimum of the set given as first argument in the partially ordered set given as the second argument. We start with simplifying the goal with the definition of `isglb`, and get three subgoals. First we prove that the concept argued as the infimum is in (`ConceptLattice K`), which means to prove that it is a formal concept of the context K. Then we prove that it is a lower bound by showing that it is less than or equal to all other formal concepts in S. As the last subgoal we prove that it is the greatest lower bound. The proof is totally 29 steps not including the number of steps of the auxiliary lemma used. It is stored as inf_cl for further use.

Correspondingly, the argument about the supremum is formalized as:

Goal "[| S <= (ConceptLattice K).<A> |] ==>
  islub S (ConceptLattice K) (| extent = (common_objects
  (common_attributes (UN C : S . C.<E>) K) K) ,
  intent = (INT C : S . C.<I>) |)";

Similar remarks as for the preceding argument apply here. The proof is totally 32 steps without counting the number of steps of the auxiliary lemmata used. It is named and stored as sup_cl for further use.

Next we prove the argument about the isomorphism. First, we prove the *only if* direction of the double implication. We formalized the statement as:

Goal "[| V : CompleteLattice |] ==>
  (isomorphic (ConceptLattice K) V) -->
  (? gamma mu . (supremum_dense (gamma ' (K.<OS>)) V) &
  (infimum_dense (mu ' (K.<AS>)) V) &
  (! g : K.<OS> . ! m : K.<AS> . ((g,m) :
  K.<IR>) = (((gamma g),(mu m)) : V.<r>)))";

For the special case $V = \mathfrak{B}(G, M, I)$, we first prove that $\tilde{\gamma}(G)$ is supremum-dense and $\tilde{\mu}(M)$ is infimum-dense in $\mathfrak{B}(G, M, I)$, and gIm is equivalent to $\tilde{\gamma}g \le \tilde{\mu}m$ for all $g \in G$ and all $m \in M$. The first two proofs are stored as the lemmata gamma_sup_dense and mu_inf_dense respectively. Later we prove these three properties for the general case V is isomorphic to $\mathfrak{B}(G, M, I)$ using the lemmata above together with the lemmata sup_dense_preserved and inf_dense_preserved. This completes the proof of the *only if* direction of the theorem. Without counting the steps of the auxiliary lemmata used, the proof is 70 steps long. It is stored as the lemma basic_thm_fwd.

Next we proceed with the proof of the *if* direction of the theorem. We formalized the statement as:

Goal "[| V : CompleteLattice |] ==>
  ? phi psi . ? gamma mu . (supremum_dense (gamma ' (K.<OS>)) V) &
  (infimum_dense (mu ' (K.<AS>)) V) & (! g : K.<OS> .
  ! m : K.<AS> . ((g,m) : K.<IR>)=(((gamma g),(mu m)) : V.<r>)) -->
  (order_preserving phi (ConceptLattice K) V) &
  (order_preserving psi V (ConceptLattice K)) &
  (my_inv phi psi ((ConceptLattice K).<A>) (V.<A>))";

(For this direction, the fact that isomorphism implies the order-embedding property is implicitly used in the book. But we proved this formally and stored as the lemma iso_imp_embd.) We start with proving that the maps φ and ψ are order-preserving. Then we prove that φ and ψ are inverse functions. We prove

Table 1. Notation index

Math. Notation	Isabelle Notation	Definition
$\prime$ (polymorphic)	common_attributes	Common Attributes of an object set
$\prime$ (polymorphic)	common_objects	Common Objects of an attribute set
(G, M, I)	K	Context K
$\mathfrak{B}(G, M, I)$	(ConceptLattice K)	Concept Lattice of the context K
$\bigwedge_{t \in T}(A_t, B_t)$	(glb S K)	Infimum of S in K
$\bigvee_{t \in T}(A_t, B_t)$	(lub S K)	Supremum of S in K
$\in$	:	In
$\wedge$	&	Conjunction
$\vee$	|	Disjunction
$\longrightarrow$	-->	Implication
$\forall t \in T.P(t)$	! t : T . (P t)	Universal Quantifier
$\exists t \in T.P(t)$	? t : T . (P t)	Existential Quantifier
$\subseteq$	<=	Subset or equal
$\bigcup_{t \in T} A_t$	UN t : T . (F t)	Indexed set union
$\bigcap_{t \in T} A_t$	INT t : T . (F t)	Indexed set intersection

this in two parts; first we show that ψ is the left-inverse of φ, then we show that it is also the right-inverse of φ. Having proved that φ and ψ are order-preserving inverse maps, we proved that φ is a lattice isomorphism. This completes the if direction of the proof. It is stored as the lemma basic_theorem_bwd. It is 286 steps without counting the steps of the auxiliary lemmata used.

4 Conclusion and Discussions

Although mathematics texts typically do not give the proofs in whole detail, they are understandable by human reader. In an informal proof, some details of the proof can be skipped relying on human intuition. But for a proof to be machine-checkable, every single step of it has to be stated formally. There should not be any gaps between proof steps, however minor they might be.

During our formalization, we noticed some of these kinds of gaps in the proofs. We have already mentioned the implicit treatment of empty index sets, empty object sets and empty attribute sets in the book. Furthermore, for connecting the proofs of the *only if* and *if* parts of the basic theorem, a lemma from lattice theory is used but it is not mentioned clearly, since it is supposedly well-known to mathematicians.

Separately, we examined the proof of basic theorem in the formal concept analysis chapter of a well-known book [2]. There, in the proof of *only if* direction of the basic theorem on page 71, we have uncovered a mistake apparently arising from misuse of overloaded symbols. It is written that the statement 'gIm if and only if $\tilde{\gamma}(g) \leq \tilde{\mu}(m)$ is in $\mathfrak{B}(G, M, I)$, for all g in G and for all m in M' is proved in 3.7. But the proof in 3.7 corresponds to the proof of the third subgoal of the *only if* direction of the Basic Theorem in the special case **L** is equal to $\mathfrak{B}(G, M, I)$. So it does not constitute a proof in the general case $\mathfrak{B}(G, M, I)$ is isomorphic to **L**. We think this part of the proof should be generalized to the isomorphism case. This is a testimony to the utility of formalization in revealing hidden gaps in published proofs.

Acknowledgments

The authors appreciate the help they received from the members of the isabelle-users mailing list, particularly Larry Paulson and Tobias Nipkow.

References

1. Berghofer, S.: Program extraction in simply-typed higher order logic. LNCS, Vol. 2646, Springer-Verlag (2002)
2. Davey, B.A., Priestley, H.A.: Introduction to lattices and order. 2nd edition. Cambridge University Press (2002)
3. Ganter, B., Wille, R.: Applied lattice theory: formal concept analysis. (1997) http://www.math.tu-dresden.de/ ganter/concept.ps
4. Ganter, B., Wille, R.: Formal concept analysis—Mathematical foundations. Springer-Verlag, Heidelberg (1999)
5. Kammueller, F.: Theory Tarski. http://isabelle.in.tum.de/library/HOL/ex/Tarski.html (1999)
6. Krohn, U., Davies, N.J., Weeks, R.: Concept lattices for knowledge management. BT Technology Journal **17** (1999)
7. Nipkow, T., Paulson, L.C., Wenzel, M.: A proof assistant for higher-order logic. LNCS, Vol. 2283, Springer-Verlag (2002)
8. Nipkow, T., Paulson, L.C., Wenzel, M.: Isabelle's logics: HOL. http://isabelle.in.tum.de/doc/logics-HOL.pdf
9. Park, Y.: Software retrieval by samples using concept analysis. Journal of Systems and Software **1** (2000)
10. Paulson, L.C.: Isabelle: A generic theorem prover. In: Odifreddi, P. (ed.): Logic and Computer Science, Academic Press (1990) 361–386
11. Paulson, L.C.: The Isabelle reference manual. http://isabelle.in.tum.de/doc/ref.pdf
12. Puitg F., Dufourd, J.F.: Formalizing mathematics in higher-order logic: A case study in geometric modelling. Theoretical Computer Science **234** (2000)
13. Rudnicki, P.: An overview of the Mizar project. http://mizar.org/project/bibliography.html
14. Schwarzweller, C.: Mizar formalization of concept lattices. Mechanized Mathematics and its Applications **1** (2000)
15. Sertkaya, B.: Proof of the basic theorem on concept lattices in Isabelle/HOL. M.Sc. thesis, Department of Computer Engineering, Middle East Technical University, Ankara, Turkey (2003)
16. Wenzel, M.: Isabelle/Isar reference manual. http://isabelle.in.tum.de/doc/isar-ref.pdf
17. Wenzel, M.: Isabelle/Isar—A versatile environment for human-readable formal proof documents. PhD thesis, Institut für Informatik, Technische Universität München, (2002) http://tumb1.biblio.tu-munchen.de/publ/dis/in/2002/wenzel.html
18. Wille, T.: Concept lattices and conceptual knowledge systems. Computers & Mathematics with Applications (1992)

System BV without the Equalities for Unit

Ozan Kahramanoğulları

Computer Science Institute, University of Leipzig
International Center for Computational Logic, TU Dresden
ozan@informatik.uni-leipzig.de

Abstract. System BV is an extension of multiplicative linear logic with a non-commutative self-dual operator. In this paper, we present systems equivalent to system BV where equalities for unit are oriented from left to right and new structural rules are introduced to preserve completeness. While the first system allows units to appear in the structures, the second system makes it possible to completely remove the units from the language of BV by proving the normal forms of the structures that are provable in BV. The resulting systems provide a better performance in automated proof search by disabling redundant applications of inference rules due to the unit. As evidence, we provide a comparison of the performance of these systems in a Maude implementation.

1 Introduction

The calculus of structures is a proof theoretical formalism, like natural deduction, the sequent calculus and proof nets, for specifying logical systems syntactically. It was conceived in [6] to introduce the logical system BV, which extends multiplicative linear logic by a non-commutative self-dual logical operator. Then it turned out to yield systems with interesting and exciting properties for existing logics and new insights to proof theory [1,12]. In [14], Tiu showed that BV is not definable in any sequent calculus system. Bruscoli showed in [2] that the non-commutative operator of BV captures precisely the sequentiality notion of process algebra, in particular CCS.

In contrast to sequent calculus, the calculus of structures does not rely on the notion of main connective and, like in term rewriting, it permits the application of the inference rules deep inside a formula (structure) which are considered equivalent modulo different equational theories (associativity, commutativity, unit, etc.). This resemblance allows us to express systems in the calculus of structures as term rewriting systems modulo equational theories [8].

In [9], we presented a Maude [3,4] implementation of system BV. The language Maude allows implementing term rewriting systems modulo equational theories due to the built in very fast matching algorithm that supports different combinations of associative, commutative equational theories, also with the presence of units. However, we observed that, often, units cause redundant matchings of the inference rules where the premise and conclusion at the application of the inference rule are equivalent structures.

In this paper, we present systems equivalent to BV where rule applications with respect to the equalities for unit are made explicit. By orienting the equalities for unit, we disallow redundant applications of inference rules. Then, in order to preserve completeness, we add structural rules that are instances of the rules of system BV. This way, resulting systems, depending on the length of the derivations, perform much better in automated proof search in our Maude implementation.

The rest of the paper is organized as follows: we first summarize the notions and notations of the calculus of structures and system BV. We then present the systems that result from removing the equalities for unit from system BV. After comparing the performance of these systems in our Maude implementation, we conclude with discussions and future work.

2 The Calculus of Structures and System BV

In this section, we shortly present the calculus of structures and the system BV, following [6].

In the language of BV atoms are denoted by $a, b, c, \ldots$ Structures are denoted by $R, S, T, \ldots$ and generated by

$$S ::= \circ \mid a \mid \langle \underbrace{S; \ldots; S}_{>0} \rangle \mid [\underbrace{S, \ldots, S}_{>0}] \mid (\underbrace{S, \ldots, S}_{>0}) \mid \bar{S} \quad ,$$

where $\circ$, the *unit*, is not an atom. $\langle S; \ldots; S \rangle$ is called a *seq structure*, $[S, \ldots, S]$ is called a *par structure*, and $(S, \ldots, S)$ is called a *copar structure*, $\bar{S}$ is the *negation* of the structure S. Structures are considered equivalent modulo the relation $\approx$, which is the smallest congruence relation induced by the equations shown in Figure 1[1]. There R, T and U stand for finite, non-empty sequence of structures. A *structure context*, denoted as in $S\{\ \}$, is a structure with a hole that does not appear in the scope of negation. The structure R is a *substructure* of $S\{R\}$ and $S\{\ \}$ is its *context*. Context braces are omitted if no ambiguity is possible: for instance $S[R, T]$ stands for $S\{[R, T]\}$. A structure, or a structure context, is in *normal form* when the only negated structures appearing in it are atoms, no unit $\circ$ appears in it.

There is a straightforward correspondence between structures not involving seq and formulae of multiplicative linear logic (MLL). For example $[(a, b), \bar{c}, \bar{d}]$ corresponds to $((a \otimes b) \mathbin{\bar{\otimes}} c^\perp \mathbin{\bar{\otimes}} d^\perp)$, and vice versa. Units 1 and $\perp$ are mapped into $\circ$, since $1 \equiv \perp$, when the rules mix and mix0 are added to MLL. For a more detailed discussion on the proof theory of BV and the precise relation between BV and MLL, the reader is referred to [6].

In the calculus of structures, an *inference rule* is a scheme of the kind $\rho \dfrac{T}{R}$, where ρ is the *name* of the rule, T is its *premise* and R is its *conclusion*. A

---

[1] In [6] axioms for context closure are added. However, because each equational system includes the axioms of equality context closure follows from the substitutivity axioms.

Associativity	Commutativity	Negation
$\langle R;\langle T\rangle;U\rangle \approx \langle R;T;U\rangle$	$[R,T]\approx[T,R]$	$\bar{\circ}\approx\circ$
$[R,[T]]\approx[R,T]$	$(R,T)\approx(T,R)$	$\overline{\langle R;T\rangle}\approx\langle\bar{R};\bar{T}\rangle$
$(R,(T))\approx(R,T)$	**Units**	$\overline{[R,T]}\approx(\bar{R},\bar{T})$
Singleton	$\langle\circ;R\rangle\approx\langle R;\circ\rangle\approx\langle R\rangle$	$\overline{(R,T)}\approx[\bar{R},\bar{T}]$
$\langle R\rangle\approx[R]\approx(R)\approx R$	$[\circ,R]\approx[R]$	$\bar{\bar{R}}\approx R$
	$(\circ,R)\approx(R)$	

Fig. 1. The equational system underlying BV

typical (deep) inference rule has the shape $\rho\,\dfrac{S\{T\}}{S\{R\}}$ and specifies the implication $T\Rightarrow R$ inside a generic context $S\{\ \}$, which is the implication being modeled in the system[2]. When premise and conclusion in an instance of an inference rule are equivalent, that instance is *trivial*, otherwise it is *non-trivial*. An inference rule is called an *axiom* if its premise is empty. Rules with empty contexts correspond to the case of the sequent calculus.

A (formal) *system* $\mathscr{S}$ is a set of inference rules. A derivation Δ in a certain formal system is a finite chain of instances of inference rules in the system. A derivation can consist of just one structure. The topmost structure in a derivation, if present, is called the *premise* of the derivation, and the bottommost structure is called its *conclusion*. A derivation Δ whose premise is T, conclusion is R, and inference rules are in $\mathscr{S}$ will be written as $\begin{array}{c}T\\ \Delta\|\mathscr{S}\\ R\end{array}$. Similarly, $\begin{array}{c}\\ \Pi\|\mathscr{S}\\ R\end{array}$ will denote a *proof* Π which is a finite derivation whose topmost inference rule is an axiom. The *length* of a derivation (proof) is the number of instances of inference rules appearing in it.

A rule ρ is *derivable for a system* $\mathscr{S}$ if for every instance of $\rho\,\dfrac{T}{R}$ there is a derivation $\begin{array}{c}T\\ \|\mathscr{S}\\ R\end{array}$. Two systems $\mathscr{S}$ and $\mathscr{S}'$ are *strongly equivalent* if for every derivation $\begin{array}{c}T\\ \Delta\|\mathscr{S}\\ R\end{array}$ there exists a derivation $\begin{array}{c}T\\ \Delta\|\mathscr{S}'\\ R\end{array}$, and vice versa. Two systems $\mathscr{S}$ and $\mathscr{S}'$ are *weakly equivalent* if for every proof of a structure T in system $\mathscr{S}$, there exists a proof of T in system $\mathscr{S}'$, and vice versa. They are *strongly (weakly) equivalent with respect to normal forms* if the above statements hold for a normal form of T.

[2] Due to duality between $T\Rightarrow R$ and $\bar{R}\Rightarrow\bar{T}$, rules come in pairs of dual rules: a down-version and an up-version. For instance, the dual of the $\mathsf{ai}\!\downarrow$ rule in Figure 2 is the cut rule. In this paper we only consider the down rules which provide a sound and complete system.

$$\circ\downarrow \frac{}{\circ} \qquad \mathsf{ai}\downarrow \frac{S\{\circ\}}{S[a,\bar{a}]} \qquad \mathsf{s}\frac{S([R,T],U)}{S[(R,U),T]} \qquad \mathsf{q}\downarrow \frac{S\langle[R,U];[T,V]\rangle}{S[\langle R;T\rangle,\langle U;V\rangle]}$$

Fig. 2. System BV

The system $\{\circ\downarrow, \mathsf{ai}\downarrow, \mathsf{s}, \mathsf{q}\downarrow\}$, shown in Figure 2, is denoted BV and called *basic system* V, where V stands for one non-commutative operator[3]. The rules of the system are called *unit* ($\circ\downarrow$), *atomic interaction* ($\mathsf{ai}\downarrow$), *switch* (s) and *seq* ($\mathsf{q}\downarrow$).

3 System BVn

The system shown in Figure 3 is called BVn. Structures on which system BVn is defined are as in the previous section, with the only difference that the equalities for unit do not apply anymore.

Proposition 1. *Every* BV *structure* S *can be transformed to one of its normal forms* S' *by applying only the rules* $\{\mathsf{u}_1\downarrow, \mathsf{u}_2\downarrow, \mathsf{u}_3\downarrow, \mathsf{u}_4\downarrow\}$ *in Figure 3 bottom-up and the equalities for negation in Figure 1 from left to right.*

Proof: Observe that applying the rules $\{\mathsf{u}_1\downarrow, \mathsf{u}_2\downarrow, \mathsf{u}_3\downarrow, \mathsf{u}_4\downarrow\}$ bottom up corresponds to applying the equalities for unit in Figure 1 from left to right. The result follows from the fact that the corresponding term rewriting system is terminating and confluent, and applicability of these rules contradicts with a structure being in normal form. □

Proposition 2. *The rules* $\mathsf{q}_1\downarrow$, $\mathsf{q}_2\downarrow$, $\mathsf{q}_3\downarrow$, *and* $\mathsf{q}_4\downarrow$ *are derivable for* $\{\mathsf{q}\downarrow\}$. *The rules* s_1 *and* s_2 *are derivable for* $\{\mathsf{s}\}$.

Proof:

- For the rule $\mathsf{q}_1\downarrow$ take the rule $\mathsf{q}\downarrow$.
- For the rule $\mathsf{q}_2\downarrow$, $\mathsf{q}_2\downarrow$, $\mathsf{q}_4\downarrow$, respectively, take the following derivations, respectively:

$$\mathsf{q}\downarrow \frac{=\frac{\langle R;T\rangle}{\langle[R,\circ];[\circ,T]\rangle}}{\frac{[\langle R;\circ\rangle,\langle\circ;T\rangle]}{=[R,T]}} \qquad \mathsf{q}\downarrow \frac{=\frac{\langle[R,T];U\rangle}{\langle[R,T];[\circ,U]\rangle}}{\frac{[\langle R;\circ\rangle,\langle T;U\rangle]}{=[R,\langle T;U\rangle]}} \qquad \mathsf{q}\downarrow \frac{=\frac{\langle T;[R,U]\rangle}{\langle[\circ,T];[R,U]\rangle}}{\frac{[\langle\circ;R\rangle,\langle T;U\rangle]}{=[R,\langle T;U\rangle]}}$$

- For the rule s_1 take the rule s.
- For the rule s_2 take the following derivation:

$$\mathsf{s}\frac{=\frac{(R,T)}{([\circ,T],R)}}{\frac{[(\circ,R),T]}{=[R,T]}} \qquad \qquad □$$

---

[3] This name is due to the intuition that W stands for two non-commutative operators.

$$\circ\downarrow \frac{-}{\circ} \qquad \mathsf{ai}\downarrow \frac{S\{\circ\}}{S[a,\bar{a}]} \qquad \mathsf{s}_1 \frac{S([R,T],U)}{S[(R,U),T]} \qquad \mathsf{s}_2 \frac{S(R,T)}{S[R,T]}$$

$$\mathsf{q}_1\downarrow \frac{S\langle[R,T];[U,V]\rangle}{S[\langle R;U\rangle,\langle T;V\rangle]} \qquad \mathsf{q}_2\downarrow \frac{S\langle R;T\rangle}{S[R,T]} \qquad \mathsf{q}_3\downarrow \frac{S\langle[R,T];U\rangle}{S[R,\langle T;U\rangle]} \qquad \mathsf{q}_4\downarrow \frac{S\langle T;[R,U]\rangle}{S[R,\langle T;U\rangle]}$$

$$\mathsf{u}_1\downarrow \frac{S\{R\}}{S[R,\circ]} \qquad \mathsf{u}_2\downarrow \frac{S\{R\}}{S(R,\circ)} \qquad \mathsf{u}_3\downarrow \frac{S\{R\}}{S\langle R;\circ\rangle} \qquad \mathsf{u}_4\downarrow \frac{S\{R\}}{S\langle\circ;R\rangle}$$

Fig. 3. System BVn

Theorem 1. *For every derivation* $\Delta \Vert \mathsf{BV}$ *there exists a derivation* $\Delta' \Vert \mathsf{BVn}$ *where* W' *is a normal form of the structure* W. (with W over Q on left, W' over Q on right)

Proof: Observe that every derivation Δ in BV can be equivalently written as a derivation where all the structures are in normal form. Let us denote with Δ these derivations where there are only occurrences of structures in normal form. From Proposition 1 we get a normal form Q' of Q going up in a derivation. With structural induction on Δ we will construct the derivation Δ'

- If Δ is $\circ\downarrow \frac{-}{\circ}$ then take $\Delta' = \Delta$.

- If, for an atom a, $\mathsf{ai}\downarrow \frac{S\{\circ\}}{S[a,\bar{a}]}$ is the last rule applied in Δ, then by Proposition 1 and by the induction hypothesis there is a derivation $\overset{W'}{\underset{T}{\Vert}}\mathsf{BVn}$ where T is a normal form of $S\{\circ\}$. The following cases exhaust the possibilities.

- If $S[a,\bar{a}] = S'[P,[a,\bar{a}]]$ then take the following derivation.

$$\mathsf{u}_1\downarrow \frac{S'\{P\}}{\mathsf{ai}\downarrow \frac{S'[P,\circ]}{S'[P,[a,\bar{a}]]}} \quad .$$

- If $S[a,\bar{a}] = S'(P,[a,\bar{a}])$ then take the following derivation.

$$\mathsf{u}_2\downarrow \frac{S'\{P\}}{\mathsf{ai}\downarrow \frac{S'(P,\circ)}{S'(P,[a,\bar{a}])}} \quad .$$

- If $S[a,\bar{a}] = S'\langle P;[a,\bar{a}]\rangle$ then take the following derivation.

$$\mathsf{u}_3\downarrow \frac{S'\{P\}}{S'\langle P;\circ\rangle}$$
$$\mathsf{ai}\downarrow \frac{}{S'\langle P;[a,\bar{a}]\rangle}$$

- If $S[a,\bar{a}] = S'\langle[a,\bar{a}];P\rangle$ then take the following derivation.

$$\mathsf{u}_4\downarrow \frac{S'\{P\}}{S'\langle\circ;P\rangle}$$
$$\mathsf{ai}\downarrow \frac{}{S'\langle[a,\bar{a}];P\rangle}$$

- If $\mathsf{s}\dfrac{P}{Q}$ is the last rule applied in Δ where $Q = S[(R,T),U]$ for a context S and structures R, T and U, then by induction hypothesis there is a derivation $\begin{array}{c}W'\\\|\mathsf{BVn}\\P\end{array}$.
The following cases exhaust the possibilities:
  - If $R \neq \circ$, $T \neq \circ$ and $U \neq \circ$, then apply the rule s_1 to Q'.
  - If $R = \circ$, $T \neq \circ$ and $U \neq \circ$ then $Q' = S'[T,U]$ where S' is a normal form of context S. Apply the rule s_2 to Q'.
  - Other 6 cases are trivial instances of the s rule. Take $P = Q'$.

- If $\mathsf{q}\downarrow\dfrac{P}{Q}$ is the last rule applied in Δ where $Q = S[\langle R;T\rangle,\langle U;V\rangle]$ for a context S and structures R, T, U and V, then by induction hypothesis there is a derivation $\begin{array}{c}W'\\\|\mathsf{BVn}\\P\end{array}$. The following cases exhaust the possibilities:
  - If $R \neq \circ$, $T \neq \circ$, $U \neq \circ$ and $V \neq \circ$, then apply the rule $\mathsf{q}_1\downarrow$ to Q'.
  - If $R = \circ$, $T \neq \circ$, $U \neq \circ$ and $V \neq \circ$ then $Q' = S'[T,\langle U;V\rangle]$ where S' is a normal form of context S. Apply the rule $\mathsf{q}_4\downarrow$ to Q'.
  - If $R \neq \circ$, $T = \circ$, $U \neq \circ$ and $V \neq \circ$ then $Q' = S'[R,\langle U;V\rangle]$ where S' is a normal form of context S. Apply the rule $\mathsf{q}_3\downarrow$ to Q'.
  - If $R \neq \circ$, $T \neq \circ$, $U = \circ$ and $V \neq \circ$ then $Q' = S'[\langle R;T\rangle,V]$ where S' is a normal form of context S. Apply the rule $\mathsf{q}_4\downarrow$ to Q'.
  - If $R \neq \circ$, $T \neq \circ$, $U \neq \circ$ and $V = \circ$ then $Q' = S'[\langle R;T\rangle,U]$ where S' is a normal form of context S. Apply the rule $\mathsf{q}_3\downarrow$ to Q'.
  - If $R \neq \circ$, $T = \circ$, $U = \circ$ and $V \neq \circ$ then $Q' = S'[R,V]$ where S' is a normal form of context S. Apply the rule $\mathsf{q}_2\downarrow$ to Q'.
  - Other 10 cases are trivial instances of the $\mathsf{q}\downarrow$ rule. Take $P = Q'$. □

Corollary 1. *System* BV *and system* BVn *are strongly equivalent with respect to normal forms.*

Proof: From Proposition 2 it follows that the derivations in BVn are also derivations in BV. Derivations in BV are translated to derivations in BVn by Theorem 1. □

Remark 1. From the view point of bottom-up proof search, rule s_2 is a redundant rule since the structures in a copar structure can not interact with each other. Hence, it does not make any sense to disable the interaction between two structures by applying this rule in proof search. However, in order to preserve completeness for arbitrary derivations this rule is added to the system.

4 System BVu

With the light of the above remark and observations that we made while proving Theorem 1, it is possible to improve further on the rules of system BVn: the system BVu in Figure 4, like system BVn, does not allow the application of the equalities for unit. Furthermore, in this system, we merge each one of the rules for unit $\{u_1\downarrow, u_2\downarrow, u_3\downarrow, u_4\downarrow\}$ in ¡Figure 3 with the rule $ai\downarrow$ since the rules for unit are used only after rule $ai\downarrow$ is applied in a bottom-up proof search. This way we get the rules $\{ai_1\downarrow, ai_2\downarrow, ai_3\downarrow, ai_4\downarrow\}$.

$$ax \frac{}{[a,\bar{a}]} \qquad s_1 \frac{S([R,T],U)}{S[(R,U),T]}$$

$$ai_1\downarrow \frac{S\{R\}}{S[R,[a,\bar{a}]]} \qquad ai_2\downarrow \frac{S\{R\}}{S(R,[a,\bar{a}])} \qquad ai_3\downarrow \frac{S\{R\}}{S\langle R;[a,\bar{a}]\rangle} \qquad ai_4\downarrow \frac{S\{R\}}{S\langle[a,\bar{a}];R\rangle}$$

$$q_1\downarrow \frac{S\langle[R,T];[U,V]\rangle}{S[\langle R;U\rangle,\langle T;V\rangle]} \qquad q_2\downarrow \frac{S\langle R;T\rangle}{S[R,T]} \qquad q_3\downarrow \frac{S\langle[R,T];U\rangle}{S[R,\langle T;U\rangle]} \qquad q_4\downarrow \frac{S\langle T;[R,U]\rangle}{S[R,\langle T;U\rangle]}$$

Fig. 4. System BVu

Corollary 2. *System* BV *and system* BVu *are equivalent with respect to normal forms.*

Proof: It is immediate that the rules $ai_1\downarrow$, $ai_2\downarrow$, $ai_3\downarrow$, $ai_4\downarrow$ and ax are derivable (sound) for system BVn. Completeness follows from the proof of Theorem 1 and Remark 1. □

The following proposition helps to understand why BVu provides shorter proofs than BVn.

Proposition 3. *Let* R *be a* BV *structure in normal form with* n *number of positive atoms. If* R *has a proof in* BVn *with length* k, *then* R *has a proof in* BVu *with length* $k - n$.

Proof: (Sketch) By induction on the number of positive atoms in R, together with the observation that while going up in the proof of R in BVn, each positive atom must be annihilated with its negation by an application of the rule $ai\downarrow$ and then the resulting structure must be transformed to a normal form by equivalently removing the unit o with an application of one of the rules $u_1\downarrow, u_2\downarrow, u_3\downarrow$ and $u_4\downarrow$. In BVn these two steps are replaced by a single application of one of the rules $ai_1\downarrow, ai_2\downarrow, ai_3\downarrow$ and $ai_4\downarrow$. □

5 Implementation and Performance Comparison

In an implementation of the above systems, the structures must be matched modulo an equational theory. In the case of system BV this equational theory is the union of the AC1 theory for par, the AC1 theory for copar and A1 theory for seq structures, where 1 denotes the unit ∘ shared by these structures. However, in the case of BVn the equalities for unit become redundant, since their role in the rules is made explicit. This way, in contrast to the BV structures, the equivalence class of BVn structures become finite and redundant matchings of structures with rules are disabled. This results in a significant gain in the performance in automated proof search and derivation search.

In [8], we showed that systems in the calculus of structures can be expressed as term rewriting systems modulo equational theories. Exploiting the fact that the Maude System [3, 4] allows implementing term rewriting systems modulo equational theories, in [9], we presented a Maude implementation of system BV. There we also provided a general recipe for implementing systems in the calculus of structures and described the use of the relevant Maude commands. Then, we implemented the systems BVn and BVu. All these modules are available for download at http://www.informatik.uni-leipzig.de/~ozan/maude_cos.html.

Below is a comparison of these systems in our implementation of these systems on some examples of proof search and derivation search queries. (All the experiments below are performed on an Intel Pentium 1400 MHz Processor.)

Consider the following example taken from [2] where we search for a proof of a *process structure*.

```
search in BV  : [a,[< a ; [c,- a] >,< - a ; - c >]] =>+ o .
search in BVn : [a,[< a ; [c,- a] >,< - a ; - c >]] =>+ o .
search in BVu : [a,[< a ; [c,- a] >,< - a ; - c >]] =>+ [A,- A] .
```

	finds a proof		search terminates	
	in # millisec.	after # rewrites	in # millisec.	after # rewrites
BV	1370	281669	5530	1100629
BVn	500	59734	560	65273
BVu	0	581	140	15244

When we search for the proof of a similar query which involves also copar structures we get the following results.

```
search [- c,[< a ; {c,- b} >,< - a ; b >]] => o .
```

	finds a proof		search terminates	
	in # millisec.	after # rewrites	in # millisec.	after # rewrites
BV	950	196866	1490	306179
BVn	120	12610	120	12720
BVu	10	1416	60	4691

It is also possible to search for arbitrary derivations. For instance, consider the derivation

$$\langle d; e \rangle$$
$$\| \text{BVn}$$
$$[\bar{a}, \langle a; d; \bar{b} \rangle, \langle b; e; \bar{c} \rangle, c]$$

with the query below, which results in the table below.

```
search [ - a , [ < a ; < d ; - b > > , [ < b ; < e ; - c > > , c ]]]
                                                        =>+ < d ; e > .
```

	finds a proof		search terminates	
	in # millisec.	after # rewrites	in # millisec.	after # rewrites
BV	494030	66865734	721530	91997452
BVn	51410	4103138	51410	4103152
BVu	10090	806417	10440	822161

In all the above experiments it is important to observe that, besides the increase in the speed of search, number of rewrites performed differ dramatically between the runs of the same search query on systems BV, BVn and BVu.

6 Discussion

We presented two systems equivalent to system BV where equalities for unit become redundant. Within a Maude implementation of these systems, we also showed that, by disabling the redundant applications of the inference rules, these systems provide a better performance in automated proof search.

Our results find an immediate application for a fragment of CCS which was shown to be equivalent to BV in [2]. Furthermore, we believe that the methods presented in this paper can be analogously applied to the existing systems in the calculus of structures for classical logic [1] and linear logic [12], which are readily expressed as Maude modules.

However, termination of proof search in our implementation is a consequence of BV being a multiplicative logic. Although, the new systems presented in this paper improve the performance by making the rule applications explicit and shortening the proofs by merging rule steps, due to the exponential blow up in the search space, an implementation for practical purposes that allows "bigger structures" will require introduction of strategies at the Maude meta-level [5], in the lines of uniform proofs [11] and Guglielmi's *Splitting Theorem* [6].

System NEL [7] is a Turing-complete extension of BV [13] with the exponentials of linear logic. In [10], we employed system NEL for concurrent conjunctive planning problems. Future work includes carrying our results to NEL and linear logic systems in the calculus of structures [12].

Acknowledgments

This work has been supported by the DFG Graduiertenkolleg 446. I would like to thank Alessio Guglielmi, Steffen Hölldobler, Roy Dyckhoff, and anonymous referees for valuable remarks and improvements.

References

1. Brünnler, K.: Deep inference and symmetry in classical proofs. PhD. Thesis, Technische Universität Dresden (2003)
2. Bruscoli, P.: A purely logical account of sequentiality in proof search. In: Stuckey, P.J. (ed.): Logic Programming, 18th International Conference. LNCS, Vol. 2401. Springer-Verlag (2002) 302–316
3. Clavel, M., Durán, F., Eker, S., Lincoln, P., Martí-Oliet, N., Meseguer, J., Talcott, C.: The Maude 2.0 system. In: Nieuwenhuis, R. (ed.): Rewriting Techniques and Applications, Proceedings of the 14th International Conference. (2003)
4. Clavel, M., Durán, F., Eker, S., Lincoln, P., Martí-Oliet, N., Meseguer, J., Talcott, C.: Maude 2.1 manual. Technical Report, Computer Science Laboratory, SRI International, http://maude.cs.uiuc.edu/manual/ (2004)
5. Clavel, M., Durán, F., Eker, S., Meseguer, J., Stehr M.-O.: Maude as a formal meta-tool. In: Wing, J.M., Woodcock, J., Davies, J. (eds.): FM'99 — Formal Methods, World Congress on Formal Methods in the Development of Computing Systems, Toulouse, France, September 20–24, 1999 Proceedings, Volume II. LNCS, Vol. 1709, Springer-Verlag (1999) 1684–1703
6. Gugliealmi, A.: A system of interaction and structure. Technical Report, WV-02-10, TU Dresden (2002)
7. Guglielmi, A., Straßburger, L.: A non-commutative extension of MELL. In: Baaz M., Voronkov, A. (eds.): LPAR 2002. LNAI, Vol. 2514. Springer-Verlag (2002) 231–246
8. Hölldobler, S., Kahramanoğulları, O.: From the calculus of structures to term rewriting systems. Technical Report, WV-04-03, TU Dresden (2004)
9. Kahramanoğulları, O.: Implementing system BV of the calculus of structures in Maude. In: Proceedings of the ESSLLI-2004 Student Session, Université Henri Poincaré, Nancy, France. (2004)
10. Kahramanoğulları, O.: Plans as formulae with a non-commutative operator. Technical Report, TU Dresden (2004)
11. Miller, D., Nadathur, G., Pfenning, F., Scedrov, A.: Uniform proofs as a foundation for logic programming. Annals of Pure and Applied Logic **51** (1991) 125–157
12. Straßburger, L.: Linear logic and noncommutativity in the calculus of structures. PhD. Thesis, TU Dresden (2003)
13. Straßburger, L.: System NEL is undecidable. In: De Queiroz, R., Pimentel, E., Figueiredo, L. (eds.): 10th Workshop on Logic, Language, Information and Computation (WoLLIC). Electronic Notes in Theoretical Computer Science **84** (2003)
14. Tiu, A.F.: Properties of a logical system in the calculus of structures. Technical Report, WV-01-06, TU Dresden (2001)

Comparison of Different Variable and Value Order Strategies for the Optimum Solution of a Single Machine Scheduling Problem with Sequence-Dependent Setups*

Seyda Topaloglu and Irem Ozkarahan

Department of Industrial Engineering, Dokuz Eylul University, 35100 Izmir, Turkey
{seyda.topaloglu,irem.ozkarahan}@deu.edu.tr

Abstract. The job sequencing problem for a single machine with sequence-dependent setups is solved using the constraint programming (CP) and mixed-integer programming (MIP) approaches. For the CP search, ten different variable and value ordering heuristics are tested using both the CP model and/or the combined model of the MIP and CP formulations. Some of these heuristics exploit problem specific data like setup cost and due date. Others rely on hybrid strategies that use the linear programming (LP) solver within the CP search or direct the search using the initial feasible solution obtained from the MIP model. A comparative analysis of the search heuristics and the CP and MIP solvers has been given with respect to the solution times. The research results indicate that the CP solver finds the optimum solution in a very short time compared to the MIP solver as the number of jobs to be scheduled increases.

1 Introduction

This is a single machine problem with sequence-dependent setups between the consecutive jobs. Jobs are grouped into different families according to the similarity of their operations so that all the jobs in a particular family need the same or similar setup. It should be noted that no setup is required for a job if it belongs to the same family of the previously processed job. On the other hand, a setup time is required at the start of the schedule when the machine switches from processing jobs in one family to jobs in another family. Batching means the grouping of jobs of one family together. Large batches have the advantage of high machine utilization because the number of setups is small. On the other hand, large batches may increase inventory as well as delay the delivery time of a job belonging to a different family. The fundamental planning problem here is to find a tradeoff between productivity and customer service quality in order to achieve a good schedule. For this reason, the problem can be referred to as the *batch sequencing problem* (BSP). As the name characterizes, not only the sequence of jobs needs to be determined, but also the grouping of jobs into batches is to be considered.

---

*This research project has been partially supported by the Dokuz Eylul University under research project #0922.01.01.04.

The BSP is a combinatorial scheduling problem which is NP-hard as shown in Monma and Potts [1]. MIP and CP are two alternative approaches to modeling and solving combinatorial optimization problems (COPs). In both cases, the solution process involves a tree search and the key to success is to adopt a good branching strategy where the search can be completed relatively quickly [2]. In MIP, an LP solver is required for solving the relaxation of the problem, giving either infeasibility or a lower bound on the objective function. Most of the modern software (e.g. CPLEX, XPRESS) applies the branch and bound technique for solving MIP problems. The most influential strategic choices for this method are the selections of which variable and which node to branch on next. Today, modern MIP solvers include built-in variable and node choice strategies such as *maximum integer feasibility* and *maximum cost evaluation* for variable choice strategies, and *minimum deterioration value in objective function* and *minimum number non-integer variables* for node choice strategies.

As indicated in Harjunkoski et al. [3], the effectiveness of the MIP methods also depends on the size of LP subproblems, and on the gap between the objective value for the optimal solution and the initial LP subproblem. To strengthen the relaxation gap, branch and cut algorithms are used in which extra cuts are added to the MIP problem.

CP has a complete search mechanism based on enumeration that produces a search tree over the solution space. It has a user-defined search strategy based on the variable choice and the order in which values are assigned during enumeration. This process is repeated until all variables are assigned values. Here, the key to success is to find efficient variable and value orderings that exploit problem specific features and complement the underlying constraint solver's own searching techniques. The search reduction in CP is based on constraint propagation through local consistency techniques [4]. These techniques logically exclude in advance certain assignments to variables that have not yet been enumerated.

Darby-Dowman and Little [2] and Puget and Lustig [5] worked on a number of models for different COPs, and they presented an analysis of the performances of MIP and CP approaches with respect to the problem and model characteristics. Accordingly, MIP is very efficient when relaxation is tight and the models have a structure that can be effectively exploited. It may be difficult to solve a MIP problem if the feasible linear region cannot identify the feasible integer region. Besides, the size of a MIP model is generally a factor that affects its performance, whereas for CP, the size of a model is not a particular relevant concept; rather it is the size of the search space and the effectiveness of constraints that reduce this search space.

MIP has the advantage of evaluating the effect of all constraints simultaneously and has the ability to detect global infeasibility, which CP lacks. The global linear consistency is checked at every node in MIP. On the other hand, CP evaluates the effects of constraints sequentially by communicating through the domains of the variables. The initial preprocessing done to define variable bounds in MIP is a form of domain reduction and constraint propagation.

CP allows treating the problem variables as computer programming variables and a variable selection strategy can be specified using information from the model of the problem. However, in MIP no information can be used. Instead, there exist several heuristics that are used to choose the variable to branch based on the solution of the LP relaxation that is solved at each node.

The prospects of CP are good on those problems related to known problem types for which good solution heuristics are available. However, a good heuristic will only lead to a good first solution that is not necessarily optimal and the overall performance will be affected by the extent to which the first solution reduces the search space. Thus, the combination of a search strategy based on a good heuristic and a tight formulation is a strong indicator of CP success. The attempts to find a good solution strategy using MIP are based on the mathematical properties of the model and not on the original problem. Therefore, if it succeeds, this can be attributed to the strength of the methods developed independent of the specific problem being addressed. But, when the attempts fail, it will be a disadvantage that the important features of the original problem cannot be used to direct the search for a solution.

The remainder of this paper is as follows: In Section 2, the MIP and CP models for the given problem are presented and the combined MIP/CP model is described. Section 3 presents the proposed CP search procedures. Section 4 provides a comparative analysis of the performances of the search procedures and the CP and MIP solvers with respect to the solution times obtained. Finally, in Section 5 concluding remarks are given.

2 Model Formulations

In this section, MIP, CP, and combined MIP/CP models are given. The proposed MIP model is developed using the batch sequencing model of Jordan and Drexl [6] and the TSP-based model in Brandimarte and Villa [7], which minimizes the total weighted completion time on a single machine with sequence-dependent setups. The formulation of the MIP model is as follows:

$$\text{Minimize} \sum_{j=1}^{J} e_j (d_j - C_j) + \sum_{i=0}^{J} \sum_{j=1}^{J} SC_{ij} X_{ij} \quad (1)$$

Subject to the constraints:

$$\sum_{\substack{i=0 \\ i \neq j}}^{J} X_{ij} = 1 \quad \text{for } j = 0, \ldots, J \quad (2)$$

$$\sum_{\substack{j=0 \\ i \neq j}}^{J} X_{ij} = 1 \quad \text{for } i = 0, \ldots, J \quad (3)$$

$$C_i + ST_{ij} + p_j \leq C_j + M(1 - X_{ij}) \quad \text{for } i = 0, \ldots, J \text{ and } j = 1, \ldots, J, i \neq j \quad (4)$$

$$C_j \leq d_j \quad \text{for } j = 1, \ldots, J \quad (5)$$

$$C_0 = 0 \tag{6}$$

$$X_{ij} = 0 \ (i > j, i, j \in F_m; m = 1, \ldots, N), \tag{7}$$

where
- N number of job families
- J number of jobs
- m index for the job family, $(m = 1, \ldots, N)$
- j index for the job, $(j = 0, 1, \ldots, J)$ (job 0 is a dummy job that comes first in the sequence and is associated with the current state of the machine)
- F_m set of jobs belonging to the job family m
- e_j earliness penalty per unit time of job j
- d_j due date for job j
- p_j processing time for job j
- st_{mn} setup time between job families m and n, $(m = 0, \ldots, N, n = 1, \ldots, N)$
- sc_{mn} setup cost between job families m and n, $(m = 0, \ldots, N, n = 1, \ldots, N)$
- ST_{ij} an $(N+1) \times N$ matrix, where it is 0 for $i, j \in F_m$, st_{mn} for $i \in F_m, j \in F_n, m \neq n$, and st_{0m} for $i = 0, j \in F_m$
- SC_{ij} an $(N+1) \times N$ matrix, where it is 0 for $i, j \in F_m$, sc_{mn} for $i \in F_m, j \in F_n, m \neq n$, and sc_{0m} for $i = 0, j \in F_m$
- M big number
- X_{ij} binary decision variable which is 1 if job j is scheduled immediately after job i and zero otherwise
- C_j decision variable that indicates the completion time of job j

Jobs are ordered in each job family in the ascending deadline order, so that $\forall i, j \in F_m$ and $i < j$, we have $d_i < d_j$.

The objective function (1) seeks to minimize the sum of sequence-dependent setup costs between the jobs and the earliness penalties for each job completed before its deadline. Constraints sets (2) and (3) are assignment constraints stipulating that each job has one predecessor and one successor in the sequence. Constraint set (4) assigns the correct completion times under the assumption that there is no preemption of jobs and that the machine cannot be shared. This constraint set provides a correct sequence on the machine ensuring that the completion time of job j is equal to or greater than the completion time of the previous job i plus the setup time between job i and job j and its processing time. Constraint (5) ensures that no job is completed after its deadline. The completion time of the dummy job 0 that is used to find the complete sequence of jobs is assigned zero by constraint (6). Due to the ordering in job families, some of the sequencing variables X_{ij} are fixed in advance by constraint set (7).

In the following, the CP model for the BSP is given, which is based on the work of Jordan and Drexl [6], but has been improved by adding global constraints (14) and (15).

$$\text{Minimize} \sum_{j=1}^{J} e_j (d_j - CT_j) + SC_{[job_{j-1}, job_j]} \quad (8)$$

Subject to the constraints:

$$job_{[pstn_j]} = j \quad \text{for } j = 1, \ldots, J \quad (9)$$

$$CT_{[job_{k-1}]} + ST_{[job_{k-1}, job_k]} + p_{[job_k]} \le CT_{[job_k]} \quad \text{for } k = 1, \ldots, K \quad (10)$$

$$CT_j \le d_j \quad \text{for } j = 1, \ldots, J \quad (11)$$

$$CT_0 = 0, job_0 = 0 \quad (12)$$

$$pstn_i < pstn_j \quad (i < j, i, j \in F_m; m = 1, \ldots, N) \quad (13)$$

$$all-different\{job_0, \ldots, job_K\} \quad (14)$$

$$all-different\{pstn_0, \ldots, pstn_J\}, \quad (15)$$

where k is the index for the position of a job in the sequence, $k = 0, \ldots, K$ ($K = J$); job_k, the finite domain integer variable that indicates the job at position k; $pstn_j$, the decision variable that indicates the position of job j in the sequence, ($j = 0, \ldots, J$); and CT_j, the decision variable that indicates the completion time of job j.

The objective function (8) minimizes the sum of early completion and setup costs as objective function (1) does. Constraint set (9) is used to relate the variables job_k and $pstn_j$. This set guarantees that each job is assigned to only one position in the sequence and that each position in the sequence has only one job assigned. Constraint set (10) accounts for a correct job sequence on the machine. Accordingly, the completion time of a job at position k should be equal to or greater than the completion time of the previous job at position (k-1) plus its processing time and the setup time between the two jobs. Constraints (11) are the demand constraints that assure the completion of each job before its due date. The job sequence is initialized by constraint (12). Constraint set (13) sequences the jobs in a family in the ascending deadline order. Constraints (14) and (15) represent the global constraint *all-different*. They are used to indicate that the arrays of variables ($job_0,\ldots,job_K$) and ($pstn_0,\ldots,pstn_J$) all take distinct values in their domain sets respectively.

In addition to the above models given, a combined MIP/CP model has been developed for the proposed hybrid strategies that are created by importing the LP solver into the CP solver. The combined model incorporates both the MIP and CP formulations. In addition, it includes the equivalence constraints that provide the translation of information between the formulations. These are:

$$X_{[job_{k-1}, job_k]} = 1 \quad \text{for } k = 1, \ldots, K \quad (16)$$

$$C_j = CT_j \quad \text{for } j = 0, \ldots, J \tag{17}$$

Constraint (16) is used to connect the MIP variables X_{ij} and the CP variables job_k. Similarly, the MIP variables C_j and the CP variables CT_j are connected by constraint (17). The solution algorithm for the combined model primarily uses the CP model and involves solving the LP relaxation of the MIP model at each node of the search tree to determine a lower bound for the objective function or to find out that the LP relaxation is inconsistent, in which case the processed node should be pruned since there is no feasible solution down that branch of the tree.

3 Proposed Search Procedures for the CP Approach

Once the CP and combined MIP/CP formulations are declared, the constraint solver will propagate the constraints of these formulations to reduce the domains of the variables. However, we need to develop appropriate search procedures that involve the use of a criterion in determining the order in which variables and values are tried during the CP search process. Variable and value orderings have profound effect on the efficiency of this process. In this section, a number of heuristic search procedures are proposed and their performances are compared with each other regarding the computation times. The CP search is executed by assigning possible jobs to the CP variable job_k in a non-deterministic way.

1. Search Procedure (SP1): This strategy is based on the first-fail principle that first chooses the variable job_k with fewest possible values in its domain for value assignment. The order of the jobs that are assigned non-deterministically to this variable is the order in its given domain.

2. Search Procedure (SP2): The second proposed heuristic search involves the calculation of a c_j value for each job. The c_j value of job j is equal to the sum of maximum setup costs that can be incurred by its possible predecessor and successor in the sequence. The order of variables for instantiation is sequential and therefore static, and the jobs are tried in the order of their ascending values of c_j for assignment to the chosen variable.

3. Search Procedure (SP3): This heuristic uses the setup cost data between the consecutive jobs to identify the order of jobs for assignment to the variable job_k. The variables are instantiated sequentially as in *SP2*. The jobs are tried for the variable job_k in the increasing order of the setup costs they incur when scheduled immediately after the job at position (k-1).

4. Search Procedure (SP4): This search procedure is an example of nested search, which enables collecting additional information during the search by trying some hypotheses and analyzing their effects. Here, the basic idea is to try out a hypothesis and to evaluate its effect on the objective function value. Our hypothesis is based on choosing the job j for assignment to the variable job_k, which causes the minimum cost increase in the objective function value. The variable ordering is static as in *SP2*.

5. Search Procedure (SP5): Here, we use nested search to tighten the lower and upper bounds of the variable job_k so that the search space is pruned.

6. Search Procedure (SP6): The ordering of the variables is done according to the first-fail principle and the jobs are tried in the increasing deadline order, i.e. the job with the earliest due date should be tried first.

7. Search Procedure (SP7): The combined MIP/CP model is solved by applying *SP2*.

8. Search Procedure (SP8): Here, the basic idea is to derive information from the LP relaxation of the problem, which will help decide on the order of variable and value choices inspired by the hybrid strategy of Little [8]. Naturally, this search procedure uses the combined MIP/CP formulation. In the LP relaxation of the MIP model, the set of X_{ij} variables associated with job i can have two or more variables with fractional values. Each CP variable associated with this set should be searched over those associated with the set of X_{ij} variables in which only one of the variables is assigned to one and the others are assigned to zero. The order of the jobs to be tried for the CP variable should be identified by their associated fractional variables X_{ij} in the ascending value order.

9. Search Procedure (SP9): To apply this search procedure, we propose to take the initial best solution found from the MIP model and to use this information in the CP model to determine the first job that will be assigned to the CP variables at the start of the search process. Afterwards, SP2 is applied to complete the CP search.

10. Search Procedure (SP10): This heuristic search is same as SP9 except that the combined MIP/CP model is used this time.

4 Computational Results

The MIP, CP, and combined MIP/CP models are all coded in Optimization Programming Language (OPL) and solved through ILOG CPLEX and ILOG Solver optimizers of ILOG OPL Studio 3.5 [9], which use the branch and bound technique to solve the MIP model and the constraint solving algorithms to solve the CP model respectively, and both of them to solve the combined MIP/CP model. The models are implemented on an 800 MHz, Pentium III microcomputer. The test data taken from Jordan [10] has been expanded with 2 more problem classes in addition to available 8 problem classes. The problem classes can be shown with the number of job families N and jobs J in $(N, J) \in \{(2,10), (2,14), (3, 9), (3, 12), (3, 18)\}$ and for high (H) and low (L) capacity utilization. The lower capacitated problems are generated by multiplying the deadlines of higher capacitated problems with 1.4. In each problem class, 3 different setup structures are used so that in total we get 5 x 2 x 3 = 30 test problems.

While MIP could not solve three of the problems optimally, CP found the optimum solution for all of them as illustrated in Table 1. The MIP solution times are bigger for high capacity utilization than for low capacity utilization. The CP solver for all the search procedures is always faster than the MIP solver for problems with high capacity utilization since constraint propagation works effectively for these problems and search space is small. The maximal solution time for high (low) capacity utilization is 3166.89 (642.49) seconds for the MIP solver and 32.52 (286.33) seconds for the CP solver. SP1, which is the default search procedure of the ILOG Solver, can be noted as the least effective among all other search procedures because it does not incorporate any problem specific information into the search. Devising an effective solution strategy for the CP search process is especially important when the number of jobs to be scheduled increases. With a little intuition embedded in the search process, solution times can be reduced a great deal. As illustrated in Table 1, the average solution time for SP1 is 3137.58 seconds for high capacity utilization, whereas it is 19.37 seconds for SP2. SP2 and SP3 have nearly the same performance. The nested search algorithms SP4 and SP5 yield worse solution times compared to SP2 and SP3 especially when the number of jobs increases. On the other hand, SP6 achieves comparable solution times with respect to SP2 and SP3. Since SP2, SP3 and SP6 involve using specific data from the application domain such as setup cost and due date, these procedures have been found successful at finding optimal solutions in reasonable time. Additionally, the rate of increase in solution times as the number of jobs increases is not as big as that of MIP.

As it is known, SP7 and SP8 use the combined MIP/CP model to integrate the LP solver within CP search. On contrary to the findings of Little [8] for the flow aggregation and crew scheduling problems, SP7 and SP8 do not improve the performance of CP over the CP-only search like SP2 and SP3.

Table 1. Average solution times in seconds for each problem class

N	J	Data Set	MIP	SP1	SP2	SP3	SP4
2	10	H	0.76	0.13	0.06	0.08	0.69
		L	0.37	5.28	3.98	4.14	11.01
2	14	H	10.78	2.40	0.50	0.82	1.45
		L	1.68	13.18	9.36	10.95	22.32
3	9	H	1.86	0.61	0.22	0.23	0.77
		L	0.71	2.37	1.76	2.05	4.64
3	12	H	50.39	13.02	1.52	1.52	6.77
		L	2.69	19.29	10.43	9.03	32.27
3	18	H	[a]	3137.58	19.37	20.13	119.54
		L	619.98	3695.79	222.67	186.25	658.63[b]

N number of families, J number of jobs
[a] None of the problems solved optimally by MIP
[b] 2 of 3 problems could not be solved by SP4

Table 1. (cont.)

N	J	Data Set	SP5	SP6	SP7	SP8
2	10	H	0.72	0.08	0.33	0.37
		L	5.86	3.39	0.62	0.69
2	14	H	1.00	0.46	0.68	0.73
		L	15.17	7.77	1.96	2.07
3	9	H	0.56	0.34	0.60	0.76
		L	2.45	3.24	1.31	1.54
3	12	H	4.22	1.85	3.54	3.57
		L	17.50	14.73	7.88	7.93
3	18	H	67.92	23.31	37.95	47.45
		L	443.56	271.70	217.77	242.79

SP9 and SP10 have been especially tried on the last problem class for low capacity utilization. The average solution time obtained by SP10 is almost one fourth of the average solution time required by MIP (159.28 seconds compared to 619.98 seconds).

In this particular problem type, the most effective search procedure for the BSP with a large number of jobs has been found as SP10 which uses the initial feasible solution found from the MIP solver and executes the combined MIP/CP model with a search heuristic that is guided by the information (c_j) obtained from the setup costs.

5 Conclusion

The single machine batch sequencing problem has been solved using the MIP and CP solvers of ILOG OPL Studio. The CP model uses the variables job_k to determine the positions of jobs in the sequence, instead of using the binary variables X_{ij} defined in the MIP model. By this way, the number of variables used in the CP model is reduced significantly as well as the number of constraints required. The CP formulation takes advantage of the CP language by using variables as indexes and by accommodating global constraints. To provide a comparable performance analysis between MIP and CP, and between different solution strategies used in CP, ten different search procedures have been developed. It has been seen that CP that is equipped with a clever solution strategy is more successful than MIP, when the number of families and the jobs to be scheduled increases. The success of CP is attributed mainly to its ability to cope with specific constraints on one hand, on the other hand, its support for mixed initiative problem solving where the user is supported by the system rather than being replaced by it.

As noted in Smith et al. [11], CP will do better if each constraint involves only a small number of variables, and if there are global constraints as in our case. Using the global constraint "all-different" has enhanced constraint propagation and domain reduction for a more efficient CP search. It is also easy to devise good solution strategies for the problem by taking advantage of the fact that the CP model represents the problem much more directly than the MIP model. Indeed, in the MIP model it is not easy to see that the problem is essentially one of assigning each job to a position in the sequence. The majority of the variables are binary variables, introduced solely to model the capacity constraints, and the fact that each job should be assigned to exactly one position is expressed implicitly in the constraints. In the CP model, on the other hand, it is easy to see the essentials of the problem because the principle variable job_k represents the assignment of a job to one position in the sequence. This allows a solution strategy to be devised around reasoning about these assignments. Hence, considering the more explicit nature of the CP model, we have easily derived search heuristics from application specific knowledge and obtained better solution times compared to MIP. Therefore, it is valid to state that if corresponding global constraints are available and a right search strategy is used, CP is very efficient.

References

1. Monma, C.L., Potts, C.N.: On the Complexity of Scheduling with Batch Setup Times. Operations Research **37** (1989) 798–804
2. Darby-Dowman, K., Little, J.: Properties of Some Combinatorial Optimization Problems and Their Effect on the Performance of Integer Programming and Constraint Logic Programming. INFORMS Journal on Computing **10** (1998) 276–286
3. Hajunkoski, I., Jain, V., Grossmann, I.E.: Hybrid Mixed-Integer/Constraint Logic Programming Strategies for Solving Scheduling and Combinatorial Optimization Problems. Computers and Chemical Engineering **24** (2000) 337–343
4. Mackworth, A.K.: Consistency in Networks of Relations. Artificial Intelligence **8** (1977) 99–118
5. Puget, J.F., Lustig, I.: Constraint Programming and Maths Programming. The Knowledge Engineering Review **16** (2001) 5–23
6. Jordan, C., Drexl, A.: A Comparison of Constraint and Mixed-Integer Programming Solvers for Batch Sequencing with Sequence-Dependent Setups. ORSA Journal on Computing **7** (1995) 160–165
7. Brandimarte, P., Villa, A.: Advanced Models for Manufacturing Systems Management. CRC Press, Boca Raton Florida (1995)
8. Little, J.: Enhancing the Performance of Constraint Programming through the Introduction of Linear Programming. Journal of the Operational Research Society **52** (2001) 82–92
9. ILOG OPL Studio 3.5: Language Manual. ILOG SA, Gentilly, France (2001)
10. Jordan, C.: Batching & Scheduling: Models and Methods for Several Problem Classes. Ph.D. Thesis, Christian-Albrechts University (1996)
11. Smith, B.M., Brailsford, S.C., Hubbard, P.M., Williams, H.P.: The Progressive Party Problem: Integer Linear Programming and Constraint Programming Compared. Constraints, An International Journal **1**(1/2) (1996) 119–138

Author Index

Acan, Adnan   41, 430
Ahn, JinHo   533
Akarun, Lale   363
Akaydin, Oyku   810
Akhan, M. Bilgay   381
Aksay, Anil   381
Albayrak, Sahin   480
Alcaraz, Salvador   615
Alhajj, Reda   470
Almeida, Luis   876
Aluru, Srinivas   503
Anar, Koray   157
Arıca, Nafiz   391
Aydos, Murat   278
Aydın, Tolga   62
Aykanat, Cevdet   801

Bahk, Saewoong   321
Ballarini, Paolo   553
Ballhysa, Elton   966
Baños, Raul   779
Barili, Antonio   648
Barth, Dominique   238
Bartolini, Novella   594
Bayilmis, Cuneyt   299
Belli, Fevzi   907
Bezerra, Eduardo A.   917
Bilgin, Orhan   761
Bingol, Haluk   688
Bononi, Luciano   627
Bortolas, Daniel O.   917
Bostan-Korpeoglu, Burcin   72
Bracuto, Michele   627
Buchholz, Peter   217
Bür, Kaan   187
Buscaglia, M.   729
Buttazzo, Giorgio   845
Buzzi, Marina   638

Çağlayan, M. Ufuk   278
Calzarossa, Maria Carla   648
Cambazoglu, Berkant Barla   801
Campegiani, Paolo   594
Cantini, Davide   866
Capra, Lorenzo   553

Carthy, Joe   837
Casalicchio, Emiliano   594
Ceken, Celal   299
Celikel, Ebru   21
Cervin, Anton   855
Cetin, A. Enis   381
Çetinoğlu, Özlem   761
Çetintaş, Erhan   278
Chae, Heung Seok   897
Chae, Yu Sik   110
Chang, Byeong-Mo   945
Chiang, Cheng-Chin   90
Cho, Eun-kyung   167
Choi, Heejin   136
Choi, Jin-Ghoo   321
Choi, Jong-Deok   945
Choi, Yong-Hoon   207
Chu, Kuo-Chung   311
Chung, Insang   887
Chung, Sang-Hwa   198
Cirinei, Michele   866
Coen-Porisini, Alberto   706
Cohen, Johanne   238
Conti, Marco   638

Dalkılıç, Mehmet Emin   21
D'Ambrogio, Andrea   584, 696
Danese, Giovanni   729
D'Angelo, Gabriele   627
D'Aprile, Davide   543
de Ga, Michael   470
Deliç, Hakan   331, 363
De Lotto, Ivo   729
de Nitto Personé, Vittoria   584
de Oliveira, Flavio M.   917
Devrim, Deniz   267
Dinçer, B. Taner   771
Distefano, Salvatore   564
Doğan, Atakan   827
Donatelli, Susanna   543
Donatiello, Lorenzo   627
Donmez, Mehmet Yunus   289
Dönmez, Meryem Pınar   751
Doukhnitch, Evgueni   267

Author Index

Eom, Young Ik   167
Erdoğan, Nadia   927
Ersoy, Cem   187, 289, 363
Erturk, Ismail   299
Evans, Michael P.   676

Facchinetti, Tullio   876
Ferikoglu, Abdullah   31
Fourneau, Jean-Michel   257
Franceschinis, Guiliana   553
Furia, Carlo A.   718

Gai, Paolo   866
Gallo, Ignazio   706
Gastal, Lynda   238
Gelenbe, Erol   1, 667
Gianni, Daniele   696
Gil, Concolación   779
Gilly, Katja   615
Gilmore, Stephen   523
Golconda, Kavitha S.   827
Gregori, Enrico   638
Großschädl, Johann   935
Guidi, Giacomo   845
Güldalı, Barış   907
Güler, Nilgün   51
Gulez, Kayhan   410
Güneş, Salih   11
Gürgen, Fikret S.   51
Gusak, Oleg   228
Güvenir, Halil Altay   62

Halici, Ugur   400
Henriksson, Dan   855
Hillston, Jane   513
Hsieh, Hsien-Hsi   90, 100
Hsu, Chih-Kang   100
Hu, Shiyan   440
Hyusein, Byurhan   837

Iazeolla, Giuseppe   584
Isik, Sinan   289
Isik, Zerrin   82

Jeong, Hyunku   176
Juiz, Carlos   615
Jung, In-Hyung   198

Kahramanoğulları, Ozan   986
Kang, Yong-hyeog   167

Kantarcı, Aylin   157
Kaptan, Varol   667
Karaoğlan, Bahar   771
Karasan, Ezhan   247
Kholmatov, Alisher   373
Kim, Beomjoon   207
Kim, Chul Hong   897
Kim, Hyeon Soo   897
Kim, Jin-Soo   176
Kim, Jongho   351
Kloul, Leila   523
Knottenbelt, William J.   789
Ko, Kwangsun   167
Koç, Çetin Kaya   278
Kodaz, Halife   11
Koker, Rasit   31
Kose, Mehtap   41
Kwon, Dong-Soo   136
Kwon, Koo-Joo   118
Kyung, Ki-Uk   136

Leblebicioglu, Kemal   400
Lee, Ben   198
Lee, Eun-Ju   176
Lee, So Myeong   198
Lee, Taekeun   167
Lenzini, Luciano   604
Leporati, Francesco   729
Levi, Albert   278
Lin, Frank Yeong-Sung   311
Lin, Huai-zhong   341
Little, Jim   470
Lopes, L. Seabra   876

Mancina, Antonio   866
Marinoni, Mauro   845
Martorini, Linda   604
Matta, Andrea   718
Mautor, Thierry   238
Mercimek, Muharrem   410
Millea, Timothy A.   676
Milosevic, Dragan   480
Mingozzi, Enzo   604
Montoya, M.G.   779
Moon, Jongsub   351
Morzy, Mikolaj   493

Newman, Richard   676
Nott, David   257

Oflazer, Kemal   147, 751, 761
Oğuztüzün, Halit   976
Oliver, Neal   228
Onur, Ertan   363
Ortega, Julio   779
Özbek, Nükhet   157
Özcanlı, Özge Can   449
Özgüç, Bülent   126
Özgül, Barış   331
Özgüner, Füsun   827
Özgür, Arzucan   688
Ozkarahan, Irem   996
Oztoprak, Abdullah Y.   810
Özyer, Tansel   470

Paci, Daniele   564
Pagnin, Davide   638
Palopoli, Luigi   866
Panchenko, Andriy   217
Park, Jaesung   207
Park, Sejin   198
Pedreiras, Paulo   876
Pembe, F. Canan   741
Piazza, Davide   523
Polat, Kemal   11
Puigjaner, Ramon   615
Puliafito, Antonio   564
Putnam, Timothy   676

Ramadan, Omar   810
Ribaudo, Marina   513
Rossi, Matteo   718
Rousseau, Stéphane   238

Şahan, Seral   11
Sahillioğlu, Yusuf   126
Salamah, Muhammed   267, 810
Santos, Frederico   876
Say, Ahmet Celal Cem   741, 966
Say, Bilge   761
Scarpa, Marco   564
Selçuk, Yunus Emre   927
Sengezer, Namik   247
Seo, Jungtaek   351
Seo, Jungwoo   351
Sertkaya, Barış   976
Sevilgen, Fatih Erdogan   503
Sezerman, Ugur   82
Shin, Byeong-Seok   110, 118

Shon, Taeshik   351
Silva, Valter   876
Sohraby, Khosrow   228
Son, Seung-Woo   136
Sproston, Jeremy   543
Stea, Giovanni   604

Tai, Wen-Kai   90, 100
Talay, A. Cagatay   819
Tansel, Abdullah Uz   459
Tessera, Daniele   648
Tillich, Stefan   935
Tola, Ömer Önder   391
Topaloglu, Seyda   996
Töreyin, B. Uğur   381
Toygar, Önsen   430
Trifunovic, Aleksander   789
Tucci, Salvatore   594
Tunalı, Turhan   157
Turk, Ata   801
Turri, Rafaella   729

Ulusoy, Ilkay   400

Varpaaniemi, Kimmo   574

Walker, Andrew   676
Wang, Yu   667
Wojciechowski, Marek   493
Wu, Zhao-hui   341

Xiong, Feng   420

Yang, Mau-Tsuen   90
Yanikoglu, Berrin   82, 373
Yarman-Vural, Fatoş   391, 449
Yazici, Adnan   72
Yılmaz, Yasin   147
Yolum, Pınar   955
Yoon, Hyeon-Ju   176
Yoon, In-Su   198

Zakrzewicz, Maciej   493
Zanero, Stefano   657
Zanzi, Antonella   706
Zhang, Jun   420
Zheng, Kou-gen   341
Zheng, Zeng-wei   341
Zorzo, Avelino F.   917

Lecture Notes in Computer Science

For information about Vols. 1–3185

please contact your bookseller or Springer

Vol. 3305: P.M.A. Sloot, B. Chopard, A.G. Hoekstra (Eds.), Cellular Automata. XV, 883 pages. 2004.

Vol. 3293: C.-H. Chi, M. van Steen, C. Wills (Eds.), Web Content Caching and Distribution. IX, 283 pages. 2004.

Vol. 3287: A. Sanfeliu, J.F.M. Trinidad, J.A. Carrasco Ochoa (Eds.), Progress in Pattern Recognition, Image Analysis and Applications. XVII, 703 pages. 2004.

Vol. 3286: G. Karsai, E. Visser (Eds.), Generative Programming and Component Engineering. XIII, 491 pages. 2004.

Vol. 3284: A. Karmouch, L. Korba, E.R.M. Madeira (Eds.), Mobility Aware Technologies and Applications. XII, 382 pages. 2004.

Vol. 3280: C. Aykanat, T. Dayar, İ. Körpeoğlu (Eds.), Computer and Information Sciences - ISCIS 2004. XVIII, 1009 pages. 2004.

Vol. 3274: R. Guerraoui (Ed.), Distributed Computing. XIII, 465 pages. 2004.

Vol. 3273: T. Baar, A. Strohmeier, A. Moreira, S.J. Mellor (Eds.), <<UML>> 2004 - The Unified Modelling Language. XIII, 454 pages. 2004.

Vol. 3271: J. Vicente, D. Hutchison (Eds.), Management of Multimedia Networks and Services. XIII, 335 pages. 2004.

Vol. 3270: M. Jeckle, R. Kowalczyk, P. Braun (Eds.), Grid Services Engineering and Management. X, 165 pages. 2004.

Vol. 3269: J. López, S. Qing, E. Okamoto (Eds.), Information and Communications Security. XI, 564 pages. 2004.

Vol. 3266: J. Solé-Pareta, M. Smirnov, P.V. Mieghem, J. Domingo-Pascual, E. Monteiro, P. Reichl, B. Stiller, R.J. Gibbens (Eds.), Quality of Service in the Emerging Networking Panorama. XVI, 390 pages. 2004.

Vol. 3265: R.E. Frederking, K.B. Taylor (Eds.), Machine Translation: From Real Users to Research. XI, 392 pages. 2004. (Subseries LNAI).

Vol. 3264: G. Paliouras, Y. Sakakibara (Eds.), Grammatical Inference: Algorithms and Applications. XI, 291 pages. 2004. (Subseries LNAI).

Vol. 3263: M. Weske, P. Liggesmeyer (Eds.), Object-Oriented and Internet-Based Technologies. XII, 239 pages. 2004.

Vol. 3262: M.M. Freire, P. Chemouil, P. Lorenz, A. Gravey (Eds.), Universal Multiservice Networks. XIII, 556 pages. 2004.

Vol. 3261: T. Yakhno (Ed.), Advances in Information Systems. XIV, 617 pages. 2004.

Vol. 3260: I.G.M.M. Niemegeers, S.H. de Groot (Eds.), Personal Wireless Communications. XIV, 478 pages. 2004.

Vol. 3258: M. Wallace (Ed.), Principles and Practice of Constraint Programming - CP 2004. XVII, 822 pages. 2004.

Vol. 3257: E. Motta, N.R. Shadbolt, A. Stutt, N. Gibbins (Eds.), Engineering Knowledge in the Age of the Semantic Web. XVII, 517 pages. 2004. (Subseries LNAI).

Vol. 3256: H. Ehrig, G. Engels, F. Parisi-Presicce, G. Rozenberg (Eds.), Graph Transformations. XII, 451 pages. 2004.

Vol. 3255: A. Benczúr, J. Demetrovics, G. Gottlob (Eds.), Advances in Databases and Information Systems. XI, 423 pages. 2004.

Vol. 3254: E. Macii, V. Paliouras, O. Koufopavlou (Eds.), Integrated Circuit and System Design. XVI, 910 pages. 2004.

Vol. 3253: Y. Lakhnech, S. Yovine (Eds.), Formal Techniques, Modelling and Analysis of Timed and Fault-Tolerant Systems. X, 397 pages. 2004.

Vol. 3250: L.-J. (LJ) Zhang, M. Jeckle (Eds.), Web Services. X, 301 pages. 2004.

Vol. 3249: B. Buchberger, J.A. Campbell (Eds.), Artificial Intelligence and Symbolic Computation. X, 285 pages. 2004. (Subseries LNAI).

Vol. 3246: A. Apostolico, M. Melucci (Eds.), String Processing and Information Retrieval. XIV, 332 pages. 2004.

Vol. 3245: E. Suzuki, S. Arikawa (Eds.), Discovery Science. XIV, 430 pages. 2004. (Subseries LNAI).

Vol. 3244: S. Ben-David, J. Case, A. Maruoka (Eds.), Algorithmic Learning Theory. XIV, 505 pages. 2004. (Subseries LNAI).

Vol. 3243: S. Leonardi (Ed.), Algorithms and Models for the Web-Graph. VIII, 189 pages. 2004.

Vol. 3242: X. Yao, E. Burke, J.A. Lozano, J. Smith, J.J. Merelo-Guervós, J.A. Bullinaria, J. Rowe, P. Tiño, A. Kabán, H.-P. Schwefel (Eds.), Parallel Problem Solving from Nature - PPSN VIII. XX, 1185 pages. 2004.

Vol. 3241: D. Kranzlmüller, P. Kacsuk, J.J. Dongarra (Eds.), Recent Advances in Parallel Virtual Machine and Message Passing Interface. XIII, 452 pages. 2004.

Vol. 3240: I. Jonassen, J. Kim (Eds.), Algorithms in Bioinformatics. IX, 476 pages. 2004. (Subseries LNBI).

Vol. 3239: G. Nicosia, V. Cutello, P.J. Bentley, J. Timmis (Eds.), Artificial Immune Systems. XII, 444 pages. 2004.

Vol. 3238: S. Biundo, T. Frühwirth, G. Palm (Eds.), KI 2004: Advances in Artificial Intelligence. XI, 467 pages. 2004. (Subseries LNAI).

Vol. 3236: M. Núñez, Z. Maamar, F.L. Pelayo, K. Pousttchi, F. Rubio (Eds.), Applying Formal Methods: Testing, Performance, and M/E-Commerce. XI, 381 pages. 2004.

Vol. 3235: D. de Frutos-Escrig, M. Nunez (Eds.), Formal Techniques for Networked and Distributed Systems – FORTE 2004. X, 377 pages. 2004.

Vol. 3232: R. Heery, L. Lyon (Eds.), Research and Advanced Technology for Digital Libraries. XV, 528 pages. 2004.

Vol. 3231: H.-A. Jacobsen (Ed.), Middleware 2004. XV, 514 pages. 2004.

Vol. 3230: J.L. Vicedo, P. Martínez-Barco, R. Muñoz, M. Saiz Noeda (Eds.), Advances in Natural Language Processing. XII, 488 pages. 2004. (Subseries LNAI).

Vol. 3229: J.J. Alferes, J. Leite (Eds.), Logics in Artificial Intelligence. XIV, 744 pages. 2004. (Subseries LNAI).

Vol. 3226: M. Bouzeghoub, C. Goble, V. Kashyap, S. Spaccapietra (Eds.), Semantics for Grid Databases. XIII, 326 pages. 2004.

Vol. 3225: K. Zhang, Y. Zheng (Eds.), Information Security. XII, 442 pages. 2004.

Vol. 3224: E. Jonsson, A. Valdes, M. Almgren (Eds.), Recent Advances in Intrusion Detection. XII, 315 pages. 2004.

Vol. 3223: K. Slind, A. Bunker, G. Gopalakrishnan (Eds.), Theorem Proving in Higher Order Logics. VIII, 337 pages. 2004.

Vol. 3222: H. Jin, G.R. Gao, Z. Xu, H. Chen (Eds.), Network and Parallel Computing. XX, 694 pages. 2004.

Vol. 3221: S. Albers, T. Radzik (Eds.), Algorithms – ESA 2004. XVIII, 836 pages. 2004.

Vol. 3220: J.C. Lester, R.M. Vicari, F. Paraguaçu (Eds.), Intelligent Tutoring Systems. XXI, 920 pages. 2004.

Vol. 3219: M. Heisel, P. Liggesmeyer, S. Wittmann (Eds.), Computer Safety, Reliability, and Security. XI, 339 pages. 2004.

Vol. 3217: C. Barillot, D.R. Haynor, P. Hellier (Eds.), Medical Image Computing and Computer-Assisted Intervention – MICCAI 2004. XXXVIII, 1114 pages. 2004.

Vol. 3216: C. Barillot, D.R. Haynor, P. Hellier (Eds.), Medical Image Computing and Computer-Assisted Intervention – MICCAI 2004. XXXVIII, 930 pages. 2004.

Vol. 3215: M.G.. Negoita, R.J. Howlett, L.C. Jain (Eds.), Knowledge-Based Intelligent Information and Engineering Systems. LVII, 906 pages. 2004. (Subseries LNAI).

Vol. 3214: M.G.. Negoita, R.J. Howlett, L.C. Jain (Eds.), Knowledge-Based Intelligent Information and Engineering Systems. LVIII, 1302 pages. 2004. (Subseries LNAI).

Vol. 3213: M.G.. Negoita, R.J. Howlett, L.C. Jain (Eds.), Knowledge-Based Intelligent Information and Engineering Systems. LVIII, 1280 pages. 2004. (Subseries LNAI).

Vol. 3212: A. Campilho, M. Kamel (Eds.), Image Analysis and Recognition. XXIX, 862 pages. 2004.

Vol. 3211: A. Campilho, M. Kamel (Eds.), Image Analysis and Recognition. XXIX, 880 pages. 2004.

Vol. 3210: J. Marcinkowski, A. Tarlecki (Eds.), Computer Science Logic. XI, 520 pages. 2004.

Vol. 3209: B. Berendt, A. Hotho, D. Mladenic, M. van Someren, M. Spiliopoulou, G. Stumme (Eds.), Web Mining: From Web to Semantic Web. IX, 201 pages. 2004. (Subseries LNAI).

Vol. 3208: H.J. Ohlbach, S. Schaffert (Eds.), Principles and Practice of Semantic Web Reasoning. VII, 165 pages. 2004.

Vol. 3207: L.T. Yang, M. Guo, G.R. Gao, N.K. Jha (Eds.), Embedded and Ubiquitous Computing. XX, 1116 pages. 2004.

Vol. 3206: P. Sojka, I. Kopecek, K. Pala (Eds.), Text, Speech and Dialogue. XIII, 667 pages. 2004. (Subseries LNAI).

Vol. 3205: N. Davies, E. Mynatt, I. Siio (Eds.), UbiComp 2004: Ubiquitous Computing. XVI, 452 pages. 2004.

Vol. 3204: C.A. Peña Reyes, Coevolutionary Fuzzy Modeling. XIII, 129 pages. 2004.

Vol. 3203: J. Becker, M. Platzner, S. Vernalde (Eds.), Field Programmable Logic and Application. XXX, 1198 pages. 2004.

Vol. 3202: J.-F. Boulicaut, F. Esposito, F. Giannotti, D. Pedreschi (Eds.), Knowledge Discovery in Databases: PKDD 2004. XIX, 560 pages. 2004. (Subseries LNAI).

Vol. 3201: J.-F. Boulicaut, F. Esposito, F. Giannotti, D. Pedreschi (Eds.), Machine Learning: ECML 2004. XVIII, 580 pages. 2004. (Subseries LNAI).

Vol. 3199: H. Schepers (Ed.), Software and Compilers for Embedded Systems. X, 259 pages. 2004.

Vol. 3198: G.-J. de Vreede, L.A. Guerrero, G. Marín Raventós (Eds.), Groupware: Design, Implementation and Use. XI, 378 pages. 2004.

Vol. 3196: C. Stary, C. Stephanidis (Eds.), User-Centered Interaction Paradigms for Universal Access in the Information Society. XII, 488 pages. 2004.

Vol. 3195: C.G. Puntonet, A. Prieto (Eds.), Independent Component Analysis and Blind Signal Separation. XXIII, 1266 pages. 2004.

Vol. 3194: R. Camacho, R. King, A. Srinivasan (Eds.), Inductive Logic Programming. XI, 361 pages. 2004. (Subseries LNAI).

Vol. 3193: P. Samarati, P. Ryan, D. Gollmann, R. Molva (Eds.), Computer Security – ESORICS 2004. X, 457 pages. 2004.

Vol. 3192: C. Bussler, D. Fensel (Eds.), Artificial Intelligence: Methodology, Systems, and Applications. XIII, 522 pages. 2004. (Subseries LNAI).

Vol. 3191: M. Klusch, S. Ossowski, V. Kashyap, R. Unland (Eds.), Cooperative Information Agents VIII. XI, 303 pages. 2004. (Subseries LNAI).

Vol. 3190: Y. Luo (Ed.), Cooperative Design, Visualization, and Engineering. IX, 248 pages. 2004.

Vol. 3189: P.-C. Yew, J. Xue (Eds.), Advances in Computer Systems Architecture. XVII, 598 pages. 2004.

Vol. 3188: F.S. de Boer, M.M. Bonsangue, S. Graf, W.-P. de Roever (Eds.), Formal Methods for Components and Objects. VIII, 373 pages. 2004.

Vol. 3187: G. Lindemann, J. Denzinger, I.J. Timm, R. Unland (Eds.), Multiagent System Technologies. XIII, 341 pages. 2004. (Subseries LNAI).

Vol. 3186: Z. Bellahsène, T. Milo, M. Rys, D. Suciu, R. Unland (Eds.), Database and XML Technologies. X, 235 pages. 2004.